THE OXFORD HANDBOOK OF

MODERN IRISH FICTION

THE OXFORD HANDBOOK OF

MODERN IRISH

FICTION

Edited by
LIAM HARTE

OXFORD
UNIVERSITY PRESS

UNIVERSITY PRESS

Great Clarendon Street, Oxford, OX2 6DP,
United Kingdom

Oxford University Press is a department of the University of Oxford.
It furthers the University's objective of excellence in research, scholarship,
and education by publishing worldwide. Oxford is a registered trade mark of
Oxford University Press in the UK and in certain other countries

Published in the United States of America by Oxford University Press
198 Madison Avenue, New York, NY 10016, United States of America

British Library Cataloguing in Publication Data
Data available

Library of Congress Control Number: 2020944057

ISBN 978-0-19-875489-3

Printed and bound by
CPI Group (UK) Ltd, Croydon, CR0 4YY

Links to third party websites are provided by Oxford in good faith and
for information only. Oxford disclaims any responsibility for the materials
contained in any third party website referenced in this work.

In memory of my parents, Tom (1929–2019) and Frankie (1930–2020)

ACKNOWLEDGEMENTS

....

I wish to express my warmest gratitude to Jacqueline Norton of Oxford University Press for commissioning this volume, and to her editorial team for their expert support and guidance in seeing it into print. I also extend my heartfelt thanks to the *Handbook*'s thirty-four contributors, both for their dedication in producing such superb chapters and for their forbearance while this book came to final fruition. Dr Niall Carson provided steadfast editorial assistance at an important stage in the volume's development, for which I thank him sincerely. I am grateful, too, to my friends and colleagues in the Department of English, American Studies, and Creative Writing at the University of Manchester for their support and advice at various points along the way. I thank the School of Arts, Languages, and Cultures for granting me a period of study leave in 2018–19 that enabled me to complete work on this volume, and my Head of Department, Professor Hal Gladfelder, for generously providing funding for the index, which was expertly compiled by Julitta Clancy. On the home front, I thank Yvonne, Oisín, and Síofra for their unfailing love, patience, and understanding while I laboured over my keyboard during evenings, weekends, and school holidays, when I could have been having (more) fun with them.

Contents

PART IV AFTER THE REVIVAL, IN JOYCE'S WAKE

PART V FICTION IN THE MODERNIZING REPUBLIC AND THE TROUBLED NORTH

PART IX CONTEMPORARY IRISH FICTION

PART X CRITICAL EVALUATIONS

LIST OF CONTRIBUTORS

Susan Cahill is Associate Professor of Irish Literature in the School of Irish Studies, Concordia University, Montréal. She is the author of *Irish Literature in the Celtic Tiger Years 1990–2008: Gender, Bodies, Memory* (Continuum, 2011), co-editor with Claire Bracken of *Anne Enright* (Irish Academic Press, 2011), and co-editor with Eóin Flannery of *This Side of Brightness: Essays on the Fiction of Colum McCann* (Peter Lang, 2012).

Gregory Castle is Professor of English and Irish Literature at Arizona State University. His monographs include *Modernism and the Celtic Revival* (Cambridge University Press, 2001), *Reading the Modernist Bildungsroman* (University Press of Florida, 2006), and *The Literary Theory Handbook* (Wiley Blackwell, 2013). He has edited *A History of the Modernist Novel* (Cambridge University Press, 2015) and co-edited two volumes with Patrick Bixby, *Standish O'Grady's Cuculain: A Critical Edition* (Syracuse University Press, 2016) and *A History of Irish Modernism* (Cambridge University Press, 2018).

Michael G. Cronin is Lecturer in English at Maynooth University. He is the author of *Impure Thoughts: Sexuality, Catholicism and Literature in Twentieth-Century Ireland* (Manchester University Press, 2012) and the editor of a 2013 *Irish Review* special issue on Irish criticism in the wake of the 2008 financial crisis.

Louis de Paor is Director of the Centre for Irish Studies at the National University of Ireland, Galway. His publications include *Faoin mBlaoisc Bheag Sin* (Coiscéim, 1991), a study of the short fiction of Máirtín Ó Cadhain, critical editions of the poems of Máire Mhac an tSaoi, Liam S Gógan, and Michael Davitt, and a bilingual anthology of twentieth-century poetry in Irish, *Leabhar na hAthghabhála: Poems of Repossession*, published by Bloodaxe Books with Cló Iar-Chonnachta in 2016.

Gregory Dobbins is an Associate Professor of English at the University of California, Davis. He is the author of *Lazy Idle Schemers: Irish Modernism and the Cultural Politics of Idleness* (Field Day Publications, 2010) and essays on Irish modernism, J. M. Synge, and James Connolly and anti-imperialist Marxism.

Jane Elizabeth Dougherty is Associate Professor of English and Women, Gender, and Sexuality Studies at Southern Illinois University Carbondale. She has published articles on Anthony Trollope, Nuala O'Faolain, Edna O'Brien, Lady Morgan, and Mary Robinson.

Sally Barr Ebest is Professor Emerita in the Department of English at the University of Missouri-St Louis. She is the author of *The Banshees: A Literary History of Irish American*

Women's Writing (Syracuse University Press, 2013). She has edited, with Kathleen McInerney, *Too Smart to be Sentimental: Contemporary Irish American Women Writers* (University of Notre Dame Press, 2008) and, with Ron Ebest, *Reconciling Catholicism and Feminism? Personal Reflections on Tradition and Change* (University of Notre Dame Press, 2003).

Melissa Fegan is an Associate Professor in the Department of English at the University of Chester. She is the author of *Literature and the Irish Famine 1845–1919* (Oxford University Press, 2002) and *Wuthering Heights: Character Studies* (Continuum, 2008).

Jack Fennell is a writer, editor, translator, and researcher. He is the author of *Irish Science Fiction* (Liverpool University Press, 2014) and *Rough Beasts: The Monstrous in Irish Fiction, 1800–2000* (Liverpool University Press, 2019). He is the editor of *A Brilliant Void: A Selection of Classic Irish Science Fiction* (Tramp Press, 2018) and was a contributing translator to *The Short Fiction of Flann O'Brien* (Dalkey Archive Press, 2013).

Elizabeth Grubgeld is Regents Professor of English at Oklahoma State University. She is the author of *George Moore and the Autogenous Self: The Autobiography and Fiction* (Syracuse University Press, 1994), which was awarded the American Conference for Irish Studies Prize for Literary and Cultural Criticism, *Anglo-Irish Autobiography: Class, Gender, and the Forms of Narrative* (Syracuse University Press, 2004), which received the American Conference for Irish Studies Robert E. Rhodes Prize, and *Disability and Life Writing in Post-Independence Ireland* (Palgrave Macmillan, 2020).

Derek Hand is Professor of English and Head of the School of English at Dublin City University. He is the author of *John Banville: Exploring Fictions* (Liffey Press, 2002) and *A History of the Irish Novel* (Cambridge University Press, 2011), and editor, with Eamon Maher, of *Essays on John McGahern: Assessing a Literary Legacy* (Cork University Press, 2019). He has edited two special editions of the *Irish University* Review, the first on John Banville in 2006 and the second, with Anne Fogarty, on Benedict Kiely in 2008.

Liam Harte is Professor of Irish Literature at the University of Manchester. His publications as author and editor include *A History of Irish Autobiography* (Cambridge University Press, 2018), *Reading the Contemporary Irish Novel 1987–2007* (Wiley Blackwell, 2014), *The Literature of the Irish in Britain: Autobiography and Memoir, 1725–2001* (Palgrave Macmillan, 2009), *Modern Irish Autobiography: Self, Nation and Society* (Palgrave Macmillan, 2007), and *Contemporary Irish Fiction: Themes, Tropes, Theories* (Macmillan, 2000; co-edited with Michael Parker).

Allan Hepburn is James McGill Professor of Twentieth-Century Literature at McGill University in Montréal. He is the author of *Intrigue: Espionage and Culture* (Yale University Press, 2005), *Enchanted Objects: Visual Art in Contemporary Literature* (University of Toronto Press, 2010), and *A Grain of Faith: Religion in Mid-Century British Literature* (Oxford University Press, 2018). He co-edits the Oxford Mid-Century Series at Oxford University Press.

Heather Ingman is Adjunct Professor in the School of English, Trinity College Dublin. Her publications include *Ageing in Irish Writing: Strangers to Themselves* (Palgrave Macmillan, 2018), *Irish Women's Fiction from Edgeworth to Enright* (Irish Academic Press, 2013), *A History of the Irish Short Story* (Cambridge University Press, 2009), *Twentieth-Century Fiction by Irish Women: Nation and Gender* (Ashgate, 2007), and *Women's Fiction Between the Wars: Mothers, Daughters and Writing* (Edinburgh University Press, 1998). She is co-editor with Clíona Ó Gallchoir of *A History of Modern Irish Women's Literature* (Cambridge University Press, 2018).

Jarlath Killeen is Associate Professor of Victorian Literature and Head of the School of English at Trinity College Dublin. His publications include *Gothic Ireland* (Four Courts Press, 2005), *The Faiths of Oscar Wilde* (Palgrave Macmillan, 2005), *The Fairy Tales of Oscar Wilde* (Ashgate, 2007), *Gothic Literature, 1825–1914* (University of Wales Press, 2009), and *The Emergence of Irish Gothic Fiction: History, Origins, Theories* (Edinburgh University Press, 2013). He has also edited collections on three major Irish Gothic writers, *Oscar Wilde* (Irish Academic Press, 2010), *Bram Stoker: Centenary Essays* (Four Courts Press, 2013), and, with Valeria Cavalli, *'Inspiring a Mysterious Terror': 200 Years of Joseph Sheridan Le Fanu* (Peter Lang, 2016).

Stefanie Lehner is Lecturer in Irish Literature in the School of Arts, English and Languages at Queen's University Belfast and Fellow at the University's Senator George J. Mitchell Institute for Global Peace, Security and Justice. She is the author of *Subaltern Ethics in Contemporary Scottish and Irish Literature: Tracing Counter-Histories* (Palgrave Macmillan, 2011).

Caroline Magennis is Reader in Twentieth and Twenty-First Century Literature at the University of Salford. She is the author of *Sons of Ulster: Masculinities in the Contemporary Northern Irish Novel* (Peter Lang, 2010).

Fiona McCann is Professor of Postcolonial Literature at the Université de Lille SHS and a Junior Fellow at the Institut Universitaire de France. Her monograph, *A Poetics of Dissensus: Confronting Violence in Contemporary Prose Writing in the North of Ireland*, was published by Peter Lang in 2014. She is the editor of *The Carceral Network in Ireland: History, Agency and Resistance* (Palgrave Macmillan, 2020) and has edited or co-edited several issues of *Commonwealth Essays and Studies* and *Études Irlandaises*.

Gerardine Meaney is Professor of Cultural Theory and Director of the Centre for Cultural Analytics at University College Dublin. She is the author of *Gender, Ireland, and Cultural Change* (Routledge, 2010), *Nora* (Cork University Press, 2004), and *(Un) like Subjects: Women, Theory, Fiction* (Routledge, 1993). She co-wrote *Reading the Irish Woman: Studies in Cultural Encounters and Exchange, 1714–1960* (Liverpool University Press, 2013) with Mary O'Dowd and Bernadette Whelan, and was one of the major co-editors of *The Field Day Anthology of Irish Writing, Volumes IV and V: Irish Women's Writing and Traditions* (Cork University Press, 2002).

Sinéad Mooney is Senior Lecturer in English at De Montfort University, Leicester and a founder member of the Irish Women's Writing Network. Her publications include *A Tongue Not Mine: Beckett and Translation* (Oxford University Press, 2011), which won the American Conference for Irish Studies Robert E. Rhodes Prize, *Samuel Beckett* (Northcote House, 2006), and *Edna O'Brien: New Critical Perspectives* (Carysfort Press, 2006), co-edited with Kathryn Laing and Maureen O'Connor.

Sinéad Moynihan is Associate Professor in American and Atlantic Literatures at the University of Exeter. She is the author of *Passing into the Present: Contemporary American Fiction of Racial and Gender Passing* (Manchester University Press, 2010), *'Other People's Diasporas': Negotiating Race in Contemporary Irish and Irish-American Culture* (Syracuse University Press, 2013), and *Ireland, Migration and Return Migration: The 'Returned Yank' in the Cultural Imagination, 1952 to the Present* (Liverpool University Press, 2019).

James H. Murphy is Professor of English and Director of Irish Studies at Boston College. He is the author or editor of fourteen books, which include *Catholic Fiction and Social Reality in Ireland, 1873–1922* (Greenwood Press, 1997), *Irish Novelists and the Victorian Age* (Oxford University Press, 2011), and *The Oxford History of the Irish Book, Volume 4: The Irish Book in English, 1800–91* (Oxford University Press, 2011).

Neil Murphy is Professor of English at Nanyang Technological University in Singapore. He is the author of *Irish Fiction and Postmodern Doubt* (Edwin Mellen Press, 2004) and *John Banville* (Bucknell University Press, 2018), and editor of *Aidan Higgins: The Fragility of Form* (Dalkey Archive Press, 2010). With Keith Hopper, he has edited *The Short Fiction of Flann O'Brien* (Dalkey Archive Press, 2013) and a four-book series related to the work of Dermot Healy, comprising a scholarly edition of *Fighting with Shadows* (2015), *Dermot Healy: The Collected Short Stories* (2015), *Dermot Healy: The Collected Plays* (2016), and *Writing the Sky: Observations and Essays on Dermot Healy* (2016), all with Dalkey Archive Press.

Tony Murray is Director of the Irish Writers in London Summer School and Curator of the Archive of the Irish in Britain at London Metropolitan University. He is the author of *London Irish Fictions: Narrative, Diaspora and Identity* (Liverpool University Press, 2012) and the editor, with Ellen McWilliams, of a 2017 *Irish Studies Review* special issue on Irishness and the culture of the Irish abroad.

Brian Ó Conchubhair is Associate Professor of Irish Language and Literature and Director of the Centre for the Study of Languages and Cultures at the University of Notre Dame. He is the author of *Fin de Siècle na Gaeilge: Darwin, An Athbheochan agus Smaointeoireacht na hEorpa* (An Clóchomhar, 2009). He has edited, with Jefferson Holdridge, *After Ireland: Essays on Contemporary Irish Poetry* (Wake Forest University Press, 2017) and, with Amber Handy, *The Language of Gender, Power and Agency in Celtic Studies* (Arlen House Press, 2013). His other edited works include *Pádraic Breathnach: Rogha Scéalta* (Cló Iar-Chonnacht, 2014), *The Midnight Court/Cúirt an*

Mheán Oíche: A Critical Edition (Syracuse University Press, 2011), and *Gearrscéalta Ár Linne* (Cló Iar-Chonnacht, 2006).

Laura O'Connor is Associate Professor in the Department of English at the University of California, Irvine. She is the author of *Haunted English: The Celtic Fringe, the British Empire, and De-Anglicization* (Johns Hopkins University Press, 2006).

Pádraig Ó Siadhail is holder of the D'Arcy McGee Chair of Irish Studies at Saint Mary's University, Halifax, Nova Scotia. His publications include *Stair Dhrámaíocht na Gaeilge, 1900–1970* (Cló Iar-Chonnacht, 1993), a history of Irish-language theatre, and two biographies, *An Béaslaíoch: Beatha agus Saothar Phiarais Béaslaí 1881–1965* (Coiscéim, 2007) and *Katherine Hughes: A Life and a Journey* (Penumbra Press, 2014). Cló Iar-Chonnacht has published four of his novels, *Parthas na gCleas* (1991), *Éagnairc* (1994), *Peaca an tSinsir* (1996), and *Beirt Bhan Mhisniúla* (2011), as well as a collection of short stories, *Na Seacht gCineál Meisce agus Finscéalta Eile* (2001).

Eve Patten is Professor of English at Trinity College Dublin. She is author of *Samuel Ferguson and the Culture of Nineteenth-Century Ireland* (Four Courts Press, 2004) and *Imperial Refugee; Olivia Manning's Fictions of War* (Cork University Press, 2012), and editor of *Irish Literature in Transition, Volume 5: 1940–1980* (Cambridge University Press, 2020). Her co-edited books include, with Aidan O'Malley, *Ireland, West to East: Irish Cultural Connections with Central and Eastern Europe* (Peter Lang, 2014) and, with Jason McElligott, *The Perils of Print Culture: Book, Print and Publishing History in Theory and Practice* (Palgrave Macmillan, 2014).

Kevin Rockett is Fellow Emeritus, Trinity College Dublin, where he was Professor of Film Studies until 2015. He is the author or co-author of nine books, including *The Irish Filmography* (Red Mountain Media, 1996); *Irish Film Censorship: A Cultural Journey from Silent Cinema to Internet Pornography* (Four Courts Press, 2004); with Luke Gibbons and John Hill, *Cinema and Ireland* (Croom Helm, 1987); and with Emer Rockett, *Neil Jordan: Exploring Boundaries* (Liffey Press, 2003), *Magic Lantern, Panorama and Moving Picture Shows in Ireland, 1786–1909* (Four Courts Press, 2011), and *Film Exhibition and Distribution in Ireland, 1909–2010* (Four Courts Press, 2011). A former Chairman of the Irish Film Institute, he is Director of Irish Film and TV Research Online (www.tcd.ie/Irishfilm).

Ian Campbell Ross is Emeritus Professor of Eighteenth-Century Studies and Fellow Emeritus at Trinity College Dublin. His works include *Laurence Sterne: A Life* (Oxford University Press, 2001), an edition of Sterne's *Tristram Shandy* (Oxford University Press, 2009), and *Umbria: A Cultural History* (Volumnia, 2020).

Frank Shovlin is Professor of Irish Literature in English at the Institute of Irish Studies, University of Liverpool. His publications include *The Irish Literary Periodical 1923–1958* (Clarendon Press, 2003), *Journey Westward: Joyce, 'Dubliners' and the Literary Revival* (Liverpool University Press, 2012), and *Touchstones: John McGahern's Classical Style* (Liverpool University Press, 2016).

Sam Slote is Associate Professor in the School of English at Trinity College Dublin. He is the author of *Joyce's Nietzschean Ethics* (Palgrave Macmillan, 2013) and co-editor of five volumes on James Joyce, including, with David Hayman, *Probes: Genetic Studies in Joyce* (Rodopi, 1995); with Luca Crispi, *How Joyce Wrote 'Finnegans Wake': A Chapter-by-Chapter Genetic Guide* (University of Wisconsin Press, 2007); with Daniel Ferrer and André Topia, *Renascent Joyce* (University Press of Florida, 2013); and, with Andrew J. Mitchell, *Derrida and Joyce: Texts and Contexts* (State University of New York Press, 2013). His edition of all-new annotations to *Ulysses* was published in 2012 by Alma Classics.

Gerry Smyth is Professor of Irish Cultural History at Liverpool John Moores University and is also a playwright and musician. His books include *The Judas Kiss: Treason and Betrayal in Six Modern Irish Novels* (Manchester University Press, 2015), *Music and Irish Identity: Celtic Tiger Blues* (Routledge, 2016), *Space and the Irish Cultural Imagination* (Palgrave Macmillan, 2001), and *The Novel and the Nation: Studies in the New Irish Fiction* (Pluto Press, 1997).

Norman Vance is Emeritus Professor of English Literature and Intellectual History at the University of Sussex and Visiting Professor at Ulster University. He is a Fellow of the English Association and of the Royal Historical Society. His books include *Irish Literature since 1800* (Longman, 2002), *Bible and Novel: Narrative Authority and the Death of God* (Oxford University Press, 2013), and *The Oxford History of Classical Reception in English Literature, Volume Four: 1790–1880* (Oxford University Press, 2015), edited with Jennifer Wallace.

Pádraic Whyte is Associate Professor of English at the School of English, Trinity College Dublin. He is the author of *Irish Childhoods: Children's Fiction and Irish History* (Cambridge Scholars, 2011) and editor, with Keith O'Sullivan, of *Children's Literature and New York City* (Routledge, 2014) and *Children's Literature Collections: Approaches to Research* (Palgrave Macmillan, 2017).

Editorial Note

Where known, the biographical dates of writers born on the island of Ireland, writers born elsewhere who settled in Ireland, and writers of Irish heritage born abroad are given in parentheses after their names occur in the main text of each chapter. The dates of significant Irish political, social, economic, and cultural events are also provided, where relevant. The publication dates of individual works of fiction cited in the main text of each chapter refer to a work's first appearance in book form.

PART I

INTRODUCTION

CHAPTER 1

....

MODERN IRISH FICTION

Renewing the Art of the New

....

LIAM HARTE

IRELAND has, since the late nineteenth century, produced a roll call of distinguished literary novelists and short story writers whose collective contribution to world literature has been far out of proportion to the country's size and population. A summary listing extends from James Joyce (1882–1941), father of the international modernist revolution of the early twentieth century, through his immediate successors, Samuel Beckett (1906–89), Elizabeth Bowen (1899–1973), and Flann O'Brien (1911–66), whose formal and thematic choices bear the imprint of Joyce's towering example, to the more recent accomplishments of John McGahern (1934–2006), Edna O'Brien (1930–), John Banville (1945–), Roddy Doyle (1958–), Colm Tóibín (1955–), and Anne Enright (1962–), each of whom has enriched and extended the scope of what has been called 'the prime national art of Ireland'.[1] For much of the past century, critical practice struggled to keep pace with this sustained novelistic productivity, as evidenced by the fact that it was not until the late 1980s that the first synoptic history of the Irish novel appeared.[2] In fact, there has been, until recently, a paradoxical and inverse relationship between, on the one hand, the voluminous production of works of literary fiction by modern Irish novelists and short story writers of international stature and, on the other, the intermittent publication of critical scholarship appraising these texts. That this has now changed, to the point where there is a very sizeable number of scholars engaged in critical work on Irish fiction, means that the present is an opportune moment in which to produce an *Oxford Handbook of Modern Irish Fiction*.

This *Handbook* collects, in one volume, thirty-four substantial new essays by leading experts on modern Irish prose fiction, a category that includes Irish-themed works by authors of Irish heritage who were born abroad and fiction by foreign-born authors

---

[1] Rolf Loeber and Magda Loeber, 'Introduction', in Rolf Loeber and Magda Loeber with Anne Mullin Burnham, *A Guide to Irish Fiction 1650–1900* (Dublin: Four Courts Press, 2006), xlix.

[2] James Cahalan, *The Irish Novel: A Critical History* (Dublin: Gill and Macmillan, 1988).

domiciled in Ireland. By combining breadth with depth, each chapter aims to meet the needs of different categories of reader, from the undergraduate or graduate student in search of a secure grounding in a topic to the specialist looking for authoritative guidance. In addition to being a primary point of scholarly reference, the *Handbook* represents a collaborative attempt to conceptualize the field of modern Irish fiction studies in a way that poses subtle challenges to critical assumptions and stimulates fresh thinking and debate. The book's overarching aim is to provide a reliable and critically perceptive guide to the principal strands of modern Irish fiction as they have evolved in the English and Irish languages since the nineteenth century, a time frame that expands where required to facilitate discussion of literary trends, modes, and authors from earlier periods. Accompanying aims include the provision of instructive overviews, written from a variety of analytical perspectives, of modern Irish novelists' experiments and innovations in genre, form, and theme; critical assessments of the significance of individual writers' achievements and their contributions to the wider tradition; and examinations of the different historical circumstances that have fertilized and shaped the development of the Irish novel and short story, both in Ireland and beyond. While it would be foolhardy to aspire to inclusive coverage of a literary corpus that is as vast as it is diverse, it is my hope that this *Handbook* will fulfil its critical and intellectual objectives and in doing so inspire consequential new scholarship.

In pursuing its objectives, the *Handbook* builds on a number of recent monographs and essay collections that have reinvigorated the study of Irish fiction, chief among which is the magisterial two-volume *Cambridge History of Irish Literature* (2006), edited by Margaret Kelleher and Philip O'Leary, which contains excellent scholarly essays that provide a thoroughgoing and robust contextualization of the tradition. The year 2006 also saw the publication of *The Cambridge Companion to the Irish Novel*, edited by John Wilson Foster, which comprises fourteen cogent overviews of the history of Irish fiction from Jonathan Swift (1667–1745) to John Banville and beyond. A series of insightful and authoritative period-specific studies followed quickly in the wake of these publications. Among the most notable of these were Emer Nolan's *Catholic Emancipations: Irish Fiction from Thomas Moore to James Joyce* (2007); Foster's *Irish Novels 1890–1940: New Bearings in Culture and Fiction* (2008); James H. Murphy's *Irish Novelists and the Victorian Age* (2011); Claire Connolly's *A Cultural History of the Irish Novel, 1790–1829* (2012); and George O'Brien's *The Irish Novel 1960–2010* (2012) and *The Irish Novel 1800–1910* (2015), each of which administered a powerful, disruptive stimulus to settled views of the Irish novelistic tradition.

To this shelf of distinguished works must be added Derek Hand's critically nuanced *A History of the Irish Novel* (2011), Heather Ingman's wide-ranging *Irish Women's Fiction from Edgeworth to Enright* (2013), and Ingman's much-needed *A History of the Irish Short Story* (2009), work on which topic has been further enriched by Elke D'hoker's *Irish Women Writers and the Modern Short Story* (2016). The impressive contents of the Oxford History of the Irish Book series have been valuably augmented by *A Guide to Irish Fiction 1650–1900* (2006), a superlative feat of bibliographic retrieval undertaken by Rolf Loeber and Magda Loeber with Anne Mullin Burnham, which has transformed understanding of pre-1900 Irish fiction by itemizing and providing commentaries on almost six thousand works by approximately fifteen hundred authors, with accompanying biographical notes. Among other things, these studies have enabled readers to appreciate anew the ways in which the Irish novel and short story—neither of them specifically native forms—have functioned as sites for the discussion and deconstruction of normative systems and as vehicles for the elaboration of alternative stories of becoming and belonging.

Inspired by such excellent scholarship, and working from the premise that there is no single interpretive framework or principle that makes modern Irish fiction comprehensible at once, this *Handbook* is organized around a select range of topics within a loose chronological framework. The nine sections that follow this one, each of which is introduced below, is designed to capture a sense of the heterogeneity and vitality of modern Irish fiction by combining coverage of key phases in its development with critical analyses of influential novelists, distinctive thematic and formal concerns, prominent literary trends and genres, and significant aesthetic agendas. The persistent influence of Ireland's political, social, and economic history on its novelists and short story writers dictates that the dynamic relationship between individual texts and their contexts is a governing concern of the volume. Although a minority of chapters focus on a major or particularly important novelist such as James Joyce or Elizabeth Bowen, contributors, on the whole, have been encouraged to write comparatively and diachronically wherever possible. Structuring the volume in this way is intended to make the experience of reading the *Handbook* stimulatingly varied rather than seamlessly linear, although I am conscious that my approach will not please all. Knowledgeable readers will doubtless imagine alternative ways of mapping the field, using different thematic and generic coordinates, and this is perhaps as it should be, since the ground of Irish fiction is subject to continual expansion and redefinition.

Like the adjacent terrain of the theory of the novel, the expansive domain of Irish prose fiction exists as 'a rich problematic rather than a monolithic idea'.[3] In it, all manner of flora flourish, from exotic fantasies and pungent satires at one end to displays of austere classicism and subdued realism at the other. As with any body of literature, the urge to search for nationally defining characteristics is irresistible, even though the process of their formation is still unfolding, and plenitude and diversity invariably complicate efforts to systematize. Of the many attempts to identify the essential qualities of Irish fiction, one of the most perceptive is that of a practitioner, the novelist and playwright Thomas Kilroy (1934–), who in 1972 made the following observation:

> At the centre of Irish fiction is the anecdote. The distinctive characteristic of our 'first' novel, *Castle Rackrent*, that which makes it what it is, is not so much its idea, revolutionary as that may be, as its imitation of a speaking voice engaged in the telling of a tale. The model will be exemplary for the reader who has read widely in Irish

---

[3] Dorothy J. Hale, 'General Introduction', in Dorothy J. Hale (ed.), *The Novel: An Anthology of Criticism and Theory 1900–2000* (Malden, MA: Blackwell Publishing, 2006), 2.

fiction: it is a voice heard over and over again, whatever its accent, a voice with a supreme confidence in its own histrionics, one that assumes with its audience a shared ownership of the told tale and all that this implies: a taste for anecdote, an unshakeable belief in the value of human action, a belief that life may be adequately encapsulated into stories that require no reference, no qualification, beyond their own selves.[4]

This incisive assessment only begins to tell the story, of course. The 'Hibernian Tale' Kilroy cites is a highly complex narrative delivered by an eccentric Irish Catholic narrator, Thady Quirk, an 'illiterate old steward' whose 'vernacular idiom' Maria Edgeworth (1767–1849), an English-born Anglo-Irish Protestant, ventriloquizes to satirize her own class.[5] In the process, she not only mediates Thady's monologue for the benefit of English readers by means of paratextual materials (preface, notes, glossary) prepared by a learned 'Editor' but also sanitizes and, at times, undermines and mocks him. By means of such mimicry and ambiguity, Castle Rackrent (1800) audaciously usurps expectations and denies readers the comforts of sincere disclosure and moral clarity. Nor was this the first occurrence in Irish fiction of a provocatively ironic narrative voice intent on exposing the constructed nature of the reality that the novel form purported to present; those fellow saboteurs of convention, Swift's Lemuel Gulliver and Laurence Sterne's (1713–68) Tristram Shandy, prove that Thady was, so to speak, no quirk.

The revolutionary force of these subversively parodic fictional creations lies in their ingenious elaboration of textual and interpretive cruxes that support multiple indeterminate readings. Anchored to varying degrees in the native Irish oral storytelling tradition, Castle Rackrent, Gulliver's Travels (1726), and Tristram Shandy (1759–67) artfully shatter the pretensions of Enlightenment modernity and the claims of its attendant literary form, the novel, to provide what Daniel Defoe in Robinson Crusoe (1719)—arguably the first English novel—called 'a just History of Fact'.[6] 'Perhaps that is the Irish influence', observes Derek Hand of Sterne's masterpiece, 'a distrust of the medium itself—a playful attitude to it, mocking it—or taking the Mick out of it, gently alerting the reader to its limits and its impossibilities',[7] while at the same time loading it with profound insights into the infinite complexity of human consciousness and experience. These special truths would endure, as would the influence of these novelists' radical incredulity towards established representational modes. Among the grateful beneficiaries of their example was James Joyce, who acknowledged his debt to Sterne when explaining the genesis of Finnegans Wake (1939), arguably the most challenging work of fiction ever produced:

---

[4] Thomas Kilroy, 'Tellers of Tales', Times Literary Supplement, 17 March 1972, 301.

[5] Maria Edgeworth, Castle Rackrent, ed. George Watson (Oxford: Oxford University Press, 1995), 3, 4. The full title of Edgeworth's anonymously published novel is Castle Rackrent, An Hibernian Tale Taken from Facts, and from the Manners of the Irish Squires, Before the Year 1782.

[6] Daniel Defoe, The Life and Strange Surprizing Adventures of Robinson Crusoe of York, Mariner (London: W. Taylor, 1719), unpaginated preface.

[7] Derek Hand, A History of the Irish Novel (Cambridge: Cambridge University Press, 2011), 47–8.

I might easily have written this story in the traditional manner....Every novelist knows the recipe....It is not very difficult to follow a simple, chronological scheme which the critics will understand....But I, after all, am trying to tell the story of this Chapelizod family in a new way....Time and the river and the mountain are the real heroes of my book....Yet the elements are exactly what every novelist might use: man and woman, birth, childhood, night, sleep, marriage, prayer, death....There is nothing paradoxical about this....Only I am trying to build many planes of narrative with a single esthetic purpose....Did you ever read Laurence Sterne...?[8]

If this tells us anything, it is that the novel, the literary genre with newness at its etymological core, continually renews itself by absorbing, dethroning, and transforming precedent. Or, in Wakean terms, each novel begins 'The seim anew.'[9]

NINETEENTH-CENTURY CONTEXTS AND LEGACIES

With such dynamics in mind, Part II of this *Handbook*, 'Nineteenth-Century Contexts and Legacies', lays the background for the volume as a whole by providing authoritative accounts of three key aspects of the pre-twentieth-century Irish novelistic tradition (fiction by Gothic, Catholic, and women writers respectively) that are important to understandings of what came after, including the fiction composed during the Irish Literary Revival, the value and significance of which is examined in Part III. It is appropriate that we should begin with a chapter devoted to Gothic fiction, an anti-realist form originating in the 1760s, if only because the very diffuseness of the Gothic mode (or form, or register, or subgenre—the terminology is a matter of scholarly debate[10]), which, it has been claimed, 'permeates virtually all Irish writing',[11] underlines the difficulty of establishing definitive temporal parameters that differentiate 'modern' Irish fiction from that which preceded it. Regarded by some critics as the defining fictional form of nineteenth-century Ireland, the predominantly Protestant predilection for writing 'supernatural fiction'[12] is one of the most marked and influential literary legacies of Ireland's colonial

---

[8] Eugene Jolas, 'My friend James Joyce', in *Eugene Jolas: Critical Writings, 1924–1951*, ed. Klaus H. Kiefer and Rainer Rumold (Evanston, IL: Northwestern University Press, 2009), 399. This essay originally appeared in the *Partisan Review* in March–April 1941.

[9] James Joyce, *Finnegans Wake*, ed. Robbert-Jan Henkes, Erik Bindervoet, and Finn Fordham (Oxford: Oxford University Press, 2012), 215: 23.

[10] See Christina Morin and Niall Gillespie, 'Introduction: De-limiting the Irish Gothic', in Christina Morin and Niall Gillespie (eds), *Irish Gothics: Genres, Forms, Modes, and Traditions, 1760–1890* (Basingstoke: Palgrave Macmillan, 2014), 1–12.

[11] Vera Kreilkamp, review of *The Gothic Family Romance* by Margot Gayle Backus, *Victorian Studies* 43, no. 4 (2001), 648.

[12] R. F. Foster, 'Protestant Magic: W. B. Yeats and the Spells of Irish History', in *Paddy and Mr Punch: Connections in Irish and English History* (London: Penguin, 1995), 212–32.

history. Synonymous with transgression, transformation, and disruption, and replete with an excess of sentiment and subjectivity, Irish Gothic has been widely read as an expression of the fears and anxieties of a privileged but embattled social caste, the once-dominant Anglo-Irish elite, bearers of a literary imagination characterized as 'ineluctably haunted, cloven into duality by the cleavage in Irish society between expropriated and expropriators',[13] whose future became more and more uncertain as a lower middle-class Catholic ascendancy of strong farmers and shopkeepers emerged.[14] Hence the recurring preoccupation of this 'already in-between'[15] class with themes of fragmented identity, illegitimate inheritance, miscegenation, disputed land ownership, cursed families, and irresistible decline, in a lineage that stretches from the late eighteenth-century novels of Regina Maria Roche (1764–1845), through the *fin-de-siècle* supernaturalist fiction of Oscar Wilde (1854–1900) and Bram Stoker (1847–1912), to the modernist ghost stories of Elizabeth Bowen and beyond. In examining the cultural and political import of this spectral subgenre in Chapter Two, Jarlath Killeen highlights the ways in which Gothic novels function as 'weapons in an ideological attack on the representational politics of the "Celtic fringe"' in the hands of Anglican writers who were politically and intellectually committed to the modernization of a (mainly Catholic) culture long denigrated as intractably 'backward', impoverished, and anti-modern. The result, he argues, is an anti-Gothic Gothic aesthetic characterized by 'the authorial undermining of the form even as it is being perpetuated'.

Despite Irish Gothic being seen as a largely Protestant phenomenon, and notwithstanding its close association with anti-Catholic polemic, a strain of 'Catholic or Catholic-nationalist Gothic'[16] has been traced to the early nineteenth-century tales of John Banim (1798–1842), William Carleton (1794–1869), and James Clarence Mangan (1803–49).[17] This seam also extends in a forward direction. After the partition of the island in 1920 and the emergence of a partially independent Irish state in 1922, a number of novelists and short story writers of Catholic background turned to Gothic conventions for a variety of reasons, whether as a means of understanding inherited psychological wounds, contextualizing recurrent political violence, or interrogating the creation of national mythologies. Killeen identifies Frank O'Connor's (1903–66) short story, 'Guests of the Nation' (1931), as a pre-eminent example of Gothic tropes being used to amplify a post-revolutionary disillusionment with the betrayal of emancipatory

---

[13] Julian Moynihan, 'The Politics of Anglo-Irish Gothic: Maturin, Le Fanu and the Return of the Repressed', in Heinz Kosok (ed.), *Studies in Anglo-Irish Literature* (Bonn: Bouvier Verlag, 1982), 48.

[14] See, for example, the chapter entitled 'Form and Ideology in the Anglo-Irish Novel' in Terry Eagleton's *Heathcliff and the Great Famine: Studies in Irish Culture* (London: Verso, 1995), 145–225.

[15] John Paul Riquelme, 'Toward a History of Gothic and Modernism: Dark Modernity from Bram Stoker to Samuel Beckett', *Modern Fiction Studies* 46, no. 3 (2000), 591.

[16] Seamus Deane, *Strange Country: Modernity and Nationhood in Irish Writing since 1790* (Oxford: Clarendon Press, 1997), 126.

[17] See Richard Haslam, '"Broad Farce and Thrilling Tragedy": Mangan's Fiction and Irish Gothic', *Éire-Ireland* 41, nos. 3–4 (2006), 215–44 and 'Maturin's Catholic Heirs: Expanding the Limits of Irish Gothic', in Morin and Gillespie (eds), *Irish Gothics*, 113–29. See also Luke Gibbons, *Gaelic Gothic: Race, Colonization, and Irish Culture* (Galway: Arlen House, 2004).

nationalist ideals. For later novelists, it is not only the ghosts of the colonial past that trouble and shape their fictions. The culpability of the postcolonial nation-state itself for victimizing its most vulnerable citizens is a notable theme of recent neo-Gothic renditions of destructive personal pasts, some of which dramatize the return of repressed histories to rupture the fabric of the national historical narrative. The intimate harm perpetrated by agents of authoritarian political and religious dogmas is harrowingly laid bare in the work of Patrick McCabe (1955–) and Eimear McBride (1976–), both of whom Killeen discusses. In contrast to O'Connor's realist recreation of the spiritually disfiguring effects of retributive violence in a time of war, McCabe's *The Butcher Boy* (1992) and McBride's *A Girl is a Half-formed Thing* (2013) exhibit a striking narrative experimentalism when evoking the enduring effects of familial and institutional abuse and deprivation, many of whose victims were hidden in plain sight. In these and other recent novels that incorporate neo-Gothic elements, language and form are made to serve immersive ends as authors seek to connect readers to the visceral experience of trauma, while simultaneously revealing the extent to which the cast aside remain constitutive, uncanny presences in the Irish cultural imaginary, akin to what Freud called 'that class of the terrifying which leads back to something long known to us, once very familiar'.[18] Far from being anti-realist, contemporary Irish usages of the Gothic mode testify to its efficacy as a heightened form of social and psychological realism, a means of affording readers a more intense engagement with intensely troubled states of mind.

The retrieval of works of Gothic fiction from a position of marginality to a more central place in the Irish literary canon has been one of the notable critical developments of the past thirty years or so. With increased scholarly attention has come a more discriminating understanding of this distinctive field of fiction, as exemplified by Siobhán Kilfeather's conceptualization of the Gothic as 'an extra dimension apparent in many works of Irish fiction',[19] Joe Cleary's critique of 'the tendency to isolate Ascendancy Gothic as *the* defining nineteenth-century Irish alternative to English realism',[20] and Christina Morin and Niall Gillespie's reframing of eighteenth- and nineteenth-century Irish Gothic as multi-generic and cross-sectarian.[21] The malleability of the Gothic mode is instantiated by the fiction of Charlotte Riddell (1832–1906), the Carrickfergus-born novelist whose 1867 short story, 'Hertford O'Donnell's Warning', provides a point of departure in Chapter Three for Gerardine Meaney's mapping of the affinities and continuities between Victorianism and modernism in works by late nineteenth- and early twentieth-century Irish women writers. This story is one of several by Riddell that feature supernatural plots, a strand of her work that complemented her pioneering social realist novels set in the

---

[18] Sigmund Freud, 'The Uncanny', in *On Creativity and the Unconscious*, trans. Alix Strachey (New York: Harper and Row, 1958), 123–4.

[19] Siobhán Kilfeather, 'The Gothic Novel', in John Wilson Foster (ed.), *The Cambridge Companion to the Irish Novel* (Cambridge: Cambridge University Press, 2006), 86.

[20] Joe Cleary, 'The Nineteenth-Century Irish Novel: Notes and Speculations on Literary Historiography', in Jacqueline Belanger (ed.), *The Irish Novel in the Nineteenth Century: Facts and Fictions* (Dublin: Four Courts Press, 2005), 204. Original emphasis.

[21] Morin and Gillespie, 'Introduction: De-limiting the Irish Gothic', 1–12.

burgeoning milieu of London commerce and finance. Many of these stories are haunted house narratives that revolve around the nexus of gender, wealth, property ownership, and the paranormal, such as those collected in her *Weird Stories* (1882), which was preceded by four Gothic novellas penned by Riddell in the 1870s. Riddell's ghost stories were intended to instruct as well as entertain; she was one of a number of late Victorian women writers who reworked Gothic conventions to air ethical concerns about social and economic inequalities, using 'the ghost story as a way to critique the economic problems in both the impoverished streets and wealthy ancestral homes of England, as well as to shine a light on the emotional grievances existing behind closed doors'.[22] Unlike other Victorian practitioners of ghost fiction, Riddell's supernatural tales refuse to subordinate the social to the sensational to achieve their ghostly effects.

Riddell is one of a significant cohort of once-popular Irish novelists of the Victorian and Edwardian eras—others include L. T. Meade (pseudonym of Elizabeth Thomasina Toulmin Smith, 1844–1914), Sarah Grand (pseudonym of Frances Clarke McFall, 1854–1943), M. E. Francis (pseudonym of Mary E. Sweetman, 1859–1930), and Katherine Cecil Thurston (1875–1911)—who until recently have been occluded in literary histories and surveys. Many were female, of middle-class origin, and prolific producers of generically varied popular fictions, including romances, country house novels, social problem novels, science fiction mysteries, novels about the Land War of 1879–82, and New Woman fiction that critiqued patriarchal norms and culturally defined gender roles. As Meaney observes, the recuperation of these neglected voices 'subverts a teleological construction of Irish literary history as a long march towards modernism'. Their restoration to the canon also modifies accounts of the nineteenth-century Irish novelistic tradition that centre on the limitations of social realism in a country marked by uneven socio-economic development, and illuminates the expansive creativity of novelists in the period between the end of the Famine and the publication of *Ulysses* in 1922.

The fact that Riddell forged her literary career in England—she moved to London with her widowed mother in 1855 and remained there until her death—makes her doubly exemplary of this largely female line for, as Meaney goes on to note, the experience of migration was a central feature of many of these novelists' careers, albeit one that meant that 'they were often excluded from Irish literary histories because they were seen not only to write for a non-Irish audience, but also to be concerned more with issues of women's education and experiences than with debates about Irish national literature'.[23]

---

[22] Melissa Edmundson, 'The "Uncomfortable Houses" of Charlotte Riddell and Margaret Oliphant', *Gothic Studies* 12, no. 1 (2010), 52.

[23] Rolf Loeber and Magda Stouthamer-Loeber, 'Literary Absentees: Irish Women Authors in Nineteenth-Century England', in Belanger (ed.), *The Irish Novel in the Nineteenth Century*, 168. The changing commercial realities of post-Union publishing were a key factor in the relocation of generations of nineteenth-century Irish novelists to London. As David Goldie succinctly states, 'In the 1830s Irish titles were as likely to be published in Dublin as in London; by the 1890s London was publishing eight Irish titles to every one published in Dublin'. 'Scottish, Irish, and Welsh Fiction in the Late Nineteenth Century', in Patrick Parrinder and Andrzej Gąsiorek (eds), *The Oxford History of the Novel in English, Volume 4: The Reinvention of the British and Irish Novel 1880–1940* (Oxford: Oxford University Press, 2011), 166.

The recalibration of the critical lenses to take fuller account of overlooked or unknown spheres of Irish literary activity and influence in England during the long nineteenth century has retrained eyes on the cross-cultural affinities and national inter-relationships that cut across the colonial binaries of centre and periphery, metropole and margin.[24] The opening up of such archipelagic and transnational perspectives has also given fresh visibility to novels that provide access to a gendered history too often obscured by the male-dominated Literary Revival, thus enabling, in Meaney's words, 'new modes of imagining what it is to be a woman, a writer, a migrant moving between countries and classes'.

That expatriate Irish women novelists were not the only group cast into shadow by the towering achievements of the Revival generation is attested by James H. Murphy in his discussion of Catholic fiction written between the 1870s and 1920s in Chapter Four. Although the fictional practice of contemporary Irish novelists is manifestly different from that of their late nineteenth- and early twentieth-century predecessors, Murphy identifies a thematic continuity between them. Shame and anger at the country's socio-cultural belatedness and underdevelopment, he argues, are the creative stimuli that link novels by writers such as Gerald O'Donovan (1871–1942), William Patrick Ryan (1867–1942), and, to an extent, James Joyce to those by the post-Joycean generation of Edna O'Brien and John McGahern. In the work of the earlier of these generations, such emotions find expression in plots and scenarios that dramatize the struggle between the forces of conservatism and liberalism for the soul of the nascent nation.

The chief object of these Catholic intelligentsia novelists' disdain in the decades prior to 1922 was the stultified torpor of a society seen as being increasingly dominated by clerical, rural, and authoritarian mindsets, whose puritanical Catholicism impeded modernization in the eyes of activist-writers such as O'Donovan and Ryan. We therefore encounter in these novelists' autobiographically inflected works variations on the figure of the defeated social reformer whose progressive ideals gain little traction in a provincial society in thrall to vested interests represented by the triumvirate of priest, shop-keeper, and strong farmer. Other novels, such as *Children of the Dead End* (1914) by Patrick MacGill (1890–1963) and *The Valley of the Squinting Windows* (1918) by Brinsley MacNamara (1890–1963), exposed the grinding poverty, economic exploitation, religious hypocrisy, and moral judgementalism that lurked beneath pastoral façades, thereby drawing the wrath of those who regarded rural communities as the spiritual centre of the nation-in-waiting. The abrasive realism of such works does not tell the whole story, however, as Murphy goes on to highlight in his discussion of works by Edward MacLysaght (1887–1986), Aodh de Blácam (1890–1951), and Eimar O'Duffy (1893–1935) that offer a more nuanced account of a Catholic culture that, for all its many shortcomings, is portrayed as being preferable to the Anglicized alternative promoted by the politically dominant partner in the Union with Britain.

---

[24] The extensive research that informs John Wilson Foster's *Irish Novels 1890–1940: New Bearings in Culture and Fiction* (Oxford: Oxford University Press, 2008) and James H. Murphy's *Irish Novelists and the Victorian Age* (Oxford: Oxford University Press, 2011) has been complemented by Tina O'Toole's *The New Irish Woman* (Basingstoke: Palgrave Macmillan, 2013) and Whitney Standlee's *'Power to Observe': Irish Women Novelists in Britain, 1890–1916* (Bern: Peter Lang, 2015).

In his preface to the first American edition of *The Valley of the Squinting Windows*, MacNamara looked back to the fiction of William Carleton, Gerald Griffin (1803–40), Samuel Lover (1797–1868), Charles Lever (1806–72), and Charles J. Kickham (1828–82), and concluded that 'somehow between them, between those who wrote to degrade us and those who have idealized us, the real Irishman did not come to be set down. From its fiction, reality was absent, as from most other aspects of Irish life.'[25] In seeking to contextualize what he regarded as a new receptivity on the part of the novel-reading public to a faults-and-all realism in post-Rising Ireland, MacNamara was rehearsing a familiar refrain of nineteenth- and early twentieth-century Irish fiction writers, one that Carleton himself invoked when he declared that his *Traits and Stories of the Irish Peasantry* (1830–33) was written 'neither to distort his countrymen into demons, nor to enshrine them as suffering innocents and saints—but to exhibit them as they really are.'[26] The challenge to classic realism was a shared preoccupation of the two literary-cultural movements that dominated the intellectual climate in which MacNamara wrote, Irish revivalism and international modernism, neither of whose adherents felt beholden to verisimilitude but rather endeavoured to create their own versions of reality. Earlier conceptions of these broadly coeval movements as antithetical have been revised by recent scholarship that has identified synergies between them, as well as bringing to light the wide diversity of viewpoints and multivalent tensions that energized each of these cultural phenomena.[27] Rather than disambiguate them, therefore, I consider it more productive to bring revivalism and modernism into critical proximity in Part III of this volume and approach them as overlapping, dialectically entwined movements that produced highly differentiated bodies of writing that were at once distinctive and mutually nurturing components of an ambitious project of national regeneration that stretched from the 1880s to the 1930s.

IRISH REVIVALISM AND IRISH MODERNISM

The place that the Literary Revival occupies in Irish cultural history is neither simple nor settled. For some, it is a celebration of the ancient Irish past; for others, an elitist appropriation of indigenous culture by scions of a class on the verge of cultural eclipse, who 'turned to literature to forge in new circumstances identities that were no longer

---

[25] Brinsley MacNamara, 'Prefatory Note', in *The Valley of the Squinting Windows* (New York: Brentano's, 1919), x.

[26] William Carleton, 'Preface', in *Traits and Stories of the Irish Peasantry* (Dublin: William Curry, Jnr. and Co., 1830), vol. 1, ix.

[27] For a useful account of the development of the critical debate, see Rónán McDonald, 'The Irish Revival and Modernism', in Joe Cleary (ed.), *The Cambridge Companion to Irish Modernism* (Cambridge: Cambridge University Press, 2014), 51–62. See also *Irish University Review. Special Issue: New Perspectives on the Irish Literary Revival* 33, no. 1 (2003) and *Irish Studies Review. Special Issue: Remapping Irish Modernism* 26, no. 3 (2018).

secured in material and social realities.[28] Yet neither explanation fully satisfies our need to understand a movement that embraces a broad spectrum of beliefs and ideologies concerning Ireland and the Irish nation. Far from naïve nostalgia for a pre-colonial past, the Revival, like modernism at large, produces a dynamic sense of the past in the present. As Joe Cleary points out, modernism and revivalism shared a similar impetus: 'to reject the immediate past as almost wholly compromised; to create a new art that would find its rightful place not in the degraded present but in some renovated future of a transformed nation or a new era'.[29] Newness in art, of course, is historically specific, taking different forms and meanings in different times and places. Accentuating the self-conscious rejection of literary precedent runs the risk of making modernism and revivalism seem *ex nihilo* phenomena, thus obscuring their subtle Victorian rootlets. We are perhaps too accustomed to associating the 'shock of the new' with the 'radical breaks and unprecedented innovations'[30] of avant-garde high modernism (after all, realism in fiction was itself once a revolutionary phenomenon). Considered on their own terms, the 1880s and 1890s were no less electrifying creative epochs, not least in the liberation from stylistic constraint offered by a cluster of *fin-de-siècle* artistic trends, notably impressionism, naturalism, and aestheticism, that redefined the novel's status as an art form and expanded its scope and purpose in myriad directions.[31]

Arguably, the Irish novelist whose imagination was most energized by these beckoning possibilities was George Moore (1852–1933). Moore's overriding aesthetic quest was for a means of expressing that which eluded the conventions of mid-Victorian realism: the deeper, more intense levels of consciousness, the shifting desires and unruly instincts of the unconscious mind. It was a search that would lead this most mercurial of novelists from the Zolaesque naturalism of *A Mummer's Wife* (1885), the frankness of which brought him into direct confrontation with the English circulating-library system, to the psychological realism of *The Lake* (1905), in which he sought to give expression to 'that vague, undefinable, yet intensely real life that lies beneath our consciousness, that life which knows, wills and perceives without help from us'.[32] Through his focus on gender and sexuality, Moore explored his abiding interest in the struggles of individuals to understand and create their own lives within the restraints and obligations of the larger society. Despite setting most of his novels in England, the site of the only viable future for many of his protagonists, he has been characterized by the most recent historian of the Irish novel as 'the writer haunting Irish prose fiction, and specifically the Irish novel,

---

[28] Adrian Frazier, 'Irish Modernisms, 1880–1930', in Foster (ed.), *The Cambridge Companion to the Irish Novel*, 121.

[29] Joe Cleary, 'Introduction', in Cleary (ed.), *The Cambridge Companion to Irish Modernism*, 11.

[30] Chris Baldick, *The Oxford English Literary History, Volume 10: The Modern Movement: 1910–1940* (Oxford: Oxford University Press, 2004), 3.

[31] For a lucid guide to theoretical debate about the novel in late nineteenth-century England, see Jesse Matz, 'Impressionism, Naturalism, and Aestheticism: Novel Theory, 1880–1914', in Parrinder and Gąsiorek (eds), *The Oxford History of the Novel in English, Volume 4*, 539–54. See also Adam Parkes, *A Sense of Shock: The Impact of Impressionism on Modern British and Irish Writing* (Oxford: Oxford University Press, 2011).

[32] George Moore, 'Since the Elizabethans', *Cosmopolis* 4 (1896), 57.

during the Revival period.'[33] He has also had his credentials as the co-father (with Joyce) of Irish modernism reaffirmed by his biographer, Adrian Frazier, who states that 'The fictions of Yeats, Wilde, Bram Stoker, Somerville and Ross and James Stephens exhibit one or two aspects of modernist style; Moore's novels have the full complement.'[34] This latter view is endorsed by Elizabeth Grubgeld, who in Chapter Five characterizes Moore's fiction as being foundational for Irish modernism. She contends that Moore drew on his deep reading of Flaubert, Dostoevsky, and other continental writers to transform the scope and subject matter of the Irish novel, 'pushing it beyond political melodrama, retellings of folklore, and the Anglo-Irish Gothic'. His efforts to render the unconscious through experimentation in narrative voice and structural framing, Grubgeld suggests, coupled with his bold adaptations of medieval tales that deviated from cultural nationalist ortho-doxy, serve to demonstrate Moore's significance as Ireland's first modernist novelist.

In addition to being a promiscuous, if passionate, embracer of diverse modes of artis-tic expression, George Moore was a novelist of many fictional methods, the common thread of which was his zeal for literary authenticity. His preoccupation with making the English novel more responsive to the social and political realities of a fast-evolving modern milieu, and to the apprehension of these realities by the inner reality of the mind, inspired him to pioneer fresh approaches to the art of novelistic storytelling, approaches that include a subtle self-consciousness about the act of storytelling itself, as Grubgeld notes. In the early 1900s, the prose fiction of the Irish Revival became the bene-ficiary of Moore's narrative innovations when he forsook a London of 'empty material-ism' to take a prominent role in the 'literary and national adventure' then unfolding in Dublin, hoping to unite the tributaries of cosmopolitanism and regionalism.[35] Keen to devote his energy to the new school of creative writing that was being nurtured by W. B. Yeats (1865–1939) and his fellow instigators of cultural renaissance, the returned novelist regenerated conceptions of fictional realism with *The Untilled Field* (1903), his collection of thirteen interlinked stories that became the foundational text of the modern Irish short story tradition and served as a generative template for Joyce's *Dubliners* (1914).

In Chapter Six, Gregory Castle reads these two seminal instalments in Ireland's moral history, with their shared theme of social and cultural inertia, alongside works by Shan F. Bullock (1865–1935), Emily Lawless (1845–1913), and Yeats himself, as exemplars of a hybrid form of Revival realism that sought to resignify Irish culture and summon up a more progressive vision of futurity. Working from a strongly naturalist standpoint, these authors articulate a chief concern of the Revival—the representation of the past and its orientation towards 'coming times'—and, in the process, challenge the conven-tions of both realism and idealism. Revival realisms, Castle argues, do not seek to revive an idealized past in the name of the Irish nation. Rather, they strategically repurpose the past as part of a critical reflection on that nation and its uncertain future.

---

[33] Hand, *A History of the Irish Novel*, 127. Original emphasis.
[34] Frazier, 'Irish Modernisms, 1880–1930', 114.
[35] George Moore, *Hail and Farewell*, ed. Richard Allen Cave (Gerrards Cross: Colin Smythe, 1985), 222, 235.

The interpenetration of fictional modes produced by the confluence of revivalist and modernist impulses and discourses noted by Castle underlines the difficulty of seeking to confine Irish novelists of this era to singular categories of writing. As Rónán McDonald reminds us, 'it was the intensity of the clash between the modern and the non-modern elements in Irish society that stimulated both revivalist and modernist projects alike',[36] and it is this same intensity that accounts for the intermixing of styles that distinguishes novelists' departures from the protocols of realism during and after the Revival. In Chapter Seven, this theme of generic and stylistic hybridity is taken up by Gregory Dobbins in his discussion of the representational ethos of James Stephens (1880–1950) and Eimar O'Duffy, whose fiction he locates within 'a distinct trajectory in twentieth-century Irish prose that falls somewhere between modernism and realism but presents something different'. The name Dobbins gives to these novelists' incorporation of fabulist elements into ostensibly naturalist depictions of contemporary realities is magic naturalism, a mode constituted at the conjunction of the modern medium of the novel and the archaic convention of the oral tale. For both Stephens and O'Duffy, the blending of the modern and the mythological served a dual purpose. Ideologically, their magic naturalist fictions sought to re-route the energies of cultural nationalism towards socially progressive ends, into the creation of a new kind of community. At the same time, Dobbins argues, they mounted a challenge to 'the developmental trajectory of the Irish novel by introducing a different narrative mode, sourced in the fantastic and centred on the scene of storytelling, that stresses the degree to which the seemingly "natural" consequences of modernity demand at the very least an imaginative response that exceeds the ideological limits of conventional realist logic'. The result is a specifically Irish version of modernism that has a place for radical political positions concerning capitalism, gender, sexuality, and the transition from colonial subjection to postcolonial sovereignty.

The distinctive character of Irish—and international—modernism was indelibly reconfigured by the linguistic exuberance and profane, anarchic energy unleashed by James Joyce's experimental rupturing of the novel genre. In making 'the activity of thought...the central concern and the determining influence on the form'[37] of *Ulysses*, the master document of the modernist movement, Joyce effected 'a yoking of ancient saga to modern novel',[38] thus showing himself to be as adept a raider of tradition as any cultural revivalist. Yet the intense particularity of Joyce's demystifying realism and the mock-heroic inflections of his avant-garde aesthetics were inimical to the sincere Celtic romanticism that was the revivalists' lodestar. As a socialist-minded cosmopolitan Dubliner who spoke no Irish, the question of Joyce's 'belonging' to the Irish Revival and the cultural and political constructions of Irishness that it fostered has vexed generations of critics and readers alike, not least because the very culture he avowedly turned

---

[36] McDonald, 'The Irish Revival and Modernism', 58.

[37] Seamus Deane, 'Joyce and Stephen: The Provincial Intellectual', in *Celtic Revivals: Essays in Modern Irish Literature 1880–1980* (London: Faber and Faber, 1985), 76.

[38] Declan Kiberd, 'Introduction', in James Joyce, *Ulysses: Annotated Students' Edition*, ed. Declan Kiberd (London: Penguin, 1992), xxv.

his back on never ceased to be the engine of his art and the focus of his reflections. There is no doubt that Joyce, whose elevated place in the pantheon is unassailable and whose vast, enduring influence surfaces in several essays in this volume, could be stinging in his critiques of the Revival's ideological deficiencies and scornful of the monocular pretentions of some of its leading figures, as exemplified by his satirical portraits of them in the first and ninth chapters of *Ulysses*. Religion, class, and culture played important roles in Joyce's alienation, the Catholic nationalist in him seeing the Anglo-Irish-led Revival as the latest manifestation of a Protestant intelligentsia staking 'its monopolizing claim on Irish culture, to define the national culture, as it had done since the seventeenth century'.[39] His antipathy was also fuelled by personal slights and disappointments, such as his omission from George Russell's (1867–1935) poetry anthology, *New Songs, a Lyric Selection* (1904), and, more woundingly, the protracted failure of the revivalist publishing house, Maunsel and Company, to publish *Dubliners* for fear of causing offence.

Yet Joyce's repudiation of the Revival was by no means absolute, nor were his artistic formation and innovations in form, technique, and subject matter untouched by its influence. The invective of his 1904 broadside, 'The Holy Office', in which he, 'unafraid, / Unfellowed, friendless and alone', distanced himself from 'The shamblings of that motley crew',[40] among whom he numbered Yeats, Russell, and J. M. Synge (1871–1909), was tempered by later expressions of shared artistic purpose, as in a letter of 1912: 'I am one of the writers of this generation who are perhaps creating at last a conscience in the soul of this wretched race'.[41] And while he held fast to his conviction that an aesthetic of uncompromising realism was essential to reveal the cultural and spiritual predicament of 'the most belated race in Europe',[42] as Emer Nolan points out, 'Joyce's forward-looking modernism, so concerned with consumption and excess, can never entirely be divorced from the supposedly regressive, nostalgic impulses that gave rise to other forms of revivalist writing'.[43]

In Chapter Eight, Sam Slote approaches *Ulysses* and *Finnegans Wake* through the prism of Joyce's complex and contested relationship to literary revivalism. Characterizing him as 'an Irish writer translated elsewhere, effecting, *pace* Pound, a dialogue between the parochial and the cosmopolitan', Slote situates Joyce's experimental challenge to the traditional plot-driven novel within the intellectual and artistic debates involving those of his peers who sought to reinvigorate the nation's culture. Slote pays particular attention to the views expressed by George Sigerson in his address to the first

---

[39] Len Platt, *Joyce and the Anglo-Irish: A Study of Joyce and the Literary Revival* (Amsterdam: Rodopi, 1998), 13.

[40] James Joyce, 'The Holy Office', in *The Critical Writings of James Joyce*, ed. Ellsworth Mason and Richard Ellmann (London: Faber and Faber, 1959), 152.

[41] James Joyce, *Letters*, ed. Richard Ellmann (New York: Viking Press, 1966), vol. 2, 311. Quoted in Clare Hutton, 'The Irish Revival', in John McCourt (ed.), *James Joyce in Context* (Cambridge: Cambridge University Press, 2009), 196.

[42] James Joyce, 'The Day of the Rabblement', in *Occasional, Critical, and Political Writing*, ed. Kevin Barry (Oxford: Oxford University Press, 2000), 50.

[43] Emer Nolan, 'Modernism and the Irish Revival', in Joe Cleary and Claire Connolly (eds), *The Cambridge Companion to Modern Irish Culture* (Cambridge: Cambridge University Press, 2005), 166.

meeting of the Irish Literary Society in 1892, in which he eulogized the distinctly hybrid nature of the country's literary heritage and urged that it be evaluated on its intrinsic artistic merits. Slote identifies in Sigerson's hypothesis a pre-echo of Mikhail Bakhtin's definition of the novel genre as 'a diversity of social speech types (sometimes even diversity of languages) and a diversity of individual voices, artistically organized',[44] which chimes in turn with Joyce's ludic method in *Ulysses*, his self-described 'chaffering allincluding most farraginous chronicle',[45] and the *Wake*. Joyce's exuberant assault on conventional literary English in *Ulysses* led the writer and critic Shane Leslie to liken the results to 'an attempted Clerkenwell explosion in the well-guarded, well-built, classical prison of English literature'.[46] Slote contends that such literary Fenianism is the means by which Joyce becomes Ireland's Shakespeare, revaluing both the nation and the bard in the process. Joyce's poetics of transvaluation extend to the novel form itself, his infusions of Hiberno-English inventiveness transforming it into a genre uniquely capable of orchestrating a seemingly limitless number of styles, idioms, and perspectives. Yet, as Slote shows, there are limits to Joyce's heteroglossia in *Ulysses*, while the very elasticity of this concept is tested to breaking point in the *Wake*.

One of the passages in *Ulysses* that features in Slote's discussion stages an encounter that is freighted with historical and cultural symbolism. It is a scene that rehearses themes that govern Joyce's entire oeuvre and reverberate through the fiction of his immediate heirs: the crisis of subjectivity under colonialism, the quest for a language and form in which to decolonize the mind and give literary expression to the Irish experience. It occurs in the opening 'Telemachus' episode when a 'poor old woman'[47] delivers milk to the Martello tower in Sandycove where Stephen Dedalus, Buck Mulligan, and Haines, a visiting Englishman and Gaelic enthusiast, are breakfasting. Assuming that he is the presence of a native speaker because of her menial status, Haines addresses the woman in Irish, a language she does not speak. Her timorous remark—'I'm told it's a grand language by them that knows'[48]—sharpens Joyce's satirization of Haines and the revivalism to which he is in thrall, while at the same time underscoring the milkwoman's loss of linguistic and cultural heritage as a subject of empire. That her dispossession is also Stephen's has previously been established by his conversation with the English Jesuit priest and university dean about the meaning of the word 'tundish' in the final section of *A Portrait of the Artist as a Young Man* (1916), which crystallizes Stephen's linguistic subordination and acute self-consciousness about his capacity, as an Irish artist manqué, to become the author of his own story. The pressing divergences that are borne in upon him during this encounter—his feeling like a foreigner in his first language, his sense of being

---

[44] Mikhail Bakhtin, *The Dialogic Imagination: Four Essays*, ed. Michael Holquist, trans. Caryl Emerson and Michael Holquist (Austin, TX: University of Texas Press, 1981), 262.

[45] Joyce, *Ulysses*, 554.

[46] Quoted in Andrew Gibson, *James Joyce* (London: Reaktion Books, 2006), 65.

[47] Joyce, *Ulysses*, 15.

[48] Ibid., 16.

unmothered by a mother tongue he has never known—are the consequences of colonialism felt upon the pulse:

> The language in which we are speaking is his before it is mine. How different are the
> words *home*, *Christ*, *ale*, *master*, on his lips and on mine! I cannot write or speak
> these words without unrest of spirit. His language, so familiar and so foreign, will
> always be for me an acquired speech. I have not made or accepted its words. My
> voice holds them at bay. My soul frets in the shadow of his language.[49]

For Joyce as for Stephen, his autobiographical alter ego, one possible response to this
humiliating predicament was to pursue authentic self-expression in the usurped ancestral language. That Joyce instead embraced his fractured linguistic inheritance and
found a freedom to remake the canonical English novel by dismantling 'd'anglas lan-
dadge'[50] attests both to his scepticism towards the ideology of cultural revival and to the
absence of a modern prose literature in the Irish language to which he might turn for
stylistic models. A host of interrelated factors, including the rupture of colonialism, the
lack of access to printing presses, the absence of an extensive readership, and the limited
exposure of Irish-speakers to higher education, inhibited the emergence of the novel in
Irish, such that no work of Irish-language prose fiction appeared in print during the
seventeenth and eighteenth centuries.[51] The early 1800s brought forth a small quantity
of fiction, but the second half of the nineteenth century is 'a complete blank, in terms of
prose writing of any kind',[52] up until the advent, around the time of Joyce's birth in 1882,
of the language revival movement, from which emerged the first recognized novel in
Irish, *Séadna* (1904), by Peadar Ó Laoghaire (Peter O'Leary, 1839–1920). Yet even as this
work was being read and reviewed, Gaelic revivalists were engaged in lively debate about
the appropriate language in which a modern literary Irish should be written. Whereas
many traditionalists advocated the value of the folktale as a model, more progressive-
minded practitioners, including Ó Laoghaire and Pádraig Pearse (1879–1916), argued
that new writing should be based on *caint na ndaoine* (the speech of the people), the
idiom and vocabulary of contemporary native speakers of Irish, and be receptive to outside influences and innovations.[53] So while modernist novelists elsewhere were pur-
posely undermining the normative conventions of nineteenth-century realist fiction,

---

[49] James Joyce, *A Portrait of the Artist as a Young Man*, ed. Seamus Deane (London: Penguin, 1992),
205. For a deft analysis of the linguistic predicament of Irish writers in the late nineteenth and early
twentieth centuries, see Barry McCrea, 'Style and Idiom', in Cleary (ed.), *The Cambridge Companion to
Irish Modernism*, 63–73.

[50] James Joyce, *Finnegans Wake* (London: Faber and Faber, 1969), 485.

[51] Cathal G. Ó Háinle, 'The Novel Frustrated: Seventeenth- to Nineteenth-Century Fiction in Irish', in
Cathal G. Ó Háinle and Donald E. Meek (eds), *Unity in Diversity: Studies in Irish and Scottish Gaelic
Language, Literature and History* (Dublin: School of Irish, Trinity College Dublin, 2004), 138.

[52] Ibid., 127.

[53] For an authoritative account of these debates, see Philip O'Leary, *The Prose Literature of the Gaelic
Revival, 1881–1921: Ideology and Innovation* (University Park, PA: Pennsylvania State University Press,
1994), especially chapter two.

their Irish-language counterparts faced more fundamental challenges, as novelist and critic Alan Titley (1947–) explains:

> The writer of Irish had more than two hundred years of desert to cross, with only the chatter of his neighbours in his ears for guidance. Most writers in this first generation of the Revival had never read a book in Irish until they reached adulthood. It was this fashioning anew that gave literature in Irish its particular flavour: the fact that every novelist had not only to create a story and people it with characters, but had also to 'create' the language itself.[54]

These circumstances help contextualize the slow and fitful emergence of modernism in Irish-language fiction in the early twentieth century, which Brian Ó Conchubhair surveys in Chapter Nine. As he explains, an incipient Irish-language modernism was further arrested in the years after 1922, when 'the demands of cultural nation-building and language learners' needs, as well as literary and linguistic reconstruction, took precedence over innovation and experimentation'. Ó Conchubhair shows how the authors of landmark texts such as Pádraic Ó Conaire's (1882–1928) *Deoraíocht* (Exile, 1910) and Seosamh Mac Grianna's (1900–90) memoir-cum-fictionalized autobiography, *Mo Bhealach Féin* (My Own Route, 1940), eschewed the homely idioms of archaic literary forms in order to give expression to the complex subjectivities wrought by the experience of modernity, whether on outlying western islands or in the tenebrous backstreets of Dublin and London. One of the hallmarks of these attempts to break free from what Ó Conaire described as 'the false Gaelicism that has sprouted in our own time'[55] is a generic instability that pitches these works into an intermediate zone between fiction and autobiography, their formal hybridity reflecting the quintessentially modernist belief that established conventions were no longer sufficient to capture breakdown and vulnerability or accommodate the prevailing dislocations of mind, body, and spirit.

AFTER THE REVIVAL, IN JOYCE'S WAKE

In his determination to break with time-honoured folk idioms and refusal to succumb to 'the nativist myth of a rural Gaelic utopia he knew to be nonexistent',[56] Pádraic Ó Conaire anticipated the artistic agendas of Máirtín Ó Cadhain (1906–70) and Flann O'Brien, both of whom deplored 'the hypocrisy of those who would celebrate the symbolic value of Gaeltacht life while turning a blind eye to its destruction', as Louis de Paor notes in his comparative analysis of their fiction in Chapter Ten, which begins Part IV of this *Handbook*. Unlike many of the most accomplished Irish modernists, Ó Cadhain and O'Brien possessed a detailed scholarly knowledge of the Irish language and its

---

[54] Alan Titley, 'The Novel in Irish', in Foster (ed.), *The Cambridge Companion to the Irish Novel*, 173.
[55] Quoted in O'Leary, *The Prose Literature of the Gaelic Revival, 1881–1921*, 108.
[56] Ibid., 136.

particular narrative traditions, which leant additional authority to their expansion of the range and scope of Irish-language fiction beyond the nativist folkloric aesthetic endorsed by cultural nationalists. Their relationship with the language and its oral and written literatures is central to their literary experiments and critical engagements with the inherited uses of narrative style, form, and technique. The scathing critique of state bureaucracies in their fiction and journalism derives from direct experience of the Irish civil service and from the disillusion of a post-revolutionary generation that witnessed the collapse of cultural and political idealism in the aftermath of the establishment of a new Irish state in 1922. While O'Brien, who wrote in English and Irish under multiple pseudonyms, was at the height of his achievements between 1939 and 1945, Ó Cadhain was interned in the Curragh military prison as a result of his subversive activities with the IRA. His time in 'Ireland's Siberia' had a transformative impact on his writing, which moved from a form of socialist realism, influenced by Maxim Gorky, to a more satirical style, tending towards surrealism and fantasy and invigorated by a strong current of sardonic anti-pastoralism. As de Paor shows, formal experiment in both Ó Cadhain and O'Brien owes as much to the particular circumstances of Irish culture, politics, and language in the middle decades of the twentieth century as it does to European modernism and postmodernism, although these latter critical frames remain central to an appreciation of these two writers' respective achievements in prose fiction.

Whether categorized as late modernists, postcolonial modernists, or postmodernists *avant la lettre*, O'Brien and Ó Cadhain are key transitional figures in the passage from modernism to postmodernism in Irish- and English-language fiction. Absurdist techniques, a riotous linguistic playfulness, a Rabelaisian delight in skewering cant, and a fierce hostility towards the idealized vision of rural and Irish-speaking communities promoted by orthodox nationalism distinguish their artfully subversive tours de force. O'Brien's *At Swim-Two-Birds* (1939) is a dissonant amalgam of myth and 'blather',[57] to use one of the author's favourite expressions, while Ó Cadhain's *Cré na Cille* (Graveyard Clay, 1949) is a novel that is literally all talk, uttered by corpses who in reality cannot speak. These two novelists were joined in their deconstructive enterprise by Samuel Beckett who, despite his different social, religious, and cultural origins, worked, like O'Brien, athwart two languages to produce a fiction that interrogates narrative process and negates any authoritative source of meaning, while sustaining a complicated relationship with the Irish Revival and with Joyce, in whose imposing shadow Beckett came to artistic maturity.

As Joyce's friend and sometime amanuensis in late 1920s Paris during the long gestation of *Finnegans Wake*, Beckett directly entered the sphere of influence of his surrogate literary father. Later, after Joyce's death in 1941, Beckett would commit the necessary act of filial estrangement by choosing to write prose fiction and drama in French, while retaining a deep indebtedness to, and abiding admiration for, his mentor's 'heroic work,

---

[57] In the mid-1930s, O'Brien was the moving force behind a short-lived humorous magazine of this name. See Anthony Cronin, *No Laughing Matter: The Life and Times of Flann O'Brien* (New York: Fromm International Publishing Corporation, 1998), 72–4.

heroic being.'[58] Beckett crystallized the defining distinction between his own aesthetic and that of his older compatriot when he explained: 'we are diametrically opposed because Joyce was a synthesizer, he wanted to put everything, the whole of human culture, into one or two books, and I am an analyser. I take away all the accidentals because I want to come down to the bedrock of the essentials, the archetypal.'[59] His trilogy of novels, *Molloy* (published in French in 1951; in English in 1955), *Malone Dies* (1951; 1958), and *The Unnamable* (1953; 1959), exemplifies this subtractive method. The first of these is sustained by a plot and some characters; the second contracts to an immobilized protagonist discharging his deathbed soliloquy in a confined space; the third, to an unplaceable disembodied voice. Beckett's artifice-stripping fiction thus extends to narrators and characters the Joycean injunction that the artist be 'refined out of existence.'[60] History and culture are also blotted out; whereas Stephen Dedalus's linguistic entrapment is finely contextual, the Unnamable's possession by compulsive utterance is radically denuded of all historical and geographical specificity:

> It is not mine, I have none, I have no voice and must speak, that is all I know, it's round that I must revolve, of that I must speak, with this voice that is not mine, but can only be mine, since there is no one but me, or if there are others, to whom it might belong, they have never come near me.[61]

Yet, like Joyce, whom he characterized as a 'biologist in words,'[62] Beckett's *déraciné* ear remained attuned to literary and political developments in the country from which he was self-exiled and with which he carried on a fraught long-distance dialogue. Whereas for most of his lifetime Beckett was commonly regarded as an accentless author, unconscriptable to national canons and unencumbered by ties to place—a view encouraged by his own declaration that 'The artist who stakes his being is from nowhere, has no kith'[63]—the decades since his death in 1989 have witnessed his gradual absorption into an expanded Irish literary pantheon, a process aided by a reappraisal of his relationship to Irish writing that does not seek to deny the challenges to assimilation his oeuvre presents.[64] As Emilie Morin puts it, 'reviewing the forms of displacement, erasure and negation surrounding Beckett's representations of Ireland brings to light a paradox central

---

[58] Quoted in James Knowlson, *Damned to Fame: The Life of Samuel Beckett* (London: Bloomsbury, 1996), 105.

[59] Samuel Beckett to Martin Esslin, quoted in James and Elizabeth Knowlson (eds), *Beckett Remembering, Remembering Beckett: Uncollected Interviews with Samuel Beckett and Memories of Those Who Knew Him* (London: Bloomsbury, 2006), 47–8.

[60] Joyce, *A Portrait of the Artist as a Young Man*, 233.

[61] Samuel Beckett, *The Unnamable*, in *The Beckett Trilogy: Molloy, Malone Dies, The Unnamable* (London: Picador, 1979), 281.

[62] Samuel Beckett, *Disjecta: Miscellaneous Writing and a Dramatic Fragment*, ed. Ruby Cohn (London: John Calder, 1983), 31.

[63] Ibid., 149.

[64] For informed analyses of Beckett's relationship to Irish literature, see Seán Kennedy, 'Irish Literature', in Anthony Uhlmann (ed.), *Beckett in Context* (Cambridge: Cambridge University Press, 2013), 205–17 and Emilie Morin, *Samuel Beckett and the Problem of Irishness* (Basingstoke: Palgrave Macmillan, 2009).

to his writing, namely that its apparent autonomy from an Irish context finds articulation only in relation to its residual attachment to Irish culture and history'.[65]

However, as Sinéad Mooney observes in Chapter Eleven, Beckett's Irish recuperation has been primarily driven by a renewed attention to the Irish dimensions of his plays, which perennially overshadow his achievements in prose fiction. Mooney shows how Beckett's particular brand of modernism was shaped in important ways by his formative encounter with Joyce and by his reading of the literature of the Revival, despite his scalding criticisms of its guiding ideology. She contends that the Irish traces left lingering with intent in Beckett's oeuvre have a conceptual significance insofar as they determine the ways in which meaning is produced and challenged, and inform the processes that allow the questioning of identity via an oblique but unabating engagement with Ireland and ideas of the nation. As well as considering the various understandings of Irish modernism that have accommodated Beckett's fiction, Mooney pays close attention to his persistent engagement, via criticism, translation, and pastiche, with Joyce's fiction. She also examines Beckett's career-long self-definition as a specialist in ignorance and impotence, whose work offered a self-impoverished flipside to Joyce's protean expansiveness. The outsiders, exiles, and refugees who are Beckett's disintegrating narrators are read in terms of their sins against narrative orthodoxy, their assaults against discourse being situated in the context of specifically Irish post-independence cultural anxieties. Beckett's transgressive approach to the practice of translation forms a key part of these assaults, which are most strikingly exemplified by his 1950s trilogy, a work that, Mooney argues, 'constructs out of an acute sense of futility and a deep distrust of the word a *via negativa* which nonetheless allows a faltering on of the novel'.

Such faltering on can also be applied to the fate, in post-partition Ireland, of the prosperous Protestant class and culture from which Beckett came. Maud Ellmann, in her study of another of this class, Beckett's contemporary, Elizabeth Bowen, reads the closing words of *The Unnamable*—'I can't go on, I'll go on'[66]—as an epitaph to the Anglo-Irish Ascendancy, whose hostility to Irish sovereignty placed them in a vulnerable position after the end of British rule in 1922.[67] There is no better evocation of the death-in-life condition of this colonial caste than Bowen's second novel, *The Last September* (1929). Set in Cork in 1920 during the War of Independence or Anglo-Irish War (1919–21), the novel elegizes the doom-laden last days of Sir Richard and Lady Naylor and their insular social circle, whose entombed fate is sealed long before the burning by republican militants of Danielstown, the country manor that is the novel's most enigmatic presence. Once read primarily as a novelist of manners in the tradition of Jane Austen and Henry James, Bowen has in recent years been reassessed in relation to her Gothic affinities with predecessors such as Joseph Sheridan Le Fanu (1814–73) and re-evaluated as a key figure in the development of the Irish novel after Joyce and in the evolution of

---

[65] Morin, *Samuel Beckett and the Problem of Irishness*, 3.
[66] Beckett, *The Unnamable*, 382.
[67] Maud Ellmann, *Elizabeth Bowen: The Shadow Across the Page* (Edinburgh: Edinburgh University Press, 2003), 15.

twentieth-century fiction more broadly. This is not to say that her mastery of social comedy or the Victorian Gothic genre has been critically downgraded but rather that there is now a growing understanding of the way Bowen's work adds nuance to different genealogies of Irish and international prose fiction through her complex relationship to modernist precepts and textual practices. While her realist inheritance is evident in her formal conservatism and liking for tightly constructed plotlines, her modernist responsiveness to significant changes in personal and social life takes diverse forms, including her 'awareness of the fluidity of sexual identity';[68] her 'hallucinatory treatment of objects';[69] her 'merging of surrealist techniques with an Anglo-Irish Gothic tradition';[70] and her dissolution of 'the very grounds of "character", what it is to "be" a person, to "have" an identity, to be real or fictional'.[71]

In Chapter Twelve, Allan Hepburn examines another manifestation of Bowen's modernist sensibility, her subtle use of narrative obliquity, which he identifies as a signature of her short story style. Over the course of her career, Bowen published approximately one hundred short stories. At the same time, she was a constant reader of other writers' stories and a close observer of developments in short story technique by Irish, British, and American contemporaries. In reviews and essays, Bowen often commented on the art of the short story, with an emphasis on visual clarity, style, and situation. Hepburn shows how Bowen's comments, although unsystematic, comprise a poetics of the short story. Drawing on archival research, he contends that her most concerted and comprehensive thinking about the form appears in unpublished notebooks that she kept for an undergraduate class taught at Vassar College in New York between February and May 1960. With examples drawn from a range of international modernist writers, Bowen offered insight in these notebooks into the formal, poetic, dramatic, reportorial, and uncanny elements of the short story form. She also devoted attention to the imprint of nationality in stories by three of her Irish contemporaries, Frank O'Connor, Seán O'Faoláin (1900–91), and Mary Lavin (1912–96), asking her students to consider whether these writers impress their Irishness on short fiction through dialogue, outlook, idiom, unconscious judgements, or other clues. Hepburn goes on to explore how in her own short stories, few of which are set in Ireland, Bowen works out an aesthetics of oblique representation of Irish history, which, he argues, she confronts with 'a tactic of indirection and diversion' that 'allows repressed material to assert itself by other means than the frontal'.

Although critical reappraisals of Bowen as a (late) modernist outstrip postcolonial readings of her fiction, her recurring engagement with the legacies of Ireland's history of colonial occupation and subjugation marks her out as a bedfellow of Joyce as much as she

[68] Heather Ingman, *Irish Women's Fiction from Edgeworth to Enright* (Sallins, Co. Kildare: Irish Academic Press, 2013), 87.

[69] Ellmann, *Elizabeth Bowen*, xi.

[70] Keri Walsh, 'Elizabeth Bowen: Surrealist', *Éire-Ireland* 42, nos. 3–4 (2007), 129.

[71] Andrew Bennett and Nicholas Royle, *Elizabeth Bowen and the Dissolution of the Novel: Still Lives* (Basingstoke: Macmillan, 1995), xvii. See also the essays in *Textual Practice. Special Issue: Elizabeth Bowen and Textual Modernity* 27, no. 1 (2013).

is one of Virginia Woolf. Her Joycean affinities are arguably most evident in her persistent interest in one of the most enduring of these legacies, betrayal in its multiple forms. Bowen's acutely perceptive treatment of this theme in works such as *The Heat of the Day* (1949) gains an added frisson from our knowing that she had first-hand experience of covert political activism during the Second World War, when she wrote secret reports on events in neutral Ireland for the British government. Bowen's clandestine activities would doubtless have intrigued Joyce, who observed that 'in Ireland, just at the crucial moment, an informer appears'.[72] Ever since Richard Ellmann established betrayal as a core feature of Joyce's life and art in his monumental 1959 biography, critics have probed the novelist's exploration of this theme in its political, historical, psychological, sexual, and linguistic dimensions. In Chapter Thirteen, Gerry Smyth traces the emergence of betrayal as a defining preoccupation in Joyce's early work, with particular reference to *Dubliners*, the signal achievement of which, he asserts, lies in Joyce's 'astonishingly nuanced management of private and public realms, and his insight into the ways and the extent to which these realms have thoroughly converged, with betrayal—of self by self, and of citizen by nation—the linking factor throughout'. Smyth goes on to track the evolving afterlife of public and private betrayal in subsequent Irish fiction, finding in short stories by Elizabeth Bowen, Frank O'Connor, Edna O'Brien, Bernard MacLaverty (1942–), Colm Tóibín, and Anne Enright ample evidence to support his thesis that betrayal is 'a radical deconstructive act in relation to the binary principles upon which any society, including that of modern Ireland, is built: male/female, public/private, active/passive'.

All of the writers Smyth discusses are distinguished exponents of the short story, which established such a rich lineage in Ireland during the twentieth century that it came to be seen as 'the quintessential Irish literary genre', as Heather Ingman notes in Chapter Fourteen. Ingman's subject is 'the curious phenomenon of three Irish writers who, internationally successful in the short story genre, fell short in the novel form'. The writers in question—Frank O'Connor, Sean O'Faoláin, and Mary Lavin—were in the vanguard of those who found the modern short story to be the medium most suited to capturing the mediocrity of the post-revolutionary state-building era, a time when, in O'Faoláin's view, 'patriotism became infected by chauvinism and true religious feeling by what most Irish writers after 1921 tended to call "puritanism"'.[73] As practitioner and theorist of the shorter form, O'Connor's influence was extensive and would endure beyond his death in 1966, particularly on creative writing programmes in the United States, where his *The Lonely Voice* (1962) 'has enjoyed a glorious afterlife as the definitive study of the modern short story for aspirant writers and the professionals who teach them'.[74] If O'Faoláin's *The Short Story* (1948) rather lacks this level of institutional cachet, it may be because it has been overshadowed by the polemical force of the wide-ranging cultural criticism that established him as the most astringent of the first generation of

---

[72] James Joyce, 'Fenianism: The Last Fenian', in *Occasional, Critical, and Political Writing*, 138.

[73] Seán O'Faoláin, 'Fifty Years of Irish Writing', *Studies: An Irish Quarterly Review* 51, no. 201 (1962), 96.

[74] Adrian Hunter, *The Cambridge Introduction to the Short Story in English* (Cambridge: Cambridge University Press, 2007), 105.

post-independence intellectuals, wager of a 'moral war'[75] against the unremittingly doctrinaire forces that restricted freedom of thought and expression, even though he, like O'Connor, respected the nationalist idealism that inspired the revolution.[76]

In their respective pronouncements on the short story, O'Faoláin and O'Connor linked its flourishing in Ireland to cultural deficiencies to which they were especially attuned as postcolonial writers and former combatants in the independence struggle, as around them a 'sectarian, utilitarian (the two nearly always go together), vulgar and provincial'[77] society took shape, in which the Catholic and nationalist puritanism that so dismayed O'Faoláin was institutionalized in the draconian censorship of books and films from the 1920s onwards. O'Faoláin argued that 'the more firmly organized a country is the less room there is for the short-story, for the intimate close-up, the odd slant, or the unique comment',[78] and attributed the genre's popularity to the fact that 'Irish life in our period does not supply the *dramatis personae*...without which dramatic themes for the novel are missing.'[79] O'Connor's argument in *The Lonely Voice* relies upon a similar genre-based distinction, the novel being for him an inherently communal form nurtured by 'normal' or 'civilized' societies (terms he stopped short of defining), whereas 'the short story remains by its very nature remote from the community—romantic, individualist, and intransigent', the preserve of 'submerged population groups'.[80] Mary Lavin, for her part, viewed the short story as 'a powerful medium for the discovery of truth', particularly as far as the emotional lives of Irish women were concerned, and objected to its being characterized as a minor form: 'At its greatest it magnifies life in much the same way that a snow flake under a microscope or a smear under a slide is seen to have an immensely complex design.'[81] Lavin's sustained exploration of the enigmatic complexities of solitary lives and human affections makes nationalist concerns an oblique presence in her fiction. This made her perspectives 'too exclusively feminine'[82] for O'Connor's liking, although he and O'Faoláin share her thematic interest in the nature of loneliness and states of inner exile.

O'Faoláin, O'Connor, and Lavin were also united by their adherence to a realist aesthetic when confronted by 'the difficulties of writing in a country where the policeman and the priest are in a perpetual glow of satisfaction'.[83] Each interpreted and practised literary realism according to their lights, and evolved their respective styles by absorbing the influences of a gallery of exemplars, Ivan Turgenev, Henry James, Anton

[75] Seán O'Faoláin, *Vive Moi! An Autobiography* (London: Sinclair-Stevenson, 1993), 181.

[76] Paul Delaney, *Seán O'Faoláin: Literature, Inheritance and the 1930s* (Sallins, Co. Kildare: Irish Academic Press, 2014), 27.

[77] Frank O'Connor, 'The Future of Irish Literature', *Horizon* 5, no. 25 (1942), 61.

[78] Sean O'Faolain, 'The Secret of the Short Story', *United Nations World* 3 (1949), 37–8; quoted in Charles E. May (ed.), *Short Story Theories* (Columbus, OH: Ohio University Press, 1976), 245.

[79] O'Faoláin, 'Fifty Years of Irish Writing', 102.

[80] Frank O'Connor, *The Lonely Voice: A Study of the Short Story* (Hoboken, NJ: Melville House Publishing, 2004), 17, 20.

[81] Maurice Harmon, 'From Conversations with Mary Lavin', *Irish University Review* 27, no. 2 (1997), 288.

[82] O'Connor, *The Lonely Voice*, 196.   [83] O'Faoláin, 'Fifty Years of Irish Writing', 103.

Chekhov, Guy de Maupassant, Virginia Woolf, and Katherine Mansfield among them. None of the three were unalloyed realists, however, not even O'Connor, whose unswerving affinity for the oral storytelling mode and corresponding antipathy towards the values and techniques of experimental modernism were deep set.[84] While recent reappraisals of O'Faoláin's and Lavin's engagements with the thematics of international modernism have contributed to a wider recognition that Irish fiction continued to develop in diverse and interrelated directions after Joyce,[85] it remains the case nonetheless that modernist experimentalism was confined to a small minority of Irish novelists in the period between the 1930s and the 1960s, when, as Terence Brown observes, 'disillusioned, post-revolutionary literary Ireland seems to have thrown out the Modernist baby with the Romantic bathwater of the Literary Revival'.[86]

The size of this minority shrinks to miniscule proportions when one looks across the border at the fiction produced in the new Northern Ireland, which Norman Vance surveys in Chapter Fifteen. As Vance notes, 'in general Ulster fiction has tended to favour more or less conventional realism, with an unspoken assumption that experimental narrative technique and the lessons of modernism belong somewhere else', although he cautions against equating mimetic realism with unquestioning forms of art. The institutional, intellectual, and artistic conditions in which Northern Irish novelists worked were markedly different from those that obtained south of the border. Although a high proportion of Ulster writers and intellectuals were prominent in the Irish Revival, the hegemony of unionist culture in the North inhibited attempts to forge distinctive modes of Irish writing, and the cultural vibrancy generated by the Revival did not energize Ulster as sustainedly as it did other parts of Ireland.[87] As Richard Kirkland explains:

> When compared to the monumental cultural achievements of the movement in the South, the Revival in the North was fragile in its existence and uncertain in its aims. If the Irish Revival proper takes its place as part of an independence narrative, its role having been to provide canonical texts upon which assertions of national

[84] For O'Connor's responses to literary modernism, see Carol Taaffe, 'Coloured Balloons: Frank O'Connor on Irish Modernism', in Hilary Lennon (ed.), *Frank O'Connor: Critical Essays* (Dublin: Four Courts Press, 2007), 205–17.

[85] See, for example, Mark Quigley, *Empire's Wake: Postcolonial Irish Writing and the Politics of Modern Literary Form* (New York: Fordham University Press, 2013), 65–121; Anne Fogarty, 'Discontinuities: *Tales from Bective Bridge* and the Modernist Short Story', in Elke D'hoker (ed.), *Mary Lavin* (Sallins, Co. Kildare: Irish Academic Press, 2013), 49–64; Delaney, *Seán O'Faoláin: Literature, Inheritance and the 1930s*, 1–39.

[86] Terence Brown, 'Ireland, Modernism and the 1930s', in *The Literature of Ireland: Culture and Criticism* (Cambridge: Cambridge University Press, 2010), 99.

[87] P. J. Mathews, 'Theatre and Activism 1900–1916', in Nicholas Grene and Chris Morash (eds), *The Oxford Handbook of Modern Irish Theatre* (Oxford: Oxford University Press, 2016), 59. An early acknowledgement of northern difference was sounded in the 1904 manifesto of the Ulster Literary Theatre, which spoke in terms of 'the Ulster and the Leinster schools' of drama, the talent of the former being 'more satiric than poetic'. 'Manifesto of the Ulster Literary Theatre', quoted in Declan Kiberd and P. J. Mathews (eds), *Handbook of the Irish Revival: An Anthology of Irish Cultural and Political Writings 1891–1922* (Dublin: Abbey Theatre Press, 2015), 94.

cultural autonomy could be guaranteed, the Northern Revival, in contrast, found itself hopelessly compromised by the very different narrative of partition in 1920, an event which ran counter to all the activity of the Revival and one to which it seemingly had no answer. Perhaps it is for this reason that ... when we search for its cultural achievements, we find sporadic and often inconclusive activity that ultimately collapses into a post-partition despair.[88]

So whereas leading novelists in the Irish Free State set about demythologizing the Revival-inspired rural imaginary and critiquing the tenacious conservatism of the new social order, much Ulster fiction from 1920 onwards was concerned with exploring regional distinctiveness (geographical and social) and multiple identities (urban and rural) with varying degrees of celebration, irony, or edginess. Underlying the problematic of regional identity in a state where the unionist governing elite held political power for fifty-one unbroken years until 1972 was the intractable reality of sectarianism, the by-product of what Sam Hanna Bell (1909–90) in 1951 characterized as the province's 'antique conflict, resolved long ago in Western Europe—the conflict of religious dogmas, encrusted with loyalties, prejudices, and racial aspirations'.[89] In such a polarized society, where history was 'still warm from the hands of zealots',[90] the individual's search for meaning and fulfilment, as depicted in the fiction of Bell, Janet McNeill (1907–94), Brian Moore (1921–99), and others, was, as Vance shows, often inseparable from the larger crisis of political identity that would tilt the province into full-scale civil conflict in the late 1960s.

FICTION IN THE MODERNIZING REPUBLIC AND THE TROUBLED NORTH

In Part V, 'Fiction in the Modernizing Republic and the Troubled North', critical attention shifts to the achievement of three major novelists from the Republic—John McGahern, Edna O'Brien, and John Banville, the last two of whom continue to publish critically acclaimed work—and to fiction by Northern Irish women writers composed during and after the Troubles, the eruption of which forced writers to re-evaluate their aesthetic choices and ideological suppositions. Born in the early 1930s and therefore lacking direct experience of the political turmoil that attended the foundation of the state, O'Brien and McGahern began their publishing careers in the early 1960s at a time when the Republic was embarking on a process of modernization that was at once belated, accelerated, and highly uneven in its effects. If, as Seamus Deane argues, 'the entity called Ireland had

---

[88] Richard Kirkland, *Cathal O'Byrne and the Northern Revival in Ireland, 1890–1960* (Liverpool: Liverpool University Press, 2006), 3.

[89] Sam Hanna Bell, 'A Banderol: An Introduction', in Sam Hanna Bell, Nesca A. Robb, and John Hewitt (eds), *The Arts in Ulster: A Symposium* (London: Harrap, 1951), 14.

[90] Ibid., 17.

somehow failed to appear'[91] in the fiction of the Revival novelists or in that of their immediate heirs, then the essence of that entity proved no less resistant to complex articulation for the first generation of post-independence novelists, whether it was a 1950s Ireland that, in McGahern's view, was 'a theocracy in all but name'[92] or its 1980s successor, a place of 'rampant individualism and localism dominating a vague, fragmented, often purely time-serving, national identity'.[93] In their attempts to render the manifold effects of the intellectually stifling atmosphere in which they came of age, McGahern and O'Brien both looked to Joyce as their lodestar. From him they derived artistic confidence and authority as young writers, McGahern responding powerfully to the dispassionate exactitude of *Dubliners*, O'Brien to *Ulysses*' taboo-breaking evocation of women's sexual and emotional lives. Yet neither writer relied solely on the instrument of Joycean realism 'to tear away the cloak of hypocrisy, the lies and cant that passed for truth'[94] in the poverty-stricken and Church-dominated rural locales that are the settings of their early novels. As critics have noted, O'Brien's searing realism 'is but a thin veneer covering an underlying symbolic structure, which dramatizes recurrent psychic patterns and processes',[95] while 'Mimetic tendencies are frequently formally complicated by symbolic or allegorical structures beneath the surface of McGahern's work.'[96]

The mythic patterning of mundane experience and the revelation of the emblematic through the particular are signal features of O'Brien's *The Country Girls* trilogy (1960–64) and McGahern's *The Dark* (1965), the furious Irish reception of which had punitive personal consequences for both writers. These seminal *Bildungsromane* established a predominant theme of their respective oeuvres: the individual's painful psychological struggle to break free from the limiting scripts of gender and sexuality in a repressive culture of shame and fear, to live according to the dictates of character rather than convention. In Chapter Sixteen, Jane Elizabeth Dougherty examines Edna O'Brien's representation of the toll this complicated emotional labour takes on the inner lives of youthful female protagonists who are by turns needy and bold. Dougherty's analysis of the dynamics of Irish female belatedness in O'Brien's work, career, and critical reception develops the hypothesis that her fictions 'present female characters whose maturation is in some way belated—repetitive, ambiguous, inconclusive—as a result of a profoundly disempowering iconicity that the culture foists upon them'. She goes on to show how the textual interchange between O'Brien and Joyce is more subtle than many critics have allowed, arguing that O'Brien's interweaving of his work with hers 'often functions not

---

[91]   Deane, *Strange Country*, 163.

[92]   John McGahern, *Memoir* (London: Faber and Faber, 2005), 210.

[93]   John McGahern, 'Dubliners', in *Love of the World: Essays*, ed. Stanley van der Ziel (London: Faber and Faber, 2009), 200.

[94]   Mike Murphy, 'Edna O'Brien', in Clíodhna Ní Anluain (ed.), *Reading the Future: Irish Writers in Conversation with Mike Murphy* (Dublin: Lilliput Press, 2000), 208.

[95]   Elke D'hoker, *Irish Women Writers and the Modern Short Story* (Basingstoke: Palgrave Macmillan, 2016), 147.

[96]   Aaron Kelly, *Twentieth-Century Irish Literature: A Reader's Guide to Essential Criticism* (Basingstoke: Palgrave Macmillan, 2008), 128.

merely as homage but also as critique, not only of Joyce but of male-authored fiction of female maturation more generally'.

The patriarchal paradigm of masculine power that O'Brien indicts in her fiction is also a foremost concern of McGahern's novels and short stories. Although the obstacles O'Brien's female characters must overcome to achieve a measure of self-worth in a structurally misogynistic society are more intractable than those faced by McGahern's male protagonists, the latter's victimization by the normative ideologies of gender is shown to have profound consequences for their identities and behaviour as youths and men. The damaged masculinities that populate his fiction are stark testaments to the degradations inflicted by the moralities of a hide-bound, censorious society, of which he wrote in 1991:

> The old fear of famine was confused with terror of damnation. The confusion and guilt and plain ignorance that surrounded sex turned men and women into exploiters and adversaries. Amid all this, the sad lusting after respectability, sugar-coated with sanctimoniousness and held together by a thin binding of religious doctrine and ceremony, combined to form a very dark and explosive force that, generally, went inwards.[97]

In Chapter Seventeen, Frank Shovlin traces the development of McGahern's critique of this failed state, finding that the novelist moved from scornful reproof to a kind of 'entente with Ireland', insofar as 'the jaundiced, sometimes embittered, portrait of the country found in the early fiction is replaced with something approaching acceptance, even sometimes admiration' in his final novel, *That They May Face the Rising Sun* (2002).

Despite being one of the most garlanded of contemporary novelists, John Banville's work has never quite fitted within a strictly Irish cultural framework, least of all within the lineage of realist fiction. While his artful prose is replete with Joycean and Beckettian traces, it eschews explicit engagement with the social, emotional, and ideological constraints that agitate the imaginations of Enda O'Brien, John McGahern, and other Irish novelists of the later twentieth century. Banville chooses instead to cultivate 'a special kind of persona, that of a "man of letters" who discriminates strongly between competing definitions of "great" art, a writer who uses interviews and reviews to proclaim the gospel of an art without attitude'.[98] Just as Banville himself has repeatedly resisted attempts to house his novels within the confines of a national tradition, many critics prefer to consider his fiction as late modernist or postmodernist in character, or as an Irish example of European counter-realism.[99] In Chapter Eighteen, Neil Murphy traverses several of these critical frames while arguing that Banville's work is, above all, a complex, embedded

---

[97] John McGahern, 'Introduction to *The Power of Darkness* [1991]', in *Love of the World*, 281–2.

[98] Joseph McMinn, 'Versions of Banville: Versions of Modernism', in Liam Harte and Michael Parker (eds), *Contemporary Irish Fiction: Themes, Tropes, Theories* (Basingstoke: Macmillan, 2000), 79.

[99] Banville has been particularly well served by his Irish critics. See, for example, Joseph McMinn, *The Supreme Fictions of John Banville* (Manchester: Manchester University Press, 1999); Derek Hand, *John Banville: Exploring Fictions* (Dublin: Liffey Press, 2002); John Kenny, *John Banville* (Dublin: Irish Academic Press, 2009); Mark O'Connell, *John Banville's Narcissistic Fictions* (Basingstoke: Palgrave Macmillan, 2013); and Neil Murphy, *John Banville* (Lewisburg, PA: Bucknell University Press, 2018).

discourse about the significance of art and the aesthetic pursuit of beauty, the defining feature of which is 'an extremely sophisticated form of self-reflexive novelistic practice'.

Murphy presents the case that Banville's fiction is an elaborate, coded account of his relationship with art in general, while also focusing on the deeply self-referential art-world that his novels create. In order to demonstrate how Banville's work has consistently sought to explore the relationship between the mysteries of aesthetic experience and the nature of being, Murphy examines his early engagements with metafiction in *Long Lankin* (1970), *Nightspawn* (1971), and *Birchwood* (1973); his erection of a complex set of scientific-artistic parallels in the science tetralogy of novels, *Doctor Copernicus* (1976), *Kepler* (1981), *The Newton Letter: An Interlude* (1982), and *Mefisto* (1986); his overt consideration of art in his Frames trilogy, which comprises *The Book of Evidence* (1989), *Ghosts* (1993), and *Athena* (1995); and his relentless fascination with the relationship between art and being in his post-2000 fiction, most notably in the Man Booker Prize-winning *The Sea* (2005), in which 'Banvillean narrative perspective becomes radically shaped and influenced by visual art'. In tracing a developmental trajectory across Banville's major novels, Murphy also shows how his primary aesthetic fascination finds expression in his translations of Heinrich von Kleist's plays and in the crime novels of Banville's alter ego, Benjamin Black.

The commitment to art over rhetoric that John Banville fastidiously maintains in his fiction could all too easily strike novelists in post-1969 Northern Ireland as an enviable, southern luxury. The perception of the North as a stagnant backwater that history had bypassed, 'a society characterized—in fiction as in everyday speech—as morbidly immutable',[100] was shattered by the recrudescence of political violence at the end of the 1960s. At a stroke, questions of nationhood, identity, territory, and displacement, and the role of the artist in their cultural negotiation, acquired a charged urgency. The aesthetic and ethical dilemmas presented by the horrors of sectarian killing elicited such a large and heterogeneous body of novelistic responses, encompassing romance plots, black farces, and feminist critiques, that by the 1980s Northern Ireland was arguably the world's most narrativized region, having become a fecund spawning ground for the so-called Troubles thriller, a subgenre that for the most part peddled risible stereotypes and perpetuated a reactionary view of the conflict as inherently irresolvable.[101] This generic diversity was not matched by formal inventiveness, however, at least not until the emergence of a younger generation of novelists in the late 1980s and early 1990s, some of whom were keen to harness the playful, ironic strategies of postmodernism to challenge engrained sectarian ideologies. However, Elmer Kennedy-Andrews rightly counsels against overestimating 'the transformative effect of postmodernism since most Troubles fiction, even that written in the '80s and '90s (with certain notable exceptions),

---

[100] Glenn Patterson, 'I am a Northern Irish Novelist', in Ian A. Bell (ed.), *Peripheral Visions: Images of Nationhood in Contemporary British Fiction* (Cardiff: University of Wales Press, 1995), 151.

[101] For a study of this literary phenomenon, see Aaron Kelly, *The Thriller and Northern Ireland since 1969: Utterly Resigned Terror* (Aldershot: Ashgate, 2005).

continues to adhere to a basically Realist aesthetic, though often incorporating elements of postmodernist style'.[102]

Much of the fiction examined by Caroline Magennis in Chapter Nineteen conforms to this pattern. She analyses works composed by Northern Irish women novelists and short story writers during two specific periods—the early-to-mid 1980s and the decade from 2006 to 2016—to ascertain how different generations of writers depict the impact of violence and brutality on women's bodies and minds. Magennis's findings temper expectations that the landmark changes that occurred in the political sphere in the interval between these two periods might be replicated in the realm of private experience. Soberingly, women's victimization by 'the intermeshed codes of patriarchy, misogyny, violent sectarianism, and the military response of the British state', which is such a persistent concern of writers such as Linda Anderson (1949–), Una Woods, Brenda Murphy (1954–), and Anne Devlin (1951–) in their 1980s fiction, cannot be confined to that particular historical moment. Rather, as Magennis demonstrates, similar concerns resurface in the twenty-first-century narratives of Bernie McGill (1967–), Lucy Caldwell (1981–), and Jan Carson (1980–), thus proving that 'the coercive force of patriarchal values and attitudes remains strong. And while the Troubles may be over, women's experience of male-dominated public spaces is still characterized by fear and trepidation.'

IRISH GENRE FICTION

The *Handbook*'s broadly chronological pattern is interrupted in Part VI, where the focus shifts to Irish crime fiction, science fiction, and children's fiction, categories of writing that, although historically under-considered and often dismissed as frivolous or unserious, include many works of impressive narrative and linguistic complexity. In gathering these chapters under the homogenizing rubric of 'genre fiction', I do so with caveats and reservations. It cannot go unnoticed that the category of 'literary' fiction is itself a genre, not all of whose practitioners axiomatically produce work of high quality, as is sometimes assumed. Nor should we forget John Frow's observation that genre is 'a universal dimension of textuality'[103] or John Mullan's point that 'Types of fiction do not constitute some set of pigeonholes into one of which every novel must fit. Sometimes only parts of a novel belong to a special type of writing.'[104] I am mindful, too, that by grouping these chapters in a discrete section I risk perpetuating the perceived ghettoization of these particular types of fiction, analysis of which is often confined to specialist collections and journals. Quarantining is not my intention, however, any more than it is the objective of the chapter authors. To the contrary, their analyses remind us of how porous are

---

[102] Elmer Kennedy-Andrews, *Fiction and the Northern Ireland Troubles since 1969: (De-)constructing the North* (Dublin: Four Courts Press, 2003), 9.

[103] John Frow, *Genre* (London: Routledge, 2006), 2.

[104] John Mullan, *How Novels Work* (Oxford: Oxford University Press, 2006), 108.

the divisions between different categories of fiction, at the same time as they deepen understandings of Irish fiction's diversity and the dynamic interactions between its component strands. So while this section's coverage extends at times to formulaic works that would fail traditional tests of 'literariness' and invite critical condescension,[105] it also features authors who, in reimagining aspects of the Irish past and present through a hypothetical or counterfactual lens, often imbue their writing with a stylistic sophistication and seriousness of purpose that engages readers at a deep intellectual level.

The popularity of contemporary Irish crime and mystery fiction is well recognized. Dubbed 'emerald *noir*' by some, this populous category, which feeds off the social disruption, greed, and corruption that attended Ireland's recent boom-and-bust economic development, embraces a wide variety of narrative types, from forensic thrillers and police procedurals to historical who-dunnits and even Gaelic *noir*. Crime narratives have long been part of Irish writing, however, as Ian Campbell Ross demonstrates in Chapter Twenty. From the early nineteenth century to the early twentieth, novelists and short story writers, including Gerald Griffin, Joseph Sheridan Le Fanu, Oscar Wilde, and Patrick Pearse, contributed to the emerging genre of crime fiction, as, after 1922, did Liam O'Flaherty (1897–1984) and Frank O'Connor. Yet these writers and their work have generally been subsumed into broader histories of Irish literature, while popular and influential crime writers such as L. T. Meade, M. McDonnell Bodkin (1850–1933), and Freeman Wills Crofts (1879–1957) have, conversely, been incorporated into assessments of 'English' crime fiction, their Irish identity ignored. A similar fate befell successors such as L. A. G. Strong (1896–1958) and Nicholas Blake, the pseudonym of Cecil Day-Lewis (1904–72). Only towards the end of the twentieth century and the beginning of the twenty-first, with the emergence of internationally acclaimed crime writers such as Ken Bruen (1951–), John Connolly (1968–), and Tana French (1973–), did notable commercial success stimulate critical engagement with Irish crime fiction as a distinctive body of writing. An engagement with the phenomenon of the Celtic Tiger, along with a prescient alertness to the Tiger's imminent demise, has been much noted by critics, boom-time Ireland having 'reproduced the social conditions that created crime fiction as a mass genre'.[106] This, however, as Ross shows, is but one feature of fiction more broadly characterized by remarkable thematic and stylistic flexibility and by varied geographical and chronological settings, in Ireland and beyond.

A comparable heterogeneity characterizes the rarely acknowledged seam of Irish fiction that deals in the narration of imaginative and speculative alternative worlds, many of which are set in the future. Jack Fennell's wide-ranging survey of this neglected tradition in Chapter Twenty-One begins with an argument for re-labelling Jonathan Swift's *Gulliver's Travels* and Samuel Madden's (1686–1765) *Memoirs of the Twentieth Century* (1733) as works of science fiction, after which he traces the impact of events from the Act

---

[105] For a recent example of the controversy that remarks about genre fiction can provoke, see Martin Doyle, 'Crime writers mystified by Colm Tóibín's criticism', *Irish Times*, 23 July 2019.

[106] Fintan O'Toole, 'From Chandler to the "Playboy" to the contemporary crime wave', *Irish Times*, 21 November 2009, 9.

of Union in 1800 to the establishment of the Irish Free State in 1922 on the alternative-world scenarios of novelists including Fitz-James O'Brien (1828–62), Robert Cromie (1855–1907), Charlotte McManus (1853–1944), and Art Ó Riain (1893–1968), the last of whom wrote under the pseudonym Barra Ó Caochlaigh. Insisting that 'the best science fiction does not dwell on technological gewgaws for their own sake but rather exploits their potential to address contemporary themes and concerns', Fennell charts the dominant anxieties that are registered by these authors, from the attenuation of the British Empire in unionist-inflected works to fears of a British recolonization of independent Ireland in those of a nationalist hue. More contemporary political and cultural concerns inform dystopian novels such as *The Bray House* (1990) by Eilís Ní Dhuibhne (1954–), *Dark Paradise* (1991) by Catherine Brophy (1941–), and *City of Bohane* (2011) by Kevin Barry (1969–), all of which fall within Fennell's purview. And just as Ross finds that much Irish crime fiction appropriates and Hibernicizes the styles and techniques of American hard-boiled detective fiction, Fennell concludes that Irish science fiction has largely 'limited itself to tackling Anglo-American tropes from an "authentically" Irish standpoint'.

Whereas the genres of science fiction and crime fiction still struggle to gain critical esteem, children's literature has in recent years become an established part of literary culture, a respected discipline within academia, and an essential component of a national literature. Significant strides have been made since the late 1990s in exploring the variety and complexity of modern Irish fiction for children and in elucidating the cultural contexts of its production.[107] A key contextual feature was highlighted by Emer O'Sullivan in 1997 when she noted that 'There is scarcely another European literature whose level of involvement in the production of reading matter for its young was so slight as Ireland's until the 1980s. Before then children's literature was almost exclusively imported, Irish children's reading material almost entirely British.'[108] The implications of this situation for the kinds of works read by Irish children, and the impact of the belated development of a native children's books industry, are among the topics addressed by Pádraic Whyte in Chapter Twenty-Two, in the course of his analysis of changing representations of home, land, and family life in touchstone works of Irish fiction for children and young readers since the late nineteenth century. Whyte first examines how the contrasting domestic spaces of the Big House and the peasant cottage act as pivotal sites for the promulgation and contestation of imperialist and nationalist ideologies in works by notable children's authors including L. T. Meade, Padraic Colum (1881–1972), Patricia Lynch (1898–1972), Maura Laverty (1907–66), and Eilís Dillon (1920–94). His focus then shifts to post-1970 works to determine how they utilize the motif of home to mediate the splintering of conventional family structures and the intrusion of malign forces that have made the recent experience of childhood in Ireland precarious and, for some, deeply traumatic. What emerges strongly from Whyte's analysis is how, far from being a sealed-off realm of

---

[107] See, for example, Valerie Coughlan and Keith O'Sullivan (eds), *Irish Children's Literature and Culture: New Perspectives on Contemporary Writing* (London: Routledge, 2011); Nancy Watson, *The Politics and Poetics of Irish Children's Literature* (Dublin: Irish Academic Press, 2009).

[108] Emer O'Sullivan, 'The Development of Modern Children's Literature in Late Twentieth-Century Ireland', *Signal* 81 (1996), 192.

innocence, childhood in Irish children's fiction has been continually framed and reframed by prevailing cultural discourses and ideological currents.

FACT INTO FICTION, FICTION INTO FILM

Part VII, 'Fact into Fiction, Fiction into Film', is concerned with the complex relation between history and its representation, with particular reference to the issues in play when Irish historical events are textualized in fictional narratives and fictional texts adapted for cinema and television. Chapters Twenty-Three and Twenty-Four are respectively concerned with novelists' literary imagining of two convulsive interconnected episodes in the nation's past, the Great Famine of the 1840s and the 1916 Easter Rising, both of which ushered in new social orders. As the commemorative activities surrounding the sesquicentennial of the Famine in 1995 and the centenary of the Rising in 2016 attested, these seismic events still possess richly ambivalent political and cultural afterlives, both in Ireland and in its British and North American diaspora.

Recent scholarship on literary expressions of the Famine has decisively overturned the durable identification of the calamity with novelistic silence.[109] As Marguérite Corporaal explains, although this national trauma was believed by many nineteenth-century writers to be 'too distressing to address explicitly' and 'unrepresentable in several respects',[110] this did not prevent a substantial corpus of Famine fiction taking shape from the mid-1840s onwards. This still-expanding corpus, which extends from Victorian-era novels that aspire to historically accurate representations of the Famine to texts influenced by the postmodern aesthetics of the so-called new historical fiction, is the subject of Melissa Fegan's critical scrutiny in Chapter Twenty-Three.[111] Fegan considers Irish novelists' persistent return to Famine themes and the different kinds of political agendas and cultural questions the reimagining of the catastrophe has attracted, from authors who thematized it while it was still a living memory to more recent novelists who examine the conjunction of the Great Hunger with other historical events and time frames. Her argument that 'Famine fiction frequently emerges at moments of conflict or change in the present' is most clearly demonstrated by the amount of post-Celtic Tiger fiction that invokes the cataclysm of the 1840s to express 'long-lasting fears about the precariousness of Irish modernity'.

[109] Notable works include Christopher Morash, *Writing the Irish Famine* (Oxford: Clarendon Press, 1995); Margaret Kelleher, *The Feminization of Famine: Expressions of the Inexpressible?* (Durham, NC: Duke University Press, 1997); Melissa Fegan, *Literature and the Irish Famine 1845–1919* (Oxford: Clarendon Press, 2002); and Marguérite Corporaal, *Relocated Memories: The Great Famine in Irish and Diaspora Fiction, 1846–1870* (Syracuse, NY: Syracuse University Press, 2017).

[110] Corporaal, *Relocated Memories*, 9.

[111] For a discussion of new historical fiction, see Martha T. Rozett, *Constructing a World: Shakespeare's England and the New Historical Fiction* (Albany, NY: State University of New York Press, 2003), 1–26.

Whereas the Famine was long thought to be the great aporia of modern Irish litera-ture, the Easter Rising has suffered the opposite fate. 'The whole event has been remorse-lessly textualized', claimed Declan Kiberd in 1995, 'for it—more than any of its individual protagonists—became an instantaneous martyr to literature.'[112] This is an argument that, as John Brannigan points out, 'alludes not just to the transformation of the Rising into theatre, poetry, spectacle, narrative and myth but also to the already textual nature of the Rising itself', its having been 'pieced together from the texts of ancient Irish folk-lore and mythology' to become 'the great, shocking text of Irish modernism'.[113] The transformation of the Rising into fiction is the theme taken up in Chapter Twenty-Four by Laura O'Connor, for whom it is of significant critical import that the most prominent literature of 1916 is not fiction but rather poetry and plays. These genres exerted a forma-tive influence on the ideological underpinnings of the Rising, and, as Yeats's 'Easter, 1916' cannily anticipates, the symbolic capital of the 'poets' rebellion' secured a privileged role for poetry and drama in subsequent commemorative literature. By contrast, to depict the Rising as 'fictional', and by extension to take artistic licence with historical fact, risks censure for distorting or denying the historicity of the week-long rebellion and ques-tioning the authority of 'history' as we know it. O'Connor explores this hazardous ter-rain by contextualizing 1916 fiction in relation to 'the Story of Ireland', a term adopted by historian Roy Foster to depict a master narrative of Irish historiography. Drawing on a wide gamut of Irish- and non-Irish-authored works, from those written soon after the Rising, before the event became indelibly coloured by Civil War politics, to recent mil-lennial fiction, O'Connor traces the ways in which both the cultural memory of the insurrection and 'the Story of Ireland' have been shaped and reshaped in a continuous dialogue with fictional and factual approaches.

The reshaping of fictional texts for the screen is the subject of Kevin Rockett's analysis in Chapter Twenty-Five, in which he addresses defining aspects of the adaptation of Irish literary fiction during the past century. From the single-reel historical drama, *Rory O'More* (1911), to the Oscar-nominated *Brooklyn* (2015), Irish fiction has supplied national and international cinema with a plethora of well-crafted stories that have become the basis for critically and commercially successful films. Cinema has in turn inspired successive generations of Irish novelists—several of whom have written specif-ically for the large or small screen—and provided them with a variety of narrative tech-niques and structuring devices. Indeed, a recurring debate within Irish film studies centres on whether literature has featured *too* prominently in the output of Irish cinema at the expense of original screenplays.

Yet Ireland is not unique in the influence literary fiction has on its cinematic profile. What perhaps distinguishes the canon of Irish literary cinema is the frequency with which such adaptations have engaged with key historical, social, and cultural processes.

[112] Declan Kiberd, *Inventing Ireland: The Literature of the Modern Nation* (London: Jonathan Cape, 1995), 213.
[113] John Brannigan, '"The Battle for the GPO": Literary Revisionism in Roddy Doyle's *A Star Called Henry* and Jamie O'Neill's *At Swim, Two Boys*', in Munira H. Mutran and Laura P. Z. Izarra (eds), *Kaleidoscopic Views of Ireland* (São Paulo: Humanitas/FFLCH/USP, 2003), 118–19.

Whether it was the cinematic recasting of the Famine on the eve of the War of Independence (*Knocknagow*, 1918) or the diverse reflections on that conflict in subsequent films (*Guests of the Nation* and *The Informer*, both 1935), adaptations have contributed to often uncomfortable national debates. The shift from grand historical epics to more intimate, psychologically explorative narratives is a feature of adaptations from the 1960s onwards, as exemplified by the filmed versions, in 1964 and 1983 respectively, of Enda O'Brien's *The Lonely Girl* (1962) and *The Country Girls* (1960). Film has also inserted itself into many novels, from the influence of cinematic form on Joyce's *Ulysses*, to the erotic adventures in a Dublin cinema of Liam O'Flaherty's Mr Gilhooley in his 1926 novel of that name, to the role Cold War science fiction films play in the psychological unravelling of Francie Brady in Neil Jordan's 1997 adaptation of Patrick McCabe's *The Butcher Boy*. As Rockett demonstrates, the image of Ireland on screen cannot be separated from its fictional canon, while many novels are unimaginable without the cinema, which, we should remember, was itself regarded as a form of writing by its earliest practitioners and audiences.[114]

CROSSINGS AND CROSSCURRENTS

Processes of adaptation and transference are also central to the chapters in Part VIII, 'Crossings and Crosscurrents', which interrogate the connections between collective and individual forms of identity and experiences of migrancy and transnationalism. The writer Blake Morrison's observation that 'To "belong" in Ireland is to leave'[115] pithily encapsulates the deeply engrained importance of migration and diaspora to Irish culture, society, and self-understanding across many centuries. Wherever we fix the pin on the map we find evidence of upheaval and dispersal, both before and after the nation-defining decade of the Famine and its mass migrations, right up to the cultural reclamation of Ireland's worldwide diasporic communities in the 1990s, which coincided with the Republic becoming a country of net immigration by the turn of the millennium. Joyce himself stands before us as the archetype of the restless artist in exile, advocate and exemplar of the view that emigration can be a portal to greater understanding of one's self and one's homeland. This is crystallized towards the end of *A Portrait*, when Stephen Dedalus records in his diary a conversation he had with his friend Davin shortly before he himself departed Dublin. In it, Stephen cryptically notes that truth is better grasped at a distance, thus placing premium value on the sharpened perspectives that geographical dislocation bestows: '3 *April*: Met Davin at the cigar shop opposite Findlater's

---

[114] David Trotter and Andrew Shail, 'Cinema and the Novel', in Parrinder and Gąsiorek (eds), *The Oxford History of the Novel in English, Volume 4*, 372.

[115] Blake Morrison, *Things My Mother Never Told Me* (London: Chatto and Windus, 2002), 71.

church. He was in a black sweater and had a hurleystick. Asked me was it true I was going away and why. Told him the shortest way to Tara is via Holyhead.'[116]

Whereas the link between voluntary expatriation and creative insight was central to Joyce's self-mythologization, those writers who have had exile foisted upon them by economic privation have often drawn inspiration from the all-too-real anguish and alienation engendered by the ruptures of displacement, while others have fashioned protagonists who revel in their escape from the trammels of social and religious conformism at home. The importance of place of settlement, social class, gender, and generational specificity to the types of emigration narrative writers create is attested by the significant variations that characterize the bodies of fiction produced in different parts of 'our greater Ireland beyond the sea.'[117] For example, the phenomenon of 'ethnicity as liberating doubleness' that Charles Fanning identifies as being 'one of the most valuable accomplishments of contemporary Irish-American writers'[118] is a much less prominent feature of the fiction of Irish and Irish-descended writers in contemporary Britain, a good deal of which expresses a diasporic sensibility akin to that described by the British-based Caribbean-born intellectual Stuart Hall, who spoke of 'belonging to more than one world, of being both "here" and "there", of thinking about "there" from "here" and vice versa; of being "at home"—but never wholly—in both places, neither fundamentally the same, nor totally different.'[119]

In Chapter Twenty-Six, Tony Murray examines the ways in which novelists and short story writers have mediated what has historically been the most politically problematic of all Irish emigrant journeys, the crossing to England. One measure (and legacy) of this difficult history is the absence of an accepted designation for the body of fiction that Murray discusses. Whereas the terms 'Irish-American' and 'Irish-Australian' have long since achieved normalized usage, the questionable legitimacy of 'Irish-English' and 'Irish-British' as literary or cultural categories is habitually signalled by the use of quotation marks. As Eamonn Hughes has noted, this semantic crux derives from the countries' acrimonious history and has 'led to a sense that "Irish-Britain" is not and may never be a satisfactory label in the way that "Black-British" or "Asian-British" are, even if only for pragmatic reasons'.[120] This terminological deficit has been compounded by the critical neglect, until very recently, of a fictional corpus that contains a wide spectrum of literary styles and sensibilities, and includes many works that explore emigrants' literal and metaphorical search for accommodation.[121] In his analysis of two centuries of

---

[116] Joyce, *A Portrait of the Artist as a Young Man*, 273.

[117] Joyce, *Ulysses*, 427.

[118] Charles Fanning, *The Irish Voice in America: 250 Years of Irish-American Fiction* (Lexington, KY: University of Kentucky Press, 2000), 378.

[119] Stuart Hall with Bill Schwarz, *Familiar Stranger: A Life Between Two Islands* (London: Penguin, 2017), 140.

[120] Eamonn Hughes, ' "Lancelot's Position": The Fiction of Irish-Britain', in A. Robert Lee (ed.), *Other Britain, Other British: Contemporary Multicultural Fiction* (London: Pluto Press, 1995), 143.

[121] Murray's *London Irish Fictions: Narrative, Diaspora and Identity* (Liverpool: Liverpool University Press, 2012) is one of two recent monographs that have begun to address this neglect, the other being Whitney Standlee's aforementioned *'Power to Observe': Irish Women Novelists in Britain, 1890–1916*.

fiction by English-domiciled writers of Irish birth and descent, Murray tracks a line of development from 'work with a predominantly public-facing and sometimes didactic motivation', such as that written by Maria Edgeworth and other early nineteenth-century Anglo-Irish novelists, to contemporary migration-themed novels by Edna O'Brien, Leland Bardwell (1922–2016), and Eimear McBride that are 'primarily inward-looking and psychological in complexion'. In mapping the evolution of this tradition through to the present day, Murray notes the emergence of recent novels that, by addressing the experience of mixed-race Irishness in multicultural English cities, chart a fresh course within the subgenre of Irish multigenerational fiction.

A different web of cultural, political, and linguistic interactions within the British and Irish archipelago forms the backdrop for Stefanie Lehner's discussion of shifting cross-currents in contemporary Irish and Scottish fiction in Chapter Twenty-Seven. The confluence of several interrelated developments in recent decades informs this chapter's rationale: the increasing interest in the historical, political, and economic synergies between Scotland, Northern Ireland, and the Republic of Ireland; the evolving devolutionary political frameworks in Northern Ireland and Scotland since the late 1990s; the rise of Irish-Scottish studies as a distinct inter-discipline (itself a devolutionary act); the ongoing application of archipelagic paradigms to cultural practices on these islands; and, last but not least, the remarkable literary renaissance that has occurred in Ireland and Scotland since the late 1980s, particularly in the area of prose fiction. Whereas contemporary Scottish culture has been commonly seen as a surrogate for political autonomy, recent Irish and Northern Irish literature has been framed against debates about how to deal with troublesome national and local histories. At the same time, all three polities have witnessed the renegotiation of presiding constructions of national culture under the pressure of far-reaching constitutional, political, and socio-economic change. Lehner argues that the work of the post-1980 generations of Irish, Northern Irish, and Scottish novelists addresses concerns that transgress and exceed national borders and forge provocative cross-border affiliations. Interpreting devolution not only as a function of territorial politics but as 'a process of transition that concerns the personal spaces in Scotland and both parts of Ireland', she provides detailed readings of nine indicative works of Irish and Scottish fiction that 'establish *affiliations* that counter their *filiative* containment within national paradigms'.

Like their emigrant cousins in Britain, cultural definition for Irish Americans has long been a problematic affair, the narrative representation of which has produced a distinctive set of enduring characteristics in Irish-American fiction, a corpus that, despite its variousness and vibrancy, is too often ignored within the field of Irish literary studies. As a contribution to redressing this neglect, Sally Barr Ebest in Chapter Twenty-Eight examines one particular seam of this tradition, post-war Irish-American domestic novels, the most notable characteristics of which are 'an overwhelming desire for assimilation on the part of their protagonists, a move away from religious and clerical themes, and a growing preoccupation with sex and sexuality as it pertains to the rights of women and LGBTQ (lesbian, gay, bisexual, transgender, and queer) people, and the wrongs perpetrated against them'. Ebest's chapter serves as a corrective to categorizations of

Irish-American literature that have had the effect of excluding from the canon female-authored novels about private lives, whose characters are often Catholic women. A less schematic approach, such as Ebest adopts, reveals a more fluid picture. Although some of the best-known novels by Irish-American male writers have focused on themes of violence, war, and masculinity, an equal number of lesser-known works recount stories of intimate relationships, sexual longing, and family dysfunction. Similarly, while the majority of female writers choose domestic settings, their novels often include scenes of turbulence and conflict as well. Gender difference notwithstanding, Ebest argues that Irish-American domestic fiction by, among others, Maeve Brennan (1917–93), Mary McCarthy (1912–89), and Alice McDermott (1953–), 'paint realistic portraits of their ethnic communities, debunk the myth of the sainted matriarch, commiserate with their self-immolated daughters, and reveal the ways in which marginalized groups and individuals have been silenced by society, politics, and religion'.

Whereas Ebest seeks to modify the critical lens through which the fiction of Irish America is viewed, Sinéad Moynihan argues for a more radical revisioning of the domain of Irish transnational fiction in Chapter Twenty-Nine. Taking her bearings from the emergent field of transatlantic literary studies, Moynihan purposefully sets out 'to dislodge Irish America as the dominant referent in discussions of Irish transnationalism and investigate a substantial tradition that positions Spain as an important space in the Irish transnational imagination'. She does this by teasing out the network of textual and thematic reverberations between three novels in particular: *Mary Lavelle* (1936) by Kate O'Brien (1897–1974), *No More Than Human* (1944) by Maura Laverty, and Colm Tóibín's *Brooklyn* (2009). In addition to paying close attention to these novels' explicit engagements with cis-Atlantic geography, Moynihan productively draws on recent work in queer diaspora studies to interrogate the connections between national identity, migration, gender, and sexuality in each text. If, as Anne-Marie Fortier claims, queer configurations of home as a site that is 'always in the making, endlessly deferred' suggest 'a radical discomfiture of the idea of "home" as a space of coherence and continuity',[122] then, as Moynihan shows, Irish transnational fictions of Spain encourage readers to rethink the heteronormative 'grand narrative' of Irish, and Irish-American, literary and cultural relations.

CONTEMPORARY IRISH FICTION

In seeking to map developments in Irish fictional practice over the past three decades or so, Part IX of this *Handbook*, 'Contemporary Irish Fiction', critically examines the role of the novel and short story in mediating the accelerated changes that have taken place across the island under the pressures of intersecting local and global forces. As such, the

---

[122] Anne-Marie Fortier, 'Queer Diasporas', in Diane Richardson and Steven Seidman (eds), *Handbook of Lesbian and Gay Studies* (London: Sage, 2002), 189.

section is shadowed by the problem that Peter Boxall identifies as besetting 'all efforts to capture the contemporary: that is, that the time we are living through is very difficult to bring into focus, and often only becomes legible in retrospect'.[123] Not that this temporal limitation has deterred scholars and commentators from producing a plethora of analyses of the nature, meaning, and impact of the multifaceted changes in the cultures and societies of the Irish Republic and Northern Ireland since the early 1990s, to which the chapters assembled here contribute.

Certain social and political developments necessarily feature prominently in each contributor's analysis. Critical appraisals of this era have already taken shape around two phenomena that have assumed epochal status because they have materially altered the course of subsequent history: the Republic's emergence as one of the most globalized counties in the world by the early 2000s and the North's transition from a thirty-year civil conflict to a negotiated political settlement. The epicentre of the economic resurgence that transfigured Irish society (albeit unevenly) in the period between the mid-1990s and 2008 was Dublin. Here, in Joyce's great word-city, the boom-fuelled material, behavioural, and attitudinal changes were experienced in concentrated form. Yet this was only the latest 'new' Dublin to be recast and remoulded by precipitous change, and it, like its predecessors, presented novelists with potent representational challenges and opportunities. In Chapter Thirty, Derek Hand argues that 'The inherent instability and malleability of the novel form made it a particularly suitable vehicle for capturing this moment of transformation, ambivalence, and contradiction, and for giving expression to the anxieties that perplexed many Dubliners during this unprecedented period in the history of their city and country.' He examines how novelists including Roddy Doyle, Paul Murray (1975–), Deirdre Madden (1960–), and Anne Enright refracted the shifting social and spatial contours of the capital during and after the years of economic expansion, finding in their work a deconstructive energy that replaces 'monolithic views of the city's history and its meaning' with visions of Dublin as a plural, fluid space, 'a work in progress where the evolving combinations of the local and global present fresh challenges to those who live and work there'.

The certainty with which one can date the start of the calamitous financial crisis that abruptly silenced the Celtic Tiger's roar—the spotlight falls on a 'panicked all-night meeting'[124] of 29–30 September 2008, at which the government was forced to agree to a multi-billion euro recapitalization of the insolvent domestic banking sector—is harder to replicate when it comes to identifying when exactly Northern Ireland became a 'post-conflict' society. This may seem ironic, given that the Troubles were formally ended by an international peace treaty signed in Belfast on Good Friday, April 1998 and ratified by simultaneous referenda in both parts of Ireland in May. Yet the single worst incident in

---

[123] Peter Boxall, *Twenty-First-Century Fiction: A Critical Introduction* (Cambridge: Cambridge University Press, 2013), 1.

[124] Blanaid Clarke and Niamh Hardiman, 'Ireland: Crisis in the Irish Banking System', in Suzanne J. Konzelmann and Marc Fovargue-Davies (eds), *Banking Systems in the Crisis: The Faces of Liberal Capitalism* (London: Routledge, 2013), 107.

the history of the conflict occurred within three months of these watershed develop-ments, when twenty-nine people were killed by a bomb in Omagh, County Tyrone planted by dissident republicans opposed to the accord. This and subsequent, less bar-barous events tempered sanguine narratives of radical socio-political transformation and suggested instead that the inertia of protracted conflict would be replaced by the dynamics of protracted transition.

A sensitivity towards such complexities informs Fiona McCann's survey in Chapter Thirty-One of Northern Irish fiction published in or after 1998, a body of writing that, as she acknowledges, calls into question the accuracy of the designation 'post-Troubles', given that all of her chosen authors 'engage to some extent with the violent past and its ongoing legacies in a still deeply divided society'. Drawing on the theories of French philosopher Jacques Rancière, McCann investigates the means by which long- and short-form fiction by four Northern Irish writers (Glenn Patterson (1961–), Anna Burns (1962–), Mark Mulholland, and Jan Carson) and one from the border town of Clones (Patrick McCabe) exploit a range of 'dissensual' approaches to interrupt and disrupt established ways of seeing Northern society, whether by unsettling entrenched patterns of division or undercutting fixed assumptions about identity. The challenge facing these and other novelists of the post-Troubles (and imminently post-Brexit) dispensation is to imagine, without descending into blunt polemic, alternative narratives of belonging amid the stark, continuing realities of religious sectarianism and systemic social inequality.

The struggle against the stigmatization of homosexuality and gay people in Irish society has forced many contemporary gay and lesbian writers to voice criticisms and critiques that are no less dissensual than those expressed in the works discussed by McCann. Although homosexual themes and homoerotic desires have long inhabited the Irish novel, albeit often in oblique and liminal ways, it was not until the closing years of the twentieth century that fictional representations of same-sex desire began to proliferate, many of them written by gay-identified authors. After the decriminalization of male homosexuality in the Irish Republic in 1993, and the consolidation of the lesbian and gay movement that had been taking shape since the 1970s, a new generation of avowedly queer authors emerged to create a distinctively Irish strain of the les-bian and gay novel, the evolution of which Michael G. Cronin tracks in Chapter Thirty-Two.

Cronin's analysis centres on two plot types, the temporal and the spatial, the first of which is the more common and takes several forms. One is the coming-out novel, in which the arc of the narrative usually follows the contours of individual biography. Among the examples Cronin discusses are works by Tom Lennon, Mary Dorcey (1950–), Emma Donoghue (1969–), and Jarlath Gregory (1978–). A second form, exemplified in fiction by Colm Tóibín and Keith Ridgway (1965–), positions lesbian and gay characters within a generational family narrative that is woven into the national narrative. In addition, authors such as Donoghue, Jamie O'Neill (1962–), and Denis Kehoe (1978–) use the historical romance genre to imaginatively create an archaeology of same-sex desires.

Cronin's survey concludes with an examination of novels by Ridgway, Micheál Ó Conghaile (1962–), and Barry McCrea (1974–), whose plots are organized spatially rather than temporally and are notable for their incorporation of non-realist tropes within a realist frame. His analysis demonstrates how contemporary Irish gay and lesbian fiction provides an imaginative space in which to reflect on the diversity of queer identities and experiences, while at the same time grappling with the unfulfilled promise of sexual freedom in the time of late capitalism. At its best, Cronin argues, this fictional strand illuminates a utopian desire to create a transformed future, a desire that the present generation calls queer and which an earlier one called liberation.

The inclusion in Cronin's chapter of Micheál Ó Conghaile's debut novel, *Sna Fir* (Among Men, 1999), which delves into the experiences of a young gay man from the Connemara Gaeltacht, serves as a reminder that the transformative journey undertaken by Irish queer fiction in recent decades bears similarities to that taken by fiction in the Irish language. A willingness on the part of Irish-language novelists to engage with sexual and social topics formerly considered taboo was already in evidence by the time Ó Conghaile published his first gay-themed short story in the late 1980s, which, he recalled, was met with 'outrage in certain sections of society which referred to it as *brocamas* or dirt. Ireland and Conamara have come a long way since then, of course, but not without pain and suffering.'[125] In Chapter Thirty-Three, Pádraig Ó Siadhail takes stock of the distance travelled during this period by the novel in Irish, which he deems to be 'as heterogeneous in its genres, themes, narrative styles, and settings as its equivalents in world literature', despite the challenges of writing in an endangered language with a small readership and declining literacy standards.

Ó Siadhail begins by examining the contrasting fortunes of novelists who emerged in the 1970s and 1980s, notably Breandán Ó hEithir (1930–90) and Séamas Mac Annaidh (1961–), who sought to escape the shadow of Máirtín Ó Cadhain, whose death in 1970 deprived Irish-language fiction of its most accomplished voice. Noting that 'a central feature of contemporary fiction in Irish is the issue of language itself', he goes on to discuss the work of Pádraig Standún (1946–) and Alan Titley, leading exponents of the two main strands of modern fiction in Irish, the popular and the literary. The achievement of writers who have worked athwart these strands, such as Diarmaid Ó Gráinne (1950–2013) and Pádraic Breathnach (1942–), is also considered, as are other recent trends, including the appearance of the popular Gaelic *noir* subgenre; the emergence of the transnational novel, whose exponents include Ó Siadhail himself; the paucity of Irish-language comic fiction; the relative scarcity of women novelists; the rise to prominence of the historical novel; and the evolution of experimental Irish-language fiction. Given that there have been, in Ó Siadhail's words, 'almost as many Irish-language novels published in the last quarter century as in the previous 100 years', unevenness of quality is to be expected. Yet this creative bourgeoning also signifies that the Irish-language novel is on 'as tentatively

---

[125] Cited in Pádraig Ó Siadhail, 'Odd Man Out: Micheál Ó Conghaile and Contemporary Irish Language Queer Prose', *Canadian Journal of Irish Studies. Special Issue: Queering Ireland* 36, no. 1 (2010), 144–5.

secure a footing as any lesser-used language can hope to be in order to cater to its diverse readership'.

Unsurprisingly, certain of the trends and themes that Cronin and Ó Siadhail identify as integral to the development of contemporary queer and Irish-language fiction reappear in Susan Cahill's survey in Chapter Thirty-Four of twenty-first-century fiction by writers from the Republic. In a period marked by 'an extraordinary renaissance in Irish fiction, featuring novels that are stylistically experimental, ethically engaged, and pointed in their social, cultural, and political critiques', the impetus towards diversification and democratization has been pronounced. Novelists' determination to envision a more pluralist and humane vision of Irish society has, Cahill argues, led to a growing desire 'to make room for the marginalized, the silenced, the alienated, and the discriminated against, including those whose voices and experiences have been elided from standard accounts of the nation's past'. While the revisioning of the master narratives of national history is neither a new nor a uniquely Irish phenomenon—Boxall notes that the post-war English novel 'has returned obsessively to the question of the mutability of the past'[126]—novelists' larger project of engendering a fresh collective self-understanding in a time of previously unimaginable change has produced distinctive fictional responses to acute crises, from Donal Ryan's (1977–) evocation of the devastating human cost of the post-2008 economic recession in *The Spinning Heart* (2012) to the humane environmentalism of Sara Baume's (1984-) *Spill Simmer Falter Wither* (2015). Cahill is especially appreciative of the achievements of post-millennial Irish women novelists, particularly those whose feminism has powered some of the most stinging critiques of the inequities of neoliberal capitalism and inspired them to articulate previously hidden aspects of women's experience.

CRITICAL EVALUATIONS

This *Handbook* concludes with an evaluation by Eve Patten of the role and significance of the Irish novelist as critic and anthologist over the past century. From Katharine Tynan (1859–1931) to Anne Enright, Irish novelists and short story writers have used the acts of literary criticism and anthology compiling to serve various ends, whether it be to proclaim an artistic credo, assemble a literary inheritance, stake out an aesthetic position, intervene in cultural debate, or contribute to the making and unmaking of literary reputations. Yet one has only to browse the essays and reviews of Elizabeth Bowen or John McGahern, for instance, to appreciate that literary criticism is also, more fundamentally, 'a creative activity in its own right—a writer's way of describing how other writers handle language and what it is that makes them unique'.[127] Novelists' evaluative

---

[126] Boxall, *Twenty-First-Century Fiction*, 46.
[127] Al Alvarez, *The Writer's Voice* (London: Bloomsbury, 2005), 10.

discriminations as critics and anthologists are therefore not only revealing of their literary politics but also cast light on their own practice as writers.

Alert to these contexts, and attentive to the intersecting vectors of literary inheritance and theoretical subtext, Patten examines the ways in which writers have positioned themselves, through the content of their fiction and critical writing, in relation to Irish traditions of the novel and the short story, particularly the problematic social realist tradition. Her focus falls on two countervailing trends in the literary-critical discourse: on one side, a long-standing 'strategic scepticism towards the novel tradition, even as that tradition flourished on an international stage', and on the other, 'the positive consolidation of an Irish fictional lineage' spearheaded by the publication of influential anthologies of Irish fiction in 1993 and 1999 by Dermot Bolger (1959–) and Colm Tóibín respectively. Patten postulates that while each editor pursued a distinctive agenda—Bolger advancing the cause of a new urban realist aesthetic, Tóibín foregrounding novelists' capacity to work creatively with domestic and cosmopolitan influences—the combined effect of their interventions has been to refocus attention on the Irish novel's dynamic responsiveness to changing conditions and place the Irish novelist 'firmly at the political and cultural vanguard of the changing nation'.

By reminding us of the novel's protean character and inherent ability to accommodate a seemingly limitless plurality of voices, perspectives, and experiences, Eve Patten's concluding remarks obliquely echo those made by Thomas Kilroy almost fifty years ago, when he said of the two novelists who interested him most at that time, Aidan Higgins (1927–2015) and John Banville, that 'Their achievement, whatever its merits, is a kind of freedom for the future. And the future is open.'[128] Now as then, all we can hazard with any certainty about the future is that its unknowable possibilities will stimulate Irish novelists, yet again, to renew the art of the new and distinguish themselves in a literary form that, as Mikhail Bakhtin insisted, has always been fortified by the disparate and capricious energies of the contemporary moment: 'The novel comes into contact with the spontaneity of the inconclusive present; this is what keeps the genre from congealing. The novelist is drawn toward everything that is not yet completed.'[129] It is entirely conceivable that many, if not most, of Ireland's future novelists and short story writers will continue to find in inherited fictional modes an effective means of posing fundamental questions about truth, identity, and existence that reach across generations. It is no less plausible that others will wish to unseat convention or seek out alternative ways of approaching through language the mysteries of the inconclusive present and the unquiet past. As I conclude this essay in July 2019, recent examples of these differing approaches lie on my desk. I select two from the pile, both published inside the last

---

[128] Kilroy, 'Tellers of Tales', 302.
[129] Mikhail Bakhtin, *The Dialogic Imagination*, 27.

twelve months, and briefly consider what they might portend for the future of Irish fiction.

Sally Rooney's (1991–) multi-award-winning second novel, *Normal People* (2018), explores the individual psychologies and fluctuating relationship of two young millennials who come of age in post-boom Ireland. This same cultural moment forms the backdrop to *This Hostel Life* (2018), a slim volume of short stories by Nigerian-born Melatu Uche Okorie (1975–), who arrived in Ireland as an asylum seeker in 2006. These stories, which provide snapshots of the Irish lives of immigrant African women, are framed, in a manner that recalls *Castle Rackrent*, by an author's preface and a contextualizing essay by a legal scholar. *Normal People* bears many of the hallmarks of conventional realism, including a traditional narrative form, transparent prose, and linear third-person narration by a voice that offers searching character insights—qualities that would not be out of place in a Victorian realist classic. Indeed, Rooney signals her literary orientation through an epigraph from George Eliot's *Daniel Deronda* (1876), which brings with it a tacit assurance that *Normal People* will not attempt to alter conceptions of what a novel is or how it achieves its effects but will rather draw instructive inspiration from canonical antecedents. By contrast, Okorie's title story displays a striking linguistic inventiveness. A polyphony of voices, previously unheard in the Irish short story, speak a patois that blends African dialects with standard and colloquial English, thus plunging the reader into a milieu that Frank O'Connor would readily recognize as that of a 'submerged population group': asylum seekers confined within the Republic's Direct Provision system. Despite its strong tang of authenticity, the author has explained that her characters' idiom 'is a completely made up one', created from 'a mixture of Englishes'.[130] Expressing themselves in this invented tongue, Okorie's asylum seekers speak powerfully of the legal injustices and intimate humiliations they must endure, screened from public view, in a twenty-first-century Ireland that likes to think of itself as liberal and progressive.

The acclaim afforded *Normal People* has consolidated Sally Rooney's meteoric rise to the status of 'the first great millennial author', a 'Salinger for the Snapchat generation', a 'Jane Austen for the precariat'.[131] The significance of Melatu Uche Okorie's work is also beginning to be recognized, albeit on a more modest scale; certainly, the publication of *This Hostel Life* marks an important milestone in the emergence of a black Irish fiction.[132] As contrasting examples of how contemporary authors appropriate and adapt fictional forms and generic conventions to accommodate the telling of new and untold stories, *Normal People* and *This Hostel Life* suggest two of the many possible trajectories of the Irish novel and short story in the twenty-first century and beyond. We cannot

---

[130] Sara Martín-Ruiz, 'Melatu Okorie: An Introduction to her Work and a Conversation with the Author', *LIT: Literature Interpretation Theory* 28, no. 2 (2017), 181.

[131] Sian Cain, 'At last, a gifted literary voice for a generation', *Guardian*, 5 September 2018, 5.

[132] In addition to attracting praise from Sebastian Barry, Roddy Doyle, and others, *This Hostel Life* was shortlisted for a 2018 Irish Book Award in the Newcomer of the Year category.

second-guess the future, but if history is any guide, we might reasonably expect Irish fiction in the coming years to be characterized by an enlivening panorama of meditations on cultural change and shifts in personal and social identity; the posing of newly disruptive questions about the perplexities of nationality, gender, sexuality, religious belief, and other markers of difference; the display of powerful moral insights into the fluctuating psychic rhythms of life in Ireland and elsewhere; an ever-widening diversity of theme and subject matter; greater formal, linguistic, and stylistic adventurousness in both traditional and electronic formats—and a constant capacity to surprise as well as to delight.

PART II

NINETEENTH-CENTURY CONTEXTS AND LEGACIES

CHAPTER 2

··

IRISH GOTHIC FICTION

··

JARLATH KILLEEN

IN 1887, Oscar Wilde (1854–1900) tried to give the Gothic a decent send off in his amusing short story, 'The Canterville Ghost'. The plot concerns the misadventures of Sir Simon de Canterville who has haunted Canterville Chase since 1584 and has a proud reputation as a great spectral performer. At one point he nostalgically recalls his many triumphs on the phantasmal stage over a 'brilliant and uninterrupted career of three hundred years', reminiscing with 'the enthusiastic egotism of the true artist' about 'his last appearance as "Red Reuben, or the Strangled Babe", his *début* as "Gaunt Gideon, the Blood-sucker of Bexley Moor", and the *furore* he had excited one lovely June evening by merely playing ninepins with his own bones upon the lawn-tennis ground'.[1] Sir Simon is a kind of one-man Gothic show, able to perform the standard monsters of the tradition (the ghost, the vampire, the animated skeleton, the poltergeist) with the aplomb of a ham actor. However, while he was certainly effective enough in his time, he is apparently completely out of date at the end of the nineteenth century. So outmoded is Sir Simon, and the genre he represents, that when the Chase is purchased by the American Otis family they do not believe he could possibly exist.

Ghosts had been banished before, of course, declared impossible at the time of the Reformation, which, as Peter Marshall explains, was 'virtually predicated on an absolute rejection of the assumption that had granted space to ghosts and ghost stories in medieval Christianity',[2] with the reformers insisting that after death souls went either to heaven or hell, and did not hang around to pester the living. Ghosts, in short, were something believed in only by the feebleminded and the superstitious—code words for Catholics. While the Otises are indeed Episcopalians, though, they dismiss ghosts on pragmatic rather than theological grounds. As Mr Otis explains when purchasing the Chase, 'I come from a modern country, where we have everything that money can

---

[1] Oscar Wilde, 'The Canterville Ghost', in *The Complete Works of Oscar Wilde, Volume VIII: The Short Fiction*, ed. Ian Small (Oxford: Oxford University Press, 2017), 87.

[2] Peter Marshall, 'The Ghost Story in Post-Reformation England', in Helen Conrad O'Briain and Julie Anne Stevens (eds), *The Ghost Story from the Middle Ages to the Twentieth Century* (Dublin: Four Courts Press, 2010), 20.

buy…I reckon that if there were such a thing as a ghost in Europe, we'd have it at home in a very short time in one of our public museums.'[3] Notwithstanding Sir Simon's best attempts to scare the Otis family, and despite his reactivation of as many of the old Gothic conventions as he can remember, he ends up being more frightened by them than they are of him, as they relentlessly pursue him and his corny props with a variety of up-to-the-minute gizmos, gadgets, and lotions, such as Pinkerton's Champion Stain Remover (to clean a bloodstained carpet), the Rising Sun Lubricator (to oil his clanking chains), and Dr Dobell's tincture (to clear up his disturbing laugh). At one point the Otis twins construct an artificial phantom with an ironic sign around its neck, 'YE OTIS GHOSTE./ Ye Onlie True and Originale Spook./ Beware of Ye Imitationes./ All others are Counterfeite,'[4] thus highlighting the dependence of Sir Simon, and the genre in which he belongs, on repetition, reproduction, and artifice. Eventually, the weakened anachronistic ghost admits defeat and begs the virginal daughter of the house—the contemporary manifestation of the maidens pursued by lecherous old patriarchs like himself in Gothic novels of the eighteenth century—to put him (and, by implica-tion, the Gothic itself, with all its creaky conventions, ludicrous plot devices, and musty formal furniture) out of his misery: 'for three hundred years I have not slept, and I am so tired.'[5] At this moment the hitherto absurd Sir Simon attains a modicum of dignity, and after he enters the Garden of Death there is a suitably solemn funeral service, culminat-ing in 'a large cross made of white and pink almond-blossoms'[6] being laid on his coffin. 'The Canterville Ghost' could well be considered a parable of closure for a genre that inherently resists such strategies, a genre which Michelle Massé has called a 'serial writ large,'[7] given its addiction to repetition, sequels, continuities, its tendency to just never go away. With Sir Simon and everything he represents laid to rest, surely the world—and Irish writers in particular—could now move on to new genres?

This chapter will argue that, like 'The Canterville Ghost', Irish Gothic fiction often employs strategies of closure, while at the same time articulating a suspicion of, or disil-lusionment with, the Gothic. Indeed, many of the major texts in the 'canon' or 'tradi-tion'[8] of Irish Gothic fiction were written by those with an intellectual and political commitment to the modernization of Ireland, a revolution predicated in part on dispel-ling rather than perpetuating an image of the country as a non-modern space, a land of outdated superstitions, ghosts, and ghouls associated with a passé eighteenth-century form.[9] For such writers, Gothic fiction often functioned as one way in which the atavistic

---

[3] Wilde, 'The Canterville Ghost', 82.

[4] Ibid., 91. For the importance of imitation in the genre, see Jerrold Hogle, 'The Ghost of the Counterfeit in the Genesis of the Gothic', in Allan Lloyd Smith and Victor Sage (eds), *Gothick Origins and Innovations* (Amsterdam: Rodopi, 1994), 23–33.

[5] Ibid., 97.   [6] Ibid., 102.

[7] Michelle Massé, *In the Name of Love: Women, Masochism, and the Gothic* (Ithaca, NJ: Cornell University Press, 1992), 20.

[8] Whether or not Irish Gothic fiction amounts to a 'tradition' has been much debated. See Jarlath Killeen, *The Emergence of Irish Gothic Fiction: History, Origins, Theories* (Edinburgh: Edinburgh University Press, 2014), 18–27.

[9] For Ireland and the 'non-modern', see David Lloyd, *Irish Times: Temporalities of Modernity* (Cork: Field Day, 2008), 73–99.

monsters of the past could be exorcized or banished, thus opening a clearing in which civilized modernity could be established. Irish Gothic fiction, then, can be read as often working against itself, calling to mind all the associations that the genre and mode bring with it, but only to launch a war with these associations and eradicate them ... forever.

EARLY IRISH GOTHIC: SLAYING MONSTERS FROM WITHIN

In 'The Canterville Ghost', Wilde certainly appears to be sabotaging the Gothic from within, like a sceptic at a Victorian séance exposing the emptiness of the experience to a credulous audience, although the tonal switch from hilarity to solemnity also indicates that with the end of the Gothic comes an evacuation of pleasure as well. Of course, Irish writers had good reasons to harbour misgivings about the Gothic and to sincerely desire its demise. After all, one explanation for the popularity of Gothic fiction in the eighteenth and early nineteenth centuries has been that it repeatedly reinforced to an English reading public the normality of England compared with the abnormality, if not the sheer perversity, of just about everywhere else. As has been emphasized by many historians, the horrific imagery of John Foxe's *Book of Martyrs* (1563) reminded English Protestants that during the reign of Queen Mary they had survived a trial by purification presided over by agents of Satan himself, and that their existence remained precarious while threatened by Catholic enemies on the continent.[10]

The eighteenth-century Gothic novel capitalized on this puritanical understanding of history by codifying it in (barely) secularized fictions in which innocence is constantly pursued by lascivious (and usually foreign and Catholic) evil. Indeed, in *Northanger Abbey* (1817), Jane Austen provides, through the rational Henry Tilney, a warning against any attempt to apply a Gothic interpretation to even tyrannical English patriarchs, insisting that the Gothic could only operate elsewhere, in other places. Henry famously clarifies to Catherine Morland (an enthusiastic fan of the work of Anne Radcliffe) that while the Gothic is an acceptable mode to employ when thinking about people and places on the edge of the civilized world, it cannot work when applied to England: 'Remember that we are English, that we are Christians. Consult your own understanding, your own sense of the probable, your own observation of what is passing around you.'[11] Henry's observation dismantles Catherine's 'visions of romance' for the 'midland counties of England', and she learns to reserve them for 'the Alps and Pyrenees ... Italy, Switzerland and the South of France', and, 'if hard pressed ... the northern and western extremities' of Britain.[12] As Darryl Jones points out, the 'northern

---

[10] See William Haller, *Foxe's Book of Martyrs and the Elect Nation* (London: Cape, 1967) and William Lamont, *Godly Rule: Politics and Religion, 1603–1660* (London: Macmillan, 1969).

[11] Jane Austen, *Northanger Abbey*, ed. John Davie (Oxford: Oxford University Press, 1990), 159.

[12] Ibid., 161.

and western extremities' that Isabella Thorpe excludes from her tour of normality incorporates 'what are still in some circles known as the "Celtic fringe" [Ireland, Scotland and Wales], and Austen's implication figures the marginal as the locus of weirdness'.[13] Austen was merely recycling a very common idea, however, since, as Joep Leerssen points out, in popular culture the so-called Celtic fringe 'is a place of stasis, a place where time moves slowly or stands still. It is also a place at the very edge of the real world'.[14] It is for these reasons that the fringe always works well as a site of horror and irrationality, as the very antithesis of the 'real'. In popular culture, Ireland has for centuries been an unreal space where anything could, and probably did, happen.[15]

Such a version of Ireland as a locus of chaos was not particularly helpful to moderniz-ing Irish thinkers and writers who were determined to re-make Ireland as a site of 'pro-gressive' rather than 'backward' thinking, and therefore the Gothic, as one powerful mode which reiterates to the point of banality the difference between normal England and the abnormal other, had to be tackled and deconstructed—from within. One way to challenge such Manichean thinking is through destroying the genre which facilitates it in the first instance, and 'The Canterville Ghost' was far from the first Irish attempt to decommission the Gothic. Some early Irish Gothic writers tried to parody the genre to death: *Castle Belmont* (1790) by Theobald Wolfe Tone (1763–98) and 'divers hands' and Mrs F. C. Patrick's *More Ghosts!* (1798) are interesting attempts to temper the enthusiasm for a genre that had, since its emergence in the 1760s, already grown tired and stale as far as the critics were concerned, even though the reading public continued to consume Gothic fiction in large numbers.

Maria Edgeworth's (1767–1849) *Ennui* (1809) is also, from one perspective, a power-fully anti-Gothic narrative, which indulges in moments of Gothic melodrama only to subsequently undermine them. The novel follows the bored Lord Glenthorn in his travels from his English home in Sherwood Park to his Irish estate in a desperate attempt to make his life more meaningful, encountering along the way the standard stereotypes that were believed to populate Ireland and a number of Gothic plot twists considered natural to life there. The ostensible lesson of this moral tale is that while it seems like a lot of fun to be in a Gothic novel, it is not economically advantageous for the welfare of the country, and that it would be better for Ireland if its inhabitants became enthusiasts of Adam Smith rather than Horace Walpole. As Richard Haslam astutely points out, *Ennui* sometimes adopts a Gothic tone only to deflate it immediately in order to dissuade the reader from indulging their predilections for such a debased genre. 'By adopting a mildly parodic tone', he contends, 'Edgeworth deftly subverts any incipient Gothic

---

[13] Darryl Jones, 'National Character and Foreclosed Irishness: A Reconsideration of *Ennui*', in Heidi Kaufman and Chris Fauske (eds), *An Uncomfortable Authority: Maria Edgeworth and her Contexts* (Newark, NJ: University of Delaware Press, 2004), 129. See also Andrew McInnes, ' "English Verdure, English Culture, English Comfort": Ireland and the Gothic Elsewhere in Jane Austen's *Emma*', *Romantic Textualities: Literature and Print Culture, 1780–1840* 22 (2017), 66–77.

[14] Joep Leerssen, *Remembrance and Imagination: Patterns in the Historical and Literary Representation of Ireland in the Nineteenth Century* (Cork: Cork University Press, 1996), 191.

[15] See Killeen, *The Emergence of Irish Gothic Fiction*, 1–11.

mood and thereby reassures rather than unsettles her early nineteenth-century reader'[16]—although, given readers' Gothic-obsessed tastes, this strategy would more likely have frustrated than pleased them. Either way, the Gothic here is apparently something to be dispelled rather than indulged. Glenthorn must stop being a kind of Catherine Morland, hoping to find ghosts around every corner, and instead become a good middle-class professional by the story's end, in an Ireland without phantoms (or even banshees, since the closest thing to one, the crone Ellinor, is dead) but which still needs to be purged of its medieval Catholic remnants. Even Waterford-born Regina Maria Roche (1764–1845), who made her name as a writer of Gothic romances, had no qualms about mocking the genre. In *The Monastery of St Columb* (1813), for example, one of her most ridiculous minor characters is the hack Gothic novelist Miss Elmere, who preposterously turns every minor incident in her tedious real life into grist for the Ann Radcliffe-lite drivel she churns out.

Ennui, More Ghosts!, Belmont Castle, and *The Monastery of St Columb* are representative examples of much early Irish Gothic fiction, which can be read as a response to the popular cultural characterization of Ireland as a site of irrational anti-modernity and an attempt to exploit popular interest in a particular genre—ideology and commerce working in tandem. Such novels figure as weapons in an ideological attack on the representational politics of the 'Celtic fringe', a battle which was waged in literature as much as it was in politics by organizations like the United Irelanders, who were firmly committed to Enlightenment rather than 'traditional' values.[17] With the example of Edgeworth, the ideological reasons behind Irish novelists' opposition to the Gothic become clearer. Lord Glenthorn grows as a character as he comes to reject Gothic melodrama and reappraise his initial delight at finding Ireland a crucible of Gothic conventions (banshees, haunted castles, sublime landscapes). Instead, he adopts the view of his land agent Mr McLeod, a figure straight out of the Scottish Enlightenment, who urges the slow but steady reconstruction of the country through the introduction of new agricultural techniques, the education of the Catholic peasantry in non-denominational schools (which will eventually turn them into Protestants), and the encouragement of industry (in the process sounding very like Edgeworth's father, Richard Lovell). McLeod wants to move Ireland gently from the plot of a Gothic to a realist novel, and Edgeworth appears to agree with him.

Given the association between Catholic irrationality and perversity in the canonical Gothic novels of the eighteenth century, it is no surprise to find that the major works of Irish Gothic fiction were written in periods when the forces of Catholicism appeared to be waxing rather than waning. Recent interpretations of the Gothic as an Enlightenment rather than a counter-Enlightenment genre help explain why it was that much Irish Gothic fiction emerged when the energies associated with the atavistic

---

[16] Richard Haslam, 'Irish Gothic: A Rhetorical Hermeneutics Approach', *Irish Journal of Gothic and Horror Studies* 2 (2007). http://irishgothichorrorjournal.homestead.com/index.html. Accessed 12 August 2018.

[17] See Kevin Whelan, *The Tree of Liberty: Radicalism, Catholicism and the Construction of Irish Identity, 1760–1830* (Cork: Cork University Press in association with Field Day, 1996), 59.

past were revitalized in political terms. Chris Baldick and Robert Mighall, for example, insist that it is a mistake to read the Gothic as at all sentimental or nostalgic about the past, insisting instead that Gothic fiction 'gratefully endorses Protestant bourgeois values as "kinder" than those of feudal barons' and 'delights in depicting the delusions and iniquities of a (mythical) social order and celebrating its defeat by modern progressive values'.[18] These Enlightenment energies can be detected in the novel sometimes deemed to be the 'first' Irish Gothic novel proper (though the quest for *an* 'origin' rather than multiple 'origins' of Irish Gothic fiction, and Gothic fiction itself, should be discouraged).[19] *Longsword, Earl of Salisbury* by Thomas Leland (1722–85), Anglican historian and Trinity College professor of oratory, appeared in 1762, soon after the formation of the Catholic Committee in 1760 and at a time when the Whiteboys, a Munster-based secret society of agrarian agitators, were considered by some observers to be party to an international Catholic conspiracy to undermine Anglican hegemony in Ireland.[20] *Longsword*'s monster is the nefarious Father Reginald, who would later be reincarnated in the stereotypically malevolent monks of the Gothic tradition, from Matthew G. Lewis's Ambrosio and Ann Radcliffe's Schedoni onwards.

Other periods of intense Irish Catholic political activity also witnessed the publication of classics of Irish Gothic fiction. Regina Maria Roche's *The Children of the Abbey* (1796) and *Clermont* (1798) appeared when Anglican anxiety about 'Catholic' secret societies was at fever pitch; Charles Robert Maturin's (1780–1824) *Melmoth the Wanderer* (1820) was published at the beginning of the so-called 'Second Reformation'; Joseph Sheridan Le Fanu's (1814–73) 'Passage in the Secret History of an Irish Countess' (1838), which eventually mutated into *Uncle Silas* (1864), emerged at the end of the Tithe War, during which his own family were directly targeted; Bram Stoker (1847–1912) began work on *Dracula* (1897) in the aftermath of the Fenian bombing campaign of the 1880s. Faced with what many perceived as the danger of the country being dragged back into a medieval mire, Irish Anglicans produced a consistent narrative of modernity menaced by monstrous survivals from the past.[21]

[18] Chris Baldick and Robert Mighall, 'Gothic Criticism', in David Punter (ed.), *A Companion to the Gothic* (Oxford: Blackwell, 2000), 214, 220.

[19] This is a point fundamentally misunderstood by Richard Haslam in 'Investigating Irish Gothic: The Case of *Sophia Berkley*', *Gothic Studies* 19, no. 1 (2017), 41.

[20] Thomas Bartlett, *The Fall and Rise of the Irish Nation: The Catholic Question, 1690–1830* (Dublin: Irish Academic Press, 1992), 68–71.

[21] The argument that there is an important relationship between Irish Gothic texts and their socio-political contexts is not meant to suggest that the fascination of Irish writers for the Gothic was not also strongly influenced by changes in print culture more generally. For example, the interest in European (especially German) supernatural and Gothic literature manifested in the *Dublin University Magazine* during the editorship of Joseph Sheridan Le Fanu (1861–69) was generated as much by commercial as ideological or aesthetic concerns. See Gaïd Gerard, 'Growing a Voice: Le Fanu and the Laboratory of the *Dublin University Magazine*', in Jarlath Killeen and Valeria Cavalli (eds), *'Inspiring a Mysterious Terror': 200 Years of Joseph Sheridan Le Fanu* (Bern: Peter Lang, 2016), 155–75. Ideology and commerce need not cancel each other out.

Irish Gothic fiction, then, can be read as a fundamentally anti-Gothic 'tradition'. Rather than being an expression of Irish writers' commitment to a version of Ireland as a place out of time, Irish Gothic fiction often served as a way to purge that image of Ireland from within. Christopher Morash has persuasively argued that even when Irish Gothic novels such as *Dracula* are not set in Ireland they are invariably about the country 'because they are obsessive studies of anachrony',[22] an anachrony exemplified by monsters like ghosts and vampires, whose eradication at the end of these narratives represents a vanquishing of the past and the true beginning of the present, the modern. Since the Gothic is a means by which to deal with the continuing influence of the atavistic past in the present, modernizers who wanted to overcome such atavism through the reform of Ireland often worked in the Gothic genre so as to confront as directly as possible the primitive forces that were keeping the country from taking its place in the pantheon of modern nations, and in confronting these forces, destroy them as well.

Sir Simon de Canterville is allowed a much more dignified death than many of the far more famous monsters that populate Irish Gothic fiction, whose demise at the plot's end signals the defeat of these remnants from the past, a dénouement central to what Robin Wood, in his study of 1970's horror cinema, calls the 'basic formula' of the genre.[23] As Wood explains, the function of the monster is to disrupt the status quo briefly before being expelled at the climax when the agents of normality restore familiarity and regularity.[24] This plot is so basic to Gothic fiction that it stretches from the self-styled origin text of the genre, Horace Walpole's *The Castle of Otranto* (1764), to late twentieth-century slasher films. It is a formula certainly much in evidence in the masterworks of Irish Gothic fiction: Melmoth is dragged kicking and screaming off to hell by the Devil; Carmilla is staked and decapitated before her body is burned; Dorian Gray manages to stab himself (by mistake) and his shrivelled-up corpse is found by servants who can recognize him only by the rings on his fingers; Count Dracula dramatically disintegrates after a bowie knife is thrust into his side, (Anti-)Christ-like, and he is decapitated. But the deaths of these fiends do more than bring the narratives they have troubled to an abrupt conclusion. They are also possibly symptomatic of a desire to bring the Gothic genre itself to an end, and such a desire helps to explain why the landmarks of the Irish Gothic canon were predominantly written by Anglicans, from Maturin, Le Fanu, and Stoker to Lord Dunsany (1878–1957) and Elizabeth Bowen (1899–1973).

[22] Christopher Morash, 'The Time is Out of Joint (O Curséd Spite!): Towards a Definition of a Supernatural Narrative', in Bruce Stewart (ed.), *That Other World: The Supernatural and the Fantastic in Irish Literature and its Contexts* (Gerrards Cross: Colin Smythe, 2003), 135.

[23] The terms 'horror' and 'Gothic' will be used interchangeably in this chapter. The relationship between them is the basis of a great deal of discussion in Gothic studies, but there is no space to enter into this debate here. See Clive Bloom, 'Horror Fiction: In Search of a Definition', in Punter (ed.), *A Companion to the Gothic*, 155–66.

[24] Robin Wood, *Hollywood from Vietnam to Reagan...and Beyond* (New York: Columbia University Press, 2003), 71–2.

These writers were, of course, surrounded by a host of others of different denominations.[25] Indeed, for some critics, practically every major and minor Irish writer from the eighteenth century onwards used Gothic conventions, such that 'the marginalized Gothic mode' paradoxically 'permeates virtually all Irish writing'.[26] Yet, despite the discursive ubiquity of Gothic tropes and themes, it is significant that in the nineteenth century, the major Irish Gothic texts (major in the sense that they slipped their temporal and cultural moorings and went global) were the product of Irish Anglicans in whose works the genre itself is intensely problematized and its disappearance often longed for as a blessed release from the ghosts of the past. As Morash puts it in a discussion of the most famous vampire stories of the Irish Gothic, Le Fanu's 'Carmilla' (1871–72) and Stoker's *Dracula*, 'the ideological project of the vampire story is an assertion of absolute modernity, in that it makes its audience long for an end to the existence of the past in the present'.[27] Just as the monsters of the Gothic must be despatched by the end of these stories, so too the version of Ireland (and, by implication, its Catholic inhabitants) as atavistic must be banished and Protestant modernity ushered in. If Irish Anglican writers produced so much Gothic fiction, it was not because they wanted to perpetuate the popular cultural version of Ireland as a wild and untamed place inhabited by freaks. Rather, it was because they wished to explode that myth, even though in killing off these Gothic monsters they would be denying readers the pleasures they so obviously craved.

Viewed in this context, certain otherwise odd aspects of these texts become rather more explicable. One such convention is the authorial undermining of the form even as it is being perpetuated. For example, in the preface to *Melmoth the Wanderer*, Maturin protests that he would rather do anything other than write this kind of fiction and insists that he only does so because of financial pressures:

> I cannot again appear before the public in so unseemly a character as that of a writer of romance, without regretting the necessity that compels me to it. Did my profession furnish me with the means of subsistence, I should hold myself culpable indeed in having recourse to any other, but—am I allowed the choice?[28]

Maturin then goes on, at the start of the novel, to disparage certain clichés of the Gothic which he associates with Irish Catholic culture, as embodied by Biddy Brannigan, a grotesque old shrew who comes to tell John Melmoth the story of his family. Maturin makes her into a hideous and possibly evil female version of Edgeworth's slippery retainer

---

[25] For an excellent examination of the full range of early Irish Gothic fiction, see Christina Morin, *The Gothic Novel in Ireland, c.1760–1839* (Manchester: Manchester University Press, 2018). See also Richard Haslam, 'Maturin's Catholic Heirs: Expanding the Limits of Irish Gothic', in Christina Morin and Niall Gillespie (eds), *Irish Gothics: Genres, Forms, Modes, and Traditions, 1760–1890* (Basingstoke: Palgrave Macmillan, 2014), 113–29.

[26] Vera Kreilkamp, review of *The Gothic Family Romance* by Margot Gayle Backus, *Victorian Studies* 43, no. 4 (2001), 248.

[27] Morash, 'Time is Out of Joint', 137.

[28] Charles Robert Maturin, *Melmoth the Wanderer*, ed. Chris Baldick (Oxford: Oxford University Press, 1989), 6.

Thady Quirk, 'a withered Sibyl, who prolonged her squalid existence by practicing on the fears, the ignorance, and the sufferings of beings as miserable as herself'.[29] Biddy ekes out a living by telling horror stories, tormenting and terrifying 'her victims into a belief of that power which may and has reduced the strongest minds to the level of the weakest'.[30] As an example of the dangerous rhetorical power of the kinds of stories she tells, the narrator instances 'the cultivated sceptic, Lord Lyttleton', who, having listened to such tales, 'yelled and gnashed and writhed in his last hours', and was reduced to the epistemological condition of 'the poor girl who, in the belief of the horrible visitation of the vampire, shrieked aloud, that her grandfather was sucking her vital blood while she slept, and expired under the influence of imaginary horror'.[31] In this analogy, the Gothic mode, in the *wrong* (Catholic?) hands, can degrade even the sceptical male Protestant to the credulous condition of an ignorant Irish girl. The Gothic is hazardous material that needs to be quarantined.

The depiction of Biddy Brannigan as a squalid purveyor of cheap horrors echoes Maturin's attempt to distance himself from what he calls in his preface the 'Radcliffe-Romance' style of writing, one deeply dependent upon 'startling adventures one meets with in romances'.[32] Instead he dedicates himself to a new form of horror writing, one closer to realism than romance, constituted by 'that irritating series of petty torments which constitutes the misery of life in general'.[33] That Maturin was actually living in a country in which daily life seemed to him like an extreme version of Radcliffean Gothic might have been one of the major incentives for attacking that form here. He claimed in *The Milesian Chief* (1812) that Ireland was the 'only country on earth, where, from the strange existing opposition of religion, politics, and manners, the extremes of refinement and barbarism are united, and the most wild and incredible situations of romantic story are hourly passing before modern eyes'.[34] If living in Ireland made you into a character in a Radcliffe-Romance, then the shifting geographical boundaries of *Melmoth the Wanderer* can be better understood: anxious to escape from Irish Gothic conventions, the plot moves from a haunted house in County Wicklow—one of the counties which, during the 1798 rebellion, was the site of violence and atrocity more appropriate to a literary romance than to real life—to England, Spain, and the South Sea Islands.[35] As exotic as some of the locations are, they were at least geographically distanced from the Radcliffe-Romance of Ireland, and therefore (or so Maturin may have felt) a potential site for the development of a new register for horror focusing on 'realistic' rather than romantic incidents.[36]

---

[29] Ibid., 10.   [30] Ibid., 11.   [31] Ibid.

[32] Ibid., 5.   [33] Ibid.

[34] Charles Robert Maturin, *The Milesian Chief*, ed. Robert Lee Wolff (New York: Garland Publishing, 1979), vol. 1, v.

[35] See Siobhán Kilfeather, 'Terrific Register: The Gothicization of Atrocity in Irish Romanticism', *boundary 2* 31, no. 1 (2004), 49–71.

[36] For an astute examination of the intrusion of 1798 in the novel, see Laura Doyle, 'At the World's Edge: Post/Coloniality, Charles Maturin and the Gothic Wanderer', *Nineteenth-Century Literature* 65, no. 4 (2011), 530–1.

It may now seem difficult to believe that the islands of the South Seas appeared less alien and strange to an Irishman of the early nineteenth century than his own country, but since 1798 many Irish Protestants had complained that they seemed to be trapped in a horror story without end. Unsurprisingly, however, atrocity scenes from recent Irish history keep invading *Melmoth*, despite Maturin's attempts to banish them to the margins by including such historical information in footnotes. For example, after an incident describing the violence and extremity of a riot in Spain, a footnote intervenes to inform the reader of an incident during the 1803 insurrection of Robert Emmett, when 'Lord Kilwarden, in passing through Thomas Street, was dragged from his carriage, and murdered in the most horrid fashion. Pike after pike was thrust through his body, till at last he was *nailed to a door*'.[37] Far-fetched (though true to life) Irish Gothic breaks in here to disrupt the narrative of banal horror. Gothic literature is also depicted as a distraction from far more important reading. Early in the novel John Melmoth finds the document containing the story of Stanton 'among some papers *of no value*, such as manuscript sermons, and pamphlets on the improvement of Ireland, and such stuff'.[38] This is a deeply ironic sentence, as it suggests that the hackneyed 'found manuscript' of Gothic fiction is more interesting than sermons or socio-political tracts about the future of the country. Much of the irony derives from the fact that the novel itself originated in one of Maturin's own sermons which, he slyly confesses in the preface, 'it is to be presumed very few have read'.[39] Concealed behind this parenthetical remark is the fact that Maturin had been trying unsuccessfully for many months to convince his publishers, Constable, to bring out a volume of his sermons.[40] By the time that *Melmoth* was finally issued, the public's appetite for Gothic melodrama trumped any possibility of Maturin's being accepted in a genre that was much more suitable to his clerical profession (his work in the Gothic having been one of the reasons why he did not advance as a clergyman). There is additional irony in the fact that the author himself further compounds the problem by indulging readers' tastes at the expense of advancing the case for Irish modernization. The reference to valueless papers suggests that there are many more significant texts that the reader could and probably should be perusing, but stories of torture, imprisonment, and Satanic pacts regrettably excite the reading public far more than works of intellectual, moral, or social edification.[41]

---

[37] Maturin, *Melmoth the Wanderer*, 257.   [38] Ibid., 21. Emphasis added.

[39] Ibid., 5.

[40] For Maturin's persistent attempts to convince Constable to undertake publication of his sermons, see Sharon Ragaz, 'Maturin, Archibald Constable, and the Publication of *Melmoth the Wanderer*', *Review of English Studies* 57, no. 230 (2006), 361–3.

[41] For different interpretations of this passage, see Haslam, 'Irish Gothic' and Christina Morin, *Charles Robert Maturin and the Haunting of Irish Romantic Fiction* (Manchester: Manchester University Press, 2011), 149–50. Bram Stoker certainly shared Maturin's modernizing outlook. See Jarlath Killeen, 'Remembering Stoker', in Jarlath Killeen (ed.), *Bram Stoker: Centenary Essays* (Dublin: Four Courts Press, 2014), 15–36.

IRISH CATHOLIC GOTHIC AFTER 1922:
RESURRECTING THE MONSTROUS

Despite Gothic being a fundamentally anti-Catholic, Protestant genre,[42] the moderniz-ing project of eighteenth- and nineteenth-century Irish Anglican exemplars is also evi-dent in the work of Catholic writers, especially after the foundation of the Irish Free State in 1922. For many such writers, the new state quickly squandered its revolutionary potential and committed itself to an intellectual and cultural conservativism that was so stultifying and regressive that it risked trapping Ireland in a time warp. As Emmet Larkin has argued, the wealthier farmers who survived the Great Famine, and who embraced both the English language and the rigours of Tridentine Catholic devotion (and therefore adopted a rigid sexual morality), were the group which then went on to campaign for Home Rule and eventually formed the governing elite in the Free State.[43] This class also supplied the personnel for the Catholic Church in the post-Famine period, so that the interests of one social class became both orthodox and hegemonic, effectively marginalizing all other voices. The theologically orthodox priest found a per-fect ally in the socially conservative farmer and his middle-class professional equivalent, and together they maintained a political and ideological stranglehold over the country for most of the twentieth century.[44] In the wake of partition, many Catholic writers and intellectuals who felt stifled by Free State orthodoxy turned, like their Anglican prede-cessors, to the Gothic as a means of attacking the forces of this political and religious conservatism by imaging them as monstrous. As Catholic nationalism atrophied it soon came to be depicted by disillusioned Catholic artists as an anachronistic and spectral presence that was out of place in the twentieth century.

The Gothic permeates much of the long and short fiction of post-independence Catholic writers. Counter-revivalist Frank O'Connor's (1903–66) short story, 'Guests of the Nation', a putatively realist text, stands out as an early example. Published in 1931, it concerns the execution in a bog of two British soldiers by their two IRA captors during the War of Independence (1919–21), an execution made traumatic by the fact that the four men had formed a kind of friendship during their brief period of acquaintance. Through his depiction of this barbaric act O'Connor dramatizes his own disenchant-ment with the violence inherent to the nationalist struggle. As Eugene O'Brien observes,

---

[42] See Victor Sage, *Horror Fiction in the Protestant Tradition* (New York: St Martin's Press, 1988); Patrick O'Malley, *Catholicism, Sexual Deviance, and Victorian Gothic Culture* (Cambridge: Cambridge University Press, 2006), 32.

[43] Emmet Larkin, *The Historical Dimensions of Irish Catholicism* (Dublin: Four Courts Press, 1997), 92, 113–14.

[44] For an analysis of clerical power and influence in post-independent Ireland, see Tom Inglis, *Moral Monopoly: The Rise and Fall of the Catholic Church in Modern Ireland* (Dublin: University College Dublin Press, 1998). See also J. J. Lee, *Ireland 1912–1985: Politics and Society* (Cambridge: Cambridge University Press, 1989).

through their murder, the nation's 'guests' are transformed into its ghosts, preserved in a liminal state by the bogland that becomes their grave.[45] As such, they are destined to haunt their executioners, a haunting that takes on ontological significance in the final paragraph of the story:

> It is so strange what you feel at times like that that you can't describe it. Noble says he saw everything ten times the size, as though there were nothing in the whole world but that little patch of bog with the two Englishmen stiffening into it but with me it was as if the patch of bog where the Englishmen were was a million miles away, and even Noble and the old woman, mumbling behind me, and the birds and the bloody stars were all far away, and I was somehow very small and very lost and lonely like a child astray in the snow. And anything that happened me afterwards, I never felt the same about again.[46]

The narrator experiences a cosmic dread and existential emptiness which drains the nationalist project of legitimacy. Although the bog suddenly seems very distant, in effect it has sucked all meaning and purpose from the narrator's life and from the nationalist ideals for which he fought. Whereas at the end of Stoker's *The Snake's Pass* (1890) the 'quaking bog' of the mythological past slides into the sea in order to make room for a development scheme to reclaim the marshland and transform the west of Ireland into an economic hub, such futuristic projections are denied in O'Connor's story as the bog expands to take over the universe.[47]

O'Connor's short story, a realist text disrupted by a powerful Gothic moment of cosmic crisis, indicates that the new certainties of the independent state were even at that early stage becoming a mirror image of the oppressive colonial power structures they had replaced. The story has had a powerful cultural afterlife; for example, its shadow hangs over Neil Jordan's (1950–) film, *The Crying Game* (1992), where we encounter a latter-day IRA volunteer haunted by his role in the death of a British soldier during the Troubles. In other texts, the violence of the Troubles is represented as barbaric and tribal, the product of a monstrous history which must be rejected if the recurring sacrifice of new generations to old ideologies is ever to be stopped.[48] In Siobhan Dowd's (1960–2007) *Bog Child* (2008), set in the 1980s, the discovery of the preserved Iron Age body of a martyred child in a County Tyrone bog is paralleled by the threatened sacrifice of a young RUC police officer by the IRA, suggesting that nothing much has changed in the centuries between these two events, and that Ireland is stuck in a primeval cycle of

---

[45] Eugene O'Brien, 'Guests of a Nation; Geists of a Nation', *New Hibernia Review* 11, no. 3 (2007), 115.

[46] Frank O'Connor, 'Guests of the Nation', in Frank O'Connor (ed.), *Classic Irish Short Stories* (Oxford: Oxford University Press, 1985), 187.

[47] For a different but incisive reading of the bog in 'Guests of the Nation', see Derek Gladwin, *Contentious Terrains: Boglands, Ireland, Postcolonial Gothic* (Cork: Cork University Press, 2016), 107–13.

[48] For an examination of Irish Gothic as a genre that is deeply concerned with child sacrifice, see Margot Gayle Backus, *The Gothic Family Romance: Heterosexuality, Child-Sacrifice and the Anglo-Irish Colonial Order* (Durham, NC: Duke University Press, 1999).

horror. Bogland is an appropriate location for this and other texts, since it has for long been regarded by modernizers as a symbol of a backward-looking Ireland, the kind that needed to be eliminated if the nation was to enter fully the modern world.[49] Memorably, in Maria Edgeworth's *Castle Rackrent* (1800), bogland is rendered as both comic (as in the 'bog of Allyballycarricko'shaughlin'[50]) and terrifying (it is where rebels and subversives hide). In John B. Keane's (1928–2002) play, *Sive* (1959), the heroine dies during her flight from her emotionally stifling peasant home by falling into a boghole and drowning, as if the past itself had reached out to thwart her capacity to act. The bog of secrets and lies, and of sacrificial victims, acts as an agent of primordial darkness in such texts.

By the middle of the twentieth century many Irish Catholic intellectuals and writers had become deeply disillusioned with the way politics and society fixated on a nostalgic version of a Gaelic peasantry as the epitome of authentic nationhood. In such a repressive atmosphere, the Gothic narratives of a corrupt Catholic Church and a backward-facing populace popularized by nineteenth-century Irish Anglican novelists were repurposed by Catholic writers who wished to challenge attempts to 'prevent the future'.[51] Certainly, much of the best Gothic fiction produced in late twentieth-century Ireland takes aim at forms of anachrony that can be read as updated versions of those battled by Maturin and Stoker. For example, Patrick McCabe's (1955–) 'bog Gothic'[52] novel, *The Butcher Boy* (1992), together with Jordan's 1997 film adaptation, powerfully reproduce the anti-Catholic paranoia of Anglican Gothic in their depiction of 1960s Catholic Ireland as a place of violence, prejudice, and perverse sexuality. The novel delights in rendering monstrous many of the cherished symbols of Catholic nationalism. McCabe merges the image of Ireland as mother, so beloved of Revival writers and conservative nationalists, with James Joyce's (1882–1941) memorable description of the nation as a 'sow who eats her farrow'.[53] The protagonist, Francie Brady, a deranged schoolboy, hallucinates that his perceived nemesis, Mrs Nugent, is a pig he must (and does) slaughter. In bludgeoning her to death, Francie is effectively trying to obliterate the puritanical state and society that have been partly to blame for the destruction of his own family, coming as he does comes from a dysfunctional household which represents the underside of the newly-minted middle-class prosperity incarnated by the Nugents.

The disorder of Francie's family is partially blamed on those institutions that embodied the Catholic ethos of the state for much of the twentieth century, especially the religious-run industrial schools which were used to quarantine those deemed to have

---

[49] For an excellent examination of the importance of the bog as a space in Irish Gothic literature, see Gladwin, *Contentious Terrains*.

[50] Maria Edgeworth, *Castle Rackrent*, ed. George Watson (Oxford: Oxford University Press, 1995), 27.

[51] See Tom Garvin, *Preventing the Future: Why was Ireland so Poor for so Long?* (Dublin: Gill and Macmillan, 2004).

[52] For a discussion of this controversial term, see Ellen McWilliams, 'Patrick McCabe', in William Hughes and Andrew Smith (eds), *The Encyclopedia of the Gothic* (Oxford: Blackwell, 2013), 431–3.

[53] James Joyce, *A Portrait of the Artist as a Young Man*, ed. Seamus Deane (London: Penguin, 1992), 220.

failed to abide to the prescribed moral standards.[54] As Laura Eldred convincingly argues, in *The Butcher Boy*, the platitudes of Irish patriotism are systematically punctured: 'the family is a site of madness, alcoholism, suicide, and abuse; religion is no good for anyone except some paedophile priests',[55] and when the 'heroes' of Irish nationalism are referenced they are depicted as either comic or alien figures who are of little use to those suffering in the independent Ireland they fought to achieve. To Francie, Daniel O'Connell, the great icon of nineteenth-century Catholic nationalism, is simply a 'big grey statue mouthing about something in the middle of the street and birds shitting all over his head'.[56] McCabe deploys the Gothic mode to attack the reactionary forces that drove citizens of independent Ireland to psychic extremes merely in an effort to live there.

In Neil Jordan's *doppelgänger* novel, *Mistaken* (2011), Irish writers are criticized for constantly Gothicizing the period from the 1940s to the 1960s, but a more recent novel, Eimear McBride's (1976–) *A Girl is a Half-formed Thing* (2013), set mostly in Mayo, turns its attention to the Ireland of the 1980s and early 1990s as still stuck in nightmare modes. The novel ironically participates in a public discourse, evident since the days of the Celtic Tiger, in which 'the years from 1973 to 1994...are sometimes treated like an impossibly distant era, one barely relevant to today's Ireland'.[57] This was a view that had much appeal in the affluent and increasingly liberal late 1990s and early 2000s, even though its roots lay in the era itself, which earned the shorthand acronym GUBU (grotesque, unbelievable, bizarre, unprecedented) after writer and politician Conor Cruise O'Brien used these adjectives to describe a series of political events in 1982 that led to the resignation of the Attorney General during the premiership of Charles J. Haughey.[58]

McBride's unnamed female narrator certainly seems to be trapped in a GUBU state of being, as well as a social and geographical hell. The plot concerns the psychological journey of a girl beset on all sides by a variety of Gothic menaces, including a deeply abusive mother under the influence of the Manichean morality of kitsch Catholic charismatics, a lascivious and predatory uncle, and, more generally, a culture whose deeply repressive attitude to human sexuality so inhibits natural impulses that they emerge only in perverted forms. The girl becomes a kind of allegorical figure for Ireland—unsurprisingly, perhaps, for a novel set in a period when the bodies of women were routinely conflated with the body of the nation in referenda on abortion and debates about sexual and personal morality.[59] The family at the centre of the narrative, like the Bradys in *The Butcher*

---

[54] For the industrial schools as forms of moral quarantine, see Harry Ferguson, 'Abused and Looked After Children as "Moral Dirt": Child Abuse and Institutional Care in Historical Perspective', *Journal of Social Policy* 36, no. 1 (2007), 123–39.

[55] Laura Eldred, 'Francie Pig vs. the Fat Green Blob from Outer Space: Horror Films and *The Butcher Boy*', *New Hibernia Review* 10, no. 3 (2006), 64.

[56] Patrick McCabe, *The Butcher Boy* (London: Picador, 1992), 37.

[57] Eamonn Sweeney, *Down Down Deeper and Down: Ireland in the 70s and 80s* (Dublin: Gill and Macmillan, 2010), 1.

[58] Ibid., 251.

[59] On the allegory of Ireland as a woman, and its ideological implications in the 1980s, see Gerardine Meaney, *Sex and Nation: Women in Irish Culture and Politics* (Dublin: Attic Press, 1991).

Boy, are in one sense a collection of freakish stereotypes—the 'wild' Irish girl, the suffocating mother, the menacing uncle—whose oddness is emphasized by their eating habits, their compulsive daily recitation of the rosary, and a reiterated obsession with sexual purity. Through this simultaneously comic and terrifying cast of characters, McBride indicts a culture in which women in particular are reduced to performing pre-scripted roles in an apparently unending and warped national romance.

A Girl is a Half-formed Thing establishes the west of Ireland as a psychologically scarring and emotionally stunted site of abuse and oppression. In her claustrophobic imagination, the central character associates the landscape with fantasies and nightmares of drowning. The mythological clashes with the real, trapping the protagonist in a horrific version of everlasting youth. The waters of the west, mythologized in works such as W. B. Yeats's (1865–1939) poems, 'He Reproves the Curlew' and 'The Wild Swans at Coole', are transformed into the murky, boggy lake water which eventually overwhelms the protagonist, as if Stoker's quaking bog has returned with a vengeance:

> Hear the curlews and the gab of swans not far from me....Much more warm now than I wanted or had thought would be. This crevice lake could be my ocean if I was...I sink baptise me now oh lord and take this bloody itch away for what am I the wrong and wrong of it always always far from thee. Ha. My nose fill with that bog water. It's run a long brown hill to get into me.[60]

Thus we can see that Irish Catholic writers such as McBride, McCabe, and O'Connor have taken a genre with a distinct anti-Catholic lineage and appropriated it for their own purposes, to critique the conservative Catholicism of the state from within and, like their Irish Anglican predecessors, further expedite the modernization of Irish society.[61]

Irish Gothic fiction, then, can persuasively be read as an anti-Gothic phenomenon, unsentimental about the past and desirous of a rational and progressive future. However, as credible as this argument about the 'meaning' of Irish Gothic is, the genre's resilience and ubiquity, as well as the fact that Irish writers tend to return to the same modes repeatedly, suggest that any representation of the 'tradition' as an expression only of a desire to release the nation from anachrony into modernity cannot be the full story. After all, if the Gothic is the problem, why do authors (and audiences) return to it so routinely? Less than three years after Wilde wrote 'The Canterville Ghost' he revisited the form with *The Picture of Dorian Gray* (1891). Likewise, while Maturin does indeed inveigh against the Gothic in *Melmoth the Wanderer*, from the outset he was planning a sequel, so that even though he appears to have been vanquished at the end of the plot, the author intended that his protagonist would return.[62] Moreover, even Edgeworth's

---

[60] Eimear McBride, *A Girl is a Half-formed Thing* (Norwich: Galley Beggar Press, 2013), 55.

[61] That Catholic authors have successfully written Gothic fiction does not cancel out claims that the Gothic is a Protestant genre (any more than the commercial success of, for example, white rappers means that rap and hip-hop are not African American forms). For an alternative view, see Haslam, 'Maturin's Catholic Heirs', 28–9.

[62] Ragaz, 'Maturin, Archibald Constable, and the Publication of *Melmoth the Wanderer*', 368.

realism in *Ennui* may be built on mythical and legendary foundations in which the dead heroes of the past come to life again and triumph in the present—a very Gothic return of the repressed.[63] Stoker, too, was unable or unwilling to leave the Gothic behind; he revised his original conclusion to *Dracula*, which had Castle Dracula destroyed by a convulsion of the earth, so that the building was left standing, with 'every stone of its broken battlements…articulated against the light of the setting sun'.[64] Framed thus, it appears as terrifying at the end as at the start, which suggests that the author may have planned to revisit it to continue the story.[65]

Killing the monsters in these texts does not really bring them to an end at all, therefore, because they are highly entertaining as well as terrifying. Nor does it help to destroy the genre from which they emerged. Rather, it releases these demons into the cultural ether. Much of the power of the Gothic stems from the fact that it is repetitious, clichéd, comforting (despite the horror), attractive, enjoyable—and never-ending. At the conclusion of 'The Canterville Ghost', Virginia's husband asks her what she got up to with Sir Simon when she was helping to ease him into the Garden of Death. In place of an answer, 'Virginia blushed'.[66] This highly suggestive reaction resonates with the sense that the lure of illicit thrills keeps the Gothic genre very much undead in Irish fiction and culture.

Further Reading

Backus, Margot Gayle. *The Gothic Family Romance: Heterosexuality, Child-Sacrifice and the Anglo-Irish Colonial Order*. Durham, NC: Duke University Press, 1999.

Foster, R. F. 'Protestant Magic: W. B. Yeats and the Spell of Irish History'. In *Paddy and Mr Punch: Connections in Irish and English History*. London: Penguin, 1995: 212–32.

Gibbons, Luke. *Gaelic Gothic: Race, Colonization, and Irish Culture*. Galway: Arlen House, 2004.

Hansen, Jim. *Terror and Irish Modernism: The Gothic Tradition from Burke to Beckett*. Albany, NY: State University of New York Press, 2009.

Haslam, Richard, 'Irish Gothic'. In Catherine Spooner and Emma McEvoy (eds), *The Routledge Companion to Gothic*. London: Routledge, 2007: 83–94.

Haslam, Richard. 'Irish Gothic: A Rhetorical Hermeneutics Approach'. *Irish Journal of Gothic and Horror Studies* 2 (2007). http://irishgothichorrorjournal.homestead.com/index.html. Accessed 12 August 2018.

Kilfeather, Siobhán, 'The Gothic Novel'. In John Wilson Foster (ed.), *The Cambridge Companion to the Irish Novel*. Cambridge: Cambridge University Press, 2006: 78–96.

---

[63] See Marilyn Butler, 'Edgeworth's Ireland: History, Popular Culture, and Secret Codes', *Novel* 34, no. 2 (2001), 267–92; Jarlath Killeen, 'Irish Gothic Revisited', *Irish Journal of Gothic and Horror Studies* 4 (2008) http://irishgothichorrorjournal.homestead.com/index.html. Accessed 12 August 2018.

[64] Bram Stoker, *Dracula*, ed. Maurice Hindle (London: Penguin, 2003), 401.

[65] For a sober assessment of the possibility that Stoker was planning a sequel, see Elizabeth Miller, *Sense and Nonsense* (Southend-on-Sea, Essex: Desert Island Books, 2006), 90–1.

[66] Wilde, 'The Canterville Ghost', 105.

Killeen, Jarlath. *The Emergence of Irish Gothic Fiction: Histories, Origins, Theories*. Edinburgh: Edinburgh University Press, 2014.

McCormack, W. J. 'Irish Gothic and After (1820–1945)'. In Seamus Deane (gen. ed.), *The Field Day Anthology of Irish Writing*, Volume 2. Derry: Field Day Publications, 1991: 831–949.

Morash, Christopher. 'The Time is Out of Joint (O Curséd Spite!): Towards a Definition of a Supernatural Narrative'. In Bruce Stewart (ed.), *That Other World: The Supernatural and the Fantastic in Irish Literature and its Contexts*. Gerrards Cross: Colin Smythe, 2003: 123–42.

Morin, Christina. *The Gothic Novel in Ireland, c.1760–1829*. Manchester: Manchester University Press, 2018.

Morin, Christina and Niall Gillespie (eds). *Irish Gothics: Genres, Forms, Modes, and Traditions, 1760–1890*. Basingstoke: Palgrave Macmillan, 2014.

CHAPTER 3

....

NATION, GENDER, AND GENRE

Nineteenth-Century Women's Writing and the Development of Irish Fiction

....

GERARDINE MEANEY

[A] low, sobbing, wailing cry echoed mournfully through the room. No form of words could give an idea of the sound.... As the summer wind comes and goes amongst the trees, so that mournful wail came and went—came and went. It came in a rush of sound, like a gradual crescendo managed by a skilful musician, and it died away like a lingering note, so that the listener could scarcely tell the exact moment when it faded away into silence. I say faded away, for it disappeared as the coast line disappears in the twilight, and there was utter stillness in the apartment.[1]

THE dark romance of the west; the inescapability of the past; the tension between modernity and tradition; urban alienation and dangerous atavism; fascination with folklore: Charlotte Riddell's (1832–1906) short story, 'Hertford O'Donnell's Warning', anticipates many of the themes which have become definitive of modern Irish fiction, even if the sentimental and moral ending is pure Victoriana. First published in 1867 and frequently anthologized, the story adapted elements of the banshee tradition to the conventions of the Victorian ghost story with an uncannily familiar plot. A successful middle-aged Irish professional man finds his ambitions for assimilation into the imperial bourgeoisie disturbed by a devastating echo of the past and the west of Ireland. While Gabriel Conroy in 'The Dead' finds his comfortable life haunted by his wife's dead lover, Dr Hertford O'Donnell is troubled by a combination of supernatural and familial forces.

---

[1] Charlotte Riddell, 'Hertford O'Donnell's Warning', in *Frank Sinclair's Wife, and Other Stories* (London: Tinsley Brothers, 1874), vol. 3, 268–9.

He has been parted from his pregnant first love by Irish sectarianism and family feuding. He is called to their son's deathbed by the O'Donnell's familial herald of death (otherwise known as a banshee), who follows father and son through London's streets and even hospital corridors. If the body of the story anticipates Gothic modernism, the ending manages to resolve intractable political and religious differences, contain supernatural forces, and fulfil the moral requirements of popular Victorian fiction through the device of an appropriate marriage. Although O'Donnell fails to save the life of his ill-fated son, he does marry the boy's mother. The heiress he had pursued in London proves herself a woman of high moral character by supporting this moral redemption of her suitor and accepting that another woman has prior claim on his affections.

Despite its rehearsal of many of the key themes of the Irish Literary Revival, this aspect of Riddell's work was rarely the subject of critical commentary until Margaret Kelleher's stirring 2000 essay, which argued that a century after her death, 'a number of her works deserve more critical attention than they have received. For readers and critics still seeking adequate models for understanding the complex processes of women's literary production, or their "struggles for fame", the case of Charlotte Riddell—life, work, and reputation—is certainly worthy of notice.'[2] Riddell's role in developing the petit bourgeois as a proper subject of fiction in English, which she pioneered in *George Geith of Fen Court* (1864), remains a footnote in accounts of the evolution of both English and Irish social fiction, though Riddell's work usually included Gothic or sensational elements even in the most quotidian locations.[3] *George Geith of Fen Court*'s detailed mapping of the streets and trade of the City of London forms part of a current of Irish urban fiction. This trend runs through May Laffan Hartley's (*c.*1850–1916) stories of Dublin society, whose themes range from destitute children through to the corrupt political class, on into its twentieth-century apotheosis in the fiction of James Joyce (1882–1941) and the meticulous mapping of both Irish and English urban settings in the work of Norah Hoult (1898–1984) and Elizabeth Bowen (1899–1973).[4] The combination of Gothic narrative and scrupulous social and geographical detail in Riddell is readily comparable to Bowen's modernist deployments of both elements, particularly if one starts with their short fiction.

Twenty-first-century criticism is much more attuned to the role of short stories in the development of new forms, styles, and subjects. For example, Heather Ingman's study of the Irish short story shifts the focus away from 'the form's alliance with realism' towards

[2] Margaret Kelleher, 'Charlotte Riddell's *A Struggle for Fame*: The Field of Women's Literary Production', *Colby Quarterly* 36, no. 2 (2000), 130.

[3] See Silvana Colella, *Charlotte Riddell's City Novels and Victorian Business: Narrating Capitalism* (New York: Routledge, 2016) for an extended discussion of Riddell's narrative mapping of the topography of capitalism, primarily the City of London.

[4] For analysis of the significance of Laffan's work, see Helena Kelleher Kahn, *Late Nineteenth-Century Ireland's Political and Religious Controversies in the Fiction of May Laffan Hartley* (Greensboro, NC: ELT Press, 2005) and Jill Brady Hampton, 'Ambivalent Realism: May Laffan's "Flitters, Tatters, and the Counsellor"', *New Hibernia Review* 12, no. 2 (2008), 127–41.

'playfulness and subversion' and 'experimentation and modernity',[5] and Elke D'hoker argues that proper critical attention to women's writing undermines the paradigm of the short story in Ireland as 'a traditional form, rooted in a common Gaelic heritage and general storytelling culture'.[6] D'hoker's identification of the experimental George Egerton (pseudonym of Mary Chavelita Dunne, 1859–1945) and the comic Edith Somerville (1858–1949) and Martin Ross (pseudonym of Violet Martin, 1862–1915) as the 'mothers of the Irish short story'[7] indicates how the radical expansion of the canons of Irish literature is reshaping literary periodization and our understanding of the relationships between genres. These trajectories and pathways indicate that the work of Irish women writers is an important element in understanding the transitions, continuities, and connections between Victorian and modernist fiction which is currently the focus of much critical attention.[8] This new critical context offers a particularly welcome corrective to the joint legacy of cultural nationalism and high modernism which long obscured the complexity and strength of nineteenth-century Irish fiction and continues to distort critical understanding, despite the flourishing over the last quarter of a century of critical studies of nineteenth-century Irish literature.[9] The centrality of modernism in the canon of Irish fiction is overdetermined by its concurrence with the emergence of the independent Irish state and the international importance of Joyce, W. B. Yeats (1865–1939), and Samuel Beckett (1906–89). In effect, these writers offer irresistible signposts in the landscape of the world's literature, such that even the most comprehensive recovery project maps earlier writers on to them (as I have done in this chapter's opening paragraph) in the interests of intelligibility.

Attention to the legacy of Irish women's writing in the 1800s subverts a teleological construction of Irish literary history as a long march towards modernism. It simultaneously challenges the characterization of nineteenth-century Irish fiction as incapable of social realism and driven into the arms of Gothic by the socio-politics of the country. By far the most challenging aspect of this fiction for literary history understood in national terms is the experience of migration, particularly to England, by so many women authors of the period—Riddell included—and their participation in a global publishing industry, where they worked as editors as well as authors in London-based

---

[5] Heather Ingman, *A History of the Irish Short Story* (Cambridge: Cambridge University Press, 2009), 12.

[6] Elke D'hoker, *Irish Women Writers and the Modern Short Story* (Basingstoke: Palgrave Macmillan, 2016), 3.

[7] Ibid., 21–50.

[8] See, for example, Louise Kane and Deborah Mutch (eds), *Victorian into Modern: Suturing the Divide, 1875–1935* (New York: Routledge, 2017) and the proceedings of the 'Transitions: Bridging the Victorian-Modernist Divide' conference, University of Birmingham, 9–10 April 2018.

[9] The publications of the Society for the Study of Nineteenth Century Ireland since 1994 give an excellent overview of the interdisciplinarity and energy of the field (http://ssnci.com/publications/). *Nineteenth-Century Ireland: A Guide to Research* (Dublin: University College Dublin Press, 2005), edited by Laurence M. Geary and Margaret Kelleher, summarized research to 2005 and laid the groundwork for a decade of further activity. James H. Murphy's *Irish Writers and the Victorian Age* (Oxford: Oxford University Press, 2011) is the first really comprehensive survey of Irish Victorian fiction.

periodicals and sometimes commanded lucrative deals with American publishers.[10] Riddell's resurrection in the canon of Irish fiction has been primarily driven by interest in her three-volume autobiographical *Künstlerroman, A Struggle for Fame* (1883), which is increasingly the subject of critical debates about the nineteenth-century novel and women's place in it.[11] A portrait of the artist which maps her rise and fall, from brilliant young literary woman to early, exhausted, and disillusioned death, the novel anticipates the preoccupation of New Woman fiction in its portrayal of women as artists, though Riddell's portrayal of her heroine, Glenarva Westley, is more pragmatic and less concerned with aesthetics and politics than later treatments of the topic by Katherine Cecil Thurston (1875–1911) and Sarah Grand (pseudonym of Frances Clarke McFall, 1854–1943). Ultimately, however, *A Struggle for Fame* is as pessimistic as later modernist treatments of women's ambitions for autonomy, such as Bowen's *The Last September* (1929).

Described as 'one of the finest Victorian novels about writing Victorian novels',[12] *A Struggle for Fame* brilliantly satirizes the less able writers who forge a career from following literary fashion, while scorning its heroine for her success with a broad readership. Linda Petersen has argued convincingly that Glenarva is both the writer's surrogate in the novel and an interrogation of the myth of the woman novelist as Romantic genius propagated by Elizabeth Gaskell's life of Charlotte Brontë. The novel's relationship to autobiographical content, the cult of literary genius, and the late nineteenth-century marketplace is strategically ambivalent. This is a critical *Künstlerroman*: its obvious descendants in canonical twentieth-century fiction are Joyce's *A Portrait of the Artist as a Young Man* (1916) and Kate O'Brien's (1897–1974) *The Land of Spices* (1941), if either author could contemplate their precocious alter egos as disillusioned middle-aged geniuses destroyed by fame. Tonally, the closest work to the last volume of *A Struggle for Fame* in twentieth-century Irish writing is probably 'The Best Butter', a 1966 short story by Una Troy (1910–93), which deals with the lonely old age of a young woman who has fled small-town Ireland for a brilliant literary career that brings her recognition from those who once despised her but also leaves her impoverished and isolated.[13]

---

[10] See Linda H. Peterson, *Becoming a Woman of Letters: Myths of Authorship and Facts of the Victorian Market* (New Jersey, NJ: Princeton University Press, 2009).

[11] See, for example, Linda H. Peterson, 'Charlotte Riddell's *A Struggle for Fame*: Myths of Authorship, Facts of the Market', *Women's Writing* 11, no. 1 (2004), 99–115; Patrick Maume, 'Works, Righteousness, Philanthropy, and the Market in the Novels of Charlotte Riddell', in Anna Pilz and Whitney Standlee (eds), *Irish Women's Writing, 1878–1922: Advancing the Cause of Liberty* (Manchester: Manchester University Press, 2016), 17–32; Kyriaki Hadjiafxendi and Patricia Zakreski (eds), *Crafting the Woman Professional in the Long Nineteenth Century: Artistry and Industry in Britain* (New York: Routledge, 2016). *A Struggle for Fame* was republished in 2016 by Tramp Press, the powerhouse of twenty-first-century Irish experimental fiction.

[12] John Sutherland, *The Longman Companion to Victorian Fiction* (Harlow: Longman, 1989), 620.

[13] See Una Troy, 'The Best Butter', *Kilkenny Magazine* 14 (1966), 48–61. Beset by the constraints of Irish censorship, Troy, who also wrote under the pseudonym Elizabeth Connor, had a very different life experience to Riddell but a similar trajectory in terms of reputation, with increasing interest in her work from contemporary critics.

Riddell was for a time a highly successful literary editor, successor to Dublin-born Anna Maria Hall (1800–81) at *St James Magazine*. Like Hall, Riddell's writing challenges the revivalist and modernist myths of a fallow field of Irish literary fiction left uncultivated after Maria Edgeworth's (1767–1849) *Castle Rackrent* in 1800 allegedly made the impossibility of Irish realism manifest.[14] Politically, the successful Irish women writers of the mid-nineteenth century were both too much at home in London and too critical of Ireland, though Riddell is very astute about anti-Irish prejudice. Hertford O'Donnell's superiors in Guy's Hospital distrust him because 'he was Irish—not merely by the accident of birth, which might have been forgiven, since a man cannot be held accountable for such caprices of Nature, but by every other accident and design which is objectionable to the orthodox and respectable and representative English mind'.[15] O'Donnell's capacity to treat his patients without regard to class or social distinction and 'to talk cordially to corduroy and fustian'[16] is presented as his positive Irish inheritance in the story. Ireland's failings are nonetheless evident in his parents' desire to foist an arranged marriage on him and the bitter feuding that ruins young lives in a society 'divided by old animosities and by difference of religion'.[17]

Riddell was herself unfashionable and impoverished in later life. The reservations of nineteenth-century reviewers in relation to her work is typical of the objections to many of her female contemporaries. For example, a review of *The Race for Wealth* (1886) commented that she had 'taken to parodying herself', adding:

> This is much to be regretted, for Mrs. Riddell has shown how well she can delineate both scenery and character. She stands out from the herds of novelists by her poetical feeling and dramatic power. In the former she is alone surpassed by 'George Eliot.' 'The Race for Wealth' does not do her justice. The reason, however, is not difficult to find.... One sermon a week is thought too much for a clergyman, and certainly two novels in twelve months are too much for any author.[18]

This decline in popularity and critical credibility is reflected in the fate of Glenarva. Already under financial pressure because of the business failures of her husband, Mordaunt Logan-Lacere, she receives news from her publisher that her book sales are falling, at which point we are told that 'if ever there was a literary woman who paced the London pavements in a fine frenzy of despair, that woman was Glenarva Logan-Lacere'.[19]

At a time when writing was the only middle-class profession which allowed a woman to support her family, women writers were frequently both excused their professional ambition on the basis of familial duty and portrayed as doomed in their artistic ambition for the same reason. Paradoxically, despite the sad end of Riddell's *Künstlerroman*

---

[14] See Derek Hand, *A History of the Irish Novel* (Cambridge: Cambridge University Press, 2011), 69.
[15] Riddell, 'Hertford O'Donnell's Warning', 252.   [16] Ibid., 251.
[17] Ibid., 291.   [18] Anonymous, 'Belles Lettres', *The Westminster Review* 86, no. 169 (1866), 526.
[19] Charlotte Riddell, *A Struggle for Fame* (London: Richard Bentley, 1883), vol. 3, 317. Kathryn Laing has recently analysed the gendered dimension of this type of critique. See her 'Hannah Lynch and the Narratives of the Irish Revival', *New Hibernia Review* 20, no. 1 (2016), 42–57.

and career, Victorian women writers had much stronger role models of women's success in the literary world than their equivalents a century later. This success was often transitory, but its scale made writers particularly vulnerable to the accusations of deficient aesthetic seriousness and preoccupation with the English literary marketplace. Several of the most popular Irish woman writers, such as Riddell, Katharine Tynan (1859–1931), and Rosa Mulholland (1841–1921), were dauntingly prolific. While Tynan and Mulholland identified with Irish nationalism and were admired by key cultural revivalists, they appear to have been too much at ease in the metropolitan literary world to please later nationalist critics, who considered both literary merit and national purity to be predicated on distance from that milieu and rejection of assimilation into the traditions of English realism. While Hall and Riddell use folk elements in their fiction, by the early twentieth century a clear division between commercial popular culture and authentic folk culture had evolved to the point where Yeats and J. M. Synge (1871–1909) could dismiss Emily Lawless's (1845–1913) *Grania: The Story of an Island* (1892) for its lack of authenticity.

Bookended by *Castle Rackrent* and Somerville and Ross's *The Big House of Inver* (1925), the long nineteenth-century tradition of Big House fiction was both continued and challenged by modernism (notably in Bowen's *The Last September*) and given an occasional postmodern twist, as in Edna O'Brien's (1930–) provocative *House of Splendid Isolation* (1994). Above all, the Big House novel bequeathed an allegorical tradition, whereby the domestic is always political and the boundaries between the familial and the national dissolve in complex patterns of kinship and betrayal. One of the most striking elements of the trajectory from *Castle Rackrent*'s narrative of the decline of one class (the landed gentry) and emergence of another (the Catholic middle class) is the deeply pessimistic national narrative which offers no viable future to either class in *The Real Charlotte* (1894) and *The Big House of Inver*.[20] If the inability of the Anglo-Irish gentry to control their environment is played out in Somerville and Ross's short stories as comedy, notably in *Some Experiences of an Irish R.M.* (1899), *Further Experiences of an Irish R.M.* (1908), and *In Mr Knox's Country* (1915), their decline is treated as tragedy in the novels, even if the tragedy is satirized and richly deserved. However unenthusiastic Somerville and Ross may have been about the Revival and cultural nationalism, these narratives embody the national in the familial in ways which are structured by nationalist mythology and symbolism. Charlotte Mullen in *The Real Charlotte* is a conniving Éire seeking the not-so-young man who will revive her fortunes in the form of the corrupt Roddy Lambert. In *The Big House of Inver*, destruction is wrought through the ambivalent figure of Shibby Pindy, the illegitimate daughter of an Ascendancy family whose decline in fortune and status is accompanied by an increase in such illegitimate descendants on and around its estate. Desire and descent connect the landed gentry and their tenants in a way which completely undermines the notion of aristocratic entitlement associated with Christopher Dysart in *The Real Charlotte* and grotesquely parodied in the two Kits

---

[20] Martin Ross had died by the time of the latter publication, but Somerville insisted on publishing her later fiction under their dual pseudonym.

of *The Big House of Inver*. Beauty Kit is an aristocratic ancestor whose 'looks and his fortune were as good as his morals were bad'[21]; his dissolute and illegitimate descendent and namesake ruins all his sister's plans to restore the family fortune.

Somerville and Ross bridge the divide between nineteenth- and twentieth-century fiction. *The Big House of Inver* is followed sixteen years later by *Two Days in Aragon* (1941) by Molly Keane (pseudonym of M. J. Farrell, 1904–96), where the transition of the Big House narrative from Edgeworth's tales of decline (*Castle Rackrent*) or renewal (*The Absentee*) to metaphor for the stillbirth of a nation is complete. The trope of the woman of the house who protects the past at the expense of the present and thus destroys or imperils her children and their future is more prevalent in twentieth-century theatre than in fiction, and is most notably represented by John B. Keane's (1928–2002) play, *Big Maggie* (1969). It has some very strong echoes in twenty-first-century Gothic fiction, however, particularly Tana French's (1973–) *Broken Harbour* (2012), in which the tragedy of a family clinging on to a house they can no longer afford is played out on a post-Celtic Tiger ghost estate. The power of the family home as metaphor for the troubles of a class or a nation is a residue of both the Big House tradition and cultural nationalism, and the popularity of French's novel shows that this trope continues to attract a large readership to women's writing which challenges the boundaries between popular and literary fiction.

In the absence of any overt acknowledgement of a tradition of Irish nineteenth-century social realism by twentieth-century Irish fiction writers, the clearest evidence of continuity lies in these writers' treatment of landscape, folklore, and, above all, the Gothic elements in Victorian fiction. This is most famously embodied in Joyce's uses of Sheridan Le Fanu's (1814–73) *The House by the Churchyard* (1863) in *Finnegans Wake* (1939). The residual influence of women's fiction from the nineteenth and early twentieth centuries is detectable primarily in the work of lesser known and lesser analysed writers, however. Tina O'Toole's and Whitney Standlee's astute comparisons of the Ibsenist allegiances, social milieu, sexual openness, and, above all, stylistic experiments of George Egerton and James Joyce represent important insights into Irish literary history.[22] The long project of feminist recovery has frequently pioneered within Irish literary studies the paradigm shifts in literary history which create new contexts for the understanding of modern fiction. These have included critical interest in the transition from Victorianism to modernism focused on connectivity rather than rupture; the re-positioning of modernism along a continuum of cultural practices from avant-garde art to popular culture; a new emphasis on cultural exchange and the complex interplay of literary networks and global marketplaces; and a fresh understanding of the symbiosis

[21] Edith Somerville and Martin Ross, *The Big House of Inver* (London: William Heinemann, 1925), 3.
[22] See Tina O'Toole, *The Irish New Woman* (Basingstoke: Palgrave Macmillan, 2013) and Whitney Standlee, 'George Egerton, James Joyce and the Irish *Künstlerroman*', *Irish Studies Review* 18, no. 4 (2010), 439–52. O'Toole has recently extended her analysis to uncover the structural commonalities between Egerton and Elizabeth Bowen. See her 'Unregenerate Spirits: The Counter-Cultural Experiments of George Egerton and Elizabeth Bowen', in Elke D'hoker, Raphaël Ingelbien, and Hedwig Schwall (eds), *Irish Women Writers: New Critical Perspectives* (Bern: Peter Lang, 2011), 227–45.

and dialogue between short stories and novels. If the Revival pre-empted the fusion of social and national narrative, in many respects both modernist writing (especially the early Joyce) and a broader grouping of Irish writing across popular, genre, and literary fiction exhibit the persistence of the marriage of the quotidian and the fantastic, the economic and the mythic, which is a marked feature of Irish women's nineteenth-century fiction. Standlee and O'Toole have made different but equally persuasive arguments for an understanding of Egerton as an important predecessor with whose work Joyce, with his broad interest in experimental fiction and decadence, was likely to be familiar. The more we know and understand about the legacy of nineteenth-century Irish women's fiction, the more we will appreciate the complex context of Irish fiction in the twentieth century and the intricate webs that connect Victorian and modern.

The prevalence of the *Künstlerroman* among late nineteenth- and early twentieth-century Irish women writers is significant. As a genre it is self-reflexive about the writing of fiction and the writing of self. Its narrative structure is inherently unstable, for the *Künstlerroman* narrates the conditions of its own production. It is a natural medium for mapping out transitional cultural spaces, and the *Künstlerromans* of Riddell, Egerton, Grand, and Thurston trace the instabilities of gender experienced by women transitioning from domestic to public and aesthetic to economic roles, sometimes in the space of a single sentence. Long before the fetishization of exile as the preferred locale of the modernist artist, these novelists chronicled the experience of migrating back and forth between Ireland, Britain, and beyond. The move to London is a key prelude to a literary career for Riddell, Egerton, and Grand's protagonists, and in *A Fair Emigrant* (1888) and *The Return of Mary O'Murrough* (1908), Rosa Mulholland explores the social phenomenon of the 'female Yank' who returns to rural Ireland with American domestic expectations and (powerful) American money.[23]

Katherine Cecil Thurston further expands the geographical and metaphorical scope of these themes. Anna Solny, the heroine of her first novel, *The Circle* (1903), is already an immigrant from eastern Europe before she embarks on her career as an actress in London. In her final novel, *Max* (1910), a Russian noblewoman moves from St Petersburg to Paris and from one gender identity to another to train as an artist. A merchant's daughter like Thurston herself, Anna rises through the ranks of one of the very few other professions which offered such opportunities, the stage. Thurston was careful to avoid any autobiographical comparisons to Anna, a young Russian Jewish woman who begins life in more modest circumstances than her creator. It is tempting nonetheless to imagine that her heroine's sense of claustrophobia in her sheltered life in her father's shop reflects some of Thurston's frustration with the life she left behind in Cork. Of Anna, we are told: 'Life in the curio shop, in the little parlour behind it, in the cramped bedroom upstairs, was one persistent waiting—for something that never came.'[24] Anna escapes this life with

---

[23] See Bernadette Whelan's discussion of this phenomenon in Gerardine Meaney, Mary O'Dowd, and Bernadette Whelan, *Reading the Irish Woman: Studies in Cultural Encounter and Exchange, 1714–1960* (Liverpool: Liverpool University Press, 2013), 102–3.

[24] Katherine Cecil Thurston, *The Circle* (New York: Burt, 1903), 2.

the help of a remarkable woman who combines the attributes of a Svengali and a fairy godmother. The novelist, in contrast, left Cork already married to Ernest Temple Thurston, initially to further his literary ambitions in London rather than her own. *Max* recounts a young woman's escape from her tempestuous marriage and from the gender restrictions of Tsarist Russia by cross-dressing as an aspirant male artist. Another of Thurston's characters seeking escape from the constraints of femininity into a life of creativity and artistic achievement, Max/Maxine's odyssey raises many questions about the possibility of a truly equal partnership between a man and a woman and the compatibility of artistic and sexual freedom. The intense seriousness with which Thurston's novels treated art and creativity was typical of her time and milieu, and is also indicative of the continuities between decadent, Gothic, New Woman, and modernist aesthetics.

It is impossible to define the writing of late nineteenth- and early twentieth-century Irish women in any kind of opposition to modernist experiment. They may not all take stylistic risks, but a great many of them challenge boundaries and enable new modes of imagining what it is to be a woman, a writer, a migrant moving between countries and classes. Their novels are scrupulous in their mapping of the economic conditions of existence. The forthrightness about the need to make a living is quite different in tone from both the modernist and naturalist traditions which later emerged in Irish fiction. Perhaps one of the reasons Yeats insisted Lawless missed the Celtic spirit is that she embodied it in *Grania* in a woman who is both an idealized relic of a lost culture and an impoverished peasant trying to make a living selling her livestock. Even authentic personifications of Gaelic Ireland must eat, in Lawless's worldview. This is partly due to an affiliation to social realism which is evident even in the fiction of those nineteenth- and early twentieth-century Irish women writers who worked in non-realist genres. Riddell realizes the working life of Hertford O'Donnell in such detail that the minutiae of surgical procedure are as present as folklore and melodrama. Like Thurston, Grand, and Egerton, she also maps the complex interrelations of commerce and aesthetics, individualism and networking that defined the working life of writers long after the transition from Victorianism to modernism.

To understand the relationship between nineteenth- and early twentieth-century Irish women's writing and the development of Irish fiction in the twentieth and twenty-first centuries it is necessary to acknowledge the elisions performed by both modernist and nationalist canon formation. Contemporary criticism has the advantage of a very wide digital panorama of texts and contexts which will ultimately enable a much more nuanced understanding of the relationship between Victorian and modern, the web of interdependencies between Gothic and multiple shades of realism and naturalism, and the evolution of the Revival from genres, modes, and cultural practices against which it would define its national project. One of the earliest and most effective uses of new digital tools in Irish literary history was the Munster Women Writers project, which was very much ahead of its time in producing an online searchable database as well as a published volume.[25] The Women in Modern Irish Culture Database followed, identifying

---

[25] Tina O'Toole (ed.), *Dictionary of Munster Women Writers* (Cork: Cork University Press, 2005).

over nine thousand writers working across every possible genre from 1800 to 2005.[26] Margaret Kelleher's work in creating an electronic version of Rolf and Magda Loeber's astonishingly comprehensive survey of Irish writing between 1650 and 1900 (written in collaboration with Anne Mullin Burnham) is not gender specific, but it does illuminate just how rich and varied is the heritage of Irish women's writing.[27] Current digital projects such as 'Nation, Gender and Genre' and 'Contagion: Biopolitics and Cultural Memory' seek to move from creating databases and bibliographies to using text-mining techniques to create an overview of what was actually written and read, explore how that writing engaged with social, political, and aesthetic topics, and recover texts which have been buried under the sediment of literary prejudice.[28] Kathryn Laing's work on the social networks of Irish women users of the British Library is not itself a digital project, but her collaboration with Sinéad Mooney has created a rapidly developing online resource via the Irish Women's Writing Network.[29]

The impact of these initiatives on the general understanding of literary history is a work in progress. Eric Hayot has argued that the impact of digital humanities has been radically diminished because it 'segregates these questions almost entirely from the work most literature scholars do'.[30] This division is beginning to break down, however. Irish literary history, particularly our understanding of the legacy of women writers submerged by canon and syllabus formation, has a huge amount to gain by taking up Andrew Stauffer's challenge that 'we all must be "double agents," able to mine large digital resources while also attending closely to textures of language only perceptible to a human reader'.[31] On the debit side, the rapid expansion of authors and texts which need to be integrated into an account of the nineteenth-century contexts of modern Irish fiction has created some degree of critical disorientation and fragmentation.

The posthumous career of Emily Lawless offers a fascinating case study which it is instructive to consider in some detail here. Lawless upsets attempts at categorization. Her paternal family was nationalist, her maternal family's allegiances unionist. She was personally opposed to Home Rule and the Land Acts, yet her historical fiction was resolutely sympathetic to Gaelic Ireland and unflinching about the atrocities committed by English forces against it. Consequently, Lawless's literary reputation has continually ebbed and flowed in response to national and cultural politics. Yeats's dismissal of *Grania* on the basis of its demonstration of an 'imperfect sympathy with the Celtic

---

[26] See https://warwick.ac.uk/fac/arts/history/irishwomenwriters/. Accessed 30 July 2018.

[27] The online Loeber Guide to Irish Fiction project is ongoing and is scheduled to become available in late 2020.

[28] See www.nggprojectucd.ie and www.contagion.ie. Accessed 30 July 2018.

[29] See https://irishwomenswritingnetwork.com. Accessed 30 July 2018. See also Kathryn Laing's paper, 'Late Nineteenth-Century Irish Women Writers, London Literary Networks and the Spaces and Places of "Making it New"', delivered at the 'Transitions: Bridging the Victorian-Modernist Divide' conference, University of Birmingham, 10 April 2018.

[30] Eric Hayot, 'Scale, Data, and World Literature'. http://erichayot.org/wp-content/uploads/2013/11/scaledata.pdf. Accessed 3 August 2018.

[31] Andrew Stauffer, 'Introduction: Virtual Victorians', in Veronica Alfano and Andrew Stauffer (eds), *Virtual Victorians: Networks, Connections, Technologies* (Basingstoke: Palgrave Macmillan, 2015), 3.

nature'[32] is well known. Yet John Brannigan has pointed out the irony that Yeats preferred the more authentic Celtic femininity of Fiona Macleod, later unmasked as a pseudonym of William Sharp. Brannigan also makes a convincing case for the unacknowledged influence of Lawless, particularly her characterization of Old Durane in *Grania*, on Yeats and more especially Synge.[33]

Lawless created in Grania a character who was an Irish peasant version of the New Woman precisely because she also embodied a kind of eternal tragic feminine. She signed her mentor Margaret Oliphant's infamous 1889 letter opposing women's suffrage, yet her fiction was unwavering in its depiction of the social constraints that limited and shortened women's lives. Grania confronts *avant la lettre* the dissonance a fully realized, active, female protagonist causes in the mythic landscape of the west of Ireland imagined by the Revival writers, even those as subtle and linguistically powerful as Synge. Grania speaks for herself, in her own language, manages her farm, and owns her place in the world. She is destroyed by two parallel, gendered networks wherein tradition and modernity, far from being antithetical, operate in fatal complicity. Her inadequate father, her restless fiancé with grand tales and little initiative, the marketplace where a woman without a man is cheated on her livestock: these comprise a failed yet lethal cocktail in which traditional prejudice against a woman farmer and the patriarchal values of modern commerce conspire to make Grania's future very bleak indeed. Just as this world of male precedence dooms her efforts, the feminine networks which offer her connection and warmth smother Grania in responsibilities and unachievable expectations. Struggling under the burden of care for her pious invalided sister, Grania eventually drowns in a doomed effort to bring the priest to give her the last rites. Grania's death identifies her with her seafaring namesake Gráinne O'Malley and suggests that such a woman can no longer keep her head above water in a modern world dominated by men like her fiancé Murdough Blake, who cares only 'for the house and the beasts and the bit of money...—that and himself'.[34]

Grania does not in any way mourn romantic Ireland or fetishize folkloric culture and peasant ways, however. Rather, the novel offers an unusually clear-eyed account of how folklore functioned in a subsistence economy to justify the repudiation of sickly or disabled children as changelings. Grania's independence and strange ways lead to comparisons with the unfortunate Katty O'Callaghan, who 'held to it that it was her own child, not changed at all, only sick',[35] when her neighbours and mother-in-law insist her ailing baby is a changeling. Katty is driven to violence by their taunts and laughter, and eventually leaves her husband and the island to bury her dead infant. There is a strong resonance here with Le Fanu's haunting 'The Child that Went with the Fairies' (1870), as well as a

---

[32] W. B. Yeats, 'Irish National Literature, II: Contemporary Prose Writers', in *Uncollected Prose by W. B. Yeats, Volume One: First Reviews and Articles 1886–1896*, ed. John P. Freyne (New York: Columbia University Press, 1970), 369.

[33] John Brannigan, '"On a Wet Rock in the Atlantic": J. M. Synge and Ethnographies of the Irish Revival', *Modernism/Modernity* 24, no. 2 (2017), 340–1.

[34] Emily Lawless, *Grania: The Story of an Island* (London: Smith, Elder and Co., 1892), vol. 2, 134.

[35] Emily Lawless, *Grania: The Story of an Island* (London: Smith, Elder and Co., 1892), vol. 1, 244–5.

striking rebuke to Yeats's romanticization of changeling lore in 'The Stolen Child' in *The Wanderings of Oisin and Other Poems* (1889). Lawless, unlike Le Fanu, does not hint that the history of famine and deprivation made rejection or infanticide of the weak inevitable and its normalization in folklore a defence mechanism. Nor does she suggest that the twilight world of fantasy offers relief from a world 'full of weeping', as 'The Stolen Child' has it. The change in tone between Le Fanu and Lawless may be related to changes in the function of changeling beliefs. The novel came out just three years before the infamous Bridget Cleary case, where changeling belief functioned to enforce social regulation of women and block social change rather than justify rejection of those who would become a burden on the community.[36] Lawless's dark example of the cruel orthodoxy of traditional beliefs is in striking contrast to Riddell's terrifying but truth-bearing banshee and Jane Barlow's (1856–1917) lyrical and gentle *Irish Idylls* (1892), a collection of short stories in which folk belief offers a primitive form of social security for widows and orphans.

In Lawless, the deconstruction of any opposition between tradition and modernity is allied to a deep-rooted antagonism towards the discourse of authenticity. Reviewing two translations from ancient Gaelic literature by Whitley Stokes and Standish O'Grady (1846–1928) in 1897, she made the following observation:

> A good deal of talk goes on in these days about the Celtic spirit, but does anyone really know what that spirit is? Has anyone ever tracked it to its secret home; ascertained where it was born, and of what elements it was originally composed? If we look at it closely and quite dispassionately, is it not nearly as much a topographical as either a philological or an ethnological spirit? Certainly if 'the breath of Celtic eloquence' is not also to some degree the breath of the Atlantic, I should be puzzled to define what it is. So soft, and so loud; so boisterous, and so heady; extremely enervating, according to some people's opinion, but Oh how subtly, how fascinatingly intoxicating, it is certainly not the property of any one creed, age, or condition of life, any more than it is of any one set of political convictions. We can only say of it that like other breaths it bloweth where it listeth. There is no necessary connection between it and the Clan-na-Gael, any more than there is between it and Landlords' Conferences or Diocesan Synods.[37]

It is not difficult to trace here an unease with lazy, uncritical thinking and a mischievous undermining of stereotypes which are reminiscent of the dramatic work of Oscar Wilde (1854–1900) and George Bernard Shaw (1856–1950). Lawless's incisive views on the ethics of literary forgery were little read during the twentieth century, except in feminist literary circles. Nevertheless, this interrogation of received categories and celebration of fluid identities chimes with the preoccupations of much twenty-first-century Irish fiction, finding peculiar echoes in writers as diverse as Kevin Barry (1969–), Anne Enright (1962–), and Sara Baume (1984–).

---

[36] See Angela Bourke, *The Burning of Bridget Cleary: A True Story* (London: Pimlico, 1999).

[37] Emily Lawless, 'A Note on the Ethics of Literary Forgery', *The Nineteenth Century and After: A Monthly Review* 41, (1897), 92.

Lawless's contribution to the long-term development of Irish fiction has a certain sub-terranean quality to it. In her powerful and unjustly overlooked historical fiction, we can trace an engagement with protracted historical processes rooted in an intensely obser-vant and sympathetic attention to the natural world which is very different to John McGahern's (1934–2006) rural naturalism, yet related to it. In *Maelcho* (1894), set during the Desmond rebellion in late sixteenth-century Munster, the narrator disingenuously regrets that Shakespeare did not encounter the great tragedies unfolding in Ireland dur-ing his lifetime: 'Surely then the world would have been made richer by one great tragedy the more, and Pity, divine but slow moving Pity, might have opened her wings in a little less niggardly fashion than she did?'[38] The novel's engagement with Elizabethan literature rehearses a preoccupation of English-language modernism, exemplified in the discourse on Hamlet in *Ulysses* (1922). The earnest literary Irishmen who measure levels of cultural attainment, difference, and assimilation against this English literary icon are also engaged in distinguishing themselves from the popular feminine in the figure of Maria Corelli, who is satirized in the same conversation.[39]

Lawless is engaged in a parallel exercise, with additional layers of political complexity. 'Wanting the poet', she tells us, 'the whole of Munster and the counties adjoining to it became that year a sort of hell',[40] as the rebellion of 1579–83 was savagely repressed. The early modern period is a relatively infrequent topic for modern Irish historical fiction; Walter Macken's (1915–67) three novels, *Seek the Fair Land* (1959), *The Silent People* (1962), and *The Scorching Wind* (1964), and Ronan Bennett's (1956–) *Havoc in its Third Year* (2004) are fascinating exceptions. In making Maelcho—a *seanchaí* (oral storyteller) and follower of Sir James Fitzmaurice of Desmond—the hero of her tale, Lawless was setting herself very much at odds with the unionist tradition in historical fiction. She was also departing from the approach she took in her partisan Land War novel, *Hurrish* (1886), which is much more in tune with pro-landlord novels such as Anthony Trollope's *Castle Richmond* (1860) and Letitia McClintock's (1835–1917) *A Boycotted Household* (1881).

The polymathic Lawless was a popular historian as well as a popularizer of natural science, and she was paid the ultimate compliment available to a historical novelist when her *With Essex in Ireland* (1890) was mistaken for an edition of an authentic journal of the time. *Maelcho* is written from a very different perspective and fuses her recurrent concerns with landscape, history, and culture. The novel denaturalizes both the political and the natural worlds of the early twentieth century, situating them as a product of long-term historical processes that profoundly affected both nature and culture and the relationship between them, as territory was annexed, populations dis-placed, forests felled, and agriculture completely transformed. The novel does not shirk from the atrocities committed by Queen Elizabeth I's forces in Ireland. After the wordsmith Maelcho is driven mad by imprisonment in silence and isolation, he

---

[38] Emily Lawless, *Maelcho: A Sixteenth Century Narrative* (London: Methuen, 1895), 344.
[39] James Joyce, *Ulysses* (Harmondsworth: Penguin, 2000), 254.
[40] Lawless, *Maelcho*, 344–5.

emerges to find his world has collapsed. Fitzmaurice is defeated and his wife and her adored daughters are massacred:

> 'The Queen of England's soldiers came; they came in hundreds and thousands! We had hidden them in the cave yonder; yes, in the cave with the other women and children, and in the innermost part of all, in the safest part of all. Could we do more than that? What more was there for us to do? What more could we do, say, Oh man returned from the grave? How could we fight? We were only a few men—nine, ten, twelve of us—and some young boys.'[41]

In the twenty-first-century context of ecocriticism, Lawless's fiction is already beginning to be read within new and exciting frameworks, and it is easy to see her as a precursor of landscape writers from Tim Robinson (1935–2020) to Sara Baume.

The conservative turn in literary taste did not extend to popular genres. Dealing sympathetically with adultery, female gambling addiction, and opium addiction in the high realms of government, Katherine Cecil Thurston is a fascinating link between nineteenth-century women's writing and both the modernist and 'domestic' fiction of the first half of the twentieth century. In 1910, the Cork-born novelist was one of the most popular authors in the USA and England. Newspapers and ladies' magazines reported on her clothes, her jewels, her wit, and her vivacious personality. Her novels, which were fast-paced, full of glamour, and extremely popular, dealt with radical ideas and impulsive artistic characters who did not conform to respectable society. The world of her books was populated by addicts, impersonators, actresses, artists, impresarios, romantics, and villains. She wrote of women like herself who took their careers seriously and tried with great difficulty to combine sexual, economic, and personal freedom. This combination obviously appealed to a broad audience at the beginning of the twentieth century. Her last novel, the aforementioned *Max*, which seems daring even today in its depiction of a woman cross-dressing in order to study and work as an artist, rose to fourth in the US bestseller lists. The international distribution, consumption, and adaptation of Thurston's literary output and artistic persona challenges the assumption that the global success of Irish women's popular fiction is a late twentieth-century phenomenon. Anticipating by many decades the strategies of multi-platform celebrity marketing, the Thurston industry enhanced the novelist's image and appeal by means of magazine articles, interviews, avid reporting of her personal life, and dramatizations of her novels, with film adaptations following almost as soon as the new medium of cinema became available.[42]

Thurston promoted an image of herself which combined sophistication and native charm, dividing her time between the metropolitan world of London society and her country house in the seaside town of Ardmore in County Waterford. She was repeatedly referred to in both the London *Times* and *New York Times* as an 'Irish lady of letters'. The more negative connotations of Irish 'wildness' became to some extent attached to her

---

[41] Ibid., 325.

[42] *The Compact*, the first of two screen versions of *John Chilcote M.P.* (1904), was made in 1912 by American Pathé, directed by Joseph A. Golden.

image after her acrimonious divorce in 1910 and in the lurid reporting of her mysterious death, aged thirty-six, the following year. Thurston is now best known for *The Fly on the Wheel* (1908), the only one of her novels reprinted by Virago and championed by Colm Tóibín (1955–) in *The Penguin Book of Irish Fiction* (1999). The novel is set in Waterford, much closer to home than most of Thurston's other fiction, and the claustrophobic middle-class society it depicts offers much more restricted options than those explored in the London and Paris of her other novels. The prominence of this uncharacteristically realist and pessimistic novel has to some extent distorted perceptions of Thurston's work and life. Her heroine's choice of suicide rather than conformity is a grand gesture which rebukes her married lover's cowardice and conventionality. Paradoxically, given Thurston's own success in literary London, the novel's conclusion fuelled speculation that her unexplained early death in a Cork hotel was suicide, while her family claimed medical misadventure or even murder. The decline in interest in her work, her exclusion from the canon, her erasure from literary histories, and the extent to which her death is more visible than her life's work in our digital age makes Thurston iconic of the fate of much nineteenth- and early twentieth-century writing by women.[43]

Thurston's divorce from her novelist husband was reported in great detail. The case was in effect fought by Ernest Temple Thurston as a contest between the claims of decadent art and those of the New Woman. At the divorce proceedings, Katherine accused Ernest of desertion and adultery; it was reported that he responded by stating that 'it was necessary for his literary work that he should descend into the depths of society'.[44] Ernest took himself very seriously as a writer and did not conceal how much he resented the fact that his wife was much more successful than him, though he was careful to present this as commercial rather than artistic success on her part. The newspaper coverage of the Thurstons' divorce was duly scandalized by Ernest's attitude to adultery and slumming, which confirmed every Edwardian stereotype of decadent artistic types. Nonetheless, the picture Ernest painted of Katherine as a domineering woman whose professional triumphs made her unbearable was potentially hugely damaging for her and fitted another stereotype, that of the successful woman writer. The story of a woman's success costing her her marriage went down well in the prevailing context of ongoing fierce resistance to the idea of married women working outside the home. Writing remained one of the few careers in which a clever woman could be really successful in 1910. Katherine's image as a grand lady of letters might have been tarnished by her divorce, but the scandal does not appear to have diminished her books' popularity or made her more cautious in her subject matter. A little notoriety may actually have appealed to Thurston's readers.

---

[43] Even the Women's History Network blog remarks: 'Far from us be it to deflect attention from the work of women writers to their lives. But the circumstances are intriguing: the new man in Thurston's life, his medical knowledge, the parallel (if the death was suicide) with her own book, all suggest something more sensational, more like her own plots, than death from an already-diagnosed medical condition.' https://womenshistorynetwork.org/katherine-cecil-thurston-from-a-will-to-a-death/. Accessed 30 July 2018.

[44] *The Times*, 8 April 1910, 3.

Writers as diverse as Katherine Cecil Thurston, Rosa Mulholland, and Katharine Tynan flourished within the world of popular fiction in *fin-de-siècle* London. Tynan in particular seems to have struggled with the emerging boundaries between recognizably national and literary writing, which was highly esteemed by her peers, and commercial fiction. She argued that her poetry represented her 'real' work, while her novels were 'potboilers, useful for keeping the family pot boiling at home, but not likely to be remembered'.[45] This self-deprecation represents an internalization of the distinction between literary and popular fiction, which Margaret Kelleher has analysed as a key inhibitor of the continuity of tradition and canon formation among women writers, despite recovery projects from the late nineteenth century onwards.[46] It also reflects the economic pressures faced by women writers of the time. Literature was literally the only profession open to women for much of this period and, however successful, women novelists were subject to severe financial restrictions for much of the twentieth century, especially if they were married. Tynan's husband's alcoholism put her under enormous pressure as she tried to provide for her large family and, as Linda Peterson notes, Riddell lost ownership of the copyright of her groundbreaking and critically admired *George Geith of Fen Court* when it was used to guarantee a mortgage on her husband's business.[47] As such examples demonstrate, issues of class and gender could intersect in unexpected ways with the business of publishing, often to the detriment of late nineteenth- and early twentieth-century women writers.

All of the women novelists discussed above had cultural and social resources as well as their own talents at their disposal, but they had limited control over their own assets, business, and even income. Moreover, as commercial success increasingly came to be seen as antithetical to literary excellence, their high sales made it easy for critics to dismiss them as merely popular. Sometimes this became a self-fulfilling prophecy as public demand and the speed of magazine and serialized publication required writers to sustain a prodigiously prolific output to keep that pot boiling. Arguably, these women's precarious finances and often irregular social positions gave them freedom to work, while simultaneously constraining the nature and occasionally the quality of the work they produced. Few had the independent means and rooms of their own which Virginia Woolf would stipulate as the requirements for women writers of the modernist age to fulfil their creativity. None had the patronage which would support uncommercial modernists of no means, such as Joyce, though in their dependence on multiple literary income streams and susceptibility to lapses in respectability there are analogies with Wilde. George Egerton, for example, suffered a severe reversal of fortune as a result of the turn against decadence of all kinds in the aftermath of the Wilde case in the late 1890s, not least because the two shared a publisher.

Play with genre; cross-fertilization between short stories and novel forms; complex relationships between literary and popular fiction; the tensions implicit in writing *about*

---

[45] Katharine Tynan, *The Middle Years* (London: Constable, 1916), 353.
[46] Kelleher, 'Charlotte Riddell's *A Struggle for Fame*', 117.
[47] Peterson, 'Charlotte Riddell's *A Struggle for Fame*', 110.

the local and national while writing *for* an international readership: these characteristics of nineteenth-century women's fiction remain common features of the latter-day Irish literary landscape. It is perhaps at these levels rather than that of style or genre that the continuities are most striking. The entanglement of the domestic, familial, and political which was characteristic of Irish women's writing in the half century before independence continued to shape the Irish novel after 1922. From popular Gothic to New Woman fiction and beyond, these writers in their very different ways grappled with the tension between women's aspirations and opportunities, and especially with the relationship between sexual and aesthetic freedoms. Paradoxically, very little of the stylistically revolutionary fiction that followed was remotely as adventurous in its treatment of gender until the later years of the twentieth century.

FURTHER READING

Bourke, Angela, Siobhán Kilfeather, Maria Luddy, Margaret MacCurtain, Gerardine Meaney, Máirín Ní Dhonnchadha, Mary O'Dowd, and Clair Wills (eds). *The Field Day Anthology of Irish Writing, Volumes IV and V: Irish Women's Writings and Traditions*. Cork: Cork University Press, 2002.

Colella, Silvana. *Charlotte Riddell's City Novels and Victorian Business: Narrating Capitalism*. New York: Routledge, 2016.

D'hoker, Elke. *Irish Women Writers and the Modern Short Story*. Basingstoke: Palgrave Macmillan, 2016.

Ingman, Heather and Clíona Ó Gallchoir (eds). *A History of Modern Irish Women's Literature*. Cambridge: Cambridge University Press, 2018.

Kelleher, Margaret. 'Charlotte Riddell's *A Struggle for Fame*: The Field of Women's Literary Production'. *Colby Quarterly* 36, no. 2 (2000): 116–31.

Kelleher, Margaret. 'Writing Irish Women's Literary History'. *Irish Studies Review* 9, no. 1 (2001): 5–14.

Laing, Kathryn. 'Hannah Lynch and the Narratives of the Irish Revival'. *New Hibernia Review* 20, no. 1 (2016): 42–57.

Meaney, Gerardine. *Gender, Ireland, and Cultural Change*. New York: Routledge, 2010.

Meaney, Gerardine, Mary O'Dowd, and Bernadette Whelan. *Reading the Irish Woman: Studies in Cultural Encounter and Exchange, 1714–1960*. Liverpool: Liverpool University Press, 2013.

Murphy, James H. *Irish Writers and the Victorian Age*. Oxford: Oxford University Press, 2011.

O'Toole, Tina (ed.). *Dictionary of Munster Women Writers*. Cork: Cork University Press, 2005.

O'Toole, Tina. *The Irish New Woman*. Basingstoke: Palgrave Macmillan, 2013.

Peterson, Linda H. *Becoming a Woman of Letters: Myths of Authorship and Facts of the Victorian Market*. New Jersey, NJ: Princeton University Press, 2009.

Pilz, Anna and Whitney Standlee (eds). *Irish Women's Writing, 1878–1922: Advancing the Cause of Liberty*. Manchester: Manchester University Press, 2016.

Standlee, Whitney. 'George Egerton, James Joyce and the Irish *Künstlerroman*'. *Irish Studies Review* 18, no. 4 (2010): 439–52.

CHAPTER 4

···

SHAME IS THE SPUR

Novels by Irish Catholics, 1873–1922

···

JAMES H. MURPHY

SHAME has been one of the spurs to Irish social modernization since the 1960s. This has relied on a view of Ireland as a poor, backward, rural, Catholic country, pivoting towards urbanization, modernization, and prosperity but needing to shed such a regressive image in the face of international derision. However, one need only think of an area such as southern Italy, which has traditionally been similarly characterized as poor, Catholic, and backward, and yet has also been perceived as exotic and glamorous, in spite of, or perhaps even because of, its reputation for criminality, to realize that an empowering shame may actually be a chosen rather than an inevitable attitude. In Ireland, shame has served as a means of energizing an agenda for social change, while also being invoked to dismiss opposition as simply regressive conservatism.

Fiction has been one of the forums in which this empowering shame has been registered and indeed fostered. The leading novelists of the 1960s, such as John McGahern (1934–2006) and Edna O'Brien (1930–), saw themselves as refugees from a backward rural Ireland. Although of modest socio-economic background, they were enabled as writers by a greater access to education. Their fiction charts the rejection of inherited mores and an embrace of a new liberalism that, consonant with the international trend of the times, tended to focus on sexual freedom. For the first time, poorer Irish people of rural Catholic background became both the authors and the subjects of fiction. This was in contrast to earlier phases of Irish fiction with an identifiably Catholic social dimension in which poorer rural Catholics—'peasants', as they were often called—tended to be written about by urban novelists. Empowering shame (the emotion of the insider), or at least its antecedent, urban disdain (the attitude of the outsider), had already been established in Irish fiction by the time McGahern and O'Brien began their careers. In part, this shame came from British and Protestant (particularly evangelical) depictions of Irish Catholics as superstitious and backward. But its principal roots were in earlier fiction by Irish Catholic authors.

There were three phases or waves of Irish Catholic fiction during the time of the Union with Britain, of which the second and particularly the third are the subjects of this chapter, inasmuch as they are part of the raising of the curtain onto modern Irish fiction, which is the subject of this work. Each of these phases coincided with important periods of socio-political crisis and transition, namely, Catholic Emancipation (1829), the Land War (1879–82), and the Irish Revival (1891–1922), the latter term used here as a general designation for a variety of movements for reform and renewal in Ireland. However, in order to understand the contribution of these phases to more recent Irish fiction, which I have characterized as a literature of empowering shame, one must first understand the paradoxical relationship between the urban and the rural in Irish Catholicism since the Reformation.[1]

Much of what people understand about Irish Catholicism is wrong or only partly true. For example, Irish Catholicism's perceived cultural identification with rural Ireland dates only from the nineteenth century. During the eras of the Reformation and Counter-Reformation, in the sixteenth and seventeenth centuries, the vanguard for a renewed and vigorous Catholicism found its locus among the Palesmen and the Old English of the east of Ireland and its towns. For two and a half centuries, Catholic priests, denied an education at home, were trained in centres of cosmopolitan culture in Spain, France, Italy, and the Low Countries. At the end of the eighteenth century the strength of Counter-Reformation or Tridentine Catholicism in Ireland lay in the towns of the east and in some of the more prosperous farming areas of Leinster and Munster. Catholic religious practice in the poorer western parts of Ireland was patchy at best. The nineteenth century, however, witnessed the so-called 'devotional revolution', whose major achievement was the bringing of rural Ireland within the ambit of Counter-Reformation or Tridentine Catholicism.[2] As a result, Catholicism's cultural centre moved from the urban to the rural and became a factor in bolstering a form of social and economic modernization unusual in otherwise urban, industrial Europe because it centred on the family rather than the individual.

As the century progressed, Ireland became a society anxious to enforce the social and sexual mores that assured the survival of the family farm, through legitimate, single-heir, mostly male inheritance. The subdivision of farms had been one of the reasons the Famine of the 1840s had taken such a toll. Families living on smaller and smaller holdings became more and more susceptible to the failure of the potato crop which was the staple of their diet. After the Famine, building up the family farm and passing it on to one heir became a priority. Non-heirs who did not emigrate, enter religious life, or find a job in the locality could remain on the family homestead as celibate farm workers. As a result, just before the First World War a quarter of people in Ireland aged fifty

---

[1] See James H. Murphy, *Ireland: A Social, Cultural and Literary History, 1791–1891* (Dublin: Four Courts Press, 2003), 70–4.

[2] Emmet Larkin, 'The Devotional Revolution in Ireland', *American Historical Review* 80 (1975), 625–52.

were unmarried.[3] A puritanical Catholic sexual code thus suited the interests of this society; but a Catholic disapproval of excessive consumption of alcohol did not, as celibate farm workers needed an outlet. Rural Ireland's embrace of a particular form of Catholicism was thus always partial and self-serving, in spite of the often robust and assertive presence of the institutions of the Church and its professional workers. To outsiders, particularly to disdainful, liberal urban dwellers, this situation had ironically and wrongly the appearance of a long-rooted conservatism in which the Church had an independent, coercive power. In private, Cardinal Paul Cullen, often considered the mastermind of the devotional revolution, suffered from intense anxiety that his condemnation of Irish revolutionaries, a group inured to clerical instruction, would lose the Church popular support.

Overall, then, it can be argued that the devotional revolution was the first and much the most successful revival movement in an Ireland that was preparing itself for a post-British-rule existence. It provided an Irishness based on religion that held sway into the late twentieth century. For the majority Irish population, demoralized by the Famine and bereft of the resources of a functioning Gaelic culture, a vibrant Catholicism provided an empowering sense of both communal pride and individual self-discipline. Modes of national identification based on race, ethnicity, culture, language, and romantic nationalism were to have their own vigour, but all had to negotiate with a reinvigorated Irish Catholic identity.

When it comes to Catholics and fiction in Ireland in the nineteenth century, two issues are noticeable. First, although many Catholics wrote novels, the writing of fiction did not have as important a role in Ireland as it did in Protestant Victorian Britain, where realism in fiction reached its zenith. There, as for example in the moral realism of George Eliot, fiction became a substitute forum for making sense of life during an era in which established religion had been shaken by a number of factors, including Darwinism. In Ireland, the religious imaginary strengthened rather than weakened, and fiction was less relevant. This is reflected, albeit in satiric form, in *Father Ralph* (1913) by the former priest Gerald O'Donovan (1871–1942), where the fact that 'Catholics write true stories about Lourdes and St Aloysius and the like'[4] is proffered as the reason why Irish Catholics had not produced anyone of the stature of the great British Victorian novelists. In addition, the publishing industry was itself largely British, and British culture, in both its Protestant and later secular guises, was largely hostile to Catholicism, although this explains the ready market for third-wave Irish Catholic fiction, which was so critical of the putative faults of Catholic Ireland. Secondly, the devotional revolution was not matched by any great assertiveness concerning Catholicism in fiction, except by a number of literary priests, such as Canon P. A. Sheehan (1852–1913), who had worked abroad and were concerned by the perceived struggle internationally between Catholicism and modernity. At home, the strengthening protective culture of Catholic Ireland seemed to

---

[3] David Fitzpatrick, 'Marriage in Post-Famine Ireland', in Art Cosgrove (ed.), *Marriage in Ireland* (Dublin: College Press, 1985), 117.

[4] Gerald O'Donovan, *Father Ralph* (Dingle: Brandon Press, 1993), 28.

render such anxiety less urgent; *Knocknagow* (1873) by Charles Kickham (1828–82) came, partially wrongly, to be seen as a token of such a world. The heroes of Sheehan's fiction, many of them priests, often find themselves torn between the allure of that protective culture and a middle-class intellectualism, although the strategy of embracing intellectualism in order to defend the faith often turns into a subtle obstacle to it.

Undoubtedly, the issue of the land was the most significant one for Irish fiction in the nineteenth century, not only because the relationship between landlords and tenants was important in itself but because British people thought of Ireland principally in terms of its perceived persistent rural turmoil. Portraying the Irish rural Catholic population was thus a critical issue. If not always writing for a British audience, Irish Catholic writers were always acutely aware that their work was subject to a British gaze. Each of the three waves of nineteenth-century Irish Catholic fiction mentioned above focused on perceptions of the rural Catholic population. In each case, the authors involved can be broadly construed as urban, as in varying degrees relatively well off (though perhaps less so in the case of the third phase), and as having a stake in Catholicism, whether religiously or socially. In the case of the first two waves, the concern of these authors is with British perceptions of Ireland, knowing that how the 'peasantry' was presented was key to that perception. Ironically, third-wave authors who were more focused on an intramural struggle for the future of Irish culture and society were the best received in Britain because they were so critical of Ireland. A review in the *Times Literary Supplement* thus waxed lyrical about *Father Ralph*: 'The picture of the seminary in this book is terribly vivid and the worst of it is that it is true.'[5]

The first phase of nineteenth-century Catholic fiction, produced in the 1820s and 1830s at the end of the era of Irish romanticism, when the emancipation of Catholics was such a dominant issue, is associated with Gerald Griffin (1803–40) and the brothers Michael (1796–1874) and John Banim (1798–1842). Their novels are ones of expeditions by urban, sophisticated Catholics into an untamed rural society. They embrace something of the anthropological and folkloric stance of much of the other Irish fiction of the time, yet their purpose, in part, is to undermine the authority of Protestant Ascendancy depictions of the Catholic peasantry in genres like the national tale, written by authors such as Maria Edgeworth (1767–1849) and Sydney Owenson (c.1783–1859). Their work is at times far from sentimentalizing, as John Banim's *The Nowlans* (1826) attests. Equally robust and negative depictions of the Irish Catholic community are portrayed in the work of the ex-Catholic writer William Carleton (1794–1869), whose origins in the peasantry gave his fiction a patina of authenticity at the time.[6]

The second phase, in the late nineteenth century, was the work of urban, upper middle-class, British-assimilationist novelists intent on establishing the Victorian respectability of Irish Catholicism, a task that involved them in demonstrating that rural Ireland was now tamed. Many of these were women writers, clustered around the *Irish*

---

[5] *Times Literary Supplement*, 8 May 1913, 197.

[6] Helen O'Connell's *Ireland and the Fiction of Improvement* (Oxford: Oxford University Press, 2006) shows how Carleton's work relies more on established literary tropes than has generally been thought.

Monthly, a review founded in Dublin in 1873 by the Jesuit litterateur Matthew Russell. They included M. E. Francis (pseudonym of Mary E. Sweetman, 1859–1930), Attie O'Brien (1840–83), and Katharine Tynan (1859–1931), though May Laffan Hartley (*c*.1850–1916) derided Catholic pretensions to respectability. By the 1880s, some of these novelists were projecting a conclusion to the Land War conducive to their class interests. *Marcella Grace* (1886) by Rosa Mulholland (1841–1921), one of the most important of these Catholic gentry novels, imagines the advantages in a time of agrarian crisis of a new class of Catholic landlords who would have a greater sense of identification with the peasantry. Its heroine, a poor Dublin Catholic girl, inherits a large estate and manages it well in the face of opposition from almost all shades of political opinion. Marcella Grace finds herself surrounded by a variety of examples of what is deemed to be bad landlordism in practice, from absenteeism to confrontation to complete abdication of the role in favour of tenant ownership. All of these the novel subjects to a searching scrutiny. Many of the landlords in question are themselves Catholics, an indication that Mulholland was not simply advocating Catholic landlords but Catholic landlords with the sympathy of someone like Marcella.

When compared with the work of third-wave Catholic novelists, the social meliorism of Mulholland and her like may appear tepid. Yet in terms of feminism and gender, her work, although it ultimately remains cautious on the subject, is certainly in advance of third-wave novelists, all of whom were men. Marcella Grace encounters a good deal of hostility in the exercise of her role of landlord because she is a woman. There is a nervous unease in the novel around gender roles, both an awareness of the mechanisms by which they are sustained but also an unwillingness to examine those mechanisms too closely. Ultimately, Marcella is shown to be in need of male moral guidance and the novel ends with her stepping into what is seen as the publicly subordinate role of wife. Although Mulholland's novels often advocate relatively advanced views concerning the role of women, she ultimately baulks in this novel at allowing Marcella Grace's exercise of power to continue. The success of a woman in such a situation can thus be gauged by her return to a traditional role, often involving marriage, once the crisis that has summoned her to a position of authority has passed or has been resolved. Ultimately, Mulholland's proto-feminist inclinations are always sacrificed to the interests of her class agenda.

The 1890s were years of transition both in Irish society and in the writing of Irish fiction.[7] With politics somewhat in the background after the fall of Charles Stewart Parnell and the split in the Irish Parliamentary Party in 1890–91, a collection of movements began to develop that would eventually become the Irish Revival. They included the Gaelic League, the co-operative movement, and the Anglo-Irish Literary Revival, and they would come to have enormous influence in debates about the future of Irish society and culture in the first decades of the twentieth century, up to the revolution and the achievement of independence in 1922. The 1890s were also marked by a great variety of new types of fiction and the transition between the second and third waves of Irish

---

[7] For a fuller account of the changes witnessed during this decade, see James H. Murphy, *Irish Novelists and the Victorian Age* (Oxford: Oxford University Press, 2011), 215–44.

Catholic fiction, although until recently the latter has been under the shadow of the literary output of W. B. Yeats (1865–1939), J. M. Synge (1871–1909) and other writers of the Anglo-Irish Literary Revival who worked mostly in drama and in poetry.[8]

The change between upper middle-class Catholic writers and Catholic intelligentsia writers was at one level a generational shift of the type described by Franco Moretti.[9] But equally, the coming settlement of the land question, and with it the advent of tenant ownership, reduced the centrality of that issue. There was also the sense that Ireland (outside Ulster) now had its own internal dynamic which was less dependent on its links with Britain. In the decades before Irish independence, novelists from the majority religiously-identified tradition on the island tested imagined future Irelands in their fiction. They did so within the context of the challenges and obstacles they perceived around them. Even as the institutions of the Union with Britain continued, the debate about Irish society became a more intramural affair. Sometime after the beginning of the twentieth century a group of novelists emerged from an educated, generally urban context which valued liberal individualism. They included Gerald O'Donovan, W. P. (William Patrick) Ryan (1867–1942), Patrick MacGill (1890–1963), Seumas O'Kelly (c.1875–1918), Brinsley MacNamara (1890–1963), Aodh de Blácam (1890–1951), Edward MacLysaght (1887–1986), Eimar O'Duffy (1893–1935), and, to a degree, James Joyce (1882–1941). The realities to be tested were those within their own society, one dominated by a vision of a rural, small-farmer, family-aspirational, faith-sustained solidarity. It was that vision which many of these intelligentsia novelists, who worked as priests, teachers, political activists, writers, and journalists, sought to challenge as they promoted an intelligentsia critique of the dominant communitarianism of the Ireland of their day. The frequent disappointment of their hopes often led to a note of disdain and anger in their works towards the rural Ireland they had been unable to change.

In the period between the decline of upper middle-class fiction and the full flowering of intelligentsia fiction, there was a time when various writers anticipated the coming developments. Two works in particular are worth mentioning. The first is *When We Were Boys* (1890) by William O'Brien (1852–1928), a nationalist politician and Land War agitator. The novel is a romance and a Fenian adventure story, with some of the features of a Catholic gentry novel. However, its greatest significance lies in its disdainful portrayal of rural society in terms of a social claustrophobia, clerical authoritarianism, and mean-spirited materialism, tropes that would become standard in the depiction of rural Ireland in the twentieth century (although there is a notable irony in O'Brien criticizing the mores of the very society he was helping to bring about). Farmers and shopkeepers from the lower middle class are the objects of particular odium. One character is described as 'a vile gombeen man', the term for someone engaging in shady business

---

[8] For an examination of the several hundred Catholic novels written during this period, see James H. Murphy, *Catholic Fiction and Social Reality in Ireland, 1873–1922* (Westport, CT: Greenwood Press, 1997). See also John Wilson Foster, *Irish Novels 1890–1940: New Bearings in Culture and Fiction* (Oxford: Oxford University Press, 2008).

[9] Franco Moretti, *Graphs, Maps, Trees: Abstract Models for Literary History* (London: Verso, 2005), 21.

transactions, while another is characterized as 'one of those strong farmers who emerged from the Great Famine fat with the spoils of their weaker brethren'.[10]

The second significant novel is *The Lake* (1905) by George Moore (1852–1933), along with its companion collection of short stories, *The Untilled Field* (1903).[11] Moore was from an Irish Catholic aristocratic background and had already been a prominent cultural and literary figure in France and England before coming to Ireland to make a contribution, as he saw it, to the Literary Revival. His work anticipates that of the two most important Catholic intelligentsia novelists, Ryan and O'Donovan, and, indeed, a version of Moore appears as a character in *The Plough and the Cross* (1910), Ryan's *roman à clef* (published under the name William Patrick O'Ryan). However, Moore's relatively exalted social position protected him from the ill effects of agitation and rebellion, factors that help explain why *The Lake* lacks the intensity of O'Donovan and Ryan's work and shows none of their initial concern with reforming Catholic Ireland. And like the work of James Joyce, Moore's fiction also differs from Catholic intelligentsia fiction in being more about personal and sexual freedom than social reform. In this respect, Moore and Joyce anticipate the preoccupations of Irish Catholic fiction from the 1960s onwards more than they reflect that of their contemporaries.

With Moore's typical flair for provocation, the central character in *The Lake* is a priest, Father Oliver Gogarty, who is in part based on O'Donovan, although Banim's *The Nowlans*, eight decades before, also featured a sexually frustrated cleric. Gogarty engages in a correspondence with a young woman from which he learns much. He had forced her to leave his parish where she worked as a teacher because she was pregnant and unmarried, an action he later regrets. His involvement with her moves from concern for her faith—especially as she works for a literary figure who is an atheist—to an acknowledgement of the human emptiness of his own existence. He has nothing to look forward to but 'the Mass and the rosary at the end of his tongue, and nothing in his heart'.[12] Losing his faith and acknowledging his love for her, he comes to believe that 'there is no moral law except one's own conscience'.[13] The novel ends with Gogarty's dramatic bid for freedom, staging his own apparent drowning in a lake so that he can escape to become a journalist in New York. Moore had initially intended the story to cap *The Untilled Field*, in which both peasants and members of the intelligentsia struggle against the common strictures of Catholic Ireland.

In the work of O'Donovan, Ryan, and other third-wave novelists, Catholic protagonists of liberal, personally autonomous, and socially progressive outlook venture once more into rural Ireland. This time, however, they present it as being in thrall to a controlling clerical hegemony, in novels whose characters enact the same social mission as that advocated by their authors. Indeed, these third-wave novelists often wrote novels whose characters enact a process of engagement with Catholic Ireland that mirrored, to a degree, the experiences of their authors. Generally beginning as enthusiastic

[10] William O'Brien, *When We Were Boys* (London: Longmans, Green, 1890), 375, 16.
[11] In 1921, Moore published a substantially revised edition of *The Lake*.
[12] George Moore, *The Lake* (Gerrards Cross: Colin Smythe, 1980), 124.   [13] Ibid., 173.

progressive Catholics, they often end in disillusion. In depicting rural Catholic culture, they often resort to satire and caricature, drawing on the tropes of Protestant evangelical fiction in the process and laying the foundations for the empowering shame evident in late twentieth-century fiction. Irish Catholicism is thus portrayed as shamefully backward and consequently as an object of disdain, as can be seen in Joyce's *A Portrait of the Artist as a Young Man* (1916) in Stephen Dedalus's contemptuous imagining of 'the shaven gills of the priests',[14] even after his conversation with the urbane and cultured Jesuit director of studies. The agenda of authors and their characters was not anthropological insight but social transformation, defying a corrupt 'old Ireland', identifying the essence of 'true Ireland', often within the hearts of the reformers, and from it seeking to forge a progressive 'new Ireland'. These novels portray their progressive heroes as being treated with hostility by the clergy, who seek to defend the culture of rural Catholicism against what they see as a corrosive pagan and foreign secularism.

These third-wave Catholic writers, like their predecessors and successors, were formed by the mores of their times, in this case European liberalism, progressive Catholicism, and the Irish Revival. Among the movements and contemporary causes their novels look to for transformation are the revived Irish language, advanced Irish nationalism, the Anglo-Irish Literary Revival, the Irish-Ireland movement, greater education for lay people, free debate, the empowerment of women (though the novels were almost always principally about men), socialism, theological modernism, and the agricultural co-operative movement. The strongest driving force behind Catholic intelligentsia fiction, however, was in fact a theological one. This is evident in what might be called the two foundational Catholic intelligentsia novels, Ryan's *The Plough and the Cross* and O'Donovan's *Father Ralph*.[15]

In the early twentieth century, there was a new, more open spirit in Catholic theology which was allied with the openness on social issues that had been inaugurated by Pope Leo XIII, who had addressed the issue of workers' rights in his encyclical, *Rerum Novarum* (1891). In theology, scholars such as Alfred Loisy pioneered novel ways of reading the Bible and there was much interest in immanentism, the notion that the divine was discovered through experience of the world. In 1907, however, in the encyclical, *Pascendi Dominici Gregis*, Pope Pius X condemned such trends, grouping them together under the term modernism. The new hostile climate casts its shadow in both novels. Although both reflect the cultural spirit of revival, renewal, and reform of the times, they have as protagonists Catholic intellectual reformers who end in defeat, disillusion, and alienation from the Church. The dramatic conclusion of the modernist controversy provides a novelistic climax that did not quite match the life experiences of the authors, however, particularly in the case of O'Donovan, who was nationally known as a progressive cleric before he abandoned the priesthood in 1908 and, after some successful years as an author, spent much of the rest of his life in a disappointing lassitude.

---

[14] James Joyce, *A Portrait of the Artist as a Young Man*, ed. John Paul Riquelme (New York: W. W. Norton, 2007), 141.

[15] Like *A Portrait*, *Father Ralph* is a *Bildungsroman*, whereas *The Plough and the Cross* focuses on the crises which bring about the end to its hero Fergus O'Hagan's hopes for reform.

Although none of the three novels discussed above is a reliable guide to the life of its author, the principal characters were all based on their creators. During this time, the novel came to be seen as a vehicle for fictionalized autobiographical renditions of the struggle between different versions of Ireland, struggles that often ended in various forms of failure, as Catholic Ireland proved to be more intractable than had been imagined. This autobiographical dimension was the reason for the great success of *Father Ralph*, which follows the education of Ralph O'Brien, a member of a relatively wealthy family who becomes a priest of the fictional diocese of Bunnahone and then leaves the priesthood in disillusionment. The clergy, with a few notable exceptions, are boorish, unintelligent, venal, and aligned with the interests of the stronger farmers and shopkeepers. Ralph is sustained for a time by his friendship with a number of pastorally-minded intellectual priests and far-sighted laymen. One of the priests wants to build 'a Church that feels and voices the aspirations of every man of good-will in the world'.[16] Meanwhile, the editor of a radical newspaper hopes to 'make religion intelligible in the light of progress'.[17] Ralph's own efforts at reform, however, and especially the club for working men which he founds, are crushed and the progressive theology which has sustained him is condemned as modernism by the Pope. His suspension over the theology issue and subsequent departure from the priesthood are greeted with incomprehension by his clerical colleagues: 'If it was drink now, or women, there'd be some meaning in it! But theology!'[18] Ralph rejects the idea of holding onto the ideal of true Ireland/Church in face of the reality of old Ireland/Church: 'He saw a vision of an ideal Church with which he was at one. . . . It faded away almost at once, and his mind dwelt on the actual Church as he knew it. His one hope for its regeneration had been crushed.'[19] The novel ends with Ralph on the boat for Holyhead, declaring: 'I have found myself at last.'[20] The departure into exile of the defeated reformer, but free individual, would become a standard plot resolution in such books, not least in Joyce's *A Portrait*.

Father Ralph was a publishing sensation, particularly in a Britain always eager for adverse views of Catholic Ireland. It made a much greater impact than *The Plough and the Cross* and not only because it was produced by a major publishing house, Macmillan, whereas Ryan had had to self-publish his work, though it had previously been serialized in his own newspaper. O'Donovan was an ex-priest and was thus perceived to be closer to the heart of things. In both novels, the line between fiction and autobiography was seen to be almost invisible, in spite of the great differences between the life of Ralph O'Brien and that of his creator. Ryan was in reality a radical journalist and the kind of religious and social reformer whom O'Donovan imagines in his novels. In an early novel, *Starlight Through the Roof* (1895), published under the pseudonym Kevin Kennedy, Ryan imagines popular action limiting the power of the clergy and their coming out in favour of reform. Later, however, one of his newspapers was closed under pressure from the Archbishop of Armagh on account of its radical views. Fergus O'Hagan, a newspaper editor and hero of *The Plough and the Cross*, is a thinly disguised

---

[16] O'Donovan, *Father Ralph*, 252.   [17] Ibid., 211.   [18] Ibid., 367.   [19] Ibid., 369.
[20] Ibid., 376.

self-portrait. O'Hagan mixes with theosophists, altruistic industrialists, and reforming priests interested in social Christianity and immanentism. He sets forth his agenda thus:

> The great modern task of freeing Catholicism in Ireland from formalism and literalism, on the one hand, and of patronage or forgetfulness of the poor rather than love of them, on the other, and making it a profoundly moving and enlightening spiritual and social force again, demanded the most subtle delicacy as well as courage.[21]

One character wisely senses that the reformers' social agenda ('applied Christianity') will be more initially appealing than their theological programme: 'The majority of our people are still far from the stage at which Modernism could interest them and they are quite unconcerned about matters of Church history and organization. But applied Christianity would move them profoundly and would give the Church an august new meaning and would revolutionize Irish life.'[22]

Nonetheless, an important concern of the novel remains the need for a real intellectual engagement with religion. As one reformer laments, 'A man with a fair intellect must really turn away in despair or weariness from the majority of Irish sermons and the generality of stuff that is called "Catholic literature." '[23] This is confirmed by the sinister bishop who warns off O'Hagan after the publication of an 'unsound and unIrish'[24] article. The bishop privately admits that the article is 'bold and cruelly true', knowing that 'our religion in Ireland has been emotional and in a measure sentimental'.[25] But education will disturb the social order and O'Hagan stands 'in the way of episcopal and British and Vatican policy in Ireland'.[26] Although ultimately defeated, O'Hagan remains in Ireland in a sort of internal exile, rendered possible by his immanentist views: 'the great Ireland is in ourselves, and it is full of beauty, divine activity and boundless hope. The outer Ireland, agitated or stagnant, is something incidental to keep our souls in training.'[27]

It should be clear that there are certainly congruences between the work of Ryan and O'Donovan and Joyce's A Portrait, which has so often been seen in the past as sui generis. In some ways, Joyce's novel was only one—albeit the only one we now remember—of a number of novels that constituted a distinctive genre dealing with the struggle of the individual for freedom in what he (and all these novelists were male) perceives to be the confining culture of Catholic Ireland. The main difference between A Portrait and those other novels is that Stephen Dedalus is principally an artist/writer, whereas the heroes of the other works are primarily social activists intent on building a new Ireland.[28] Their authors are only in a secondary sense artists, having taken to novel writing to record

---

[21] William Patrick Ryan, The Plough and the Cross: A Story of New Ireland (Dublin: Irish Nation Office, 1910), 3.

[22] Ibid., 174.   [23] Ibid., 177.   [24] Ibid., 254.   [25] Ibid., 311, 304.   [26] Ibid., 312.

[27] Ibid., 373.

[28] In spite of a brief youthful interest in socialism, Joyce was never a social or political activist in the cause of reforming Catholic Ireland, although A Portrait is certainly influenced in terms of genre by the Catholic intelligentsia fiction that was being produced in the early years of the twentieth century.

their disdain for the society that had spurned them and express their frustration at the rejection of their plans for social transformation. This latter point may help to explain the apparent oddity of Stephen's final declared intention of pursing the rather public project of creating his race's conscience, in a work which has hitherto largely been about the winning of a private space for personal artistic creativity. So while *A Portrait* may be claimed as a Catholic intelligentsia novel in a modified sense when compared with the aforementioned novels by Ryan and O'Donovan, Joyce fits in more easily within the wider group of Catholic intelligentsia writers, many of whom were not actively interested in religion and saw Catholicism simply as a power system without any progressive possibilities.

Other Catholic intelligentsia novels of this period engage with the condition of Ireland through different modes and approaches. Many are satires of the inertia of a Catholic Ireland resistant to progressive change, one dominated by farmers, shopkeepers, and priests. This was the Ireland that Joyce had chosen not to depict when he abandoned his idea of writing a short story collection to be called *Provincials*, as a sequel to *Dubliners* (1914). Perhaps *A Portrait* was itself an influence on the secularization of the genre, though not in its anticlericalism, which is already strongly present in Ryan and O'Donovan. Indeed, the use of the term Catholic intelligentsia throughout this discussion indicates a sociological origin rather than any necessary religious commitment. Written after the suppression of modernism, these later novels display varying degrees of optimism or pessimism about the prospect for reform and the development of a progressive Church. Indeed, in some, reform barely registers in their disdainful depictions of a bleak reality. The novels of six other novelists are thus worth mentioning to illustrate the variety of possible attitudes and approaches. Like *A Portrait*, they follow in the wake of *The Plough and the Cross* and *Father Ralph*, which are the exemplar novels of the genre because of the prominence of their authors as social reformers prior to them becoming published novelists. Some of these novels, however, themselves caused controversy and were thus their authors' means of public intervention in debates about Ireland's present and future.

Born into poverty in County Donegal, from which he escaped to work as a navvy in Scotland in the early 1900s, Patrick MacGill became a poet, journalist, and novelist who wrote from a socialist perspective. He is excoriating in his depiction of social deprivation in novels such as *Children of the Dead End* (1914) and *The Rat Pit* (1915), a theme rarely touched upon in Joyce's work. As with O'Donovan, the manifest closeness of his fiction to real life was one reason for its phenomenal success. *Children of the Dead End*, for example, sold ten thousand copies in the space of fifteen days at the time of its publication.[29] MacGill's socialism and anticlericalism won him enemies as he recounts in the semi-autobiographical *Glenmornan* (1919), in which a reformer, Doalty Gallagher, is driven from his local area for being outspoken and for having reportedly lost his faith. Here is the angry shame concerning backward Catholic Ireland that would decades later become such a powerful force for social change: 'Doalty knew that words were futile

---

[29] *Irish Book Lover* 5 (1914), 179.

against the smug, self-possessed priest. He was an over fed, blatant tyrant whom the people obeyed like sheep! Poor people, poor, silly, stupid people!'[30]

The novels of Brinsley MacNamara (the pen name of John Weldon) are highly critical of Irish society on the brink of independence. *The Valley of the Squinting Windows* (1918) caused a furore of indignation on its publication because of its hostility against the clergy. In it, the debilitating effects of Irish Catholic marital mores become a generalized social malaise, as personal frustration leads to a mean-spirited bitterness and a desire to destroy the possibility of happiness for others. Thus, Father O'Keeffe 'was still a man of clay and loved the rich grass and fine cattle it produced', which leads him to ensure that 'the gombeen-man, the auctioneer and the publican were enabled to proceed with their swindle of the poor by maintaining his boon companionship'.[31] An even more pervasive corruption is seen to be at work in MacNamara's *The Clanking of Chains* (1920), where the nationalist idealism of the period after 1916 is confronted with the cynical realities of small-town gombeen life, as vested interests commandeer the hope that had been engendered by the Rising. Michael Dempsey, a hapless republican idealist, is an embarrassment to his employer until nationalism comes into vogue in 1916 and he turns into a business asset. Dempsey, however, does not understand the *realpolitik* of the new situation. When he protests that the shopkeepers have automatically assumed control of the recently formed committee to resist the conscription of Irishmen into the British forces fighting the First World War, they accuse him of treachery and force him to leave the town. The novel thus highlights the establishment's capacity to retain control while adjusting its rhetoric in response to changes in popular ideology. The *Times Literary Supplement* aptly noted that the novel's characters are 'actuated by every motive except patriotism'.[32] MacNamara's next novel, *The Mirror in the Dusk* (1921), charts the careers of four young people who choose to marry for reasons that accord with lower middle-class Catholic expediency rather than for romantic love, and whose choices return to haunt them, as they find themselves unable to do without true human love and fulfilment. Financial imperatives mean that three of the protagonists marry unhappily and one of the three ends up murdered as a result. The novel concludes with the fourth protagonist reflecting that 'The fields had beaten the loves of all of them, for it was the queer way they had married.'[33]

Two novels by the Abbey playwright, short story writer, and Sinn Féin journalist Seumas O'Kelly carry this pessimistic analysis further, to the extent of being apathetic about the value of even an attempted progressive intervention. Both *The Lady of Deerpark* (1917) and *Wet Clay* (1922) target a destructive greed as the characteristic vice of Catholic Ireland, although O'Kelly's work did not attract the same degree of hostility as the novels of MacGill and MacNamara. In the first, illusions are exploited and the old class system appears on the verge of collapse, though without positive benefits. A well-born though

[30] Patrick MacGill, *Glenmornan* (London: Herbert Jenkins, 1919), 262.
[31] Brinsley MacNamara, *The Valley of the Squinting Windows* (Dublin: Anvil Press, 1989), 102.
[32] *Times Literary Supplement*, 25 March 1920, 200.
[33] Brinsley MacNamara, *The Mirror in the Dusk* (London: Maunsel and Roberts, 1921), 250.

emotionally inarticulate woman marries a vulgar horse-dealer in a disastrous union which leaves the principal characters dead at the end of the novel. In *Wet Clay*, a whole community destroys the naïve idealism of a young American, Brendan Nilan, a devotee of the poetry of Walt Whitman, who arrives at his grandmother's farm with notions of helping to improve the country. One character sees his grandmother in these terms: 'She's ignorant and narrow-minded, and her life must be sordid, hobbling round a kitchen chopping cabbages for pigs, saying cutting things, hating to see a young woman well dressed. There's the peasant, the ignorant peasant.'[34] Nilan's attitude, however, is very different. ' "Wrong, all wrong!" cried Brendan Nilan with some excitement. "Margaret Mulvehill is a splendid, a rare old woman, a seer, a philosopher, a female intelligence, a will, a holder of power, a ruler." '[35] His arrival provokes a paroxysm of anxiety in the family over the question of who will inherit the land. Not only does his presence disrupt established land inheritance patterns, his working practices disrupt settled agricultural work patterns and his romantic attachments disrupt marriage expectations. All of these factors become motives for his murder. No individual escapes into freedom in either of these novels by O'Kelly.

Gerald O'Donovan added to this more simply critical phase of Catholic intelligentsia fiction in several novels, including *Waiting* (1914) and two very directly satirical works, *Conquest* (1920) and *Vocations* (1921). In *Waiting*, at least there is an idealistic hero, although his independence of mind draws the ire of the local clergy. In *Conquest*, the Daly family is obsessed and embittered by its struggle to recover ancestral land of which it had been dispossessed. All is manoeuvring for political advantage, although Arabella Daly, in conversation with Father Lysaght, affects an apparent naïvety about a bishop's participation in a controversial funeral:

> 'I don't criticize my priests,' Arabella said ironically, adding more seriously, 'Anyhow I forgive them a lot for the beautiful sermon the bishop preached today. It was wonderful.'... 'It was,' Father Lysaght said with a chuckle. 'It was reported that the bishop had a convenient cold and intended to snub Pierce Daly by not attending his brother's funeral. That big gathering of people...was partly a political meeting in honour of Pierce, and partly a snub to the bishop....Father Carberry got wind of the demonstration, and the bishop made a marvellous recovery from his cold. Even Mallon, the grocer, who organized the funeral, admits that the bishop carried off all the honours.'[36]

In *Vocations*, Winnie Curtin's desire to become a nun is encouraged by her class-conscious mother, who had been unsuccessful in her own attempt. 'The nuns were sympathetic but prudent. The manner necessary for Drumbawn convent could only be acquired at a high-class boarding school; and a vow of poverty was only possible when backed by a comfortable balance at the bank.'[37] Winnie confuses repressed sexuality

---

[34] Seumas O'Kelly, *Wet Clay* (Dublin: Phoenix Publishing Company, 1922), 199–200.
[35] Ibid., 200.   [36] Gerald O'Donovan, *Conquest* (New York: G. P. Putnam's Sons, 1921), 116–17.
[37] Gerald O'Donovan, *Vocations* (New York: Boni and Liveright, 1921), 37.

with sanctity, especially as far as her relationship with the curate Father Burke is concerned. She fantasizes bringing him his breakfast each morning in the convent, while she sees herself as a saint in a holy picture, 'hanging up yet in every convent in the world with *age quod agis* in old English lettering stamped on her exposed heart'.[38]

Not every perspective was as polarized, however, as three further novels, each with a clear autobiographical origin, demonstrate. When it became clearer that Catholic Ireland was not about to signal defeat in the foreseeable future, another group of intelligentsia writers, who adopted a more nuanced approach to the existence of Catholic Ireland, emerged in the run-up to independence in 1922. Their new Ireland is a less Edenic and a more pragmatic one than the ones we have so far examined. The regressive is balanced by the progressive and the new is prepared for a compromise with the old. The novels in question are *The Gael* (1919) by English-born agricultural reformer and cultural revivalist Edward MacLysaght (who published it under the name Edward E. Lysaght), *Holy Romans* (1920) by London-born Sinn Féin journalist and Catholic convert Aodh de Blácam (Hugh Saunders Blackham), and *The Wasted Island* (1920) by the English-educated writer and political activist Eimar O'Duffy.

In all three texts, a qualified hope for a new Ireland is tempered by a contextualized awareness of existing conditions. In *The Gael*, the efforts of rural reformer Con O'Hickie are frustrated by the vested interests in a small town, though he also has allies, including among the clergy, and the prospects for change are not entirely bleak. However, the novel ends with O'Hickie swept up into the War of Independence and into an ambivalence as to the value of such political engagement when compared with social reform:

> His story is the story of many Irishmen, drawn against their will into the vortex of destructive politics, deflected from constructive activity by the effects of the political system upon their lives as individuals, and the greater the work of one man in the service of the nation the more certain his distraction from the personal to the public sphere.[39]

Just as Patrick Pearse (1879–1916) and James Connolly left their educational and socialist work, 'so Con was taken from his plough and his mill and from his gropings towards a newer and a better rural life.'[40]

In *Holy Romans*, a gombeen man promotes an Irish college for financial gain, against the wishes of the people who want to invest in a co-operative. One character laments, 'If only the Church would give a lead to the people instead of stumbling along behind the moneybags we might make Ireland the grandest country on earth.'[41] No such grand vision emerges from *The Wasted Island*, which paints a negative view of post-Rising Ireland. Yet for the protagonists of all three of these novels Catholic nationalist Ireland, with all is flaws, is better than the Anglicized existence from which they have escaped.

---

[38] Ibid., 116. Her motto is Latin for 'Do your duty'.
[39] Edward E. Lysaght, *The Gael* (Dublin: Maunsel and Company, 1919), 335.   [40] Ibid.
[41] Aodh de Blácam, *Holy Romans: A Young Irishman's Story* (Dublin: Maunsel and Company, 1920), 282.

Con O'Hickie in *The Gael* has an Irish republican upbringing in England and comes to Ireland in order to make it his home; Shane Lambert in *Holy Romans*, like the novel's author, was born in England and is a convert both to Irish nationalism and to Catholicism; and *The Wasted Island*'s Bernard Lascelles embraces the nationalist cause after escaping from a stifling upper middle-class milieu.

Although defeated by the partisans of the lower middle class at an election, O'Hickie is not disheartened. Gaelicism, the co-operative movement, and republicanism remain forces of undiminished strength. He is supported by a priest who is an opponent of materialism and an advocate of change. Above all, the lower middle class is not as overwhelmingly powerful as it is in the novels of O'Donovan and MacNamara. *Holy Romans*, a convincingly rendered *Bildungsroman*, is the most interesting of the three novels whose contexts mitigate the negativities of Catholic Ireland. Like *The Gael*, it adopts a critical intelligentsia version of lower middle-class Ireland. Unlike *The Gael*, however, it sees the clergy as being in league with the new establishment: 'They [the middle classes] rule everything. They even dictate to the Church. You never hear a sermon on the sins of the rich.'[42] Shane Lambert grants the truth of such comments yet this does not prevent him from becoming a convert because, most significantly, the society he embraces is one which includes within it those who rebel against its oppressive aspects. Among his friends are a man who is a Marxist and evolutionist, a second who is a mystic, and a third who is a trade unionist and anticlericalist. For Shane, far from being outcasts from Catholicism, these men are all part of its living embodiment: 'In Fergus the scientist he had seen that the Church could be modern. Old Peter, the mystic, had shown him that a Catholic could be a visionary and a dreamer. Faragal Faal had taught him that a man could be a devoted Catholic and no slave.'[43] It is this contextualized Catholic Ireland, and the new Ireland it entails, that Shane embraces and looks to with such hope at the end of the novel. Perhaps only a convert could see things this way. Most Catholic intelligentsia dissidents of the time tended to feel that they had been denied any legitimate voice on account of their oppositional stance. MacLysaght, de Blácam, and O'Duffy offered a balanced approach to rural Catholic society that would certainly not be adopted by their successors in the later twentieth century.

Catholic intelligentsia fiction was a complex and evolving phenomenon. With roots in the economic and social change of the late nineteenth century, and a prolepsis in the work of William O'Brien and George Moore among others, its principal energy came from disillusion at the apparent failure of a theologically inspired social vision for Ireland. This disillusion expressed itself in a negative portrayal of Catholic Ireland, albeit one that could also be tempered. Although their social agendas did not carry forward, and although they lacked the focus on sexual freedom of later writers, Catholic intelligentsia novelists were nonetheless foundational cultural influences in the discourse of disdain for rural Catholic Ireland. The disdain of such writers, who viewed rural society from the imagined superiority of mostly urban backgrounds, became an empowering

---

[42] Ibid., 244.   [43] Ibid., 233.

shame in the minds of later writers of rural origin. Their work in turn became a powerful cultural force in Irish social change from the 1960s onwards.

FURTHER READING

Candy, Catherine. *Priestly Fictions: Popular Irish Novelists of the Early Twentieth Century.* Dublin: Wolfhound Press, 1995.

Foster, John Wilson. *Irish Novels 1890–1940: New Bearings in Culture and Fiction.* Oxford: Oxford University Press, 2008.

Frazier, Adrian. *George Moore, 1852–1933.* New Haven, CT: Yale University Press, 2000.

Larkin, Emmet. 'The Devotional Revolution in Ireland'. *American Historical Review* 80 (1975): 625–52.

Murphy, James H. *Catholic Fiction and Social Reality in Ireland, 1873–1922.* Westport, CT: Greenwood Press, 1997.

Murphy, James H. *Ireland: A Social, Cultural and Literary History, 1791–1891.* Dublin: Four Courts Press, 2003.

Murphy, James H. *Irish Novelists and the Victorian Age.* Oxford: Oxford University Press, 2011.

O'Brien, George. *The Irish Novel 1800–1910.* Cork: Cork University Press, 2015.

O'Connell, Helen. *Ireland and the Fiction of Improvement.* Oxford: Oxford University Press, 2006.

PART III

IRISH REVIVALISM AND IRISH MODERNISM

CHAPTER 5

···

GEORGE MOORE

Gender, Place, and Narrative

···

ELIZABETH GRUBGELD

GEORGE Moore (1852–1933) was a prolific writer who perpetually reinvented himself, so much so that it can be difficult to settle decisively upon either the genre of his prose works or the period to which they are best assigned. In addition to his many works of non-fiction, Moore published six novels between 1883 and 1889, three in the 1890s, five between 1901 and 1918, and five adaptations of classical and medieval texts during the last decade of his life. He also produced extensive revisions of earlier novels, four books of interrelated short stories, and periodical fiction. His autobiographical writings flaunt their fictive anecdotes and dialogue, and even Moore himself could not decide until the second English edition of 1889 whether *Confessions of a Young Man* (1888) was a novel about Edwin (or Edward, or Edouard) Dayne or a memoir about George Moore. His *A Story-Teller's Holiday* (1918), the most generically multifaceted of all his writings, embeds tales based on medieval Irish materials and a modern novella within its overtly fictionalized autobiographical frame-tale and its self-referential outer framing. Across this wide and prodigious career, he returned repeatedly to matters of sexual behaviour and gender roles, as well as to exploring how narrative might extend beyond the protocols of genre to accommodate an ever-changing understanding of identity, nationality, and the act of narrative itself.

Moore's Irish fiction draws from his wide reading in continental literature and pro-pels the Irish novel into the twentieth century, pushing it beyond political melodrama, retellings of folklore, and the Anglo-Irish Gothic. The work he produced during his ten-year repatriation in Ireland (1901–11) is both international and distinctly regional in sub-ject matter, diction, and form, anticipating the fiction of later writers like Frank O'Connor (1903–66), Mary Lavin (1912–96), and Edna O'Brien (1930–), while to his reworking of Irish medieval materials he brought a more complex agenda than the cultural nationalism of earlier prose adaptations. Moore's innovations in what Ford Madox Ford later named 'literary impressionism'[1] and his foregrounding of the act of

---

[1] Ford Madox Ford, 'On Impressionism', in *Critical Writings of Ford Madox Ford*, ed. Frank McShane (Lincoln, NE: University of Nebraska Press, 1964), 33–55.

recollection align him with English modernists like Ford, Joseph Conrad, and Virginia Woolf, while creating a narrative space in which he could most fully integrate a multiplicity of Irish voices into his fiction.

THE NINETEENTH-CENTURY NOVEL: SEX AND METHOD

In order to examine Moore's importance to the modern Irish novel, it will be necessary first to address his nineteenth-century novels, including those with primarily English characters and locales. His reading of continental fiction and philosophy has been much studied, and little question remains that he was among the first to incorporate into English-language fiction the ideas of Balzac, Zola, Flaubert, Schopenhauer, and Wagner, ideas he imbibed during the six years he spent in Paris in the 1870s.[2] After land agitation in his native Mayo rendered any continuation of his protracted education in the cafés of Montmartre financially untenable, he settled in London to begin the disciplined routine of daily writing that he would follow through the rest of his life. In *Confessions of a Young Man*, he reflects that he left Paris in the autumn of 1879 'as covered with "fads" as a distinguished foreigner with stars. Naturalism I wore round my neck, Romanticism was pinned over the heart, Symbolism I carried like a toy revolver in my waistcoat pocket, to be used on an emergency.'[3] In the flurry of books that followed his return to London, Moore tested these and other modes of writing.

The novels *A Modern Lover* (1883), *A Mummer's Wife* (1885), *A Drama in Muslin* (1886), *A Mere Accident* (1887), *Spring Days* (1888), *Mike Fletcher* (1889), *Vain Fortune* (1891), and *Esther Waters* (1894) present Moore's experiments with naturalism, realism, the psychological artist-novel, studies of sexual variance and masculine decadence, and the large-scale Victorian social novel. But no matter how much Moore looked over his shoulder at his continental and English models, each effort presents a distinct departure from its precedent, and he was much too interested in the unusual or rebellious character, the odd tale, and the peculiar turn of speech ever really to be a naturalist, a label he attempted to shake off soon after he had adopted it. From the French realists Moore learned to avoid sentimentality while allowing the precise details of embodied experience to articulate the internal effects of class and gender conflict as well as the economic and social dynamics of a fictional world. Without exception, these novels challenged the boundaries of British convention with their frank portrayals of sexual desire and class struggle, and in their often satiric critique of gender roles and the abuses of power. Such boldness was not without costs. His battles with the circulating libraries, booksellers,

---

[2] Such studies are far too numerous to cite here and include books and articles on Moore's literary and biographical relationships with many French writers and the impact of Wagner, Schopenhauer, Dostoevsky, Chekhov, and Turgenev on his work.

[3] George Moore, *Confessions of a Young Man*, ed. Susan Dick (Montreal: McGill-Queen's University Press, 1972), 149.

litigious crusaders, and groups like the National Vigilance Association commenced with *A Modern Lover* and did not cease until 1918, after which he increasingly turned towards privately published limited editions.

Moore's concern with the nature of sexual desire, the ambiguities of sexual and gender identity, and the inherent inequalities of marriage trouble the structure of the marriage plot that had for generations dominated the British novel. In Moore's fiction, men and women marry for money or cannot marry because they have no money. Some refuse marriage for multiple psychological and social reasons, and bisexual and homosexual individuals struggle with the pressures of social conformity and religious doctrine. The marriage of novel-reading Kate Ede and her sickly husband mirrors the stultifying conformity of lower middle-class life in *A Mummer's Wife*, while the cheap romance of her elopement with an actor mirrors the melodrama of the stage as the only alternative to that life she can imagine. The moribund world of upper-class Ireland in *A Drama in Muslin* is reflected in the horrors of the marriage market and the aspirations of the emergent New Woman in its earnest protagonist. Rose Leicester (later rewritten as Nora Glynn) functions less as a character in *The Lake* (1905; revised in 1921) than as an incarnation of the natural world as interpreted through Vitalist theories of instinctive force, although she leads Father Oliver not towards marriage but towards self-discovery and a life of wandering. Other works in turn probe the complex psychology of both desire and its lack.

In *A Mummer's Wife* and *A Drama in Muslin*, Moore vividly depicts lower middle-class existence in an English pottery town, the life of a travelling theatre troupe, and Irish landlord society in decline. The three novels that followed study human sexuality as singular case studies informed by the pessimistic philosophy of Schopenhauer but without the rich social context of the earlier books. *A Mere Accident*, *Spring Days*, and *Mike Fletcher*, like the stories and novella of *Celibates* (1895), were read for the most part as sensational melodrama, and Moore himself was dissatisfied with all three novels, forbidding the republication of the latter two and self-mockingly disowning them as 'the work of a disciple—Amico Moorini I put forward as a suggestion'.[4] Yet despite its failures, the trilogy offers a daring exploration of the relationship between sex, art, religion, and ethics. Each addresses a crisis in nineteenth-century masculinity, and, as Adrian Frazier argues, despite the collapse of its ambitious intentions, the brilliance of *Mike Fletcher* lies in its 'cold, ruthless, ugly portrait' of male privilege and 'male rapacity'.[5] Additionally, Moore pursues the class analysis of sexual behaviour he had instigated in two earlier works set in Ireland, *A Drama in Muslin* and the partially fictive sketches of *Parnell and His Island* (1887). Mike Fletcher's origins as the son of a governess and a small farmer in rural Ireland fuel his class anger, and yet because he enacts that anger through sexual violence (his having 'been the ruin of hundreds',[6] as one of his friends

---

[4] George Moore, 'Preface', in *The Lake* (Gerrards Cross: Colin Smythe, 1980), xi.
[5] Adrian Frazier, *George Moore, 1852–1933* (New Haven, CT: Yale University Press, 2000), 197–8. The crisis of masculinity is discussed in Mark Llewellyn, 'Masculinity and the Introjected Self in George Moore's *Mike Fletcher*: "I'm Weary Playing at Faust"', *English Literature in Transition, 1880–1920* 48, no. 2 (2005), 131–46.
[6] George Moore, *Mike Fletcher* (London: Ward and Downey, 1889), 4.

attests), it produces boredom and despair but no exclusion from the elite English society he increasingly despises.

Regardless of Moore's disappointment in the results of his labours, he could not abandon the questions he had raised. The figure of the cynical womanizer and would-be artist who first appeared as *A Modern Lover* and again in the trilogy continues to haunt his fiction, as do variously named incarnations of *A Mere Accident*'s John Norton, a pious, repressed homosexual man torn between aestheticism and a rejection of the senses that, Moore implies, is as much the manifestation of his sadomasochistic eroticism as religiously motivated renunciation. A similarly sophisticated understanding of diverse sexualities underlies the story of the protagonist of the eponymously titled novella that opens *Celibates*, 'Mildred Lawson'. Obsessed with chastity, the flirtatious Mildred cannot bear to be touched but enjoys her power over men, imagining herself as 'a dainty morsel'[7] to tempt a man's appetite. She compulsively gazes at herself in the mirror and fantasizes about the gaze of others; even when alone, she performs for herself, shedding a constricting undergarment in order to take a pensive attitude of sadness. She is not without desire, but she is incapable of desiring anyone but herself. Written during the peak of late Victorian treatises in sexology, *Celibates*, like the trilogy, maintains a direct focus on sexual psychology bolder than anything being produced in Ireland at the time.

The sexual body again figures prominently in Moore's next novel, but aware of the need to try different narrative strategies he turned towards the Victorian social novel. What he discovers through the writing of *Esther Waters* is crucial to the difficult conceptual and technical challenges he would take up later in *The Lake*, perhaps the first modernist novel to have been written in and about Ireland. *Esther Waters* Moore proclaimed to be 'as characteristically English as *Don Quixote* is Spanish',[8] although the novel draws upon his upbringing in Mayo for its vivid depiction of the stable yards and the world of horse-racing; his reading of Balzac for its large cast of characters and the precision of its urban geography; and his admiration of Zola for its portrayal of working-class conditions, prostitution, and childbirth. As *Esther Waters* evolved from its serial version to the first revision of 1899, he continued to search for a way to represent not only the social world in which Esther lives but also the workings of the unconscious and an embodied phenomenology of experience. Similarly, the concept of 'instinct' that Moore had defined as his own guiding light in *Confessions of a Young Man*, and which would figure pre-eminently in *The Lake*, begins to coalesce in the pages of *Esther Waters*.

It may have been conceived as a consummate Victorian novel, but *Esther Waters* inverts the genre in many ways. Sold as a single volume instead of the triple-decker format favoured by booksellers and the lending libraries, it eschews the conventional triple plot in which the upper-class characters play the major roles. Instead, the story attends with a singular focus to the inner life and outward travails of an illiterate female servant. Rather than perishing ignominiously (the typical fate of the unwed mother in Victorian

---

[7]   George Moore, *Celibates* (London: Walter Scott, 1895), 95.
[8]   George Moore, 'Preface', in *Esther Waters* (New York: Boni and Liveright, 1922), vi.

fiction), Esther is victorious in her struggle to raise her infant son to adulthood. She rejects the religious man who proposes marriage in favour of the more physically attractive man (a former footman turned publican and bookmaker) who seduced and impregnated her years before, and the two are happily married until his death. By force of an instinct that she neither chooses nor inherits from her parents, Esther suffers great hardship but remains undamaged by the degradations of her situation. While repudiating the moralizing of sentimental fiction, the novel thus questions the inevitability of its own relentless insistence on the absolute force of environmental and hereditary conditioning.

Although Esther functions within her society exclusively as a tool of others—a labourer, an object of sexual assault, a potential prostitute, and a wet nurse for the children of the rich—the narrative never lets the reader experience her exclusively as a body to be acted upon. Instead, numerous scenes focalized through a close third-person narration articulate her own embodied perspective, whether she is dizzy with hunger and exhaustion or ecstatic in the embrace of her newborn son. In revising the novel from its initial serial version, Moore came to see Esther's instinctual drive as more than unconscious desire or the result of inherited traits.[9] Instead of being entirely subject to biological and environmental determinism as Zola's experimental novel would dictate, Esther's body and its instincts lead her towards a strong sense of her individuality, her creative impulse, and a conviction of her life's meaning. As Moore wrote to his friend Lena Milman in 1893, 'We must discriminate between what is mere inclination and what is instinct. All my sympathies are with instincts and their development. Instinct alone may lead us aright.'[10] While drawing even further away from naturalism, Moore also continues to undermine the marriage plot. Only a stage in Esther's story, the marriage itself receives little consideration, and the novel concludes as the widowed Esther tells her story to her first employer, also now a widow, with whom she will live out her days as a companion and helper.

Celibacy, rather than marriage, continues to be Moore's subject in his later Irish fiction and in that which immediately followed *Esther Waters*'s critical and commercial success. In addition to *Celibates* (the first of three collections of fiction on the subject), the paired novels *Evelyn Innes* (1898) and *Sister Teresa* (1901) consumed Moore's attention in the last years of the nineteenth century. The works gave him immense trouble, and shortly after the initial appearance of *Evelyn Innes* he confessed to Edouard Dujardin his fear that he 'had given three years to the concoction of an imbecility'.[11] Unable to abandon the project, he published four substantial revisions and two rewritten versions of its sequel, *Sister Teresa*. Although he never succeeded in eliminating the technical problems (and in both

[9] See Jay Jernigan, 'The Forgotten Serial Version of George Moore's *Esther Waters*', *Nineteenth-Century Fiction* 23 (1986), 99–103 and Nathalie Saldou-Welby, '"The Soul with a False Bottom" and "The Deceitful Character": Analyzing the Servant in the Gouncourts' *Germinie Lacerteux* and George Moore's *Esther Waters*', in Christine Huguet and Fabienne Dabrigeon-Garcier (eds), *George Moore: Across Borders* (Amsterdam: Rodopi, 2013), 206–26.

[10] George Moore, *George Moore in Transition: Letters to T. Fisher Unwin and Lena Milman, 1894–1910*, ed. Helmut E. Gerber (Detroit, MI: Wayne State University Press, 1968), 71.

[11] George Moore, *Letters from George Moore to Ed. Dujardin, 1886–1922*, ed. and trans. John Eglinton (New York: Crosby Gaige, 1929), 43.

cases the originals are the superior versions), the sequence represents a critical transitional stage in his turn towards a fiction of interiority. The 'wonder and mystery of life', he asserts in an 1896 article, is to be found in 'that vague, undefinable, yet intensely real life that lies beneath our consciousness'. 'It is in the underlife,' he continues, 'that a great novelist finds his inspiration, and the business of his art.'[12] In choosing as his subject matter the 'underlife' of a gifted Wagnerian soprano who defies convention in order to pursue the fulfilment of her sexual desire, her professional ambitions, and an inherent mysticism that cannot always align itself with dogma, Moore proved a powerful influence on D. H. Lawrence's portrait of the Brangwen sisters; Lawrence was in fact an admirer of Moore's work and especially of *Evelyn Innes*.[13] Evelyn's vanity, however, constrains her efforts to express her sensuality without selfishness, her duties to others without abnegation, and her musical gifts and spiritual aspirations without such self-conscious theatricality that she doubts her ability to live a life of integrity, free of the constraints of external discipline. Repudiating any sort of sexual life, she retires to a convent where, her magnificent voice broken, she also relinquishes her art.

Beyond *A Drama in Muslin*, which ends with its heroine's departure from Ireland in the company of a humble doctor who draws her respect and affection if not her passion, the stories of George Moore conclude in celibacy or the prediction of only brief happiness for the couple who have come together in their pages. Although an early novel, *A Drama in Muslin* is also the first and last fiction that he would write on the subject of the declining Big House and the history of its family, a topic that dominates the fiction of Anglo-Ireland from the nineteenth-century Gothic romance to the work of writers like Aidan Higgins (1927–2015), William Trevor (1928–2016), and Jennifer Johnston (1930–) in the late twentieth century. The subject remains an autobiographical preoccupation for Moore and leads him to produce some of the finest autobiographical writing to come out of Ireland, but it never again arises in his stories or novels. Adam Parkes has suggested that Moore's repudiation of the family as a fictional unit comprises a foundational component of his modernist internationalism, positioned in opposition to the familial rhetoric of nationalism and its corresponding ideology of blood relation. Instead of the family, Parkes argues, Moore returns in one way or another to the kind of homosocial fraternity of single men he found in Paris, privileging their independence while, I would add, openly acknowledging that his masculine autonomy and mobility rests on both the labour of the Irish tenants whose rents allow him to pursue literature and on the contributions of other friends, family, and collaborators, particularly women.[14]

---

[12] George Moore, 'Since the Elizabethans', *Cosmopolis* 4 (1896), 57.

[13] Lawrence admired Moore since his time as a schoolteacher in Croydon and, according to Jessie Chambers, was 'extremely enthusiastic' about *Evelyn Innes*, which he sent her as a gift, along with *Esther Waters and Sister Teresa*. Emile Delavenay, *D. H. Lawrence: The Man and his Work. The Formative Years: 1885–1919* (Carbondale, IL: Southern Illinois University Press, 1972), 93.

[14] Adam Parkes, *A Sense of Shock: The Impact of Impressionism on Modern British and Irish Writing* (Oxford: Oxford University Press, 2011), 77–98. From *Parnell and His Island* in 1887 to the conclusion of *A Story-Teller's Holiday* in 1918, Moore explicitly acknowledges that his freedom to pursue literature had been bought by tenant labour.

Modernist Metropolitanism
and the Regional Subject

With the family histories of the Irish landlord class diverted for the most part to memoir, Moore continued to address the failures of the family unit in the cycle of short fiction published in 1903 as *The Untilled Field*. Although Moore's interest in celibacy as a form of sexual variance is not exclusive to those works with an Irish setting, *The Untilled Field* reflects what Emer Nolan diagnoses as a pervasive cultural reaction to the Famine and its aftermath: 'the social phenomenon of celibacy obsessively represented in a literature that took it as the key to all political and ideological mythologies'.[15] In the case of Peter Phelan, from the story 'The Exile', antipathy to marriage with the girl who loves him emanates from traits peculiar to his character: a generalized fecklessness in worldly matters and an inability to maintain an interest in anything, be it farming, the priest-hood, or women. Yet as with all of Moore's Irish fiction, the story is sociological as well as psychological: Peter's capable and passionate brother James must emigrate to America because he cannot imagine marrying any woman other than the one who loves Peter and, without a wife, he cannot take charge of his father's farm, apparently the only source of work for him in the remote countryside. The psychology of the story, much of it told in close third-person narration or indirect discourse from the perspective of the widowed father of both young men, is inseparable from its sociology, and its sociology is rooted in the economic deprivations resultant from colonial exploitation and the inadequacies of the land redistribution acts of the late nineteenth century.

With the exception of the talkative, thesis-driven stories about repatriated artists that conclude the volume, *The Untilled Field* depicts the effects of poverty, isolation, and authoritarian religion with irony and restraint. Modelled on Turgenev's *A Sportsman's Sketches* (1852), *The Untilled Field* achieves a spare understated style of the kind Moore describes in his 1888 essay in praise of Turgenev as 'a bare narrative' in which factual details, brief conversations, closely focalized perception, free indirect discourse, and an 'absolute impersonality of diction' reveal the depths of inarticulate characters who hardly know themselves.[16] At moments the book is gently humorous, as in the sympathetic treatment of Father MacTurnan, an idealistic priest from a remote area of northern Mayo who writes a letter to Rome in which he reluctantly proposes to renounce celibacy in order to repopulate his parish, which is too poor to support its young people. In a subsequent story, 'A Playhouse in the Waste', the priest unsuccessfully attempts the building of a playhouse to bring a potential source of income to the emigration-ravaged community. However comic some of these elements may be, in their probing of the effects of social conformity and religious repression upon the lives of young people, and

---

[15] Emer Nolan, *Catholic Emancipations: Irish Fiction from Thomas Moore to James Joyce* (Syracuse, NY: Syracuse University Press, 2007), 137.

[16] George Moore, 'Turgueneff', *Fortnightly Review* 49 (1888), 248, 249.

on women in particular, the stories bristle with an undercurrent of resistance that anticipates James Joyce's (1882–1941) *Dubliners* (1914) and the mid-century fiction of Mary
Lavin and Edna O'Brien.

'A Playhouse in the Waste' deserves special attention for its treatment of the meagre
opportunities available to those in the remote regions of the west of Ireland and its
exposure of the effects of sexual repression and the suffering of women. Yet its deeper
significance lies in the way Moore addresses and complicates his subject matter through
the narrative framing that creates a polyphony of voices within the story, each of which
is subject to silent ethical scrutiny, as is the reader's identification with one or more of
those voices. All of this Moore accomplishes in the deceptive guise of a very familiar
genre, that of the strange tale of folk belief as told to a gentleman traveller. In addition to
the framing structure offered by the narration of a local jarvey and Father MacTurnan
himself, in his 1914 revision of the story Moore further frames 'A Playhouse in the Waste'
by establishing a first-person narrator who identifies its existence as a literary text drawn
from the oral discourse of a group of Dublin gentlemen, each of whom has a different
level of engagement with the lives and language of the rural working class.

The story begins as the men enjoy some amusing gossip about the odd case of the
priest whose letter to Rome has somehow become a subject of discussion, although the
letter's details remain unclear. Eventually,

> out of the talk a tall gaunt man emerged, in an old overcoat green from weather and
> wear, the tails of it flapping as he rode his bicycle through the great waste bog that
> lies between Belmullet and Crossmolina. His name! We liked it. It appealed to our
> imagination. MacTurnan! It conveyed something from afar like Hamlet or Don
> Quixote. He seemed as near and as far from us as they.[17]

The narrator is not a stranger from another land; his first utterance—'"It's a closed
mouth that can hold a very good story", as the saying goes'[18]—signals his easy familiarity
with idiom, although he establishes distance from its origin by identifying the phrase as
an adage. His group of friends, too, use Irish-inflected speech patterns such as 'And why
would he be building a playhouse…and he living in a waste?'[19] Despite their linguistic
familiarity, MacTurnan seems 'near' only as a species of literary character might be, and
they delight in his strangeness much as Joyce's John Alphonsus Mulrennan is fascinated
by an old man with whom he speaks Irish in a mountain cabin. Moore thus foregrounds
his alienation, and presumably that of his intended readership, from the very people
who were the subject of much Revival writing. Moore began *The Untilled Field* with the
intention that it would be translated into Irish and, he hoped, become part of Irish-
language literature; but as he wrote each story, he became increasingly aware that his
tales were perceived as offensive and unsympathetic. By the time of this 1914 revision, he
had returned to London and completed the last volume of *Hail and Farewell* (1911–14), in

---

[17] George Moore, 'A Playhouse in the Waste', in *The Untilled Field* (Gerrards Cross: Colin Smythe,
1976), 150.
[18] Ibid.   [19] Ibid., 151.

which he envisages himself in Dublin as a Don Quixote, like Father MacTurnan, on an impossible quest to rescue his country from itself.

Yet another narrator, Pat Comer, an organizer for the Irish Agricultural Organization Society (IAOS) founded by Sir Horace Plunkett, joins the group and, having just returned from the area, relates the story of the playhouse as told to him by a jarvey and Father MacTurnan himself. As his role in the IAOS might suggest, Pat is one step closer to the world of his character, as his speech reflects both his education and a much greater degree of idiom. He holds the floor for the remainder of the story, barring two short interjections. The first comes from the frame narrator when he identifies himself as someone who exists beyond that Dublin fireside, a writer who lives in a world shared with the reader and who has written the story we now read. Moore thus acknowledges the literary object that the oral narrative has become, an object that is part of the economy of publication and distribution. Later, Pat remarks that jarveys are good storytellers, and one of the men in the group compliments him on his abilities as well. Through the two interjections, Moore undercuts the illusion of documentary authenticity, a concern that had emerged as a point of vehement contention among various factions of the Revival even before the controversies surrounding the 1903 production of *In the Shadow of the Glen* by J. M. Synge (1871–1909).

Providing one short description of the ragged clothes and starving faces he sees in the parish, Pat otherwise permits his informants to tell the story and, like his author, permits the details of what he sees and hears to communicate that which he thinks and feels. The mood turns as the story concludes with the jarvey's explanation of what destroyed the playhouse. A local girl named Margaret, who takes the part of Good Deeds in a passion play that Father MacTurnan has translated from Latin to Irish, finds herself 'wake [ill] coming home from the learning of the play' and her illness turns out to be of the worst sort for an unmarried female. The jarvey continues:

> 'And when the signs of her wakeness began to show, the widow Sheridan took a halter off the cow and tied Margaret to the wall, and she was in the stable till the child was born. Then didn't her mother take a bit of string and tie it round the child's throat, and bury it near the playhouse; and it was three nights after that the storm rose, and the child pulled the thatch out of the roof.'[20]

Others claim to have seen a 'white thing' by the roadside, including the priest who blesses it with water from a boghole in an effort to subdue it through an impromptu baptism. Mesmerized by the supernatural aspects of his story, none of the narrators or listeners remark at all on the suffering of Margaret or the cruelty of her elders, and, like the infanticide, the story's critical realism disappears into the genre of ghost story for the narrators, listeners, and the reader who has been similarly lured. Instead of relying on authorial commentary, Moore has deployed narrative framing and a variety of discourse registers to articulate the effects of absentee landlordism, generalized agricultural distress, restrictive religion, and gender oppression, while simultaneously he scrutinizes cultural revivalists and agricultural reformers, as well as the curious reader who holds the book in her hands.

[20] Ibid., 162–3.

Like *The Lake* and most of *A Story-Teller's Holiday*, *The Untilled Field* is set in Galway and in Mayo, where Moore came of age and retained ownership of Moore Hall on Lough Carra and the remainder of what had been a vast estate. The life and landscape of western Ireland are his fictional materials, along with the suburbs and slums of England, even though Moore lived exclusively in Paris and London, apart from his decade-long Dublin sojourn. Despite his guarded optimism that Dublin could become an artistic centre—and in actuality he enjoyed ten years of literary friendships, collaborations, and the writing of some of his best work there—by 1903 he had acknowledged to Dujardin that 'I have entirely renounced my Celtic aspirations,'[21] and five years later declared that the anticipated artistic renaissance 'does not exist, it is a myth'.[22] The centre–periphery model of modernist internationalism advocated by writers like Ezra Pound and literary historians for decades since has been subject to many challenges by theorists of transnational culture, but Moore appears to have accepted it as doctrine even if his practice suggests a more nuanced understanding.

Apart from two more collections of stories concerning celibacy, Moore's fiction after *The Untilled Field* and the first version of *The Lake* continues to be set in areas remote from the metropolitan centre or in the distant past. In addition to his non-fiction and revisions of some earlier works, he focused most of his time on a complete rewriting of *The Lake*, which appeared in 1921, the controversial but well-received Jesus-novel, *The Brook Kerith* (1916), and *A Story-Teller's Holiday*, which frames its stories of medieval Ireland within an auto-fictional journey to and from Moore Hall. Although he was only very briefly intrigued by the reworking of Irish folklore as a regenerating beacon for a national culture, this attention to the distant past should not be read as mere escapism or as symptomatic of modernist melancholy and belatedness. By drawing from the medieval rather than the ancient Irish past, Moore engages Catholicism on his own terms. As John Wilson Foster rightly argues, his bawdy tales of sexual temptation, which were variations on the translations of Douglas Hyde (1860–1949) and Kuno Meyer, paganize Catholicism without the guise of anthropology or history and present a 'counterblast' to the desexualized stories of works like Hyde's *Legends of Saints and Sinners* (1915).[23]

Like *The Brook Kerith* and *A Story-Teller's Holiday*, the adaptations of other medieval tales that preoccupied Moore's last years revisit the past for the sake of the present, although not in the service of cultural nationalism. In *The Brook Kerith*, the newly converted Paul must decide his future after a chance encounter with a Jesus who, rescued from the cross by Joseph of Arimathea, has lived on as a simple Essene shepherd, repudiating the egotism that made him seek disciples and, although still celibate, espousing an acceptance of sexuality as part of a pantheistic love of the natural world. For Moore, the attraction of ancient and medieval settings was not just that their atmosphere suited the oral method of composition and the framework of the oral tale to which he had been

---

[21] George Moore to Edouard Dujardin, quoted in Joseph Hone, *The Life of George Moore* (New York: Macmillan, 1936), 245.

[22] Moore, *Letters from George Moore to Ed. Dujardin, 1886–1922*, 65.

[23] John Wilson Foster, *Fictions of the Irish Literary Revival: A Changeling Art* (Syracuse, NY: Syracuse University Press, 1987), 273–6.

devoted since acquiring the services of a stenographer shortly after his arrival in Dublin. Moore was reclaiming early Christian history and the stories of 'the land of saints and scholars' in support of his lifelong concerns with the vagaries of human desire, the search for vocation, and the need for intellectual independence.

Narrating Gender and Place

Moore's writing in the first two decades of the twentieth century represents the culmination of his thinking on gender and sexuality, Ireland as idea and place, and the possibilities of voice and the structure of narrative. As in 'A Playhouse in the Waste', Moore drew further away from overt authorial commentary, replacing that and interior monologue with focalized third-person narration and, most particularly, indirect discourse. As Luke Gibbons maintains, indirect discourse plays a distinct and highly significant role in Irish fiction. Speaking both of Joyce and of Irish literary history more generally, he posits that

> Though free indirect discourse was characteristically used in modernism to register the psychological, inner world of a character, the regular recourse to colloquial idioms and elements of performance to signal its presence in Irish literature opens onto wider social vistas, as if a voice can only make its presence felt by means of the culture that speaks through it.[24]

Through what Gibbons calls 'vernacular modernism', Ireland 'achieves articulation not only as subject matter or content but also as form'.[25]

By shifting from the interior monologues of *Evelyn Innes* and *Sister Teresa* to free indirect discourse and to the focalized narration, oral structure, and framing that characterize his Irish fiction, Moore too signals the 'wider social vistas' beyond the psychological interiority at which he had been directing his efforts for years. In 'The Exile', for example, the descriptive language with which a paragraph begins reveals itself as the perception of the character rather than the omniscient narrator:

> The mare trotted gleefully; soft clouds curled over the low horizon far away, and the sky was blue overhead; and the poor country was very beautiful in the still autumn weather, only it was empty. He passed two or three fine houses that the gentry had left to caretakers long ago. The fences were gone, cattle strayed through the woods, the drains were choked with weeds, the stagnant water was spreading out into the fields, and Pat Phelan noticed these things, for he remembered what this country was forty years ago. The devil a bit of lonesomeness there was in it then.[26]

---

[24] Luke Gibbons, *Joyce's Ghosts: Ireland, Modernism, and Memory* (Chicago, IL: University of Chicago Press, 2015), 81.

[25] Ibid., xiv.   [26] George Moore, 'The Exile', in *The Untilled Field*, 20.

The shift to Pat's idiom in the paragraph's last sentence is preceded by subjective descriptors and observations about the current state of the countryside by one who knows it sufficiently well to note cattle straying into the woods and recall why certain houses are empty. The spatialized consciousness of the old man moves down the road, seeing past and future as he surveys the present. The passage is suffused with an intimate knowledge of local history and a deeply felt topophilia, saying much about Pat's bewilderment and sorrow but doing so in terms of the economic and political landscape in which he lives.

This approach reaches its apogee in the completely rewritten 1921 edition of *The Lake*. Within the topical, digressive, and often stilted epistolary first edition of 1903, Moore found the core of a story that would probe his complex and contradictory feelings about the land of his birth and explore the pantheistic spirituality that increasingly attracted him, and the independence of thought he believed integral to a full human life. In his preface to the new edition, Moore confesses his partiality to the novel, explaining that

> my reason for liking 'The Lake' is related to the very great difficulty of the telling, for the one vital event in the priest's life befell him before the story opens, and to keep the story in the key in which it was conceived, it was necessary to recount the priest's life during the course of his walk by the shores of a lake, weaving his memories continually, without losing sight, however, of the long, winding, mere-like lake, wooded to its shores, with hills appearing and disappearing into mist and distance.[27]

His conception of the story, he writes, was 'the essential rather than the daily life of the priest', coupled with the desire to capture the 'drama [that] passes within the priest's soul' and 'the weaving of a story out of the soul substance without ever seeking the aid of external circumstance'.[28] This mastery of technique, of which Moore was so proud, owes much to the precedent of *Hail and Farewell*, his three-volume autobiography. *Hail and Farewell* may be full of incident and comic in ways *The Lake* never attempts, but its full embrace of subjectivity, its structural dependence upon the narrator's peregrinations around Dublin and journeys elsewhere, and its open delight in the diversity of speech among its characters prefigure the kind of culturally inflected impressionism Moore would take up in revising his novel.

Impressionism is a term coined in this usage by Ford Madox Ford, whose admiration for Moore's non-fiction led him to identify him in *The March of Literature* (1938) as 'the father of Anglo-Saxon Impressionism'[29] (although also, more accurately, 'an Irishman trained by the French'[30]). Ford's sense of Moore's nationality appears confused, but the point is that Ford sees Moore as an outsider, like Joseph Conrad, undervalued and out of the mainstream of a British tradition exemplified by Arnold Bennett, and thus able to take new and exciting approaches to literature. Ford's 1914 manifesto, 'On Impressionism', sets forth an

---

[27] Moore, *The Lake*, x.   [28] Ibid.

[29] Ford Madox Ford, *The March of Literature: From Confucius' Day to Our Own* (Normal, IL: Dalkey Archive Press, 1994), 840.

[30] Ford Madox Ford, *Thus to Revisit: Some Reminiscences* (New York: E. P. Dutton, 1921), 32.

understanding of narrative as akin to Impressionist painting: as a matter of *style*, it is a system of verbal brushstrokes by which a reader may see consciousness, as the Impressionist painting strives to replicate the eye's experience of light. The Impressionist, he continues, 'gives you nothing but the pleasure of coming in contact with his temperament',[31] and while here Ford is referring to the temperament of the authorial persona, his comments apply equally to a protagonist who is as much the subject of tightly focalized narration as Father Oliver of *The Lake*. For Moore as for Ford, 'the pleasure of coming in contact with his temperament' results from the writer's commitment to four features of storytelling: a narrative voice that moves seamlessly among memory, invention, and meta-commentary on the storytelling process; a voice that speaks from the story's diegetic plane of action rather than the recollective vantage point we associate with an authoritative narration; a narrative that follows the meanderings of the mind instead of a chronology of action; and prose that renders an impression of the world as an entryway to 'personality' and some significant truth about the surrounding world.

Ford's own digressive progression through the thought process of a character was much maligned by Theodore Dreiser in a review of *The Good Soldier* published shortly after the novel's appearance in 1915. Dreiser cites what he calls 'a good explanation of a bad method',[32] but it is such an apt explanation of Ford's very good methodology that it bears repeating, and most importantly, because it also describes precisely what Moore achieves in *The Lake*. From one of the several apologies Ford's narrator offers and retracts in a single gesture, this one is, as Dreiser notices, the most descriptive of the novel's own procedure:

> I have, I am aware, told this story in a very rambling way so that it may be difficult for anyone to find their path through what may be a sort of maze. I cannot help it. I have stuck to my idea of being in a country cottage with a silent listener, hearing between the gust of the wind and amidst the noises of the distant sea, the story as it comes. And, when one discusses an affair—a long, sad affair—one goes back, one goes forward. One remembers points that one has forgotten and one explains them all the more minutely since one recognizes that one has forgotten to mention them in their proper places and that one may have given, by omitting them, a false impression. I console myself with thinking that this is a real story and that, after all, real stories are probably told best in the way a person telling a story would tell them. They will then seem most real.[33]

Here is the encounter with personality, the representation of a consciousness that resides in numerous temporal zones. Here too is a structure of telling that follows the action of the mind, exactly as both *Hail and Farewell* and *The Lake* rest on a loose chronological

[31] Ford, 'On Impressionism', 35.

[32] Theodore Dreiser, 'The Saddest Story', *The New Republic* 3, no. 28 (1915), 155.

[33] Ford Madox Ford, *The Good Soldier* (London: Penguin, 1946), 167. Although Moore had corresponded with Ford as editor of the *English Review*, which published selections from *Hail and Farewell*, no evidence exists that Moore was familiar with Ford's novel.

architecture but are plotted through long walks during which the meditative consciousness moves from an ever-changing moment to amble among pasts remembered and those openly invented.

Like Moore's other autobiographical works and much of his fiction, *The Lake* also engages in conversation with the life and speech of the community in which it takes place and from which it arises. Its subtle depiction of a man's growing consciousness of his need for a personal life—'that intimate exaltation that comes to him who has striven to be himself, and nothing but himself'[34]—depends much less on internal monologue in the sense of fully formed thoughts than on the natural world as seen and felt by him; it is his impression of the external world that reveals his interiority. In 'Mr Bennett and Mrs Brown', Virginia Woolf decried fiction's emphasis on sociological detail; nevertheless, she knew that Clarissa Dalloway's reaction to Miss Kilman's ever-present green macintosh would say much about Clarissa's longings, desires, and fears, perhaps even more than the garment says about Miss Kilman's own.[35] Moore, like Ford and others of the period, also writes that inner life through an aesthetic of exteriority, finding in the outlines of the human body and the quirks of speech and dress the surest signposts of the life within.

Finally, *A Story-Teller's Holiday* finds Moore at the outer reaches of fiction as a fixed genre. Unstable as to the mode, tone, and the identity of its speaking voice, and structurally unlike anything else, *A Story-Teller's Holiday* is a novel, an autobiography, a collection of short fiction, and a fantastic parody of the documentary Irish folklore collections fashionable during the Revival period. The book begins with Moore's evocation of his readership, a select group who will appreciate the erotic and arcane elements of the beautifully produced and privately printed limited edition of the book they hold in their hands; the public author, 'thy friend, George Moore',[36] is conflated then with the autobiographical narrator who returns to Mayo on matters of business. The narrator implausibly enters into a storytelling exchange with Alec Trusselby, a reed-gatherer whose speech and habits bear little resemblance to the rural people depicted in *The Untilled Field*, and who is assuredly a caricature whose very improbability satirizes the folklore gatherers of the early Revival period. At the conclusion of their exchange, the autobiographical narrator pulls away from the realm of fiction to a poignant recollection of his family history, the death of his parents, and his need to reject the actual places of the past—not only Moore Hall but the Montmartre of his youth—in order to sustain them in what are for him the more generative spaces of memory and narration.

Among the stories told, most of which refer to the pursuit of love in medieval Ireland and a rejection of religious strictures, 'Albert Nobbs' arises as a memory from the narrator's childhood, and by the manner of its telling reinscribes his sense of the irretrievability and even the unknowability of the past. A hotel waiter who lives a lonely life disguised

---

[34] Moore, *The Lake*, 175.

[35] Virginia Woolf, 'Mr Bennett and Mrs Brown', in *Collected Essays* (London: Hogarth Press, 1966), vol 3, 319–37.

[36] George Moore, *A Story-Teller's Holiday* (London: Privately printed for subscribers only by Cumann Sean-eolais na hÉireann, 1918), 2.

as a man and whose gender is unknown to anyone other than Hubert, another cross-dressing woman she meets only once, Albert's inner life is finally undefinable, a subject of speculative fictionalizing by a narrator who has already identified himself as having been a young child during the time of the story he tells. Albert's birth name is never given and her gender is uncertain even to herself, as are her erotic orientations, having once been in love with a male employer and unable to kiss the woman she is courting in hopes of companionship and a home of her own, yet attracted to that woman and not another because of the shape and appearance of her body. Albert's body, in turn, is a subject of curiosity and pronominal confusion after her death. Throughout the novella, Moore repeatedly marks moments of failed communication and missed opportunities, and physical movement through the city of Dublin, or up and down the labyrinths of stairs within the hotel, leads to isolation rather than revelation. Just as Hubert falls asleep during Albert's revelation and others misunderstand or cannot hear, so Alec proves himself a bad listener of the narrator's story, unable or unwilling to understand what he has heard.

On the one hand, 'Albert Nobbs' speaks to the unsettled nature of gender and sexuality and to the gendered violence and inequitable employment that drives Albert into disguise; in this sense, it reflects Moore's abiding concerns with sexual variance and the restrictive conditions of women's lives in both England and Ireland. On the other, its very form relays the profound connections between Moore's sense of the ambiguity of identity and Irish traditions of oral discourse and the origins of story in the voices of a wider community. It is a tale told by a speaker who is partly historical, partly a literary persona, and partly an invention of another speaker who is himself a figure of memory and fantasy. The tale contains multiple speakers spinning their own versions of an experience they cannot properly name and whose origins are somewhere in rumour and speculation. 'Albert Nobbs', like the whole of *A Story-Teller's Holiday*, appears as Father MacTurnan comes riding on his bicycle, 'out of the talk'. Although a habit of rushing too much work into print prematurely, personal animosities, particularly with W. B. Yeats (1865–1939), and the sheer breadth of his career placed Moore at the margins of the Irish tradition for all too long, his fiction proves itself to be at the heart of Irish modernism.

FURTHER READING

Brunet, Michel, Fabienne Gaspari, and Mary Pierse (eds). *George Moore's Paris and his Ongoing French Connections*. Bern: Peter Lang, 2015.

Cave, Richard. *A Study of the Novels of George Moore*. Gerrards Cross: Colin Smythe, 1978.

Foster, John Wilson. *Fictions of the Irish Literary Revival: A Changeling Art*. Syracuse, NY: Syracuse University Press, 1987.

Frazier, Adrian. *George Moore, 1852–1933*. New Haven, CT: Yale University Press, 2000.

Frazier, Adrian and Conor Montague (eds). *George Moore: Dublin, Paris, Hollywood*. Dublin: Irish Academic Press, 2012.

Gibbons, Luke. *Joyce's Ghosts: Ireland, Modernism, and Memory*. Chicago, IL: University of Chicago Press, 2015.

Grubgeld, Elizabeth. *George Moore and the Autogenous Self: The Autobiography and Fiction*. Syracuse, NY: Syracuse University Press, 1994.

Heilmann, Ann and Mark Llewellyn (eds). *George Moore: Influence and Collaboration*. Newark, NJ: University of Delaware Press, 2014.

Huguet, Christine and Fabienne Dabrigeon-Garcier (eds). *George Moore: Across Borders*. Amsterdam: Rodopi, 2013.

Joyce, Simon. *Modernism and Naturalism in British and Irish Fiction, 1880–1930*. Cambridge: Cambridge University Press, 2014.

Lanigan, Liam. *James Joyce, Urban Planning and Irish Modernism: Dublins of the Future*. Basingstoke: Palgrave Macmillan, 2014.

Parkes, Adam. *A Sense of Shock: The Impact of Impressionism on Modern British and Irish Writing*. Oxford: Oxford University Press, 2011.

Pierse, Mary and Maria Elena Jaime de Pablos (eds). *George Moore and the Quirks of Human Nature*. Bern: Peter Lang, 2014.

CHAPTER 6

....

REVIVAL FICTION

Proclaiming the Future

....

GREGORY CASTLE

In Shan F. Bullock's (1865–1935) short story, 'The Haymakers', one of his *Irish Pastorals* (1901), the narrator describes a field filled with men 'strong as young bulls', in 'a very feast of work, a mad riot of sweet toil'.[1] While the weather had been toying with them for months, they are now 'stealing a march upon it', and even as the sun leaves 'for his kingdom beyond the mountain',[2] the workers strive to overcome all obstacles, to see their own toil in an ideal light, as something other than what it is. But on the other side of the harvest, in the future it makes possible, a new recognition will make up for this necessary misprision, one that allows them to prepare 'for the great time when radiantly we should point to work well done and jeeringly ask of the enemy to do its worst'.[3] Here we find inscribed, in no uncertain terms, the temporality of Revival, the logic of the future perfect, in which the hardship of labour holds within it the promise of its necessity, a promise that can be fulfilled only afterwards. We find, in short, a moment of recognition, cast into 'coming times', that makes up for what has been endured. The future is the promised land where all present efforts are leading, even those efforts that appear to head in the opposite direction, towards the comforts of the past, which, on this view, takes on the contours of a place that can be revisited in order to confirm its, and one's own, authenticity. If Bullock misrecognizes the romanticism he mobilizes in his portrayals of Irish country life, he does so in the service of the future. But the precariousness of the trope—an idealized Ireland subjected to the 'reality principle'—underscores the fragility of what it represents: 'Yes; that great time was coming: but when? Who could tell? Poor Ireland's weather goddess, even at best, was a fickle jade; who could tell what torrents of tears lay deep behind the flash of her smile?'[4]

Like the weather goddess, Revival occupies a complex and contradictory place in the Irish cultural imaginary. On the one hand, it signifies the cultural renaissance associated

[1] Shan F. Bullock, 'The Haymakers', in *Irish Pastorals* (London: Grant Richards, 1901), 96.
[2] Ibid.   [3] Ibid.   [4] Ibid.

with an Anglo-Protestant literary coterie led by W. B. Yeats (1865–1939), J. M. Synge (1871–1909), and Lady Augusta Gregory (1852–1932) that had wide influence in Ireland, England, North America, Japan, and many other places; it often stood (and sometimes continues to stand) accused of the colonialist appropriation of authentic Gaelo-Catholic folklore, legend, mythology, and local traditions in order to engage in deliberately false perceptions and to commodify and market the 'Irish peasant' and other bogus forms of Irish cultural capital.[5] As a result, works of the Literary Revival were often misunderstood and sometimes dismissed as exoticism, primitivism, naïve sentimentalism, ethnographic fabrication, or historical distortion—mired in a 'borrowed aesthetic', as Frantz Fanon puts it in *The Wretched of the Earth* (1963), a 'concept of the world discovered under other skies'.[6] On the other hand, Revival (without the modifying 'Literary') has come to signify a wide array of indigenous cultural practices and traditions. For contemporary critics, the questions of cultural authenticity and the status of the past lead either in the direction of investigations into neglected social movements, people, and works,[7] or towards a critique of the Revival's ethnographic imagination, particularly the discourse of the primitive that recent critics have argued is a crucial touchstone for Revival attitudes towards the past, Irish culture, and Irish Catholic identity.[8]

In the deep background of much Revival discourse is an assumption that the past is in need of redemption in Walter Benjamin's sense of being bound *necessarily* to the future. According to Benjamin,

> The past carries with it a temporal index by which it is referred to redemption. There is a secret agreement between past generations and the present one. Our coming was expected on earth. Like every generation that preceded us, we have been endowed with a weak Messianic power, a power to which the past has a claim. That claim cannot be settled cheaply. Historical materialists are aware of that.[9]

I believe that revivalists too were aware of this 'temporal index', aware that the past must be understood for what it can tell us not about *past time* (understood as a *space of time*

---

[5] Still pertinent on the issue of representing 'authentic' Ireland is Edward Hirsch's 'The Imaginary Irish Peasant', *PMLA* 106 (1991), 1116–33.

[6] Frantz Fanon, *The Wretched of the Earth*, trans. Richard Philcox (New York: Grove Press, 2004), 159. This seminal work was first published in French in 1961.

[7] See P. J. Mathews, *Revival: The Abbey Theatre, Sinn Féin, the Gaelic League and the Co-operative Movement* (Cork: Cork University Press, 2003); Karen Steele, *Women, Press and Politics During the Irish Literary Revival* (Syracuse, NY: Syracuse University Press, 2007); Catherine Morris, *Alice Milligan and the Irish Cultural Revival* (Dublin: Four Courts Press, 2012); and Declan Kiberd and P. J. Mathews (eds), *Handbook of the Irish Revival: An Anthology of Irish Cultural and Political Writings 1891–1922* (Dublin: Abbey Theatre Press, 2015).

[8] See Gregory Castle, *Modernism and the Celtic Revival* (Cambridge: Cambridge University Press, 2001); Sinéad Garrigan Mattar, *Primitivism, Science, and the Irish Revival* (Oxford: Oxford University Press, 2004); and Maria McGarrity and Claire A. Culleton (eds), *Irish Modernism and the Global Primitive* (New York: Palgrave Macmillan, 2009).

[9] Walter Benjamin, 'On the Concept of History', in *Selected Writings*, ed. Marcus Bullock and Michael W. Jennings (Cambridge, MA; Belknap-Harvard University Press, 1996), vol. 4, 390.

cordoned off from the present) but about the future it promises (a 'weak' power over time), a future 'expected on earth', if not in any heaven: a *horizon*, not a *place*. The past, no matter how miserable, is bound to this future *as that which will have been redeemed*. A crucial part of this redemptive process is a logic of misrecognition that turns a rectifying gaze on colonial and nationalist misconceptions of Ireland and its history. This healing misprision serves the ends of a cultural revolution that seeks to reveal the promise of coming times. Revival thus relies on wilful errors about the Irish past serving, in James Joyce's (1882–1941) ripe phrase, as 'the portals of discovery'[10] opening onto an Irish future.

In general, then, Revival seeks to overcome the misapprehensions that exoticism and nostalgia put into play, both in history and in memory, by the tactical reuse of rhetorical tropes and images, which are often misrecognized as signs of inauthenticity, in the service of a sovereign Irish future.[11] However, for over a century, the critical discussion has tended to focus on drama, poetry, history, Irish language and translation, design, music, and other cultural practices. Fiction is rarely adduced—still less *realist* fiction—as evidence, to argue, one way or the other, about the social, cultural, and political significance of Revival.[12] But I believe that in writers as diverse as Bullock, Emily Lawless (1845–1913), George Moore (1852–1933), W. B. Yeats, and James Joyce we find dramatic instances of a logic of misrecognition that lays bare the dialectics of redemption and the promise of coming times subtending so much of Revival discourse. It goes without saying that a fiction based on such a logic has little in common with the nineteenth-century realist novel tradition (particularly in England and France), in part because in this tradition realism amounted to the imitation of social conditions (the primary role of mimesis) and to the tacit acceptance, even approval, of those conditions. We do not see such tacit acceptance in Revival fiction, even though we see clearly that such fiction sanctions and celebrates the local communities it presents to the reader. It rejects, however, the conditions of life that people in such communities are forced to endure (poverty, ignorance, violence, inequality, injustice), which are at times so bleak and intractable that they come to appear as *natural*. In Revival fiction, formal hybridity frees realist representation from the burden of merely imitating such conditions and moves it in the direction of a critical account of social realities *and* of the romanticism so often mobilized in literary and artistic accounts of Irish culture and the Irish past.

Emer Nolan's examination of the Irish realist tradition has paved the way for my argument. Nolan speaks of a 'largely uncritical commitment on the part of many Irish writers to realism as the sovereign form of the novel. Nevertheless, there is an underacknowledged Catholic tradition in nineteenth-century Irish letters—one that sporadically recognizes the limitations of realism, even though it remains in thrall to its prestige and

---

[10] James Joyce, *Ulysses* (New York: Vintage-Random House, 1990), 190.

[11] On this critical and tactical use of tropes, see Gregory Castle, 'Irish Revivalism: Critical Trends and New Directions', *Literature Compass* 8, no. 5 (2011), 292, 295–8.

[12] An important exception to this general assessment is John Wilson Foster's *Fictions of the Irish Literary Revival: A Changeling Art* (Syracuse, NY: Syracuse University Press, 1987).

popularity.'[13] Unlike the 'sovereign form' of realism to which she refers, Revival fiction is subject to hybrid formations in which a naturalist intention to reveal underlying social and familial conditions is wedded to a form of vernacular realism that is both selective (description is not mere notation) and romantic. Simon Joyce, following Nolan, regards Ireland's violent colonial history, economic instability, and sectarian tensions to be well suited to naturalist analysis, as opposed to the 'collective political agency' subtending the 'totalizing ambitions' of realism.[14] As a standpoint, orthodox naturalism (objective, non-selective point of view; exact and 'specialized' description; a reportorial or 'anti' style; a focus on ordinary life) is critical and subversive of social norms; it seeks to uncover the social conditions and human relationships that conventional realism represses or occludes.[15] If Revival fiction, like Synge's drama, tends to romanticize its depiction of these conditions and relations, it does so by using compromised temporal tropes (nostalgia, primitivism, the timeless ethnographic present[16]) in a naturalist mode of storytelling that gives them new and surprising potential to illustrate what *will have to be overcome* when the Irish nation finds its own historical moment of recognition, its own time for revival.

EMILY LAWLESS'S *HURRISH* AND *GRANIA*

Emily Lawless's novels, *Hurrish: A Study* (1886) and *Grania: The Story of an Island* (1892), Shan Bullock's short story collections, *Ring o' Rushes* (1896) and *Irish Pastorals*, and George Moore's collection, *The Untilled Field* (1903), are the main exemplars of Revival realism in its pastoral or romantic naturalist mode. These works consistently shift the balance between naturalist objectivity and romantic idealization, and thereby challenge the dominant form of novelistic realism. Lawless's work is an early example of what will become a common Revival practice. In *Hurrish*, she uses romantic tropes of the noble peasant to articulate, in precise naturalist descriptions, complex ideas about how the

---

[13] Emer Nolan, *Catholic Emancipations: Irish Fiction from Thomas Moore to James Joyce* (Syracuse, NY: Syracuse University Press, 2007), xiii.

[14] Simon Joyce, *Modernism and Naturalism in British and Irish Fiction, 1880–1930* (New York: Cambridge University Press, 2014), 84.

[15] On naturalism and its relation to realism, see Joyce, *Modernism and Naturalism*, 11–23. Conventional literary realism, of the sort that Georg Lukács championed against naturalism, deals with the dynamic relationships of the individual in society. In the realist novel, larger social patterns and destinies are projected onto characters and their relationships, and while language is used in its imitative capacity to give a faithful depiction of the social world, that world is the result of authorial and narratorial selection and exclusion. The narrator's point of view typically serves as the moral and intellectual centre of the narrative.

[16] On the ethnographic present, see Johannes Fabian, *Time and the Other: How Anthropology Makes its Object* (New York: Columbia University Press, 1982), 8off. On primitivism, see Mattar, *Primitivism, Science, and the Irish Revival*, introduction and chapter one; on nostalgia, see Declan Kiberd, 'The Perils of Nostalgia: A Critique of the Revival', in Peter Connolly (ed.), *Literature and the Changing Ireland* (Totowa, NJ: Barnes and Noble, 1982), 1–24.

geography and social conditions of the Burren in County Clare—'strange, remote, indescribable'[17]—impact personality; but she does not explicitly critique the 'structures of feeling'[18] that shape and limit Hurrish O'Brien's romantic destiny and heroic nobility. In *Grania*, she employs the same set of tropes but in a more persistently tactical way that enables her protagonist to overcome the limitations placed on her aspirations. The two novels are interlocking and self-correcting fictions. Hurrish cannot overcome the narrative in which he emerges morally triumphant; Grania, in pursuing her own desire in an isolated and fiercely patriarchal society, creates a new kind of narrative, for otherwise *her* triumph would be unrecognizable. If *Hurrish* sets up the ideal, *Grania* overcomes it and points us towards a future beyond its failure to be realized.

Lawless is well regarded for her detailed landscape descriptions, but she is equally adept at suggesting the utter strangeness of landscape through the same descriptive means. As Heidi Hansson has observed, Lawless 'attempted to balance the search for authenticity with descriptions of a landscape that could accommodate differences'.[19] Behind her 'descriptions of animal and plant life' lay 'a respect for the individuality and complexity of things in nature'.[20] Her romantic naturalist style captures a complex geotemporality in which a contemporary landscape evokes a primeval epoch, an *elsewhere* that is also *right here*, an indigenous present moment in which the eternal cohabits with the everyday. Thus, *Hurrish* evokes a certain primitivism even as it locates Hurrish firmly and authentically within his own historical moment. He is an 'elementary and elemental type', a 'genuine Celt', a 'broad-shouldered, loose-limbed, genial faced-giant'.[21] The novel takes place during the Land War of the early 1880s, but Hurrish, who possesses a robust 'primitive patriotism', refuses to rise to nationalist provocations. 'There was too much earnest about it all',[22] he says of the nationalists leading the agitation. They 'killed one another for *reasons*, not from pure love and friendliness'.[23] He condemns ideological reasons for violence but not violence itself, so long as it emerges organically from the community in the form of 'faction fights, scrimmages, and "divarsions"' like those 'of a generation or two ago'.[24]

Hurrish's encounter with Mat Brady, a local gombeen man who threatens to take over the farm of an evicted family, begins as just such a diversion, but Lawless's narrator makes clear that there is a 'gloomier side of things': 'The fun, it is true, is on the surface, the bitterness, discord, misery down at the roots, in a distracted present and an unforgotten past.'[25] When Mat is found dead, Hurrish is brought to trial for murder, though he acted in self-defence. The real villain of the piece is Mat's brother, Maurice, who had informed on Hurrish and thereby incurred the anger of the local republicans. Hurrish's

---

[17] Emily Lawless, *Hurrish: A Study* (New York: Garland Publishing, 1979), vol. 1, 4.

[18] In *The Long Revolution* (New York: Columbia University Press, 1961), Raymond Williams asserts that a 'structure of feeling' registers a 'whole way of life', 'the particular living result of all the elements in the general organization' (48).

[19] Heidi Hansson, *Emily Lawless 1845–1913: Writing the Interspace* (Cork: Cork University Press, 2007), 59.

[20] Ibid. 79.   [21] Lawless, *Hurrish*, vol. 1, 38–9, 9.   [22] Ibid., 86.

[23] Ibid. Original emphasis.   [24] Ibid., 85–6.

[25] Emily Lawless, *Hurrish: A Study* (New York: Garland Publishing, 1979), vol. 2, 83.

intended, Alley Sheehan, comes upon Maurice while he is in hiding, brandishing a gun in a 'flash of lightning' that 'flung its melodramatic illumination over the whole scene'.[26] But she is too late to warn her beloved. In death, Hurrish confronts the utter strangeness of his circumstances, in which nothing is as it appears:

> *To believe yourself in a natural world, to find yourself in an unnatural one*, to take up a fruit and to find a stone, to stretch out a hand to a friend and to receive back a dagger in your heart, faintly describes the sort of vortex of mystery into which his soul was plunged.[27]

His life ends in a martyrdom, which he does not understand, 'to a long and an ugly past' and to an 'ill-governed' land where 'Hate of the Law is the birthright and the dearest possession of every native son of Ireland'.[28]

In *Hurrish*, the protagonist, even in the midst of moral triumph, cannot move beyond the constraints of his own romanticization, in which he is formed into a martyr, 'though he knew it not'.[29] *Grania* pursues this same dynamic, though the natural and the unnatural tend to come together in a way that makes legible Grania O'Malley's more private martyrdom. Subtitled 'The Story of an Island', *Grania* takes the form of a Gothic romance presided over by the Atlantic, the 'wild nurse, mother, and grandmother of storms', with the potential for 'heaven only knows how many unborn tempests for ever and for ever brooding within her restless old breast'.[30] In her dedication, Lawless notes that Inishmaan has more than its 'full share' of gloom: 'This is an artistic fault no one can doubt, yet there are times—are there not?—when it does not seem so very easy to exaggerate the amount of gloom which life is any day and everyday quite willing to bestow'.[31] Lawless artfully misrecognizes the relation between reality and representation by suggesting that she exaggerates in fictional form in order to *make more real* a reality that she fears her readers will doubt.

This technique of exaggeration lends the novel a Gothic romanticism that is in keeping with the protagonist's struggle with her own inner life, which is linked to elemental forces in ways she does not yet comprehend. Grania's aspirations for love and for the future far outstrip the traditional values of her natal community, particularly those of her devout sister, Honor, which means that her burgeoning self-awareness can only be misrecognized as an *affliction*—'this strange unrest, this disturbance' that discombobulates her thought, 'a queer, dim process, very strange in its methods, very mysterious often in its results'.[32] Her queer awakening is suitably represented in a romantic naturalist style that depicts human and natural 'disturbance' as falling within a continuum of elemental forces to which she is linked in a strange relation of storyteller and listener:

---

[26] Ibid., 202–3.   [27] Ibid., 241. Emphasis added.   [28] Ibid., 247.   [29] Ibid.

[30] Emily Lawless, *Grania: The Story of an Island* (New York: Garland Publishing, 1979), vol. 1, 25.

[31] Ibid., unpaginated dedication.

[32] Emily Lawless, *Grania: The Story of an Island* (New York: Garland Publishing, 1979), vol. 2, 137, 140.

'the whole drama of the sky'[33] tells its story to her, as do the droplets of water that run down the oar blades, as if 'telling her stories; some of them old stories but others quite new—stories that she had certainly never heard or never understood before'.[34]

Grania's radical cognitive and imaginative conjunction with her environment, figured in the image of a listener who craves intimate stories, renders her queer in ways that prove fatal. She quarrels with Murdough, the man she is meant to marry, who articulates what she recognizes but cannot yet say: that she is 'an unaccountable product, one that made him feel vaguely uneasy; who seemed to belong to a region in which he had never travelled; who was "queer," in short; the last word summing up concisely the worst and most damning thing that could be said of anyone in Inishmaan'.[35] One way of accounting for this queer development is to read Grania's formative quest, as Hansson does, in terms of spatiality rather than temporality. On this view, 'Grania's initial experience of the sea can be seen to develop her autonomy', which means that her death by drowning enacts the sea's 'promise of liberation'.[36] Figured as self-sacrifice, her death is yet another canny and deliberate misrecognition: she surrenders to the sea, with 'a long-drawn sigh of satisfaction, falling into the laminaria', which supported her then 'loosen[ed] its long sashlike strands'.[37]

In death, Grania sustains the sense of intermingling with the earth that has been a vital part of her life. The earth's primeval benefaction, in the simple form of kelp, rushes to greet her and supports her, abstracting her from life into an 'all-pervading dreaminess,...a dream too deep and apparently too satisfactory to be ever again disturbed or broken in upon by anything from without'.[38] The romanticization of Grania's death, particularly its juxtaposition to her sister's deathbed vision of a heavenly future 'approaching fast, coming near and nearer every moment',[39] constructs a complex dialectical misprision in which a queer alternative, like the laminaria, becomes entangled with Honor's equally romantic surrender to a Christian vision of what is to come. And while Grania, like the narrator, might imagine such a heaven as 'unthinkable, untenable, all but impossible', for Honor it is 'no phantom, no mirage, but the soberest and solidest of solid realities; the thing for which they live, the hope for which they die'.[40] The sisters come together on the shifting ground of an unknown future, which is, in their different ways of apprehending it, a solid reality.

SHAN BULLOCK'S *RING O' RUSHES* AND *IRISH PASTORALS*

Like his counterparts in the Dublin-based Revival, Shan Bullock sought to represent the 'solid realities' of Irish life, even those that were 'unthinkable, untenable, all but impossible'. His realist pastorals, which owe some of their surface lustre to a long tradition of Celtic romanticism, attempt to convey the authentic environment of rural Ireland, whose

[33] Lawless, *Grania*, vol. 1, 202.   [34] Lawless, *Grania*, vol. 2, 92.   [35] Ibid., 194.
[36] Hansson, *Emily Lawless*, 78.   [37] Lawless, *Grania*, vol. 2, 299.   [38] Ibid., 300.
[39] Ibid., 302.   [40] Ibid., 303.

small farmers, Catholic and Protestant alike, live unperturbed lives in an environment that is suffused with tradition, stories, and local gossip. *Ring o' Rushes*, set in Bullock's native region of south Fermanagh, on the border with Cavan, exemplifies the curious and vulnerable romantic idyll at the heart of Revival fiction.[41] In his prologue, the author describes the town of Bunn (based on Belturbet, County Cavan) and the surrounding area and invites the reader to 'linger awhile' and admire 'the book-stall, the brawny corduroyed porters, the pigs and cattle in the vans, picturing to yourself, maybe, Mary the emigrant standing there weeping by her old yellow trunk.'[42] Although Mary occupies a tenuous position ('maybe' we will recognize her as the emigrant she is), she is structurally vital to the community—*as it is understood by the people of Bunn.*[43] Emigrants mingle with townspeople in a romanticized picture of an organic community: we find 'many worthy souls' who 'live happily among those barren hills, and love them steadfastly; some, exiles in this bustling outer world, have left their hearts there.'[44] All seem content, but contentment is earned on sufferance, for emigration creates a unique form of trauma, a form of exile in which leaving or not having left becomes an indelible part of one's being. In 'The Emigrant', for example, Bullock depicts a young woman who 'could do nothing at home. Sure, it was better to go [to New York] than to be a burden on them all.'[45] Mary is persuaded by a young man to stay, but within hours she is abandoned. Bullock turns the screw on the emigration theme in a way that looks forward to Joyce's 'Eveline', for in both stories the main point is seemingly the trauma of leavetaking. But whereas the protagonist of Joyce's story is too frightened to leave, Mary is left with no one to try to stop her, for it is the young man who ends up staying, 'drunk and asleep'[46] on the platform.

If the experience of emigration is often traumatic in Bullock's fiction, the experience of return is rarely healing. Too often, when the emigrant returns and revisits his homeland, his hopes are cruelly undermined by the fact that 'old Ireland' has not, as he has, improved itself. 'His Magnificence', the opening story in *Ring o' Rushes*, concerns the return of Tommy Burke, 'a whole live gentleman all the way from America.'[47] Burke passes through a landscape that only the narrator seems to register: 'the river tumbling gloriously among the boulders and rushing carelessly past a world of quiet beauty on its banks', the whole scene 'crowding away towards his Majesty the mountain.'[48] When he arrives at his mother's hovel, the contrast between the bucolic region and the life of its inhabitants could not be more stark. He finds her sitting in the 'smoke and gloom of the home of his ancestors' and is forced to recognize that 'his splendour' was 'down in the dirt with his own mother.'[49]

---

[41] On the real-life counterparts to Bullock's fictional places, see Patrick Maume, 'The Margins of Subsistence: The Novels of Shan Bullock', *New Hibernia Review* 2, no. 4 (1998), 133–46.

[42] Shan F. Bullock, 'Prologue', in *Ring o' Rushes* (New York: Stone and Kimball, 1896), ix.

[43] In this regard, Bullock follows the naturalist precept to focus on ordinary life. Maume credits Bullock with a 'faithful reproduction of Fermanagh dialect and rural life' ('The Margins of Subsistence', 133), but whereas he sees Bullock as part of a national revival movement, Foster does not. See Foster, *Fictions of the Irish Literary Revival*, xxiii, 175–6.

[44] Bullock, 'Prologue', xii–xiii.   [45] Shan F. Bullock, 'The Emigrant', in *Ring o' Rushes*, 207.

[46] Ibid., 215.   [47] Shan F. Bullock, 'His Magnificence', in *Ring o' Rushes*, 28.

[48] Ibid., 6–7.   [49] Ibid., 18.

Bullock's pastoralism differs from forms of pastoral found in ancient times, when the vital contrast at work was between *locus amoenus* (lovely place) and the corrupt and overly cultured *polis*. His main concern is the *unlovely* place and the poverty, ignorance, and suffering of the people who inhabit it. This is especially true of the stories in *Irish Pastorals*, which are arranged according to what people do—planters, turf-cutters, mowers, haymakers, reapers, diggers, herders—and their reflections on the world in which they labour. For example, in 'The Diggers', James Daly, lost in 'the joys of thought' while on a break, thinks about 'the *curiousness* and *onknowableness* of things, the strangeness and mystery of them'.[50] But a 'cloud of gloom' dissipates the joy: 'Wherever he looked he saw signs of misery, or of coming misery.... The world was all wrong. Heaven was unjust. The past was a failure; the present a misery; the future unthinkable'.[51] We meet characters drawn with a romantic flourish—Lizzie Dolan in 'The Turf Cutters', for example, 'young, fresh, bouncing, the belle of the bog'—but we often find, on the very same page, an undercutting description: 'you might have weighed—and valued—the bulk of [the villagers] against half a ton of hay'.[52] In 'The Reapers', the narrator invites the reader to expect a Celticist fantasy of country life, but this expectation is quickly quashed when the narrative moves seamlessly into a naturalist description of the wretched conditions on which 'my Lord the Sun' shines, the 'sodden haycocks, and flattened laps and whole acres of meadow lying rotten in the swath'.[53] In each of these instances, Bullock deconstructs the very tropes that sustain his romanticizations; in tactical misrecognitions of rural Irish life, he lifts the veil of illusion surrounding it but simultaneously remobilizes, often through the agency of unreliable narrators or storytellers, the trope of the veil.

This deconstructionist manoeuvre, however, is not meant to do away with romanticism but to temper it with a rectifying gaze, to incorporate and resignify it. The result is a vision of traditional life, with all of its suffering, that is ultimately redemptive. 'The Mowers', a paean to simple bucolic labours, sustains this vision in a mood of buoyant reflection not often seen in Revival fiction. We read that 'The scythes found a merrier note, a sharper twang as they met the grass. Even the mowers, down in their stolid depths, felt something stir responsive to that sudden change in things'.[54] The landscape is extravagantly beautiful yet it is far from being a mere romantic backdrop to 'a great commotion of work'.[55] In Bullock's vividly realist depiction, life and work, joy and hardship merge in a single expression of belonging, a structure of feeling that accommodates every element of the social and natural environment. He situates romanticism in a dialectical relation with naturalism, the very mode of representation meant to unveil it. Thus we find that the mowers accept the 'burden of work... unmurmuringly; accepting it as they accepted most things—hunger and cold, pain and trouble, life and death—with air of sullen indifference, of philosophic resignation to the inevitable—the inevitable before which your sapient ran cheerfully nor lingered to be kicked'.[56] This odd image, in which the 'sapient ran cheerfully' before life's brute inevitability, captures the futural

---

[50] Shan F. Bullock, 'The Diggers', in *Irish Pastorals*, 203. Original emphasis.   [51] Ibid., 203.
[52] Shan F. Bullock, 'The Turf Cutters', in *Irish Pastorals*, 47.
[53] Shan F. Bullock, 'The Reapers', in *Irish Pastorals*, 146.
[54] Shan F. Bullock, 'The Mowers', in *Irish Pastorals*, 72.   [55] Ibid., 72.   [56] Ibid., 85.

state posited generally in Revival fiction, the idea that present hardship, chase us as it will, finds its promise in coming times. Now, I want to be clear that this promise does not always hold open the possibility of bounty and riches, health and happiness. To assert as much would be to fall into the trap of naïve (or 'bad') revivalism. Yet even when the weather is harsh and the landscape a dire threat to health and well-being, there is a sense that 'my Lord the mountain'[57] offers to the inhabitants of this corner of Ireland something more reliable to look forward to than the usually absent figure of the landlord. In his deconstruction of romanticism, Bullock constructs a new template of futurity, *a structure of feeling for what is to come.*

GEORGE MOORE'S *THE UNTILLED FIELD*

As a Catholic landowner, George Moore occupied a unique position in the largely Anglo-Irish and Protestant Literary Revival, and he used this position to write *The Untilled Field*, 'in the hope of furnishing the young Irish of the future with models'.[58] What he provided was a form of naturalism that influenced, among others, James Joyce.[59] Like Bullock and Lawless, Moore admits the *onknowable* into his naturalist accounts in *The Untilled Field*—witness, for example, the 'solid reality' of the fairies in 'Julia Cahill's Curse' or the mysticism of 'The Window'—and he uses Celtic romanticism tactically in several stories, pre-eminently 'The Wild Goose'. His main concern, however, is exposing the bullying, meddlesome authority of the clergy and the spectre of emigration that is for him organically connected to it. 'The Wedding Feast', which focuses on the union of Peter and Kate, deals directly with the tensions arising between an impoverished young woman who faces a negated future and a marriage market governed by clerical edict. When Kate rebels and claims she's going to America, it is clear to her where the fault lies: 'Yes, that was the priest's doing and mother's and I thought they knew best. But I'm thinking one must go one's own way, and there's no judging for oneself here. That's why I'm going.'[60] Mary M'Shane's artful dodge on the question of Father Maguire's power—'there is plenty in the parish who believe he could turn them into rabbits at the light, though I don't take it on myself to say it's the truth or lie'[61]—is a form of sly civility, a cagey accommodation of beliefs that remains non-committal on the matter

---

[57] Ibid., 72.

[58] George Moore, *The Untilled Field* (London: William Heinemann, 1914), v. This edition differs from others, primarily in excluding 'The Way Back', which in other editions is the final story. 'The Way Back' continues the narrative of the novella 'The Wild Goose', which concludes the 1914 edition. I have chosen the 1914 edition because the arrangement of stories strikes me as superior to others and because it includes an important preface by Moore. On these matters, see Jane Roberts, 'George Moore: A Wild Goose's Portrait of His Country', *Irish University Review* 22, vol. 2 (1992), 305–18.

[59] For a good summary of the criticism of Joyce and Moore as naturalists, see Joyce, *Modernism and Naturalism*, 107–8 and note 47.

[60] George Moore, 'The Wedding Feast', in *The Untilled Field*, 100.   [61] Ibid., 90.

of their truth or validity—an accommodation that is, in effect, a form of going 'one's own way', for those who stay.[62]

Moore's critique of emigration fantasies—America as a utopian *elsewhere*—lies primarily in his ability to convey the sense of desperation that gives birth to them. In 'The Exile', for example, Catherine refuses one Phelan brother, James, because she prefers the other, Peter, who has begun to train for the clergy at Maynooth. Once Peter decides not to take orders, James pleads with him to marry Catherine in order to free him to emigrate: 'I want to get to America. It will be the saving of me.'[63] The possibility of emigrating becomes a defining aspect of Catherine's character, even though she stays behind to marry and live an Irish future. Like the protagonist of Joyce's 'Eveline', she is defined as *the one who stayed*, who has forgone the experience of a future *elsewhere*.

Emigration promotes anxiety about the future: should one stay and face what is *onknowable* (weather, love, politics, family) or face the future abroad? This dread is recorded in 'Home Sickness', which, like Bullock's 'His Magnificence', relates the return of a successful Irish emigrant and describes the contrast between American plenty and the impoverished villages that he now sees *as if for the first time*. Not only has James, the prodigal son, found an Irish fiancée, Margaret, but his presumptive father-in-law 'was learning him how to buy and sell cattle. The country was mending, and a man might become rich in Ireland if you only have a little capital.'[64] Although he has acquired all he needs for a successful Irish future, James longs for his former American life and 'the smell of the Bowery slum',[65] so he abandons Margaret and returns to New York. As an old man, he surrenders himself to nostalgia, to a 'vague tender reverie' of Ireland that moves from bitter memories of 'little fields divided by bleak walls' to rosy ones of 'the green hillside, and the bog lake and the rushes about it'.[66] In passages like these, Moore resembles Lawless in pairing very different styles to depict the same landscape—not only as it *appears* (the task of conventional realism) but as it appears in the romantic imagination.

The emphasis on emigration in Moore, as in Bullock, allows a certain kind of question to be asked about time, namely, where does one find a better future? 'The Wild Goose' tries to answer this question by showing how an Irish success story, built upon Irish capital and Irish politics, can lead ultimately to the same end: emigration and the possibility of a future *elsewhere*. Ned Carmady, having emigrated with his family and later returned, becomes one of the 'shmart young fellars'[67] that Hurrish O'Brien denigrates, 'a young man that the people knew nothing about, who would voice the new ideas for them'.[68] Ned's political interests spring entirely from his fundamental misrecognition of the Irish as a people incapable of explaining themselves. He is strongly influenced by his wife Ellen, who teaches

---

[62] See Homi K. Bhabha, 'Sly Civility', in *The Location of Culture* (London: Routledge, 1994), 93–101. Simon Joyce sees in such artful dodges a 'bifurcated consciousness' or 'cognitive split' (*Modernism and Naturalism*, 104–5).

[63] George Moore, 'The Exile', in *The Untilled Field*, 18.

[64] George Moore, 'Home Sickness', in *The Untilled Field*, 44.   [65] Ibid., 45.

[66] Ibid., 46, 49.

[67] Lawless, *Hurrish*, vol. 1, 157.   [68] George Moore, 'The Wild Goose', in *The Untilled Field*, 259.

him 'that the new Ireland was an entirely Gaelic Ireland, an Ireland that for centuries had sought refuge underground like a river, but was coming up again'.[69] His downfall begins the moment his borrowed passion for Celtic romanticism—'tales of heroism and chivalry' that he learned from Ellen, which were 'all vision and dream but none the worse for that'[70]—is overtaken by his heartfelt desire to revive Ireland by modernizing its clergy. He comes to believe that Catholic Ireland is being reduced by emigration and clerical celibacy to 'one vast monastery'; 'In five-and-twenty years the last of Ireland would have disappeared in America', he warns his audience, and 'Ireland would become a Protestant country'.[71] Ned's attack on the Church turns out to be a profound miscalculation and he finds his political career in ruins even before it properly begins. On board the ship taking him away again, 'He stood watching the green waves tossing in the mist, at one moment ashamed of what he had done, at the next overjoyed that he had done it.'[72]

Ned Carmady's ambivalence establishes a new ground for romanticism, one that modernists like Joyce will later scrupulously explore. In 'The Wild Goose', the future is no longer beholden to a past in need of safeguarding through mindless adherence to tradition and clerical authority. We may not trust Ned's intentions—it is uncertain if he knows or trusts them himself—but we have to admire his ability to posit the future in a way that resists the pressures of a predictable outcome, one that would settle all debates, realign all data, and nullify all alternatives in advance. In *The Untilled Field*, George Moore depicts a romanticized vision of Ireland in such a way that retains the romanticism but not the vision of the future that it typically evokes.

W. B. Yeats's *The Secret Rose* and James Joyce's *Dubliners*

If Lawless, Bullock, and Moore represent the range and variety of Revival fiction, Yeats and Joyce give us some sense of its limits. In Joyce's *Dubliners* (1914), naturalism prevents Revival tropes from taking root in the stories by suppressing both realism and romanticism, while in Yeats's fiction, romantic expressionism overwhelms realism and provides a new ground of recognition for the reality of the faery *otherworld*. As Frank Kinahan has noted, Yeats did not regard the 'attractions of faery as dangerous because illusory'; he 'saw them as dangerous because real'.[73] More than any other Revival prose writer, Yeats veered towards folklore and folktales. By the mid-1890s, he had already published two collections of tales, which were complemented by *The Celtic Twilight* (1893), which

---

[69] Ibid., 239.   [70] Ibid., 257.

[71] Ibid., 304, 299–300. Ned shares this belief with Father MacTurnan, who expresses similar sentiments in 'A Letter to Rome'.

[72] Ibid., 316. The 1903 edition ends with a different version of 'The Wild Goose' followed by 'The Way Back', in which Ned, still deeply set against Catholicism, reappears at a tea party in London on his way to South Africa. I believe the 1914 edition leaves us with a sense of futurity that is not bound by Ned's teleological scepticism but by a general openness to an unknown, but vital, future.

[73] Frank Kinahan, *Yeats, Folklore, and Occultism: Contexts of the Early Work and Thought* (Boston, MA: Unwin Hyman, 1988), 64.

contains folk material and contemporary poetry, including some of his own, and has been described by Edward Hirsch as a generic anomaly, a 'curious hybrid of the story and the essay, the accurate notation of the folklorist and the fictional reminiscence of the imaginative writer'.[74]

The most compelling examples of Revival fiction in Yeats's prose canon are the stories featuring Red Hanrahan in *The Secret Rose* (1897),[75] which come closest to embodying the representational ethos we have seen so far: the naturalist inclination to critique what the realist wishes to champion and the accommodations made to romanticism, which serve a tactical purpose in the struggle to resignify Irish culture. As Lawless does in *Hurrish*, Yeats shows the hard life of an Irishman given to self-romanticizing. Hanrahan is an 'Old lecher with a love on every wind', a man with 'but broken knees for hire' who struggles not only with his own weaknesses but with a community that has increasingly little use for him.[76] In 'The Twisting of the Rope', a woman declares that 'if you would put a poet of the Gael out of the house, he would put a curse on you that would wither the corn in the fields and dry up the milk of the cows, if it had to hang in the air seven years'.[77] The power of the 'curse-making bards', who 'bring shame and sorrow' to those they target, suggests that bards, like priests, have power *over the future*.[78] The cruel reality of Hanrahan's position in the community is communicated in the manner in which the traditional task of rope twisting is used to get him to leave on his own accord, 'twisting the rope always till he came to the door that was open behind him, and without thinking he passed the threshold and was out on the road'.[79] He later writes a song about his banishment and falls into a dreamy reverie amid 'mist and shadows': 'And then it seemed to him as if the rope had changed in his dream into a great water-worm that came out of the sea, and that twisted itself about him, and held him closer and closer'.[80] But unlike Grania, raptured in a similar manner by the laminaria, Hanrahan escapes the dream mist and passes into the land of 'the Sidhe, the ancient defeated gods', who offer him 'beauty that is as lasting as the night and the stars'.[81]

If Yeats tests the limits of Revival fiction by giving prominence to the supernatural and mystical elements of folklore, Joyce's *Dubliners* confronts a different set of limits, for it reveals an uneasy accommodation of romanticism in a set of stories whose naturalist agenda, both in the text and in Joyce's comments on it, minimizes in advance even the tactical use of romantic tropes.[82] Instead we find stark depictions of contemporary

---

[74] Edward Hirsch, 'Coming out into the Light: W. B. Yeats's *The Celtic Twilight* (1893, 1902)', *Journal of the Folklore Institute* 18, no. 1 (1981), 13. For a discussion of Yeats's engagement with folkloric and anthropological discourses, see Castle, *Modernism and the Celtic Revival*, chapter two.

[75] With Lady Augusta Gregory's assistance, Yeats rewrote the Hanrahan stories in 1907 and they were published six years later under the title *Stories of Red Hanrahan, The Secret Rose, Rosa Alchemica*.

[76] These lines come from Yeats's 'The Tower' (1928), which includes a long section recounting Hanrahan's career and his importance for Yeats's oeuvre. See *The Collected Works of W. B. Yeats: Volume 1: The Poems*, ed. Richard J. Finneran (New York: Macmillan, 1989), 196–7.

[77] W. B. Yeats, 'The Twisting of the Rope', in *Mythologies* (New York: Macmillan, 1959), 230.

[78] W. B. Yeats, 'Red Hanrahan's Curse', in *Mythologies*, 242, 240.

[79] Yeats, 'The Twisting of the Rope', 231.   [80] Ibid., 232.

[81] W. B. Yeats, 'Hanrahan's Vision', in *Mythologies*, 249, 251.

[82] For Joyce's comments on his naturalist intentions, see his letters excerpted in James Joyce, *'Dubliners': Text, Criticism, and Notes*, ed. Robert Scholes and A. Walton Litz (London: Penguin, 1996), 253–69, 276–7.

inner-city Dublin ('a stubbornly recalcitrant lived reality'[83]) that are all the more powerful for their apparent refusal to romanticize. Yet Joyce's stories engage the issues of Revival in a compelling if surreptitious way by making micro-accommodations for the very forms and modes (romanticism, folklore, fantasy) that his 'scrupulous meanness'[84] ought, on principle, to have disallowed. This frequently occurs at the point of epiphany, the point at which scrupulous critique comes to a standstill, for in the epiphanic moment we find the same dynamic of mutual undermining that is characteristic of Revival fiction, only in the condensed form of a dialectical image.[85]

A good example is 'Eveline', in which emigration (to Argentina) provokes in the protagonist a pathological desire *not* to leave. Joyce's naturalist portrayal of an abused young woman whose life is testimony to the benefits of going *elsewhere* conforms to what we see in Lawless, Bullock, and Moore. A romantic trope is undermined by a naturalist's eye on the 'real' event: Joyce's story builds up the romantic opportunity that awaits Eveline, only to undercut it *from within her own heart*. The last image of Eveline clutching the rails at the quay, as her intended boards ship, leaves no room for doubt that, for the protagonist, the future will be a duplication of the present, that in fact there will be *no future*. The epiphany in this story is a dialectical image of the future emptying out: 'She set her white face to him, passive, like a helpless animal. Her eyes gave him no sign of love or farewell or recognition.'[86] And yet, an alternative to her present circumstances springs from her failure to escape from them. The strange last words of her mother ('Derevaun Seraun!'[87]) signals the possibility of the *elsewhere* she seeks, but it remains in the story a complete mystery, nothing at all like the familiarity of the 'Unfamiliar' that advances on Honor O'Malley at her death.

In *Dubliners*, the future is curiously off-stage, a place to which one wishes to go but to which one has been debarred entry. We see the struggle of individuals, like Little Chandler in 'A Little Cloud', who imagines himself a successful and fashionable writer like Yeats: 'The English critics, perhaps, would recognize him as one of the Celtic school by reason of the melancholy tone of his poems; besides that, he would put in allusions.'[88] His desire for recognition, however, is all but snuffed out by his failure to recognize himself. He consistently undercuts his own aspirations, in part because they are so comically distant from his way of life, which he likens to living 'on the hire system'.[89] He is utterly estranged from his wife, whose eyes in a photograph reflect his own despairing look. He passes judgement on himself, seeing himself as 'a prisoner for life', and sheds 'tears of remorse' for his inauthenticity.[90] How different is Little Chandler's journalist friend Gallagher, the returned emigrant who brags about the future he has achieved and will continue to enjoy abroad. He truly proclaims the future because he has, in effect, written it for himself. But he is a rare being in *Dubliners*. Against such a success story, we have

---

[83] Joyce, *Modernism and Naturalism*, 110.

[84] See Joyce's letter to Grant Richards, in Joyce, *'Dubliners': Text, Criticism, and Notes*, 262.

[85] On the unscrupulous nature of the epiphany, see Kevin J. H. Dettmar, 'The *Dubliners* Epiphany: (Mis)reading the Book of Ourselves', in *The Illicit Joyce of Postmodernism: Reading Against the Grain* (Madison, WI: University of Wisconsin Press, 1996), 76–105.

[86] James Joyce, *Dubliners*, ed. Jeri Johnson (Oxford: Oxford World's Classics, 2000), 29.

[87] Ibid., 28.   [88] James Joyce, 'A Little Cloud', in *Dubliners*, 55.   [89] Ibid., 63.

[90] Ibid., 64–5.

not only sad sacks like Little Chandler but also the 'shmart young fellars' in 'After the Race', most of whom squander their future potential in a gamble for even more potential; they are capitalists of time who suffer reversals, and for whom the future is nothing more than a false brightness, 'a shaft of grey light'.[91]

According to Simon Joyce, Joyce's 'introjected naturalism', whereby 'external determinations get internalized', allows him to focus on the inner life of his characters, which is where tensions arise in the midst of social paralysis.[92] This focus is especially acute in troubling, ambivalent stories like 'A Painful Case' and 'The Dead'. In the former, we see, closely and intimately, how James Duffy fails the test of his mettle; he cannot overcome his own ambivalence and so loses the opportunity to chose an *onknowable* future with Emily Sinico. He is stuck with his 'bottle of lager beer and a small trayful of arrowroot biscuits', stuck with the bitter knowledge that his future will be at best a remembered thing: 'He gnawed the rectitude of his life; he felt that he had been outcast from life's feast'.[93] 'The Dead' offers a more sensational form of this same self-gnawing rectitude in the ghostly figure of Michael Furey, who looms over Gabriel Conroy's complacent meditations about his wife. Joyce explores Gretta Conroy's past life with Michael in the idiom of the ghost story, particularly of the kind found in Irish folklore, and thereby reuses in a tactical and ambivalent way the very tropes of Revival that the story otherwise calls into question.[94] Granted, Joyce's fiction refuses to allow 'my Lord the Sun' to shine, as Bullock's does, but we find in 'The Dead' a glimmer of that light, for in the epiphany at its conclusion Joyce offers an opportunity for ambivalence to register the persistence of hope. Even the feelings of 'anguish and anger'[95] that paralyse the first-person narrator of 'Araby' ultimately point to the future in which he will be able to look upon himself and his experience more wisely, for the protagonist *has outlived the crisis he narrates*. The logic of misrecognition coded in this narrative distance similarly motivates the free indirect style of 'The Dead', in which we find a protagonist continually second-guessing himself, correcting his responses and belittling his own anticipatory fantasies. Missing, however, is the wisdom we sense in the opening stories, the wisdom of a future *that has already arrived*. In this respect, 'The Dead' is a premier example of romantic naturalism but one in which it is uncertain whether romanticism has been resignified in any healthy and forward-looking way.

In 'The Dead', the deceased remain persistently alive—in memory and memorials, in images, in stories, in ghostly visitations—and the future opens up in a way that is uncharacteristic of *Dubliners* as a whole. One wonders whether the final glorious paragraphs, wherein Gabriel meditates on his wife, on Michael Furey, on the landscape outside his window, contains an epiphany or an elaborate ruse.[96] In a collection that delves into the complexities of Irish urban life with the 'scrupulous meanness' of the naturalist,

[91] James Joyce, 'After the Race', in *Dubliners*, 35.
[92] Joyce, *Modernism and Naturalism*, 108–18.
[93] James Joyce, 'A Painful Case', in *Dubliners*, 83, 89.
[94] On Joyce's *Dubliners* and the critique of Revival, see Castle, *Modernism and the Celtic Revival*, 178–88.
[95] James Joyce, 'Araby', in *Dubliners*, 24.
[96] The debate surrounding the conclusion of 'The Dead' continues, but a good summary of the major points from a critical theory perspective can be found in Vincent Pecora, '"The Dead" and the Generosity of the Word', *PMLA* 101 (1986), 233–45.

'The Dead' stands out for overcoming the naturalist mode from within it. The story is called 'The Dead' in part because the Irish Catholic imagination translates the terror of death into an expectation of an *afterlife* in heaven. But in Gabriel's vision of futurity, something more terrifying is on offer, for whether or not he becomes truly generous with himself and others, his future is a march into a realm where there is no longer a distinction between himself and anyone else, for 'His own identity was fading out into a grey impalpable world: the solid world itself which these dead had one time reared and lived in was dissolving and dwindling.'[97] Like so many characters in Revival fiction, Gabriel's future hinges on whether or not he can overcome his own complicity in the foreclosure of coming times brought about by an unhealthy and unproductive romanticism. Seeing himself for what he *thinks* he is—'a pennyboy for his aunts, a nervous well-meaning sentimentalist'[98]—is an important first step. But he also must learn to accept and accommodate this pennyboy—albeit, a far cry from 'my Lord the Sun'—if he ever hopes to know himself and the world in which he lives.

FURTHER READING

Beaumont, Matthew (ed.). *A Concise Companion to Realism*. Malden, MA: Wiley-Blackwell, 2010.

Cahalan, James M. *Double Visions: Women and Men in Modern and Contemporary Irish Fiction*. Syracuse, NY: Syracuse University Press, 1999.

Deane, Seamus. *Celtic Revivals: Essays in Modern Irish Literature 1880–1980*. London: Faber and Faber, 1985.

Edwards, Heather. 'The Irish New Woman and Emily Lawless's *Grania: The Story of an Island*: A Congenial Geography'. *English Literature in Transition, 1880–1920* 51, no. 4 (2008): 421–38.

Finneran, Richard J. *The Prose Fiction of W. B. Yeats: The Search for 'Those Simple Forms'*. Dublin: Dolmen Press, 1973.

Foster, John Wilson. *Fictions of the Irish Literary Revival: A Changeling Art*. Syracuse, NY: Syracuse University Press, 1987.

Frawley, Oona (ed.). *A New and Complex Sensation: Essays on Joyce's 'Dubliners'*. Dublin: Lilliput Press, 2004.

Grubgeld, Elizabeth. *George Moore and the Autogenous Self: The Autobiography and Fiction*. Syracuse, NY: Syracuse University Press, 1994.

Ingman, Heather. *A History of the Irish Short Story*. Cambridge: Cambridge University Press, 2009.

Kiberd, Declan and P. J. Mathews (eds). *Handbook of the Irish Revival: An Anthology of Irish Cultural and Political Writings 1891–1922*. Dublin: Abbey Theatre Press, 2015.

O'Leary, Philip. *The Prose Literature of the Gaelic Revival, 1881–1921: Ideology and Innovation*. University Park, PA: Pennsylvania State University Press, 1994.

Trevor, William. *A Writer's Ireland: Landscape in Literature*. London: Thames and Hudson, 1984.

---

[97] James Joyce, 'The Dead', in *Dubliners*, 176.   [98] Ibid., 173.

CHAPTER 7

THE MATERIALIST-FABULIST DIALECTIC

James Stephens, Eimar O'Duffy, and Magic Naturalism

GREGORY DOBBINS

THE archival turn evident in Irish literary studies over the last two decades has largely overlooked James Stephens (1880–1950) and Eimar O'Duffy (1893–1935).[1] Though once highly regarded, Stephens's critical reputation has diminished over time and is overshadowed by the historical anecdote that James Joyce (1882–1941) chose him to complete the composition of *Finnegans Wake* (1939) if it proved beyond Joyce's capabilities.[2] Eimar O'Duffy has received almost no scholarly attention. Part of the reason for such critical neglect lies in the diversity of these writers' prose, which varies so widely in aesthetic quality that it resists synoptic assessment. The initial basis for a comparison between the two writers originates in their shared tendency to draw upon Irish mythological material. While that practice was not unusual in the immediate aftermath of the Irish Literary Revival, its originality for these two writers lay in their transposition of fabulist elements into a contemporary context in order to juxtapose the tension between the modern and the archaic. In an 'appreciation' of Stephens first

---

[1] For recent work on Stephens, see in particular Joseph Lennon, *Irish Orientalism: A Literary and Intellectual History* (Syracuse, NY: Syracuse University Press, 2004), 290–323 and Joseph Valente, *The Myth of Manliness in Irish National Culture, 1880–1922* (Urbana, IL: University of Illinois Press, 2011), 129–39. On O'Duffy, see Gregory Dobbins, *Lazy Idle Schemers: Irish Modernism and the Cultural Politics of Idleness* (Dublin: Field Day Publications, 2010), 122–49 and Frances Flanagan, *Remembering the Irish Revolution: Dissent, Culture, and Nationalism in the Irish Free State* (Oxford: Oxford University Press, 2015), 50–81. The older work of Vivian Mercier, Hilary Pyle, Robert Hogan, Augustine Martin, and John Wilson Foster, cited in the Further Reading section below, continues to provide the basis for criticism of these writers.

[2] Richard Ellmann, *James Joyce* (Oxford: Oxford University Press, 1983), 591–2.

published in 1965, Denis Donoghue suggested that this practice had links to a certain conversational quality of the work:

> I have touched on a commonplace, that modern Irish literature is a wordy business. We have had our solid novels, tracts for the times, beasts of burden, but they are not indigenous. The native product tends to be runic, archaic, pedantic, a caprice of words alone.... I have in mind books like *At Swim-Two-Birds*, Eimar O'Duffy's *King Goshawk*, Brinsley MacNamara's *Various Lives of Marcus Igoe*, Austin Clarke's *The Sun Dances at Easter*. Stephens is a crucial figure in this tradition. In such books the motto is: keep talking, and it can't happen. Life is suffered only in the cracks between the words.[3]

On the one hand, Irish novels which approximate those from other national literary traditions are 'solid' but lose their 'indigenous' specificity; on the other hand, if they depart from those same conventions they become wordy, 'archaic', and not, ultimately, very much like novels. Given what Donoghue asserts about Stephens throughout the rest of his brief essay, these 'indigenous' qualities implicitly specify those qualities that make it 'second-rate'[4] literature.

Donoghue's remarks are part of a long critical tradition that has grappled with the erratic history of the Irish novel.[5] For better or worse, this ongoing endeavour suggests, Ireland lacked the social stability that could foster a realist tradition in the nineteenth century comparable to other national traditions. Ultimately—and after even greater political instability in the beginning of the twentieth-century—the chaotic form of the modernist novel would emerge to better capture the particularities of life in Ireland in a period of profound political transformation. Yet the writers and texts Donoghue identifies blur the distinctions between realist and modernist prose through the incorporation of a fabulist dimension in which speech seems to undermine the fixity of the written word. Donoghue's aside suggests the existence of a distinct trajectory in twentieth-century Irish prose that falls somewhere between modernism and realism but presents something different. It is not just that Stephens, O'Duffy, Flann O'Brien (1911–66), Brinsley MacNamara (1890–1963), and Austin Clarke (1896–1974)—or similar writers like Darrell Figgis (1882–1925) and Mervyn Wall (1908–97)—blend the modern and the mythological in order to represent Irish culture as simultaneously contemporary and ancient; it is that they also avail of the conventions of storytelling. Perhaps it is better to regard them as part of a local variation of what would later be called magic realism in Latin American literature.[6] Certainly,

---

[3] Denis Donoghue, 'James Stephens', in *We Irish: Essays on Irish Literature and Society* (Berkeley, CA: University of California Press, 1986), 207.

[4] Ibid., 205.

[5] On the critical history of the Irish novel and its perceived deficiencies, see David Lloyd, *Anomalous States: Irish Writing and the Post-Colonial Moment* (Durham, NC: Duke University Press, 1993), 125–62 and Joe Cleary, *Outrageous Fortune: Capital and Culture in Modern Ireland* (Dublin: Field Day Publications, 2006), 36–57.

[6] Terry Eagleton argues that Stephens's writing in particular anticipates magic realism; see his *Crazy John and the Bishop and Other Essays on Irish Culture* (Cork: Cork University Press, 1998), 228.

the works of each of the novelists in question offer 'a transfigured object world in which fantastic events are also narrated', drawing upon 'a kind of narrative raw material derived essentially from peasant society, and drawing in sophisticated ways on the world of village or even tribal myth', thus producing 'not a realism to be transfigured by the "supplement" of a magical perspective but a reality which is already in and of itself magical or fantastic'.[7] Yet simply to identify the works of these writers as magic realists *avant la lettre* proves problematic beyond the difficulties that result from the anachronistic transposition of a representational trajectory rooted elsewhere onto prior Irish literary history.

While folkloric and fabulist qualities are abundant in the works of the writers in question, it is much more difficult to casually assert that these novels are also grounded in realism, for the object world they depict tends to be inflected in a particularly pessimistic manner that departs from objective mimesis. The non-magical side of these novels tends to be governed by a 'general narrative paradigm, which could be described as the trajectory of decline and failure', as Fredric Jameson argues of naturalism, a 'sub-genre' of realism that 'seems rather to breathe a kind of *Stimmung* or affect associated with pessimism or melancholy'.[8] As Joe Cleary convincingly argues, naturalism was as prominent, influential, and persistent as any other mode throughout the course of twentieth-century Irish fiction, even if it eventually fell into a condition of critical neglect as it came to be eclipsed in reputation and perceived importance by modernism.[9] According to Cleary, the central point of coherence for Irish naturalism was 'its constitutive problematic: namely, how to conceive of meaningful human agency in a world where action and understanding, comprehension of the forces that shape society and meaningful intervention into society, are always perceived to thwart and compromise each other'.[10]

Ultimately, this hallmark of naturalism also presents a fundamental aporia. On the one hand, if it stressed that human agency could never overcome the impersonal social and political forces it was pitted against, naturalism ran the risk of asserting that the social world and all of its inequalities and injustices were unchangeable, static, and natural. On the other hand, if naturalism depicted situations in which humans somehow triumphed over those conditions which were the basis for their misery, it risked underplaying the grave strength and force of that which it opposed and of lapsing into sentimentalism or romanticism. James Stephens and the other writers identified by Donoghue offer a solution to this representational problem: the dilemma could be resolved by magic, primarily delivered through the incursion of mythological and folkloric material into what otherwise look like naturalist novels. Rather than presenting a series of stylistic aberrations, perhaps the unique qualities and contradictions of works like Stephens's *The Charwoman's Daughter* (1912), *The Crock of Gold* (1912), *Here Are Ladies* (1913), and *The Demi-Gods* (1914), and O'Duffy's Cuanduine trilogy (1926–33) suggest the basis for a different categorical

---

[7] Fredric Jameson, *Signatures of the Visible* (New York: Routledge, 1992), 128–9, 138.
[8] Fredric Jameson, *The Antinomies of Realism* (London: Verso, 2013), 149, 148.
[9] See Cleary, *Outrageous Fortune*, 84–137.   [10] Ibid., 94.

identification altogether—magic naturalism—to describe that trajectory of Irish fiction which begins with Stephens and continues at least until the 1950s.[11]

Since it bears a formal debt to storytelling, the theorization of magic naturalism begins with its apparent 'spoken' qualities. In 'The Storyteller' (1936), Walter Benjamin considers at length the differences between story and novel. Benjamin argues that the novel, rooted in 'the individual in his isolation', is both the genre which best registers 'experience' (the sharing of which through storytelling he believed had 'fallen in value' since the First World War), while at the same time failing to make complete sense of it.[12] By 'experience' (*die Erfahrung*), Benjamin means a coherent, sequential understanding of the past and present that comes closer to a grasp of social totality than a more immediate sense of the present moment and all of its sensations (what Benjamin refers to elsewhere as *das Erlebnis*). Since its emergence as a genre coincided historically with processes of modernization, in which the 'wisdom' of experience gradually came to be displaced by the increasingly overwhelming sensory details of the present, the novel proved to be particularly adept at representing *das Erlebnis* but deficient at registering *die Erfahrung*: 'To write a novel is to take to the extreme that which is incommensurable in the representation of human existence. In the midst of life's fullness, and through the representation of this fullness, the novel gives evidence of the profound perplexity of the living.'[13]

By contrast, the much older oral genre of the story exists in the first place to document *die Erfahrung*. Stories originate in collective memory, which 'creates the chain of tradition which transmits an event from generation to generation', thus creating the conditions of possibility for a record of 'experience' itself.[14] Moreover, the story inevitably 'contains, openly or covertly, something useful. In one case, the usefulness may lie in a moral; in another, in some practical advice; in a third, in a proverb or maxim. In every case the storyteller is a man who has counsel for his audience.'[15] While the very idea of having such a purpose, Benjamin concedes, may seem 'old-fashioned', this is not because that motive is in itself no longer valid but because those situated within the context of modernity have lost the capacity to apprehend *die Erfahrung*: 'the communicability of experience is decreasing. In consequence, we have no counsel either for ourselves or for others.'[16] The disappearance of storytelling as a prominent narrative mode is part of modernization itself, yet the 'usefulness' provided by experience does not simply disappear as the narratives which bear it become residual. If what had once been useful now seems useless, the very persistence of its traces could retain a subversive potential

---

[11] In *Unauthorized Versions: Irish Menippean Satire, 1919–1952* (Washington, DC: Catholic University of America Press, 2000), José Lanters identifies these writers as practitioners of an Irish variation of what Mikhail Bakhtin called 'Menippean' satire, a dialogic form in which writers draw from medieval sources in order to address contemporary concerns. By focusing on the origins of this literary practice in naturalism, the term magic naturalism attempts to reconceptualize the archaic *and* the modern dimensions of their fiction.

[12] Walter Benjamin, 'The Storyteller: Observations on the Works of Nikolai Leskov', in *Selected Writings: Volume Three, 1935–1938*, trans. Edmund Jephcott, Howard Eiland, and others, ed. Howard Eiland and Michael W. Jennings (Cambridge, MA: Belknap Press of Harvard University Press, 2002), 142, 146.

[13] Ibid., 146.   [14] Ibid., 154.   [15] Ibid., 145.   [16] Ibid.

to unsettle a logic that regards it as obsolete. Magic naturalism appears to evade the anti-nomical distinction Benjamin draws between story and novel by having it both ways at once. A dialectical contradiction between a narrative frame derived from the more modern medium of the novel (and its associations with the 'perplexity' of contemporary modernity) and the conventions of storytelling (and its retention of some archaic form of 'usefulness') provides the structural crux of magic naturalism.

The Writers' Background and Intellectual Formation

In the prose fiction of both James Stephens and Eimar O'Duffy, the 'usefulness' which motivated their writing originated in their personal histories and encompassed a commitment to progressive socio-political transformation that both encapsulated and went well beyond anti-imperialist nationalism. The facts of Stephens's birth remain unclear, and while he often claimed to have been born in Dublin on 2 February 1882 (the same day as Joyce and the supposed reason the latter chose Stephens to complete *Finnegans Wake*), evidence suggests that he was born two years earlier, that his supposed father died when he was a child, and that he was possibly illegitimate.[17] His childhood was split between a Protestant orphanage and periods living with a family who employed his mother as a servant, and he began working as a clerk while still in his adolescence. By 1905, he was working as a scrivener in Dublin, and in that year published his first short story in the *United Irishman*, after which he began to contribute to it and its successor, *Sinn Féin*. Through these connections, Stephens acquired the patronage and friendship of Arthur Griffith and George Russell (1867–1935), who introduced him to Hinduism, Buddhism, and socialism.

As Stephens rose to prominence during the Revival (including the publication of poetry, articles concerning Irish politics in several nationalist publications, and work for various dramatic venues), his personal life took a turn which was contrary to the mores of the time. In 1907, he entered into what became a lifelong relationship with Millicent Kavanagh, who was at that time pregnant and separated from her husband, and assumed paternity of her unborn child. Stephens's relationship with Cynthia, as he called Millicent, would inspire an opposition to the oppressive social consequences of the institution of marriage in Ireland, a recurring theme in his fiction (and quite possibly the more logical explanation why the similarly inclined Joyce became interested in Stephens as a potential collaborator). By 1912, Stephens's writing had attracted the attention of Macmillan, which published in quick succession his first four prose works. After a period spent living in Paris, he returned to Dublin and took employment as registrar of

---

[17] See Hilary Pyle, *James Stephens: His Work and an Account of His Life* (London: Routledge and Kegan Paul, 1965).

the National Gallery of Ireland. By 1916, Stephens stood as a unique figure within the Dublin literary scene: a committed nationalist attracted to the Irish language movement and even more so to Sinn Féin but wary of the more sectarian republican movements that had emerged by then; a non-practising Protestant living openly with a Catholic woman who was still married to someone else; a self-educated working-class socialist enthused by the political militancy of James Connolly but who nevertheless longed for a movement that had room for the mystical possibilities offered by Hinduism and Buddhism; and a writer of increasing prominence who had very close links to many of the influential figures of the Revival.

Born a little more than a decade after Stephens in 1893, Eimar O'Duffy had a comparatively privileged upbringing.[18] His father was a prominent Dublin dentist fervently loyal to both the Catholic Church and the British crown. Due to paternal insistence, O'Duffy's education included qualification as a dentist from the National University, but he rebelled against his background and became interested in socialism, militant republicanism, and the literary world of the Revival. After the outbreak of the First World War, he refused his father's demand that he enlist and instead joined the Irish Volunteers. O'Duffy took a leadership role in that organization, wrote about military tactics for various nationalist publications, and was eventually inducted into the Irish Republican Brotherhood (IRB) in early 1916. Even in the personal accounts of those who considered themselves his friends, O'Duffy appears to have had a remarkably difficult and uncompromising personality, and in both the cultural sphere of the Revival and the conspiratorial context of militant republicanism he tended to take unyielding, divisive positions. O'Duffy did not object to revolutionary violence but insisted that the only argument for force was the rational viability of military success. He was absolutely opposed to any of the mythological or symbolic justifications for self-sacrifice that would later come to be associated with the rhetoric of Patrick Pearse (especially when expressed by personal enemies like Joseph Mary Plunkett). In April 1916, O'Duffy strongly supported Eoin MacNeill's countermanding order to postpone the Easter Rising. Through the rest of his life he retained his vitriolic opposition to what he regarded as the waste brought about by the insurrection and became only more polemical as the ideological aura of the event grew in the wake of the executions of its leaders. When Éamon de Valera began to reorganize the IRB a year later, O'Duffy was excluded and did not participate thereafter in any of the movements committed to armed struggle.

Each writer's political and social views originated squarely within the Irish nationalist movement and both initially attempted to work for progressive goals within the Irish Free State. Stephens continued to work at the National Gallery, while O'Duffy worked as a literary editor for the *Irish Volunteer* and as a publicist in the Department of External Affairs in the new civil service. Both became frustrated with the increasingly conservative nature of the newly independent country and in particular opposed the influence of the Catholic Church on social policy. Coincidentally, both lost their respective positions

---

[18] The chapter on O'Duffy in Frances Flanagan's aforementioned *Remembering the Irish Revolution* is the most comprehensive account of his life, to which my biographical summary is indebted.

around the same time after quarrels with superiors that were partly personal and partly political, and departed Ireland for Britain permanently in 1925 in attempts to re-launch their respective literary careers. Neither was especially successful in their endeavours. Stephens never published another new work of prose fiction after he left Ireland, though he continued to publish poetry and ultimately found success in the two decades before his death in 1950 through BBC broadcasts in which he played the role of a modern *sean-chaí* (oral storyteller) by telling his stories rather than writing them.

Success proved more elusive for O'Duffy. After alienating many of his former comrades through his hostile representation of the Rising in his first novel, *The Wasted Island* (1919), and publishing two romantic comedies and a historical novel about sixteenth-century Ireland inspired by Alexander Dumas, O'Duffy appeared to have realized his potential when Macmillan published *King Goshawk and the Birds*, the first novel of the Cuanduine trilogy, in 1926. Perhaps that novel was a little too close in some ways to Stephens's writing, as George Russell argued in an otherwise positive review which nevertheless suggested that O'Duffy had plagiarized his old protégé.[19] Macmillan went on to publish *The Spacious Adventures of the Man in the Street* (1928), the second novel of the trilogy, and a revised version of *The Wasted Island* in 1929, but none of the books sold in significant numbers. By that point O'Duffy's youthful interest in a vaguely defined socialism had been displaced by a fervent commitment to the Social Credit movement, and a press identified with that cause, Putnam's, published his economic tract, *Life and Money* (1932), as well as *Asses in Clover* (1933), the third novel in the trilogy.[20] O'Duffy attempted to generate income by writing mystery novels despite his professed hatred for the genre, but all three were unsuccessful. He died suddenly and in relative obscurity in 1935, aged forty-one.

The Easter Rising presents the central contextual link between the two writers, even if most of Stephens's fiction was written before and all of O'Duffy's novels after that event. Stephens's publication in late 1916 of *The Insurrection in Dublin*, a section from his personal journal, provided the first extended non-fiction account of the Rising. The book is interesting in literary terms for its immediacy (Stephens emphasizes the chaos and uncertainty of the moment rather than the details of historical fact discovered later) and includes a poignant lament for the dead, while its conclusion argues for a non-sectarian nationalism that could become the basis for a collective local redress to deeper social problems.[21] Stephens's fictional works published before 1916 clearly anticipate this position and his subsequent works maintain it, even if an earlier enthusiasm for socialism diminished in relation to an increasingly mystical dimension inspired by Hinduism and Buddhism.[22] By contrast, O'Duffy's embittered view of the Rising and personal grievances against some of its participants informed his representation of it in *The Wasted Island*.

---

[19] Russell's review was published in the *Manchester Guardian* on 12 November 1926. O'Duffy aggressively denied the charge in a response published four days later.

[20] Social Credit, an anti-capitalist economic theory developed in the 1920s by Major C. H. Douglas, proposed the abolition of money in favour of a form of credit that would be distributed equally throughout all of society.

[21] James Stephens, *The Insurrection in Dublin* (Gerrards Cross: Colin Smythe, 1978), 111.

[22] On Stephens's gradual shift from socialism to mysticism, see Lennon, *Irish Orientalism*, 307–10.

Despite these differences in perspective, both writers were convinced that the underlying poverty and uneven economic development of Ireland were more pressing issues for the would-be nation, and would need to be the focus of any subsequent movement towards political independence. Whether in Stephens's writing before 1916 or in O'Duffy's novels published a decade later, both writers frequently made thematic use of the circumstances of physical deprivation in order to interrogate Irish poverty and the ideological forces which benefit from and sustain it, while still retaining some fidelity to the mythological sources evident in their fiction. In the works of both writers, the movement back and forth between the corporeal and the fantastic—between naturalist conditions and fabulist possibilities—was directed towards a greater, 'useful' goal: the redirection of cultural nationalism towards large-scale social transformation.

ESTABLISHING THE PROTOTYPE: JAMES STEPHENS'S EARLY MAGIC NATURALIST FICTION

A work by another influential Irish writer also inspired by the aftermath of the Easter Rising offers a vantage point from which to identify the emergence of magic naturalism as a unique trajectory within the history of Irish prose. In *A Story-Teller's Holiday* (1918), a narrative which openly straddles the line between autobiography and fiction, George Moore (1852–1933) provides a record of a journey he made to Ireland in the summer of 1916 to visit his family and personally apprehend the political changes that had recently taken place. Ultimately, Moore remains ambiguous about the Rising's aftermath and never makes it to his ancestral home in Mayo, although he does end up doing a lot of unanticipated literary work. Most of the text concerns a series of encounters with a fictitious local eccentric named Alec Trusselby, a fern-gatherer and storyteller who fascinates Moore. A storytelling competition develops between them and becomes the primary focus of the narrative. In the end, there is no clear winner, and the contest concludes when Moore withdraws, ostensibly because he is disappointed by Trusselby's reception of a story taken from Turgenev but implicitly because he has simply run out of things to talk about. Quite literally, Moore and the narrative mode from which he draws, which is rooted in the European literary tradition, are exhausted, while the older form of storytelling practised by Trusselby has the capacity to resume at any moment and continue the conversation, endlessly. Moore was an astute enough stylist to realize that Trusselby's language, technique, and subject matter might not seem very convincing if he were to depict it himself, so in 1916 he reached out for collaborative assistance to the promising young Stephens in order to help make the language of Trusselby's stories 'poetical but highly sexed'.[23] It is not entirely clear how much of *A Story-Teller's Holiday* was actually written by Stephens, but

[23] Cited in Adrian Frazier, 'Irish Modernisms, 1880–1930', in John Wilson Foster (ed.), *The Cambridge Companion to the Irish Novel* (Cambridge: Cambridge University Press, 2006), 128.

his influence upon it is prominent whenever Trusselby opens his mouth. Indeed, the exhaustion felt by Moore at the end of the narrative and his subsequent departure from the site of storytelling might present the symbolic moment in which the first wave of Irish naturalism acknowledges the arrival of a now ascendant magic naturalism.

The 'highly sexed' dimension to Stephens's writing which impressed Moore originated in a broader concept of physical desire centered on the motif of hunger. Hunger was a fundamental, recurring point of focus for Stephens, and his representation of it was by turns literal (in regard to the possibility of starvation as a consequence of widespread poverty), metaphorical (in respect to desire, the existential consequences of sexual frustration, and the role played by the institution of marriage in perpetuating internalized repression), and, ultimately, spiritual (in reference to the need for a visionary dimension which would accompany the progressive movements like socialism, feminism, and Irish nationalism that Stephens enthusiastically endorsed in his criticism and journalism— and then transcend once the immediate political objectives they sought had been attained). In all three cases, hunger is a form of misery that it is necessary to overcome. It also presents an initial negative condition that raises the possibility of achieving a more progressive, utopian goal, if one can endure and move beyond hunger.

As the name of the novel's primary character, Mary Makebelieve, suggests, *The Charwoman's Daughter* clearly draws upon the fairy tale genre, and its generically appropriate finale, in which mother and daughter are unexpectedly saved from poverty through an inherited fortune, obscures the otherwise realistic description of urban squalor which provides its focus. Yet the novel's status as one of the first extended fictional representations of Dublin slum life aligns it at least in part with naturalism, and the sense of dissonance between form and content brought about by its conclusion only stresses the degree to which materialist problems demand something more than well-intentioned fabulist solutions. If Stephens were to produce a more critical account of hunger, a manifestation of poverty intrinsic to a seemingly 'natural' and unchangeable understanding of modernity, he would require something 'useful' which both evaded the imaginative limits created by the practical logic of the present and offered genuine utopian possibilities that would at least formulate theoretical propositions of a better world. Stephens founds these possibilities in ancient Irish mythology and folklore, which are largely absent from *The Charwoman's Daughter* but in his later fiction provide a means of stridently challenging a social reality otherwise best captured through the pervasive abjection of naturalism.[24] In these works, the magical qualities of tradition are usually directly summoned by a storyteller figure who inhabits a marginal position in the modern world. The reality of hunger tends to be a recurring point of departure for all else that follows.

In Stephens's fiction, to be hungry signals an implicitly politicized condition of revolutionary potential. It also provides a legitimate moral justification for breaking laws

[24] This not to suggest that local folklore is entirely absent from *The Charwoman's Daughter*. As Joseph Valente's ingenious reading of the novel argues, Stephens's treatment of the marriage plot manages to echo the gendered sovereignty myth so prevalent throughout the Revival and to satirize its emphasis on blood sacrifice, thereby suggesting its fundamental inability to bring about progressive political transformation. See *The Myth of Manliness in Irish National Culture*, 136–9.

which guarantee the stability of an unjust social order, as one of the angels in *The Demi-Gods* suggests. Yet hunger could also serve as a necessary precondition to an awareness of the hidden history of Ireland embedded within folklore and myth. In 'The Story of Tuan Mac Cairill', the opening tale in *Irish Fairy Tales* (1920) and the symbolic introduction to the sequence of stories which follows, Stephens addresses the survival of pagan culture through a story about the title character's conversion to Christianity. As both a corporeal condition and the consequence of a social system that overwhelms individual agency, the physicality of hunger identifies it with a material reality consistent with naturalism. Occasional forays into the translation of older Irish-language sources aside, Stephens tends to represent the objective nature of hunger and the modern form of poverty which produces it through a narrative technique that originates precisely in that bleaker approach to realist prose. Yet the trope of hunger not only registers Stephens's objection to a social order which permits it to become a normalized facet of modernity in the first place. It also signals a necessary condition of absence that will be satisfied by the imaginative sustenance of transformative, utopian possibilities that are registered in folklore and which can inspire political, sexual, economic, and spiritual liberation.

In *The Crock of Gold*, Stephens's most celebrated novel, the Greek god Pan appears in modern Ireland in order to initiate a magical transformation that will culminate in the simultaneous realization of both national sovereignty and egalitarian socialism. For all of that to happen in the final pages of the novel, however, Pan must be replaced by the local god Angus Óg, who has been summoned back to Ireland through the intervention of a character named the Philosopher, an eccentric figure who possesses a definitive understanding of ancient folklore and is given to long digressive parables and stories about any matter that presents itself. The novel contains so many narrative strands (including a fabulist parable concerning the innocence of children, a comic depiction of a conflict between an oppressive group of policemen and a rebellious gang of leprechauns, and a contemporary recasting of Blake's *The Four Zoas*) that it seems a disservice to emphasize one in particular. Yet Stephens's movement back and forth between different forms of hunger and a magic drawn from mythology constitutes the primary structural foundation for a trajectory in twentieth-century Irish fiction that this work more than any other inaugurated. Stephens links the literal hunger of starvation to the metaphorical condition of unfulfilled desire through Pan's courtship of a young woman named Caitilin Ni Murrachu. The relationship that develops between them becomes a means for Stephens to launch an attack on a collective sense of sexual repression rooted in both Victorian moralism and Catholic Jansenism.

A magical dialectical transformation of a naturalist condition lies behind this aspect of *The Crock of Gold* and provides its narrative centre. Young Caitilin, who shares a first name with the most common personification of national sovereignty in Revival writing, inhabits a modern Ireland characterized by an overwhelming collective hunger. Union with Pan offers a negation of that hunger and the enablement of personal freedom, but Caitilin's preference for Angus extends to collective liberation and leads to the utopian vision described in the conclusion of the novel. The novel's dialectical model in turn offers a paradigm of what will become the basis for the magical naturalist trajectory in twentieth-century Irish fiction in general. The types of hunger which arise from poverty

or sexual repression, two of the most common points of focus within naturalism, register the oppressive disenchantment of what Benjamin calls *das Erlebnis* and refer to larger
social forces which appear unchangeable due to their monolithic power. Yet narrative
digressions within the novel, often brought about by the appearance of a character who
is a latter-day incarnation of the traditional *seanchaí* or oral storyteller, permit the
arrival of personae and other elements drawn from ancient Irish tradition which provide the means to satisfy a hunger that limits the possibility of agency. This is not an end
in itself, however, for there is ultimately something more 'useful' at stake. Through this
fabulist dimension, Stephens introduces a latent form of *die Erfahrung* which, though it
may appear to belong to a distant past long disconnected from the present, conjures up a
mythological tradition filled with parables and concepts that offer progressive alternatives to an oppressive present. As in *A Story-Teller's Holiday*, narratives committed to the
naturalistic documentation of contemporary reality are crossed with mythological tales
that bear archaic but 'useful' knowledge.

In Stephens's writing, marriage is one of the primary means through which the limits
of the present are suffered and reproduced. While he was writing *The Crock of Gold* in
1912, he contributed a series of articles entitled 'The Populace Mind' to the suffragist
periodical the *Irish Citizen* that indicate his feminist sympathies and the motivations
behind his representation of marriage.[25] Although the term is unwieldy, by 'populace
mind' Stephens means something like the ideological forces, rooted in social convention, which determine what is 'natural' and what is 'unnatural'. For Stephens, supposedly
'natural' conditions like marriage, and the conventional forms of social performativity
they require, in actuality reproduce the power imbalances which are inherent to modernity, such that *The Crock of Gold* demands the institution of marriage be dismantled to
create equality between partners. Stephens's short stories, however, extensively document the miseries of marriage to a degree which is much more naturalist than magical.

His first collection, *Here Are Ladies*, possesses an elaborate organizational structure
which anticipates the 'schema' Joyce would draw upon in *Ulysses* (1922). The collection
consists of six triadic sequences of narratives comprising an introductory poem, character sketches, and a story organized around variations on a general theme: the existential
hunger of life in a society in which conventional marriage is an inescapable 'natural'
condition. Rather than presenting a 'contrapuntal comedy of the sexual life',[26] much of
the collection is relentlessly bleak in comparison to Stephens's longer fictional works.
The different triads allow him to present a critique of marriage from a variety of perspectives, including those for whom the romantic ideology of marriage can never be
realized in actuality, those who have had their romantic expectations defeated by marital realities, and even children whose imaginative innocence will dissipate once they
understand that adulthood will involve the inevitability of marriage. There is little of the

---

[25] James Stephens, 'The Populace Mind', in *Uncollected Prose of James Stephens: Volume One, 1907–1915*,
ed. Patricia McFate (Dublin: Gill and Macmillan, 1983), 97–106.
[26] Augustine Martin, 'Introduction', in James Stephens, *Desire and Other Stories*, ed. Augustine Martin
(Dublin: Poolbeg Press, 1980), 9.

magic of fabulist possibility to alleviate the anatomy of metaphorical hunger depicted in the different sections of the collection. It is at least qualified by a lengthy concluding section entitled 'There is a Tavern in the Town', which provides a literal depiction of storytelling through the random ruminations of an 'old gentleman', a Dublin pubgoer who recalls the character of the Philosopher and digressively expounds at length on a variety of subjects. If this character is unable to summon myth and magic like his counterpart in *The Crock of Gold* does, he at least serves as an archaic reminder of an older mode of narrative production, the source of 'useful' knowledge, which stands in juxtaposition to the accounts of metaphorical hunger in the rest of the collection.

In the works Stephens published after 1916, the integration of magical possibility and naturalist reality is less evident. *Irish Fairy Tales, Deirdre* (1923), which once more depicts the tragic consequences of a socially prescribed marriage at the expense of sexual freedom, and *In the Land of Youth* (1924) all retain their ostensibly archaic frames without directly referring to contemporary reality, even if the substance of the tales Stephens chooses to reproduce implicitly continue his interrogation of the categories of the 'natural' and the 'unnatural' in regard to modern Ireland. Since it assembles previously uncollected short fiction, Stephens's final prose work, *Etched in Moonlight* (1928), lacks the structural design of *Here Are Ladies* and *Irish Fairy Tales*, but the stories it includes, most of which are focused on grim social realities, suggest that the Irish Free State would ultimately prove inimical to mythically informed utopian transformation.

Two stories in particular stand out as examples of his best work, their titles signifying the degree to which they extend Stephens's earlier narrative concerns. 'Desire' utilizes a vaguely supernatural conceit to present an eerie dream sequence that foreshadows a husband's sudden death, which becomes inevitable because he has placed his own interests ahead of his wife's needs. 'Hunger', possibly the grimmest piece of fiction in the history of Irish naturalism, depicts the gradual starvation of an impoverished Dublin tenement family. By the end of the story, each family member has died except for the mother, who has slowly become insane as a consequence, and a disabled child who will never be able to care for himself without his family. Neither story bears any trace of the fabulist dimension present in Stephens's earlier writing, and even though they were written several years before their publication in 1928, their bleakness suggests that the magic had run out.

REVISING THE PROTOTYPE: EIMAR O'DUFFY'S CUANDUINE TRILOGY

By 1928, Eimar O'Duffy had published the first two volumes of the Cuanduine trilogy, and magic naturalism had entered into a new phase. George Russell's observation that O'Duffy's debt to Stephens in *King Goshawk and the Birds* bordered on plagiarism was much closer to the truth than O'Duffy was willing to concede, as large parts of the narrative draw directly from *The Crock of Gold*. O'Duffy's first character of importance is named the Philosopher of Stoneybatter, and is virtually identical to Stephens's similarly named character, had he relocated to Dublin and continued to live in a particularly dystopian version of the Irish Free State a few decades after 1922. As the trilogy begins, the American millionaire Goshawk, controller of the world's food supply, purchases all birds in existence as a gift for his wife, an act which transforms the meaning of 'nature' by assigning it a financial value. After the Philosopher's opposition to this act of privatization is violently rebuked by his fellow Dubliners, he sets out on a quest which summons mythological assistance in the shape of Cuchulainn (who earlier reappeared in a modern guise in Stephens's *The Demi-Gods*) to battle global capitalism.

Importantly, however, the novel differs from Stephens's earlier work in that none of the magical processes initiated by the Philosopher successfully overcome the naturalist qualities of modernity. Cuchulainn proves comically incapable of making any sense of modern Ireland and departs in frustration one-third of the way through the first novel of the trilogy. While on earth he fathers a son named Cuanduine (the Hound of Man) who comes very close to achieving the goals set in motion by the Philosopher but ultimately proves unsuccessful. By the end of *Asses in Clover*, Cuanduine defeats Goshawk but spares the life of his economic advisor Slawmey Candor, thus permitting capitalism to reconstruct itself; he opens the cages to free the birds, but they have become so accustomed to imprisonment that they lack the ability to recognize the possibility of freedom and remain confined. Cuanduine renounces humanity and departs from the world just as his father did, and nothing like the utopian apocalypse at the end of *The Crock of Gold* takes place. Instead, after a lengthy subplot concerning the failed colonization of the moon, an economic depression brings about the collapse of civilization and humanity destroys itself.

A final observation by one of the gods in *Asses in Clover* regarding the extinction of 'a strange creature called Man' neatly summarizes the central premise of naturalism:

> 'At first he was truly interesting, but he reached his zenith too quickly, and then rapidly declined. During his last few hundred years, when he was already far gone in decay, he achieved a mastery of natural forces that was marvellous in a race so stupid, but his wickedness and folly were such that it did him more harm than good.'[27]

Such a conclusion suggests that the material circumstances of reality ultimately prevent the possibility of fabulist transformation, and that the thousand pages of O'Duffy's trilogy are as much a parody of Stephens's fiction as a novelistic exposition of the principles of Social Credit. Yet the statement quoted above is part of a conversation between two distant gods who exist outside of material reality; if it reiterates the principles of naturalism, it is spoken from a perspective that is already magical. The extended nature of O'Duffy's recurring narrative tangents (and moreover, their frequently obsessive tone in which a given satirical point is repeated ad infinitum) often obscure the structural

---

[27] Eimar O'Duffy, *Asses in Clover* (London: Putnam's, 1933), 330.

complexity of the trilogy as a whole. The various tensions present in Stephens's writing—between spoken story and novel, objective actuality and mythological possibility, *die Erfahrung* and *das Erlebnis*—do not disappear from O'Duffy's refashioning of the magical naturalist narrative model but merely function differently in order to propose a 'useful' position more appropriate to a disparate historical moment for Ireland and, by extension, all of the capitalist world order. The failure of Cuchulainn, emblematic icon of that 'wasted' political moment in 1916 towards which O'Duffy retained such deep enmity, suggests that Stephens's formulation of the fabulist dialectic would not be enough, and actual social transformation would require a much stronger form of magic than that which the mythological tradition alone could provide.

In *The Spacious Adventures of the Man in the Street*, the second novel of the trilogy, O'Duffy refashions Stephens's model of magic naturalism even further by reversing the function of its foundational principles. In that novel, a modern Dubliner named Robert Emmett Aloysius O'Kennedy (whose physical form had momentarily been borrowed by Cuchulainn in *King Goshawk and the Birds*) travels to a planet called Rathé located in an alternate dimension of reality committed to the principles of Social Credit. Most of the narrative concerns O'Kennedy's account of the differences between Rathean life and the more familiar conventions of capitalist modernity. While O'Duffy goes to great lengths to stress the enlightened superiority of Rathé (it is a classless society free of inequality and poverty, where feminism and socialism are unnecessary because patriarchy and capitalism have never existed), he filters it through the confusion and shock O'Kennedy feels towards such 'unnatural' instances of impracticality and immorality. Yet O'Kennedy's perspective also enables O'Duffy to engage satirically with the limits of what Stephens called 'the populace mind' by redeploying both the narrative content and structural form of Stephens's prototypical magic naturalism for the purposes of ideological demystification.

While O'Duffy's representation of life in 'Bulnid', the Rathean version of Dublin, is clearly superior to its counterpart on Earth, it is not without its own ideological limits when it comes to constructs of 'nature' and 'reality'. Using the motif of hunger, O'Duffy both subverts and extends the critique of moralism that is also present in Stephens's writing. The metaphorical form of hunger which Stephens identifies with the overwhelming frustration of unconsummated sexual longing does not exist on Rathé. However, in a transposition of the consequences of guilt onto the satisfaction of a different kind of hunger, typicalRatheans have the same kind of relationship to eating that Irish people do to sexual pleasure. In their youth, and before they have had much opportunity to develop their palates through exposure to different tastes, Ratheans choose one type of food they enjoy and must remain faithful to it for the rest of their lives by eating nothing else. This conceit of a monophagous society allows O'Duffy to make the satirical point that the collective anxiety about 'unnatural' practices associated with sexual freedom in conservative Ireland might seem just as arbitrary and ridiculous from a different angle, but the ideological limits of his central character's perspective allows him to go even further in his critique.

Since O'Kennedy's sense of the world originates in the social realities of the Irish Free State, his understanding of the 'natural' is shaped by the same conditions typically depicted within naturalism as the familiar conventions of modernity. To elaborate upon this point, O'Duffy introduces two additional societies that O'Kennedy visits in his travels. Harpaxe, the least evolved area of the planet and the only part of Rathé controlled by a 'work-state' similar to that found on Earth, presents a dystopian representation of capitalism in which O'Duffy rewrites the conventions of naturalism for brutally satirical purposes. By contrast, inhabitants of the utopian Isles of the Blest, the most evolved part of Rathé, are shown to have attained an advanced level of intelligence and are no longer bound by the material world. Since the Blest, freed from the obligation to work, devote their existence to intellectual and creative contemplation, they have discovered magical powers which permit them to exist in a transcendental condition that brings the possibility of eternal life beyond their physical embodiment. From O'Kennedy's perspective, the Isles of the Blest are the dullest and least interesting place imaginable, while Harpaxe is so agreeable to him that it not only serves as the highlight of his journey but presents the one location on Rathé possibly superior to Earth.

In the final section of the novel, O'Kennedy's time on Rathé ends and, after meeting a procession of gods and supernatural entities, he arrives back to Earth to inhabit his own body now that Cuchulainn is no longer in need of it. If the first and third novels of the trilogy offer lengthy digressive narratives in which a magical presence associated with Irish myth enters into a dystopia characterized by the satirical extension of the conventions of naturalism, *The Spacious Adventures of the Man in the Street* evokes a version of reality more appropriate to a naturalist novel by depicting a seemingly magical context in which Social Credit is an impractical political fantasy. Importantly, in each case O'Duffy represents the ultimate failure of perspectives which originate from elsewhere to overturn the conventions of actual or alternative realities. Despite a fabulist capacity for agency rooted in their mythic origins, neither Cuchulainn nor Cuanduine are able to defeat a version of modernity which has accepted injustice and social impoverishment as inevitable and intractable. But no less importantly, O'Kennedy's assumptions regarding the 'natural' inevitability of capitalism are not enough to defeat the values of an alternative reality which has actualized magical possibility.

Dialectical terms clarify the difference between Stephens's prototypical form of magical naturalism and O'Duffy's revision of it. For Stephens, fabulist and folkloric motifs which originate in the stories of socially marginal characters disrupt a narrative frame that is otherwise concerned with the representation of the seemingly unchangeable pathologies of modernity. In this manner, the 'useful' magic of Irish tradition transforms a naturalist depiction of reality, producing a visionary synthesis which at once challenges the ideological limits of 'the populace mind' with regard to what might be feasible or 'natural' and prophesizes the utopian and progressive potential of revolution. In O'Duffy's refashioning of the dialectic between magic and naturalism, the two never synthesize; irrespective of which direction they encounter each other, thesis and antithesis persist in mutual contradiction. Yet that does not mean that the progressive potential of magic naturalism evident in Stephens's version of it disappears altogether in O'Duffy's fiction. As Louis Althusser hypothesized, if a given contradiction appears to be stable and fixed within the conventional terms of the dominant ideology, such certainty only indicates that it possesses an even greater latent potential for revolutionary transformation.[28] Moreover, as Fredric Jameson argues of Brecht's tendency to depict dramatic situations where opposed principles fail to resolve themselves in the interest of a conclusion, an unsynthesized contradiction presents an initial moment of ideological demystification and initiates a process of critique that demands a seemingly impractical or 'unnatural' solution that will inevitably contribute to the imagination of utopian possibility.[29]

The achievement of Irish independence and the onset of a global economic depression that occurred in the brief period between Stephens's publication of his most influential novels and O'Duffy's composition of the Cuanduine trilogy meant that O'Duffy was confronted by a transformed historical moment. By that point, the subversive elements of Irish tradition celebrated by Stephens had become symbols of ideological limits themselves, and from O'Duffy's perspective were now complicit with the perpetuation of an unjust social order. This did not mean that the power of magic had expired, as it appeared to have in Stephens's later prose fiction published during the same period; it only meant that a different form of magic would be required to move beyond the structural contradiction which provides the formal basis for the Cuanduine trilogy. In its most coherent form (that is, the materialist economic theories of C. H. Douglas rather than the anti-Semitic, proto-fascist rants of figures associated with the movement, such as Ezra Pound), Social Credit does not seem very magical in its goals or imagery. As *Life and Money* indicates, however, O'Duffy's positions regarding Social Credit were not exactly coherent in the first place. One of the more unusual positions he takes in that work concerns his defence of his own ignorance of economics; from his perspective, he was ideally suited to launch a critique precisely because his lack of detailed knowledge made him immune to the potential threat of false consciousness which a more orthodox understanding of capitalism might entail. For O'Duffy, it was enough to believe in the magical possibilities Social Credit could provide, rather than delineate the practical processes through which they might be implemented.

In his discussion of the development of Irish naturalism, Joe Cleary argues that in its formative pre-1922 phase it provided a sceptical perspective on the romanticism of the Revival, while also advocating progressive political change. As it evolved in the 1920s and 1930s, however, naturalist writers' expressions of 'domestic dissent and social critique...were elaborated essentially in terms of a desire for normalization, not radical transformation'.[30] As my analysis here suggests, the development of Irish magic naturalism follows a similar historical trajectory. Neither James Stephens's nor Eimar O'Duffy's formulation of magic naturalism presented viable or feasible solutions to actual social and political problems in Ireland. But neither did more familiar forms of naturalist fic-

---

[28] Louis Althusser, *For Marx* (London: Verso, 1990), 87–128.

[29] Fredric Jameson, *Valences of the Dialectic* (London: Verso, 2009), 280–1.

[30] Cleary, *Outrageous Fortune*, 108.

tion that were committed to the documentation of those same problems. Ultimately, magic naturalist fiction serves an additional purpose: to challenge the developmental trajectory of the Irish novel by introducing a different narrative mode, sourced in the fantastic and centred on the scene of storytelling, that stresses the degree to which the seemingly 'natural' consequences of modernity demand at the very least an imaginative response that exceeds the ideological limits of conventional realist logic.

In Stephens's *The Demi-Gods*, three angels, all of whom have ancestral origins rooted in Irish legend, descend to Earth, take human form, and join a group of Travellers. As they journey through Ireland, much of the text is devoted to the various stories they tell each other. Roughly halfway through the narrative, the group meets a character who had once been a greedy landowner until he renounced wealth and became an itinerant musician. After his new companions respond warmly to the story of his life, Billy the Music states:

> 'It's because the stories were good ones that they were well told, for that's not my trade, and what wonder would it be if I made a botch of it? I'm a musician myself, as I told you, and there's my instrument, but I knew an old man in Connaught one time, and he was a great lad for the stories. . . . . He was a gifted man, for he would tell you a story about nothing at all, and you'd listen to him with your mouth open and you afraid that he would come to the end of it soon, and maybe it would be nothing more than the tale of how a white hen laid a brown egg. He would tell you a thing you knew all your life, and you would think it was new thing. There was no old age in that man's mind, and that's the secret of story-telling.'[31]

Allowing for colloquial differences, Walter Benjamin would not have put it much differently. While the impression a story makes upon an audience depends on the skill of the storyteller, the cumulative force of the narrative depends upon its familiarity and connection to a broader understanding of a world rooted in knowledge of the past. The story evokes a living collective memory which connects the act of remembrance to a wider appreciation of social totality, which in turn can become the basis for a critical opposition to forms of domination and exploitation.

In the novels discussed in this chapter, the conversations and the stories they reveal are rooted in an older, longer temporality that appears obsolescent but nevertheless lurks beneath the surfaces of modernity. It is through these stories that 'archaic' material makes its way into the texts, often on the flimsiest pretexts, such as when mythological, supernatural, or fantastic elements suddenly interrupt ostensibly social realist narratives, thereby creating a discordance that is the sign of transformative potential. At the very least, James Stephens, Eimar O'Duffy, and the other 'wordy' writers identified by Denis Donoghue as producers of 'second-rate' prose not only deserve a reappraisal of their 'spoken' qualities; their obscured imaginative potential also merits further critical re-evaluation.

---

[31] James Stephens, *The Demi-Gods* (London: Macmillan, 1914), 207–8.

FURTHER READING

Bramsback, Birgit. *James Stephens: A Literary and Bibliographical Study*. Cambridge, MA: Harvard University Press, 1959.

Dobbins, Gregory. *Lazy Idle Schemers: Irish Modernism and the Cultural Politics of Idleness*. Dublin: Field Day Publications, 2010.

Flanagan, Frances. *Remembering the Irish Revolution: Dissent, Culture, and Nationalism in the Irish Free State*. Oxford: Oxford University Press, 2015.

Foster, John Wilson. *Fictions of the Irish Literary Revival: A Changeling Art*. Syracuse, NY: Syracuse University Press, 1987.

Frankenberg, Lloyd (ed.). *A James Stephens Reader*. New York: Macmillan, 1962.

Frankenberg, Lloyd (ed.). *James, Seumas, and Jacques: Unpublished Writings of James Stephens*. New York: Macmillan, 1964.

Hogan, Robert. *Eimar O'Duffy*. Lewisburg, PA: Bucknell University Press, 1972.

Lanters, José. *Unauthorized Versions: Irish Menippean Satire, 1919–1952*. Washington, DC: Catholic University of America Press, 2000.

Lennon, Joseph. *Irish Orientalism: A Literary and Intellectual History*. Syracuse, NY: Syracuse University Press, 2004.

McFate, Patricia. *The Writings of James Stephens: Variations on a Theme of Love*. New York: Macmillan, 1979.

McFate, Patricia (ed.). *Uncollected Prose of James Stephens*. London: Macmillan, 1983. 2 vols.

Martin, Augustine. *James Stephens: A Critical Study*. Dublin: Gill and Macmillan, 1977.

Mercier, Vivian. 'The Satires of Eimar O'Duffy'. *The Bell* 12, no. 4 (1946): 325–36.

Pyle, Hilary. *James Stephens: His Work and an Account of His Life*. London: Routledge and Kegan Paul, 1965.

Quintelli-Neary, Marguerite. *Folklore and the Fantastic in Twelve Modern Irish Novels*. Westport, CT: Greenwood Press, 1997.

CHAPTER 8

···

EPIC MODERNISM

Ulysses and Finnegans Wake

···

SAM SLOTE

JAMES Joyce (1882–1941) occupies a complex position in respect to the Irish Revival, literary and otherwise, and one which has been debated ever since *Ulysses* was first published in February 1922. When introducing Joyce and *Ulysses* to the French literary public on the eve of the novel's publication in Paris, Valery Larbaud contextualized Joyce largely in terms of French literary traditions. This was certainly an appropriate strategy considering his audience, and the French influences that Larbaud signals, especially Gustave Flaubert, are certainly apposite. Larbaud's critical gesture is one of assimilation, the placing of Joyce within a specific continental European context: 'He is what we call a pure "Milesian": Irish and Catholic of old stock, from the Ireland that benefits from some affinities with Spain, France, and Italy, but for whom England is a strange land which cannot be made closer even by the commonality of language.'[1] Larbaud then goes on to claim that 'with Joyce's work…Ireland makes a sensational re-entry into European literature'.[2] *Grace à* Joyce, Ireland becomes a nation again within the world republic of letters, which is, as per Larbaud's argument, the only terrain in which he can be properly evaluated.

Larbaud was hardly the only critic making such claims. Writing in the *New Age* in 1915, Ezra Pound stated that Joyce 'writes as a European, not as a provincial'.[3] While Pound does not ignore an Irish comportment to Joyce's writing, he subordinates it to Joyce's continental notions. There is, then, a traceable line of interpretation between Pound and Larbaud on the one hand and Richard Ellmann's 1959 biography on the other, where Joyce is canonized within a European corpus. Ellmann's Joyce fits in perfectly with the New Criticism, in that any focus on the historical contexts or cultural

---

[1] Valery Larbaud, 'James Joyce', *La Nouvelle Revue Française* 103 (April 1922), 387. My translation.

[2] Ibid., 389.

[3] Ezra Pound, 'The Non-Existence of Ireland', in *Pound/Joyce: The Letters of Ezra Pound to James Joyce, with Pound's Essays on Joyce*, ed. Forrest Read (New York: New Directions, 1967), 32–3.

specificities of Joyce's works was deemed inessential to an appreciation of Joyce's modernist, international grandeur. Certainly, such a deracinated critical stance was useful to scholars, typically American at this time, who would have been, among other things, somewhat oblivious to the nuances of Irish history and culture. Of course, there was dissent to this construction of Joyce. Irish scholar Ernest Boyd felt that he needed to counter Larbaud in the revised edition of his book on the Irish Literary Revival, which first appeared in 1916. He claimed that Joyce could only be understood in the context of Irish literature and, specifically, the Literary Revival: 'The fact is, no Irish writer is more Irish than Joyce; none shows more unmistakably the imprint of his race and traditions.'[4] He also chided Larbaud for granting Joyce 'a prematurely cosmopolitan reputation.'[5] This in turn prompted a tetchy retort from Larbaud, where he did little more than assert his (considerable) credentials as a literary critic.[6]

If anything, Larbaud and Boyd are both correct: Joyce operates within both Irish and continental contexts. Indeed, Joyce would not be the only writer associated with the Irish Literary Revival who harboured continental aspirations. Even in exile and even in disdain, Joyce remains an Irish writer; or, perhaps, as Friedhelm Rathjen put it, 'not an Irish writer but an ex-Irish writer';[7] or perhaps, a *translated* Irish writer—an Irish writer translated elsewhere, effecting, *pace* Pound, a dialogue between the parochial and the cosmopolitan.

Joyce's position in relation to the various debates within the Irish Revival finds its metonym with Stephen Dedalus in the 'Scylla and Charybdis' episode of *Ulysses*: an outsider trying to ingratiate himself into the elite through force of will and intellect but entirely on his own terms. That is, he is trying to translate himself into the clique even as he redefines the nature of that clique. The immediate topic of Stephen's literary negotiation is the various ages and stages of Shakespeare, and, specifically, the question of how a writer might represent, epitomize, and metonymize a nation. At one point, uncharacteristically, Stephen stands silent as two Trinity-educated librarians, who appear under their own names— T. W. Lyster and John Eglinton (the pseudonym of William Kirkpatrick Magee)—exchange gossip and observations about the unfolding literary scene in Dublin, during which they refer to the views of Dr George Sigerson, physician, translator, and president of the National Literary Society from 1893 to 1925: 'Our national epic has yet to be written, Dr Sigerson says. Moore is the man for it.... We are becoming important, it seems.'[8] Willard Potts is perfectly representative of the common temptation within Joycean exegesis to take this statement at face value as a mocking reference to the novelist George Moore (1852–1933): 'Occurring in a

---

[4] Ernest A. Boyd, *Ireland's Literary Renaissance* (New York: Alfred A. Knopf, 1922), 405.

[5] Ibid., 404.

[6] Valery Larbaud, 'À propos de James Joyce et de *Ulysses*: Réponse à M. Ernest Boyd', *La Nouvelle Revue Française* 108 (January 1925), 5–17.

[7] Friedhelm Rathjen, 'Silence, Migration, and Cunning: Joyce and Rushdie in Flight', *James Joyce Quarterly* 39, no. 3 (2002), 556.

[8] James Joyce, *Ulysses*, ed. Hans Walter Gabler with Wolfhard Steppe and Claus Melchior (London: Bodley Head, 1993), 9.309–13. As per convention, the Gabler edition will be cited hereafter by episode followed by the line number.

book titled *Ulysses*, the question of who would write the national epic also is clearly self-reflexive. By 1922 it would have been obvious that Moore was most certainly not "the man for it", leaving Joyce as the likely claimant.[9] So *Ulysses*, following this line of reasoning, would be, in one way, the apotheosis of the Irish Literary Revival but also something different and apart, a new dispensation.

What such a reading misses is that George Sigerson's claim is being misrepresented, albeit in an instructive way. Sigerson did not quite call for an Irish national epic, but what he did solicit was in some ways closer to Joyce's ambition, insofar as he opposed theories of racial and cultural purity and instead drew attention to the heterogeneity of the Gaelic literary tradition. In a lecture on the history of Irish literature delivered to the Irish Literary Society in 1892, Sigerson asserted that ancient Irish literature, while as majestic as any ancient epic, is fundamentally distinct and unrelated to any classical norms. He states that Greek epic arose out of conditions specific to ancient Greek culture: 'That Epic stands alone, nor should we desire to have ideas cast in the same mould. Such desire is the defect of stereotyped thought, which does not understand that to have something diverse and original is to possess a treasure.'[10] In effect, he is arguing that Irish literature—whatever it might have been and whatever it might become—does not need its own national epic but something else, something of its own: 'Our ancient literature must be judged by itself, on its intrinsic merits as the articulate expression of independent humanity. If a standard is required, let it be compared with the non-classic literatures of the western world.'[11] Ireland, in short, is too *sui generis* for epic.

Superficially, Sigerson's paean for a truly Irish literature might be seen to resemble a kind of literature of Irish Ireland, hearkening back to an unsullied, pure Gaelic form. But this is not how he ends his talk. Rather, he concludes by arguing that a contemporary Irish literature needs to recapture its ancient, protean, independent vitality:

> Irish literature is of many blends, not the product of one race but of several. It resembles the great oriel of some ancient cathedral, an illumination of many beautiful colours, some of which can never be reproduced, for the art is lost. We possess an unique treasure in that ancient literature which grew up from a cultured people, self-centred, independent of Roman discipline.[12]

Sigerson's final plea is to reanimate this faithful departed spirit of old. Marvelling at the power of words to 'survive the mightiest monarch and outlast the lives of empires', he expresses a fervent hope for renewal: 'Yet out of the Dead Past speaks still the Living Voice. So, to-day, we may be illumined by the light of a star which perished a thousand years ago.'[13] The distinctiveness of Irish literature is a function of a unique and specific mélange.

---

[9] Willard Potts, *Joyce and the Two Irelands* (Austin, TX: University of Texas Press, 2000), 166.
[10] George Sigerson, 'Irish Literature: Its Origin, Environment, and Influence', in Charles Gavan Duffy, George Sigerson, and Douglas Hyde, *The Revival of Irish Literature* (London: T. Fisher Unwin, 1894), 69.
[11] Ibid.   [12] Ibid., 109.   [13] Ibid., 111.

Stripped of its nostalgia, Sigerson's hypothesized Irish literature of the future is one that is independent of the classical genres, such as epic, and is thus mixed and mongrel and hybrid. In describing what an Irish literature should be, it is almost as if Sigerson were describing the novel—at least the novel as defined by Bakhtin, a genre apart from both mythical time and prescribed canonical form, a genre that is pointedly *not* epic. For Bakhtin, the novel is 'by its very nature, not canonic. It is plasticity itself. It is a genre that is ever questing, ever examining itself and subjecting its established forms for review.'[14] While this is not what Sigerson is explicitly or consciously calling for, his lecture is not so much an appeal for a national epic but rather a national novel, the translation or transvaluation of both epic and nation (and even, as with all good transvaluation, of the novel genre itself) into a new, hybrid form.

While prose works were not unknown in the Irish Literary Revival, drama was its primary medium, as W. B. Yeats (1865–1939) clearly signals in his acceptance speech for the 1923 Nobel Prize, in which he specifically assigns theatre the role of merging the English and Irish languages in the manner of the Galway peasantry, 'who told stories in a form of English which has much of its syntax from Gaelic, much of its vocabulary from Tudor English.'[15] Here and elsewhere, Yeats sees drama as the conduit for forging a new and distinctive Irish identity as a fusion of older forms. On the other hand, George Moore would have been one of the few dissenters to the Revival's privileging of drama over other genres and so the naming of him as the preferred author of the Irish national epic in 'Scylla and Charybdis' is, even if a case of Joycean bait-and-switch, a nod in the direction of the novel form.

While Bakhtin perceived the novel form as standing apart from a prescribed and prescribing canonicity, he also understood it to exist within a canon, albeit a self-generating one. However, Bakhtin's conception of the novel is distinct from Anglophone understandings of its evolution. The tradition of the Anglophone novel begins with Daniel Defoe and has two key features that Bakhtin would not consider essential: psychological realism and a single organic plot, what Ian Watt calls 'formal realism.'[16] In distinction, Bakhtin regards Miguel de Cervantes's *Don Quixote* (1605, 1615) as the first novel and sees it as a work that has clear, direct antecedents in the Greek romances of the second century. This means that Bakhtin's conception of the novel is far looser and more diverse, both in terms of individual novels and groups of them, than that proposed by Anglophone critics: 'The novel can be defined as a diversity of social speech types (sometimes even diversity of languages) and a diversity of individual voices, artistically organized.'[17] Of course, a novel is a flimsy mechanism upon which to build a nation. Yet, as Bakhtin recognized, it is nonetheless all too easy

---

[14] Mikhail Bakhtin, *The Dialogic Imagination*, ed. Michael Holquist, trans. Caryl Emerson and Michael Holquist (Austin, TX: University of Texas Press, 1981), 39.

[15] W. B. Yeats, 'The Irish Dramatic Movement: A Lecture Delivered to the Royal Academy of Sweden', in *The Collected Works of W. B. Yeats, Volume III: Autobiographies*, ed. William H. O'Donnell and Douglas N. Archibald (New York: Scribner, 1999), 411.

[16] Ian Watt, *The Rise of the Novel* (London: Chatto and Windus, 1957), 32.

[17] Bakhtin, *The Dialogic Imagination*, 262.

to conscript the novel into the consolidation of a new form and identity or the renova-
tion of belated or neglected forms and identities:

> The novel senses itself on the border between the completed, dominant literary lan-
> guage and the extraliterary languages that know heteroglossia; the novel either
> serves to further the centralizing tendencies of a new literary language in the pro-
> cess of taking shape (with its grammatical, stylistic and ideological norms), or—on
> the contrary—the novel fights for the renovation of an antiquated literary language,
> in the interests of those strata of national language that have remained (to a greater
> or lesser degree) outside the centralizing and unifying influence of the artistic and
> ideological norm established by the dominant literary language.[18]

In Bakhtinian terms, therefore, Sigerson's plea is for a literature that is both centralizing
and decentralizing. Such tension is the general predicament in which Joyce wrote
Ulysses, the tension between the weight of inherited tradition and the novelty that issued
from the creative rancour generated by the different voices within the Revival, from
Yeats to D. P. Moran to J. M. Synge (1871–1909) to John Eglinton to Michael Cusack to
James Connolly to Maud Gonne, and so on to no last term. One of the informing contexts of Joyce's art, therefore, is the fractiousness of various creative forces pulling with
and against each other in the maelstrom of erstwhile Irish cultural revivification.

To be sure, Bakhtin's idea of the novel is mostly antithetical to the staid and formulaic
Victorian novel. By mixing modes, by presenting multiple perspectives through multiple
styles, Joyce is moving close to Bakhtin's idea of the novel as a space in which to experiment with ideas and realize different interpretive possibilities. Indeed, *Ulysses'* Homeric
structure and use of epic allusions better place it within the Bakhtinian register and are
broadly compatible with Sigerson's claim that Irish literature should be read and evaluated apart from classical norms. This is because Joyce ironizes the Homeric analogies and
allusions even as he invokes them: the novel is titled *Ulysses*, not Odysseus, which is not
just the translated Latin name of the Greek hero but the post-classical Latin version of the
name (the Roman Latin being *Ulixes*). By using the name *Ulysses* as his title, Joyce is suggesting all the versions of Odysseus that stand between us and Homer, thereby evoking,
but also ironizing, the 'epic distance' requisite to epic.[19] Joyce's epic is therefore a *translated* one. The novel, according to Bakhtin, transvalues or even repudiates epic, and that
is precisely what Joyce does in *Ulysses*, overlaying epic distance onto a map of Dublin,
thereby translating distance into proximity, or rather, a simulated proximity.

Joyce's solution to the centralizing/decentralizing dialectic is not entirely programmatic, therefore. Rather than downplay the heterogeneity of discourses associated with the Revival, he exults in the heteroglossia afforded by the novel. *Ulysses*
finesses the problem of tradition and novelty, if only partially, through a welter of
multiple, intercalated perspectives. Whilst writing *Ulysses*, Joyce described his task
as one of 'writing a book from eighteen different points of view and in as many styles,

---

[18] Ibid., 67.   [19] Ibid., 13.

all apparently unknown or undiscovered by my fellow tradesmen'.[20] This figure of eighteen different perspectives can either be seen as an exaggeration or an understatement. With select exceptions, the earlier episodes of *Ulysses* proceed largely from the same formal frame, a combination of free indirect discourse and internal monologue, what Joyce called the book's 'initial style'.[21] Only from 'Wandering Rocks' does each episode have a distinct, identifiable style and idiom. But the figure of eighteen could also be understood as an understatement because the rubric 'distinct, identifiable style' could be better phrased as 'distinct, identifiable set of stylistic protocols', since these later episodes—especially 'Cyclops', 'Circe', and 'Ithaca'—deploy more than just the one style.[22]

A key part of Joyce's talent as a writer can therefore be said to lie in his ability to represent various characteristically identifiable voices—which is to say that Joyce is a writer fluent in a multiplicity of styles. Already in the earliest-written stories of *Dubliners* (1914), Joyce modulates style to the individual temperaments represented. With *A Portrait of the Artist as a Young Man* (1916), he expands this stylistic variability into a sophisticated form of free indirect discourse and with *Ulysses* takes this a step (or two) further. For example, the absence of quotation marks—or 'perverted commas'[23] as Joyce styled them—and discursive markers, such as the phrase 'he said', are signs of Joyce's confidence in his ability to differentiate characters purely on the basis of their own individuating and identificative patois, as well as of his faith in his readers' interpretive prowess.

In his 1907 lecture, 'Ireland: Island of Saints and Sages', Joyce characterizes the hybridity of Irish identity in terms not dissimilar from Sigerson (before him) and Larbaud (after):

> Our civilization is an immense woven fabric in which very different elements are mixed, in which Nordic rapacity is reconciled to Roman law and new Bourgeois conventions to the remains of a Syriac religion. In such a fabric, it is pointless searching for a thread that has remained pure, virgin and uninfluenced by other threads nearby. What race or language (if we except those few which a humorous will seems to have preserved in ice, such as the people of Iceland) can nowadays claim to be pure? No race has less right to make such a boast than the one presently inhabiting Ireland.[24]

Here, Joyce's conception of Ireland, like the novel as theorized by Bakhtin, is mixed and mongrel. In light of this passage, it is tempting to see a political cast to Joyce's multifarious art of style, especially in an episode like 'Cyclops'. The plurality of style indicates an already-latent plurality within Irish identity. Just as Yeats highlighted the synthesis of

---

[20] James Joyce, *Letters of James Joyce*, ed. Stuart Gilbert (New York: Viking Press, 1957), vol. 1, 167.

[21] Ibid., 129.

[22] See Karen Lawrence, *The Odyssey of Style in 'Ulysses'* (Princeton, NJ: Princeton University Press, 1981).

[23] James Joyce, *Letters of James Joyce*, ed. Richard Ellmann (New York: Viking Press, 1966), vol. 3, 99.

[24] James Joyce, *Occasional, Critical, and Political Writing*, ed. Kevin Barry (Oxford: Oxford University Press, 2000), 118.

the English and Irish languages as evinced in the folk-speech of Galway as the vector for cultural revival, Joyce also works within a meeting of the two linguistic streams.

However, Joyce practises a different type of linguistic combination to that of Yeats. Rather than write in British English, he consistently writes in Hiberno-English. This extends not merely to the reportage of individual characters' speech but also to the diegetic voices in *Dubliners* and *A Portrait*. Furthermore, *Ulysses* consistently deploys Hiberno-English idioms and spellings, such as 'rere' for the word 'rear', as in, 'He trod the worn steps, pushed the swingdoor and entered softly by the rere.'[25] Terence Dolan writes that Joyce 'dismantled English and deconstructed it as a Tower of Babel, with many component parts, led by English and Irish, in the form of Irish-English'.[26] As I will discuss in the second part of this chapter, Joyce's Babelian, Hibernicized English is not without consequence for *Finnegans Wake* (1939), his most advanced work of fiction. Subtly, from the start, Joyce decentres and combines—pluralizes, even—the literary and linguistic traditions of Ireland. His use of Hiberno-English is exactly the conduit through which he attempts to become the national poet, the Irish Shakespeare, doing so in a way that transvalues both Ireland and Shakespeare. One of the names in the mock heroic list of 'Irish heroes and heroines of antiquity' in 'Cyclops', 'Patrick W. Shakespeare', yokes together England's national poet with Patrick Weston Joyce, the scholar of Irish history and literature and author of the foundational study of Hiberno-English, *English as We Speak it in Ireland* (1910).[27] The name Joyce thus becomes the hinge between Shakespeare and (the seminal scholar of) Hiberno-English.

Joyce's art of amalgamation and substitution extends to more than just names and languages: his remaking and remodelling of the genre of the novel also depends upon combination and recombination. *Ulysses* begins with Buck Mulligan's theatrics, comprising his mock-sermon whilst shaving and his reconscription of the Sandycove Martello Tower, an erstwhile military garrison, into symbolic duty (or mock-symbolic duty—with Mulligan such a distinction hardly matters) as the 'omphalos'[28] of a new, literary, neo-pagan Ireland. It thus comes as no surprise that when the elderly milkwoman comes in, she too is enlisted into various symbolic duties. From a simple, perhaps even unconscious, approbation of the milk, the old woman earns two epithets customary to Ireland, silk of the kine and the poor old woman (*sean bhean bhocht*), and thus takes on an overloaded symbolic, even Yeatsian, cast:

> He watched her pour into the measure and thence into the jug rich white milk, not hers. Old shrunken paps. She poured again a measureful and a tilly. Old and secret she had entered from a morning world, maybe a messenger. She praised the goodness of the milk, pouring it out. Crouching by a patient cow at daybreak in the lush field, a witch on her toadstool, her wrinkled fingers quick at the squirting dugs. They lowed about her whom they knew, dewsilky cattle. Silk of the kine and poor old

[25] Joyce, *Ulysses*, 5.338–9.

[26] Terence Dolan, 'Joyce: Babble or Babel?', in Anne Fogarty and Fran O'Rourke (eds), *Voices on Joyce* (Dublin: University College Dublin Press, 2015), 102.

[27] Joyce, *Ulysses*, 12.176, 12.190–1.   [28] Ibid., 1.176.

woman, names given her in old times. A wandering crone, lowly form of an immortal serving her conqueror and her gay betrayer, their common cuckquean, a messenger from the secret morning. To serve or to upbraid, whether he could not tell: but scorned to beg her favour.[29]

In a 1911 essay, John Eglinton castigated the Revival's penchant for figuring Ireland as an old woman, attributing it to 'the addled masculine brain of the Irish idealist', 'brooding over Ireland's wrongs'.[30] Joyce's criticism of this figuration in this passage is not quite as stark as Eglinton's since he allows for multiple perspectives to emerge from this act of symbolic appropriation by characterizing the symbolism as being just another mode of menial servitude imposed on the poor old woman ('A wandering crone, lowly form of an immortal serving her conqueror and her gay betrayer'). Furthermore, she is not utterly denied a degree of agency. While the milkwoman does not speak Irish and cannot even recognize the language when it is spoken by Haines, the Englishman, she is perfectly fluent in Hiberno-English ('I'm told it's a grand language by them that knows'[31]) and she is more than fluent in calculating what she is owed: 'Well, it's seven mornings a pint at twopence is seven twos is a shilling and twopence over and these three mornings a quart at fourpence is three quarts is a shilling. That's a shilling and one and two is two and two, sir.'[32]

The milkwoman's appearance in the opening 'Telemachus' chapter indicates an interplay or, even, a tension between realism and symbolism. Such tension can really only be sustained within novelistic discourse since the novel allows for various kinds of stylistic and perspectival layering and intermixing. With *Ulysses*, the symbolism is a function of the realism. For example, the language of the closing scene in 'Nestor', in which the anti-Semitic schoolteacher Mr Deasy walks away from Stephen having delivered his parting sally in their conversation about Irish history, appears symbolic even though it is perfectly naturalistic: 'On his wise shoulders through the checkerwork of leaves the sun flung spangles, dancing coins.'[33] The image of the dancing coins is an entirely legitimate description of a physical phenomenon and as such precedes any symbolic force that it carries. Such an optical occurrence is occasioned by the fact that the sun is not a single point of light but a disk. Any gap between the leaves of a tree allows for the projection of a

---

[29] Ibid., 1.397–407. The woman's praise of milk directly invokes George Russell's programme for an Irish dietary revival, specifically his championing of the consumption of this pure, rural form of sustenance, as set out in a 1906 article he wrote for the *Irish Homestead* entitled 'In Praise of Milk': 'Pure milk is the best all round food anyone could take.... We will go so far as to say that if it comes to a matter of food values that the farmer who would exchange threepence worth of milk for sixpence worth of any other kind of food be a loser by the exchange. Here is our country with tuberculosis afflicting its inhabitants like a leprosy almost, a disease which is traceable to bad air and bad food, and for which the cure is good air, and good food which means milk and eggs, and our people sell all and buy inferior stuff like bacon from America, as unhealthy a food as one could well eat.' George Russell, *Selections from the Contributions to 'The Irish Homestead'*, ed. George Summerfield (Gerrards Cross: Colin Smythe, 1978), vol. 1, 70. Quoted in Helen O'Connell, '"Food Values": Joyce and Dietary Revival', in John Nash (ed.), *James Joyce in the Nineteenth Century* (Cambridge: Cambridge University Press, 2013), 132–3.

[30] John Eglinton, *Anglo-Irish Essays* (Dublin: Talbot Press, 1917), 88. Joyce refers to this passage in the 'Scylla and Charybdis' episode. See *Ulysses*, 9.312.

[31] Joyce, *Ulysses*, 1.434.   [32] Ibid., 1.442–5.   [33] Ibid., 2.448–9.

sharp image of that disk and multiple gaps allow for a plurality of displaced and dappled sunlight spots, hence the illusion of dancing coins. Thus, a natural phenomenon is described in figurative, symbolically charged language while still remaining empirically accurate. Realism and symbolism are, as it were, two sides of the same coin, or, as Frank Budgen puts it, 'Joyce's realism verges on the mystical.'[34] Yet Joyce also provides a telling counter-example, in which there is no such synergy between symbol and reality. At several points in the novel, Leopold Bloom thinks of the incongruity in the symbolism of the masthead to the *Freeman's Journal*, which shows a sun rising over the Bank of Ireland, formerly the Irish Houses of Parliament, which supposedly suggests a dawn for a new era of Irish self-government. The problem is that this political symbolism contravenes the geographical rising and setting points of the sun, and so what the masthead really depicts is 'a homerule sun rising up in the northwest' or even a 'Homerule sun setting.'[35]

The languages of *Ulysses*, then, are mixed and multiple, as are its proliferating modes and perspectives. In this, *Ulysses* is much like a pantomime: a famous, classic story (in this case, Homer's *Odyssey*) is retold, remade, and remodelled with nods and winks, splashes of local colour, bursts of scenic splendour, and plenty of topical allusions. The 'Cyclops' episode, which unfolds in Barney Kiernan's pub, provides a good example of how multiple styles and perspectives rest within what would ostensibly be a single, unifying mode, specifically (but not exclusively) one associated with the Literary Revival. That is, within this episode Joyce presents a range of perhaps irreconcilable styles jostling against each other. A particularly complex example of intertwined perspectives occurs when the Citizen, who is loosely based on Michael Cusack, founder of the Gaelic Athletic Association, reads from a skit in the nationalist *United Irishman* about an African potentate visiting the United Kingdom:

> —A delegation of the chief cotton magnates of Manchester was presented yesterday to His Majesty the Alaki of Abeakuta by Gold Stick in Waiting, Lord Walkup of Walkup on Eggs, to tender to His Majesty the heartfelt thanks of British traders for the facilities afforded them in his dominions. The delegation partook of luncheon at the conclusion of which the dusky potentate, in the course of a happy speech, freely translated by the British chaplain, the reverend Ananias Praisegod Barebones, tendered his best thanks to Massa Walkup and emphasised the cordial relations existing between Abeakuta and the British empire, stating that he treasured as one of his dearest possessions an illuminated bible, the volume of the word of God and the secret of England's greatness, graciously presented to him by the white chief woman, the great squaw Victoria, with a personal dedication from the august hand of the Royal Donor. The Alaki then drank a lovingcup of firstshot usquebaugh to the toast *Black and White* from the skull of his immediate predecessor in the dynasty Kakachakachak, surnamed Forty Warts, after which he visited the chief factory of Cottonopolis and signed his mark in the visitors' book, subsequently executing an old Abeakutic wardance, in the course of which he swallowed several knives and forks, amid hilarious applause from the girl hands.[36]

---

[34] Frank Budgen, *James Joyce and the Making of 'Ulysses'* (Oxford: Oxford University Press, 1989), 71.
[35] Joyce, *Ulysses*, 4.101–2, 13.1079.   [36] Ibid., 12.1514–33.

The basis of this parody is the visit of the Alake (leader) of the western Nigerian province of Abeokuta to England in May and June 1904, during which he had an audience with King Edward VII. The Alake also spoke at a reception given by the committee of the Church Missionary Society, where he remarked that Queen Victoria had sent a Bible to his father some years before. While the *United Irishman* did run parodic skits, this one derives from the reportage of the speech in the London *Times*, which Joyce then elaborated and embellished into a politically provocative pastiche. In this way, Joyce, in the words of John Nash, moulds 'the *Times* into its direct opposite, a humorous and anti-imperial newspaper'.[37]

Nash's verdict implies that Joyce is being polemical in this passage, which he is, but in a more oblique manner, perhaps, than Nash suggests, for there is more to Joyce's reworking of his source material than simply shifting the ideological valence to its seeming contrary. The report in the *Times* reads as follows:

> The Alake spoke at some length, and at the close his secretary informed the committee of the tenor of his remarks. He said it was a red letter day in his life to meet the committee, for the history if Abeokuta was closely bound up with that of the C. M. S. [Church Missionary Society]. His father, who was the Alake nearly 60 years ago, gave the land on which the church in the Ake township of Abeokuta was built, and he had had the honour of laying the foundation-stone of the present church, built as a memorial of the missionaries Townsend and Wood. In Townsend's time his father had sent a letter to Queen Victoria, and through Lord Chichester the Queen had sent him back two bound volumes of the Word of God, saying that that book was the secret of England's greatness.[38]

The parodied version hews to the source text while adding in details that emphasize English ridiculousness, such as 'Gold Stick in Waiting, Lord Walkup of Walkup on Eggs' (the office, formally named the Captain and Gold Stick of His Majesty's Body Guard, is real; Lord Walkup, sadly, is not); the 'reverend Ananias Praisegod Barebones', whose name comes from Praisegod Barebones, an English millenarian preacher and member of Cromwell's 1653 parliament; and 'Cottonopolis', the nickname for Manchester.[39] Furthermore, the fact that the gift—to which so much value is accorded—is a Bible emphasizes the religious divide that pervades Irish nationalism, since Protestantism derives from a veneration of the Bible whereas Catholicism privileges the teachings of the institutional Church. The characterization of the Alake incorporates various racist tropes, exemplified by his ostentatious 'wardance'. However, two of the terms used

---

[37] John Nash, '"Hanging Over the Bloody Paper": Newspapers and Imperialism in *Ulysses*', in Nigel Rigby and Howard J. Booth (eds), *Modernism and Empire: Writing and British Coloniality, 1890–1940* (Manchester: Manchester University Press, 2000), 189.

[38] *The Times*, 15 June 1904, 10.

[39] Joyce even manages to tuck into this passage a phrase—the affected expression 'partook of luncheon'—lifted from Queen Victoria's published diary, *Leaves from the Journal of Our Life in the Highlands* (1868). See Ronan Crowley, 'The Queen is Not a Subject: Victoria's *Leaves from the Journal* in *Ulysses*', in Nash (ed.), *James Joyce in the Nineteenth Century*, 201.

derive from different racist contexts: the honorific 'Massa', which is used in racist depictions of African-American, but not African, speech, and 'squaw', which is typically applied by Indians to white women. The racism is therefore both endemic and generic. These modifications displace the dry, pro-imperial reportage of the *Times* into an anti-imperial lampoon that condescends to both colonizer and colonized alike.

Joyce thus effects a multi-angled, prismatic parody, both of British religious and imperial colonization and nativist Irish nationalism. Even though 'Cyclops' is a multi-perspectival episode, shifting between the nameless narrator's pub-tale and the various intruding burlesques, this one individual passage alone—the Citizen's recitation from the paper—is itself multi-perspectival. Furthermore, this text is presented in a nested manner: the *Times'* coverage is parodied through a parody of the *United Irishman*, which is itself read aloud by the Citizen within the action of 'Cyclops', which is an episode with a complex narrative structure. Even at a basic level, then, the parody is a parody of a parody. Joyce's intertextuality works as a kind of multi-modal translation whereby different fragments, transferred and recontextualized variously, multiply. Joyce's poetics of citation and recontextualization is thus, ultimately, more than mere satire; it is a poetics of transvaluation.

It is, of course, all too easy to give Joyce more credit than he deserves for being multi-perspectival since there are limits to the range of viewpoints *Ulysses* represents. The novel primarily captures a fairly tight band of outlooks and experiences within the Dublin middle class, with occasional glimpses into upper- and lower-class lives. Through the latter, Joyce is able to suggest the squalid conditions endured by the poor and destitute, as in this moment at the start of the 'Lotus-Eaters' episode: 'By Brady's cottages a boy for the skins lolled, his bucket of offal linked, smoking a chewed fagbutt. A smaller girl with scars of eczema on her forehead eyed him, listlessly holding her battered caskhoop.'[40] Brady's Cottages was a sub-tenement infill housing development located off Lime Street in the docklands area of the city, consisting of houses little better than shanties.[41] The anonymous boy is collecting potato skins for pigfeed, a common job for poor children in early twentieth-century Dublin. While some of these details would be unknown to readers, the general demeanour of the boy and girl suffices to create an impression of the poverty prevalent in the Dublin of this time. But it is only an *impression*, as registered by Bloom as he is walking through the city. Despite the polyphony of styles and the seeming comprehensiveness of *Ulysses*, only three perspectives predominate, those of Bloom, Stephen, and Molly. There are instances where the free indirect discourse allows for the intrusion of other consciousnesses, such as those of Blazes Boylan, Father John Conmee, and Gerty MacDowell, but these are rare. The most substantial such intrusion by a minor character occurs in the tenth episode, 'Wandering Rocks', when young Patsy Dignam tries to comprehend how his father's death will

[40] Joyce, *Ulysses*, 5.5–6.
[41] Jacinta Prunty, 'Improving the Urban Environment: Public Health and Housing in Nineteenth-Century Dublin', in Joseph Brady and Anngret Simms (eds), *Dublin Through Space and Time (c.900–1900)* (Dublin: Four Courts Press, 2007), 189–90.

change his life. Here, snippets of discourse, representing what the boy thinks he should be feeling, stand in for fuller representation:

> Never to see him again. Death, that is. Pa is dead. My father is dead. He told me to be a good son to ma. I couldn't hear the other things he said but I saw his tongue and his teeth trying to say it better. Poor pa. That was Mr Dignam, my father. I hope he is in purgatory now because he went to confession to father Conroy on Saturday night.[42]

Joyce is thus not necessarily as perfectly omniscient as his magnum opus might make it seem. In 'Scylla and Charybdis', Stephen haughtily proclaims: 'A man of genius makes no mistakes. His errors are volitional and are the portals of discovery.'[43] This is a particularly shrewd line on Joyce's part since it absolves him, as the author—and a *soi disant* man of genius—of making any mistakes. Since a genius makes no mistakes, anything that *seems* like a mistake in *Ulysses* must actually be something ingenious that can only be discerned by a suitably astute reader. With this line, then, Joyce shunts the responsibility for error from the author to the reader by saying, in effect, that there are no mistakes in this text, just artistic brilliance that may or may not be properly apprehended. By the same token, Joyce cannot quite capture *all* perspectives, rich and poor, male and female. Indeed, Sandra Gilbert and Susan Gubar's critique of his androcentrism, while it can be challenged and nuanced, cannot be completely dispelled.[44] Joyce's heteroglossia has its limits.

If *Ulysses* is an encyclopaedia, then, it is a limited one in that it only provides the simulation or appearance of comprehensiveness. The question-and-answer format of the 'Ithaca' chapter is a perfect example of this in that the more information it provides in its weird, tangential, proliferating responses, the more it indicates the information that has not been revealed. For example, the description of the unexpected moving of the furniture in the Blooms' living room—which has inspired much speculation about who might have been able to move all of this furniture[45]—is far less detailed than it initially seems:

> A sofa upholstered in prune plush had been translocated from opposite the door to the ingleside near the compactly furled Union Jack (an alteration which he had frequently intended to execute): the blue and white checker inlaid majolicatopped table had been placed opposite the door in the place vacated by the prune plush sofa: the walnut sideboard (a projecting angle of which had momentarily arrested his ingress) had been moved from its position beside the door to a more advantageous but more perilous position in front of the door: two chairs had been moved from right and left of the ingleside to the position originally occupied by the blue and white checker inlaid majolicatopped table.[46]

---

[42] Joyce, *Ulysses*, 10.1169–74.   [43] Ibid., 9.228–9.

[44] See Sandra M. Gilbert and Susan Gubar, *No Man's Land: The Place of the Woman Writer in the Twentieth Century, Volume 1: The War of the Words* (New Haven, CT: Yale University Press, 1988), 261–3.

[45] See, for example, Hugh Kenner, 'Molly's Masterstroke', *James Joyce Quarterly* 10, no.1 (1972), 19–28.

[46] Joyce, *Ulysses*, 17.1281–90.

This certainly seems comprehensive and thorough, but close inspection shows this not to be the case. As Ian Gunn and Clive Hart note, 'The reader is told the original and final positions of the sofa and sideboard, but only the original position of the two chairs and the final positions of the table and piano.'[47] The fact of there being a *gap* in the information is hidden precisely because there is so much information provided.

If anything, *Finnegans Wake* is a stranger book than *Ulysses*. Fundamentally, its very status as a novel is in question: certainly it stretches Bakhtin's idea of heteroglossia and linguistic diversity to what might be its limit. Finn Fordham writes: 'Joyce takes bits of language from anywhere, as small as a letter or as large as a story, and fuses them. More than any novel before, the novel plays with the novel's form as something that oscillates between being unified (self-joining) and falling apart (self-dividing).'[48] But of course, following on from Bakhtin, the history of the novel is precisely a negotiation between formal possibility and constraint. The linguistic and formal malleability of the novel allows for the expression of something new through varied forms and styles. In *Finnegans Wake*, Joyce achieves this through the intercalation of multiple perspectives and diverse languages, what he calls a 'parapolylogic',[49] that is, a language suggestive of various senses in tandem, sometimes harmonious, sometimes discordant, often both. Any Wakean passage is susceptible to multiple and incommensurable readings, and each reading is a fractal or partial metonym of some imagined yet non-present asymptotic whole. The plurality of patterns that can be adduced—the puns that can be parsed, the estranged words that can be translated, the syntax that can be construed, and (even) the characters that can be named—make it seem as if there could be an overall guiding structure, a figure in the carpet. But the rampant proliferation of these clues also interferes with the possibility of a tidy synthesis without remainder, so that the carpet remains messy and littered. No pattern is definitive, yet all that can be read are these partial and incomplete series of signs and traces that take the place of answers, as 'the infinisissimalls of her facets becomes manier and manier'.[50] The convoluted Wakean style is a vehicle for a multitude of concurrent perspectives.

Inverting a formula popular in these ecologically-sensitive times, Joyce thinks locally yet acts globally in *Finnegans Wake*. That is to say, he filters something like an amalgamation of all world histories, languages, cultures, arts, sciences, religions, myths, and so forth through a distinctly local, Irish prism. Through Ireland, Joyce, somehow, represents the whole world, but in so doing he retains the specificity of his Irish home. When Joyce refers to 'Howth Castle and Environs',[51] the environs are as global as they are Hibernian, as if the whole world were a suburb of Dublin.

[47] Ian Gunn and Clive Hart, *James Joyce's Dublin: A Topographical Guide to the Dublin of 'Ulysses'* (London: Thames and Hudson, 2004), 72.

[48] Finn Fordham, *Lots of Fun at 'Finnegans Wake': Unravelling Universals* (Oxford: Oxford University Press, 2007), 49.

[49] James Joyce, *Finnegans Wake* (London: Faber and Faber, 1975), 474.05. As per convention, the *Wake* will be cited hereafter by page number followed by the line number.

[50] Ibid., 298.31–2.   [51] Ibid., 3.03.

Six times in the *Wake* Joyce cites, with varying degrees of distortion, a sentence that he called 'beautiful',[52] which comes from *Introduction à la philosophie de l'histoire de l'humanité* (1857) by the French philosopher of history, Edgar Quinet. Joyce's immediate source was not the original Quinet, however, but rather a quotation of him by Léon Metchnikoff in his *La Civilisation et les grands fleuves historiques*, published in 1889.[53] Quinet writes of the effects of historical change, and so the variations that Joyce inflicts on his sentence are exemplary of the very processes of history that Quinet is describing. In the first chapter of Book II of the *Wake*, we read:

> Since the days of Roamaloose and Rehmoose the pavanos have been strident through their struts of Chapelldiseut, the vaulsies have meed and youdled through the purly ooze of Ballybough, many a mismy cloudy has tripped taintily along that hercourt strayed reelway and the rigadoons have held ragtimed revels on the platau-plain of Grangegorman; and, though since then sterlings and guineas have been replaced by brooks and lions and some progress has been made on stilts and the races have come and gone and Thyme, that chef of seasoners, has made his usual astewte use of endadjustables and whatnot willbe isnor was, those danceadeils and cancanzanies have come stimmering down for our begayment through the bedeaf-dom of po's taeorns, the obcecity of pa's teapucs, as lithe and limbfree limber as when momie mummed at ma.[54]

As with Joyce's other versions of the Quinet sentence, the temporal marker at the beginning is altered. Instead of Quinet's ancient historians, Pliny and Columella, Joyce substitutes the mythological founders of Rome, Romulus and Remus. Furthermore, Quinet's flowers have become dances (pavan, valses, and rigadoons), an appropriate metamorphosis for this chapter in which the Maggies dance around Shem as he attempts to guess their colour. The point here seems to be that the dance endures through decay and entropy, much as children's games have lasted throughout history. The games of children are, on the one hand, fleeting; by definition one (usually) grows out of them. On the other hand, they have persisted throughout the ages; individual players may grow up, but they will always be replaced by subsequent generations, thereby allowing for the continuation of the game.

In addition, in this particular variation on Quinet's theme, Joyce substitutes Chapelldiseut for Quinet's 'les Gaules', thereby returning, in this game, Isolde back to Ireland from France. In so doing, Joyce places Chapelizod at the centre of the myth of historical continuity and change. With the Phoenix Park, 'the most extensive public park in the world',[55] Chapelizod thus takes on the status of a kind of pastoral Hibernian Eden in *Finnegans Wake*, not an Eden that has been abandoned, but

---

[52] Joyce, *Letters*, vol. 1, 295.

[53] This source was discovered by Ingeborg Landuyt and Geert Lernout and is discussed in their article 'Joyce's Sources: *Les grands fleuves historiques*', *Joyce Studies Annual* 6 (1995), 99–138.

[54] Joyce, *Finnegans Wake*, 236.19–32.   [55] Ibid., 140.12–13.

one that has grown and evolved. Joyce frequently conflates Chapelizod with the town of Lucan, which is further to the west, in neologisms such as 'Lucalizod' and 'unlucalised'.[56] Even as Joyce universalizes the local—thereby 'un-localizing' it—it retains its local colours. In many ways, the use and abuse Joyce inflicts on Chapelizod is a microcosm of his treatment of history and language in *Finnegans Wake*: as something eminently, universally fungible, yet, somehow, ineluctably Irish. He makes the local universal while it still retains the traces and character of its locality, its own private Lucalizod, as it were.

Despite inevitable limitations—many of which are self-consciously indicated—James Joyce's *Ulysses* and *Finnegans Wake* are, in appropriately different ways, novels that encompass the vast impersonality of epic as well as the deeply personal and local geographies of the home place, the point of origin. Whether fairly or not, for Bakhtin, epic is the genre of monoidealism; it is monoperspectival, with a singular focus. Such an assessment obviously neglects various formal and thematic discontinuities within the epic tradition but is nonetheless a reasonable assessment of how epic has come to stand, in a tautological manner, as the story of epic heroes from an epic past. Such monoidealism is eminently amenable for conscription into ideological service. Put bluntly, epic is prone to propagandize. In contrast, the Joycean text—however imperfectly—embraces 'plurabilities' of style and perspective and the necessary corollary of ambivalence that accompanies multiple meanings and voices. That is, Joyce translates and transvalues both the global and the local through collage and the interplay of perspectives and styles: the global becomes local becomes global. Beyond the (merely) ideological issues of an Irish Revival, Joyce's texts are concerned with the fungibility of styles and perspectives. They are epics whose grandeur is the art of metamorphosis, metamorphosis of even epic itself, in that epic distance can itself become intimate. Joyce finds space for a 'loose cellarflap' under 'the apathy of the stars' into which 'allotted human life formed a parenthesis of infinitesimal brevity'.[57]

FURTHER READING

Crispi, Luca. *Joyce's Creative Process and the Construction of Characters in 'Ulysses': Becoming the Blooms*. Oxford: Oxford University Press, 2015.

Fordham, Finn. *Lots of Fun at 'Finnegans Wake': Unravelling Universals*. Oxford: Oxford University Press, 2007.

Gibbons, Luke. *Joyce's Ghosts: Ireland, Modernism, and Memory*. Chicago, IL: University of Chicago Press, 2015.

Gibson, Andrew. *Joyce's Revenge: History, Politics, and Aesthetics in 'Ulysses'*. Oxford: Oxford University Press, 2002.

Hand, Derek. *A History of the Irish Novel*. Cambridge: Cambridge University Press, 2011.

Hofheinz, Thomas C. *Joyce and the Invention of Irish History: 'Finnegans Wake' in Context*. Cambridge: Cambridge University Press, 1995.

---

[56] Ibid., 32.16, 87.18.   [57] Joyce, *Ulysses*, 4.77, 17.2226, 17.1055–56.

Lawrence, Karen. *The Odyssey of Style in 'Ulysses'*. Princeton, NJ: Princeton University Press, 1981.

Lernout, Geert. *Help My Unbelief: James Joyce and Religion*. London: Continuum, 2010.

Nolan, Emer. *James Joyce and Nationalism*. London: Routledge, 1995.

Rabaté, Jean-Michel. *James Joyce and the Politics of Egoism*. Cambridge: Cambridge University Press, 2001.

Senn, Fritz. *Inductive Scrutinies: Focus on Joyce*, ed. Christine O'Neill. Dublin: Lilliput Press, 1995.

Van Mierlo, Chrissie. *James Joyce and Catholicism: The Apostate's Wake*. London: Bloomsbury, 2017.

CHAPTER 9

....

THE PARALLAX OF IRISH-LANGUAGE MODERNISM, 1900–1940

....

BRIAN Ó CONCHUBHAIR

MODERNISM emerged slowly and sluggishly in Irish-language prose fiction and auto-biography, despite the critical contributions of James Joyce (1882–1941), Samuel Beckett (1906–89), and Flann O'Brien (1911–66) to European modernism. Standard accounts mark the appearance of Máirtín Ó Cadhain's (1906–70) *Cré na Cille* (Graveyard Clay, 1949) and his later short story collections as heralding the formal emergence of literary high modernism in the prose fiction of Northern Europe's oldest vernacular literary language. Arguably, the acme of Irish-language fictional modernism remains Eoghan Ó Tuairisc's (1919–82) *Dé Luain* (Doomsday, 1966), a richly imaginative reconstruction of the twelve hours leading up to the 1916 Easter Rising that partially subscribes to Virginia Woolf's injunction that novelists 'consider the ordinary mind on an ordinary day'.[1] The narrative emerges through the stream of consciousness of the Rising's main protagonists and antagonists—Pádraig Pearse (1879–1916), James Connolly, Eoin MacNeill, and Sir Matthew Nathan, the British Under-Secretary for Ireland—on anything but an ordinary day. It captures the uncertainty and confusion of the final fateful hours, from the news of Roger Casement's arrest reaching Dublin Castle to frantic efforts to undo MacNeill's debilitating countermanding order. Part fiction, part recreated chronicle, *Dé Luain* employs contemporary newspaper accounts and official documents to recreate the confusion and excitement of the hours prior to the declaration of the Republic outside the General Post Office.

   If *Dé Luain* approximates the techniques and styles of high modernism, so also does Ó Cadhain's *Fuíoll Fuine* (Dregs of the Day, 1970), a novella published in the collection *An tSraith Dhá Tógáil* (The Swathe Being Raised), which concerns the experiences of N.,

---

[1] Virginia Woolf, 'Modern Fiction', in Vassiliki Kolocotroni, Jane Goldman, and Olga Taxidou (eds), *Modernism: An Anthology of Sources and Documents* (Chicago, IL: University of Chicago Press, 1998), 397.

whose job in the civil service not only dominates his life but has obliterated his personality. Excused from work to plan his wife's funeral, N. suffers from debilitating anxiety, a fear of failing at work, and an inability to act or perform. Dreading his two sisters-in-law who await his return home, his chief task is to locate an undertaker. Unable to make any decision regarding the funeral, in case he errs or fails to meet expectations, he wanders the city seeking a cut-price deal.[2] Irish-language prose modernism also flourishes in the work of Diarmaid Ó Súilleabháin (1932–85), particularly in *An Uain Bheo* (The Living Instant, 1968) and *Caoin Tú Féin* (Cry for Yourself, 1967), and in Pádraig Ó Ciobháin's (1951–) *Desiderius a Dó* (The Second Desiderius, 1995), which is structured musically with an overture and a *caidéinse* (cadence), and which derives its title from *Scáthán an Chrábhaidh* (The Mirror of Piety), Flaithrí Ó Maolchonaire's 1616 translation of the Spanish post-Reformation text, *Desiderius*.[3] We must also mention here Pádraic Breathnach's (1942–) sustained engagement with the evolving Irish experience in fiction that uses modernist techniques and styles, which is an impressive achievement and an important component in the story of Irish-language modernism in the latter half of the twentieth century.[4]

If modernism in Irish has flourished in the later twentieth century, what of its surprisingly slow start? Modernists and cultural nationalists, despite the many issues that divided them, viewed language as a potential key to revealing an alternative, more authentic perspective on life and reality.[5] While modernists believed that language blocked 'true' consciousness, cultural nationalists subscribed to a theory that English thwarted 'true' Irish consciousness and inherent potential. The challenge for both cohorts was to create conditions where language could be emancipated from its imprisoning everyday forms to express 'pure consciousness'.[6] In the 1920s, the leading advocate of the literary use of vernacular speech (*caint na ndaoine*) in Irish-language texts, Father Peter O'Leary (1839–1920), also known as An tAthair Peadar Ó Laoghaire, identified a core cultural and linguistic distinction when he declared:

> These fundamental principles of Irish thought were built and shaped long centuries before the principles which have fashioned English thought and speech were dreamt of . . . [T]he Irish mind had no consciousness whatever of the manner in which English thought worked out its own modes of expression in subsequent ages. . . . Some people seem to imagine that thought is essentially the same in the minds of all

---

[2] *Fuíoll Fuine* is often compared to Ó Cadhain's novella, *An Eochair* (The Key), trans. Louis de Paor and Lochlainn Ó Tuairisg (Mclean, IL: Dalkey Archive Press, 2015).

[3] See Philip O'Leary, 'Sea Stories and Soul Searching: Vocation in the Novels of Diarmaid Ó Súilleabháin', *Proceedings of the Harvard Celtic Colloquium* 4 (1984), 9–38. See also Iarla Mac Aodha Bhuí, *Diarmaid Ó Súilleabháin: Saothar Próis* (Baile Átha Cliath: An Clóchomhar 1992).

[4] See Brian Ó Conchubhair, 'Pádraic Breathnach: Moderniste Mhaigh Chuilinn', in Brian Ó Conchubhair (ed.), *Pádraic Breathnach: Rogha Scéalta* (Indreabhán: Cló Iar-Chonnacht, 2014), 7–32.

[5] Barry McCrea, *Languages of the Night: Minor Languages and the Literary Imagination in Twentieth-Century Ireland and Europe* (New Haven, CT: Yale University Press, 2015), 29.

[6] Raymond Williams, *The Politics of Modernism: Against the New Conformists*, ed. Tony Pinkney (London: Verso, 1989), 73.

human beings, and that difference of language is only a mere accidental difference in the mode of expressing the thought. That is a most egregious mistake. There are extensive fields of thought, constantly formed in the Irish mind, and as constantly expressed in Irish speech, which cannot be formed in English speech. The English mind is not only ignorant of those fields of thought, but utterly incapable of reaching them.[7]

The overall focus for Irish-language writers, then, was to express and cultivate that specific *aigne Gaelach* (Irish mindset), an attitude, rooted in the western peripheries of the island, that many envisioned as not only rural and traditional but also Catholic and socially conservative.

Despite such commonalities between modernists and cultural revivalists, modernism in early twentieth-century Irish-language prose fiction remained rare, especially that vertiginous English-language high modernism which reached its apotheosis in the 1920s, the decade of Joyce's *Ulysses* (1922), Woolf's *To the Lighthouse* (1927), Ford Madox Ford's *The Last Post* (1928), and the first English translation of Marcel Proust's *À la recherche du temps perdu* (1913–27). In the new Free State, the demands of cultural nation-building and language learners' needs, as well as literary and linguistic reconstruction, took precedence over innovation and experimentation. Thus, the development of modernism in Irish-language prose fiction resembles the modernist turn in other non-metropolitan and understudied regions of the world, attention to which destabilizes 'the centrality of Europe within narratives of global modernism while providing alternative understandings of the meaning and function'[8] of modernism within its aesthetic, cultural, linguistic, and national contexts. While most European modernists turned away from their literary inheritances when confronted by the challenge of capturing in art the lived experience of modernity, their Irish counterparts came of age during a linguistic and cultural revival that sought to reanimate the older traditions. Rather than turn to the Orient or Africa, Irish-language authors contended with cultural nationalist fervour at home. Such conditions certainly favoured provincialism but not among all writers, and it is in the work of such nonconformists that we find the modernist strain.[9]

While modernist critics' attitudes to Ireland have changed to such an extent that there is no longer 'an implicit oxymoron in "Irish modernism"',[10] the same does not always hold for attitudes toward literature written in Irish, where, too often, the focus remains on the clash between a high European cosmopolitan modernism and a cultural nationalism perceived as insular. In this context, Pádraic Ó Conaire's (1882–1928) *Deoraíocht: Úrscéal ar an Aimsir seo atá i Láthair* (Exile: A Novel about the Present Time, 1910),

---

[7] Peter O'Leary, *Papers on Irish Idiom*, ed. T. F. O'Rahilly (Dublin: Browne and Nolan, n.d.), 71.

[8] Rachel Adams, 'Tradition', in Eric Hayot and Rebecca L. Walkowitz (eds), *A New Vocabulary for Global Modernism* (New York: Columbia University Press, 2016), 234.

[9] See Douglas Mao and Rebecca L. Walkowitz, 'The New Modernist Studies', *PMLA* 123, no. 3 (2008), 737–48. See also Susan Stanford Friedman, 'Planetarity: Musing Modernist Studies', *Modernism/ Modernity* 17, no. 3 (2010), 471–99.

[10] Julian Murphet and Rónán McDonald, 'Introduction', in Julian Murphet, Rónán McDonald, and Sascha Morrell (eds), *Flann O'Brien and Modernism* (New York: Bloomsbury Academic, 2014), 4.

Tomás Ó Criomhthain's (1856–1937) *An t-Oileánach: Scéal a Bheathadh Féin* (The Islander: His Life Story, 1929), and Seosamh Mac Grianna's (1900–90) *Mo Bhealach Féin* (My Own Route, 1940) and Dá mBíodh Ruball ar an Éan (Had the Bird a Tail, 1940) merit careful consideration as texts that mark the emergence of literary modernism in Irish. In addition to serving as precursors to later modernist works such as the aforementioned *Cré na Cille, Dé Luain, Caoin Tú Féin,* and *An Uain Bheo,* as well as Flann O'Brien's *An Béal Bocht* (The Poor Mouth, 1941) and Ó Cadhain's *An Braon Broghach* (The Grimy Globule, 1948), *Cois Caoláire* (Alongside the Seashore, 1953), and *An tSraith ar Lár* (The Shorn Swath, 1967), these texts capture the fictive responses of authors writing in a marginalized European vernacular to profound changes in human experience and consciousness. In their embrace of modernist techniques to articulate the ruptures wrought by modernity, Ó Conaire, Ó Criomhthain, and Mac Grianna interrogate cultural and linguistic nationalism and evince an awareness that the old models and genres will no longer suffice.

PÁDRAIC Ó CONAIRE'S *DEORAÍOCHT*: THE DISINTEGRATION OF A DISPLACED BEING

Without leaving the prodigious myths that surround Pádraic Ó Conaire aside, it is nigh impossible to distinguish where the romantic, bohemian alcoholic ends and the modernist, socialist agitator begins.[11] As a young civil servant in London in the early 1900s, Ó Conaire joined the Gaelic League, taught language classes, lectured in Irish history, and successfully competed at the Oireachtas, the annual Irish-language literary and cultural festival founded in 1897. As a well-educated Irish-speaker (the product of Rockwell College in Tipperary and Blackrock College in Dublin) living in the imperial capital, yet fully immersed in the Irish cultural nationalist project, Ó Conaire complicates the standard narrative that equates modernism with leaving Ireland and things Irish behind, a trajectory epitomized by the literary career of the Francophile Samuel Beckett.[12] Ó Conaire challenges such versions of modernist practice. Not only did he write in Irish while living in London, *Deoraíocht* eschews nostalgic visions of a romantic return to Ireland and the generic conventions of the folktale and the oral tradition, both of which are so deeply intertwined in the Irish-language literary tradition.

Throughout his short story collections, Ó Conaire probes, in pre-Freudian fashion, the complexity of human behaviour and motivation through motifs such as the *doppelgänger* and the window and its refracted images, especially in 'Nora Mharcais Bhig'

---

[11] See Eibhlín Ní Chionnaith, *Pádraic Ó Conaire: Scéal a Bheatha* (Indreabhán: Cló Iar-Chonnacht, 1995), Pádraigín Riggs, *Pádraic Ó Conaire, Deoraí* (Baile Átha Cliath: An Clóchomhar, 1994), and Aindrias Ó Cathasaigh, *An t-Athrú Mór: Scríbhinní Sóisialacha le Pádraic Ó Conaire* (Baile Átha Cliath: Coiscéim, 2007).

[12] Megan Quigley, 'Ireland', in Pericles Lewis (ed.), *The Cambridge Companion to European Modernism* (Cambridge: Cambridge University Press, 2011), 171. See also Pascale Casanova, *The World Republic of Letters*, trans. M. B. DeBevoise (Cambridge, MA: Harvard University Press, 2004), 304–5.

(Nora, Daughter of Small Marcus), 'Neill', 'Teatrarc na Gaililí' (The Tetrarch of Galilee), 'Aba-Cána-Lú', and 'Anam an Easpaig' (The Bishop's Soul).[13] Such stories not only explore weighty and controversial social issues—alcoholism, rape, spousal abuse, mental illness, prostitution—but also crises of conscience, pathologies, and moral dilemmas. Ó Conaire does so, however, in a more naturalistic manner than his Irish-language contemporaries Conán Maol (pseudonym of Pádraig Ó Séaghdha, 1855–1928), Pádraig Pearse, Séamus Ó Grianna (1889–1969),[14] Pádraig Ó Siochfhradha (1883–1964), Micheál Ó Siochfhradha (1900–86), and Seosamh Mac Grianna.[15] His 1909 short story, 'Páidín Mháire' (Páidín, Son of Máire), is often read as a precursor to Deoraíocht yet it is notably less modernist in style. Unlike the story, the novel deconstructs a first-person narrative into a journal or diary and then reconstructs it as a mature work lacking a beginning and a conclusion, making Deoraíocht both larva and moth of 'Páidín Mháire'. In this regard, the novel epitomizes Walter Benjamin's distinction between the modern novel and the folktale. Whereas a teller of tales repackages experiences for listeners, the modern novelist is isolated and alienated from community and society: 'The birthplace of the novel is the solitary individual, who is no longer able to express himself by giving examples of his most important concerns, is himself uncounseled, and cannot counsel others. To write a novel means to carry the incommensurable to extremes in the representation of human life.'[16]

Set almost entirely in London, Deoraíocht details the exploits of Micheál Ó Maoláin, a Galwegian who is permanently maimed following a traffic accident not long after his arrival in the capital. Critics acknowledge the plot's 'magic elasticity' and the manner in which it 'bend[s] the realistic premise', and concur that 'it is much more a symbolic rendering of the fate of the Irish in exile than a documentary telling'.[17] Indeed, James Cahalan considers it 'the most innovative, forward-looking Irish novel in either language during this period before the arrival of Joyce as a novelist'.[18] The loss of a leg and a hand, as well as major damage to Micheál's face, mirror the psychological trauma he endures as a rural emigrant in an urban setting. A grotesquerie of deformity, he is stripped of his identity, physically as well as culturally, and thus becomes a rootless citizen of the modern world, confiding his jagged, confused emotions to his diary.[19] Having frittered away the financial

[13] See Brian Ó Conchubhair, 'What Happened to Literary Modernism in the Irish-Language Short Story?', in Elke D'hoker and Stephanie Eggermont (eds), The Irish Short Story: Traditions and Trends (Bern: Peter Lang, 2014), 121–47.

[14] Ó Grianna, brother of Seosamh Mac Grianna, was one of the most prolific authors of this period and arguably the master documentarian of the quotidian Gaeltacht experience. If there comes a moment in every novelist's career where they must decide whether to plough the same furrow that earned them success or explore new pastures, Ó Grianna never experienced that moment, or if he did, remained content to follow his plough fastidiously.

[15] See Aisling Ní Dhonnchadha, An Gearrscéal sa Ghaeilge, 1898–1940 (Baile Átha Cliath: An Clóchomhar Tta., 1981) and Máirín Nic Eoin, An Litríocht Réigiúnach (Baile Átha Cliath: An Clóchomhar Tta., 1982).

[16] Walter Benjamin, Illuminations, trans. Harry Zohn (London: Jonathan Cape, 1970), 87–8.

[17] Alan Titley, 'The Novel in Irish', in John Wilson Foster (ed.), The Cambridge Companion to the Irish Novel (Cambridge: Cambridge University Press, 2006), 174; James M. Cahalan, The Irish Novel: A Critical History (Boston, PA: Twayne, 1988), 122.

[18] Cahalan, The Irish Novel, 117.

[19] Cahalan sees similarities to Brecht, Beckett, Flannery O'Connor, and Carson McCullers in Ó Conaire's expressionistic depiction of Micheál's physical and psychological condition. See The Irish Novel, 118.

compensation from his accident, Ó Maoláin performs as a freak in a travelling circus. The circus manager, 'an Fear Beag Buí' (the Little Yellow Man), contrives a marriage between Micheál and his daughter, the Fat Lady, as a joint new attraction. Later, when the circus tours Ireland, Micheál encounters former friends in Galway. When his past and present collide, Ó Maoláin destroys the circus in a rage. Destitute once again, he returns to London, rejecting all efforts to rescue him. Once more his past and present collide when the Fat Lady, the socialist Big Red-haired Woman, and his former romantic attachment from Galway gather to save him; but, again, he cannot reconcile the various strands of his life and experience. Ultimately, Micheál dies in a park in London under suspicious circumstances. Only then do we learn that the narrator, à la Flann O'Brien's *The Third Policeman* (1967), has been dead all along.[20]

Deoraíocht may be read, as it was by early critics, as a cautionary tale of the perils of emigration or as Ó Conaire's attempt to capture the uprooted individual's experience of urban modernity and its effect on human dignity and sensibility. Certainly, the novel offers a searing critique of modernity's impact on the organic community spirit and traditional way of life of rural people in early twentieth-century Ireland. It also elucidates the emigrant's interior life, vividly recreating his wretched displacement and his alienating and alienated experience in a capitalist bureaucratic system. Ó Conaire's most modernist and most intense work, the novel persistently returns the reader to the narrator's felt reality, to his pain, confusion, and frustration. Yet, such is the narrator's egomaniacal solipsism that he is eminently dislikeable and readily detestable. A prime candidate for the title of first anti-hero in Irish-language prose fiction, Micheál's loathsomeness results from the revelation of his inner thoughts and emotional reactions to the world around him.

Deoraíocht, a fictional narrative without a clear start or end, is an episodic novel based, we later learn, on a series of letters and diaries written by the main character and compiled for our benefit by an unknown friend. Bram Stoker (1847–1912) in *Dracula* (1897) and Joseph Conrad in *Lord Jim* (1900) employed a similar organizing principle, and like the latter, *Deoraíocht* comprises a fragmented series of events narrated by an unreliable, unpredictable, and unsavoury individual. The use of a narrator who finds the cripple's diary indicates a Marlow-like awareness of the limits of the novel and narrative structure; it also denotes a clear rejection of the omniscient narrative voice in the emerging Irish-language novel, as practised by Peadar Ó Laoghaire, Úna McClintock Dix (1880–1958), Liam Ó Rinn (1886–1943), Seán Ó Ruadháin (1883–1966), Séamus Ó Grianna, Micheál and Pádraig Ó Siochfhradha, Éamonn Mac Giolla Iasachta (1887–1986), and Seán Mac Maoláin (1884–1973). The voice that narrates *Deoraíocht* stands between the reader and the events narrated, opening up a distance—and a space for interpretation—that is notably absent from the fictional works of Ó Conaire's aforementioned contemporaries. In artistic terms, the narrator's position is similar to that of the *Rückenfigur* (literally meaning 'back figure') in pictorial art, the figure who is simultaneously part of and apart from the painted landscape, more mediator than actor.

---

[20] Cahalan, *The Irish Novel*, 118.

Moreover, the broken syntax and disjointed thought patterns in chapter four gesture towards a proto-stream of consciousness style which, while somewhat suggestive of Joyce, is much more in line with the alternative form identified by Franco Moretti as a stream of consciousness 'for exceptional circumstances: fainting, delirium, suicide, death-agony (or, more innocuously: walking, drunkenness, sleeplessness, panic).'[21] This technique, argues Moretti, 'is a system, a signal but little more. Before Leopold Bloom is reached, there is still a long way to go.'[22]

The verbal and temporal swings that characterize the book's style embody the modernist attitude whereby style 'is no longer merely the expression of meaning but rather a process that makes meaning possible in the first place.'[23] If, as Moretti observes of T. S. Eliot, 'thinking in fragments' marks 'the characteristic feature of the modern individual', then the novel's diaristic form may be seen as symptomatic of 'the contemporary disorder' wrought by modernity.[24] Ó Conaire's narrator, unable to integrate his life experiences into a unified whole, is himself a fragment, physically, emotionally, psychologically, and linguistically. Division and duality shadow him throughout, whether in the form of his struggles to reconcile his present with his past or his bilingualism (he speaks both Irish and English in London and Galway). When we glimpse the world through his bitter eyes and comprehend it through his tormented mind, we see flashes of a disturbing reality, one which, to cite Jonathan Jones on Vincent Van Gogh, 'is not an objective record of a misfortune but, in its hypnotic intensity, a portrait of the artist both martyred and liberated by madness.'[25]

The novel's 'untidiness' may therefore be read as a central element of its design rather than an unintended result of Ó Conaire's stylistic choices. Style, Remy de Gourmont suggested in 1902, is a question of physiology: 'we write, as we feel, as we think, with our entire body'.[26] It follows that a one-handed, one-legged, unbalanced man will not provide a steady linear narrative. Rather, the textual gaps and omissions are features of form and personality. Micheál, as Maud Ellmann says of Stephen Dedalus, is 'dismembering, not developing but devolving, not achieving an identity but dissolving into a nameless scar'.[27] Louis de Paor underlines this link between form and theme when he says of the novel:

> The physical disintegration of the central character is accompanied by an existential crisis of identity as he descends into the grotesque underworld of a travelling freak show. Despite the clumsiness of its structure, the novel's interrogation of dislocation

[21] Franco Moretti, *Modern Epic: The World System from Goethe to García Márquez*, trans. Quintin Hoare (New York: Verso, 1996), 174.

[22] Ibid., 170.

[23] Ben Hutchinson, *Modernism and Style* (Basingstoke: Palgrave Macmillan, 2011), 35.

[24] Moretti, *Modern Epic*, 186. See also Angela Bourke, 'Legless in London: Pádraic Ó Conaire and Éamon a Burc', *Éire-Ireland* 38, nos. 3–4 (2003), 54–67.

[25] Jonathan Jones, 'The whole truth about Van Gogh's ear, and why his "mad genius" is a myth', *Guardian*, 12 July 2016.

[26] Quoted in Hutchinson, *Modernism and Style*, 33.

[27] Maud Ellmann, 'Disremembering Dedalus: *A Portrait of the Artist as a Young Man*', in Robert Young (ed.), *Untying the Text: A Post-Structuralist Reader* (London: Routledge and Kegan Paul, 1981), 194.

and despair, of marginalization and isolation, is in keeping with the central preoccu-pations of European modernism.[28]

Ó Conaire's portrait of this crippled Irishman, then, represents the first effort, intel-lectually and stylistically, to engage with modernity and the concerns of modernism in the Irish-language novel. He finds beauty and humanity not in nature, history, or myth, as favoured by folklorists and his literary peers, but in ugly, degenerate London and its freak shows. As a novel marked by the stylistic, thematic, and generic concerns of early modernism, *Deoraíocht* offers what Ford Madox Ford called 'the impression not the corrected chronicle';[29] which is to say, it provides life as experienced in the moment rather than subsequently reordered, sequenced, and intellectualized. For Ó Conaire, as for Georg Lukács, the modernist experience is one of disconnection: external reality is unintelligible and in turn reinforces an internal sense of inalterabil-ity. Human action is both ineffectual and insincere. All that remains is an unpredictable world, one dominated by angst, regret, fear, and uncertainty.[30] The constant anxiety that grips Micheál Ó Maoláin echoes both Søren Kierkegaard's *The Concept of Anxiety* (1844) and Fyodor Dostoevsky's *Notes from the Underground* (1864). The London of this book—and, for that matter, the Galway—lacks any sense of commu-nity. The temporary sanctuary that the working men's hostel and the circus provide is illusionary. In this world, the past with its traditions and rituals is irrevocably sun-dered from the senseless, disjointed present. Ó Conaire leaves us with a perspective on humanity that echoes that of Schiller in *On the Aesthetic Education of Man* (1795): 'Everlastingly chained to a single little fragment of the Whole, man himself develops into nothing but a fragment.'[31]

While *Deoraíocht* explores concerns that would later animate Joyce and Beckett, the novel is in some respects closer to the less formally experimental work of Conrad, Lawrence, and Forster. Certain elements of *Deoraíocht* are clearly derived from Conrad—*The Nigger of the 'Narcissus'* (1897) as much as *Almayer's Folly* (1895), as well as the aforementioned *Lord Jim*—and the novel also shares similarities in tone and style with Knut Hamsun's *Sult* (Hunger, 1890). Stephen Matthews argues that such authors, while pursuing a version of realism found in the nineteenth-century novel and offering key insights into 'the social, imperial and industrial realities of their time', also explored 'the psyche of those entrapped by these modern realities' and 'displayed a focus that they held in common with many more technically-experimental modern-ist writers and modernist thinkers'.[32] With *Deoraíocht*, Ó Conaire became part of this

[28] Louis de Paor, 'Irish Language Modernisms', in Joe Cleary (ed.), *The Cambridge Companion to Irish Modernism* (Cambridge: Cambridge University Press, 2014), 164.

[29] Ford Madox Ford, *Critical Writings of Ford Madox Ford*, ed. Frank MacShane (Lincoln, NE: University of Nebraska Press, 1964), 41.

[30] See Georg Lukács, *The Theory of the Novel*, trans. Anna Bostock (Monmouth: Merlin Press, 2006), 36.

[31] Friedrich Schiller, *On the Aesthetic Education of Man, in a Series of Letters*, trans. Elizabeth M. Wilkinson and L. A. Willoughby (Oxford: Clarendon Press, 1967), 35.

[32] Steven Matthews (ed.), *Modernism: A Sourcebook* (Basingstoke: Palgrave Macmillan, 2008), 26.

continuum of Edwardian experimental modernist writers. Like them, he sought to express the immediate impact of modernity on the individual, relying less on traditional plot and sentimentality—as understood in the English-language novel and the emerging Irish-language novel tradition—and more on unreliable narration and experimental techniques. Whereas Ó Conaire's Irish-language contemporaries focused on linguistic preservation and were closely attuned to meeting readers' expectations, his novel marks the moment when the Irish-language novelist becomes aware of his alienation from the dominant values of bourgeois culture and seeks to expand the reader's perceptual and symbolic horizons. *Deoraíocht* marks the advent of a critical self-consciousness within the twentieth-century Irish-language prose fiction tradition.

SUBALTERN ORACLES SPEAK: THE RISE OF THE GAELTACHT AUTOBIOGRAPHY

Despite such a promising start, literary modernism subsequently made little headway in Irish. The publication of Arnold Ussher's translation of Brian Merriman's (*c*.1750–1805) eighteenth-century poem, *Cúirt an Mheán Oíche* (The Midnight Court), in *Klaxon* in 1923 ostensibly marks the first formal contact in print of the Irish language with European high modernism in the newly declared Irish Free State.[33] *Klaxon*, edited by A. J. Leventhal, with a 'Brancusi-like cover device and a "Negro sculpture in wood" as frontispiece',[34] was the first, short-lived little magazine published in the new state. Its origins lay in Séamus O'Sullivan's failed attempt to publish a lengthy review article on *Ulysses* in the *Dublin Magazine*, which Dollard's, one of the largest printing houses in Dublin, promptly refused to publish. With its Vorticist-like cover, this Irish *Blast* illustrated the concerns of some of Ireland's young intellectuals; it signified, claimed George Russell (1867–1935), the voice of 'Irish youth . . . trying desperately to be wild and wicked without the capacity to be anything else but young'.[35] The editorial of the first (and only) issue in the winter of 1923 brashly claimed: 'We railed against the psychopedantic parlours of our elders and their old maidenly consorts, hoping the while with an excess

---

[33] In 'The Best Irish Poem', published in *Dana* in February 1905, John Eglinton had already identified Merriman's poem as a text that 'registered both the discontinuities in Ireland's cultural tradition and the country's present circumstances'. See Dathalinn M. O'Dea, 'Modernist Nationalism in *Dana*: An Irish Magazine of Independent Thought', *Éire-Ireland* 45, nos. 3–4 (2010), 105. The poem has been translated into English, Esperanto (1980), Scots-Gaelic (1985), German (1905, 1986), French (2000), and Japanese (2014). See Brian Ó Conchubhair (ed.), *The Midnight Court/Cúirt an Mheán Oíche: A Critical Edition* (Syracuse, NY: Syracuse University Press, 2011), 107–22.

[34] Tim Armstrong, 'Muting the Klaxon: Poetry, History, and Irish Modernism', in Patricia Coughlan and Alex Davis (eds), *Modernism and Ireland: The Poetry of the 1930s* (Cork: Cork University Press, 1995), 43.

[35] Cited in William T. O'Malley, 'Modernism's Irish *Klaxon*' (2003). Technical Services Department Faculty Publications. Paper 19. http://digitalcommons.uri.edu/lib_ts_pubs/19. Accessed 29 June 2018.

of Picabia and banter, a whiff of Dadaist Europe to kick Ireland into artistic wakefulness.'[36]

Although it might seem incongruous alongside articles on Joyce and Picasso, there was a certain logic to the inclusion of Ussher's translation. *Cúirt an Mheán Oíche* is the dream account of a man who is summoned to a subterranean court, convened at midnight, where women and men give voice to sexual frustrations and interrogate social practices involved in courtship, mating, and social intercourse in late eighteenth-century Ireland. At the poem's conclusion, the female judge orders the narrator, found guilty of being single despite his age, to be stripped and whipped by the available women. With that, he awakes, just in time, from his dream fantasy. In addition to psychoanalytical readings of the poem as expressing the author's unconscious desires and suppressed anxieties, it is also considered a possible inspiration for both the 'Circe' episode in *Ulysses* and Molly's closing soliloquy.[37] *Klaxon* lasted but one issue; the potential for marrying the older Irish-language tradition with modernism would have to wait until the 1950s and Máire Mhac an tSaoi's (1922–) landmark poem, 'Ceathrúintí Mháire Ní Ógáin' (Mary Hogan's Quatrains).

Little of sustained and serious merit appeared in Irish-language prose fiction in the intervening decades, during which folkloric models re-emerged to dominate the literature of the 1920s and 1930s. An Gúm (the Scheme), the official Irish-language publisher, produced texts committed to nation-building and linguistic retrieval.[38] Established in 1926 and charged with publishing textbooks and original fiction in Irish, it soon turned to the translation of classic and contemporary texts to provide popular reading, including *Béal na hUaighe agus Scéalta Eile* (The Mouth of the Grave and Other Stories, 1927),[39] *An Fuadach* (Kidnapped, 1931), *Dracula* (1933), *Árda Wuthering* (Wuthering Heights, 1933), and *Scéal Lorna Doone* (Lorna Doone, 1934).[40] Original works in Irish published by An Gúm at this time embodied the belief that Irish peasant life contained the basis for a harmonious, rational, humane society, a utopian view that was far removed from the wretched reality of those who lived it. They included *Fánaí* (Wanderer, 1927) by Seán Óg Ó Caomhánaigh (1885–1946); *Lucht Ceoil* (Music People, 1932) by Barra Ó Caochlaigh (pseudonym of Art Ó Riain, 1893–1968); *Cailín na Gruaige Duinne* (The Brown Haired Girl, 1932) by 'Brenda', the pen-name of Úna McClintock Dix; and *Lá agus Oidhche* (Day and Night, 1929) by Mícheál Mac Liammóir (pseudonym of Alfred Willmore, 1899–1978). Most of these texts, both original and those translated into Irish, fall into Clement Greenberg's

---

[36] Armstrong, 'Muting the Klaxon', 43.

[37] See James A. W. Heffernan, 'Joyce's Merrimanic Heroine: Molly vs. Bloom in Midnight Court', *James Joyce Quarterly* 41, no. 4 (2004), 745–65.

[38] See Philip O'Leary, *Gaelic Prose in the Irish Free State, 1922–1939* (Dublin: University College Dublin Press, 2004), Alan Titley, *An tÚrscéal Gaeilge* (Baile Átha Cliath: An Clóchomhar Tta., 1991), and Gearóidín Uí Laighléis, *Gallán an Ghúim* (Baile Átha Cliath: Coiscéim, 2017).

[39] Translated by Leon Ó Broin, this volume includes translations of works by Prosper Mérimée, Émile Souvestre, Alphonse Daudet, Edmond About, Guy de Maupassant, A. S. Pushkin, and Jerome K. Jerome.

[40] See Brian Ó Conchubhair, 'An Gúm and the Irish Language Dust-Jacket', in Linda King and Elaine Sisson (eds), *Ireland, Design and Visual Culture: Negotiating Modernity, 1922–1992* (Cork: Cork University Press, 2011), 93–113.

category of kitsch or Georg Lukács's notion of entertainment. Few, if any, could be described as avant-garde, serious, or representative. Despite their tremendous linguistic and anthropological value, they tend to be plot-driven, sentimental, and cliché-ridden.

Aside from these works, the major contribution to Irish-language prose literature in this period was the Gaeltacht autobiography.[41] Written by rural, Catholic native-speakers of Irish—the new state's most cherished citizens—these insider accounts from the western littoral were read as exemplary embodiments of the nation's spirit that pre-figured a cultural unity to be shared by all, their depiction of poverty and deprivation notwithstanding.[42] Materially poor but spiritually, linguistically, and culturally rich, these sententious texts quickly resonated with the public, offering readers access to a seemingly enchanted world and allowing them to engage vicariously in a narrative of communal suffering for a greater good. Many are postcards from a place and society that never existed but which created a caricature that stuck, for better and worse. Such respite from reality was in short supply during the depressed 1930s and 1940s.

The key text here is Tomas Ó Criomhthain's *An t-Oileánach*. Completed in 1923, it was published by the Talbot Press in 1929 in a version edited by Pádraig Ó Siochfhradha, who wrote under the sobriquet 'An Seabhac' (the Hawk). The first English translation by Robin Flower appeared five years later.[43] Readers, still coming to terms with the slaugh-ter and wide-scale destruction wrought by the First World War on the continent and the turmoil of revolution and civil war at home, found solace in a heroic story of self-sufficiency, perseverance, and daily struggle played out in a hostile, primeval landscape. So successful was it that it inaugurated what in Jamesonian terms could be described as 'a whole aesthetic of repetition',[44] exemplified by works such as Muiris Ó Súilleabháin's (1904–50) *Fiche Bliain ag Fás* (Twenty Years A-Growing, 1933), Peig Sayers's (1873–1958) *Peig* (1939), and Séamus Ó Grianna's *Nuair a Bhí Mé Óg* (When I was Young, 1942). Largely lacking a unique authorial signature, such works were fetishized by the Free State. Such was their sway that they rose to the level of national paragon, at which Flann O'Brien took satiric aim in his weekly *Irish Times* column and in *An Béal Bocht*.

Recent scholarship, however, has challenged the received interpretation of *An t-Oileánach* and *Fiche Bliain ag Fás*. Mark Quigley provocatively reads these autobiog-raphies less as expressions of naïve autoethnography and more as works of late modern-ism that resist the reifying demands of official state nationalism, which sought to frame the

---

[41] See Declan Kiberd, *Irish Classics* (Cambridge, MA: Harvard University Press, 2001), 521–42, Irene Lucchitti, *The Islandman: The Hidden Life of Tomás O'Crohan* (Bern: Peter Lang, 2009), and Máirín Nic Eoin, *An Litríocht Réigiúnach* (Baile Átha Cliath: An Clóchomhar Tta., 1982).

[42] David Lloyd, *Nationalism and Minor Literature: James Clarence Mangan and the Emergence of Irish Cultural Nationalism* (Berkeley, CA: University of California Press, 1987), 160–5.

[43] Oifig An tSoláthair/Muinntir C. S. Ó Fallamhain Teo. published Ó Siochfhradha's edited version *An t-Oileánach: Scéal a Bheathadh Féin* in 1929. The book was extensively reprinted in subsequent dec-ades and it also went through many English-language editions, most of them under the imprint of Oxford University Press. *An t-Oileánach* appeared in German as *Die Boote fahren nicht mehr aus* in 1960, in French as *L'Homme des îles* in 1994, and in Danish as *Manden på øen* in 1996. Garry Bannister and David Sowby published an unabridged English-language translation in 2012.

[44] Fredric Jameson, *The Antinomies of Realism* (London: Verso, 2013), 144.

rugged islander as the emblem of postcolonial primitivism.[45] As such, he contends, they not only muddle modernism's ontological and aesthetic orderings but 'shatter the division between anthropological object and observing subject that organizes the artistic consciousness of the earlier generation of modernists shaped by a late-imperial age'.[46] Relying less on the pyrotechnic literary techniques of high modernism, *An t-Oileánach* 'highlights the generic pressures of postcolonial autobiography' through Ó Criomhthain's 'ongoing frustration of the genre's demand for disclosure. He thus effectively turns the genre upon itself to produce an autobiography of "tradition" rather than of himself'.[47] Instead of positing the native speaker as the salvation of a dissociated subjectivity, as early modernists attempted, Quigley recasts Ó Criomhthain as a writer who critiques the modern postcolonial subject from a late modernist perspective, thus prefiguring the mid-century fiction of Samuel Beckett.[48] Nevertheless, *An t-Oileánach*'s success not only inaugurated but validated an anthropological and sociological turn in Irish-language writing.

The fetishization of such literary images of Gaeltacht life and native speakers posed challenges to Irish-language writers. Such was the success of these autobiographies and the widespread acceptance of the typologies they offered that they threatened to flatten and generalize the diversity of Irish speakers' individual identities and experiences. The sanitized, non-controversial version of rural life presented in *An t-Oileánach* perversely became the typical representation of the Irish-speaking world. The challenge those authors who rejected the cultural-nationalist paradigm faced was to capture the Gaeltacht experience without sensationalizing, emotionalizing, or making an anecdote of it. Modernism would ironically provide the answer for native speakers and Gaeltacht-born writers who had left their western coastal homes and travelled to Dublin and beyond, where they came of age in a violent and politically unstable period of world history.

As modernists internationally sought newer, more innovative forms that would allow them to mould, shape, and share their perceptions and immediate experiences, many began to reject the genre of autobiography, or at least that version of autobiography that comprised a 'description of reality in the form of the coherent interpretation of a succession of events starting from a given beginning to a predictable end'.[49] But as modernism developed, the role of the artist advanced, to the point where 'the artist was increasingly envisaged as a manipulator of reality—a myth maker—rather than as someone concerned with faithfully representing the actual'.[50] With this came new approaches to life-writing, among them the rise of 'fictionalized autobiography preoccupied with the shift from early experience towards a more alienated and unsettled maturity within modernity',[51] exemplified by Gertrude Stein's *The Autobiography of Alice B. Toklas* (1933), which elevated the

---

[45] Mark Quigley, *Empire's Wake: Postcolonial Irish Writing and the Politics of Modern Literary Form* (New York: Fordham University Press, 2013), 18.

[46] Ibid., 2.   [47] Ibid., 32.

[48] Ibid., 2–3. See also Gregory Castle, *Modernism and the Celtic Revival* (Cambridge: Cambridge University Press, 2001).

[49] Mirjana M. Knežević, 'Postmodernist Approach to Biography: *The Last Testament of Oscar Wilde* by Peter Ackroyd', *Facta Universitatis, Linguistics and Literature* 11, no. 1 (2013), 47–54.

[50] Paul Poplawski, *Encyclopedia of Literary Modernism* (Westport, CT: Greenwood Publishing Group, 2003), 272.

[51] Matthews (ed.), *Modernism*, 4.

genre to the level of a legitimate and intricate art form. So while An Gúm continued to churn out Gaeltacht stories, certain Irish-language authors began to chart their own routes through which to map their particular late modernist experiences.

SEOSAMH MAC GRIANNA: A DISRUPTIVE ARTICULATION OF BEING

If Ó Criomhthain, as documentarian of the quotidian, successfully raised his insider's account of daily island life, devoid of interiority, to mythic levels, few if any of his imitators matched his achievement. *An t-Oileánach* sparked a slew of imitations from native speakers in other Irish-speaking regions but moved certain others to tell their individual experiences in different forms, forms that were neither traditional nor in keeping with national expectations but which were in line with modernist trends and styles. Collectively, these writers provided powerful counter-testimony to that offered by the island authors whose work the nascent state idealized. One such writer was Liam O'Flaherty (1897–1984)—a native speaker from the Aran Islands, a British Army First World War veteran, a socialist, and a participant in the Irish Civil War—who emerged in the 1920s as a daring novelist and short story writer in English as well as in Irish. In partial response to *An t-Oileánach*'s success, he penned *Two Years* in 1930 and *Shame the Devil* in 1934, two non-traditional memoirs.

Another was Seosamh Mac Grianna, whose 1940 memoir-cum-fictionalized autobiography, *Mo Bhealach Féin*, was also inspired by *An t-Oileánach*.[52] Born in Ranafast in the Donegal Gaeltacht into a family of storytellers, Mac Grianna, who initially wrote as 'Iolann Fionn', was a more polished and nuanced writer than his brother, Séamus Ó Grianna, who wrote under the sobriquet 'Máire'. After an erratic second-level education, he qualified from St Patrick's College in Drumcondra as a primary schoolteacher in 1921. During the Civil War he was interned as a republican combatant. From 1933, he worked for many years as a translator for An Gúm, years that exerted a costly creative and psychological toll. Mac Grianna was attuned to the pervasive sense of disenchantment and the crisis engulfing Irish and European culture in the 1930s. Bereft and solitary, his personal life was unconventional. The mid-1930s found him in Grangegorman psychiatric hospital; by the 1950s, he was living in dire conditions in Clontarf. In 1959, his only son drowned in Howth and his wife later allegedly committed suicide. Having entered St

---

[52] For criticism, see Fionntán de Brún, *Seosamh Mac Grianna: An Mhéin Rúin* (Baile Átha Cliath: An Clóchomhar Tta., 2002), 117–39; Declan Kiberd, '*Mo Bhealach Féin*: Idir Dhá Thraidisiún', *Scríobh 5* (1981), 224–39; Liam Ó Dochartaigh, '*Mo Bhealach Féin*: Saothar Nualitríochta', *Scríobh 5* (1981), 240–7; and Brian Ó Conchubhair, 'Seosamh Mac Grianna: A Bhealach Féin', in John Walsh and Peadar Ó Muircheartaigh (eds), *Ag Siúl an Bhealaigh Mhóir: Aistí in Ómós don Ollamh Nollaig Mac Congáil* (Baile Átha Cliath: Leabhair Chomhar, 2016), 126–53. *Báire na Fola*, Mac Grianna's long-lost novel about the Invincibles and the informer James Carey, has recently been discovered and displays a range of literary styles and narrative strategies.

Conal's Psychiatric Hospital in Letterkenny, Mac Grianna disappeared from public view while undergoing treatment for schizophrenia. He died in care in 1990.[53]

None of his early life experiences—neither his upbringing, his distinguished family background, his college years, nor his period of political activism—find their way into *Mo Bhealach Féin*, a first-person account of living in rented accommodation in 1930s Dublin by 'a character that bears some resemblance'[54] to Mac Grianna himself. The book describes the narrator's involvement with landladies, the IRA, and the Salvation Army. It also recounts his theft of a small boat in which to sail to Wales, where he proceeds to lead a black resistance movement in Cardiff. Comparable to O'Flaherty's *Two Years* and George Orwell's *Down and Out in London and Paris* (1933) and *The Road to Wigan Pier* (1937), *Mo Bhealach Féin* is a profoundly honest and often scathing critique of the stulti-fying intellectual climate of the Free State, in which Mac Grianna examines the role of the nonconformist artist in the pursuit of truth. Written prior to the author's tragic men-tal breakdown, it provides a frightening insight into a brilliant and bellicose but also a dark and unbalanced mind. For Seamus Deane, the view of Mac Grianna that emerges is that of 'a man deeply disturbed by his creative gift, by its own peremptory nature, and by the double sense of estrangement and superiority which it bequeathed to him'.[55]

Whereas many authors published by An Gúm sought to recover the lost qualities of a vestigial Gaeltacht and envisioned native culture as a panacea for modernity, Anglicization, and urbanization, Mac Grianna, like Ó Conaire, recognized that the old patterns and beliefs no longer sufficed. Cultural nationalism and adherence to political dogma, like the-ology, could only take one so far. Thus, *Mo Bhealach Féin* eschews standard tropes and immerses the reader in the *demi-monde* of backstreet Dublin. Unconcerned with early life experiences, it focuses instead on adult alienation. The narrator, permanently on edge, alternately cowed and violent, is all too recognizable as 'a mind at war with the world, act-ing the part of the superior artist but ultimately suffering for it'.[56] *Mo Bhealach Féin* exists as part of the European trend towards fictionalized autobiography, exemplified by such canonical modernist texts as D. H. Lawrence's *Sons and Lovers* (1913), Katherine Mansfield's *Prelude* (1916), Joyce's *A Portrait of the Artist as a Young Man* (1916), and E. M. Forster's *A Passage to India* (1924), all of which reflect upon personal experience from an estranged and estranging perspective. Drawing on a variety of genres, including crime *noir*, murder mysteries, travelogues, adventure narratives, and espionage fiction, Mac Grianna's style is as changeable and transient as his narrator. Furthermore, he refashions autobiographical material throughout and combines it with wholly fictional matter. If the extent to which specific parts of *Mo Bhealach Féin* are factual or fictional is unknown and a matter of debate, this should not overly concern us for, as Hélène Cixous asserts, there is little if any

---

[53] For a fuller biographical account, see Pól Ó Muirí, *Seosamh Mac Grianna: Míreanna Saoil* (Indreabhán: Cló Iar-Chonnacht, 2007) and *A Flight from Shadow: The Life and Work of Seosamh Mac Grianna* (Belfast: Lagan Press, 1999).

[54] Titley, 'The Novel in Irish', 179.

[55] Seamus Deane, '*Mo Bhealach Féin*', in John Jordan (ed.), *The Pleasures of Gaelic Literature* (Dublin: Mercier Press, 1977), 54.

[56] Titley, 'The Novel in Irish', 179.

difference between biography, autobiography, and other narrative forms: they all 'tell one story in place of another'.[57]

Mo Bhealach Féin chimes with modernist life narratives that explore failure: failure at the level of social integration but also the failure to meet or accept 'a goal recognized as valuable by the community' or nation, which 'is itself a kind of success'.[58] The book's coruscating preface is in many ways a modernist manifesto rather than an explanatory foreword. It places the work formally in an Irish context, where An Gúm, the official state publishing house, dominated literary production. In the narrative proper, Mac Grianna's narrator asserts 'his own absolute freedom from convention'[59] and in the process becomes not only a spokesperson for alienated urban Irish-speakers—Gaeltacht expats, so to speak—but also for those who, regardless of language, nation, or cultural affiliation, felt isolated, deracinated, and disaffected in 1930s Europe. As in *Deoraíocht*, we encounter an outsider angrily rejecting the world, a protagonist estranged from a bourgeois culture he finds oppressive.

Mo Bhealach Féin concludes with the narrator's optimistic statement that 'Tá an saol mór lán den fhilíocht ag an té dar dual a tuigbheáil, agus ní thráfaidh an tobar go deo na ndeor' (The great world is full of poetry for the person able to understand it, and the well will never run dry).[60] Such optimism proved short-lived in reality, however. In the summer of 1935, Mac Grianna abandoned the novel on which he was working, *Dá mBíodh Ruball ar an Éan*. The text trails off dramatically with a stark admission: 'Thráigh an tobar sa tsamhradh, 1935. Ní scríobhfaidh mé níos mó. Rinne mé mo dhícheall agus is cuma liom' (The well ran dry in the summer, 1935. I will write no more. I did my utmost and I don't care).[61] Thus the narrative stalls, unresolved and irresolvable, leaving the reader with nothing but bitterly human distress. Despite its incomplete status, the novel, in which the journal narrator discovers the secret diary of an artist held prisoner by political subversives, was published as an appendix to *Mo Bhealach Féin* in 1940 and reprinted in 1941.

Dá mBíodh Ruball ar an Éan questions the commitment to artistic freedom in places such as the Irish Free State, where the tension between Romantic and Enlightenment values is replayed in the friction between nationalism and individualism: national liberation transposes individual freedom to a collective plane but in doing so risks curtailing it.[62] Commencing and concluding abruptly without a traditional start or finale, the plot centres on a visual artist who abandons his existing romantic techniques in favour of a 'cubist-classical' style. In addition to expressing his artistic dilemmas through painting, the artist records his inner thoughts and feelings in his diary, portions of which form the

---

[57] Hélène Cixous, *Rootprints: Memory and Life Writing* (London: Routledge, 1997), 178.

[58] John Paul Riquelme, 'Modernist Transformations of Life Narrative: From Wilde and Woolf to Bechdel and Rushdie', *Modern Fiction Studies* 59, no. 3 (2013), 466.

[59] de Paor, 'Irish Language Modernisms', 165.

[60] Seosamh Mac Grianna, *Mo Bhealach Féin* (Baile Átha Cliath: Oifig an tSoláthair, 1965), 173.

[61] Seosamh Mac Grianna, *Dá mBíodh Ruball ar an Éan* (Baile Átha Cliath: An Gúm, 1992), 94–5.

[62] On this point, see Terry Eagleton, *Heathcliff and the Great Hunger: Studies in Irish Culture* (London: Verso, 1996), 235.

novel's text. Mac Grianna's use of a confessional voice, constantly alternating perspectives, and adaptation of cinematic techniques associated with *film noir*, detective movies, and thrillers mark *Dá mBíodh Ruball ar an Éan* out as a modernist text, as does its perspective on the artist's role and function in 1930s society.[63] One contemporary commentator remarked: 'In mood and texture it reminded me constantly of French novelists, now of Mauriac's *Le Noeud de Vipères*, again of Duchamel. This style, with all the substance which has made it and for which it has been made, I take to be one of the indisputable achievements of modern Gaelic letters.'[64]

Mac Grianna shares Beckett's antipathy to art and literature being conscripted to serve political agendas and state ideologies. He also questions whether, in the politically turbulent 1930s, artists should concede authority to the new political formations that emerged to challenge the status quo or allow their work, beliefs, and manifestos to be debauched for ideological or material gain.[65] In its call for literature to cease day-tripping to the Gaeltacht, its rejection of ideologically aligned art, and its refreshingly novel use of a contemporary vernacular, *Dá mBíodh Ruball ar an Éan* adumbrated aspects of *An Béal Bocht* and paved the way for *Cré na Cille* less than a decade later. In comparing the philosophical and ethical similarities shared by the works of Beckett and Ó Cadhain—that writing could itself exist as the afterlife of expression, with momentous consequences for the novel and for drama—Fintan O'Toole notes that 'something of the same notion was brewing in the minds of writers whose social, linguistic, and political backgrounds were completely different from Beckett's.'[66] One such writer was Seosamh Mac Grianna.

If it may be argued that Tomás Ó Criomhthain furtively turned the traditional autobiography upon itself to acknowledge an experience freighted with modernity, Pádraic Ó Conaire and Seosamh Mac Grianna firmly turned to mainstream European literary modernism to express their and others' experiences of dislocation, fragmentation, and isolation. Modernism is the literary, cultural, and intellectual context that shapes the works discussed here and links them with later Irish-language modernists such as Máirtín Ó Cadhain, Eoghan Ó Tuairisc, and Diarmuid Ó Súilleabháin. It should not surprise that Mac Grianna saw in Ó Conaire a kindred spirit and literary mentor, as is evident from his 1936 collection, *Pádraic Ó Conaire agus Aistí Eile* (Pádraic Ó Conaire and Other Essays).[67] Both writers felt alienated and estranged from mainstream society. Both fell foul of the state and authorities on whom they heavily relied for survival as artists. Both refused to participate in the project of producing literature as cultural, nationalist, or linguistic propaganda. Both had creative work censored and considerably delayed. Both resolved not to repeat the confused and half-thought-through actions of their predecessors, which, far from shedding light on the human condition, only muddied the waters. And both rejected the mode of writing—as demanded by An tAthair

---

[63] See de Brún, *Seosamh Mac Grianna*, 159–82.
[64] Roibeard Ó Faracháin, 'Seosamh Mac Grianna', *The Bell* 1, no. 2 (1940), 64.
[65] Quigley, *Empire's Wake*, 73–4, 140.
[66] Fintan O'Toole, 'Finding a Lost Ireland', *New York Review of Books*, 17 December 2015.
[67] See de Brún, *Seosamh Mac Grianna*, 141–58.

Peadar—that tells a smooth story with a beginning, a middle, and an end, and which in the process assuages and reassures.

Being modern, according to Roland Barthes, means knowing that some things can no longer be done. Ó Conaire and Mac Grianna each recognized and felt that reality. Consequently, their styles and modes of writing differ radically from those of writers that preceded them, in that they retreat from the polemics of cultural nationalism, eschew rural linguistic purity, and reject the comforts of certainty in their exploration of the complexities of modern existence. Their novels refuse to fetishize those on the geographical or cultural margins or validate idealism through affirmations of sacrifice and suffering. Instead of retreating into a past that never was, they open their confused minds to us. Their texts are deeply implicated in the advent of a critical self-consciousness within the Irish-language prose tradition. In contrast to almost all other prose texts of the period from 1880 to 1940, the writings of Pádraic Ó Conaire and Seosamh Mac Grianna return the reader to life more violently, making them more aware and alert to the moment and the experience of modern living.

FURTHER READING

de Brún, Fionntán. *Seosamh Mac Grianna: An Mhéin Rúin*. Baile Átha Cliath: An Clóchomhar Tta., 2002.

Kiberd, Declan. *Irish Classics*. Cambridge, MA: Harvard University Press, 2001.

Lucchitti, Irene. *The Islandman: The Hidden Life of Tomás O'Crohan*. Bern: Peter Lang, 2009.

Ní Chionnaith, Eibhlín. *Pádraic Ó Conaire: Scéal a Bheatha*. Indreabhán: Cló Iar-Chonnacht, 1995.

Ní Dhonnchadha, Aisling. *An Gearrscéal sa Ghaeilge*. Baile Átha Cliath: An Clóchomhar Tta., 1981.

Nic Eoin, Máirín. *An Litríocht Réigiúnach*. Baile Átha Cliath: An Clóchomhar Tta., 1982.

Ó Cathasaigh, Aindrias. *An tAthrú Mór: Scríbhinní Sóisialacha le Pádraic Ó Conaire*. Baile Átha Cliath: Coiscéim, 2007.

Ó Conchubhair, Brian. *Fin de Siècle na Gaeilge: Darwin, An Athbheochan agus Smaointeoireacht na hEorpa*. Indreabhán: An Clóchomhar, 2009.

O'Leary, Philip. *The Prose Literature of the Gaelic Revival, 1881–1921: Ideology and Innovation*. University Park, PA: Pennsylvania State University Press, 1994.

O'Leary, Philip. *Gaelic Prose in the Irish Free State, 1922–1939*. Dublin: University College Dublin Press, 2004.

O'Leary, Philip. *Irish Interior: Keeping Faith with the Past in Gaelic Prose, 1940–1951*. Dublin: University College Dublin Press, 2010.

Ó Muirí, Pól. *A Flight from Shadow: The Life and Work of Seosamh Mac Grianna*. Belfast: Lagan Press, 1999.

Quigley, Mark. *Empire's Wake: Postcolonial Irish Writing and the Politics of Modern Literary Form*. New York: Fordham University Press, 2013.

Titley, Alan. *An tÚrscéal Gaeilge*. Baile Átha Cliath: An Clóchomhar Tta., 1991.

Uí Laighléis, Gearóidín. *Gallán an Ghúim*. Baile Átha Cliath: Coiscéim, 2017.

PART IV

··

AFTER THE
REVIVAL, IN
JOYCE'S WAKE

··

CHAPTER 10

LETHAL IN TWO LANGUAGES

Narrative Form and Cultural Politics in the Fiction of Flann O'Brien and Máirtín Ó Cadhain

LOUIS DE PAOR

On 15 September 1939, six months after Brian Ó Nualláin's (1911–66) debut novel *At Swim-Two-Birds* was published in London under the pseudonym of Flann O'Brien, Máirtín Ó Cadhain (1906–70) was arrested under the Offences Against the State Act at his workplace in the Dublin office of Conradh na Gaeilge (the Gaelic League). He was detained without formal charges in Arbour Hill Prison until his release in December but was arrested again in April 1940 after delivering a graveside oration at the funeral of Tony D'Arcy, a republican prisoner from east Galway who had died on hunger strike. Ó Cadhain was interned without trial and spent the rest of the war years in Tintown, the Curragh military prison. During his confinement in 'Sibéir na hÉireann' (Ireland's Siberia), Ó Cadhain read voraciously in several languages, taught classes on Irish language and literature to fellow internees, and developed his writing to the point where his subsequent work is almost unrecognizable from the apprentice work contained in his first collection of stories, *Idir Shúgradh agus Dáiríre* (Half in Earnest, Half in Jest, 1939). Although it has little to recommend it apart from the author's prodigious facility with language, the book sold sufficiently well to be reprinted in 1947 with the addition of a glossary for readers who might otherwise struggle with the author's encyclopaedic knowledge of Irish.

In sharp contrast, and despite its initial success on the home front, where it outsold *Gone With the Wind* in Dublin bookshops for a week in April 1939, only 244 copies of Flann O'Brien's *At Swim-Two-Birds* had been sold when the publisher's warehouse in London was firebombed in the autumn of 1940 and all stocks destroyed.[1] For all the

---

[1] Anne Clissmann, *Flann O'Brien: A Critical Introduction to His Writings* (Dublin: Gill and Macmillan, 1975), 80; Anthony Cronin, *No Laughing Matter: The Life and Times of Flann O'Brien* (New York: Fromm International Publishing Corporation, 1998), 99.

excitement generated by *At Swim-Two-Birds* among critics and other writers, including James Joyce (1882–1941), Dylan Thomas, William Saroyan, and Graham Greene, Flann O'Brien's reputation as a novelist would not be revived until the reissue of the novel in America in 1951 and in Britain in 1960, and the posthumous publication of *The Third Policeman* (1967), which he completed in 1940. This chapter will explore some of the parallels and disjunctions between the lives and writings of O'Brien and Ó Cadhain and the extent to which their work can be read as a response to the dramatic changes that took place in Ireland in the first half of the twentieth century. The relationship with language, a key element in European modernism and postmodernism, is central to the work of both writers, as is their knowledge of Irish and the Irish-language literary tradition.

Ó Cadhain's internment coincided with the most productive period of Brian Ó Nualláin's literary career, during which he published under various pseudonyms as both novelist and newspaper columnist. Having graduated with an MA in Modern Irish from UCD and taken up an appointment as a civil servant in the Department of Local Government in 1935, he wrote three of the most remarkable Irish novels of the twentieth century and became the country's best-known satirist during the course of the following decade. The newspaper column, 'Cruiskeen Lawn', that Ó Nualláin began writing for the *Irish Times* under the pseudonym Myles na gCopaleen (also Myles na Gopaleen) on 4 October 1940 was familiar to readers in the Curragh prison camp, as Ó Cadhain himself confirmed.[2] Ó Cadhain's response to Ó Nualláin's only novel in Irish, *An Béal Bocht* (The Poor Mouth, 1941), was less than favourable, however. In a letter to Tomás Bairéad penned on Christmas Eve 1941, he wrote:

> Ní baol air gob ar bith a thabhairt don Ghaeilge oifigiúil ná do bhéarlagair lucht an údaráis. Cluinim go bhfuil sé féin in a bhó mhór i gceann de na ranna rialtais. Sin í an tslosaíocht chéanna i gcónaí. Magadh a dhéanamh faoi chuile shórt ach faoin rud atá contúirteach duit féin, agus is iondúil gurb shin é an díol magaidh is mó ar fad agus is géire a dteastaíonn é a ionsaí.[3]

> He makes no attempt to poke fun at official Irish or the jargon of those in power. I hear he himself is a big shot in one of the government departments. The same toadyism again. Making fun of everything except that which is dangerous to yourself and as often as not that is the biggest joke of all and the one most needing to be attacked.

In his review of a new edition of *An Béal Bocht* in 1965, Ó Cadhain remained sceptical. Despite declaring it one of the great prose satires of the Irish language, to be ranked

---

[2] Máirtín Ó Cadhain, *As an nGéibheann: Litreacha chuig Tomás Bairéad* (Baile Átha Cliath: Sáirséal agus Dill, 1973), 80.

[3] Ibid., 88. Ó Cadhain's criticism anticipates Carol Taaffe's discussion in *Ireland Through the Looking Glass: Flann O'Brien, Myles na gCopaleen and Irish Cultural Debate* (Cork: Cork University Press, 2008) of the extent to which Ó Nualláin's satire is both enabled and disarmed by his ambivalent relationship to his own historical circumstances. Observing that 'in some senses he embodied the very values that he mocked', Taaffe describes Ó Nualláin as 'a writer whose idiosyncratic humour was at once in conflict with, and wholly indebted to, the charged cultural debates of the Irish Free State and its successor' (2).

alongside the seventeenth-century *Pairlement Chloinne Thomáis* (Parliament of Clan Thomas) and the twelfth-century *Aislinge Meic Conglinne* (The Vision of MacConglinne), he argued that the denizens of Corca Dorcha, the Gaeltacht area where the novel is set, were less true to life than the Yahoos in *Gulliver's Travels* (1726) and the pigs in *Animal Farm* (1945).[4] Interestingly, Ó Cadhain's verdict is not dissimilar to Daniel Corkery's (1878–1964) critique of Ó Cadhain's own most famous work, *Cré na Cille* (Graveyard Clay, 1949), as expressed in his 1950 review of the novel:

> Dá bhféadfaimis—rud ná féadaimid—ár n-eolas féin ar mhuintir na Gaeltachta do chur ar ceal, d'fhéadfaimis suim do chur i muintir an scéil seo mar dhaoine a bhí ar aon dul leo san atá ann fós. Ach ní raibh na daoine seo beo riamh. Ní chreidimid go ndúradar riamh aon fhocal eile ach amháin iad san a tugadh dóibh le rá. Ar ádhmharaí an tsaoil tá píosa de theangain na Gaeltachta againn ná déanfar é a shárú go ceann i bhfad.[5]

> If we could do the impossible and suspend our knowledge of those who live in the Gaeltacht, we might be interested in the characters of this story as people who were similar to those who still live in Irish-speaking communities. But these people never existed. We don't believe they ever spoke a single word other than those they were given to speak. Fortunately, we have an example of the language of the Gaeltacht which will not be surpassed for a long time.

There is a telling paradox here. *An Béal Bocht* and *Cré na Cille* challenge the idealization of the Gaeltacht in Irish literature and political discourse, yet the satirical edge of these works, in which inflation, exaggeration, and humour are deployed to expose the rift between rhetoric and reality, is blunted by readings that insist the writer's verbal manipulation has severed the connection between language and truth, word and world. This paradox is at the heart of Ó Nualláin's work, in which the capacity of language to unhinge itself from actuality is countered by a fierce nostalgia for a world in which language remains unalienated.

That the language of *Cré na Cille* should pass the reality test while the characters who speak it should not is a nice conundrum. Yet the extent to which Ó Cadhain's use of Irish is both exemplary and reckless is a characteristic of his writing that has been acknowledged by critics and by the author himself: 'An uirnís liteartha is fearr a fuair mé ó mo mhuintir an chaint, caint thíriúil, caint chréúil, caint chraicneach a thosaíos ag damhsa orm scaití, ag gol orm scaití, de mo bhuíochas' (The best literary device I got from my people was their talk, rough, earthy, salty speech that starts dancing on me sometimes, crying on me other times whether I like it or not).[6] The poet Seán Ó Ríordáin (1916–77) identified linguistic excess and a delight in the absurdity of language as defining features of Rabelaisian writers, among whom he included Myles na gCopaleen and Ó Cadhain, along with Aristophanes, Machiavelli, Cervantes, Erasmus, Joyce, Beckett, Brian Merriman (*c.* 1750–1805), and the author of *Pairlement Chloinne Thomáis*. In addition to

---

[4] Máirtín Ó Cadhain, 'Leabhar atá ar Aora Móra Phróis na Gaeilge', *Feasta* 18, no. 1 (1965), 25–6.

[5] Domhnall Ó Corcora, 'Cré na Cille', *Feasta* 3, no. 2 (1950), 15.

[6] Máirtín Ó Cadhain, *Páipéir Bhána agus Páipéir Bhreaca* (Baile Átha Cliath: An Clóchomhar Tta a d'fhoilsigh do Chumann Merriman, 1969), 15.

celebrating the ludic dimension of language, the Rabelaisian attitude was characterized, according to Ó Ríordáin, by ferocious independence from established conventions; an unscrupulously satirical and mercilessly destructive approach to human folly; a relentless assault on pretension; and a determination 'to destroy the official picture of events',[7] as Mikhail Bakhtin put it. For all the verbal pyrotechnics, there is also a savage indignation in the work of both Ó Cadhain and Ó Nualláin as they deploy their linguistic ingenuity to speak truth to power. Ó Cadhain once described himself as lethal in the two official languages of the Irish state—'bheadh sé cho maith dhom a rá go gcreidim go bhfuil mé marfach—dúnmharfach b'fhéidir—i gceachtar den dá theanga oifigiúil' (I might as well say that I believe I am lethal—murderous, even—in either of the two official languages)[8]—and the same might be said of Ó Nualláin.

Much has been made of Brian Ó Nualláin's misfortune as an unlucky writer whose novels in English failed to find an audience at a time when critical and popular success might have provided further stimulation for his work. The rejection of *The Third Policeman* by Longmans in 1940 and the delay in reissuing *At Swim-Two-Birds* occurred at a critical moment in his life and in his development as a writer. His most successful novel on its initial publication was *An Béal Bocht*, which was reprinted within months of its first printing in November 1941 and sold 1100 copies in the following twelve months.[9] As suggested by Ó Cadhain in his review of the later edition, Ó Nualláin's most successful period as a novelist occurred before modern writing in Irish entered its most productive phase in the immediate aftermath of the Second World War. This meant that Ó Nualláin had more or less abandoned the language in his own writing by the time the transformation of literature in Irish occurred, effected in poetry by Ó Ríordáin, Máirtín Ó Direáin (1910–88), and Máire Mhac an tSaoi (1922–), and by Ó Cadhain and Eoghan Ó Tuairisc (1919–82) in prose from the early 1940s through to the end of the 1960s.

By the time Ó Direáin published his first collection of poems, *Coinnle Geala* (White Candles), in 1942, Ó Nualláin had already begun the move from Irish to English as the principal language of his journalism and novels; he wrote almost exclusively in English from 1943. The reasons for rejecting Irish will be explored a little later in this chapter, but the absence of a substantial body of significant work by other writers in Irish in the 1930s as he began his own experiments with form and language should be mentioned as a contributing factor. The most successful works in Irish in the 1920s and 1930s were the Blasket autobiographies, which engaged the attention of both Ó Nualláin and Ó Cadhain. The critical response of both writers to the misrepresentation, in literature and in political rhetoric, of community life in the rural Gaeltacht, and to the misreading of the work of Tomás Ó Criomhthain (1856–1937), Muiris Ó Súilleabháin (1904–50), and Peig Sayers (1873–1958), owes something to their very different personal circumstances.

Máirtín Ó Cadhain was born in 1906 in the Connemara Gaeltacht at a time of considerable economic hardship that remained more or less undiminished following the

---

[7] Quoted in Stiofán Ó Cadhla, *Cá bhfuil Éire? Guth an Ghaisce i bPrós Sheáin Uí Ríordáin* (Baile Átha Cliath: An Clóchomhar Tta., 1998), 141.

[8] Ó Cadhain, *Páipéir Bhána*, 34.

[9] Breandán Ó Conaire, *Myles na Gaeilge: Lámhleabhar ar Shaothar Gaeilge Bhriain Uí Nualláin* (Baile Átha Cliath: An Clóchomhar Tta., 1986), 112.

transition from British rule to Irish self-government in 1922. Having trained at St Patrick's Training College in Dublin, he began working as a primary schoolteacher in Connemara and joined the local battalion of the IRA shortly afterwards. He identified the poverty and inequality he had witnessed in his own community as the primary justification for the subversive activities that eventually saw him elected to the Army Council of the IRA in 1938 and imprisoned during the Second World War. While in the Curragh military prison, he transformed his style of writing from the uncomplicated plots and characterization of the earlier stories to a form of social realism, heavily influenced by the revolutionary romanticism of Maxim Gorky, in which the tension between established social conventions and the emotional needs of individual characters is explored. While many of his most perceptive critics insist there is no evidence of Ó Cadhain's political engagement in his fiction, it might be argued that his sympathetic portrayal of individual characters whose emotional lives are stunted by poverty is part of a lifelong struggle for economic justice for his own community. Although he withdrew from active involvement in the IRA following his release from prison in 1945, Ó Cadhain's commitment to left-wing republicanism continued throughout his life and he was active in the Gaeltacht Civil Rights movement in the year before his death in 1970.

Brian Ó Nualláin was born in Strabane, County Tyrone in 1911 into a middle-class family steeped in Irish cultural nationalism. Having served as a customs and excise officer in the British administration, his father was promoted under the new Free State government and the family moved to Dublin in 1923. From the outset, the young author's relationship with both Irish and English was complicated. Irish was the language of domestic intimacy and family holidays in the Donegal Gaeltacht of Cloughaneely. English was the language of the broader community and of other children with whom the Ó Nualláins were discouraged from socializing. It was also a book language, part of the literature which the young Ó Nualláins read from an early age across several genres in both Irish and English. According to his brother Gearóid, Brian's extraordinary ability as a mimic and *pasticheur* in both languages was evident from an early age.[10] But his strange bookish bilingualism may also have contributed to a deep scepticism of language and its capacity to engage reality authentically, 'evidence of his having opened perhaps too many books at too early an age'.[11] In both the novels and the newspaper columns, there is an undertow of nostalgia for an unalienated language capable of bridging the gap between word and world, a sense that the scorn directed at those who misuse words, wilfully or otherwise, is at least partly directed at the author's own inability to move beyond pastiche to discover a more stable relationship between the ludic tendency of his bilingual imagination and an autonomous reality beyond the unreliable mediation of language. That nostalgia is a defining element of Ó Nualláin's work, which provides its own idiosyncratic response to the mid-century crisis of confidence in language following the convulsions of two world wars. In his most accomplished work, the author's comic ability to exploit the capacity of language to misrepresent and distort the

[10] Cronin, *No Laughing Matter*, 18.

[11] John Wyse Jackson, 'Introduction', in *Myles Before Myles: A Selection of the Earlier Writings of Brian O'Nolan*, ed. John Wyse Jackson (London: Paladin Grafton Books, 1989), 13.

empirical world is cut through with an awareness of the chaotic, anti-human consequences of counter-factual verbal indulgence.

LANGUAGE, FORM, AND TRADITION

Bríona Nic Dhiarmada has drawn attention to a dystopian element in Irish-language writing from the middle decades of the twentieth century that challenges the deep attachment to the rural home place, which is one of the most persistent features of the Irish literary imagination.[12] Ó Cadhain's critique of the extent to which this aspect of the Irish tradition facilitated the political and economic neglect of Irish-speaking communities in the west of Ireland is as scathing as Myles na gCopaleen's representation of the visiting language enthusiasts in *An Béal Bocht*, who continue their endless speeches about the virtues of truly Gaelic Gaels while the natives drop dead 'most Gaelically'[13] from malnourishment:

> Is aoibhinn le Gaeil áirithe cumraíocht bhéalchráifeach mhídhaonna a dhéanamh de na carraigí nár scuab an Éire stairiúil léi ag trá dí. Is daoine a d'fhoghlaim an teanga cuid mhór de léitheoirí na Gaeilge. Mí shaoire a chaitheamh dóibh i gceantar Gaeltachta. An forchraiceann a fheiceáil faoi scéimh an tsamhraidh, Nuair
> *Is aoibhinn teacht féar agus fonn*
> *Agus tormán na dtonn le Lios na Sí.*
> An t-eidheann síorghlas ar chúl na gcarraigí a dhiúl le béal pógchíocrach. Ní féidir 'síorthragóid na beatha' a shamhlú le Tír na hÓige![14]

> Some Gaels like to make a mealy-mouthed inhuman construction from the rocks that historical Ireland did not wash away with her as her tide receded. Many readers of Irish are people who have learned the language. They spend a month in a Gaeltacht area and see its outer skin [foreskin] in the prettiness of summer when 'The coming of grass and desire is sweet / and the crash of the waves at Lios na Sí'. To suck the evergreen ivy behind the rocks with a kiss-hungry mouth. The 'perpetual tragedy of life' cannot be imagined in the Land of Youth!

In Ó Cadhain's rural stories, individual characters are formed and deformed by their interaction with the local geography. Their patterns of speech and thought, even their physical characteristics, betray the influence of a physical environment that has made them in its own likeness. If there is occasional satisfaction to be gained from their ability to reap some reward from working land and sea, it is the destructive impact of their economic dependence on unproductive holdings that is foregrounded in his stories, as it is,

---

[12] Bríona Nic Dhiarmada, 'Utopia, Anti-Utopia, Nostalgia and Ó Cadhain', *Canadian Journal of Irish Studies* 4, no. 1 (2008), 58–64.

[13] Flann O'Brien, *The Poor Mouth*, trans. Patrick C. Power (London: Picador, 1975), 5.

[14] Máirtín Ó Cadhain, 'Saothar an Scríbhneora', *Scríobh* 3 (1978), 75.

indeed, in *An Béal Bocht*, which Sean O'Casey (1880–1964) described as 'a vicious bite at the hand that never fed it'.[15]

Yet for all their bleakness, Ó Cadhain's early stories do not share the relentless pessimism of Ó Nualláin's novel. In the best of his stories from the 1940s and early 1950s, it is the oppressive nature of social structures determined by economic necessity rather than any personal failure on behalf of the central characters that frustrates their attempts at self-fulfilment. In their struggle with adversity, Ó Cadhain's female characters are heroic representatives of the human capacity for endurance. Their emotional resilience and unarticulated protest against apparently immutable social conditions and economic laws provide the basis for a sympathetic portrayal of human beings oppressed by historical circumstances but finally undefeated by them. For Ó Cadhain, as indeed for Gorky, such optimism was a necessary precondition for revolutionary action: 'Sé an dóchas an maidhmiú cuartach, an *chain detonation* a fheicim ariamh anall i stair na tíre. Na géaga giniúna: an dóchas ag gint an mhisnigh agus an misneach ag gint an ghnímh' (Hope is the chain detonation I see right through the history of the country. The genealogy of generation: hope begetting courage and courage begetting action).[16]

The most impressive stories in Ó Cadhain's *An Braon Broghach* (The Dirty Drop, 1948) and *Cois Caoláire* (Beside the Bay, 1953) excavate the emotional lives of women at moments of transformation and personal crisis. We see the separation of a mother and daughter by emigration in 'An Bhliain 1912' (The Year 1912); the displacement and alienation of a young woman on the occasion of her arranged marriage in 'An Bhearna Mhíl' (The Hare Lip); the tension between a young woman, who has spent ten years in America before returning to Ireland, and her new husband, as she proves incapable of fulfilling her obligations to family and community through incompetence at harvesting seaweed in 'An Taoille Tuile' (Floodtide); the near hallucinogenic state, brought about by extreme hunger, of a woman who discovers that her husband has committed suicide in 'Ag Dul ar Aghaidh' (Going On); the sexual frustration of an unmarried woman in early middle age in 'Ciumhais an Chriathraigh' (The Edge of the Bog); and the gradual breakdown of a woman who has had five stillborn children in 'An Strainséara' (The Stranger).

The writing in these stories is clumsy in places as Ó Cadhain struggles to reconcile his political anger and psychological insight with the free indirect style that allows him to reveal pre-verbal and non-verbal aspects of the characters' unarticulated thoughts and feelings. Occasionally the line between the voice of the narrator and the interior voice of the character is breached and the author intervenes to press home the moral and political dimensions of the characters' plight, reminding readers that his characters are representative of a community on the brink of economic destruction. The struggle with form and technique is evident in much of Ó Cadhain's early work as he tries to reconcile his prodigious linguistic ability with the formal constraints of the European short story and his own particular insight into the predicament of the individual in a traditional

---

[15] Quoted in Cronin, *No Laughing Matter*, 129.
[16] Máirtín Ó Cadhain, *An Aisling* (Baile Átha Cliath: Coiste Cuimhneacháin Náisiúnta, 1966), 28.

peasant society. While Gorky provided a catalyst for the best of his work in the 1940s by demonstrating that such a life could provide material for literature, whether among the Cossacks on the River Don or in the Connemara Gaeltacht, Ó Cadhain insisted that Sigmund Freud was the most significant influence in twentieth-century prose. Narrative fiction, he argued, provided unique access to the subconscious mind, a way of revealing the tensions between conscious thought, speech, and behaviour on the one hand and pre-verbal patterns of thought and feeling on the other.[17]

If Ó Cadhain's short stories are characterized by deep empathy with the predicament of women in traditional peasant societies, emphasizing their emotional strength and resilience, his most successful novel is a dystopian representation of a community which, even in death, is characterized by envy, pretension, and unrelieved malevolence. The construction of a Gaeltacht community in *Cré na Cille* is at odds with the state-sponsored dream of traditional rural community life as superior to the modern urban world contaminated by Anglicization and British imperialism. It is also a corrective to a heroic reading of the Blasket autobiographies that emphasizes stoic masculinity, passive femininity, social cohesion, and Christian fatalism, while ignoring the economic injustices that made these values necessary for the survival of the community. In death, there is no longer any need to conceal the more destructive aspects of human nature that had to be suppressed above ground in a community where co-operation and interdependence were preconditions for survival, and the tensions between individuals could not be given free rein.

While Ó Cadhain's formal innovation and technical virtuosity are more evident in the novel than in any of the shorter fiction he produced in this period, the linguistic plenitude of *Cré na Cille* is undermined by the obsessive repetition of key phrases, linguistic tags that seem to be the only remnants of individual identity that are left to the dead. Caitríona Pháidín's endless ranting against her sister and her neighbours is tethered to endless repetition and eventually reduced to the same exclamatory phrase, devoid of semantic content, a surrender to helpless inarticulacy: 'Ab ba búna'. The exuberance of Ó Cadhain's language is undercut by the location of his anti-novel in a graveyard and the sense that effervescence of language is all that is left to the dead. The static condition of the corpses, their physical disintegration and impotence, provides a dark counterpoint to their verbal jousting in dialogue charged with frustrated ambition incapable of realization. The linguistic excess of *Cré na Cille* is a measure of the helplessness of those who have nothing left except language, a dead world in which words are bereft, incapable of engagement with reality.

In Myles na gCopaleen's *An Béal Bocht*, language itself is diminished, reduced to the relentless recycling of clichés sanctioned by the authority of traditional precedent. The dialect of Corca Dorcha consists of predetermined patterns of speech, a linguistic straitjacket constraining the individual's capacity for independent thought and action so that each generation is condemned to repeat and regenerate the stereotypes laid down in the immutable laws and language of 'Gaelic tradition'. The relationship between *An Béal Bocht* and the autobiographies of native Irish speakers is often misinterpreted, although Ó Nualláin made

---

[17] Ó Cadhain, *Páipéir Bhána agus Páipéir Bhreaca*, 30–1.

his intentions clear with regard to Tomás Ó Criomhthain's *An t-Oileánach* (The Islandman, 1929) in particular, explaining: 'In one week I wrote a parody of it called *An Béal Bocht*. . . . My prayer is that all who read it afresh will be stimulated into stumbling upon the majestic book upon which it is based.'[18] For Ó Nualláin, Ó Criomhthain's book was 'a private grief', 'a thing not to be seen or talked about and certainly not to be discussed with strangers'.[19] It was, he wrote, 'the superbest of all books', one he 'regarded . . . with awe. (Not, as is customary, with "Aw".)'.[20] 'Against it', he added, 'about ninety per cent of books in English, with their smear of sophistication, fall into the ordained bin of trash.'[21] The target of his own satirical parody of the style and structure of 'native autobiography'[22] was not the authors but the sentimental misreading ('Aw') of their work by those whose idealization of peasant life in the west of Ireland was so ideologically powerful that material poverty and spiritual richness became inextricably linked in their rhetorical constructions of the Gaeltacht. His book, he said, was 'a ferocious and highly technical assault on the Gaels', 'an honest attempt to get under the skin of a certain type of "Gael", which I find the most nauseating phenomenon in Europe. I mean the baby-brained dawnburst brigade who are ignorant of everything, including the Irish language itself.'[23]

The satirical thrust of *An Béal Bocht*, and the author's determination to draw attention to the hypocrisy of those who would celebrate the symbolic value of Gaeltacht life while turning a blind eye to its destruction, are evident again in a newspaper column on *An t-Oileánach* four years after the evacuation of the Great Blasket in 1953:

> The man who wrote the remarkable book, Tomás Ó Criomhthain, is dead, and the Great Blasket is utterly deserted. Nothing now lives there except rabbits. Mr [J. A.] Brooks says 'it is a nostalgic book'. So it is. It is the symbol of a Gaelic order gone under for good. But it is an extremely noble salute from them about to go away. From another view, it is the apotheosis of native government. It conforms in detail with the contemporary political jest of having a Minister for the Gaeltacht. The lads are now gone, their tongues at rest, their faces baked in salt water.[24]

In different modes, the newspaper column and *An Béal Bocht* offer a searing critique of the extent to which the rhetoric of cultural nationalism was implicated in the failure of those in power to alleviate the poverty of those whose 'truly Gaelic' suffering had provided such a powerful example of the qualities of self-reliance, self-sacrifice, and Christian stoicism that were central to Ireland's self-imaging in the decades after the establishment of the Free State in 1922.[25] Part of the horror of *An Béal Bocht* is the way in which rhetoric trumps reality and language forces its own tyrannical authority on the world. The central character, Bónapart Ó Cúnasa, makes every effort to escape his

---

[18] Myles na Gopaleen, 'Islanding', in *The Hair of the Dogma: A Further Selection from 'Cruiskeen Lawn'*, ed. Kevin O'Nolan (London: Hart-Davis, MacGibbon, 1977), 181.

[19] Ibid., 180–1.   [20] Ibid., 180.   [21] Ibid., 181.

[22] See John Eastlake, 'Native American and Irish Native Autobiography: A Comparative Study'. Unpublished PhD thesis, NUI Galway, 2008.

[23] Quoted in Clissmann, *Flann O'Brien*, 234, 238.   [24] na Gopaleen, 'Islanding', 180.

[25] Taaffe, *Ireland Through the Looking Glass*, 120–1.

'literary fate', but his personality and behaviour, even the language he speaks, must conform to the way they are represented in the 'good books', the final authority on all aspects
of the life of Corca Dorcha. Ó Nualláin indicts editors, teachers, government officials,
and finally the inhabitants themselves, who have internalized the stereotypes imposed
on them by colonists and nationalists alike, so that their own self-representation conforms to prefabricated patterns they seem incapable of correcting or resisting. Trapped
by the 'carceral logic'[26] of the text, they are condemned to a cycle of endless repetition
that makes progress or escape impossible.

Ó Cadhain's accusation that Myles na gCopaleen chose soft targets for his satire and
omitted self-criticism from his assault is mistaken, as Brian Ó Nualláin was himself a
product of the ideology he lampooned so mercilessly in *An Béal Bocht*. It might be
argued that his rejection of the political and cultural beliefs of his own upbringing and
family, and of the state he served, was central to his decision to abandon writing in Irish
after 1943, despite the success of the novel among a readership which could hardly have
failed to see that they themselves stood, with the author, among the ranks of the accused.
Carol Taaffe has suggested that the regeneration of the Irish revival movement in the
early 1940s contributed to the popularity of the 'Cruiskeen Lawn' newspaper column,
but that the xenophobic and fascist tendencies of more extreme elements in new groupings such as Ailtirí na hAiséirí (Architects of the Resurrection) and Glún na Buaidhe
(the Victorious Generation) contributed to Ó Nualláin's decision to abandon writing in
Irish.[27] Ó Nualláin's distaste for the chauvinism of these organizations, which grew and
declined with almost equal rapidity during the war years, is evident in his columns from
the period. That his older brother Ciarán—with whom he shared a bedroom for many
years, as well as literary ambitions and collaborations, and the only person to whom he
spoke Irish in his later years—was involved with Glún na Buaidhe and edited its newspaper until his death in 1979, indicates the extent to which Ó Nualláin's dispute with the
revivalism of the 1940s was a disenchanted reaction against a defining element of his
own personal and literary formation.

At Swim-Two-Birds satirizes the pretensions of narrative fiction by drawing attention
to the conventions of genre that facilitate the production of counterfeit models the
writer passes off as reality. An alternative to such 'despotic' practices would allow that 'a
satisfactory novel should be a self-evident sham to which the reader could regulate at
will the degree of his credulity'.[28] By mixing competing registers of language and narrative modes—'some thirty-six styles and forty-two extracts',[29] including cowboy stories
and court proceedings, the advice of racing tipsters and early Irish sagas, translations
from Latin, school textbooks, extracts from a novel in progress, and an account of the
principal narrator's interaction with family and friends—the conventional nature of
narrative is foregrounded and the presumption to truth of any form of writing, including
the realistic novel, ridiculed. Ó Nualláin draws the reader's attention to the fictionality of

[26] Sarah McKibben, 'The Poor Mouth: A Parody of (Post) Colonial Manhood', *Research in African Literatures*, 34, no. 4 (2003), 96.

[27] Taaffe, *Ireland Through the Looking Glass*, 91–119.

[28] Flann O'Brien, *At Swim-Two-Birds* (London: Penguin, 1967), 25.

[29] Clissmann, *Flann O'Brien*, 86.

fiction and the extent to which all modes of writing are constrained by the conventional nature of language itself. While demonstrating his own extraordinary capacity for parody and pastiche, his anti-novel makes the suspension of disbelief required by all forms of narrative ludicrous.

As noted by several critics, particularly Eva Wappling, the treatment of early Irish literature in *At Swim-Two-Birds* draws directly on Ó Nualláin's postgraduate research to provide a tragic counterpoint to his comic critique of linguistic and narrative self-referentiality.[30] In his MA thesis, the young scholar identified 'Celtic realism' among the principal characteristics of early Irish poetry, a form of truth-telling that integrated precision and economy of language with sharp observation of the natural world, the autonomy of which the poets acknowledged, thus avoiding the pathetic fallacy Ó Nualláin associated with English poetry.[31] For Ninian Mellamphy, the novel is

> a monument to human failure, especially to this 'failure' in terms of man's awareness of his alienation from the wholeness of life celebrated in epic literature. . . . O'Brien shows that the epic vision, or what it symbolizes, is to modern man as grotesquely improbable as it is nostalgically attractive; this we see in his 'humorous or quasi-humorous' treatment of Finn, the Gargantuan non-thinker who gets wisdom from the sucking of his thumb.[32]

Despite being 'twisted and trampled and tortured for the weaving of a story-teller's book-web',[33] the medieval hero Finn McCool is a more integrated human being than any of his twentieth-century associates, comfortable with the carnal dimension of human existence, determined to use language only to speak of the world as he has known it through direct sensory experience. The figure of Sweeny, 'a huddle between the earth and heaven',[34] who has become unhinged by war and an encounter with a saint representing the new Christian order in which the authority of the book usurps that of the native pagan oral tradition, represents 'the very heart of the matter'.[35] That the warrior king is murdered on account of a false story emphasizes again the despotic capacity of language and narrative to distort and control reality. For Finn, the tyranny of language and a narrative imagination unrestrained by fidelity to the empirical world is the ultimate nightmare:

> Indeed, it is true that there has been ill-usage to the men of Erin from the book-poets of the world and dishonour to Finn, with no knowing the nearness of disgrace

---

[30] See Eva Wappling, 'Four Irish Legendary Figures in *At Swim-Two-Birds*: A Study of Flann O'Brien's use of Finn, Suibhne, the Pooka and the Good Fairy'. Unpublished PhD thesis, Uppsala University, 1984. See also Clissmann, *Flann O'Brien*, 122–50 and J. C. C. Mays, 'A Literalist of the Imagination', in Timothy O'Keeffe (ed.), *Myles: Portraits of Flann O'Brien* (London: Martin Brian and O'Keeffe, 1973), 77–119.

[31] Brian Ó Nualláin, 'Nádúir-fhilíocht na Gaedhilge: Tráchtas maraon le Duanaire'. Unpublished MA thesis, University College Dublin, 1935.

[32] Ninian Mellamphy, 'Aestho-autogamy and the Anarchy of Imagination: Flann O'Brien's Theory of Fiction in *At Swim-Two Birds*', in Rüdiger Imhof (ed.), *Alive Alive O! Flann O'Brien's 'At Swim-Two-Birds'* (Dublin: Wolfhound Press, 1985), 150. Melamphy's article was first published in 1978.

[33] O'Brien, *At Swim-Two-Birds*, 19.   [34] Ibid., 314.

[35] Mellanphy, 'Aestho-autogamy and the Anarchy of Imagination', 153.

or the sorrow of death, or the hour when they may swim for swans or trot for ponies or bell for stags or croak for frogs or fester for the wounds on a man's back.[36]

Where *At Swim-Two-Birds* undermines the pretensions of literature to represent reality, *The Third Policeman* introduces readers to a nightmare world, 'exhilarating and wrong,'[37] in which the self-referential logic of science is unhinged from reality and language fails to get a grip on the empirical world. The nameless narrator is trapped in a world no longer governed by the laws of common sense as his obsessive quest for scientific omniscience leads him to murder, plunging him into a parallel universe, 'an unalleviated nightmare of infinite recession', where the 'ultimate assertion of unmitigated selfhood' leaves him impotent, incapable of agency, in a hell of his own making.[38] It is a diabolical inhuman world in which boundaries are constantly transgressed, where conventional laws of time and space are destabilized and confused, where characters and voices merge, and the categorical distinctions between animate and inanimate objects blur and disintegrate. Human reason and scientific logic prove incapable of restoring order and equilibrium.

The promiscuous infidelity of language is central to the book as words fail to establish meaningful relationships with their referents. Anthony Cronin suggests the flat style of the first-person narrator in *At Swim-Two-Birds* 'had given the impression that English was being written as if it were a dead language', while *The Third Policeman* 'often reads like a translation from the Irish'.[39] In both novels, a strangely depersonalized anti-style might be read, he says, as 'an expression of surprise that such a language as English exists and can be made to express facts or describe appearances and feelings'.[40] While the linguistic anxiety in Ó Nualláin's work has been quite properly read as a response to the modernist and postmodernist predicaments, it also owes something to his own particular experience of Ireland's skewed bilingualism. As in the case of his contemporary, Seán Ó Ríordáin, there is a sense in Ó Nualláin's work of a fractured verbal imagination not fully at home in either Irish or English, despite its unusual facility in both languages.

Critics Keith Brooker, Flore Coulouma, and others have rejected the tendency among earlier scholars to see Ó Nualláin's change of primary medium from novels to journalism as precipitating a decline in his work, one aggravated by personal circumstances and the pressure of newspaper deadlines.[41] For Claud Cockburn, there are clear patterns of continuity between the novels and the 'Cruiskeen Lawn' columns, and John Wyse Jackson makes a compelling case for considering the best of Ó Nualláin's *Irish Times* contributions 'as some unidentified subspecies of the fiction family, a random, episodic, wildly innovative rough beast of a "novel", in which the novel form itself has been stretched to screaming point and beyond'.[42] Jackson also points to the crucial relation-

---

[36] O'Brien, *At Swim-Two-Birds*, 20.   [37] Mays, 'A Literalist of the Imagination', 95.
[38] Ibid., 90–2.   [39] Cronin, *No Laughing Matter*, 106.   [40] Ibid., 107.
[41] Joseph Brooker, *Flann O'Brien* (Tavistock: Northcote House, 2005); Flore Coulouma, 'Tall Tales and Short Stories: *Cruiskeen Lawn* and the Dialogic Imagination', *Review of Contemporary Fiction: Flann O'Brien Centenary Essays* 31, no. 3 (2011), 162–77.
[42] Claud Cockburn, 'Introduction', in Flann O'Brien, *Stories and Plays*, ed. Claud Cockburn (London: Paladin Grafton Books, 1991), 13; John Wyse Jackson, 'Introduction', in Flann O'Brien, *Flann O'Brien at War: Myles na gCopaleen 1940–1945*, ed. John Wyse Jackson (London: Duckworth, 1999), 11.

ship between the column and its predominantly male readership, 'the new Irish intelligentsia', the chief architects and principal beneficiaries of the new state: 'Like a funfair mirror, "Cruiskeen Lawn" reflected their own beliefs and preconceptions back at them, with the boundaries distorted and certainties doubtful.'[43] The accumulated effect of his assault on the conventionality of language in his newspaper column was such that Hilton Edwards complained in a letter to Ó Nualláin: 'I find it almost impossible to write a letter to you because your friend Myles na Gopaleen's dissertations on clichés have so unnerved me.'[44] The rehabilitation of the best of the columns adds considerably to an appreciation of Ó Nualláin's achievements as a writer of prodigious formal dexterity who transgresses the boundaries of established literary conventions. It also clarifies the extent to which his most accomplished work was written in the course of a long decade that stretched from the late 1930s through to the early 1950s.

In a 1952 radio broadcast, Máirtín Ó Cadhain spoke of the need to renovate the inherited resources of Irish to explore the predicament of men diminished and emasculated by the despotism of modern bureaucracy.[45] The challenge of representing such a world which, like Ó Nualláin, he himself had inhabited for a time, working as an official government translator, was to develop a register of Irish appropriate to material previously beyond the reach of Irish-language fiction. That the Irish civil service included native speakers and secondary speakers with varying degrees of proficiency in the language enabled Ó Cadhain to forge a plausible literary dialect that is sufficiently flexible to integrate urban office-speak with more traditional rural idioms. From the early 1950s through to his death in 1970, Ó Cadhain refurbished the Irish language to articulate the experience of deracinated men, alienated from their physical environments, from meaningful sexual relationships and the solidarity of community, from their own attenuated selves.

Two late collections, *An tSraith ar Lár* (The Fallen Sheaf, 1967) and *An tSraith dhá Tógáil* (The Gathered Sheaf, 1970), give evidence of a significant shift in Ó Cadhain's manipulation of language, style, and form to match this change in subject matter. In them, there is a greater degree of assurance in his engagement with the European short story and with free indirect style but also greater technical dexterity and formal diversity as he moves to a more surreal style better suited to the absurdity of a world ruled by bureaucracy. Irony gradually hardens into satire in Ó Cadhain's treatment of compromised masculinity in the later stories, replacing the empathetic treatment of female resilience in the earlier stories. *An tSraith ar Lár* includes an almost impenetrable Joycean satire of the institutionalized Irish language movement, a surreal parable in which houses begin mysteriously to assault each other, and a sequence of connected stories about a Gaeltacht community in transition to Anglicization and modernity, in which characters migrate from one story to another. The recurrent motif of a hearse in which a woman gives birth clarifies the tension between life and death, fertility and impotence, which is at the heart of the sequence. That tension is also central to 'An Eochair' (The Key)

[43] Jackson, 'Introduction', 10.

[44] Quoted in Monique Gallagher, 'Flann O'Brien: Myles from Dublin', in Marc Poitou (ed.), *The Princess Grace Irish Library Lectures*, 7 (Gerrards Cross: Colin Smythe, 1991), 17.

[45] Ó Cadhain, 'Saothar an Scríbhneora', 80.

and the two most impressive stories in *An tSraith dhá Tógáil*, 'Fuascailt' (Release), and 'Fuíoll Fuine' (Sunset Dregs), in which Ó Cadhain explores the anxieties of male characters whose physical and social impotence leads ultimately to their deaths.

While Ó Cadhain's later work confirms his own prodigious linguistic ability and the capacity of Irish to renew itself, the fraying of language in the speech and thought patterns of the straw men who inhabit the late stories is directly linked to their capitulation to the 'paperocracy'. The cyclical repetition of precedent, protocol, and procedure inhibits action in 'An Eochair', where J., a junior clerk locked into an office on a bank holiday weekend, dies as a result of his own inability and that of his more powerful seniors, including government ministers and ecclesiastical authorities, to break down the door in the absence of any appropriately sanctioned instructions. The influence of Flann O'Brien might be detected in the posthumously published 'Ag Déanamh Páipéir' (Turning to Paper), in which the body of a clerk who devoted his life to paperwork gradually turns to paper. As in Ó Nualláin's *An Béal Bocht* and *The Third Policeman*, the world of Ó Cadhain's late stories is grim and out of kilter; characters are deprived of agency and language impedes access to reality rather than enabling it. 'Fuíoll Fuine', the final story in *An tSraith dhá Tógáil*, follows the central character N. as he wanders around Dublin, unable to make the necessary arrangements for his wife's funeral. The blurring of distinctions between the real and the unreal is matched by an unravelling of language that corresponds to the ennui and impotence of the central character, who seems as incapable of registering guilt or empathy as the unnamed narrator of *The Third Policeman*. After numerous encounters with individuals and agencies unable or unwilling to relieve him of his responsibilities, he ends up drinking with a sailor who promises to arrange passage for him on a ship to Valparaiso. The story ends obliquely with a suggestion that N. has drowned.

LEGACIES AND AFTERLIVES

In an RTÉ documentary recorded shortly before he died in October 1970, Ó Cadhain spoke of a work in progress that readers might take from their shelves now and again, if he was given time to complete it 'ón uaigh áibhéileach sin in Ard Jerome ina bhfuil mo bhean curtha' (by that monstrous grave in Mount Jerome where my wife is buried).[46] Ó Cadhain's writing life coincided with an extraordinary flourishing of new poetry, fiction, drama, criticism, and historical writing in Irish. His era also witnessed the emergence in Irish of ambitious small journals, a national book club, a writers' association, new publishing houses, and advances in the design, marketing, and distribution of books to a substantial readership. The collapse of that literary infrastructure in the closing decades of the last century, coupled with the incremental decline in the readership

---

[46] Aindrias Ó Gallchóir, 'Turas ar an nGealchathair', *Scríobh* 3 (1978), 85. The work in progress was *An tSraith dhá Tógáil*.

available for work that is formally or linguistically challenging, suggest that Ó Cadhain's work is more likely to be read in other languages than the Irish of his collected stories and novels. The extraordinary critical response to *Cré na Cille* in two recent English translations,[47] and the expectation that those versions, along with an earlier rendering by Joan Trodden Keefe, will provide the basis for translations into other languages in the near future, suggest that Ó Cadhain is more likely to find a new audience in transla-tion than from within a diminished Irish language readership. In Irish, *Cré na Cille* has reached a more substantial audience through stage and screen adaptation than it has on the printed page. From a literary perspective, it may be that the reworking of classic texts in this manner is neither regrettable nor abnormal. However, for a writer committed to the maintenance and regeneration of a minority language, the success of his work in translation is mitigated by the failure to sustain a significant readership for it in the lan-guage in which it was written.

The revival of interest in Brian Ó Nualláin's novels and journalism that has flared sporadically from the 1960s onwards has been kickstarted again in the early decades of this century, which have witnessed sustained growth in scholarship on his work from disparate disciplines and theoretical perspectives in several languages. A fleeting refer-ence to *The Third Policeman* in the American television series *Lost* contributed to the renewal of popular interest in a writer whose work continues to speak to a world implod-ing under the burden of its own delusions, accelerated by the failure of language to honour its responsibility to reality. Ó Nualláin's writing also provides insights into the predicament of a bilingual writer unwilling or unable to inhabit fully the received pat-terns of either Irish or English. Something of this predicament is captured by an anec-dote about the first occasion the young Brian spoke English to his family. On being rebuked in Irish by his father for mimicking the accents of Offaly people, Brian responded: 'And as for you, sir, if you do not conduct yourself, I shall do you a mischief.'[48] A similar dissonance is audible in a letter of condolence Ó Nualláin sent to a man mourning the death of his nephew, which Ó Nualláin's friend, Niall Montgomery, quoted from in a tribute published the day after his death in April 1966:

> Cúis doilghis et dímheanmnan dhúinn leithshiúr bhur n-onóra bheith ar mí-charáiste mháthardha; ocus isé ár nguidhe-ne an Coimhdhe bheith anois feasta ag neartú na mnásan maille le sláinte do dheonadh di et fós an tí bec nach maireannn do bhreith slán co flaithis Dé agus do chumhdach go deo ar bhuandorchadas shuthain.[49]

> It is a cause of sorrow and dejection to us that your honourable [half-] sister should be in a state of maternal despair; and it is our prayer that the Creator will henceforth strengthen that woman and grant her health and also that the little person who has died should be brought safely to heaven and be protected forever from perpetual and everlasting darkness.

---

[47] Cló Iar-Chonnacht and Yale University Press published Alan Titley's version, *The Dirty Dust*, in 2015. A second translation, by Liam Mac an Iomaire and Tim Robinson, entitled *Graveyard Clay*, was published by Yale in 2016.

[48] Cronin, *No Laughing Matter*, 18.

[49] Niall Montgomery, 'An Aristophanic sorcerer', *Irish Times*, 2 April 1966.

While the formality of expression is suitably dignified and restrained, the use of the Latin conjunction 'et' and strange amalgam of Old, Middle, Early Modern, and Modern Irish suggest an inability to deploy the resources of the living language to communicate directly with the bereaved. The inconsistency of Ó Nualláin's writing, the alleged absence of a defining myth or set of preoccupations, has been overstated, but his extraordinary ability as a *pasticheur* may also indicate a difficulty in moving beyond imitation: the nightmare of the ventriloquist who finds himself incapable of speaking directly without mask or mimicry. 'What of my own problem', Myles na gCopaleen asks in one of his columns, 'that of a creative writer who has nothing original to say, whose sole contribution to the terrestrial literatures has been to refute each and every claim to originality on the part of other writers?'[50]

There are significant differences and notable parallels between the lives and works of Máirtín Ó Cadhain and Brian Ó Nualláin. Both writers suffered from difficult personal circumstances, aggravated by ill-health and the vagaries of the literary marketplace; both also offer a bleak portrayal of a world in transition and a scathing critique of Ireland's self-fashioning in the middle decades of the twentieth century. For writers whose work is so intimately connected to the time and place in which it was written, so clearly addressed to its own contemporary audience, their capacity to speak to a twenty-first-century audience in Ireland and elsewhere is as remarkable as their prodigious ability with language and form. Ó Cadhain's insight into lives blighted by economic injustice and bureaucratic tyranny has lost little of its political urgency in the half-century since his death, while Ó Nualláin's work continues to deride a world in which absurdity insists on being taken seriously and the distortion of language is a defining attribute of power.

FURTHER READING

Clissmann, Anne. *Flann O'Brien: A Critical Introduction to his Writings*. Dublin: Gill and Macmillan, 1975.

Cronin, Anthony. *No Laughing Matter: The Life and Times of Flann O'Brien*. New York: Fromm International Publishing Corporation, 1998.

de Paor, Louis. *Faoin mBlaoisc Bheag Sin*. Baile Átha Cliath: Coiscéim, 1991.

de Paor, Louis (ed.). *Canadian Journal of Irish Studies. Special Issue: Máirtín Ó Cadhain* 4, no. 1 (2008).

Denvir, Gearóid. *Cadhan Aonair: Saothar Liteartha Mháirtín Uí Chadhain*. Baile Átha Cliath: An Clóchomhar Tta., 1992.

Hopper, Keith. *A Portrait of the Artist as a Young Post-Modernist*. Cork: Cork University Press, 1995.

Mays, J. C. C. 'A Literalist of the Imagination'. In Timothy O'Keeffe (ed.), *Myles: Portraits of Flann O'Brien*. London: Martin Brian and O'Keeffe, 1973: 77–119.

Ó Cadhain, Máirtín. *Páipéir Bhána agus Páipéir Bhreaca*. Baile Átha Cliath: An Clóchomhar Tta a d'fhoilsigh do Chumann Merriman, 1969.

[50] Myles na gCopaleen, 'Cruiskeen Lawn', *Irish Times*, 4 June 1945.

Ó Cathasaigh, Aindrias. *Ag Samhlú Troda: Máirtín Ó Cadhain 1905–70*. Baile Átha Cliath: Coiscéim, 2002.

Ó Conaire, Breandán. *Myles na Gaeilge: Lámhleabhar ar Shaothar Gaeilge Bhriain Uí Nualláin*. Baile Átha Cliath: An Clóchomhar Tta., 1986.

Taaffe, Carol. *Ireland Through the Looking Glass: Flann O'Brien, Myles na gCopaleen and Irish Cultural Debate*. Cork: Cork University Press, 2008.

Wappling, Eva. 'Four Irish Legendary Figures in *At Swim-Two-Birds*: A Study of Flann O'Brien's use of Finn, Suibhne, the Pooka and the Good Fairy'. Unpublished PhD thesis, Uppsala University, 1984.

CHAPTER 11

EFFING THE INEFFABLE

Samuel Beckett's Narrators

SINÉAD MOONEY

'WHERE now? Who now? When now?'[1] The three questions with which Samuel Beckett's (1906–89) *The Unnamable* (1953) begins are generally read as specific to the denatured, ailing, yet weakly persistent narrative voice which utters them, the barely-present successor to what was already in 1953 a long line of Beckettian protagonists for whom the body is a disintegrating hulk, subjectivity a befuddled memory, and meaning a haunting void. The questions might, however, be applied to Beckett's work as a whole. Where, if anywhere, does Beckett's oeuvre properly belong? Should it be seen as part of European high modernism, alongside the works of Marcel Proust and James Joyce (1882–1941), both of whose writing elicited appreciative critical essays from the young Beckett during the 1920s and early 1930s? Is it more accurately placed as postmodernist, his linguistic scepticism and representational *mise-en-abyme* grouping him with writers such as Borges and Calvino? Or are all such attempts to 'place' Beckett essentially mistaken, and his work considered *sui generis*, as Beckett himself suggested in his 1954 tribute, 'Homage to Jack B. Yeats', in which he claimed, famously, that the true artist is 'from nowhere' and 'has no kith', and therefore that, as he would later phrase it, art is merely the result of an impossible but undeniable human 'obligation to express'?[2] If the latter, we are then left with the question of what to make of the weak but persistent echoes of Irish names and landscapes which appear to be simultaneously incorporated into and rejected from his mature work, traces which are never entirely evacuated from its dynamics of abstraction and subtraction.

As a writer who began his career in the shadow of Joyce's *Finnegans Wake* (1939), Samuel Beckett's vehement refusal of tradition, coupled with his internationalist stance and distrust of all national cultural projects, means that his placement within the canon

---

[1] Samuel Beckett, *The Unnamable*, in *The Beckett Trilogy: Molloy, Malone Dies, The Unnamable* (London: Picador, 1979), 219.

[2] Samuel Beckett, *Disjecta: Miscellaneous Writing and a Dramatic Fragment*, ed. Ruby Cohn (London: John Calder, 1983), 149, 139.

of Irish fiction has never been a straightforward matter. Affinities to Irish writers from Jonathan Swift (1667–1745) onwards were frequently suggested by earlier Beckett critics such as Vivian Mercier, but influences, still less inheritances, were almost impossible to evidence, particularly in the face of the withering scorn so often vented on the Irish literary scene in Beckett's letters and early criticism. His bilingualism, his reluctance to engage overtly or consistently with Irish politics, culture, and society, and his proximity to the European avant-garde meant that his work has never fitted easily into conventional narratives, or indeed syllabi, of Irish literature. Neither does he sit easily in the French canon; *The Cambridge Companion to the French Novel from 1800 to the Present* (1997) provides two cursory mentions of Beckett in relation to the *nouveau roman*.[3] For much of the history of Beckett studies, its scholars only occasionally registered Beckett's Irish background, while Irish studies, for its part, though not infrequently making gestures towards the consideration of Beckett as a leading European writer of Irish origins, tended to handle him with as much brevity as it did reverence. The liminal, inconclusive nature of Beckett's work foiled easy incorporation into the somewhat reductive binary of Irish modernism where so often, as Seán Kennedy puts it, 'the dubiously messianic narrative of Irish literary history whereby a right-wing and nationalist Yeats gives way to an emancipatory, pluralist and internationalist Joyce'[4] has held sway.

And yet, as many recent studies have shown, Beckett's linguistic self-consciousness and extreme fictions of failure, diminishment, and death are deeply coloured by his culture of origin. If Beckett has, ultimately, been most convincingly placed between high modernism and postmodernism as a 'late' modernist, suspicious of politically engaged art, recognizing the problems of representation—what *Watt* (1953) sees as a doomed attempt to 'eff the ineffable'[5]—and eventually self-distanced from the stance of high modernism, his positioning does not take place in a socio-cultural void. The particular modernism of Beckett—his deep-rooted scepticism at the notion of any truth or subjectivity being accessible through or in language, his investment in destabilizing in literature what he called in 1937 the 'old lazy ways' long abandoned by music and the visual arts, his exploration of an 'art of failure'[6]—was in many ways conditioned by both his exposure to the literature of the Irish Literary Revival and its aftermath and his formative early encounter with the work of Joyce. Despite his vigorous denunciation of the Revival as 'antiquarian'[7] in early broadsides such as 'Recent Irish Poetry' (1934) and 'Censorship in the Saorstat' (1935), and his satirical sideswipes at the Abbey Theatre, Irish mythology, and literary censorship in *Murphy* (1938), *Watt*, and *Mercier et Camier* (written 1946), Beckett's career-long search for a 'literature of the unword'[8] would involve an inventive exploration of the relationship between language, culture, and meaning. Disturbing their conventional alignment enabled him to evolve a narrative mode that thrived on its antagonism towards the requirements of classical realism.

---

[3] Timothy Unwin (ed.), *The Cambridge Companion to the French Novel from 1800 to the Present* (Cambridge: Cambridge University Press, 1997), 139–40, 157.
[4] Seán Kennedy (ed.), *Beckett and Ireland* (Cambridge: Cambridge University Press, 2010), 27.
[5] Samuel Beckett, *Watt* (London: Faber and Faber, 2009), 51.   [6] Beckett, *Disjecta*, 172, 123.
[7] Ibid., 70.   [8] Ibid., 173.

His prose, if it jumbles together Irish place and proper names with the French language, and sets compulsively-narrating creatures in movement through indistinct and indecipherable terrain, nonetheless stages a set of oblique but insistent relationships between Ireland and modernist experimentation.

Beckett's Irishness was, however, for a long time regarded as an ironic or paradoxical by-product of his status as a cosmopolitan or 'world writer' who wrote profoundly deracinated works that dealt with 'a generalised cultural condition'.[9] Rootless, hermetic, and radically linguistically dislocated, Beckett was the type of T. S. Eliot's 'abstract European', 'a blank face speaking every language with neither a native nor a foreign accent'.[10] His work was apparently endlessly hospitable to transcendental humanist readings which aligned the deracination and non-specificity of Beckett's settings and his two languages with the timeless and universal qualities for which the Nobel Prize citation praised him in 1969. This entrenched view was left largely untroubled by Beckett studies' embrace of deconstructionist and postmodernist criticism during the 1980s, which, in focusing on formal and linguistic questions, left some of the ahistoricist and decontextualized assumptions of humanist Beckett criticism undisturbed. Scholars were reluctant to engage in what was viewed, when it was considered at all, as a reductive squeezing of a metropolitan or European writer into a national tradition.

In more recent years, an increasingly historicist turn in Beckett studies, a more nuanced consideration of the various spaces and times of modernism, and reconsiderations of the parameters of Irish literature have facilitated Beckett's gradual assimilation into the Irish canon, aided in part by a corresponding popular transformation of him into an increasingly visible marketable cultural icon. However, the popular 'reclamation' of the 'Irish Beckett', within Ireland at least, has primarily been of Beckett the dramatist, spearheaded as it was by the Gate Theatre's 1991 Samuel Beckett Festival and its subsequent international remountings, and further bolstered by the 2001 Beckett on Film project. If, by the time of the Beckett centenary celebrations in Dublin in 2006, the 'Irish Beckett' no longer seemed a contradiction in terms, this was largely a recognition of the Irish concerns of Beckett's drama, which—mostly written in English after En attendant Godot (Waiting for Godot, 1953) and Fin de partie (Endgame, 1957), and often written for the voices of Irish actors such as Patrick Magee—was always more hospitable to Irish-centric readings, particularly given the author's own expressed admiration for the plays of J. M. Synge (1871–1909), Sean O'Casey (1880–1964), and certain late plays of W. B. Yeats (1865–1939). Simply put, Beckett is easier to see as an Irish dramatist than as an Irish novelist.

His more elliptical, difficult, and deracinated prose, written chiefly in French after the Second World War and self-translated into his native English, is far less liable to what some commentators have viewed as the dangers of empty commodification by the Irish culture industry.[11] Nor, precisely because of his writing in French and reliance on self-

---

[9] Peter Boxall, 'Samuel Beckett: Towards a Political Reading', Irish Studies Review 10, no. 2 (2002), 160.

[10] T. S. Eliot, 'Goethe as Sage', in On Poetry and Poets (London: Faber and Faber, 1957), 216.

[11] See Patricia McTighe, '"Getting Known": Beckett, Ireland and the Creative Industries', in Fintan Walsh (ed.), That Was Us: Contemporary Irish Theatre and Performance (London: Oberon Books, 2013), 157–72.

translation, can his prose fiction be assimilated to any falsely normative relationship to Irish culture and to national novelistic traditions and tendencies. In dealing with Beckett's prose we need to accommodate several elements: a comparative paucity of specific reference, the manner in which his work both posits and resists reference to Ireland (Irish place names clashing eerily with French voices), and the oblique ways in which, in Peter Boxall's influential contention, a 'semi-autobiographical drama of cultural belonging and alienation'[12] is played out across Beckett's narrators' wanderings, and is written into the very texture of his fictional spaces. Much of his work remains in dialogue with Irish landscapes and includes satiric but purposeful networks of allusion to modes of Irish writing, mythology, and historiography. It also frequently derives its energies from oppositions to or reworkings of Irish predecessors, particularly James Joyce, and often parodies modes and discourses of the Revival and post-Revival eras by bringing them into contact with the *nouveau roman*.

BECKETT AND JOYCE

Beckett, of course, is not Joyce, whose work it is impossible to consider in isolation from its embeddedness in the social, economic, and political ferment of Irish culture at the turn of the twentieth century. All of *Ulysses* (1922), *A Portrait of the Artist as a Young Man* (1916), and even the less formally complex stories of *Dubliners* (1914) emerge as thoroughly imbricated, formally and through their notoriously dense tissue of allusion and parody, with the colonial Ireland of the period. In them, formal and aesthetic innovations emerge as inseparable from the works' registering of the rich complexities of local geographies, political catchphrases, and advertizing slogans. Yet Beckett, whose work begs to be read in terms of its derivation from, and fruitful opposition to, the work of Joyce, simply cannot sustain the kind of detailed cultural archaeology which supports Joyce studies. As David Lloyd notes, 'Working on Beckett is peculiarly difficult, and therefore, perhaps, instructive to cultural studies, because of his notorious formal recalcitrance to the referential tendencies of the field.'[13]

But the Joyce from which Beckett's work derives is not the Joyce of *Ulysses* but, crucially, the Joyce of the dazzlingly multilingual acquisitiveness of 'Work in Progress', later *Finnegans Wake*. During the young Beckett's unhappy peregrinations before he settled in Paris in 1937—'a young man with nothing to say and the itch to make',[14] as he later said dismissively of his youthful self—Joyce was swiftly established as his ideal of the omnipotent, consummately dedicated author-god when he met him through Thomas MacGreevy (1893–1967). In 1929, when he was a temporary lecteur at the École Normale

---

[12] Boxall, 'Samuel Beckett: Towards a Political Reading', 162.

[13] David Lloyd, 'Frames of *Referrance*: Samuel Beckett as an Irish Question', in Kennedy (ed.), *Beckett and Ireland*, 39.

[14] Quoted in Lawrence Harvey, *Samuel Beckett: Poet and Critic* (Princeton, NJ: Princeton University Press, 1970), 273.

Supérieure and already helping to translate the thousand or more river names woven through 'Anna Livia Plurabelle', Beckett published his first essay, an impassioned defence of 'Work in Progress', in the journal *transition*. The same issue contained his first published short story, the conspicuously Joycean 'Assumption', which appeared under the pseudonym Andrew Belis. His 'Dante . . . Bruno. Vico . . . Joyce' (1929) defends Joyce's experimentalism from an implied reader's hostility, preaching the need to reinvigorate an overly 'sophisticated' English he perceives as in danger of being 'abstracted to death' by a new writing which will 'recognise the importance of treating words as something more than polite symbols'.[15] He argues that Joyce, who has 'desophisticated language', has arrived at 'direct expression', a 'savage economy of hieroglyphics'; his is a mode of writing in which 'form *is* content, content *is* form', and in which writing 'is not *about* something' but '*is that something itself*'.[16] In 1930, Beckett, along with his École Normale Supérieure colleague Alfred Péron, was commissioned by Joyce to translate part of this 'direct expression', a section of 'Anna Livia Plurabelle', into French. It is this nexus, more than anything else, that forms Beckett's work's constitutive encounter with that of Joyce, and which would direct the course of the pre-war novels Beckett wrote in English, an influence that would continue more obliquely into the self-impoverished French work of the post-war years.

That the 'Anna Livia Plurabelle' translation was in some sense a quasi-Oedipal encounter is an inescapable conclusion, especially as the translation by Beckett and Péron, entitled 'Anna Lyvia Pluratself', was ultimately rejected by Joyce in favour of a heavily revised version by a hand-picked group which included Philippe Soupault, Eugène Jolas, Paul Léon, and Joyce himself.[17] If, as John P. Harrington argues, Beckett's 'Recent Irish Poetry' is in some sense 'the work of an angry young man repudiating his elders', staging an aggressively Oedipal break with the fathers of the Revival, then Joyce eventually becomes an alternative, and problematic, father figure.[18] Beckett's frustration at what he saw as 'the chasm of feeling and technique between [Joyce's] hieroglyphics and our bastard French',[19] his sense of his own inadequacy as a translator of a revered, if almost untranslatable, work of dense, morphological inventiveness, and the eventual bruising rejection of the translation, is obvious in his correspondence; it is also a key moment in the establishment of his mature aesthetic of lessness, failure, and inadequacy. From his involvement with 'Work in Progress' Beckett derived his sharp sense of Joyce as a maximalist, a 'superb manipulator of material . . . making words do the absolute maximum of work', and his own oppositional and belated sense of being a 'non-knower', as he would tell Israel Shenker in 1956.[20]

---

[15] Beckett, *Disjecta*, 28.   [16] Ibid., 27-28. Original emphasis.

[17] James Joyce, 'Anna Livie Plurabelle', trans. Samuel Beckett, Alfred Péron, Philippe Soupault, Yvan Goll, Adrienne Monnier, Eugène Jolas, and Paul Léon, in collaboration with the author, in *La Nouvelle Revue Française* 19, no. 212 (1931), 633–46. Beckett and Péron's translation was eventually published in Jacques Aubert and Fritz Senn (eds), *Cahier James Joyce* (Paris: Éditions de l'Herne, 1985), 417–22.

[18] John P. Harrington, *The Irish Beckett* (Syracuse, NY: Syracuse University Press, 1991), 29.

[19] Samuel Beckett, *The Letters of Samuel Beckett, Volume 1: 1929–1940*, ed. Martha Dow Fehsenfeld and Lois More Overbeck (Cambridge: Cambridge University Press, 2009), 24–5, 41.

[20] Israel Shenker, 'Moody Man of Letters', *New York Times*, 5 May 1956, 2, 1, 3.

In 1932, Beckett would offer his story, 'Sedendo et Quiesciendo', to Chatto and Windus, with a note that demonstrated his rueful awareness of the extent to which he was still helplessly ventriloquizing Joyce: 'Of course it stinks of Joyce, in spite of my most earnest endeavours to endow it with my own odours.'[21]

In Beckett's first published fiction, the 'odours' of 'Work in Progress' are most obvious in the density of allusion and multilingual wordplay, as well as in a somewhat weary sense of his own manifold belatedness. The unfinished novel, *Dream of Fair to Middling Women*, written in 1932 in Paris but published only posthumously in 1992, has been aptly summed up by John Pilling as a 'pot-pourri of irreconcilable elements, part-autobiography, part-fiction, and part loose-leaf folder for any passing expressive gesture'.[22] Made up largely of second-hand nuggets of knowledge and turns of phrase from his omnivorous reading, it was mined by Beckett shortly after its composition for his short story collection, *More Pricks Than Kicks* (1934). Furiously choleric in tone, and heavily reliant on the omnivorous note-taking to which Beckett was addicted in the 1930s, both novel and stories concern the life and loves of the feckless Dubliner Belacqua Shuah, a shambling, solipsistic combination of clown and scholar whose ability to confront and delimit reality is conspicuously deficient, and who already foreshadows a line of successors. At best, *Dream of Fair to Middling Women* and *More Pricks Than Kicks*, both with the artist as central character and offering revised, darker 'portraits of the artist', manifest a fierce iconoclasm towards anachronistic literary pieties and a determination to move beyond what *Dream* disdainfully calls the 'chloroformed world'[23] of the well-made story. At worst, they are clotted, derivative, and floridly over-written, expending their textual energies on post-Joycean linguistic exhibitionism and consciously belated and weary gestures of dissent. After all, as James McNaughton argues, Beckett, arriving 'late to the Irish revival, and late to modernism', as well as late to the political upheavals of early twentieth-century Ireland, was establishing himself within a familiar field of literary possibilities: 'after Joyce, it was not exactly heroic to reject social realism or bourgeois novels that celebrate marriage, property and children' in favour of experimental linguistic scepticism and modernist detachment and irony.[24]

If Beckett lambasted most writers and artists active in Ireland in the 1930s, and played the stereotypical modernist by rejecting Irish parochialism and backwardness in favour of artistic devotion and political aloofness, his contemporary fiction was already examining such high modernist posturing and subjecting it to a somewhat jaded satire, as when 'A Wet Night' in *More Pricks Than Kicks* mocks a group of perambulating Trinity College students for obsessing about the 'essential difference'[25] between Einstein and

[21] Beckett, *The Letters of Samuel Beckett*, 81.

[22] John Pilling, 'Beckett's English Fiction', in John Pilling (ed.), *The Cambridge Companion to Samuel Beckett* (Cambridge: Cambridge University Press, 1994), 20.

[23] Samuel Beckett, *Dream of Fair to Middling Women*, ed. Eoin O'Brien and Edith Fournier (Dublin: Black Cat Press,1992), 119.

[24] James McNaughton, 'The Politics of Aftermath: Beckett, Modernism, and the Irish Free State', in Kennedy (ed.), *Beckett and Ireland*, 57.

[25] Samuel Beckett, *More Pricks Than Kicks* (London: Picador: 1974), 63.

Henri Bergson and exhibiting a trite, second-rate, and belated interest in modernist thought. Beckett is almost equally suspicious of both the provincial 'accredited' nationalist thematics he attacks in 'Recent Irish Poetry' and the belated provincial striving after modernism, which is merely another form of 'accreditation'.[26]

For Beckett in the 1930s, the new is not, after all, so new. James McNaughton points to how, after undergoing analysis under Wilfred Bion, Beckett acknowledged the psychological toll of an earlier period of reclusiveness, during which he immersed himself in 'a crescendo of disparagement of others and myself' and indulged in a 'negation of living' which he himself linked to the terrible psychosomatic symptoms that eventually drove him to protracted analysis in London.[27] For McNaughton, it is 'As if [Beckett's] life were a parody of Stephen Dedalus'[28] in its internalization of high modernism's stance of superiority, which superseded commitment to anything, even to writing itself. Fictional versions of this internal drama are played out in the figure of Belacqua and, more obviously, in the eponymous protagonist of *Murphy*. In these early works, the narrators satirize as dangerous and ridiculous their characters' solipsistic retreat from the world, and delineate a pathology of smug subjectivity and withdrawal associated with the progressive avant-garde.

Murphy is best known for its broad satire of revivalist iconography and questioning of hegemonic cultural values. The novel stages a series of savage set-pieces, including the satiric one-man protest of Neary's beating of his head against the buttocks of Oliver Sheppard's statue of the mythic Cuchulain on the 'holy ground'[29] of Dublin's General Post Office; Murphy's will directing the disposal of his ashes to take place during a performance at the Abbey Theatre, locus of national ideological investment; the burlesque of Austin Clarke (1896–1974) as the pot poet Austin Ticklepenny; the fascination with Eastern mysticism of George Russell (1867–1935) and Yeats; and the prostitute Celia's construction as a parody of revivalist representations of Ireland. Equally derided, however, are attitudes and behaviours that are the flip side of these: Murphy's solipsistic indifference to society and other people, his search for a refuge in which he can perform his peculiar meditations, and the depiction of an aloof, fastidious aesthetic sensibility which abhors the material world and chooses instead a withdrawal to the padded cells of a psychiatric hospital as a form of modernist retreat to the nirvana of the isolated ego.

Like his predecessor Belacqua Shuah, another *flâneur* and 'chronic emeritus'[30] obsessed with achieving the correct state of consciousness, Murphy dies by gas. His ashes never make it to their post-mortem protest in the toilets at the Abbey but end up on the floor of a London pub and are eventually 'swept away with the sand, the beet, the butts, the glass, the matches, the spits, the vomit',[31] his grandiose aspirations reduced to rubbish. If Irish cultural nationalism is comprehensibly derided in Beckett's early fiction,

---

[26] Beckett, *Disjecta*, 76.   [27] McNaughton, 'The Politics of Aftermath', 65.   [28] Ibid.

[29] Samuel Beckett, *Murphy* (London: Pan, 1973), 28. A few months before Beckett wrote this scene, Sheppard's statue was newly dedicated by Éamon de Valera in 1935 as part of a renegotiation of a contentious recent past into a cohesive national mythos. See Patrick W. Bixby, 'Beckett at the GPO: *Murphy*, Ireland and the "Unhomely"', in Kennedy (ed.), *Beckett and Ireland*, 78–95.

[30] Beckett, *Murphy*, 16.   [31] Ibid., 154.

so too are what are viewed as trite and belated modernist postures of aloofness and aestheticism. *Murphy* is in some sense still a Joycean *Bildungsroman*, heavily dependent upon what Emilie Morin calls 'coded satire'[32] and interspersed with allusions to Irish revivalist literature refracted through the lens of *A Portrait* and *Ulysses*. If Stephen Dedalus, from a paralysed colonial Dublin, viewed exile as the essential precondition for his renewed encounter with 'the reality of experience' and his forging of 'the uncreated conscience of my race',[33] *Murphy* moves the post-Dedalian protagonist to London, where exile offers no opportunity for meaningful encounter or creativity, only increasingly parodic forms of solipsism and self-seclusion. If Beckett's youth growing up in Ireland during the revolutionary period taught him a disgust for the ways in which art was appropriated to political ends to bolster competing narratives of Irish identity, then his exposure to Nazi racial ideology and censorship during his travels in Germany in 1937 and 1938 after he finished *Murphy* made him even more certain that art should be 'free to be derided (or not) on its own terms and not those of the politicians'.[34]

The Turn to French

Beckett's enormously fertile 'siege in the room'[35] period that lasted from approximately 1946 until the early 1950s, during which he wrote four short stories, four novels, and two plays in French, is in some ways the most mysterious episode of all in his career, and the most subject to mythologization and critical speculation. Clearly, the turn to French liberated something in a writer for whom composition had always been difficult. This turn has been variously linked to a self-conscious aesthetic of self-impoverishment, weakness, and reduction; a self-liberation from the overweening influence of Joyce and Irish literature; a recovery from the linguistic breakdown of his wartime novel, *Watt* (a literary artefact so odd that the manuscript was impounded as suspicious by the War Office when Beckett travelled through London to Dublin in the spring of 1945); a final renunciation of the accumulative, consciously derivative techniques of writing he had employed for much of his pre-war career; and an ultimate embrace of the position of the 'non-knower'. Moreover, the turn to French is seen by many critics as a crucial moment in the self-impoverishing development of Beckett's writing career along a teleology from reference to referencelessness, from history to ahistoricity, a journey whereby, as Anna McMullan puts it, 'all specificities of class, nation, or geography . . . give way to abstracted and formalised spaces of representation'.[36] Ireland, conventionally, has been seen as one

---

[32] Emilie Morin, *Samuel Beckett and the Problem of Irishness* (Basingstoke: Palgrave Macmillan, 2009), 50.

[33] James Joyce, *A Portrait of the Artist as a Young Man*, ed. Seamus Deane (London: Penguin, 1992), 275–6.

[34] Beckett, *Disjecta*, 91.

[35] Quoted in Deirdre Bair, *Samuel Beckett: A Biography* (London: Jonathan Cape, 1978), 346.

[36] Anna McMullan, 'Irish/Postcolonial Beckett', in Lois Oppenheim (ed.), *Palgrave Advances in Beckett Studies* (Basingstoke: Palgrave Macmillan, 2004), 99.

of the elements lost in Beckett's adoption of a foreign language, but in fact Beckett's trilogy in both its languages can be understood as a tissue of historico-cultural allusions precisely by virtue of its flaunting of its own non-nativeness and translatedness.

As Sam Slote notes, 'Beckett's linguistic turn is more akin to a series of blurry zigzags'[37] than anything that implies an intentional movement towards a fixed and final destination. Beckett did not relinquish his mother tongue completely, as Vladimir Nabokov did; no sooner had he embarked upon writing in French than he almost immediately began to translate his own French prose back into English, so that virtually all of his works have two, often non-identical, texts. Moreover, the trilogy of novels *Molloy* (1951), *Malone meurt* (1951), and *L'Innommable* (1953), which were self-translated as *Molloy* (1955), *Malone Dies* (1956), and *The Unnamable* (1958), were underwritten by the fact that Beckett was still, during their composition, working as a jobbing translator, making a living by translating vast amounts of what *The Unnamable* would dub 'others' words'.[38] Also, as late as 1946 Beckett's name was being approved by Harriet Shaw Weaver as a member of a potential translation team for a French *Finnegans Wake*.[39] This lending out of his voice, and the voicing of other people's words, is closely related to the trilogy's problematization of voice itself, of the origin and propriety of utterance, and of the apparent impossibility of speaking of and for oneself—'I say what I hear, I hear what I say, I don't know, one or the other, or both'[40]—which contributes largely to Beckett's mature work constituting something of an outlier or alien presence within the history of the Irish novel.

Key to an understanding of the linguistic and temperamental strangeness of Beckett's work is his interest in eschewing the narrative strategies of the traditionally omnipotent author for the less masterful practices which cluster around the shadowy, ambivalent figure of the translator—even when these two figures are combined in the same person. Many of his mature stylistic signatures derive from what he learned from his translations of the work of others, and which he then put into practice in the narrative dynamics of his own work. These include the lack of topographical specificity; the citational subjectivity of his narrators; his preoccupation in prose as well as drama with voices severed from bodies; his particular sense that language will always be found wanting; and, ultimately, his desire for a 'literature of the unword', in which language does not disappear but instead is turned back repeatedly against itself in an enactment of the unwording or denunciation of literary discourse that his pre-war novels thematized. This characteristically late modernist linguistic subversion (as distinct from the commitment to a renewal of language by high modernists such as Joyce or Pound), combined with Beckett's rejection of a conventional intelligibility which he viewed as spurious in the aftermath of the Second World War, was symptomatic of his desire to find a post-Joycean way of writing which would accommodate what he viewed as 'the

---

[37] Sam Slote, 'Bilingual Beckett: Beyond the Linguistic Turn', in Dirk Van Hulle (ed.), *The New Cambridge Companion to Samuel Beckett* (Cambridge: Cambridge University Press, 2015), 114.

[38] Beckett, *The Unnamable*, in *The Beckett Trilogy*, 355.

[39] Letter from Harriet Shaw Weaver to Lionel Munro, 15 July 1946, quoted in John Pilling, *A Samuel Beckett Chronology* (Basingstoke: Palgrave Macmillan, 2006), 98.

[40] Beckett, *The Unnamable*, in *The Beckett Trilogy*, 380.

mess'[41] of contemporary existence. Writing in a foreign language, and only then seeking a deliberately self-impoverished and insecure niche for his novels in his native language, allowed Beckett a shadowy, subversive way of moving forward, despite a crippling loss of faith in language and in the possibility that art could offer either transfiguration or transcendence.

Conventionally, of course, translators tend to be self-effacing textual presences and translations themselves do not draw attention to their secondary status to the 'original' texts. Norman Shapiro epitomizes this traditional view when he defines translation as 'the attempt to produce a text so transparent that it does not seem to be translated'.[42] 'A good translation', he writes, 'is like a pane of glass. You only notice that it's there when there are little imperfections—scratches, bubbles. Ideally, there shouldn't be any. It should never call attention to itself'.[43] If the English-language editions of the trilogy often appear to fail as novels by imperfectly concealing their textuality behind a satisfactory 'story' and their heterogeneous materials beneath the illusion of a stable subjectivity, it is a failure achieved with a deliberate *gaucherie*, one designed to flout the conventional doctrine of the 'invisibility' of the translator and overturn the hierarchy of original and translation.

Of course, the French 'originals' are already themselves radically unconventional texts, obsessed with the destitution of words and things and with an ontological homelessness well served by the mismatch of Irish proper names and French language. They present a savagely reduced world in which wanderers who mispronounce their French make their way across an indistinct terrain in prose which always already feels like an eccentric translation into French from some non-existent Hiberno-English original, with obtrusively non-French proper names, currencies, and systems of measurement. In translation, however, far from 'domesticating' the trilogy so that it might become an exclusively Irish trio of novels—become the Irish trilogy it seems to be aspiring towards in the original French but for the apparent accident of the language of composition— Beckett makes the translated text appear still more disconcertingly foreign. While early criticism of the trilogy often admired Beckett's skill in finding equivalent textual effects in his other language, his self-translations in fact frequently refuse equivalence. Texts which are already in their original forms mined with narrative and linguistic deviations, gaps, and incongruities, develop in translation further unsettling linguistic markers or references to another linguistic universe, reneging still further on the realist contract.

In the trilogy, the conventionally 'invisible' practices of translation are traceable throughout, dominated as it is by linguistically located speakers who are both polyglot and studiously ventriloquistic, uneasily straddling languages and cultures, frequently referring to other language or languages. The voice of *The Unnamable* seems to remember an illustrated dictionary, or perhaps a schoolchild's language textbook, and the

[41] Quoted in Thomas F. Driver, 'Interview with Samuel Beckett', in Lawrence Graver and Raymond Federman (eds), *Samuel Beckett: The Critical Heritage* (London: Routledge and Kegan Paul, 1979), 219.
[42] Quoted in Lawrence Venuti, *The Translator's Invisibility: A History of Translation* (London: Routledge, 1995), 1.
[43] Ibid.

experience of being taught worryingly arbitrary words, 'on lists, with images opposite, I must have forgotten them, I must have mixed them up, these nameless images I have, these imageless names, these windows I should perhaps rather call doors, at least by some other name'.[44] Molloy works out a sadistic bodily code of translation, thumping his elderly mother's skull in order to indicate 'yes', 'no', and the crucial 'money'.[45] By drawing attention to its own language via inconsistencies, foreign words, and a refusal to conceal the fact of *translatedness*, Beckett's English-language trilogy transgresses against representation and the conventional invisibility of the translator, an invisibility which works in a way that is cognate to mimesis's effacement of its own processes.

Often, the implied translator becomes visible in ironic moments of unconcealed hesitation as to his accuracy in rendering the original, such as when the French Macmann, having decided to lie down in the rain so as not to get wet all over, 'allait pouvoir se lever dans dix minutes un quart d'heure, le devant poussiéreux'. A faithful English translation of this passage would simply register Macmann's 'dusty front', but the translator jokes at his own uncertain reading of the original, dithering about 'his front, no, his back, white with, no, front was right, his front white with dust'.[46] A conventional translation would conceal its hesitation before the original, but Beckett ironically highlights his own tentativeness and secondariness as a self-translating author. All of Beckett's trilogy narrators could therefore be more accurately conceived of as translators of various kinds, recounting narratives which may in fact be someone else's autobiography entirely, worrying endlessly about accuracy—worries which they nonetheless emphasize to puncture the illusion of transparency—and actively disowning stories which appear to be their own. Creatures compulsively tell stories which may or may not be theirs, or cite as a translator would testimonies from another source—'I say it as I hear it',[47] as the speaker of *How It Is* (1964) periodically insists—so that to speak, in Beckett's mature work, often appears to be the same as ventriloquizing the words of another. What is said, or heard, or repeated appears to need to be interpreted or translated as if from an alien source. Speakers draw attention to their own foreignisms, linguistic oddities, and mispronunciations—'awful English this',[48] as the narrator of *From an Abandoned Work*, first published in 1956, remarks—deictically making language visible *as* language and as *a* language.

Common to virtually all criticism of the trilogy is an acknowledgement of its assault on the order of discourse, its disintegration of the traditional narrative conventions of the novel, and its attack on certainty and knowledge. Beckett's wandering tramps, or deathbed moribunds mouldering in their solitary rooms, huts, or ditches, recall, for David Watson, Foucault's *fous*, marginalized by the dominant discourse of reason, forced to account for themselves by *recounting* their stories to the forces of law and order and other powers-that-be, who clearly regard these errant storytellers as anti-social

---

[44] Beckett, *The Unnamable*, in *The Beckett Trilogy*, 375.

[45] Beckett, *Molloy*, in *The Beckett Trilogy*, 18.

[46] Samuel Beckett, *Malone meurt* (Paris: Editions de Minuit, 1951), 108; *Malone Dies*, in *The Beckett Trilogy*, 219.

[47] Samuel Beckett, *How It Is* (New York: Grove Press, 1964), 7.

[48] Samuel Beckett, 'From an Abandoned Work', in *The Complete Short Prose 1929–1989*, ed. S. E. Gontarski (New York: Grove Press, 1995), 164.

elements requiring surveillance.[49] Just as Beckett's speakers are regularly rebuked by the forces of authority for not being able to walk, rest, or recall their own names *comme tout le monde*, the irregular, ragged stories to which they are driven in order to fulfil the narrative imperatives to which they are subject invariably transgress the rules of narrative and are not *vraisemblant* or *convenable*. His stories appear to be written in ignorance of the laws of conventional storytelling, not least in the way that they refuse the reader the illusion of being immersed in the story, living through the plot, identifying with the characters. Like the uncouth tramp Molloy, who claims he has never been taught 'the guiding principles of good manners' and thus parades 'in public certain habits such as the finger in the nose, the scratching of the balls, digital emunction and the peripatetic piss', the narrative appears to be in a condition of 'doubting the possibility of systematic decorum'.[50]

Realist mimesis, of which the nineteenth-century novel is of course the classic instance, presupposes the purpose of language is to directly and *transparently* express an extra-linguistic 'reality' which pre-exists the text itself. What Barthes dubs the 'doxa'[51]— the contractual tissue of codes incorporating expectation and probability, to which any text must defer to be *vraisemblable*—supports the relations of reader and writer and attempts to ensure and police the unproblematic transmission of this agreed 'reality'. Beckett's trilogy, however, flagrantly offends against this realist mimetic supposition of unproblematic representation and the instrumentality of language. The reader's attempt to 'make sense' of its narratives is frustrated by the text's refusal to set up a stable referential relationship between itself and an intelligible extralinguistic reality. Beckett, therefore, uses the figure of the translator, and the doxa of transparency to which the 'invisible' translator is, like the realist novelist, subject, in order to conduct his aporetic assaults on the novel and on language, *through* language.

At times, as when Molloy describes the speech he hears as 'pure sounds, free of all meaning',[52] there is a disturbingly complete absence of relationship between sound and sense. The 'icy words . . . icy meanings'[53] that hail down on him suggest a self-estranged subject assailed by a stubbornly material and opaque language which comes unsettlingly close to mere noise, of the kind that continually haunts the edges of Beckett's discourse, as in the Unnamable's 'mewl, howl, gasp and rattle' and his promises to fix the alien 'gibberish' he has been taught by improvising onomatopoeic nonsense: 'I'll practise, nyum, hoo, plop, psss, nothing but emotion, bing bang, that's blows, ugh, pooh, what else.'[54] Not surprisingly, for a writer who comes to French with habits and linguistic impulses formed in English (or Hiberno-English), Beckett's writing consistently constructs itself in terms of an untranscendable materiality of language. The limits of this language are shaped by its essential foreignness in relation to speaking subjects who attempt, compulsively, to construct themselves within it in a series of never-ending, unsettling skirmishes

[49] David Watson, *Paradox and Desire in Beckett's Fiction* (Basingstoke: Macmillan, 1991), 1ff.
[50] Beckett, *Molloy*, in *The Beckett Trilogy*, 25.
[51] Roland Barthes, *S/Z: An Essay*, trans. Richard Miller (Oxford: Blackwell, 1990), 200.
[52] Beckett, *Molloy*, in *The Beckett Trilogy*, 47.
[53] Ibid., 31.   [54] Beckett, *The Unnamable*, in *The Beckett Trilogy*, 308, 376.

with words. If the work of Joyce constituted for Beckett a form of 'apotheosis of the word',[55] then the trilogy constructs out of an acute sense of futility and a deep distrust of the word a *via negativa* which nonetheless allows a faltering on of the novel.

THE TRILOGY, TRANSLATION, AND IRELAND

Beckett's bilingualism has contributed largely to the characterization of his post-war French work as hermetic, monastic, and without politics or any reference to a world outside the monadic space of the writing itself. This characterization, however, looks increasingly naïve. Just as Beckett, when he left Ireland permanently in 1937, certainly did not leave the country behind imaginatively, neither can his choice of French as a language of prose composition or his career-long self-translation be completely divorced from Free State cultural and ideological anxieties of the 1930s concerning deanglicization, censorship of foreign publications, and the promotion of translation into the Irish language as a filter against pernicious foreign influence. As his 'Censorship in the Saorstat' and 'Recent Irish Poetry' demonstrate, Beckett, writing (albeit with disdain) about the post-Yeatsian poetry of his contemporaries, was well aware of the centrality of literary translation to the laying of the cultural-political basis of Irish nationhood.[56] In fact, his complaints about the lingering influence on 1930s Irish poetry of the '*Gossoons Wunderhorn* of that Irish Romantic Arnim-Brentano combination, Sir Samuel Ferguson and Standish O'Grady',[57] indicate a consciousness of Ferguson's influential belief in the importance of fluent translation into English of the Gaelic literature of the past. In a context of increasing Anglicization and mounting nationalism, Ferguson's curiously inhibited English translations were produced with the intention that, as Francis Mulhern puts it, 'the spirit of an unriven other world, reincarnated in canonical forms of the English-language poetic, would foster an irenic Irish identity and so assist political healing.'[58] After independence, policing translation—whether into English or Irish—was an element in a larger ideological project aimed at the creation of a more conservative national culture, a view typified by Aodh de Blácam's (1890–1951) statement (issued around the time that Beckett was worrying about the consequences of translating de Sade's *Les cent-vingt jours de Sodom* in an increasingly puritan post-independence literary culture) that 'All great writing is conservative. After all, the very purpose of the writing is to conserve.'[59]

---

[55] Beckett, *Disjecta*, 172.

[56] See Matthijs Engelberts and Everett Frost with Jane Maxwell (eds), *Samuel Beckett Today/ Aujourd'hui. Special Issue* 16 (2006). *Notes Diverse Holo: Catalogues of Beckett's Reading Notes and Other Manuscripts at Trinity College Dublin, with Supporting Essays.*

[57] Beckett, *Disjecta*, 76.

[58] Francis Mulhern, 'Translation: Re-writing Degree Zero', in *The Present Lasts a Long Time: Essays in Cultural Politics* (Cork: Cork University Press, 1998), 168.

[59] Aodh de Blácam, 'The World of Letters: Poison in the Wells', *Irish Monthly* 65 (1937), 280. De Blácam was condemning literary modernism and objecting to government funds being spent on An Gúm's translation into Irish of 'foreign detective stories'.

The trilogy sets its face against a conservation agenda. Impurities of various kinds, including obscenities and more straightforwardly linguistic impurities, form an important part of its thematics and style. The An Gúm translators, acting under the auspices of the Department of Education and tasked with providing a supply of Irish-language material to aid the revival of Irish, were anxious to respect the prescription against Anglicisms, leading to an extreme reluctance to import unusual, non-standard, or foreign forms into Irish. Post-independence translators were also intimately involved in the standardization of Irish orthography and grammar which was essential if Irish was to function as a working language in a modern society.[60] Beckett's trilogy takes a very different course, exploiting 'translatedness' in both its languages and actively flaunting its impurities and linguistic hesitations. With its promiscuous admixture of Irish names— Molloy, Moran, Malone, Macmann, Quin, Christy—and such un-Irish references as horse butchers, aspects of French topography, Bastille Day, and the Bank of England, the trilogy makes play with the self-proclaimed lack of fluency of the implied translator. For example, the French Molloy makes a pantomime of being unsure of what gender the noun 'existence' is, and apologizes for the 'awfulness' of his language;[61] Moll's love-letter to Macmann in *Malone Dies* offers for the original French 'tête-beche' (literally 'head to toe' but metaphorically the sex act at which they intermittently labour) the mangled, mispronounced 'tetty-beshy'[62]; and the Irish language is satirically introduced into the translation in terms of insult and incomprehensibility—'Les pleurs et les ris, je ne m'y connais guère' becomes 'tears and laughter, they are so much Gaelic to me'.[63]

If we consider the trilogy as a set of pseudo-translations, produced in awareness of a specifically Irish set of national anxieties, the novels also play subversively with notions of translation as a dangerous source of the cultural 'rot' that censorship was designed to check. Beckett's sardonic remark in a 1933 letter to Thomas MacGreevy on the subject of a 'phallic tower on Inishmore', formerly referred to by the islanders as '*penis erectus* in Gaelic but now out of newly acquired prudery . . . the *upright thing*',[64] suggests his awareness of translation as part of a project which would consolidate notions of the ancientness of Ireland and bolster a crusade for sexual propriety. In fact, as Michael Cronin points out, 'transforming readers of Irish into members of the English Victorian urban middle class, while at the same time extolling the virtues of a ruggedly independent rural Ireland'[65] is one of the more familiar contradictions of nationalism in Ireland. Beckett, through his enthusiasm for Synge, would have had at least some knowledge of Irish mythological tales from plays such as *Deirdre of the Sorrows* (1910), and his 'Recent Irish Poetry' shows him on nodding terms with 'Oisin, Cuchulain, Maeve, Tir-nanog, the Táin Bo Cuailgne, Yoga, the Crone of Beare'.[66] Unlike anything Synge produced, however, the trilogy combines a gleeful despatch of the bowdlerization of Irish myths in

---

[60] Michael Cronin, *Translating Ireland: Translation, Languages, Cultures* (Cork: Cork University Press, 1996), 155.

[61] Beckett, *Molloy* (Paris: Editions de Minuit, 1951), 62.

[62] Beckett, *Malone meurt*, 146; *Malone Dies*, in *The Beckett Trilogy*, 240.

[63] Beckett, *Molloy*, 48; *Molloy*, in *The Beckett Trilogy*, 35.

[64] Samuel Beckett to Thomas MacGreevy, 7 September, 1933 (TCD MS 10402).

[65] Cronin, *Translating Ireland*, 152.   [66] Beckett, *Disjecta*, 71.

translation with a satirical investment in *dinnseanchas*, the lore associated with Irish place names and one of the pieties of Revival and post-Revival literature.

Molloy's excremental topography combines a mocking nod to the Revival's fetishizing of place and a transgression of the bowdlerization of bawdy early Irish texts in translation. The French *Molloy* features journeys in the vicinity of Bally (whose name is, as Hugh Kenner notes, 'half Irish cliché, half English obscenity'[67]), Shit, Shitba, and Hole, while the English text, itself mildly self-censoring, given a putative Anglophone audience, renders the first two of these place names as the more Anglo-Saxon Turdy and Turdyba. On the other hand, both French and English texts throughout flaunt a close attention to physical grotesqueries, bawdiness, and bodily functions, elements which also characterize early Irish texts but which were frequently deliberately lost in translation by their Victorian and Edwardian translators. The tales of the Ulster and Fenian cycles of Irish myth pay great heed to sexualities, physical oddities, and the frequently grotesque deaths of their human and superhuman fighters and lovers—a tendency removed in translation by translators such as Augusta Gregory (1852–1932) in her *Cúchulain of Muirthemne* (1902) and *Gods and Fighting Men* (1904). In contrast, while Molloy remarks that people are 'extraordinarily reserved, in my part of the world, about everything connected with sexual matters',[68] the preceding passage describes in detail his paid encounters with the grotesque sheela-na-gig physicality of a fellow-haunter of rubbish dumps, Edith or Ruth, who may have been in fact an old man somehow concealing his testicles. In a similar vein, Malone records the spectacle of his creature and alter ego Macmann, whose family are 'sprung from the same illustrious ball', 'trying to bundle his sex into his partner's like a pillow into a pillow-slip, folding it into two and stuffing it in with his fingers'.[69]

Far from being 'reserved', then, the trilogy evinces a Swiftian relish in ageing sexuality and bodily flaws and fluids, and savagely rejects the norms of romantic love. While, occasionally, an obscene joke itself relies on a putatively bilingual reader—as in the schoolboy joke about the ancient French town of Condom being situated on the River Baise—in general the English text is the more gleefully scabrous. The comically mealy-mouthed interjection in which Molloy apologizes for the anality of his prose—'I apologize for having to revert to this lewd orifice, 'tis my muse will have it so'[70]—draws attention to an obsessive recounting of excremental, urinary, and ejaculatory processes, as well as characteristically appalled and appalling evocations of the experience of being born, and of 'her who brought me into the world, through the hole in her arse if my memory is correct. First taste of the shit'.[71]

The adulterated, hybrid subject of the trilogy constitutes a rebuttal of the ideal subject of Irish cultural nationalism—what David Lloyd characterizes as the 'individual's ideal continuity with the nation's spiritual origins'—and of nationalism's Romantic concern with

---

[67]   Hugh Kenner, *Samuel Beckett* (London: John Calder, 1960), 57.
[68]   Beckett, *Molloy*, in *The Beckett Trilogy*, 55.
[69]   Beckett, *Malone Dies*, in *The Beckett Trilogy*, 238.
[70]   Beckett, *Molloy*, in *The Beckett Trilogy*, 73.   [71] Ibid., 17.

the capacity of original 'genius' to depict and embody the 'spirit of the nation'.[72] The trilogy's active recalcitrance towards the monologic demands of literary nationalism for a total identification with the nation means that it circles thematically and stylistically around adulteration as the constitutive anxiety of nationalism, like the 'Cyclops' episode of *Ulysses*. As we have seen, translation was crucial to this preoccupation with linguistic and cultural recovery in revivalist literature and its aftermath. The six texts of the trilogy, however, are defiantly problematic in their irreducibility to a single or stable national identity or language in which either author or narrators might be 'at home'. As such, they challenge the notions of authenticity and legitimacy which the new Irish state and its 'official' translators promoted. Instead of homogeneity, Beckett's trilogy performs something akin to the adulteration of interpenetrating discourses of *Ulysses* and *Finnegans Wake* by multiplying, in translation, its rampant internal heterogeneities. The result is a Bakhtinian multiplicity of contending, ill-integrated linguistic universes which stand in direct contradistinction to a desired unified national identity as defined and represented in a national literature.

If, ultimately, the defiant non-representivity of the novelistic forms in which Beckett worked cannot easily be understood in relation to prior traditions of Irish fiction, apart from the defining high modernist 'apotheosis of the word' of James Joyce, they are nonetheless far from devoid of Irish content. Beckett's decision to write his novels primarily in French after the war did not require an absolute 'rupture of the lines of communication'[73] between his fiercely denatured prose and antagonism to representation on the one hand, and his Irish origins on the other. Considering *Molloy*, *Malone Dies*, and *The Unnamable* as pseudo-translations which exploit the 'impotent' and belated position of the translator illuminates Beckett's work's complex relationship to Ireland by the culturally specific ways in which he engages with what he calls 'the nature of what has so happily been called the unutterable or ineffable, so that at any attempt to utter or eff it is doomed to fail'.[74] Suspicious of the idea of tradition or national canons as reifying, Beckett's work mobilizes, as Adorno influentially argued of his *Endgame*, shreds and remnants, the 'innumerable allusions and cultural tidbits'[75] of a world that has lost its capacity to integrate.

FURTHER READING

Boxall, Peter. 'Samuel Beckett: Towards a Political Reading'. *Irish Studies Review* 10, vol. 2 (2002): 159–70.

Cronin, Michael. *Translating Ireland: Translation, Languages, Cultures*. Cork: Cork University Press, 1996.

Engelberts, Matthijs and Everett Frost with Jane Maxwell (eds). *Samuel Beckett Today/ Aujourd'hui*. Special Issue 16 (2006). *Notes Diverse Holo: Catalogues of Beckett's Reading Notes and Other Manuscripts at Trinity College Dublin, with Supporting Essays*.

[72] David Lloyd, *Anomalous States: Irish Writing and the Post-Colonial Moment* (Dublin: Lilliput Press, 1993), 88.

[73] Ibid., 70.   [74] Beckett, *Watt*, 51–2.

[75] Theodor W. Adorno, 'Trying to Understand *Endgame*', in *Notes to Literature*, ed. Rolf Tiedemann, trans. Sherry Weber Nicholsen (New York: Columbia University Press, 1991), vol. 1, 241.

Harrington, John P. *The Irish Beckett*. Syracuse, NY: Syracuse University Press, 1991.

Kennedy, Seán (ed.). *Beckett and Ireland*. Cambridge: Cambridge University Press, 2010.

McMullan, Anna. 'Irish/Postcolonial Beckett'. In Lois Oppenheim (ed.), *Palgrave Advances in Beckett Studies*. Basingstoke: Palgrave Macmillan, 2004: 89–109.

Mooney, Sinéad. *A Tongue Not Mine: Beckett and Translation*. Oxford: Oxford University Press, 2011.

Morin, Emilie. *Samuel Beckett and the Problem of Irishness*. Basingstoke: Palgrave Macmillan, 2009.

Pilling, John (ed.). *The Cambridge Companion to Samuel Beckett*. Cambridge: Cambridge University Press, 1994.

Pilling, John (ed.). *A Samuel Beckett Chronology*. Basingstoke: Palgrave Macmillan, 2006.

Shenker, Israel. 'Moody Man of Letters'. *New York Times*, 5 May 1956, 2, 1, 3.

Slote, Sam. 'Bilingual Beckett: Beyond the Linguistic Turn'. In Dirk Van Hulle (ed.), *The New Cambridge Companion to Samuel Beckett*. Cambridge: Cambridge University Press, 2015: 114–25.

Venuti, Lawrence. *The Translator's Invisibility: A History of Translation*. London: Routledge, 1995.

CHAPTER 12

....

OBLIQUITIES

Elizabeth Bowen and the Modern Short Story

....

ALLAN HEPBURN

ELIZABETH Bowen's (1899–1973) understanding of the short story is remarkably consistent from her earliest theorizations in the 1930s to her essays on fictional technique in the 1940s and 1950s. In reviews and essays, Bowen develops a poetics of the modern short story that emphasizes visual impact, style, nationality, and obliquity. With European and American examples in mind, she promotes a view of the short story as a highly structured, impersonal art form, not one that descends from folktales, ghost stories, or other oral traditions, even when it draws upon supernatural effects. Frank O'Connor (1903–66) calls the short story 'a piece of artistic organization'.[1] Bowen holds the same view. Motivated by the inner necessity of its subject, the short story has no essential form, nor any set length or style. In her critical observations about short stories, she invariably gives precedence to situation over character or scene. Unlike novels, which have passages during which tension eases off, 'the short story revolves round one crisis only—one might call it, almost, a crisis in itself. There (ideally) ought to be nothing in such a story which can weaken, detract from, or blur the central, single effect.'[2] In Bowen's stories, the central crisis is not always named, although in 'Her Table Spread', 'A Love Story 1939', and 'Sunday Afternoon', all of which are set in Ireland, the unnamed crisis pertains either to Irish revolutionary history or to the Second World War. Conscious of her divided allegiances—she saw herself simultaneously as Irish, Anglo-Irish, British, and European—Bowen approached the subject of national belonging obliquely.

---

[1] Frank O'Connor, *The Lonely Voice: A Study of the Short Story* (London: Macmillan, 1963), 37.

[2] Elizabeth Bowen, 'Stories by Elizabeth Bowen', in *Afterthought: Pieces about Writing* (London: Longmans, 1962), 78.

A Poetics of the Short Story

In the first half of her career, between 1920 and 1945, Bowen wrote dozens of short stories. In the second half of her career, from 1945 until her death in 1973, she wrote just a handful of stories but commented extensively on short story technique, both her own and others'. These comments, not formalized into a theory per se, nevertheless comprise a poetics of short fiction. Bowen's acquaintance with late nineteenth- and early twentieth-century short fiction was formidably broad. She had a particular affection for and insight into stories by Maxim Gorky, Guy de Maupassant, Anton Chekhov, Katherine Mansfield, James Joyce (1882–1941), Somerset Maugham, D. H. Lawrence, Frank O'Connor, Eudora Welty, Seán O'Faoláin (1900–91), and Mary Lavin (1912–96). In her introduction to *The Faber Book of Modern Stories* (1936), Bowen praises Maupassant's realist astringency—the exactingness of his detail—and credits Chekhov with making subjectivity 'edit and rule experience and pull art, obliquely, its way'.[3] As she understands it, the short story begins as a European genre whose lessons and techniques can be adapted to national requirements, whether French, Russian, or Irish.

In 1951, Bowen wrote an introduction to the twenty-one stories selected as finalists for a competition run by the *Observer* newspaper. Praising the imaginative range of these stories, mostly written by amateurs, Bowen summarizes her views on the craft and aims of short fiction in general:

> No other prose form can, without distortion, let itself be so rich in fantasy, or concentrate so much sensation into few pages, or be stamped to such an extent by vision. The narrative can be shaped to the ruling idea, suited to, soaked in the prevailing mood; indeed, this form has inherent freedom.[4]

Freedom, as Bowen specifies in other contexts, refers to the choice of subject and the flexibility of form. Nothing predetermines the length, the situation, or the structure of a story. Unlike novels and drama, the short story is not hemmed in by a long tradition that limits its range of subjects. Compactness is a virtue, not a constraint, insofar as it distils vision, sensation, or mood.

By concentrating on a single action or crisis, the short story approaches poetry, which Bowen treats as synonymous with concision, intensity, and style. 'Poetic tautness and clarity' are essential to the short story, which is 'an affair of reflexes, of immediate susceptibility, of associations not examined by reason: it does not attempt a synthesis'.[5] It has to convey the effect of spontaneity, even if it is subject to scrupulous arrangement and stylistic control. To succeed it cannot slacken its pace. To some degree, tautness

---

[3] Elizabeth Bowen, 'The Faber Book of Modern Short Stories', in *Collected Impressions* (London: Longmans, 1950), 39.

[4] Elizabeth Bowen, 'Introduction to *The Observer* Prize Stories', in *People, Places, Things: Essays by Elizabeth Bowen*, ed. Allan Hepburn (Edinburgh: Edinburgh University Press, 2008), 319.

[5] Bowen, 'The Faber Book of Modern Short Stories', 38.

depends on reactions to unexpectedness—'reflexes' and 'immediate susceptibility'. The short story may begin in ordinary experience, but it defamiliarizes that experience and therefore revitalizes it. The modernity of the short story lies in its very brevity or its poetic condensation of material: it conveys the abruptness of a shock. When she refers to the poetic element of short fiction, Bowen usually means density of material, though she also means something like the sudden disclosure of another dimension of experience, akin to Joyce's epiphanies.[6]

The modernity of the short story also resides in its visual appeal. 'The story should be as composed, in the plastic sense', Bowen states, 'and as visual as a picture'.[7] As the equivalent of a picture, the short story conjures up the sharpest possible image of a situation, visible to the author and transmissible to a spectator. The image has to be both distinct and distinctive; its vividness, whether in terms of colour, contrast, perspective, scale, or subject, leaves an imprint on the reader's imagination. In the preface to *Ivy Gripped the Steps and Other Stories* (1945), Bowen claims that her wartime stories are 'disjected snapshots'[8] rather than coherent pictures of what was happening around her. Although grabbed by force from the chaos of war, these stories appeal to the eye, not so much reportorial as surreal in their visual content. Having studied for two terms at the London County Council School of Art when she was twenty, and having a disposition to think in visual terms, Bowen understands the short story as a sketch; in its brevity, it remains suggestive. At the same time, the sketch should not be taken as preliminary to a larger work: it has its own integrity, which owes something to its spontaneity and its dimensions. When her first two volumes of short stories, *Encounters* (1923) and *Ann Lee's and Other Stories* (1926), were conjoined into one volume under the title *Early Stories* (1950) for publication in the USA, Bowen cast a critical eye over her youthful accomplishments and, by and large, approved of them: 'The stories have build, style, and occasional felicities of expression which I must say startle me. Their strong point is visual clarity'.[9] For Bowen, then, the short story works best when it projects a shape or situation as a central picture to the reader, like a projector flashing an image on the screen of the reader's mind.

The analogy between short story and picture invites any number of subsidiary metaphors. Short stories spotlight details—gestures, objects, faces—in order to heighten drama. Bowen has a fondness for the image of spotlights trained upon human dramas. A story, she states, 'confers importance: characters in it are given stature, and are moreover spotlit, so that their gestures are not only clearly seen but cast meaningful shadows'.[10]

---

[6] In her short story course at Vassar College in 1960, Bowen likened 'poetry' to illumination, visual effects, the inner nature of man, symbolism, and unanswerable queries (HRC 7.3 Notebook, 13). To illustrate her points Bowen assigned Joyce's 'The Dead' and prompted students to think about speech rhythms, topographical references, and vocabulary. Citations from the Vassar notebooks at the Harry Ransom Centre refer to box and folder number; Bowen numbered some notebook pages by hand, but not all.

[7] Bowen, 'The Faber Book of Modern Short Stories', 43.

[8] Elizabeth Bowen, 'Preface', in *Ivy Gripped the Steps and Other Stories* (New York: Knopf, 1946), xiv. In the USA, Knopf published *The Demon Lover and Other Stories* (1945) as *Ivy Gripped the Steps*. Bowen's preface appeared only in the American edition.

[9] Elizabeth Bowen, 'Preface', in *Early Stories* (New York: Knopf, 1951), x.

[10] Elizabeth Bowen, 'Rx for a Story Worth the Telling', in *People, Places, Things*, 326.

Drawn to non-heroic characters, she notes her own tendency of 'spotlighting faces or cutting out gestures that are not even the faces or gestures of great sufferers'.[11] The metaphor of the spotlight evokes lighting effects in *film noir* or theatre, where stark contrasts confer significance. The spotlight aggrandizes certain gestures and forces the eye to pick out details, even shadows, as meaningful in comparison with what is cast into the background or lost in darkness. Or gestures may be cut out, like figures and forms in Henri Matisse's *découpages*, reduced to elemental forms and primary colours.

The short story necessarily has an angle of vision, much like the perspective in a picture or the tilt of a camera in a film or a photograph. 'Where is the camera-eye to be located?' Bowen demands in 'Notes on Writing a Novel'.[12] Building upon the metaphor of the camera-eye, she often describes the short story as impassive, neutral, perhaps not quite documentary in its realist grasp of detail but still capable of recording visual effects with the sensitivity of a painter or the all-seeingness of the camera. Nonetheless, pictures are ultimately not the same as stories: 'A story moves, advances, and it not only can and does do this, but it must. If it stood still, it would cease to be a story and become a picture.'[13] Although intensely visual if not photographic, the dominant picture that a story projects should not freeze characters or actions into immobility.

In a shrewd assessment of Katherine Mansfield's artistry, Bowen insists on visuality as constitutive of brevity: 'the short story, by reason of its aesthetics, is not and is not intended to be the medium either for exploration or long-term development of character. Character cannot be more than *shown*—it is there for use, the use is dramatic. Foreshortening is not only unavoidable, it is right.'[14] Whereas drama in the theatrical sense relies on monologue and dialogue, drama in the visual sense relies on sudden glimpses into the unexpected. Drama emerges from the mute picture; the glimpse or snapshot suggests an action that is not, and cannot be, lengthened visually but can be unfolded in narrative. 'Foreshortening', as a technical term in visual art, refers to a reduced scale or distance that depends on perspective or angle of vision. In foreshortening, perspective causes some objects—a fist in front of a face, for example—to appear larger or closer than it is. Foreshortening occludes some elements from the picture when space is telescoped. While bearing that visual sense in mind, Bowen means that Mansfield's stories in particular and the short story in general aggrandize details through foreshortening. She also means that the time scale of the short story—its temporal rather than its spatial dimension—is reduced to intensify dramatic impact.

In her statements about fiction, Bowen always differentiates short stories from novels. The short story is by no means an aborted novel. Nor is it an outtake or an extract from a longer work. The short story dwells on an impression, an atmosphere, an event, a mood, or a situation that is not nor cannot be developed to the proportions of a novel. Due to the scale of the subject, the short story admits no subplot. 'The first necessity for the short story, at the set out, is *necessariness*', Bowen claims. 'The story, that is to say, must

---

[11] Bowen, 'Preface', in *Ivy Gripped the Steps*, xiv.
[12] Elizabeth Bowen, 'Notes on Writing a Novel', in *Collected Impressions*, 257.
[13] Bowen, 'Rx for a Story Worth the Telling', 326.
[14] Elizabeth Bowen, 'Stories by Katherine Mansfield', in *Afterthought*, 71. Original emphasis.

spring from an impression or perception pressing enough, acute enough, to have made the writer write.'[15] For this reason, the short story concentrates on one critical situation and eliminates all material that is superfluous to that situation.

Like James Joyce's gnomic technique or Katherine Mansfield's ellipses, Bowen's concept of the story depends upon the suppression or exclusion of information. A story should 'have implications which will continue'[16] beyond its end-point, she asserts, and follows this injunction in much of her own short fiction. As a case in point, in 'In the Square', a story about a man named Rupert who returns to a fashionable house owned by Magdela in war-time London, Bowen lets questions resonate without furnishing answers. Where has Rupert been? Why does he return? To whom does Magdela speak on the phone and why does this conversation make her feel happy? Will Gina, Magdela's husband's mistress who lives on the ground floor, leave Magdela's house now that she has found a new boyfriend? Will the old times and everything that goes with them—the iron palings around the square, gossipy dinners, Magdela's husband—return when the war ends or will the 'great change'[17] that Magdela foresees come to pass? Offering only the thinnest slice of temporality, fined down to an hour or two on a hot July evening during the war, the story suspends answers to all these questions. Because of its suppression of any material that is superfluous to it, the story bears a whiff of unfinishedness. Gnomic inconclusiveness allows the short story to make its effects felt beyond its conclusion. Modernist style requires the calculated omission of information in order to create implications.

Nowhere is Bowen's modernism felt more fully than in her commitment to style as an end in itself. In her book reviews, Bowen often zeroes in on stylistic flaws and felicities in writers' prose. In a review of Somerset Maugham's novel, *Theatre* (1937), for instance, she observes that he has impersonalized his style to the point of cruelty: 'Maugham anatomizes emotion without emotion; he handles without pity a world where he finds no pity.'[18] His style is 'neutral, functional, and fully efficient, the servant, not the mistress of the writer's imagination'.[19] On the one hand, Bowen admires impersonality and consistency in style; on the other, she intimates that Maugham's detached and remote style solidifies into a habit, a style not entirely free of workmanlike sameness. There is a principle concealed within this observation, namely, that style has to remain subordinate to the subject of the story. The situation dictates the style, not vice versa. For this reason, Bowen likes the 'vitality, aptness, structure and inherent beauty of Mr [Aldous] Huxley's style'.[20] His is a lively style adaptable to different subjects. By contrast, she dislikes the facility of Harold Nicolson's prose because he is 'prey to his own good writing'.[21] As she told Charles Ritchie, Nicolson's prose is 'a perfect example of someone who you c[oul]d see smiling complacently over his own phrases', whereas Bowen herself 'in accordance with Proust's maxim always tried to eliminate passages that gave her that complacent

[15] Bowen, 'The Faber Book of Modern Short Stories', 42. Original emphasis.

[16] Elizabeth Bowen, 'Gorki Stories', in *Collected Impressions*, 153.

[17] Elizabeth Bowen, 'In the Square', in *The Collected Stories of Elizabeth Bowen*, ed. Angus Wilson (New York: Ecco Press, 1989), 615.

[18] Elizabeth Bowen, 'A Straight Novel', in *Collected Impressions*, 135.   [19] Ibid., 132.

[20] Elizabeth Bowen, 'Mr Huxley's Essays', in *Collected Impressions*, 147.   [21] Ibid., 143.

sensation.'[22] Self-expression and sentiment have to be expunged to create a truly modern literary style. Modern style at its best ought to be precise, modulated, and surprising; from unexpectedness, it draws its vitality. This principle holds true for all fiction, whether novel or short story, although the sheer length of the novel may cause lapses of style to be overlooked. The short story affords no such negligence.

In her commitment to a scrupulous, objective style, Bowen turned time and again to Gustave Flaubert's dicta about style as guides to her own understanding of literary art. Like Flaubert, she aspired to write a book that could 'sustain itself by the inner force of its style'.[23] In a speech delivered at Harvard University in 1953, Bowen appealed to Flaubert's definition of style as 'not just a matter of sentence formation, of pleasing sounds or effective words, but that it really arises in the first place from the whole sight, view, and conception of which the author has of his subject and of his scenes'.[24] In *The Death of the Heart* (1938), when the novelist St Quentin muses to Anna, 'you cannot write without style',[25] he recalls, as Maud Ellmann notes, the derivation of the word 'style' from the Latin *stilus*, a stake or a paling, 'a pointed instrument used for cutting letters or for stabbing flesh'.[26] As Flaubert proposed and Bowen seconded, style has a point. It cuts and stabs.

Yet style bears, more often than not, an oblique relation to subject matter. As Flaubert notes, style is an angle of vision, a manner of expressing a point of view. If style is 'an absolute manner of seeing'[27]—a phrase from Flaubert's correspondence that Bowen quotes with approval—it cannot be dissociated from the subject. In literature, style is a matter of cadence, clauses, and arrangement of words, in addition to being everything that the writer thinks worthy of notice. The angle of vision may be panoramic and aerial, abridged and microscopic, or anything in between. Because of the shortness of short stories, style has to be immediately apprehensible; otherwise, it risks depleting momentum or distracting from the subject. With Flaubert's commitment to impersonality in mind, Bowen thinks of style as the dissolution of language: it is the medium in which plot, character, and description liquefy.

In 1960, Bowen taught a class on the short story to twenty-five students at Vassar College in Poughkeepsie, New York. In preparatory notes for the class, she brings together her theories of the short story in telegraphic jottings that she likely elaborated during the course itself. Despite their cursoriness, these notes offer Bowen's most systematic thinking about the purposes and techniques of short fiction. She divided the class into weekly headings: form, uniqueness, contemporaneity, drama, poetry, reportage, 'the inside view and the outside view', character, plot, primitivism, scene, regional-

---

[22] Charles Ritchie Papers, Thomas Fisher Rare Book Library, University of Toronto. MS Coll. 00626. Box 1. Diary entry, 14 November 1941.

[23] Elizabeth Bowen, 'Fiction', in *The Weight of a World of Feeling: Reviews and Essays by Elizabeth Bowen*, ed. Allan Hepburn (Evanston, IL: Northwestern University Press, 2017), 86.

[24] Ibid., 22.   [25] Elizabeth Bowen, *The Death of the Heart* (New York: Anchor, 2000), 8.

[26] Maud Ellmann, *Elizabeth Bowen: The Shadow Across the Page* (Edinburgh: Edinburgh University Press, 2003), 145.

[27] This phrase comes from an 1852 letter from Flaubert to Louise Colet. Bowen cites it in 'The Flaubert Omnibus', in *Collected Impressions*, 34 and 'The Technique of the Novel', in *The Weight of a World of Feeling*, 22.

ism, satire, 'national imprint', uncanniness, and limitations of the genre.[28] Each week she assigned readings to illustrate these topics. There were some traditional choices (Hemingway, Chekhov, Maupassant, Poe, Mansfield, Joyce, Maugham, Lawrence) and some up-to-date works to appeal to American students (Irwin Shaw, Eudora Welty, J. D. Salinger, Katherine Anne Porter, Wallace Stegner, Flannery O'Connor). As the semester proceeded, Bowen eliminated some authors and topics while modifying others. Choices were both informed and wide-ranging. Welty's 'First Love' was used to demonstrate the dramatic element in short fiction, while Maupassant's 'Boule de Suif', Angus Wilson's 'The Wrong Set', and Katherine Mansfield's 'In a German Pension' were discussed in light of their varying degrees of irony and invective.[29]

For a lesson on primitivism, Bowen asked the Vassar students to read three stories: Lawrence's 'Tickets, Please', Porter's 'Pale Horse, Pale Rider', and Stegner's 'The Women on the Wall'. Primitivism, which draws upon emotion and instinct, may be better suited to some subjects than to others: break-ups, death, surprising encounters, ghostliness, war. Lawrence's story may seem slightly old-fashioned alongside Porter's account of the Spanish flu epidemic and Stegner's story about wives in California waiting for news of their husbands fighting overseas, but Bowen always thought of Lawrence as her contemporary. She included 'You Touched Me' in *The Faber Book of Modern Stories* and she ranked 'The Fox' as his best work of fiction.[30] During the Second World War, she states, 'Lawrence was the one artist whom I, for one, constantly had in mind', in part because his handling of primitive feeling—intuition, reactions, impulses—spoke most directly to the 'merciless, scorching propinquity' that wartime conditions forced upon people in England.[31] He pioneered new subject matter in human relations and a style that spoke to the primacy of emotions in those relations.

According to Bowen's notes for the class at Vassar, the short story 'does better with the elemental rather than the subtle'.[32] Primitivism is often an attribute of characters who are the subjects, not the masters, of their passions. In a similar manner, Seán O'Faoláin praises Bowen's characters as 'the modern, sophisticated, naturalistic novelist's versions of primitive urges', who are, sometimes against their will, 'conscripted by passion into fate'.[33] Their primal feeling, which O'Faoláin aligns with passion, is their strength. In Bowen's stories, characters' rationality takes second place to their emotions and unconscious urges. They react not according to social codes but according to instinct and impulse. Intuition matters more in 'Look at All Those Roses', 'The Disinherited', 'Attractive Modern Homes', and Bowen's other stories with barely suppressed murder plots than does reason.[34] As Bowen told her students at Vassar, the short story ought to

[28] Bowen, HRC 7.3 Notebook, 19, 43.   [29] Ibid., 39.   [30] Ibid., 159.

[31] Elizabeth Bowen, 'D. H. Lawrence', in *Collected Impressions*, 158.

[32] Bowen, HRC 7.3 Notebook, 29.

[33] Seán O'Faoláin, *The Vanishing Hero: Studies in Novelists of the Twenties* (London: Eyre and Spottiswoode, 1956), 173, 172.

[34] For a lesson on 'mystery and detection', Bowen noted that 'enigmatic behaviour' and 'uncertain outcome' are inherent in all short stories, not just those, such as Arthur Conan Doyle's, that focus on crime (HRC 7.3 Notebook dated 26 April).

shy away from small touches—details, elaborations—that are better suited to the novella or the novel, because they reduce the impact of elemental feeling. In her thinking about modern primitivism, Bowen compares the short story to acts of violence. In general, 'the short story cannot simply be an *Explosion*. As a rule, it does best when we are caused to feel the explosive element beneath the surface.'[35] As the metaphor of a depth charge implies, the violence of the short story is best felt at a slight distance, a distance from which aftershocks can be registered and damage assessed.

National Imprint and the Irish Short Story

At Vassar, Bowen asked her students to consider 'national imprint' by reading short stories by Frank O'Connor, Seán O'Faoláin, and Mary Lavin. She does not specify which stories by these authors were assigned for this lesson, though she subsequently refers in her notes to O'Faoláin's 'The Man Who Invented Sin', the title story of his 1948 collection. Throughout her career, Bowen kept a keen eye on developments in contemporary Irish fiction. For her weekly book column in *The Tatler and Bystander* she reviewed, to name just a few examples, Lavin's *The House in Clewe Street* (1945), O'Connor's *The Common Chord* (1947), O'Faoláin's *Teresa and Other Stories* (1947), Liam O'Flaherty's (1896–1984) *Two Lovely Beasts* (1948), as well as countless Irish histories, memoirs, and picture books. Like O'Faoláin in *The Short Story* (1948) and O'Connor in *The Lonely Voice* (1963), Bowen usually judges Irish short fiction alongside European and American works to demonstrate the universality and adaptability of the short story form.

In her discussion of 'national imprint', Bowen proposed a thought experiment: '*If you read* 3 pages of a Short Story from which *all personal names* and *place-names* had been deleted, how would you—or, Would you?—guess at the Nationality of the author.'[36] Dialogue, scene, and the outlook of the writer, which she defines as 'unconscious judgements,'[37] may provide clues to an author's national identity. Yet nationality remains elusive: 'In so far as Frank O'Connor is an outstanding IRISH writer, in what would you find his 'Irishness' to consist?'[38] Bowen poses the same question about O'Faoláin. In both cases, the question has an a priori answer: both are Irish, so their national traits must be evident in some aspect of their style. O'Connor's and O'Faoláin's Irishness may, ultimately, consist in a saturation in vernacular language, topical references, local atmosphere, and the literary stylization of experience.

Bowen often expresses perplexity about how to position modern Irish fiction vis-à-vis international literature. In *The Faber Book of Modern Stories*, she excludes American and Russian stories but includes a cluster of four Irish stories: Joyce's 'Araby', O'Connor's

---

[35] Bowen, HRC 7.3 Notebook, 30.   [36] Ibid., n. p. Original emphasis and orthography.
[37] Ibid., n. p.   [38] Ibid., n. p.

'Peasants', O'Faoláin's 'The Bombshop', and O'Flaherty's 'The Wounded Cormorant'. In an essay called 'The Short Story in England' (1945), Bowen mentions these four writers again but sets them aside as being 'outside my present scope'[39] because they are Irish. Although they are exemplary modernists who write in English, they are not English. In her Vassar notebooks, she does not isolate vernacular language or unconscious judgements among French, American, or British writers. For writers of those national origins, such traits are a given and express themselves in and through their fiction.

As Barry McCrea comments, Irish writers express national differences through language itself, there being 'an ideological dissonance between the language people actually spoke—overwhelmingly English—and the language they felt they ought to be speaking'.[40] For exactly this reason, in *A Portrait of the Artist as a Young Man* (1916), Stephen Dedalus frets over the distinction between the Irish word 'tundish' and the English word 'funnel'.[41] During the Irish Revival, the perception of English as a foreign language, along with the clash between national political concerns and international literary currents, 'produced an unusual focus in Irish writing on questions of style and idiom'.[42] As McCrea points out, Hiberno-English bears the ghostly traces of obliterated syntax and vocabulary; to write in English at all is therefore to make a political choice. In Bowen's phrase, 'national imprint' is not the mark on the paper but the missing language—Gaelic—that leaves a ghostly impression on the rhythms, cadences, and style of English.

Bowen was not alone in viewing the Irish short story as a unique category. Frank O'Connor begins his introduction to the anthology, *Irish Modern Short Stories* (1957), with a credo: 'I believe that the Irish short story is a distinct art form.'[43] Especially in the 1920s and 1930s, as in O'Connor's *Guests of the Nation* (1931) and O'Faoláin's *Midsummer Night Madness and Other Stories* (1932), the short story became the paradigmatic literary form for representing 'the limitations of the Irish nation as embodied in the Irish state'.[44] In this period, short story writers dwell on discrepancies between Irish social and cultural realities and the conservative, censorious, and Catholic proscriptions of the state. The title stories in both O'Connor's and O'Faoláin's books address Irish revolutionary history and its human costs. John, the first-person narrator in 'Midsummer Night Madness', feels ambivalent about burning Henn's Big House; he cannot bring himself to answer the Protestant landowner's jeering question, 'I suppose you're another one of our new patriots? Eh? Eh?'[45] The narrator in O'Connor's 'Guests of the Nation' positions himself as a storyteller who cannot find the appropriate language to describe the murder of two English hostages: 'It is strange what you feel at such moments, and not to be

[39] Elizabeth Bowen, 'The Short Story in England', in *People, Places, Things*, 312.

[40] Barry McCrea, 'Style and Idiom', in Joe Cleary (ed.), *The Cambridge Companion to Irish Modernism* (Cambridge: Cambridge University Press, 2014), 64.

[41] James Joyce, *A Portrait of the Artist as a Young Man*, ed. Jeri Johnson (Oxford: Oxford University Press, 2008), 158.

[42] McCrea, 'Style and Idiom', 63.

[43] Frank O'Connor (ed.), *Modern Irish Short Stories* (Oxford: Oxford University Press, 1957), ix.

[44] Heather Ingman, *A History of the Irish Short Story* (Cambridge: Cambridge University Press, 2009), 116.

[45] Seán O'Faoláin, *Midsummer Night Madness and Other Stories* (London: Cape, 1932), 15.

written afterwards.'[46] In this sense, the tumultuous history of the War of Independence, the Civil War, and the establishment of the Irish Free State finds its expression in literature almost by indirection, in the concise, even fragmentary, form of the short story.

For O'Connor and O'Faoláin, as for Bowen, the short story has the benefit of approaching history through a universal form. In *The Lonely Voice*, O'Connor locates the essence of the short story in its temporality. Whereas the novelist has time to represent 'the chronological development of character or incident', with all the sequences of cause and effect implied by the leisurely pace of development, the short story writer 'must be forever selecting the point at which he can approach [human life], and each selection he makes contains the possibility of a new form as well as the possibility of a complete fiasco'.[47] In other words, the brevity of the short story forces the hand of the writer, who must choose an angle of approach and a temporality suited to the subject. Because each choice has never been tried before—unless, of course, the story is a rehash or a pastiche—the result may be either a triumph or a failure. Only the subject and the angle of approach can determine the appropriate form. O'Connor sums up his argument in an aphorism: 'the form of the novel is given by the length; in the short story the length is given by the form'.[48] O'Connor evades the question of historicity, and more particularly the implication of Irish literature in revolutionary history, by defining the short story as an art form whose inherent capacity for irony and ambiguity elevate it above history altogether. The closest he comes to making a political statement is his influential observation that short fiction concerns 'submerged population groups', among whom he counts 'tramps, artists, lonely idealists, dreamers, and spoiled priests'.[49] According to O'Connor, the defining concern of the short story is an existential human loneliness that may be local in its setting but universal in its application.

O'Faoláin, too, thinks of the short story as a universal art form. In 1942, he broadcast a series of talks on Radio Éireann that were subsequently published in five instalments in *The Bell* under the title 'The Craft of the Short Story' (1943). Five years later, these essays were further revised for his critical study, *The Short Story*, with extensive excisions and expansions. The short story, O'Faoláin declares, is neither an anecdote nor a character sketch. Modern storytellers 'aim to make situation and construction merge into a single movement and when they succeed they bring the short-story to its peak of technical achievement'.[50] To illustrate this point, O'Faolain notes the compression of Bowen's 'Her Table Spread', in which 'the situation, the group, the place, [and] the atmosphere'[51] are welded together in such a way that one cannot be extricated from the other.

In the interval between publishing 'The Craft of the Short Story' and *The Short Story*, O'Faoláin clearly read Bowen's 'Notes on Writing a Novel', which first appeared in *Orion* in 1945 and was reprinted in *Collected Impressions* in 1950. In that essay, Bowen expounds her theory of the camera angle in cinema as analogous to the visual and moral angle assumed by the narrator (or author) in fiction. 'In a good film', Bowen states, 'the camera's

[46] Frank O'Connor, *Collected Stories*, ed. Richard Ellmann (New York: Knopf, 1981), 12.
[47] O'Connor, *The Lonely Voice*, 21.   [48] Ibid., 27.   [49] Ibid., 17, 20–1.
[50] Seán O'Faoláin, *The Short Story* (New York: Devin-Adair, 1951), 201–2.   [51] Ibid., 203.

movement, angle and distance have all worked towards one thing—the fullest possible realization of the director's idea, the completest possible surrounding of the subject.'[52] In a passage that he added between the publication of 'The Craft of the Short Story' and *The Short Story*, O'Faoláin applies the term 'camera-angle' to 'Her Table Spread' to describe 'how the mental camera moves, withdraws to a distance to enclose a larger view, slips deftly from one character to another, while all the time holding one main direction of which these are only variations.'[53] Like Bowen, O'Faoláin admires the narrative mobility that this cinematic technique enables: as with the shifting point of view induced by cinematic shots, focalization in textual narrative can shift fluidly from character to character within the general structure of the story.

In 'Her Table Spread', the mental camera moves from Alban, an Englishman visiting an Irish castle owned by Valeria, who is variously described as 'abnormal' and 'impulsive,'[54] to scenes of guests conversing over dinner or listening to piano music. Sometimes the focalization is personal, as when it filters Valeria's delusional perspective or Alban's frustration; sometimes the narrator pans over a group of characters neutrally or impassively without alignment to any individual. In this way, the narrative, like the mobile camera in film, surrounds its subject in the completest possible way. In O'Faoláin's assessment, the movement of the camera indicates what the story is about. In 'Her Table Spread', Valeria, who fancies that she will marry one or another English navy officer whom she has never met, makes others bend to the force of her delusion. Her delusion has everything to do with an Anglo-Irish dependence on, and romance with, Britain as a military state. Valeria's table is spread for some young navy officer, but it is not spread for Alban, the potential husband invited to the castle.

Bowen's short stories, like her novels, display their Irish national imprint in the indirect representation of politics. Joe Cleary argues that Irish literature expresses 'a traumatic sense of modernity-as-catastrophe.'[55] In modernist Irish works, politics and history find their outlet in formal experimentation (*The Third Policeman*) and erudition that sometimes slides into pedantry (*Finnegans Wake*).[56] By comparison, Bowen's modernity, while it shares experimental qualities, especially in the convolutions of her prose and the temporally disjunctive organization of her plots, represents historical upheaval obliquely. In *The Last September* (1929), set during the War of Independence, the Anglo-Irish make it a policy not to notice what is happening, despite the ubiquity of British soldiers and IRA fighters around the countryside. At a party held by the British, Moira Ralte worries that the IRA will fire in at the windows, but such random acts of violence, she thinks, might add an element of fun to the get-together. 'It takes two to make a war.... *We're* not fighting,'[57] says her host, Mrs Rolfe, meaningfully. In this view, the Black and Tans are not suppressing IRA insurgents but keeping the peace. Laurence, an Oxford student prone to uttering ironic *bon mots* like a latter-day Wilde, comes closer to stating the reality of the situation, albeit glazed with Anglo-Irish regret:

[52] Bowen, 'Notes on Writing a Novel', 257.   [53] O'Faoláin, *The Short Story*, 204.
[54] Bowen, 'Her Table Spread', in *The Collected Stories of Elizabeth Bowen*, 418, 420.
[55] Joe Cleary, 'Introduction', in Cleary (ed.) *The Cambridge Companion to Irish Modernism*, 9.
[56] Ibid., 10.   [57] Elizabeth Bowen, *The Last September* (New York: Anchor, 2000), 209.

'It would be the greatest pity if we were to become a republic and all these lovely troops were taken away.'[58] Laurence's irony troubles a direct statement of allegiance. Is it only the departure of the British that would make a republic regrettable? Would it be the greatest pity or just one of many? The political content of the novel, filtered through the speech and actions of the Anglo-Irish, remains contained when not outright ignored. Derek Hand, commenting on *The Last September*, draws attention to Bowen's 'art of constant deflection and deferral', which causes her 'to redirect any decisive moment of confrontation'.[59] Bowen meets Irish history with a tactic of indirection and diversion—an aesthetics of obliquity.

OBLIQUITY

V. S. Pritchett claims that Elizabeth Bowen, an unofficial historian of the contemporary moment, represents history with the 'obliquity'[60] of a dispossessed poet. As Pritchett suggests, obliquity is both a narrative mode and a literary style in Bowen's fiction—an approach brought about by dislocation or by inhabiting a zone outside what is customary. In Bowen's novels and short stories, obliquity allows repressed material to assert itself by other means than the frontal. For example, in her first novel, *The Hotel* (1927), Sydney Warren calls herself a realist and finds that, as a result, her imagination 'was able to revenge itself obliquely upon her'[61] for having been so savagely repressed. Obliquity in this instance asserts a counter-truth or different kind of wisdom than realism permits. In fact, all Bowen's fiction operates on the principle of obliquity: topics that cannot be confronted directly can be approached slantwise the better to disclose their vulnerabilities.

According to the *OED*, the word 'obliquity', with its evocations of geometry and astronomy, refers to 'a slanting direction or position'. In grammar, there are oblique cases, which are all those except the nominative and vocative. In military usage, obliquity refers to a sideways movement or march that protects the rearguard. In its colloquial sense, obliquity conveys something roundabout, something that does not go straight to the point. In her various styles of obliquity, Bowen conjures up all of these definitions in turn. Oblique movement is not perpendicular, parallel, or true in the mathematical sense. Whereas a point is a crux or a target, obliquity designates a movement in the direction of, or an approach to, that point. More often than not, Bowen assumes obliquity as a form of not knowing or as a tactic of surprise. In narrative, obliquity implies that the angle of representation is aslant actual events, as if deliberate obscurity of meaning were the only way to arrive at the heart of the matter.

---

[58] Ibid., 30–1.
[59] Derek Hand, *A History of the Irish Novel* (Cambridge: Cambridge University Press, 2011), 182.
[60] V. S. Pritchett, 'The Future of English Fiction', *Partisan Review* 15, no. 10 (1948), 1066.
[61] Elizabeth Bowen, *The Hotel* (Chicago, IL: University of Chicago Press, 2012), 25.

In her introduction to the *The Faber Book of Modern Stories*, Bowen singles out 'oblique narration',[62] along with cinematic cutting and the unlikely placing of emphasis, as hallmarks of modern short story technique. Elaborating this point, she notes that the short story allows for breaks and inconclusiveness and thus, unlike the novel, may come closer to 'aesthetic and moral truth. It can, while remaining rightly prosaic and circumstantial, give scene, action, event, character a poetic new actuality. It must have had, to the writer, moments of unfamiliarity, where it imposed itself.'[63] In other words, the poetic core of the short story, which relies on brevity to achieve its aesthetic effect and communicate its moral truth, may be discoverable only from an oblique angle. When Pritchett describes Bowen as a dispossessed poet whose particular gift is obliquity, he has in mind this contradiction between a dramatic crux and the aesthetic means by which that dramatic crux, compelled by necessity, unfolds in narrative.

For Bowen, obliquity is a signature of Irish style. In a review of Joseph Hone's *The Moores of Moore Hall* (1939), she comments that 'to dream of Ireland is one thing, to live there another. Ireland broke each of the Moores, in her oblique way.'[64] In the case of the Moores, defeat is not attributable to any specific cause and may be a gradual wearing down rather than a sudden breaking of morale. In another review, Bowen refers to 'tactful Irish obliqueness',[65] in which obliquity keeps up the appearance of tact while asserting an alternative truth. Obliquity pries the lid off commonplace situations and reactions in order to show what might be hidden within them. In this sense, obliquity is the manifestation of Bowen's modernity: what cannot be breached directly can be sidled up to and taken by surprise.

Very few of Bowen's stories are set in Ireland, but those that are tend to display deflection and obliquity as political strategies. In 'Sunday Afternoon', Henry Russel travels from wartime London to the peaceable outskirts of Dublin. Elders sitting about a lawn where a slight wind frets the trees resist knowing about the war as best they can. They do not care to hear that Henry lost all his objects and artworks when his flat was bombed during an air raid. The elders keep up a habit of deflection and not knowing, although the narrator sometimes slyly insinuates that they may know more than they let on. They watch Maria wipe up spilt tea—'this little bit of destruction', it is called—with 'appeasement'.[66] The word 'appeasement' buzzes with historical allusiveness, specifically to Chamberlain's policy toward Hitler, widely perceived to be a concession to Nazi aggression during the Munich crisis of 1938, and the futility of that appeasement as proven by the Nazis' subsequent invasion of the Sudetenland. In 'Sunday Afternoon', the reference to 'appeasement' aligns Bowen's elderly characters with a policy of ignoring the obvious and making concessions where none are warranted.

Bowen uses style and idiom in 'Sunday Afternoon' to register an ambiguous view of Irish neutrality during the war. Certainly, she satirizes the inertia of the genteel

---

[62] Bowen, *The Faber Book of Modern Stories*, 38.   [63] Ibid., 43.
[64] Elizabeth Bowen, 'The Moores of Moore Hall', in *Collected Impressions*, 161.
[65] Elizabeth Bowen, 'Hamilton Rowan', in *Collected Impressions*, 165.
[66] Elizabeth Bowen, 'Sunday Afternoon', in *The Collected Stories of Elizabeth Bowen*, 620.

Anglo-Irish, who dither and drink tea when they ought to be, at the very least, interested in news about the war. Maria complains that nothing ever changes in her cosy Dublin suburb with its distant view of mountains. Contradicting Maria, who is outspoken and modern, Henry defends the elders, with 'their little fears and their great doubts'.[67] According to Henry, they give life a point of view and a principle; despite their refusal to hear about the war, they tacitly acknowledge the forces of fate that operate on every individual. With some wistfulness and not a little force—he dissuades Maria from running off to London to join the war effort, at least for the time being—Henry asks, 'Where shall we be when nobody has a view of life?'[68] In this regard, Bowen balances a commitment to action against a commitment to tradition. The elderly people who dissociate themselves from the war remain true to their country and their customs. They live in an 'eternalized Sunday afternoon'[69] without progress or movement. Suspended in time, they do not feel compelled to face catastrophic modernity, if that modernity is understood as global warfare happening somewhere other than suburban Dublin. In its handling of different temporalities, the story approaches the question of history obliquely, as if sharing the elders' point of view. For his part, Henry is about to return to 'the zone of death'[70] and has not the least idea of whether he will survive the war. Maria notices that the war is not yet in history books because it is still going on. By contrast, Henry dispenses with the question of temporality by asking 'what the importance of time could be'.[71] In 'Sunday Afternoon', the Anglo-Irish habit of not noticing generalizes into a condition of suspending the question of history and time altogether, as a means of denying the importance of modernity-as-catastrophe.

Compression in the short story favours obliquity. Under the obligation to leave motives and material unelaborated, the short story creates opportunities for surmise. The crisis in 'A Love Story 1939'—the death of an RAF pilot in the early days of the war, and the emotional consequences that arise from his death—is never stated outright. Even the Irish setting of the story has to be inferred from details. A waiter with 'a Kerry face'[72] brings drinks. Linda, overseeing a fuss in the hotel lobby, placidly comments that 'the Irish are exhibitionists'.[73] Mrs Massey wishes she were proud of her country (Britain), but she is ashamed of 'this country'[74] (Ireland). The story refuses to mention the war directly or even acknowledge that its subject is Irish neutrality during the war.

'A Love Story 1939' is constructed around various couples and their private lives. The couples do not necessarily interact with each other; their contact is circumstantial rather than consequential. Mrs Massey harangues her daughter Teresa as they enter the hotel for drinks, a scene that Linda and Frank observe as they pass through the lobby. Frank deviously calls Linda his cousin, but in fact the couple are lovers who have come to the hotel for a romantic getaway. Clifford and Polly, a wedded but mismatched pair, are honeymooning in Ireland when the war breaks out; they keep to themselves, except when Clifford, out of politeness, volunteers to drive Mrs Massey and Linda home, with

---

[67] Ibid., 621.   [68] Ibid., 622.   [69] Ibid., 616.   [70] Ibid., 621.   [71] Ibid., 621.
[72] Elizabeth Bowen, 'A Love Story 1939', in *The Collected Stories of Elizabeth Bowen*, 498.
[73] Ibid., 499.   [74] Ibid., 509.

Frank gamely in tow. The story ends with Clifford tactfully rejecting Frank's invitation for the couples to socialize over drinks. The couples are not meant to blend.

Despite its title, the story does not disclose whose love story this is. At the same time, the story is specifically about the conditions that animate love affairs in 1939. Polly— guilty of 'styleless, backgroundless dullness'[75]—enervates her younger husband. She leaps up to light him a cigarette and wraps her arms around his neck while he is writing. Nonplussed, he unfastens her arms 'with as little emotion as a woman undoing a boa'.[76] If Clifford feels effeminized in the marriage, Polly is infantilized. She curls up 'childishly'[77] with a book, props a stuffed panda on her desk, and wears her hair like a fourteen-year-old. Clifford escapes from Polly by sitting in their parked car while she mopes in their hotel room. If this love story is theirs, it is not destined to happiness.

Other couples fare no better. Although Frank says that he loves catering to Linda's every wish, his eye roves to other women. After noticing Teresa in the lounge of the hotel, he clumsily tries to embrace her and puts his hands on her shoulder blades while she sobs. Linda, fully aware of Frank's philandering, writes a letter—possibly to her husband, possibly to another suitor—to explain her whereabouts. In Frank's absence, she wonders whether she ought to have written a warmer letter just in case the escapade with Frank does not work out. All these couples and couplings are a distraction from the true emotional centre of the story: Teresa's grief for the dead aviator. Although Mrs Massey carries on histrionically about the dead man, Teresa's muted reaction indicates the depth of her feeling. Without ever acknowledging that Teresa and the aviator are romantically paired, the story intimates in its oblique fashion that death has made them more permanently a couple than either Polly and Clifford or Frank and Linda.

Although 'A Love Story 1939' hews closely to a narrow band of time—an autumn evening—it drops insinuations about possible futures for the characters that resonate beyond the conclusion. Clifford stalks about with a gun during the day; he feels pent up in Ireland and longs to go to war. Frank, a veteran of the last war, intends to stay out of it and sell cars in Cork. He and Linda, after their interlude, may go their separate ways. Teresa contemplates leaving her mother and Ireland: 'An idea of going away for ever lifted and moved her heart, like a tide coming in.'[78] All of these possible outcomes are oblique insofar as they have no realization within the temporality of the story itself. They are vectors, possibilities, advances, and outcomes glimpsed beyond the strictures of the story itself.

Obliquity may be another term for irony. Elizabeth Bowen's irony, operative in both her short stories and her novels, takes into account the differences between present and past, modernism and tradition, Ireland and Britain. As a strategy of representation, obliquity leaves room for puzzlement about national history. By deflecting violence and confrontation, the oblique writer gains ground. In an interview published in *The Bell* in 1942, Bowen claimed that no outsider could write effectively about Ireland: 'This country's different from the other countries in Europe. It's so much more complex. It requires such an enormous amount of knowledge and experience before the foreigner begins to

[75] Ibid., 500.   [76] Ibid.   [77] Ibid., 499.   [78] Ibid., 501.

make an impression—even on the rim of things.'[79] If insularity causes foreigners to approach the complexities of Ireland by indirection, that indirection is reciprocated: Irish writers take an oblique approach to modernism in all its foreign guises by adapting short story technique to their own purposes. In her consideration of short story technique, Bowen implies that insularity leaves a national imprint on Irish short stories and that the universality of the form redeems, or at least moderates, the effects of insularity. For Bowen, the short story achieves its aesthetic effects obliquely while maintaining its commitment to visuality, style, and national imprint.

FURTHER READING

Brooke, Jocelyn. *Elizabeth Bowen*. London: Longmans, 1952.

Corcoran, Neil. *Elizabeth Bowen: The Enforced Return*. Oxford: Oxford University Press, 2004.

D'hoker, Elke. *Irish Women Writers and the Modern Short Story*. Basingstoke: Palgrave Macmillan, 2016.

Ellmann, Maud. *Elizabeth Bowen: The Shadow Across the Page*. Edinburgh: Edinburgh University Press, 2003.

Glendinning, Victoria. *Elizabeth Bowen: A Biography*. New York: Anchor, 2005.

Jordan, Heather Bryant. *How Will the Heart Endure: Elizabeth Bowen and the Landscape of War*. Ann Arbor, MI: University of Michigan Press, 1992.

Lassner, Phyllis. *Elizabeth Bowen: A Study of the Short Fiction*. New York: Twayne, 1991.

Teekell, Anna. *Emergency Writing: Irish Literature, Neutrality, and the Second World War*. Evanston, IL: Northwestern University Press, 2018.

Towheed, Shafquat. 'Territory, Space, Modernity: Elizabeth Bowen's *The Demon Lover and Other Stories* and Wartime London'. In Susan Osborn (ed.), *Elizabeth Bowen: New Critical Perspectives*. Cork: Cork University Press, 2009: 113–31.

Trotter, David. 'Dis-enablement: Subject and Method in the Modernist Short Story'. *Critical Inquiry* 52, no. 2 (2010): 4–13.

Walshe, Éibhear (ed.). *Elizabeth Bowen*. Dublin: Irish Academic Press, 2009.

---

[79] 'Meet Elizabeth Bowen', *The Bell* 4, no. 6 (September 1942), 426.

CHAPTER 13

THE ROLE AND REPRESENTATION OF BETRAYAL IN THE IRISH SHORT STORY SINCE *DUBLINERS*

GERRY SMYTH

JAMES Joyce's (1882–1941) first composition of note was a poem (now lost) entitled 'Et Tu, Healy' in which he adapted that famous Shakespearean phrase to indict the treachery of Timothy Healy, quondam trusted lieutenant of Charles Stewart Parnell. Another piece of Joycean juvenilia is entitled 'Trust Not Appearances', a reflection on the discrepancy between outward appearance and underlying reality.[1] These early writings anticipate a career in which the idea of betrayal featured as one of the presiding influences on the author's artistic, psychological, and political profile. Joyce saw betrayal everywhere he looked: in Irish history, in literature, and in his own life. Already apparent in his debut publication, *Chamber Music* (1907), and the abandoned *Stephen Hero* (posthumously published in 1944), Joyce's major work represents a relentless dissection of the anatomy of betrayal in all its shapes and forms. This obsession, moreover, was to have a lively afterlife in subsequent Irish literary discourse as generations of writers returned to this theme time and again until, following the economic, civic, and ethical crises of the early twenty-first century, Irish society at large learned to speak the Joycean language of betrayal.[2]

Much of the evidence for Joyce's fixation with betrayal is adduced from *Ulysses* (1922), and it is easy to understand why. At the heart of that remarkable novel is a simple story

---

[1] Richard Ellmann quotes a section of the poem in his 1959 biography; see *James Joyce* (Oxford: Oxford University Press, 1983), 33. The essay may be found in James Joyce, *Occasional, Critical, and Political Writing*, ed. Kevin Barry (Oxford: Oxford World's Classics, 2000), 3.

[2] These issues are fully engaged in my book, *The Judas Kiss: Treason and Betrayal in Six Modern Irish Novels* (Manchester: Manchester University Press, 2015).

about adultery.[3] As such, it belongs to a well-established nineteenth-century European tradition in which marital infidelity features as an explicit threat to the legal and moral bases of bourgeois society—that form of society, in other words, from which the novel itself emerged and in which it flourished.[4] At the same time, the ghost of political betrayal stalks the pages of *Ulysses*, not only in the form of Parnell but also in the figures of Hamlet, Dermot Mac Murrough, and many others, including the arch-betrayer himself, Judas Iscariot. As I have already suggested, however, Joyce's fixation with betrayal existed before *Ulysses*, and in this chapter I want to examine some of the contexts within which this singular fixation was established and explored in the earlier part of his career, with particular reference to the short story collection *Dubliners* (1914). Proceeding by way of an overview of what is still widely regarded as a 'minor' literary form, the latter part of the chapter will then focus on the re-emergence of that theme in a selection of indicative post-Joycean Irish short stories.

THE SHORT STORY: A MINOR FORM?

The short story has attracted much scholarly attention since it began to emerge in its modern form in the middle of the nineteenth century. Through one process or another, various ideas have come to be associated with this 'modest art',[5] and it has become a favourite testing ground for a range of aesthetic, philosophical, and moral theories. Indeed, attempting to *define* the short story represents a recurring gesture in its own right, a gesture which many great practitioners and critics have made over the years since Edgar Allan Poe's review of Nathaniel Hawthorne's *Twice-Told Tales* in 1842. Poe famously stressed compression and focus, a unity of affect in which 'patterns of detail [mesh] closely with plot and characterization toward a concerted impact'.[6] This theory remains influential, engaging as it does with what would seem to be the form's defining feature: its shortness. Indeed, its brevity compared to the novel has led some critics to regard the short story as a kind of poem, characterized by precision of imagery and concision of expression. In this regard, the craft of the short story lies in its tightly controlled movement towards a particular effect or impression.

Other theories have emerged to complement and qualify Poe's thesis. For some, the short story is regarded as the modern articulation of an inherent turn to narrative, especially character- and event-based narrative. Its genealogy lies in myth and legend, fable

---

[3] According to Ellmann, the Bloom strand, concerning a Jewish Dubliner rescuing a young man in difficulties, was originally conceived as a short story for inclusion in *Dubliners* (*James Joyce*, 230).

[4] See Tony Tanner, *Adultery in the Novel: Contract and Transgression* (Baltimore, MD: Johns Hopkins University Press, 1979).

[5] See T. O. Beachcroft, *The Modest Art: A Survey of the Short Story in English* (London: Oxford University Press, 1968).

[6] Quoted in R. C. Feddersen, 'Introduction: A Glance at the History of the Short Story in English', in Erin Fallon, R. C. Fedderson, James Kurtzleben, Maurice A. Lee, and Susan Rochette-Crawley (eds), *A Reader's Companion to the Short Story in English* (London: Greenwood Press, 2001), xviii.

and parable, anecdote and essay, sketch and ballad.[7] Its historical practitioners include William Congreve, William Painter, Geoffrey Chaucer, and a host of anonymous writers and storytellers stretching back into prehistory. Some maintain that the form's basis in oral anecdote rather than written narrative renders it the most democratic of forms, locked in to everyday experience in ways that adjacent forms (drama, poetry, and the novel) can never truly be.[8] In her introduction to *The Faber Book of Modern Stories* (1937), Elizabeth Bowen (1899–1973) likened the 'heroic simplicity'[9] of the modern short story to that of the cinema (although she was surely mistaken to claim that neither form was sponsored by a tradition).

As the short story matured around the turn of the twentieth century, two principal trends, each with its basis in Poe's early intervention, came to be emphasized in both practice and commentary. These trends have many names, but in essence they are often regarded as operating along a continuum running between the realism associated with the French writer Guy de Maupassant and the impressionism associated with the Russian Anton Chekhov. The former connotes ideas of linearity, effect, and irony, the narrative *coup* which speaks especially to Poe's emphasis on craftsmanship and concision. The Chekhovian trend introduces ideas of spatiality, tonal affect, atmosphere, and perspectivism; it also de-emphasizes 'story' in favour of suggestion, mood, and tone, which are ultimately made to serve a greater sense of reality than that available to mere realism. According to Bowen, Maupassant was a writer of 'primary colours . . . energetic, ruthless, nervous, plain', whereas 'Tchehov stands . . . for an emancipation of faculties, for a romantic distension of the form of the story to let in what might appear inchoate or nebulous'.[10] The 'story' is not so much a coherent tale as a fragment snatched from reality; its animating 'crisis' is symbolic and casual rather than concrete or dramatic. Perhaps the principal formal effect of Chekhovian style is the epiphany, described by Mary Rohrberger as 'a point of frozen energy operating just beyond understanding'.[11]

With Chekhov we have approached the gates of modernism; and with the introduction of the epiphany we observe the figure of James Joyce hoving into view.[12] But Joyce's aesthetic composition had an alternative genealogy—Ireland—and therein lies a range of alternative (or at least complementary) considerations. Most historians of the short story have noted the existence of a distinctive Irish tradition in which Joyce's fifteen stories in *Dubliners* form a watershed of sorts. After Joyce, in Walter Allen's typical canon, the twentieth-century Irish short story encompasses two distinct moments: an earlier

---

[7] See H. E. Bates, *The Modern Short Story* (London: Thomas Nelson and Sons, 1943), 13.

[8] Beachcroft, *The Modest Art*, 3.

[9] Elizabeth Bowen, 'Introduction: The Short Story', in Elizabeth Bowen (ed.), *The Faber Book of Modern Stories* (London: Faber and Faber, 1937), 7. In *Scribbling Women and the Short Story Form: Approaches to American and British Women Writers* (New York: Peter Lang, 2008), literary historian Ellen Burton Harrington points to the 'rich periodical culture on both sides of the Atlantic in the nineteenth century' (14) as the seedbed for the development of the form.

[10] Bowen, 'Introduction: The Short Story', 9–10.

[11] Quoted in Harrington, *Scribbling Women and the Short Story Form*, 7.

[12] Quoting Herbert Gorman, Ellmann claims that Joyce had not read Chekhov when he wrote the stories in *Dubliners* (*James Joyce*, 166).

one including Daniel Corkery (1878–1964), Michael McLaverty (1904–92), Liam O'Flaherty (1897–1984), Seán O'Faoláin (1900–91), and Frank O'Connor (1903–66); and a later one featuring Brian Friel (1929–2015), John Montague (1929–2016), Edna O'Brien (1930–), and Julia O'Faoláin (1932–).[13] Allen's overview missed a later, equally brilliant generation in which the form has continued to evolve and thrive down to the time of this volume's publication.

If all this activity has led the short story to be considered 'the pre-eminent Irish prose form',[14] there is another sense in which it has never managed to shed its irreducibly 'minor' status. The claim would be that, because of various sociological and cultural factors—the predominantly agricultural basis of society, the absence of a strong public sphere, the prevalence of an oral tradition of storytelling, and what H. E. Bates described as 'a natural genius for dramatizing life'[15]—the short story historically *belonged* to Irish cultural history in a way that the novel never could; moreover, it *belonged* to Irish cultural history in a way that it could never *belong* to British cultural history in all its stratified complexity.[16] This is in essence the thesis developed by both Seán O'Faoláin and Frank O'Connor in their influential studies—a minor form for a minor, unformed society that was 'uncongenial to the novel form'.[17] At the same time, the short story is often regarded as a quintessentially modern—sometimes modernist—form, one that comes into its own in terms of the Maupassant/Chekhov stand-off noted above. While the 'Irish school' might retain deep discursive links with an ancient storytelling tradition, the modern short story is in essence a literary form and thus fundamentally removed from the oral tale in terms of their respective methods and assumptions. One might say in this regard that the oral tradition is both an opportunity and a limitation for the Irish writer. To anyone enculturated in an Irish context (on the island or elsewhere), the spoken tradition remains a powerful resource; amongst other things, it represents a means of exploring formative ideas relating to community, memory, and identity. On the other hand, the written story offers the glamour of artifice in all its precision and irony; more important still, it offers the Irish writer an *escape* from community, a chance to experiment with individual subjectivity outwith the bonds of memory and received identity.

The short story offers the Irish writer an opportunity, in other words, to adopt 'the lonely voice' identified by Frank O'Connor as the form's defining effect. Lacking a 'hero' as such, the short story speaks for and to the solitary individual—'outlawed figures

---

[13] Walter Allen, *The Short Story in English* (Oxford: Clarendon Press, 1981), 210–8, 388–94. Invariably in such accounts there are honourable mentions for Mary Lavin and Elizabeth Bowen, although the latter's Irishness, as we shall see, remains a problematic quality.

[14] Heather Ingman, *A History of the Irish Short Story* (Cambridge: Cambridge University Press, 2009), 1.

[15] Bates, *The Modern Short Story*, 148. Bates goes on to identify George Moore's *The Untilled Field* (1903) as the inaugural moment of the properly modern Irish story, a judgement with which Frank O'Connor concurs in his seminal 1963 study, *The Lonely Voice: A Study of the Short Story*.

[16] Ingman points out that in his influential anthology, *Great Irish Short Stories* (1964), Vivian Mercier emphasized the link between the oral tradition and the modern literary short story by including translations and adaptations from folktales by J. M. Synge, Lady Gregory, Douglas Hyde, and Gerald Griffin, before commencing his selection of literary examples proper with the work of William Carleton (*A History of the Irish Short Story*, 8).

[17] Ingman, *A History of the Irish Short Story*, 5. The studies in question are O'Faolain's *The Short Story* (1948) and O'Connor's aforementioned *The Lonely Voice*.

wandering about the fringes of society'[18]—and what it offers those figures is a perspective on their own solitude, their own marginal status, ultimately their own loneliness. The acquisition of such a voice represents a dubious achievement, perhaps, but its value remains clear and attractive to the writer looking to escape the deadly bonds of *Gemeinschaft*. Herein (despite O'Connor's scepticism towards his predecessor's achievement) emerges the profile of the Joycean short story, populated as it is with a range of lonely, marginal 'heroes' struggling to escape the confines of the traditional community. And herein, also, is perhaps the basis of the Irish short story's links with the figure of betrayal.

When attempting to illustrate what he describes as the 'three necessary elements in a story—exposition, development, and drama', O'Connor writes: 'Exposition we may illustrate as "John Fortescue was a solicitor in the little town of X"; development as "One day Mrs Fortescue told him she was about to leave him for another man"; and drama as "You will do nothing of the kind," he said.'[19] It is interesting to note that O'Connor's apparently throwaway example relays the adulterous three-cornered romance that is at the heart of so much modern literature (including *Ulysses*). We presume John Fortescue resists his wife's demand because he feels betrayed: someone with whom he was legally and sentimentally bonded entertained an alternative secret desire. We note also that Fortescue possesses a professional public profile (he is a solicitor in a small town), so there is scope for the development of elements of political intrigue, ideological competition, and civic trust betrayed. In essence: the exposition describes the way things *apparently* are; the development reveals how things *really* are; the drama describes the consequences of this disconnection. The gap between 'exposition' and 'development' is animated by a discourse of betrayal, which is to say, by the powerful emotional response to the realization of a hidden reality at odds with established reality. As O'Connor's example illustrates, there are two principal spaces or modes wherein this drama unfolds: the private home, with its emphasis on interpersonal treachery, and the public sphere, where different groups vie for the right to describe competitors as 'traitors' in respect of a true, antecedent reality. Such a model brings us back to Joyce once again.

Joyce's pivotal status with regard to modern Irish experience is encapsulated in his abbreviated short story-writing career, and in ways which fully anticipate his turn to longer fiction. The stories in *Dubliners* operate with reference to a series of binaries broached throughout this section, each element of which is charged with a range of moral, aesthetic, political, and social values: old/new; oral/literary; tradition/modernity; community/individual; nationalism/cosmopolitanism; private/public; Romantic/modernist; event/impression. It is the very existence of the binary that allows for the emergence of a discourse of betrayal, as each element vies for dominance over a competitor to which it is, paradoxically, symbiotically related. In Joyce's own work, to which I now briefly turn, this tendency was repeatedly thematized in terms of the two modes described in the previous paragraph: public political betrayal of (and by) the abstract nation and private personal betrayal of one individual by another.

---

[18] Frank O'Connor, *The Lonely Voice: A Study of the Short Story* (Hoboken, NJ: Melville House Publishing, 2004), 18.

[19] Ibid., 25.

BETRAYAL IN *DUBLINERS*

In 'Two Gallants', the sixth story in *Dubliners*, the character Lenehan describes his acquaintance Corley as a 'Base betrayer!'[20] What is intended as a joking compliment resonates throughout the story and the collection as a whole: Corley *is* a base betrayer, primed for treachery by the society in which he lives and the history which has produced him. Corley betrays the servant girl with whom he is walking out; moreover, he implicates her in the same practice, as it seems clear that her acquisition of the 'small gold coin'[21] involves a breach of trust of some kind or degree. But Lenehan is a traitor also: he has betrayed his own youth, his own potential and future. Even the putative relationship with a future partner is conceived in an exploitative mode, as he fantasizes about 'a good simple-minded girl with a little of the ready'.[22] His relationship with Corley is, likewise, a pretence of friendship, for all the while an inimical reality, based on acquisition and greed, lurks behind the semblance of friendship. 'Ivy Day in the Committee Room' exemplifies another form of betrayal that stalks the pages of *Dubliners*. In it, the character Joe Hynes recites a poem in which he likens the late Charles Stewart Parnell to Christ betrayed:

> *He dreamed (alas, 'twas but a dream!)*
> *   Of Liberty: but as he strove*
> *To clutch that idol, treachery*
> *   Sundered him from the thing he loved.*
>
> *Shame on the coward caitiff hands*
> *   That smote their Lord or with a kiss*
> *Betrayed him to the rabble-rout*
> *   Of fawning priests—no friends of his.*[23]

This recitation takes place within a setting that is both public and heavily politicized: local government elections in the period after the death of 'the Chief'. The allegiances in the Committee Room are tentative and divided; the atmosphere is suspicious and strained; if the ghost of Parnell is in the building, so too is that of Judas, ready as always to hand over his Lord with a treacherous kiss.

Dubliners has traditionally been regarded as a text in which the *paralysis* of contemporary Irish life constitutes the underlying linking reality of each character in each story. 'Two Gallants' fits easily with such a thesis: the characters *appear* to be moving as they walk the city streets, but in fact they are merely circling ceaselessly around a kind of hell from which there is no escape. Paralysis is but one symptom of a much more malign underlying reality, however, one that blights the lives of all the characters in a more

---

[20] James Joyce, 'Two Gallants', in *Dubliners*, ed. Jeri Johnson (Oxford: Oxford World's Classics, 2000), 39.
[21] Ibid., 45.   [22] Ibid., 43.
[23] James Joyce, 'Ivy Day in the Committee Room', in *Dubliners*, 104.

insidious and destructive way. In each story, betrayal is the reality behind the representation, the secret behind the semblance, the ill will behind the apparent good humour. Betrayal is the enemy who passes as a friend, the subject who owes allegiance according to one or another discursive regime (family, friend, confessor, age, spouse, lover, ally) but who eschews that allegiance in the name of some other expedient. *Dubliners*, in short, is populated by a series of characters (themselves representative of the race) who inhale an atmosphere of betrayal that is operating at large throughout Irish society.

In all fifteen stories, the act of betrayal oscillates between public and private contexts. Although one 'scene' may dominate ('Ivy Day in the Committee Room' is clearly more public than 'Eveline', for example), the sense of movement between dual locations is implicit throughout. Each story, moreover, works to expose the complex interpenetration of these contexts and the ways in which the betrayals perpetrated in each converge in time and space. 'A Little Cloud' provides an obvious example. Little Chandler becomes over-excited during his rendezvous with old friend Ignatius Gallagher. When he insists rather too pointedly that Gallagher will indeed marry, despite the latter's demurral, Little Chandler becomes aware 'that he had betrayed himself'.[24] The word functions here in a Freudian sense: despite our conscious and unconscious attempts to keep the secret (whatever it may be), betrayal, as Freud famously put it, 'oozes out of [us] at every pore'.[25] Just so in this instance: Little Chandler has been feeling oppressed by Gallagher's breeziness, his freedom, and his apparent success, and this accentuates the feelings of resentment, entrapment, and failure that he would normally repress. Finding himself in unusual public circumstances, however, and under the influence of alcohol and tobacco, these repressed desires and fears burst through the masking defences of his consciousness to reveal a different reality beneath, one haunted by feelings of failure and inadequacy. Little Chandler's encounter with Gallagher, and his fantasies about leaving Dublin to become a poet, resonate in relation to a discourse of national identity—which is to say, a public, performative discourse in which the category of contemporary 'Irishness' is indicted for its stultifying inadequacies.

Having once established this insidious presence, moreover, Joyce goes on to show how deeply and how destructively it has penetrated the world of contemporary Ireland. When he returns home, Little Chandler experiences feelings of frustration and resentment—towards his house, his job, his family, towards the kind of life that he is living in this particular city at this particular time. The scene of betrayal has moved indoors, in other words, from a public political context to a private interpersonal one. The expanding field of betrayal comes clearly into focus: from an innocent baby, to Little Chandler, to the surrounding city, to the country itself. As it stretches outwards in space to encompass the nation's colonial status, it also reaches backwards in time towards a history that is itself littered with both the victims and the perpetrators of betrayal.

---

[24] James Joyce, 'A Little Cloud', in *Dubliners*, 61.
[25] Sigmund Freud, 'Fragment of an Analysis of a Case of Hysteria (Dora)', in *The Pelican Freud Library, Vol. 8: Case Histories I: 'Dora' and 'Little Hans'*, trans. Alix and James Strachey, ed. Angela Richards (Harmondsworth: Penguin, 1983), 114. It is not coincidental that one of the cornerstones of Freudian discourse is the notion of self-betrayal.

The pattern in which a treacherous public encounter reverberates within a private context is repeated throughout *Dubliners*. In 'After the Race', Jimmy Doyle has a private moment of regret after the foolishness of his public performance, whereas in 'Counterparts', Farrington is betrayed by his alcohol addiction into making a public error, only to reproduce that treachery in his own home with an assault on his son. The pattern culminates (as so much else does) in 'The Dead', a story which works to reveal the bad faith upon which both the public and the private lives of its principal protagonist, Gabriel Conroy, is founded. Joyce's brilliance in these stories lies in his astonishingly nuanced management of private and public realms, and his insight into the ways and the extent to which these realms have thoroughly converged, with betrayal—of self by self, and of citizen by nation—the linking factor throughout.

Public Betrayal after Joyce

As with so many of his formal and thematic concerns, Joyce's obsession with betrayal reverberated throughout subsequent Irish literary history, albeit in the altered forms determined by changing socio-political circumstances. Such a claim might not seem immediately apparent in relation to one of the most famous of Irish short stories, Frank O'Connor's 'Guests of the Nation' (1931), which, in terms of setting, theme, and stylistic treatment, is some considerable way removed from the stories in *Dubliners*. The action is set during the War of Independence or Anglo-Irish War (1919–21) and is narrated by Bonaparte, a young IRA volunteer who, with his comrade Noble, is guarding two captured British soldiers, 'Awkins and Belcher, in an isolated farmhouse. Along with the old woman who owns the property, the four men form a kind of family characterized by spatial intimacy and shared habits. The unit commander, Jeremiah Donovan, arrives with the news that the two hostages are to be shot in reprisal for the execution of four IRA volunteers. The men are taken out to the bog behind the house where they are dispatched and buried.

The two young IRA men are intensely conflicted about their role in this development. Having lived and socialized with their 'enemies', they find themselves caught between an apparently natural empathy towards fellow humans and their duty to oppose, to the point of violence and death, particular kinds of humans—which is to say, their political competitors. Issues of affinity and affiliation are subtly plotted throughout the story, with Jeremiah Donovan representing an alien presence within the complex quartet formed by the Noble/'Awkins and Bonaparte/Belcher pairings. Within the imaginary space formed by this quartet, values (such as 'Awkins's avowed political anarchism) and practices (such as Irish dancing and card-playing) have started to become enmeshed; and as with any breaching of the border between 'essentially' different categories, familiarity with the other creates a moral and psychological responsibility for his or her fate.

The word 'chum' is repeated eighteen times throughout the story, becoming a kind of leitmotif across the score of the text. Like 'mate' or 'pal', 'chum' was a throwaway word in contemporary English vernacular; in a story about the limits of interpersonal friendship against a backdrop of political strife, however, it takes on a heavily weighted resonance. '[The] word lingers painfully in my memory',[26] remarks Bonaparte, no doubt tormented by his role in what feels like the betrayal of his erstwhile 'chums'. For always with the possibility of friendship, as Joyce showed so thoroughly and so painfully, comes the possibility of betrayal. Walking towards his death, 'Awkins offers to desert the British Army and take up arms for the cause of his 'chums', but everyone present—friend *and* enemy, Irish *and* English—hears this for what it is: a desperate bargain to save his life. The responsibilities of friendship are always mitigated by powerful external forces—society, ideology, culture, law, and so on. Bonaparte does not want to shoot his 'chums', but neither can he countenance, from either a practical or a moral point of view, dissenting from his own 'side': 'Because there were men on the Brigade you daren't let nor hinder without a gun in your hand, and at any rate, in those days disunion between brothers seemed to me an awful crime. I knew better after'.[27] The cynicism of the last sentence indicates a narrative perspective from after the Civil War, itself a large-scale, protracted example of 'disunion between brothers'.

Back in the 'proper' war, Bonaparte is deeply traumatized by the experience—a trauma, he paradoxically writes, 'not to be written afterwards'.[28] After the deed is done, he stands at the back door of the farmhouse, staring at the heavens, unable to accede to the prayers of Noble and the old woman, and coming to the realization that he has been profoundly and permanently damaged by the events. Bonaparte's experience provides an early example of what would come to be described as the revisionist turn in modern Irish history: the painful insight that the situation was not, never had been, as dominant nationalist–republican ideology claimed it to be. The concept of betrayal is in fact embedded within all shades of Irish history at a deep structural level: fear of being betrayed, certainly, but fear also that one must inevitably be regarded as a traitor in relation to the great variety of moral and political discourses vying for one's allegiance.

Issues resonating at a theoretical and philosophical level in other parts of the island impacted on the day-to-day lives of people living in Northern Ireland during the period known as 'the Troubles', stretching from the late 1960s to the late 1990s. In 'A Trusted Neighbour' in his 2006 collection, *Matters of Life and Death*, Bernard MacLaverty (1942–) tells the story of a young Catholic family, Ben and Maureen and their two children, who move to a religiously mixed Belfast neighbourhood. Ben learns that his neighbour, Dawson Orr, is a Protestant policeman. Although somewhat overbearing, Dawson appears friendly enough, even giving his 'trusted neighbour'[29] lifts into the city in the morning on the back of his motorcycle. Dawson's deeply entrenched bigotry gradually emerges, however, culminating in his assertion that Catholic families in another part of the city torched their own houses in order to implicate the Protestant loyalist community. Dawson starts to park his car in front of Ben's house, and although this is

[26] Frank O'Connor, 'Guests of the Nation', in *Collected Stories* (New York: Vintage, 1982), 9.
[27] Ibid., 7.   [28] Ibid., 12.
[29] Bernard MacLaverty, 'A Trusted Neighbour', in *Matters of Life and Death* (London: Vintage, 2007), 72.

initially put down to drunkenness, the truth emerges after the Orr family moves away. Another neighbour informs Ben that the policeman had warned all the Protestant families in the neighbourhood that he, Dawson, was under threat, and that they should move their children out of the front bedrooms, away from any possible attack. Not only had Dawson not informed his Catholic neighbour, but in knowing that Ben and Maureen's two young children slept in the front bedroom, he had deliberately parked his car outside Ben's house so as to confuse any potential attacker.

'A trusted neighbour' is an ironic description of the failure of friendship, and the responsibilities that come with it, in a divided community. Ben is not 'involved' in the conflict, although he knows people who probably are, and his Catholic identity is enough to implicate him in the eyes of a Protestant community experiencing what it perceives to be a sustained attack upon its existence. During a late-night drinking session, Dawson rehearses the platitudes of communitarian philosophy: 'It takes all sorts, eh? We are all thrown together whether we like it or not. Gotta make the best of it. You're a nice guy. . . . If only they were all like you.'[30] Behind this apparent commitment to shared values, however, Dawson's paranoia leads him to emphasize difference rather than commonality, and thus to betray his neighbour. This revelation seems to orient MacLaverty's story in a particular direction, one associated with a realist tradition: the narrative turns on a *coup* whereby the semblance of reality is stripped away to reveal an underlying truth.

In keeping with MacLaverty's technique, however, 'A Trusted Neighbour' incorporates subtleties of rhythm and imagery which belie any simplistic or straightforward reading. Ben's embrace of Dawson during their early morning motorcycle rides is replicated in the image of his embrace of Maureen, as he '[puts] his hands on her back like he was her pillion passenger'; Ben is kept awake at the end of the story by the image of an injured girl whom he had encountered during a hospital visit described at the outset.[31] This in itself is a reflection of the complexity of the situation MacLaverty is attempting to describe. In a community lacking a common frame of reference, 'truth' is always going to be a matter of perspective. 'Truth', moreover, is always haunted by its symbiotic ghost—betrayal—and this is something that the short story form is eminently equipped to reveal.

The two defining developments of early twenty-first-century Ireland were the financial crisis which signalled the end of the Celtic Tiger and the abuse scandals which so thoroughly undermined the foundations of the Catholic Church. The situation was similar in each case: institutions and practices which *appeared* to be one thing (a responsible economic programme on the one hand, a cogent ethical system on the other) were actually something else—were, indeed, in some senses the *opposite* of what they appeared. Faced with irresponsible self-serving financiers on the one hand and morally bankrupt religious on the other, it is no wonder that the idea of betrayal loomed so large in Irish life during this period. Moreover, although each has been in its way a form of public betrayal, the consequences of each penetrated deeply into the fab-

---

[30] Ibid., 72.   [31] Ibid., 87–8.

ric of modern Irish life. Such a context is highly amenable to the short story format in a number of respects, not least, the narrative 'turn' in which large public developments may be observed to reverberate at the level of banal quotidian experience.

Colm Tóibín's (1955–) *Mothers and Sons* (2006) recalls *Dubliners* insofar as it is a collection of stories linked by a specific theme, in this case, the complex emotional relationships that develop between women and their male offspring. One of those stories, 'A Priest in the Family', tells of Molly O'Neill, an elderly widow living in a small Irish town. Molly's life is as full and meaningful as she can make it: she has plenty of acquaintances and some close friends. Her two daughters live nearby, and she is particularly attached to her four grandsons, who visit her once a week. Molly is intelligent and independent; she is a Catholic though not an unquestioning one, as we see her debating the use of prayer with a priest named Father Greenwood in the opening section of the story.

Molly's life is ripped asunder when she learns that her son Frank, a priest, is to face abuse charges deriving from an earlier stage of his career. Tóibín prepares the reader for this revelation with hints about the 'old school' piety that Frank inherited from his father; and, as Molly attempts to acquire an internet account in the local library, a friend's comment that 'You never liked missing anything, Molly. You'll get all the news from that now'; and again, the 'look of pain' that spreads across her sister-in-law's face when Molly inquires if Frank has visited her.[32] This is a community—small, intergenerational, linked by common concerns and a common cultural inheritance—in which Molly feels fully integrated: 'She knew all about them, she thought, and they about her.'[33] Such, however, proves not to be the case; the devastating news obliges Molly to regard herself and all her relationships anew.

The issue appears to be not what Frank did but how Frank's actions reflect on her and on her life in the community. When the reality of the situation dawns, her response is to say that 'You've all made a fool out of me!',[34] immediately displacing the pain of Frank's guilt elsewhere. Molly feels betrayed by those (the priest, her daughters, and sister-in-law) who she believes should have informed her of the truth, and by the community at large which allowed her to interact with them as if things were not entirely different after the emergence of such information. Such is the nature of betrayal: the initial act reverberates outwards, encompassing wider and wider circles of acquaintance, family, community, and eventually the society within which that initial act takes place. In the final scene, Frank visits his mother to inform her of the impending trial and to encourage her to take a holiday so as to escape at least some of the imminent revelations. The actual cause of all this pain is never broached, however, and the story ends uncertainly with Molly watching from the window of her house as Frank drives away. Her response to the news of Frank's crime—moving through denial, shame, and eventually a kind of stunned acceptance of guilt by association—is of a piece with modern Irish society's traumatized response to the evidently compromised moral foundations upon which its house had been raised.

---

[32] Colm Tóibín, 'A Priest in the Family', in *Mothers and Sons* (London: Picador, 2006), 152, 155, 157.
[33] Ibid., 155.   [34] Ibid., 161.

PRIVATE BETRAYAL AFTER JOYCE

Gabriel Conroy's great fear is that his wife has been or is being unfaithful to him—if not physically or consciously, then emotionally or subconsciously; if not *since* their meeting and marriage, then *before*. This latter charge appears entirely unreasonable to modern sensibilities: how can it be fair to impugn a lover for liaisons which predate our acquaintance? To Gabriel and to his creator, however, such was part of the complex politics of interpersonal relationships, in which questions of commitment, affiliation, and fidelity follow no laws of logic or reason. 'The Dead' casts a long shadow over modern Irish culture; it might be said, indeed, that the memory of 'The Dead' reverberates throughout much subsequent literary discourse, and that Joyce's transposition of a crisis of national identity into a story of love and betrayal becomes a recurring motif within the Irish literary imagination. The issue of interpersonal treachery has had a particularly dynamic afterlife in the form so brilliantly exploited by Joyce in this foundational statement.

Elizabeth's Bowen's relationship with Ireland was as conflicted and as complex as Joyce's. I should say 'Anglo-Ireland', because Bowen, both in her life and in her work, exemplified the ambivalence associated with that community. This condition was pushed to a point of crisis by the onset of the Second World War, the early years of which Bowen passed as an Air Raid Precautions warden in London. Having survived the Blitz during the years 1940 and 1941, Bowen was recruited by the British secret service to return to Ireland in order to compile a report on the country's mood—in particular, how it might respond to enforced occupation of the three Atlantic ports (Berehaven, Cobh, and Lough Swilly), sovereignty over which had been ceded to Éire by Britain in 1938. This was the background against which the 1941 short story, 'Summer Night', was written and published.

Bowen's narrative is an affront to the aesthetic tradition which emerged from Poe and which found its exemplary articulation in Maupassant, insofar as it signally fails to observe a unity of focus or setting. Instead, it conjoins a number of different story lines as focalized by a range of different characters. In the opening strand, a woman named Emma drives through the Irish countryside towards the house of her lover. Emma has left her husband the Major at home with their two children, Di and Vivie, and an elderly relative known as Aunt Fran. Emma stops at a hotel to telephone Robinson, her lover, and speaks briefly with the proprietress who is reading in her newspaper about an 'an awful air battle'.[35] The focus then switches to Robinson's house where he is entertaining two people: a deaf woman from the local town named Queenie Cavey and her brother Justin, on holiday from Dublin. The action switches again, this time to the house of the Major sixty miles away. We observe him taking a telephone call from Emma, a few miles down the road from her previous call, and we learn from the children that he is 'disappointed'[36] about the war. Vivie wanders the house naked until she is sent back to bed by Aunt Fran, who we then follow back to her own bedroom where she broods on her own

---

[35] Elizabeth Bowen, 'Summer Night', in *The Collected Stories of Elizabeth Bowen* (London: Vintage, 1999), 585.

[36] Ibid., 596.

loneliness and the evil that seems to inform her every perception: 'You cannot look at the sky without seeing the shadow, the men destroying each other. What is the matter tonight—is there a battle? This is a threatened night.'[37] After a brief scene in which Justin Cavey takes offence at Robinson's apparent desire for his visitors to leave, Emma arrives. The lovers discuss their respective families (he is separated from his wife and two children) as they take a walk in the flower garden, and Emma begins to sense something of the banality of their affair. The final two scenes are dedicated to the Caveys. The first is a letter written by Justin to Robinson, breaking their friendship—a kind of love letter haunted by the ghost of homosexual desire.[38] Finally, as Queenie settles down for the night she recalls her single romantic encounter from another summer night twenty years earlier, and fantasizes a similar encounter with Robinson.

'Summer Night' is a perfect illustration of Bowen's dictum that '[poetic] tautness and clarity are so essential to [the short story] that it may be said to stand at the edge of prose.'[39] The story's brilliance lies in its author's management of a complex cast of characters and scenes, and in her appreciation of the ability of language to create dense, overlapping layers of meaning and inference. Fear of treachery stalks all but one of these characters—treachery of self by other, and of self by self—all against a background of Ireland's wanton (from Bowen's perspective) abstention from an international alliance of right-minded nations against the Nazi terror. The only person to escape Aunt Fran's 'infected zone' is a deaf woman who inhabits a 'sphere of silence that not a word clouded'.[40] Her estrangement from language renders Queenie impervious to the treacheries of desire and betrayal that are the very condition of language. 'Contemplative, wishless, almost without an "I"',[41] the deaf woman embodies a kind of resistance to language's remorseless drive towards identity, and to the inevitable betrayals that ensue from such a vain pursuit.

Whereas the reader is allowed only glimpses into the mind and motivation of Joyce's Gretta and Bowen's Emma, the perspective in Edna O'Brien's 'The Love Object' (1968), the title story of her first short story collection, is dominated throughout by a first-person narrator named Martha. Having made her reputation in the early 1960s writing about the restricted circumstances of contemporary Irish women, O'Brien had broadened her scope later in the decade with two novels—*August is a Wicked Month* (1965) and *Casualties of Peace* (1966)—featuring non-Irish settings. 'The Love Object' is of a piece with these texts inasmuch as there appears to be no recognizably 'Irish' dimension to the plot, other than the author's profile and the sense that her understanding of the morphology of desire has been decisively shaped by her upbringing. Martha is a successful thirty-year-old television presenter living in 'swinging' London. She is also a divorcee with two young sons attending boarding school at the insistence of their father. Martha begins an affair with an 'elderly' ex-soldier, now a lawyer, to whom she refers as

---

[37] Ibid., 599.

[38] On the perceived links between treason and homosexuality during the Second World War and the Cold War, see my chapter on Bowen's novel, *The Heat of the Day* (1949), in *The Judas Kiss*, 115–34.

[39] Bowen, 'Introduction: The Short Story', 7.

[40] Bowen, 'Summer Night', 599, 607.   [41] Ibid., 607.

'the love object'.[42] Part of the same successful London set, he is on his third marriage and has grown-up children of his own. The story follows the contours of that affair through a series of stages, from initial seduction, through intense sexual expression and emotional dependence (and the pain that ensues therefrom), on to a noncommittal ending in which the affair looks set to continue intermittently.

As ever, O'Brien's theme is the radical irrationalism of the heart. In some senses, Martha is a classical instance of 'the other woman'; unlike so many of her literary mothers, however, she feels no remorse or guilt. Nor does she feel pity or sorrow for Helen, the 'real' wife, whom she regards as a mere figure within the 'real' world. For despite the unlikeliness of this particular liaison, Martha finds herself increasingly powerless to resist the emotional energies which insist that *this* man and no other is the one with whom she *must* be. She experiences love and tenderness but also jealousy, anger, hatred, and eventually depression. At one point, Martha suspects 'an element of betrayal'[43] in her lover's actions; and when he ends the affair, she contemplates a very half-hearted suicide. She is saved from breakdown by a local plumber who talks her down, and by the arrival of her ill children to whom she must tend. After a reconciliation of sorts, Martha ponders the nature of her relationship with the love object, coming to a realization that as lovers they occupy a space outwith the contours of normal life and normal behaviour. Each inheres within the other in a mysterious communion of physical, emotional, and mental capacities. The power of love, it seems, lies in its resistance to the terrible 'nothing'[44] from which human consciousness snatches its possibility. This is a world in which bourgeois notions of adultery have no purchase, and the only betrayal worth contemplating is that relating to the conjoined roles of lover and love object.

Anne Enright (1962–) is O'Brien's natural heiress inasmuch as the recurring theme of each writer has been the complexity of modern love against a socio-cultural backdrop warped by the exigencies of (post)colonial dependence. As practitioners of both long and short fiction, they also share an interest in language, form, and style—in particular, the discrepancy (as just observed) between objective and subjective reality. As with Tóibín, Enright's writing brings us within view of a present that is caught up in traditions of betrayal, inherited most evidently from Joyce, while at the same time being prey to new treacheries operating at large throughout modern Irish society.

'Until the Girl Died', from Enright's second collection, *Taking Pictures* (2008), is another variation on the story of marital infidelity. The unnamed narrator lives in an affluent area of Dublin with her husband Kevin and their three children—prime territory, we surmise, for what Enright described as 'the usual betrayal story'[45] in the title story of her debut collection, *The Portable Virgin* (1991). Kevin is 'a fantastic man'[46] who happens to cheat on his wife intermittently. His latest lapse has been with a twenty-four-year-old IT technician named Samantha whom he met at work. The story opens with news of Samantha's death in a car accident in Italy, and the narrator's realization that her husband's

---

[42] Edna O'Brien, 'The Love Object', in *The Love Object: Selected Stories* (London: Faber and Faber, 2013), 169.

[43] Ibid., 182.   [44] Ibid., 197.

[45] Anne Enright, 'The Portable Virgin', in *The Portable Virgin* (London: Vintage, 2002), 81.

[46] Anne Enright, 'Until the Girl Died', in *Taking Pictures* (London: Jonathan Cape, 2008), 190.

grieved response is not that of a friend or colleague but of a lover. Enright's story poses the question of what the modern Irish woman should do in the face of such a betrayal. She feels rage towards Kevin, but she also feels pity for the fact that as an Irish man he is singularly ill-equipped to deal with the emotional fallout from his own actions. She identifies the residual Catholic guilt which ravages him after each affair, but she experiences similar feelings in relation to her own behaviour towards her grieved husband. With her children starting to suffer and Kevin threatening to disappear within this spiral of guilt and sorrow, the narrator realizes that she must be the one to take control; the ghost of the other woman needs to be exorcized before the family can move on. And so she dons appropriate clothing, buys some lilies, and makes her way to a graveyard on the far side of the city. There, she makes a gesture on behalf of her careless, emotionally inept husband: she makes peace with the dead girl by telling her 'that she mattered'.[47] Burying her own anger and pain, the narrator somehow finds a range of positive resources—love, forgiveness, pity—which will enable the family to begin some kind of healing process. On her return from the cemetery, she says to Kevin, 'Let's do something for Easter, what do you think. Something nice. Where would you like to go?'[48]

It will have escaped nobody's notice that the three stories discussed under the rubric of 'public betrayal' are by male writers, while the three chosen for the final section of this chapter have been by women. This might be regarded as unfortunate insofar as it appears to underpin the gendered division of modern Irish life into masculine and feminine realms, and all the disabling practices emerging from such a treacherous split. No doubt there are many short stories which belie the stereotypes upon which such a division has been created and maintained—many of them, indeed, by the authors upon whom I have focused in this chapter. I stand by the selection, however, both inasmuch as it reflects an important aspect of Irish socio-cultural experience in the century since the publication of *Dubliners* but also, and more significantly, insofar as it exposes the deep interpenetration of public and private realms in modern Irish life—the fact that betrayal is in itself a radical deconstructive act in relation to the binary principles upon which any society, including that of modern Ireland, is built: male/female, public/private, active/passive. Inspired by Joyce's example, the modern Irish short story exhibits a recurring pattern in which public/political treachery comes home to roost, so to speak, whereas private/interpersonal betrayal leaves home for the big city. Somewhere near the border they meet and recognize each other for what they are: brothers in arms, sisters under the skin. It is Ireland's great good fortune to be endowed with so many writers who have sensed this consanguinity, and who have found so many compelling ways to explore its consequences.

FURTHER READING

Allen, Walter. *The Short Story in English*. Oxford: Clarendon Press, 1981.
Averill, Deborah M. *The Irish Short Story from George Moore to Frank O'Connor*. Lanham, MD: University Press of America, 1982.

[47] Ibid., 198.   [48] Ibid.

Bates, H. E. *The Modern Short Story*. London: Thomas Nelson and Sons, 1943.

Beachcroft, T. O. *The Modest Art: A Survey of the Short Story in English*. London: Oxford University Press, 1968.

D'hoker, Elke. *Irish Women Writers and the Modern Short Story*. Basingstoke: Palgrave Macmillan, 2016.

D'hoker, Elke and Stephanie Eggermont (eds). *The Irish Short Story: Traditions and Trends*. Bern: Peter Lang, 2012.

Fallon, Erin, R. C. Fedderson, James Kurtzleben, Maurice A. Lee, and Susan Rochette-Crawley (eds). *A Reader's Companion to the Short Story in English*. London: Greenwood Press, 2001.

Harrington, Ellen Burton. *Scribbling Women and the Short Story Form: Approaches to American and British Women Writers*. New York: Peter Lang, 2008.

Ingman, Heather. *A History of the Irish Short Story*. Cambridge: Cambridge University Press, 2009.

O'Connor, Frank. *The Lonely Voice: A Study of the Short Story*. Hoboken, NJ: Melville House Publishing, 2004.

O'Faoláin, Seán. *The Short Story*. London: Collins, 1948.

Smyth, Gerry. *The Judas Kiss: Treason and Betrayal in Six Modern Irish Novels*. Manchester: Manchester University Press, 2015.

Storey, Michael L. *Representing the Troubles in Irish Short Fiction*. Washington, DC: Catholic University of America Press, 2004.

Tanner, Tony. *Adultery in the Novel: Contract and Transgression*. Baltimore, MD: Johns Hopkins University Press, 1979.

CHAPTER 14

··

ARROWS IN FLIGHT

*Success and Failure in Mid-Twentieth-Century
Irish Fiction*

··

HEATHER INGMAN

FRANK O'Connor (1903–66), Seán O'Faoláin (1900–91), and Mary Lavin (1912–96) were
the writers who arguably did most in the years between 1930 and 1960 to establish the
short story as the quintessential Irish literary genre. All three writers paid close attention
to the form, revising their stories many times, sometimes even after publication.
O'Connor's influential work, *The Lonely Voice: A Study of the Short Story* (1963), and
O'Faoláin's role as founder of *The Bell*, the literary magazine he edited from 1940 to 1946,
gave these writers the opportunity to shape the Irish short story of this period. Yet in
conjunction with their work on the short story, all three writers published novels that, in
the view of critics as well as the writers themselves, were failures. Various reasons have
been adduced for this failure: their resistance to modernist experimentation; the primacy of the short story in Ireland due to the oral storytelling tradition; the chaotic
nature of the times that proved an obstacle to encapsulation in the novel form. The connections, both personal and professional, between O'Connor, O'Faoláin, and Lavin were
many, and this chapter aims to explore the curious phenomenon of three Irish writers
who, internationally successful in the short story genre, fell short in the novel form.

All three writers had a complex relationship with Ireland. Born in Massachusetts to
Irish parents, Mary Lavin spent her early years in America before her parents re-
emigrated to Ireland in 1922, when she was ten. Although she spent the rest of her life in
the country, settling and raising a family in Bective, County Meath, she observed and
wrote about it with the critical eyes of an outsider. Seán O'Faoláin and Frank O'Connor
(the pen name of Michael O'Donovan), born in Cork city in the opening years of the
twentieth century, participated in the struggle for independence and did not wish to turn
their backs on their country after its liberation from British rule. At the same time, they
felt that independence had been only partly achieved and both became disenchanted
with the narrowly defined nationalism, puritanical religion, and literary censorship that
marked the newly independent state. The banning for alleged obscenity of a novel as

subtle and sensitive as Kate O'Brien's (1897–1974) *The Land of Spices* (1941) and of Eric Cross's collection of Tim Buckley's traditional Irish tales, *The Tailor and Ansty* (1942), were only two examples of the repressive attitudes of the authorities to literature during these years, attitudes that were to directly affect the working lives of both O'Connor and O'Faoláin. Despite their commitment to Ireland as a theme, both writers spent considerable amounts of time outside the country and both sought an international readership.

It was to realism and its close associate, naturalism, that all three writers turned in their efforts to portray emerging Catholic middle-class life in post-independence Ireland. As the energies sparked by the years of cultural and political revolution faded in the more repressive and provincial atmosphere of mid-century Ireland, Yeatsian romanticism, although useful for inspiring a revolution, no longer seemed adequate to portray the realities of Irish life. At the same time, O'Faoláin and O'Connor were not alone among their contemporaries in having difficulties with the precedent set by James Joyce (1882–1941). O'Connor admitted that it took him years to get to grips with Joyce's achievement and, when he did, found he could not use it for his own literary purposes.[1] In his cultural history, *The Irish* (1947), O'Faoláin expressed regret that his generation had not tackled Joyce earlier.[2] Although modernist influences may be detected in certain short stories by O'Faoláin and Lavin, the primary commitment of these mid-century writers was not so much to language and form as to the lives of their own people, to realism, and to the ordinary reader.

O'Connor, O'Faoláin, and Lavin were acutely aware of the Irish tradition of storytelling. O'Connor sought to preserve elements of the warm speaking voice of the storyteller in his work, while Lavin wove Irish folk motifs into some of her stories and novels. In other ways, too, their work was marked by an essential Irishness. Because of the recent revolution and subsequent fallout from the Irish Civil War (1921–22), O'Faoláin and O'Connor regarded their society as out of step with other Western societies and argued that it could not achieve the stable, universalized view of human life they believed the novel demanded. For this reason they maintained that the Irish novel was a recent phenomenon. 'Irish prose literature has hardly yet as much as begun,'[3] O'Faoláin claimed. As other chapters in this volume show, Ireland does have a lengthy tradition of the novel and, indeed, writers such as Elizabeth Bowen (1899–1973), Kate O'Brien, and Molly Keane (pseudonym of M. J. Farrell, 1904–96) were producing distinguished novels about Ireland at mid-century. What matters for the purposes of this chapter, however, is that O'Faoláin and O'Connor, at least, had doubts about the possibility of producing a novel that accurately depicted Irish life, and in turn these doubts impinged on their handling of the novel form itself.

---

[1] Frank O'Connor, *The Lonely Voice: A Study of the Short Story* (Hoboken, NJ: Melville House Publishing, 2004), 150. For more on O'Connor's resistance to Joyce, see Carol Taaffe, 'Coloured Balloons: Frank O'Connor on Irish Modernism', in Hilary Lennon (ed.), *Frank O'Connor: Critical Essays* (Dublin: Four Courts Press, 2007), 205–17.

[2] Seán O'Faoláin, *The Irish* (Harmondsworth: Penguin, 1980), 140–1.

[3] Seán O'Faoláin, 'The Emancipation of Irish Writers', *Yale Review* 23 (1934), 488. Quoted in Paul Delaney, *Seán O'Faoláin: Literature, Inheritance and the 1930s* (Sallins, Co. Kildare: Irish Academic Press, 2014), 141.

FRANK O'CONNOR

'They had all read the Russians,[4] V. S. Pritchett remarked after meeting Irish writers, including O'Connor and O'Faoláin, in 1920s Dublin. Describing himself as 'an aspiring young writer who wanted to know Ireland as Gorky had known Russia,[5] O'Connor read not only Gorky but Chekhov, Turgenev, and Gogol. In *The Lonely Voice*, he begins by quoting from Gogol's 'The Overcoat' in order to illustrate his own view of the modern short story as pivoting on a central crisis that alters a person's life forever. The social context of Turgenev's *Sketches from a Hunter's Album* (1852) and its evocative descriptions of the Russian landscape chimed with Irish nationalist feeling about the land, and O'Connor claimed Turgenev as an influence on his first short story collection, *Guests of the Nation* (1931).[6] As for Chekhov, Constance Garnett's thirteen volumes of translations of the Russian author, which appeared between 1916 and 1922, were influential in the English-speaking world, and it was W. B. Yeats (1865–1939) who named O'Connor 'the Irish Chekhov'.[7]

All this is slightly misleading, however. O'Connor did study the Russians, but in his short stories—he published eight major collections between 1944 and 1969—his attention was focused on Ireland, Irish literary traditions, and Irish readers. He explained: 'I prefer to write about Ireland and Irish people merely because I know to a syllable how everything in Ireland can be said.'[8] O'Connor's insistence on the primacy of life and his resistance to artistic experiment meant that whilst the setting of his stories was often Chekhovian—the tedium and philistinism of provincial life—he neglected Chekhov's disciplined emphasis on mood and feeling, his lyricism, and his open-endedness. In the hands of writers like Turgenev and Chekhov, and French writers such as Flaubert and Maupassant, the short story was developing irony and complexity, as writers began to exploit the form's potential as a self-consciously stylized work of art as opposed to a mimetic portrayal of life. This was not O'Connor's aim, however. His wish to recreate the speaking voice of Irish oral tradition in the modern short story reveals that his overriding concerns were to forge a bond with his readers similar to that between the *seanchaí* (oral storyteller) and his audience and to elicit an immediate emotional response. As Roger Chatalic puts it, 'He objected to the cult of form for its own sake, because to him it meant turning one's back on the reader.'[9] So while O'Connor did read Russian and

---

[4] Ben Forkner and Philippe Sejourne, 'Interview with V. S. Pritchett', *Journal of the Short Story in English* 6 (1986), 12.

[5] Frank O'Connor, *An Only Child* (London: Macmillan, 1961), 197.

[6] For further discussion of O'Connor's reading of the Russians, see Hilary Lennon, 'Frank O'Connor's 1920s Cultural Criticism and the Poetic Realist Short Story', in Elke D'hoker and Stephanie Eggermont (eds), *The Irish Short Story: Traditions and Trends* (Bern: Peter Lang, 2015), 149–70.

[7] See Roger Chatalic, 'Frank O'Connor and the Desolation of Reality', in Patrick Rafroidi and Terence Brown (eds), *The Irish Short Story* (Gerrards Cross: Colin Smythe, 1979), 189–204.

[8] Quoted in Thomas Flanagan, 'The Irish Writer', in Maurice Sheehy (ed.), *Michael/Frank: Studies on Frank O'Connor with a Bibliography of his Writing* (Dublin: Gill and Macmillan, 1969), 150.

[9] Chatalic, 'Frank O'Connor and the Desolation of Reality', 197.

French authors, he did not take all he could from them; indeed, early reviews of his work characterized his stories as old-fashioned storytelling.[10]

In some of the stories in *Guests of the Nation*, O'Connor's focus on the voice of the narrator speaking directly to the reader results in a conversational tone that, as Terence Brown has suggested, does not entirely resonate with a modern readership.[11] In the title story, however, which centres on an act of retributive violence during the War of Independence, O'Connor's use of a narrator moves beyond mere storytelling to trace the narrator's gradual disillusionment with the violence perpetrated in the name of the Irish nation. The focus on a moment of crisis in the narrator's life makes this a paradigmatic O'Connor story and the ending conveys a profound sense of alienation as the deaths of the two British soldiers lead the narrator to understand how easily home and human affections may be destroyed. Traces of the oral storytelling tradition are still present in O'Connor's third collection, *Crab Apple Jelly* (1944), in stories such as 'The Grand Vizier's Daughters', while several others, such as 'The Long Road to Ummera', 'The Cheapjack', and 'The Luceys', have openings that suggest a story arising out of a community. Unlike the storyteller of the oral tradition, however, these narrators, unreliable and often limited in their point of view, cannot be straightforwardly equated with O'Connor's own voice. The evolution in O'Connor's understanding of the short story form during these years was influenced by his first-reading agreement with the *New Yorker* magazine, which encouraged him to move away from reliance on oral storytelling techniques into a more complex literary story suited to his new reading public.[12] Although he never entirely abandoned his attempt to incorporate the speaking voice of oral tradition into the modern short story, he reduced or ironized the role of the narrator and focused on character, producing story cycles centred on particular figures, such as Father Fogarty and Larry Delaney.

As a consequence of the financial hardship he suffered during the 1940s, when his trenchant criticisms of Irish life led to his unofficial blacklisting during the Second World War, O'Connor spent most of the 1950s in the United States, where his career flourished.[13] His feelings of alienation from the Ireland that had developed after 1922 helped to shape his view of the short story form as being fundamentally concerned with marginalized social groups and lonely rebels. *The Lonely Voice*, published after his return to Ireland, identifies these themes as especially suited to a society in which restrictive socio-economic conditions had increased the number of disaffected loners. His own stories deal sympathetically with the isolation of priests in rural communities in the Father Fogarty stories; the marginalization of the elderly ('The Long Road to Ummera'); the loneliness of those affected by the shift from rural to urban life ('Uprooted'); and those who in increasing numbers in this period chose emigration ('Darcy in the Land of Youth'). At a time when the Catholic Church was emphasizing the evils of sexuality

---

[10] See Robert C. Evans, 'Frank O'Connor's American Reception: The First Decade (1931–41)', in Lennon (ed.), *Frank O'Connor*, 71–86.

[11] Terence Brown, 'Frank O'Connor and a Vanishing Ireland', in Lennon (ed.), *Frank O'Connor*, 41–52.

[12] See James Alexander, 'Frank O'Connor in *The New Yorker*, 1945–1967', *Éire-Ireland* 30, no. 1 (1995), 130–44.

[13] James Matthews, *Voices: A Life of Frank O'Connor* (Dublin: Gill and Macmillan, 1983), 188–90.

outside marriage, children born out of wedlock also suffered social exclusion, and stories such as 'The Babes in the Wood' and 'The Weeping Children' are heartbreaking portrayals of children farmed out to indifferent carers. Religious and class differences are frequently depicted as obstacles to romance in his stories of the provincial middle classes ('Legal Aid', 'My First Protestant', 'The Cheat', 'The Corkerys'), and sexual repression also plays its part in hindering the development of mature relationships ('The Mad Lomasneys', 'The Cheapjack', 'The Sorcerer's Apprentice', 'Judas'). Despite their often light-hearted tone, these stories link thwarted love with the characters' oppressive social circumstances in a way that underpins O'Connor's central theme of human loneliness.

O'Connor's view that the short story prospers at times of social upheaval and was therefore more suited than the novel to portraying mid-century Irish life did much to establish the short story as the pre-eminent Irish literary form in this period. He argued: 'There has been no development comparable with the development of the short story, such as would even make it possible for a critic to speak of the Irish novel.'[14] Realist novelists, he suggested, had been defeated by the fact that, historically, Ireland lacked a stable, settled society such as was conducive to the flourishing of the novel in nineteenth-century England. This is to take a restricted view of the novel, and in *A History of the Irish Novel* (2011), Derek Hand indicts both O'Connor and O'Faoláin for their narrowness in ignoring Joyce's artistic achievements and indeed the picaresque origins of the form. In *The Mirror in the Roadway: A Study of the Modern Novel* (1955), O'Connor sees the novel primarily as a vehicle for moral and social critique and criticizes the shift, evident in fiction from Henry James onwards, to what he saw as the self-absorbed prioritizing of art over life. Such views, Hand argues, prevented O'Connor from exploiting to the full the resources of the form.[15]

In telling the parallel stories of Mary Kate, child of a prostitute raised in Cork's tenements, and her friend Phil, who undergoes a Dostoeveskian descent into religious mania, O'Connor's debut novel, *The Saint and Mary Kate* (1932), conforms to his preference for the nineteenth-century realist form. Indeed, at one point the narrator interrupts the narrative to call himself a 'chronicler ... of the realist school'.[16] Although the novel received a favourable reception in America and Britain as an honest portrayal of slum life, a contemporary review in the *Catholic World* criticized the sordid nature of the novel's Zolaesque realism.[17] More troubling, perhaps, is the fact that *The Saint and Mary Kate* is very much a novel written by a short story writer: the tone O'Connor adopts is similar to that of his storytellers, tragicomic with an edge of jauntiness that does not always suit his subject matter. The rather static portrait of tenement life in the opening pages is intended to capture, in naturalist mode, the environment of Mary Kate's childhood with her mother and her aunt in their slum dwelling called, with a nod to Ibsen, 'Dolls' House'. A series of episodes provide life lessons for Mary Kate and Phil, with the narrator, like his omniscient counterpart in works of Victorian realism, commenting on their moral development. Although the novel may not rank very highly when compared to the experiments of his

[14] O'Connor, *The Lonely Voice*, 199.
[15] Derek Hand, *A History of the Irish Novel* (Cambridge: Cambridge University Press, 2011), 3.
[16] Frank O'Connor, *The Saint and Mary Kate* (Belfast: Blackstaff Press, 1991), 141.
[17] Evans, 'Frank O'Connor's American Reception', 75–7.

modernist predecessors, O'Connor's commitment to portraying his own people led to the inclusion of what was, for the times, radical subject matter: poverty, drunkenness, insanity, domestic violence, infanticide, and children born out of wedlock.

O'Connor's second novel, *Dutch Interior*, published in 1940 and banned in July of the same year, deals with emerging middle-class Catholic lives and is even more episodic than his first. The title anticipates O'Connor's comparison of Dutch genre painting and the Victorian realist novel in *The Mirror in the Roadway*. In a series of loosely related chapters, intended, as in a Vermeer painting, to display the light and dark (but mainly the dark) of Irish provincial society, the novel expresses O'Connor's anger at the circumstances of Irish life that thwart individual talent. His portrait of Cork society is developed in a series of dramatized episodes centred on Peter Devane, his younger brother Gus, and their friends. Part one, dwelling on the youth of the protagonists, though playing to O'Connor's gift for portraying childhood, lacks pace and tension. There are many painterly passages describing the city of Cork in different lights but very little interiority and some intrusive narratorial interventions. This first part ends with Gus escaping Cork to embrace new ideas—psychoanalysis, Walt Whitman, Buddhism—and marry a Russian, while Peter remains behind, sunk in lethargy, having abandoned his dreams of becoming a musician. Their friend Stevie's feelings of entrapment draw on the frustration felt by O'Connor and other writers at being stranded in neutral Ireland during the war years. In part two, the energy of the returned Gus contrasts sharply with the disillusionment and apathy of his friends left behind in Cork, who disguise their deepest feelings in banter and drink. Yet in the end Gus too is defeated by the corruption and hypocrisy of a country run by ex-gunmen and the Catholic Church—themes that would often recur in late twentieth-century Irish fiction and public discourse.

Frank O'Connor's resistance to modernist experimentation did not necessarily hinder him in the short story form, which already had an established indigenous tradition, but it was a disadvantage for his novel writing. There is no doubt that it was the short story that absorbed his attention as a writer: his comments in *The Lonely Voice* indicate that he regarded the novel as the less pure art form. In a telling letter to Nancy McCarthy in the midst of writing *The Saint and Mary Kate*, he complained: 'Why didn't I stick to short stories which I know I can do on my head instead of mucking about with a form of which I know nothing and for which I care less?'[18]

SEÁN O'FAOLÁIN

The late 1920s and early 1930s were the years when Frank O'Connor and Seán O'Faoláin worked most closely together, as thematic similarities between the former's 'September Dawn' and the latter's 'Fugue' bear out.[19] Between 1932 and 1975, O'Faoláin published

---

[18] Quoted in Eavan Boland, 'The Innocence of Frank O'Connor', in Sheehy (ed.), *Michael/Frank*, 78.
[19] See Deborah M. Averill, *The Irish Short Story from George Moore to Frank O'Connor* (Lanham, MD: University Press of America, 1982), 274.

eight short story collections. Set during the period of the struggle for independence and civil war, the stories in his first, *Midsummer Night Madness and Other Stories*, which was published by Jonathan Cape in 1932 and immediately banned in the Irish Free State, are more extended than those of O'Connor and move the Irish short story more firmly towards modernist techniques of irony, indirection, and interiority. The collection's title story, which is narrated by an idealistic young republican rebel in Cork, is shaped not by external events, such as the burning down of the ancestral home of Henn, a Protestant landowner, by IRA commandant Stevey Long, but by skilful exploration of the gunmen's psychology and the narrator's partial consciousness, so that the speaking voice of oral tradition becomes transformed into the subjectivity of the modernist narrator. Other modernist traits in this collection include the musical counterpointing of 'Fugue' and the intermittent interiority of stories such as 'The Small Lady' and 'The Patriot'. Such modernist traces point forward to O'Faoláin's next collection, *A Purse of Coppers* (1937), where the fractured dialogues of stories like 'Admiring the Scenery' and 'A Broken World' oblige the reader to supply the meaning.

Many of the stories in *Midsummer Night Madness and Other Stories* that are based on O'Faoláin's experiences of fighting on the republican side during the revolutionary period, though retaining elements of romantic nationalism, particularly in the lyrical descriptions of the Cork countryside, displayed sufficient disillusionment with republican politics to anger the IRA. The volume's final story, 'The Patriot', which portrays the dehumanizing effect of violence, marks a break with the past as the public world of political involvement is replaced by the private world of the self and the warmth of a human relationship. The focus on gunmen, bomb-makers, informers, and revolutionaries creates tension and interest, but the stories are as much a comment on current debates on Irish society in the late 1920s and early 1930s as they are a reflection on the Troubles. In 'Midsummer Night Madness', for example, Henn's flight to Paris indicates the direction O'Faoláin believed Ireland should turn to renew its cultural and literary life. This willingness to critique post-independence Ireland lends O'Faoláin's stories historical importance. 'A Broken World' is a particularly effective depiction of the lingering effects of colonization, while stories like 'A Born Genius' and 'Kitty the Wren' highlight wasted talent and thwarted lives. Several stories ('A Meeting', 'There's a Birdie in the Cage') focus on women's domestic confinement, thus highlighting the forced retreat from the political sphere of women who had previously participated in the independence struggle. The many portraits of priests, not all of them unsympathetic, reflect the dominance of the Catholic Church over all aspects of Irish life during this period.[20]

O'Faoláin's work as a short story writer was complemented by his influential role as editor of *The Bell*, a magazine he founded in 1940 with the aim of combating Ireland's cultural isolationism and raising the level of intellectual debate in the country. O'Connor became poetry editor. O'Faoláin's editorials railed against censorship, provincialism, middle-class complacency, the power of the clergy, and Éamon de Valera's isolationist economic policies. Editorship of *The Bell* also gave O'Faoláin the chance to help younger

---

[20] For analysis of the priest figure in *A Purse of Coppers*, see Delaney, *Seán O'Faoláin*, 227–52.

writers, and through his comments on the short story form he redirected Irish exponents of it towards realistic portrayals of contemporary urban and rural life. His views
were incorporated into his critical study, *The Short Story* (1948), wherein he endeavoured to distinguish the modern short story from the loosely structured tale of oral
tradition by associating the form with concision, irony, and open-endedness and by
stressing that the modern version differed from the tale or anecdote in being chiefly 'an
adventure of the mind'.[21]

O'Faoláin's own stories from this period, in *Teresa and Other Stories* (1947), *The Finest
Stories of Seán O'Faoláin* (1957), and *The Stories of Seán O'Faoláin* (1958), display an
uneven application of his theories. Rather than focusing on psychological exploration,
many of them are taken up with satirizing aspects of Irish life, employing a comic tone
that has not always worn well and an intrusive narrative commentary that prevents his
stories from achieving the artistry of Chekhov. O'Connor described Irish literature in
these years as being 'diverted'[22] by the realities of Irish life, and stories such as 'The Man
Who Invented Sin' express O'Faoláin's barely contained resentment against the claustrophobic nature of society and the role of the Church in hampering individual fulfilment.
The comedy of a story such as 'Unholy Living and Half Dying' does not disguise the fact
that mid-century Ireland is still as much a place of stagnation and paralysis as it was in
the stories of George Moore (1852–1933) and James Joyce, while the poignant 'Lord and
Master' portrays a small-town society riven by greed, factionalism, and self-interest. In
'Lady Lucifer', three representatives of the intelligentsia—a priest, a bank clerk, and a
doctor—debate whether they should stay in a country where so many lead lives of quiet
despair. In O'Faoláin's finest stories of the period, social commentary is subordinate to
the exploration of states of mind. 'Lovers of the Lake' suggests the psychological cost of
the conflict between tradition and modernity as Jenny, a disaffected middle-class wife,
alternates between residual religious belief and sexual desire for the married Bobby
Flannery, a Dublin surgeon, with whom she travels to Lough Derg to make a penitential
pilgrimage. O'Faoláin's lengthy probing of Jenny's state of mind and detailed depiction
of the changing moods of the two lovers mark 'Lovers of the Lake' as a technically skilled,
emotionally intense modern short story.

The more favourable economic circumstances that followed Seán Lemass's appointment as taoiseach in 1959 resulted in the emergence of a younger, more cosmopolitan
generation open to global influences. For O'Faoláin, too, although his principal place of
residence remained Dublin, teaching spells in various American universities had given
him a more international outlook, as reflected in the collections *I Remember! I
Remember!* (1961) and *The Heat of the Sun: Stories and Tales* (1966), which contain stories featuring Irish characters in Europe and the USA. Some, such as the skilful and subtle 'A Shadow, Silent as a Cloud' and 'A Touch of Autumn in the Air' in *I Remember! I
Remember!*, reveal uneasiness about the cost of progress, echoing contemporary debates
over whether Ireland's distinctive culture, traditions, and language were being too

---

[21] Seán O'Faoláin, *The Short Story* (Cork: Mercier Press, 1948), 213.
[22] Frank O'Connor, *The Backward Look: A Survey of Irish Literature* (London: Macmillan, 1967), 227.

readily sacrificed to the desire to modernize.[23] *The Heat of the Sun* marked the beginning of a decline in O'Faoláin's fiction, however, as he moved away from the compact short story to what he called in his preface the 'Tale',[24] a longer, more digressive form with more incidents and more changes of mood. This was not always successful, but it does indicate a frustration on O'Faoláin's part with the restrictions of the short story form.[25]

The difficulties O'Faoláin experienced in trying to capture Irish life are evident in his first novel, *A Nest of Simple Folk* (1934), in which he attempts to encompass Ireland between 1854 and 1916 through the stories of several individuals, principally Leo O'Donnell and his nephew Denis. The novel is divided into three sections as Leo moves from his upbringing in rural Limerick to the small town of Rathkeale and finally to Cork city. The third section, portraying Denis's upbringing, draws heavily on O'Faoláin's own childhood. The novel borrows its title from Turgenev's *Home of the Gentry* (1859), sometimes translated as *A Nest of the Gentry*, in which Turgenev, like O'Faoláin, portrays his own class. But whereas Turgenev's intense and compact novel, depicting the Russian intelligentsia in the 1840s, achieves a delicate balance between social concern and psychological insight, in *A Nest of Simple Folk* the reader has the impression of a writer struggling to contain the vast time scale of his historical backdrop.

In *Home of the Gentry*, Turgenev focuses on a small number of protagonists and significant turning points in their emotional lives, with the result that they emerge as fully rounded characters in a way that O'Faoláin's do not. *A Nest of Simple Folk*, while containing lyrical descriptions of the Irish countryside and Cork city, remains sprawling and diffuse, its action scattered between too many different characters. The minor figures seem hastily sketched and even the major ones lack the subtlety of Turgenev's portraits. Denis, torn between a policeman father who is loyal to the British and the first stirrings of rebellion, is a potentially interesting character, but the novel ends too abruptly for this conflict to be developed in any depth. Denis's incipient interest in the theatre provides a missed opportunity to expand on the *Bildungsroman* element of this third section. In Turgenev, everything—description, setting, dialogue, ideological debate—is subordinate to the gradual revelation of character, whereas in O'Faoláin's fiction, as Patrick Walsh notes, there is a recurring and disabling tension between engagement with the subjective experience of his characters and the more didactic presentation of them as social types.[26]

O'Connor and O'Faoláin blamed the provisional nature of Irish society for the failure of the Irish novel. Turgenev, too, was conscious of working in a context that lacked a tradition of realist fiction and expressed doubts as to whether Russia's social environment was favourable to the form, yet between the years 1856 and 1862 he expanded the

---

[23] See Terence Brown, *Ireland: A Social and Cultural History 1922–2002* (London: Harper Perennial, 2004), 254–96.

[24] Seán O'Faoláin, *The Heat of the Sun: Stories and Tales* (London: Rupert Hart-Davis, 1966), 5.

[25] See Roy Foster's comments in the *Irish Times*, 16 April 1976, 10.

[26] Patrick Walsh, 'Seán O'Faoláin's *Midsummer Night Madness and Other Stories*: Contexts for Revisionism', in Kathleen Devine (ed.), *Modern Irish Writers and the Wars* (Gerrards Cross: Colin Smythe, 1999), 141.

short story form of his *Sketches* to produce a series of artistically convincing novels.[27] Again, we are brought back to aesthetic failure in the case of mid-twentieth-century Irish fiction. O'Faoláin seems unsure of the kind of novel he wants to write: echoes of other styles permeate *A Nest of Simple Folk*—Dickensian caricature, Hardyesque fatalism, Arnold Bennett's attention to material surroundings, George Eliot's broad social canvas, Walter Scott's historical sagas—at the expense of an individual voice.

Bird Alone (1936), banned on publication, possesses similar uncertainties of tone. The lively Cork dialogue and the use of the digressive storyteller mode sits uneasily with the genuine tragedy of Elsie Sherlock's internalization of a particularly harsh and punitive post-Famine Catholic ideology and that of Corney Crone's loneliness, brought on by being unable to share his people's beliefs and hence their way of life. The novel is held together by recurrent references to the Faust myth, connected both to Corney and his Parnellite grandfather. Yet despite possessing greater unity than *A Nest of Simple Folk*, *Bird Alone* does not avoid the pitfall of episodic looseness.[28] The long stretches of dialogue and the debates about Ireland before and after the death of Parnell divert attention from Corney, and, until the quickening of tension in Elsie's story towards the end, the novel dissolves into a series of character sketches—of Corney's grandfather and Virginia, Christy, and Stella, all of whom influence Corney's development. *Bird Alone* has the material to fashion a great Catholic novel around themes of sin, redemption, and rebellion, but neither the portrait of the two very different families—the Crones and the Sherlocks—nor the love affair between Corney and Elsie are explored with sufficient subtlety. Nevertheless, Corney's anguish at his isolation from his own people, while being unable to throw off residual Catholic thinking, is genuinely moving.

If *A Nest of Simple Folk* and *Bird Alone* are set at a distance of several decades from the time of writing, *Come Back to Erin* (1940) engages directly with Irish life in the 1930s and a state which, in its drive for stability and middle-class respectability, has no place for the old republican fighter Frankie Hannafey. The novel displays psychological insight into the mental conflicts of an ex-gunman in a lethargic and bourgeois post-revolutionary society which is shown to be indifferent to Frankie's dream of a social revolution that would free the economy from dependence on British bankers. The sustained interiority of *Come Back to Erin* deepens the characterization, not only of Frankie but also of his brothers: Michael with his sexual repressions and St John with his manic spiritual torments over his marriage to an American Episcopalian. Unable to implement the social renewal he desires, Frankie flees to the States where his life immediately opens out, intellectually through plays, books, and concerts, and sexually in his affair with Bee, whom he marries. The novel is not entirely clear as to why, knowing that he will be unable to bring about a similar creative renewal in Ireland, Frankie feels he has to return. The reader is forced to adduce extra-literary considerations connected with O'Faoláin's belief that his generation, having grown up during a time of revolutionary violence,

[27] For Turgenev's development of the Russian novel, see Richard Freeborn, *Turgenev: The Novelist's Novelist* (Oxford: Oxford University Press, 1960), 37–133.
[28] For a detailed analysis of the Faust motif in *Bird Alone*, see Delaney, *Seán O'Faoláin*, 198–226.

could not simply turn their back on their country. After his stimulating life in America, Frankie settles down, bathetically, to a job as a warble-fly inspector, his salary paid by the state he once ran from.

Joe Cleary suggests that Seán O'Faoláin's work offers 'a seriously limited, indeed quite conservative conception'[29] of the possibilities available to the fiction writer in post-revolutionary Ireland. It is true that social and moral analysis, rather than aesthetic experimentation, is the keynote of O'Faoláin's novels and even of his short stories. Nevertheless, the best of his fiction is valuable for its exploration of the tensions of Irish life at mid-century and the emotional, intellectual, and spiritual conflicts of individuals trapped in a repressive society.

MARY LAVIN

In his chapter on Mary Lavin in *The Lonely Voice*, Frank O'Connor's association of the short story with the romantic outsider leads him to argue that Lavin's concentration on the family and the community in her stories shows her to be essentially a novelist. His argument exposes the flaws both in his definition of the short story (writers like Jane Barlow (1856–1917) and Edith Somerville (1858–1949) and Martin Ross (1862–1915) produced stories portraying lives within a community, as Elke D'hoker has pointed out[30]) and of the novel (the nineteenth-century realist novel may depict lives in a community, but the modernist novel focuses on the consciousness of one or two individuals). Furthermore, in his criticism of Lavin's use of flashback, O'Connor reveals his instinctive resistance to modernist elements in her stories. Lavin began her writing career by abandoning a doctoral thesis on Virginia Woolf, and her employment of modernist indeterminacy, ellipsis, and ambiguity in her first collection, *Tales from Bective Bridge* (1942), has been noted.[31] In the metafictional 'A Story with a Pattern', written in the late 1930s and published in the collection *A Single Lady and Other Stories* (1951), Lavin obliquely signalled her intention to abandon the well-made short story packed with incident for a looser structure, more suited to probing beneath surfaces and exploring states of mind. The story is narrated by a female short story writer who is introduced at a party to an overbearing middle-aged man who is keen to dispense unsolicited literary advice. His insistence that she get more plot and pattern into her work is met with a steely defence of modernist technique by the writer: 'Life in general isn't rounded off like that at the edges; out into neat shapes. Life is chaotic; its events are unrelated.'[32] Lavin

---

[29] Joe Cleary, *Outrageous Fortune: Capital and Culture in Modern Ireland* (Dublin: Field Day Publications, 2007), 148.

[30] Elke D'hoker, 'Complicating the Irish Short Story', in D'hoker and Eggermont (eds), *The Irish Short Story*, 7.

[31] See Anne Fogarty, 'Discontinuities: *Tales from Bective Bridge* and the Modernist Short Story', in Elke D'hoker (ed.), *Mary Lavin* (Sallins, Co. Kildare: Irish Academic Press, 2013), 49–64.

[32] Mary Lavin, *In a Café*, ed. Elizabeth Walsh Peavoy (Dublin: Town House, 1995), 225.

later defined the short story as 'an arrow in flight'[33] without a definite beginning or end, being a revelation rather than an explanation of life's unpredictability.

In her preface to her *Selected Stories* (1959), Lavin formulated an artistic credo that challenges O'Connor's view of the short story as structured around a single epiphany: 'Because of this conviction that in a true story, form and matter are one, I cannot attach the same importance as the critics to brevity and relevance. It is surely significant that the great short stories of the world have often been studded with irrelevancies.'[34] This rejection of neat plot solutions in favour of capturing some of life's uncertainty led to length being an issue in several of her stories and a particular problem when trying to get them placed with the *New Yorker*.[35] 'The Becker Wives', the title story of her 1946 collection, is sufficiently long to qualify as a novella, while the five stories focusing on the middle-class Grimes family ('A Visit to the Cemetery', 'An Old Boot', 'Frail Vessel', 'The Little Prince', and 'Loving Memory'), published between 1951 and 1961, have been likened to a story cycle with shared settings, characters, and themes.[36] In *The Lonely Voice*, O'Connor sees the Grimes stories as proof that Lavin had attempted and failed to write a novel of provincial life, but story cycles are a separate genre, mid-way between the single story and the novel, and it is arguable that Lavin intended these to be read as such.

Lavin's stories employ a variety of styles, from the modernist interiority of 'Miss Holland', a story that has been likened to Katherine Mansfield's 'Miss Brill', to the reproduction of oral storytelling techniques in 'A Likely Story' and the use of folktale and fable in 'The Dead Soldier', 'The Green Grave and the Black Grave', and 'The Widow's Son'.[37] However, she worked predominantly in the realist mode and, despite O'Connor's misgivings, many of the themes she tackled bear resemblance to those of other mid-century Irish writers. Lavin published nineteen short story collections during her lifetime, four in the 1940s alone—*Tales from Bective Bridge*, *The Long Ago and Other Stories* (1944), *The Becker Wives and Other Stories* (1946), and *At Sallygap and Other Stories* (1947)— and, as in stories by O'Connor and O'Faoláin, materialism and deprivation are prominent themes, reflecting the economic hardships of mid-twentieth-century Ireland. She drew on her observations of her mother's shopkeeping relatives in Athenry, County Galway to feature a Catholic middle class so consumed by the need to earn a living that the death of the heart ensues. This theme encompasses both urban stories like 'The Little Prince', 'The Will', and 'The Becker Wives', and those that have a rural setting, such as 'Lilacs' and 'The Widow's Son'. As in O'Connor's stories, oppressive structures of class ('A Gentle Soul') or religion ('The Convert') are obstacles to love. In 'The Becker Wives', where the Beckers' stolid materialism is represented by their heavy furniture and stout, placid wives, Flora, Theobald Becker's new wife, seems to offer the possibility of a

---

[33] Quoted in Leah Levenson, *The Four Seasons of Mary Lavin* (Dublin: Marino Books, 1998), 54.

[34] Mary Lavin, *Selected Stories* (New York: Macmillan, 1959), unpaginated preface.

[35] See Gráinne Hurley, ' "Trying to Get the Words Right": Mary Lavin and *The New Yorker*', in D'hoker (ed.), *Mary Lavin*, 81–99.

[36] See Elke D'hoker, 'Family and Community in Mary Lavin's Grimes Stories', in D'hoker (ed.), *Mary Lavin*, 152–68.

[37] For the comparison with Mansfield, see Giovanna Tallone, 'Theatrical Trends in Mary Lavin's Early Stories', in D'hoker (ed.), *Mary Lavin*, 68.

different, more creative way of living until she turns out to be schizophrenic, an unset-tling conclusion that suggests the choice for women's lives in post-independence Ireland lies between conformity and insanity.[38] Lavin's idealistic characters resist the material-ism they see around them but often end either destitute, like Bedelia's brother Tom in 'The Little Prince', or forced to capitulate, like Stacy in 'Lilacs', a story in which Lavin fol-lows Chekhov's precept about making literature out of dung-heaps.

What distinguishes Lavin's stories from those of O'Connor and O'Faoláin is, as O'Connor points out, the absence of reference to Ireland's nationalist struggles: 'an Irishman, reading the stories of Mary Lavin, is actually more at a loss than a foreigner would be. His not-so-distant political revolution, seen through her eyes, practically dis-appears from view.'[39] That the domestic and apolitical nature of Lavin's work confused and alienated O'Connor, who remarked that her narrative perspective 'is perhaps too exclusively feminine',[40] reveals that Lavin was breaking new ground in Irish writing. Although sometimes rejecting the notion that gender played a significant part in her work ('I write as a person. I don't think of myself as a woman who writes. I am a writer. Gender is incidental to that'[41]), Lavin has been an important trailblazer for Irish women writers, introducing new themes into the Irish short story, such as conflicted mother–daughter relationships, female sexuality, and widows.

'The Nun's Mother', for example, portrays a mother and daughter so entangled in Ireland's normalizing discourse concerning women's bodies that they are unable to speak openly to one another, while 'Sunday Brings Sunday' contains early and out-spoken criticism of the sexual repressions of rural Irish life that leave a young girl dan-gerously ignorant about her own body. The suppression of the female body recurs in 'Chamois Gloves', where Mabel's liberated talk about labour pains and breastfeeding causes embarrassed silence in the convent parlour. 'A Cup of Tea' draws on Lavin's rela-tionship with her own mother to portray tensions between a university-educated daughter and a mother whose life has centred on domesticity and the family. The story ends bleakly, suggesting the emotional cost of a daughter being educated outside her mother's range. In 'A Family Likeness', conflict echoes down the generations as past mis-understandings between Ada and her mother are replicated in the complex relationship Ada has with her own daughter Laura. The portrayal of three generations of mother–daughter relationships gone awry underlines the sense of entrapment.

In the 1960s, Lavin drew on her experience of widowhood to highlight Irish society's insensitive attitude towards this marginalized group. The most notable story to broach this theme is 'In the Middle of the Fields', which portrays the life of an unnamed widow who single-handedly runs a farm in Meath (as Lavin herself did after the death of her first husband, William Walsh, in 1954) and reveals the physical and emotional vulner-ability of a woman in a male-dominated working environment. The foregrounding of women's lives differentiates Lavin's stories from those of O'Faoláin and certainly of

---

[38] See James Heaney's commentary in '"No Sanctuary from Hatred": A Re-appraisal of Mary Lavin's Outsiders', *Irish University Review* 28, no. 2 (1998), 294–307.

[39] O'Connor, *The Lonely Voice*, 195–6.   [40] Ibid., 196.

[41] Quoted in Levenson, *The Four Seasons of Mary Lavin*, 225.

O'Connor, yet her portraits of trapped masculinity in the form of celibate priests, shop-keepers, and workaholic professionals in stories such as 'The Shrine', 'Posy', and 'A Memory' are equally insightful.[42]

In the past, scholars such as Augustine Martin, Seamus Deane, and Declan Kiberd have judged Lavin to be a writer who fitted into the social consensus of the times (her work was never banned). Recent critical trends, however, exemplified by the work of Anne Fogarty and Derek Hand, have underlined the ambushing oddness and unexpected radicalism that underpin her stories of seemingly ordinary Irish lives, traits also evident in Lavin's two novels. *The House in Clewe Street* (1945) opens in the manner of a nineteenth-century realist novel, suggesting a family story of life in Castlerampart, a fictionalized version of Athenry. There is a static quality to the opening chapters as Lavin constructs a picture of small-town life dominated by class, property, and Catholicism, and of the bourgeois Coniffe family who thoroughly embrace the values of this world. The feminine atmosphere of the Coniffe household, particularly after Theodore's death, and the relationship between Theresa and Sara, with the elder sister dominating the younger, may seem to resemble an Irish version of Elizabeth Gaskell's *Cranford* (1853), but Lavin's portrait is much more critical and bitter in tone. Whereas Gaskell had a deep affection for Knutsford, Lavin was distrustful of the values of Athenry. In *Cranford*, there may be insensitivity, and even cruelty, but kindness, charity, and forgiveness win out in the end. In *The House in Clewe Street*, although Theresa's domineering traits, like Miss Jenkyns's, are the result of having domestic responsibility thrust upon her, this extenuating circumstance is scarcely explored. Instead, Theresa's vindictiveness and spite are presented as products of her environment and its harsh, uncompromising religion, so different from the deeply felt but understated faith of the Cranford inhabitants.

When *The House in Clewe Street* shifts to Theresa's nephew Gabriel and his relationship with his aunts' servant Onny, there is a move from a nineteenth-century community-based narrative perspective to a twentieth-century focus on an individual's quest for different values from those in which he was raised. For Gabriel, Onny's brightly coloured clothes express a spirit of rebellion and sensuality that his society tries to suppress. When the couple escapes to Dublin, the novel becomes dominated by Onny's sexuality as her body exerts its charms over the bohemian artists among whom she and Gabriel live. The result is an unsettling mix of Victorian realism and modern *Bildungsroman*, but the problem is that Gabriel is so trapped in the small-town values of his aunts that the *Bildungsroman* element fails to take flight. Jealous of Onny's success, Gabriel tries to assert his authority and bring her outlaw body inside the Catholic Church by marrying her. Although by now pregnant, Onny refuses to be cowed, a reversal of the situation in *Bird Alone*, where Elsie is unable to overcome her feelings of guilt and shame at her pregnancy. Rejecting ownership either by Gabriel or by the Church, Onny asserts her rights over her body, including her right to have an (illegal) abortion, the bungling of which causes her death. Yet despite the urging of his artist friends, Gabriel will not disown her, even if it means making himself, under Irish law, an

---

[42]   See Heather Ingman, 'Masculinities in Mary Lavin's Short Stories', in D'hoker (ed.), *Mary Lavin*, 30–48.

accessory to murder. Remarkably for the period, Lavin portrays an Irish woman asserting ownership of her body, deriving pride and pleasure from it in a way that anticipates
the treatment of women in the fiction of Edna O'Brien (1930–). Though Onny comes to
a tragic end, it is she who grips the reader's imagination and she who obsesses Gabriel in
his search for a different way of living, as indeed she seems to have taken over Lavin's
imagination. The ending suggests that with Onny's death, Gabriel's quest for selfhood in
the city may be about to begin.[43]

The treatment of the mother figure in Lavin's second novel, *Mary O'Grady* (1950),
similarly challenges stereotypes around Irish womanhood. Transplanted, as many were
in this period, from her rural upbringing to life in the city, the eponymous Mary is seemingly the perfect embodiment of the contemporary ideal of Catholic wife and mother, at
least she appears so to her husband Tom. After Tom's death the family idyll is increasingly undermined by tragedy and it becomes apparent that, despite Mary's struggle to
keep her family members safe, it is often her misjudgements that bring disaster on them,
her country values being at odds with, and even unhelpful in, the city.[44] Towards the end
of her story Mary reveals her doubts as to whether her mothering has been successful:
'She had spared neither toil nor sweat nor sacrifice, and yet life, that had been as sweet as
milk and honey, was souring, hour by hour.'[45] As the family home deteriorates around
her, it comes to seem not a safe haven but a place of emotional imprisonment. In *Mary
O'Grady*, Lavin's portrait of the urban family turns into something far more bitter and
angry than the prevailing Irish ideology around the family usually admitted.

Mary Lavin was a meticulous reviser of her stories, reworking them even after publication.[46] In contrast, *Mary O'Grady* was written quickly, over the course of one summer
while she was pregnant with her second child and tending to her father who had terminal cancer.[47] This suggests that she turned to the longer prose form for distraction: in
interviews, she dismissed *The House in Clewe Street* and *Mary O'Grady* as inferior novels
and wished she could cut them up into the short stories she believed they should have
been.[48] Lavin's novels are of interest, however, for their exploration of themes, such as
female sexuality and motherhood, that would be taken up in the more explicitly feminist Irish fiction of the 1970s and after. Both her short stories and her novels suggest that
Lavin was a more radical writer than is sometimes allowed.

[43] See Derek Hand, '"I Had Always Despised Him a Little": Plumbing the Depths of Feeling in Mary
Lavin's Two Irish Novels', in D'hoker (ed.), *Mary Lavin*, 139–51.

[44] See Anne Fogarty's comments on this novel in '"The Horror of the Unlived Life": Mother–Daughter
Relationships in Contemporary Irish Women's Fiction', in Adalgisa Giorgio (ed.), *Writing Mothers and
Daughters: Renegotiating the Mother in Western European Narratives by Women* (New York: Berghahn,
2002), 85–117. See also Jacqueline Fulmer, *Folk Women and Indirection in Morrison, Ní Dhuibhne, Hurston,
and Lavin* (Aldershot: Ashgate, 2007), 63–74.

[45] Mary Lavin, *Mary O'Grady* (London: Virago, 1986), 203.

[46] For Lavin's compositional methods, see Janet Egleson Dunleavy, 'The Making of Mary Lavin's
"Happiness"', *Irish University Review* 9, no. 2 (1979), 225–31.

[47] Levenson, *The Four Seasons of Mary Lavin*, 82.

[48] Derek Hand, '"I Had Always Despised Him a Little"', 139–40.

Rather than looking to their own failure to explore more deeply what the form could and could not do, Frank O'Connor and Seán O'Faoláin blamed Irish circumstances for their inability to write successful novels, and wrote novels in the classic realist tradition as if to make up for what they saw, erroneously, as the absence of the novel tradition in nineteenth-century Ireland. Mary Lavin's remarks on the novel are more concerned with her own failure and her recognition that the circumstances of her life as a widowed mother of three young daughters did not easily allow time for the longer form. In the short story, O'Connor, O'Faoláin, and Lavin are undisputed masters, responsible for its mid-century success as the predominant Irish literary form. Although sometimes revealing an uncertain relationship between modernity and tradition, all three writers produced a solid body of work reflecting what it was like to live in Ireland in the period between the 1930s and the 1960s.

FURTHER READING

Averill, Deborah M. *The Irish Short Story from George Moore to Frank O'Connor*. Lanham, MD: University Press of America, 1982.

Delaney, Paul. *Seán O'Faoláin: Literature, Inheritance and the 1930s*. Sallins, Co. Kildare: Irish Academic Press, 2014.

D'hoker, Elke (ed.). *Mary Lavin*. Sallins, Co. Kildare: Irish Academic Press, 2013.

D'hoker, Elke and Stephanie Eggermont (eds). *The Irish Short Story: Traditions and Trends*. Bern: Peter Lang, 2015.

Hand, Derek. *A History of the Irish Novel*. Cambridge: Cambridge University Press, 2011.

Ingman, Heather. *A History of the Irish Short Story*. Cambridge: Cambridge University Press, 2009.

Kilroy, James (ed.). *The Irish Short Story: A Critical History*. Boston, PA: Twayne, 1984.

Lennon, Hilary (ed.). *Frank O'Connor: Critical Essays*. Dublin: Four Courts Press, 2007.

Levenson, Leah. *The Four Seasons of Mary Lavin*. Dublin: Marino Books, 1998.

O'Connor, Frank. *The Lonely Voice: A Study of the Short Story*. Hoboken, NJ: Melville House Publishing, 2004.

O'Faoláin, Seán. *The Short Story*. Cork: Mercier Press, 1948.

Rafroidi, Patrick and Terence Brown (eds). *The Irish Short Story*. Gerrards Cross: Colin Smythe, 1979.

CHAPTER 15

'PROUD OF OUR WEE ULSTER'? WRITING REGION AND IDENTITY IN ULSTER FICTION

NORMAN VANCE

We're proud of our wee Ulster,
We'll always take a stand,
For Protestants the Union Jack
Will fly across this land.[1]

Modern 'Ulster', properly speaking the six counties of Northern Ireland rather than the nine counties of the historic province of Ulster, was born amid bitter political controversy and civil disturbances occasioned by the partition of Ireland under the Government of Ireland Act of 1920. The citizens and some of the writers of the six northeastern counties, which I shall refer to as Ulster for convenience, were left to ponder whether they and their locality were distinctly and defiantly British, as unionists insisted, or still Irish, as nationalists asserted, or something else again. The phrase 'our wee Ulster', in the entertainer James Young's tongue-in-cheek song from 1967, picks up on a specifically Protestant and unionist tradition of stubbornly defensive local or regional pride and brash affirmation of a distinctive collective identity. Issues of tradition and identity, geographical as well as historical and political, tend to recur in self-consciously 'Ulster' regional fiction, as in the fiction of other regions and countries, in part carrying on by other means an established discourse of identity politics.[2] But the necessarily selective survey which follows indicates that such concerns are often

---

[1] From James Young's song 'Gerry's Walls' (1967), quoted in Bob Purdie, *Politics in the Street* (Belfast: Blackstaff Press, 1990), 82.

[2] See Richard Kirkland, *Identity Parades: Northern Irish Culture and Dissident Subjects* (Liverpool: Liverpool University Press, 2001), 78–124.

interestingly complicated not just by unease and critical questioning but by engagements with other narratives such as demographic change, coming of age, personal ambition, and disappointment.

Identity politics on their own can be a literary liability, inviting tunnel vision and partisan rant, not to mention critical censure. With the embattled mindset of (partly) Protestant and unionist Ulster very much in mind, the poet Tom Paulin (1949–) and the critic Terence Brown have reflected critically on the historical and imaginative limitations and impoverishment of aggressively 'remember[ing] who we are.'[3] Inevitably, this kind of obsession oversimplifies matters, and few writers of Ulster fiction seek to identify themselves in crudely partisan terms as 'Protestant unionist' or 'Catholic nationalist'. Rather, they tend to share an awareness that those living in the same place may well come from different religious and political cultures, or none, and that even those of similar nurture may think differently about generational continuities. Furthermore, with changing social conditions the security of being at home in a particular place may be precarious.

The shifting balance between rural Ulster and burgeoning Belfast, which expanded rapidly from the mid-nineteenth century onwards with streams of new arrivals, both Catholic and Protestant, from the countryside, necessarily complicated the issue of regional identity and unsettled people's sense of belonging and of who they were, a theme addressed in *Lost Fields* (1942) by Michael McLaverty (1904–92). The novel opens with wind and rain and a caged lark in an urban kitchen, but the last chapter offers glimpses of a better life in the countryside, with larks singing freely, hawthorn blossom in the hedges in the spring time, and trout to be caught when it rains.[4] But evocations of an essentially (and benignly) rural homeland could also risk sentimental pastoral nostalgia of the kind represented by the chapter entitled 'The Glamour of the Gloaming' in Margaret S. Norris's volume of pious country sketches, *Glenreeba* (1939). Understandably enough, later Ulster writers such as Maurice Leitch (1933–) reacted with iconoclastic anti-pastoral, exemplified by Leitch's *The Smoke King* (1998), a novel of rural life in 1940s Ulster, which is summed up on the last page as 'this heartless place'.[5] An alternative possibility is the kind of gritty urban realism found in Leitch's earlier novel of contemporary life in Belfast, *Silver's City* (1981). Starting with a grim epigraph from St Augustine—'The Devil hath established his cities in the North'—the novel goes beyond conventional realism to suggest terminal despair of the place and its people. But this bleakness brings its own distortions.

Among the cures for tunnel vision, tried by some writers, are ironic distance, studied ambivalence, or, more ambitiously, disconcerting quasi-modernist departures from old-fashioned realism, effected by disrupting narrative coherence. In the 1950s and

[3] Tom Paulin, 'After the Summit', in *Liberty Tree* (London: Faber and Faber, 1983), 29. Quoted and discussed in Terence Brown, 'Remembering Who We Are', in *Ireland's Literature: Selected Essays* (Mullingar: Lilliput Press, 1988), 223–42.

[4] Michael McLaverty, *Lost Fields* (Dublin: Poolbeg Press, 1980), 5, 199–200.

[5] Maurice Leitch, *The Smoke King* (London: Vintage, 1999), 360. Leitch's protagonists tend to be alienated outsiders. See Barry Sloan, 'The Remains of Protestantism in Maurice Leitch's Fiction', in Elmer Kennedy-Andrews (ed.), *Irish Fiction since the 1960s* (Gerrards Cross: Colin Smythe, 2006), 260–1.

1960s, the novelists Brian Moore (1921–99) and Janet McNeill (1907–94) attempted some strategic shifting of narrative point of view, enabling the multiple perspectives, or at least binocular vision, which assist depth perception. Unconventional and sometimes devastating sidelights are provided in dialect speech, clearly distinguished from the standard English of the narrative voice, in stories such as those in *At Home in Tyrone* (1944) by 'Tullyneil', the pseudonym of R. L. Marshall (1887–1971). Marshall's terminally alcoholic Guldy soars above endemic sectarianism, impartially scathing and detached about both Orange and Green processions as they pass down the village street. Leitch's *Poor Lazarus* (1969) presents the perspective of the local protagonist, Yarr, alongside notes on particular scenes in the Canadian film director Quigley's cinematic notebook. There is something satisfyingly untidy about Quigley's perception of a 'scattering of jig-saw pieces' resisting his artistic need (and the requirement of conventional narrative) for a more or less 'perfected whole'.[6]

There are a few excursions into transcendent fantasy or dream consciousness in the novels of the Belfast suburbanite Forrest Reid (1875–1947) and in those of Reid's protégé, Stephen Gilbert (1912–2010), notably his bizarre *Ratman's Notebooks* (1968), as well as in the strange visionary novel, *Mine Eyes Have Seen the Glory* (1953), by the Antrim Presbyterian minister Hubert Quinn (1901–72). Quinn's title simultaneously recalls the first line of Julia Ward Howe's apocalyptic 'Battle Hymn of the Republic' (1862) and Fanny Parnell's romantic-nationalist poem, 'Shall Mine Eyes Behold Thy Glory, O My Country?', which is quoted in the novel as an epigraph and again in the main text.[7] The narrative links historical retrospect on the violent events of the 1916 Easter Rising with a quasi-messianic protagonist, a shepherd's son significantly named Patrick, a prophet of ultimate unity and hope in and beyond his own place, with his vision of what he calls a 'New Humanity' journeying to the 'Oneness' of the divine.[8] But in general Ulster fiction has tended to favour more or less conventional realism, with an unspoken assumption that experimental narrative technique and the lessons of modernism belong somewhere else.

Yet traditional forms can still unsettle traditional ideas. *Changing Winds* (1917), a rather sprawling early novel by Belfast-born St John Ervine (1883–1971) that responds to the political turmoil of the time, including the Easter Rising, provided literary accommodation for sharply divided and changing views on the nature and future of Ulster and of Ireland as a whole. The tradition of Romantic poetry informed the underlying mythic resonances and archetypal journeying in some of the stories of the Tyrone-born novelist Benedict Kiely (1919–2007).[9] Romantic evocations of the life of the youthful imagination recur in the work of Forrest Reid; his Tom Barber trilogy (1931–44) is concerned not just with nature and magic but with a discreet homoeroticism, as Colin Cruise has

---

[6] Maurice Leitch, *Poor Lazarus* (London: Panther, 1970), 159.
[7] Hubert Quinn, *Mine Eyes Have Seen the Glory* (London: Pentagon Press, 1953), 173–4.
[8] Ibid., 68, 46.
[9] See John Wilson Foster, *Forces and Themes in Ulster Fiction* (Dublin: Gill and Macmillan, 1974), 72–81.

argued.[10] Writers could laugh at class-consciousness among Protestants and Catholics alike, as Ruddick Millar (1907–52) does in his comic novel, *Plus-Fours and No Breakfast: A Belfast Story* (1937). Identity politics could yield to cheerfully impartial humour in the Ballygullion stories of Lynn Doyle, the pseudonym of Leslie Montgomery (1873–1961), the first of which appeared in 1908, or to tart local speech and a vivid sense of place in *Gape Row* (1934) by Agnes Romilly White (1872–1945), set in the County Down village of Dundonald, near Belfast.[11] There was sometimes an overlay of sexual repression or generational conflict, themes from an earlier life in Belfast reviewed from across the Atlantic, in Brian Moore's early fiction. Yet the theme or problematic of regional identity in a divided society pervades much twentieth-century Ulster fiction and appears in many guises, from a delight in local idiosyncrasy, to a self-mocking or satirical recoil from it, to a profound regretting of history and division.

This recurring theme goes back to earlier region-specific concerns and discourses, much older than the constitutionally separate Northern Ireland but sensitive to some of the underlying differences which culminated in the partition of the country. The earnest Belfast Society for Promoting Knowledge had fostered specifically Northern knowledge since the eighteenth century. Queen's College Belfast, one of three Irish university colleges set up under the 1845 Irish Colleges Act, played some part in stimulating local writing, particularly when it became a university in its own right in 1908. It had a curriculum which included the relatively new academic discipline of English Literature, taught to generations of local writers. Irish Presbyterians were located mainly in the North, and the ministers and their wives and daughters, well-educated and in close touch with local communities for pastoral reasons, contributed significantly to Ulster writing.

By the nineteenth century, Irish Presbyterian history, which is largely an Ulster history, could be read in locally-published work by Northern church historians such as Thomas Witherow and James Seaton Reid. The latter was a great-uncle of the novelist Forrest Reid, whose self-image as aesthete, heretic, and 'apostate'—the term he chose as the title of his 1926 autobiography—registers even as it repudiates the pervasive nature of Ulster Presbyterianism and other inherited pressures and pieties. The complexities and distinctiveness of regional history and geography, anthropology and sociology, which found subsequent expression in fiction, had been explored in publications such as *A Guide to Belfast and the Counties of Down and Antrim* (1902) by the Belfast Naturalists' Field Club, founded in 1863, while the *Ulster Journal of Archaeology*, founded in 1852, had published quasi-anthropological articles on topics such as 'The origin and characteristics of the population in the counties of Down and Antrim'.[12] The Irish Literary Revival stimulated writers' interest in 'peasant quality', largely focused on the far west and south west of the country. Northern responses included *My Lady of the Chimney Corner* (1913) and its sequel, *The Souls of Poor Folk* (1921), by Alexander Irvine (1863–1941), popular sketches of his parents' life in Antrim in the

---

[10] Colin Cruise, 'Error and Eros: The Fiction of Forrest Reid as a Defence of Homosexuality', in Éibhear Walshe (ed.), *Sex, Nation and Dissent in Irish Writing* (Cork: Cork University Press, 1997), 60–86.

[11] Ballygullion does not exist, but the name is modelled on Slieve Gullion, a mountain in south Armagh.

[12] Jonathan Bardon, *A History of Ulster* (Belfast: Blackstaff Press, 1992), 400.

1870s, which gave dignity and literary recognition to an Ulster family living in very humble circumstances.

CRITICAL CONTEXTS

Literary critics have often tended to minimize Northern distinctiveness. The editors of the ambitious and idiosyncratic five-volume *The Field Day Anthology of Irish Writing* (1991–2002) include Northern fiction but do not identify or discuss it as such, presenting it under inclusive headings such as 'Irish Fiction' and 'Contemporary Fiction'. In his sophisticated study, *Literature, Partition and the Nation State* (2002), Joe Cleary makes connections between the partition of Ireland and other politically controversial acts of division, arguing not just for the artificiality but the 'discursive invisibility' of the Irish border, and claiming that Northern Irish literature did not acquire a 'distinct aesthetic complexion' until the onset of the Troubles in the 1970s.[13] In order to make his case, Cleary is dismissive of works such as the Dutch geographer M. W. Heslinga's study, *The Irish Border as a Cultural Divide* (1962), which gives some discursive visibility to the border by reviewing cultural differences on either side of it, and he dwells on the limitations of the cultural regionalism advocated by the poet John Hewitt, a regionalism intended to move beyond political and sectarian divisions.[14] But Hewitt was hardly the only non-sectarian Ulster regionalist: the architect Denis Hanna, for example, claimed there was something rather akin to 'that illusive quality called Nationality' in 'the regional spirit of Ulster' and that 'the province has a rich personality of her own'.[15] The regional distinctiveness that is addressed, explicitly and implicitly, in some of the Ulster fictions discussed in this chapter suggests that the border's alleged discursive invisibility may have been exaggerated.

Despite the pioneering criticism of John Wilson Foster's *Forces and Themes in Ulster Fiction* (1974), until recently, Ulster fiction has not had much critical attention. It did not help that the high-minded trustees of the Linen Hall Library in Belfast refused for many years to purchase anything as frivolous as novels, and that fiction, along with the theatre, was distrusted by conservative churchmen as altogether too worldly and profane for the godly.[16] This did not prevent Ulster writers from producing novels or short fiction, but for a time they made little impression. In a 1951 volume on *The Arts in Ulster*, compiled for the Festival of Britain, there are chapters on drama and poetry, but instead of a chapter on fiction there is an account of 'Ulster Prose' by the broadcaster and dramatist John Boyd (1912–2002).[17] This does discuss the nineteenth-century Tyrone novelist William

---

[13] Joe Cleary, *Literature, Partition and the Nation State* (Cambridge: Cambridge University Press, 2002), 98, 76.

[14] Ibid., 69, 70–72, 236 n28.   [15] Denis Hanna, *The Face of Ulster* (London: Batsford, 1952), v, 1.

[16] See Norman Vance, 'Revival and Presbyterian Culture', *Bulletin of the Presbyterian Historical Society of Ireland* 22 (1993), 16–19.

[17] John Boyd, 'Ulster Prose', in Sam Hanna Bell, Nesca A. Robb, and John Hewitt (eds), *The Arts in Ulster: A Symposium* (London: Harrap, 1951), 99–127.

Carleton (1794–1869) and rather tersely surveys subsequent fiction, although the chapter title and Boyd's sometimes rather lofty tone play down the importance and extent of both novels and short stories. Fiction did not feature at all in the rather sketchy bibliography of *Causeway* (1971), an Arts Council-funded symposium which again buried Ulster fiction under the title of 'Prose' in a short and appreciative but rather drastically selective essay by John Cronin, while poetry, theatre, music, painting, and sculpture were all given more generous treatment.[18] In the same year, *Northern Ireland 1921–1971*, a lavishly illustrated government publication designed to celebrate the fiftieth anniversary of the state, gave space to a wide range of cultural and other achievements. But its sole allusion to the novel took the form of a photograph of the then-deceased Forrest Reid. There were also photographs of St John Ervine, author of seven novels, and of Joseph Tomelty (1911–95), dramatist and author of novels including *Red is the Port Light* (1948), a sombre tale of shipwreck, loneliness, and murder on the County Down coast, but both were described as men of the theatre rather than writers of fiction.

This neglect persisted in James M. Cahalan's *The Irish Novel* (1988), which gave little space to Northern writers and played down specific Northern contexts by using broader categories such as 'Women Novelists' or 'Conventional Realists'. Since then, more critical and scholarly attention has been paid to Ulster writing, particularly contemporary fiction, with perceptive essays and studies considering individual writers and exploring particular themes, notably 'Troubles fiction', aspects of which are discussed later in this volume.[19] Among these studies is Eamonn Hughes's authoritative chapter on Northern Irish fiction during the Troubles in *Stepping Stones* (2001), a successor volume to *The Arts in Ulster* and *Causeway*, which reviewed the contribution of the arts to Northern Irish society in the period from 1971 to the turn of the millennium.[20] The second volume of the substantial *Cambridge History of Irish Literature* (2006) has (very short) sub-chapters on 'Fiction from Northern Ireland' by John Wilson Foster and on 'The Novel in Northern Ireland' and 'Short Fiction in Northern Ireland' by George O'Brien.[21] But there still seems to be a certain critical embarrassment about Ulster or Northern Irish fiction as a separate descriptive category, even in studies where Northern fictions are discussed.[22]

The reasons for such critical invisibility, particularly in earlier times, may include the greater local prominence, as performance arts, of poetry and drama (not to mention dramatist-novelists remembered only as dramatists); the overshadowing of Northern Irish fiction by internationally respected Irish novelists imaginatively located in other parts of Ireland, from James Joyce (1882–1941) to John Banville (1945–); and a

[18] John Cronin, 'Prose', in Michael Longley (ed.), *Causeway: The Arts in Ulster* (Belfast: Arts Council of Northern Ireland, 1971), 71–82.

[19] See, for example, Elmer Kennedy-Andrews, *Fiction and the Northern Ireland Troubles since 1969: (De-)constructing the North* (Dublin: Four Courts Press, 2003).

[20] Eamonn Hughes, 'Fiction', in Mark Carruthers and Stephen Douds (eds), *Stepping Stones: The Arts in Ulster 1971–2001* (Belfast: Blackstaff Press, 2001), 79–102.

[21] See Margaret Kelleher and Philip O'Leary (eds), *The Cambridge History of Irish Literature, Volume 2: 1890–2000* (Cambridge: Cambridge University Press, 2006), 165–73, 436–41, 459–63.

[22] See, for example, the treatment of Northern Irish fiction in Derek Hand, *A History of the Irish Novel* (Cambridge: Cambridge University Press, 2011).

comparative critical indifference to short stories, favoured by many Ulster writers and a problem for Irish writers more generally. Part of the blame may rest on what may now seem severe and sometimes unreasonable or inappropriate critical standards encouraged by the rise of university English and Leavisite criticism, leaving almost every novel ever written seriously at risk of being deemed inadequate in some particular. Furthermore, self-respecting critics may have been reluctant to risk their reputations by over-praising or perhaps even studying 'local' fiction, intimidated, perhaps, by the influential views of those self-conscious apostles of 'culture', notably Matthew Arnold, E. M. Forster, and Forster's friend and protégé, Forrest Reid, who did much to establish the legend of indus-trial Belfast as hopelessly philistine, strictly 'workful' in the manner of Dickens's Coketown, and hostile to the imagination.[23]

It is indeed easy, but misleading, to think of specifically Ulster writing before and after partition as workful and tediously argumentative, and therefore having little or nothing to do with imaginative literature, let alone fiction. The Reverend T. M. Johnstone's *Ulstermen: Their Fight for Fortune, Faith and Freedom* (1914) and Henry Maxwell's *Ulster Was Right* (1934) may come to mind as examples. But the often prosaic interplay of place, politics, and controversy could and did feed into the novel form. The veteran Belfast-born political journalist and broadcaster John Cole (1927–2013), sensitive to local land-scape and idiom, published a thriller, *A Clouded Peace* (2001), in his retirement. Hugh Shearman (1915–99), biographer of the first unionist prime minister, Lord Craigavon, also wrote two entertaining tongue-in-cheek fictions, *The Bishop's Confession* (1943) and *A Bomb and a Girl* (1944). The musician and film-actor Richard Hayward (1892–1964) explored the region both in his well-illustrated travel-book *In Praise of Ulster* (1938) and in *Sugarhouse Entry: A Novel of the Ulster Countryside* (1936), which conveys a sense of continuity between country and city and gives its hero, Robert Dunseith, a Protestant who employs Catholics, something of the radicalism of the Ulster Protestants who joined the United Irishmen in the 1790s.

STIMULI AND INFLUENCES

There is a continuum and a creative interplay in Ulster writing between the non-fic-tional and the fictional, between historical discourse and the narrative imagination, which is too easily overlooked. The medieval scholar and translator Helen Waddell (1899–1965), daughter of an Ulster Presbyterian missionary and English graduate of Queen's University Belfast, wrote both the historical study, *The Wandering Scholars* (1927), and the bestselling novel, *Peter Abelard* (1933). Perhaps drawn to the inter-national intellectual culture of Catholic Europe in the Middle Ages and the tragedy of Abelard and Heloise in reaction against the narrow sectarianism of her native province,

---

[23] See E. M. Forster, 'Forrest Reid', in *Abinger Harvest* (London: Arnold, 1936), 75–80. This appreci-ation of Reid was first published in the *Nation* in April 1920.

Waddell was generous both in her historical sympathy and in her support of other Ulster writers, including the scholarly Presbyterian minister W. F. Marshall (1888–1959), for whose *Ballads and Verses from Tyrone* (1929) she wrote an introduction.[24] Yet another Presbyterian minister and fiction writer, Hubert Quinn, whose ministry was spent in the Antrim countryside, was interested in wandering scholars and lost souls closer to his own time and place but shared something of Waddell's broad religious sympathies. Like her, he and Patrick Adare, his ministerial alter ego in the novel *Dear Were the Days* (1934), seemed to favour the humane Abelardian theory of the Atonement, which stressed exemplary love rather than the harsher Augustinian and Calvinist versions of the doctrine which emphasize sacrifice for universal sinfulness.

Sociological, cultural, and ethnic differences in Ulster, together with other historical and political themes much explored during the Home Rule debates, had found fictional expression in *The Red Hand of Ulster* (1912) by George A. Birmingham (pseudonym of James Owen Hannay, 1865–1950), a farcical but disconcertingly prophetic novel about unionist gun-running, and in his more serious historical novel, *The Northern Iron* (1907), which is about the submerged radical tradition in Ulster represented by the eighteenth-century United Irishmen. There are similar socio-political concerns in W. F. Marshall's *Planted by a River* (1948) and in the more acerbic *Across the Narrow Sea* (1987) by Sam Hanna Bell (1909–90). These are well-crafted historical novels about early and insecure Presbyterian settlement. Biographical and autobiographical memoirs find their counterpart in fictions of wartime Belfast such as *The Last Romantic out of Belfast* (1984) by Sam Keery (1930–) and Brian Moore's earlier *Bildungsroman*, *The Emperor of Ice-Cream* (1965).[25] Natural and social history sometimes converged. There are links between *Carragloon: Tales of our Townland* (1935) by the Reverend W. R. Megaw (1885–1953), affectionate and well-observed (if slightly melancholy) fictional sketches of country people and a passing rural world, and Megaw's meticulous scientific observations on mosses and liverworts contained in his contribution to the second edition of S. A. Stewart and T. H. Corry's *The Flora of the North-East of Ireland* (1938), which he edited with Robert Lloyd Praeger. The pioneering and influential social anthropology of the Queen's-based geographer Estyn Evans, author of *Mourne Country* (1951), *Irish Folk Ways* (1957), and other studies, influenced *December Bride* (1951) and other novels, stories, articles, and regional broadcasts of his friend Bell.[26]

The aspiration of the more ambitious writers for greater public visibility was met by a burgeoning Northern publishing culture, which played its part in the rise of local fiction, particularly writing aimed mainly at an Ulster readership. There had been print works and newspapers in Strabane, Derry, Armagh, and Newry as well as in Belfast since the eighteenth century, but the rapid growth of Belfast as an industrial city in the 1800s brought with it new printing businesses, and printers and booksellers often

---

[24] Marshall's brother, R. L., quotes Waddell's cheerful translation of a medieval drinking song at the end of his *At Home in Tyrone*.

[25] See Guy Woodward, *Culture, Northern Ireland and the Second World War* (Oxford: Oxford University Press, 2015).

[26] Sean McMahon, *Sam Hanna Bell: A Biography* (Belfast: Blackstaff Press, 1999), 24.

doubled as publishers. One of the more enduring businesses was M'Caw, Stevenson, and Orr, established in 1876. Their list contained a considerable number of novels and collections of short stories, including the work of Matt Mulcaghey (pseudonym of Guy Wilson, 1875–1959), a journalist and author of *Aghnascreeby* (1934), a novel which drew on childhood memories of the Tyrone countryside and of colourful eccentrics such as the tramp who assures a little boy that he is a hailstone maker, out of work for want of snow. Not long after partition the Quota Press was established with offices in Donegall Street in Belfast. Between 1927 and 1954 it published a long list of local material, including *Carragloon*. Assisted by the Arts Council, the tradition of local literary publishing continues, represented for example by Blackstaff Press, established in 1971, which has published or reprinted the work of many Ulster writers, Hewitt and Bell among them.

Differences between the Glens of Antrim, which Hewitt loved, and north Down and Belfast, the settings of Bell's fiction, draw attention to the artificiality or oversimplification of deeming the whole of Northern Ireland to be a single region. Yet at another level the very patterns of internal difference are regionally distinctive, associated with the complicated history of Scottish and English settlement and the belated, but rapid, industrialization which had no parallel elsewhere in Ireland. When sound broadcasting was introduced, the consensus-minded BBC established a single Northern Ireland region in 1924, with a policy commitment to serve the whole of a deeply divided society. This was never easy, but regional programming proved to be a powerful stimulus to Ulster writing: the novelists Janet McNeill and Joseph Tomelty wrote radio drama and BBC features producers such as Leitch and Bell also wrote novels.[27]

A little haughty in the early days, the BBC was not particularly friendly to strong regional accents, at least partly because of worries about intelligibility over the airwaves, which led to St John Ervine's pleasant but unmistakeably Ulster accent being noted as a possible problem at the beginning of his long career as a broadcaster. Despite this, the new possibilities of recorded speech played their part in exposing listeners to linguistic and accent diversity in Northern Ireland as elsewhere. These developments both drew on and fed into local writing. W. F. Marshall gave broadcast talks on Ulster dialect in 1935 under the heading 'Ulster Speaks'. The following year he was instrumental in the broadcast of selections from *A Midsummer Night's Dream* spoken in a Tyrone accent which, he argued, was the nearest surviving approximation to Elizabethan English. Marshall was also a major contributor of Ulster examples to the *Scottish National Dictionary* (1931–75). The manuscript of his *Ulster Dialect Dictionary* was reputedly destroyed by his dog, but systematic dialect studies by various scholars, particularly the Ulster-born Robert J. Gregg, carefully documented different kinds of speech throughout the six counties, distinguishing town and country accents and tracing strong Scots influence, particularly in north Down and Antrim, with English or Gaelic influences more apparent in other areas.[28]

---

[27] See Rex Cathcart, *The Most Contrary Region: The BBC in Northern Ireland 1924–1984* (Belfast: Blackstaff Press, 1984).

[28] Robert J. Gregg, *The Scotch-Irish Dialect Boundaries in the Province of Ulster* (Port Credit, Ontario: Canadian Federation for the Humanities, 1985).

The best examples of traditional dialects tended to be found among older people less likely to have been schooled out of dialect speech and less affected by modern influences such as greater social mobility, the drift to the city, the cinema, or indeed broadcasting itself, all of which tended to weaken local distinctiveness. The sense of rapid change, not just in speech but in rural communities more generally, was itself both a literary theme and a stimulus to locally-based storytellers to draw on increasingly distant childhood memory, traditional lore, or old stories that had been handed down, before all was lost completely. Generational continuity on the land, less and less a feature of rural life, was a recurring theme in fictions such as Hubert Quinn's *The Land Remains* (1944) or Florence Davidson's story, 'The Islander', set on one of the islands in Strangford Lough, in her collection, *Loan-Ends: Stories in Ulster* (1933). A natural model for regional fiction with dialect speech was supplied in the work of the Dorset novelist and poet Thomas Hardy, a contributor to Joseph Wright's *English Dialect Dictionary* (1898–1905) and a friend of St John Ervine after he moved to England. Hardy's fictional strategy of renaming and lightly disguising particular places is often followed by Ulster writers. Belfast usually remains Belfast, though Donaghadee reappears as Donaghreagh in Ervine's novel, *The Wayward Man* (1927), and Greyabbey as Glenreeba in Norris's *Glenreeba*. Hardy's 1916 poem about stubborn continuities in the countryside, 'In Time of "The Breaking of Nations"', supplied an epigraph for *Elders' Daughters* (1942), a novel of Presbyterian life in rural Tyrone by Lydia M. Foster (1867–1943).

There were Scottish influences too, not just Presbyterianism but the poetry of Robert Burns, whose Ayrshire dialect was readily accessible to Scots-descended readers and writers in the North of Ireland: their own speech was often not very different.[29] Burns provided some of the inspiration for the so-called 'kailyard school' of Scottish fiction, popular in Ulster, offering tales of (mainly Presbyterian) life in the countryside and associated with novelists such as Ian Maclaren (pseudonym of Reverend John Watson) and J. M. Barrie.[30] Set not in rural Scotland but in Ballyclare in County Antrim, the short stories in *When Lint was in the Bell* (1897) and subsequent collections by Archibald McIlroy (1859–1915) provided a model for what might be called 'Ulster kailyard' fiction, much of it written by Presbyterian ministers or their wives and daughters. McIlroy's title, meaning 'when the flax was in bloom', was taken from a line in Burns's 'The Cottar's Saturday Night'.

But Presbyterian Scotland and the kailyard were not the only influences on Ulster fiction. There was also a visual dimension. Lydia Foster begins her novel, *The Bush that Burned: An Idyll of Ulster Life* (1931), with potato-digging on a Tyrone farm in the 1840s. The narrator comments: 'It was a scene worthy the brush of a Millet. Two backs bent over the brown earth of a potato field that was yielding up its treasure.'[31] The knowing reference

---

[29] See Frank Ferguson and Andrew R. Holmes (eds), *Revising Burns and Ulster: Literature, Religion and Politics, c.1790–1920* (Dublin: Four Courts Press, 2009).

[30] Even though the Linen Hall Library had long held out against fiction as merely frivolous, it eventually succumbed to local demand and some time in the 1890s acquired a copy of the 1893 edition of Barrie's *Auld Licht Idylls*.

[31] Lydia Foster, *The Bush that Burned: An Idyll of Ulster Life* (Belfast: Quota Press, 1934), 9.

is to the work of Jean-François Millet, famed for scenes of life on the land, such as his 1857 painting, *Les Glaneuses*. Millet's works had influenced both the rural scenes of regional writers and the Scottish and Irish painters who had studied in Paris, including the enduringly popular Ulster artist Paul Henry, whose work includes *The Potato-Diggers* (1910–11) and *The Potato Harvest* (1918–19). But Foster's protagonist has no wish to remain a picturesque figure in a pastoral landscape: his ambition, which he eventually achieves, is to leave the land and study for the ministry in Belfast. While there is much psalm-singing and solemnity in the story, there are also touches of gentle mockery, and the love poetry of Burns rather than the psalms of David concludes the narrative. In Sam Hanna Bell's novel of rural life in County Down, *December Bride*, the conflict between sanctimoniousness and sexual promptings in the Presbyterian minister Mr Sorleyson is a theme which can be traced back to Burns's 'Holy Willie's Prayer', but the epigraph and the sombre atmosphere, which refuses naïve pastoral sentimentalities, come from Hardy.

While it is natural to look for links between Ulster fictions and those of the Irish Literary Revival and the post-Revival period which are set in other parts of Ireland, the differences must also be acknowledged, chief among which is the fact that in the divided communities of Northern Irish fiction, the spectre of otherness and sectarian tension, of Orange and Green in potential confrontation, represents an unyielding constant. There are Scots-descended planters in W. F. Marshall's *Planted by a River*, at first sight a bland celebration of Presbyterian-settled Ulster. The title comes from the metrical version of the first psalm in the Scottish Psalter, which commends the righteous man as one who 'shall be like a tree that hath / Been planted by a river'. But the settlement and the implied stability and peace are fragile: the novel incorporates both recent memories of violent religious and political conflict at the siege of Derry and the Battle of the Boyne and a continuing threat of violence represented by the rapparee Shane Nugent. The narrator fears but understands the resentment of the disinherited and is uneasy about unequal laws after the Williamite wars, which have reduced the noble and courteous Colonel O'Neill to the status of a 'landless Papist'.

The Catholic sense of otherness, of Protestant order and Presbyterian righteousness as the oppressive and resented other, is present, with varying degrees of ironic distance, in the fiction of Brian Moore, secular and agnostic and yet, as Terence Brown argues, inescapably Catholic.[32] Catholic or not, for Moore there ought to be more to life, even in Belfast, than sectarian rancour. But Catholic and Protestant had been uneasy neighbours in the north-east of Ireland since Presbyterian Scots arrived in the seventeenth century—the theme of Bell's *Across the Narrow Sea*—and the problematic and contested identity of their region through its difficult history provided a background and metaphor for more or less ironic fictional explorations of personal identity and insecurity, variously confused and aggressive. This can be seen not just in novels by Moore and Bell but in Janet McNeill's *The Maiden Dinosaur* (1964) and, a generation earlier, in St John Ervine's *The Foolish Lovers* (1920). It is to the fiction of these four novelists that I will turn in the final part of this chapter.

---

[32] Terence Brown, 'Show Me a Sign: Brian Moore and Religious Faith', in *Ireland's Literature*, 174–88.

St John Ervine, Janet McNeill, Brian Moore, and Sam Hanna Bell

Born in Protestant East Belfast in 1883 within earshot of the shipyards, St John Ervine grew up with the sectarianism of Orange and Green and a rather austerely philistine version of Calvinism, which he gradually rejected. He found work as an insurance clerk in Belfast and then, from 1901, in London, where he soon fell among Fabians. On encountering H. G. Wells and George Bernard Shaw (1856–1950), Ervine became a socialist for a season and something of a sociologist after an informal higher education in the Fabian 'nursery'. Gradually, he developed his own form of socially radical constitutional nationalism, as well as establishing himself as a dramatist and man of letters. There seems to have been a radical streak in his family: his father, a printer, had died when he was two but, unlike his mother, was rumoured to have been bookish and sometimes inconveniently opinionated, and an eighteenth-century ancestor had been a United Irishman. Although he became a rather idiosyncratic unionist in later life, in England, the younger Ervine was distrustful of the unionism of industrial leaders such as the Belfast linen lords, which he felt played on sectarian differences to distract attention from oppressive labour conditions. His early Shavian problem plays such as *Mixed Marriage* (1911) and *The Orangeman* (1913) had tried to point beyond tribal sloganizing and drum-beating. But his radicalism and idealism had started to drain away by the time he wrote *The Foolish Lovers*, chastened and overtaken by extreme events which helped to polarize public opinion in Ireland, particularly the Easter Rising, which he experienced at first hand as manager of Dublin's Abbey Theatre.

Despite the self-conscious realism of his writing, something of his earlier more romantic and idealistic self, abetted by his rather vague sense of his own father, survives in *The Foolish Lovers*, which is set in small-town Ulster and in London. It is, at some level, an ironically distanced rewriting of Ervine's own early life. Like his sometimes combative protagonist, John MacDermott, Ervine was the restless only son of a long-widowed mother. Both author and protagonist discovered romance in Shakespeare at performances of *The Merchant of Venice* and *Romeo and Juliet* in a Belfast theatre. MacDermott rejects the possibility of a teaching career, as Ervine had done because of family poverty, and the option of working in the family shop, not unlike the shop run by Ervine's grandmother and uncles which had helped to support his mother and himself. Like Ervine, MacDermott is driven by youthful ambition to leave Ulster in order to make something of himself; the main difference is that Ervine eventually succeeded. Where the author seems to have been largely self-motivated, his protagonist is encouraged in his dreams and his longing for adventure by his quixotic Uncle Matthew, a bookish idealist and unsuccessful romantic, perhaps loosely modelled on Ervine's quirky father. Years previously, Matthew had lost his job as a teacher for breaking a shop window in protest against the cynical commercial exploitation of the death of Queen Victoria. This was, arguably, a noble folly, although some thought he was 'quare in the head'[33] and he never worked again, which left him reliant on the support of William, his stoically uncomplaining shopkeeper brother. The follies and literary aspirations of young John, their London-based nephew, foolish and precipitate and indeed obsessively selfish as they are, are less positively represented. John's vision of London is a fantasy, fed by Uncle Matthew's romantically literary view of a city he has never visited, but it is soon dispelled by harsh reality.

John MacDermott, brash and hot-tempered, carries about with him a particularly bumptious, indeed comic, version of Ulster chauvinism, including overweening pride in his rather unremarkable home town Ballyards, based on Newtownards in County Down. His attempt to break into journalism in London is not helped by his conviction that the provincial Ulster papers he knew from childhood were much better than anything Fleet Street could offer, indeed that 'the *North Down Herald* was far more interesting than the *Times*'.[34] His journalist friend Hinde teases him by suggesting they should start a paper for Ulstermen in London, to be called *To Hell With the Pope* or *No Surrender*. Undeterred, he tells the Ulster-born Clotworthy, editor of the *Daily Sensation*, that 'I come from Ulster where all the good men come from'[35] and is impervious to Clotworthy's dry response that he has also seen some poor specimens from the same place. His opinion that the *Sensation* would be improved by telling readers the truth instead of the usual lies, certain he will always know what the truth is, is clearly naïve and impractical, and he is told the paper has no use for John the Baptists.

Yet the satire cuts both ways: the unattractive cynicism of the newspaper world and the prosaic realities, restlessness, eccentricities, and unneighbourly loneliness of life in London gradually suggest there might be something to be said after all for the circumscribed, complacently humdrum life of Ballyards, where everyone knows everyone else. The point is reinforced towards the end of the novel when John's English wife, whom he met when she was rather joylessly working in London, finds that she greatly prefers Ballyards to the metropolis. He himself fails to find success or even satisfaction in his literary career and has to depend on modest earnings from occasional journalism and then mechanical work as a subeditor. He manages to place his first novel with an unscrupulous publisher, though he earns nothing from it, and to see his play on St Patrick performed in an obscure repertory theatre, though without much remuneration. His only literary success is a trivial comic sketch for the music halls which has had to be reworked by an experienced actor.

In the end, MacDermott is forced to choose between stubbornly continuing to chase his ambition in London and rejoining his wife and child, now living with his mother in Ballyards. In Samuel Johnson's *Rasselas* (1759), the would-be adventurer's choice of life takes him back to his starting point in the Happy Valley. *The Foolish Lovers* follows the same pattern, although for all the rather misplaced pride of its citizens, Ballyards is no Happy Valley. In a muted conclusion, MacDermott agrees to carry on the shop with the now ageing Uncle William, a more prosaic but more reliable role model than the bookish

---

[33] St John Ervine, *The Foolish Lovers* (London: W. Collins and Sons, 1920), 11.   [34] Ibid., 210.
[35] Ibid., 213.

and quixotic Uncle Matthew. Combative to the last, he resolves to fight off a ruthless competitor, rather unconvincingly exclaiming that 'there's a romance at the end of it all'.[36]

Romance and excitement seem to have even less scope in the Belfast of *The Maiden Dinosaur* by Janet McNeill, daughter of a Presbyterian minister. The narrative appears to move in tight, cramped circles around Sarah, an unmarried middle-aged classics teacher who is self-protected against too much reality. It takes in her emotionally volatile best friend Helen and the other occupants of the now subdivided suburban house where she grew up and still lives, as well as her friends from schooldays, some now married, and the restricted, conservative, male-dominated world of a rather tepidly Protestant middle-class Ulster, sustained if at all by an inherited, almost mechanical habit of faith. But exact, concise writing registering Sarah's sharply intelligent, usually unspoken perceptions, combined with an authorial sensitivity to atmosphere and fragile or transient personal relationships, probe beyond the ostensible boundaries. Crisis, desolation, and traumatic memory constantly threaten to intrude, and the apparently secure little world of the novel is riven by a friend's suicide and by Helen's own subsequent suicide attempt and departure for a new life in London.

In the opening paragraph, Sarah, unseen, observes the brisk and dapper masculinity of George, a frequent visitor to Helen's flat, as a performance, like his curiously passionless relationship with Helen. Helen drunkenly jeers at Sarah's virginal ignorance, but there is more dramatic performance and underlying desperation than fulfilment in her tumultuous emotional life. Husbands and fathers, including Sarah's father as she remembers him, are edgily presented as unsuccessful authority figures, vulnerable, inadequate, and even transgressive within their prescribed roles. Even the seagulls from Belfast Lough did not keep to their own space but 'invaded the lawn with a bold disturbance of wings'.[37] Observed Catholic otherness, as represented by early mass, features momentarily, the celebration of the Eucharist apparently leading each week to an enviable 'newly done-over soul',[38] making it appear more positive than Protestant worship.

Awareness of a more extensive, disturbingly different dimension insinuates itself into the novel and Sarah's consciousness, partly through animal imagery. The dinosaur of the title, a schoolgirl's perception of an ageing teacher, suggests something at once monstrous, grotesque, and harmlessly extinct, but the roaring of live beasts can be heard at times from the nearby zoo, a recurring metaphor for subconscious stirrings and disconcerting, even erotic, possibilities not fully confronted. Sarah's intermittent, well-hidden pride in her half-buried other life as a published poet is described as living in her 'like an animal'.[39] This pride stirs a little when she and her friend Addie go to take part in a television programme on local writers. Even before the interview, the more forthright Addie has anticipated and rejected the familiar charge that they had 'Never Really Lived'[40] or had the luridly traumatic or perverse experiences popularly thought necessary for writers, despite their fifty years of life through two world wars, bombing raids, and the Troubles of the 1920s. In the interview itself, the male interviewer is patronizing and

---

[36] Ibid., 392.   [37] Janet McNeill, *The Maiden Dinosaur* (Belfast: Blackstaff Press, 1984), 10.
[38] Ibid., 11.   [39] Ibid., 19.   [40] Ibid., 96.

incompetent, misquoting and misrepresenting Sarah's work and ignoring the classical matrix in Horace that she has mentioned. He is predictably determined to pigeonhole her as a provincial miniaturist restricted by upbringing and environment, confined to a Belfast drawing-room except for 'holidays in Irish bogland under a Paul Henry cloud',[41] as Sarah silently summarizes it, more vividly than he himself could have done. The unruly beast of Sarah's pride stays silent and private, but Addie enjoys herself by retaliating that 'comfortable and happy childhoods and only a literary acquaintance with brothels and dry-closets'[42] need not be a literary liability.

Addie's remark doubles as an oblique and partial defence of the apparently limited scope of the novel itself. *The Maiden Dinosaur* constantly if discreetly points beyond itself, and beyond its immediate setting in north Belfast and provincial Ulster, to issues of personal rather than regional or political identity. It ends with Sarah's emotional exhaustion and the sober realization that after forty-five years her long relationship with Helen is finally over. But life, and indeed human relationships, must somehow continue. George is about to come and visit her, but she is not ready for any social encounter. She quells her rising panic as she thinks of a promising pupil who bungled an examination by not attempting to answer a question from every section. Sensitive to language both as a poet and a teacher of classics, she—and the reader—can see this as a metaphor: success in life, as in examinations, calls for at least an attempt at each of the questions posed. At this, Sarah experiences silent laughter and perhaps some kind of returning confidence in herself and the future.

The Maiden Dinosaur invites comparison with Brian Moore's Belfast novel, *The Lonely Passion of Judith Hearne* (1955), which explores the mindset and increasingly disturbed inner life of a Catholic middle-class spinster, but the real point of comparison with Moore is in the negotiation of personal crisis. This is most apparent in his coming-of-age novel, *The Emperor of Ice-Cream*, in which Gavin Burke's Oedipal crisis in relation to his domineering father and his Catholic nationalist family is set against, and precipitated by, the larger crisis of wartime bombing in Belfast. Problematic personal and political identities become metaphors for each other as the people prepare for air raids and wait for something to happen. Almost too neatly, self-discovery and the discovery of a role and a significance for Belfast and Northern Ireland in time of war proceed side by side after a period of confusion and uncertainty. This neatness is assisted by historical hindsight and some tidying up of untidy events, as Patrick Hicks has demonstrated.[43]

As in *The Foolish Lovers*, there is a certain ironic detachment in time and place from the author's earlier self, on whom Gavin is partly modelled. Something of a misfit academically, Moore, like Gavin, had been born into a high-achieving middle-class Catholic family in Belfast. He began to write only after he had moved to North America in the late 1940s. Like the young Moore, the unemployed Gavin joins the ARP (Air Raid Precautions Unit), encountering there a motley collection of misfits and malcontents,

[41] Ibid., 98.   [42] Ibid., 99.
[43] Patrick Hicks, *Brian Moore and the Meaning of the Past* (Lewiston, NY: Edwin Mellen Press, 2007), 48–52.

among them timeservers, unionists, nationalists, and even a home-grown Marxist. His adolescent quarrel with his father and his upbringing is partly religious and moral, a struggle with Catholic dogmatism, guilt, and sexual repression, which he dramatizes as an inconclusive interior dialogue between his white and black angels, although it is also political, or rather anti-political.

In the opening months of the Second World War, Belfast, like the rest of Ulster, seemed a very marginal place where nothing of note was happening, of little military interest to Adolf Hitler or anyone else. On the principle of an enemy's enemy being a friend, some Irish nationalists, north and south, like some of Gavin's family, had been disposed to look to Germany for support in the continuing national struggle against British hegemony in Northern Ireland. Twenty-five years later, when Moore published his novel, the genocidal horrors of Nazism and the folly of trusting Hitler had become glaringly apparent. Moreover, the reputation of Britain's wartime leader Winston Churchill, who died in 1965, had risen from maverick politician to saviour of his country and world statesman. So when Moore makes Gavin's opinionated anti-Semitic father insist that 'the heel of John Bull' is much worse than the 'German jackboot', and dismiss Churchill as a 'military incompetent' and 'architect of the Gallipoli shambles', he wins easy sympathy for Gavin's alienation.[44] There is, however, a comic reversal in the novel when the windows of the Burke house are shattered by a German bomb blast, which prompts Gavin's father to bluster that he prefers 'the heel of old John Bull'[45] after all.

As the bombs start to fall indiscriminately on Catholic and Protestant alike, the bullying father dwindles into a badly frightened man and, for Gavin at least, 'this dull dead town'[46] becomes part of history, part of the war. Useful at last in the ARP, he refuses to flee to Dublin with his family: by staying put, he can forget his father and his own angers and frustrations as the city seems to be facing destruction. It would be too much to say that Gavin becomes a hero, since glamorous heroics belong in a different kind of wartime novel, but at last he finds something that needs to be done, and he finds himself. With an ARP friend (incidentally a Protestant) Gavin voluntarily and doggedly undertakes the job of placing mutilated corpses in coffins. He has somehow, almost accidentally, become a better man than his father, who realizes he has been a fool. The novel ends in their bomb-damaged condemned house with a kind of reconciliation and role reversal when the father weeps and seeks comfort from the son.

Moore's peacetime retrospect from the 1960s shows how the German bombs aimed at the Belfast shipyards, which threatened the whole population, could redirect a bitter legacy of internal violence and disputed identity, at least for a time. By the 1980s, however, the bombs were homemade. Sam Hanna Bell's *Across the Narrow Sea* revisits the early days of Scots settlement in Ulster in the light of renewed sectarian violence. It features Neil Gilchrist, an unsuccessful Scottish law student—another young man at odds with his father—who needs to make his own way and looks for new possibilities in County Down, not far from the settler town of Newtownards. Insecurity and tension between settlers and

---

[44] Brian Moore, *The Emperor of Ice-Cream* (New York: Bantam Press, 1966), 24, 66.
[45] Ibid., 173.   [46] Ibid., 160.

the native Irish they have dispossessed are already laying the foundations for trouble later on. An apparently casual glimpse thirty years into the future, when 'the house fell in flame and smoke',[47] anticipates the 1641 rebellion, traditionally regarded as a Catholic revolt against the Ulster plantation. Gilchrist finds employment as an arborist or woodland manager on the Ravara estate but is aware that this role stops well short of the enduring commitment to the land, to the 'Delving, sowing, reaping'[48] represented by the MacIlveen family who came from Scotland with him. They seem likely to stay for generation after generation, but he returns to Scotland and to married life with the runaway daughter of his employer. Will Scots-settled and variously-peopled Ulster, turbulent and divided, succeed or fail? Can men and women find fulfilment in it and be happy? Can they be proud of it? Since 1920, from St John Ervine to Sam Hanna Bell, Ulster novelists have pondered these questions, and usually left them unanswered.

FURTHER READING

Bardon, Jonathan. *A History of Ulster*. Belfast: Blackstaff Press, 1992.

Brown, Terence. *Ireland's Literature: Selected Essays*. Mullingar: Lilliput Press, 1988.

Cathcart, Rex. *The Most Contrary Region: The BBC in Northern Ireland 1924–1984*. Belfast: Blackstaff Press, 1984.

Cleary, Joe. *Literature, Partition and the Nation State*. Cambridge: Cambridge University Press, 2002.

Courtney, Roger. *Emancipation of the Imagination: Forgotten Writers of East Belfast*. Belfast: EastSide Partnership, 2015.

Foster, John Wilson. *Forces and Themes in Ulster Fiction*. Dublin: Gill and Macmillan, 1974.

Foster, John Wilson (ed.). *The Cambridge Companion to the Irish Novel*. Cambridge: Cambridge University Press, 2006.

Hand, Derek. *A History of the Irish Novel*. Cambridge: Cambridge University Press, 2011.

Ingman, Heather. *Irish Women's Fiction from Edgeworth to Enright*. Sallins, Co. Kildare: Irish Academic Press, 2013.

Kennedy-Andrews, Elmer (ed.). *Irish Fiction since the 1960s*. Gerrards Cross: Colin Smythe, 2006.

Vance, Norman. *Irish Literature since 1800*. London: Longman, 2002.

Walshe, Éibhear (ed.). *Sex, Nation and Dissent in Irish Writing*. Cork: Cork University Press, 1997.

Woodward, Guy. *Culture, Northern Ireland and the Second World War*. Oxford: Oxford University Press, 2015.

---

[47] Sam Hanna Bell, *Across the Narrow Sea* (Belfast: Blackstaff Press, 1987), 221.   [48] Ibid., 286.

PART V

FICTION IN THE MODERNIZING REPUBLIC AND THE TROUBLED NORTH

CHAPTER 16

EDNA O'BRIEN AND THE POLITICS OF BELATEDNESS

JANE ELIZABETH DOUGHERTY

THE critic Jed Esty has written of the protagonist of James Joyce's (1882–1941) *A Portrait of the Artist as a Young Man* (1916) that 'Stephen self-consciously assumes the mantle of the Irish artist but allocates the burden of Irish iconicity to the people around him (particularly women)'.[1] Edna O'Brien's (1930–) fiction, her career, and her critical reception have all been routinely placed within the parentheses in Esty's statement: all three testify to the continued burden of iconicity borne by Irish women, and to their difficulties in assuming the mantle of author. From her first, semi-autobiographical novel, *The Country Girls* (1960), which was banned by the Irish Censorship Board and characterized by the Archbishop of Dublin as a smear on Irish womanhood, to the fiction she continues to produce in her late eighties, O'Brien has repeatedly explored the ways in which the burdens of iconicity impinge on the development of a mature Irish female subjectivity.[2] Moreover, O'Brien herself has laboured under this burden, imposed on her in part because she is an Irish female artist following James Joyce. Indeed, so thoroughly has she been weighed down by her status as an icon of Irish femininity, the chief markers of which are her much-noted beauty and her 'stage-Irish' persona, that it has often overshadowed her artistry, making her a writer 'who regularly has her work assessed on grounds other than its literary qualities.'[3]

---

[1] Jed Esty, *Unseasonable Youth: Modernism, Colonialism, and the Fiction of Development* (New York: Oxford University Press, 2012), 155.

[2] For an overview of the censure and praise that greeted *The Country Girls*, see Maureen O'Connor, 'Girl Trouble', *Dublin Review of Books* 55 (2014). http://www.drb.ie/essays/girl-trouble. Accessed 3 June 2017.

[3] Rebecca Pelan, 'Reflections on a Connemara Dietrich', in Kathryn Laing, Sinéad Mooney, and Maureen O'Connor (eds), *Edna O'Brien: New Critical Perspectives* (Dublin: Carysfort Press, 2006), 19. See also Rebecca Pelan, 'Edna O'Brien's "Stage-Irish" Persona: An "Act" of Resistance', *Canadian Journal of Irish Studies* 19, no. 1 (1993), 49–61.

Although O'Brien has continually critiqued the distortive effects of such representations of her on her fiction and its reception, she is still not consistently recognized as a mature Irish artist.[4] That is to say, her artistry has been recognized belatedly, after years of having been viewed as a once-promising young writer who never fulfilled her potential. In this, her career trajectory echoes the plots of many of her novels and short stories, particularly her fictions of maturation, wherein we see the forces of iconicization retarding or rendering recursive female characters' attempt to develop mature subjectivities. Joyce's fictional counterpart, Stephen Dedalus, came to think of himself not only an artist but as an artist who would create an Irish national literature, as indeed Joyce himself did. Edna O'Brien, against all odds and in the face of much critical opposition, would also become an artist in Joyce's wake. Yet neither of her eponymous country girls—the feisty Bridget/Baba Brennan and the literary-minded Caithleen/Cait/Kate Brady—can imagine becoming an artist, or be imagined as one. Caithleen is instead shown to desire the position of Joycean bird-girl, to seek to become a static feminine icon—a subject, or rather an object, position which is presented by the text as her only realistic 'artistic' choice.

Nor is hers an isolated case. As I will hypothesize in what follows, many of O'Brien's fictions present female characters whose maturation is in some way belated—repetitive, ambiguous, inconclusive—as a result of a profoundly disempowering iconicity that the culture foists upon them. While this may also be true of Joyce's *Bildungsromane*, as critics such as Esty and Vincent P. Pecora have suggested, O'Brien's fictions of maturation reveal that her young heroines face additional obstacles, as for them artistry is impossible to claim and neither epiphany nor exile offers even a temporary escape from impinging social forces. The coming-of-age of her young female characters, then, is as truly belated as O'Brien's artistic maturity has been deemed to be. In this chapter, I will first discuss O'Brien's own perceived belatedness before moving on to an exploration of her depictions of Irish girls trapped in states of permanent liminality, and then end with an examination of how O'Brien's frequent Joycean intertextuality reveals a gendered intensification of what Esty identifies as 'the disruption of developmental time in reciprocal allegories of self-making and nation-building',[5] which he sees as a crucial element in Joyce's characterization of Stephen. O'Brien's work shows that to be both Irish and female is to experience enforced iconicity as an irreparable disruption of one's developmental time.

---

[4] The belated nature of the critical appreciation of O'Brien may be gauged by comparing the sometimes damning reviews of her early work with the reception afforded *The Little Red Chairs* (2015), her first novel in a decade, which garnered some of the most favourable reviews of her long and prolific career. See, for example, Patricia Craig, 'Monsters in the midst', *Independent*, 22 October 2015; Éilís Ní Dhuibhne, 'The Little Red Chairs by Edna O'Brien', *Irish Times*, 24 October 2015; Julie Myerson, 'A chilling masterpiece', *Guardian Review*, 8 November 2015; and Joseph O'Connor, 'O'Brien's fizzing, risk-taking symphony is a triumph', *Irish Independent*, 9 November 2015.

[5] Esty, *Unseasonable Youth*, 2.

GENDER, AUTHORSHIP,
AND CRITICAL RECEPTION

Edna O'Brien was always a rather unlikely author and one who has not been given enough credit for her uniqueness in late twentieth- and early twenty-first-century Irish letters, or for the prophetic nature of much of her fiction. As novelist Anne Enright (1962–) asserts, 'there is no one like her'; she has survived the 'forces that silenced and destroyed who knows how many other Irish women writers'.[6] O'Brien was born in 1930 in Tuamgraney, County Clare, into a household that was rural, Catholic, and conservative, and, indeed, into a newly independent state that was busy defining itself in relation to these three markers of difference. Although her parents had inherited wealth, by the time of Edna's birth it had been squandered by her father, whose drinking and chronic indebtedness were the cause of much marital and domestic discord, which blighted his daughter's early years. Her resultant upbringing in circumstances of 'semi-grandeur'[7] may explain why, as a fiction writer, O'Brien is a sensitive, if often overlooked, chronicler of the injuries of class. She recalls that her family home had very few non-religious books and that her mother, whom she adored, had a suspicion of literature. Nevertheless, her parents valued education enough to send their daughter to a convent school in Loughrea, County Galway, after which O'Brien moved to Dublin in the mid-1940s to train as a pharmacist, although at that time it would have been expected, and indeed was prescribed in the Irish Constitution, that her primary vocation was to be a wife and mother. In the event, O'Brien fulfilled both roles while still in her twenties, although she married the older, divorced Irish novelist Ernest Gébler (1914–98), in spite of (and partially because of) the disapproval of her parents. In 1958, the couple moved to London, where O'Brien, like many an Irish author, found exile congenial to her artistic development, even as she continued to set most of her fictions in Ireland. Written in the space of a few weeks during her first winter in London, *The Country Girls* was heavily influenced by events in O'Brien's own youth and her relationship with her parents, as she explained in her memoir, *Country Girl* (2012): 'The novel's opening paragraph centred on the fear of father. . . . But it was my mother who filled the canvas and who infused that first book.'[8]

The Country Girls proved to be controversial in some quarters, although its reception was by no means wholly critical. However, as Maureen O'Connor and Rebecca Pelan point out, the initial positive reviews often used language ('fresh', 'dewy', 'charming') that

---

[6] Anne Enright, 'Fabulous and infuriating', *Guardian Review*, 13 October 2012.

[7] Edna O'Brien, *Country Girl* (London: Faber and Faber, 2012), 61. Maureen O'Connor argues that 'class is crucial not only in approaching O'Brien's subject matter and treatment of it but also in appreciating her audience'. 'Edna O'Brien, Irish Dandy', in Laing et al., *Edna O'Brien*, 48.

[8] O'Brien, *Country Girl*, 130.

emphasized what the reviewers saw as the 'girlish' qualities of the novel and its author.[9] The book was nevertheless banned in Ireland and caused tensions between O'Brien and her mother, who was shamed by its scandalousness, and her husband, who resented his young wife's literary talent and envied her sudden commercial success, and whose rancour hastened the end of their ailing marriage. Despite his apparent disdain for his wife's artistic gifts, Gébler would nevertheless claim, in the course of their bitter divorce proceedings, that he had written not only *The Country Girls* but also her second novel, *The Lonely Girl* (1962).[10] Although Gébler may have been particularly and personally bitter, this denial of O'Brien's creativity and anger at her temerity in claiming the mantle of artist are not too dissimilar to much of the gendered criticism that greeted her fiction in the decades to come.

This is not to suggest that O'Brien's work should be immune from critique or that her creative output has been consistently excellent. My point is that some criticism of her work seems to stem from opposition towards her audacious determination to pursue a literary career on her own terms rather than acquiesce in the roles that were socially prescribed for women of her generation. As has been argued by her most perceptive critics, O'Brien's iconicity has frequently overwhelmed serious consideration of her work.[11] Indeed, many scholarly considerations of her begin by noting the relative dearth of serious academic criticism of her fiction and expressing the hope that she will soon be given the critical respect and in-depth attention that her work merits. As critics have long noted, the focus on women's private experiences in O'Brien's early work led to her being regarded as obsessive, limited, and romantic, and charged with writing poorly veiled autobiography. Later in her career, when her fiction addressed more overtly political concerns, she was criticized for violating her artistic mandate and failing to observe the apparently self-evident distinction between the public and the private. Although even in her political fictions she focuses on women's lives, the complaint that she is insufficiently feminist has often been voiced. A common thread in these criticisms is the conflation of the author with her protagonists. All of these critiques have the effect of denying O'Brien the authorial right of invention.

A recurring element in characterizations of O'Brien's early work is the widespread critical inability to see it as anything other than confessional. Stan Gebler Davies, O'Brien's nephew by marriage, may have had personal reasons for arguing that her work is 'the sort of self-indulgent drivel written by housewives seeking to escape Wimbledon', and that she has been wise to continue to take the advice of her former husband—presumably the true artist of the pair—that 'she run her diaries through the typewriter. . . . It is a literary technique well known to all scribblers, and while it may not often produce high literature, it is frequently lucrative.'[12] Yet if Davies was being particularly nasty, it is

---

[9] O'Connor, 'Girl Trouble'; Pelan, 'Reflections on a Connemara Dietrich', 12–37.

[10] O'Connor, 'Girl Trouble'.

[11] See especially Pelan, 'Reflections on a Connemara Dietrich'. See also O'Connor, 'Girl Trouble' and Amanda Greenwood, *Edna O'Brien* (Tavistock: Northcote House, 2003), particularly chapter one, which examines the gender-specific critical responses to O'Brien's fiction.

[12] Stan Gebler Davies, 'The trouble with Edna', *Evening Standard*, 19 October 1992.

nevertheless the case that his criticism of O'Brien's work as confessional rather than inventive is not unusual, even among scholarly critics.[13]

The gendered nature of this criticism is cast into wider relief when we compare the reception of her fiction with that of Irish male authors, such as her predecessor Joyce, whose *A Portrait of the Artist as a Young Man* is far more autobiographical than any of O'Brien's fictions of maturation, or her contemporary John McGahern (1934–2006), whose *Memoir* (2005) made clear just how rooted his fiction was in his own life experience. Yet as O'Connor notes, McGahern's novels 'do not draw the same accusations of over-reliance on autobiography, or of "being stuck in a rut"'[14] that O'Brien's works persistently receive. Unlike her, McGahern escaped what Amanda Greenwood has identified as O'Brien's critics' 'unrelenting conflation of author and character'.[15] This is because in identifying her work as autobiographical, critics have sought to diminish it as merely confessional. In so doing, they denigrate her status as a professional novelist and devalue her artistic achievements. This dismissal of her authorial powers of imagination is, of course, a critical fate O'Brien shares with other undervalued female writers.

Later in her career, O'Brien began to write fictions relating to more obviously political topics, through which she maintained her preoccupation with writing Irish women's lives. Yet her supposedly newfound interest in politics was also mocked, often in gendered terms, and she was criticized by some as an irresponsible interloper. Joan Smith, for example, wrote of *House of Splendid Isolation* (1994) that 'too much posing as a tragedy queen has turned [O'Brien] deaf to her own bathetic efforts'.[16] Here again, we see O'Brien's iconicity (her 'posing as a tragedy queen') set against her inadequate art (her 'bathetic efforts'). As Greenwood notes, other reviewers assumed that O'Brien's engagement with militant Irish republicanism, which is one of the themes of *House of Splendid Isolation*, 'arose not so much from concern with Irish politics and history, but rather from an attraction to the "flawed" and "emotionally unavailable" hero supposedly typified by Gerry Adams',[17] the then leader of Sinn Féin. In writing a newspaper profile of Adams, O'Brien was described as having a 'silly novelettish mentality' which made her 'the Barbara Cartland of long-distance Republicanism',[18] associating her yet again with the 'silly' women who write and read romance novels, as well as criticizing her for being insufficiently informed about the complexities of contemporary Irish politics.

Perhaps the most notable critique of O'Brien's engagement with Irish public events came from the influential cultural commentator Fintan O'Toole, who criticized the

[13] See, for example, Denis Donoghue, 'The Idiom of Stephen Dedalus in Rural Terms', *New York Times*, 3 May 1970, 5–6; Peggy O'Brien, 'The Silly and the Serious: An Assessment of Edna O'Brien', *Massachusetts Quarterly* 28, no. 3 (1987), 474–88; Tamsin Hargreaves, 'Women's Consciousness and Identity in Four Irish Women Novelists', in Michael Kenneally (ed.), *Cultural Contexts and Literary Idioms in Contemporary Irish Literature* (Totowa, NJ: Barnes and Noble, 1988), 290–305.

[14] O'Connor, 'Girl Trouble'.   [15] Greenwood, *Edna O'Brien*, 7.

[16] Joan Smith, 'Tears and terror in the wind', *Independent*, 24 April 1994, 33.

[17] Greenwood, *Edna O'Brien*, 4.

[18] Edward Pearce, 'Words with no wisdom', *Guardian Review*, 12 July 1994, 18. Quoted in O'Brien, *Country Girl*, 249.

novelist for publishing *In the Forest* (2002), which was inspired by the murders of Imelda and Liam Riney and Father Joseph Walsh by Brendan O'Donnell in 1994. As Pelan astutely points out, 'O'Toole's main problem with O'Brien's use of the factual material of the murders rests on what he sees as a very clear distinction between public and private meaning', a distinction that O'Brien muddies by writing a novel that constitutes 'an example of unethical intrusion into the private realm'.[19] As Pelan also notes, O'Toole's stated objection was that the novel would cause pain to the loved ones of O'Donnell's victims, but he does not give the same consideration to the families of those who, arguably, had equal cause to be offended by two male-authored Irish novels with real-life origins, John Banville's (1945–) *The Book of Evidence* (1989), inspired by the murderer Malcolm MacArthur, and Eoin McNamee's (1961–) *Resurrection Man* (1994), which is based on the activities of Lenny Murphy and the Shankill Butchers in 1970s Belfast.[20] Nor does it make sense to characterize the O'Donnell murders as wholly private events, given that they were among the most publicized of recent Irish criminal history, with some commentators seeing links between O'Donnell's bleak childhood and the historical maltreatment of children within families and state-sponsored correctional institutions. In this context, O'Toole's criticisms seem more concerned with her incursions onto the public, masculine realm than her intrusion onto 'private' terrain. O'Brien is thus permitted to write about the 'private' experiences of Irish women—and condescended to when she does so—but writing about public events is apparently impermissible.

As Pelan further observes, it has eluded many critics of O'Brien that she has in fact deliberately problematized the patriarchal distinction between the public and the private.[21] From her first novel, she has been posing questions about the uses and abuses of power in relation to Irish women's lives and presenting characters who are 'victims of their own general social powerlessness'.[22] In fact, it could be argued of O'Brien's early work that it is prophetic, anticipating the feminist slogan that 'the personal is political'. In view of this, it is highly ironic that her fiction has been criticized for its feminist shortcomings and she herself for her 'supine, woebegone inclinations'[23] that cause her female protagonists to fail in their fight to resist or change the conditions that oppress and divide them.

For example, Peggy O'Brien argues that the protagonist of the short story, 'Paradise', is a 'relentlessly whining, self-pitying person'[24] and that this reflects O'Brien's own emotional immaturity. This criticism of O'Brien's deficient feminism reveals not only that the novelist has been habitually conflated with her characters but that in narrating their ideological belatedness O'Brien herself has been misread as belated in her engagement with the feminist cause. What such arguments overlook is that a work of fiction is not required to present a triumph over patriarchy to be feminist; feminist fictions can also make patriarchal structures of inequality and oppression visible. In writing about an Ireland in which women were simultaneously rhetorically honoured

---

[19] Pelan, 'Reflections on a Connemara Dietrich', 12.   [20] Ibid., 13.   [21] Ibid., 14.
[22] Ibid., 18.   [23] O'Brien, *Country Girl*, 204.
[24] O'Brien, 'The Silly and the Serious', 478.

and socio-economically disempowered, O'Brien highlighted this egregious disjunction and laid bare some harsh truths about Irish women's actual everyday experiences.
That this has eluded so many readers is testament to the cultural endurance of both
the iconicization and the marginalization of women in this society, so much so that a
contemporary feminist critic is apt to read with amazement the obtuseness of some of
the early critical reactions to *The Country Girls*.

Many of the early reviewers of *The Country Girls* responded to this rather sad tale of
female subjugation as if it were a mid-twentieth-century version of *Sex and the City*. As
Greenwood argues, such critics 'fail either to acknowledge the subtext of *The Country
Girls*' "ebullience" or to recognize adolescent naïvety as a necessary component of
O'Brien's deconstructions of "femininity" and "romance".[25] However, once the second
and third novels in the trilogy, *The Lonely Girl* and *Girls in Their Married Bliss* (1964),
were published, it became impossible for critics to ignore their previous naïvety, just as it
had become impossible for Caithleen Brady to ignore hers. Now that O'Brien's country
girls had moved from innocence to experience and arrived at an understanding of their
own belatedness and profound disempowerment, critics detected a shift 'towards a
sharper, less pleasant'[26] narrative tone. In response, critic Sean McMahon decried the
feminist realism of *Girls in Their Married Bliss*, which shows its two protagonists,
although they have taken on the prescribed and supposedly natural female vocations of
marriage and motherhood, remaining unfulfilled. He wrote that 'Miss O'Brien seemed
in places to be writing a kind of neo-feminist propaganda', a 'retardation' that he hoped
would prove temporary.[27] McMahon's sexist characterization of O'Brien as retarded
was, ironically and regrettably, echoed by feminist critics like Peggy O'Brien, who also
saw her 'authorial identity' as being 'arrested'.[28]

In her artistic belatedness, Edna O'Brien has thus been characterized as being either
too feminist or not feminist enough, which is yet another version of the female double-
bind. In writing of Irish female protagonists who have finally grown up—in that they
have achieved an understanding that they can never fulfil, or indeed even recognize,
their potentialities in a patriarchal social order—O'Brien herself is perceived as having
stubbornly remained immature. Yet for the novelist as well as for her characters, this
belatedness is often attributed to some vague personal failing rather than being acknowledged as a function of a patriarchal culture and a masculine social order. To read
O'Brien as having failed to mature as a writer is to exonerate these dominant cultural
and social forces since it misses the point that her maturity lies in her critique of institutionalized male dominance and sexist values for making it nearly impossible to fulfil
one's potential as an Irish female subject. I wish to turn now to O'Brien's portrayals of
young female subjectivity in five of her novels, to explore in greater detail her fictional
interrogation of Irish female belatedness.

[25] Greenwood, *Edna O'Brien*, 23.
[26] Pelan, 'Reflections on a Connemara Dietrich', 19.
[27] Sean McMahon, 'A Sex by Themselves: An Interim Report on the Novels of Edna O'Brien', *Éire-
Ireland* 2, no. 1 (1967), 79. Quoted in Pelan, 'Reflections on a Connemara Dietrich', 20.
[28] O'Brien, 'The Silly and the Serious', 479.

LIMINALITY AND THE QUEST
FOR IRISH WOMANHOOD

Edna O'Brien has written a number of novels that can be characterized as *Bildungsromane*, although all of them also critique the genre. The list includes the afore-mentioned *The Country Girls Trilogy*, to which an epilogue was added in 1986, *A Pagan Place* (1970), and *Down by the River* (1996). Each of these works dramatizes women's dif-ficulty in achieving mature subjectivity and agency in late twentieth-century Ireland. Of course, Joyce also felt this to be the case in the late 1800s and early 1900s, but there is no escaping the overt and subtle realities of oppression for O'Brien's heroines, even if they flee postcolonial Ireland. As Kathryn Kleypas argues, O'Brien uses the *Bildungsroman* form to show that the 'vision of individual development for the female protagonist is seen in a series of clashes with an inimical milieu; these clashes often cultivate not inte-gration but withdrawal, rebellion, or even suicide. Social integration can only be achieved by severe compromise on the part of the woman.'[29] This emphasis on a form of compromise that is coercive and inimical to women means that in O'Brien's fictional universe social acceptance is dependent upon her female subjects submitting to forces of iconicization and infantilization that lead to outcomes that are themselves belated, which is to say indeterminate, unsatisfying, or ambiguous. O'Brien's depiction of the impossibility of female self-realization, therefore, stands in sharp contrast to the possi-bilities afforded male protagonists by temporary or permanent escape in Joyce's fictions of maturation.

It is striking that of the female protagonists who possess names in the novels listed above, all are associated with Irish female icons: Cathleen Ni Houlihan in the case of Caithleen Brady, St Bridget, the female patron of Ireland, in the case of Baba Brennan, and the Virgin Mother in the case of Mary MacNamara. Cathleen Ni Houlihan is of course the mythic embodiment of Ireland itself, who inspires men to fight for her free-dom. In W. B. Yeats's (1865–1939) landmark 1902 drama about her, Cathleen became his private icon, given dramatic life by Maud Gonne in the lead role. In her trilogy, O'Brien writes a grotesque parody of Irish men fighting for Ireland when Catholic vigilantes seek to forcibly send Caithleen Brady back to her father's house and in the process assault her lover Eugene Gaillard for corrupting her innocence. Although Eugene has previously dismissed Caithleen's fears of just such an event, maintaining that it cannot happen because 'it's the twentieth century', the men who assault him say they have the right to do so because 'We won our fight for freedom. It's our country now.'[30] By this measure, the spoils of independence include the circumscription of female agency by patriotic men.

---

[29] Kathryn L. Kleypas, 'Edna O'Brien's *A Pagan Place* and the Irish *Bildungsroman* Tradition', in P. J. Mathews (ed.), *New Voices in Irish Criticism* (Dublin: Four Courts Press, 2000), 60.

[30] Edna O'Brien, *The Country Girls Trilogy and Epilogue* (New York: Penguin, 1986), 286, 300.

Caithleen's friend and rival Baba is named for a saint who is 'associated with thresholds,'[31] suggesting that St Bridget is herself a figure of belatedness. This sense of permanent liminality, of being forever poised between childhood and maturity, is of course reinforced by Baba's childhood nickname, an idiomatic Irish term meaning 'baby', which she will carry into adulthood. Likewise, Mary MacNamara, the abject protagonist of *Down by the River*, is named for a religious figure poised between childhood and maturity, who embodies the paradox of being simultaneously virgin and mother. In keeping with the cultural logic of the destructive virgin/whore dichotomy, when Mary is seen as having violated the terms of her social integration by seeking an abortion after being raped and impregnated, she is transformed into a repentant prostitute and renamed Magdalene. Such women must be wholly good or wholly bad in this repressive cultural climate; there is no liveable middle ground. Similarly, when the unnamed narrator of *A Pagan Place* sees two family members kiss each other, her thoughts instantly turn to a biblical binary: 'Your aunt and your mother kissed and you thought of Mary Magdalene and her sister Martha and how one was a saint and one was a sinner, and then you thought of you and Emma.'[32] In constructing her mature self, the narrator will act according to the same zero-sum logic and choose Martha's path.

Unlike *A Pagan Place*, *The Country Girls Trilogy and Epilogue* and *Down by the River* present potential alternatives to these binary choices, but these alternatives are shown to be iconic and therefore also painfully limiting. As Elizabeth A. Chase notes, Caithleen strives to plot her own life according to that of a romantic novel, specifically *Jane Eyre* (1847), and find some emotional fulfilment in her prescribed roles as wife and mother.[33] In so doing, however, she is attempting to replace one icon of femininity with another by becoming a kind of secular, literary saint, 'the long-suffering heroine who, in the end, achieves a suitable marriage as a reward for her patience and virtue.'[34] As Chase points out, Caithleen 'tries throughout the *Trilogy* to find her own husband-God figure', but 'each relationship fails to deliver the self-annihilation it originally promises.'[35] Similarly, in *Down by the River*, an alternative to religious iconicization emerges in the form of consumer culture. Yet it too demands female suffering without paying any emotional dividends, as we see when Noni, a member of an anti-abortion group, is bitterly disappointed when her good taste and strenuous housekeeping are ignored by the fellow group members she invites to her house, and when other characters participate in the rituals of female grooming (which Mary's friend Tara calls 'trying to be grown-up'[36]) in order to seek and to retain male approval. As O'Brien shows, these rituals are themselves occasioned by the icons of contemporary femininity, the photoshopped objects of veneration which appear in women's magazines, promoting the gendered fantasy of remaining forever youthful, forever 'girlish'.

---

[31] Wanda Balzano, 'Godot Land and Its Ghosts: The Uncanny Genre and Gender of Edna O'Brien's "Sister Imelda"', in Lisa Colletta and Maureen O'Connor (eds), *Wild Colonial Girl: Essays on Edna O'Brien* (Madison, WI: University of Wisconsin Press, 2006), 107.

[32] Edna O'Brien, *A Pagan Place* (London: Penguin, 1971), 48.

[33] Elizabeth A. Chase, 'Rewriting Genre in *The Country Girls Trilogy*', *New Hibernia Review* 14, no. 3 (2010), 91–105.

[34] Ibid., 93.   [35] Ibid., 99.

[36] Edna O'Brien, *Down by the River* (London: Phoenix, 1997), 167.

This belatedness, whereby the Irish female subject remains forever poised on the threshold between girlhood and womanhood, is further reflected in the very title of *Girls in Their Married Bliss*, which should represent a contradiction in terms. In Ireland, a 'girl' traditionally meant a maiden, one who was as yet unmarried though of marriageable age, and so marriage should turn girls into women (of the house). Yet Caithleen and Baba remain girls even when they have fulfilled their designated duties by becoming wives and mothers. Eugene's renaming of Caithleen as Kate reflects this, as it at once infantilizes and 'modernizes' her by (nominally) removing her Irish identity, which he sees as immature. Throughout their relationship, Eugene vacillates between adoring and decrying his future wife's girlishness. Caithleen frequently worries that he will find her 'childish' and he does indeed call her 'a very—foolish—little girl'[37] during an argument in *The Lonely Girl*. Later, in the course of a row that will break them up temporarily, Eugene tells Caithleen, 'Young girls are like a stone, . . . nothing really touches them. You can't have a relationship with a stone, at least I can't.'[38]

Yet Caithleen Brady rightly believes that it is her girlishness that Eugene finds appealing. She hopes that when they become engaged she will 'stay young always' and Eugene tells her that the ring he gives her has to last not forever but for 'As long as you keep your girlish laughter.'[39] This proves to be prophetic, as when he becomes disappointed in Kate and their marriage begins to fail he mourns the 'simple, uncomplicated girl'[40] that he had thought she was and that he had hoped she would stay (complaints that anticipate those made by Sean McMahon about the trilogy itself, as we have seen above). Given the mixed messages that she gets from her partner about whether or not she should grow up, it is perhaps not surprising that in *Girls in Their Married Bliss* Kate wishes that the biblical Eve, and by extension all women, could have remained as a rib of Adam.[41] Eve herself is the ur-example of the pitfalls of female maturation, as acting as an agent and seeking knowledge gets her expelled from Eden by her maker and blamed by the forces of patriarchy for the downfall of mankind. For Kate, it comes to seem that annihilation is preferable to trying to achieve the unachievable and become a mature Irish woman.

A Pagan Place also explores Irish female belatedness, specifically through the idea of the 'prodigal', a word that carries strong biblical connotations. The unnamed narrator's elder sister Emma has a disastrous maturation narrative, becoming pregnant by an unknown man and giving birth to a baby whom she immediately gives up. In the aftermath of the narrator's sexual abuse by a priest—an event her mother refers to, bizarrely, as her 'debut'—her father beats her, then admits that 'he was hot-tempered but said he meant no harm, that it was for your benefit and was to instil in you good conduct. He said one prodigal in any family was enough. Maybe you had wanted to compete with Emma in iniquity.'[42] In referring to Emma here as a 'prodigal', her father pointedly associates her maturing sexuality with disobedience and with belatedness, and implies that she will in fact remain 'prodigal' indefinitely.

---

[37] O'Brien, *The Country Girls Trilogy and Epilogue*, 231, 261.   [38] Ibid., 359.
[39] Ibid., 315, 316.   [40] Ibid., 406.   [41] Ibid., 500.   [42] O'Brien, *A Pagan Place*, 179, 184.

This is a far cry from how the minor male character Ambie is treated. Although he impregnates a servant, it is she who is punished by being forced to induce a miscarriage. Indeed, Emma's so-called prodigality seems far more appealing than the other paths taken by female characters in the novel, as the 'too brainy'[43] Miss Davitt drowns herself and the narrator's mother is completely disempowered. Even the most mundane aspects of female behaviour and deportment are policed, often in explicitly patriarchal and religious terms: 'You tried to whistle. Only men should whistle. The Blessed Virgin blushed when women whistled and likewise when women crossed their legs.'[44] This regime of gendered control is further underlined when the narrator, having decided to become a nun, is given a wallet by her mother, embroidered with initials that stand for 'Enfant de Marie'.[45] Wife, mother, nun—all 'vocations' lead not to maturation but to continued infantilization and subordination.

O'Brien revisits the powerful and contradictory forces that retard the development of mature femininity in modern Ireland in *Down by the River*, which, as Christine St Peter and Sophia Hillan have argued, is a retelling of *The Country Girls*, with Mary MacNamara as Caithleen's counterpart and her friends Tara and Mona taking it in turns to play the Baba role.[46] Like Miss X, her real-life counterpart, Mary is caught between girlhood and womanhood, viewed by her father and by the Irish social order as both female child and adult woman.[47] In his first attack on Mary, her father asks her to repeat the childhood doggerel 'Sugar and spice, and all things nice / That's what little girls are made of, made of',[48] yet he subsequently assaults her because she is wearing makeup and her mother's dress. Similarly, Irish society cannot decide if Mary is girl or woman, maiden or mother, Virgin Mary or Mary Magdalene. On the one hand, she is deprived of agency by being continually referred to as 'wee' and 'little' and being forced to obtain her father's permission to be examined by a doctor or represented by a lawyer; on the other, Mary is seen as powerful enough, in her meek rebelliousness, to threaten the nation itself, producing a public anxiety that is revealed when the anti-abortion activists promise (or threaten) to 'make a true Irish girl'[49] of her. These misogynistic, contradictory responses to young womanhood are crystallized in the description of Mary as 'Some little slut about to pour piss on the nation's breast.'[50] Even those who sympathize with her recognize that her case exemplifies the disjunctions caused by competing ideas of Irish femininity.

---

[43] Ibid., 28.   [44] Ibid., 99.   [45] Ibid., 201.

[46] Christine St Peter, 'Petrifying Time: Incest Narratives from Contemporary Ireland', in Liam Harte and Michael Parker (eds), *Contemporary Irish Fiction: Themes, Tropes, Theories* (New York: Macmillan, 2000), 131; Sophia Hillan, 'On the Side of Life: Edna O'Brien's Trilogy of Contemporary Ireland', in Colletta and O'Connor (eds), *Wild Colonial Girl*, 151.

[47] 'Miss X' was the anonym given to the fourteen-year-old girl at the centre of a 1992 legal case which plunged the Republic into an abortion crisis. The girl, who was pregnant as a result of rape by a family friend, was initially prevented by the Irish High Court from travelling to Britain for an abortion. This judgement, which provoked widespread public opposition, was subsequently overturned by the Supreme Court on the grounds that there was a substantial risk to the life of the teenager, who had threatened suicide. The case led to a change in the law to allow Irish women the right to travel abroad for a termination.

[48] O'Brien, *Down by the River*, 4.   [49] Ibid., 283.   [50] Ibid., 190.

An anonymous priest, addressing Mary as 'Dear little Magdalene', writes to tell her that she has aged before she 'had even blossomed', while her lawyer reflects that

> there is really no such thing as youth, only luck, and the enormity of something which can happen, whence a person, any person, is brought deeper and more profoundly into sorrow and once they have gone there, they can't come back, they have to live in it, live in that dark, and find some glimmer in it.[51]

As in other of O'Brien's novels, then, the process of female maturation in *Down by the River* appears not as natural, inevitable, and progressive but as recursive, ambiguous, and indeterminate, leaving the protagonist in a state of seemingly permanent liminality. Both it and the other novels discussed in this section end inconclusively. *The Country Girls* and *The Lonely Girl* end up as suspended romances without concrete evidence of maturation or even a moment of Joycean epiphany. *Girls in Their Married Bliss* ends with Kate's sterilization and Baba's realization that 'she was looking at someone of whom too much had been cut away, some important region that they both knew nothing about'.[52] This indeterminacy is echoed in the conclusion of the epilogue, with Baba's dawning awareness, as she waits at the train station to receive Kate's body, that 'there are some things in this world that you cannot ask, and oh, Agnus Dei, there are some things in this world you cannot answer'.[53] As Kristine Byron notes, this open-ended conclusion leaves it to the reader 'to try to formulate the missing questions and answers'.[54] The meaning of the text, and of Kate's life, is thus belated, indefinitely deferred. If her counterpart Stephen Dedalus has not yet fulfilled his artistic destiny at the end of Joyce's narrative, he is nevertheless still alive, still full of the potential that his bird-girl epiphany revealed to him. In the final section of this chapter, I will briefly consider how O'Brien's revisions of the Joycean epiphany further underscore her explorations of the permanent liminality of the Irish female subject.

REWRITING THE JOYCEAN EPIPHANY

Many critics have recognized O'Brien's artistic debt to Joyce, but few have acknowledged that her frequent use of Joycean allusion carries with it a critical charge. In particular, O'Brien's work often highlights the dangers of Joyce's iconicization of Irish women. Indeed, one of O'Brien's most cited statements about Joyce, in which she referred to him as 'a blinding light and father of us all',[55] is hardly as complimentary as is sometimes

---

[51] Ibid., 240, 229–30.   [52] O'Brien, *The Country Girls Trilogy and Epilogue*, 508.
[53] Ibid., 532.
[54] Kristine Byron, '"In the Name of the Mother…": Reading and Revision in Edna O'Brien's *Country Girls Trilogy and Epilogue*', in Colletta and O'Connor (eds), *Wild Colonial Girl*, 27.
[55] Philip Roth, 'A Conversation with Edna O'Brien', *New York Times Book Review*, 18 November 1984. Quoted in Pelan, 'Reflections on a Connemara Dietrich', 37.

implied, in that a blinding light does not provide the best circumstance for artistic inven-tion. And given the kinds of actual and would-be fathers who have appeared in her fiction, characterizing Joyce as the ur-patriarch is not necessarily an unqualified homage. In fact, as Greenwood points out, O'Brien has given the forename James to several of her most abusive fictional fathers, including Caithleen's in *The Country Girls*, at whose hands she suffers physically, and Mary's in *Down by the River*, whose domineering behaviour and attitude stifle his daughter's subjectivity.[56] O'Brien's sense of her own literary inherit-ance, her supposed standing as Joyce's dutiful daughter, is therefore far more complex than is commonly assumed. Her use of Joycean intertextuality, particularly in her fictions of maturation, often functions not merely as homage but also as critique, not only of Joyce but of male-authored fiction of female maturation more generally.

The ending of *Down by the River* stands as an example of this. The novel culminates in a scene in which Mary MacNamara sings to a boisterous crowd in a disco, having been summoned to perform by a disc jockey who dubs her 'the little linnet'.[57] The latent Joycean allusion in this remark is amplified in the novel's penultimate paragraph, which conjures up a vision of a snow-covered Irish landscape suspended in a state of 'cladded stillness', as O'Brien's bird-girl waits 'for the face to materialise, the face that she will sing the words to, sing regardless, a paean of expectancy into the gaudy void'.[58] The final moments of *Down by the River* thus represent both a doubling and an immediate evacu-ation of two Joycean epiphanies. O'Brien's bird-girl image echoes Joyce's ironic back-ward glance at a version of his callow yet brilliant self, as embodied by Stephen in *A Portrait*, while her snow allusion explicitly references what many critics have read autobiographically as Joyce's anxious forward projection of a potential middle-aged self in the character of Gabriel Conroy in 'The Dead'. In these intertextual moments, Mary's liminality and lack of maturation are underlined as, once again, her subjectivity is defined by its relational and interstitial character.

However, unlike Joyce's male protagonists, O'Brien's heroine does not undergo a life-changing revelation. The Joycean epiphany is, by definition, momentary yet definitively transformative for those who experience it. In *Down by the River*, the epiphanic moment is even more fleeting and falls short of being transformative, as readers are given no ink-ling of how the effects of this episode will reverberate for this young woman, in part because her fate has always depended on what dwells in the souls of others. Indeed, far from marking a decisive step towards personal growth, the novel's conclusion suggests that Mary's song proves more meaningful for her listeners than for her. In singing a seemingly wordless song that is characterized as a response to the 'innermost cries'[59] of her listeners' souls, Mary functions more as an icon and catalyst than as a young woman who has mature agency over her own life.

[56] Greenwood, *Edna O'Brien*, 89.   [57] O'Brien, *Down by the River*, 297.
[58] Ibid. The linnet reference also carries Yeatsian connotations. For more on the novel's intertextual aspects, see Jane Elizabeth Dougherty, '"Never Tear the Linnet from the Leaf": The Feminist Intertextuality of Edna O'Brien's *Down by the River*', *Frontiers: A Journal of Women Studies* 31, no. 3 (2010), 77–102.
[59] O'Brien, *Down by the River*, 298.

In *The Country Girls*, Caithleen Brady undergoes an experience that bears significant similarities to that of Mary and in which Joyce's *A Portrait* is again an intertext. Late in the novel, there is a pivotal, sexually charged scene in which she is alone in her Dublin lodgings after a night out with Mr Gentleman, her older, married, and thoroughly inappropriate suitor. Emotionally needy and semi-inebriated, she responds inwardly to Mr Gentleman's utterance of her name:

> He looked at me for a long time. That look of his which was half sexual, half mystic; and then he said my name very gently. ('Caithleen.') I could hear the bulrushes sighing when he said my name that way, and I could hear the curlew too, and all the lonesome sounds of Ireland.[60]

Unlike Stephen Dedalus, whose climactic bird-girl epiphany crystallizes his artist destiny, Caithleen's apprehension of her name as a kind of bird-call suggests that she has learned to embrace a preordained iconicity as an Irish woman which forecloses the possibility of her becoming an artist herself, though she retains her artistic sensibility throughout her life. Nor will this moment of recognition last. Whereas Stephen's epiphany heralds his embrace of a definitive, mature vocation, one which combines the sacred and the profane, Caithleen's signals her pursuit of romantic fulfilment. But rather than an emotionally secure and stable domestic life, she will find instead that she compulsively seeks a repetition of her youthful moments of passionate intensity.

The Joycean snow, too, becomes symbolically ominous in relation to the romance of Caithleen and Mr Gentleman. 'Softly and obliquely' it falls when in *The Country Girls* he first kisses her, in a passage whose syntactical rhythms echo those of the celebrated closing paragraph of 'The Dead': 'It fell on hedges and on the trees behind the hedges, and on the treeless fields in the distance, and slowly and quietly it changed the colour and the shape of things, until evening outside the motorcar had a mantle of soft white down.'[61] Caithleen's intuition that Mr Gentleman is about to profess his love for her is confirmed when he stops the car and cups her face in his hands:

> And that moment was wholly and totally perfect for me; and everything that I had suffered up to then was comforted in the softness of his soft, lisping voice, whispering, whispering, like the snowflakes. A hawthorn tree in front of us was coated white as sugar, and the snow got worse and was blowing so hard that we could barely see. He kissed me. It was a real kiss. It affected my entire body. My toes, though they were numb and pinched in the new shoes, responded to that kiss, and for a few minutes my soul was lost. Then I felt a drip on the end of my nose and it bothered me.[62]

Caithleen's rapturous, quasi-spiritual response to Mr Gentleman's words and actions are clearly suggestive of an epiphanic experience, yet O'Brien determinedly refuses to allow this moment to become life-defining or life-changing. Caithleen's romantic ecstasy is interrupted by banal irritants (her pinched toes, her runny nose) which curtail her bliss.

---

[60] O'Brien, *The Country Girls and Epilogue*, 163.   [61] Ibid., 90.   [62] Ibid.

Furthermore, the romance of the snow is offset by its blinding intensity, which prevents good judgement, and by the presence of a hawthorn tree, which carries associations of ill luck in other of her fictions. There is also the symbolism of naming to consider. The snow is associated with the voice of Mr Gentleman, whose real name is Jacques, the French equivalent of the name of Caithleen's abusive father (and of O'Brien's artistic patriarch and mentor). This suggests that Caithleen is deeply in thrall to a man who is both suitor and surrogate father. A relationship that she associates with her maturation into womanhood and, subliminally, with her being 'reparented' by a more loving—and, significantly, foreign—man is in fact one which is fraught with emotional implications.

The snow that falls in *The Country Girls Trilogy and Epilogue* and *Down by the River* has an analogue in the ground frost that appears in 'Irish Revel', O'Brien's most sustained fictional revision of Joyce, which appeared in her first collection, *The Love Object and Other Stories* (1968).[63] An oblique retelling of 'The Dead' from the standpoint of a shy seventeen-year-old girl called Mary, the story moves the action from an urban to a rural space in the west of Ireland. As the only daughter of a poor farming family, Mary's life is one of relentless drudgery, a fact which makes the arrival of an invitation to attend a party at the local hotel all the more exciting. The invitation heightens Mary's memories of John Roland, an English painter who visited the area two years earlier and for whom she developed intense feelings, despite him telling her that he loved his wife and children. Mary cycles to the party with hopes of seeing him there, only to discover that she has been invited in order to act as a servant. Not only is Roland not there but the men who do attend are boorish and the rest of the partygoers pretentious and shallow. Disillusioned, Mary wishes she were at home and leaves early the next morning because she has work to do on the farm. Half a mile from home, she stops to reflect on the events of the night before:

> Frost was general all over Ireland; frost like a weird blossom on the branches, on the riverbank from which Long John Salmon leaped in his great, hairy nakedness, on the ploughs left out all winter; frost on the stony fields, and on all the slime and ugliness of the world.
>
> Walking again she wondered if and what she would tell her mother and her brothers about it, and if all parties were as bad. She was at the top of the hill now, and could see her own house, like a little white box at the end of the world, waiting to receive her.[64]

Whereas Gabriel Conroy's snow is a blanket, Mary's frost is a kind of membrane, leaving visible what the snow has covered and denying her even the illusion of transcendence or escape from 'the slime and ugliness of the world'. The frost also crystallizes Mary's grim destiny, in the shape of the coffin-like 'white box' that is her home. Although she continues to hope for a sweetheart and a romance that might transform her life, O'Brien's

---

[63] For more extended readings of this story, see Pelan, 'Reflections on a Connemara Dietrich' and Sandra Manoogian Pearce, 'Snow Through the Ages: Echoes of "The Dead" in O'Brien, Lavin, and O'Faolain', in Michael Patrick Gillespie (ed.), *Joyce Through the Ages: A Non-Linear View* (Gainesville, FL: University of Florida Press, 1999), 165–78.

[64] Edna O'Brien, 'Irish Revel', in *The Love Object and Other Stories* (London: Penguin, 1970), 113–14.

imagery implies that her young protagonist's maturation as a poor, rural, Irish woman will be characterized by stasis rather than progression.

Edna O'Brien's Joycean allusions and intertextual references reveal the extent to which his heroes are privileged in ways her heroines are not, as the epiphanies and departures of the former offer at least the illusion of transcendence and the possibility of meaningful escape. In her fiction as in her literary career, O'Brien repeatedly asks us to focus on the belatedness of Irish female maturation, highlighting the ways in which women's subjectivity has been thwarted and retarded by the combined forces of patriarchal oppression and public iconicization, including the iconicization engendered by Ireland's literary fathers. Given the many obstacles that have hampered her own progress, O'Brien's success as an Irish female artist, albeit one whose recognition as such has been belated, impels us at last to consider what a unique, pioneering, and prophetic figure she has been in Irish literary history.

FURTHER READING

Chase, Elizabeth A. 'Rewriting Genre in *The Country Girls Trilogy*'. *New Hibernia Review* 14, no. 3 (2010): 91–105.

Colletta, Lisa and Maureen O'Connor (eds). *Wild Colonial Girl: Essays on Edna O'Brien*. Madison, WI: University of Wisconsin Press, 2006.

Dougherty, Jane Elizabeth. ' "Never Tear the Linnet from the Leaf": The Feminist Intertextuality of Edna O'Brien's *Down by the River*'. *Frontiers: A Journal of Women Studies* 31, no. 3 (2010): 77–102.

Dougherty, Jane Elizabeth. 'From Invisible Child to Abject Maternal Body: Crises of Knowledge in Edna O'Brien's *Down by the River*'. *Critique: Studies in Contemporary Fiction* 53, no. 4 (2012): 393–409.

Esty, Jed. *Unseasonable Youth: Modernism, Colonialism, and the Fiction of Development*. Oxford: Oxford University Press, 2012.

Greenwood, Amanda. *Edna O'Brien*. Tavistock: Northcote House, 2003.

Laing, Kathryn, Sinéad Mooney, and Maureen O'Connor (eds). *Edna O'Brien: New Critical Perspectives*. Dublin: Carysfort Press, 2006.

Morgan, Eileen. 'Mapping Out a Landscape of Female Suffering: Edna O'Brien's Demythologizing Novels'. *Women's Studies: An Interdisciplinary Journal* 29, no. 4 (2000): 449–76.

Pearce, Sandra Manoogian. 'Snow Through the Ages: Echoes of "The Dead" in O'Brien, Lavin, and O'Faolain'. In Michael Patrick Gillespie (ed.), *Joyce Through The Ages: A Non-Linear View*. Gainesville, FL: University of Florida Press, 1999: 165–78.

Pecora, Vincent P. ' "The Dead" and The Generosity of the Word'. *PMLA: Publications of the Modern Language Association of America* 101, no. 2 (1986): 233–45.

Rooks-Hughes, Lorna. 'The Family and the Female Body in the Novels of Edna O'Brien and Julia O'Faolain'. *Canadian Journal of Irish Studies* 22, no. 12 (1996): 83–97.

St Peter, Christine. 'Petrifying Time: Incest Narratives from Contemporary Ireland'. In Liam Harte and Michael Parker (eds), *Contemporary Irish Fiction: Themes, Tropes, Theories*. New York: Macmillan, 2000: 125–44.

Weston, Elizabeth. 'Constitutive Trauma in Edna O'Brien's *The Country Girls Trilogy*: The Romance of Reenactment'. *Tulsa Studies in Women's Literature* 29, no. 1 (2010): 83–105.

CHAPTER 17

....

'HALF-ARSED MODERN'

John McGahern and the Failed State

....

FRANK SHOVLIN

ON 27 November 1967, Jimi Hendrix was presented with a birthday cake to mark his turning twenty-five. Shortly afterwards, he and his band took to the stage in the Whitla Hall in Queen's University Belfast for what would be the one and only live performance by the Jimi Hendrix Experience on the island of Ireland. The *Belfast Telegraph*'s correspondent was blown away but not necessarily impressed: 'The noise being blasted out at the Whitla Hall last night during the Jimi Hendrix concert was the loudest I have ever heard. It was so bad you could feel your insides—and even your chair—resonating.'[1] Within two years of this deafening cacophony, Belfast was experiencing a more sinister kind of noise as it became engulfed in a bitter civil war, and the carefree joys of that night in the Whitla would seem drawn from a different, more innocent time.

Three days earlier, the hall witnessed a rather more sedate event, although in its own way it was no less historic. Seamus Heaney (1939–2013), the young Derry poet whose first collection, *Death of a Naturalist*, had been published by Faber and Faber the previous year to widespread critical acclaim, introduced a lecture by John McGahern (1934–2006), whose first novel, *The Barracks*, had been issued by the same publishing house in 1963, and whose second, *The Dark*, had caused a sensation on its appearance in 1965. The lecture, on the subject of Herman Melville's 1853 short story, 'Bartleby, the Scrivener', was titled 'I Would Prefer Not To'.[2] Among the audience that day were Madeline Green, who would later become McGahern's second wife, and poet Richard Murphy (1927–2018), also of the Faber stable and a friend and correspondent of McGahern's. In his

---

[1] George Hamilton, 'Cool reception at the Whitla', *Belfast Telegraph*, 28 November 1967. On this concert, see http://novdec1967.blogspot.ie/2010/02/27-november-1967-whitla-hall-festival.html. Accessed 24 August 2016.

[2] See http://www.belfastfestivalanthology.com/media/60sArchive.pdf. Accessed 24 August 2016.

autobiography, Murphy recalls the haunting impact McGahern's lecture had on him and the Belfast audience:

> When John McGahern lectured on Herman Melville's 'Bartleby the Scrivener', he made an oral poem out of his love for the story, the style and the vision. The rhythm and sound of his Leitrim voice uttering the refrain, 'I'd prefer not to', the clarity of his obscure thought, the trembling of the piece of paper he was holding in his hand, kept me on tenterhooks, not to miss a word, hoping he'd not break down. Of course he didn't, and went on to talk about Proust's *Contre Sainte-Beuve* and to quote Bergson on laughter and Kafka's story *The Metamorphosis* about a man who turned into an insect.[3]

Murphy was not the only one there to be mesmerized by McGahern's performance. Ray Rosenfeld of the *Belfast Telegraph* was similarly enthusiastic in his report for the paper:

> Mr McGahern clearly has a profound love for the art and the thought of Melville and he revealed this so movingly that even the totally ignorant would have been drawn into an equal absorption. . . . He took sequence after sequence from the story, reading in a voice of rare beauty. He subjected them to an analysis so acute and so detailed that with any other critic it could have damaged the fabric, but with him it only revealed the quality of the work.[4]

This is not, perhaps, the John McGahern the majority of the reading public are accustomed to encountering, for McGahern, since his death in 2006, has become the subject of considerable mythmaking: gentleman farmer, chronicler of a bygone age, last great *cause célèbre* of Irish literary censorship. And yet while there are elements of truth in each of these myths, to adhere wholly to any one of them is to do a disservice to this most rigorous, learned, and committed of artists. McGahern was a writer who, in insisting on the primacy of the Western canon while at the same time casting a cold eye on the Ireland of his time, provided Irish fiction and cultural life with a chronicle of unmatched accuracy and delicacy. What allowed him to become such an acute recorder of the Ireland of his times was the fact that, unlike those leviathans who preceded him—James Joyce (1882–1941), Samuel Beckett (1906–89), and even, eventually, W. B. Yeats (1865–1939)—he decided to live out his days in the country of his birth and to bear witness to its changing social fabric from the vantage point of a tiny Leitrim parish, away from the clamour of the metropolitan centres of Dublin and London that had so often seen Irish writers compromise themselves in the past. Like Melville's Bartleby, he chose to live life entirely on his own terms and was unswerving in his devotion to bring into the light his vision of the world around and within him.

While McGahern felt able to stay in Ireland despite all its shortcomings, one of those writers he most admired—Joyce—remains the best example of an Irish artist who went

---

[3] Richard Murphy, *The Kick: A Life Among Writers* (London: Granta, 2002), 261–2.
[4] Ray Rosenfeld, 'John McGahern gives insight on Melville', *Belfast Telegraph*, 25 November 1967.

into a determined self-exile in order to forge for himself a soul and a way of life away from the constraints of his native land. Joyce's brother, Stanislaus, also became much admired by McGahern, and the Leitrim writer thinks of him when trying to come to grips with a definition of Ireland in all its colours:

> Remarkable work in the short story has come continually out of Ireland, but it is likely that its very strength is due to the absence of a strong central tradition. Stanislaus Joyce is most persuasive in his articulation of this problem for the Irish writer, if problem it be; for to live here is to come into daily contact with a rampant individualism and localism dominating a vague, fragmented, often purely time-serving, national identity.[5]

Here, McGahern is thinking of Stanislaus's unsparing descriptions of the Ireland of his youth, provided in his *Dublin Diary* (1962) and in his account of later life with James in Trieste, *My Brother's Keeper* (1958), in which he wrote:

> In Ireland, a country which has seen revolution in every generation, there is properly speaking no national tradition. Nothing is stable in the country; nothing is stable in the minds of the people. When the Irish artist begins to write, he has to create his moral world from chaos by himself, for himself. Yet, though this is an enormous dis-advantage for a host of writers of good average talent, it proves to be an enormous advantage for men of original genius, such as Shaw, Yeats or my brother.[6]

From as early as the late 1950s, John McGahern could see for himself that he too would have to make his own way without the aid of a strong national tradition. He saw, too, that he lived in a young country barely able to look after itself but with enough of interest happening across the land to feed the imagination of a dedicated and ambitious writer such as he was.

Seamus Heaney once described John McGahern as being a writer who was on a 'secret errand, a soul journey'.[7] It would be a mistake, as such, felt Heaney, to read him as a soci-ologist. Instead, right from the first sentence of *The Barracks* to the final words of *Memoir* (2005), one must take McGahern as a unified whole, a writer who, like Yeats and Joyce, spent a lifetime in a conscious act of self-creation. And if one reads McGahern in this chronological fashion, one sees a writer coming to an accommodation with life in general and, more specifically, with a life lived in a newly independent Ireland. Sergeant Reegan, the key figure, along with his terminally ill wife Elizabeth, in *The Barracks* is a garda in the very first cohort recruited by the unarmed police force of the Irish Free State. He is bitterly frustrated with his life in the new, narrow, limited state, a country

---

[5] John McGahern, 'Dubliners', in *Love of the World: Essays*, ed. Stanley van der Ziel (London: Faber and Faber, 2009), 200.

[6] Stanislaus Joyce, *My Brother's Keeper*, ed. Richard Ellmann (Cambridge, MA: Da Capo Press, 2003), 185. McGahern admired greatly the lesser-known *Dublin Diary of Stanislaus Joyce*, edited by George Harris Healey, which was published by Faber in 1962.

[7] RTÉ Radio sound archive.

which had begun with such hope and pride for those young recruits, many of whom, as IRA volunteers in the Anglo-Irish War, had fought for Irish freedom:

> The British had withdrawn. The Capital was in a fever of excitement and change. New classes were forming, blacksmiths and clerks filling the highest offices in the turn of an hour. Some who had worried how their next loaf or day might come were attending ceremonial functions. There was a brand new tricolour to wave high; a language of their own to learn; new anthems of faith-and-fatherland to beat on the drum of the multitude; but most of all, unseen and savage behind these floral screens, was the struggle for the numbered seats of power.[8]

Although McGahern is always insistent on the need to keep absolutely separate the realms of artifice and autobiography, one cannot but see in his vivid account of life in a mid-century police barracks images of what his own young life must have been like in those years after the death of his mother in 1944, and the subsequent years lived with his father, Sergeant Frank McGahern, in Cootehall barracks in County Roscommon.

The policemen of McGahern's fictionalized barracks are no longer young, and the first flush of excitement at being part of some new national adventure has dissipated:

> These police recruits walking the Phoenix Park in the evenings, or on the lighted trams that went down past Phibsboro' to the music halls, what were their dreams? They knew that lightning promotion could come to the favoured. They saw the young girls stand to watch them from the pavements as they marched to Mass on Sunday mornings.
>
> Now they sat and remembered, thirty years later, waiting to go to their homes in the rain.[9]

Sergeant Reegan, as the most intelligent of the guards in the barracks, feels the strain and tug of disappointment more acutely than the others, who manage to find solace in every-day social activities like listening to the radio, idle chat, and waiting anxiously for sports results. In many ways he is a version of McGahern's own father, as is Moran, the demoralized ex-IRA officer of *Amongst Women* (1990). The great problem for men like these is that they have known both hope and power when young and have seen these stripped away by a kind of freemasonry of mediocrity promoted in the new Ireland:

> But he'd been born into a generation wild with ideals: they'd free Ireland, they'd be a nation once again: he was fighting with a flying column in the hills when he was little more than a boy, he donned the uniform of the Garda Síochána and swore to preserve the peace of The Irish Free State when it was declared in 1920, getting petty promotion immediately because he'd won officer's rank in the fighting, but there he stayed—to watch the Civil War and the years that followed in silent disgust, remaining on because he saw nothing else worth doing. Marriage and children had

---

[8] John McGahern, *The Barracks* (London: Faber and Faber, 1983), 28.   [9] Ibid., 28–9.

tethered him in this village, and the children remembered the bitterness of his laugh the day he threw them his medal with the coloured ribbon for their play.[10]

In these three passages from *The Barracks*, McGahern covers a great deal of ground: the new flag (which would eventually be chosen for the cover image of *Amongst Women*); the new language, Irish, which becomes the medium of schoolyard coercion in *The Leavetaking* (1974); the close weaving together of Church with state as the guards march to Sunday mass. That Catholic power, merely hinted at in the description of the marching recruits, was soon to flex its muscles in an attempt to crush the young McGahern as he brought his next novel, *The Dark*, to publication.

The Dark, as well as being perhaps the most influential and best-known twentieth-century Irish *Bildungsroman* after Joyce's *A Portrait of the Artist as a Young Man* (1916), is a savage critique of power and its abuse. This abuse comes in several forms but is at its most frightening and disturbing in the unwanted sexual advances made on young Mahoney, the novel's central protagonist, first by his father and later by a priest cousin, Father Gerald. From today's vantage point the novel reads like a warning shot of what was to come, the many abuse scandals that have broken the Catholic Church's power in Ireland and accelerated secularism to a breathtaking speed. But when first published it must have seemed like an extraordinary affront to McGahern's Catholic school employers who quickly moved, under the orders of Archbishop John Charles McQuaid, to have him dismissed. The Republic of Ireland of this period was, thinks McGahern, a theocratic state in all but name. 'I believe', he argued, that 'it's not too crude to say that Church and State had colluded to bring about a climate that was insular, repressive, sectarian. Anybody with eyes or ears could see that the whole spirit of the 1916 Proclamation had been grossly subverted.'[11] And yet, in spite of these abuses, McGahern insisted, quite rightly, that the mass of Irish people got on with life as they chose to live it, paying lip service to Church and state dictums alike: 'most people were untouched by all this and went about their sensible pagan lives as they had done for centuries'.[12] Drinking, dancing, sex: none of these activities disappeared even at the height of Church power; and, in fact, if one were to use McGahern's stories and novels as historical documents, one would have to conclude that Ireland of the 1950s and 1960s was a place more of sexual adventure than of repression and abuse.

In the wake of the censorship scandal, McGahern moved to London, refusing to make a fuss or to permit organized objections by anti-censorship champions such as Owen Sheehy-Skeffington. He would not return to live in the country again for more than five years, settling at first in County Galway and later in Leitrim. That he chose to return is significant. For Joyce and Beckett, two of his artistic heroes, such a move would have been unthinkable. But McGahern remained interested in Ireland and felt that one could live a life there and remain true to one's art. He had the advantage that, by the early 1970s, things were beginning to get slightly less restrictive, and the banning of *The Dark* proved to be the last major sting of the censorship wasp. Asked towards the end of his life why

---

[10] Ibid., 109.   [11] John McGahern, 'Censorship', in *Love of the World*, 97.   [12] Ibid.

he had not rejected the Ireland that had rejected him, he answered in terms that bordered on patriotism, or at least love of country:

> I don't think you can reject anything myself. . . . This is my country, that was the weather of my life, and you make the best you can of it. There's a poem of Sappho that I like very much where she says 'Some say our infantry, some more say our cavalry, and some more say our fleet of shining oars is the finest sight on dark earth, but I say, whatever one loves, is' . . . and I say whatever one loves, is. And that's my country.[13]

While writers like Joyce and Beckett retained an interest in Ireland and used their experiences there to enrich their literary works, they chose to remain on the continent—and for the most part in its cosmopolitan nerve centre, Paris—away from the damaging insularity of their homeland.

Although McGahern, too, spent brief periods living in Paris in 1969 and in the early 1970s, it was to England he had turned first after dismissal from his post in a Dublin primary school in 1965. For people like Sergeant Reegan of *The Barracks* or Mahoney senior of *The Dark*, to have to turn to the old enemy for refuge so soon after defeating them in armed struggle was a bitter pill to swallow, yet emigration to England remained a necessity for their children's generation also. Young Mahoney knows that if he does not shine in his Leaving Certificate examination at school he will be left with the usual option: 'You can go to England if all fails. You'll work in Dagenham and they'll call you Pat.'[14] The eponymous central character of the short story, 'Eddie Mac', a clever but unlettered farm labourer, knows that England can provide a place of refuge and a new life in the aftermath of the stealing and sale of his employers' cattle. McGahern describes brilliantly the journey that was so familiar to so many of his countrymen and women:

> From Westland Row he walked to the B&I terminal on the river and bought a single ticket to Liverpool. . . . The boat would get into Liverpool in the morning. Though it would take them days yet to figure out what had happened, he would travel on to Manchester before getting a haircut and change of clothes. From Manchester the teeming cities of the North stretched out: Leeds, Newcastle-upon-Tyne, Glasgow. . . . In those cities a man could stay lost for ever and victory could still be found.[15]

Unlike Eddie Mac, by the time McGahern arrived in London in the mid-1960s to live for a sustained period he already knew the place well, having worked there on building sites in the 1950s, to make money over the summer period while studying to be a teacher in Dublin. During this period he also made the acquaintance of several writers and artists who gathered around the literary quarterly, *X* (McGahern's first publisher), in the early 1960s. London, and English society more generally, are typically portrayed in a very positive light by McGahern. He was at the vanguard of the first generation of writers born

[13] Interview with Myles Dungan, 'Rattlebag', RTÉ Radio 1, 2002. RTÉ Radio sound archive.
[14] John McGahern, *The Dark* (London: Faber and Faber, 1983), 137.
[15] John McGahern, 'Eddie Mac', in *Creatures of the Earth: New and Selected Stories* (London: Faber and Faber, 2007), 277–8.

into an independent state and was insistent that Ireland's problems could no longer be blamed on Britain. 'In fact', he recalled, 'certain British institutions, like Penguin Books, the BBC, the *Observer*, the *Sunday Times*, the *Listener*, became our windows on the world, and without them this place would have been far darker than it was.'[16]

Elizabeth Reegan of *The Barracks* nurses in London through the war years and comes to consciousness through an ultimately unhappy love affair with Michael Halliday, an English doctor in her hospital. While her memories of the affair are bittersweet, the images of London life that come to her in her final lonely days, married to a thwarted, ever-complaining husband in the fishbowl of a tiny rural Irish community, are warm and vivid: 'Names came. The London Hospital Tavern, The Star and Garter, The Blind Beggar in Whitechapel Road; the prettier pubs of the city with always the vases of red and yellow on the counter, their names like The Load of Hay enough to remember.'[17] And again, as the novel comes towards its close, the memories of a life of joyful anonymity amid London's streets return to give succour to Elizabeth:

> And she didn't think she could go on only for the fact that often when she was alone her sense of the collapsing rubble of this actual day faded, and processions of dead days began to return haunting clear, it seems as compensation. Her childhood and the wild smell of the earth in the evenings after spring rain and the midges swarming out of the trees; streets of London at all hours, groping for the Jewish names on the lintels—Frank, Levine, Lerner, Goldsberg, Botzmans—above the awnings in the little market off Commercial Road, and did the sun still glitter so on the red-stained glass over the little Yiddish Theatre, the left side of the road as you came from Aldgate, *Grand Palais*.[18]

Elizabeth never associates the teeming streets of the city with loneliness; rather it is the inward-looking quietude of her Irish country home that fills her with a sense of isolation. McGahern himself loved the life of the London pub, and the East London he describes in *The Barracks* is where he lived for a period in the 1960s with two of his sisters who, like Elizabeth, were nurses. Writing to a friend in 1965, he describes his life there in affectionate terms:

> It's a lovely Easter, this house is full of building workers, a huge Victorian house of 14 rooms and a long garden with white pear tree and the forsythia and apple bloom in the hedges, and they are all on holiday, and I spend all my time drinking beer with them down in the Three Blackbirds, a dark old coaching inn the same for over 200 years beside the Midland railway, and it is all light and happy, even the drunkenness is frivolous bellylaughing and hearty shouts that bear neither relation to before or after, and middling happy there I often wonder why there's always some ugliness in some way about all literary gatherings and drinkings? And not here for some other reason.[19]

---

[16] McGahern, 'Censorship', 97.   [17] McGahern, *The Barracks*, 86.   [18] Ibid., 186.
[19] Letter to Patrick Gregory, 1965. This letter will be included in *The Letters of John McGahern*, ed. Frank Shovlin (London: Faber and Faber, forthcoming).

It is in his third novel, *The Leavetaking*, that McGahern puts this time away from Ireland to greatest use in his fiction and promulgates the idea that England, and London in particular, is a place of calm and refuge away from the restrictions of Irish conservative Catholicism. The novel, split into two parts, centres around Patrick Moran, an Irish schoolteacher fleeing to London to escape an unhappy love affair, only to find himself falling for a young American divorcée. They marry in a registry office, he returns to Ireland with her, and is dismissed from his post in a Catholic boys' primary school because of his marriage outside of the Catholic Church. Part One sees Patrick in his final day in the schoolyard before dismissal, thinking of his beloved mother's last illness, death, and funeral. The school is portrayed as an ugly and brutal place where discipline is strict and the Irish language is used as the lexicon of control. Patrick uses the language to speak to his 'Old fanatical peasant'[20] headmaster. 'I prefer to thank him in the patriotic and official idiom', he tells us, 'since in it I am unable to betray shades of feeling.'[21] And there will be no feeling or solidarity for the boys in his charge either:

> 'Anybody moving after the bell goes straight to the office,' the headmaster is outside the swing door, shouting into the voracious shrieking of the gulls. The second bell drowns his voice. They run to their lines. 'No talking after the bell,' I hear him shout as some murmur rises into the gull shriek.
> 'Lamha suas,' I say and the lines stretch out as they put hands on each other's shoulders. 'Lamha sios,' their hands slap their sides.
> 'Lamha sios.'
> 'Lamha suas.'
> 'Iompaigi,' for the last time and they turn, the headmaster moving among the lines as some brownsuited cormorant scanning water.[22]

There is a monotonous and wearying militarism about all of this that will be familiar to many Irish readers born before 1980, and we are left in no doubt that this school, this place, is the product of a failed state: 'The lavatories and schoolrooms are flatroofed and concrete, the single arm of the assembly hall alone v-roofed. Ragged rose bushes hang limp under its windows, a strip of black earth in concrete, the concrete beginning to crack after ten years, half-arsed modern as the rest of the country.'[23] It is a description born of disappointment rather than hate. There is no doubt that some details in these portraits of a Dublin school are taken from personal experience, as is made plain in a letter McGahern wrote to fellow schoolteacher and writer, Michael McLaverty (1904–92), in 1960:

> Although most of the children in the school where I teach come from comfortable homes there is a small slum in the middle of Clontarf. This year I happen to have ten from there—eight to nine years old—and what I learn shakes me. Any scar will nearly always fester. <u>I notice how they huddle apart from the other children</u> in the

---

[20] John McGahern, *The Leavetaking* (London: Faber and Faber, 1974), 12. This novel was substantially revised and reissued in 1984.

[21] Ibid.

[22] Ibid., 19. These orders, although slightly misspelled, translate as 'hands up', 'hands down', 'hands up', 'turn'.

[23] Ibid., 10.

playground. It is strange that while their shoes are leaking that they can always muster money for drill costumes or a shining new red tie and blue suit for First Communion—any outward show. Why I probably tell you these things is that only today I discovered that the sweaty smell of decay, nauseatingly strong from some of them, comes from them sleeping in their clothes. It is difficult to reconcile the desire to do nothing but write ('I intend to give up this scribbling', Byron said in one of his letters), even a cushioned civil service life, with all the human suffering about us.[24]

For all of that, however, it would be remiss not to point out that McGahern found his own schooldays, particularly his secondary schooling with the Presentation Brothers in Carrick-on-Shannon, where love of reading and learning was encouraged, to be 'a time of grace'.[25]

Patrick Moran of *The Leavetaking* escapes his 'half-arsed' native land to the exciting anonymity of London. Ireland's very size is regretted, 'where everybody who is not related knows someone who knows someone else you share an enemy or friend with'.[26] By contrast, and much to his relief, he finds in England that the 'thronged vastness of London was the natural element of my need to be alone and slowly I was seeing that for the first time in my life I was free'.[27] He gets a job as a barman with a landlord named Mr Plowman—a kind of decent English everyman—and there meets Isobel, the young American with whom he falls in love. *The Leavetaking* is unique among McGahern novels in that he decided several years after its publication to rewrite it, thinking in part that he was, to use one of his favourite criticisms of others, too close to the material. One of the more notable additions is a greater expansiveness given to his descriptions of Plowman who, we are told in the 1984 revised edition, is 'a tall, courteous Englishman who had served in the R.A.F.'.[28] Both Plowman and his wife are exceptionally generous in their treatment of Patrick and Isobel, a generosity of spirit that is markedly lacking in Patrick's Irish employers when the couple moves back to Dublin, and Patrick recalls with shame the obsequiousness which marks the Irish teacher's life in a remembered exchange with a school inspector: 'I blush still as I hear the slavish caution of my whole forever overmastered race in my voice.'[29] One hears in this sentence an echo of Joyce and the 'gratefully oppressed'[30] spectators of his short story, 'After the Race'. England would again become a place of refuge and escape in both *The Pornographer* (1979) and *Amongst Women*, although by the closing years of his writing life McGahern appears to have come close to some sort of rapprochement with his homeland.

A further, consistent complaint that McGahern, both in his fiction and in his essays, makes about independent Ireland is that, almost as soon as it achieved its freedom, it

[24] Letter to Michael McLaverty, 9 March 1960, in John Killen (ed.), *Dear Mr McLaverty: The Literary Correspondence of John McGahern and Michael McLaverty 1959–1980* (Belfast: Linen Hall Library, 2006), 20. Original emphasis.

[25] John McGahern, 'Schooldays: A Time of Grace', in *Love of the World*, 103.

[26] McGahern, *The Leavetaking*, 182.   [27] Ibid., 108.

[28] John McGahern, *The Leavetaking* (London: Faber and Faber, 1984, rev. ed.), 102.

[29] Ibid., 174.

[30] James Joyce, 'After the Race', in *Dubliners*, ed. Terence Brown (London: Penguin, 1992), 35.

merely replaced one group of oppressors with an equally—perhaps even more—avaricious and controlling ruling elite. *Amongst Women*, with the tyrannical ex-IRA commander Michael Moran at its heart, is particularly acute in its criticism of what Frantz Fanon, in another postcolonial context, described as the national bourgeoisie, a class whose 'innermost vocation seems to be to keep in the running and to be part of the racket'.[31] Such an outcome, in Fanon's view, is common to a range of states that have fought to free themselves of colonial dominion: 'National consciousness, instead of being the all-embracing crystallization of the innermost hopes of the whole people, instead of being the immediate and most obvious result of the mobilization of the people, will be in any case only an empty shell, a crude and fragile travesty of what it might have been.'[32]

McGahern's is an Ireland that has entirely betrayed the high ambitions and ideals of the country's founding fathers. In 1991, on the occasion of the seventy-fifth anniversary of the Easter Rising, he commented: 'I think that the 1916 Rising was not considered to be of any great importance in the country I grew up in. In fact, it was felt secretly to have been a mistake. "What was it all for?" was a puzzlement as widespread as the Rosary.'[33] Instead of a country cherishing all of its children equally, Ireland, in his view, got 'a new class' which comprised 'the chosen few, and their bounty, more often than not, was enclosed in individual families. They grew rich in sanctimoniousness as well as in power and money. They were the new horsemen.'[34] Moran of *Amongst Women* refuses to claim the IRA pension to which he is entitled, disgusted as he is by the new state run by teachers, priests, doctors, and the children of the privileged. When his daughter Sheila confesses her ambitions to be a doctor, it is too much for him to bear:

> Sheila could not have desired a worse profession. It was the priest and doctor and not the guerrilla fighters who had emerged as the bigwigs in the country Moran had fought for. For his own daughter to lay claim to such a position was an intolerable affront. At least the priest had to pay for his position with celibacy and prayer. The doctor took the full brunt of Moran's resentment.[35]

With Church and state in cahoots to uphold the power of a small elite, corruption across all ranks of society is an inevitable consequence, and McGahern shows himself sensitive to the vagaries of such a world in stories such as 'High Ground', 'The Recruiting Officer', and 'Crossing the Line'.

Prime among McGahern's many corrupt characters is the local gombeen man of 'High Ground', Senator Eddie Reegan:

> He had come poor to the place, buying Lynch's small farm cheap, and soon afterwards the farmhouse burned down. At once, a bigger house was built with the insurance

---

[31] Frantz Fanon, *The Wretched of the Earth*, trans. Constance Farrington (London: Penguin, 2001), 120.
[32] Ibid., 119.
[33] John McGahern, 'From a Glorious Dream to Wink and Nod', in *Love of the World*, 125.
[34] Ibid., 125–6.   [35] John McGahern, *Amongst Women* (London: Faber and Faber, 1991), 88.

money, closer to the road, though that in its turn was due to burn down too, to be replaced by the present mansion, the avenue of Lawson cypresses now seven years old. Soon he was buying up other small farms, but no one had ever seen him work with shovel or with spade. He always appeared immaculately dressed. . . . He set up as an auctioneer. He entered politics. He married Kathleen Relihan, the eldest of old Paddy Relihan's daughters, the richest man in the area, Chairman of the County Council.[36]

This story has a predictability that is all too familiar to observers of post-independence Irish politics. Moreover, Reegan's fictional antics have a real-life echo in the absurd political dance conducted in Fenagh, the nearest village to McGahern's Leitrim home, which he himself remembered in wry, if perplexed, terms:

> Two bars watch one another across a road, one Fianna Fáil, the other Fine Gael. The site of the one public telephone was a major focus. For some years now it stands outside the Fianna Fáil bar, but once it used to move with every change of government, all of thirty yards to the other side of the road.[37]

Reegan's political manoeuvrings have a more sinister edge than the comedy of Fenagh's moving telephone kiosks as he tries to have Leddy, the local schoolmaster, removed from his post to be replaced with young Moran, the story's narrator. Moran despises the wheedling Reegan but has a residual love and admiration for the alcoholic but kindly Leddy. In remembering a conversation he had with Leddy on a previous visit to his house, Moran—and McGahern—are clear in their preference for how we ought to read and live in the world: ' "None of my own family were clever," he confided. "It was a great disappointment. And yet they may well be happier for it. Life is an extraordinary thing. A very great mystery. Wonderful . . . shocking . . . thing." '[38] Reegan, like so many other McGahern characters—John Quinn in *That They May Face the Rising Sun* (2002), Guard Harkin in 'Love of the World'—seems on the surface to do very well materially, but in failing to recognize the mystery and majesty of life, he fails to come to consciousness, to be fully human. *Amongst Women's* Michael Moran, perhaps McGahern's finest character study, is similarly blinded by the trappings of the visible world. Only at the very end of his life are we told that he 'had never realized when he was in the midst of confident life what an amazing glory he was part of'.[39] It is not until *That They May Face the Rising Sun* that McGahern appears to provide a workable antidote to his protagonists' materialistic worldviews.

When McGahern's sixth and final novel was published in 2002, it was greeted with almost unanimous acclaim. The novel examines the lives of Joe and Kate Ruttledge on their return from London to a quiet rural Irish community, the members of which live around a lake and include a set of neighbours, among them their dearest friends Jamesie and Mary, who we come to know intimately. McGahern knew this would be his final

---

[36] John McGahern, 'High Ground', in *Creatures of the Earth*, 191–2.
[37] John McGahern, 'County Leitrim: The Sky Above Us', in *Love of the World*, 25.
[38] McGahern, 'High Ground', 197.   [39] McGahern, *Amongst Women*, 179.

novel and it carries within it a hushed sense of valediction. Despite its several shocking moments of cruelty—most notably the public rape of a new bride on her wedding day by John Quinn—the novel is as close as McGahern comes to writing what one might call an optimistic book. Seamus Deane in his *Guardian* review saw McGahern as having solved a puzzle set by Joyce some eighty years earlier in *Ulysses* (1922): 'at last an Irish author has awakened from the nightmare of history and given us a sense of liberation which is not dependent on flight or emigration or escape'.[40] It is as if McGahern has reached an entente with Ireland, and the jaundiced, sometimes embittered, portrait of the country found in the early fiction is replaced with something approaching acceptance, even sometimes admiration.

England still works as a type of 'not Ireland' in the novel, and is still admired. But it is not so straightforward anymore. While Jamesie praises a pruning shears as 'Pure Sheffield. Great steel', he also points to a downside: 'You can't get meat in England'.[41] As in other of McGahern's fictions, we find in Johnny, Jamesie's brother, a key character who has escaped to England to forget heartbreak. But the escape is not nearly so beneficial as it was in *The Leavetaking*. The portrait of his life working in the Ford factory in Dagenham—a fate predicted for young Mahoney in *The Dark*—is rather lonesome, and there is a poignancy in his annual summer trip home, the sense that he has somehow lost his place in paradise. McGahern had first given us a hint of this side of emigrant life in his 1975 short story, 'A Slip-up', in which we get a snapshot of Michael and Agnes, an elderly Irish couple who have given up their small Irish farm to move to England. Their English life is a regimented one, punctuated by trips to Tesco and bottles of Bass in the Royal. Michael's inner, secret life has become so increasingly stuck in his Irish farming past that he has begun to forget and wander. But that inner life is far more vivid and appealing than the dull urban life to which they have moved:

> This morning as he walked with Agnes he decided to clear the drinking pool which was dry after the long spell of good weather. First he shovelled the dark earth of rotted leaves and cowshit out on the bank. Then he paved the sides with heavy stones so that the cattle would not plough in as they drank and he cleared the weeds from the small stream that fed it. . . . For all that time he was unaware of the shopping bag, but when all the water flowed down towards the pool he felt it again by his side. He wondered what was keeping Agnes. He'd never finished such a long job before outside Tesco's. Usually he'd counted himself lucky if he was through with such a job by the time he'd finished his bottle of Bass in the Royal by ten to one.[42]

Like many Irish migrants before and since, Michael has never really left Ireland at all.

That They May Face the Rising Sun represents a real break with the expected direction of McGahern emigrants in that the Ruttledges successfully move to rural Ireland from

---

[40] Seamus Deane, 'A new dawn', *Guardian*, 12 January 2002.

[41] John McGahern, *That They May Face the Rising Sun* (London: Faber and Faber, 2002), 3, 4.

[42] John McGahern, 'A Slip-up', in *Creatures of the Earth*, 86. This story was first published in *Strand* in June 1975 and first collected in *Getting Through* (1978).

London. There is no grand dramatic reason for the move, as becomes clear in an exchange between Joe Ruttledge and the local auctioneer, publican, undertaker—and IRA man—Jimmy Joe McKiernan:

> 'How do you find England?' 'We have jobs. The life is easy and comfortable. We'd hardly be looking at places here if we were entirely happy.' 'What do you find wrong with England?' 'Nothing but it's not my country and I never feel it's quite real or that my life there is real. That has its pleasant side as well. You never feel responsible or fully involved in anything that happens. It's like being present and at the same time a real part of you is happily absent.'[43]

The choice the Ruttledges have made is for a life of contemplation over a life of action, and it is a decision that has worked for them, with Joe Ruttledge by far the happiest and most content of all the central characters of McGahern novels. McGahern himself described the life he returned to in rural Leitrim as being particularly well fitted to the writerly vocation. As with the Ruttledges, his ideal is 'a life of no excitements' in which the world of the imagination takes primacy over the world of action and material gain.[44]

Many readers and critics have commented on the sense of timelessness in *That They May Face the Rising Sun*, with its deliberate lack of chapters and circling seasons.[45] Only two brief markers are laid down to give us a sense of when all of this is taking place—a mention of Jamesie's liking for the popular television show *Blind Date* and a reference to the bombing by the Provisional IRA of the Remembrance Sunday ceremony in Enniskillen, County Fermanagh in November 1987. The use of the latter event as a sign-post is no accident, and it is worth noting that McGahern chooses in the closing twenty pages of this, his final novel, to comment openly for the first time in his fiction about what is euphemistically termed 'the national question'. Johnny dies on one of his ritual trips home from England and there comes a point when, against his wishes and better judgement, Joe Ruttledge has to spend time alone with Jimmy Joe McKiernan, as they wait over Johnny's body before its removal to the local church:

> The two men had not been alone together and had not spoken other than the daily courtesies whenever they met in passing since Jimmy Joe had sold them the farm above the lake all those years before. They had met in passing many times, especially in bars, where Jimmy Joe sold *An Phoblacht*. There were a few who bought it out of active sympathy, and more still, like Jamesie, out of a desire to please and keep all sides happy. There were also a few like Ruttledge who refused to buy the newspaper because they disapproved of violence and the aims of that violence. . . . 'A lot has happened since I sold you that place across the lake.'
> 'More to you than me,' Ruttledge said as he offered whiskey.

---

[43] McGahern, *That They May Face the Rising Sun*, 19.
[44] A point of view expressed by McGahern in the documentary about his life, *John McGahern: A Private World*, directed by Pat Collins (Hummingbird/Harvest Films, 2005).
[45] See, for example, Denis Sampson, '"Open to the World": A Reading of John McGahern's *That They May Face the Rising Sun*', *Irish University Review. Special Issue: John McGahern* 35, no 1 (2005), 136–46.

There were the explosions in towns he had been linked to, kidnappings, the making and carrying of bombs, murders, maimings, interrogations, executions, the years in Long Kesh; it was a source of some surprise—but finally none—that such a man should be declining the whiskey so courteously. Easier still to imagine him on hunger strike and proceeding to the final self-effacement with a quiet, unbreakable resolve. Others he would use pitilessly as tools.[46]

Although McGahern's father Frank had served as an IRA volunteer with pride during the Anglo-Irish War of 1919–21, his son saw nothing worth honouring in the Provisionals of his own times. Yet, like Ruttledge, his innate sense of courtesy and manners allows him to go no further in condemnation than the passage above.

Living in Leitrim, it was frequently convenient for the McGaherns to shop over the border in Enniskillen, that town so devastated by the Remembrance Sunday bombing that did more than almost any other atrocity of the modern Troubles to pull public support away from militant republicanism. Courtesy is again to the fore in a marvellous essay about Leitrim that includes a poignant, funny vignette of the vexed history of Anglo-Irish relations, as McGahern recalls an occasion when the depersonalized atmosphere of a British Army checkpoint was humanized by an unexpected request:

Only once were the assembly-line formalities broken. As the soldiers were checking our identification, an officer appeared and asked if we were going to Enniskillen. His upper-class English accent defined his rank; an Irish officer would have had much the same accent as his men. When we told him that we were on our way to Enniskillen and would be returning within a few hours, he asked us if we would bring him two loaves of wholewheat bread. On our return, as we proffered the brown parcel, the soldiers were edgy, their machine guns at the ready. 'Just a few loaves of wholewheat bread,' we said in as conciliatory a tone as possible. 'Your officer asked us to bring them.'

'Oh, that nutcase,' a soldier said, just as the officer himself appeared, pulling money from inside his combat jacket. 'Thank you very much indeed. We were completely out of wholewheat bread.' When the money was refused—'with the compliments of the country'—he looked at a loss for a moment, before coming to attention and honouring us with one of the sharpest salutes I have ever seen, out there beneath the mountains, in the middle of the wilderness. I wish the whole commerce of Northern Ireland could be as simple as that human request.[47]

Within a decade of that border encounter, peace had come to Northern Ireland, although the border remains steadfast. But for that brief exchange between Ruttledge and McKiernan in the upstairs bedroom of Jamesie's house, one might never have guessed that as McGahern wrote his finest works, a bitter guerrilla war was defining the political life of his country. But that should come as no surprise really, as the journey that captured McGahern's attention, and which he spent a working life trying to dramatize through his fiction, was always inward rather than outward, to the domain of the imagination rather than to that of the observable world.

[46] McGahern, *That They May Face the Rising Sun*, 283–4.
[47] McGahern, 'County Leitrim', 21–2.

FURTHER READING

Joyce, Stanislaus. *My Brother's Keeper: James Joyce's Early Years*, ed. Richard Ellmann. Cambridge, MA: Da Capo Press, 2003.

Kiberd, Declan. 'John McGahern's *Amongst Women*'. In Maria Tymoczko and Colin Ireland (eds), *Language and Tradition in Ireland: Continuities and Displacements*. Amherst, MA: University of Massachusetts Press, 2003: 195–213.

Kiberd, Declan. 'Introduction'. In John McGahern, *Love of the World: Essays*, ed. Stanley van der Ziel. London: Faber and Faber, 2009: xi–xxiii.

Killen, John (ed.). *Dear Mr McLaverty: The Literary Correspondence of John McGahern and Michael McLaverty 1959–1980*. Belfast: Linen Hall Library, 2006.

McKeon, Belinda. '"Robins Feeding with the Sparrows": The Protestant "Big House" in the Fiction of John McGahern'. *Irish University Review* 35, no. 1 (2005): 72–89.

Maher, Eamon, *John McGahern: From the Local to the Universal*. Dublin: Liffey Press, 2003.

Sampson, Denis, *Outstaring Nature's Eye: The Fiction of John McGahern*. Washington, DC: Catholic University of America Press, 1993.

Sampson, Denis, *Young John McGahern: Becoming a Novelist*. Oxford: Oxford University Press, 2012.

Shovlin, Frank, 'Secular Prayers: Catholic Imagination, Modern Irish Writing and the Case of John McGahern'. In Oliver P. Rafferty (ed.), *Irish Catholic Identities*. Manchester: Manchester University Press, 2013: 321–32.

Van der Ziel, Stanley. *John McGahern and the Imagination of Tradition*. Cork: Cork University Press, 2016.

Whyte, James. *History, Myth, and Ritual in the Fiction of John McGahern: Strategies of Transcendence*. Lewiston, NY: Edwin Mellen Press, 2002.

CHAPTER 18

....

JOHN BANVILLE'S
FICTIONS OF ART

....

NEIL MURPHY

THIS chapter will situate the novels of John Banville (1945–) in the context of his oft-repeated claim that his fictions are works of art and his related insistence that the pursuit of beauty is the primary aim of the artist and therefore one of his foremost concerns.[1] Specific novels—notably *Birchwood* (1973), *Mefisto* (1986), *The Book of Evidence* (1989), *Eclipse* (2000), and *The Sea* (2005)—will be highlighted as key moments in his development as an artist, and the crime novels written under the pseudonym Benjamin Black will be considered in the same critical context. Banville's claim that a work of art 'is not about something, it is something'[2] posits that an artwork does not reflect a desire to represent a notional model of material reality but rather establishes an independent aesthetic storyworld with its own rules and values. In interview, he has argued that there is a fundamental difference between what he terms the 'translatable content' (or meaning) of art and its significance. He rejects the prioritization of translatable content, arguing: 'Nothing is translatable really. I don't think anything has meaning, in the sense that I define it.'[3] For Banville, 'meaning' amounts to a mode of knowable representation—or art as a vehicle for comment, opinion, or social engagement—against which he sets his face. Instead, he believes that art's primary 'significance' lies in its capacity to 'make vivid for the reader the mysterious predicament of being alive'.[4] In order to achieve this aim, the artist seeks to 'go beyond mere human *doing* to the question of what it is to *be*, the question of being in the world'.[5]

---

[1] See, for example, Belinda McKeon, 'John Banville, The Art of Fiction No. 200', *Paris Review*, no. 188 (2009), 132–53.

[2] Cited in Travis Elborough, 'Fully Booked: Q & A with John Banville', 29 June 2012. https://www.panmacmillan.com/blogs/literary/fully-booked-q-a-with-john-banville. Accessed 8 April 2016.

[3] Hedwig Schwall, 'An Interview with John Banville', *European English Messenger* 6, no. 1 (1997), 15.

[4] Cited in Elborough, 'Fully Booked'.

[5] Hugh Haughton and Bryan Radley, 'An Interview with John Banville', *Modernism/Modernity* 18, no. 4 (2011), 865. Original emphasis.

As will be evident hereafter, these artistic preoccupations frequently find expression in Banville's evolving deployment of the self-reflexive mode, from the use of metafictional pranks and overt self-reflexive observations about language, memory, and writing in the early novels to the more sophisticated development of metaphorical parallels in the science and art novels published between the mid-1970s and the late 1990s. Similarly, his recurring use of mirror images, intertextual references, and figurative fictional modes characterizes the formal artistic style that progressively emerges. In fact, Banville's increasingly nuanced self-reflexive commentaries on art are central to the development of the fiction of one of the most sophisticated exponents of the self-conscious mode in all of contemporary writing. Banville's particular use of the metafictional model represents a very particular aesthetic decision that is essentially counter-realist and yet simultaneously indicative of his desire to radically develop beyond the limits of that model.

Banville's first three works, *Long Lankin* (1970), *Nightspawn* (1971), and *Birchwood* (1973), are all modelled on metafictional narrative forms.[6] 'The Possessed', the novella in *Long Lankin* narrated by the novel's central character, Ben White, seeks to convey his artistic aspirations—'I think I might write a book. I could tell a story about the stars and what it's like alone up there'[7]—even though the plot fails to offer sufficient coherence to support such ruminations. Similarly so with *Nightspawn*, which is essentially a parody of a crime novel that seeks to double-up as a self-reflexive commentary on the significance and difficulties of art. Although the novel is clearly written under the influence of classical metafictional novels such as those by Samuel Beckett (1906–89), Flann O'Brien (1911–66), and Vladimir Nabokov, it does not reach their level of artistic sophistication. As with *Long Lankin*, the plot fails to offer adequate metaphorical scaffolding for the artistic commentary, with the result that its value as direct artistic statement and formal exemplum is limited. The interrogative mode in the Big House novel, *Birchwood*, is more fluidly absorbed into the fabric of the telling, rendering the novel more convincing both as a fiction and as a commentary on the creative act. As Vera Kreilkamp suggests, *Birchwood*, although a 'fulfilment of the tradition as well as a parody and subversion of it', transforms 'a literary symbol of political and economic loss into a haunting image of the failure of memory and the inaccessibility of the past',[8] and thus positions an epistemological concern at its centre. Historical reference becomes literary metaphor and metaphor turns back on itself in self-parody.

Birchwood's implicit rejection of the forms of realist fiction is exemplified by Gabriel Godkin's return to his ancestral home in the latter stages of the novel, revealing, through metaphor, the *re-constituted* importance of the traditional fictional model:

> Perhaps I shall leave here. Where would I go? Is that why they all fought so hard for Birchwood, because there is nowhere else for them to be? Outside is destruction and

[6] In *John Banville* (Dublin: Irish Academic Press, 2009), John Kenny observes that Banville's first two works 'can be read as a kind of aesthetic autobiography' (41).

[7] John Banville, *Birchwood* (London: Secker and Warburg, 1970), 188.

[8] Vera Kreilkamp, *The Anglo-Irish Novel and the Big House* (Syracuse, NY: Syracuse University Press, 1998), 249.

decay. I do not speak the language of this wild country. I shall stay here, alone, and live a life different from any the house has ever known.[9]

Banville's metaphorical substitution of an isolated house for the act of fiction writing extends throughout his work. In this instance, Gabriel implies the importance of some aspects of the realist mode, and it is therefore at this point in Banville's oeuvre that an essentially hybrid form of realism and metafiction is established. Gabriel here suggests that some form of continued belonging to the established tenets of storytelling must be retained, although in modified form. In fact, Banville has stated that Gabriel's claim that he will stay and 'live a life different from any the house has ever known' is 'The only direct statement I've ever made in any book.'[10] Gabriel repeatedly stresses this metaphorical positioning during the final pages of the novel: 'Now the white landscape was empty. Perhaps it is better thus, I said, and added, faintly, I might find some other creatures to inhabit it. And I did, and so I became my own Prospero, and yours.'[11] As he concludes his account, Gabriel self-reflexively notifies us that he has 'cleared out the attic, boarded the windows.'[12]

Thus, *Birchwood* represents a pivotal moment in Banville's development as a novelist because it shows him adopting a hybrid form in which he combines the essence of realist plot formation (something explicitly abandoned by many postmodern writers) with a self-reflexive artistic progress statement that issues from Gabriel's role as a creative teller of his own tale. This remains his preferred model throughout his subsequent work. Rather than mimic the example of pure avant-garde experimentation, Banville instead chose to keep faith with the realist plot as part of his narrative response to the formal cul-de-sac that postmodernism had arguably created for the novel. The two historical novels that immediately follow *Birchwood*, *Doctor Copernicus* (1976) and *Kepler* (1981), concretize this aesthetic declaration by representing modified versions of the house of fiction.

Banville's science tetralogy encompasses four novels: *Doctor Copernicus, Kepler, The Newton Letter: An Interlude* (1982), and *Mefisto* (1986). The first two of these represent a post-*Birchwood* artistic shift, but they are not philosophically dissimilar to it and the preceding works. The self-reflexive observations about the limits of language, the treachery of memory, and the hazards of locating a fixed version of truth are all classical Banvillean preoccupations. Banville has admitted that with respect to *Doctor Copernicus* and *Kepler*, 'science, history and mathematics are no more important to those books than the *Odyssey* is to *Ulysses*.'[13] Instead, science is presented in both books as primarily a creative pursuit, wherein lies its true significance for Banville. More specifically, the scientific processes of Copernicus and Kepler are continually conflated with activities that metaphorically resonate with the act of creative writing. In this respect, Mark O'Connell suggests that Banville's 'metafictional strategy in *Doctor Copernicus* is to surreptitiously write about writing whilst appearing to write about science. There are

[9] Banville, *Birchwood*, 174.   [10] Schwall, 'An Interview with John Banville', 19.
[11] Ibid., 172.   [12] Ibid., 174.
[13] Cited in John McKenna, 'Rage for order', *In Dublin*, 13 November 1986, 17.

passages in which it is difficult to avoid the suspicion that Banville is engaging in a kind of covert auto-representation.'[14] These two historical novels also represent relatively subversive variations on the genre, given that they contain anachronistic quotations from modern scientists (Albert Einstein, Arthur Eddington, Max Planck) and writers (Søren Kierkegaard, Franz Kafka, and Wallace Stevens, among others). In addition, both novels are set up as deeply self-conscious works that implicitly interrogate the validity of their scientists' intellectual and creative quests to such an extent that they raise significant questions about the attainment of intellectual truth more generally. Thus, in Banville's specific deployment of the historical novel genre, historical reconstruction is far less important than the self-reflexive artistic process.

The unnamed historian of *The Newton Letter*, although not a scientist like Copernicus or Kepler, is also presented as a creator. While his role as a failed historian is significant, it is his inability to accommodate within his intellectual systems the complexity of living that indicates his primary significance. He retreats from history because the immediacy of the world distracts him: 'Shall I say, I've lost faith in the primacy of the text? Real people keep getting in the way now, objects, landscapes even. Everything ramifies.'[15] He is also depicted as a detached academic who is continually frustrated by the fluid nature of external reality and by his inability to apply significance to real objects by means of his defining systems: 'I had bought guide books to trees and birds, but I couldn't get the hang of them. The illustrations would not match up with the real specimens before me.'[16] As a result, he is compelled to recalibrate his imaginative response to reality. *The Newton Letter* also differs significantly from *Birchwood* in that it does not simply avail of a parodic, metafictional form, nor does it draw on stock literary characters. Rather, it echoes Banville's own movement away from the historical novel form by overtly subverting the efforts of its narrator, who admits that he had sought to write the history of a great scientist—a parodic rendition of what Banville himself does in the earlier historical fictions. *The Newton Letter* does, however, create the narrative model—one that appears to seek an accommodation with a recognizable contemporary reality—which would be more fully accomplished in the final part of the tetralogy, *Mefisto*.

Although *The Newton Letter* has proven to be an attractive proposition with some critics because of its overt use of the Irish Big House genre, *Mefisto* is a far more aesthetically adventurous novel which revisits many of the fascinations of Banville's earlier novels but radically refashions them within a very complex narrative structure. Gabriel Swan's transformation from adhering to a specific mathematical system to seeking a less programmatic method of understanding the phenomenal world self-consciously mirrors Banville's own artistic development in terms of his movement beyond the quasi-historical novel form. In the first half of the novel, Gabriel views the world exclusively in mathematical terms, whereas in part two, material reality fractures his artificial order to such a degree that 'A panic of disconnected numbers buzzed in my head. Grass, trees,

---

[14] Mark O'Connell, *John Banville's Narcissistic Fictions* (Basingstoke: Palgrave Macmillan, 2013), 149.
[15] John Banville, *The Newton Letter: An Interlude* (London: Panther Books, 1984), 9.
[16] Ibid., 13.

railings, the road.'[17] In his newly forged understanding, a more profound sense of the integrity of objects, rather than their designated signifiers, asserts itself: 'Things crowded in, the mere things themselves. One drop of water plus one drop of water will not make two drops, but one. Two oranges and two apples do not make four of some new synthesis but remain stubbornly themselves.'[18] Whereas Gabriel had once relied on mere mathematics, as always with Banville, deeper engagement with the complex essences of experiential reality renders all systems of thought inadequate.

While each of Banville's science novels dwells upon the difficulty of bridging the gap between phenomenal reality and human-made systems of investigation or interpretation, there are marked differences between them. *Mefisto*, for example, engages with the concept of strangeness for the first time in his work, a development Banville associates with a significant change in his artistic practice:

> *Mefisto* was a big shift for me. I began to write in a different way. I began to trust my instincts, to lose control, deliberately. It was exciting and it was frightening. The writer who wrote *Mefisto* was a writer in deep trouble. He didn't know what he was doing.[19]

Like several of his other novels (*Birchwood*, *The Book of Evidence*, *The Sea*), *Mefisto* represents a moment of crucial artistic development for Banville. The novel sought to fold the fluidity of imaginative response (as opposed to the more systematic scientific method) into the formal process of narration in a way that poses a significant challenge to readers. The novel represents a fictional model of reality that might demonstrate the tentative grasp one has on the real, rather than attempt a direct representation of the world. This deeply self-reflexive mode paved the way for future works. After *Mefisto*, and even allowing for relatively traditional plot-driven novels like *The Book of Evidence* and *The Untouchable* (1997), Banville's fiction evolves in a direction where the content primarily becomes the subject of its own self-reflexive investigations. The novels of the past three decades of his career increasingly place art at their plotted centres, freeing Banville from the somewhat strained metaphorical parallels that had defined much of the early work.

Banville's fascination with the principle of literature as art, and with the visual arts more generally, is derived in part from his sense of a very particularized literary lineage that is frequently associated with 'high autonomous art'.[20] This lineage includes authors such as Heinrich von Kleist, Flaubert, Beckett, Stevens, Nabokov, and Kafka, all of whom confronted ideas of authorship, art, the problem of representation, the distinction between form and content, and, in many cases, an aesthetic need for objectivity. Banville is fond of citing Kafka's dictum that 'The artist is the man who has nothing to say',[21] thus

---

[17] John Banville, *Mefisto* (London: Paladin, 1987), 139.   [18] Ibid., 233.

[19] McKeon, 'John Banville, The Art of Fiction No. 200'. Banville has indicated that he views the quality of 'strangeness' to be the 'mark of art' and has often returned to this theme in interviews. See, for example, Hedda Friberg, 'John Banville and Derek Hand in Conversation', *Irish University Review* 36, no. 1 (2006), 200.

[20] Kenny, *John Banville*, 16.

[21] John Banville, 'The Personae of Summer', in Jacqueline Genet and Wynne Hellegouarc'h (eds), *Irish Writers and Their Creative Process* (Gerrards Cross: Colin Smythe, 1996), 119.

indicating his commitment to an autonomous art form that refuses to accommodate the representational mirroring of reality and instead draws attention to the surface texture of the compositional design of the words. Even though he acknowledges that literature is essentially a linguistic rather than a sensual art form, Banville is drawn to the visual qualities of stillness, the obsessed gaze, and the paradox of surface and depth that informs his increasingly detailed descriptions of the ways things appear. Reflecting on his teenage desire to be a painter, he remarked: 'I loved the idea of working on the surface, because I think, on the surface, that's where the real depth is.'[22]

The trilogy of novels that features Freddie Montgomery—*The Book of Evidence*, *Ghosts* (1993), and *Athena* (1995)—is constructed around paintings, forgeries, and the fatal impact of imaginative failure on the lives of the characters. Freddie's assertion that 'failure of imagination is my real crime, the one that made the others possible',[23] defines the artistic momentum of all three novels. The murder of Josie Bell, he suggests, was made possible by a more fundamental failure of imaginative awareness and, as such, its significance extends far beyond the trope of murderer and victim. Like Gabriel Swan, Freddie has abandoned scientific method and rejected moral codes. But since he has not yet located or developed an alternative model of coherence, his imaginative processes are not refined enough to respond to the world without the aids of scientific or moral systems.

The ostensible shift from scientific method to an awareness of the need for direct imaginative engagement with one's experiences is evident in many ways. A plethora of references to the visual arts are apparent in the trilogy, which in turn generate a very distinct surface texture in the novels, as when Freddie describes living in California 'amid those gentle paintbox colours, under that dome of flawless blue'.[24] Furthermore, many scenes allude to particular artists and artworks, not all of them real, as exemplified by the invented Jean Vaublin, whose work lies at the centre of *Ghosts*: 'Wonderful prospect from this lofty crest, the near green and the far blue and that strip of ash-white beach holding up an enormity of sea and sky, the whole scene clear and delicate, like something by Vaublin himself, a background to one of his celebrated *pèlerinages* or a delicate *fête galante*.'[25] Jean Vaublin is a near-anagram of John Banville and, in a classical shift across ontological levels, a Banville landscape is here compared to a Vaublin/Banville painting, transgressing the limits of the surface plot. Vaublin is modelled on the French artist Jean-Antoine Watteau, while his painting *Le Monde d'or* is actually based on at least two Watteau paintings, *Gilles* (1718–19) and *L'Embarquement pour Cythère* (1717). This technique is emblematic of Banville's narrative innovation throughout the trilogy: the imaginative conflation of Banville, Vaublin, and Watteau; the artistic mirroring of the novel, *The Book of Evidence*, with the painting that Freddie steals; the self-referential deployment of seven fake paintings in *Athena*—all generate purely invented universes with distinctive painterly textures.

---

[22]   Cited in Cody Delistraty, 'John Banville on the Utter Mystery of Writing', *New Yorker*, 18 September 2015.
[23]   John Banville, *The Book of Evidence* (London: Secker and Warburg, 1989), 215.   [24]   Ibid., 67.
[25]   John Banville, *Ghosts* (London: Secker and Warburg, 1993), 30.

A key example of such textual blending is the manner in which the murder of Josie is framed. Several critics have suggested that Freddie fails to see the girl's humanity until just before he kills her, arguing that his claims that he had never before 'felt another's presence so immediately and with such raw force', and that he saw her as 'somehow radiant' are genuine.[26] However, Freddie also imagines that he is able to see clean through Josie's head, which is hardly an overt sign of his humane empathy for her. Similarly, while he insists that he feels her presence, he both fails to describe her with any great clarity and persists with the habit he exhibits throughout the novel of embalming her in clichés (she is 'wide-eyed, like a rebuked child', they are like 'a married couple having a fight'[27]). Freddie's claims are further undermined by his later assessment of what he considers to be his most fundamental failing:

> This is the worst, the original sin, I think, the one for which there will be no forgiveness: that I never imagined her vividly enough, that I never made her be there sufficiently, that I did not make her live. Yes, that failure of imagination is my real crime, the one that made the others possible. What I told that policeman is true—I killed her because I could kill her, and I could kill her because for me she was not alive.[28]

It is thus far more likely that Freddie's initial claim that he genuinely empathized with his victim before murdering her is no more plausible than any of his other inventions and fantastical claims. Thereafter, he is far less prone to misconceptions about people. His subsequent claim that his failure was primarily imaginative is more convincing as a reflective self-evaluation of his crime. Freddie does not consider the murder to be a result of moral failure. Rather, his moral lack was made possible by an imaginative failure and is thus a symptom, not a cause. He furthermore insists that he did not make a conscious decision to kill Josie: 'There is no moment in this process of which I can confidently say, there, that is when I decided she should die. Decided?—I do not think it was a matter of deciding. I do not think it was a matter of thinking, even.'[29] Without a moral imperative, Freddie's actions are inexplicable, and so his assertion that his was an imaginative lapse represents a philosophical solution for him.

The detailed use of artistic allusions in *The Book of Evidence* is further intensified in *Ghosts* and *Athena*. In *Ghosts*, Freddie, now released from prison, is acting as an assistant to one Professor Kreutznaer, an expert on the work of Vaublin and an inhabitant of an unnamed island. The novel's main narrative frame is predicated on at least two paintings by Watteau, and the ontological status of the characters repeatedly shifts between

---

[26] Banville, *The Book of Evidence*, 113. See Elke D'hoker, 'Portrait of the Other as a Woman with Gloves: Ethical Perspectives in John Banville's *The Book of Evidence*', *Critique: Studies in Contemporary Fiction* 44, no. 1 (2002), 27 and Tony E. Jackson, 'Science, Art, and the Shipwreck of Knowledge: The Novels of John Banville', *Contemporary Literature* 38, no. 3 (1997), 520.

[27] Banville, *The Book of Evidence*, 112, 113, 111.

[28] Ibid., 215. Freddie also compares the first time he saw Josie 'in the open French window with the blue and gold of summer at her back' with the moment when he 'hit her again and again', claiming that on *both* occasions there had 'been no more of her there, for me, than there was in the newspaper stories' (215).

[29] Ibid., 151.

fictional and allusory planes. For example, Flora dreams of the golden world (mirroring Vaublin's *Le Monde d'or*) and of 'worlds within worlds. They bleed into each other. I am at once here and there, then and now, as if by magic.'[30] Her dream effectively articulates the integrated moving surface that is the ontological frame of the novel, while also offering self-reflexive commentary on the narrative as both itself and other—as both novel and painting simultaneously.

With *Athena*, we partly return to the ekphrastic mode, via a sequence of catalogue-style responses to the seven fictional paintings. However, the presence of the figure A, a quasi-personified expression of Art itself, greatly complicates the novel's engagement with art, as does the fact that the seven paintings are fakes (with an eighth allegedly real). The artistic commentaries of Morrow (the Freddie figure) on the fake paintings are synonymous with a commentary on Banville's own work. The paintings are attributed to artists whose names are anagrams or near-anagrams of John Banville or J. Banville, including one Johann Livelb, Gabriel's circus stage name in *Birchwood*. Furthermore, as critics have noticed, Morrow's commentaries correspond to various qualities in Banville's own fiction, such as the 'highly worked, polished textures' of Giovanni Belli's work and the 'remoteness and classical stillness' of Job van Hellin's.[31] One could argue, however, that the catalogue entries and extended discussions on art in *Athena* render the fictional frame less fluid than *The Book of Evidence* and *Ghosts*, and leave it too heavily laden with ideas. At many points in the artistic commentaries and in the descriptions of Morrow's own aesthetic reactions to his immediate surroundings (particularly those that focus on his response to the metaphorical figure A), the narrative offers extensive elaboration of purely theoretical points without adequately integrating them into the texture of the fiction.

Eclipse (2000), *Shroud* (2002), and *Ancient Light* (2012) all feature characters named Alex Cleave, Cass Cleave, and Axel Vander, who are variously associated with acting, puppetry, and impersonation (Alex is a theatre actor, as is Dawn Devonport in *Ancient Light*, and Axel is an impersonator). In *Eclipse*, Alex complains that he has 'lived amid surfaces too long', and when later the surface plot recedes he feels as if he has 'stepped through the looking-glass into another world where everything is exactly as it was and at the same time entirely transformed.'[32] In *Ancient Light*, Alex entertains the possibility of 'a world next to this one, contiguous with it, where there might linger somehow the spirits of those no longer here and yet not entirely gone, either.'[33] This motif of doubling is Banville's way of suggesting how imaginative constructs of reality commingle, somehow, with the real world. Indeed, the characters' awareness of their curiously doubled natures is frequently emphasized, as in *Eclipse*, when Alex's wife Lydia (or Leah) calls him a ghost and it does not surprise him in the slightest. Similarly, Cass Cleave in *Shroud* claims that she 'saw herself as a puppet, with lacquered cheeks and fixed mad grin,

[30] Banville, *Ghosts*, 55.
[31] John Banville, *Athena* (London: Minerva, 1996), 75, 103. See Kenny, *John Banville*, 166 and O'Connell, *John Banville's Narcissistic Fictions*, 171–4.
[32] John Banville, *Eclipse* (London: Picador, 2000), 23, 121.
[33] John Banville, *Ancient Light* (London: Viking, 2012), 20.

popping up in front of him, look at me, look at me!'[34] Other figures from Banville's by now familiar intertextual repository also make allusive appearances. Cass identifies with the 'the one-eyed glare and comically spavined gait'[35] of the Harlequin, previously mentioned in *Ghosts*. These harlequins, puppets, and other artificial figures are frequently blended with 'real' characters in the novels, as when Vander admits to his own puppet status, acknowledging that he is 'all frontage; stroll around to the back and all you will find is some sawdust and a few shaky struts and a mess of wiring'.[36]

These examples form part of an increasingly familiar pattern in Banville's work which speaks to yet another way of acknowledging the deep duality of all things. Even casual scenic descriptions are forever on the verge of becoming something else: 'the mountains in the distance, pale blue and flat, as if they had been painted on the sky in a weak wash of lavender'.[37] The world to which the narrator refers is the world of pure artifice, which in turn defines his relationship with material reality. The self-referentiality here, however, is distinctly unlike that in Banville's earlier works, which seek to draw our attention to the limits of language and offer a self-conscious commentary of the novels' own making. The Cleave trilogy of novels extends this commentary to questions of being that are framed within overtly aestheticized universes. The characters are openly aware of their fictional nature and appear to possess intertextual consciousnesses that give them insight into Banville's extended fictional universe, which includes a by now familiar host of literary, philosophical, and visual arts influences. When they ask metaphysical questions, it is to this invented sphere that they refer.

Given that they inhabit such deeply self-reflexive fictive worlds, these characters' questioning is inevitably linked to their own ontological status and to the specific characteristics of the aestheticized contexts that they inhabit. Alex Cleave admits to such an aesthetic fascination when he spies on a naked girl from his window: 'the unadorned grave beauty of her movements was, it pained the performer in me to acknowledge, inimitable: even if I spent a lifetime in rehearsal I could not hope to aspire to the thoughtless elegance of this girl's most trivial gesture'.[38] What most enthrals this narrator is the absence of self-consciousness in the girl, a detail that reflects Banville's fascination with the German playwright Heinrich von Kleist, including his 1810 essay, 'The Puppet Theatre'. For Kleist, the marionette was a perfect example of unconscious aesthetic expression, which he contrasted with the clumsiness of human dancers: 'when consciousness has, as we might say, passed through an infinity, grace will return; so that grace will be most purely present in the human frame that has either no consciousness or an infinite amount of it, which is to say either in a marionette or in a god'.[39] Banville's appropriation of Kleist in this instance is directly related to his privileging of the reconfigured, aestheticized world over the material world from which it has been drawn.

With his Man Booker Prize-winning *The Sea*, Banville attained a level of technical achievement beyond anything he had previously managed, creating a fluent

---

[34] John Banville, *Shroud* (London: Picador, 2002), 313.   [35] Ibid., 4.   [36] Ibid., 329.
[37] Banville, *Ancient Light*, 17.   [38] Banville, *Eclipse*, 101.
[39] Heinrich von Kleist, 'The Puppet Theatre', in *Heinrich von Kleist: Selected Writings*, ed. and trans. David Constantine (Indianapolis: Hackett Publishing Company, 2004), 416.

interdependency of the novel's myriad components (temporal, ontological, intertextual). *The Sea* exemplifies how Banville typically constructs a secondary allusive ontology beside the primary surface reality of plot by imbuing characters and events with multiple layers of significance. The novel also uses a variety of narrative methods to suggest the way time operates in a non-linear, episodic fashion. These methods act as indicators of temporal shifts, which in turn reflect the multi-temporal context for protagonist Max Morden's imagining mind, which repeatedly transgresses the three time zones featured in the novel. *The Sea* details key events from Max's childhood, recounted in old age, when he has returned to the seaside town where he spent time as a child. His accounts of his present and past experiences are interspersed with his memories of his wife Anna's terminal illness. As I will outline below, the novel's most striking feature is its assimilation of a range of sophisticated strategies drawn from the visual arts. Nowhere in Banville's earlier works are paintings integrated into the narrative to the degree that they are in *The Sea*, even in a novel like *Ghosts*, which repeatedly alludes to Watteau's work. With *The Sea*, Banvillean narrative perspective becomes radically shaped and influenced by visual art.

The presence of a secondary textual frame in *The Sea*, which is drawn from classical mythology, is evident from the outset. Carlo Grace, father of the twins Chloe and Myles, is described as being both man and deity. He is 'the one who appeared to be in command over us all, a laughing deity, the Poseidon of our Summer', yet he is also a 'grinning goat god' and a satyr.[40] His children are simultaneously children and the Graces of Greek myth; Myles, for example, is both a 'godling' and a 'malignant sprite'.[41] In addition, Max is a 'lyreless Orpheus',[42] trying to imaginatively recover his dead wife. These metaphorical parallels are so pervasive that the primary ontological frame of the novel is frequently punctured, as when Constance Grace transforms from woman to daemon and back to woman in adolescent Max's sexualized delirium. The impact of such persistent allusive doublings creates what Rüdiger Imhof calls 'an echo chamber of literary quotations and allusions',[43] such that the characters and their environment are perpetually themselves and other. This sense of the multiplicity of things extends at times to Max's engagement with phenomenological reality, as when he feels that everything 'seemed to be something else'.[44]

Max is writing a book on the French artist Pierre Bonnard, whose intertextual presence in *The Sea* resonates with aesthetic significance. Allusions to the artist are strewn throughout the text, and Max himself frequently draws our attention to them, as when he playfully observes that Bonnard 'would have caught that texture exactly, the quiet sheen and shimmer of it'.[45] More important, perhaps, is the way in which Max embeds subtle allusions in the fabric of his story, as when he recalls his first visit to the Cedars, the home of the Grace family: 'So there I am, in that Edenic moment at what was suddenly the centre of the world, with that shaft of sunlight and those

---

[40] John Banville, *The Sea* (New York: Alfred A. Knopf, 2005), 123, 125, 233.   [41] Ibid., 61, 226.
[42] Ibid., 24.
[43] Rüdiger Imhof, '*The Sea*: "Was't Well Done?"', *Irish University Review* 36, no. 1 (2006), 167.
[44] Banville, *The Sea*, 65.   [45] Ibid., 43.

vestigial flowers—sweet pea? all at once I seem to see sweet pea.'[46] As Monica Facchinello has observed, *Sweetpeas* is the title of a 1912 painting by Bonnard.[47] More revealingly, Max, in recalling Chloe as a child, sees a similarity between her facial features and those of a spectral figure in a still life by Bonnard: 'She wore [her hair] in a pageboy style, with a fringe at the front overhanging her handsome, high-domed, oddly convex forehead—like, it suddenly strikes me, remarkably like the forehead of that ghostly figure seen in profile hovering at the edge of Bonnard's *Table in Front of the Window*.'[48] The presence of a barely visible human figure is significant because while such figures in Bonnard's work bear some vague resemblance to life, they also speak of an otherness, of presence beyond precise conception and representation. That is to say, they are not about something, they are that something, thus echoing Banville's own artistic credo.

Bonnard's painting of his wife Marthe, which Max refers to as *Nude in the Bath, with Dog*, occupies a position of central significance in *The Sea*.[49] Max's ekphrasis of this work in part two of the novel reveals as much about his emotional response to Anna as it does about the painting itself. In fact, Imhof suggests that Bonnard's painting 'provides an exact correlative to the narrative'[50] of *The Sea*. The immediate connections between Bonnard's and Max's female subjects are clear from Max's reference to Marthe's dying within a year of the painting being initiated. Furthermore, Max states that he is reminded of Anna when he looks at the painting: 'Her right hand rests on her thigh, stilled in the act of supination, and I think of Anna's hands on the table that first day when we came back from Mr Todd, her helpless hands with palms upturned.'[51] The novel's artistic focus thus mirrors Bonnard's aesthetic images, while the painter's aesthetic views resonate with Banville's ideas on art and representation. For example, Bonnard argued that while one 'always speaks of submitting to the demands of nature', there is also 'the demands of the picture' to consider, and noted that the painter's 'principal subject is the surface which has its colour, its laws, over and above those of objects'.[52] The 'demands of the picture' make similar claims on Banville, as is evident in his prioritization of form above content and surface above 'meaning'.

John Banville's aesthetic appropriation of Pierre Bonnard is similar to his assimilation of writers like Wallace Stevens and Rainer Maria Rilke in the earlier novels, and of Kleist throughout his career. His decision to adapt three of Kleist's plays—*Der zerbrochne Krug* (1811), *Amphitryon* (1807), and *Penthesilea* (1808)—as *The Broken Jug* (1994), *God's Gift*

---

[46] Ibid., 89.

[47] Monica Facchinello, '"The Old Illusion of Belonging": Distinctive Style, Bad Faith and John Banville's *The Sea*', *Estudios Irlandeses* 5 (2010), 39.

[48] Banville, *The Sea*, 137.

[49] The title Max ascribes to the paining is a minor variation on its correct title, *Nude in the Bath with Small Dog* (or *Nu dans le bain au petit chien*), which Bonnard began in 1941 and completed five years later. While this may be an error, it is more likely that Banville sought to allude to other Bonnard paintings, many of which feature a similar dog. See, for example, *Woman with Dog*, *Dressing Table and Mirror*, and *The Bathroom*, all of which include a dachshund.

[50] Imhof, '*The Sea*', 176.   [51] Banville, *The Sea*, 153.

[52] Quoted in Karen Wilkin, 'Pierre Bonnard's Late Interiors', *New Criterion* 27, no. 7 (2009), 43.

(2000), and *Love in the Wars* (2005) respectively, is therefore unsurprising.[53] Kleist's work appears to be of interest to Banville primarily because of a shared sense of the essential strangeness of human existence, what Kleist referred to as 'confusion'.[54] Banville finds in Kleist a fellow champion of the idea that existence is defined by how we negotiate the labyrinths of confusion rather than by how we resolve confusion into apparent order.[55] Both Banville's and Kleist's works depict the confusion of self and the overt strangeness of being. In a sense, all of Banville's work—and, arguably, that of his alter ego Benjamin Black—can be seen to grapple with these essentially ontological questions. In *God's Gift* and *The Infinities*, one can clearly discern many of Banville's familiar traits: playfulness, profound self-consciousness, the language of acting, the imagery of forgery and imitation, the duplicity of phenomenal reality, and an extension of his grand artistic metaphor to include the Greek gods as emblems of doubling, otherness, and strangeness.

Banville's decision, as he entered his seventh decade, to write crime novels under a pen name appeared to mark a significant new artistic departure. Yet while the eight Quirke novels published to date—*Christine Falls* (2006), *The Silver Swan* (2007), *Elegy for April* (2010), *A Death in Summer* (2011), *Vengeance* (2012), *Holy Orders* (2013), *Even the Dead* (2015), and *Prague Nights* (2017)—offer a sophisticated reconstitution of his literary focus, the aesthetic rationale may not be as dramatically different as it initially seems. Banville's novels, after all, have always been built around a variant of the detective genre—the philosophical detection quest—and therefore the narrative mode is not too dissimilar to that employed in the Quirke novels, with their intellectual mystery games, stock criminals, and seemingly irresolvable crimes. Banville's philosophical detection quests are always related to aspects of the creative process via an engagement with language, memory, the imagination, creative-scientific pursuits, the visual arts, and acting, while Black's detection quests are more closely related to the stock features of resolving crimes. Nevertheless, the detection process in the Quirke series frequently raises epistemological questions that recall those interrogated in Banville's non-detective fiction. More pertinently, perhaps, the kinds of imagery deployed by Black and Banville often strike echoing notes that chime with each other, as do their allusive frames and styles of characterization, as evidenced by the increasing similarities between Phoebe Quirke and Cass Cleave.

In the Black novels, Quirke, the chief pathologist at the Hospital of the Holy Family in 1950s Dublin, is repeatedly drawn into criminal plots along with his sidekick, Inspector Hackett, while his adoptive father is apparently connected to several crimes involving the Catholic Church. The novels' ostensibly socio-political plotlines mark an important fundamental difference between Black's novels and those of Banville, even though the

[53] In a further appropriative twist, *God's Gift*, Banville's rewriting of *Amphitryon* (which was itself inspired by Molière's 1668 comic version of the Greek myth) appeared in a prose rendition as *The Infinities* in 2009.

[54] Cited in David Constantine, 'Introduction', in *Heinrich von Kleist: Selected Writings*, xxi.

[55] I discuss the influence of Kleist on Banville's work in greater length in 'John Banville and Heinrich von Kleist: The Art of Confusion', *Review of Contemporary Fiction* 34, no. 1 (2014), 54–70.

novelist himself is somewhat resistant to this reading of his work. For instance, when asked by Hugh Haughton 'if, under the name of Benjamin Black, there is a more politically conscious writer about the historical Ireland' at work, Banville disagreed, saying: 'I really believe that any writer who imagines he has a social voice is in trouble. If you mix politics and art, you get bad politics and bad art. . . . For art, subject is always incidental, or at least secondary, to the work itself.'[56] Such observations are consistent with others Banville has made about the social realist novel throughout his career, in which he has insisted that subject matter—or 'meaning'—is secondary to form and style. And yet, the fact that many of the crimes and corrupt practices with which Quirke becomes embroiled are connected in circuitous ways to the institutional Church and organizations with which it was closely associated in the 1950s has led some critics to discern clearer political subtexts in the Black novels than one finds in Banville's more 'literary' offerings.[57] Moreover, a note of socio-political critique can be heard in some of Banville's reflections on the Quirke series, such as when he likens mid-century Irish Catholic repression to that of post-war totalitarian regimes:

> Of course, we were under the yoke of an iron ideology. We were told in those days that the Soviet satellite countries, behind the Iron Curtain, they are not free there. We are free. . . . The church and state were hand in hand just as the state and party were hand in hand there. And our lives were completely un-free.[58]

This view finds its way into the novels, with Quirke warning Phoebe about the nature of the Catholic Church in *Even the Dead*: 'They're just the same as the Communists they're always warning us about—two sides of the same coin.'[59]

Despite such sentiments, Banville disagrees that the Quirke novels have political intent and instead insists that the Church-centred plots are 'just material'.[60] Refuting the suggestion that he has 'a crusading social purpose' in these novels, he maintained in one interview that he 'just wanted to write a novel, and the scandals that had just begun to be revealed at that time seemed ideal for my purpose'.[61] Yet in another he admitted that the growing public awareness of the historical crimes committed by Irish Catholic clerics 'was preying on my mind'.[62] Nonetheless, while the subject matter of the Quirke novels may be more socially recognizable than the preoccupations of Banville's other fiction, in the author's own terms it remains incidental. Whether as Banville or Black, his chief aim is to create works of art, not rhetoric. Denis Donoghue's distinction

[56] Haughton and Radley, 'An Interview with John Banville', 867–8.

[57] See, for example, Haughton and Radley, 'An Interview with John Banville', 857.

[58] Cited in Jim Ruland, 'Guest Profile: Benjamin Black Interview Parts 1-4', *The Elegant Variation: A Literary Weblog*, 8 December 2008.

[59] Benjamin Black, *Even the Dead* (London: Penguin, 2016), 194.

[60] Erin Mitchell, 'Q & A with Benjamin Black', *Crimespree Magazine*, 27 January 2016. http://crimespreemag.com/qa-with-benjamin-black/. Accessed 1 June 2016.

[61] Ibid.   [62] Ruland, 'Guest Profile'.

between eloquence and rhetoric is useful here: rhetoric 'has an aim, to move people to do one thing rather than another', while eloquence 'has no aim: it is a play of words or other expressive means. It is a gift to be enjoyed in appreciation and practice. The main attribute of eloquence is gratuitousness.'[63] So although some of Banville's interviews, essays, and reviews contain rhetorical statements about the Catholic Church, no such rhetorical purpose is *foregrounded* in the Quirke novels, despite their being in accord with many contemporary readers' sense of injustice and outrage at the ethical contagion that the Church came to represent in late twentieth-century Ireland.

Whether we encounter Banville's anxious intellectual adventurers or the erstwhile Quirke struggling through the grime of Dublin's criminal culture, the disinterested self-containment is similar. Arguably, Benjamin Black's fictive worlds are simply those of John Banville recreated in modified form. The same sense of the 'veiled and deceptive nature of things'[64] persists, and as Morrow tells us in *Athena*, citing Adorno, 'works of art recall the theologoumenon that in a state of redemption everything will be just as it is and yet wholly different'.[65] This aesthetic imperative governs the shift from Banville to Black. The characters in Black's detective novels inhabit an intertextually framed universe just as their near relatives do in Banville's novels. The use of the detective form in the Black novels may initially be misleading, given the usual generic expectations, but Banville's deployment of the form extends beyond such expectations. It represents an elaborate intellectual playfulness because it mirrors the unresolved intellectual quest motif that governs so much of Banville's work.

In all, the Benjamin Black novels amount to a formal reconstitution of the philosophical and poetic framing that characterizes John Banville's entire oeuvre. Banville's fictions are distinguished by an aestheticized surface veneer and so too are the Quirke novels, replete with marionette figures and intertextual frames. In both cases, such overt declarations of fictionality offer ample evidence of an extremely sophisticated form of self-reflexive novelistic practice, which has been the defining feature of Banville's aesthetic from the outset, and which has become progressively complex and varied over time. Rather than simply recycle the anti-epistemological focus that characterizes the metafictional novel, however, his work has always revolved around an almost traditional model of aesthetic value, particularly with respect to the visual arts. Painters like Watteau, Bonnard, Fragonard, Van Gogh, and several other French and Dutch still-life painters do not sit comfortably with a poetics of postmodernism, and yet they offer a key to the specific nature of Banville's variation on the self-conscious mode. At the centre of his narrators' obsessions lies a perpetual engagement with the value and feasibility of art in what is surely one of the most innovative variations on the self-reflexive form in contemporary literature.

---

[63] Denis Donoghue, *On Eloquence* (New Haven, CT: Yale University Press, 2008), 3.
[64] Black, *Even the Dead*, 112.   [65] Banville, *Athena*, 105.

Further Reading

Banville, John. 'Survivors of Joyce'. In Augustine Martin (ed.), *James Joyce: The Artist and the Labyrinth*. London: Ryan Publishing, 1990: 73–81.

Banville, John. 'Making Little Monsters Walk'. In Clare Boylan (ed.), *In The Agony and the Ego: The Art and Strategy of Fiction Writing Explored*. Harmondsworth: Penguin, 1993: 105–12.

Banville, John. 'The Personae of Summer'. In Jacqueline Genet and Wynne Hellegouarc'h (eds), *Irish Writers and Their Creative Process*. Gerrards Cross: Colin Smythe, 1996: 118–22.

Donoghue, Denis. *Speaking of Beauty*. New Haven, CT: Yale University Press, 2003.

Hand, Derek. *John Banville: Exploring Fictions*. Dublin: Liffey Press, 2002.

Haughton, Hugh and Bryan Radley. 'An Interview with John Banville'. *Modernism/Modernity* 18, no. 4 (2011): 855–69.

Imhof, Rüdiger. *John Banville: A Critical Introduction*. Dublin: Wolfhound Press, 1997.

Kenny, John. *John Banville*. Dublin: Irish Academic Press, 2009.

McMinn, Joseph. *The Supreme Fictions of John Banville*. Manchester: Manchester University Press, 1999.

McMinn, Joseph. 'Ekphrasis and the Novel: The Presence of Paintings in John Banville's Fiction'. *Word and Image: A Journal of Verbal/Visual Enquiry* 18, no. 3 (2002): 137–45.

Murphy, Neil. *John Banville*. Lewisburg, PA: Bucknell University Press, 2018.

O'Connell, Mark. *John Banville's Narcissistic Fictions* (Basingstoke: Palgrave Macmillan, 2013).

Schwall, Hedwig. 'An Interview with John Banville'. *European English Messenger* 6, no. 1 (1997): 13–19.

Smith, Eoghan. *John Banville: Art and Authenticity*. Bern: Peter Lang, 2014.

Watkins, Nicholas. *Bonnard*. London: Phaidon Press, 1994.

CHAPTER 19

....

SEX AND VIOLENCE
IN NORTHERN IRISH
WOMEN'S FICTION

....

CAROLINE MAGENNIS

HISTORICALLY, fiction by Northern Irish women writers has often served to fill the representational lacunae left by the frequently stereotypical images found in the work of their male counterparts on both sides of the Irish Sea. This has certainly been the case for much of the period since the early 1970s, particularly during the thirty-year-long conflict that preceded the Belfast or Good Friday Agreement of 1998. Traditionally, literary portrayals of women tended to fall into one of two categories, either 'angels of the home, their political involvement confined to . . . providing shelter for the fugitive'[1] or sexualized *femme fatales*, beautiful but deadly. Needless to say, these twin stereotypes greatly simplify women's complexity as human beings and their agency as social and political actors, yet their dichotomized nature can itself be read as a function of an intensely polarized political conflict. Linda Anderson's (1949–) 1984 novel, *To Stay Alive*, presented an early rebuke to such simplistic views, as when a police officer observes: 'Women, in this country at any rate, are as ruthless and as vicious as the men.'[2] Gerardine Meaney pursued this line in more detail in her 1991 LIP pamphlet, arguing that Irish women are not

> essentially more peaceable, less dogmatic, uninfected by bloodthirsty political ideologies. Women have been actively involved in every possible variant of both nationalism and unionism. They too have been prejudiced and brought up their

---

[1] Margaret Ward, *The Missing Sex: Putting Women into History* (Dublin: Attic Press, 1991), 7. Jayne Steel has interrogated the terrorist *femme fatale* stereotype in late twentieth-century Irish and British fiction. See her 'Vampira: Representations of the Irish Female Terrorist', *Irish Studies Review* 6, no. 3 (1998), 273–84 and *Demons, Hamlets and Femme Fatales: Representations of Irish Republicanism in Popular Fiction* (Bern: Peter Lang, 2007).

[2] Linda Anderson, *To Stay Alive* (London: Bodley Head, 1984), 23.

children to be prejudiced. Women have supported and carried out violent actions. They have gained and lost from their involvement. If patriarchal history has portrayed us as bystanders to the political process, it has lied. We have always been implicated, even in our own oppression.[3]

As a negotiated political settlement painstakingly began to take shape in the years following the 1994 paramilitary ceasefires, the hitherto limited understanding of the role of women in the conflict was expanded by feminist scholars who began to analyse previously unacknowledged realities, including 'the often silenced experiences of wives and mothers following the imprisonment and/or deaths of their husbands and sons . . .; the violence orchestrated against women and the rupturing of private spaces and traditional boundaries . . .; the participation of women in public protests and peace-building . . .; and, more recently, the involvement of women in paramilitary activity'.[4] As this scholarship continues apace, this is an opportune moment to revisit fiction produced during the 1980s, when the conflict was in full spate, before considering works written in the years since the Belfast Agreement, specifically those published between 2006 and 2016, during which time the North has been slowly transitioning into a 'post-conflict' society.[5]

Both of these periods produced some remarkably vibrant works of long- and short-form fiction which attend to markedly different political and social circumstances. Given the transformations that have occurred since the 1980s, differences of thematic emphasis are to be expected, yet shared preoccupations also emerge, particularly with regard to the treatment of the effects of violence on Northern Irish women's psychic, emotional, and sexual lives, which will be the main focus of this chapter. As we shall see, female novelists and short story writers in these respective eras share a lineage of using fiction to voice the hidden, the stigmatized, and the unspoken. Rather than present the personal sphere as somehow immune from political and sectarian conflict, they dramatize the ways in which the zone of war traverses embodied subjectivities and extends into the realm of private experience. Their work punctures the veneer of domestic civility conferred by the veneration of the nuclear family in Northern Irish life and shows intimacy between the sexes to be characteristically dark, troubling, and fraught with danger for women, despite the transformations mentioned above. Analysing these respective literary corpuses alongside each other illuminates the embodied and affective impact of violence on the lives of particular women in particular places and times.

---

[3] Gerardine Meaney, *Sex and Nation: Women in Irish Culture and Politics* (Dublin: Attic Press, 1991), 15.

[4] Sara McDowell, 'Commemorating Dead "Men": Gendering the Past and Present in Post-conflict Northern Ireland', *Gender, Place and Culture* 15, vol. 4 (2008), 335.

[5] The term 'post-conflict' is used in this chapter because while the major paramilitary groups in Northern Ireland have been on ceasefire since 1998, sporadic violence still occurs, particularly during the summer months. Furthermore, the suspension of the Northern Ireland Assembly in January 2017 as a result of a row between the two governing parties, the Democratic Unionist Party (DUP) and Sinn Féin, coincided with a rise in dissident republican activity, which created international headlines in April 2019 when journalist Lyra McKee was killed during riots in Derry/Londonderry.

'WHAT IS THE COLOUR OF SHAME?': LIVING WITH EXTREMES OF LOVE AND HATE DURING THE TROUBLES

This section will focus on fiction written in the years between the republican hunger strikes in the Maze Prison during 1980 and 1981, which marked a pivotal turning point in the political strategy of the republican movement, and the Anglo-Irish Agreement signed by the British and Irish governments in November 1985, which provoked unprecedented levels of unionist opposition. As the political ground shifted radically during this period, Northern Irish women's fiction engaged directly with the impact of street violence, incarceration, social taboos, and other oppressive realities. Rebecca Pelan notes of this period that women writers in the North 'seem to be much less concerned with who is at fault than they are with representing the effects of the political conditions on women's lives',[6] an observation which highlights a key distinguishing feature of writers who sought to capture the crushing, gendered impact of violence and not merely its symbolic significance. As we shall see, their work is often unflinching in its representation the abject horror and brutality of violence during the Troubles, exhibiting a persistent concern with the effects of pain on women's bodies and minds and the impact of violence on families, neighbourhoods, and the wider community. It is significant that violence is shown to be enacted in private as well as in public spaces. By doing so, female authors complicate the association of domesticity with maternal femininity and question the extent to which home can be considered a place apart, a place of refuge, let alone the cherished, inviolable space envisioned by many traditionalists. Home functions as a complex metonym in this body of fiction, a site of sanctuary for some and a site of pleasure for others. No less commonly, home appears as an unsafe site in which domestic abuse and sexual assault are perpetrated in secret and where women's domestic autonomy is curtailed by the overwhelming force of patriarchal authority.

In *The Dark Hole Days* (1984), Belfast writer Una Woods presents the parallel lives of Joe and Colette, two Belfast youths from either side of the sectarian divide, who do not know each other and never meet but whose mutual entrapment by their social and political circumstances culminates in a tragic event in which their lives converge. The novella takes the form of alternate diary entries by the two central protagonists, whose first-person ruminations and accounts of their activities become intermixed with a third-person narrative voice as their stories unfold. Woods presents the Troubles as part of a broader picture of life in Northern Ireland during the 1980s for these restless, disenfranchised youngsters, whose desire for self-realization and intimacy is constrained by the ever-present reality of the political conflict. Colette yearns to escape Belfast and redefine herself, yet the alternative futures she imagines are shut down by the all-pervasive nature

---

[6] Rebecca Pelan, *Two Irelands: Literary Feminisms North and South* (Syracuse, NY: Syracuse University Press, 2005), 59.

of the conflict: 'All the people's thoughts. Ideas floating and clashing and breaking and falling and out of the dust another spark, another thought. Another man was shot today.'[7] In this context, the act of keeping a diary becomes a kind of proxy for living a more satisfying life elsewhere:

> With writing this I feel they [possibilities] may be opening up. And if I never do anything, at least I'll have this. It's an extra me. I've created an extension. Sometimes I think I love it so I can escape into its meaning. But in another way I'm ashamed of it, like I'm ashamed to cry or I'd be humiliated if somebody walked into my room and I had nothing on. How can I describe it? The rawness or something. You know what I mean?[8]

Joe is also profoundly affected by the climate of fear, violence, and uncertainty, but unlike Colette he chooses to look within his community for direction. He seeks a purpose by gravitating towards paramilitarism, consolidating his sense of masculinity through a rhetoric of righteous defence: 'Protection was a word he understood. It referred to people, to territory, to ideas. To be the protector, not the aggressor was to be on the side of right.'[9] But behind his macho public persona lies an emotional vulnerability and a craving for intimacy. Joe develops a strong attraction to a young woman who works in his local dole office, not only because he is painfully lonely but also because she treats him with dignity. There is no evidence that his feelings for her are reciprocated, however. Instead, we see Joe project his intense longings onto the woman and weave a fantasy from his perfunctory weekly interactions with her. While the overwrought emotionalism of his imaginings are reminiscent of a popular romance novel, some are inflected by disturbing signs of a latent need to inflict pain: 'I would make her cry just to watch her tears and to protect her. And then she would sleep with her hair falling all over the white pillow and she would know that I was there, so that a silent peace would rest on her lips.'[10] Such passages suggest that Joe's involvement with the agents of violence has caused his grasp on reality to break down, a process accelerated by his living in terror of his erstwhile associates as a result in his absconding from the scene of a random sectarian murder. The fact that the victim was Colette's father means that her hopes of starting a new life as a civil servant in England are ruined, leaving her in a 'pit of mourning': 'We're stamped as victims now. We'll always be the victims of the troubles, and I thought I was before. But it was the knowledge that I could be.'[11]

To Stay Alive also deals with the violence and brutality of the Troubles through a juxtaposition of the experiences of men and women, particularly the reproductive bodies of women and the victimized bodies of men. The sense of disaffection that pervades Woods's novella is strongly present in this juxtaposition, as is a perception of the sheer ubiquity of violent death. Colette's bleak impression of Belfast as a city where 'unimportant people were killing equally unimportant people'[12] is echoed by Anderson's narrator,

---

[7] Una Woods, *The Dark Hole Days* (Belfast: Blackstaff Press, 1984), 18.   [8] Ibid., 22.
[9] Ibid., 45.   [10] Ibid., 33.   [11] Ibid., 58.   [12] Ibid., 51.

who, following the novel's opening scene in which a dog is shot for target practice, reflects: 'Death. Nothing but death. The whole fucking city. A necropolis.'[13] Rosaleen's dissatisfaction with her shotgun marriage to Danny, a medical student, is magnified as the loyalties of their small community close in around them and she seeks succour in the arms of Gerry, a British soldier. Throughout, Anderson highlights Rosaleen's physical desires and shows how she must temper them to assuage her husband's ego: 'It was her lovemaking that made him uneasy. There was a physical readiness in her, something frank and voluptuous. He liked to hold her for a long time with her clothes on. He wanted some resistance.'[14]

Rosaleen's sexual desire is considered as much of a destabilizing force in the couple's lives as the political conflict. She herself is often preoccupied with the disjuncture between her feigned coyness and her authentic, raw sexuality. Sex and violence are acutely conflated in her relationship with Gerry, whose obsession with her begins when he sees her picture at a security briefing and becomes heightened as he hears stories of the dangers of taboo encounters: '"Irish men piss on soldiers' tarts", he remembered, and in that moment, desire flooded him. His prick stiffened and twitched like a divining rod over sudden water.'[15] Their lovemaking is fierce and impulsive and often takes the reader by surprise, as when they initiate intercourse in a cemetery. Yet Gerry develops genuine love for Rosaleen and, in one of the few depictions of cunnilingus in Northern Irish fiction, is determined to please her sexually: 'He dropped to his knees and raised her night-dress, covering her thighs with kisses and then gently pressing his mouth to her vulva.'[16] This intimate, caring interlude is all too fleeting, however, in a novel that is otherwise deeply unsentimental about depicting the most grotesque violence in 'the terrible bloody North of Ireland'.[17]

One year after the publication of *The Dark Hole Days* and *To Stay Alive*, an anthology of women's writing was produced to mark the tenth anniversary of the Northern Ireland Women's Rights Movement. *The Female Line* (1985) was edited by Ruth Hooley (1953–), later Ruth Carr, who in her brief introduction explains that, although the volume 'is not putting forward a particular viewpoint or political slant', it is avowedly feminist in being 'a women-only publication'.[18] One might go further and argue that the project's feminism is also signalled by the inclusion of a diverse range of female experiences, many of which shatter social and moral taboos. Hooley notes that while home, family, and personal relations are predominant preoccupations, the contributions also move beyond the 'limitations of the domestic situation' towards themes 'of escape, of the imagination, and more particularly the birth of the self as an independent, political being'.[19] The anthology, then, aspired to engage with local concerns—Hooley acknowledges that the Troubles are never 'very far from the door'—while at the same time gesturing towards experiences that are common to women across cultures: 'What emerges most readily

---

[13] Anderson, *To Stay Alive*, 7.   [14] Ibid., 12.   [15] Ibid., 27.
[16] Ibid., 191.   [17] Ibid., 192.
[18] Ruth Hooley, 'Introduction', in Ruth Hooley (ed.), *The Female Line: Northern Ireland Women Writers* (Belfast: Northern Ireland Women's Rights Movement, 1985), 1.
[19] Ibid., 2.

from these writings are mixed feelings of dis-satisfaction, alienation, affection and humour: a sense of belonging and disowning.'[20]

Many of the contributions in *The Female Line* emphasize the oppressive double bind of Northern Irish women during the 1980s, compelled as they were to navigate the intermeshed codes of patriarchy, misogyny, violent sectarianism, and the military response of the British state. This is perhaps best exemplified by the three short stories in the volume by Brenda Murphy (1953–). The first, 'A Curse', focuses on a young woman being held in a cell awaiting interrogation. Throughout the Troubles, there were persistent complaints, mainly from within the Catholic nationalist population, about the brutality of the interrogation techniques adopted by the British Army and the Royal Ulster Constabulary (RUC).[21] Yet Murphy immediately wrong-foots the reader by showing her nameless protagonist in the throes of severe period pain, the intensity of which is graphically evoked. This opening sets the scene for a work that foregrounds the gender-specific privations of women who experience the brunt of a harsh police and prison system. The woman's mere mention of menstruation prompts a disgusted male police officer to brand her as shameless, which prompts her to wonder: 'What is the colour of shame? All she could see was red as it trickled down her leg.'[22] Alone and distressed, the woman's appeal for empathy from a policewoman is met with further brusqueness, thus demonstrating that, in this deeply divided society, political loyalties take precedence over gender solidarity. As Pelan notes, as well as 'an intense sense of confinement and powerlessness, Murphy's story addresses two problematic aspects of gender politics in Northern Ireland: what women are permitted to speak about, and the failed notion of female solidarity.'[23] At no point does the narrator explain what part she has taken in the conflict, though we learn that this is not her first time in an interrogation room. 'A Curse' sheds light on those experiences which are outside received narratives of 'the struggle' and offers an insight into what women had to endure while keeping their mouths shut.

In 'Happy Birth Day', Murphy dramatizes the acute pain and pleasure of the maternity ward. The excruciating agony of a woman in labour—'I feel it will rip open the seams of my skin. . . . I am consumed now by the urge to push and eject'[24]—is sharply contrasted with the overwhelming sensations of seeing her baby girl's tiny hands and feeling her latch on to her breast for the first time. Such a juxtaposition of intense pain and spontaneous love subverts the trope of sainted Irish motherhood and gives expression to the visceral immediacy of the physical and emotional extremes a woman experiences when giving birth. Murphy's final story, 'Limbo', which is barely half a page long, shows that she can represent the exquisite ache of desire as well as the torment of the maternity ward and interrogation cell. As before, the narrative is focused around intense

---

[20] Ibid.

[21] See Allen Feldman, *Formations of Violence: The Narrative of the Body and Political Terror in Northern Ireland* (Chicago, IL: University of Chicago Press, 1991) and Huw Bennett, ' "Smoke Without Fire"? Allegations against the British Army in Northern Ireland, 1972–5', *Twentieth Century British History* 24, no. 2 (2013), 275–304.

[22] Brenda Murphy, 'A Curse', in Hooley (ed.), *The Female Line*, 40.   [23] Pelan, *Two Irelands*, 72.

[24] Brenda Murphy, 'Happy Birth Day', in Hooley (ed.), *The Female Line*, 93.

feelings rendered in graphic detail. Here, an unnamed narrator speaks of powerful emotions that are changeable and contradictory. Murphy conveys a woman in a troubled, unsettled state of mind, one who is agitated and fearful yet also capable of remarkable passion: 'This human skin I'm in contains all those emotions, good and bad. It can still surprise me with sudden outbursts of love and lust. Lust for the same person I've loved for years.'[25] As in 'Happy Birth Day', female embodiment offers pleasure and possibility alongside the traditional narrative of suffering. All three stories foreground the diverse ways in which women's experiences of living in a time of intense community conflict are mediated corporeally as well as psychologically, showing the female body to be a protean site of duress, vulnerability, need, and resilience.

In Anne Devlin's (1951–) contribution to *The Female Line*, 'Five Notes After a Visit', a Catholic Northern Irish woman returns to Belfast from England after her Protestant partner gets a teaching job in the city. Like *The Dark Hole Days*, the story adopts a diaristic form, with three of the five eponymous notes being precisely dated. Two potent shadows hang over the narrative: the narrator's lover's ex-wife, who is depicted as emotionally unstable, and the omnipresent hum of the Troubles, within which the narrator feels imprisoned. Devlin emphasizes the quotidian ways in which conflict impacts on the narrator's family—'There is barbed wire on the flowerbeds in my father's garden. A foot patrol trampled his crocuses last spring'[26]—and her constant alertness to possible danger. Her worst fears are realized when she receives an anonymous death threat, which prompts her to return to England alone, only to find that there is no immunity from the Troubles there either. Her postman tells her that his son is serving in the British Army in Northern Ireland; her local shopping centre endures its third bomb scare in a week. Hope is glimpsed in the sight of a busker playing a love song and a woman who refuses to discriminate on the grounds of nationality. Yet the tone and content of the final note are grave: 'Noday. Nodate 1984. I keep myself awake all night so I am ready when they come.'[27] The narrator's distorted syntax, hyper-vigilance, and allusion to a non-specific 'they' suggest a mind so deeply affected by the Troubles that its very sanity is now in question.

Attempts to 'read' the conflict take on a literal aspect in Fiona Barr's 'The Wall-Reader', a short story that offers further insights into the insidious forms of social control that operated within communities during the worst years of the conflict. In this story, the malaise of the post-war housewife, as detailed by Betty Friedan in *The Feminine Mystique* (1963), collides with a middle-class fetishism of the violence of the Troubles. The story concerns a Belfast couple, Mary and Sean, whose ordered life is rent asunder as a result of the wife's transgression of the social codes imposed upon women in this fractured society. The narrative begins with Mary on a taxi journey, silently pondering the origins and meaning of 'Belfast's grim graffiti'[28] and, by extension, the conflict itself. Although the city is depicted as a dystopian landscape, Mary and Sean are relatively insulated by

---

[25] Brenda Murphy, 'Limbo', in Hooley (ed.), *The Female Line*, 136.
[26] Anne Devlin, 'Five Notes After a Visit', in Hooley (ed.), *The Female Line*, 61.   [27] Ibid., 67.
[28] Fiona Barr, 'The Wall Reader', in Hooley (ed.), *The Female Line*, 82.

their class status and daily routine. Yet this same routine has become oppressive for this new mother, who hankers for something more.

It is unclear whether the cause of Mary's disaffection lies in the suffocating confines of a patriarchal society or in the quietism that is central to staying safe during this time of violent conflict. Whatever its cause, tedium and a lack of fulfilment have driven Mary to develop an eccentric hobby ('Respectable housewives don't read walls!') and she longs to see her own name daubed on concrete, thus 'declaring her existence worth while'.[29] It is not her name, however, but the word 'tout' that appears on the wall of her driveway, put there by those who have observed her in regular covert dialogue with an on-duty British soldier, with whom she forms a tentative platonic bond by sharing experiences of child-rearing. Within hours of this message appearing, the couple makes plans to relocate to Dublin, with Mary's thoughts now exclusively focused on her infant daughter's future: 'She was her touchstone, her anchor to virtue. Not for her child a legacy of fear, revulsion or hatred.'[30] Thus, like 'Five Notes After a Visit', 'The Wall-Reader' ends with a woman's departure from the troubled North in an attempt to escape a culture of fear, surveillance, and the policing of female behaviour by sinister forces.

'She was Always Bracing Herself': Navigating Intimacy in 'Post-Conflict' Northern Ireland

Although overshadowed at the time of its publication by other works that were taken to be more representative of Northern Irish life in the 1980s, *The Female Line* represented an important literary intervention, insofar as it inserted women's creative voices into a male-dominated literary sphere and asserted the specificity of their experiences in a society dominated by masculinist discourses of violent struggle. In her preface to the 2016 digital reprint of the anthology, Ruth Carr reflects:

> in that bleak era of Thatcherism and conflict dominated by issues of national iden-tity, taboo-breaking fiction, poetry and drama was lifting the lid on still closer oppressions in women's lives. There was a distinct sense of 'can do'—most likely trickling down, somewhat belatedly, from more dynamic cultural centres elsewhere in the world.[31]

Carr goes on to review the changed literary landscape for Northern Irish women writers in the twenty-first century, noting that it has taken a full thirty years for a second all-female anthology to appear. The work in question, *The Glass Shore: Short Stories by Women Writers*

---

[29] Ibid., 83.   [30] Ibid., 87.
[31] Ruth Carr, *The Female Line: Northern Ireland Women Writers* (Belfast: Herself Press, 2016), no pagination.

from the North of Ireland (2016), edited by Sinéad Gleeson, is a fiction-only volume that offers a diversity of viewpoints and narrative techniques and, importantly, allows lines of connection to be drawn between contemporary Northern Irish lives.[32]

Critic Rónán McDonald has argued, with reference to Troubles fiction, that 'the short story form both reflects the problems of articulation and representation within that fractious political situation and, with its characteristically wry, elliptical point of view, can be a subversive strategy of understatement'.[33] This imperative, while palpable during times of extreme violence, is arguably as vital in this 'post-conflict' era as Northern Irish women writers respond to political and social shifts in works that probe the changing condition of women as embodied subjects in a culture and society still deeply scarred by sectarian violence. This section will consider the treatment of emotional and sexual intimacy in works by three writers who have come to prominence in the 'new' Northern Ireland—Bernie McGill (1967–), Jan Carson (1980–), and Lucy Caldwell (1981–)— whose short stories and novels are deeply revealing of the continuities as well as the changes being witnessed in the aftermath of the Troubles.

Among the qualities that distinguish Bernie McGill's potent debut collection, *Sleepwalkers* (2013), are its outward-looking perspectives and its variety of cultural settings and scenarios. Landscapes are vividly rendered, from Ancona and Andalusia to the Northern Irish coast. While loss is often at the centre of McGill's stories, they are also, in places, ripe with sensuality. Food, sex, and everyday pleasures are explored alongside pain and haunting. For example, the opening story, 'Home', tells of a woman who seeks solace from a personal tragedy by escaping to the French coast and having an affair with a younger American man. Her sensual pleasure is set against a vivid retelling of the family accident that has psychically scarred her. The past also intrudes on the present in 'The Language Thing', in which a young teaching assistant from Belfast meets with a friend from Ireland while they are both on a European placement. The protagonist's displacement is compounded by the flashes of violence she sees in dispatches from home: 'She doesn't have much Italian but the pictures need no translating. You see a body on the ground, a priest on his knees, catch the word "Belfast", before the boys close in.'[34] The women attempt to distract some persistent suitors by speaking prayers in Irish to each other, but the images continue to intrude. In 'No Angel', a daughter is haunted by thoughts of her dead brother and father. The latter spectre is keener on dispensing mundane fatherly advice than rattling chains, yet insists on his son having an open casket following his violent death so that mourners can 'look and know what animals we're living amongst'.[35] McGill's stories are not conventional Troubles narratives; indeed, one has to read the signifiers carefully in some of them to recognize the legacies

---

[32] *The Glass Shore* followed the success of *The Long Gaze Back: An Anthology of Irish Women Writers* (2015), also edited by Gleeson, which largely comprises new stories by contemporary writers from both sides of the Irish border.

[33] Rónán McDonald, 'Strategies of Silence: Colonial Strains in Short Stories of the Troubles', *The Yearbook of English Studies* 35 (2005), 249.

[34] Bernie McGill, 'The Language Thing', in *Sleepwalkers* (Belfast: Whittrick Press, 2013), 35.

[35] Bernie McGill, 'No Angel', in *Sleepwalkers*, 43.

they bear. *Sleepwalkers* is a book of aftermaths, one that probes what happens in the wake of illness, bereavement, and love. A recognition of the need to bear witness to violence and accept its repercussions coexists with a determination to embrace all that the present and future have to offer. McGill's stories echo what the narrator of 'Islander' imagines her unborn child is telling her: 'We carry the living, and we do whatever it takes to wake the dead.'[36]

Ballymena-born Jan Carson's remarkable short story collection, *Children's Children* (2016), explores themes of birth, adolescence, sex, and death. The stories are playful and experimental in style and range from the lightly absurdist to the dazzlingly fantastical. In general, the stories are difficult to place temporally, but it is clear that they are mostly set in and around Belfast, where Carson works as a community arts officer. Problems associated with intimacy are present throughout and childhood and child-rearing are simultaneously demystified and made fantastical. In 'We've Got Each Other and That's a Lot', scammers exploit infertile couples to the soundtrack of Bon Jovi; in 'Contemporary Uses for a Belfast Box Room', a couple use the eponymous room to store their first-born child. Parents haunted by dead children appear in 'In Feet and Gradual Inches', 'How They Were Sitting When Their Wings Fell Off', and 'Alternative Units'. In the last of these, the supernatural exists side by side with the domestic banality of IKEA tubs in the utility room, and the bearing of an everyday spectre is parsed as 'I didn't ask for a ghost child. It's not an ideal situation.'[37]

The opening story, 'Larger Ladies', focalizes a range of themes—immigration, loneliness, single parenthood, women's internalization of sexist values—through the eyes of Sonja, a young Polish single mother. Sonja works in a Belfast clinic that specializes in extreme weight loss therapy for women, where patients are sedated for extended periods and subjected to vibration treatment until they achieve their target weight. Whereas Sonja feels a degree of compassion for the women in her charge, she loathes 'the husbands who drove them to the clinic and picked them up afterwards, in low-flying weekend cars'.[38] If we were expecting the culturally defined experience of women in Northern Ireland to have been transformed since the 1980s, the outsider perspective provided by Sonja suggests that the coercive force of patriarchal values and attitudes remains strong. And while the Troubles may be over, women's experience of male-dominated public spaces is still characterized by fear and trepidation: 'Living in Belfast made her twitchy. There were noises everywhere: helicopters, sirens, young men swearing at each other sharply in the street. She was always bracing herself.'[39] This latent sense of menace colours Sonja's bond with her young son Dylan, of whom she is fiercely protective, the absence of a father in his life making her at once fearful for and fearful of the kind of man he may become. These anxieties are heightened at the story's close by the arrival of the first 'larger gentleman' at the clinic. Dylan's curiosity about him both intensifies Sonja's 'hunger for her son that was too sharp to bear sharing with anyone else'[40] and deepens her feelings of vulnerability and unsettlement. Yet again, a

[36] Bernie McGill, 'Islander', in *Sleepwalkers*, 71.
[37] Jan Carson, 'Alternative Units', in *Children's Children* (Dublin: Liberties Press, 2016), 159.
[38] Jan Carson, 'Larger Ladies', in *Children's Children*, 22.   [39] Ibid., 20.   [40] Ibid., 24.

female-authored Northern Irish short story ends with an image of a fearful woman in flight from the province.

Yet while macho masculinity excites fear and loathing in 'Larger Ladies', other stories in *Children's Children* brim with affection for the men of Belfast. 'Swept', a story that explores the changing nature of matrimonial dynamics in later life, exhibits a distinct empathy for the recently retired Bill, who is now a housebound husband. The funeral of Jim, a former shipyard worker, in 'Dinosaur Act' brings into focus the repressed emotional lives of 'big men with damp skin and proper suits, kept good for funerals and marching',[41] who come to pay their respects. 'Every one of them was thick with the need to cry, and not just about Jim', yet they 'were not the kind of men who cried, even over a dead wife—though a child might have been the exception'.[42] This story is also a closely observed study of the impact of an all-consuming grief on the Protestant faith of Jim's bereaved wife Sandra. Without Jim's 'quiet faith', which she both envied and despised, Sandra is prey to the religious doubt that has long shadowed her, and she now struggles to conceal the extent of her unbelief: 'The words had never held for Sandra and they did not hold now. She was too proud or stubborn, too bound to those truths you could prove with your eyes or your holding hands'.[43]

In Carson's stories, extremes of pain and pleasure often sit comfortably alongside the supernatural and the quotidian. 'Floater' opens with a female narrator informing her daughter that she was conceived in an airplane bathroom. The first-person voice laconically discloses intimate details of what was a decidedly unromantic encounter, thus creating the expectation of a frank confessional tale. These expectations are immediately dashed, however, by the revelation that this mother keeps her daughter 'anchored to the backyard fence by a single piece of purple ribbon'.[44] 'Shopping' is a comic tour de force which tells of an unconsummated 'supermarket love affair'[45] between two strangers, both married, who meet every Tuesday in Knocknagoney Tesco in Belfast. Their intimacy is conducted through putting items in each other's baskets, their hands fleetingly touching in the dairy aisle. Lust is kept in check by pragmatism: 'We never forgot, even for one heady second, that the shopping came first. It would have been ludicrous to return home without the hand soap or the mandarin oranges we'd set out for'.[46] The emotional peak of their unconventional dalliance coincides with its demise. He grabs her by the wrists in the frozen desserts aisle and rips open a box of ice creams; she realizes he 'was a civil servant in a BHS pullover, getting the groceries in. He was somebody's husband, much like my own, but thinner'.[47]

At one point in 'Shopping', the narrator compares herself and the object of her desire to 'compass points',[48] she sitting at the north-east corner of a café table, he at the south-west. This symbolically suggestive scenario is replicated in the title story of the collection, a parable about a woman from 'the south' and a man from 'the north' who, as the last of their kind, have accepted their fate, which is to be 'married for the good of the island, both

---

[41] Jan Carson, 'Swept', in *Children's Children*, 169.   [42] Ibid., 169–70.
[43] Ibid., 179, 182.   [44] Jan Carson, 'Floater', in *Children's Children*, 117.
[45] Jan Carson, 'Shopping', in *Children's Children*, 149.   [46] Ibid., 149.   [47] Ibid., 151.
[48] Ibid., 146.

northern and southern sides'.[49] The island is a place where people who are essentially the same as each other repress this knowledge and cleave to the zero-sum thinking of a partitioned state: 'On the island you were north or south, or you left for the mainland.'[50] The couple's willingness to overcome their inbred mutual suspicion of each other is thwarted by their inability to agree a side of the border on which to live. Since to move north or south would imperil the island's precarious balance, they remain apart, silently wondering 'if they loved the island enough to be neither north nor south, foreigner or familiar, but rather a brave new direction, balanced like a hairline fractured in the centre of everything.'[51] This ending captures the desire to jettison shibboleths in favour of more generative ways of living on a changing island, and the fragility of such hopes. As such, it is emblematic of the deeper mood of *Children's Children*, which balances the weight of historical legacies against the lightening possibilities of a transformed future.

Similar dual-faced perspectives are detectible in the fiction of another singular voice to emerge in this period, Belfast-born Lucy Caldwell, who has lived in England for most of her adult life. Her first novel, *Where They Were Missed* (2006), examines the violence of the Troubles through the eyes of two young girls, Daisy and Saoirse, whose adolescent longings are set against the backdrop of a political violence that they barely understand. The novel is also an exploration of mental illness and a young protagonist's attempt to make the disparate facets of her memories and identity cohere. The early chapters offer a sharp contrast between the 'harsh sounds of bombs and guns and ballyclavas'[52] and the Irish songs and stories the daughters' mother communicates in a hushed voice. The girls are only ever given a partial glimpse of the violence as they overhear stories told by adults or see media images of 'men dressed all in black with big black balaclavas pulled down over their faces and only little slits for their eyes.'[53] As the violence spirals, so too does their mother's descent into madness. The escapist fairytales she tells grow increasingly dark as she becomes more and more detached from reality, haunted by 'some great, unspeakable sadness' that 'lingered and clung in corners, pooling like mist in the spaces that people left behind as they turned their backs.'[54] In the second part of the novel, set in Donegal, Saoirse seeks to make sense of her mother's mental illness while she convalesces in a former Anglo-Irish Big House among women who 'have had terrible traumas in their pasts,'[55] while simultaneously grappling with her own desire to reconcile herself to her mixed-religious background. Saoirse, whose name translates as 'freedom', achieves a measure of liberation when she refuses the stories told by and about her family and instead sets about creating a new, integrated version of her identity which is grounded in her complex past but oriented towards a new horizon.

Caldwell's second novel, *The Meeting Point* (2011), deals with themes of faith, fidelity, and sensuality set against the violent conflict between the West and the Middle East that followed the attacks of 11 September 2001. A Protestant couple from Northern Ireland and their young daughter move to Bahrain, where, in small, intimate ways, their

---

[49] Jan Carson, 'Children's Children', in *Children's Children*, 184.
[50] Ibid., 186.   [51] Ibid., 190.
[52] Lucy Caldwell, *Where They Were Missed* (London: Viking, 2006), 41.   [53] Ibid., 24.
[54] Ibid., 46.   [55] Ibid., 177.

relationship begins to unravel. As Euan Armstrong sets about his missionary work in this majority Muslim country, his wife Ruth feels increasingly detached and alienated, as if 'Something in her has cracked. A hairline fissure, invisible to the eye.'[56] As their once passionate relationship stagnates into infrequent lovemaking, Ruth develops an attraction for a young local man, Farid. Caldwell's depiction of their interactions is playful and sensual, particularly her description of Ruth's experiences of Middle Eastern foods and street markets.

Often, Irish narratives of sexual guilt are rendered in a Catholic context; Caldwell demonstrates how deep-rooted such repressive taboos are within the Northern Irish Protestant evangelical community also. Desire and pain commingle in the novel's vivid depiction of Ruth's sexual reawakening far from home as her feelings of intense physical attraction for the Muslim other cut across her religious conditioning and make her question her faith. One encounter with Farid and a pomegranate leaves her obsessively thinking about knowledge and betrayal in the Genesis myth, yet her visceral lust for him is overwhelming: 'She feels it low in her sacrum, her pelvis, dark, hidden places: a dull, pulsing ache. She has never felt desire like this before. She has never been so miserable in her life.'[57] All of Caldwell's novels are concerned with aftermaths, and *The Meeting Point* also registers the extent to which lost loves have an embodied afterlife. After leaving Bahrain and Farid behind, a fierce pain remains, one which Ruth comes to see as 'not a real wound: just the ghost of an old one.'[58]

The international canvas and multicultural colouration of *The Meeting Point* are replicated in Caldwell's third novel, *All the Beggars Riding* (2013), which is set in London but takes in experiences from Belfast, Chernobyl, and the West Indies. Like several of her other works, the plot centres on a woman's attempt to construct a coherent personal narrative in the wake of trauma and involves the uncovering of a secret which has both painful and cathartic consequences. 'Even our own stories, we're unequipped and essentially unable to tell',[59] reflects protagonist Lara Moorhouse, a woman nearing forty who lost her Belfast-born father when she was a child and is now nursing her dying mother. Memory is an unstable, volatile force in the novel, one quite distinct from the process of crafting fiction. As Lara begins to understand her past, the impulse to recreate it precisely falls away and she turns instead to the story of her neighbour Mr Rawalpindi and his experiences of immigration from the West Indies, which include covert homosexual encounters. Thus, *All the Beggars Riding* extols the virtues of turning outwards from a solipsistic preoccupation with one's own narrative towards a reconsideration of the humanity of others. Ironically, the catalyst for Lara is a trip to Belfast, a place that once represented so much pain and trauma for her family but which she now sees in a fresh light: 'If you don't know Belfast, if all you know of it is the litany of murders and maimings, the annual images of marching and rioting, the hardened male voices defending or accusing on the radio, there's nothing to prepare you for how beautiful it is.'[60]

---

[56] Lucy Caldwell, *The Meeting Point* (London: Faber and Faber, 2011), 43.   [57] Ibid., 189.
[58] Ibid., 279.   [59] Lucy Caldwell, *All The Beggars Riding* (London: Faber and Faber, 2014), 89.
[60] Ibid., 209.

Although the short stories in *Multitudes* (2016) are loosely focused on the theme of coming-of-age and have associations with Northern Ireland, they represent a steep departure from Caldwell's earlier work and indeed from previous Troubles fiction by women, insofar as the conflict is barely registered in many of them. This characteristic more than any other justifies placing *Multitudes* in the subcategory of 'post-conflict' Northern Irish fiction. Dense in nostalgic period detail, these stories exhibit an acute eye for the violence of adolescence and the complex process of negotiating a burgeoning female sexuality. 'Thirteen', for example, is a bittersweet account of the heartache and tantalizing joy of adolescent longing which is redolent of 1990s teenage girlhood. When the narrator is peer-pressured into kissing a group of boys and then sexually assaulted, she is ostracized for this supposedly promiscuous behaviour and forms a friendship with a fellow social outcast, Jacqueline Dunne. Throughout, the girls' sexuality is uncertain and performative, often based on information and advice contained in teen magazines such as *More!*. When they meet some young men in a local park, one takes advantage of Jacqueline being intoxicated and the reader is unsure whether the narrator is physically ill because of alcohol consumption or unwanted digital penetration. 'Thirteen' is not a diatribe against the perils of teenage sexuality, however. Rather, the story traces the complexities of the young narrator's developing sense of herself as a sexual being and the confusing effects of her internalization of normative notions of gender behaviour, as evidenced by her ambivalent inner responses to her homoerotic feelings for Jacqueline. Other stories in the collection also depict female sexual and romantic awakening in ways that refuse to privilege heterosexuality as the cornerstone of sexual relationships. One such is 'Here We Are', which represents lesbian sexuality as a joyous, unselfconscious pleasure. Asked about her treatment of female sensuality in this work, Caldwell remarked:

> It was evident to me that there needed to be a sex scene: the relationship is a sexual one, and consummation of the relationship seemed essential. The fact of writing a sex scene between two schoolgirls, such an 'obvious' trope of male, heteronormative fantasy, made me very wary of being, or seeming, titillating; at the same time, I didn't want to be coy.[61]

Caldwell's exploration of non-normative sexual identities reaches its apotheosis in 'Through the Wardrobe', a story narrated in the second-person in which a transgender woman recalls her Belfast childhood and adolescence in a developing male body that she repudiates. 'It starts with the Belle dress', she begins, thus highlighting her fetishistic boyhood yearning for the one item of clothing that would somehow ensure safety from 'something inside'.[62] Later, as a teenager, she seizes a secret moment to rifle though her sisters' shared wardrobe, which 'is almost pulsing, bursting with sheer essence of girl',[63] for a particular gold dress. Seeing her reflection in the mirror crystallizes the feminine

---

[61] Lucy Caldwell in email interview with author, May 2016.
[62] Lucy Caldwell, 'Through the Wardrobe', in *Multitudes* (London: Faber and Faber, 2016), 97, 91.
[63] Ibid., 96.

identity the narrator has been craving since the age of six: 'A sudden flash comes to you of the Belle dress, from all those years ago, and you realise it's the memory you've been reaching for, the thing that hovers at the edge of your dreams, and everything, all at once, makes a terrifying, intoxicating sort of sense.'[64] Throughout the long and arduous process of transitioning that is to follow, this image will exist in her mind's eye as 'a sort of talisman', ensuring that 'no matter what it takes and no matter how long it takes, you will come through.'[65]

This transgender narrator's statement of resolve in the face of adversity speaks to the defiant determination that characterizes many of the female protagonists in the works discussed in this chapter, which span a period from the darkest days of the Troubles to the contemporary 'post-conflict' moment. In bearing witness to the palpable effects of violence, fear, oppression, and powerlessness, these protagonists refuse to relinquish resilience and hope. Their bodies have been possessed, penetrated, and monitored, yet those same bodies never cease to have the capacity for pleasure, however transient or qualified. Without ever losing sight of the concrete specificities of these women's embodied experiences, or resuscitating the cultural nationalist iconography that posited an idealized feminine figure as the personification of the nation, it may not be too far-fetched to draw an analogy between the resilience of these fictional beings and the resourcefulness necessary to build a positive future for the wider body politic of Northern Ireland.

Further Reading

Aretxaga, Begoña. *Shattering Silence: Women, Nationalism, and Political Subjectivity in Northern Ireland*. Princeton, NJ: Princeton University Press, 1997.

Connolly, Linda. *The Irish Women's Movement: From Revolution to Devolution*. Basingstoke: Palgrave Macmillan, 2002.

Kennedy-Andrews, Elmer. *Fiction and the Northern Ireland Troubles since 1969: (De-)constructing the North*. Dublin: Four Courts Press, 2003.

Magennis, Caroline. ' "My Narrative Falters, as it Must": Rethinking Memory in Recent Northern Irish Fiction'. In Chris Andrews and Matthew McGuire (eds), *Post-Conflict Literature: Human Rights, Peace, Justice*. London: Routledge, 2016: 43–55.

Magennis, Caroline. 'Fiction from Northern Ireland'. In Heather Ingman and Cliona Ó Gallchóir (eds), *A History of Modern Irish Women's Literature*. Cambridge: Cambridge University Press, 2018: 365–82.

Meaney, Gerardine. *Sex and Nation: Women in Irish Culture and Politics*. Dublin: Attic Press, 1991.

Parker, Michael. *Northern Irish Literature, 1956–2006: The Imprint of History*. Basingstoke: Palgrave Macmillan, 2007. 2 vols.

Patten, Eve. 'Women and Fiction 1985–1990'. *Krino* 8, no. 9 (1990): 1–7.

---

[64] Ibid., 93. As this set-piece scene makes clear, 'Through the Wardrobe' is an intertext of *The Lion, the Witch and the Wardrobe* (1950), Belfast-born C. S. Lewis's famous fantasy novel for children, which he wrote for his goddaughter, Lucy Barfield.

[65] Caldwell, 'Through the Wardrobe', 99.

Peach, Linden. *The Contemporary Irish Novel: Critical Readings*. Basingstoke: Palgrave Macmillan, 2004.

Pelan, Rebecca. *Two Irelands: Literary Feminisms North and South*. Syracuse, NY: Syracuse University Press, 2005.

St Peter, Christine. *Changing Ireland: Strategies in Contemporary Women's Fiction*. Basingstoke: Palgrave Macmillan, 2000.

Steel, Jayne. 'Vampira: Representations of the Irish Female Terrorist'. *Irish Studies Review* 6, no. 3 (1998): 273–84.

PART VI

IRISH GENRE FICTION

CHAPTER 20

....

IRISH CRIME FICTION

....

IAN CAMPBELL ROSS

CRIME fiction, in the work of some fifty currently active writers, is the most popular form of Irish writing today. Such fiction, whether focusing on criminals or those investigators—police, private, or amateur—who pursue them, has long been important, however. Irish authors have notably contributed to, and even anticipated, the body of writing that originated in the three 'tales of ratiocination'[1] Edgar Allan Poe published between 1841 and 1845: 'The Murders in the Rue Morgue', 'The Mystery of Marie Rogêt', and 'The Purloined Letter'. The chapter that follows attempts to survey the broad spectrum of writing that 'crime fiction' occupies; to indicate some of the most significant works that lie along it; and, in so doing, to reveal the plurality of 'Irish' crime fiction over the course of 180 years.

In the 1840s, Poe's three stories of the Chevalier C. Auguste Dupin introduced tropes recognized as important in crime fiction. The Chevalier is 'the double Dupin': both mathematician and poet, he combines the creative and the resolvent, an aristocrat in post-revolutionary France who inhabits a decaying Gothic mansion in Paris. The first Dupin story, 'The Murders in the Rue Morgue', takes the form of one of crime fiction's most enduringly popular forms: the locked room mystery. This had been anticipated three years earlier by Joseph Sheridan Le Fanu (1814–73) in 'Passage in the Secret History of an Irish Countess', published in the *Dublin University Magazine* in November 1838. Subsequently revised as 'The Murdered Cousin' (1851), the story was expanded to become Le Fanu's best-known novel, *Uncle Silas* (1864), one of the most significant crime novels of the mid-nineteenth century, alongside Charles Dickens's *Bleak House* (1851) and Wilkie Collins's *The Moonstone* (1868). The original short story is set in Ireland, but by the time of the novel's publication, Le Fanu's English publisher had insisted that his fiction should be of 'an English subject and in modern times',[2] in contrast to the author's early preference for Irish subjects in a contested past. Like many

---

[1] Edgar Allen Poe to Philip Pendleton Cooke, 9 August 1846, in *The Letters of Edgar Allen Poe*, ed. John Ward Ostrum (Cambridge, MA: Harvard University Press, 1948), vol. 2, 328.

[2] Richard Bentley to Joseph Sheridan Le Fanu, 26 February 1863, quoted in W. J. McCormack, *Sheridan Le Fanu and Modern Ireland* (Oxford: Clarendon Press, 1980), 140.

later Irish writers, Le Fanu deferred to the much larger and financially rewarding readership across the water.

The first novel Le Fanu wrote in line with his publisher's direction was *Wylder's Hand* (1864); this, like other sensation novels of the 1860s, draws on Gothic tropes, but the central mystery of the novel, an investigation into the disappearance of Mark Wylder, anticipates much subsequent crime fiction. Like *Bleak House* and *The Moonstone*, the novel was first published in serial form—in the *Dublin University Magazine*—and it was in the magazines of the late nineteenth century that detective fiction emerged as a distinctive kind of popular literature.[3] In the 1890s, Conan Doyle's Sherlock Holmes stories appeared in *The Strand*. Among Irish authors who found a ready readership in this and similar magazines were L. T. Meade (the pen name of Elizabeth Thomasina Toulmin Smith, 1844–1914) and M. McDonnell Bodkin (1850–1933). Meade, a notable feminist who made a pioneering contribution to literature for girls, including the magazine *Atalanta*, was also well known for her crime fiction, written independently or in collaboration with, variously, Dr Clifford Hawkins and Robert Eustace. With Hawkins, she wrote twenty-four medical mysteries, first published in *The Strand* and later collected as *Stories from the Diary of a Doctor* (1893). Challenging male hegemony in the medical profession, these stories initiated a strand of crime writing still popular today.[4] Meade also created one of the best known of Victorian female investigators, Florence Cusack, whose adventures, published in *Harmsworth's*, began with the much-anthologized 'The Arrest of Captain Vandaleur' (1894). Although the story is set in England, there is a powerful Irish resonance in the name of the villain, for the tenant evictions of 1888–1900 on the County Clare estate of the absentee landlord Captain Hector S. Vandeleur were notorious.[5]

Meade's contemporary, Matthias McDonnell Bodkin, also located his crime fiction in England, a fact especially noteworthy since Bodkin—a lawyer, writer, and MP for Roscommon from 1892 to 1895—had strong nationalist sympathies. Author of historical fiction on Irish themes, including *Lord Edward Fitzgerald* (1896) and *The Rebels* (1899), McDonnell Bodkin created a popular and distinctive series of detective stories, beginning with *Paul Beck: The Rule of Thumb Detective* (1899) and including *Dora Myrl, The Lady Detective* (1900), *The Capture of Paul Beck* (1909)—in which the gun-toting Dora, a New Woman forced to abandon her first choice of career in medicine, 'captures' Beck in matrimony—and *Young Beck, A Chip off the Old Block* (1911), in which the couple's son takes up his parents' calling. As a 'rule of thumb' detective who muddles along in his cases, Beck is a parody of the Great Detective personified by Sherlock Holmes, anticipating such 'ordinary' detectives as Baroness Orczy's Old Man in the Corner, G. K. Chesterton's Father Brown, and Agatha Christie's Miss Marple. Bodkin's crime fiction consisted mainly

---

[3] See, for example, Richard D. Altick, *The English Common Reader: A Social History of the Mass Reading Public, 1800–1900* (Chicago, IL: University of Chicago Press, 1957) and Josephine M. Guy and Ian Small, *The Textual Condition of Nineteenth-Century Literature* (London: Routledge, 2012).

[4] Christopher Pittard, *Purity and Contamination in Late Victorian Detective Fiction* (London: Routledge, 2011), 147–58.

[5] For Vandeleur, see Joseph V. O'Brien, *William O'Brien and the Course of Irish Politics, 1881–1918* (Berkeley, CA: University of California Press, 1976), especially 65–6.

of short stories, the earliest appearing in *Pearson's Magazine*. *The Capture of Paul Beck*, however, was a novel—a sign of changing patterns of publication—that allowed Bodkin more scope to remind readers of his nationality and political views. In it, Beck and Myrl find themselves on opposite sides of a case that requires a journey to Ireland. It is Dora's first visit and, though she has heard terrible stories of the 'wild Irish', she 'found Dublin very much to her taste', staying in the Shelbourne Hotel on St Stephen's Green and taking in the tourist sights, including the former Houses of Parliament on College Green, 'the temple of Irish liberty', now darkly noted as being thronged with the money-changers of the Bank of Ireland.[6] Before she concludes her whirlwind tour of the country, Dora Myrl has 'found salvation' and become 'a convinced Home Ruler, in love with Ireland and things Irish'.[7]

Not all early Irish crime fiction used English settings or was shaped by English models. In the year of Catholic Emancipation, Gerald Griffin's (1803–40) *The Collegians* (1829) fictionalized the notorious 1819 murder of the young Ellie Hanley as a tale of murder by two Trinity College Dublin students in the 1770s, confronting English readers with inequalities and injustices in the west of Ireland. Griffin was a Limerick-born Roman Catholic; William Carleton (1794–1869) was a Catholic from County Tyrone who converted to Anglicanism as a young man. Carleton's 'Wildgoose Lodge' (1830), first published as 'Confessions of a Reformed Ribbonman: An Owre True Tale' in the *Dublin Literary Gazette*, is based on a real-life episode that took place in 1816, leading to the execution of sixteen Ribbonmen. Here, the narrator both participates in and is repelled by the murder of eight people burned alive in the lodge of the title, anticipating the ways in which much crime fiction involves doubling, implicating not only its characters but also readers in questions of innocence and guilt. 'Wildgoose Lodge' was collected in *Traits and Stories of the Irish Peasantry* (1830). Samuel Lover's (1797–1868) *Legends and Stories of Ireland* (1831) includes 'The Priest's Story', which tells of a Roman Catholic priest who, discovering the identity of his brother's murderer under the seal of the confessional, is unable to act—although the murderer admits his guilt and is hanged a decade after the crime. In *Ancient Legends, Mystic Charms, and the Superstitions of Ireland* (1887), Jane Wilde (1821–96), writing as Lady Wilde ('Speranza'), included 'The Holy Well and the Murderer', in which the killer's guilt is revealed by the magic of the well, a recurrent feature of Irish folklore.[8]

That nineteenth-century Irish crime writing differed from fiction in Great Britain may be understood not only in relation to the power of the English market but also in the context of very different attitudes towards 'crime' and those charged with detecting and punishing it. The evictions of the Great Famine years and following decades saw the Royal Irish Constabulary (RIC) involved in actions that many, both in Ireland and England, found repugnant. Nor did the courts help. The notorious Maamtrasna murders

---

[6] M. McDonnell Bodkin, *The Capture of Paul Beck* (London: T. Fisher Unwin, 1909), 237.

[7] Ibid.

[8] Modern crime fiction that evokes an older Ireland includes Peter Tremayne's Sister Fidelma series and Cora Harrison's Mara, Brehon of the Burren books, set in the seventh and sixteenth centuries respectively.

of 1882, when a family of five, including children, were gruesomely slaughtered, resulted in an English-language trial following which one of the defendants, Myles Joyce, was found guilty and hanged, though he was a monoglot Irish-speaker who almost certainly understood virtually nothing of the proceedings.[9] In 1895, the burned body of Bridget Cleary was uncovered in a shallow grave outside of Clonmel in County Tipperary. Married to Michael Cleary, she had fallen ill and had been visited by a priest, while her family attempted to cure her with folk remedies, one of which caused her death. In the apparent belief that Bridget had been taken by the fairies, Michael Cleary burned what he claimed to think was the body of a changeling. In the murder trial that followed, deeply rooted Irish folk beliefs came up against the very different assumptions of English law. The case was widely covered in the press and the eventual conviction of Cleary for manslaughter satisfied neither his accusers nor defenders.[10]

Understandably, perhaps, Irish crime fiction of the last two decades of the nineteenth century tended to steer well clear of crime close to home. Kathleen O'Meara (1839–88) combined Roman Catholic piety with a warning against the spread of revolution in her tale of intrigue and murder, *Narka the Nihilist* (1888), set in Russia and France. *Dracula* (1897), Bram Stoker's (1847–1912) Gothic invasion novel, finds Van Helsing drawing on theories associated with the founder of modern criminology, Carlo Lombroso, to create a criminal profile of the Romanian count. In 1890, *Lippincott's Magazine* published the first version of Oscar Wilde's (1854–1900) *The Picture of Dorian Gray* (1891), while 'Lord Arthur Savile's Crime', a first version of which appeared in *The Court and Society Review* in 1887, gave its name to the volume Wilde published in 1891 as *Lord Arthur Savile's Crime and Other Stories*. While few did, or would now, consider *Dorian Gray*—a novel replete with crimes, including murder—as crime fiction, 'Lord Arthur Savile's Crime' is a story incomprehensible outside of the context of contemporary magazine crime fiction, on which it offers an oblique, comic commentary. A rare exception in using Irish settings was Richard Dowling (1846–98), a former journalist with *The Nation* and author of several Irish regional novels, who featured a London private investigator, George Tufnell, in *A Baffling Quest* (1891) but also wrote *Old Corcoran's Money* (1897), a dark tale of miserly greed set in Ballymore, usually taken as a fictionalized Waterford.

A decade later, George A. Birmingham (1865–1950) domesticated international conspiracy theory in *The Search Party* (1909), whose villain, the shadowy Mr Red, head of the Anti-Militarist Brotherhood of Anarchists, takes a house in Connacht and proceeds to kidnap a number of locals along with two visiting British MPs. A comic novel, *The Search Party* has a sharp political edge, especially in the depiction of the two English politicians who, having studied the Irish Question for a fortnight, now 'thoroughly understood'[11] the problem. Birmingham was the pen name of James Owen Hannay, a Church of Ireland clergyman in Westport, County Mayo. A member of the Gaelic

[9] See Margaret Kelleher, *The Maamtrasna Murders: Language, Life and Death in Nineteenth-Century Ireland* (Dublin: University College Dublin Press, 2018). Myles Joyce (Maolra Seoighe) received a posthumous pardon from the President of Ireland, Michael D. Higgins, in April 2018.

[10] See Angela Bourke, *The Burning of Bridget Cleary: A True Story* (London: Pimlico, 1999).

[11] George A. Birmingham, *The Search Party* (London: Bodley Head, 1973), 128.

League, he was variously influenced, in matters of land reform and politics, by Horace Plunkett and Arthur Griffith. Contemporary Ireland remained a problematic location for writers of popular fiction, however. Gaelic revivalists, demanding an authentic national literature, had little time for crime fiction, while the continuing struggle for Home Rule did not lend itself to easy representation in crime (or comic) fiction. In Patrick Pearse's (1879–1916) dark story, 'An Bhean Chaointe' (The Keening Woman, 1916), the reader's sympathy is predictably invoked not for the forces of law and order but for the naïve young lad from the west of Ireland, framed for murder by a shadowy government agent and a perjured 'peeler', and for his aged mother, the keening woman of the title—a figure drawn from Irish folklore—whose efforts to secure her son's release fail in the face of indifference on the part of the authorities both in Dublin and London.[12]

Language, location, and attitudes to law and order all marked differences between Ireland and England, along with the latter's vastly greater readership. Irish-language crime fiction nevertheless emerged in the early years of the Free State. An tAthair Seoirse Mac Clúin (1894–1949) looked to Holmes and Watson in creating Séamas de Barra and his partner Antoine Ó Briain in short stories that appeared in *An Sguab* (The Brush) in 1922 and 1923. Micheál Ó Gríobtha's Toirdhealbhach Ó Briain appears in three stories set in Dublin, in a volume entitled *Lorgaireacht* (Detection, 1927). The earliest Irish-language crime novels were Ciarán Ó Nualláin's (1910–83) *Oidhche I nGleann na nGealt* (A Night in the Glen of the Madmen, 1939) and Seoirse Mac Liam's *An Doras do Plabadh* (The Door That was Slammed, 1940). Ó Nualláin's brother Brian O'Nolan (1911–66), better known as Flann O'Brien or Myles na gCopaleen, published under many aliases but used his own name, Brian Ó Nualláin, in writing 'Eachtraí Shearluic' (Adventures of Sherlock), a Holmesian parody in which the Great Detective is consulted by a disguised Moriarty, claiming to be Oisín in search of the Fianna. In true Mylesian fashion, Holmes, Watson, and Moriarity all end up in the Grangegorman psychiatric hospital.[13]

Much Irish-language crime fiction was published by An Gúm, the state-sponsored publishing house set up as part of the Department of Education in 1926. Best-known among its authors was the English-born Cathal Ó Sándair (1922–96), whose very popular *Réics Carló* series appeared between the 1950s and the 1970s. Whether Irish readers, especially children, should be encouraged to read crime fiction was, however, debatable, for surely exposure to criminal activity could only encourage readers to try it out for themselves, a view the Censorship Board espoused in systematically banning true crime magazines between the 1930s and 1960s—although crime fiction itself seems only to have been fitfully banned. While the language question divided writers, the legacy of Ireland's recent past—the War of Independence, followed by the Civil War and the establishment of the Free State—generally proved too bitter to encourage crime fiction.

[12] See Máire Ní Fhlatúin, 'The Anticolonial Modernism of Patrick Pearse', in Howard J. Booth and Nigel Rigby (eds), *Modernism and Empire: Writing and British Coloniality, 1890–1940* (Manchester: Manchester University Press, 2000), 156–74 and Anne Markey, 'Introduction', in *Patrick Pearse: Short Stories*, ed. Anne Markey, trans. Joseph Campbell (Dublin: University College Dublin Press, 2009), vii–xlv.

[13] See Philip O'Leary, *Gaelic Prose in the Irish Free State, 1922–39* (University Park, PA: Pennsylvania State University Press, 2004), 193–9, to which the foregoing paragraph is indebted.

Robert Brennan (1881–1964), who led the 1916 Rising in Wexford, wrote fiction that sought to provide entertainment in difficult days, beginning with *The False Finger Tip: An Irish Detective Story* (1921), published under the name Selskar Kearney; six short stories set in France, which appeared in the American *Detective Fiction Weekly*; and the London-published *The Toledo Dagger* (1927). Liam O'Flaherty (1897–1984), though, set both *The Informer* (1925) and *The Assassin* (1928) in Dublin shortly after the Civil War, describing the former as 'a sort of high-blown detective story',[14] while Frank O'Connor's (1903–66) 'Guests of the Nation' (1931) and Rearden Conner's (1907–91) *Shake Hands with the Devil* (1933) are set in the War of Independence.

The most influential modern Irish writer of crime fiction, Freeman Wills Crofts (1879–1957), published, between 1920 and 1957, over thirty novels and many short stories, which sit at the very heart of Golden Age crime fiction. Dublin-born but Belfast-educated, Crofts spent his early professional life working as a railway engineer in the northern counties of Ireland before settling in England, where he co-founded the Detection Club in 1930 with other prominent authors such as Agatha Christie and Dorothy L. Sayers. His detective novels mostly feature Inspector Joseph French of the London Metropolitan Police force, the first police detective hero in crime fiction. As such, French marks a shift away from the Great Detective, epitomized by Sherlock Holmes, or the overlooked amateur, such as Chesterton's Father Brown, who had dominated earlier crime fiction, often at the expense of slow-witted policemen, reliant on the superior minds of consulting or amateur detectives to solve their cases.

In *The Cask* (1920)—published in the same year as Christie's first novel, *The Mysterious Affair at Styles*, which introduced readers to Hercule Poirot—Crofts featured a Scotland Yard detective, Inspector Burnley, one of several investigators in an ingeniously plotted murder case that moves back and forth between London and Paris. Raymond Chandler damned Crofts with faint praise as 'the soundest builder of them all'.[15] Croft's novels are certainly meticulously plotted, but the unpredictability of plot development gives continuing interest to them. French does not appear until the fourth chapter of *Inspector French and the Starvel Tragedy* (1927), enters belatedly in *Fatal Venture* (1939), and is seen only in the second half of *Antidote to Venom* (1938), an example of the 'inverted mystery', in which the commission of the crime and the nature of the criminal are the initial centre of interest, with the detective's attempts to unravel a mystery already known to the reader forming the matter of the second part.

As a railway engineer, Crofts had a strong interest in travel of all kinds. Trains (running strictly to the published timetable), boats, and cars feature variously in the plots of many novels, including *The Cask*, *Sir John Magill's Last Journey* (1930), and *The 12.30 from Croydon* (1934). So do elaborate, and sometimes illustrated, mechanical devices for the commission of crime, as in *Antidote to Venom* and *Sir John Magill's Last Journey*. Crofts set much of his fiction in England, yet like other, earlier Irish writers he often includes Irish scenes or sets books partly, or principally, in Ireland. As early as 1925, soon

[14] Liam O'Flaherty, *Shame the Devil* (London: Grayson and Grayson, 1934), 189.
[15] Raymond Chandler, *The Simple Art of Murder* (London: Hamish Hamilton, 1950), 325.

after partition, when visiting Barcelona in *Inspector French's Greatest Case* (1925), French describes (perceived) differences between the inhabitants of southern Spain and the 'more go-ahead and enterprising' Catalans, commenting: 'That sounds a bit like Ireland. . . . I've been both in Belfast and in the south, and the same thing seems to hold good', though he quickly adds that 'Dublin is a fine city, and no mistake'.[16]

By the time of his death in 1957, the style of Freeman Wills Crofts's novels was a throw-back to a departed age. While none of his mid-century successors equalled his renown, they included such notable writers as Nicholas Blake, pen name of the future poet laureate Cecil Day-Lewis (1904–72), and Nigel Fitzgerald (1906–81), along with L. A. G. Strong (1896–1958), Sheila Pim (1909–95), and Eilís Dillon (1920–94). Between 1935 and 1966, Blake published twenty crime novels, most featuring the amateur detect-ive Nigel Strangeways, reputedly modelled on W. H. Auden, and set in England. Arguably his best Strangeways novel, *The Beast Must Die* (1938), later became one of Claude Chabrol's finest films, *Que la bête meure* (1969). Born in what was then the Queen's County (County Laois), Day-Lewis was taken to England as a very young child but retained close contact with Ireland, and one of his stand-alone novels, *The Private Wound* (1968), set in the west of Ireland, deals with themes of belonging and alienation close to the heart of a writer who, at the end of his life, sought out his Irish roots.

English-born but with an Irish family background and lifelong interests in the coun-try and its literature, L. A. G. Strong was a prolific novelist, poet, critic, and director of the publishing house of Methuen. Although Irish settings and themes feature in other of his books, Strong's well-regarded crime fiction, from *Slocombe Dies* (1942) to *Treason in the Egg* (1958), featuring Inspector Ellis McKay of Scotland Yard, offers puzzle-mysteries in English locations. Conversely, Nigel Fitzgerald wrote a dozen detective novels, most with Irish settings, featuring Inspector Duffy of the 'Civic Guard' and the actor-manager Alan Russell. While his earliest novel, *Midsummer Malice*, dates only from 1953, Fitzgerald's work follows the model of the Golden Age puzzle-mystery, complete—as in his much-admired *Suffer a Witch* (1958)—with a map of the fictional small town of Dun Moher and a timetable, to assist readers attempting to solve the murder before the detective. The Dublin-born and Cambridge-educated Sheila Pim, biographer of Irish botanist Augustus Henry, made use of her extensive horticultural knowledge—not least the toxic properties of plants—in four crime novels set in an Irish village, starting with *Common or Garden Crime* (1945) and ending with *A Hive of Suspects* (1952). Eilís Dillon, meanwhile, wrote three crime novels that employ Irish settings—*Death at Crane's Court* (1953), *Sent to His Account* (1954), and *Death in the Quadrangle* (1956)—set respectively in the west of Ireland, County Wicklow, and a not-too-fictional Dublin university. While the best of these, *Sent to His Account*, acknowledges deep-seated tensions between Dublin and the countryside, and within the Wicklow village where the local landowner is murdered, there is little to indicate the strong nationalist sympathies of the author.

---

[16] Freeman Wills Crofts, *Inspector French's Greatest Case* (London: Penguin, 1953), 72–3.

Freeman Wills Crofts, Nicholas Blake, and Nigel Fitzgerald were published by Collins, the most influential English publisher of crime fiction; Dillon's novels appeared from the more 'literary' house of Faber. Although a seeming indication of the enhanced status of crime writing, not all readers were impressed. 'I cannot help feeling that, if Miss Dillon is so good a writer, perhaps she should be encouraged to launch in the wider seas of the real novelist',[17] opined an *Irish Times* reviewer. Crime fiction's dubious reputation encouraged Brian Moore (1921–99), future author of the literary thrillers *The Colour of Blood* (1987) and *Lies of Silence* (1990), to publish seven pulp-fiction titles, including *Wreath for a Redhead* (1951) and *A Bullet for My Lady* (1955), under the pen names Bernard Mara and Michael Bryan. Given crime fiction's low status, it comes as a surprise to find the *Irish Times* in 1953 publishing a serial work of crime fiction, *The Scarperer*, trailed as a 'fascinating' depiction of Dublin's underworld by Emmet Street, the unlikely pseudonym of a young Brendan Behan (1923–64).[18]

The 1950s marked the beginning of a near-forty year hiatus in the writing of crime fiction by Irish authors. Among rare exceptions were writers living abroad, most notably Patricia Moyes (1923–2000)—more recognizably Irish as Patricia Pakenham-Walsh—author of twenty English-based police procedurals featuring CID Inspector Henry Tibbett, published between 1959 and 1993. From the 1980s, the journalist and historian Ruth Dudley Edwards (1944–) pioneered a return to crime fiction, with a dozen novels featuring Robert Amiss and Baroness Ida (Jack) Troutbeck, from *Corridors of Death* (1981) to *Killing the Emperors* (2013). Set in England, these often sharply satirical novels do not entirely overlook Ireland, as in *The Anglo-Irish Murders* (2000).

It was only in the 1990s, however, that Irish crime fiction again began to flourish. Although it has recently been argued that 'Virtually all twenty-first-century Irish crime fiction is derived from the tradition of the American hardboiled',[19] the truth is more complicated. Far from revealing a 'striking lack of diversity, in terms of subgenres and models',[20] one of the most notable features of contemporary Irish crime fiction is the various forms it takes, both in English and in the much smaller market of Irish-language fiction. Although, like their counterparts elsewhere, contemporary Irish crime writers have been significantly influenced by the American hard-boiled writing that originated with Dashiell Hammett, Raymond Chandler, and Ross McDonald, their output includes not only private-eye mysteries (the hard-boiled form par excellence) but police investigations set in a remarkable range of locations; amateur sleuths; crime comedy; psychological crime novels; historical fiction (set both in Ireland and elsewhere); crime fiction for children and young adults; and stand-alone works that often cross the disputed boundaries between 'genre' and 'literary' fiction.

---

[17] *Irish Times*, 26 June 1954, 8.

[18] See John Brannigan, ' "For the Readies": Brendan Behan, Crime Fiction, and the Dublin Underworld', *Éire-Ireland* 49, nos. 1–2 (2014), 92–105.

[19] Maureen T. Reddy, 'Contradictions in the Irish Hardboiled: Detective Fiction's Uneasy Portrayal of a New Ireland', *New Hibernia Review* 19, no. 4 (2015), 126.

[20] Ibid.

Among writers whose work flaunts the influence of hard-boiled fiction, Declan Hughes (1963–) is notable. Ed Loy—his name a sharp-edged gesture towards one of Irish literature's most celebrated (would-be) murderers, Christy Mahon in J. M. Synge's (1871–1909) *The Playboy of the Western World* (1907), as well as Hammett's Sam Spade— features in five crime novels, beginning with *The Wrong Kind of Blood* (2006). Later books take the PI from the coastal south Dublin suburbs to the heart of the capital and to California, his former home. As with Ross McDonald—an important influence— Hughes's plots expose the hidden secrets of dysfunctional families.[21] Declan Burke's (1969–) crime writing also foregrounds hard-boiled influences—particularly Raymond Chandler—in *Eightball Boogie* (2003) and its follow-up, *Slaughters Hound* (2013), both featuring Harry Rigby and set in Sligo. Elsewhere, though, Burke's writing is more notable for its screwball humour, as in *The Big O* (2007) and *Crime Always Pays* (2013), while the surreal comedy and metafictionality of *Absolute Zero Cool* (2011) suggests a modern take on Flann O'Brien's *The Third Policeman* (1967).

Like Seamus Smyth in *Quinn* (1999), Ken Bruen (1951–) reworks the hard-boiled tradition in Irish settings with great élan. The ferocious, hard-drinking, drug-taking for- mer garda Jack Taylor features in over a dozen Galway-set novels from *The Guards* (2001) to *Galway Girl* (2019), parodying as much as imitating hard-boiled models. Prolific and open to diverse literary influences, Bruen subverts anodyne English police procedurals with his memorably vicious and unscrupulous south-east London police- man, Inspector Brant, while referencing the occult fictions of Dennis Wheatley in *The Devil* (2010). Among stand-alone novels, *London Boulevard* (2001) is a persuasive reworking of Billy Wilder's classic *film noir, Sunset Boulevard* (1950). As editor of *Dublin Noir* (2006), a collection of nineteen stories by European and North American writers set in the Irish capital, Bruen insisted on the global reach, as well as the popularity, of crime fiction.[22]

So much is obvious in the writing of the most successful contemporary Irish crime novelist, John Connolly (1968–). In a compelling series of eighteen novels, from *Every Dead Thing* (1999) to *A Book of Bones* (2019), featuring the former NYPD cop, now PI, Charlie Parker, Connolly has developed a distinctive prose style, richly allusive and capable of great poetic force. Most particularly, Connolly's pervasive use of Gothic tropes suggests close affinities with Irish predecessors, going back through Bram Stoker and Sheridan Le Fanu to Charles Robert Maturin (1780–1824). The setting of the Charlie Parker series in Maine reminds readers that from Poe onwards, crime fiction has inhabited borderlands. Maine is a liminal zone, not only the most northerly of the United States, bordering on Canada, but a maritime state whose main settlements lie on a heavily indented Atlantic shoreline, while its largely uninhabited interior is a space where civilization and untamed nature coexist uneasily.

---

[21] Declan Hughes, 'Irish Hard-Boiled Crime: A 51st State of Mind', in Declan Burke (ed.), *Down These Green Streets: Irish Crime Writing in the 21st Century* (Dublin: Liberties Press, 2011), 161–8.

[22] The international series now includes Adrian McKinty and Stuart Neville (eds), *Belfast Noir* (New York: Akashic, 2014).

Parker remains tormented by his failure to protect his wife and child, murdered before the series begins, and throughout Connolly's fiction past and present are woven inextricably together. The spectral presence of sinister figures such as the Travelling Man or the Collector, who cross time and space, opens up the novels' sharply realistic depiction of contemporary settings—perversely lightened by the menacing presence of Parker's gay sidekicks, the hit-men Angel and Louis—to a much broader, timeless engagement with questions concerning the origin and nature of evil. Such fundamental questions seem sometimes to embarrass writers of contemporary crime fiction. Connolly invites the reader to face them by means of compelling and unsettling narratives and by the immensely skilful deployment of epigraphs and mottoes, including that which opens *A Song of Shadows* (2015), taken from Mikhail Bulgakov's *The Master and Margarita* (1966–67): 'What would your good do if evil didn't exist, and what would the earth look like if all the shadows disappeared?'. Seeming to have turned its back on Ireland, Connolly's fiction, pervaded by deep-rooted religious and racial hatreds, forces readers to confront the buried truths of Irish history and the pressing need to come to terms with them.[23]

Connolly combines elements of American hard-boiled fiction with Irish, as well as American, Gothic; Hughes, Bruen, and Burke transplant American hard-boiled to Ireland. Other private-eye fiction is of a more domestic, less overtly violent kind. Vincent Banville (1940–) is author of a pioneering series, beginning with *Death by Design* (1993), set in Dublin and featuring the private detective John Blaine. In her second novel, *False Intentions* (2005), Arlene Hunt (1972–) created QuicK Investigations, featuring the Dublin partnership of John Quigley and Sarah Kenny, who appear much less as outsiders and, especially in the case of Kenny, are shown to be closely involved in family relationships. Hunt nevertheless engages seriously with contemporary Irish social issues in popular form, exposing corruption behind the façade of middle-class respectability in novels including *Black Sheep* (2006), *Undertow* (2008), and *Blood Money* (2010).[24]

Central to Irish experience in recent decades, and influential in effecting sweeping social change, has been the bringing to light of crimes long concealed, sometimes as wilful acts of national amnesia: violence against women and children within the home; child abuse by priests and other religious; the enforced adoptions of children born to unmarried mothers; the confinement of those mothers and other unfortunates to Magdalene laundries; the violence perpetrated against children in the industrial schools; the burgeoning gang-controlled drug and sex trades, along with widespread financial corruption extending through the worlds of politics, banking, and property. In exposing unwelcome truths about the nation today, crime writers have necessarily confronted its past.

Nineteenth-century Catholic distrust of the RIC and late twentieth-century republican hatred for the Royal Ulster Constabulary (RUC) in Northern Ireland militated

---

[23] See John Connolly, 'No Blacks, No Dogs, No Crime Writers: Ireland and the Mystery Genre', in Burke (ed.), *Green Streets*, 39–57.

[24] See Arlene Hunt, 'A Shock to the System', in Burke (ed.), *Green Streets*, 270–81.

against the writing of police procedurals. Several novelists have recently attempted to explain and fill this void in historical crime fictions. Conor Brady, former editor of the *Irish Times*, member of the Garda Síochána Ombudsman Commission (2005–11), and author of histories of the Garda Síochána, has written four well-researched novels—*A June of Ordinary Murders* (2012), *The Eloquence of the Dead* (2013), *A Hunt in Winter* (2016), and *In the Dark River* (2018)—set in the late 1880s and featuring Sergeant Joe Swallow of the Dublin Metropolitan Police, touching on events including Queen Victoria's golden jubilee, land evictions, and the fall of Parnell.[25] Kevin McCarthy has done something similar for a later period and a different location, the War of Independence in County Cork, in *Peeler* (2010), whose central character, Acting Sergeant Seán O'Keeffe, reappears in *Irregulars* (2013), set during the Civil War. Adrian McKinty's (1968–) outstanding DI Sean Duffy series features a Catholic officer in the overwhelmingly Protestant RUC in the 1980s.

Among the first contemporary writers to introduce Irish police officers to crime novels was Hugo Hamilton (1953–), in *Headbanger* (1996) and *Sad Bastard* (1998), two blackly humorous works featuring Garda Pat Coyne, which, at the outset of the Celtic Tiger years, combined exposure of Irish criminality of different kinds—including gangsterism and clerical child sexual abuse—with an interrogation of the increasingly hybrid nature of modern Irish identity. Subsequent Garda Síochána officers have included Jim Lusby's (1951–) DI Carl McCadden from Waterford; Brian McGilloway's (1974–) Inspector Benedict Devlin of Lifford; Niamh O'Connor's DS Jo Birmingham from Dublin; Julie Parsons's (1951–) retired DI Michael McLoughlin, most recently in the intricate and powerful *The Therapy House* (2017); and Dervla McTiernan's (1976–) DS Cormac Reilly in a promising debut novel, *The Ruin* (2018).

In Northern Ireland, Eugene McEldowney's (1943–) Superintendent Cecil Megarry serves in the RUC in Belfast, Adrian McKinty's DI Sean Duffy in Carrickfergus, while Stuart Neville's (1972–) Inspector Jack Lennon and Brian McGilloway's DS Lucy Black are with the Police Service of Northern Ireland (PSNI), which replaced the discredited RUC in 2001. Paul Charles's (1949–) DI Christy Kennedy, an Ulsterman, works in London, as does Jane Casey's (1977–) DS Maeve Kerrigan. Variations on the serving police officer include the consultant pathologist Quirke in Benjamin Black's popular series set in 1950s Dublin; Cormac Millar's (1950–) Séamus Joyce, acting director of the (fictional) Irish Drug Enforcement Agency; Louise Phillips's (1967–) criminal psychologist Dr Kate Pearson, working with the Garda Síochána; and Claire McGowan's (1981–) forensic psychologist Dr Paula McGuire of the PSNI.

Imaginative in conception, increasingly complex in execution, and stylistically confident are six novels by Tana French (1973–) featuring different members of the Dublin Murder Squad and set in a revealing range of locations in and around the Irish capital: the south Dublin suburbs, the inner-city, a bleak estate on Dublin's northern fringes, and an expensive south Dublin girls' school. The range of police investigators, from

---

[25] See Conor Brady, *Guardians of the Peace* (Dublin: Gill and Macmillan, 1974) and *The Guarding of Ireland: The Garda Síochána and the Irish State, 1960–2014* (Dublin: Gill and Macmillan, 2014).

Detective Cassie Maddox of *In the Woods* (2007) and *The Likeness* (2008) to detectives Antoinette Crowley and Stephen Moran of *The Secret Place* (2014) and *The Trespasser* (2016), is a notable strength of French's books—one possible solution to the risk, experienced by all writers of crime series, of uncritical repetition—whose key themes include friendship and family, which are also central to her stand-alone novel, *The Wych Elm* (2019). French's work also engages with the difficulties experienced by female officers of sustaining both a personal and a professional life, especially in an environment so traditionally hostile to women as the police service.[26] A similar concern runs through much women's crime fiction, including Sinéad Crowley's novels featuring the married DS Claire Boyle in Dublin and Jane Casey's London-based novels, from *The Burning* (2010) to *Cruel Acts* (2019), in which DS Maeve Kerrigan's ambivalent feelings towards her policeman live-in boyfriend Rob and her work partner, the thoroughly misogynistic DI Josh Derwent, complicate her feminist ideals.

While the Troubles in Northern Ireland did not generally prove conducive to writing crime fiction in Ireland itself, exceptions of different kinds are to be found in Benedict Kiely's (1919–2007) *Proxopera* (1977), Bernard MacLaverty's (1942–) *Cal* (1983), and Brian Moore's *Lies of Silence*. Pioneered by Eugene McEldowney, Eoin McNamee (1961–), and Colin Bateman (1962–), contemporary work originated with authors who began to publish in the years between the Anglo-Irish Agreement (1985) and the Good Friday Agreement (1998). The difficulties of writing crime fiction constructed around police figures is indicated in a Northern Irish context by the work of Bateman, a comic crime writer. Exceptionally prolific, he has written just two such novels, *Murphy's Law* (2002) and *Murphy's Revenge* (2005)—based on a TV series he created—featuring an undercover policeman who, following the death of his young son in an IRA bombing, is reassigned to London. Bateman's other fiction is notably wide-ranging, with series variously featuring Dan Starkey, a journalist (like Bateman himself) and the owner of a crime bookshop in Belfast, who appears in four titles beginning with *The Mystery Man* (2009). Author of many stand-alones, including *Mohammed Maguire* (2001), which offers an outsider's bleakly comic perspective on Northern Ireland, Bateman is capable of fiercely funny writing. Readers of crime fiction have often fought shy of humour, even black humour, but Bateman's is a major and distinctive voice in contemporary Irish crime writing.

In the 1990s, the Belfast-born *Irish Times* journalist Eugene McEldowney wrote a series of four novels featuring RUC Superintendent Cecil Megarry, which attempted to depict a Northern Ireland suffering not just from political crime but from 'ordinary' crime too. The latter dominates *A Kind of Homecoming* (1993), while *A Stone of the Heart* (1995) focuses on a vulnerable young working-class Catholic, Sean Maguire, drawn slowly into an IRA plot to kidnap the young daughter of a British intelligence officer. While highlighting the godfathers of violence, McEldowney's work is notable for its clear-eyed but sympathetic evocation of a society in which almost everyone is in some way a victim of the continuing political situation. Unlike Megarry, Adrian McKinty's

---

[26] See Brady, *The Guarding of Ireland*, 9; Catherine Clancy, '50 Years Later: Women in Policing', *Communiqué: An Garda Síochána Management Journal* (2009), 22–8.

Sean Duffy of the RUC does not entirely break out of the hard-boiled private eye mould. Yet while the stubbornly insubordinate detective finds familiar refuge in drink and drugs—enlivened by a stimulatingly eclectic taste in music—Duffy's particular demons arise from his being among a small minority of Roman Catholic officers during the Troubles, a minority often despised, even by Protestant fellow officers. With his dark humour and undisguised intelligence, Duffy is a compelling character in six novels with Tom Waits-inspired titles, from *Cold, Cold Ground* (2012) to *Police at the Station and They Don't Look Friendly* (2017).

Stuart Neville's Inspector Jack Lennon features in four fictions set in Northern Ireland, mainly Belfast, published between 2009 and 2014, to which Neville has added a new series whose central character is Lisburn-based DCI Serena Flanagan. Despite the presence of Lennon, the real focus of Neville's remarkable first novel, *The Twelve* (2009), is Gerry Fegan, a republican paramilitary killer haunted by the ghosts of the twelve people he has murdered: soldiers, members of the Ulster Defence Regiment, the RUC, loyalist paramilitaries and four civilians, 'in the wrong place, at the wrong time'.[27] Fegan hopes to exorcize his demons by killing the godfathers of the crimes he has committed, against the background of a city and province slowly changing after the Good Friday Agreement, but the past will not go away: 'it was the civilians whose memories screamed the loudest'.[28]

From *Borderlands* (2007) to *The Rising* (2010), Brian McGilloway's novels—featuring Garda Detective Inspector Ben Devlin in Lifford, County Donegal, which lies across the River Foyle from Strabane in County Tyrone, home to the PSNI's Inspector Hendry—literalize the idea that crime fiction's defining location is a liminal zone. The border here, the books suggest, is an arbitrary one and as easily crossed by post-Troubles criminals as by paramilitaries. The lack of co-operation between the Garda Síochána and the RUC in the decades before the Good Friday Agreement is seen as gradually, if uneasily, improving as the peace process slowly progresses. McGilloway's newer series, set in Northern Ireland, features DS Lucy Black, most recently in *Bad Blood* (2017).

Also working with the PSNI is forensic psychologist Paula Maguire in six novels by Claire McGowan, the most recent of which is *The Killing House* (2018). In *The Dead Ground* (2014), Maguire's life seems to be falling apart when she discovers herself to be pregnant, uncertain which of two recent lovers fathered the child. Its plot constructed around cases concerning missing children and the murder of a lesbian doctor who runs a family planning clinic, this London-published novel confronts English readers with the notion that, in legal, moral, and political matters, the idea of the United Kingdom is a fiction. Here, abhorrence of abortion and homosexuality unites otherwise divided hard-line republicans and unionists. The daughter of a Catholic policeman father passed over for promotion in favour of a less competent Protestant, with whom she now works, and of a mother who remains one of the 'disappeared', Maguire must unwillingly accept the need for, and inevitability of, compromise in personal as well as political life.

---

[27] Stuart Neville, *The Twelve* (London: Harvill Secker, 2009), 4.   [28] Ibid.

The best known, and arguably the best, crime fiction writer from Northern Ireland is Eoin McNamee. *Resurrection Man* (1994) is a chilling, lightly fictionalized account of the Shankill Butcher murders carried out between 1975 and 1982, in which a small group of Protestant killers, led by Lenny Murphy (reimagined here as Victor Kelly), snatched random Catholics, or those they believed to be Catholics, from the streets of Belfast to beat them before cutting their throats. Unflinching yet never gratuitously brutal, *Resurrection Man* depicts a psychopathic killer trapped in the inescapable sectarian topography of Belfast. It was the first in a cluster of novels that disinter episodes from a Northern Ireland troubled long before 1969. McNamee's (unplanned) Blue trilogy offers different perspectives on the life of Lancelot Curran, a Northern Ireland High Court judge, Ulster Unionist Party MP, and father of Patricia Curran, a nineteen-year-old student murdered in a frenzied knife attack in 1952. *The Blue Tango* (2001) revisits that murder and the resulting miscarriage of justice that led to the conviction of Iain Hay Gordon in 1953 (Gordon was cleared of the crime in 2000). The trial of Robert McGladdery for the murder of the nineteen-year-old Pearl Gamble in 1961 is the focus of *Orchid Blue* (2010); the judge was Curran, who passed a sentence of death on McGladdery, the last person to be hanged in Ireland. *Blue is the Night* (2015) returns to an earlier murder case in which Curran was prosecutor, allowing the backroom machinations designed to ensure the prosecution fail—in order not to endanger Curran's emerging political career—to expose the corruption endemic in the stultifying Northern Ireland of the 1950s. McNamee's most recent novel, *The Vogue* (2018), likewise focuses on Northern Ireland, while embracing American and English locations, in a racially and religiously charged narrative extending from the Second World War to the beginning of the twenty-first century.

Eoin McNamee's outstanding novels are not easily contained within an idea of genre fiction. Among similarly evasive works are John Banville's *The Book of Evidence* (1989), Patrick McCabe's (1955–) *The Butcher Boy* (1992), William Trevor's (1928–2016) *Felicia's Journey* (1994), Joseph O'Connor's (1963–) *Star of the Sea* (2002), Aifric Campbell's *The Semantics of Murder* (2008), Emma Donoghue's (1969–) *Room* (2010), and Neil Jordan's (1950–) *The Drowned Detective* (2016), three of which are based on real-life cases. Carlo Gébler (1954–), too, has used historical crimes as the basis of unconventional novels whose titles, including *How to Murder a Man* (1999), consciously evoke crime fiction. *The Dead Eight* (2011) is a sure-paced reworking of the events leading up to the 1940 murder of Mary McCarthy in Tipperary and to the hanging of an innocent man, Harry Gleeson, who was given a posthumous pardon by President Michael D. Higgins in 2015. Here, the crime and its (known) outcome are related only close to the end of the novel, whose focus is on social, religious, political, and sexual tensions within the repressed rural society of the 1920s and 1930s.

Gébler, Brady, McCarthy, McKinty, and McNamee, together with Joe Joyce (1947–) in his three *Echoland* novels (2013–15) located in Ireland during the Emergency, and Benjamin Black in his Quirke series set in Dublin of the 1950s, have sought to bring the Ireland of the past into modern crime fiction. In two ingenious Irish-language short story collections, Biddy Jenkinson (1949–) features the Jesuit lexicographer and historian

Patrick S. Dinneen S.J., compiler of the Irish–English dictionary *Foclóir Gaedhilge agus Béarla* (1904). Writers who use the language to engage with modern Ireland include Éilís Ní Dhuibhne (1954–) in *Dúnmaharú sa Daingean* (Murder in Dingle, 2000) and *Dún an Airgid* (The Silver Fort, 2008), and Anna Heussaff (1957–), whose third novel, *Scáil an Phríosúin* (The Shadow of the Prison, 2015), features a female investigative journalist and a male garda, disgruntled at being transferred from Dublin to County Cork, thus engaging with contemporary urban–rural tensions. Heussaff adapted her second novel, *Buille Marfach* (The Deadly Blow, 2010), into English as *Deadly Intent* (2014), in marked contrast to Jenkinson, who prefers not to allow her work to be translated into English: 'a small rude gesture to those who think that everything can be harvested and stored without loss in an English-speaking Ireland'.[29]

A focus on organized crime in Dublin characterizes four novels by Gene Kerrigan (1950–)—*Little Criminals* (2005), *The Midnight Choir* (2008), *Dark Times in the City* (2009), and *The Rage* (2011)—whose grimly convincing rendering of an urban underclass owes much to the author's experience as a crime journalist and author of admired true-crime books. Kerrigan has described his own fiction as paralleling shifts in Irish society that occurred between 2005 and 2011, noting that 'Crime is often a distorted version of the behaviour held in high regard within a society. Ambitious and able people who never learned the skills of capitalist buccaneering become ghetto entrepreneurs.'[30] His impressive fiction goes some way to justifying Fintan O'Toole's assertion that 'Irish-set crime writing…has become arguably the nearest thing we have to a realist literature adequate to capturing the nature of contemporary society'.[31] The link between the capitalist buccaneering of the Celtic Tiger years and crime also informs Alan Glynn's (1960–) prescient *Winterland* (2009), which eerily foresaw the slump that followed. Yet while Glynn's later novels, *Bloodland* (2011) and *Graveland* (2013), rehearse the theme of corporate greed, they extend their range beyond Ireland to the United States and Africa, in what the writer himself has termed his 'globalization' trilogy.

Globalization is already changing Irish crime fiction. The Irish diaspora underpins Adrian McKinty's Michael Forsythe trilogy, starting with *Dead I Well May Be* (2003), whose hero, an illegal immigrant escaping from paramilitaries who want to kill him, soon encounters plenty of criminals who want to do the same thing in the United States. In her debut novel, *The Fall* (2012), Claire McGowan offered an unflinching picture of contemporary London, riven by class and racial mistrust. Yet the literary marketplace remains important, as it was for London-bound Irish writers of the nineteenth century. Although the success of Irish writing has led publishers, including Penguin and Hachette, to set up Irish subsidiaries, many writers discussed above publish in England. The lure of a wider readership has also led to authors using international settings. William Ryan's (1965–) Captain Alexi Dimitrevich Korolev works in the USSR of the

---

[29] Biddy Jenkinson, 'A Letter to an Editor', *Irish University Review* 21, no. 1 (1991), 34. For advice on contemporary Irish-language crime fiction, I am greatly indebted to Dr Anne Markey.

[30] Gene Kerrigan, 'Brutal, Harrowing and Devastating', in Burke (ed.), *Green Streets*, 261.

[31] Fintan O'Toole, 'From Chandler to the "Playboy" to the contemporary crime wave', *Irish Times*, 21 November 2009, 9. This article is reproduced in Burke, *Green Streets*, 358–61.

1930s, and Conor Fitzgerald's (1964–) Commissario Alex Blume in modern-day Rome. Ken Bruen in three novels, Benjamin Black in *The Lemur* (2008) and in the 'Philip Marlowe' pastiche, *The Black-eyed Blonde* (2014), Eoin Colfer (1965–) in *Plugged* (2011) and *Screwed* (2013), and Arlene Hunt in *The Chosen* (2011) are among those to have set works in the United States. Alex Barclay (1974–), the pen name of Yve Morris, whose two Joe Lucchesi novels feature an NYPD detective transplanted to Ireland, soon moved in the opposite direction, developing the increasingly convincing Denver police detective Ren Bryce in five novels from *Blood Runs Cold* (2008) to *The Drowning Child* (2016).

Strikingly, two debut novels, otherwise very different, suggest new, though as yet unrealized, possibilities for Irish crime fiction. Frankie Gaffney's *Dublin Seven* (2015) recounts the downward spiral towards death of the young Shane Laochra, trapped in the microcriminality fostered by drug abuse in inner-city Dublin, from the (acknowledged) standpoint of an author brought up in the same environment. Lisa McInerney's (1981–) *The Glorious Heresies* (2015), a tale of murderous mayhem in a drug-ridden Cork, is formally much more accomplished but similarly describes, in darkly comic tones, life in the 'arse end of Ireland' as experienced by a writer who knows something of what she writes.[32]

Over a decade ago, it was suggested that 'Early twenty-first-century Irish criticism finds identity everywhere, constantly, going back as far as the critical eye can see, and stretching across all texts.'[33] Irish crime fiction, though, has still only rarely found a place in criticism, literary history, or anthologies, so that any true critical engagement with it must first place that fiction, in all its diversity, within the wider body of Irish writing.[34] With its deliberately broad sweep, this chapter has not tried to evade the question of whether, by adopting an uncritical identity politics, pluralism merely 'blunt[s] the critical faculties which give a shape to Irish literature'.[35] It has, rather, attempted to set up appropriate conditions for addressing that very issue.

FURTHER READING

Blake, Nicholas. 'The Detective Story—Why?'. In Howard Haycraft (ed.), *The Art of the Mystery Story: A Collection of Critical Essays*. New York: Grossett and Dunlap, 1946: 398–405.
Brannigan, John. '"For the Readies": Brendan Behan, Crime Fiction, and the Dublin Underworld'. *Éire-Ireland* 49, nos. 1–2 (2014): 92–105.

---

[32] Lisa McInerney, *The Glorious Heresies* (London: John Murray, 2015), 292. See also her second novel, *The Blood Miracles* (2017). McInerney wrote an unarchived blog entitled 'Arse End of Ireland' for several years prior to the publication of her debut novel.

[33] Colin Graham, 'Literary Historiography, 1890–2000', in Margaret Kelleher and Philip O'Leary (eds), *The Cambridge History of Irish Literature, Volume 2: 1890–2000* (Cambridge: Cambridge University Press, 2006), 591.

[34] See, however, Ian Campbell Ross and William Meier (eds), *Éire-Ireland. Special Issue: Irish Crime Since 1921* 49, nos. 1–2 (2014), Elizabeth Mannion (ed.), *The Contemporary Irish Detective Novel* (Basingstoke: Palgrave Macmillan, 2016), and Brian Cliff, *Irish Crime Fiction* (Basingstoke: Palgrave Macmillan, 2018).

[35] Graham, 'Literary Historiography, 1890–2000', 591.

Burke, Declan (ed.). *Down These Green Streets: Irish Crime Writing in the 21st Century*. Dublin: Liberties Press, 2011.

Burke, Declan. http://crimealwayspays.blogspot.ie

Cliff, Brian. *Irish Crime Fiction*. Basingstoke: Palgrave Macmillan, 2018.

Connolly, John. *Parker: A Miscellany*. Dublin: Bad Dog Books, 2016.

Evans, Curtis. *Masters of the Humdrum Mystery: Cecil John Charles Street, Freeman Wills Crofts, Alfred Water Stewart, and the British Detective Novel, 1920–1961*. Jefferson, NC: McFarland, 2012.

Kincaid, Andrew. ' "Down these Mean Streets": The City and Critique in Contemporary Irish Noir'. *Éire-Ireland* 45, nos. 1–2 (2010): 39–55.

King, Stewart and Stephen Knight. 'The Challenge of Global Crime Fiction: An Introduction'. *Clues: A Journal of Detection* 32, no. 2 (2014): 5–7.

Mannion. Elizabeth (ed.). *The Contemporary Irish Detective Novel*. Basingstoke: Palgrave Macmillan, 2016.

Millar, Cormac. 'Crimes and Contradictions: The Fictional City of Dublin'. In Lucy Andrews and Catherine Phelps (eds), *Crime Fiction in the City: Capital Crimes*. Cardiff: University of Wales Press, 2013: 47–64.

O'Leary, Philip. *Gaelic Prose in the Irish Free State, 1922–39*. University Park, PA: Pennsylvania State University Press, 2004.

Panek, Leroy Lad. *An Introduction to the Detective Story*. Bowling Green, OH: Bowling Green State University Popular Press, 1987.

Panek, Leroy Lad. *After Sherlock Holmes: The Evolution of British and American Detective Stories, 1891–1914*. Jefferson, NC: McFarland, 2014.

Reddy, Maureen T. 'Contradictions in the Irish Hardboiled: Detective Fiction's Uneasy Portrayal of a New Ireland'. *New Hibernia Review* 19, no. 4 (2015): 126–40.

Ross, Ian Campbell and William Meier (eds). *Éire-Ireland. Special Issue: Irish Crime Since 1921* 49, nos. 1–2 (2014).

Rzepka, Charles J. 'Introduction: What is Crime Fiction?'. In Charles J. Rzepka and Lee Horseley (eds), *A Companion to Crime Fiction*. Oxford: Wiley-Blackwell, 2010: 1–9.

Schaffer, Rachel (ed.). *Clues: A Journal of Detection. Special Issue: Tana French and Irish Crime Fiction* 32, no. 1 (2014).

CHAPTER 21

IRISH SCIENCE FICTION

JACK FENNELL

THE Irish *Old Moore's Almanac* (not to be confused with the English publication of the same name) typically carries an idiosyncratic mix of practical data, such as calendars, tide charts, and household tips, as well as more esoteric content, such as horoscopes and predictions. The 2015 edition contains articles on improving silage quality, knitting, and gardening in winter, alongside features on reincarnation, psychic communication with animals, and farming on Mars. It also offers month-by-month predictions for 2015, grouped into Irish and world events. In the latter category, the *Almanac* predicted an 'exciting dinosaur discovery', self-regulating artificial hearts, agricultural robots, and flying cars, and held out the prospect that increased human emigration to outer space would give rise to a new breed of attorney, 'the celestial solicitor'.[1] The predicted events for Ireland, however, were markedly less sensational: low-level celebrity drama for the most part, accompanied by predictions of political scandal, education reform, additional taxes, and extreme weather. From this, it seems that Ireland and 'the world' are largely separate entities, with divergent futures in store.

These predictions by the venerable *Almanac* illustrate a major characteristic of much Irish science fiction: the sentiment that 'the future' was something that happened to other people, somewhere else. Academic discussions of science fiction invariably begin with, or return to, the ongoing debate regarding definition. More often than not, science fiction critics disagree on the question of what exactly characterizes the genre. At one end of the spectrum is the somewhat vague notion of a 'sense of wonder'; at the other, the more rigorous definition, first put forth by the renowned theorist Darko Suvin in 1979, that science fiction is the literature of 'cognitive estrangement'.[2] By this he means that in science fiction the reader is immersed in a world that has been altered by the presence of a strange new thing, which Suvin calls the 'novum', and must therefore navigate this altered world using their cognitive abilities, logic, and scientific principles.

---

[1] See the sections entitled 'Old Moore Predicts' for the months from May to October in *Old Moore's Almanac 2015* (2014), 9–14.

[2] Darko Suvin, *Metamorphoses of Science Fiction* (Bern: Peter Lang, 2016), 20.

Cognitive estrangement is generally accepted to be the most useful theorization of this genre, since it neatly encapsulates the quality that distinguishes science fiction from other genres such as fantasy or horror. Science fiction portrays itself as being somewhat consonant with the rules of the world we live in, and thus projects an aura of 'plausibility', even when it breaks those rules. For example, faster-than-light travel is impossible according to the laws of physics as we currently understand them; in science fiction, however, it can be assumed that given enough time, science will find a way around such limitations.

Differences of opinion still abound, however, on the question of when science fiction first appeared. Various seminal texts and publications are proposed, such as Hugo Gernsback's magazine *Amazing Stories*, launched in 1926, the short stories of Edgar Allen Poe, and Mary Shelley's *Frankenstein; or, The Modern Prometheus* (1818), to name but a few. Some critics argue that science fiction could not have existed prior to the Enlightenment, while others trace the genre back to Lucian's *True History*, written in the second century. My own opinion is that science fiction emerges from the admixture of tradition and modernity, and is particularly likely to flourish in places where the transition from one to the other has been contested, violent, or unsettled. 'Tradition' can be conceived of as a set of pre-existing cognitions, coded as folk wisdom or even simple 'common sense', that people often rely on to fill in the gaps in their knowledge or understanding of a given subject. To take one mundane example, if one does not know how viruses spread, it might 'stand to reason' that the common cold spontaneously appears in low temperatures. The use of analogy to explain complicated scientific precepts to lay audiences can also give rise to misunderstandings, as such analogies typically omit a great deal of data in the interests of getting the essence of a theory across, leaving gaps to be filled in with prior beliefs, many of which are culturally informed. For example, the phrase 'global warming', while technically accurate in describing the nature of climate change, led many non-scientists to assume that the world is simply getting hotter, which does not reflect the actual complexity of the phenomenon.

Historically, rapid paradigm shifts create moments or epochs in which traditional and modern practices and phenomena exist side by side, and out of this coexistence arise syncretic 'myths' of the kind that inform science fiction. In Ireland, such paradigm shifts have included the end of the Gaelic nobility, the end of the clan system, and the Great Famine of the 1840s, each of which involved the sudden rupturing of tradition by the forces of economic or political modernity. The fact that Ireland remained mostly unindustrialized until the twentieth century meant that scientific knowledge, to the extent that it was taught at all, was often perceived to be of equivalent value to folk wisdom. These are, I maintain, excellent conditions for the emergence of a science-fictional imagination, as amply demonstrated in the pioneering work of Jonathan Swift (1667–1745).

Swift's *Travels into Several Remote Nations of the World* (1726), generally known as *Gulliver's Travels*, is sometimes denounced as being 'anti-science', partly because it satirizes scientific endeavour in part three, which describes the activities of the Academy of Lagado (extracting sunbeams from cucumbers, turning human waste back into food, and such like).[3] This is not the complete picture, however, because the text relies on scientific principles to a huge extent. Seamanship and navigation were the primary sciences of Swift's age, and Lemuel Gulliver is very invested in them, so much so that his cousin Richard Sympson, in a foreword, admits to having excised 'innumerable passages' relating to winds, tides, and related topics in order 'to fit the work as much as possible to the general capacity of readers'.[4] Indeed, Gulliver is something of a know-it-all, offering his assistance to European cartographers in correcting their maps and charts of the Pacific, and elsewhere in the text he demonstrates his sound knowledge of ship design and constructs boats with the help of the locals. The story is also littered with mathematical jokes, such as the one that sees Lilliput and Brobdingnag cast as human countries respectively divided and multiplied by a factor of twelve,[5] and the movements of the floating island of Laputa are described with reference to Isaac Newton's *Principia Mathematica* (1687).[6] Thus, the work cannot be entirely dismissed as anti-scientific. At the same time, however, Gulliver encounters necromancers, ghosts, immortals, and talking horses. Carl Freedman ascribes this mixture of the scientific and the fantastical to the age in which Swift lived: the early eighteenth century, he argues, was a time in which 'it was still possible . . . for a serious mind to refuse to take science seriously'.[7] In other words, there was an equivalent value between science and magic, and even if the latter no longer 'worked' in the heart of the British Empire, it was feasible that somewhere out beyond the frontier the supernatural still held sway.

Somewhat less surreal than Swift's work, Samuel Madden's (1686–1765) part-satirical, part-utopian epistolary novel, *Memoirs of the Twentieth Century* (1733), describes approximately 260 years of future history which generally follows an upward trajectory of reform and social improvement. The text is presented as correspondence between the Lord High Treasurer and various British ambassadors, written between 1997 and 1999. As might be expected from correspondents such as these, the history described is mainly focused on macropolitics and strategic Europe-wide alliances. Germany is not yet united, France is no longer a military power to be reckoned with, Russia is fast becoming one of the most advanced nations on Earth, and the Vatican has set its sights on conquering all of Europe. The King of Britain has established scholarships and seats of learning for geography, meteorology, and the mechanical arts, and among the scientific discoveries benefiting twentieth-century humanity is a medicinal cure for unrequited love. While on the surface Madden is giving us a down-to-earth science fiction tale, we are told at the outset that these letters from the future were delivered to Madden by his

---

[3] A number of critics have objected to the novel's classification as science fiction on these grounds. See, for example, Brian Aldiss and David Wingrove, *Trillion Year Spree* (Thirsk, Yorkshire: House of Stratus, 2001), 81 and Brian Stableford, *Algebraic Fantasies and Realistic Romances: More Masters of Science Fiction* (Rockville, MD: Borgo Press/Wildside Press, 1995), 48.

[4] Jonathan Swift, *Travels into Several Remote Nations of the World; By Lemuel Gulliver, First a Surgeon, and then a Captain of Several Ships* (London and Edinburgh: Smith and Hill, 1819), xi–xii.

[5] Adam Roberts, *The History of Science Fiction* (Basingstoke: Palgrave Macmillan, 2007), 70.

[6] Robert M. Philmus, *Into the Unknown: The Evolution of Science Fiction from Francis Godwin to H. G. Wells* (Berkeley, CA: University of California Press, 1970), 10–12.

[7] Carl Freedman, *Critical Theory and Science Fiction* (Hanover, NH: Wesleyan University Press, 2000), 4–5.

guardian angel in 1728, and that he spent the next five years translating them from late twentieth-century English into the language of his own time.

From these examples, it is clear that at a certain point in history, tradition and modernity were held to have equivalent value or utility. While this equivalence soon faded in other societies, in Ireland, folk beliefs persisted well into the nineteenth century. The tumultuous events of that century brought this particular cultural logic into collision with the industrialized modern world. It is to the fallout from this collision that we will now turn.

THE NINETEENTH CENTURY

Irish identity was impacted, altered, and renegotiated in a variety of ways in the first half of the nineteenth century. The Act of Union of 1800 formally ended the country's legislative independence, while legal reforms and Catholic Emancipation in 1829 eventually enabled the emergence of a new Catholic middle class. These changes had further consequences when the Famine of the 1840s, arising out of laissez-faire economic policies, brought about a swift and violent transition from tradition to modernity. Nationalist sentiment grew stronger in the aftermath of the Famine, and revolutionary movements were augmented by a wealthy, educated, politically engaged Catholic middle class that attributed the disaster to British mismanagement of Irish affairs. Post-Famine nationalism came to be partly characterized by romantic gestures and symbolism, and partly by violence and assassination. A further development was the 'New Departure' arrived at in 1879, whereby parliamentary Irish nationalists at Westminster—participants in a modern bureaucratic institution—coordinated their efforts with those of revolutionary groups such as the Fenian Brotherhood, whose militancy was sanctioned by appeals to national identity, history, and tradition.

The oral Gaelic tradition, meanwhile, had been practically wiped out through starvation and emigration, and for those who survived and remained, socio-economic factors incentivized the abandonment of the Irish language altogether. With the widespread loss of the language, a sizeable amount of the native Irish culture was lost as well. To correct this damage, the constituent elements of the Gaelic Revival—a heterogeneous movement encompassing literary, linguistic, musical, and sporting organizations—attempted the painstaking reconstruction of an 'authentic' Irish identity from the 1880s onwards. As Joe Cleary points out, however, these efforts were hindered by the absence of 'a high Gaelic intelligentsia' or a 'vernacular post-Renaissance high culture' to draw from; thus, at a time when European artistic expression was developing in modernist directions, Irish cultural revivalists instead turned to folk culture, mythology, and pagan epics.[8]

---

[8] Joe Cleary, *Outrageous Fortune: Capital and Culture in Modern Ireland* (Dublin: Field Day Publications, 2007), 90.

One recurring motif of nineteenth-century Irish science fiction is the mixture of science and spiritualism, as a number of authors explicitly combined the scientific and the supernatural without acknowledging any contradiction between them. This kind of writing is exemplified in the work of Fitz-James O'Brien (1828–62), whose short stories include 'The Diamond Lens' (1858), in which a microscopist consults the ghost of a dead scientist for advice and thus constructs the most powerful microscope ever devised, and 'What Was It?' (1859), in which a group of people subdue an invisible predator and try to account for it in scientific, occult, and legal terms. Both stories were published in the collection *The Diamond Lens and Other Stories* (1887). Writing under the pen name of Antares Skorpios, Jane Barlow (1856–1917) employs mysticism to very cynical effect in *History of a World of Immortals Without a God* (1891), wherein a misanthropic Earthman uses Tibetan magic to transport himself to the planet Venus, a utopian world populated by immortals who await the appearance of their 'Unseen God'. The protagonist describes Earth and the rest of the cosmos to them, and his misanthropic description plunges the immortals into an existential despair from which, being immortal, they can never escape.

The turn to mysticism is even more explicit in 'The Story of a Star' (1894) by George (Æ) Russell (1867–1935), in which the narrator recalls memories of a past life as one of the Persian magi. As a mage, he seeks to advance his knowledge of astronomy by means of astral projection beyond the confines of Earth. On these time travels, he notices a mysterious planet that appears and disappears according to a particular cycle, and after learning this cycle's pattern through repeated observation he is eventually able to predict the time of its next appearance. He is thus able to witness the 'birth' of the planet, a mystical process whereby it comes into existence from nothingness. The mage learns that the planet is the creation of godlike beings from a higher plane of existence, so vast that he can only perceive 'the outer verge of their spiritual nature'.[9] He asks them for the meaning of life; they respond that 'The end is creation, and creation is joy',[10] and inform him that our world will eventually become like theirs—in other words, a realm of pure thought. When he awakes from his dream, he is bitterly disappointed to discover that he cannot accurately translate the enormity of his experience into written words.

These authors may have simply been more temperamentally inclined towards mixing the scientific with the occult than their British and continental contemporaries, with the ghost and fairy lore of Irish folk culture running in parallel to the malevolent spirits of the Anglo-Irish Gothic novel. But whatever the impetus, this outright mixture of the positivist and the paranormal waned somewhat towards the end of the nineteenth century, to be superseded by more 'robust' kinds of science fiction. Using the pseudonym Luke Netterville, Standish O'Grady (1846–1928) employed the trope of magical transportation to dubious ends in *The Queen of the World; or, Under the Tyranny* (1900), a 'yellow peril' story wherein an Irish medical student transports himself to the year 2179 through occult means. There, he discovers that the villainous Chinese have conquered the entire world and he joins an 'Anglo-Saxon' rebel movement led by the former King of

---

[9] Æ, 'The Story of a Star', in *Imaginations and Reveries* (Dublin: Maunsel and Company, 1915), 192–3.
[10] Ibid., 193.

England. Although it is largely without merit, this novel demonstrates one strand of Irish science fiction dovetailing into another, as the mystical trappings are used to set the scene for a 'future war' narrative.

Following the publication of George Tomkyns Chesney's *The Battle of Dorking* (1871), there was a vogue throughout Europe for 'historical' accounts of imminent and terrible wars. Unsurprisingly, the Irish variant of this subgenre dealt with internal struggles rather than international strife, and various anonymous and pseudonymous authors wrote detailed accounts of successful rebellions or valiant reconquests of the country. Generally, these texts tended to be published whenever an Irish Home Rule bill was proposed, and they are for the most part quite forgettable. Their one distinctive aspect was a reluctance to rely on the super-weapons indulged in other strands of future-war fiction, with one or two noteworthy exceptions: the anonymously authored *The Battle of the Moy; or, How Ireland Gained Her Independence, 1892–1894* (1883), for example, makes use of a spring-loaded nitroglycerine cannon. Elsewhere, the majority of nineteenth-century science fiction texts focused on engineering rather than 'science' per se, with geniuses building machines with practical goals in mind. This kind of science fiction is obviously indebted to Jules Verne, and in Ireland it was very much influenced by the political strife of the day.

Robert Cromie (1855–1907), a Belfast writer whose work is somewhat reminiscent of Verne, produced adventure narratives from a strongly unionist, pro-imperial viewpoint, with heroic British explorers as protagonists. His most famous works are *A Plunge into Space* (1890) and *The Crack of Doom* (1895).[11] In the former, the discovery of a means to suspend the law of gravity allows a team of seven adventurers (a scientist, a renowned explorer, an Irish politician, a financier, a writer, a newspaperman, and an artist) to travel to Mars. There, they discover a utopian society without laws, disease, money, or conflict; in short, a society where, for all practical intents and purposes, there is no material scarcity. While on Mars, the Earthlings succumb to boredom and attempt to 'improve' this idyllic society by reintroducing politics and capitalism; consequently, they are expelled by the Martians. Tragically, a Martian girl has fallen in love with one of the Earthmen, the writer character, and attempts to stow away on their ship. In order to maintain a sufficient air supply, the Earthmen jettison her into outer space. Upon their return to Earth, the broken-hearted writer commits suicide. Of particular note is Cromie's description of how the Martian hegemony came to be. Not only is the capital situated on the same line of latitude as London, but the dominant Martian culture once had an empire comparable in size and power to the British one. The big difference is that the Martian empire did not restrain itself from eradicating anyone who stood in its way, and it is heavily implied that the current utopia was created by means of multiple genocides.

---

[11] *A Plunge into Space* came with a preface supposedly written by Verne, but there is compelling evidence to suggest that it was fraudulent. Most notably, none of Cromie's works was ever translated into French, and Verne, by his own admission, could not read English. See Robert M. Philmus, 'H. G. Wells, Robert Cromie and Literary Crime' and Arthur B. Evans, 'Wells, Cromie and Verne: An Addendum', both in *Science Fiction Studies* 20, no. 1 (1993), 137–8 and 138–9 respectively.

In *The Crack of Doom*, a young Englishman named Arthur Marcel joins the *Cui Bono* society in order to woo the beautiful Natalie Brande. Natalie's brother Herbert, a brilliant scientist, has come to the conclusion that suffering and injustice are the organizing principles of the material universe and has founded this secret society with the aim of destroying Earth. Even more unfortunately for Marcel, members of the society are possessed of considerable telepathic powers and use these abilities to kill anyone who tries to leave. The narrative contains a plethora of fascinating allusions to end-of-empire anxiety, as well as a prolonged meditation on masculinity and gender. The female protagonists begin the narrative as quasi-transvestite 'evolved women' before returning to conventional femininity at the end; at the same time, every male character is evaluated according to their manliness.

The engineering tale is approached from a different political perspective in Thomas Greer's (d. *c.*1895) one science fiction novel, *A Modern Daedalus* (1885), which concerns an Irish engineer's invention of a flying machine and his subsequent induction into the fight for Irish freedom. Having been fascinated as a child by the flight of seagulls in his native Donegal, John O'Halloran spends his life in pursuit of a means to enable human flight. Returning home to his father and brothers after a spell at university in Belfast, he manages to invent such a machine, which is apparently no more difficult to use than a bicycle. His family pressures him to use this invention to aid the nationalist cause, but his personal pacifism and abhorrence of bloodshed leave him no option but to refuse. Banished from his family home, O'Halloran manufactures an improved model of his flying machine and flies to London with the intent of making his invention available to the general public. When he does so he is arrested, to be held prisoner until such time as he agrees to build a flying army for the crown, a turn of events that causes the young man to develop greater sympathy for the Irish nationalist cause. When his brother helps him to escape, he returns to Ireland to take part in a nationwide uprising that liberates the country. In a forward, Greer distances himself from the 'dynamite party' and emphasizes that the story that follows is mere fantasy, but his protestations seem disingenuous when weighed against the novel's descriptions of the cruelties endured by the Irish peasantry at the hands of the British.

REVOLUTION AND INDEPENDENCE

As a consequence of the Gaelic Revival, one of the more pronounced elements of early twentieth-century Irish nationalism was an emphasis on 'authenticity', sometimes constructed as an apparent wish to rewind and replay Irish history from a time prior to its colonial disruption. As Terence Brown puts it, authors turned to rural Ireland for 'an unsullied tradition . . . which suggested an undying continuity, an imperviousness to change, an almost hermetic stasis that transcended history'.[12] Douglas Hyde's

---

[12] Terence Brown, *Ireland: A Social and Cultural History 1922–1985* (London: Fontana Press, 1985), 87.

(1860–1949) seminal lecture of 1892, 'The Necessity for De-Anglicising Ireland', would set the tone not just for the Revival but for early twentieth-century Irish nationalism more generally. An interesting work to consider in this context is *The Professor in Erin* (1918) by Charlotte ('L') McManus (1853–1944). Originally serialized in Arthur Griffith's *Sinn Féin* newspaper in 1912, the story follows the Celtologist and philologist Professor Schliemann as he tries to navigate a parallel universe in which Hugh O'Neill defeated the English at the Battle of Kinsale in 1601. In this alternate world, Ireland is a constitutional monarchy with a thriving economy and a number of scientific achievements to its credit. Society is based as far as possible on the old clan system and Irish is the primary language of the people. As Schliemann tries to find a way home, he becomes embroiled in a number of intrigues and is accused of being a spy as Ireland prepares to go to war with Germany.

The dream of Irish national resurrection came at a time of massive social change across the West. Changing means of production and increased proletarian agitation antagonized the Irish landowning classes, which went to extraordinary lengths to ensure the continuation of an almost feudal economic system. The growing strength of the mass media, eyed with trepidation by the Catholic hierarchy, challenged established ideologies and demagogues around the world. Engineering and invention were supposed to increase efficiency in every aspect of modern life, even war: new weapons would bring every conflict to a speedy conclusion, thus lowering the death toll and making war more humane.[13] The unprecedented slaughter of the First World War demonstrated how grossly ill-founded this optimism turned out to be. At the same time, there was the philosophical crisis triggered by quantum mechanics' challenge to Newtonian physics, which had largely reflected humanity's common-sense view of the world and provided a rational foundation for the concepts of historical and economic change.

The doomed Easter Rising of 1916 resulted in a sea-change in Irish public opinion. In the immediate aftermath of the Rising, the rebels were mocked and denounced by many Dubliners. However, following the executions of the leading participants, including the gravely wounded James Connolly, support for the republican cause increased exponentially and fuelled the War of Independence, which ended with the divisive Anglo-Irish Treaty of 1921, which copper-fastened the partition of the island into a twenty-six-county Free State and a six-county Northern Ireland. From 1922, the contest between tradition and modernity in Ireland would become much more pronounced. On one hand, independence (of a sort) had been achieved; on the other, the cocoon of the British Empire was gone, and Ireland (minus most of Ulster) had to look to its own resources and take care of its own defences.

An Tost (Silence) by Art Ó Riain (1893–1968), writing as Barra Ó Caochlaigh, a five-part novella published in 1927, reflects the possibilities and uncertainties of this new era as it models the transition from the colonial past to an independent future. Part one is set in 1914 and concerns Seán Ó Suíbhne, a young Dublin Castle employee who loses his

---

[13] See I. F. Clarke, *Voices Prophesying War, 1763–1984* (London: Oxford University Press, 1966) on 'future war' narratives of the mid- to late nineteenth century.

job and the respect of the woman he loves after taking part in an Irish Republican Brotherhood manoeuvre. Part two is set in the aftermath of the Rising, when the two are reunited in a hospital and their love rekindled as Máire helps Seán to escape the British. Part three takes place in 1921, when Seán and Máire are married and have an infant son, Fionnbarra. Seán is by now a commander on the anti-Treaty side in the Civil War and rescues his family from a cruel opponent. The fourth section is set in 1938, when Fionnbarra is a medical student. He is given the opportunity to pursue music as a career, thanks to his fine tenor voice, but is also committed to healing the sick of Dublin's slums, where he contracts diphtheria and loses his ability to sing. The final section moves forward to 1975, when Britain and Japan declare war on the Americas. Ireland declares it will remain neutral, despite an ultimatum from the British, who promptly invade, intent on seizing a colossal stockpile of oil and minerals held in a secret location. Fionnbarra by this time has become Minister for Air Travel and has been entrusted with a secret map which he must conceal from the invaders. The closing section of the novella includes references to futuristic inventions, such as coin-operated public radios on every street corner, and a description of torture by laser.

An Tost registers a certain fear of infiltration that independence ushered in. Economically underdeveloped and still recovering from a bitter civil war, Ireland's place in the modern world seemed vulnerable and open to attack. *Marbhán* (Corpse), a two-part detective story by the pseudonymous 'Conán' set in the year 2000, published in the *Connacht Tribune* newspaper in March and April 1933, illustrates this paranoid mood perfectly. In the future world of the story, the disestablishment of the British monarchy has given rise to a British republic and a united Ireland. There is, however, an underground society dedicated to the reinstitution of the monarchy, known as the *Screacháin Roilige* (the Owls), and it transpires that they are active in Galway. A secret agent known only as Marbhán infiltrates one of the organization's cells, which leads to the arrest of the subversive group's ultimate leadership, who are masquerading as an ordinary family living in the countryside.

Even as some authors used futuristic settings to criticize the Free State government, others regarded tradition as a safe refuge. The conflict between tradition and modernity is especially evident in Seosamh Ó Torna's short stories, 'Duinneall' and 'Ceithre Bhuille an Chluig', both published 1938. The titular creature in 'Duinneall'—a portmanteau of *duine* (person) and *inneall* (engine)—is a human being that has been transformed into a machine-like thing through environmental exposure to the modern world, specifically by working in a factory. It does not understand beauty or compassion, and its instinct is to empower the powerful and eradicate the powerless. The narrator warns that thousands of these things exist around the world, insinuating themselves into political and civic life, and that only the 'truth' is capable of defeating them. As in similar science fiction texts, such as Jack Finney's *The Body Snatchers* (1955), the tone of the story is ambiguous—the narrator could be a paranoid fantasist, but there is also the implication that the danger is real. This text is interesting in that it (perhaps unconsciously) appropriates Marxist teaching in defence of the 'Gaelic' way of life. The Duinnealls are workers who have been alienated from their human nature by the labour conditions of modern industry. Their aims are the eradication of traditional life, literature, music, freedom, and even the human soul, and the tell-tale signs of their activities are an increase in aeroplanes and the proliferation of jazz music.

In 'Ceithre Bhuille an Chluig' (Four Strikes of the Bell), an Irish lay missionary returns from Africa to discover that a utopia has been established in his absence. Scientists have discovered that Einstein was wrong—space is not curved but straight, and thus human beings should be morally 'straight' as well. Nevertheless, a secret underground movement of former robber barons wants a return to the profitable days of greed and sin. The narrator awakes at the story's climax, revealing that all that went before was a prophetic vision received while under hypnosis. Ordinarily, the 'it-was-just-a-dream' ending would disqualify the story from being science fiction at all, but its use in Irish tales is subtly different, since in each case it is treated ambiguously. At the end of McManus's *The Professor in Erin*, it is revealed that the never-colonized world of Erin was a dream provoked by a head injury, but the professor himself regards it not as a fantasy but a prophecy. Likewise, 'Ceithre Bhuille an Chluig' ends with an assertion that the world of the dream was somehow more real than waking life.

This use of the dream ending harks back to the traditional Irish belief in prophetic visions, particularly when the dreamer is in a liminal state, such as being close to death. A feature of Irish legend, this trope would later form the basis of seventeenth-century *aisling* poetry, in which visions of a beautiful woman inspire the poet-dreamer to support the Jacobite cause. The earnestness of these dream-stories was lampooned by a young Brian Ó Nualláin (1911–66), who would become better known as Flann O'Brien, in his short story, 'Díoghaltas ar Ghallaibh 'sa Bhliadhain 2032!' (Revenge on the English in the Year 2032!), whose narrator finds himself transported in a dream to a twenty-first-century Gaelic-speaking Ireland. There, his nationalist zeal leads him to teach a series of vile Gaelic insults to an English tourist, under the pretext of helping him to ask for directions, which leads to the hapless tourist receiving a terrible beating from a taxi driver. This would set the tone for a great deal of Irish science fiction to come.

The prevailing mood of paranoia would change in the aftermath of the Second World War, which was euphemistically referred to as 'the Emergency' in Ireland. Possibly as a reaction against the security measures and enforced self-sufficiency of the war years, which included universal rationing, widespread censorship, and unaccountable government inspectors (particularly the 'glimmer men', who covertly policed household use of natural gas), some Irish authors started to pour scorn on tradition and the seemingly arbitrary denunciation of modern culture. One such example is Seán Mac Maoláin (1884–1973), whose unnamed narrator in *Algoland* (1947) finds himself in the titular country in a dream, having eaten stale seafood before bedtime. He befriends the local poet laureate who takes it upon himself to guide the narrator around the capital city, La Primabura. The city is underground and the inhabitants, who speak a language similar to classical Latin, wear skin-tight clothing and travel around on motorized roller-skates. The most interesting aspect of this work is the way in which it satirizes socially conservative nationalism by means of an interview with Algoland's oldest citizen, who lives in the island's last remaining cottage and has an unrivalled knowledge of folklore and folk wisdom. While the authorities do their best to keep him and his wife *in situ* to preserve his precious knowledge, their efforts prove futile. Being old enough to remember the hardship and toil of everyday life in the old days, the elderly couple are fans of modern technology, such that the old man rarely plays traditional tunes on his fiddle anymore and is instead a devotee of jazz music, to which he listens on his gramophone.

The ambivalent relationship between the past and the present is particularly noticeable in Samuel Beckett's (1906–89) *Endgame* (1957) and *Krapp's Last Tape* (1958), both of which could be considered science fiction as well as absurdist works. *Krapp's Last Tape*, after all, is set thirty years in the future and has the eponymous protagonist listening to tapes he recorded in his youth. At the time of the play's composition, the tape recorder had only recently become commercially available. Beckett extrapolates upon the social impact of this technology, using it to make larger points about the dissolution of youthful optimism, thus exemplifying the point that the best science fiction does not dwell on technological gewgaws for their own sake but rather exploits their potential to address contemporary themes and concerns. *Endgame* is more ambiguous in this regard, but it is not hard to see how it might be read science-fictionally, given its post-apocalyptic setting. We learn from Hamm, the master of the last remaining Big House in this shattered world, that the surrounding countryside is full of refugees; he has denied their pleas for food by telling them: 'Use your head can't you, use your head, you're on earth, there's no cure for that!'[14] This line establishes that whatever happened, it happened to the world we live in: *Endgame* is set in our future. The precise nature of the apparent apocalypse is never made explicit. Hamm asks his servant Clov to report on the state of the world from the window, but the most we learn is that the sea is tideless and the sky sunless. Not only has the order of nature broken down, but language itself has become almost wholly arbitrary.

There were still some authors who sought refuge in the past, though, and among these was Edward John Moreton Drax Plunkett (1878–1957), better known as Lord Dunsany. While known primarily for his works of fantasy, Dunsany also penned two novels that were extraordinarily hostile to the post-war world. *The Last Revolution* (1951) depicts an uprising of sapient machines, against whom the natural world seems to rally to the side of humanity. The novel is especially noteworthy for a farcical scene in which a scientist's fiancée is kidnapped by a sapient motorcycle, as sympathetic birds and animals look on, powerless to help. *Pleasures of a Futuroscope*, written in 1955 and published posthumously in 2005, centres on a device that allows the user to see into the future. The narrator looks forward 600 years into the future to see a rural England that has returned to nature. Following a nuclear cataclysm, London is now a water-filled crater and humans have reverted to a neolithic state of being. The narrator decides to follow the fortunes of one particular family, recording their encounters with wolves, a wild man, and a band of dastardly gypsies. The most notable aspect of this novel is the attention Dunsany devotes to the depiction of nature. His utopia is a wild wood from which machinery and heavy industry are absent and forgotten.

---

[14]   Samuel Beckett, *Endgame and Act Without Words* (New York: Grove Press, 1958), 53.

REVIVAL AND RECESSION

The economic transformation of the 1960s, bolstered by the policies of Seán Lemass's Fianna Fáil government, meant that many Irish people began to enjoy higher levels of disposable income and develop more liberal attitudes, fuelled by their growing exposure to Anglo-American popular culture and lifestyles. While these developments perturbed some social conservatives, writers such as Cathal Ó Sándair (1922–96) drew inspiration from these expanding horizons. Born in Weston-super-Mare in Somerset to an English father and an Irish mother, Ó Sándair was the author of the *Captaen Spéirling* series of children's books, which includes *Captaen Spéirling agus an Phláinéad do Phléasc* (Captain Spéirling and the Planet that Exploded, 1960), *Leis an gCaptaen Spéirling go Mars* (Captain Spéirling Goes to Mars, 1961), and *Captaen Spéirling, Spás Phíolóta* (Captain Spéirling, Space Pilot, 1961). In these stories, Ó Sándair depicts a future Ireland where people drive uranium-powered cars on an autobahn running the entire length of the island, the Ministry of Defence maintains a military unit of space pilots, and the government ensures its popularity by spraying chemicals into the stratosphere to make it snow every Christmas. The world of tomorrow is one of interplanetary commerce, where trade and regime change go hand in hand. Spéirling flits around the solar system, abolishing slavery on Venus and Mars, preventing a third world war on Earth, and developing telepathic powers in time to repulse an alien invasion. These stories are obviously imitative of British and American series such as Dan Dare and Buck Rogers, but this derivativeness is beside the point. Spéirling is not only an Irish speaker but also a practising Catholic who can quote the Sanctus in Latin. Essentially, Ó Sándair is appropriating popular culture to demonstrate the continuation of tradition into the future, thus impressing upon his target audience of children that there was no necessary contradiction between being Irish and reaching for the stars. Having a respectful regard for the past did not preclude living in the kind of glorious future depicted in American pulp magazines.

The first half of the twentieth century was the golden era of cheap fiction magazines (termed 'pulps' on account of the cheap paper on which they were printed), which emphasized sensationalism and melodrama over characterization, subtlety, and nuance. Pulp writers were hacks who wrote in a number of different genres, often mixing and matching plots and clichés between westerns, science fiction, and detective stories. Although this was the era that gave rise to the iconic 'space opera' formula, which featured valiant space pilots in high-stakes armed conflict with alien monsters, the influence of the pulps would not be felt in Irish science fiction until after mid-century. The main authors of American-style space operas on the island of Ireland, James White (1928–99) and Bob Shaw (1931–96), were both from Belfast. Unfortunately, at the time they were producing their best work, sectarian animosity in Northern Ireland escalated into an ethnic conflict that would continue for three decades. Shaw and White were very well received by science fiction readers, many of whom had no idea that they were not

American. Reading them in context, however, it is impossible to miss the looming influence of the Troubles in their invented worlds.

White is best known for the Sector General series (1962–99), a space opera set on a hospital space station, which takes a resolute stance against warmongering and bigotry. The series is also inspired by White's (unachieved) ambition to become a doctor. There are plenty of weird aliens on display, but none of them are evil invaders; there are in fact no real villains, other than the greedy and the tragically misguided. Bob Shaw wrote dozens of novels, most of which were stand-alone adventure stories. Among his linked titles, the Ragged Astronauts sequence and the Orbitsville series stand out. The former is set on a pair of planets that are close enough to each other to have overlapping atmospheres. When ecological disaster threatens the inhabitants of 'Land', they must migrate to the uninhabited 'Overland' by hot-air balloon. The Orbitsville series is set inside a 'Dyson sphere', a colossal shell surrounding a star, with a breathable atmosphere and an internal surface area equivalent to five billion Earths, where competition over territory or resources is unthinkable.[15] Both series depict groups of migrants arriving in places with no history, where a fresh start can be made. The villains are those who have profited politically or economically from historical circumstance on the old world, and now seek to take over the new one. Tellingly, Shaw moved his family from Northern Ireland to England in 1973 to get away from the intensifying political violence.

An interesting novel to consider alongside these is Ian McDonald's (1960–) *Sacrifice of Fools* (1996), which explicitly addresses the Troubles by imagining the consequences of a large-scale extraterrestrial settlement in Belfast, a colony partially initiated by cynical politicians trying to unite Catholics and Protestants by introducing a third 'other'. The plan is not successful: shared distrust of the aliens does not diminish the locals' mutual sectarian hatred and paramilitary groups covertly plot the appropriation of extraterrestrial weaponry. The plot unfolds as a murder mystery, with a social worker (and former getaway driver for a loyalist hit squad) trying to track down a serial killer who may or may not be human. In his other works, the award-winning Manchester-born McDonald, who has lived in Belfast since early childhood, has become known for setting other science fiction tropes in locations that are often ignored by Western science fiction, such as alien life in Africa (*Chaga*, 1995), artificial intelligence in India (*River of Gods*, 2004), quantum computing in a Brazilian slum (*Brasyl*, 2007), and nanotechnology in Turkey (*The Dervish House*, 2010).

By the 1980s, the economic revival inaugurated by the Lemass government of the early 1960s was a distant memory and the Republic was enduring a lengthy recession. Perhaps unsurprisingly, dystopian narratives resonated with Irish readers during these years, many of which feature bleak urban landscapes, authoritarian overlords, and worn-out modernization projects (particularly the Lemassian tactic of rehousing the inner-city urban poor in high-rise tower blocks). A prime example of such narratives is

---

[15] This kind of structure, which would capture the entire energy output of a star, is named after the physicist and mathematician Freeman Dyson, based on an essay published in the journal *Science*. The first description of such a sphere, however, is credited to the English science fiction author Olaf Stapledon.

Mícheál Ó Brolacháin's (1960–2009) *Pax Dei* (1985), an Irish-language novella set in a dystopian urban future, where corporations have taken the place of nation-states. There are two parallel storylines. The first concerns a young boy called Rurc who lives with his mother in a colossal block of flats; when she dies, Rurc is forced to fend for himself. His exploration of the tower block brings him into contact with another little boy and a psychopathic gangster. The second plot strand concerns P. X. Winterbottom, an executive in one of the multinationals, who is frantically preparing for the arrival of the company's chairman. The grim story of the two young boys is written in the present tense, making their suffering immediate and inescapable, whereas the more comic bungling of the company men is placed at a comfortable distance through the use of the past tense. The antics of the powerful beget tragedies for the powerless, as Winterbottom saves his own skin by ordering the bombing of the tower block, thereby eradicating the cost of upkeep—and the residents themselves.

This dystopian streak in Irish science fiction continued into the early 1990s. In Eilís Ní Dhuibhne's (1954–) *The Bray House* (1990), Ireland is buried under radioactive ash following a nuclear disaster. Robin, a Swedish researcher whose Irish husband was visiting his family when the catastrophe occurred, leads an expedition to Bray in County Wicklow five years later. There, the archaeologists excavate the contents of a typical middle-class home. While the fragments of the lives of the now-dead McHugh family are pored over and catalogued, Robin struggles to get along with her team. The novel is not entirely successful, mostly because five years is too short a time for the prevailing culture to have been completely forgotten, yet Ní Dhuibhne's science fiction approach to contemporary Irish society is both defamiliarizing and perspicacious. The focus on the family home is of particular note, as traditional notions of family life were increasingly being debated and contested in the Irish public sphere at the time of the novel's publication.

Dark Paradise (1991) by Catherine Brophy (1941–) is set on the planet Zintilla, where a humanoid species has evolved into two distinct types: natural humans who live rustic lives in the wilderness and 'Crystal Beings' who have altered their bodies over the generations through genetic engineering and eugenics. The Crystal Beings, who lack legs, reproductive organs, and excretory appendages, live beneath the Cowl—a colossal roof covering a large portion of the planet's surface—in a society devoted to knowledge and logic, where emotions are abhorred as 'chaos'.[16] Somewhat predictably, a group of young Crystal Beings manages to escape from the Cowl with the help of the unevolved 'bipeds' and form a rebel movement to end the joyless, antiseptic Zintillian hegemony. At the end of the novel, however, an exiled Crystal Being, who has been drifting through space for the majority of the story, is abruptly reborn as an infant on planet Earth, thus recasting the preceding story as a dramatization of the provenance of human life. This particular issue would become the subject of a heated public debate on abortion in the Republic the following year, following the disclosure of the facts of the infamous 'X' case. Read in this context, *Dark Paradise* can be situated in the same anxious transitional social moment as *The Bray House*.

---

[16] Catherine Brophy, *Dark Paradise* (Dublin: Wolfhound Press, 1991), 52–3.

HUNTING THE TIGER

Figured as an unprecedented upsurge in prosperity, the hedonism and conspicuous consumption of the Celtic Tiger period of the late 1990s and early 2000s gave rise to a number of texts that tried to ape the styles and techniques of hard-boiled American science fiction and techno-thrillers in Irish settings, usually without irony and often with risible results. Although American cyberpunk fiction—near-future dystopian science fiction focusing on information technology and corporate dominance—was largely a spent force by the time Irish authors started writing it, the narrative possibilities offered by scenarios featuring self-aware computers in Irish locales gave rise to some interesting works that commented on the economic boom and even seemed to gleefully foretell its downfall.

Tim Booth's bombastic *Altergeist* (1999) is set in a fractious 'New Ireland' where the Catholic Church, the Russian Army, and an American media corporation compete with the remnants of the Irish government for control over the state. The plot follows Misha Ploughman, a cadet at the 'DizBee' Learning Centre for Advertising Design, who goes on the run after top-secret software is downloaded into her brain, one consequence of which is the 'Altergeist Effect'—for reasons unknown, the software triggers personality changes in young women, accompanied by phenomenal telekinetic powers. A thematically similar work is *Welcome To Coolsville* (2004) by Jason Mordaunt, a satire set in a future Dublin suburb called Maymon Glades, where multinational corporations wield extraordinary political power and practically everything has been privatized. The story is a rats' nest of characters and plotlines, including the development of a chemical agent that makes people docile and compliant, a *Charlie's Angels*-style sisterhood of warrior nuns established by a rogue Jesuit, the establishment of a museum of popular culture, genetic engineering, and the search for immortality. The influence of Anglo-American science fiction, particularly that of the television and film variety, is clearly visible in both these novels, which privilege action over introspection and rely on a number of familiar tropes and images from popular culture. To a degree, the comedy of these stories arises from locating these tropes and images in the Irish landscape.

Mike McCormack's (1965–) *Notes from a Coma* (2005) takes a less frenetic approach to the future of Ireland. The (absent) protagonist is one John Joe O'Malley, the adopted son of a farmer in the west of Ireland, who volunteers to enter a medically-induced coma. This is a feasibility test funded by the European Union, to determine whether congestion in the prison system can be eased by placing criminals into comas for the duration of their sentences. In the background, the volunteers progress from being the latest reality TV sensation to being almost deified by the general population. By setting this science fiction experiment against the backdrop of Killary Harbour in County Galway, McCormack articulates the unease and discomfort of many Irish people with their country's place in an increasingly globalized world.

The bubble economy produced by the years of market-led globalization did not survive the 2008 financial crash, and the inequities at the heart of the boom were exposed by the economic bloodbath that followed. As was the case with the 1980s recession, the popular mood swung back towards anger and an appreciation of the dystopian. Set in the 2050s in a fictional city in the west of Ireland, Kevin Barry's (1969–) *City of Bohane* (2011) is a novel that is perhaps just as pessimistic as Ó Brolacháin's and at the same time as gleefully nihilistic as the aforementioned works by Booth and Mordaunt. Bohane is a bleak urban environment ruled by gangsters, where crime and murder are part of the fabric of everyday life and where the most lucrative trades revolve around prostitution and opium. The plot follows various gangland players and local power brokers prior to, during, and after a gang war to establish ownership over the most profitable areas of the city. The most striking aspects of the novel are Barry's use of language, which has drawn just comparisons with that of James Joyce (1882–1941) and Anthony Burgess, and his unabashed incorporation of images and motifs taken from 'lowbrow' science fiction sources, such as *Mad Max* and the British comic-book *2000AD*, to tell a story that is quintessentially Irish.

To a large extent, Irish science fiction has limited itself to tackling Anglo-American tropes from an 'authentically' Irish standpoint. However, there are signs that changes are afoot in how Irish people imagine the future. The 2016 edition of *Old Moore's Almanac* is less flamboyant in its predictions than its 2015 counterpart and certainly more pessimistic, foretelling worldwide economic hardship, political instability, and a new cold war between Russia, China, and the USA. On the plus side, human beings in general will demand a more egalitarian world economy, corruption will be exposed at all levels of politics and business, and 'Amazing acts of humanitarian understanding will hit the news.'[17] Predicted technological developments include medical breakthroughs that make surgery obsolete, cheap gene-sequencing, holographic phone calls, and robots to pick and sort fruit. Once again, the predictions for Ireland are mostly unremarkable, but this time we are told that the country will launch its own space probe at some point during the year.

Twenty-first-century Irishness, to a degree at least, now allows for active participation in forging the future rather than simply consuming it. The likelihood is that Irish science fiction authors will continue to repurpose standard genre tropes and filter them through a national consciousness. While the outcomes may be of dubious literary quality, the evidence to date suggests that the tension between tradition and modernity in Irish culture will continue to yield results that are, at the very least, worthy of further study.

FURTHER READING

Bould, Mark, and Sherryl Vint. *The Routledge Concise History of Science Fiction*. Abingdon: Routledge, 2011.

Brown, Terence. *Ireland: A Social and Cultural History 1922–1985*. London: Fontana Press, 1985.

[17] 'Old Moore Predicts: Media Themes for 2016', *Old Moore's Almanac 2016* (2015), 4.

Cahill, Susan. *Irish Literature in the Celtic Tiger Years 1990–2008: Gender, Bodies, Memory*. London: Continuum, 2011.

Fennell, Jack. *Irish Science Fiction*. Liverpool: Liverpool University Press, 2014.

Freedman, Carl. *Critical Theory and Science Fiction*. Hanover, NH: Wesleyan University Press, 2000.

James, Edward. 'The Anglo-Irish Disagreement: Past Irish Futures'. *Linen Hall Review* 3, no. 4 (1986): 5–8.

Langer, Jessica. *Postcolonialism and Science Fiction*. Basingstoke: Palgrave Macmillan, 2011.

Maume, Patrick. 'Futures Past: The Science Fiction of Bob Shaw and James White as a Product of Late-Industrial Belfast'. In Paddy Lyons and Alison O'Malley-Younger (eds), *No Country for Old Men: Fresh Perspectives on Irish Literature*. Bern: Peter Lang, 2009: 193–214.

Rieder, John. *Colonialism and the Emergence of Science Fiction*. Middletown, CT: Wesleyan University Press, 2008.

Wills, Clair. *That Neutral Island: A Cultural History of Ireland During the Second World War*. London: Faber and Faber, 2007.

CHAPTER 22

HOUSE, LAND, AND FAMILY LIFE

Children's Fiction and Irish Homes

PÁDRAIC WHYTE

ALTHOUGH not usually identified as a genre—any more than the category of 'literature for adult readers' might be considered a genre—children's literature is generally understood as a body of literature defined by its readership. Children's fiction encompasses everything from fiction for the very young up to and including teenage fiction, and embraces a wide range of forms and genres of texts, from picturebooks to Young Adult novels.[1] Critics have identified a number of common tropes within this corpus, chief among which is the concept of home, which Jane Carroll defines as 'the centre of human identity', a hallowed space that 'acts as a nexus between the world and the Self'.[2] Pauline Dewan notes that 'throughout children's literature, houses dominate the novels in which they are found' and that for children, 'home is charged with great emotional significance'.[3] The recurrence of this trope has particular significance when examining children's fiction found within the broader category of Irish fiction, where houses, and the activities that take place within them, often carry much symbolic weight. Representations of home, as well as those elements inextricably linked to ideas of home, such as land and family life, have often facilitated the exploration of complex social and political forces within Irish culture. Indeed, this can be seen in the text which is often a touchstone for discussions of the origins of Irish children's fiction, *The History of Harry Spencer; Compiled for the Amusement of Good Children; And the Instructions of Such as Wish to Become Good* (1794)

---

[1] Traditionally, because of recurring tropes, themes, and motifs found within such fiction, Young Adult fiction is considered a discrete genre within teenage fiction. See Pádraic Whyte, 'Young Adult Fiction and Youth Culture', in Valerie Coghlan and Keith O'Sullivan (eds), *Irish Children's Literature and Culture: New Perspectives on Contemporary Writing* (London: Routledge, 2011), 71–84.

[2] Jane Carroll, *Landscape and Children's Literature* (London: Routledge, 2012), 20.

[3] Pauline Dewan, *The House as Setting, Symbol, and Structural Motif in Children's Literature* (Lewiston, NY: Edward Mellen Press, 2004), 2–3.

by James Delap.[4] Ideas of home are to the fore throughout the narrative, which opens with the protagonists leaving home and concludes with the return of a family member to a new home.[5]

This chapter examines the representations of house, land, and family life in a number of significant texts from the late nineteenth century to the present day, tracing developments and trends in modern Irish fiction for children and identifying the many ways in which these manifestations of home are in dialogue with each other. With a focus on realist fiction written in English, the chapter identifies notable touchstones and examines specific depictions of home, from the Big House to the thatched cottage; from gender construction to the collision of traditional and modern forces within the domestic sphere; from diverse family structures in urban homes to fractured family lives during the conflict in Northern Ireland; and from the interweaving of private and public histories to the creation of sanctuaries for young adults. The following chronological survey of changing conceptions of home and family life reveals the complicated cultural and social discourses at play in modern Irish children's fiction.

THE LATE NINETEENTH AND EARLY TWENTIETH CENTURIES

In the latter part of the nineteenth century and the early part of the twentieth, numerous Irish writers engaged with contrasting ideas of house and home. These included the motifs of the nation-as-house, the peasant cottage as a national symbol, and varying representations of the culture of the Big House. Often, these motifs were vehicles for the exploration of tensions between landlords and tenants, ascendancy figures and peasants, Protestants and Catholics, and between English and Irish cultures. Flora L. Shaw's (1852–1929) *Castle Blair: A Story of Youthful Days* (1878) is a landmark text in the history of Irish children's fiction, 'the nearest we have in children's literature to the "big house" novel of much Irish literature'.[6] Shaw, who was born in England and later became known

---

[4] The children's book collector Mary 'Paul' Pollard was the first to identify this novel, which was published under the pseudonym Philanthropos, as the earliest known work of fiction for children written by an Irish author and first printed in Ireland. See the entry for Delap in Ralph Loeber and Magda Loeber with Anne Mullin Burnham, *A Guide to Irish Fiction 1650–1900* (Dublin: Four Courts Press, 2006), 358. A substantial portion of Delap's text is directly taken from Henry Brooke's five-volume *The Fool of Quality* (1765–70) and Thomas Day's *A History of Sandford and Merton*, published in three volumes between 1783 and 1789.

[5] Using home as a guiding analytic allows us to see the extent to which Delap's text conforms to the traditional 'home/away/home' model that Perry Nodelman identifies as central to many, but not all, children's texts in *The Pleasures of Children's Literature* (New York: Longman, 1992).

[6] Robert Dunbar, 'Rebuilding *Castle Blair*: A Reading of Flora Shaw's 1878 Children's Novel', in Celia Keenan and Mary Shine Thompson (eds), *Studies in Children's Literature 1500–2000* (Dublin: Four Courts Press, 2004), 32. For a discussion of the Big House subgenre, see Vera Kreilkamp, 'The Novel of the Big House', in John Wilson Foster (ed.), *The Cambridge Companion to the Irish Novel* (Cambridge: Cambridge University Press, 2006), 60–77.

as Lady Lugard, spent her childhood summers in Kimmage House in Dublin, home of her grandfather Sir Frederick Shaw. It was his estate that was used as the inspiration for *Castle Blair*, which engages with the culture of the late nineteenth-century Land Wars. In Shaw's narrative, a French cousin, Nessa, arrives to live with the Blair children and the Big House is established as something uniquely Irish, in contrast to the manors of Europe. 'Irish ways', the reader is informed, 'certainly seemed different from any that she knew.'[7] The parents of the Blair children live in India and the children are represented as unruly and wild but also loving and affectionate and in need of the civilizing force that Nessa brings. This process is demonstrated through the lessons they learn, as well as through the transformation of domestic space, as Nessa brings order to the schoolroom located within the house, thus figuring the reshaping through education of personality, temperament, and identity.[8]

The main tension in the novel is that between the eldest of the Blair children, Murtagh, and the hated land agent Mr Plunkett. For much of the narrative, it appears that Murtagh and his siblings are sympathetic to the plight of the Catholic tenants who are being evicted. Yet despite such sympathies, the cabin-dwellers are ultimately shown to be responsible for their own misfortune, and the reader's attention is continually drawn to their laziness, alcoholism, and violent treatment of their children. By the end of the novel, Murtagh, on realizing that he is now heir to Castle Blair, is represented as having arrived at a greater understanding of the complexity of landlord–tenant relations. He recognizes the need for kindness and compassion under certain circumstances but also acknowledges the motivations for the land agent's actions and the need to bring discipline and order to the estate. As a result, the reader is encouraged to dismiss the Fenians' account of events and the hearsay that tenants may have genuine grievances. Instead, the actions of Mr Plunkett are presented as justified and for the good of those in the cabins as well as those in the castle.

The late nineteenth century saw an increase in the volume of fiction produced both for boy and girl readers, and a large number of Victorian children's authors wrote tales similar in tone to that of Shaw. Significantly, many of the stories targeting a young female readership explored Irish–English relationships through representations of domestic spaces, drawing upon a tradition where such an environment was associated with women and childhood. Among these stories is Josephine Callwell's (d. 1935) tale of a young Irish girl negotiating her relationship with her new English stepfather, which was published as *Timothy Tatters: A Story for the Young* in 1890. That Callwell presents Irish homes as uncivilized and inferior to the orderly homes and gardens of the English is evident from the narrator's description of Castlefogarty: 'The garden, doubtless, was not very trimly kept . . . but few people in Ireland, and certainly no one in Castlefogarty, would have troubled themselves about such small drawbacks.'[9] The representation of both house and garden as wild functions as a metaphor for the Irish people, regardless of class or background, a trope common in much of the literature of the period.

---

[7] Flora Shaw, *Castle Blair* (Oxford: Oxford University Press, 1929), 20–1.   [8] Ibid, 103.
[9] Josephine Callwell, *Timothy Tatters: A Story for the Young* (London: T. Nelson and Sons, 1890), 31.

A similar treatment of domestic space can be found in the work of Cork-born L. T. Meade (pseudonym of Elizabeth Thomasina Toulmin Smith, 1844–1914), one of the most prolific children's authors of all time.[10] Meade's *Light o' the Morning; or, The Story of an Irish Girl* (1899) follows the adventures of a character named Nora who goes to great lengths to save her ancestral home in Kerry from being sold; the novel concludes with her English uncle buying the property. Throughout, Irish and English identities are constructed in opposition to each other, with the English represented as overly self-disciplined and the Irish shown to be lacking in manners and social graces. On a visit to England, Nora longs to be free of the confined built environment, while back in Kerry, her father eschews the comforts of the house to sleep in the barn. The novel suggests that, even with the benefits of education, the Irish are impervious to change, yet so too are the English for that matter, which leaves amicable coexistence as the only viable way forward. Despite this, Meade's final representation of the Irish as being more at home in spaces associated with animals is extremely problematic, complicit as it is with dehumanizing colonial discourses.

These, however, were not the only authors of the period writing child-centred narratives about Ireland within the contexts of nationalist protest and agrarian unrest. Jeanette Condon argues that writers such as Rosa Mulholland (1841–1921) in *The Girls of Banshee Castle* (1895) and Katharine Tynan (1859–1931) in *A Girl of Galway* (1902) 'subtly challenged if not entirely subverted'[11] the imperialist ideologies found in the novels of Shaw, Meade, and Callwell. In these novels, which targeted a young, female, English middle-class readership, Mulholland and Tynan acknowledge tenant grievances, advocate investment for the improvement of conditions, and espouse the transformative potential of benevolent landlordism, while simultaneously upholding and legitimizing the existing class hierarchy. At the end of *A Girl of Galway*, the changes wrought by the initiatives of a younger generation of landowners have transformed the woods surrounding the Corofin estate into 'something of a marvel' and made them as 'Beautiful as fairyland'.[12]

Many of the English publications for young male readers during this period focused on ideas of imperial expansion, often portrayed through adventure narratives. Such publications were widely read by Irish boys (and girls), prompting cultural revivalists to offer counter-narratives drawn from Ireland's history and heritage. This trend was inaugurated by a committed unionist, Standish O'Grady (1846–1928), whose *The Coming of Cuculain* (1894) 'marked the beginning of a process that was to gain momentum during the Literary Revival and continue to the present day—the retelling of

---

[10] See Carole Dunbar, 'The Wild Irish Girls of L. T. Meade and Mrs George de Horne Vaizey', in Keenan and Thompson (eds), *Studies in Children's Literature 1500–2000*, 38–43 and Beth Rogers, *Adolescent Girlhood and Literary Culture at the Fin de Siècle: Daughters of Today* (Basingstoke: Palgrave Macmillan, 2016).

[11] Janette Condon, '"Victoria's Own"? Discourses of Cultural Imperialism and Nationalist Resistance in Nineteenth-Century Children's Literature in Ireland'. Unpublished PhD thesis, NUI, Galway, 1999, 198.

[12] Katharine Tynan, *A Girl of Galway* (London: Blackie and Son, 1902), 384.

Ireland's ancient myths and legends for children'.[13] O'Grady's tales popularized the image of Cuchulain, inspiring writers such as Lady Augusta Gregory (1852–1932), Eleanor Hull (1860–1935), and Patrick Pearse (1879–1916), whose interest in Irish myth, fairy lore, and folklore was shared by many others, including Ethna Carbery (pseudonym of Anna Johnston MacManus, 1864–1902), her husband Seamus MacManus (1869–1960), Padraic Colum (1881–1972), George (Æ) Russell (1867–1935), his wife Violet Russell (1869–1932), James Stephens (1880–1950), W. B. Yeats (1865–1939), and Ella Young (1867–1956), with artists such as Beatrice Elvery, Maud Gonne, and Jack B. Yeats providing illustrations for their works.[14]

In his introduction to the 1919 edition of *The Coming of Cuculain*, Russell invokes the popular revivalist nation-as-house motif when he praises O'Grady as a man 'who rushes into a burning mansion and brings out its greatest treasure', adding: 'When I read O'Grady I was as such a man who suddenly feels ancient memories rushing at him, and knows he was born in a royal house, that he had mixed with the mighty of heaven and earth and had the very noblest for his companions.'[15] Whereas Russell's comments associate the cultural treasures of the nation with socially privileged dwellings, other writers of this period continued to invoke the established trope of the peasant cottage as the source of enriching myths and folktales. These tales were pointedly linked to an oral tradition located within the family home—usually a rural cottage—which 'became a national symbol of an independent, natural, morally upright, and more spiritual way of life than was available in the overcrowded cities'.[16] Thus, the motif of stories heard by the fireside introduced young readers to a range of Irish myths and folktales, and was central to many early twentieth-century works of children's fiction, notably those of a writer who was one of the most prolific and popular children's authors of the period, Padraic Colum, author of approximately twenty-six works for children, three of which—*The Golden Fleece and the Heroes that Lived Before Achilles* (1921), *The Voyagers: Being Legends and Romances of Atlantic Discovery* (1925), and *The Big Tree of Bunlahy: Stories of My Own Countryside* (1933)—received Newbery Honor citations in recognition of their distinguished contribution to children's literature in the USA.[17]

[13] Ciara Ní Bhroin, 'Recovering a Heroic Past: The *Táin* Retold', in Mary Shine Thompson (ed.), *Young Irelands: Studies in Children's Literature* (Dublin: Four Courts Press, 2011), 68.

[14] Myths, legends, fairytales, and folktales have featured prominently in Irish writing and illustrations for children throughout the twentieth century and right up to the present day, as evidenced by the work of authors such as Máirín Cregan, Sinéad de Valera, Malachy Doyle, Marie-Louise Fitzpatrick, Marie Heaney, P. J. Lynch, Eileen Ó Faoláin, Michael Scott, and Niamh Sharkey.

[15] Æ, 'Introduction', in Standish O'Grady, *The Coming of Cuculain* (Dublin: Talbot Press, 1919), xx, x.

[16] Brian P. Kennedy, 'The Traditional Irish Thatched House: Image and Reality, 1793–1993', in Adele M. Dalsimer (ed.), *Visualizing Ireland: National Identity and the Pictorial Tradition* (Winchester, MA: Faber and Faber, 1993), 173.

[17] I discuss Padraic Colum's Newbery Honor books in detail in 'A Place in the Canon: Padraic Colum's Newbery Books and the Development of American Children's Literature', in Timothy Young (ed.), *Story-Time: Essays on the Betsy Beinecke Shirley Collection of American Children's Literature* (New Haven, CT: Yale University Press, 2016), 139–55.

The skills of vivid storytelling that are central to these writings for children stemmed from Colum's childhood experience of listening to his aunts and uncles in his native Longford, one of whom 'told his stories in the evening; he told them by the light of a candle and a peat fire'.[18] *The Big Tree of Bunlahy*, the dedication to which acknowledges the 'wise and witty discourse'[19] that Colum heard by the hearth in his aunt's home, contains a frame narrative of the author/narrator's return to the village of his childhood and his recollection of the tales he heard under the eponymous tree. In this instance, the tree replaces the hearth as the centre of the storytelling experience and the rural village becomes a symbol of home. When read in autobiographical terms, and taking into account Colum's move to New York with his wife in 1914, the village of Bunlahy functions as a metonym for Ireland, and the collection itself gives expression to an emigrant's nostalgic view of his homeland. The author's homecoming and recollection of tales demonstrates Colum's use of memory to access the myths and legends heard during his youth in Ireland, which in turn became sources of inspiration for his later works, which were composed and published in the USA and aimed at a predominantly American readership. For the implied American child reader, Ireland is presented in romantic terms as the home of not simply the best stories but also the best storytellers. More significantly, while the account in *The Big Tree of Bunlahy* of the young Colum discovering riches in the bogland of Bunlahy establishes treasure as a metaphor for story, it also ensures that the bog, and the landscape more broadly, is linked inextricably to Irish heritage and identity. As a result, Colum's depiction of his Irish home is a romantic nationalist idealization of a premodern culture suffused with the lore of an ancient past.

THE 1930S AND 1940S

In many children's books published in the 1930s and 1940s, the home of the protagonist is often located adjacent to or in the middle of a bog, a pastoral setting that had the effect of further romanticizing Irish home life of the period. Notable examples include Patricia Lynch's (1898–1972) *The Turf-Cutter's Donkey* (1934), Maura Laverty's (1907–66) *The Cottage in the Bog* (1945), and Mary Flynn's (1911–84) once popular but now largely forgotten *Cornelius Rabbit of Tang* (1944) and its three sequels, *Cornelius on Holiday* (1945), *Cornelius in Charge* (1946), and *Danny Puffin* (1947). As with *The Big Tree of Bunlahy*, these texts represent the bog as an almost magical site for the discovery of ancient artefacts that have been preserved for millennia. But they go further by engaging with weighty social and political discourses of the newly independent state. Lynch's book asserts a nationalist ideology that intertwines the cottage, the land, and the nuclear family; Flynn engages with the gender politics of the period; while Laverty takes a

---

[18] Padraic Colum, 'Story Telling, New and Old', in *The Fountain of Youth* (New York: Macmillan, 1927), 193.
[19] Padraic Colum, *The Big Tree of Bunlahy: Stories of My Own Countryside* (New York: The Macmillan Company, 1933), unpaginated dedication.

postcolonial approach, demonstrating the newfound power of the cottage-dwellers to retrieve for the nation treasures withheld by the owners of the Big House.

All six of these children's texts were published in a cultural climate where the dominant political figure of the postcolonial nation, Éamon de Valera, advocated the frugal surroundings of the cottage as an appropriate residence for citizens of the new Ireland, even though most rural-dwellers themselves desired more modern housing.[20] *The Turf-Cutter's Donkey* is in keeping with the taoiseach's bucolic vision; indeed, it was first published in serialized form in the *Irish Press* newspaper, which de Valera founded in 1931. Lynch published over fifty books for children and won numerous literary awards. Her work was hugely popular throughout the twentieth century and *The Turf-Cutter's Donkey* in particular is often regarded as a classic of Irish children's fiction. Illustrated by Jack B. Yeats, the book features child protagonists Eileen and Seamus who live 'in a cabin just beyond the crossroads at the edge of the great bog. The cabin was so low and the thatch so covered with grass and daisies, that a stranger would never have found it only that the walls were whitewashed.'[21] Whereas the proximity of Irish cabins and their inhabitants to the land carried predominantly negative connotations in children's fiction of the nineteenth century, in Lynch's work, such proximity betokens an organic, family-centred rootedness that pre-empts the idealized view of Irish society expressed in de Valera's oft-cited radio broadcast of St Patrick's Day, 1943. The romantic simplicity of the life of the turf-cutter, who 'knew so many songs to sing and so many tunes to whistle that he hadn't a deal of time for turf-cutting,'[22] may be a fantasy, but in ideological terms it represents a deliberate attempt to redeem an Irish rural lifestyle as something to be admired rather than pilloried. This is further reinforced by the manner in which the story privileges the nuclear family as the ideal unit, thus anticipating the 1937 Constitution, and highlights the necessity of a knowledge of myth and folklore for survival, in contrast to earlier cabin-centred works that emphasize the importance of education to facilitate commerce and industry. Throughout Lynch's prolific career as a children's writer, which spanned four decades, different kinds of dwellings are represented, including caravans, urban houses, and thatched cabins, but the idealization of a closely integrated family structure remains a constant.[23]

Flynn's *Cornelius Rabbit of Tang* also engages with aspects of de Valera's Constitution and reveals the workings of conservative cultural ideologies within the domestic sphere. In this anthropomorphic tale, one of Cornelius's more interesting adventures shows him attempting to assume the duties of the notably nameless Mrs Rabbit and cook dinner for the family, an episode that can be read as an oblique commentary on the gendered nature of domestic labour that had recently been enshrined in Article 41.2 of the Constitution, which states that 'By her life within the home, woman gives to the State a

---

[20] Kennedy, 'The Traditional Irish Thatched House', 174–6.

[21] Patricia Lynch, *The Turf-Cutter's Donkey* (Dublin: Poolbeg Press, 1988), 7.   [22] Ibid., 7.

[23] Leeann Lane links the idealization of family and home in Lynch's children's fiction to the early loss of her father and her subsequent nomadic childhood. See Leeann Lane, ' "In My Mind I Build a House": The Quest for Family in the Children's Fiction of Patricia Lynch', *Éire-Ireland* 44, nos. 1–2 (2009), 169–93.

support without which the common good cannot be achieved.'[24] On discovering that work in the kitchen is much more difficult than he had imagined, Cornelius resorts to making a salad. While the depiction of his culinary failure acknowledges the arduous nature of domestic labour, this episode also reinforces gender stereotypes by suggesting that such work comes more naturally to women than to men. Thus, while Flynn goes some way towards challenging engrained attitudes, the outcome of this episode ultimately perpetuates the stereotypical thinking and social conservatism of the era.

Whereas the works by Lynch and Flynn are primarily concerned with the social realities of post-independence Irish culture, Laverty's *The Cottage in the Bog* dramatizes the changing power relations between the owners of the Big House and the inhabitants of a thatched cottage. The novel focuses on the adventures of three cottage-dwelling children, Essie, Con, and Mike, who, like Eileen and Seamus in *The Turf-Cutter's Donkey*, have unique access to Irish myths and legends. The children discover that the new owner of the local Big House is trying to steal and profit from an ancient treasure buried at a rath, or fort, that is now on his property. The treasure, it transpires, is that of the legendary Fionn Mac Cumhail, but before the evil McFadden can melt it down, the children rescue it and present it to the National Museum. In this instance, the Big House has fenced off valuable hidden treasure from the local community; it is then recovered by the young and preserved for future generations. The story ends with a party, complete with 'music that drifted over the bog',[25] to mark this triumph, which ensures that the riches of the land will no longer be held and controlled by those occupying the Big House. Like Lynch, Laverty's romanticized representation of rural Irish society, which bears echoes of de Valera's vision of a nation of 'cosy homesteads', gives succour to a conservative nationalist agenda.

THE 1950S AND 1960S

Irish children's fiction of the 1950s and 1960s continued to address and comment upon contemporary social and political issues, frequently using the motif of home as a guiding analytic. As Ireland entered a period of rapid modernization, Galway-born Eilís Dillon's (1920–94) representations of home often explored transformations in society and identity, displaying in the process an openness towards the potential benefits of these changes rather than casting them as an unqualified threat to traditional ways of life. Dillon, described by Mary Shine Thompson as 'the doyenne of Irish children's literature',[26] was one of the most successful Irish children's authors of the twentieth century. Her adventure stories, as Ciara Ní Bhroin notes, 'use a genre more typically

---

[24]   See https://www.gov.ie/en/publication/d5bd8c-constitution-of-ireland/. Accessed 30 May 2016.
[25]   Maura Laverty, *The Cottage in the Bog* (Dublin: Townhouse, 1992), 124. The book was illustrated by the author's daughter, Barry Castle.
[26]   Mary Shine Thompson, 'A Sense of Place in Irish Children's Books', in Valerie Coghlan and Celia Keenan (eds), *The Big Guide 2: Irish Children's Books* (Dublin: Children's Books Ireland, 2000), 99.

associated with the British Imperial adventure to create a decolonising, distinctly Irish literature', whereby the island 'can be read as a metaphor for Ireland and the community as a microcosm of the larger Irish community'.[27] This is evident in tales such as *The Lost Island* (1952), *The Fort of Gold* (1961), *The Coriander* (1963), and *The Sea Wall* (1965), in which the adolescent male protagonist, in a transitional stage of life, is often used to represent a changing Ireland.

The work of Dillon's that perhaps best exemplifies her use of the spaces of home to dramatize shifting attitudes is *The House on the Shore* (1955), in which young Jim O'Malley makes the journey to his uncle's Big House by the coast, only to discover that the local community of farmers believes that Uncle Martin has absconded with their money, a plot twist that echoes Ireland's colonial history of landlord–tenant relations. Cloghanmore House, which is falling into ruin, is juxtaposed with the warmth and friendliness of the traditional cottage of the Faherty family, suggesting a tendency towards idealization that echoes that found in the writings of Patricia Lynch and Maura Laverty. However, the Fahertys' abode is far from frugal as they have profited from the introduction of an irrigation scheme that Mr Faherty has learned about in France. This innovation has transformed the local farmland and motivated the locals to raise funds to establish a seaweed factory, developments which imply that modern techniques can enhance traditional practices and improve the quality of life.

With the help of a friend, Jim manages to recover the stolen money and return it to the community, but not before they burn the Big House, an act reminiscent of the burning of almost two hundred Ascendancy houses by republican militants in the early 1920s. Once the Big House is destroyed, the money returned, and progressive ideas embraced by the workers, the whole community prospers, suggesting a defining moment of cultural transition. The community is no longer dependent upon a relationship with the Big House for its survival, nor is it shown to need economic protectionism. Rather, it thrives as a result of looking to Europe for new ideas and drawing on its collective resources to revitalize local industry. In political terms, the narrative trajectory supports a move away from the isolationist policies of de Valera's governments towards the economic expansionism that would eventually materialize in the 1960s under the premiership of Seán Lemass. Similar themes can be found in one of Dillon's last novels, *The Island of Ghosts* (1990), a sophisticated narrative that addresses the tensions encapsulated in ideas of progress and change.

While Dillon presents the reader with nuanced and complex representations of the reality of home in a modern world, many children's texts continued to represent the Irish thatched cottage in nostalgic light, as a place of sanctuary from the ills of the modern world and a beacon of homeliness, particularly for the emigrant Irish, as epitomized in John Ford's film, *The Quiet Man* (1952), and the idealized tourist postcards of John Hinde. This tendency is evident in Walter Macken's (1915–67) *Flight of the Doves* (1968), which follows the story of Finn and Derval Dove as they escape from their

---

[27] Ciara Ní Bhroin, 'Forging National Identity: The Adventure Stories of Eilís Dillon', in Keenan and Thompson (eds), *Studies in Children's Literature 1500–2000*, 113.

abusive stepfather in Liverpool and journey to the west coast of Ireland to their grand-mother's 'white cottage close to the sea with the whitewashed stone wall surrounding it'.[28] Such romantic imagery does not obscure all social realities, however. As is the case in many of Patricia Lynch's novels, *Flight of the Doves* features child protagonists encoun-tering members of the Travelling community, thus providing young readers with a sense of Ireland as place of some cultural diversity. But while some Travellers are depicted as benevolent, offering the children food and welcoming them to their caravans, others are represented as lazy and greedy and their caravans unclean, to the extent that *Flight of the Doves* ultimately perpetuates problematic stereotypes of Traveller culture. Patrick Duggan's (1934–) *The Travelling People* (1964) offers a more positive representation of Travellers by focusing on events and experiences from within their own community. The tensions between the lifestyles and perspectives of settled people and those of the nomadic Travellers are directly addressed and 'the complexity of discrimination is fre-quently recognised'.[29] Duggan's exposure of such social complexities is rare in mid-twentieth-century Irish children's fiction, however, where romantic representations of rural home life predominate.

THE LATE TWENTIETH AND EARLY TWENTY-FIRST CENTURIES

In the closing decades of the twentieth century dramatic changes occurred in the rep-resentations of Irish homes in children's fiction. Writing in 2011, Pat Donlon noted that 'children's literature in Ireland over the last three decades has witnessed something lit-tle short of a miraculous revival from near extinction in the 1960s to thriving industry in the late 1990s'.[30] Initiatives that supported the development of children's literature included the decision of the O'Brien Press in the late 1970s to publish children's titles; the hosting of the Loughborough Conference on Children's Literature by Trinity College Dublin in the early 1980s; the awarding of Arts Council grants for works of children's literature for the first time in 1981; the establishment of the Children's Literature Association of Ireland in 1986 and the Irish Children's Book Trust in 1989, organizations that eventually merged in 1997 to become Children's Books Ireland; and the founding in 1998 of *iBbY Ireland*, the Irish section of the International Board on Books for Young People.[31]

---

[28] Walter Macken, *Flight of the Doves* (London: Macmillan, 1968), 130.
[29] Ciara Gallagher, database entry for *The Travelling People*, National Collection of Children's Books website. https://nccb.tcd.ie/exhibit/bg257f32c. Accessed 25 March 2016.
[30] Pat Donlon, 'Books for Irish Children', in Clare Hutton and Patrick Walsh (eds), *The Oxford History of the Irish Book, Volume V: Irish Book in English 1891–2000* (Oxford: Oxford University Press, 2011), 383.
[31] For a further discussion of these developments, see Emer O'Sullivan, 'Insularity and Internationalism: Between Local Production and Global Marketplace', in Coghlan and O'Sullivan (eds), *Irish Children's Literature and Culture*, 183–96 and Donlon, 'Books for Irish Children', 383.

Other developments in Irish culture during the early part of the twenty-first century further reflected a desire to take children, their experiences, and the literature produced for them more seriously. An Ombudsman for Children was established in 2003 and in 2011 the government created the cabinet post of Minister for Children. In 2010, Siobhán Parkinson (1954–) became Ireland's first Children's Laureate/Laureate na nÓg, and has been succeeded, at two-yearly intervals, by Niamh Sharkey (1972–), Eoin Colfer (1965–), P. J. Lynch (1962–), and Sarah Crossan (1981–). Such significant changes in the cultural production and understanding of children's fiction facilitated a wider and more varied representation of Irish home life, which includes depictions of urban and suburban homes, an engagement with the conflict in Northern Ireland, an interrogation of the Irish past, and an exploration of the realities of young adult experiences. The remainder of this chapter will examine a selection of recent works in which the implied child reader is introduced to often contentious social and political issues through the lens of home life and familial experience. What unites many of these texts is their desire to humanize abstract social and political issues for young readers and foster in them an empathetic awareness of their import and effects at the level of the individual and the family.

In *My Friend Specs McCann* (1955), originally broadcast on the BBC Northern Ireland *Children's Hour*, Janet McNeill (1907–94) sets some of Spec's adventures in a boarding school and some in Belfast city. However, it was not until the 1970s and 1980s that authors writing about Northern Ireland for children began to move away from the rural representations of the region, such as those found in the work of Meta Mayne Reid (1905–90), and engage directly with urban home life. This trend is particularly evident in the work of writers who portray life during the Troubles, the most famous of whom is Edinburgh-born Joan Lingard (1932–), who spent her childhood years in Belfast. Her extremely popular five-book series aimed at a teen readership, published between 1970 and 1976, features Kevin McCoy and Sadie Jackson, Catholic and Protestant teenagers whose love for each other is tested by a host of obstacles. In the first novel in the series, *The Twelfth Day of July* (1970), Kevin and Sadie are living in terraced houses in Belfast, on either side of the sectarian divide. Apart from the fact that Kevin's family reveres the Pope and Sadie's honours King William of Orange, the teenagers' home lives are described in almost identical terms, which is Lingard's attempt at emphasizing the cross-religious similarities that the bloody conflict often obscured. However, this approach results in an overly simplistic representation of the deeply entrenched political and religious divisions within Northern Ireland that belies any sort of nuance or complexity.

In later years, authors such as Maeve Friel (1950–), Carlo Gébler (1954–), Sam McBratney (1943–), Tom McCaughren (1936–), Kate MacLachlan, and Martin Waddell (1941–) engaged with the conflict in a more sophisticated manner.[32] Published under his *nom de plume* Catherine Sefton, Waddell's Troubles trilogy is particularly noteworthy for complicating simplistic binaries as it skilfully examines the multiple divisions within communities. In all three novels, the fractured home lives of children mirror the

---

[32] For a discussion of Troubles fiction for children and young people, see Celia Keenan, 'The Troubled Fiction of the "Troubles" in Northern Ireland', in Coghlan and Keenan (eds), *The Big Guide 2*, 111–16.

dysfunctional nature of Northern Irish society. Teenager Kathleen's old family farmhouse in *Starry Night* (1986) is located in a republican community close to the border with the Republic, and during attempts to repair it is revealed to be rotten to the core. This parallels Kathleen's experiences within the home, which is a toxic environment with stifling ideologies that prevent the teenager from forming her own identity. By the end of the narrative she must choose whether to escape to a new bungalow or to return to the farmhouse and change her circumstances from within. Waddell uses the farmhouse as an explicit metaphor for Northern Ireland, a place that presents its youth with the options of fleeing to a strife-free existence elsewhere or staying and contributing to positive social change from within.

The second novel in the trilogy, *Frankie's Story* (1988), features a girl who lives in the ironically named Unity Estate in a house where 'you slam a door somewhere, and the whole world knows about it.'[33] Caught in the middle of her parents' acrimonious separation, Frankie tries to do the right thing at home and in her Catholic community but becomes an innocent victim of the Troubles when she is erroneously branded an informer and a petrol bomb is thrown into her home. Unlike Kathleen in *Starry Night*, Frankie has no option but to abandon her home and seek refuge in England. Brian, the wheelchair-using protagonist of the final novel, *The Beat of the Drum* (1989), watches as a Catholic family is chased from their home in his Protestant neighbourhood. A victim of the Troubles himself—he was injured in a bomb attack that killed his parents—Brian tries to understand the opposing perspectives of his aunt and uncle with whom he now lives, as exchanges within the domestic space introduce the reader to competing justifications of pacifism and violence in Northern Ireland. Rather than abandoning home, Brian firmly decides to remain with his aunt and uncle, noting that 'I am responsible. That's why I am staying here.'[34] Waddell ends his trilogy, written at the height of the conflict and during a period of increased emigration, by issuing an explicit call for young people to remain at home and work to transform their society for the better.

Although the home life of young people in rural Ireland continued to be represented, the increased focus on urban and suburban settings from the 1980s onwards was part of a broader trend among authors to explore the heterogeneous nature of Irish childhood experience, which coincided with a boom in children's publishing. In particular, Irish children's fiction saw a significant increase in narratives centred on domestic spaces in Dublin, from the inner-city dwellings in Carolyn Swift's (1923–2002) Robbers series (1981–92) to Fowl Manor, a converted medieval castle on the outskirts of the capital, in Eoin Colfer's Artemis Fowl series (2001–12). Much of Siobhán Parkinson's groundbreaking work is distinguished by the use she makes of domestic spaces in suburban Dublin to explore social and attitudinal change, including changing forms of family life and family values. For example, *Sisters . . . No Way!* (1996), which comprises the back-to-back diaries of two teenagers who become stepsisters, addresses the reality of parental

---

[33] Catherine Sefton, *Frankie's Story* (London: Teens Mandarin, 1990), 6.
[34] Catherine Sefton, *The Beat of the Drum* (London: Hamish Hamilton, 1989), 105.

loss, alcoholism, and the interpersonal dynamics within a non-traditional family unit; *Breaking the Wishbone* (1999) dramatizes the hardships of youth homelessness and life on the city streets; and *The Love Bean* (2002) tackles issues of immigration and identity through the experiences of Irish twins Julia and Lydia, as well as those of a young African boy named Tito, who seeks refugee status in Ireland while living in a hostel in south County Dublin.

Parkinson's desire to present her young readers with socially realistic portraits of twenty-first-century family life is shared by Roddy Doyle (1958–), whose 2007 novel, *Wilderness*, centres on the relationship between teenage Gráinne, who lives with her father, half-brothers, and stepmother, and the mother who abandoned her to pursue a life in New York. This strand of contemporary Irish children's fiction gives vivid expression to the diverse configurations of family and challenges any preconception that the conventional nuclear family might be the norm. However, despite such developments, many contemporary urban-based texts for children often lack representations of diversity, particularly in relation to race, ethnicity, same-sex-parent families, and transgender childhood experiences.

An exception to the pattern of using urban locales to examine the changing nature of Irish society and the impact of secularizing forces on children's home lives can be found in Kate Thompson's (1956–) *The New Policeman* (2005). Set in Kinvara, County Galway, the novel explores the clash between the forces of tradition and modernity during the Celtic Tiger period, as well as the accelerated pace of life that was one of the by-products of the boom years. These tensions can be seen in microcosm in the family of the teenage protagonist, JJ Liddy, whose unmarried parents have rejected Catholicism yet are avid devotees of traditional Irish music, with JJ himself being an accomplished fiddler. By hosting regular *céilís* in their home, the unconventional Liddys—JJ's surname is that of his mother, not his father—are carrying on a family tradition which in an earlier generation led to conflict between the boy's grandfather and a local priest, who associated dancing with immoral behaviour, and whose disappearance following his confiscation of the grandfather's precious flute led to rumours that he was murdered by him. Through this thematic strand, Thompson represents the Catholic Church's waning social influence and the loosening of its control over people's minds and morals. The antithetical pulls of fairy lore and Catholic theology are reflected in JJ's moving between the material world of Kinvara and Tír na nÓg, the mythical land of eternal youth, as he tries to uncover the mystery of time's disappearance and give his beleaguered mother the gift of time for her birthday. Even though Thompson offers a somewhat sentimental representation of myth and music as the solutions to contemporary problems, *The New Policeman* is nevertheless a sophisticated narrative that deconstructs the Church's influence in Irish society and its attempt to control and regulate life within the home.

As Irish society was changing in the 1990s, so too were approaches to, and understandings of, Irish history. This was a period in which academic debates about historical revisionism had entered mainstream culture, prompting many children's authors to unpick the seamless linearity of traditional nationalist historiography and turn a spotlight on neglected and forgotten aspects of the country's past.[35] Indeed, such was the dramatic growth of historical fiction for children and young people that Celia Keenan estimated in 1997 that 'approximately one quarter of all Irish books for children consists of those of predominantly historical interest'.[36] John Quinn's (1949–) *The Summer of Lily and Esme* (1991) is one such book, the focus of which is a hitherto much-ignored topic not only in Irish children's fiction but in twentieth-century Irish culture more generally: the Irish involvement in the First World War. Set in contemporary Ireland, it follows the progress of eleven-year-old Alan and his family, which is Catholic, as they move from the city to the countryside when his businessman father buys Glebe House, 'glebe' being the name once used for Church of Ireland rectories.[37] The move to this new home provides Alan with the opportunity to uncover histories of Ireland previously unknown to him. Through his interaction with two elderly middle-class Protestant neighbours, Lily and Esme, Alan gains access to private histories that, through memory, are often lived out in the present. He also learns of the women's father's involvement in the British Army during the war and reads the poetry of Francis Ledwidge, who was killed at the Battle of Passchendaele in 1917. By these means, Quinn explores the latent legacies of this occluded history in contemporary Irish culture. As the ghost of ten-year-old Albert in the attic and the circumstances of his death are slowly revealed, the author suggests the necessity of acknowledging the complexities of the past, working through them, and then laying ghosts to rest.

Quinn was not alone in engaging with lesser-known aspects of the Irish past and interweaving public and private histories for an implied child reader. Whereas his novels are set in the present, other writers, such as Marita Conlon-McKenna (1956–), Aubrey Flegg, Sam McBratney, Tom McCaughren, Éilís Ní Dhuibhne (1954–), Joan O'Neill, Mark O'Sullivan (1954–), Siobhán Parkinson, and Gerard Whelan (1957–), produced works of fiction for children set during significant historical moments. For example, Parkinson's *Amelia* (1993) and its sequel, *No Peace for Amelia* (1994), which are set in Dublin during the years between 1913 and 1916, dismantle grand narratives of Irish history and, through representations of experiences of domesticity, encourage an implied child reader to think about the role played by women in Ireland's past and relate those struggles for equality to contemporary cultural debates. In many ways, Parkinson's work was pioneering, as there was hitherto limited engagement in children's fiction with the experiences and activities of politically aware women from different class backgrounds during epoch-defining events.

---

[35] Pádraic Whyte, *Irish Childhoods: Children's Fiction and Irish History* (Newcastle upon Tyne: Cambridge Scholars, 2011), xxvii.

[36] Celia Keenan, 'Reflecting a New Confidence: Irish Historical Fiction for Children', *The Lion and the Unicorn* 21, no. 3 (1997), 369.

[37] Valerie Coghlan, '"What Foot Does He Dig With?" Inscriptions of Religious and Cultural Identity', in Coghlan and O'Sullivan (eds), *Irish Children's Literature and Culture*, 60. Quinn's 2005 novel, *Bill and Fred?*, offers another perspective on this aspect of Ireland's cultural heritage in an era of global marketing by showing how a dilapidated Big House is saved from ruin by becoming a location for the shooting of an American TV series.

Published as the Northern Irish peace process was gaining momentum, Mark O'Sullivan's *Melody for Nora* (1994) also broke new ground by being one of the first Irish novels, for adults or children, to interrogate in detail the events of the Irish Civil War. In it, the conflict itself and its memory in the contemporary moment are represented as forms of personal and cultural paralysis, captured in Nora's own private trauma and the paralysis she suffers after a fall at home. Whereas domestic space become a metonym for the Irish nation in this novel, in *Daisy Chain War* (1990), Joan O'Neill uses a fictional personal memory to explore a collective cultural memory of Irish childhood experiences of the Second World War and its aftermath. The home of the young protagonist, Lizzie Doyle, becomes a locus for the exploration of public debates related to the war when her cousin Vicky, an evacuee from the London Blitz, and her grandmother, a de Valera supporter from rural Ireland, come to stay with the Doyle family in Dun Laoghaire. Issues of neutrality and government policies, the impact of the Blitz on the lives of ordinary people, food rationing in Dublin, and accounts from the front line are examined through the personal encounters and perspectives of these characters in the Doyle home. In both these novels, the experiences of child protagonists in domestic spaces are used to introduce the complexity and impact of more abstract cultural debates to younger readers.

More recent events in Irish history are explored in the groundbreaking novels of Siobhan Dowd (1960–2007). In *Bog Child* (2008), which Éilís Ní Dhuibhne notes 'is essentially about an individual struggling in the nightmare of history',[38] the harsh realities of the 1981 IRA hunger strikes intrude on the Northern Irish home of teenager Fergus as his brother Joe becomes a hunger striker in Long Kesh prison. This is a skilfully crafted narrative in which, once again, the private and the public are intertwined. In one episode, Fergus encourages his mother to bake a tart as a gift for Joe. Her apolitical, instinctively nurturing response—'If that son of mine is starving himself, my rhubarb tart will have him eating again'[39]—heightens the poignancy of their naïve search for hope in a grim situation. However, Joe's refusal to eat the tart signifies the preeminence of his commitment to political struggle over family bonds. In *A Swift Pure Cry* (2006), set in Cork in 1984, Dowd again positions a very personal tale against the backdrop of shocking public events, namely, the deaths of fifteen-year-old Ann Lovett and her baby while giving birth in secret and the Kerry Babies controversy, which exposed the sexual life of Joanne Hayes to national scrutiny. Dowd's pregnant protagonist, Shell Talent, whose mother has died and whose alcoholic father has neglected his children, is let down by the education system, the Catholic Church, and a local community that chooses not to interfere in the girl's home life. In showing Shell's home to be a place where the threat of paternal abuse is very real, Dowd encourages the reader to understand Shell's predicament within the context of contemporary debates regarding children's abuse and neglect, and suggests that such iniquity is not confined to a distant past.

---

[38] Éilís Ní Dhuibhne, 'Borderlands: Dead Bog and Living Landscape', in Coghlan and O'Sullivan (eds), *Irish Children's Literature and Culture*, 34.
[39] Siobhan Dowd, *Bog Child* (Oxford: David Fickling Books, 2008), 72.

Dowd was one of a number of Irish authors during this period whose work can be classified as Young Adult fiction, a specific genre that originated in 1940s America and falls within the broader category of children's literature. In recent years the number of Irish Young Adult texts has increased significantly, a welcome development that has provided a space for older children to read about themes and issues traditionally deemed inappropriate for younger readers. Authors including Sarah Crossan, Margrit Cruickshank (1942–), Claire Hennessy (1986–), Tom Lennon, Geraldine Meade, Jane Mitchell, Éilís Ní Dhuibhne, Louise O'Neill (1985–), Mark O'Sullivan, Deirdre Sullivan, and Sheena Wilkinson (1968–) have written novels that address the complex relationships many young people have with their homes and families, and how home often fails to offer security and protection. Oftentimes, as well as dealing with universal themes of suffering, isolation, and identity formation, many of these novelists address weighty issues such as mental health problems, self-harm, racism, xenophobia, homophobia, and various forms of abuse.

One such example is Louise O'Neill's controversial *Asking For It* (2015), in which young Emma O'Donovan undergoes a gruesome ordeal at a house party in her small rural community when she is raped by a number of young men. Her parents find her unconscious and exposed on the porch of their family home, a moment that is tellingly symbolic of the girl's threshold location, almost safe within her home yet vulnerable to the intrusive communal gaze. O'Neill shows Emma trying to hide from the world by staying at home, only to find that no such sanctuary is possible in the digital era, as images of her taken during her assault are circulated on social media and are accessible from her bedroom. O'Neill explores the multiple effects of the girl's violation, from the horrific to the mundane, and creates a character who obsessively relives her trauma and comes to define herself in relation to the 'pink flesh'[40] of her body in the photographs. In terms of Irish Young Adult fiction, *Asking For It* is a pioneering novel that does not censor the realities of sexual violence but rather invites implied readers to think about issues of consent and question their own position in, and complicity with, a culture in which violence against women is commonplace. While the narrative could be read as a form of nihilistic fiction that offers little hope, it may also provoke an angry response that facilitates empowerment on the part of the reader.

Sheena Wilkinson's *Still Falling* (2015), set in contemporary Belfast, provides a more reassuring narrative about resilience and survival. A new foster home offers the possibility of safety for teenage Luke who, through his friendship with Esther, begins to come to terms with his disturbing childhood experiences. While Esther also has problems at home, it is Luke's story—the struggle of living with his mother and her boyfriend, through to his finally getting the support he needs while staying with Sandra and Bill— that drives the narrative. Although different types of homes are represented in the novel, Wilkinson suggests that, regardless of its makeup, home should be a place where those within can trust, support, and believe one another. Read alongside other children's fiction that has documented the effects of abuse and the failures of the adult world,

---

[40] Louise O'Neill, *Asking for It* (London: Quercus, 2015), 169.

Still Falling offers a more hopeful account of how the (Northern Irish) foster care system can help to transform young people's lives for the better.

From the Land Wars of the late nineteenth century to the invasion of private space by digital media in the twenty-first, Irish children's fiction has repeatedly engaged with the complexities of social, political, and cultural change through the prism of home. The imperialist ideology that informs the treatment of the domestic culture of the Protestant Big House in works by Flora L. Shaw and L. T. Meade contrasts sharply with the postcolonial perspectives Maura Laverty and Eilís Dillon bring to bear on the motif of home in order to dramatize the changing power dynamics between landowners and tenants after independence. Home in twentieth-century Irish nationalist rhetoric is at once the house that holds the stories or treasures of the nation and the peasant cottage that embodies authentic national experience. However, the traditional cottage could also symbolize conservative values and repressive ideologies that were inimical to many late twentieth-century children's authors, whose work seeks to engage young readers through socially realistic and often provocatively explicit accounts of childhood experience in Ireland, north and south. This arc of transition is beautifully captured in Margrit Cruickshank's *Circling the Triangle* (1991) when Stephen, a Dublin teenager, removes a picture of a thatched cottage from the wall, suggesting that such depictions of home and Irishness are no longer relevant to his generation.[41] Arguably, this representational trend gave the false impression that 'urban' was synonymous with progress, whereas 'rural' indicated a culture stuck in the past. Works such as Dillon's *The House on the Shore* and Kate Thompson's *The New Policeman* provide more nuanced perspectives that disrupt such binary thinking by suggesting that tradition and modernity can coexist in rural Ireland. In these and other narratives, home acts as an interface between the child and the wider world, and is often portrayed as a sanctuary where children can learn the skills that will aid their social progress. Elsewhere in contemporary Irish fiction for children, the notion of home as a safe space is shown to be unable to withstand the many harsh realities that intrude on it, as documented in the work of Louise O'Neill, Siobhan Dowd, Sheena Wilkinson, and others, which recognizes the diversity and complexity of Irish childhood experience. In the twenty-first century as in the nineteenth, contested ideas of house and home remain centrally important components of Irish children's fiction, engagement with which has enabled successive generations of authors to create original and sophisticated representations of selfhood and cultural identity, past and present.

FURTHER READING

Catlett Anderson, Celia and Robert Dunbar (eds). *The Lion and the Unicorn. Special Issue: Irish Children's Literature* 21, no. 3 (1997).

Children's Books Ireland/Inis. Dublin: Children's Books Ireland, 1989–present.

---

[41] See Robert Dunbar, 'Rarely Pure and Never Simple: The World of Irish Children's Literature', *The Lion and the Unicorn* 21, no. 3 (1997), 309–19.

Coghlan, Valerie. 'Ireland'. In Peter Hunt (ed.). *The International Companion Encyclopedia of Children's Literature*. London: Routledge, 2004: 1099–103.

Coghlan, Valerie and Celia Keenan (eds). *The Big Guide to Irish Children's Books*. Dublin: Irish Children's Books Trust, 1996.

Coghlan, Valerie and Celia Keenan (eds). *The Big Guide 2: Irish Children's Books*. Dublin: Children's Books Ireland, 2000.

Coghlan, Valerie and Keith O'Sullivan (eds). *Irish Children's Literature and Culture: New Perspectives on Contemporary Writing*. London: Routledge, 2011.

Coghlan, Valerie and Siobhán Parkinson (eds). *Irish Children's Writers and Illustrators 1986–2006: A Selection of Essays*. Dublin: Children's Books Ireland and Church of Ireland College of Education Publications, 2007.

Donlon, Pat. 'Books for Irish Children'. In Clare Hutton and Patrick Walsh (eds), *The Oxford History of the Irish Book, Volume V: The Irish Book in English 1891–2000*. Oxford: Oxford University Press, 2011: 367–89.

National Collection of Children's Books catalogue and database. https://nccb.tcd.ie.

O'Sullivan, Emer. 'The Development of Modern Children's Literature in Late Twentieth-Century Ireland'. *Signal* 81 (1996): 189–211.

O'Sullivan, Keith and Pádraic Whyte (eds). *Children's Literature Collections: Approaches to Research*. Basingstoke: Palgrave Macmillan, 2017.

Shine Thompson, Mary (ed.). *Young Irelands: Studies in Children's Literature*. Dublin: Four Courts Press, 2011.

Shine Thompson, Mary and Valerie Coghlan (eds). *Divided Worlds: Studies in Children's Literature*. Dublin: Four Courts Press, 2007.

Shine Thompson, Mary and Celia Keenan (eds). *Treasure Islands: Studies in Children's Literature*. Dublin: Four Courts Press, 2006.

Watson, Nancy. *The Politics and Poetics of Irish Children's Literature*. Dublin: Irish Academic Press, 2009.

Whyte, Pádraic. *Irish Childhoods: Children's Fiction and Irish History*. Newcastle upon Tyne: Cambridge Scholars, 2011.

Whyte, Pádraic. 'Children's Literature'. In James H. Murphy (ed.), *The Oxford History of the Irish Book, Volume IV: The Irish Book in English 1800–1891*. Oxford: Oxford University Press, 2012: 518–28.

PART VII

FACT INTO FICTION, FICTION INTO FILM

CHAPTER 23

....

THE GREAT FAMINE IN FICTION, 1901–2015

....

MELISSA FEGAN

THE Irish Famine has been identified by Oona Frawley as a 'memory crux', a cata-strophic event which, as the initiator of major cultural change, is endlessly returned to and which raises 'intensely problematic' questions about the country's relationship to its past.[1] In 1995, the year of the one hundred and fiftieth anniversary of the start of the Famine, Terry Eagleton raised the issue of why such a crucial moment in history had not inspired 'a major literature': 'There is a handful of novels and a body of poems, but few truly distinguished works. Where is the Famine in the literature of the Revival? Where is it in Joyce?'.[2] He returned to the question in a review of Joseph O'Connor's (1963–) Famine novel, *Star of the Sea* (2002):

> The Irish famine of the 1840s was the greatest social catastrophe of 19th-century Europe, yet inspired surprisingly little imaginative writing. There is a powerful novel by Liam O'Flaherty and a starkly moving drama by the contemporary play-wright Tom Murphy. But in both Yeats and Joyce it is no more than a dim resonance. It is as though African-Americans were to maintain an embarrassed silence about the slave trade.[3]

Eagleton was certainly not alone in thinking there was a strange paucity of material. The pioneering scholar of Famine literature, Christopher Morash, recalls that when he men-tioned his work to colleagues in the mid-1980s, 'the response was almost always the same. I would get a quizzical look, followed by: "There's not much to study, is there?"'[4]

[1] Oona Frawley, 'Introduction: Cruxes in Irish Cultural Memory: The Famine and the Troubles', in Oona Frawley (ed.), *Memory Ireland, Volume 3: The Famine and the Troubles* (Syracuse, NY: Syracuse University Press, 2014), 2.

[2] Terry Eagleton, *Heathcliff and the Great Hunger: Studies in Irish Culture* (London: Verso, 1995), 13.

[3] Terry Eagleton, 'Another country', *Guardian Review*, 25 January 2003, 26.

[4] Christopher Morash, 'An Afterword on Silence', in George Cusack and Sarah Goss (eds), *Hungry Words: Images of Famine in the Irish Canon* (Dublin: Irish Academic Press, 2006), 300.

Morash and others, such as Margaret Kelleher, have since proved that the Famine has been an abiding concern in Irish literature from the 1840s onwards, and anthologies such as Morash's *The Hungry Voice: The Poetry of the Irish Famine* (1989) and *Recollecting Hunger: An Anthology* (2012), edited by Marguérite Corporaal, Christopher Cusack, and Lindsay Janssen, have collected significant examples. The essays in George Cusack and Sarah Goss's *Hungry Words: Images of Famine in the Irish Canon* (2006) also demonstrate that the Famine is much more than a 'dim resonance' in the works of W. B. Yeats (1865–1939), James Joyce (1882–1941), Samuel Beckett (1906–89), and others. In fact, cataloguing the number of writers who have responded to the Famine, both during the event and in the generations that followed, confirms the endless return that Frawley describes, and testifies to what Morash characterizes as 'a tradition of Famine writing, which, if it was not always overt, was nonetheless sustained'.[5]

However, if writers of Famine fiction are part of a tradition, they seem largely unaware of it. When twentieth- or twenty-first-century Famine novelists look back to their forebears, it is to a limited canon of William Carleton (1794–1869), Liam O'Flaherty (1897–1984), and Walter Macken (1915–67)—although Macken's *The Silent People* (1962) is not in fact about the Great Famine—or to poets such as James Clarence Mangan (1803–49) and Lady Wilde (1821–96), or to Tom Murphy's (1935–2018) play *Famine* (1968). Joseph O'Connor said that when he read Eagleton's comments in *Heathcliff and the Great Hunger*, he 'felt it implicitly threw down a challenge',[6] suggesting that *Star of the Sea* was written in part to compensate for a general fictional neglect. Yet it may be that the very diversity of Famine fiction occludes the sense of a tradition.

Famine fiction is transnational: alongside Irish, British, Canadian, and American authors (some of Irish origin), other writers with no personal connection to the country have been drawn to the event as a setting. Grace Neville has also pointed out that many French writers have published novels dealing either briefly or at length with the Famine, including *Les Dames à la licorne* (1974) by René Barjavel and *Eléazar ou la source et le Buisson* (1996) by Michel Tournier.[7] The Famine has also attracted those for whom writing fiction is not their primary profession, such as the former ITN senior foreign correspondent Michael Nicholson, the British Conservative politician Nadine Dorries, and the Irish songwriter Brendan Graham. Furthermore, Famine fiction has been produced in a wide range of genres, including historical fiction, historiographical metafiction, Gothic horror, popular romance, queer fiction, children's fiction, and crime fiction. Bernhard Klein suggests that the further we get from the Famine temporally, the less scrupulous novelists become about historical accuracy or sensitivity.[8] While many of those who have produced Famine fictions are intensely conscious of their ethical

---

[5] Ibid., 303.

[6] José Manuel Estévez-Saá, 'An Interview with Joseph O'Connor', *Contemporary Literature* 46, no. 2 (2005), 163.

[7] Grace Neville, 'Remembering and Forgetting the Great Famine in France and Ireland', *New Hibernia Review* 16, no. 4 (2012), 80–94.

[8] Bernhard Klein, *On the Uses of History in Recent Irish Writing* (Manchester: Manchester University Press, 2007), 52.

responsibilities when representing one of the most traumatic periods in Irish history, for others it is a conveniently sensational setting, as in Scott Mariani's thriller, *The Forgotten Holocaust* (2015), the tenth novel in his series about Ben Hope (described as 'James Bond meets Jason Bourne with a historical twist'[9]), which 'reveals' that the Famine was deliberately caused by a scientifically-minded Anglo-Irish landlord who disseminated potato blight on the orders of the British government.

Morash argues that the literature of the Famine is 'a process of claiming the dead',[10] an appropriation that changes according to when the texts were written and by whom. The earliest Famine fiction was written in the heat of the moment; William Carleton's *The Black Prophet* was published serially in the *Dublin University Magazine* in 1846, appearing in book form the following year, and Mary Anne Hoare (*c.*1818–72) began publishing her short stories about the Famine in periodicals in the same year, before collecting them in *Shamrock Leaves* (1851). For both, the motivation was to call attention to the people's suffering—Carleton in the hope of awakening the government to the need to take action immediately, Hoare to encourage charitable donations. Anthony Trollope wrote his Famine novel, *Castle Richmond* (1860), as a farewell to Ireland and as a defence of government policy. For writers in the following decades, the Famine was both historical, because it described a world that had been swept away, and present, because the landscape was scarred with ruined cabins and unfinished roads, outbreaks of hunger and starvation persisted in the west of Ireland, and the mismanagement of the catastrophe was prime evidence in the political campaign for Home Rule. Margaret Brew (1850–*c.*1905), daughter of a County Clare landowner, dedicated her three-volume Famine novel, *The Chronicles of Castle Cloyne* (1884), to Lady Florence Dixie, an outspoken opponent of the Land League, and aimed to show that 'Peer and peasant, landlord and tenant, the home of the great, and the cabin of the lowly'[11] were collectively affected by the Famine.

At the beginning of the twentieth century, the need to preserve the memory of the Famine became an important consideration. Justin McCarthy (1830–1912), author of *Mononia: A Love Story of 'Forty-Eight* (1901), had been a journalist on the *Cork Examiner* during the 1840s and as such was a rare living witness. Most subsequent writers would be reliant on second-hand testimony and would be depicting a world that felt increasingly alien in a modernizing Ireland. In *The Wizard's Knot* (1901), William Barry (1849–1930) sees the Famine as the death of a distinctively Irish culture:

> Fiddling and dancing stopped dead; there was no sound of the old fairy music from rath or hillside; sports fell extinct among the myriads who looked, in a fever-dream of despair, upon the fields which had turned to plague-spots. Rooted in their sorrow to the soil, what could they do but shroud their heads at last and die speechless?[12]

---

[9] See http://www.scottmariani.com/bio.html. Accessed 8 June 2016.

[10] Christopher Morash, *Writing the Irish Famine* (Oxford: Clarendon Press, 1995), 187.

[11] Margaret Brew, *The Chronicles of Castle Cloyne; or, Pictures of the Munster People* (London: Chapman and Hall, 1885), vol. 1, viii.

[12] William Barry, *The Wizard's Knot* (New York: The Century Co., 1901), 331–2.

The London-born son of Irish emigrants, Barry described the novel in his *Memoirs and Opinions* (1926) as 'my mother's own fairy-tale' and an attempt to capture 'that ancient folk-lore which lives under all outward change,'[13] an urgent task while that change was accelerating.

In *Glenanaar* (1905), Canon Patrick Sheehan (1852–1913) depicts a present-day Ireland that was economically 'not yet up to the normal standard of living' but far enough from the 1840s to 'ask ourselves in amazement how did the people then live.'[14] Yet, he notes, even the word 'blight' could still terrify a supposedly modern Irishman and blight was still occurring in western counties as he wrote. Famine, 'civilization's hungry double,'[15] still lurks. The insecurity of development is signalled in the shift into present tense when Sheehan's narrative reaches the social and demographic catastrophe itself:

> It is an appalling picture, that which springs up to memory. Gaunt spectres move here and there, looking at one another out of hollow eyes of despair and gloom. Ghosts walk the land. . . . Mothers try to still their children's cries of hunger by bringing their cold, blue lips to milkless breasts. Here and there by the wayside a corpse stares at the passers-by, as it lies against the hedge where it had sought shelter. The pallor of its face is darkened by lines of green around the mouth, the dry juice of grass and nettles. All day long the carts are moving to the graveyards with their ghastly, uncoffined loads.[16]

As Morash notes, this cannot be a 'memory' for Sheehan, given his date of birth, except in the sense of the 'semiotic system of representations which had replaced the Famine'[17]: spectres and walking skeletons, mothers unable to feed their babies, corpses by the roadside, the desperate search for food, the mass grave. In *The Hunger* (1910), Mildred Darby (1867–1932) asserted that the pressures of modernity threatened to eclipse the memory of the Famine. 'Life is too crowded to remember the events of the nineteenth in this busy twentieth century', she wrote, adding that beyond the 'passing curiosity' aroused by ruined dwellings, or the 'vague uneasiness' at strangely mounded cemeteries, the Famine did not intrude on the minds of the young in a peaceful and prosperous Ireland.[18] Yet these blithe youths coexist with an older generation who 'gaze back through the happier sunshine of the present to the thick darkness of the past', exposing the 'blood-red scars of [their] memories' in hatred of 'the Governmint'.[19]

---

[13] William Barry, cited in Rolf Loeber and Magda Loeber with Anne Mullin Burnham, *A Guide to Irish Fiction 1650–1900* (Dublin: Four Courts Press, 2006), 123–4.

[14] Canon Patrick Augustine Sheehan, *Glenanaar: A Story of Irish Life* (London: Longmans, Green, and Co., 1905), 197.

[15] Morash, *Writing the Irish Famine*, 51.   [16] Sheehan, *Glenanaar*, 198–9.

[17] Morash, *Writing the Irish Famine*, 4.

[18] Mildred Darby, *The Hunger, Being Realities of the Famine Years in Ireland 1845 to 1848* (London: Andrew Melrose, 1910), 1–2.

[19] Ibid., 3.

Famine fiction frequently emerges at moments of conflict or change in the present. Darby, the English-born mistress of Leap Castle, dedicated *The Hunger* to 'all the Children of the British Empire, and to our Cousins in the United States'. Her strident defence of the Union at the end of the novel, in spite of her consciousness that the mismanagement of the Famine strongly suggested that Ireland would be better off governing herself, points to her desire to exorcize the past at a time when Home Rule looked increasingly likely. Louis J. Walsh's (1880–1942) *The Next Time: A Story of 'Forty-Eight* (1919) implicitly connects the failed 1848 rising with the Easter Rising—after which Walsh shifted from constitutional nationalism to militant republicanism—and the War of Independence, which began in its year of publication. Walsh's hero, forced to rebel due to 'the maddening scenes of 'Forty-Six and 'Forty-Seven', dies asking: 'We won't fail the next time, Jim—sure we won't?'[20] Sometimes, however, the conjunction is not specifically Irish; L. T. Meade (pseudonym of Elizabeth Thomasina Toulmin Smith, 1844–1914) begins *The Stormy Petrel* (1909) with a glance at the contemporary suffrage movement and a comparison with the position of women during the Famine: 'A girl did not dare to be original in 1846.'[21]

The association between Famine fiction and present-day crises continued in the post-independence era. Derek Hand argues that O'Flaherty's *Famine* (1937) is 'a displaced critique of the contemporary world',[22] a reminder of the still-pressing need for justice and civil equality in an independent Ireland in the year of the Irish Constitution. Less displaced is Flann O'Brien's (1911–66) *An Béal Bocht* (1941), where the 'hard times' are perpetuated by the romantic sentimentalism of Gaelic scholars for whom 'poverty, hunger and distress'[23] are essentially Irish and to be celebrated. Gentlemen motor from Dublin 'to inspect the paupers' and are particularly taken with Sitric O'Sanassa: 'they never saw anyone who appeared so truly Gaelic.... There was no one in Ireland comparable to O'Sanassa in the excellence of his poverty; the amount of famine which was delineated in his person.'[24] John Banville's (1945–) *Birchwood* (1973) collapses history, so that the protagonist experiences the War of Independence and the Famine simultaneously. The butler Fogarty in William Trevor's (1928–2016) 'The News from Ireland' (1986) predicts bloodshed as a result of the Famine—'it is the future that's withering now'[25]—a prophecy played out during the War of Independence and the Civil War in his *Fools of Fortune* (1983) and *The Silence in the Garden* (1988). More recently, Colum McCann's (1965–) *TransAtlantic* (2013) links the Famine, the American Civil War, the Troubles, and the Northern Ireland peace process across four generations of women. *Star of the Sea* ends with the significant date of Easter Saturday 1916, but O'Connor also gestures ironically towards the treatment of refugees and immigrants in contemporary

---

[20] Louis J. Walsh, *The Next Time: A Story of 'Forty-Eight* (Dublin: M. H. Gill and Son, 1919), 183, 227.

[21] L. T. Meade, *The Stormy Petrel* (London: Hurst and Blackett, 1909), 2.

[22] Derek Hand, *A History of the Irish Novel* (Cambridge: Cambridge University Press, 2011), 176.

[23] Flann O'Brien, *The Poor Mouth*, trans. Patrick C. Power (Normal, IL: Dalkey Archive Press, 1998), 88.

[24] Ibid., 88–9.

[25] William Trevor, 'The News from Ireland', in *Ireland: Selected Stories* (London: Penguin, 1995), 164.

Ireland, as when the ship's captain asserts: 'if Ireland were a richer land and other nations now mighty were distressed; as certain as I know that the dawn must come, the people of Ireland would welcome the frightened stranger with that gentleness and friendship which so ennobles their character'.[26] Nuala O'Faolain's (1940–2008) *My Dream of You* (2001) uses a divorce case from the 1840s to examine the patriarchal subjugation and sexual exploitation of women in twentieth-century Ireland and Britain. Her protagonist wonders: 'Could I move beyond some momentary imagining of the past towards finding a meaning for it? Not an explanation, but a meaning? And not a meaning in history but in my own life?'[27] This is a question which preoccupies most serious Famine fiction.

It is hardly surprising then that there has been a resurgence in literary interest in the Famine in the 1990s and early decades of the twenty-first century, given the aforementioned anniversary commemorations and the corresponding explosion in Famine historiography. This is due not only to the greater exposure of the Famine in public discourse but also to a revival of insecurities that seemed to belong to the past. Fintan O'Toole has described the forces that destroyed the Celtic Tiger as 'nineteenth-century revenants, come back to haunt its dreams of twenty-first-century success',[28] and many Irish novels set in the post-crash period invoke the memory of Famine as the acme of ruin. In Donal Ryan's (1977–) *The Spinning Heart* (2012), for example, a young man planning to leave for Australia is aggrieved because his friends who had gone in previous years had been objects of envy for the 'unreal craic' they had gone for, whereas he will be 'a tragic figure, a modern incarnation of the poor tenant farmer, laid low by famine, cast from his smallholding by the Gombeen Man, forced to choose between the coffin ship and the grave. Matty Cummins and the boys were blackguards; I am a victim.'[29] The extraordinary excess of Constance Madigan's Christmas 2005 food shopping in Anne Enright's (1962–) *The Green Road* (2015)—'four hundred and ten euros, a new record. She thought she should keep the receipt for posterity. Dessie would be almost proud'[30]—is underlined by numerous references to the Famine here and elsewhere in the novel. The chapter is called 'The Hungry Grass', in reference to a superstition that the fairies make hungry grass grow where generosity has failed to be shown, and anyone who walks on it will begin to starve, while those who relieve them will be rewarded.[31] Constance remembers to buy Camembert and Parma ham, Prosecco, mangoes, melon, and all manner of exotic fare, but when she leaves the supermarket for the second time, she realizes that she has forgotten potatoes and 'thought about pulling over to the side of the road and digging some out of a field, imagined herself with her

[26] Joseph O'Connor, *Star of the Sea* (London: Vintage, 2003), 279.

[27] Nuala O'Faolain, *My Dream of You* (London: Penguin, 2001), 64.

[28] Fintan O'Toole, *Ship of Fools: How Stupidity and Corruption Sank the Celtic Tiger* (London: Faber and Faber, 2009), 214.

[29] Donal Ryan, *The Spinning Heart* (London: Doubleday Ireland, 2014), 57.

[30] Anne Enright, *The Green Road* (London: Jonathan Cape, 2015), 230.

[31] See William Carleton, 'Fair Gurtha; or, The Hungry Grass. A Legend of the Dumb Hill', *Dublin University Magazine* 47, no. 280 (1856), 414–35.

hands in the earth, scrabbling around for a few spuds. Lifting her head to howl.'[32] Although fleeting, the fantasized degeneration from relatively wealthy cosmopolitan consumer to Famine victim is eloquent of long-lasting fears about the precariousness of Irish modernity.

The search for the meaning of the Famine leads to questions of culpability. While there is a general consensus in modern Famine fiction that the British government failed dismally in its duties, accusations range from genocide to more measured suggestions of incompetence and negligence. In O'Flaherty's *Famine*, the 'tyranny' of a 'feudal government', which responds 'with brutal force when the interests of the landowner were threatened, even to the extent of plundering the poor people's property', is to blame.[33] For Louis J. Walsh, responsibility lies with 'the cruel Government-produced Famine'.[34] However, Elizabeth Byrd (1912–89) depicts relief efforts as essentially well-intentioned but idiotic in *The Famished Land* (1972), citing as evidence pamphlets in English for the illiterate or Irish-speaking populace advising them to use implements they have no access to and cannot afford to buy; the Duke of Norfolk's suggestion that they live on curry powder; a public works canal built through porous rock; the distribution of turnip seed when turnips were expected; rice provided with no cooking instructions, which kills a child; and skimpy clothing sent by an English charity fit only for 'the climate of hell'.[35] While some suspect a deliberate policy to poison or taunt, the local priest Father O'Leary says, 'It's their old sin—negligence, indifference ... what was sent to help us was sent, not in malice, but in ignorance.'[36]

The public works scheme, which was instigated in the neediest areas during 1846 and 1847, is a recurring motif of mismanagement. Barry's eponymous wizard ends up breaking stones on the roads, much to the shock of a neighbour: 'Wisha! wisha! did you ever hear tell of the like of that? And he the finest scholar in Munster! Oh, God help us!'[37] Tim Murphy in Darby's *The Hunger* starves to death while working on the roads, along with many others; the engineer hides the corpses which are 'fatal evidences that someone in the pay department had blundered'.[38] In Seán Kenny's time-travel narrative, *The Hungry Earth* (1995), a Dublin accountant in the 1990s bumps his head and wakes in County Mayo in the late 1840s, where he is immediately identified as a relief works inspecting officer, and in a reflection which says much about Ireland in the age of global capitalism, wonders: 'Surely they should hire the fittest labourers, finish the road at minimum cost and distribute the profit they made to the poor, if that's what this was all about, keeping, say, ten per cent for themselves as a management fee?'[39]

The workhouses are usually represented as places of terror rather than refuge, a last resort when death is imminent. For example, in Marita Conlon-McKenna's (1956–) *Under the Hawthorn Tree* (1990), the children escape from a group being herded to the

---

[32] Enright, *The Green Road*, 232.   [33] O'Flaherty, *Famine*, 324.
[34] Walsh, *The Next Time*, 228.
[35] Elizabeth Byrd, *The Famished Land: A Novel of the Irish Potato Famine* (London: Pan Books, 1974), 143.
[36] Ibid., 115, 133.   [37] Barry, *The Wizard's Knot*, 350.
[38] Darby, *The Hunger*, 225.   [39] Seán Kenny, *The Hungry Earth* (Dublin: Wolfhound Press, 1995), 70.

workhouse, being all too aware of their reputation: 'the places are full of disease . . . you can hear the people screaming when you walk by'.[40] In a similar vein, the Master in Eugene McCabe's (1930–) *Tales from the Poorhouse* (1999) says: 'This place has become a kind of Public School for the impoverished. Their only lesson? How to die, and I am death's headmaster.'[41] 'Attie and his Father' (1912) by the pseudonymous 'Slieve Foy' evades many of the usual motifs of Famine-centred texts. It does not represent the coming of the blight, no landlord or agent threatens the Sullivans with eviction, and when John finds work on a relief project in Dublin, he makes enough in three weeks to spend on toys for his young son. Furthermore, John's elderly mother voluntarily goes into the workhouse with her grandchildren so that her son can find work, a solution which ignores the reality of harsh regulations that meant the whole family had to enter the workhouse together, giving up their land. But this mother is well aware of the probable consequences of her decision, and goes to bed the night before leaving home 'with a feeling akin to what she might have experienced had she descended alive into an open grave, and heard the clink of spades that were seen to cover her with clay'.[42] Both she and her little grandson die quickly in the workhouse.

The condemnation of food exportation during the Famine, which is still a contested area in the historiography, is a constant in Famine fiction. Walsh's hero—a disciple of John Mitchel, like Walsh himself—claims: 'There was no famine in the country at all. . . . A national Government would have at once closed all the ports till its own people were preserved from starvation.'[43] Darby claims that 'the very oats grown in Ireland were exported and imported again three and four times over, each time bearing more profits and expenses, before they were bought at a purely fictitious value for the perishing people who had originally grown them!'[44] The loaded cart on the way to the port guarded by soldiers or attacked by the famished populace is a recurring motif. There are two such scenes in quick succession at the end of O'Flaherty's *Famine*. A half-naked wretch yells at soldiers guarding a convoy of carts: 'Robbers! . . . Ye are stealing our corn and we dying of hunger. We are laid low now but we will rise again. We'll crush the tyrants that suck our blood.'[45] At the port, both the emigrants on the ship and the crowd gathered to wish them farewell curse and wail at the sacks of grain being loaded for transport to England, and young men 'held up their clenched fists and threatened the soldiers with cries of future vengeance.'[46] Even the son of the Landlord in McCabe's *Tales from the Poorhouse* says: 'No famine here. . . . Plenty of food. Ports should be closed and people fed', while his father asks: 'How? . . . Who'd pay?'[47] The Mother curses England for sending the Irish 'gravel and shite' to eat, 'and their great ships sailin' from our ports half foundered with

[40] Marita Conlon-McKenna, *Under the Hawthorn Tree: Children of the Famine* (Dublin: O'Brien Press, 1990), 48.

[41] Eugene McCabe, *Tales from the Poorhouse* (Oldcastle: Gallery Press, 1999), 46.

[42] Slieve Foy, *Stories of Irish Life Past and Present* (London: Lynwood and Co., 1912), 45.

[43] Walsh, *The Next Time*, 167.   [44] Darby, *The Hunger*, 13.

[45] O'Flaherty, *Famine*, 443.   [46] Ibid., 445.

[47] McCabe, *Tales from the Poorhouse*, 100.

food from every townland of Ireland to feed their murderin' armies. . . . May they suffer some day for what they done to us.'[48]

Charles Trevelyan, Assistant Chief Secretary to the Treasury during the Famine, has become a particular hate figure in popular fiction. In Elaine Crowley's (1927–2011) *Dreams of Other Days* (1984), Charlotte, daughter of Lord Kilgoran, says of Trevelyan: 'Apparently he's one of those dreadful people who always thinks they are right. Papa said people like that are dangerous.'[49] Later, when the promised Indian corn is withdrawn, Father Bolger announces:

> All the work of Charles Edward Trevelyan, Assistant Secretary at the Treasury—he's the rock on which Ireland will perish. He hasn't an ounce of compassion. . . . He's blind to everything except pennies and pounds, and balancing books. A man with no doubts, cold and conscientious, who takes duty beyond the bounds of reason, and into the bargain dislikes the Irish.[50]

In Brendan Graham's *The Whitest Flower* (1998), there is extreme hardship when the relief works are held up because a letter from Trevelyan has not arrived, and when they resume, pay is delayed 'until Trevelyan himself gave Treasury approval for the funds to be released.'[51] Michael Nicholson also identifies Trevelyan as 'the villain' in his 2015 novel, *Dark Rosaleen*. Prior to writing it, he intended to demonstrate that 'we English had been badly judged', but in the course of his research, which included reading Tim Pat Coogan's *The Famine Plot* (2012), he became convinced the Famine was 'a deliberate policy of imposed starvation'.[52]

Matthew Schultz argues that it is only in the twenty-first century that generous landlords and honest tradesmen appear in 'nonsectarian Famine narratives'.[53] However, most twentieth-century Famine novels are more historically and ideologically astute than this suggests. Absentee or rapacious landlords and vicious mercenary agents are certainly apparent in many texts. The lecherous Sir Richard Pakenham of *The Whitest Flower* evicts the heroine's family on Christmas Eve. In O'Flaherty's *Famine*, the drunken, bestial, impotent English agent Chadwick, whose spoiling of Ellie Gleeson can only take the form of suckling at her breast ('half his shame' was cut off by the 'heathens' in India), is utterly ruthless: 'Let them starve. Good riddance, I say. . . . Why should we help them? Let them die.'[54] However, not all landlords in *Famine* are malign; when Chadwick hires a gang of ruffians to eject tenants in arrears, the narrator interjects: 'I must remark at this point that Colonel Bodkin [a resident landlord] did everything in his power to dissuade Chadwick from this course.'[55]

---

[48] Ibid., 122.   [49] Elaine Crowley, *Dreams of Other Days* (Harmondsworth: Penguin, 1985), 300.
[50] Ibid., 403.
[51] Brendan Graham, *The Whitest Flower* (London: HarperCollins, 1999), 222.
[52] Michael Nicholson, 'Famine novel changed my mind on England's guilt', *Irish Times*, 14 December 2015.
[53] Matthew Schultz, *Haunted Historiographies: The Rhetoric of Ideology in Postcolonial Irish Fiction* (Manchester: Manchester University Press, 2014), 37.
[54] Liam O'Flaherty, *Famine* (Dublin: Wolfhound Press, 1992), 291, 75.   [55] Ibid., 259.

Margaret Kelleher has noted that several twentieth-century Big House novels, including Edith Somerville's (1858–1949) *The Big House of Inver* (1925) and Trevor's *Fools of Fortune*, employ the death of a benevolent female ancestor during the Famine to legitimate a Protestant Ascendancy under threat of dissolution, 'her martyrdom constituting her descendants' strongest claim to an Irish identity'.[56] This can also be seen in O'Connor's *Star of the Sea*, as David Merridith's mother, Lady Verity, died of fever during a previous famine, a fact remembered by his tenants, who desecrate his father's grave but leave his mother's untouched. It is notable that the 'claim to an Irish identity' is frequently complicated in Famine narratives by the protagonists' hybridity. In nineteenth-century novels such as Trollope's *Castle Richmond* and Annie Keary's (1825–79) *Castle Daly* (1875), the protagonists are the children of Irish fathers and English mothers. The emblematic and enigmatic Famine victim of *Star of the Sea*, Mary Duane, is the illegitimate daughter of the elder Lord Kingscourt, and Mary Kilmartin in *Famine* is the granddaughter of an English sailor; indeed, her mother's maiden name, Crampton, is the same as that of the English officer inspecting the relief works.

In Barry's *The Wizard's Knot*, the English absentee landlords are certainly criticized, yet so too are the resident Irish Catholic landlords (the half-Russian Lisaveta O'Connor and half-English Sir Philip Liscarroll), in spite of their efforts to save tenants. Indeed, Lisaveta's mixed heritage enables her to compare the poverty of Russian serfs and Irish peasants, and to see clearly the role her class has played: 'We are all to blame; none of us can get off. But the people, who have sinned a thousand times less than ourselves, will suffer most.'[57] Another Catholic landlord, David Quinn in Conal O'Riordan's (1874–1948) *Soldier's End* (1938), dedicates himself to Famine relief in memory of his nationalist half-English wife. Protestant landlords are also frequently represented as committed to saving their tenants. Merridith in *Star of the Sea* is forced to become a Famine emigrant himself, having paid for the passage of seven thousand tenants to Quebec. Even his murderer acknowledges that, though a landlord, Merridith is a victim rather than a perpetrator of starvation and death. In their reflection of a wide variety of landlord types, Famine novels accord with the depiction of landlords as 'the good, the bad and the ugly' in the folklore of the catastrophe.[58]

The most odious figures in Famine folklore are those from within the community who seek to profit from their neighbours' distress, particularly those who grabbed land from the evicted and the shopkeepers and gombeen men who pushed up prices during the catastrophe.[59] In *Star of the Sea*, Pius Mulvey commits the unforgivable sin of grabbing land from his own brother, while in Carol Birch's (1951–) *The Naming of Eliza Quinn* (2005), Eliza Vesey, coveting her neighbours' land, plants a gun on it and then informs on them to the authorities in order to have them evicted. The shopkeeper Johnny Hynes in O'Flaherty's *Famine* is the epitome of the gombeen man: the son of an informer, he has a withered hand, foxy eyes, thin lips, and a hooked nose. Flourishing under the law's protection of free trade,

---

[56] Margaret Kelleher, *The Feminization of Famine: Expressions of the Inexpressible?* (Durham, NC: Duke University Press, 1997), 134.

[57] Barry, *The Wizard's Knot*, 192.

[58] Cathal Póirtéir, *Famine Echoes* (Dublin: Gill and Macmillan, 1995) 9.   [59] Ibid.

Hynes makes a fortune through a dynastic alliance with an importer of yellow meal: 'Like a vulture, that soars in ecstasy over a battlefield, he took delight in the people's misery, since that misery was going to put money into his pocket. . . . "God bless this famine!" thought Hynes.'[60] However, some Famine narratives oppose the representation of merchants as misers preying on the misery of the starving. In Darby's *The Hunger*, there is a remarkable reversal; Tony O'Donoghue, the son of parsimonious shopkeepers who is supposed by his neighbours to be a miser, is in fact a saintly figure. Distressed at what the yellow meal does to his customers, he provides oatmeal instead, and eventually secretly gives away all of his money and goes into the poorhouse. His last six pounds, which he kept to cover the costs of his own burial, he gives to a man who has murdered a bailiff, so that he can emigrate. Paddy the Pawn in Byrd's *The Famished Land* is a Jekyll-and-Hyde figure, cruel during the day but kindly at night; his neighbours know to approach him for food or money after dark.

Historian Peter Gray has pointed to the remarkable ideological potency of the widely held belief among those in power that the Famine was providential in origin, such as the Home Secretary, Sir James Graham, who described 'the pestilence, and famine' as 'instruments of [God's] pleasure' in a letter to Prime Minister Peel in October 1845.[61] Trevelyan saw the Famine as a 'great intervention of Providence' to 'restore the energy and the vast industrial capabilities of that country'.[62] Yet even those vehemently opposed to the government's management of relief conceded providentialism. In 1847, Isaac Butt spoke of 'the fearful blight with which it has pleased an all-wise God to visit the food of her people', while John Mitchel's famous dictum of 1858 that 'the English created the famine' is preceded by the admission that 'The Almighty, indeed, sent the potato blight'.[63] Nor were such views confined to politicians and activists. Many of those interviewed by the Irish Folklore Commission in the 1930s and 1940s recorded the belief that the catastrophe was a providential punishment for a previous waste of food.[64] Brian Kilmartin in *Famine* shares the peasant belief—'God sends famine to remind us of our sins'—yet his daughter-in-law takes a more enlightened view:

> There was no God for her or the other poor people, who were starving to death. God belonged to the rich, among whom there was no hunger and no understanding of hunger. To be afflicted with hunger was considered, in the world of the rich, a crime which placed the sufferers outside the bounds of humanity.[65]

The providential theory is thus exposed as hypocritical and easily manipulated to validate complacency and ideological positions, including various forms of nationalism. Mrs Delaney, the middle-class Dublin Catholic in Walsh's *The Next Time*, claims the

[60] O'Flaherty, *Famine*, 178.

[61] Sir James Graham, cited in Peter Gray, *Famine, Land and Politics: British Government and Irish Society, 1843–50* (Dublin: Irish Academic Press, 1999), 99.

[62] C. E. Trevelyan, *The Irish Crisis* (London: Longman, Brown, Green and Longmans, 1848), 1, 8–9.

[63] Isaac Butt, 'The Famine in the Land. What has been Done, and What is to be Done', *Dublin University Magazine* 29 (1847), 501; John Mitchel, *The Last Conquest of Ireland (Perhaps)* (Glasgow: R. and T. Washbourne, 1882), 219.

[64] Póirtéir, *Famine Echoes*, 38.   [65] O'Flaherty, *Famine*, 273–4, 420.

Famine is 'a visitation from Providence … for the country's ingratitude to "the Liberator" and for the wickedness and infidelity preached by the *Nation* writers', while Father Geelan in *Famine* says it is 'because the people shirked the fight'.[66]

The inaction of the Catholic clergy during the crisis comes under greater scrutiny in twentieth- and twenty-first-century Famine fiction. During the nineteenth-century devotional revolution, religion in Famine novels often meant accusations of proselytism against Protestant clergymen or the representation of Catholic priests as sacrificial martyrs. A hardening of attitudes is clear in later work. The nationalist Father Geelan's attempt to break the police blockade of the food depot to save the people from starvation in *Famine* is thwarted by the conservative Father Roche, who realizes too late that 'it was the policy of "peace at any price," preached by him and by all the other priests and politicians in command of the great Repeal Association, that had produced this catastrophe'.[67] The Protestant rector Mr Coburn is much more strident in his challenge to authority but is unfairly traduced by the paranoia of proselytism, stoked by Kitty Hernon's desperate offer of her children to him. In Graham's *The Whitest Flower*, Ellen calls Father O'Brien 'Pontius Pilate' for his failure to intervene against the landlord. Her husband adds:

> The bishops will always line up with the Crown to get more money for Maynooth, and more power for themselves. And come the day when we're all lying stretched with the hunger, and no one to give us a decent burial, the Church and the Crown will still be saying, 'What can *we* do? It's the will of God.'[68]

In *Under the Hawthorn Tree*, a priest fails to help the vulnerable children, fearing they carry disease. Father Galligan in *Tales from the Poorhouse* castigates Roisin for her impurity in a time of hunger, but his hypocrisy is evident in 'his grand shiny boots, and the shine of good feedin' on his face and the proud stance of him, and the belly on him like there were twins in it at least'.[69]

Central to Famine fiction is the dehumanizing effect of starvation, an excessive abjection David Lloyd refers to as the 'indigent sublime'.[70] Under the stress of famine conditions, the mutual reliance of family and neighbours disintegrates into competition for food, and reverence for the dead gives way to the mass grave and the hinged coffin, or the consumption of corpses by pigs, dogs, and rats. In O'Flaherty's *Famine*, Brian Kilmartin insists on spending money the family can ill afford on proper funerals for his son Michael and Patrick Gleeson, and he himself dies in the effort to bury his wife. But Mary's mother is put 'into a common hole, in a wild field, like an animal'.[71] In *Star of the Sea*, when a woman dies shortly after embarking, her family mutilate her face with a blade to avoid the shame of her body washing up on the shore and being identified. Ellen

---

[66] Walsh, *The Next Time*, 144; O'Flaherty, *Famine*, 163.   [67] O'Flaherty, *Famine*, 327.

[68] Graham, *The Whitest Flower*, 130.   [69] McCabe, *Tales from the Poorhouse*, 28–9.

[70] David Lloyd, 'The Indigent Sublime: Specters of Irish Hunger', *Representations* 92, no. 1 (2015), 152–85.

[71] O'Flaherty, *Famine*, 430.

in *The Whitest Flower* discovers the body of her husband tossed on the death cart outside the workhouse and drags it many miles so that she can bury him in the family plot. She later finds the bodies of her neighbours, partially eaten by their dog. Even in *Under the Hawthorn Tree*, a children's book, there is no evasion of horror. Eily O'Driscoll is sickened by the macabre gossip she hears:

> 'The poor old priest went calling on four of the cottages and found all in them dead of the famine fever and huge rats swarming the place. They had to open a burial pit a mile outside the village to throw all the bodies of those that died into it.' The women continued, with each story worse than the one before.[72]

The children are attacked by a pack of dogs clearly used to human flesh, see 'four or five skeleton-like bodies, their bare skin and bones showing through the rags,'[73] being dragged on a slide, and come across the rotting body of a man in a ditch. They pray for him and make a wooden cross to mark the spot.

The care shown by the O'Driscoll children is unusual; the hardening of hearts in the midst of hideous sights is more commonly depicted. In Andrew Pepper's crime novel, *Bloody Winter* (2011), Martha mentions casually, 'I forgot to tell you. I came across a body yesterday. . . . Birds had pecked out the eyes. . . . It wasn't anyone I knew.'[74] At the end of the novel, Knox finds a rotting corpse being feasted on by maggots and 'a large mongrel, carrying what looked like human flesh in its jaws. He noted these things without outrage or moral indignation: this was just the way it was.'[75] One of the most affecting stories is Seosamh Mac Grianna's (1900–90) 'Ar an Trá Fholamh' (On the Empty Shore, 1929), in which Cathal, carrying the corpse of his friend, waits in line for soup to give him strength to bury him. No one pays attention to the body until Cathal tries to take advantage of two women fighting to reach into the cauldron; he is pulled back by a man who threatens: 'If you don't stay out, I'll stuff that corpse down into the cauldron.'[76] The fact that they are all well-known to each other enhances the shocking cruelty.

Worse than indifference is the sacrificing of loved ones in the attempt to survive. Mary and Martin in *Famine* divest themselves of the older generation, in a primitive impulse of survival inherited from 'nomadic days, when the aged were sacrificed in time of need by the young and vigorous'.[77] The Master in *Tales from the Poorhouse* rejects his own sister and her child, and is tormented by their deaths. The neighbours in Birch's *The Naming of Eliza Quinn* board the living Peadar into a cabin with his dead wife's body, terrified of the fever. In both Trevor's 'The News from Ireland' and Nicholson's *Dark Rosaleen*, parents mark their baby with stigmata to attract aid, while in *Famine* and *Star of the Sea* a parent commits infanticide.

---

[72] Conlon-McKenna, *Under the Hawthorn Tree*, 89.   [73] Ibid., 69.

[74] Andrew Pepper, *Bloody Winter* (London: Weidenfeld and Nicolson, 2011), 53, 124.

[75] Ibid., 262.

[76] Seosamh Mac Grianna, 'Ar an Trá Fhoilimh', trans. Séamus Ó Néill, in Seamus Deane (gen. ed.), *The Field Day Anthology of Irish Writing* (Derry: Field Day Publications, 1991), vol. 3, 849.

[77] O'Flaherty, *Famine*, 347.

Most texts reflect the desperate eating practices that arose during the Famine—consuming cats, dogs, and rats, mouths stained green with grass, stealing blood from cattle. Eliza Quinn wryly notes of her neighbour, who has butchered his dog Mick: 'Poor old Mick... I'll bet they were picking him out of their teeth for days.'[78] Cormac Ó Gráda has referred to cannibalism as 'famine's darkest secret, a taboo topic',[79] yet it is frequently referred to in modern Famine fiction, often as a dark rumour, sometimes a certainty. In *The Famished Land*, Moira discovers her little brothers eating their baby sister and slowly comes to terms with and understands their actions, but they bury the memory and never speak of it again. Kenny's *The Hungry Earth* ends with the protagonist's anguished discovery that his ancestor survived the catastrophe by stealing and eating babies. In Éilís Ní Dhuibhne's (1954–) 'Summer Pudding' (1997), the narrator recalls her father telling her, after he has lost his job on the relief works, 'Kill me and eat me. I will die soon enough anyway.'[80]

Kelleher has argued that Famine literature's great strength is 'its potential to individualize the crisis', and that the spectacle of famine is predominantly portrayed through the starving body of a woman, most frequently that of a mother.[81] In many of these texts, there is an emblematic moment when the protagonist encounters a starving woman and her children. In *Famine*, Dr Hynes's exaltation at Father Geelan's call to 'Learn to love this Irish earth, as your real mother'[82] is immediately undercut by the cry for help of a real mother, on her way to the workhouse ten miles away and fearful that her child will starve before they get there. In Colum McCann's *TransAtlantic*, Frederick Douglass and Richard Webb encounter a woman on the road to Cork, dragging the body of her child on a bundle of twigs. Incapable of grasping that her child is dead, she begs for help, even urging them to take the child. The men can only offer useless coins, which she drops to the ground, and they leave her. When Douglass tells this story to Isabel Jennings the next morning, she immediately sets out to look for and help the woman, thus underlining the insufficiency of the men's response.

However, women in Famine fiction are also frequently portrayed as indomitable survivors prepared to do anything to save themselves and their families. Graham's *The Whitest Flower* even came with the endorsement of the then taoiseach, Bertie Ahern, who described its heroine, Ellen Rua O'Malley (one of many red-haired heroines in popular Famine fiction), as 'the resurrection of the new Ireland rising out of starvation and disease, the embodiment of the hope that kept our people going'.[83] The heroines of Michael Mullen's *The Hungry Land* (1986) and Nicholson's *Dark Rosaleen* are spoilt, headstrong, wealthy women who sacrifice security for rebellion. Mary in *Famine* and Moira in *The Famished Land* prove themselves strong and capable when husbands and fathers are taken from them. Mary Duane in *Star of the Sea* and Roisin in *Tales from the Poorhouse*

[78] Carol Birch, *The Naming of Eliza Quinn* (London: Virago, 2005), 207.

[79] Cormac Ó Gráda, *Eating People Is Wrong, and Other Essays on Famine, Its Past, and Its Future* (Princeton, NJ: Princeton University Press, 2015), 14.

[80] Éilís Ní Dhuibhne, *The Inland Ice and Other Stories* (Belfast: Blackstaff Press, 1997), 59.

[81] Kelleher, *The Feminization of Famine*, 5, 8.   [82] O'Flaherty, *Famine*, 124.

[83] Bertie Ahern, cited in Graham, *The Whitest Flower*, ii.

know that their only resource is their bodies; prostitution as a survival strategy, absent in nineteenth-century fiction, is acknowledged in contemporary fictional accounts.

The ethical and aesthetic challenge of representing the Famine has always been apparent. Kelleher notes that a recurring question in Famine literature is 'can the experience of famine be expressed; is language adequate to a description of famine's horrors?', before going on to argue that in spite of the difficulties, 'questions about language's competence give way to a detailed attempt at representation'.[84] This is in contrast to most visual representations made during and immediately after the Famine, which generally avoided the horrendous scenes described in literature. As Luke Gibbons notes, 'It is as if words could go into places where images feared to tread.'[85] The pre-existence of literary modes to accommodate horror, most notably the Gothic, provided established paradigms.[86] And yet several recent novels have returned to the difficulty of expressing the true horror of death by starvation and disease, contrasting textual and visual representation by inserting into the narrative the figure of the artist, and in particular the Cork-born artist James Mahony, whose 'Sketches in the West of Ireland' appeared in the *Illustrated London News* in February 1847.

One notable example of this trend is Nicholson's *Dark Rosaleen*, which opens with the English heroine destroying a copy of the *Illustrated London News* in her fury at her father's demand that she accompany him to Ireland: 'But she could not touch the drawing of the boy, thin and almost naked, standing defiantly by the bodies of his mother and sisters.'[87] The image seems to be based on Mahony's frequently reproduced 'Boy and Girl at Cahera', in which a ragged boy stares at the viewer, while an equally ragged girl reaches for a potato on the ground. But, as Emily Mark-Fitzgerald argues, Mahony's most affecting sketches, such as 'Boy and Girl at Cahera' and 'Woman begging at Clonakilty', in which a woman carrying her dead baby begs for money to bury it, are outnumbered by 'scenic views' and are reliant on the surrounding text to expose the horror. A horrific description of the tearing to pieces of the putrefying body of a man by dogs is accompanied by a sketch of a cabin with two melancholy figures outside, leaving the scene of horror to the imagination, so that 'the viewer escapes a visual assault and responds with an indignant imagination, the sensibilities of the audience simultaneously offended and protected'.[88] The scene Nicholson describes could not be accommodated within the conventions of nineteenth-century illustration.

This theme also features in O'Connor's *Star of the Sea*, as when the American journalist, Grantley Dixon, recalls a 'middle-aged Corkman', clearly based on Mahony, who is

[84] Margaret Kelleher, 'Irish Famine in Literature', in Cathal Póirtéir (ed.), *The Great Irish Famine* (Dublin: Mercier Press, 1995), 232.

[85] Luke Gibbons, *Limits of the Visible: Representing the Great Hunger* (Quinnipiac, CT: Ireland's Great Hunger Museum, 2014), 13.

[86] See Robert Smart, *Black Roads: The Famine in Irish Literature* (Quinnipiac, CT: Ireland's Great Hunger Museum, 2015).

[87] Michael Nicholson, *Dark Rosaleen* (Dublin: History Press Ireland, 2015), 13.

[88] Emily Mark-Fitzgerald, *Commemorating the Irish Famine: Memory and Monument* (Liverpool: Liverpool University Press, 2013), 46.

'commissioned by a London newspaper to go to Connemara and make pictures of the Famine' at Clifden workhouse:

> He was weeping very quietly as he tried to draw. . . . His hands were trembling as they attempted to form shapes. And Dixon had been afraid to look at whatever was happening in the room. . . . Now he looked at some of the sketches he had torn from the London journals. . . . The emaciated faces and twisted mouths. The tormented eyes and outstretched hands. . . . Shocking the images: but nothing to what he had seen. They were not even close to what he had seen.[89]

There is a disjunction here not just between the reality Dixon witnesses and the sketches but between the sketches Dixon describes and the ones which actually appeared in the *Illustrated London News*, which could not portray the 'twisted mouths' and 'tormented eyes' of the dead and dying. But the artist has at least achieved an approximate representation, whereas Dixon cannot: 'The Famine could not be turned into a simile. The best word for death was death.'[90]

Recent novels choose narrative techniques that reinforce the aesthetic challenge of representation. McCabe's *Tales from the Poorhouse* offers four widely differing perspectives on the Famine: those of Roisin and Mary Brady, the poorhouse Master, and the Landlord. In Niall Williams's (1958–) *The Fall of Light* (2001), the Famine is only experienced second-hand: Teige Foley, safe on Scattery Island, has a vision of what his brother, Tomas, witnesses in Cork. Another brother, marooned with his troupe of gypsies in central Europe, encounters a spectral Irishman who 'told of those who ate the grass and the nettles and the green leaves of the hedgerow. . . . He told of a man in delirium who cut off his arm and cooked it in a fire to feed to his son.'[91] Many of these novels demonstrate the 'intense self-consciousness (both theoretical and textual) about the act of narrating in the present the events of the past',[92] which is the defining feature of historiographic metafiction. Dixon in *Star of the Sea* is a journalist and aspiring novelist whose Famine novel fails to find a publisher. 'Morbid type of thing', one tells him. 'Fine for the newspapers. You'd *expect* it in the newspapers. But the reader of fiction wants something else.'[93] The non-fiction book Kathleen plans in *My Dream of You* mutates into a novel due to the impossibility of discovering the truth by other means. As Miss Leech ironically points out, her story 'does exactly what a lot of the highbrow fiction coming into the library these days does—it keeps changing as you look at it. You don't know what to believe. Our readers hate that, of course.'[94] Yet the fact that it is possible to trace a sustained tradition of Famine fiction from the 1840s to the present suggests both a wide acceptance and enjoyment of its rich ambivalence and multiplicity, and a continuing fascination with the suffering and survival strategies of the characters these texts depict.

---

[89] O'Connor, *Star of the Sea*, 128, 130.   [90] Ibid., 129.
[91] Niall Williams, *The Fall of Light* (London: Picador, 2002), 246–8.
[92] Linda Hutcheon, *The Politics of Postmodernism* (London: Routledge, 2002), 68.
[93] O'Connor, *Star of the Sea*, 122. Original emphasis.   [94] O'Faolain, *My Dream of You*, 381.

FURTHER READING

Corporaal, Marguérite, Christopher Cusack, and Lindsay Janssen (eds). *Recollecting Hunger: An Anthology. Cultural Memories of the Great Famine in Irish and British Fiction, 1847–1920*. Dublin: Irish Academic Press, 2012.

Corporaal, Marguérite, Christopher Cusack, Lindsay Janssen, and Ruud van den Beuken (eds). *Global Legacies of the Great Irish Famine: Transnational and Interdisciplinary Perspectives*. Bern: Peter Lang, 2014.

Crowley, John, William J. Smyth, and Mike Murphy (eds). *Atlas of the Great Irish Famine, 1845–52*. Cork: Cork University Press, 2012.

Fegan, Melissa. *Literature and the Irish Famine 1845–1919*. Oxford: Clarendon Press, 2002.

Fegan, Melissa. '"That Heartbroken Island of Incestuous Hatred": Famine and Family in Joseph O'Connor's *Star of the Sea*'. In Marie-Luise Kohlke and Christian Gutleben (eds), *Neo-Victorian Families: Gender, Sexual and Cultural Politics*. Amsterdam: Rodopi, 2011: 321–41.

Frawley, Oona (ed.). *Memory Ireland, Volume 3: The Famine and the Troubles*. Syracuse, NY: Syracuse University Press, 2014.

Kelleher, Margaret. 'Irish Famine in Literature'. In Cathal Póirtéir (ed.), *The Great Irish Famine*. Dublin: Mercier Press, 1995: 232–47.

Kelleher, Margaret. *The Feminization of Famine: Expressions of the Inexpressible?* Durham, NC: Duke University Press, 1997.

Klein, Bernhard. *On the Uses of History in Recent Irish Writing*. Manchester: Manchester University Press, 2007.

Lloyd, David. 'The Indigent Sublime: Specters of Irish Hunger'. *Representations* 92, no. 1 (2005): 152–85.

Morash, Christopher (ed.). *The Hungry Voice: The Poetry of the Irish Famine*. Dublin: Irish Academic Press, 1989.

Morash, Christopher. *Writing the Irish Famine*. Oxford: Clarendon Press, 1995.

Póirtéir, Cathal. *Famine Echoes*. Dublin: Gill and Macmillan, 1995.

Schultz, Matthew. *Haunted Historiographies: The Rhetoric of Ideology in Postcolonial Irish Fiction*. Manchester: Manchester University Press, 2014.

Smart, Robert. *Black Roads: The Famine in Irish Literature*. Quinnipiac, CT: Ireland's Great Hunger Museum, 2015.

CHAPTER 24

THE 1916 RISING IN THE STORY OF IRELAND

LAURA O'CONNOR

IRELAND's troubled history is legendary. A useful prelude to any discussion of Irish historical fiction is to consider the ambiguities of this claim. It suggests that Ireland's eventful past is common knowledge. It may also indicate that some of what passes as fact may be fanciful pseudohistory, and it implies that the narrative trajectory of Irish history makes for a good story. The storyness of Irish history, with its familiar masterplot of an oppressed yet unvanquished nation throwing off the colonial yoke, is critiqued by Roy Foster in his analysis of popular Irish histories bearing the 'Story of Ireland' title.[1] Irish historiography needs to avoid the Romantic trappings and partisan allegiances of the Story-of-Ireland topos, Foster argues, and cultivate dispassionate scepticism instead. Yet the bid to inoculate 'history' against the incursions of 'legend' obscures the commingling of *story* and hi*story*. Historical novels are useful for theorizing the cross-fertilization between 'fact' and 'fiction' because their authors constantly negotiate between the two. The Story-of-Ireland topos informs the prior knowledge and curiosity that readers bring to bear on Irish historical fiction. Its legibility generates opportunities to bring alternative and supplemental stories (and histories) to the fore. Moreover, and crucially, the insurrectionists who imagined, planned, and conducted the 1916 Easter Rising did so with a view to making it pivotal in the 'Story of Ireland' and also to shaping how it would be remembered and narrated in the future. In addition to covering the events of Easter week, historical novelists explore how the Rising's literary and symbolic provenance reinforces its pre-eminence in the ongoing 'Story of Ireland'.

Within Ireland's storied past, the Rising occupies a privileged place. A classroom poster of Ireland's historical timeline encapsulates the trajectory: the line-graph displays peaks marking St Patrick's arrival in Ireland in 432, the 1014 Battle of Clontarf, and, at the apex, the 1916 Rising. The rebellion began a series of tumultuous events that led to the

---

[1] R. F. Foster, *The Irish Story: Telling Tales and Making It Up in Ireland* (London: Allen Lane/Penguin, 2001).

partitioning of the island in 1921, the foundation of the Irish Free State in 1922, and the Civil War of 1922–23 and its turbulent aftermath. Internationally recognized as foundational, equivalent in import if not in magnitude to the American Declaration of Independence in 1776 and the creation of India and Pakistan in 1947, the Rising set an inspiring precedent for other British colonies seeking independence in the twentieth century. Yet in many ways the Rising was a hapless revolution. It had no chance of military success; it didn't inaugurate insurrection nationwide or win popular support; and the confusion over timing and the crossed chains of command and communication meant that it unfolded haphazardly.

The secret organization of the Irish Republican Brotherhood (IRB), a caucus within the Irish Volunteers, planned a nationwide uprising for Easter Sunday 1916, which fell on 23 April. When the Irish Volunteer leader Eoin MacNeill belatedly learned of the clandestine plan, he countermanded the order to assemble. The IRB cabal, along with the socialist Irish Citizen Army led by James Connolly, decided to proceed anyway. On Easter Monday, they occupied and fortified key sites in Dublin. Standing outside their headquarters at the General Post Office (GPO), Patrick Pearse (1879–1916) read the Proclamation of the Irish Republic to a bemused public. The Proclamation presents the Rising as one in a series of rebellions, both a culmination of past events and a precursor to future assertions of freedom, destined to be repeated until sovereign independence is attained:

> In every generation the Irish people have asserted their right to national freedom and sovereignty; six times during the past three hundred years they have asserted it in arms. Standing on that fundamental right and again asserting it in arms in the face of the world, we hereby proclaim the Irish Republic as a Sovereign Independent State, and we pledge our lives and the lives of our comrades in arms to the cause of its freedom, of its welfare, and of its exaltation among the nations.

Six days later, after almost 500 people, mostly civilians, were killed and the bombarded city centre lay in ruins, the rebels surrendered. Over the following weeks, public opinion turned strongly in favour of the republican cause; the execution of fifteen leaders by the British authorities led to their lionization as martyrs.

Historicizing the Rising is complicated not only by partisanship, which hardened after the Civil War, but also by the conflictual, yet often coexistent, modes of historical imagining at play in recollecting and interpreting it. The salience of these divergent modes of historical consciousness may be illustrated in relation to Sir Walter Scott's enduring influence on historical fiction. Critics concur with James Cahalan's assertion that 'an understanding of the Irish historical novel must begin with Walter Scott because Irish historical novelists began with him'.[2] In an international context, Georg Lukács's influential treatment of Scott's historical fiction as exemplary in *The Historical Novel*,

---

[2] James Cahalan, *Great Hatred, Little Room: The Irish Historical Novel* (Syracuse, NY: Syracuse University Press), 1.

first published in 1937, stimulated materialist criticism of the genre and enhanced Scott's twentieth-century critical stature. According to Lukács, Scott 'has a deeper, more genuine and differentiated sense of historical necessity than any writer before him', which 'allow[s] his characters to express feelings and thoughts about real, historical relationships in a much clearer way than the actual men and women of the time could have done'.[3] By portraying a 'middling'[4] protagonist caught in a historical crisis, Lukács argues, historical novels explore the competing forces of that crisis and capture what it was like to live through it. The primary historical personages feature as peripheral or cameo characters, appearing only at significant junctures to convey 'artistically the connection between the spontaneous reaction of the masses and the historical consciousness of the leading personalities'.[5]

Scott's enduring contribution to the demand for an aestheticized Scottishness and Celticism, begun by *Ossian* in the 1760s and continued in nineteenth-century Ireland by Maria Edgeworth (1767–1849), Thomas Moore (1779–1852), Lady Morgan (c.1783–1859), Standish O'Grady (1846–1928), and W. B. Yeats (1865–1939), had more far-reaching consequences than his example as a novelist, however. Together these writers transformed the Celtic periphery into an imagined 'fringe', an alluring touristic, cinematic, and literary setting associated with wistful moods and melancholy reverie.[6] For Scott, the war between Jacobites and Hanoverians and the Scottish and English nations was safely concluded sixty years previously at Culloden, and the romantic setting of the Highlands references a bygone era. By contrast, for eighteenth-century Gaelic poets, Young Irelanders of the 1840s, the IRB, and early twentieth-century Irish cultural revivalists, Jacobite poetry and song, especially the Gaelic genre of the *aisling* (dream-vision poem), was a means of reiterating the imperative to recover Irish sovereignty. The Irish Jacobite tradition inculcates a typological cast of historical consciousness, one where present oppression shall issue oppositional revolt in the future, and the current regime is regarded as an anomalous interlude in the nation's 'destiny'. The separatist 'dream' of the future restoration of native sovereignty eschews the mainstream linear logic of incremental reform in favour of an 'as once, so again' pattern of recurrence and return that approximates the cyclical temporality of myth.[7]

In the years immediately after 1916, the political history and symbolism of the Rising were cultivated, disseminated, and interpreted through literature, and they have continued to be interpreted in this way. Historians cite literary sources as evidence, making the boundaries between 'fiction' and 'history' even more porous than usual. Essays and speeches by Pearse and Connolly, widely circulated after the Rising, led to serious engagement with their respective ideologies. Pearse, Thomas MacDonagh (1878–1916),

---

[3] Georg Lukács, *The Historical Novel*, trans. Hannah and Stanley Mitchell (Lincoln, NE: University of Nebraska Press, 1983), 58, 63.

[4] Ibid., 33.   [5] Ibid., 44.

[6] On this transformation, see my *Haunted English: The Celtic Fringe, the British Empire, and De-Anglicization* (Baltimore, MD: Johns Hopkins University Press, 2006), 15–20.

[7] See Murray Pittock, *Celtic Identity and the British Image* (Manchester: Manchester University Press, 1999), 2–3.

and Joseph Mary Plunkett (1887–1916) composed poetry and plays in the Jacobite *aisling* tradition, in which a female personification of Irish sovereignty—known by clandestine code-names like Cathleen Ni Houlihan—obliges the poet-speaker to urge his country-men to defend her honour, which the colonial usurper has violated. Their posthumously published poetry, much of it composed in elegiac and prophetic registers, became a commemorative staple.

The controversy over the Rising's timing goes to the heart of the myth/history dichot-omy. It raises fascinating 'what if' speculation and is key to understanding how the Rising's apparent haphazardness derives from deep ideological differences. Had the rebels waited, to follow one line of speculation, would unfolding events, such as the 1918 conscription crisis, have perhaps precipitated nationwide insurrection and mutiny among the ranks of the 200,000 Irish soldiers at the Western Front? While such issues are foremost for political pragmatists and strategists, for fervent cultural nationalists who envisioned the Rising as a mythopoeic and symbolic as well as a military event, other considerations may have taken precedence. For them, the messianic symbolism of the Easter timing was essential to the Rising's efficacy. The messianic mythos draws on Christian symbolism and also on the rhetoric of recurrence and rebirth—evident in the Proclamation's citation of a generational series of uprisings—espoused by republicans. Moreover, it aligns with the coeval movements to regenerate Ireland's literary culture, the Gaelic Revival and the Irish Literary Renaissance.

'The Coming Revolution' (1913), Pearse's essay espousing 'bloodshed [as] a cleansing and a sanctifying thing',[8] works a religious variation on pro-war propaganda about redemptive blood-sacrifice in Europe. The symbolic appeal of Pearse's cult of founda-tional sacred violence for Irish nationalism is evinced by how the insurgents were not heroized as warriors but rather apotheosized as martyrs after they were executed by the British. The Proclamation's opening self-authorization, 'In the name of God and of the dead generations', exploits and boosts frameworks of Irish social memory—songs, stories, elaborate funerals, commemorative rituals—which cumulatively nourish the underlying messianic mythos. Michael Collins's oft-cited remark that the Rising 'had the air of Greek tragedy about it'[9] applies not only to the theatrical delivery of the Proc-lamation against the porticoed backdrop of the GPO and the spectacular conduct of some insurgents; it also implicates the cultic violence that lies at the origins of tragedy and the inauguration of new epochs heralded in the refrain of Yeats's 'Easter, 1916': 'All changed, changed utterly: / A terrible beauty is born.'[10] 'Myth' and 'story' are more than the disparaged 'other' of history in a context where the Rising's leaders strove to inscribe themselves into the myth of messianic republicanism they inherited and bequeathed.

Novels composed soon after the Rising, often by witness-participants, were written and read in dialogue with the posthumous writings of the executed leaders during the

---

[8] Pádraig Pearse, 'The Coming Revolution', in *Collected Works of Pádraig H. Pearse: Political Writings and Speeches* (Dublin: Phoenix, 1916), 99.

[9] Clair Wills, *Dublin 1916: The Siege of the GPO* (London: Profile Books, 2009), 87.

[10] W. B. Yeats, 'Easter, 1916', in *W. B. Yeats: A Critical Edition of the Major Works*, ed. Edward Larrissy (Oxford: Oxford University Press, 1997), 85.

Anglo-Irish War of 1919–21, when the Rising's political outcome was very uncertain. Post-independence novelists tend not to perceive the Rising as a singular event, by contrast, but rather as an episode in the tumultuous decade between the 1913 Lockout and the mid-1920s. After the Civil War—fought between nationalists who accepted the Anglo-Irish Treaty of 1921, which granted dominion status to a twenty-six-county Irish Free State, and the anti-Treaty minority who opposed settling for anything less than a thirty-two-county sovereign republic—it became almost impossible to refer to the Proclamation's republican ideal without re-opening unresolved disputes over the Treaty. This chapter first considers novels written in the Rising's immediate aftermath, which stand apart because they are not mediated through Civil War hindsight and show a striking reliance on the *Bildungsroman* form. Later novelists are at a generational remove, both in temporal terms and in the sense that the Rising is filtered through their family and community memories and stories, as well as through broader cultural narratives. To display their diversity, range, and common themes, I have grouped my chosen texts into three categories: novels that focus on combat, including the convergence of 1916 with the First World War; the family saga, which marks and bridges temporal distances, and dominates mid-twentieth-century writing; and novels that merge the story of the Rising with emancipatory homosexual narratives that, until recently, were largely omitted from the 'Story of Ireland' and from narratives centred on the patriarchal institution of 'family'.[11]

EARLY FICTIONAL RESPONSES TO THE RISING

The publication in 1916 of James Joyce's (1882–1941) *A Portrait of the Artist as a Young Man*, the classic literary treatment of the individual and the nation's interrelated transformations from dependency to autonomy, seems almost too timely, given its influence on Rising-inspired fiction. When read alongside contemporaneous works about the rebellion, the continuities between *A Portrait* and nineteenth-century Irish fiction become apparent, however. The emphasis on literary formation in *A Portrait* resonates with a staple of Irish historical novels since Maria Edgeworth's *The Absentee* (1812): scenes in which the hero/heroine is morally and politically enlightened by reading Irish history. The pedagogical scenario implies that few people could read Irish history without becoming radicalized by it. This also accounts for the partisan nature of nineteenth- and twentieth-century Irish historical novels noted by Cahalan: instead of moderating their outlook, like Scott's heroes, Irish protagonists typically evolve in the reverse direction, from an Anglo-oriented or non-aligned stance to one of committed nationalism.[12]

---

[11] The brevity of this chapter precludes full consideration of the numerous novels about 1916 published since the 1920s. For further guidance, see the annotated bibliography in Wills, *Dublin 1916*, 227–41 and Danine Farquharson's ongoing online bibliography of novels about 1916 at http://www.mun.ca/easter1916/index.php. Accessed 23 June 2017.

[12] Cahalan, *Great Hatred, Little Room*, 18.

By roundly refusing to affiliate to the nationalist cause and resolving instead to 'fly by those nets' of 'nationality, language, religion', Stephen Dedalus's *non serviam* inaugurates a counter-example to the nationalist conversion narrative.[13]

Because the Rising was a surprise coup, many nationalists felt wrongfully excluded from it. George Russell's (1867–1935) *The Interpreters* (1919) responds with a symposium airing a range of diverse takes on revolution, while Eimar O'Duffy's (1893–1935) *roman à clef*, *The Wasted Island* (1919), seeks to set the record straight by telling an 'other' side of Volunteer history, one that champions Stephen Ward (a.k.a. Bulmer Hobson, who was imprisoned by IRB leaders to prevent him from derailing the Rising) and lambastes Austin Mallow (a.k.a. Plunkett) in ways that were bound to provoke censure, and did. O'Duffy had informed MacNeill about the clandestine plan and was present when he and Hobson confronted Pearse about it. The concluding chapter depicting the Rising is ominously entitled 'The Catastrophe'. In it, the (semi-autobiographical) Bernard Lascelles and his circle of UCD students attend the inaugural Rotunda meeting of the Irish Volunteers in November 1913. They are elated when its membership increases sevenfold in early 1914, and appalled when John Redmond offers unconditional support for the British war effort in August 1914 without leveraging the crisis to advance the nationalist cause.[14] Most Volunteers enlisted.

Lascelles's circle, who debate issues like re-forestation with gusto, worry about the IRB's increasing influence among the remaining Volunteers and mistrust the poet-revolutionaries 'martyromania'.[15] In a scene in which Mallow extols martyrs' blood and is impressed by the 'genius' of a hastily composed parody of Plunkett's messianic verse— significantly entitled 'Aisling'—Lascelles observes his 'emaciated body' (Plunkett had tuberculosis) 'jerk for the blood-lust of the restless tortured spirit it harboured, [and] realise[s] he might as well argue with a lunatic'.[16] As the days go by and the *Helga* gunboat bombards the city, Lascelles can no longer endure being a bystander and joins the insurrectionists. He bayonets a British soldier, is thrown into a dungeon, and spirals into despair and madness. In his delirium, he feels 'a recrudescence of violent anger against the authors of the calamity and the things they had done to enforce their will'.[17] Given the consistent emphasis on his circle's rationality, the sudden incoherence of Lascelles's descent into insanity presents a peculiar, as well as an unsatisfactory, conclusion to the novel. A notable because evidently unintentional irony is that O'Duffy's avatar becomes a 'wasted' 'lunatic', an embodiment of what he most abhors about his nemesis, Plunkett.

The 'wasting' theme resurfaces in *The House of Success* (1922) by Darrell Figgis (1882–1925). Jeremiah O'Hare, an affluent self-made businessman, has suppressed memories of boyhood poverty and homelessness. There are few chinks in O'Hare's energetic worldly demeanour, aside from anguished talk in his sleep and a habit of always addressing his namesake son, Jerry, as Diarmuid O'Hara, the name he once bore as a Gaelic-speaking peasant boy in Connemara. Anxious that his son not be educated

---

[13] James Joyce, *A Portrait of the Artist as a Young Man*, ed. Seamus Deane (London: Penguin, 1992), 220.
[14] Eimar O'Duffy, *The Wasted Island* (New York: Dodd, Mead, and Company, 1920), 269.
[15] Ibid., 148.   [16] Ibid., 274.   [17] Ibid., 525.

into dull conformity, he sends him to an experimental school resembling St Enda's, the secondary school for boys established by Pearse in 1908. The father wants Jerry to 'build' the flourishing business he began; the son wants to 'smash' Ireland's exploitative economy and oppressive ethos; each 'taunts' and then 'haunts' the other.[18] Fear overwhelms the father when Jerry participates in the Rising, 'translating [him into] a lifeless hulk'.[19] Working a *doppelgänger* variation on the Cathleen Ni Houlihan conceit of a crone metamorphosing into a queen, the son's valour saps the vigour out of the father and his capitalist success. The juxtaposed 'wasted' trope in both novels limns a typology of the one ascendant at the other's expense. The precursor is dethroned by the *Bildung's* hero; Plunkett is exalted in history's annals at Hobson's expense; and events foreclose alternative futures.

In St John Ervine's (1883–1971) *Changing Winds* (1917), the education of Henry Quinn is arranged by his unconventional father, a colourful Protestant unionist landowner who wants his son to prosper among the Anglo elite without distancing himself from his Irish roots. Before he rejoins his public-school friends in London, Henry is educated at Trinity College Dublin and tutored by John Marsh, an ardent cultural nationalist who is subsequently killed in the Rising. Mortified by an unmanly cowardice that makes him baulk at enlisting, Henry is surprised to feel no fear as a bystander during the Rising. He decides to enlist after his upcoming marriage, certain that he shall die, like his friends, at the Western Front. The role of the Irish insurrection in stiffening a man's resolve to join the Allies' cause also features in *The Tree of Heaven* (1918) by English novelist and pro-war feminist May Sinclair (pseudonym of Mary Amelia St Clair, 1863–1946). Michael Harrison is attracted to the grassroots nature of Irish nationalism because it is the antithesis of the Great War's industrial scale, but, like Quinn, he eventually reconciles himself to dying for what his peers regard as the greater cause.

It is noteworthy that most of the early 1916 novels are written by Protestant or Northern nationalists. The Catholic ethos of 1916 commemorations and much republican rhetoric, compounded by the 1921 sectarian partitioning of Ireland, would soon marginalize them as a group. Annie M. P. Smithson's (1873–1948) *Her Irish Heritage* (1917) has an Edgeworthian premise: Clare Castlemaine, raised a freethinker by her late father in London, knows as little about her long-dead mother's Catholic relatives in Ireland 'as she did of the North Pole'.[20] Admiring how her relatives' Catholicism is a '*living* faith',[21] Clare gravitates towards Mary Carmichael, a Catholic convert. When Mary's faith is imperilled by her fiancé's inexplicable abandonment of her, Clare makes its resilience a test case for herself. Notwithstanding the romantic plot—Clare is engaged to a worthy Irish suitor—the abiding impression left by the novel is of the existential loneliness of those for whom religious faith is not a given.

Brinsley MacNamara's (1890–1963) *The Clanking of Chains* (1920), which pits the dedicated and naïve idealist Michael Dempsey against the begrudgery of his native

---

[18] Darrell Figgis, *The House of Success* (Dublin: The Gael Co-operative, 1922), 259.
[19] Ibid., 275.   [20] Annie M. P. Smithson, *Her Irish Heritage* (Dublin: Talbot Press, 1945), 10.
[21] Ibid., 110. Original emphasis.

village of Ballycullen, explores the gap between a small community's nationalist self-image and its narrow-minded attitudes. Even as they wax sentimental over Dempsey's performance as Robert Emmet in a local drama, the villagers resent how the role ennobles the shop-boy's stature and set about taking him down. Dempsey functions much like a Billy Budd, a moral innocent whose sincere idealism highlights by contrast the malicious envy and 'shoneenism'[22] of his community. *The Clanking of Chains* is a sequel to MacNamara's aptly titled *The Valley of the Squinting Windows* (1918), which was publicly burned on its publication by the people of Delvin in County Westmeath, the author's birthplace and the thinly disguised setting for both novels.

Gaelic novelist Pádraic Ó Conaire (1882–1928) departs from the individualist focus of the *Bildungsroman* to portray the Rising's countrywide impact in *Seacht mBua an Éirí Amach* (Seven Traits or Triumphs of the Rising), his 1918 cycle of short stories. The breakdown of communication and the localization of the Rising to Dublin city meant that news of it spread nationwide through hearsay. Ó Conaire's stories explore the hidden desires motivating a series of people whose lives were disrupted by the insurrection: the mother and fiancée of a slain rebel each try to hide the truth from the other; an authoritarian bishop is stirred to humane leadership; a vengeful woman is tormented with fear that her son will learn that she had blinded his father; and a woman flirts with a spy to protect a rebel she admires. The story-cycle form creates a prismatic impression of the Rising's ramifying effects across the country, and the seven stories cumulatively convey the attitudinal shifts that turned public opinion in favour of the republican cause.

Eoghan Ó Tuairisc (1919–82) adopts a similar radiating structure in his 1966 novel, *Dé Luain* (Monday), although the latter's narrative technique is more experimental than O'Conaire's storytelling style. *Dé Luain* captures the befuddling impact of a bitter morning-after realization that Sunday's Rising has been cancelled, the confusion being compounded by the subsequent call for insurgents to re-mobilize swiftly, despite the cancellation. Doubt and uncertainty over whether or not the mobilization is for real strengthens Ó Tuairisc's strategy of representing the Rising as it would have unfolded in the present for its participants. The montage of gathering insurgents, isolated by private thought even as they steel themselves for concerted action, evokes a temporality of discrepant simultaneity. *Dé Luain* ends with Pearse's Proclamation, not the text itself but diffuse interpretations of it, including Pearse's thoughts as he listens to his voice proclaiming what seems to him to be scripted by a stranger. The performative core of the Rising becomes spectral, and the provisional ('sealadach'[23]) nature of the Proclamation's thereby constituted government is emphasized. The spectral palimpsestic effect is evoked by the combination of historical exactitude in reconstructing life in Dublin on a given day and the ghosting of the insurgents' steps in the sort of ritualized re-enactment undertaken by Bloomsday or *via dolorosa* pilgrims.

---

[22] Brinsley MacNamara, *The Clanking of Chains* (Tralee: Anvil Books, 1965), 61.
[23] Eoghan Ó Tuairisc, *Dé Luain* (Dublin: Sáirséal, 1966), 222.

Dé Luain was part of an upsurge of historical fiction and historiography that coincided with the celebration of the jubilee of the Rising in 1966. Indeed, its blend of renewed historical rigour and ritualistic remembrance is characteristic of commemorative milestones, which rouse the public to explore 'what actually happened' and to contemplate the present's indebtedness to historical struggle. People became more educated about a past made freshly legible by popular histories, historical novels, and documentary broadcasts, and attuned to the impact of supplementary school curricula, commemorative parades, and memorabilia on the formation of Irish common memory and cultural identity. The controversies over how to commemorate Easter week demonstrates the public's vigilance in shaping how the Rising, and its role in the 'Story of Ireland', gets represented. Critiques of the republican cult of martyrdom mounted in the run-up to the jubilee and became more passionate during the Troubles, when the IRA cited republican ideology to justify the armed struggle to undo partition. Although these debates stimulated prolonged historiographical discourse over the 'revisionist' turn envisaged in Foster's 'Story of Ireland' critique, they exerted little influence on the subject matter of contemporary historical novels.[24] Instead, the most notable pattern in mid-century fiction is the preponderance of family sagas. Before turning to them, however, I would like to examine some exceptions to the general trend: novels that recreate the violence of Easter week and address its First World War context.

THE RISING AND THE FIRST WORLD WAR

Although early fiction about 1916 deals with the impact of the First World War, and with the mixed response toward the Rising-within-the-War from a public which already had deeply opposed views about Irish participation in the British war effort, the World War context is sidelined in later fiction because novelists adopted the restricted purview of Free State Ireland. Irish Volunteers who survived the horrors of trench warfare arrived home to be treated as veterans of the wrong war in the nationalist south and as heroes in the unionist north. The Rising is conspicuously overlooked north of the border, where '1916' became shorthand for commemorations of the Battle of the Somme that were subsequently folded into the July Orange parades as a counter-myth to it. The post-Rising partitioning of the island is replicated in the unilateral provenance of literature about it.

Liam O'Flaherty's (1897–1984) action novel, *Insurrection* (1950), portrays a group of snipers charged with delaying the British troops' march on the city. Apart from the likeable captain, Michael Kinsella, they are a rag-tag bunch: George Stapleton, a garrulous aesthete eager to experience the extremity of war; Tommy Colgan, a truculent,

---

[24] For critical perspectives on the Rising seventy-five years after the event, see Máirín Ní Dhonnchadha and Theo Dorgan (eds), *Revising the Rising* (Derry: Field Day Publications, 1991).

cowardly youth; and the hero, Bartly Madden. The dull-witted and aimless Madden—at best the 'middling' hero envisioned by Lukács—is an accidental recruit, manoeuvred into the conflict by Mrs Colgan to protect Tommy. Hearing Pearse read the Proclamation embeds 'an abstract idea' that for the first time in Madden's life 'lit the fire of passion in his soul', a star-struck enrapture to 'the Idea' which also extends to his captain.[25] Madden's peasant brawn and devotion to the (always capitalized) Idea brings him to 'the ecstasy of the warrior'[26] more than once. O'Flaherty refashions the battle frenzy (*riarstradh*) of medieval epic in the primitivist garb of D. H. Lawrence: 'Madden's nostrils kept expanding and contracting as he looked down at [Kinsella's] corpse . . . like a wild stallion of the western desert that stops dead in his tracks before his herd of mares and rises up with forelegs bent, taut like a compressed spring, to stamp upon a coiled rattlesnake'.[27] Flat characterization restricts full treatment of the erotic drive behind the Rising's violence, however. By representing the ordinary proletarian rather than the exceptional or dashing soldier, O'Flaherty counters idealizations of the 'glory' of heroism, as he previously did in his 1929 novel about the trenches, *The Return of the Brute*.

The competing claims of the Rising-within-the-War is the subject of Sebastian Barry's (1955–) *A Long Long Way* (2005), which details the squalid and brutish experience of Private Willie Dunne from his birth in Dublin in 1896 to his death in Flanders in October 1918. Crushed that his short stature prevents him from following his father, a Castle Catholic, into the Dublin Metropolitan Police, Willie joins the Royal Dublin Fusiliers. In late April 1916, as Willie and his regiment are about to return to the Front after their furlough, they are suddenly ordered to disembark at the Dublin docks and counterattack an unidentified enemy in the city centre. Surrounded by dead Tommies at Mount Street Bridge, Willie and his comrades are bewildered. 'Is it us against us?' one asks in angry consternation when he reads the Proclamation's reference to 'our gallant allies in Europe', and another weeps when he realizes that members of his own regiment are mowing down 'our fellas'.[28] Willie himself comforts a dying young rebel, whose blood leaves an indelible stain on his uniform. Two days later, back at the Front, Willie kills a German soldier who comes over the top during a gas attack at Hulloch; most of his battalion is wiped out. When Willie expresses sympathy for the insurrectionists in a letter home, his father shuns him. Divided allegiances are focalized through Willie's relationship with Jesse Kirwan, court-martialled and shot for conscientious abstention in support of the Rising. The enormity of the Great War dwarfs the comparatively minor losses of the Rising. The disparity between the furore over executing the Rising's leaders and the summary execution enacted against Kirwan (and shell-shocked deserters) is left to speak for itself.

The indirect yet devastating impact of war on women's lives was complicated by mixed allegiances toward the competing claims of the Rising and the World War. Furthermore, the gender divide between male combat and women's auxiliary roles

[25] Liam O'Flaherty, *Insurrection* (Boston, MA: Little, Brown, 1951), 30.   [26] Ibid., 168.
[27] Ibid., 233.   [28] Sebastian Barry, *A Long Long Way* (New York: Penguin, 2005), 90.

was exacerbated by the distance between the British and Irish 'home fronts' and the trenches in Europe. Lia Mills's *Fallen* (2014) is a 'testament of youth' complicated by the Rising. Katie is almost undone by the gulf separating the genteel constraints of her own life from the harrowing accounts of trench warfare in her slain twin's letters. The 'fallen' conceit couples her brother's possibly suicidal death with her half-witting, stricken attempt to contact a commensurate 'reality' through the loss of virginity. Against the unfolding insurrection, her growing intimacy with an angry wounded veteran enables a reckoning with the dark convergence of Eros and Thanatos enveloping them. Katie's first-person narration facilitates the indirect assimilation of historical fact into fiction, albeit at a cost of registering women's hardship as collateral damage. In Sheena Wilkinson's (1968–) *Name Upon Name* (2015), the polarizing impact of the Rising-within-the-War on the fifteen-year-old Helen's maternal Catholic and paternal Protestant relatives belatedly enables her to piece together the sectarian history behind the opaque righteous silences and veiled slights she has observed between them over the years. Her youthful point of view and fierce determination to maintain intimacy with both sides of her family credibly exposes the intractability of Northern sectarianism and the gulf separating rival nationalist and unionist versions of '1916'.

Women from *Cumann na mBan* (a paramilitary women's council) were key organizers of the Rising, and although several women were combatants, the paternalistic Volunteers succeeded in restricting most of them to auxiliary roles.[29] The Gifford sisters, the subject of Marita Conlon-McKenna's (1956–) *Rebel Sisters* (2016), chafe against the restrictive alternatives of subaltern or domestic angel. They include Nellie, a member of the Irish Citizen Army who fights with Countess Constance Markievicz at St Stephen's Green; Muriel, Thomas MacDonagh's wife; and Grace, who marries Joseph Plunkett on the eve of his execution. However, the rather flat characterization and Conlon-McKenna's reluctance to probe the sisters' ambivalences about their respective situations means that the novel reads more like a fictionalized group biography than an autonomous work of fiction.

Countess Markievicz features prominently as a combatant leader in fictional and historical representations of the Rising. That said, her cameo appearances in historical novels tend to emphasize her glamorous celebrity in ways that compound her outlier status when compared with the authoritative cameos of her male counterparts. A founding member of Na Fianna Éireann (a paramilitary scouting organization) and the Irish Citizen Army, and a garrison captain at St Stephen's Green, Markievicz was condemned to death with the other leaders. Because her death sentence was commuted due to her sex, however, she is excluded from the highest strata of the heroic pantheon. This chivalric exclusion renders the sacrificial martyrdom that transforms the citizen into a founding 'father' as an exclusively male prerogative, and elides women's contribution to the Rising.

[29] See Margaret Ward, *Unmanageable Revolutionaries: Women and Irish Nationalism* (London: Pluto Press, 1989).

THE RISING AND THE FAMILY SAGA

The family saga allows jubilee novelists of the mid-1960s to bridge the intervening fifty years and to explore how family and national histories enmesh. Legends flourished about the Rising even before it concluded, making it a storied event when first encountered by many people. The Rising first intrudes on the Galway Duane family in Walter Macken's (1915–67) *The Scorching Wind* (1964) when the Fenian schoolmaster-father is wrongfully (and, for him, flatteringly) arrested as a suspected organizer. Duane had clashed with his sons over their resistance to his republican zeal, but they are radicalized by Black and Tan violence and their father's untimely death. The restoration of filial ideological continuity is derailed by the fratricidal violence of the Civil War, however, when the anti-Treaty Dominic is killed in a shoot-out led by Dualta, a Free Stater.

The postcolonial tension surrounding changing class relations between the rising Catholic bourgeoisie and the *déclassé* Anglo-Irish caste is the dominant theme of family sagas. In Peadar O'Donnell's (1893–1986) *There Will Be Fighting* (1931), pre-war fears of oncoming change leads to the ostracism of the upwardly mobile Catholic Godfrey-Dhu family in the Orange stronghold of the Laggan. In order to impress his beloved, Nuala Godfrey-Dhu, Orangeman Sam Rowan leads his neighbours to rescue her brother from prison. The romantic outcome suggests that while it is possible, the odds are nonetheless stacked against romances-across-the-divide and neighbourly solidarity overcoming sectarian hostility.

Seán O'Faoláin's (1900–91) *A Nest of Simple Folk* (1934) and Eilís Dillon's (1920–94) *Blood Relations* (1977) imply that tribal allegiances outlast inter-denominational romances through the device of an informer. Although the informer trope recurs in novels about the Anglo-Irish War and Civil War, and may indirectly allude to the secrecy surrounding the Rising, here it represents abiding sectarian mistrust. The class fluidity produced by violent upheaval broadens the marriage prospects of the shabby-genteel Molly Gould in *Blood Relations*, yet she baulks at marrying a cultured gentleman of Connemara peasant stock. O'Faoláin's wayward and unheroic Leo Foxe-Donnel attributes his Fenian radicalism to rebelling against his maternal Anglo-Irish family's machinations to reappropriate their distaff heritage.[30] Leo's grandnephew Denis likewise feels suffocated as the object of his father's social ambition, and rebels when he learns that his father betrayed Leo. Class aspiration is seen as betraying 'true' republicanism.

Iris Murdoch's (1919–99) sole foray into historical fiction, *The Red and the Green* (1965), filters her Anglo-Irish heritage and outsider status through cousins Andrew, a visiting English officer, and Frances, who by the time she narrates the novel's 1930s coda is an expatriate with an English family. The novel focuses on the internal debates and moral dilemmas of Millie, an eccentric lady rebel; her Catholic nephew Pat Dumay,

---

[30] Seán O'Faoláin, *A Nest of Simple Folk* (New York: Carol Publishing, 1990), 158.

an Irish Volunteer; and the bumbling scholar Barney. The action reveals them to be self-isolating narcissists, blind to their self-deceptions. Millie and Pat are objects of desire for several members of this 'practically incestuous'[31] family. The climax occurs on Easter Sunday night, the interregnum between the planned and actual Rising, when four suitors converge on Millie's home. Millie deflowers Andrew. They are interrupted by Dumay, apparently intent on acquaintance rape to vent his rage over the cancelled Rising. Barney and Chris are next to arrive. Inverting the nostrum that 'England's difficulty is Ireland's opportunity', Chris vainly hopes that 'Millie's [financial] difficulty would be Christopher's opportunity'.[32] The failed orgy alludes to Raymond Queneau's *We Always Treat Women Too Well* (1947), in which Gertie Girdle, accidentally detained in the toilet of the GPO, seduces the rebels, all named after characters from *Ulysses*.[33] *The Red and the Green* inscribes Murdoch's work into Irish literature by making it densely intertextual, especially toward Joyce and Yeats, and placing it in a radical tradition through the coda's linkage of 1916 to the republican cause in the Spanish Civil War.

Macken's trilogy and the novels by O'Faoláin and Dillon extend back from 1916 to post-Famine Ireland. By contrast, Morgan Llywelyn's (1937–) *1916: A Novel of the Irish Rebellion* (1998), the first in a five-volume series on the Irish twentieth century, connects the Rising with the Troubles. Ned Halloran, an orphaned survivor of the Titanic and a former student at St Enda's, is a central witness-participant in the Rising. The transatlantic frame of *1916* offers a rare émigré perspective on the insurrection, as his sister Kathleen's changing relationship to her homeland alienates her from her uncomprehending Scotch-Irish husband. Whereas Ned is formed by the 'cult of boyhood' fostered by St Enda's and Na Fianna Éireann,[34] the boy protagonists in Rising-centred novels by Gerard Whelan (1957–) and Roddy Doyle (1958–) hail from Dublin's tenements, then the worst in Europe, and are shaped by the labour politics of the 1913 Lockout. In *The Guns of Easter* (1996), Whelan's children's novel, Jimmy dodges through the besieged city to salvage food for his family. Gazing on her sleeping son who 'had spent this week fighting in her war', Lily Conway reflects on how her 'fight to feed her children and keep her family whole and safe . . . [is] a war just as old and just as dangerous as any fought by men, and the results of losing in that war were just as terrible'.[35]

The title of Doyle's *A Star Called Henry* (1999) alludes to how Henry Smart is a replacement for a namesake brother who died in infancy. The novel accentuates the disposability of Dublin's slum children by having Henry's younger brother Victor die also. 'There should be something in there about the rights of children', Henry opines when consulted by James Connolly about the Proclamation, and 'cherishing all the children of the nation equally' is duly inserted.[36] Despite how Éamon de Valera in particular strove to

[31] Iris Murdoch, *The Red and the Green* (New York: Viking, 1965), 18.   [32] Ibid., 71.

[33] See Margaret Scanlan, *Traces of Another Time: History and Politics in Postwar British Fiction* (Princeton, NJ: Princeton University Press, 1990), 27–35.

[34] See Elaine Sisson, *Pearse's Patriots: St Enda's and the Cult of Boyhood* (Cork: Cork University Press, 2004).

[35] Gerard Whelan, *The Guns of Easter* (Dublin: O'Brien Press, 1996), 165.

[36] Roddy Doyle, *A Star Called Henry* (Toronto: Vintage, 1999), 109–10.

naturalize the new nation-state through association with the family—evident in the exaltation of the patriarchal (uppercase) 'Family' as a sacrosanct social unit in the 1937 Constitution—mid-century family sagas do not address the discrepancy between official pieties about family and the negligible resources allocated to family welfare. For Doyle, the Rising's revolutionary potential is hijacked by bourgeois Volunteers who 'detest the slummers'.[37] A plot twist clinches the anti-bourgeois polemic: Henry discovers that the men he had assassinated during the Anglo-Irish War as purported spies had been framed by a 'respectable' crime lord and Volunteer benefactor because they had married women from his brothel. By making what Samuel Beckett's (1906–89) *Murphy* (1938) lampoons as 'the holy ground'[38] of the GPO into a setting for wild sex, Doyle punctures pious nationalism with irreverent mockery. There, Henry and Miss O'Shea, his former teacher and future wife, encounter one another for the first time since he was nine. Their astonishing sexual prowess winks at the prodigious sexuality of mythic heroes and heroines, while the titillating conflation of classroom and bedroom—their tryst is peppered with exclamations of 'maithiú' (good for you)—gratifies adult–schoolchild fantasies.

THE RISING AND NARRATIVES OF HOMOSEXUAL DESIRE

The greatest recent attitudinal change in Irish society has been the rapid shift from a deeply homophobic and closeted society through the 1980s to becoming the first country to legalize same-sex marriage by popular vote in 2015. Public interest in the Rising's homoerotic overtones has grown in concert with the ongoing recuperation of hidden homosexual stories and histories.[39] A muted yet persistent rumour about a homoerotic subtext for Patrick Pearse's attraction to young boys has settled into a consensus that Pearse sublimated his probably unadmitted homoeroticism into his aspirations for St Enda's school and for Irish independence. A legible, albeit unheeded, history of lesbian insurgents, including prominent figures like Dr Kathleen Lynn and Elizabeth O'Farrell, has been edited out of the Rising's history until recently.[40] The Rising's most conspicuous homosexual story was the pillorying of international human rights advocate and nationalist separatist Sir Roger Casement, after the prosecution in his trial leaked the controversial Black Diaries, which detailed his homosexual activities.[41]

---

[37] Ibid., 117.   [38] Samuel Beckett, *Murphy* (London: Picador, 1973), 28.

[39] For a perspective relevant to Jamie O'Neill's cultural context, see Éibhear Walshe, 'Sexing the Shamrock', *Critical Survey* 8, no. 2 (1996), 159–67.

[40] See Louisa McGrath, 'It's time to acknowledge the lesbians who fought in the Easter Rising', *Dublin Inquirer*, 25 November 2015. https://www.dublininquirer.com/2015/11/25/Remembering-the-lesbians. Accessed 8 August 2017.

[41] See Lucy McDiarmid on the successive 'remoralisations' of Casement in 'The Afterlife of Roger Casement', in *The Art of Controversy* (Ithaca, NY: Cornell University Press, 2005), 167–210.

Mario Vargas Llosa's novel about Casement, *The Dream of the Celt* (2010), is a counter-example to Lukács's dictum against making a major historical figure the protagonist of a historical novel. Llosa responds to the challenge by keeping his meticulously researched fiction close to the historical record, a costly choice because the sources are such a gruelling read. Casement's reports on the horrific abuse of indigenous workers by depraved rubber barons in the Congo and Peru are repugnant to contemplate, and a comparable sense of quantitative overload is induced by the Black Diaries' shorthand logging of sexual encounters. The task of characterizing 'Roger', as Llosa refers to *Dream*'s protagonist, is complicated by the contradictory tendencies to expose and conceal, champion and exploit, in the juxtaposed archives. In a poignant example of the novelist revising history, Llosa supports his claim in the epilogue that Casement 'wrote certain things [in the Diaries] because he would have liked to live them but couldn't', by inserting unconvincing 'proof' in the novel of Roger recording fantasized non-events.[42]

Valiant Gentlemen (2016) by Australian-American novelist Sabina Murray narrates Casement's life from the perspective of his long friendship with English sculptor and colonial adventurer Herbert Ward and his wife Sarita Sanford Ward, an Argentinian-American heiress with family ties to the Sanford Exploration Expedition, in whose employ Ward and Casement first met in 1886. Murray's fictional license is that unbeknown to him, Ward was the undeclared love of Casement's life. Much of the novel is focalized through Sarita, whose frank and loving relationships with both men allow her to observe the Casement–Ward friendship with equanimity and compassion. Recounting a conversation to Casement about she and Herbert's desire to name their third son after him, for example, Sarita uses the ambiguity of her comment that 'men like [Casement] don't marry'[43] to gently convey—all without seeming to tell anything—that she knows his secret and won't divulge it to her oblivious husband.

I conclude this chapter with a discussion of Jamie O'Neill's (1962–) *At Swim, Two Boys* (2001) because this multilayered *Bildungsroman* encompasses so many features of 1916 fiction. The friendship between the sheltered Jim Mack and the working-class Doyler evolves into a loving homosexual relationship over the course of a year, during which they learn the suppressed history of their sexuality from a Wildean mentor, Anthony MacMurrough. In the spring of 1915, the boys make a pledge to swim to Muglins rock in Dublin Bay on Easter Sunday 1916, which the delayed Rising frees them to do. MacMurrough, who has returned to his Aunt Eveline's home after serving two years in prison for sodomy, is editing a treatise by his late mentor-lover Scrotes, which seeks to dismantle the association of Greek love with perversity. Eveline, a rebel aristocrat like Markievicz and Lady Jane Wilde (1821–96), seeks to rehabilitate Anthony and to restore the MacMurrough clan's patriotic reputation through nationalist activism. Watching St Enda's boys in a pageant at Eveline's garden fête, MacMurrough is laconic about Pearse's charisma 'with his own blush of boys', even as he answers his question about

---

[42] Mario Vargas Llosa, *The Dream of the Celt*, trans. Edith Grossman (New York: Picador, 2010), 355, 234.
[43] Sabina Murray, *Valiant Gentlemen* (New York: Grove Press, 2016), 231.

how Pearse 'make[s] those boys love him so' by seeking the schoolmaster's approval.[44] MacMurrough's admiration for the 'aloof' *paedeia* at St Enda's, and gratitude for how Scrotes's radical 'kindness' healed his abject sense of being 'kindless', emphasize the importance of inspirational mentoring in enabling upcoming generations to thrive.[45] *At Swim, Two Boys* offers hidden-in-plain-sight genealogies for alternative family formations. The 'cherishing all of the children of the nation equally' precept is fulfilled when Mr Mack's empathy for a fellow orphan overrules his exorbitant need for social respectability, and Jim's late brother's girlfriend and child are accepted into his family.

Sexual maturation is greatly complicated for both boys by the apparent absence of any narrative within which to situate their sexual desires or to suggest that they are not alone in experiencing them. When MacMurrough replies to Doyler's query, 'Is there many about that likes what you do?', by saying that he had a friend, Scrotes, who believed 'That we existed, he and I, and others like us', this is news even to the street-savvy Doyler.[46] Notwithstanding this invisibility, it isn't news to Doyler that homosexual relations are thoroughly interpellated by money and class: he likens his relationship with MacMurrough to that of a tart with a 'nob'.[47] When MacMurrough presses Jim on 'what is Ireland that you should want to fight for it', Jim replies, 'It's Doyler', adding: 'I know Doyler will be out, and where would I be but out beside him', with 'out' conveying more than one kind of solidarity.[48] Jim goes on to explain that 'it's like we have a language together', and then adds: 'You're a part of my country too now, MacEmm.'[49]

At Swim's distinctive vernacular is at once densely intertextual and decidedly demotic. It draws upon, and extends, an unmistakably Irish—and more specifically Dublin—literary vernacular in which Joyce, Oscar Wilde (1854–1900), and (as the title emphasizes) Flann O'Brien (1911–66) are especially prominent. *At Swim*'s variegated sociolects—the banter and in-jokes of best mates; the absurd affectations of Mr (Malaprop) Mack; MacMurrough's witty repartee with his aunt and philosophical disquisitions with Scrotes—are carefully calibrated by O'Neill. For example, Jim feigns 'do be' instead of 'does' to elide his class difference from Doyler, even as he chafes against his father's insistence that he address him as 'Papa' in order to emulate his social betters at grammar school. Markers of class, nationality, and sexual orientation commingle and interact, and sometimes transcode one another. When MacMurrough is asked if he is 'an unspeakable of the Oscar Wilde sort', he deflects and flips the question by affirming that he is Irish.[50] The quotable textual effect is reinforced by how the *cognoscenti*'s literary intertexts jostle and overlap with the vulgate's clichés, proverbial turns of phrase, and expressions of endearment. A marvellous example is how O'Neill queers the 1798 United Irishmen's clandestine passcode, 'as straight as a rush', into the boys' private language: 'Are you straight so?' 'I'm as straight as a rush.'[51] The greeting is so deliciously queer that

[44] Jamie O'Neill, *At Swim Two, Boys* (New York: Scribner, 2001), 322, 326.   [45] Ibid., 322, 269.
[46] Ibid., 280, 283.   [47] Ibid., 286.   [48] Ibid., 435.   [49] Ibid.   [50] Ibid., 309.
[51] Ibid., 337.

it has been assimilated into an international gay argot, an improbable repurposing of an eighteenth-century watchword.

At Swim retrospectively highlights the centrality of male bonding to 1916 (and to 1798's *fraternité*). Eveline has an epiphany at Easter Sunday mass when she notices the collar of a Volunteer uniform under an altar server's vestments: 'And it seemed of a sudden that [her nephew's] love should be so. Inevitable that such love should send him to war. Inevitable as war was inevitably male.'[52] Notwithstanding deep personal chagrin that she could never reach this male preserve, Eveline drifts into imagining 'Casement and Pearse and her nephew, each feasting upon this lad'[53] as they kneel before the doomed youth. While the three men's ardent 'feasting' is sexual, the onlookers' gaze is broadened by Eveline to encompass the admiring elegiac dread and ambivalent resignation with which patriotic young volunteers were regarded throughout Europe at the time. Jim's simple 'and where would I be but out beside him' (or them) was echoed by thousands of soldiers returning to the Front; by Volunteers who disagreed with the Rising's timing but joined anyway; and by the public who chose to be 'out' with the Rising's leaders once the executions began.

By entwining the boys' exploits in 1916 with Ireland's, the homosexual and national emancipatory plots each support the other, not least by disclosing how enmeshed they already were. The variegated intertextuality of *At Swim, Two Boys* displays the many allegorical levels, recurrent plotlines, and generic registers in which the Rising serves as an intertext in Ireland's culture and in literature about 1916. The boys' swim to Muglins is a means to pledge their troth and to risk their lives laying claim to a 'country' and a 'language' wherein they may 'exist'. The allegorical rite of passage queers the sovereignty plot underpinning the *aisling* that meant so much to Pearse, Plunkett, and other insurrectionists who subscribed to it. Doyler and Jim's earnest reliance on ritual and sacred symbols from their culture (the Easter date, the flag, and the proxy Starry Plough token) discloses the mythopoeic burden of their ordeal, a conjunction of story, deed, and symbol evident in the mythopoeic Rising. And the commixture of critique and sentimentality in O'Neill's frequent tonal shifts and code-switching dialogue shows the diverse repository of intertexts that together comprise the fictional, popular, and political afterlives of the Easter Rising.

FURTHER READING

Beiner, Guy. 'Making Sense of Memory: Coming to Terms with Conceptualisations of Historical Remembrance'. In Richard S. Grayson and Fearghal McGarry (eds), *Remembering 1916: The Easter Rising, the Somme and the Politics of Memory in Ireland*. Cambridge: Cambridge University Press, 2016: 13–23.

Cahalan, James. *Great Hatred, Little Room: The Irish Historical Novel*. Syracuse, NY: Syracuse University Press, 1983.

---

[52] Ibid., 543.   [53] Ibid.

Farquharson, Danine. *Novels of the Easter Rising: An Annotated Bibliography.* http://www.mun.ca/easter1916/index.php

Foster, John Wilson. *Irish Novels 1890–1940: New Bearings in Culture and Fiction.* Oxford: Oxford University Press, 2008.

Foster, R. F. *The Irish Story: Telling Tales and Making It Up in Ireland.* London: Allen Lane/Penguin, 2002.

Higgins, Róisín. *Transforming 1916: Meaning, Memory and the Fiftieth Anniversary of the Easter Rising.* Cork: Cork University Press, 2012.

Kiberd, Declan. *Inventing Ireland: The Literature of the Modern Nation.* London: Jonathan Cape, 1995.

Lacey, Brian. *Terrible Queer Creatures: Homosexuality in Irish History.* Dublin: Wordwell Books, 2015.

Lee, J. J. *Ireland 1912–1985: Politics and Society.* Cambridge: Cambridge University Press, 1989.

Leerssen, Joep. *Remembrance and Imagination: Patterns in the Historical and Literary Representation of Ireland in the Nineteenth Century.* Cork: Cork University Press, 1997.

Lukács, Georg. *The Historical Novel,* trans. Hannah and Stanley Mitchell. Lincoln, NE: University of Nebraska Press, 1983.

McDiarmid, Lucy. *The Irish Art of Controversy.* Dublin: Lilliput Press, 2005.

Ní Dhonnchadha, Máirín and Theo Dorgan (eds). *Revising the Rising.* Derry: Field Day Publications, 1991.

O'Leary, Philip. *The Prose Literature of the Gaelic Revival, 1881–1921: Ideology and Innovation.* University Park, PA: Pennsylvania State University Press, 1994.

Sisson, Elaine. *Pearse's Patriots: St Enda's and the Cult of Boyhood.* Cork: Cork University Press, 2004.

Townshend, Charles. *Easter 1916: The Irish Rebellion.* London: Allen Lane, 2005.

Wallace, Diane. *The Woman's Historical Novel: British Women Writers, 1900–2000.* Basingstoke: Palgrave Macmillan, 2005.

Ward, Margaret. *Unmanageable Revolutionaries: Women and Irish Nationalism.* London: Pluto Press, 1989.

Wills, Clair. *Dublin 1916: The Siege of the GPO.* London: Profile Books, 2009.

CHAPTER 25

IRISH LITERARY CINEMA

KEVIN ROCKETT

If evidence were needed of the importance of literature, and particularly fiction, to Irish cinema, then perusal of the 2016 Academy Award nominations reveals the continuing importance of literary adaptations. Prominent on the shortlists were the adaptations of Emma Donoghue's (1969–) 2010 novel, *Room* (2015), directed by Lenny Abrahamson, which received four nominations, including one for Donoghue herself for best adapted screenplay, and Colm Tóibín's (1955–) 2009 novel, *Brooklyn* (2015), directed by John Crowley, which was nominated for three Oscars. Both films were also in the running for the prestigious Best Picture award, although *Room*'s lead actress Bree Larsen was the only one to win an Oscar.[1] Not since 1990, when Jim Sheridan's adaptation of Christy Brown's (1932–81) autobiography, *My Left Foot* (1954), was nominated in five categories, winning two, have Irish writers been so honoured.[2] Even though in the intervening years only novelist and director Neil Jordan (1950–) has won a feature film Oscar—for his original screenplay for *The Crying Game* in 1993—such is the centrality of literary adaptation to discussions of Irish film that Cork University Press, in association with the Irish Film Institute, devoted a twelve-book series, 'Ireland into Film' (2001–07), to Irish literary adaptations for the screen.

Ironically, the critical and commercial success of most Irish literary works in the cinema has been as a result of screenplays generated by American or British writers who have otherwise not produced Irish-themed writing. For example, it was English novelist and screenwriter Nick Hornby who was nominated for an Oscar for adapting the screenplay of *Brooklyn*, while American Frank S. Nugent was the adaptor of Maurice Walsh's (1879–1964) 1933 short story that led to the landmark film, *The Quiet Man* (1952), the release date of which coincides with *Brooklyn*'s period setting.

---

[1] Worldwide, *Room* took, to April 2016, $35,401,758 at the box office, of which $14,677,654 was earned in the USA. *Brooklyn* was even more successful, taking $62,026,790 worldwide, of which $38,273,392 was collected at the US box office.

[2] For a discussion of *My Left Foot*, see Ruth Barton, *Jim Sheridan: Framing the Nation* (Dublin: Liffey Press, 2002), 15–38.

The often unacknowledged work of such literary adaptors has sometimes disguised what distinguishes a film from its literary origins because, after all, screen credits usually state that a film is *based* on a particular book or story rather than specify that it is an *adaptation* of it. Nevertheless, as Deborah Cartmell argues, the issue ought to be the separation of adaptation studies from 'fidelity criticism'.[3] Cinema's industrial dynamics and narrative conventions almost always demand something other than a faithful adaptation, as a result of which a book may or may not be true to its literary origins.

In what follows, three main themes are addressed in assessing the history of the adaptation of Irish literary fiction. The first part of the chapter examines the influence of the cinema and cinema-going on authors as recorded in their memoirs and literary output, and the influence of cinematic form on narrative structure, the latter being most evident in the later work of James Joyce (1882–1941). A second strand examines notions of female agency as they are refracted through the lens of the migrant experience in the novels of Edna O'Brien (1930–) and Maeve Binchy (1939–2012), and in Tóibín's *Brooklyn*. Finally, the post-independence legacy, as depicted in adaptations of the novels and short stories of John McGahern (1934–2006) and William Trevor (1928–2016) in particular, is discussed as a means of revealing the predicament of those who were psychically frozen during this period of economic, social, and cultural stagnation.

FORMED BY THE CINEMA

There are a number of points where the work of Irish novelists and short story writers may intersect with or be influenced by the cinema. The most obvious of these occurs when writers record their early cinema-going experiences and when these memories become the basis for plots and scenarios in their fictional works. Most transparent, perhaps, is William Trevor's memoir, *Excursions in the Real World* (1993), in which he recalls the 'magnificent array of cinemas'[4] in Cork city and cites a range of films made between 1936, when he was eight, and his turning sixteen in 1944. In recalling how he fell in love with actress Barbara Stanwyck, Trevor records how the cinema 'provided an influence that cut deeper, and has lasted longer, than schoolroom information about trade winds and the rhomboid'.[5] Such experiences later found their way into his fiction, as evidenced by 'The Death of Peggy Meehan', which was first published as 'The Death of Peggy Morrissey' in *The Distant Past and Other Stories* (1979). Set in 1936, it tells the story of a

---

[3] Cited in Lance Pettitt, 'William Trevor's Screen Fictions: "No Interest. Not Suitable for Treatment"', in Paul Delaney and Michael Parker (eds), *William Trevor: Revaluations* (Manchester: Manchester University Press, 2013), 76.
[4] William Trevor, *Excursions in the Real World* (London: Hutchinson, 1993), 10.   [5] Ibid., xv.

seven-year-old boy living in the grip of an over-protective mother who forbids him from going to the cinema. Ironically, it is only when he is left in the care of young Father Parsloe that freedom beckons. As is the case in many of Trevor's short stories, the cinema gives access to fantasies previously forbidden, even if the child finds it difficult to understand the film's narrative twists. In this story, the film features an extra-marital subplot in which a husband has an affair, but in the tradition of Hollywood's meting out of retribution to transgressors, the 'other woman' dies in a car crash, whereupon the man returns to his wife, who assures him repeatedly that all is well. Needless to say, the boy's father disapproves of the outing—the film 'wasn't suitable for a child'[6]–but this does not stop the son fantasizing about his own triangular relationship with contemporaries Claire and Peggy. The boy dreams of Peggy falling out of a car to her death, like the woman in the film, but in fact she dies of diphtheria. This event marks his later life as he retains a lifelong fascination with the dead girl, even imagining sexual relations with her as a forty-six-year-old bachelor. For the narrator of this unsettling tale, the fantasy of childhood is more vivid than present-day reality.

While this story's film reference could be applied to a range of films—it is a cross between *The Postman Always Rings Twice* (1946), in which a transgressive wife dies in a car crash, and *Brief Encounter* (1945), in which a wayward wife returns to her boring husband—the fact is that no film released in Ireland in 1936, or in 1946, when the aforementioned two films were banned, was allowed to represent extra-marital affairs.[7] Thus, the boy protagonist's—and Trevor's—memories of cinema-going need to be approached with a degree of circumspection (unless, of course, Trevor's memories are of seeing such films in England's less strict censorship environment). Such nostalgic longing for a lost youth in the cinema is not uncommon in Irish memoir and fiction, but what might be more productive to reflect on, perhaps, is how the formal orthodoxy of Hollywood film and the moral conservatism of the Irish cinema experience impacted on the type of narrative practices Trevor subsequently adopted.

In Trevor's novella, *Nights at the Alexandra* (1987), Harry, the fifty-eight-year-old narrator, looks back to his teenage years and to the opening of the town's cinema, remembering how potential patrons looking forward to seeing *Gone with the Wind* (1939), unaware of the Irish film censor's thirteen cuts to it.[8] Even truncated versions of Hollywood films offered a release from the stifling conformity of provincial Ireland in the post-independence decades of economic and ideological protectionism, where the act of cinema-going was itself a form of cultural resistance. Harry recalls how patrons would admire photographs of movie stars William Powell, Myrna Loy, and Carole Lombard on the cinema's balcony stairs, 'stopping to examine them, couples arm in arm,

---

[6] William Trevor, 'The Death of Peggy Meehan', in *The Collected Stories* (London: Penguin, 1993), 394–5.

[7] Kevin Rockett, *Irish Film Censorship: A Cultural Journey from Silent Cinema to Internet Pornography* (Dublin: Four Courts Press, 2004), 129–30.

[8] Ibid., 80–1.

the girls' voices full of wonder'.[9] 'People loved the Alexandra',[10] we are told, as much for the scarlet seats, lights that made the curtains change colour, and usherettes in uniform, as for the films themselves. Even the 'tetchiness' of the Reverend Wauchope softened 'beneath a weight of wonder', while the 'sour disposition' of his wife dissipated as she watched the real-life murder drama, *All This and Heaven Too* (1940).[11] The disturbing Gothic melodrama, *Rebecca* (1940), is the first film shown at the Alexandra, a sort of *mise-en-abyme* for its developers, the Messingers—the husband a sixty-two-year-old German, his second wife a twenty-seven-year-old Englishwoman—who find sanctuary in Ireland during the Second World War.[12] As in *Rebecca*, Harry 'knew that death was everywhere'[13] in their drawing-room, as Frau Messinger was dying, something which happens shortly after the cinema opens. Before then, she tasted 'its nights of pleasure',[14] but after her death Herr Messinger abandons the venue to Harry, who runs it until the cinema falls into disuse in the early 1960s.

Elizabeth Bowen (1899–1973), Trevor's Anglo-Irish predecessor, has more directly recorded her experience of filmic narrative and the cinema environment. Writing in 1938, she described how the cinema offered 'the delights of intimacy' with 'black-and-white personalities' on screen, and remarked that 'seldom in real-life (or so-called real life) does acquaintanceship, much less intimacy, with dazzling, exceptional beings come one's way'.[15] Indeed, such was the 'rapture' the characters on screen provoked in her that she felt that 'I not only perceive them but *am* them; their hopes and fears are my own; their triumphs exalt me'.[16] Cinema's immersive quality—a modernist concept—is perhaps what attracts writers and audiences generally, as it serves to displace the real or the mundane into a spectatorial and non-reflective experience. Bowen's reasons for going to the cinema stemmed from her desire to be 'distracted (or "taken out of myself")' and to not 'want to think'.[17] The cinema was for her 'an oblong opening into the world of fantasy' which offered the communal pleasure of sitting 'in a packed crowd in the dark, among hundreds riveted on the same thing'.[18] Yet for all the pleasure that Elizabeth Bowen and William Trevor derived from cinema-going, their cinema experiences and affinity for film did not explicitly find their way into the *form* of their writings.

The same cannot be said of James Joyce. When in December 1909 he opened the Volta cinema in Dublin, Ireland's first full-time cinema, Joyce chose as part of the inaugural programme Mario Caserini's film of that year, *The Tragic Story of Beatrice Cenci*, a retelling of a sixteenth-century Italian story of patricide, most famously explored by Percy Bysshe Shelley in his 1819 play, *The Cenci*. Giving a hint of future censorship controversies as cinema began to produce more transgressive narratives, the *Freeman's Journal*

---

[9] William Trevor, *Nights at the Alexandra* (London: Hutchinson, 1987), 64.
[10] Ibid.   [11] Ibid., 65.
[12] *Rebecca*, adapted from Daphne du Maurier's 1938 Gothic novel of that title, concerns how the second Mrs de Winter is tormented by the memory of Rebecca, Maxim de Winter's first wife, who died in mysterious circumstances.
[13] Trevor, *Nights at the Alexandra*, 53.   [14] Ibid., 57.
[15] Elizabeth Bowen, 'When I Go to the Cinema', in Charles Davy (ed.), *Footnotes to the Film* (London: Lovat Dickson, 1938), 213–14.
[16] Ibid., 214. Original emphasis.   [17] Ibid., 205.   [18] Ibid.

complained that it 'was hardly as exhilarating a subject as one would desire on the eve of the festive season'.[19] While Joyce did not stay long as manager of the Volta, his broader interest in the cinema had a lasting influence on him and his work; indeed, he noted that when obliged to keep his eyes closed following his frequent eye operations, he saw a cinematograph 'going on and on and it brings back to my memory things I had almost forgotten'.[20]

The most lasting and celebrated of these cinematic influences on Joyce has been the indebtedness of his 'stream of consciousness' mode of writing, particularly in *Ulysses* (1922), to the technique of cinematic montage. As Harry Levin put it, 'In its intimacy and its continuity, *Ulysses* has more in common with the cinema than with other fiction. The movement of Joyce's style, the thought of his characters, is like unreeling film.'[21] In this way, interior monologue could simulate cinematic montage as a means of exploring the psychic life of the characters. As Luke Gibbons notes, this was how Joyce also saw it, 'the very form of cinema acting as [a] kind of archive of the unconscious'.[22] So while Joyce sprinkled *Ulysses* and *Finnegans Wake* (1939) with film references, it is the manner in which he adopted cinematic form as part of his narrative strategy that distinguishes him from most other Irish writers, then or since. This in turn presented a challenge to those who wished to adapt his fiction for the screen. Whatever criticisms may be made of the adaptations of Joyce's work, a key measurement of success is the degree to which film-makers give effective cinematic form to the interior monologues in his fiction. While Joyce favoured the experimental Russian film director and theorist, Sergei Eisenstein, as the person best suited to adapt *Ulysses* for the screen, those who realized the Joycean challenge generally fell far short of requirements.

The adaptors of Joyce's quintessential modernist novel—most especially the 1967 version of *Ulysses* by Joseph Strick—not only failed to reimagine Joyce's text visually but also overlooked that book's foundational legacy to cinematic form itself. Only novelist Mary Manning, working with New York avant-garde artist and filmmaker Mary Ellen Bute to produce *Passages from James Joyce's 'Finnegans Wake'* (1967), envisaged a formally challenging work. Strick also made a version of *A Portrait of the Artist as a Young Man* in 1977 in which, as Gibbons points out, the director failed to relate *mise-en-scène* to narrative voice. While Strick faithfully recreated period detail, he failed to appreciate that Joyce was less interested in such faithfulness to 'inert surroundings' than to 'the points of view of those who inhabit them'.[23] Gibbons argues that one of the film's shortcomings is its 'literal textual expression' of the Parnellite subtext, something which 'is not relayed

---

[19] 'Volta Cinematograph', *Freeman's Journal*, 21 December 1909, 10. See Kevin Rockett, 'Something Rich and Strange: James Joyce, Beatrice Cenci and the Volta', *Film and Film Culture* 3 (2004), 21–34.

[20] James Joyce to Harriet Shaw Weaver, 27 June 1924, in Stuart Gilbert (ed.), *The Letters of James Joyce* (New York: Viking Press, 1957), vol. 1, 216.

[21] Harry Levin, *James Joyce: An Introduction* (London: Faber and Faber, 1960), 82. Cited in Luke Gibbons, '"The Cracked Looking Glass" of Cinema: James Joyce, John Huston, and the Memory of "The Dead"', *Yale Journal of Criticism* 15, no. 1 (2002), 127–8.

[22] Gibbons, '"The Cracked Looking Glass" of Cinema', 128.

[23] Luke Gibbons, *Joyce's Ghosts: Ireland, Modernism, and Memory* (Chicago, IL: Chicago University Press, 2015), 110.

visually as it is in Joyce's acoustic imagination', with the result that politics 'remains in the public sphere, narrowly conceived, whereas the underlying impulse of Joyce's narrative suggests that it is part of the innermost structures of feeling of the characters in the Dedalus household.'[24] It was only with John Huston's 1987 adaptation of Joyce's most famous short story, 'The Dead', that the writer's subtle political and personal themes were woven together, such that the writer's 'acoustic imagination' found its echo on screen. In his extended discussion of *The Dead*, Gibbons draws attention to the latent cinematic elements in Joyce's story that Huston brought to the surface.[25]

Unexpectedly, we can find echoes of this modernist sensibility in the most influential film of Irish migration, the aforementioned *The Quiet Man*.[26] Film studies scholarship has focused less on the story's 1920s contexts, whether political or socio-economic, than on the visual richness of Ford's reworking of the original story by Maurice Walsh. In that regard, the film's self-referentiality, even its premature postmodernism,[27] has been welcomed as a refreshingly 'modernist' destabilization of its putative romanticism and has contributed to its canonization as the most popular film ever made about Ireland and the Irish. That avant-gardist concern, which is rare when applied to a mainstream classical narrative film, puts *The Quiet Man* alongside a small collection of literary adaptations in which the form of expression breaks with the standard three-act drama of classical cinema.[28] It is to those formally more conventional, but occasionally thematically challenging, genre films we can now turn, beginning with an issue of central concern to contemporary scholarship and to feminist politics: female agency.

FEMALE AGENCY AND THE DESIRE TO ESCAPE

The cinema version of *Brooklyn* can be said to be more faithful than most to its source material. Nevertheless, the film downplays, and leaves ambiguous, elements that might be deemed to be mildly controversial in the cinema. These include the issue of race, a minor but important element in the novel, as shown when the nervous staff of the department store where Tóibín's heroine, Eilis Lacey, works have to serve African-Americans, as the shop moves to attract Brooklyn's new middle-class residents. Also, much reduced and modified in the film is the voyeuristic and even physically intrusive behaviour of the shop supervisor, the possibly lesbian Miss Fortini, who is described over three pages in the novel, as she manipulates Eilis into trying on bathing suits after

---

[24] Ibid., 111.   [25] Ibid., 112–37.

[26] As *The Quiet Man* has been extensively discussed, it hardly needs further exploration here. See especially Luke Gibbons, *The Quiet Man* (Cork: Cork University Press, 2002).

[27] See Martin McLoone, *Irish Film: The Emergence of a Contemporary Cinema* (London: British Film Institute, 2000), 52–9.

[28] Another such experimental film is *I Could Read the Sky* (1999), adapted by Nichola Bruce from the photographic novel of the same name by Timothy O'Grady and Steve Pyke, which features novelist Dermot Healy as an anonymous emigrant in England.

the store closes and observes her naked—something, of course, not permitted in this film genre. By drawing attention to these changes and omissions, the intention is not to criticize the film's sanitizing of Tóibín's rare incursions into controversial territory in his fiction but rather to highlight cinema's difference. After all, *Brooklyn* as a novel and a film is a romantic drama which, if written by a woman, might very well have been categorized (and denigrated) as 'chick lit'. Thus, it is perhaps best to approach the text within the terms of the broad genre of popular romantic drama and explore other literary adaptations which have as a central feature the issue of female agency, and in that regard *Brooklyn*'s Eilis can be contrasted with the young female protagonists in the fiction of Edna O'Brien and Maeve Binchy. What a great many of these novels have in common is their 1950s setting. *Brooklyn* is set in 1952, Binchy's *Circle of Friends* (1990) in 1949 and 1957, and O'Brien's early novels are mostly set in the 1950s and early 1960s.

On *Brooklyn*'s publication in 2009, much attention was paid to Eilis's agency and independence, as explored through Tóibín's depiction of her slowly developing self-awareness and coming of age. In the 2015 film version, actress Saoirse Ronan's facial expressions and sparse dialogue serve as the substitute for Eilis's inner (and often banal) reflections in the novel. Yet *Brooklyn* is a literary and filmic work in which Eilis's agency is hard to find as at every turn she is acted on rather being an agent of change. Her sister arranges for her to go to America; Father Flood organizes her American employment, accommodation, and night course; and her beau, Tony, expends great effort in wooing her. Eilis's passivity extends to sex, as shown when Tony's initiation and enjoyment of intercourse with her for the first time is represented as a physically painful experience for Eilis, meaning she is literally acted upon again, although the film wraps this scene in romantic trappings. Even though she is already married to Tony, on her return to Ireland Eilis drifts into a relationship with publican Jim Farrell, which could transform her social status. This relationship is only interrupted when the malicious shopkeeper, Miss Kelly, finds out about her marriage. At this critical juncture, however, Eilis finally asserts her independence to tell Miss Kelly that she had 'forgotten what this town was like', and then proudly reveals her married name—something she does not do in the novel. Nevertheless, Eilis is immediately propelled back to America, leaving the next day. Whereas there is considerable ambiguity in the heroine's re-emigration as explored by Tóibín in his novel, in Crowley's film, Eilis's memories of Jim are transformed by commercial cinema's generic convention—the happy ending—into an unambiguous embracing of Tony and the future *he* has mapped out for them in the Long Island suburbs. This ending contrasts with the novel's final reflective moments, which show Eilis on the train to the transatlantic liner, contemplating her future.

Edna O'Brien's screen heroines also remain close to the originals, not least because O'Brien adapted her own work for the screen. Her screenplays include *Girl with Green Eyes* (1964) from her 1962 novel, *The Lonely Girl*; *I Was Happy Here* (1965), a re-working of the short story, 'A Woman by the Seaside'; and *The Country Girls* (1983) from the 1960 novel of the same name. In addition to adapting her own work, O'Brien was served by directorial continuity in all three films, with director Desmond Davies also collaborating on the script of *I Was Happy Here*. In these films and works of fiction, O'Brien uses young Catholic women as mirrors in which repressive familial and clerical patriarchal norms are reflected, while at the same time depicting the painful paths to self-fulfilment, and even personal failure, encountered by these women in their relationships.

As was the case with her early novels, O'Brien's films had censorship difficulties, but as the films were being released the censorious Irish climate was changing. Since the beginnings of Irish film censorship in 1923, almost every film released had been given a general or universal certificate. Thus, when *Girl with Green Eyes* was viewed by the Irish film censor in April 1964, age classification of films had yet to be introduced to regulate viewers' access to work featuring adult themes which censors had long deemed objectionable, such as extra-marital affairs, sexual promiscuity, and depictions of female agency in general. As a result, the censor, Christopher Macken, followed his counterparts in publications' censorship and banned the film. It was, he noted in his report to the Censorship of Films Appeal Board, an 'unsavoury'[29] picture that was not fit to be shown in Ireland. The board agreed and upheld the ban, only for it to be lifted in 1970 when *Girl with Green Eyes* was awarded an over-16s certificate. Macken also banned *I Was Happy Here* in 1966 ('the whole tone of this presentation contravenes decency',[30] he wrote), but on this occasion a new appeals board overturned the decision and passed the film uncut with an over-18s certificate.

By the time *The Country Girls* was released in 1983, few films were being banned in the Republic. Although the last of the trilogy to be adapted for the screen, *The Country Girls* may be seen as the prototype of, or back story to, O'Brien's other heroines, as fourteen-year-old Kate Brady finds herself trapped on the family farm in rural Ireland with her alcoholic father and exhausted mother. Difficult as their lives elsewhere might subsequently become, Kate and her kind close off the option of returning to their home place permanently. In that regard, Kate's rejection of her father's authority, an important element in *The Lonely Girl*, is the action of a 'modernizing' and liberal-minded young woman who is looking to the future without familial, clerical, or patriarchal control. In line with commercial cinema's upward trajectory, Kate's escape to Dublin and eventually to London is seen as positive, notwithstanding the challenges that face the naïve young Clare girl as she grapples with romantic and sexual entanglements along the way. Yet O'Brien's 1986 epilogue to *The Country Girls* trilogy suggests that the heroine may not remain happy in her new urban environment (a theme also explored in *I Was Happy Here*). As in much female-centric Irish literature that has been adapted for the screen—a list that includes *Brooklyn* and *Circle of Friends*—emigration is often an uncertain avenue of escape for a pregnant, troubled, or unemployed girl.

Economic migration to England was no less urgent for a great many Irish males. Tellingly, however, a key omission in *Brooklyn*'s journey from page to screen is the

---

[29] Censor's report to Censorship of Films Appeal Board, 12 May 1964. Quoted in Rockett, *Irish Film Censorship*, 421. O'Brien's London-set novel, *Zee and Co*, adapted for the cinema in 1971, was cut due to its use of the 'f' word, a term which was only fully liberated in Irish writing with Roddy Doyle's novel, *The Commitments* (1987), the film version of which was released in 1990.

[30] Censor's report to Censorship of Films Appeal Board, 19 April 1966. Quoted in Rockett, *Irish Film Censorship*, 203.

exclusion of references to Eilis's three brothers being migrants in England, the youngest of whom comes to say goodbye to her in the novel as she awaits the boat in Liverpool that will take her to New York. *Brooklyn*'s cinematic trajectory would have had difficulty integrating into the narrative arc of this romantic drama such a raw experience of migration and the dark history of British colonialism in Ireland that was one of its drivers. By contrast, Eilis's sartorial transformation before entering America—discarding her Irish dowdiness for New World sexual attractiveness—and her radiant illumination as she leaves Ellis Island immigration station symbolize her entry into a world that will be dominated by consumerism, from lipstick and face cream to exotic foods and suburban living. In the end, Eilis's embracing of the New rather than the Old World is informed by the contrast between a parochial Irish economy and the attractions of a multicultural metropolitan society, captured in the gulf between the class-biased Enniscorthy grocery shop and the more democratic New York department store.

Maeve Binchy's *Circle of Friends*, which was adapted for the screen in 1995, is mainly set in 1957, when childhood friends Benny, Nan, and Eve experience the standard anxieties of romantic fiction, with family repression, unfaithful boyfriends, pregnancy, and hopeful futures as central ingredients. The film reflects a positive approach to female independence: pregnant Nan seeks a new life in England, while the central protagonist, Benny, not only recovers her estranged boyfriend but looks forward to a career as a writer. Notwithstanding its focus on independent female characters, the screen adaptation of *Circle of Friends* was seen as unashamedly aimed at the international film market. 'Barely a line of dialogue goes by', Ben Thompson commented, 'without a shifting backdrop of bustling period street-scene, a babbling brook or a misty hillside, while Michael Kamen's score wears its shamrock on its sleeve with almost comical commitment.'[31] Thompson added that the script by Andrew Davies, a prolific adaptor of period or heritage drama for television, 'has its fair share of tourist board Irishry',[32] while only one of the six main roles was played by an Irish actor.

Thompson raises an issue which is all too familiar in Irish film more generally: the need for a film to satisfy the demands of the commercial market, no matter how much this might neutralize or downplay culturally critical themes. Since the vast majority of big budget feature films made in and about Ireland are produced with the aid of international finance, the most obvious concession to market forces is to cast in Irish roles high profile non-Irish actors, who may not be able to capture the nuances of Irish speech. Perhaps the most grating example of this is the butchery of J. M. Synge's (1871–1909) lines by Welsh actor Gary Raymond as Christy Mahon in the 1962 film version of *The Playboy of the Western World* (1907). Furthermore, most of the films discussed here had non-Irish directors, an outcome which may occasionally have contributed to a productive distancing from the source material but which too often reveals an inability to explore the country's varied landscapes or appreciate its cultural and linguistic subtleties. The linguistic distinctiveness of a literary or dramatic source may also be modified by a non-Irish scriptwriter's transformation of local dialect into a more formal English or

---

[31] Ben Thompson, 'Circle of Friends', *Sight and Sound* 5 (1995), 42.   [32] Ibid.

American idiom, ostensibly to make it more 'comprehensible' or easier on the ear for non-Irish audiences. A further issue is the sanitization of demotic language deemed offensive to cinema audiences, a striking example of which is the translation of the politically incorrect and racially offensive word 'niggers' into 'blacks' in the film adaptation of Roddy Doyle's (1958–) 1987 novel, *The Commitments*.[33]

THE POST-INDEPENDENCE LEGACY

While 1950s and 1960s female writers sought to spirit away their protagonists from the stifling conformity of rural and small-town Ireland, John McGahern and William Trevor sought to excavate the undercurrents of the often twisted lives of those who remained behind, while at the same time exploring the psychic condition of the country. Although McGahern has garnered critical acclaim for his often forensic examination of family and community, the transfer of his work to the screen has been less assured than might have been expected. A number of his short stories and two of his novels have been adapted, mostly for the small screen. *Wheels* (1976), based on the short story of the same name and directed by Cathal Black, concerns the reluctance of a son to facilitate his father and stepmother moving to the city. McGahern's 1974 novel, *The Leavetaking*, was adapted as the forty-minute *The Lost Hour* (1982), directed by Sean Cotter, which depicts young Patrick Moran's mother's illness and death from cancer and his difficult relationship with his patriarchal policeman father. In what can be considered a sequel to *The Lost Hour*, the short story 'Bomb Box' was adapted as *The Key* (1983) and concerns Patrick's relationship with his father after his mother's death. The more prosaic *Swallows* (2000), directed by Michael O'Connell and based on the 1971 short story of the same title, focuses on the shared passion for the music of Niccolò Paganini of a rural policeman and a land surveyor.

None of these adaptations, however, had the impact of the critically acclaimed four-episode television adaptation of McGahern's *Amongst Women* (1990) in 1998. Set mainly in the 1950s, the novel explores a farming family ruled by an autocratic father, remarried widower Michael Moran, whose maxim is to expect nothing from life, materially or emotionally, a message he tries to instil in his five children, most of whom prosper with the help of their stepmother, Rose, who shields them from their father. Even when the children leave home and build lives in Dublin and London, the influence of their father is not shaken off. Yet Moran is not just an isolated, one-dimensional tyrant. An IRA volunteer during the War of Independence, he is also a product of independent Ireland and his bitterness is anchored, archetypically, in those complex experiences.

---

[33] In interview, Doyle has spoken of his unease with aspects of the adaptation of *The Commitments*. See *Irish Cinema: Ourselves Alone?* (1995), directed by Donald Taylor Black and written by Kevin Rockett. Doyle's other Barrytown novels, *The Snapper* (1990) and *The Van* (1991), were also adapted for the screen in 1993 and 1996 respectively, although *The Commitments* was to remain the more popular, and was the first film to take over one million pounds at the Irish box office.

Nor is Moran's authoritarianism absolute, as novel and film make clear. Drawing its energy, perhaps, from the emergence of a new generation of feminists in the 1980s, *Amongst Women* depicts the assertion of female agency and independence even within the constraints of a patriarchal order, in a similar manner to Brian Friel's (1929–2015) play, *Dancing at Lughnasa* (1990), the film version of which was also released in 1998.

While McGahern's earlier original screenplay for *The Rockingham Shoot* (1987) explores the legacy of violence in the post-independence era, like almost all films based on his fiction, it was produced for television. Only Cathal Black's 1995 adaptation of 'Korea' from McGahern's 1970 short story collection, *Nightlines*, was produced for the cinema. Set, like *Brooklyn*, in 1952, *Korea* explores residual Irish Civil War bitterness within the framework of the relationship of a young couple whose fathers fought on opposing sides in that conflict. John Doyle wants his son Eamon to emigrate to America, even if it means him being drafted into the US Army to fight in Korea, rather than have him continue a relationship with the daughter of his nemesis, Ben Moran, whose own son's body is returned to Ireland for burial after he is killed during the Korean War. Meanwhile, potential enlightenment for the post-independence generation is symbolized by the installation in the village of electricity, a marker of creeping modernity. A brighter, tourism-fuelled future beckons for the no-longer-isolated and 'dark' community.

Notwithstanding complaints that Irish cinema of the 1970s and 1980s was overly focused on rural social realism, what is perhaps surprising is that so few films actually dramatized social relations on the land, or even those of the Big House Anglo-Irish landlord class of an earlier era. The writer from an Anglo-Irish Protestant background who has proved most attractive to film and television producers has been William Trevor, although the literary and filmic output of the Belfast-born Catholic novelist Brian Moore (1921–99) has been no less impressive.[34] While Trevor has consistently explored the Big House world, his imagination has also been drawn to provincial Catholic society, even in the decades before those treated in McGahern's fiction.[35] Whatever the merits of his feature films and other productions, it is unquestionably the case that the greatest impact was made by Pat O'Connor's 1982 television adaptation of Trevor's 1972 short story, 'The Ballroom of Romance', winner of the Best Single Drama

---

[34] Almost half of Moore's twenty novels were adapted for the screen, although not all were concerned with Ireland. Moore was an adaptor of his own published work and a screenwriter of original material. He wrote the first draft of Alfred Hitchcock's *Torn Curtain* (1966), an experience that led to the director's unsympathetic portrayal as Bernard Boyari in Moore's 1970 novel, *Fergus*. Besides such projects, two of his novels, *The Luck of Ginger Coffey* (1960) and *The Lonely Passion of Judith Hearne* (1955), were adapted for the screen in 1964 and 1988 respectively. Although set in 1950s Belfast, *Judith Hearne*, directed by Jack Clayton, was relocated to Dublin, suggesting the malleability of literary texts in the hands of adaptors. Moore's *Catholics* (1972) and *The Temptation of Eileen Hughes* (1981) were adapted for television by Jack Gold and Tristram Powell respectively.

[35] For a list of forty-three of Trevor's film and television screenplays and adaptations, see the filmography in Delaney and Parker (eds), *William Trevor: Revaluations*, 214–15.

award at that year's British Academy of Film and Television Awards.[36] Focusing on sexual and material frustrations in 1950s rural Ireland, the ballroom is seen as an oasis of hope in the bleak lives of the central protagonists. It focuses on a spinster, thirty-six-year old Bridie, daughter of a small farmer, whose dreams of a romantic future were dashed long ago by the emigration to England of the youth she hoped to marry. By evening's end, such longing gives way to the reluctant acceptance that she will settle for a life with Bowser Egan, whose nickname alone reveals his uncouthness, while her own name adds an ironic, even mocking, twist to her marital ambitions.

Central to Trevor's oeuvre has been an exploration of the legacy of colonialism in Ireland. His 1994 novel, *Felicia's Journey*, can be read as an allegory of British–Irish relations in which the eponymous pregnant young Irish girl meets Joseph Hilditch, a serial killer rooted in Britain's imperial past, as she searches Birmingham's grim industrial landscape for Johnny Lysaght, the father of her unborn child, who unbeknownst to her has joined the British Army. Hilditch, who lures naïve Felicia into his sinister yet pathetic world, lives, ironically enough, on a road named after the first Duke of Wellington, Arthur Wellesley, the Irish-born hero of Waterloo. As she falls into the predatory trap of Hilditch, 'the embodiment of a malign residual colonialism,'[37] he convinces her to have an abortion, a decision which racks her with a guilt that is further reinforced by memories of her doctrinaire Catholic nationalist father. Nevertheless, it is Hilditch who suffers a psychotic breakdown after he fails to control the Irish girl and then becomes fearful that she is controlling him, a fear Trevor expresses in explicitly colonial terms: 'The Irish girl has invaded him, as territory is invaded.'[38] Switching places with her, he roams the streets, including visits to his childhood haunts, only to discover that they are now populated by Indians and Pakistanis. This postcolonial shock leads to the disturbance of Hilditch's long-buried memories of childhood sexual abuse by his mother, the return of a repressed past that mirrors the return of the legacies of Britain's imperial exploits overseas. In the end, both Hilditch, who commits suicide, and Felicia, who survives only to become a wandering homeless girl, are seen as victims, and in Trevor's fictional universe sympathy is extended to both of these hapless beings.

The 1999 film adaptation of *Felicia's Journey* brings into stark relief how a director with a distinctive authorial signature—in this case, Canadian filmmaker Atom Egoyan—can adapt a novel to his particular concerns, stripping out, for example, the underlying postcolonial discourse of the novel.[39] Egoyan claimed that the version of Ireland depicted in the novel was no longer evident when he was making the film in the

---

[36] For a discussion of Trevor's engagement with television, and a comparison of the story and the adaptation of 'The Ballroom of Romance', see Pettitt, 'William Trevor's Screen Fictions', 76–91.

[37] Liam Harte and Lance Pettitt, 'States of Dislocation: William Trevor's *Felicia's Journey* and Maurice Leitch's *Gilchrist*', in Ashok Bery and Patricia Murray (eds), *Comparing Postcolonial Literatures: Dislocations* (London: Macmillan, 2000), 73.

[38] William Trevor, *Felicia's Journey* (London: Viking, 1994), 179.

[39] See Richard Porton, 'The Politics of Denial: An Interview with Atom Egoyan', *Cineaste* 25, no. 1 (1999), 39–41.

late 1990s. Consequently, he produced a film which neutered the political and allegorical power of the novel, while at the same time foregrounding the director's interest in post-modern reflexivity, such that postmodernism's scepticism about the capability of 'history' or the past to exert any force other than through texts is brought to the fore, as Stephanie McBride observes in her analysis of the film.[40] In that regard, Egoyan's interest in 'showing the frame as well as the picture'[41] allows for his exploration of recurring themes such as dislocation and character motivation. Thus, the film's roaming camera movements across Hilditch's fake imperial mementoes, and its use of videotape record-ings of both his own childhood with his mother and his victims 'confessions' and dis-tress, are examples of Egoyan's postmodern interrogation of the nature of memory. At the same time, both novel and film are imbued with cinematic references, most espe-cially to the dysfunctional mother–son dynamics of another serial killer, *Psycho's* Norman Bates. Egoyan's adaptation, though, does not end with Trevor's wandering tramp but instead presents Felicia as a figure of renewal and hope, planting flower bulbs in an urban park.

While Trevor may be comfortable exploring Anglo-Irish colonial legacies allegoric-ally, he is somewhat less assured when dealing with themes related to other aspects of Irish history and politics, as is evident in the 1983 adaptation of 'Attracta', his somewhat limited short story in his 1978 collection, *Lovers of Their Time and Other Stories*. Feeding off tropes that are familiar from numerous British films which have decontextualized Irish history and politics, beginning with the adaptation of F. L. Green's *Odd Man Out* (1947), *Attracta*, directed by Kieran Hickey, reduces the Northern Ireland conflict to a case of rape by paramilitaries of a woman who later commits suicide. On reading of this woman's tragic fate, Attracta develops a deep empathy for her as she belatedly discovers the truth about the deaths of her own parents at the hands of the IRA during the War of Independence.

The story's theme was later extended in *Fools of Fortune* (1983), one of Trevor's two novels—the other being *The Silence in the Garden* (1988)—with a Big House at its core. Adapted as a feature film in 1990, *Fools of Fortune*, which was scripted by Michael Hirst, expresses a familiar concern of Trevor's: how violence in one generation is passed down to the next. The story revolves around Willie Quinton's traumatic memories of the burning of his family home by the Black and Tans during the War of Independence, which caused the deaths of his sisters, and the killing of his Protestant father, who was regarded as an IRA sympathizer—itself an overturning of conventional expectations of Irish political loyalties. Willie is tormented by an impulse to avenge his father's death and eventually does so when he shoots dead his father's killer in Liverpool. United with a former lover and the daughter whom he did not know he had with her, the trio return to the Big House, whose splendour is magically restored and happy memories recalled through the daughter's eyes.

---

[40] See Stephanie McBride, *Felicia's Journey* (Cork: Cork University Press, 2006). McBride cites Jonathan Romney's remark that 'Egoyan wants [viewers] at once to be absorbed in his dramas and to remain critically detached from them' (68).

[41] Ibid., 64.

Along with the near-contemporary adaptation of Jennifer Johnston's (1930–) Big House novel, *The Old Jest* (1979), as *The Dawning* (1988), *Fools of Fortune* can be seen as part of the 'heritage cinema' generic trend in British filmmaking, a feature of which is a sepia-toned nostalgia for a stable world of fixed social and cultural boundaries. History in such films is typically corralled off from the present, seen as a spectacle and robbed of its complexity. In Ireland's case, however, such hermetic sealing off is more difficult, not least because *Fools of Fortune* and *The Dawning* are set during the War of Independence and were made while the post-1969 war in Northern Ireland was ongoing. As a result, whatever their stylistic debts to the heritage mode, their plots, like that of *Attracta*, cannot escape the present. As John Hill points out, *Fools of Fortune*'s failure to seal off the past from the present reinforces the 'strong connections between the past and subsequent eras'[42] in modern Ireland, thus underlining the fact that nostalgia is not an option when exploring the 1919–21 period. Yet this does not mean that the political violence depicted in the melodramatic film is as adequately contextualized as it is in the restrained and elliptical novel on which it is based. Whereas nuance is a trademark of the latter, the film veers towards that tradition of British filmmaking which depicts Irish characters as being fatally flawed by violence.[43]

As is the case in *The Dawning*, the Anglo-Irish family in *Fools of Fortune* is distinguished by its attempts to cross class and religious divides but whose neighbours view them as 'traitors'[44] to their background for having supported Irish self-determination for generations. Nevertheless, with the intrusion of violence, both Trevor and Johnston seem to throw up their hands in despair at arriving at any solutions that might transcend present-day political and religious divisions. That, of course, was a common feature of films depicting Northern Ireland in the post-1969 era. Similarly, Elizabeth Bowen's *The Last September* (1929), adapted by novelist John Banville (1945–) and directed by Deborah Warner in 1999, does not engage with the complex dynamics of the Anglo-Irish generation that came under threat from republicans during the independence struggle. In this Big House novel, set in rural Cork in 1920, Sir Richard and Lady Naylor disapprove of their niece Lois's relationship with lowly-ranked British Army captain, Gerald Lesworth. Yet, like young Nancy in *The Dawning*, Lois develops in secret a relationship with an IRA leader, in her case, one Peter Connolly. As the film slides towards its inevitable violent conclusion, in which Gerald is killed by Peter, Lois is spirited away to London. As with so many such young women, she is left with only memories of what might have been.

While Trevor's forays into Irish history and its modern partitionist iterations may be challenged for their focus on intractable violence, these criticisms pale when compared

---

[42] John Hill, '"The Past is Always There in the Present": *Fools of Fortune* and the Heritage Film', in James MacKillop (ed.), *Contemporary Irish Cinema: From 'The Quiet Man' to 'Dancing at Lughnasa'* (Syracuse, NY: Syracuse University Press, 1999), 31.

[43] See John Hill, 'Images of Violence', in Kevin Rockett, Luke Gibbons, and John Hill (eds), *Cinema and Ireland* (London: Routledge, 1988), 147–93.

[44] William Trevor, *Fools of Fortune* (London: Bodley Head, 1993), 33. See Mary Fitzgerald–Hoyt, *William Trevor: Re-imagining Ireland* (Dublin: Liffey Press, 2003), 85–95.

with the decontextualizing tendency evident in so many other adaptations set in the present. From a film-analytical perspective, the most notorious of such adaptations is Pat O'Connor's version of Bernard Mac Laverty's (1942–) *Cal* (1983), a film scripted by the author. Released in 1984 at a time of heightened political and military tension in the North of Ireland, the first three scenes highlight the work's limitations. The film opens by showing Cal McCluskey as a driver for an IRA unit which kills a policeman in front of his wife. It then cuts from the escaping car to the metaphysical world of an evangelical preacher putting up a sign stating 'The end of the world is nigh' in a bleak Ulster landscape. This is followed by the appearance of the film's organizing metaphor—a butcher in an abattoir—when Cal goes to visit his father. No wonder John Hill, in his analysis of the film, borrowed his subtitle from a loyalist's observation about the Northern state: 'What a fucking country'.[45]

Of the adaptations concerned with Northern Ireland's divided society, perhaps only Thaddeus O'Sullivan's visually evocative 1991 version of Sam Hanna Bell's (1909–90) *December Bride* (1951) has captured the deeper complexities in its portrayal of a Presbyterian community on the shores of Carlingford Lough at the turn of the twentieth century. What gave O'Sullivan the freedom to explore the sexually repressive tensions within this community, as well as such fraught issues as religious sectarianism and Twelfth of July triumphalist displays, is the novel's status as historical fiction, temporally distanced from contemporary events.[46] This was also the case in the most accomplished film adaptations of literary works of the silent era. Both *Knocknagow* (1918) from Charles Kickham's (1828–82) 1873 novel of that name, and *Willy Reilly and his Colleen Bawn* (1920) from William Carleton's (1794–1869) near-eponymous novel of 1855, explored through a historical lens the still-raw issues of land reform and religious sectarianism respectively, in a manner that could help contemporaneous Irish audiences to distil them within the framework of republican discourse.[47]

For those anticipating the endgame of the 1990s peace process, Colin Bateman's (1962–) 1998 adaptation of his novel, *Divorcing Jack* (1995), gave a hint of the prevailing public mood in a future political environment. Set in 1999, the film is sceptical about the prospects for peace as its dark comic tone collapses both republican and loyalist activists into equally cynical self-serving thugs, symbolized by their blowing each other

[45] See John Hill, '*Cal*: What a Fucking Country', in Rockett et al., *Cinema and Ireland*, 181–4. The bleakness of *Cal*, which goes on to depict Cal's attempted self-redemption through a distasteful relationship with the dead policeman's widow, is also a feature of the 1998 screen adaptation of Eoin McNamee's novel, *Resurrection Man* (1994), which focuses on the murderous activities of the real-life Shankill Butchers, who targeted Catholics in Belfast during the mid-1970s and were associated with the Ulster Volunteer Force.

[46] For an extended analysis of the film, see Martin McLoone, '*December Bride*: A Landscape Peopled Differently', in MacKillop, *Contemporary Irish Cinema*, 40–53. See also Lance Pettitt, *December Bride* (Cork: Cork University Press, 2001).

[47] See Kevin Rockett, 'The Silent Period', in Rockett et al., *Cinema and Ireland*, 16–32. *Willy Reilly and his Colleen Bawn* can be viewed on YouTube, preceded by a short documentary contextualizing the film. A *Screening the Past* special issue is devoted to *Knocknagow* and includes a link to the film (www.screeningthepast.com/issue 33).

up at the film's climax.[48] This was a far cry from the heroic, if flawed, characters who populated the sparse output of Irish literary-based work during the interwar years, as writers and filmmakers explored the human and political legacy of the 1916–23 period. During the 1930s, only the somewhat amateurish adaptation by Denis Johnston of Frank O'Connor's (1903–66) humanistic short story, 'Guests of the Nation' (1931), in 1935 and John Ford's expressionistic Hollywood adaptation of Liam O'Flaherty's (1897–1984) *The Informer* (1925) in the same year had literary origins.[49] Like so much British cinema that dealt with post-partition Ireland from *Odd Man Out* onwards, *The Informer* is infused less with political subtlety than with an uncontextualized depiction of atavistic violence, the fatal and predetermined flaw of the Irish from which they cannot escape except through death.

The choices made by commercial cinema, whether in Hollywood or in Europe, have seen most literary adaptations being driven by the logic that what was popular in book form could be replicated on celluloid. Cinema history is littered with examples to support this view, from *The Birth of a Nation* (1915), based on a play, to *Gone with the Wind*, from a bestselling novel, through to later examples such as *To Kill a Mockingbird* (1962) and, more recently, the *Harry Potter* and *Lord of the Rings* franchises. While Ireland has not experienced such blockbuster books or films in the modern era due to the limited size of its markets, it is notable that two popular works of fiction, the aforementioned *Knocknagow* and *Willy Reilly and his Colleen Bawn*, provided the source material for the country's first two feature films. Moreover, the impulse behind the establishment of Ardmore Studios in Bray, County Wicklow in 1958 was the adaptation of a cycle of Abbey Theatre plays, six of which found their way on to the screen.

In more recent times, as is evident from the above discussion, literary adaptations remain central to Irish cinema's output, even if the material has no Irish characteristics beyond the nationality of the source writer or director—*Room* being the most obvious example—or the choice of an Irish-themed subject by non-Irish producers. The Americanized 2007 film version of Cecilia Ahern's (1981–) Dublin-set debut novel of 2004, *P.S. I Love You*, is evidence enough that filmmakers can disregard nationality as well as fidelity to an original work of fiction. While such fidelity ought not to be the measure of a film's worth, the logic of its funding and production can detach a work from its cultural origins. As a result, it has been argued that while the adaptations of Edna O'Brien's novels are faithful renditions of the originals, the film producers' discomfort, perhaps, at some of the thematic elements of Colm Tóibín's *Brooklyn* led to an uncritical embracing of American consumerism as a panacea for Ireland's perceived backwardness. For all that, however, the canon of Irish literary cinema constitutes a distinctive and impressive body of work. Although it may be regretted that this or that novel or short story has not been filmed, and the

---

[48]   See John Hill, '*Divorcing Jack*', in Brian McFarlane (ed.), *The Cinema of Britain and Ireland* (London: Wallflower Press, 2005), 227–36.

[49]   For analyses of these adaptations, see Kevin Rockett, '1930s Fictions', in Rockett et al., *Cinema and Ireland*, 60–2 and Patrick F. Sheeran, *The Informer* (Cork: Cork University Press, 2002).

dearth of adaptations of formally experimental works lamented, the roster of writers whose works have been adapted—Kickham to McGahern, Bowen to Tóibín, O'Brien to Binchy, Trevor to Donoghue—and the roll call of themes that have been dramatized—famine, rural isolation, patriarchal fathers, predatory clerics, independent women—testify to a cinematic canon that is broadly representative of its literary equivalent.

FURTHER READING

Barton, Ruth. *Jim Sheridan: Framing the Nation*. Dublin: Liffey Press, 2002.

Cronin, Michael. *The Barrytown Trilogy*. Cork: Cork University Press, 2006.

Gibbons, Luke. *The Quiet Man*. Cork: Cork University Press, 2002.

Gibbons, Luke. *Joyce's Ghosts: Ireland, Modernism, and Memory*. Chicago, IL: Chicago University Press, 2015.

Hill, John. '"The Past is Always There in the Present": *Fools of Fortune* and the Heritage Film'. In James MacKillop (ed.), *Contemporary Irish Cinema: From 'The Quiet Man' to 'Dancing at Lughnasa'*. Syracuse, NY: Syracuse University Press, 1999: 29–39.

McBride, Stephanie. *Felicia's Journey*. Cork: Cork University Press, 2006.

McLoone, Martin. '*December Bride*: A Landscape Peopled Differently'. In James MacKillop (ed.), *Contemporary Irish Cinema: From 'The Quiet Man' to 'Dancing at Lughnasa'*. Syracuse, NY: Syracuse University Press, 1999: 40–53.

Pettitt, Lance. *December Bride*. Cork: Cork University Press, 2001.

Pettitt, Lance. 'William Trevor's Screen Fictions: "No Interest. Not Suitable for Treatment"'. In Paul Delaney and Michael Parker (eds), *William Trevor: Revaluations*. Manchester: Manchester University Press, 2013: 76–92.

Rockett, Kevin. *Irish Film Censorship: A Cultural Journey from Silent Cinema to Internet Pornography*. Dublin: Four Courts Press, 2004.

Rockett, Kevin. 'Cinema and Irish Literature'. In Margaret Kelleher and Philip O'Leary (eds), *The Cambridge History of Irish Literature, Volume 2: 1890-2000*. Cambridge: Cambridge University Press, 2006: 531–61.

Rockett, Emer and Kevin Rockett. *Neil Jordan: Exploring Boundaries*. Dublin: Liffey Press, 2003.

Rockett, Kevin, Luke Gibbons, and John Hill. *Cinema and Ireland*. London: Routledge, 1987.

PART VIII

CROSSINGS AND
CROSSCURRENTS

CHAPTER 26

....

THE FICTION OF THE IRISH IN ENGLAND

....

TONY MURRAY

IF emigration is 'a mirror in which the Irish nation can always see its true face',[1] such a mirror is by no means flawless. It has cracks, abrasions, and missing pieces which distort our under-standing of how one of the most persistent features of Irish history has affected its people's perception of themselves. This is nowhere more evident than in the country's literary reflec-tions on migration. This is particularly true in regard to one of its nearest neighbours, England, where the presence of the Irish has long been freighted with political and cultural difficulties due to the troubled colonial relationship between the two countries. Unsurprisingly, there-fore, authors have used stories about the Irish in England to make polemical interventions in broader historical and political debates. Prose fiction, however, has a unique capacity to medi-ate the deeply textured interplay between the public and private aspects of the migrant experi-ence and, in recent times, its primary focus has been the particularities of individual immigrants' material circumstances, social interactions, and psychological states. This chap-ter aims to demonstrate how, over two centuries of fiction about the Irish in England, there has been a discernible shift of emphasis away from matters of primarily public concern to those of a more private nature, resulting in works that illuminate latent as well as manifest features of the diasporic experience and its attendant cultural allegiances and identities.

There is insufficient space here to provide a fully comprehensive survey of the fiction of the Irish in England, and many novels and short stories on the topic by established Irish writers are necessarily excluded.[2] Viewed as a whole, this literary corpus lends itself to a

---

[1] Liam Ryan, 'Irish Emigration to Britain since World War II', in Richard Kearney (ed.), *Migrations: The Irish at Home and Abroad* (Dublin: Wolfhound Press, 1990), 46.

[2] Some of these excluded texts are referred to here in passing, while others are critiqued in one or more of the volumes in the Further Reading section below. For the broader context of scholarly engagement with the critical and semantic parameters of Irish migrant culture, see Aidan Arrowsmith (ed.), *Irish Studies Review. Special Issue: Irishness in Britain* 14, no. 2 (2006); Piaras Mac Éinrí and Tina O'Toole (eds), *Éire-Ireland. Special Issue: New Approaches to Irish Migration* 47, nos. 1–2 (2012); and Ellen McWilliams and Tony Murray (eds), *Irish Studies Review. Special Issue: Irishness and the Culture of the Irish Abroad* 26, no. 1 (2018).

variety of potential angles of analysis, but three prevalent and interrelated themes provide a critical framework for the examination that follows, the focus of which will necessarily be on fiction produced by writers who are Irish by birth or descent. In the first section, I discuss works by Anglo-Irish authors whose cultural duality afforded them an interstitial perspective on the societies of both countries. In the nineteenth century, many of these authors used fiction to examine both the attractions and the limitations of English society for a class that steadily lost its political power and social privilege in Ireland after the Act of Union of 1800. In the twentieth century, as this class's status in the wake of Irish independence became even more anomalous, Anglo-Irish writers in England moved their attention away from political preoccupations to the broader and more complicated personal predicaments in which such migrants found themselves. The second section deals with the specific experiences of Irish women in England, who migrated there in larger numbers than men from the late nineteenth century onwards. Again, a public-to-private transition is apparent as we move from nineteenth-century works motivated by increasingly (proto-)feminist convictions to works of the later twentieth century, which, while no less politically aware, concentrate more on how the individual experience of displacement impacted on women's personal sense of identity. The final section addresses works that centre on second- and later-generation Irish migrants in England, most of which have been written in the last hundred years. Here, a similar change of emphasis is apparent, insofar as fictional accounts from the first half of the twentieth century tend to focus on communal questions of class and religious identity, whereas those from the post-war era are more preoccupied with their characters' individualized negotiations of race and ethnicity.

While the earliest texts examined here date from the early 1800s, novels about the Irish in England had appeared from as far back as the 1660s. Most of these were picaresque romances and as such do not qualify for inclusion within the thematic framework of this chapter (or indeed the temporal scope of this volume), but their existence proves that the subject of migration to England was a distinct feature of the earliest stages of the Irish novel's evolution.[3] It should also be noted that the presence of Irish characters in England has a long lineage in the work of non-Irish writers, a topic worthy of a separate study.[4] The Irish experience in Scotland is sufficiently distinctive in cultural and religious terms to merit discrete treatment also, although the same cannot be said of the Irish experience in Wales, which has featured little in fiction.[5] Given the city's historical

---

[3] See, for instance, Richard Head, *The English Rogue* (1665), Thomas Amory, *The Life of John Buncle, Esq.* (1756), and Charles Johnstone, *The Adventures of Anthony Varnish* (1786). For a critique of such novels, see Derek Hand, *A History of the Irish Novel* (Cambridge: Cambridge University Press, 2011), 24–59. For examples of recent historical novels by English-based Irish writers set before 1800, see Emma Donoghue, *Slammerkin* (2001) and Ronan Bennett, *Havoc in its Third Year* (2004).

[4] One of the best-known examples is the character of Phineas Finn in Anthony Trollope's *Phineas Finn, the Irish Member* (1869) and *Phineas Redux* (1874).

[5] For examples of fictional portrayals of the Irish in Scotland, see Patrick MacGill, *Children of the Dead End: The Autobiography of a Navvy* (1914) and Bernard MacLaverty, *Grace Notes* (1997). For examples of fictional, if peripheral, Irish characters in Wales, see Henry Digby Beste, *Poverty and the Baronet's Family: An Irish Catholic Novel* (1845) and Daniel Owen, *Rhys Lewis* (1885).

attraction for generations of Irish writers, novels and short stories set in London have dominated the canon, although a significant proportion feature urban locations of Irish settlement elsewhere, notably Lancashire and the West Midlands, while a handful represent the less common experience of Irish migrants in rural English settings.

ABSENCE AND ALIENATION: ANGLO-IRISH PREOCCUPATIONS

Most histories of the Irish novel identify *Castle Rackrent* (1800) by Maria Edgeworth (1767–1849) as a defining moment in its development. Twelve years later, the same author published *The Absentee* (1812), which explores the anomalous position of the Anglo-Irish in English society after the Act of Union. A central and sometimes didactic theme in Edgeworth's work is the neglect by the ruling Anglo-Irish Ascendancy of their obligations in regard to their estates and dependents in Ireland. As the title of the novel makes clear, *The Absentee* deals with an especially nefarious aspect of this subject. Lord Clonbrony, the landlord in question, has been living comfortably in London for some years on the proceeds of his Irish estate. His wife, however, struggles to establish herself in cosmopolitan high society and is ridiculed by her female English peer group for attempting to ingratiate herself with them. Despite throwing an extravagant party which impresses them, her unsuccessful endeavours to disguise her use of Hiberno-Irish idioms ensures that she continues to be regarded as an outsider.

By anchoring a novel about absentee landlordism in England, Edgeworth is able to provide a dual commentary on Anglo-Irish affairs. She not only demonstrates how the Irish peasantry are objectified by the Anglo-Irish from afar but also how the latter are themselves objectified in turn by the English in their midst. Meanwhile, a generational disjuncture is apparent when Lady Clonbrony's son becomes increasingly alienated from what he regards as his mother's 'Londonomania'[6] and urges her to moderate her obsession with the city. Unlike his parents, who have little interest in Ireland, Lord Colambre is anxious to learn more about the economic and social consequences of their neglect of their Irish estates, eventually persuading the family to return to live there. The novel suggests, therefore, how commitment to property and nation, while undermined by the migration of one generation, can, under certain circumstances, be revived by the concern and actions of a subsequent generation.

The Wild Irish Boy (1808) by Charles Maturin (1780–1824) is generally considered one of the author's less successful novels, but its attention to absenteeism is noteworthy if only because it pre-dates Edgeworth's text. Ormsby Bethel is the English-born son of an

---

[6] Maria Edgeworth, *The Absentee*, ed. W. J. McCormack and Kim Walker (Oxford: Oxford University Press, 2001), 199. For a critique of this aspect of *The Absentee*, see Claire Connolly, *A Cultural History of the Irish Novel, 1790–1829* (Cambridge: Cambridge University Press, 2012), 24–28.

Anglo-Irish landlord leading a dissolute and reckless life in London.[7] When he visits his ancestral home in Ireland, he is struck not so much by the actual absence of the landlord class as by 'a kind of mental absenteeism pervad[ing] [the] country'.[8] However, his disillusion with the behaviour of both the Catholic peasantry and the Protestant Ascendency undermines any suggestion that he might play the mediating role in Anglo-Irish affairs that Colambre does. In this regard, the novel differs radically from *The Absentee*, and, by focusing more on Ormsby's conflicted patriotism, anticipates questions of cultural allegiance more associated with much later novels about the second-generation Irish experience in England. By contrast, when absentee landlord Gerald Blount visits his estates for the first time in John Banim's (1798–1842) *The Anglo-Irish of the Nineteenth Century* (1828), his prejudices about the Irish poor evaporate, prejudices acquired years before during a visit he made to the Irish ghetto of St Giles in London, which carried a stigma of contagion and criminality propagated by hostile coverage in the English press.[9] Banim's novel, by implication, raises an intriguing question about the extent to which long-established anti-Irish racism in English society might have prejudiced the attitudes of absentee landlords to their dependants back in Ireland.[10]

'Kate Connor' (1842), a short story by Mrs S. C. Hall (Anna Maria Fielding, 1800–81), demonstrates that the morality of landlord absenteeism and its continuing political ramifications were still topical well into the nineteenth century.[11] Here, a young peasant woman makes a lone and perilous journey to England to appraise her landlord's daughter (and erstwhile confidante) about her family's recent eviction and the mistreatment of tenants by the land agent. Very much in the spirit of Edgeworth, this results in the landlord setting an example to his peers by immediately returning to his estate. However, Kate's unlikely journey across the Irish Sea is a rather cumbersome and unconvincing narrative device for illustrating how good Anglo-Irish relations might be maintained.

By the late nineteenth century, when the worst vestiges of absenteeism were largely a thing of the past, there was a shift of emphasis in the literature away from such didactic concerns towards the more personal preoccupations of Anglo-Irish characters in England. One consequence of this is that anomalies and ambiguities about the status and role of the Irish landlord class in English society tend to be explored in more psychologically nuanced ways. George Moore's (1852–1933) *A Drama in Muslin* (1886) is a good example of how the genre of the absentee novel morphed into a more modernist examination of how a younger generation of Anglo-Irish migrants were beginning to seek alternative futures to the redundant trajectories mapped out for them by their parents. Significantly, Alice Barton's eventual form of escape, as well as being a physical migration to London,

---

[7] For a later novel which echoes this theme, see Katherine Cecil Thurston, *The Gambler* (1905).

[8] Charles Maturin, *The Wild Irish Boy* (London: Longman, Hurst, Rees, and Orme, 1808), vol. 2, 311.

[9] John Banim, *The Anglo-Irish of the Nineteenth Century* (London: Henry Colburn, 1828), vol. 3, 105–7.

[10] For further discussion of this issue, see Emer Nolan, *Catholic Emancipations: Irish Fiction from Thomas Moore to James Joyce* (Syracuse, NY: Syracuse University Press, 2007), 73–6.

[11] Mrs S. C. Hall, 'Kate Connor', in *Sketches of Irish Character* (London: Frederick Westley and A. H. Davis, 1831), 189–208.

is one of class migration, since Moore's heroine chooses to marry a doctor against her aristocratic parents' wishes. Another example is provided by *Robert Thorne* (1907) by Shan F. Bullock (1865–1935). Despite being born in Devon, the eponymous hero has an Irish mother and is closely based on the author's own life in England, where he worked as a civil service clerk after emigrating from Fermanagh in 1883.[12] Like Alice Barton, Bullock's fictional alter ego transgresses a cultural divide by building a close friendship with Mrs Flynn, his Irish Catholic landlady. This is a rare example of a novel which, by portraying the relationship between a second-generation Irish Protestant and an Irish-born Catholic in England, highlights commonalities between their respective cultural backgrounds which might not otherwise be immediately apparent.

The narrative approach of *Robert Thorne* also represents a self-conscious move away from the realist fiction of the nineteenth century to the more self-reflective prose of the subsequent century. The novel is prefaced by a letter from Bullock, posing as the editor of Thorne's auto-biography, in which he apologizes to Thorne for any 'erasures—interpolations—additions'[13] in the text. He even goes so far as to insert a number of footnotes questioning the veracity of certain factual details and criticizing Thorne's prose style. In the first of these, Bullock remarks that 'It is necessary to keep in mind, whilst reading his record, that Thorne was half Irish by birth.'[14] This may just be a tongue-in-cheek jibe at Thorne's Irish background, but it might also be an indication of how Bullock (the author rather than the fictionalized editor) was prepared to question the efficacy of his own testimony, thus anticipating the postmodern playfulness of later London Irish novels such as Dónall Mac Amhlaigh's (1926–89) *Schnitzer O'Shea* (1985) and Robert McLiam Wilson's (1964–) *Ripley Bogle* (1989).

The afterlife of the Anglo-Irish Ascendancy in Ireland's literature has been most pronounced in the genre of the Big House novel, which began to emerge during the period of the land reforms of the late nineteenth century and has continued with remarkable resilience up to the present day. One of its most accomplished exponents was Elizabeth Bowen (1899–1973), who came from such a background herself. Bowen lived in the south of England for most of her life and it was arguably the objective reflection afforded by this physical distance from Ireland that enabled her to capture the nuances of Anglo-Irish life so perceptively in her second novel, *The Last September* (1929). Fictional works portraying Irish characters in Bowen's country of adoption tend to mirror this sense of distanciation, with plotlines which entail them making journeys back to Ireland to maintain their sense of Irishness rather than pursuing this through Irish associations in England. One such example is *A World of Love* (1955), in which Antonia Montefort makes regular visits to her country house in Ireland. Another is Bowen's great Second World War novel, *The Heat of the Day* (1948). Stella Rodney's life in London is lived in a constant state of contingency, not only because of the Blitz but also because of the inde-terminate nature of her relationships with two male spies with whom she is romantically involved. She is able to periodically escape her circumstances, however, by visiting

---

[12] For a slightly earlier novel about an Irish clerk in London, see W. B. Yeats, *John Sherman* (1891).

[13] Shan F. Bullock, *Robert Thorne: The Story of a London Clerk* (London: T. Werner Laurie, 1907), vii.

[14] Ibid., 1.

Mount Morris, her family estate in Ireland. In contrast to London, the estate offers Stella a seemingly tranquil and stable retreat in neutral Ireland where, as she reflects, the house 'rose to the surface in her, as though something weighting it to the bottom had let go'.[15] Here, too, she is able to reconnect with her childhood memories and find time to reconsider the complications of her personal life in England.

The plotlines of *The Heat of the Day* and *A World of Love* both exemplify a significant evolution in the fictional representation of Anglo-Irish identities. Whereas in much nineteenth-century fiction, London provides Anglo-Irish protagonists with a haven from the turmoil of their Irish estates, by the mid-twentieth century, Ireland has become a sanctuary and a place of refuge for their beleaguered descendants. This trend is also apparent in 'Sunday Afternoon' (1941), one of Bowen's few short stories about the Anglo-Irish, in which Henry Russel visits family friends in County Dublin after being bombed out of his flat in London during the Second World War. Bowen juxtaposes the horrors of life in London at this time with the Edwardian-like calm of a country house belonging to the Anglo-Irish Vesey family. By doing so, she highlights the gulf that has opened up between the anachronistic lives and worldview of the Anglo-Irish and the sterner realities of war-torn England. The dramatic tension of the story ultimately pivots around the question of migration and in particular Mrs Vesey's young niece, Maria. Here is a young woman who feels so stifled by her family circumstances that she is prepared, against the advice of Russel, to move to London and risk the Blitz for a 'new catastrophic *outward* order of life'.[16] While the obverse of Antonia Montefort's and Stella Rodney's motivation, Maria's decision reflects a long-established 'push' factor for Irish female migrants, which is examined in more detail in the next section.

Like Elizabeth Bowen, with whom she became a close friend in later life, Iris Murdoch (1919–99) was an only child, born into an Anglo-Irish Protestant family in Dublin, who grew up in England and worked in Whitehall during the Second World War. The Irishness of Murdoch's fictional Irish characters in England is, like Bowen's, often only alluded to tangentially, which possibly reflects Murdoch's life-long ambivalence about her own national identity.[17] In her partially autobiographical first novel, *Under the Net* (1954), Jake Donaghue has somewhat indeterminate Irish ancestry by way of his side-kick, the Irish-born Finn (Peter O'Finney), who he describes as 'a sort of remote cousin of mine, or so he used to claim, and I never troubled to verify this'.[18] In its existentialist preoccupations and low-key comedy, *Under the Net* shares commonalties with two important London Irish novels. On the one hand, it looks back to Samuel Beckett's (1906–89) *Murphy* (1938), a copy of which Jake possesses and the plots of which are mirrored in their respective protagonists' jobs as hospital orderlies. On the other, it anticipates the trajectory of Anthony Cronin's (1928–2016) *The Life of Riley* (1964), as its

---

[15] Elizabeth Bowen, *The Heat of the Day* (London: Penguin, 1962), 165–6.

[16] Elizabeth Bowen, 'Sunday Afternoon', in *The Collected Short Stories of Elizabeth Bowen* (London: Penguin, 1983), 620. Original emphasis.

[17] For an extended discussion of this topic, see Peter J. Conradi, *Iris Murdoch: A Life* (London: HarperCollins, 2001), 3–32.

[18] Iris Murdoch, *Under the Net* (London: Vintage, 2002), 7–8.

solipsistic anti-hero adopts a bohemian lifestyle, only to end up alone and chastened on the streets of Hampstead. The ambiguous identity of Irish characters in Murdoch's work is also evident in Pattie O'Driscoll, the housekeeper in *The Time of the Angels* (1966). Here is an early example of a mixed-race Irish character which signals the beginning of a shift of emphasis in Irish fiction in England to the more complex questions of identity discussed in the final section of this chapter.[19]

William Trevor (1928–2016) might be considered the inheritor of Bowen and Murdoch's mantel. Born into a middle-class Protestant family in Cork, he moved to London in 1952 and once described his true sense of home as being somewhere between Holyhead and Dun Laoghaire, a remark that accords with Roy Foster's characterization of Bowen as feeling 'most at home in mid-Irish Sea'.[20] In the early phase of his career, Irish characters in Trevor's novels set in England are generally unattractive figures, such as the blackmailer Mr Studdy in *The Boarding House* (1965) or the sexual predator Septimus Tuam in *The Love Department* (1966). By the early 1970s, the appearance of more complex and sympathetic characters, such as Alban Roche in *Miss Gomez and the Brethren* (1971), reflects an increasingly nuanced approach to Irishness which by *Felicia's Journey* (1994) had developed into what one critic described as Trevor's 'most comprehensive study to date of an Irish sensibility, trying—and failing—to make sense of England'.[21] As a writer renowned for his skilful treatment of the anomalous position of the Anglo-Irish in Ireland, the political and moral dilemmas that Irish people in England faced during the Northern Ireland Troubles offered Trevor similar subject matter, albeit in an altogether different context. Short stories such as 'Another Christmas' (1978) and 'Being Stolen From' (1981) clearly demonstrate how sensitively he was able to handle this. They also reveal how the complexities of Anglo-Irish political relations, so pronounced in early nineteenth-century Irish literature, were still evident at the end of the twentieth, albeit treated in less moralizing and more psychologically sophisticated ways.

REFUGE AND OPPORTUNITY: WOMEN'S JOURNEYS

As one of Ireland's closest neighbours, England has historically provided Irish women migrants with a readily accessible place of opportunity and a physical and emotional haven, albeit a sometimes uneasy one. One of the earliest fictional renditions of this

---

[19] Other England-based Irish characters in Murdoch's oeuvre include Tim Burke in *The Sandcastle* (1957), Martin Lynch-Gibbon in *A Severed Head* (1961), and Kate Gray and Gavin Fivey in *The Nice and the Good* (1968).

[20] William Trevor, 'Between Holyhead and Dun Laoghaire', *Times Literary Supplement*, 6 February, 1981, 131; R. F. Foster, 'The Irishness of Elizabeth Bowen', in *Paddy and Mr Punch: Connections in Irish and English History* (London: Allen Lane, 1993), 107.

[21] Michael W. Thomas, 'William Trevor's Other Island', *Irish Studies Review* 6, no. 2 (1998), 155.

theme occurs in Ann Hamilton's *The Irishwoman in London* (1810), an epistolary account of Ellen O'Hara, a young woman who flees an unhappy marriage in Monaghan to live incognito in London. Despite being reclaimed and repatriated by her husband, she opts once more to pursue the romantic opportunities offered by the metropolis after his death. Revealingly, it transpires that her mother had made a similar journey some years earlier when she eloped with her fiancée, something which indicates that such experiences were not unusual for Irish women of means, even in the pre-Victorian period.[22]

If moving to England, and to London in particular, in the nineteenth century was a drastic but effective way for young Irish women to assert their independence, it was also seen as a necessity by many aspiring writers keen on pursuing a career in literature and the arts.[23] Most English-based Irish female novelists of this era, such as Charlotte Riddell (1832–1906) and Emily Lawless (1845–1913), came from well-to-do Protestant backgrounds, the largest cohort being daughters of Church of Ireland ministers, such as Selina Bunbury (1802–82), who moved to Liverpool in 1830, and the highly prolific Cork-born L. T. Meade (pseudonym of Elizabeth Thomasina Meade Smith, 1844–1914), who moved to London in 1874. Notable Irish Catholic novelists whose careers followed the same course include M. E. Francis (pseudonym of Mary E. Sweetman, 1859–1930), who lived in Lancashire and Dorset, and Katharine Tynan (1859–1931), who lived for a large part of her life in London. What is most distinctive about the treatment of emigration to England in these authors' works is the correlation between the 'push' motivations of unhappy or abusive marriages at home and the 'pull' motivations of potential affairs and careers abroad.

Unsurprisingly, perhaps, the fiction produced by such writers had a strong autobiographical aspect. An early example of this is *Molly Carew* (1879) by Elizabeth Owens Blackburne Casey (1848–94). While essentially a conventional romance and product of the popular Victorian genre of sensationalist fiction, the novel's treatment of the difficulties an Irish female migrant faces in the male-dominated literary world of London makes it a precursor to works by better-known authors such as Riddell, whose *A Struggle for Fame*, her first novel, about an Irish woman in London, did not appear until 1883.[24] Its central character, Glenarva Westley, based to some extent on Riddell herself, faces deep prejudice from London publishers due to her gender. While it has been criticized for occluding the Irish dimension to its heroine's character, the novel is, nevertheless,

---

[22]   In the early to mid-nineteenth century, the topic of Irish women in England was also taken up by a number of English novelists. See Amelia Beauclerc, *Alinda, or the Child of Mystery: A Novel* (1812), Miss Mason, *Kate Gearey, or Irish Life in London: A Tale of 1849* (1853), and William Harrison Ainsworth, *Old Court: A Novel* (1867).

[23]   See Rolf Loeber and Magda Stouthamer-Loeber, 'Literary Absentees: Irish Women Authors in Nineteenth-Century England', in Jacqueline Belanger (ed.), *The Irish Novel in the Nineteenth Century: Facts and Fictions* (Dublin: Four Courts Press, 2005), 167–86 and Ciaran O'Neill and Mai Yatani, 'Women, Ambition, and the City, 1890–1910', in Anna Pilz and Whitney Standlee (eds), *Irish Women's Writing, 1878–1922: Advancing the Cause of Liberty* (Manchester: Manchester University Press, 2016), 100–20.

[24]   See also Rosa Mulholland's *Dunmara* (1864), published under the pseudonym Ruth Murray, which concerns an Irish female artist in London.

a meticulously crafted record of the practical day-to-day hurdles encountered by an ambitious but unfairly disadvantaged female writer of the time.[25]

By the latter end of the nineteenth century, such novels had become more self-consciously feminist in outlook.[26] Sarah Grand's (pseudonym of Frances Clarke McFall, 1854–1943) semi-autobiographical New Woman novel, *The Beth Book* (1897), for instance, is an account of a middle-class northern Irish woman whose burgeoning self-awareness, in the wake of a disastrous marriage in Yorkshire, fuels her ambitions to become a writer in London. Crucially, Grand conveys how the city not only provides Beth with the practical opportunity to pursue her chosen career but also the freedom and sensibility of mind necessary to write in the first place. Her rambles through London's streets teach her 'to appreciate the wonder and beauty of the most wonderful and beautiful city ever seen', as her 'eyes grew deep from long looking and earnest meditating upon it.'[27] This description contrasts starkly with representations of London as corrupt and heathen in Irish cultural discourse of the late nineteenth and early twentieth centuries. There was considerable moral and religious anxiety at this time about the potential dangers to which young London-bound women might be subjected, and this is reflected in fiction. An early example is the short story, 'A Psychological Moment at Three Periods' (1894), by George Egerton (pseudonym of Mary Chavelita Dunne, 1859–1945). It concerns an Irish woman in London who is subjected to the attentions of a sexual predator and is notable for the way it employs the early techniques of literary modernism to convey the fragmented impressions and intuitions of its heroine at a moment of personal jeopardy.[28] Journeying deeper into this fictional territory, the threat of what was referred to as the 'white slave trade' (sex trafficking in today's terms) is flagged up in two early twentieth-century novels about vulnerable young Irish women in English cities. Rosa Mulholland's (1841–1921) *The Tragedy of Chris: The Story of a Dublin Flower Girl* (1902) follows a young woman who travels to London in order to rescue her friend who has fallen into a life of prostitution. While the novel successfully captures the sense of culture shock experienced by its protagonists in London, it has been criticized for eliding 'the stark reality of the economic choices faced by poverty-stricken Irish women'[29] who had no option but to migrate there. The eponymous protagonist of *The Story of Mary Dunne* (1913) by M. E. Francis, meanwhile, escapes from the morally claustrophobic atmosphere of her rural Irish community after being criticized by her parish priest for associating with men other than her fiancée, only to be kidnapped into prostitution in Liverpool.

---

[25] James H. Murphy, *Irish Novelists and the Victorian Age* (Oxford: Oxford University Press, 2011), 6.

[26] Despite this distinctly feminist turn, a reactionary impulse is evident in the plotlines and characterizations of Irish fiction in England well into the twentieth century. See, for example, Mrs Alexander, *Kitty Costello* (1904) and Dorothea Conyers, *Rooted Out* (1923).

[27] Sarah Grand, *The Beth Book* (Toronto: George N. Morang, 1897), 536.

[28] For a slightly later and more emphatically modernist novel about a vulnerable Irish person in London, see Pádraic Ó Conaire, *Deoraíocht* (1910).

[29] Heather Ingman, 'Aliens: London in Irish Women's Writing', in Tom Herron (ed.), *Irish Writing London: Volume 2, Post-War to the Present* (London: Bloomsbury, 2013), 53.

By the mid-twentieth century, writers had developed an increasingly sceptical attitude to the supposed attractions of new lives in England and the escape trope took on a more tarnished appearance as a result. A job in a London literary publishers' office is just one of a series of short-term and unfulfilling positions for the heroine of *Rose Forbes: The Biography of an Unknown Woman* (1937) by George Buchanan (1904–89). Having fled her hometown of Bangor in Northern Ireland after the tragic drowning of her fiancée, Rose is initially attracted to an unnamed English seaside resort. She then drifts into a series of unsatisfactory affairs with men she meets in London, before finding herself trapped in a marriage with a man she does not love. In this regard, she is representative of a number of female characters in interwar Irish fiction who live unfulfilled lives on the fringes of English society, such as the prostitute Celia Kelly in Beckett's *Murphy* and the eponymous housemaid in 'Bridget Kiernan' (1928) by Norah Hoult (1898–1984).

Perhaps the best-known example of a novel about the disappointments for Irish women which result from romantic adventures in England is the ironically titled *Girls in Their Married Bliss* (1964). By the opening of this, the third part of Edna O'Brien's (1930–) *The Country Girls* trilogy, the two young heroines, Kate Brady and Baba Brennan, are both in dysfunctional relationships in London and have resorted to extra-marital affairs in an attempt to escape their unhappiness. For Baba, the more psychologically robust of the two, the nefarious effects of this are contained. Kate's sexual exploits, however, are more detrimental to her well-being. She is not as emotionally well-defended as Baba and, when an affair leads to the potential break-up of her marriage, her sense of guilt and fear of sudden abandonment lead her into increasingly self-destructive behaviour. Despite its portents, it still comes as a shock when her eventual suicide is confirmed in an epilogue to the trilogy, published in 1986. Similar conflicts are apparent in O'Brien's fifth novel, *Casualties of Peace* (1966). Although artist-protagonist Willa McCord avoids her compatriot's fate by leaving an unhappy marriage before it is too late, she ironically meets her end as the inadvertent victim of a similarly dysfunctional relationship between a London Irish couple with whom she is lodging.

That London Winter (1981) by Leland Bardwell (1922–2016) is another autobiographical novel about an Irish woman's unsuccessful attempt to find emotional escape and satisfaction through the pursuit of an extra-marital affair. Like Bowen and Murdoch, Bardwell was an Irish-born Protestant who was educated in England. Her novel is set in late 1950s London and traces the emotional decline of Nina as she resorts to heavy drinking and an increasingly debauched lifestyle to assuage her unhappiness. In contrast to Edna O'Brien's heroines, however, Nina is part of a more middle-class and trendy left-wing social set that mixes with a far wider cross-section of London's population, including other migrant groups such as Cypriots, Russians, and Tamils. The novel is not as technically accomplished as O'Brien's but nevertheless provides a rare insight into the consequences for an emotionally troubled Irish woman of mixing in the ostensibly more liberated but still male-dominated bohemian milieu of post-war Soho.[30] Nina's

---

[30] For a novel which critically portrays this milieu from an Irish male point of view, see Michael Campbell, *Oh, Mary, This London* (1959).

experiences in *That London Winter* can also be read to some extent as the unadorned flip-side to the somewhat glorified male version of this world described in Anthony Cronin's *The Life of Riley* and Iris Murdoch's *Under the Net*.

It is telling that Bardwell did not publish her novel until more than two decades after it is set. This may be related to the fact that by the 1980s, Irish women writers, with the advent of second-wave feminism, were beginning to have an even bigger impact on Irish literature than in the late nineteenth century. Fiction by and about Irish women in England played an important role in this development. This was particularly true in relation to works by a new generation of mainly Catholic Northern Irish writers in England whose fiction directly or indirectly confronted the trauma of the Troubles. Notable texts include Anne Devlin's (1951–) short story, 'Five Notes After a Visit' (1986), and Deirdre Madden's (1960–) novel, *One by One in the Darkness* (1996). Fiction by Northern Irish Protestant women is less common and until relatively recently has been somewhat overlooked by critics. Linda Anderson's (1949–) *Cuckoo* (1986) is a case in point. The novel is set in London in the early 1980s and concerns Fran McDowell, a Belfast Protestant, coming to terms with the double trauma of a forced abortion and a personal bereavement due to the Troubles.[31] Furthermore, Fran finds herself in the pre-dicament of raising a mixed-race daughter as a single mother at a time of multiple polit-ical crises, including the Irish republican hunger strikes, the Falklands War, and the cruise missile protests. It is her involvement with the last of these issues, however, which finally provides her, in the shape of the Greenham Common women's peace camp, with a dependable, if surrogate, sense of home and security after the emotional disturbances she has experienced. Fran's attempt to deconstruct her past through a series of personal and political present-day relationships involves a complex meditation on the intercon-nectedness of trauma, grief, sexuality, nationality, and memory. The formal structure and tone of the novel mirror the fragmented legacy of the protagonist's past, incorporat-ing numerous time shifts, multifocal narrative voices, and switches from prose to drama to diary-writing. It is significant that the last of these forms, the performative act of writ-ing itself, provides Fran with a means of reconciling a conflicted past in Ireland with a complicated present in England—an outcome that echoes that of her London Irish fore-bears of the late nineteenth century.

Eimear McBride's (1976–) second novel, *The Lesser Bohemians* (2016), subverts the long-established narrative of the unhappy Irish woman seeking emotional refuge through escape to England. Set in north London in the mid-1990s, it centres on Eily, an eighteen-year-old Irish drama student, who, by revealing her emotional vulnerability during the course of an extended affair with an older English actor, assuages the legacy of a traumatic childhood. The novel's critical acclaim derives in part from the manner in which it employs a variation on the uncompromising neo-modernist prose style of McBride's multi-award-winning first novel, *A Girl is a Half-formed Thing* (2013).

---

[31] There is a distinct subgenre of fiction about Irish women's experiences of abortion in London. See, for instance, Maeve Binchy's 'Shepherd's Bush' in *Central Line* (1978), Deirdre Shanahan's 'Dancehall' in *Green Ink Writers: Anthology of Short Stories* (1982), and Edna O'Brien's *Down by the River* (1996).

This allows its author to mediate her protagonist's sometimes exhilarating, sometimes disconcerting disjunctions between thought, speech, and sexual expression. Eily's experience of migration is notable for the way she embraces London and the physicality of its streets and buildings with the same sense of abandon and adventure she does her love affair. As such, *The Lesser Bohemians* is markedly different to many earlier portrayals of young Irish women in England, where the city is often perceived as overwhelming or threatening for the newcomer. McBride can also be seen as representative of a new generation of Irish women writers who are no longer cowed by the overbearing influence of patriarchal Catholic values but are writing with a self-confident vigour reminiscent of the New Woman writers of the *fin de siècle*, and bringing fresh perspectives to bear on the fiction of the Irish in England.

ASSIMILATION AND AMBIVALENCE: GENERATIONAL DIMENSIONS

Since the early twentieth century, a growing body of prose literature by the descendants of Irish migrants in England has emerged.[32] Whether published as fiction or as auto-biography, such texts provide a fertile source for exploring how the cultural identities of second- and later-generation migrants are articulated and narrativized over time and place. For male writers, this is more commonly explored in autobiography than in fiction, while the reverse is true for female writers.[33] Sociological research has found that the descendants of Irish migrants sometimes claim contrary ethnic positions according to different circumstances.[34] By threading different life events together through narrative, autobiographical fiction can be a productive site for examining how writers and their characters employ these forms of 'contingent positionality'[35] to negotiate and mediate testing questions of identity and allegiance.

Bill Naughton (1910–92) was born in Ireland but raised from the age of four in the Lancashire mill town of Bolton during the interwar years. He is best known for the novel *Alfie* (1966), which became an iconic film about 1960s London, and also wrote a critically

---

[32] There is insufficient space here to cover the expansive genre of popular family sagas which contains many characters of Irish descent in English society. Relevant works include James Hanley's *The Furys Saga* (1935–58), Catherine Cookson's *Kate Hannigan* (1950) and *Fifteen Streets* (1952), Martina Cole's *Dangerous Lady* (1992) and *Maura's Game* (2002), and Gilda O'Neill's *A Bond of Fate Trilogy* (2002–05).

[33] For critiques of this literature, see Liam Harte (ed.), *The Literature of the Irish in Britain: Autobiography and Memoir, 1725–2001* (Basingstoke: Palgrave Macmillan, 2009) and Tony Murray, *London Irish Fictions: Narrative, Diaspora and Identity* (Liverpool: Liverpool University Press, 2012).

[34] See Philip Ullah, 'Second-generation Irish Youth: Identity and Ethnicity', *New Community* 12 (1985), 310–20.

[35] Avtar Brah, *Cartographies of Diaspora: Contesting Identities* (London: Routledge, 1996), 149.

acclaimed series of memoirs in his later years.[36] Earlier in his career, Naughton published *One Small Boy* (1957), a semi-autobiographical novel about a child of immigrant Irish parents in the north of England. Significantly, religion plays a more dominant role than ethnicity in the formation of its young protagonist's identity. This is particularly true in regard to Michael M'Cloud's growing awareness of his sexuality and how this awareness is self-policed by his strong sense of Catholic guilt. This becomes apparent when Michael describes the street games he plays with his non-Catholic peers and how their guilt-free appetite for mischief not only contrasts with his own reticence but also with his 'Lucifer's sin of pride'[37] at being so judgemental about their behaviour.

Occasionally, however, Michael's struggle with his ethnicity displaces his near fixation on religion. This is encapsulated in the tension between his admiration for certain English qualities, such as tolerance, and his refusal to conform to English conventions because of the anti-Irish prejudice he encounters. The latter is graphically demonstrated during an exercise at school when, required to recite a poem aloud to the rest of his class, Michael pronounces the word 'thing' in the Irish manner as 'ting' and is repeatedly scolded and beaten by the teacher for doing so.[38] Rather than correcting his pronunciation, Michael stubbornly refuses to conform to the 'King's English', reciting to himself the words of a song about the Irish revolutionary leader Robert Emmet in order to endure the ordeal. By exploring these contradictory impulses, Naughton reveals how a dual sense of English and Irish affiliation is publicly and painfully negotiated by Michael, and how he eventually learns to deploy it strategically in different circumstances.

The Streets of Ancoats (1985) by Malcolm Lynch (1923–94) is an autobiographical novel with similar concerns in a comparable setting, this time an Irish neighbourhood in Manchester in the late 1920s. Catholicism once again plays a primary role in the story, with numerous references to the sacraments of Confession and Holy Communion, religious vocations, and sectarian gangs. Nine-year-old Kevin is more self-confident about his ethnicity than Michael M'Cloud, however, something which may be due to his growing up in a more distinctly Irish environment. This is vividly illustrated by a classroom scene which is uncannily similar to the one in *One Small Boy*. Kevin, like Michael, is physically punished by the teacher for insubordination. But in this novel, rather than humiliating the boy for having an Irish background, the teacher ameliorates the shame he feels in front of his classmates by drawing their attention to the historical contribution of Irish labourers to the physical infrastructure of their region:

> 'The Irish have been coming to Manchester for three hundred years. Their muscles and tenacity built the first railway station in the world, in this town. Against impossible odds of marshes and swamps they put the first ever railway line from here to Liverpool for Stephenson's Rocket to pull passengers on. Right now, they're building a magnificent library in Peter's Square, where Peterloo took place. In the Great War,

[36] For a critique of Naughton's autobiographies, see Liam Harte, 'Migrant Memory: The Recovery of Self in the Autobiography of Bill Naughton', *Critical Survey* 8, no. 2 (1996), 168–77.

[37] Bill Naughton, *One Small Boy* (London: MacGibbon and Kee, 1957), 111.

[38] Ibid., 149–51.

which isn't all that long ago, the Manchester Regiment was recruited almost exclusively from the Ancoats Irish—yes, the Ancoats Irish. So the Irish may claim this as an Irish town.'[39]

Compared to most fictional accounts of Irish life in England, Lynch's novel is also unusual for its attention to cross-cultural interactions between immigrant groups. In Lynch's Ancoats, the Irish and the Italian communities not only share a common neighbourhood but also a religion, which is variously a source of tension, comedy, and pathos.[40] In a touching scene in the opening chapter, Kevin puzzles over his ethnicity when attracted to Vera, an Italian neighbour who 'was not a bit like the white-faced, freckled, red-haired Irish girls whom he normally threw half-bricks at'.[41] Kevin's concern that he may not be permitted to marry Vera when he grows up reflects the influence of his national distinctiveness, but his friends' reassurance that 'it would be okay because she was a Catholic, even though she was not Irish',[42] tellingly demonstrates how a communal form of religious allegiance plays a key role in the development of his ethnic consciousness.

After London, the centre of Irish life in England most often represented in fiction is Liverpool. A key example of this is a series of short stories by Moy McCrory (1953–) collected in *The Water's Edge and Other Stories* (1985), *Bleeding Sinners* (1988), and *Those Sailing Ships of His Boyhood Dreams* (1991). Most of these stories are set in the decades immediately after the Second World War and revolve around the lives of middle-aged working-class Catholic women, the majority of whom, judging from their surnames, are either Irish-born or of Irish descent. The stories are told from a firmly feminist perspective and with a sense of humour often associated with the city in which they are set.[43] Unlike other major English cities, a marked sectarian divide between Catholics and Protestants persisted in Liverpool until the mid-twentieth century. As a consequence, religion in McCrory's work is a profoundly public marker of ethnic affiliation. This is reflected in stories such as 'Last Judgement' (1985), 'New Blood' (1985), and 'The Wrong Vocation' (1991), which playfully critique the effects of Catholic indoctrination on Liverpool Irish children. 'Touring Holiday' (1985), on the other hand, signals a shift towards more personal preoccupations and has a more distinctly Irish dimension. It concerns a teenager who visits the country of her parents' birth and, for the first time, confronts her uncertain sense of national identity. Travelling there with

---

[39] Malcolm Lynch, *The Streets of Ancoats* (London: Constable, 1985), 162. There is a sizeable subgenre of fiction about Irish construction workers in England which includes Walter Macken's *I Am Alone* (1949), J. M. O'Neill's *Open Cut* (1986), John B. Keane's *The Contractors* (1993), and Edna O'Brien's short story, 'Shovel Kings', in *Saints and Sinners* (2011).

[40] For a fictional account of an Irishman's interactions with the Jewish community in London, see French-Canadian Louis Hémon's *Blind Man's Bluff*, trans Arthur Richmond (1925).

[41] Lynch, *The Streets of Ancoats*, 13.

[42] Ibid., 14. For a fictional exploration of Irish-Italian interactions in nineteenth-century Liverpool, see John Denvir, *The Brandons: A Story of Irish Life in England* (1903).

[43] For short stories about similar themes set in London, see 'After the Dance' and 'Don't Give Nothing' in Bridget O'Connor's *Here Comes John* (1993).

her family's English neighbours, the girl initially identifies as English. However, as a consequence of her neighbours' anti-Irish attitudes and sneering provocations about her Irish habits, she returns home with a radically different sense of belonging to the one that she had set out with.

A visit or sojourn in Ireland is a common device used by authors to present characters' re-evaluations of the English and Irish aspects of their identities,[44] and bears some resemblance to the journeys made by the English-born offspring of absentee Anglo-Irish landlords discussed earlier. L. T. Meade's *The Home of Silence* (1890) and Katharine Tynan's *The River* (1929) are early examples of this subgenre. Unusually for a novel about the Irish in England, *The River* is set in a rural location, in this case a fictionalized village in Lincolnshire.[45] However, it is during the course of her alternating stays between there and the west of Ireland that Kitty Adair, a woman with mixed Catholic and Protestant parentage, learns to successfully negotiate the boundaries of religious as well as national identity. In this regard, Kitty mirrors the personality of her author, whose peripatetic lifestyle informed the preoccupations of her novels.[46]

An important development in recent years has been the emergence of a body of work exploring the lives of mixed-race Irish people growing up in England. One of the first examples of this trend is *Lara* (1997), a verse novel by London-born Bernardine Evaristo (1959–). Lara is raised in Woolwich in the 1960s and 1970s, and the novel charts her family history, in richly evocative imagery, from the late eighteenth century to the present day. As well as having German, Brazilian, and Nigerian roots, Lara is fourth-generation Irish on her mother's side. Despite her distant Irish origins, and their occlusion by successive generations of Englishness, the first half of the novel traces Lara's Irish ancestry back to the Great Famine in Tipperary. In doing so, it demonstrates how an awareness of a deeply buried family history can leave profound impressions on an individual's sense of identity. This is echoed in the plurality of literary genres and forms that Evaristo draws upon to weave the historical texture of the novel, suggesting that any single narrative mode is insufficient to adequately reflect her heroine's multiple sense of belonging. The novel also reflects a broader transition within the subgenre of Irish multigenerational fiction, away from the communal contexts of identity formation towards characters' more singular searches for a sense of self.

In terms of literary form, *Vauxhall* (2013), the debut novel by London-born Irish-Nigerian Gabriel Gbadamosi (1961–), takes a more conventional approach to mixed-race Irishness. Whereas in *Lara*, a working-class south London neighbourhood is the site of a centuries-deep excavation of ethnic heritage, in *Vauxhall*, a similar environment is the anchor for a first-person realist text set in the 1970s, in which the action is

---

[44] See, for instance, Maude Casey's *Over the Water* (1987), Brian Keaney's *Family Secrets* (1997), and Dermot Bolger's *Father's Music* (1998).

[45] For examples of texts set in other rural English locations, see L. T. Meade's *Bashful Fifteen* (1892), Dorothy Macardle's *Uneasy Freehold* (1941), Caroline Blackwood's *Corrigan* (1984), Maurice Leitch's *Burning Bridges* (1989), and Pauline McLynn's *Missing You Already* (2009).

[46] See Whitney Standlee, *'Power to Observe': Irish Women Novelists in Britain, 1890–1916* (Bern: Peter Lang, 2015), 196.

played out within the confines of its immediate location. Yet its young protagonist, Michael, embarks on a no less demanding journey of discovery than Lara as he learns about his Irish and Nigerian family inheritance. This takes place while his inner-city neighbourhood is being demolished to make way for new tower blocks in a London struggling to adjust to the realities of a post-imperial multicultural dispensation. The effects of this are evident in the abject confusion and marginalization the boy feels as a consequence of the sometimes brutal racism he and his family experience. Michael's mother, who is white and might therefore be considered an insider in British culture, is nevertheless treated as an outsider, not only because she is Irish but also because she is married to a Nigerian man. In one episode, she is subject to racial abuse by a local street vendor and an elderly passer-by, the former of whom calls her a 'black man's mattress'.[47] Meanwhile, the fact that neither of them is even prepared to acknowledge Michael's presence at the scene provokes the following reaction from the boy: 'It was like I was a wooden post. They were treating me like I wasn't real. . . . "I'm a real boy," I said. They both turned to look at me, but it didn't make any difference, they looked at each other and shook their heads and turned away.'[48] This passage exemplifies one of the novel's strengths: its evocation of the boy narrator's mounting incredulity while growing up in a contested cultural environment where racism is blatant and endemic.

A similar mother–son relationship is at the heart of *My Name is Leon* (2016), the debut novel by Birmingham-born Kit de Waal (pseudonym of Mandy Theresa O'Loughlin, 1960–), daughter of an Irish mother and an African-Caribbean father. Set against the backdrop of the 1981 Birmingham riots, it is a first-person account by a mixed-race eight-year-old boy who is under the foster care of Maureen, an Irish woman.[49] Like Gbadamosi's young protagonist, Leon experiences casual racism on a daily basis, something with which Maureen and her sister Sylvia try to help him come to terms. No less crucial to Leon's informal education are two surrogate father figures: Tufty, an Afro-Caribbean man who informs him about the provocative police tactics against black people prior to the riots, and Mr Devlin, from whom he learns about the historical reasons for the Irish republican hunger strikes taking place at the time. While both characters are secondary protagonists, their influential role in the novel subtly draws attention to the fact that issues of colour and ethnicity in multicultural England cannot be reduced to a simple matter of black and white. Rather, the novel highlights how the country's cultural heterogeneity is often prone to being overwritten by an assumed hegemonic white Englishness.[50] By revisiting the politics of Anglo-Irish allegiance explored in earlier fiction about the Irish in England, this novel of mixed-race Irishness ploughs an old furrow

---

[47] Gabriel Gbadamosi, *Vauxhall* (London: Telegram, 2013), 162.   [48] Ibid.

[49] For other texts which portray the experience of the Irish in the West Midlands, see Jonathan Coe's *The Rotters' Club* (2001), Anne Bennett's *Pack Up Your Troubles* (2000), Kit de Waal's *The Trick of Time* (2018), and William Trevor's aforementioned *Felicia's Journey*.

[50] For an examination of this topic, see Mary J. Hickman, Sarah Morgan, Bronwen Walter, and Joseph Bradley, 'The Limitations of Whiteness and the Boundaries of Englishness: Second-generation Irish Identifications and Positionings in Multiethnic Britain', *Ethnicities* 5, no. 2 (2005), 160–82.

in terms of its postcolonial preoccupations, while unearthing new and challenging dimensions at every turn.

The prose fiction examined in this chapter explores how the processes of migrant adjustment to a new society are mediated under differing historical and political conditions through a variety of cultural signifiers, including nationality, religion, race, and class. It is notable also for its formal diversity, reflecting and contributing to developments in Irish prose literature more generally, from epistolary nineteenth-century modes, through various forms of twentieth-century realism and modernism, to contemporary metafictional and omni-generic narratives. However, the primary critical purpose of this chapter has been to identify and analyse predominant themes. Here, surprising commonalities are apparent not only within but between the categories of fiction examined. This is true even across works which feature ostensibly disparate cohorts of Irish migrants. One example of this is the similarity between the anomalous position in English society of the largely privileged Anglo-Irish protagonists of nineteenth-century fiction and that of the predominantly working-class characters of Irish descent in fiction from later eras. Particularly striking are the disjunctures of cultural allegiance between parents and their offspring, regardless of when or where the novel or short story is set. The emergence of a subgenre concerned with mixed-race Irish people in England further enhances the range of the canon by raising questions about the diverse components that make up diasporic identities in the contemporary period. Yet the role played here by race and colour is in many ways similar to that played by religion and class in the working-class Irish fictions set in the north of England in the early twentieth century.

Notwithstanding its numerous specificities, therefore, these continuities highlight how remarkably interconnected this literature is. Its most significant feature over the course of the last 200 years is the transition from work with a predominantly public-facing and sometimes didactic motivation to texts that are primarily inward-looking and psychological in complexion. Of course, no single text is ever entirely one or the other, and it is frequently the dynamic tension between these poles which provides such rich insights into the lives and preoccupations of its characters. As writers adopt new modes and genres in order to capture the experience of future generations of Irish migrants in England, what is unlikely to change is the essential purpose of prose fiction to provide unique insights into the relationship between society and the individual. Moreover, the fiction of the Irish in England will surely continue to demonstrate how reflecting the 'true face' of Irish migration can be an unpredictable yet engrossing narrative venture for both authors and their readers.

FURTHER READING

Arrowsmith, Aidan. 'Inside-Out: Literature, Cultural Identity and Irish Migration to England'. In Ashok Bery and Patricia Murray (eds), *Comparing Postcolonial Literatures: Dislocations*. Basingstoke: Palgrave, 2000: 59–69.

Bolger, Dermot. 'Foreword'. In Dermot Bolger (ed.), *Ireland in Exile: Irish Writers Abroad*. Dublin: New Island, 1993: 7–10.

Duffy, Patrick. 'Literary Reflections on Irish Migration in the Nineteenth and Twentieth Centuries'. In Russell King, John Connell, and Paul White (eds), *Writing Across Worlds: Literature and Migration*. London: Routledge, 1995: 20–38.

Harte, Liam (ed.). *The Literature of the Irish in Britain: Autobiography and Memoir, 1725–2001*. Basingstoke: Palgrave Macmillan, 2009.

Herron, Tom (ed.). *Irish Writing London, Volume 1: Revival to the Second World War*. London: Bloomsbury, 2013.

Herron, Tom (ed.). *Irish Writing London, Volume 2: Post-War to the Present*. London: Bloomsbury, 2013.

Hughes, Eamonn. '"Lancelot's Position": The Fiction of Irish-Britain'. In A. Robert Lee (ed.), *Other Britain, Other British: Contemporary Multicultural Fiction*. London: Pluto Press, 1995: 142–60.

McWilliams, Ellen. *Women and Exile in Contemporary Irish Fiction*. London: Palgrave Macmillan, 2013.

Murphy, James H. *Irish Novelists and the Victorian Age*. Oxford: Oxford University Press, 2011.

Murray, Tony. *London Irish Fictions: Narrative, Diaspora and Identity*. Liverpool: Liverpool University Press, 2012.

O'Brien, George. 'The Aesthetics of Exile'. In Liam Harte and Michael Parker (eds), *Contemporary Irish Fiction: Themes, Tropes, Theories*. Basingstoke: Macmillan, 2000: 35–55.

Standlee, Whitney. *'Power to Observe': Irish Women Novelists in Britain, 1890–1916*. Bern: Peter Lang, 2015.

Ward, Patrick. *Exile, Emigration and Irish Writing*. Dublin: Irish Academic Press, 2002.

CHAPTER 27

··

DEVOLUTIONARY STATES

Crosscurrents in Contemporary Irish
and Scottish Fiction

··

STEFANIE LEHNER

THERE is a long tradition of the Irish and the Scots looking back and forth across the Irish Sea for ideological, political, economic, and cultural inspiration. In the late eighteenth century, a group of radical Irish poets attached to the United Irishman's *Northern Star* newspaper took inspiration from Robert Burns for their project of Irish cultural nationalism; in the early twentieth, Edwin Muir in his (in)famous reflections on Scottish culture evoked the example of Irish writers, in particular William Butler Yeats (1865–1939), to argue that 'Scotland can only create a national literature by writing in English'.[1] This tradition continues into the present century. In 2008, then First Minister of Scotland, Alex Salmond, outlined a vision of Scotland's future as an emulation of Celtic Tiger Ireland—a prosperous 'small independent nation'[2] that stands on its own politically and economically, both in Europe and the wider world—and he and other Scottish nationalist leaders courted the political classes in the Republic of Ireland for support in the run-up to the 2014 independence referendum. While the Republic is, of course, no longer hailed as 'a shining light and beacon to the world',[3] it is argued that proponents of Scottish independence nevertheless 'reach into Irish history' when asserting that 'Ireland and Scotland shared a common experience of "bullying" and intimidation by London governments'.[4] Interestingly, it had been exactly that focus on their 'frequently

---

[1] See Liam McIlvanney, *Burns the Radical: Poetry and Politics in Late Eighteenth-Century Scotland* (East Linton: Tuckwell Press, 2002); Edwin Muir, *Scott and Scotland: The Predicament of the Scottish Writer* (Edinburgh: Polygon Books, 1982), 111.

[2] Alex Salmond, 'Shaping Scotland's Future'. Public lecture, Trinity College Dublin, 13 February 2008, www.gov.scot/News/Speeches/Speeches/First-Minister/dublin. Accessed 30 May 2016.

[3] Ray MacSharry and Padraic White, *The Making of the Celtic Tiger: The Inside Story of Ireland's Boom Economy* (Cork: Mercier Press, 2000), 360.

[4] Henry McDonald, 'Nicola Sturgeon should be cautious in seeking Irish support: Dublin has its eye on the North', *Guardian*, 31 January 2013.

tense relationship'[5] with their larger neighbour, England, that had initially stalled Irish–Scottish comparisons.

The critic Willy Maley contends that 'it is precisely because of their different but related involvements with England that each [country] has resisted comparison with the other. Anglo-Irish and Anglo-Scottish hyphens conceal an Irish–Scottish interface.'[6] To some extent, such an interface is emblematized, culturally and politically, by Northern Ireland. However, it is notable that contemporary Scottish politicians have been keen to downplay historical links with the North, while stressing affiliations with the Republic. One example of this has been the recent upsurge in interest over the question of whether Scotland is becoming 'Ulsterized'. This question, which has drawn academic and journalistic comment, circles around the extent to which Scottish (electoral) politics have begun to mirror the divided nature of Northern Ireland's by becoming polarized into an ideological zero-sum game played out between proponents of nationalism/independence/separatism on the one hand and unionism on the other.[7] As Graham Walker notes, the fierce opposition to the notion of 'Ulsterization' among Scottish commentators exposes a notable anxiety about certain 'eschewed' connections between Scotland and Northern Ireland, not least among them the importance of residual sectarianism.[8] The resilience of the question is illustrated by its thematic appearances in works such as Andrew O'Hagan's 2006 novel, *Be Near Me*, and, through football associations, in Irvine Welsh's *Trainspotting* (1993).

What this attests to is a complex historical, political, and cultural relationship between these three 'regions' of the Atlantic archipelago, with literature functioning as 'a key crossover'.[9] Indeed, there is a long tradition of literary crosscurrents between the two islands, evident, for instance, in the ways in which the recuperation of ancient legends and myth, initiated in Scotland with the publication of James Macpherson's *Poems of Ossian* (1773), inspired the later Irish Literary Revival.[10] More recently, there has been a remarkable literary 'renaissance' that has occurred in Ireland and Scotland since the 1980s, particularly in the area of prose fiction, which is, amongst other things, characterized by the increasing emergence of many women writers and a notable tendency

---

[5] Liam McIlvanney and Ray Ryan, 'Introduction', in Liam McIlvanney and Ray Ryan (eds), *Ireland and Scotland: Culture and Society, 1700–2000* (Dublin: Four Courts Press, 2005), 15. While it is controversial to designate Scotland's historical experience as colonial, Ireland's history is widely discussed in colonial terms. For a comparative analysis of the differences between Ireland's and Scotland's relation to the Union, see Jim Smyth, 'Arguments For and Against Union: Scotland and Ireland: 1700–2000', in McIlvanney and Ryan (eds), *Ireland and Scotland*, 23–37. For a detailed discussion of postcolonial approaches in Irish and Scottish studies, see Stefanie Lehner, *Subaltern Ethics in Contemporary Scottish and Irish Literature: Tracing Counter-Histories* (Basingstoke: Palgrave Macmillan, 2011), 30–42.

[6] Willy Maley, ' "Kilt by Kelt shell Kithagain with Kinagain": Joyce and Scotland', in Derek Attridge and Marjorie Howes (eds), *Semicolonial Joyce* (Cambridge: Cambridge University Press, 2000), 205.

[7] David Torrance, 'The Ulsterisation of Scottish politics is complete', *Herald Scotland*, 9 May 2016.

[8] Graham Walker, 'Billy or Dan: why deny that Scotland is "Ulsterised"?', *Scottish Review*, 18 May 2016.

[9] Maley, ' "Kilt by Kelt shell Kithagain with Kinagain" ', 205.

[10] See, for example, Thomas M. Curley, *Samuel Johnson, the Ossian Fraud, and the Celtic Revival in Great Britain and Ireland* (Cambridge: Cambridge University Press, 2009).

towards formal and stylistic experimentation.[11] These new generations of writers emerged in a period that notably transformed the political, economic, and cultural landscapes of Ireland, Northern Ireland, and Scotland. In all three regions, change was associated with negotiating a range of political, economic, and socio-cultural fissures and pressure points.

In Scotland, the failure, from a nationalist perspective, of the 1979 devolution referendum coincided with the election of a Conservative government at Westminster, which created a democratic deficit for Scotland because it had almost no electoral mandate north of the border, and was followed by severe economic recession. In Northern Ireland, the protracted period of violent political conflict perpetuated and deepened the ethno-nationalist divide. The Troubles also continually spilled over into the Irish Republic, destabilizing consecutive governments and unsettling party political and constitutional consensus.[12] The protracted recession of the 1980s in the Republic led to renewed spikes in emigration and unemployment, whilst the climate of conservative Catholic traditionalism caused repeated clashes with liberals and feminists over issues such as access to contraception, abortion, and divorce. While the socio-cultural and political-economic landscape of the Republic had been undergoing sustained change since the 1960s, accelerated by the country's membership of the European Economic Community after 1973, it was the sudden advent of the 1990s economic boom that most radically altered its infrastructure and outlook.[13] In turn, the 1997 Scottish devolution referendum transformed the political configuration of the country by paving the way for the 1998 Scotland Act, which meant that in May 1999 a Scottish parliament was convened for the first time since its adjournment in 1707. Devolution was also part of a broader package of political reforms in Northern Ireland that consolidated the peace process, apparent, for instance, in the way in which internal power-sharing mechanisms were mandated in the 1998 Belfast Agreement, which itself represented a defining moment in the evolution of relations between the constituent parts of the British and Irish archipelago.

The rise of Irish-Scottish studies in this period has, in part, been underpinned by significant governmental funding, which itself can be read as a kind of devolutionary act.[14] Cumulatively, these changes signal a shift in the locus of decision-making and

---

[11] The term 'renaissance' is used more widely in the Scottish context. See, for example, Douglas Gifford, 'At Last—The Real Scottish Literary Renaissance?', *Books in Scotland* 34 (1990), 1–4.

[12] See Henry Patterson, *Ireland's Violent Frontier: The Border and Anglo-Irish Relations During the Troubles* (Basingstoke: Palgrave Macmillan, 2013).

[13] See, for example, Michael Parker, 'Changing History: The Republic and Northern Ireland since 1990', in Scott Brewster and Michael Parker (eds), *Irish Literature since 1990: Diverse Voices* (Manchester: Manchester University Press, 2009), 3–15.

[14] Trinity College Dublin received £400,000 from the Irish Higher Education Authority to set up a Centre for Irish-Scottish Studies in 1999, the same year in which the Research Institute of Irish and Scottish Studies (RIISS) was founded at the University of Aberdeen. In 2005, RIISS was awarded £1.34 million by the UK Arts and Humanities Research Council, the largest ever single award in the humanities at that point in time. See T. M. Devine, 'Making the Caledonian Connection', in McIlvanney and Ryan (eds), *Ireland and Scotland*, 248–57.

governance towards decentralization. As Arthur Aughey has pointed out, devolution entailed an ongoing 'modification of how the UK's component nations stand in relation to one another'.[15] Furthermore, the 'new politics' of this devolutionary movement also called for the opening of political space to civic society and the deepening of access to previously liminal voices. The embedding of these dynamics in everyday life through-out the UK and Ireland occur on a number of levels and, as Aughey suggests, they set in motion a path whose destination—like most political journeys—was and remains uncertain.[16] These devolutionary impulses are apparent in the literature of this period, which is characterized by critique of traditional power relations—whether in terms of gender hierarchies, class, or race—and a foregrounding of those marginal identities and voices that have been tacitly occluded and excluded. At the level of form, the experimentations in the works of these writers are often associated with postmodernism, through their challenge to established metanarratives and dominant national paradigms.

This chapter uses the term and concept of devolution as a lens to explore the changed literary landscape of Irish and Scottish fiction since the 1980s. Rather than consider devolution solely as a political and institutional process that concerns 'the devolving of power by central government to local or regional administration',[17] the chapter will also consider its figurative connotations, from the intransitive meanings of the verb, which connotes 'descent or passing on through a series of revolutions or stages, in time, order, etc.'.[18] This suggests a process of transition that implies a change but no radical break, evoking the sense of an inheritance that is being passed on: in short, evolution rather than revolution. One way to read this in relation to 'devolutionary fiction'[19]—that is, fiction written prior to and after devolution agreements in Scotland and Northern Ireland in the late 1990s—is by considering how such work relates to inherited literary traditions and national paradigms. I want to suggest that the works considered in this chapter can be read as devolutionary not only because they are written in a specific period but also because they rework, revise, and transform received traditions and paradigms to allow for new voices, perspectives, histories, gender relations, and forms of identity to emerge.

This cultural understanding of devolution resonates with the political meaning of the term, which posits that devolution is 'not a cessation of all power from the centre with the establishment of new states; rather it is the distribution of selected responsi-bilities, with core state power residing in the national, that is, the British, parliament'.[20] In this regard, devolution has been criticized, specifically in the Scottish context, as an

---

[15] Arthur Aughey, *The British Question* (Manchester: Manchester University Press, 2013), 61.

[16] Ibid., 55.

[17] Judy Pearsall (ed.), *Concise Oxford English Dictionary* (Oxford: Oxford University Press, 2002), 392.

[18] *OED* online, https://www.oed.com/. Accessed 4 June 2016.

[19] See Graeme Macdonald's definition of this term in 'Scottish Extractions: "Race" and Racism in Devolutionary Fiction', *Orbis Litterarum* 65, no. 2 (2010), 81.

[20] John Wilson and Karyn Stapleton, 'Introduction', in John Wilson and Karyn Stapleton (eds), *Devolution and Identity* (Aldershot: Ashgate, 2006), 2.

ultimately 'conservative political process' that is 'no more or less than an effort to re-legitimise the UK state.'[21] This reading highlights the importance of territorial politics within what Aughey refers to as the modifications set in motion by devolution. In so doing, it risks neglecting the ways that devolution affects and has insinuated itself into broader political and cultural spaces. Framing devolution as a (counter) revolutionary, conservative tactic to (paradoxically) re-legitimate the state ends in the contradiction that nationalist/separatist movements have thrived in the past two decades, politically, socially, and culturally, in the face of a neoliberal attack on welfarism. Alternatively, viewing devolution through an evolutionary lens allows us to see how devolution gives rise to the kind of spaces where alternative forms of political mobilization and cultural expression can occur. It also allows us to see devolution as precipitating accommodation as well as containment, as evidenced in the failure of the 2014 referendum to bring about an independent Scotland and the dwindling of support for reunification among Northern Irish nationalists prior to the 2016 Brexit referendum. As such, it is possible to avoid a moral judgement on devolution, while at the same time considering how it facilitates and delimits expressions of history, gender, and identity, amongst others.

This chapter will trace some of these devolutionary 'states' in Scottish and Irish literature by considering over three sections how writers are engaged in rewriting and transforming inherited literary paradigms which have proven disabling and restrictive. This specifically concerns the perception of these regions' 'failed cultural continuity',[22] in the words of Cairns Craig, a sentiment reflected in Seamus Deane's claim that Ireland has 'no continuity of cultural experience comparable to that of the nation states of France and England',[23] which is also applicable to Scotland. This heightened recognition of these states' internal divisions, dualities, and fragmentation is captured in the Gothic tradition in Irish and Scottish writing and in G. Gregory Smith's concept of 'the Caledonian Antisyzygy', which traced the distinctiveness of Scottish literature to its 'combination of opposites.'[24] It is also reflected in Northern Ireland's 'two traditions' model and Thomas Kinsella's notion of the divided Irish mind.[25] Contemporary Irish and Scottish fiction, I suggest, has been engaged in considering how these tensions and dualities can provide opportunities for creatively rethinking conceptions of history, gender relations, and

---

[21] Scott Hames, 'Introduction', in Scott Hames (ed.), *Unstated: Writers on Scottish Independence* (Edinburgh: Word Power Books, 2012), 7.

[22] Cairns Craig, 'National Literature and Cultural Capital in Scotland and Ireland', in McIlvanney and Ryan (eds), *Ireland and Scotland*, 62.

[23] Seamus Deane, *Celtic Revivals: Essays in Modern Irish Literature 1880–1980* (London: Faber and Faber, 1985), 18.

[24] See G. Gregory Smith, *Scottish Literature: Character and Influence* (London: Macmillan, 1919), 4–27. For a comparative analysis of the literary tradition of Scottish and Irish Gothic, see David Punter, 'Scottish and Irish Gothic', in Jerrold Hogle (ed.), *The Cambridge Companion to Gothic Fiction* (Cambridge: Cambridge University Press, 2002), 105–23.

[25] Thomas Kinsella, 'The Divided Mind', in David Pierce (ed.), *Irish Writing in the Twentieth Century: A Reader* (Cork: Cork University Press, 2000), 810–14. Kinsella's influential essay was first published in 1971.

identity constructions. The following discussion will explore these interrelated issues through the lenses of nine indicative Scottish and Irish novels which establish *affiliations* that counter their *filiative* containment within national paradigms.[26]

DEVOLUTIONARY HISTORIES: ALASDAIR GRAY, PATRICK MCCABE, AND ROBERT MCLIAM WILSON

This section will comparatively examine three texts that both dismantle and reimagine such divisions and dualities as have characterized the cultural history of Scotland, the Irish Republic, and Northern Ireland: *Lanark* (1981) by Alasdair Gray (1934–2019), *The Dead School* (1995) by Patrick McCabe (1955–), and *Eureka Street* (1996) by Robert McLiam Wilson (1964–). All three feature male character doubles, which is reflected in their formal division into two intersecting narrative strands. Arguably, this Gothic idiom can also be seen in these novels' mappings—prior to the more recent devolutionary transformations charted above—of their respective socio-political landscapes as traumatic, haunted, and paralysed. The power of historical repetition in these texts seems at times to be more forceful than historical change, and history itself just another uncanny repetition, a failure to deliver meaningful change. Yet all three texts counter this dynamic by their insistence on alternative perspectives which may challenge this kind of historical determinism, albeit to different degrees and extents.

Published in 1981, yet written over a period of almost thirty years, Gray's *Lanark* is generally considered one of the key texts of the Scottish 'renaissance' in the 1980s and captures the pessimism that characterized Scottish politics and culture in that period. Invoking Smith's 'Caledonian Antisyzygy', *Lanark* is split into realist and fantasy sections, which juxtapose and intersect the realist portrait of Duncan Thaw as a young artist in Glasgow with the fantastical adventures of Lanark in the dystopian city of Unthank and its related heterocosms. The realist sections of Books 1 and 2 are framed within the fantasy parts of Books 3 and 4, so that the order of the books is 3124. As Nastler, Gray's parodic postmodern projection of himself, explains in the epilogue, 'I want *Lanark* to be read in one order but eventually thought of in another.'[27]

As his double, the character of Lanark functions both as a continuation (in the form of a rebirth) and a repetition of Thaw, thus emphasizing their parallel predicaments, which can be related to the predicament of Scotland itself. Both Thaw and Lanark are characterized by a lack of confidence; they also share an inhibited sexuality that has an arrogant aspect, which is expressed in their struggle to enter meaningful personal

---

[26] See Edward Said's distinction between filiation and affiliation in *The World, the Text, and the Critic* (London: Faber and Faber, 1983), 16–20.

[27] Alasdair Gray, *Lanark* (London: Picador, 1985), 483.

relationships and find sexual fulfilment. Their psychological states are reflected in their physical diseases: while Thaw suffers from chronic asthma and eczema, Lanark develops 'dragonhide', whereby his body becomes steadily encased in 'hard insulating armour'.[28] This condition not only literalizes his metaphorical condition of emotional and sexual frigidity but, as Ozenfant, one of the doctors of the institute in which Lanark finds himself, explains, is also reflective of nations: 'Like nations losing unjust wars they convert more and more of themselves into armour when they should surrender or retreat'.[29]

This allegorical alignment of the personal with the political becomes even more pronounced in Thaw's disturbing rape fantasies, through which he often attempts to alleviate his physical afflictions. The 'state' of the raped woman—and his own implication in the act—becomes a metaphor for the 'state' of the nation, which is most forcefully expressed in Gray's subsequent novel, *1982 Janine* (1984), which uses the pornographic fantasies of a middle-aged Scotsman, Jock, to comment on contemporary Scottish politics: 'But if a country is not just a tract of land but a whole people then clearly Scotland has been fucked'.[30] As Jock realizes his own complicity in this misogynistic process of oppression, his embrace of his feminine marginality enables him to emerge as 'a new man' or, at least, 'not the same man, anyway'.[31] Yet such a transformation seems unavailable to Lanark and Thaw, who remain trapped in an all-powerful system whereby 'each escape into an alternative world is an escape leading only to repetition in another dimension of the very contradictions from which [they] sought release'.[32]

Gray's use of pathologies to dramatize the enervated condition of Scotland after 1979 is replicated by Patrick McCabe in his depiction of Ireland's troubled transition from a 'traditional' to a 'modern' 'state'. Like *Lanark*, *The Dead School* merges realism and fantasy into a Gothic tale, whose two narrative strands juxtapose and interweave the histories of schoolteachers Raphael Bell, born in 1913, and Malachy Dudgeon, born in 1956, whose life stories are narrated from their respective beginnings to their disastrous ends in 1979. Malachy's embrace of liberal values, drugs, rock music, and American consumer culture appears to supersede Raphael's rigid traditionalism and patriotic endorsement of 'all things Gaelic and Irish'.[33] However, if this suggests a period of profound transformations, it also conceals a notable sense of stasis. Despite the Lemassian project of modernization, stubborn impediments—chief among which were a Church-endorsed social conservatism and economic underperformance and recession—suggested a climate of political and cultural stagnation. As Luke Gibbons notes, 'If a Rip Van Winkle fell asleep in the 1950s and woke up in the 1980s, he could be forgiven for thinking that nothing had changed in between'.[34]

While Raphael's symbolic union with Nessa from the 'wee North' produces a stillborn son, Malachy represents a form of 'rebirth', as the progeny and heir of 'the damaging

---

[28] Ibid., 68.   [29] Ibid.

[30] Alasdair Gray, *1982 Janine* (Edinburgh: Canongate, 2003), 126.   [31] Ibid., 330.

[32] Cairns Craig, 'Going Down to Hell is Easy: *Lanark*, Realism and the Limits of Imagination', in Robert Crawford and Thom Nairn (eds), *The Arts of Alasdair Gray* (Edinburgh: Edinburgh University Press, 1991), 98.

[33] Patrick McCabe, *The Dead School* (London: Picador, 1995), 107.

[34] Luke Gibbons, *Transformations in Irish Culture* (Cork: Cork University Press, 1996), 83.

silences embedded within [Raphael's] own belief in and love of all things Irish'.[35] Despite Raphael's perception of his younger colleague as the personification of all foreign and modern evils, Malachy can be read as the product of deformed and defunct patriarchal institutions—from marriage and the Catholic Church to the wider community—that make up the social and moral fabric of the Irish Republic, and which are exposed as pathological versions of Éamon de Valera's dream vision of a wholesome bucolic nation. Both protagonists are ultimately defeated by their inability to recognize their own implication and entrapment in these discourses: McCabe's 'strongly deterministic vision',[36] like Gray's, insists that the force of repetition overpowers the possibilities for change. Yet while the characters are unable to break out of this traumatic paradigm, *The Dead School* itself raises our awareness of the destructive legacy of a system that neglects ethical responsibility towards the other by exhuming marginalized and silenced stories, such as those concerning the death of Mrs McAdoo's baby or the Dummy's suicide.[37]

Lanark also foregrounds possibilities of seeing things differently, not only by fusing alternative perspectives in Thaw's paintings but by highlighting the importance of the metaphor of triangulation for both Thaw and Lanark.[38] As a geodesic surveying method, triangulation uses two known points to determine the third point in a triangle; in this way, it insists on the necessity of dual perspectives. This method works in *Lanark* to reconcile divisions and repetitions by countering both the shared solipsistic vision of Thaw and Lanark and the determinism of the God-author-creator-conjurer Nastler, whom Lanark meets in the epilogue. Shortly before his death, Lanark has a vision of climbing a mountain with his son Sandy that both repeats and redeems Lanark's earlier life as Thaw, when he went hiking with his father. Both times, the hikers encounter a triangulation point, whose symbolic assertion that no single viewpoint suffices enables Lanark to realize that 'I am not a victim': 'I don't care what absurdity, failure, death I am moving toward. Even when your world has lapsed into black nothing, it will have made sense because Sandy once enjoyed it in the sunlight.'[39]

In a comparable manner, Robert McLiam Wilson uses double perspectives in *Eureka Street* as a means to counter determinism and violence. The novel is set in the period before and after the 1994 paramilitary ceasefires in Northern Ireland, which fostered the negotiations that led to the Belfast Agreement, thus offering a much more optimistic version of history than the two previously discussed novels. *Eureka Street* suggests a transgression of the two-community paradigm by focusing on the friendship between Chuckie Lurgan, a Protestant, and Jake Jackson, originally from the Catholic Falls Road, and by juxtaposing the intra-diegetic, first-person narration of Jake with an extra-diegetic, third-person narrator. Such refraction of viewpoints was already emphasized in Wilson's first novel, *Ripley Bogle* (1989), whose eponymous hero insists on calling

[35] Tom Herron, 'ContamiNation: Patrick McCabe and Colm Tóibín's Pathographies of the Republic', in Liam Harte and Michael Parker (eds), *Contemporary Irish Fiction: Themes, Tropes, Theories* (Basingstoke: Macmillan, 2000), 182.
[36] Ibid., 189.
[37] For a detailed discussion of these aspects of the novel, see Lehner, *Subaltern Ethics*, 67–81.
[38] On the importance of triangulation in *Lanark*, see Stephen Bernstein, *Alasdair Gray* (London: Associated University Presses, 1999), 46–57.
[39] Gray, *Lanark*, 515.

himself 'Ripley Irish British Bogle'[40] to mark his hybrid parentage and to disrupt what Edna Longley calls 'the conditioning process of the North'.[41]

Eureka Street embraces the novel genre's heteroglossia as an analogue to the city. Chapter ten offers a poetic, almost songlike metafictional description of the sleeping city of Belfast, seen from above: 'The city's surface is thick with living citizens. Its earth is richly sown with its many dead. The city is a repository of narratives, of stories. Present tense, past tense or future. The city is a novel.'[42] However, this harmonious vision is violently shattered by the bomb explosion that abruptly ends the stories of apparently minor characters such as Rosemary. The narrative voice insists: 'They all had stories. But they weren't short stories. They shouldn't have been short stories. They should have each been novels, profound, delightful novels, eight hundred pages or more.'[43] Part of the carnage of chapter eleven is the murder of narrative. The narrator here not only bears witness to the violence and the erasure of stories but also invokes empathy; indeed, *Eureka Street* insists that such imaginative empathy offers a double vision that works as a counter to violence. Reflecting on his propensity to engage in acts of violence, Jake realizes that

> It was because I had no imagination. The human route to sympathy or empathy is a clumsy one but it's all we've got. To understand the consequences of our actions we must exercise our imaginations. We decide that it's a bad idea to hit someone over the head with a bottle because we put ourselves in their position and comprehend that if we were hit over the head with a bottle, then, my goodness, wouldn't that hurt! We swap shoes. If you do this—if you can do this—then violence or harm becomes decreasingly possible for you.[44]

As Elmer Kennedy-Andrews notes, 'This is the novel's Eureka cry—to see that the Other can be enriching, rather than something to be distrusted or abominated or brought under control.'[45]

Eureka Street, like *Lanark* and *The Dead School*, charts its protagonists' respective quests for heterosexual union and emotional fulfilment. The difference is that in this novel these quests are successful. *Eureka Street* proliferates in happy endings, not only for Chuckie and Jake but also for several other characters, some of whom find happiness in more transgressive unions, such as that between Chuckie's working-class mother and her long-known female neighbour, and that between the Muslim Rajinder and his Jewish girlfriend: 'There'd been a couple of ceasefires and suddenly Belfast was the city of

[40] Robert McLiam Wilson, *Ripley Bogle* (London: Vintage, 1998), 16. Ripley Bogle's act of renaming echoes that of his creator, who was born Robert Wilson but added a middle name that approximates to the Irish translation of his surname.

[41] Edna Longley, *The Living Stream: Literature and Revisionism in Ireland* (Newcastle upon Tyne: Bloodaxe Books, 1994), 176.

[42] Robert McLiam Wilson, *Eureka Street* (London: Vintage, 1997), 215.

[43] Ibid., 231.   [44] Ibid., 62–3.

[45] Elmer Kennedy-Andrews, 'The Novel and the Northern Troubles', in John Wilson Foster (ed.), *The Cambridge Companion to the Irish Novel* (Cambridge: Cambridge University Press, 2006), 255.

love.'[46] In the end, Jake, who has spent most of the novel railing against the militant republicanism embodied by the ironically named Aoirghe Jenkins, rather surprisingly starts a sexual relationship with her, thereby symbolically enacting the domestication of her fervent nationalism through his moderate humanism.[47]

Lanark, *Eureka Street*, and *The Dead School* rewrite their respective national paradigms, neither completely abandoning 'traditional conceptions' nor remaining helplessly 'entrapped' or 'contained' within them.[48] The emphasis on alternative stories and perspectives in all three novels works to destabilize deterministic visions of history and unilateral, centralized power relations, such as that between author/narrator and character. This devolutionary impulse foregrounds the local, the marginal, the silenced, and the oppressed; yet it is notable that all three works replicate an oppressive gendered national model in which women are reduced to signs and symbols of the nation. In the rape fantasies of Thaw and Jock, as well as in the national romances between Raphael and Nessa and Jake and Aoirghe, women, treated as national allegories, remain silent ciphers without agency or voice.[49] Berthold Schoene's reading of 'the *doppelgänger* motif as a gender-specific obsession with difference' in the context of the (post)colonial male's 'fear of his own intrinsic self-and-otherness, or "effeminacy"', sheds light on the ways in which the male protagonists of all three novels attempt to assert their virility and reclaim patriarchal dominance, while suffering from their perceived (post)colonial 'effeminacy'.[50] Ultimately, the devolutionary imaginaries of *Lanark*, *Eureka Street*, and *The Dead School* remain tethered to a gendered colonial paradigm that reinstalls a system of unequal and binary gender roles and relations.

DEVOLUTIONARY ENGENDERINGS: ANNE ENRIGHT AND A. L. KENNEDY

Perhaps it was in order to pre-empt women being, once again, reduced to such voiceless symbols that Irish writer Anne Enright (1962–) and Scottish writer A. L. Kennedy

---

[46] Wilson, *Eureka Street*, 345.

[47] See Richard Kirkland, 'Bourgeois Redemptions: The Fiction of Glenn Patterson and Robert McLiam Wilson', in Harte and Parker (eds), *Contemporary Irish Fiction*, 213-31.

[48] Beat Witschi, 'Defining a Scottish Identity', *Books in Scotland* 34 (1990), 6; Alison Lumsden, 'Innovation and Reaction in the Fiction of Alasdair Gray', in Gavin Wallace and Randall Stevenson (eds), *The Scottish Novel Since the Seventies* (Edinburgh: Edinburgh University Press, 1994), 115–26.

[49] For feminist criticism of this gendered national trope in relation to Ireland, see Ailbhe Smyth (ed.), *Irish Women's Studies Reader* (Dublin: Attic Press, 1993) and Eavan Boland et al., *A Dozen Lips* (Dublin: Attic Press, 1994). For the Scottish context, see Kirsten Stirling, *Bella Caledonia: Woman, Nation, Text* (Amsterdam: Rodopi, 2008). For the Irish–Scottish comparative context, see Marilyn Reizbaum, 'Gender and Nationalism in Scotland and Ireland: Making and Breaking the Waves', in McIlvanney and Ryan (eds), *Ireland and Scotland*, 183–202.

[50] Berthold Schoene, 'The Union and Jack: British Masculinities and the Post-nation', in Glenda Norquay and Gerry Smyth (eds), *Across the Margins: Cultural Identity and Change in the Atlantic Archipelago* (Manchester: Manchester University Press, 2002), 94.

(1965–) decided in their respective 1995 novels, *The Wig My Father Wore* and *So I Am Glad*, to feature spectral males, Kennedy resurrecting the ghost of Cyrano de Bergerac, Enright, the angel of a suicide. Like their male colleagues, both authors evoke the motif of the double; here, however, the intention is to dramatize the instability of naturalized dichotomies such as body/mind, life/death, magic/realism, which in both works point to the destabilization of fixed gender categories. Such deconstructions allow for the creative reconstruction of the self and identity outside binary gendered norms. Both novels are set in the 1990s, exemplifying the profound social and economic changes taking place in Britain and Ireland at the time. They are narrated through the first-person perspectives of their female protagonists, both of whom are caught at moments of personal crisis which have been brought on by their struggles to realize themselves as independent women in patriarchal societies. And in both works, the (imaginary) relationships these women foster with ghostly and therefore non-phallic representations of masculinity enable them to rediscover sexual intimacy and nurture, which allows them in turn to engender alternative gender roles and relations.

The protagonists of both novels reject patriarchal constructions of femininity. 'I'm not a "woman",'[51] Enright's Grace tells her chauvinistic work colleagues who equate femininity with being sexually available and devoted to men. Grace also insists that 'I never was a virgin',[52] refusing the Catholic notion of the impurity of sexual desires. Yet for Grace, as for Kennedy's Jennifer Wilson, sexuality is strictly demarcated from emotions. Just as Grace intimately 'understand[s] the difference between sex and love',[53] so too Jennifer has detached intercourse from emotional engagement. Being 'intimately active instead of intimate' allows her to conceal the 'invincible lack of involvement on [her] part'.[54] This emotional detachment within these women's private lives is reflected in their professions: Grace works as a producer for the RTÉ television show, 'Love Quiz', and Jennifer as a radio announcer for the national news. Their work for the national media—a means of mass communication that constitutes what Benedict Anderson famously called an 'imagined community'[55]—exposes its negative impact as a contributor to the loneliness, atomization, and one-way communication that characterizes postmodern social relations. Both protagonists are complicit in the commodification and exploitation of human emotions and social relations. Whereas Grace's dating show uses the romantic concept of love to sell sex as an ersatz for intimacy, Jennifer allows the trained neutrality of her voice to be used to manipulate facts for commercial and ideological ends. Yet, like Grace, Jennifer ultimately has 'no say in what I say or even how I say it'.[56]

In both novels, the female narrators struggle to assert control over the capacity of their narratives to challenge the imposed system and 'false order constructed by the

---

[51] Anne Enright, *The Wig My Father Wore* (London: Jonathan Cape, 1995), 50.
[52] Ibid., 45.   [53] Ibid.
[54] A. L. Kennedy, *So I Am Glad* (London: Vintage, 1996), 4.
[55] See Benedict Anderson, *Imagined Communities: Reflections on the Origin and Spread of Nationalism* (London: Verso, 1983).
[56] Kennedy, *So I Am Glad*, 62.

authorities and regulators of [their] social world'.[57] That Enright and Kennedy employ methods of 'collage and montage' is evidenced by the episodic and fragmentary structures of their novels, which resist narrative and temporal coherence, as Grace and Jennifer both insist on 'ordering events, even altering time, to suit [their] personal chronology of emotional development'.[58] The use of fantastical elements further underlines this break with convention, as the 'magic' of Enright's Stephen and Kennedy's Savinien is offset by their reality and immediacy, thus destabilizing the distinction between the real and the fantastic.

Both texts resurrect a historically and geographically displaced male figure. The angel of Enright's story, Stephen, killed himself in Canada in 1934, while Jennifer discovers that her supposed new flatmate is in fact the seventeenth-century French writer and duellist Savinien de Cyrano de Bergerac. These long-dead figures arrive in a rather down-to-earth manner. While Savinien falls out of death (instead of rising up from it) to land in Jennifer's house, Grace recalls that her angel 'rang at my door with an ordinary face on him and asked for a cup of tea, as was his right. He revealed himself on the threshold with broad comments about my fertility. Who needs it?'[59] Whereas Grace is associated with her body from the start of the novel, Stephen is represented as acorporeal. Epitomizing the Cartesian gender divide between body and mind, Stephen impersonates the hegemonic masculine realm of the mind/spirit in opposition to Grace's body/flesh. This is underlined by his obsession with whiteness. He makes 'entirely white' meals and paints everything white, which prompts Grace to tell her mother that he has a 'virginity complex'.[60] But Stephen's attempt to implement a Catholic sexual morality is consistently undermined by Grace, who contaminates his imposed whiteness with the redness of blood, tomatoes, and blackberry jam—a colour symbolizing fertility, menstruation, and birth, and thus an affirmation of life against his virtual death.

As this chromatic imagery insinuates, alongside the transgression of the life/death distinction, *The Wig My Father Wore* destabilizes gender binaries. The male 'angel in the house'[61] becomes the feminized counterpart to the breadwinner, Grace. Through their interrelation their allocated gender identities become blurred to a point where 'each approaches the other's condition'.[62] While Stephen gains corporeality—he bleeds and even becomes ill—Grace's body returns to what she calls her 'new girl's body'.[63] This intermingling muddies gender distinctions whilst still keeping in place unique differences. Thus, Grace insists on her own corporeal uniqueness when she feels threatened by incorporation: 'I want my body back. I want my hands back and my cellulite and my

---

[57] Patricia Coughlan, 'Irish Literature and Feminism in Postmodernity', *Hungarian Journal of English and American Studies* 10, nos. 1–2 (2004), 184.

[58] David Borthwick, 'A. L. Kennedy's Dysphoric Fictions', in Berthold Schoene (ed.), *The Edinburgh Companion to Contemporary Scottish Literature* (Edinburgh: Edinburgh University Press, 2007), 265.

[59] Enright, *The Wig My Father Wore*, 1.   [60] Ibid., 37.

[61] Reflecting on the writing process, Enright compared herself to 'a Victorian male writing about a female "angel" of domesticity, virtue and grace'. See Caitriona Moloney (ed.), *Irish Women Writers Speak Out: Voices from the Field* (Syracuse, NY: Syracuse University Press, 2003), 60.

[62] Coughlan, 'Irish Literature and Feminism in Postmodernity', 185.

[63] Enright, *The Wig My Father Wore*, 163.

stupid-looking feet.'[64] And while Stephen attains a more material presence, even appearing on Grace's dating show, he nonetheless retains his 'magic': he has a halo, wings, and, like Savinien, he glows. Conversely, Jennifer's alienation from both her body and her emotions makes her initially 'an appropriate model for the masculinized Cartesian subject'.[65] As a poet and soldier, Savinien, by contrast, combines masculine and feminine traits in a way that amazes Jennifer. It is his tenderness and utter vulnerability—his feminine, non-threatening side—that make her assume responsibility for him: she pays his rent and cares for him when he is severely ill. Yet their encounter is also a demand for recognition, not only of his own true identity as Cyrano de Bergerac but also of her own uniqueness, which she finds reflected in him: 'I knew what frightened me in him was only what I recognised of me.'[66]

The act of falling in love with their doubles generates for both female protagonists a critical engagement with their repressed personal histories, in particular the place of sex and sexuality in their respective family histories. Whereas the sexual morality of Grace's family insists on the silence and secrecy of bodily pleasures, epitomized by the novel's eponymous wig,[67] Jennifer's parents never kept any secrets, which is meant literally. As a child, Jennifer was made to watch her parents having sex, which is when her detachment began: 'All I did was watch. . . . I was left alone.'[68] For both women, the process of exhuming their pasts opens up future dimensions. In *The Wig My Father Wore*, this is announced by the horoscope that Grace's angel reads to her: 'Changes are afoot Gemini! . . . Clear out the old and sing in the new.'[69] Similarly, Jennifer recalls how 'an old thing seemed to stop and a new began and I stepped through a change of time'.[70]

Sexual union with their spectral others makes both protagonists come alive to female creation and creativity. Grace becomes pregnant and moves to the west of Ireland after Stephen disappears. The novel closes with a snapshot of her cycling along a country road, leaving a trail of leaking milk in her wake. This milk trail, symbolizing nurture and prefiguring her mothering role, becomes a metaphor for ethical love relations, for a non-patriarchal, mutually satisfying relationship between two beings, self and other, and, by extension, for an integration of the past and the future. Grieving his loss, Grace understands that her guardian angel has not abandoned her:

> When I turn around I will see it on the road. I will see the trail of milk all the way up the hill and I will see Stephen at the top of the hill with the clouds behind him, looking at the milk or looking at me and he will be in love with me.[71]

It is notable that this passage is rendered in the future tense; Grace looks backwards to look forward, to embrace an indeterminate future with Stephen's love watching over her.

---

[64] Ibid., 126–7.

[65] Carole Jones, *Disappearing Men: Gender Disorientation in Scottish Fiction 1979–1999* (Amsterdam: Rodopi, 2009), 143.

[66] Kennedy, *So I Am Glad*, 248.

[67] See Coughlan, 'Irish Literature and Feminism in Postmodernity', 183.

[68] Kennedy, *So I Am Glad*, 71.   [69] Enright, *The Wig My Father Wore*, 90.

[70] Kennedy, *So I Am Glad*, 137–8.   [71] Enright, *The Wig My Father Wore*, 215.

In a similar fashion, Jennifer Wilson eventually surpasses her enclosed self and embraces the dualism of 'We. That's Savinien and I. Us. Goodbye me and welcome to we.'[72] Yet like Stephen, Savinien perishes as Jennifer comes emotionally fully alive. Whilst Grace's spectral union produces a child, Jennifer's produces a book. Through writing, Jennifer wants 'to reverse . . . the passage of time' but realizes that 'At the end of a page, a chapter, a day of work, I have to come back.'[73] While she, like Grace, mourns the loss of her lover, she also starts to understand that writing, like the ghostly other, always already belongs to the future. In concluding her memoir, Jennifer is able to embrace this unknown futurity. Her last line reads: 'I will miss this [writing] and I will miss Savinien and I will be glad.'[74]

Through their encounters with non-threatening, non-phallic spectral male figures, the female protagonists of *The Wig My Father Wore* and *So I Am Glad* experience the possibility of ethical, albeit heterosexual, gender relations. This experience enables them to exhume the past in order to open the present to an alternative future that is marked by an ethics of care, love, and responsibility for the gendered other. The devolutionary engenderings within these two novels seem to gesture towards post-patriarchal social structures; ultimately, however, theirs is not a political vision but one that remains focused on the interpersonal. In other words, while devolving voice, agency, and power to the female protagonists, and challenging allegorical constructions of femininity (as evidenced by the three male-authored novels discussed above), Enright's and Kennedy's scope remains somewhat limited to the personal and domestic spheres. The final section of this chapter considers the extent to which a responsibility for the other can be transferred to a wider community, and in the process adumbrates devolutionary forms of identity in two twenty-first-century novels.

DEVOLUTIONARY IDENTITIES: MIKE McCORMACK AND JENNI FAGAN

Mike McCormack's (1965–) *Notes from a Coma* (2005) and Jenni Fagan's (1977–) *The Panopticon* (2012) deal with unwanted others by featuring protagonists who are both orphans. McCormack's John Joe (JJ) O'Malley is bought from a Romanian orphanage by a bachelor famer and brought back to live with him in County Mayo. Fagan's fifteen-year-old Anais Hendricks has moved multiple times between different foster families and institutions; she has also been charged with 147 criminal offences. Herein, both novels signal the breakdown of the nuclear model of the family. Uncertainty about their origins poses for both JJ and Anais an 'identity problem', to use the term that is repeatedly applied to Fagan's vulnerable heroine: 'Identity problem. Funny that. Fifty odd

---

[72] Kennedy, *So I Am Glad*, 222.   [73] Ibid., 187.
[74] Ibid., 280.

moves, three different names, born in a nuthouse to a nobody that was never seen again. Identity problem? I dinnae have an identity problem—I dinnae have an identity, just reflex reactions and a disappearing veil between this world and the next.'[75]

The instability of Anais's identity is heightened by the novel's Gothic sensibility, which develops the tradition of doubles, dualities, and the merging of realism and fantasy evident in the previously discussed works. As suggested in the excerpt above, Anais inhabits a space between the real and the fantastic, the disjunction between which is enhanced by her use of drugs, such that the stone-winged cat that marks the entrance to her current institutional home can come alive and fly. In the absence of any other evidence of her heritage, she considers herself to be the product of a scientific experiment: 'In all actuality they grew me—from a bit of bacteria in a Petri dish. An experiment, created and raised just to see exactly how much, fuck you, a nobody from nowhere can take.'[76] JJ is also shadowed by a sense of eccentricity and is torn by an incommensurable, somewhat Gothic guilt. This derives partly from his being saved from the orphanage and partly from the death of Owen, his best friend and adopted brother, which impacts on his sense of self: 'He saw himself free in the universe, not in the positive sense of being able to make his own destiny but in the negative one of being cast out without love or grace.'[77]

When we encounter them, JJ and Anais are both confined in sinister all-seeing institutions. Suspected of having comatosed a police officer, Anais is brought to the eponymous Panopticon, a former Victorian prison built according to Jeremy Bentham's design to allow for constant surveillance of its inmates, which has been turned into a care home for juvenile delinquents. Throughout McCormack's novel, JJ is in a coma on a prison ship in Killary Harbour, with his every brainwave being monitored and broadcast through 'the nation's print and electronic media'.[78] Unlike Anais, who feels at the mercy of an ominous power that controls and watches her every move, JJ volunteered to be the control subject for the Somnos Project, an experiment testing deep coma as a potential option for the EU penal system. Yet whether chosen or not, the protagonists' respective situations entail a ceding of power, control, and sovereignty over their selves and their identities to invisible governmental and (supra-)state powers.

JJ's lack of control over his fate and his 'soul' is evident in the fact that he is ultimately voiceless in the rendering of his own story. The first-person narrations of his adoptive father, neighbour, girlfriend, teacher, and local TD are supplemented by a sixth voice that appears in the lengthy footnotes that run in parallel to the main text, and which McCormack likens to 'marginalia' that constitute 'the event horizon, a hopeless attempt to inscribe someone as widely as possible in the universe'.[79] Emphasizing the experimentalism of the novel as 'a hybrid of science fiction and Irish domestic realism', McCormack describes JJ as a 'flesh and blood character at the centre of this legal,

[75] Jenni Fagan, *The Panopticon* (London: Windmill Books, 2013), 99.   [76] Ibid., 31.
[77] Mike McCormack, *Notes from a Coma* (London: Jonathan Cape, 2005), 46.   [78] Ibid., 1.
[79] Val Nolan, 'Experiment or Die: An Interview with Mike McCormack', *Ariel: A Review of International English Literature* 43 (2013), 93.

technological, and familial complex of forces. They pull and drag at him, and they define him.'[80] In *The Panopticon*, Anais's constant paranoia about being watched, to the extent that she even fears 'total mind control',[81] suggests that she has internalized the defining disciplinary gaze, as Michel Foucault proposed in relation to the male subject of surveillance: 'he inscribes in himself the power relation in which he simultaneously plays both roles; he becomes the principle of his own subjection'.[82]

Following Foucault, both *Notes from a Coma* and *The Panopticon* insist that power is multidirectional and performative. This brings with it ethical responsibilities that both works locate outside of the more narrowly defined interpersonal relations considered in *The Wig My Father Wore* and *So I Am Glad*. For instance, the performativity of power is demonstrated in the private outdoor wedding ceremony that Anais and her fellow inmates perform for Isla, a HIV-positive mother of twins, and her lover Tash, who works as a prostitute to raise enough money for them to rent a flat: 'Then I declare with the power invested in me by youz, and Anais, and the island—and the swans over there— that you are now wife and wife. You may kiss the bride!'[83] This diffusion of power opens up pockets of resistance against confining and defining identity constructions. With the help of others, Anais is able to creatively refashion her own self. Her foster mother's naming her after her favourite writer, Anaïs Nin, seems to have inspired her affinity for a bohemian lifestyle and her embrace of bisexuality, and an old monk's stories about her birth in the mental asylum, in which he himself resides, enables her to imagine herself not as the result of a 'test-tube' experiment but as 'the daughter of an Outcast Queen', flying away on a winged cat.[84]

The way in which Fagan's novel deconstructs what McCormack calls the 'tradition of the sovereign autonomous individual, . . . self-sufficient of identity' by foregrounding how Anais is, in fact, constructed by others, reflects the Irish author's thesis 'that in some ways our identities are entrusted to other people. And that they safeguard them, and that they nurture them, and that they make sure we don't get injured.'[85] The different narrators of *Notes from a Coma* illustrate this as they watch over JJ with love and care, and not just voyeurism, while he is unconscious. Identity in both novels is thereby almost literally devolved to others: not only in terms of giving them power and responsibility but also in the sense of putting them in charge of passing it on through time and space, even beyond death. JJ's girlfriend Sarah remembers that after JJ lost his memory though a nervous breakdown, his retrieved memories were in fact those of Owen shortly before his death. He reflects: 'So I can hardly remember my own life but I have a detailed memory of my friend's death. My best friend, this crisis apparition, come back to haunt me.'[86] The Gothic mode gestures here not simply towards trauma but to that idea that Owen's identity—the double or other of JJ's own self—has been passed to him for

[80] Ibid., 95, 91.   [81] Fagan, *The Panopticon*, 70.
[82] Michel Foucault, *Discipline and Punish: The Birth of the Prison*, trans. Alan Sheridan (Harmondsworth: Penguin, 1991), 202–3.
[83] Fagan, *The Panopticon*, 209.   [84] Ibid., 246, 251.
[85] Mike McCormack cited in Belinda McKeon, 'Metaphysics gets a Mayo accent', *Irish Times*, 13 May 2005.
[86] McCormack, *Notes from a Coma*, 156.

safekeeping. In a comparable manner, Anais embraces and preserves her mother's identity by escaping from institutional confinement, renaming of herself Frances (meaning 'freedom'), and declaring: 'I'm getting out. So, Vive freedom. Vive Paris. . . . Vive flying cats and cigarillo-smoking Outcast Queens! . . . I—begin today.'[87]

This chapter has read devolution not just in terms of territorial politics but as a process of transition that concerns the personal spaces in Scotland and both parts of Ireland. It suggests that the devolutionary impulse of 'passing on' power, voice, agency, care, and trust is underpinned by an ethics of responsibility towards the other. In this regard, the 2016 Brexit campaign slogan, 'Take back control', with its emphasis on reclaiming sovereignty and autonomy, stands in stark contrast to the type of sub-territorial and everyday dynamics that I have traced in these devolutionary writings, where power and/or 'control' are fluid and diffuse but nonetheless meaningful. As such, these texts may be read as being directly engaged with the devolutionary impulse to disperse or pass over power and control to and from the personal level, thus empowering liminal voices and identities within society and the political realm. While the Brexit vote produced new patterns of affiliation between Scotland and Northern Ireland (and the Irish Republic, as evidenced by the almost palpable shock and anger the referendum result provoked), it also raised concerns about the peace process and brought the border, in its many forms, back into public and political discourse with a salience that devolution had largely neutered.[88] In other words, the devolutionary dynamics mapped above may yet be subject to renewed importance in the interregnum created by the EU referendum result of June 2016.

FURTHER READING

Bell, Ian A. (ed.). *Peripheral Visions: Images of Nationhood in Contemporary British Fiction.* Cardiff: University of Wales Press, 1995.

Dix, Hywel. *Postmodern Fiction and the Break-Up of Britain.* London: Continuum, 2010.

Gardiner, Michael. *The Cultural Roots of British Devolution.* Edinburgh: Edinburgh University Press, 2004.

Lehner, Stefanie. ' "Dangerous Liaisons": Gender Politics in the Contemporary Scottish and Irish ImagiNation.' In Michael Gardiner, Graeme Macdonald, and Niall O'Gallagher (eds), *Scottish Literature and Postcolonial Literature: Comparative Texts and Critical Perspectives.* Edinburgh: Edinburgh University Press, 2011: 221–33.

Lehner, Stefanie. *Subaltern Ethics in Contemporary Scottish and Irish Literature: Tracing Counter-Histories.* Basingstoke: Palgrave Macmillan, 2011.

McGlynn, Mary. *Narratives of Class in New Irish and Scottish Literature: From Joyce to Kelman, Doyle, Galloway, and McNamee.* Basingstoke: Palgrave Macmillan, 2008.

McIlvanney, Liam and Ray Ryan (eds). *Ireland and Scotland: Culture and Society, 1700–2000.* Dublin: Four Courts Press, 2005.

[87] Fagan, *The Panopticon*, 324.

[88] See, for example, Fintan O'Toole, 'The English have placed a bomb under the Irish peace process', *Guardian*, 24 June 2016 and 'Belfast Agreement is a threat to the new English nationalism', *Irish Times*, 5 July 2016.

Norquay, Glenda and Gerry Smyth (eds). *Across the Margins: Cultural Identity and Change in the Atlantic Archipelago*. Manchester: Manchester University Press, 2002.

Reizbaum, Marilyn. 'Canonical Double Cross: Scottish and Irish Women's Writing'. In Karen Lawrence (ed.), *Decolonizing Tradition: New Views of Twentieth-Century 'British' Literary Canons*. Chicago, IL: University of Illinois Press, 1992: 165–90.

Ryan, Ray. *Ireland and Scotland: Literature and Culture, State and Nation, 1966–2000*. Oxford: Clarendon Press, 2002.

CHAPTER 28

SEX, VIOLENCE, AND RELIGION IN THE IRISH-AMERICAN DOMESTIC NOVEL

SALLY BARR EBEST

THERE are few happily married couples in Irish-American domestic novels; indeed, marriage as the death of happiness might be considered their primary trait. This realistic approach can be traced to James T. Farrell (1904–79). His 1932 publication of *Young Lonigan: A Boyhood in Chicago Streets*—the first of his Studs Lonigan trilogy, which was completed by *The Young Manhood of Studs Lonigan* (1934) and *Judgment Day* (1935)— broke through the 'opposition to realism' promoted by the Catholic press, which had stymied Irish-American writers in the late nineteenth and early twentieth centuries, to re-create 'an American fictional world from Irish ethnic materials'.[1] Working against a simplistic cultural mindset desirous of respectability, between 1932 and his death in 1979 Farrell consistently portrayed and criticized the lives of lower-middle-class Irish Americans living in Chicago, providing 'a voice for the inarticulate'.[2] No discussion of Irish-American literature would be complete without him, for 'No writer is more central to the history of the American Irish than James T. Farrell'.[3] Of course, Farrell represents only half of the equation. To gain a full sense of Irish-American literature, the female voice must also be heard. Within Irish literary studies, this cohort has been 'outside history',[4] to borrow Eavan Boland's resonant term; indeed, prior to Charles Fanning's

---

[1] Charles Fanning, *The Irish Voice in America: 250 Years of Irish-American Fiction* (Lexington, KY: University of Kentucky Press, 2000), 241.

[2] Ibid., 261.

[3] William V. Shannon, *The American Irish: A Political and Social Portrait* (Amherst, MA: University of Massachusetts Press, 1989), 249.

[4] See Eavan Boland, 'Outside History', in *Object Lessons: The Life of the Woman and the Poet in Our Time* (New York: Norton, 1995), 123–53.

groundbreaking *The Irish Voice in America* (1990) Irish-American women were either seldom addressed or inaccurately portrayed by priests, scholars, historians, and critics.[5] Yet in their novels and short stories, Irish-American women writers challenge 'Catholic woman stereotypes simply by writing with intelligence and imagination'.[6] Their voices merit recognition, therefore, for they have played a key role in exposing women's issues, protecting women's rights, and anticipating and effecting change.

Who qualifies as Irish American? At one time, the primary identifier was the 'Mc' or 'O' in surnames, a characteristic that qualifies the authors Mary McCarthy (1912–89), Edwin O'Connor (1918–68), Tom McHale (1941–82), Mary McGarry Morris (1943–), and Alice McDermott (1953–) for discussion herein. But others, who can trace their heritage to ancestors who settled in Ireland during the Elizabethan and Jacobean colonization projects, and whose names lack such prefixes, also qualify. We must acknowledge, too, those writers who, despite their heritage, do not self-identify as Irish American but whose work engages with Irish- and Irish-American-inflected themes. This category includes Joyce Carol Oates (1938–), Blanche McCrary Boyd (1945–), Susanna Moore (1945–), Michael Downing (1958–), and Susan Minot (1956–), as well as more recent authors such as Jennifer Finney Boylan (1958–) and Stephanie Grant (1962–), all of whom fall within this chapter's scope. So too do Irish-born writers such as Maeve Brennan (1917–93) and Colm Tóibín (1955–) who moved to, or reside in, the USA.

The three most prominent characteristics of the writers discussed here is that their fictions of domestic life in the USA exhibit an overwhelming desire for assimilation on the part of their protagonists, a move away from religious and clerical themes, and a growing preoccupation with sex and sexuality as it pertains to the rights of women and LGBTQ (lesbian, gay, bisexual, transgender, and queer) people, and the wrongs perpetrated against them. Works by McCarthy, McDermott, Farrell, O'Connor, McHale, Maureen Howard (1930–), Elizabeth Cullinan (1933–), Mary Gordon (1949–), and Eileen Myles (1949–) also highlight their Irish Catholic heritage, although only O'Connor views it positively. Other authors reveal their ethnicity thematically through their stylistic or cultural language patterns. Oates, Howard, J. P. Donleavy (1926–2017), William Kennedy (1928–), and Mark Costello (1936–) share a proclivity for satire and linguistic experimentation. McCarthy, Oates, Myles, Donleavy, Costello, Kennedy, and O'Connor reveal the ravages of that most stereotypical Irish trait, alcoholism, whereas Maeve Brennan, Mary McGarry Morris, Matthew Thomas, Jack Dunphy (1914–92), and Edward Hannibal (1936–) shine a spotlight on unhappy marriages. With the exception of Dunphy, these authors debunk the myth of the sainted Irish mother, while Howard, McDermott, Cullinan, Gordon, McHale, Kennedy, O'Connor, and Tóibín bemoan the plight of the self-immolated daughter consigned to care for her widowed parent. The majority of these fictions can be further identified by their use of realism, regional

[5] See Mary Jo Weaver, *New Catholic Women: A Contemporary Challenge to Traditional Religious Authority* (New York: Harper and Row, 1985), 11–13.
[6] Jeana DelRosso, *Writing Catholic Women: Contemporary International Catholic Girlhood Narratives* (New York: Palgrave Macmillan, 2005), 55.

settings, explicitly Irish names, and by plots revolving around guilt, redemption, and forgiveness, the leitmotifs of an Irish Catholic identity.

To illustrate, this chapter compares post-war Irish-American domestic novels and short stories by writers of both genders, examining the influence of politics, assimilation, and ethnic identity on their plots and characters. Given the sheer volume of Irish-American fiction, this discussion is by necessity limited. It omits non-domestic novels as well as Irish-American women's third-wave and post-feminist works; instead, it focuses on approximately four representative novels per decade from the 1940s to the present. On the basis of this examination, I argue that while both male and female writers agree that married life rarely equals domestic bliss, the authors' gender identity determines their representation of the roles played by marriage, sexuality, and religion. 'Unhappily Ever After' examines the preponderance of adultery and gendered abuse; 'Opening Bedroom and Closet Doors' discusses attitudes regarding women, sex, and sexual preference; and 'Losing My Religion' traces the movement from immigrant piety to an intellectual, independent view of the Church which acknowledges its ongoing gender hierarchy. Taken altogether, this discussion not only reveals the progression of Irish Americans' fictional lives across the past seventy-five years but also examines the role of Irish-American women writers in expanding that view.

UNHAPPILY EVER AFTER

Although the Nineteenth Amendment to the Constitution gave American women the right to vote in 1920, they did not automatically gain equal rights with men. Too often limited to poorly paid 'women's work', they were essentially barred from higher education due to sexist advisors, male-only admission practices, and miniscule graduate admission quotas.[7] Not until John F. Kennedy's election as president in 1960 and the passage of the Civil Rights Act four years later were women's rights legally protected. Even then, whether they worked inside or outside the home, women were generally treated as second-class citizens. Most Irish-American domestic novels and short stories address the tension and discord created in this environment, which could escalate into coercive and abusive relationships. Regardless of gender, abuse ranges from verbal and psychological to physical and sexual. The primary difference lies in how the authors address it: as a rule, female authors set out to expose it, while male authors view it more as a given.

Dublin-born Maeve Brennan moved with her family to New York in 1934 at the age of seventeen and began writing for the *New Yorker* in 1949. Brennan is known for her *New Yorker* column, 'The Talk of the Town', and for her short stories, two collections of which were published during her lifetime. While her early stories were set in Dublin and drew comparisons with James Joyce's (1882–1941) *Dubliners* (1914), the majority of her later

---

[7] Susan Brownmiller, *In Our Time: Memoir of a Revolution* (New York: Random House, 1999), 2.

work is set in New York. Among the former, she is best known for her stories about two unhappy couples, the Derdons and the Bagots, whose verbally violent exchanges were rarely heard in fiction at the time. For example, throughout 'An Attack of Hunger' (1962), Rose and Hubert Derdon bicker. Glaring at her, he tells her to shut up and rails, 'I'm sick of you, sick of your long face, and your moans and sighs—I wish you'd get out of the room, I wish you'd go, go on, go away. I don't want any tea. All I want is not to have to look at you anymore this evening.'[8] Similarly, 'The Shadow of Kindness' (1965) suggests the attitude of the working man toward his stay-at-home wife. Martin Bagot, we are told, had warned his wife 'that she must stop forcing herself, stop *trying* to think, because her intelligence was not high and she must not put too much of a strain on it or she would make herself unhappy'.[9] This focus, which Brennan reiterates in many of her mid-century Dublin stories, reflects the culture's social and religious beliefs in hierarchical marriage which shaped domestic life in Ireland and America at that time.[10]

With the rise of second-wave feminism, Irish-American women became more out-spoken. Brennan's contemporary, Mary McCarthy, whose ancestors emigrated from Ireland to Newfoundland before heading southwest for Minnesota, is best known for her satirical attacks in *The Group* (1963), in which she examines her Vassar College class-mates' marriages to mock (among other things) their naïveté regarding gender equality. Following the tradition of Irish-American fiction, this novel uses a story set in the past—in this case the 1930s—to comment on the subjugation of women in 1960s America. As recent college graduates, most of these young wives believe themselves bound for the world of work, but repeatedly their spirits are quashed. One group member, Priss, is introduced as a political activist, but after she marries and gives birth she becomes so weak-willed that she lets her newborn scream for hours rather than disobey her paediatrician husband's orders to nurse only at the scheduled time. McCarthy's central protagonist, Kay Peterson, walks on eggshells around her volatile spouse Harald. Once he starts drinking, the venom flies. She grabs a knife; he blackens her eye. Ultimately, he commits her to a psychiatric ward against her will. *The Group* reveals the collision of hierarchical marriage with changing mores regarding a woman's roles. For Kay, the situation is exacerbated by Harald's inability to maintain a steady job and lubricated by his alcoholism. Harald feels his masculinity challenged by a working wife; he is caught in a web of his own machismo and in need of a scapegoat. Domestic violence allows him to recapture 'physical control of his wife as his cultural privilege'.[11] Susanna Moore's first novel, *My Old Sweetheart* (1982), echoes this message with the story of an isolated, fragile woman whose philandering husband moves her from New York to Hawaii (where Moore grew up), browbeats her, and then commits her to an institution because of her drug use. This husband, like Priss's, believes himself superior because he is a white, rich,

---

[8] Maeve Brennan, 'An Attack of Hunger', in *The Springs of Affection* (Dublin: Stinging Fly Press, 2016), 155.

[9] Maeve Brennan, 'The Shadow of Kindness', in *The Springs of Affection*, 235. Original emphasis.

[10] See Mark Spilka, *Eight Lessons in Love: A Domestic Violence Reader* (Columbia, MO: University of Missouri Press, 1997), 4.

[11] Ibid., 17.

male physician—factors which contribute to a sense of entitlement and, in some cases, a propensity to abuse.

Joyce Carol Oates has repeatedly addressed such feminist issues in her fiction. Oates is not generally known to be Irish American, for, like Flannery O'Connor before her, she rarely invokes her Irish roots, although the paternal Oateses immigrated to upstate New York during the Famine. In her 1960s novels, *A Garden of Earthly Delights* (1967), *Expensive People* (1968), and *them* (1969), Oates contrasts romance with reality. Relentlessly grim, these novels feature doomed heroines as hapless as McCarthy's. However, in Oates's 1970s novels—*Do With Me What You Will* (1973), *The Assassins* (1975), *The Childwold* (1975), and *Unholy Loves* (1979)—women free themselves from negative relationships. *The Childwold* is particularly uplifting, for it takes the themes and characters in Nabokov's *Lolita* (1955) and turns them on their head. Rather than portraying Lolita as a ruined nymphet, Oates's Laney Bartlett escapes and moves beyond Kasch, her rapist/seducer, expanding her mind and her world. 'You are no longer recognizable!' he laments. 'You are no longer mine.'[12]

New Englander Mary McGarry Morris drew on her experiences as a social worker to develop her first novel, *Vanished* (1988), in which she uses role reversal to comment on domestic violence. Her central protagonist, Aubrey Wallace, is so demoralized by his common-law wife's verbal abuse that he cannot find the courage or the will to leave. Likewise, Alice McDermott's award-winning *Charming Billy* (1997), set in her native Long Island, shows the effects of Billy Lynch's alcoholism on his wife Maeve as she recalls anxiously awaiting his late drunken arrivals, cleaning up his vomit, trying to drag him indoors, and enduring his tirades. But neither Morris nor McDermott stress victimization; rather, as Mark Spilka observes, they hold the perpetrators accountable by illustrating the 'enormous pressures on women to accept vulnerable positions, their openness to further battering, and to accede to their partners' views and ways, so as to protect themselves (and often their children) from even worse treatment'.[13]

More often in Irish-American fiction, domestic abuse takes the form of adultery, regardless of gender. The work of Boston native Susan Minot, who is Irish Catholic on her mother's side, features characters who betray their husbands; indeed, Minot's *Folly* (1992), *Evening* (1998), and *Rapture* (2003) are all cautionary tales about women's gullibility in extra-marital affairs. In their desire for independence, the single women in Elizabeth Cullinan's *Yellow Roses* (1977), Mary Gordon's *Final Payments* (1978), Maureen Howard's *Grace Abounding* (1982), and Diana O'Hehir's *I Wish This War Were Over* (1984) have affairs with married men. All but Cullinan's Louise Gallagher—who wisely breaks it off—pay for their sins through embarrassment or abandonment. This is not a case of female protagonists being punished for their moral errancy but a reflection of reality, for it calls attention to cultural norms still present today. Similarly, in Tom McHale's satire, *Farragan's Retreat* (1971), Arthur Farragan begins an affair after wife Muriel spurns his affections, supposedly because of a difficult childbirth. What Arthur does not realize is

---

[12] Joyce Carol Oates, *The Childwold* (New York: Fawcett, 1975), 290.
[13] Spilka, *Eight Lessons in Love*, 14.

that Muriel despises him, having learned that at the behest of his siblings he has agreed to kill his son because he has fled the country to escape the draft. Farragan is either a fool, an outlier, or a hypocrite, for he claims to love his wife and tells himself the affair is to spare her. Another outlier is John 'Fitzie' Fitzpatrick, an advertising man in Edward Hannibal's *Chocolate Days, Popsicle Weeks* (1970). This novel, which shares thematic parallels with Sloan Wilson's *The Man in the Grey Flannel Suit* (1955), illustrates Americans' Cold War anxiety and middle-class angst. Like Wilson's protagonist, Fitzie has a wife and three children and is apparently living the American dream, yet neither he nor his wife is happy. Busy climbing the corporate ladder, Fitzie is unfaithful to his wife only once. Neither Farragan nor Fitzie recognizes that they are perpetuating the patriarchal hierarchy, although in allowing Farragan's wife to avenge his duplicity his creator appears to acknowledge the double standard.

Adultery aside, *Chocolate Days* reflects the broad social trajectory of most Irish Americans in the 1970s, succeeding in business, outpacing every other ethnic group except the Jews, and moving to the suburbs.[14] But whereas the heroines of Irish-American novels of that era, such as Maureen Howard's *Bridgeport Bus* (1965) and Elizabeth Cullinan's *In the Time of Adam* (1971) and *Yellow Roses*, work to establish their independence, Fitzie works to support his family. Like Howard's and Cullinan's characters, Fitzie longs to assimilate, but his feelings are more intense and conflicted. Throughout his life, he hated his parents because they had moved to the city, shipped him to the country in the summer, sent him to parochial school, made him do homework, paid for his college education, yet insisted he live at home to save money. Returning home for his mother's funeral, he realizes his parents' sacrifices and recognizes the effects: they helped him become an American success story.

Given the realistic tenor of Irish-American urban life in Farrell's Studs Lonigan trilogy, it follows that domestic violence plays a recurring role: Lizz O'Flaherty O'Neill often fights with husband Jim about her religious extremism; Aunt Margaret O'Flaherty battles viciously with her mother during drunken arguments. But as Farrell shifts his focus to third-generation immigrants, this element diminishes. In his Bernard Carr trilogy—comprising *Bernard Clare* (1946), *The Road Between* (1949), and *Yet Other Waters* (1952)—and *The Silence of History* (1963), Farrell's central protagonists, Bernard Carr and Eddie Ryan, vacillate between two desires: to develop their intellect and to find the perfect girl, 'the right girl, the only girl, the girl who would love him, worship him, and understand him. . . . The silent voices of his spirit would become the choir of the music of his love.'[15] This silence, which Farrell found typical among Irish-American men, is Eddie's undoing. He cannot find the words or the courage to express his feelings when the opportunity arises, and so the girl drifts away.

More typical are the darker tales. Satires by Irish-American males are often presented as angry, drunken harangues. The mode was established by *The Ginger Man* (1955), the

---

[14] Timothy J. Meagher, *The Columbia Guide to Irish American History* (New York: Columbia University Press, 2005), 132.
[15] James T. Farrell, *The Silence of History* (London: W. H. Allen, 1964), 3–4.

breakthrough novel by J. P. Donleavy, who was born in New York to immigrant Irish parents and who later moved to Ireland, where he lived until his death in 2017. The novel ruffled critical and religious feathers with its Joycean shards of prose describing Sebastian Dangerfield's rancorous marriage and louche lifestyle, elements which caused America and Ireland to ban the book for obscenity.[16] Ostensibly pursuing a law degree at Trinity College Dublin, the married Dangerfield's preferred activities revolve around drinking and pursuing women. Asked by a friend whether his wife objects, he replies, 'These English wives are great. Know their proper place.'[17] But Dangerfield's relatives are from Connemara, making him lower class in his wife's eyes. Thus, arguments about money, class, and alcohol lead to abuse. Finding him passed out on the kitchen table in their filthy house, she screams: 'You're a liar. You were drinking, drinking, drinking. Look at the grease, the mess, the filth.'[18] Accusations and insults mount until she slaps him and he punches her in the face. Mark Costello's collection of interlinked short stories, *The Murphy Stories* (1973), is indebted to if not derivative of Donleavy in both style and content. The seven stories in the volume describe the unstable, ill-advised marriage of Michael Murphy, a half-mad Midwestern Catholic who alternates between violence, sentimentality, and remorse, yelling at his wife and threatening bodily harm in response to her screams and threats.

Apart from Farrell's Lizz O'Neill and her sister Margaret, female characters in these men's novels and short stories echo Boland's critique that women are 'outside history'. Donleavy and Costello neither develop their female characters nor critique politics or society. They simply reinforce male privilege by damning the 'hysterical' female, even though the men are actually venting their envy, humiliation, powerlessness, resentment, and hostility because they cannot express their feelings in words. These tamped-down emotions erupt in anger, which is socially acceptable in men. Consequently, the male writers do not hold their characters accountable for domestic violence. They do, however, satirize the angry, blustering alcoholic who has lived on as an Irish stereotype.

Bridging the gap between satire and sentiment is the New Jersey-born novelist and playwright Jack Dunphy. In his *The Murderous McLaughlins* (1988), a Yeats epigraph sets the tone: 'Cast your mind on other days / That we in coming days may be / Still the indomitable Irishry.' The novel is narrated by a young boy whose father moved out when the lad was stricken with scarlet fever. After recovering, the boy's mother sends him to beg his father to return home. Instead, the boy moves in with his grandparents, his father, and his extended family—murderous Uncle Chauncey and Uncle Tom, a Lothario who croons 'Danny Boy' in bed—all of whom try to live down the ignominy of the trigger-happy Chauncey. 'Why were we sorry for ourselves but sorrier for others? That was Irish,'[19] the boy declares. In keeping with the traditional Irish-American immigrant story, the matriarch, grandmother Mary Ellen McLaughlin, tries to make the

---

[16] Noel Shine, 'Dangerfield Lives! *The Ginger Man* at 60', *Irish America* (October/November 2015), 100-03. http://irishamerica.com/2015/10/dangerfield-lives-the-ginger-man-at-60/. Accessed 27 June 2017.

[17] J. P. Donleavy, *The Ginger Man* (New York: Grove Press, 1955), 13.   [18] Ibid., 28.

[19] Jack Dunphy, *The Murderous McLaughlins* (New York: McGraw Hill, 1988), 201.

family respectable, but the McLaughlin men will have none of it. Sensing the futility of this task, Mary Ellen turns her attention to her grandson, taking him to Atlantic City and to Galway—a rare occurrence in fiction prior to the ubiquity of transatlantic flights. Ultimately, her guidance helps her grandson not only to assimilate but also, like Hannibal's Fitzie, to realize his potential.

William Kennedy's best-known novels, *Legs* (1975), *Billy Phelan's Greatest Game* (1978), and *Ironweed* (1983), are neither sentimental nor domestic. In contrast, *Very Old Bones* (1992), narrated by Orson Purcell, is written as a memoir covering three generations of Phelan family history. Orson is the illegitimate son of Peter Phelan, both of whom reside in the family home with Peter's sisters Julia (yet another spinster who has devoted her life to her family) and Mary and their 'holy moron'[20] brother Tom. Exploring each family member's background through Peter's series of paintings, Orson tries to decipher the truth about his origins by examining the 'very old bones' of his family history. Contrary to Kennedy's previous works, *Very Old Bones* does not delve into alcoholism or domestic violence. Given the nature of Orson's birth, adultery is at the centre of the novel and the raison d'être for his search for answers. Regardless of birthright, these male characters share this search in their desire for assimilation.

Twenty-first-century novels, including those by Irish-born writers with transatlantic careers, retain many of the above traits, albeit in much smaller families. For example, Colm Tóibín's *Brooklyn* (2009) retells the immigrant's story from the point of view of young Eilis Lacey, who makes her way to and from the New World alone. Like characters in other male-authored novels, Eilis deceives her husband; unlike her male counterparts, she gets away with it because her spouse never learns of her disloyalty. More recently, Matthew Thomas's *We Are Not Ourselves* (2015) traces the marriage of Eileen Tumulty and Edmund Leary from 1951 to 2000. When Ed is in the throes of disease, Eileen succumbs to desire, quickly followed by remorse. There is plenty of anger but no domestic violence; in this case, most arguments relate to Ed's debilitating illness. Ultimately, the marriage remains intact because of Eileen's infinite patience. In this novel, as in others in this category, confrontations and adulterous encounters are lubricated with alcohol, but no one ever separates: like swans, these fictional Irish Americans mate for life.

OPENING BEDROOM AND CLOSET DOORS

When Irish-American Kate O'Flaherty Chopin's (1851–1904) *The Awakening* was published in 1899, it was condemned by the Catholic Church because it described a woman's sexual longings and extra-marital affair, a stance that underscored the Catholic association of sex with sin. Any expectations that such clerical condemnation would act as a deterrent were in vain, however, as Irish-American women—rather like their Irish

---

[20] William Kennedy, *Very Old Bones* (New York: Viking, 1992), 6.

foremothers—continued to write about sexuality and gender, as they had been doing since earlier in the nineteenth century, not for salacious or gratuitous reasons but to emphasize the wrongs perpetrated against them and to subvert traditional notions of female identity. A full understanding of Irish-American domestic fiction by women thus depends on us recognizing the longevity and persistence of their engagement with themes that crystallize women's historical disempowerment and highlight the major changes in gender dynamics ushered in by second-wave feminism and the struggle for LGBTQ rights.

Mary McCarthy's highly autobiographical *A Charmed Life* (1955) is one of the first post-war domestic novels to address sexual violence against women. In this satirical treatment of McCarthy's relationship with her second husband, the writer and critic Edmund Wilson, one of the most harrowing scenes involves the fictional Miles Murphy's rape of his ex-wife Martha Sinnott:

> 'Please don't', she begged, with tears in her eyes, while he squeezed her nipples between his fingertips. . . . . 'Stop, Miles, I beg you,' she moaned, with a terrified air of throwing herself on his mercy. . . . Compunction smote him; he ought not to have done this, he said to himself tenderly. . . . Clasping her fragile body brusquely to him, he thrust himself into her with short, quick strokes. A gasp of pain came from her, and it was over.[21]

Although McCarthy included this real-life scene for personal rather than political reasons,[22] it nonetheless calls attention to rape, an issue that received little attention in America prior to the publication of Irish-American Kate Murray Millett's *Sexual Politics* in 1969 and Susan Griffin's seminal essay, 'Rape: The All-American Crime', in 1971. Similarly, McCarthy highlights the medical profession's tendency to dismiss women's right to sexual equality in *The Group*, as exemplified when Norinne visits a doctor to seek advice about her husband's impotence, only to be told that 'Sex wasn't necessary for a woman.'[23]

McCarthy paved the way for subsequent generations of Irish-American women to use fiction not simply to publicize sexual issues but also to illustrate the pain, suffering, and trauma that women experienced as a result of sexual victimization and violence within marriage and relationships. By focusing on these inequities, Irish-American women writers carried on the tradition begun by their foremothers, battling patriarchal subjugation on three fronts: religion, which created such subjugation; society, which reinforced it; and politics, which tries to recreate and perpetuate the oppression of women. Considering that Irish-American women represent the largest and longest established group of ethnic writers, this theme underscores their role in promoting,

---

[21] Mary McCarthy, *A Charmed Life* (New York: Harcourt Brace, 1955), 201.

[22] See Carol Brightman, *Writing Dangerously: Mary McCarthy and her World* (New York: Harcourt Brace, 1992), 243.

[23] Mary McCarthy, *The Group* (New York: Harcourt Brace, 1963), 165.

protecting, and perpetuating the rights of women in the United States and around the world.

Joyce Carol Oates consistently pursues the issue of rape in her fiction. Her most overtly 'Irish' novel, *We Were the Mulvaneys* (1996)—whose title evokes her Irish great-great-grandmother, who brought her six children to America in the late 1800s after the death of her husband Dominic Oates—hints at the theme's personal relevance.[24] Believing she was date-raped when she was drunk, Marianne Mulvaney tries to return to high school as if nothing had happened; meanwhile, her father Michael is so angry that he drowns his grief in drink. Consequently, when he tells his doting wife Corinne that he cannot even look at the girl, overnight she packs up their traumatized seventeen-year-old daughter, abandons her with a distant aunt, and rarely visits thereafter, for years losing contact altogether. The multifaceted impact of rape is suggested by the past-tense title of the novel, for what had been a happy family disintegrates: the two eldest sons become estranged and the marriage itself falls apart.

After the Stonewall riots in 1969, Irish-American gay and lesbian writers began to emerge. In 1973, South Carolina-born novelist Blanche McCrary Boyd published *Nerves*, a tentative exploration of lesbian sexual desire and its effects on her heroine's husband and daughter. A decade later, lesbian writers began publishing en masse, perhaps in response to Ronald Reagan's demonization of gay people during his presidency from 1981 to 1989.[25] Between 1984 and 1987, when lesbian novels were being published at a pace of twenty-three per year, Irish-American women contributed almost half this number.[26] Unlike the 'coming out' novels published in the decades before and after Reagan's years in office, many of which featured graphic sex scenes (often enhanced by alcohol and drug use), intertextual references, and textual experimentation, 1980s novels such as Maureen Brady's (1943–) *Folly* (1982) celebrate the lesbian mother, while works by Valerie Miner, Nisa Donnelly, Lee Lynch, and Vicki P. McConnell emphasize the importance of community to underscore their 'normalcy'.

After Reagan, lesbian fiction by Irish-American authors resumed its exploration of protagonists' sexuality in often passionate relationships. In their focus on relationship misunderstandings, domestic disputes, and characters' search for identity, these works parallel those about heterosexual couples. What sets them apart are the writers' narrative strategies. Lesbian writing in the 1990s was notably intertextual, rewriting and reinterpreting earlier fictional depictions. Because these writers felt the 'lack of an authorized/authentic script for the articulation of lesbian desire',[27] they relied on

---

[24] Susanna Araújo, '"I'm Your Man": Irish American Masculinity in the Fiction of Joyce Carol Oates', in Sally Ebest Barr and Kathleen McInerney (eds), *Too Smart to be Sentimental: Contemporary Irish American Women Writers* (South Bend, IN: University of Notre Dame Press, 2008), 157.

[25] See Urvashi Vaid, 'Foreword', in Sarah Schulman, *My American History: Lesbian and Gay Life During the Reagan and Bush Years* (New York: Routledge, 1994), xi.

[26] Bonnie Zimmerman, *The Safe Sea of Women: Lesbian Fiction, 1969–1989* (Boston: Beacon Press, 1990), 207.

[27] Sonya Andermahr, '"A Person Positions Herself on Quicksand": The Postmodern Politics of Identity and Location in Sarah Schulman's *Empathy*', in Gabriele Griffin (ed.), *'Romancing The Margins'? Lesbian Writing in the 1990s* (London: Harrington Park Press, 2000), 15.

symbolic renaming and misidentification as well as on the tools of metafiction, particularly parody, fantasy, and irony. Boyd's *Revolution of Little Girls* (1992), for example, begins with hallucinations, while the intertextual *Terminal Velocity* (1997) recalls issues raised in her earlier novels. Stephanie Grant's *The Passion of Alice* (1995) and *The Map of Ireland* (2008) use the metaphors of anorexia and pyromania respectively to explore her heroines' non-heteronormative desires, while the main character in Eileen Myles's *Cool for You* (2000) is a woman named Eileen Myles who embodies real and fictional elements of the author's life.

In the twenty-first century, Irish-American women writers have further expanded the boundaries of sexuality. Jennifer Finney Boylan's bestselling memoir, *She's Not There* (2003), likens transgender sexuality to growing up in a haunted house. Boylan's trilogy, which is completed by *I'm Looking Through You* (2008) and *Stuck in the Middle With You* (2013), recalls growing up as a woman in a man's body (until 2001 the author published under the name James Boylan), as well as her attempts to ignore these feelings by marrying a woman and having children. The trilogy examines the effects of transitioning on her wife and children, with the primary stresses falling on Boylan's wife, although the couple and family remain together.

Irish-American gay men began publishing later than their lesbian counterparts. *Chasing Danny Boy* (1999), a collection of short stories by gay men from Ireland, England, Germany, and America edited by Mark Henry, was the among the first volumes of its kind. The stories by Irish-American writers in this collection parallel lesbian writers' pre- and post-Reagan-era combination of sex and politics, but they are in no way works of domestic fiction. However, with the increasing social and cultural acceptance in the USA of same-sex people and partnerships, Irish-American gay literature, like the lesbian novels of the 1980s, began to turn its focus to domestic relationships. One such work that represents this trend is *Breakfast with Scot* (1999), a comic novel by Michael Downing which dramatizes what happens when a Boston-based gay couple become the legal guardians of an eleven-year-old boy after the death of his mother. Like most couples, Sam and Ed must learn parenting skills. This rite of passage is further complicated by the fact that Scot arrives with bags of make-up, jewellery, perfume, and ladies' underwear, which he puts on at school and for which he is sent home. Yet together, this new family unit manages to adjust and successfully navigate the choppy waters of surrogate parenthood.

Breakfast With Scot contains no sex scenes, thus locating gay identity in relationships rather than in sexuality per se. Among heterosexual Irish-American male writers, however, the purpose of sex scenes varies. Edward Hannibal's Fitzie views sex as a means of procreation, although nothing happens when his wife is unhappy. His solution? Make another baby. In *Farragan's Retreat*, sex serves as a release since Farragan's wife refuses to have intercourse with him. Protagonists in *The Ginger Man* and *The Murphy Stories* use sex to dominate; not surprisingly, these scenes are often graphic. Describing Sebastian Dangerfield's relations with one of his mistresses, Donleavy writes:

> Chris's willowy fingers dug into his thighs and hers closed over his ears and he stopped hearing the soup sound of her mouth and felt the brief pain of her teeth

nipping the drawn foreskin and the throb of his groin pumping the teeming fluid into her throat, stopping her gentle voice and dripping from her chords that sung the music of her lonely heart.[28]

Mark Costello's description of Murphy's attempts to seduce his sleeping wife are no less explicit: 'When he reaches her pajama pants again, he moves his hand over her buttocks, between her legs, and begins to push her pajama pants into her with the middle finger of his right hand. She rolls and sits up facing him screaming you bastard and swings at him.'[29]

In *Writing Catholic Women*, Jeana DelRosso maintains that Irish-American males' attitudes toward sex are 'inextricably bound to representations of women'[30] in Catholic literature more broadly. Psychologist Monica McGoldrick, who has studied ethnic family relationships, agrees, noting that such ingrained attitudes are further reinforced by the tendency of Irish-American mothers to coddle their sons and scold their daughters. Consequently, the females grow up 'formidable and tenacious' and well aware that they cannot rely on a man to take care of them, while the males may develop ambivalent relationships with the opposite sex. 'From a distance, they admire [women's] fire, strength, and martyrdom, but up close they are often tense, scornful, and hostile and underneath deeply frightened of their [partner's] power.'[31] In sum, among heterosexual writers, depictions of sexual relations display clear gender differences: men dominate, women (often unwillingly) submit. Gender also determines narrative style. Sex scenes by straight authors tend to be matter-of-factly described, whereas lesbian writers are generally more graphic but less direct, relying on intertextuality and a pastiche of genres to convey their message. Regardless of gender or gender preference, these works reflect the social, political, and religious milieux in which the writers worked— influences also evident in the authors' acceptance or rejection of religious faith.

LOSING MY RELIGION

After the second Vatican Council in 1965 and the subsequent issuance of *Humanae Vitae* in 1968, many American Catholics began to lose faith in their Church. Attendance at mass dropped by 15 per cent, Catholics began to question papal infallibility, and the

---

[28] Donleavy, *The Ginger Man*, 95.
[29] Mark Costello, 'Strong is Your Hold O Love', in *The Murphy Stories* (Urbana, IL: University of Illinois Press, 1973), 50–1.
[30] DelRosso, *Writing Catholic Women*, 31.
[31] Monica McGoldrick, 'Belonging and Liberation: Finding a Place Called Home', in Monica McGoldrick (ed.), *Re-Visioning Family Therapy: Race, Culture, and Gender in Clinical Practice* (New York: Guilford Press, 1998), 28.

numbers of priests, sisters, and seminarians dropped precipitously.[32] This falling away of faith and lack of religious certainty is evident in several Irish-American novels of that era. In her study of post-conciliar American Catholic fiction, Anita Gandolfo sub-divides fictional responses to these shifts in religious belief and practice into several 'patterns of vision', her term for 'the perspective that informs the text'.[33] The final part of this chapter will draw on Gandolfo's typology to examine novels that illustrate four of these fictional patterns: visions of experience, passionate intensity, reconciliation, and alternative visions.

Memories of a Catholic Girlhood (1957), Mary McCarthy's semi-autobiographical vignettes recounting her life with Aunt and Uncle Shrivers, who took in Mary and her brothers after their parents' death, exemplifies Gandolfo's category of visions of experi-ence. The first three chapters detail the Shrivers' physical and psychological abuse of the children, actions which cause young Mary to question her faith. Whereas her mother's Catholicism had seemed beautiful and pure, these relatives make it appear cruel and hypocritical. Briefly, after she is rescued by her maternal grandparents and enters con-vent school, Mary's faith is so renewed that she fears for her Protestant grandfather's soul. Ultimately, however, after debating priests at her high school, McCarthy illustrates that for her, intellect trumps faith, an attitude Timothy Meagher characterizes as the movement from the piety of the immigrant generation of devout Irish Catholics to the more intellectually questioning mindset of later generations.[34]

This movement also can be observed in the work of James T. Farrell. The Studs Lonigan trilogy and the lesser-known O'Neill–O'Flaherty pentalogy, published between 1936 and 1953, contrast the role of faith among first-, second-, and third-generation Irish Americans living in Chicago. The first generation finds solace and certitude in the Church; the second vacillates between pragmatism (among the men) and piety (among the women); while the third, focused on in the Bernard Carr trilogy and *The Silence of History*, has moved on to a more sceptical, independent-minded position. Such move-ments parallel Farrell's own journey, whose intellectualism eventually led him to reject his faith as well as his beliefs in existentialism and communism because they interfered with his 'artistic integrity'.[35] *The Silence of History* retraces that process. When Eddie Ryan discusses his decision to attend the University of Chicago, his peers, neighbours, and even some priests advise against it for fear he will become an apostate. Their fears are realized when shortly thereafter he publicly declares that he has lost his religion and stops attending mass. Temporarily, he questions his decision during college coursework on the Middle Ages. But ultimately Eddie begins to see that although his religious upbringing clearly influenced his actions and beliefs and was a part of himself, it was

[32] Thomas J. Shelley, 'Twentieth-Century American Catholicism and Irish Americans', in J. J. Lee and Marion R. Casey (eds), *Making the Irish American* (New York: New York University Press, 2006), 574–608.

[33] Anita Gandolfo, *Testing the Faith: The New Catholic Fiction in America* (Westwood, CT: Greenwood Press, 1992), xiii.

[34] Meagher, *The Columbia Guide to Irish American History*, 78.

[35] Fanning, *The Irish Voice in America*, 260.

also 'part of his past' because 'He did not believe in the faith of his boyhood. He did not believe in the God of his boyhood. He did not believe.'[36]

Tom McHale's *Farragan's Retreat* is also influenced by experience. Like McHale, Arthur Farragan comes from a relatively large Irish-Catholic family of five: himself and siblings Stephen (deceased), John, Anna, and Edmund (a priest). In fact, the title refers both to Arthur's annual retreat at Edmund's monastery and his retreat from the promise he made to his siblings to murder his own son. Over the course of the novel, Farragan moves from believing that Catholicism is in his blood to realizing he and his siblings have lost their faith, for none of them question the morality of this mandate. Indeed, Edmund will provide an alibi since Farragan supposedly will be completing his annual retreat at his brother's monastery. But this satire also serves as commentary on the lessening influence of the Church and the concomitant weakening, after Vatican II, of the faith-based bonds that traditionally structured ethnic cultures and identities. Gandolfo notes that McHale's irony 'is expressive of Catholics whose fundamental life choices were made in the pre-Vatican II era of innocence and for whom Catholicism was part of the structure of life itself'.[37] Losing his innocence, by the novel's end Farragan dismisses his religion as 'that manure pile of platitudes'.[38] This feeling echoes the sentiments many fictional Irish-American female characters developed after Vatican II.

During this period of cultural upheaval and decline in religious commitment, many Irish-American Catholic women experienced a sense of emptiness and dislocation, outcomes revealed in autobiographical novels featuring guilt-ridden female protagonists trying to escape their suffocating socio-cultural and religious milieux. This cloud hangs over third-generation Irish writer Maureen Howard's *Bridgeport Bus*. The plot is framed by Mary Agnes ('Ag') Keeley's rejection of the Church because she associates it with her hypocritical Irish Catholic mother whom she has supported since high school. Because her mother has nothing better to do, most battles entail Church-related guilt. After escaping to New York, Ag creates a domestic lifestyle more to her liking, beginning a relationship with a co-worker, becoming friends and roommates with another young woman, and inviting artists to make her apartment their party house, 'the first place on earth, a Paradise without Adam or as yet a snake'.[39] Although this guilt-free environment is what she wants, it comes with consequences ranging from damaged property to an unplanned pregnancy. Out of a job, Ag moves home, grows increasingly out of touch with reality, and—in a scene that parodies the presentation of wine to communicants—apparently causes her mother (Mother Church?) to choke to death.

Second-generation Irish American novelist Elizabeth Cullinan also takes aim at the ultra-religious yet hypocritical mother in *House of Gold* (1969), which belongs with *Bridgeport Bus* in the category of alternative visions of preconciliar Catholicism.[40] Like Howard and Farrell, Cullinan debunks a number of stereotypes: the saintly

---

[36] Farrell, *The Silence of History*, 262.   [37] Gandolfo, *Testing the Faith*, 37.
[38] Tom McHale, *Farragan's Retreat* (New York: Viking, 1971), 282.
[39] Maureen Howard, *Bridgeport Bus* (New York: Penguin, 1965), 58.
[40] Gandolfo, *Testing the Faith*, 120–2.

Irish-American mother, Julia Devlin; Elizabeth, the self-immolated daughter caring for her widowed mother; the self sacrifice of the Devlin children—Father Phil and Mothers Mary James and Helen Marie—who devote their lives to the Church at their mother's insistence. Through these characters, Cullinan equates Julia's controlling approach to her family with the power of the Church to rule its followers' lives, as well as highlighting their shared hypocrisy. Building on the symbolism of the gold-plated possessions in the Devlin home, Cullinan underscores the disconnection between the superficially loving family gathered to mourn the passing of the matriarch and the effects of her 'repression of the human, the suppression of any expression of emotion among family members, and the lack of self-awareness that comes from reliance on pious platitudes for meaning'.[41] She does this to illustrate the need for a paradigm change in Mother Church. This change is evident in the next generation, particularly Elizabeth Devlin's daughters, who in their refusal to honour family myths suggest they will be equally sceptical of the religious mythos surrounding their parents' Church.

Change has not come quickly, however. Critiques of the Church's misogyny remain popular among late-twentieth-century Irish-American women writers. Susan Minot's *Monkeys* (1986) is a subtle example of this trend, so subtle that the *Chicago Tribune* declared that 'Few novels have so powerfully displayed the collective unity—and joy—of family life.'[42] *Monkeys* is the story of the Irish-Catholic Vincent family (the novel's title is a term of endearment for the seven children) who live on the East Coast. The narrative contrasts Mr Vincent's defiant alcoholism with his wife's devotion to motherhood and domestic order. Even after her death, everything seems great: 'Caitlin and Delilah are blabbing away in the kitchen. . . . The girls never stop talking, worrying about their boyfriends, worrying about Dad, always having fits—especially since their mother died.'[43] However, the fact that the older girls have assumed their mother's role of cooking, cleaning, and waiting on their father and brothers does not mean all is well. Rather, it implies that the Catholic structure perpetuates traditional gender hierarchies in the domestic sphere. As Jeana DelRosso puts it, 'the reproduction of these relations in consciousness, in social practice, and in ideology turns especially on the organization of family, kinship, and marriage, of sexuality, and of the division of all sorts of labor by gender'.[44]

Considerably more direct is the lesbian poet and novelist Eileen Myles. Myles grew up in Boston in an Irish-Polish family at mid-century, a time and place that contributed to her closeted homosexuality and to alcoholism, drug abuse, depression, guilt, and feelings of rejection, by-products of Myles's ambivalence about her sexuality and her strained relations with her parents. These feelings of estrangement stem both from her father's death and her mother's anger after finding her in bed with a lover, as she reveals in her autobiographical novel, *Cool for You* (2000). Analysing Myles's works, Kathleen Kremins explains: 'In an Irish-Catholic community, sex was fraught with anxiety and

---

[41] Ibid., 121–2.
[42] Laurie Hogin, 'Joys of family life on display in *Monkeys*', *Chicago Tribune*, 27 April 1986.
[43] Susan Minot, *Monkeys* (New York: Random House, 1986), 109.
[44] DelRosso, *Writing Catholic Women*, 1.

doubt, often devoid of romanticism, and associated with evil.'[45] Or as Myles puts it, 'Though my mother was Polish, the feeling was Irish. I guess it was just Catholic.'[46]

New Yorker Mary Gordon's first novel, *Final Payments* (1978), corresponds to those post-conciliar American Catholic novels that espouse a 'vision of reconciliation'.[47] Ross Labrie suggests that this novel attempts to 'record the process of female victimization within both American society and the Irish-American Catholic Church'.[48] When Isabel Moore's father catches her *in flagrante* with his star pupil, she laments, 'My sex was infecting me; my sex was a disease.'[49] After her father's death—another symbol of the Church's waning influence—Isabel tries to escape, in part by taking (married) lovers. Thus, when she is publicly exposed by the wife of one of her lovers, she becomes so mired in guilt that she atones by promising to care for and support Margaret, a bitter old woman who had hoped to marry Isabel's father. This is the worst of domestic situations. As Margaret berates and belittles Isabel, she sinks into depression, gaining weight as she seeks solace in food and sleep. Reconciliation occurs gradually. After the family priest visits, Isabel starts reading her missal. Attending Good Friday services, she reflects on the death of Christ and his ability to forgive those who betrayed him. Such thoughts lead her to realize not only that she is worthy of forgiveness but also that she needs to hear these words from her own kind, in her own Church.

Similar themes pervade Gordon's next novel, *In the Company of Women* (1980), as well as Elizabeth Savage's *A Good Confession* (1975) and Lisa Carey's *Every Visible Thing* (2006). In Carey's novel, the Furey family disintegrates after the disappearance of their eldest son, Hugh. His mother retreats to her room and her husband stops his research on angels, leaving the remaining children, Lena and Owen, to raise themselves. Without parental supervision, these two search for meaning. Lena assumes her elder brother's gender identity (and clothing) in an attempt to learn what happened to him, while Owen is so lonely that he experiments with homosexuality. After he is outed and ostracized by his peers, he refuses to attend school. To pass the time, he begins reading his father's research. When Owen's life is miraculously saved, he starts believing in guardian angels. After he is saved a second time and is 'awakened' to save his sister in a third incident, which literally awakens his parents to their children's peril, the family returns to the Church. The novel's title and closing words underscore the role of faith in this reconciliation: 'Every visible thing in this world is put in the charge of an angel.'[50]

Published shortly before Vatican II, Edwin O'Connor's Pulitzer Prize-winning *The Edge of Sadness* (1961) fits Gandolfo's characterization of novels informed by 'passionate intensity', in which 'plot and character are subordinated to the service of an authorial

[45] Kathleen Kremins, 'Blurring Boundaries: Eileen Myles and the Irish American Identity', in Ebest and McInerney (eds), *Too Smart to be Sentimental*, 191.
[46] Eileen Myles, *Cool for You* (New York: Soft Skull Press, 2000), 95.
[47] Gandolfo, *Testing the Faith*, 95.
[48] Ross Labrie, *The Catholic Imagination in American Literature* (Columbia, MO: University of Missouri Press, 1997), 253.
[49] Mary Gordon, *Final Payments* (New York: Anchor Books, 1978), 265.
[50] Lisa Carey, *Every Visible Thing* (New York: HarperCollins, 2006), 305.

thesis that has persuasive power'.[51] The narrator Father Hugh recounts the discontents of the Carmody family—Old Charlie, the widowed patriarch; convent-educated daughter Mary, yet another resentful daughter who ceded her independence to care for her father; Helen, who entered into a loveless marriage to escape her tyrannical father; John, an unhappy priest; and Dan, a ne'er do well. These characters come alive through that most Irish of conventions, talk. While Hugh is telling the Carmody's story, he is simultaneously recalling his own descent from young priest, to recovering alcoholic, to his current post in a decaying parish. These conversations with the Carmody family help him realize all he has learned over the course of his career. In the process, O'Connor illustrates the progression of Irish Americans from aspirational first-generation immigrants, to solid yet disappointed members of the middle-class, to the polished but impious third generation.

Matters of faith appear to be reconciled in Alice McDermott's aforementioned *Charming Billy*. This novel examines the role of Billy Lynch's faith, representative of that of the Irish Catholic community more widely, through the eyes of his adult niece. McDermott links Billy's alcoholism with his faith: drink allows him to elide faith and disappointment, love and loss. Bars become confessionals as he moves between faith and memories of his lost love. These convoluted beliefs are contrasted with the narrator's scepticism, for she sees the effects of drink on Billy, on his wife Maeve, and on her father, Billy's best friend and enabler. Nevertheless, by the novel's close the narrator seems to accept the redemptive power of religion, asking if 'what was actual, as opposed to what was imagined, as opposed to what was believed, made, when you got right down to it, any difference at all',[52] a complex pondering that reflects the narrator's conflicted state of mind. As Beatrice Jacobson notes, the narrator has already ' "gotten right down to it," reinscribing and revising versions of Billy and those close to him, yet this death-centered novel that is also an elegy ends with a wedding. Story, at least when it is embraced by the teller and listener, is faith.'[53]

As this chapter has sought to demonstrate, Irish-American domestic novels reflect ongoing wars between opposite sides—in this case, between the genders—for independence and control. They dramatize the struggles of women and other marginalized groups against the patriarchal forces of political and religious figures, structures, and belief systems. This is most evident in the fiction of Irish-American women writers, which has consistently exposed and critiqued the sources and modes of subjugation. As we have seen, these writers have produced highly autobiographical works exploring the origins and impact of various forms of domestic and interpersonal violence, of rape and adultery, and of personal and political oppression. These novels reflect the changing socio-cultural climates of their times. Novels of the 1960s illustrate women's domestic frustrations, thus anticipating the inevitability of the feminist movement. The

---

[51] Gandolfo, *Testing the Faith*, 50.

[52] Alice McDermott, *Charming Billy* (New York: Farrar, Straus, and Giroux, 1998), 243.

[53] Beatrice Jacobsen, 'Alice McDermott's Narrators', in Ebest and McInerney (eds), *Too Smart to be Sentimental*, 132.

disappointment that followed *Humanae Vitae* can be traced in the critical religious novels of the late 1960s and 1970s. The need for rape laws, crisis centres, and women's shelters in the USA is underscored in novels of the 1970s, while 1980s novels counter political attempts to revoke women's rights and to demonize LGBTQ individuals, efforts that have continued in the twenty-first century due to renewed incursions that began with the terrorist attacks on 9/11 and show no signs of decline.

Although the domestic fiction by Irish-American male novelists follows a slightly different path, it too is highly autobiographical and reflects the time of its composition. Prior to the election of John F. Kennedy and the growth of the Civil Rights movement, most of these writers came from working-class immigrant backgrounds and had not yet joined the ranks of the middle class; thus, pre-1960 novels tend to focus on the experiences and aspirations of blue-collar workers. As they, and their subjects, moved up the social class ladder, their fiction began to embrace a new set of preoccupations, anxieties, and frustrations during the 1960s and 1970s, a period marked by a move away from ethnic neighbourhoods to the suburbs, where economic success was of primary concern. By the 1980s, as they became more firmly ensconced in the middle class, Irish-American males grew more conservative. Many supported Ronald Reagan and were not overly disturbed by his avoidance of LGBTQ issues, as evidenced in the lack of novels exploring these topics.[54] By the 1990s, however, as befits the *fin-de-siècle* tendency toward sexual openness and equality, Irish-American gay writers were ready to come out.

Despite these differences, Irish-American domestic novels by both genders share a number of similarities. Following in Farrell's footsteps, they paint realistic portraits of their ethnic communities, debunk the myth of the sainted matriarch, commiserate with their self-immolated daughters, and reveal the ways in which marginalized groups and individuals have been silenced by society, politics, and religion. In so doing, they provide a voice to the inarticulate, regardless of gender or gender preference. Highly autobiographical, they remind readers of the class differences faced—and overcome—by their forefathers and foremothers, often drawing on the Irish bent for satire to spice up the message. Along the way, they question, critique, and sometimes abandon their Church for impeding that journey. In sum, drawing on the Irish tradition of storytelling, these writers have created powerful and provocative fictional narratives that trace the progress of the Irish and their descendants in America.

Further Reading

DelRosso, Jeana. *Writing Catholic Women: Contemporary International Catholic Girlhood Narratives*. New York: Palgrave Macmillan, 2005.

Ebest, Sally Barr. *The Banshees: A Literary History of Irish American Women Writers*. Syracuse, NY: Syracuse University Press, 2013.

Ebest, Sally Barr and Kathleen McInerney (eds). *Too Smart to be Sentimental: Contemporary Irish American Women Writers*. South Bend, IN: University of Notre Dame Press, 2008.

---

[54] Jay P. Dolan, *The Irish Americans: A History* (New York: Bloomsbury, 2008), 293.

Faderman, Lillian. *Odd Girls and Twilight Lovers: A History of Lesbian Life in Twentieth-Century America*. New York: Columbia University Press, 1991.

Fanning, Charles. *The Irish Voice in America: 250 Years of Irish-American Fiction*. Lexington, KY: University of Kentucky Press, 2000; 2nd edition.

Gandolfo, Anita. *Testing the Faith: The New Catholic Fiction in America*. Westwood, CT: Greenwood Press, 1992.

Meagher, Timothy J. *The Columbia Guide to Irish American History*. New York: Columbia University Press, 2005.

Spilka, Mark. *Eight Lessons in Love: A Domestic Violence Reader*. Columbia, MO: University of Missouri Press, 1997.

CHAPTER 29

'A SLY, MID-ATLANTIC APPROPRIATION'

Ireland, the United States, and Transnational Fictions of Spain

SINÉAD MOYNIHAN

> Let's try an outrageous generalisation, prompted by the appearance of Sebastian Barry's mesmerising *On Canaan's Side* on the longlist for the Booker Prize. It can be contradicted by a thousand qualifications and counter-examples, but it is nonetheless worth positing. It is this: that the great theme of the contemporary Irish novel is not Ireland but the US.[1]

So opined Fintan O'Toole, leading critic and cultural commentator, in 2011, citing in evidence, in addition to Barry's (1955–) novel of that year, Joseph O'Connor's (1963–) *Redemption Falls* (2007), Colm Tóibín's (1955–) *The Master* (2004) and *Brooklyn* (2009), Colum McCann's (1965–) *This Side of Brightness* (1998) and *Let the Great World Spin* (2009), Joseph O'Neill's (1964–) *Netherland* (2008), and Roddy Doyle's (1958–) *Oh, Play That Thing* (2004). O'Toole's assertion has been echoed several times, implicitly or explicitly, in reviews of contemporary Irish fiction set entirely or partially in the USA. For example, in his review of Paul Lynch's (1977–) *Red Sky in Morning* (2013), John Boland wrote that the novel's 'arduous transatlantic crossing recalls Joseph O'Connor's *Star of the Sea* and Colm Tóibín's *Brooklyn*', while 'the notion of hostile forces following their quarry from Ireland to America is familiar from Roddy Doyle's *The Last Roundup* and Sebastian Barry's *On Canaan's Side*'.[2] Sinéad Gleeson, in a review of Mary Costello's *Academy Street* (2014), proclaimed that 'From Maeve Brennan to Colm Tóibín and Colum McCann, Irish writers have an umbilical connection to America', and went on to

[1] Fintan O'Toole, 'Irish writers have yet to awake from the American Dream', *Irish Times*, 30 July 2011, 8.
[2] John Boland, 'A fine thriller emerges from a flood of adverbs and adjectives', *Irish Independent*, 5 May 2013.

note that 'readers may hear echoes of Tóibín's *Brooklyn*' in Costello's novel.[3] Similarly, Sue Gaisford was reminded of Tóibín and 'the awareness of the romantic appeal of America to those living just the other side of the Atlantic'[4] when reviewing Anne Enright's (1962–) *The Green Road* (2015).

Tóibín's novel, in particular, has acquired an iconic status as a kind of emigrant ur-narrative, which has only been reinforced and deepened by its 2015 screen adaptation, directed by John Crowley. For Mark Kermode, Crowley's *Brooklyn* taps into 'a rich seam of émigré cinema (Jim Sheridan's 2002 *In America* is a distant cousin)' and 'one sublime sequence…echoes the poetry of the Pogues' "Fairytale of New York"'.[5] Richard Brody invokes the most oft-cited representation of Irish America, John Ford's *The Quiet Man* (1952), in his much less laudatory review of the film for the *New Yorker*. Brody objects to the film's 'greenwashing' of Ireland and its 'sanitization' of Brooklyn, and finds that, by comparison, 'Whatever the townsfolk are in Ford's film—comical, bumbling, braggadocious, headstrong—they're also deeply, even tragically, in the know.'[6] Like reviews of the film, the few existing scholarly commentaries on *Brooklyn* situate the novel in relation to narratives of Irish migration ranging from George Moore's (1852–1933) *The Untilled Field* (1903), particularly 'Home Sickness', and James Joyce's (1882–1941) 'Eveline' in *Dubliners* (1914) to Edna O'Brien's (1930–) *The Light of Evening* (2006), McCann's *Let the Great World Spin*, and Barry's *On Canaan's Side*.[7] The same commentators have also discerned in *Brooklyn* traces of Tóibín's 'absorption in [non-Irish] canonical' texts, such as Jane Austen's *Pride and Prejudice* (1813) and *Mansfield Park* (1814) and Henry James's *The Portrait of a Lady* (1880–81).[8]

This chapter examines Tóibín's novel from a more oblique angle, taking its cue from Aamer Hussein's review of *Brooklyn* for the London *Independent*, in which he claims that the novel is 'like a sly, mid-Atlantic appropriation of the romantic novels of Kate O'Brian [*sic*] or Maura Laverty—about Irish girls travelling to pre-Civil War Spain in the 1930s, falling in love, and going home heartbroken.'[9] In other words, this reading of Tóibín's novel takes seriously Hussein's assertion that *Brooklyn* is more indebted to

---

[3] Sinéad Gleeson, '*Academy Street* by Mary Costello review: woman on the sidelines', *Guardian*, 25 October 2014.

[4] Sue Gaisford, '*The Green Road* by Anne Enright', *Financial Times*, 1 May 2015.

[5] Mark Kermode, '*Brooklyn* review: this *Fairytale of New York* casts a spell', *Guardian*, 8 November 2015.

[6] Richard Brody, 'The Sanitized Past of *Brooklyn*', *New Yorker*, 6 November 2015.

[7] On links between *Brooklyn* and Moore and Joyce, see Ellen McWilliams, *Women and Exile in Contemporary Irish Fiction* (Basingstoke: Palgrave Macmillan, 2013), 172–5 and Tory Young, '*Brooklyn* as the "Untold Story" of "Eveline": Reading Joyce and Tóibín with Ricoeur', *Journal of Modern Literature* 37, no. 4 (2014), 123–40. On *Brooklyn* and Edna O'Brien, see Eve Walsh Stoddard, 'Home and Belonging among Irish Migrants: Transnational versus Placed Identities in *The Light of Evening* and *Brooklyn: A Novel*', *Éire-Ireland* 47, nos. 1–2 (2012), 147–71. On *Brooklyn* and McCann and Barry, see Elizabeth Butler Cullingford, 'American Dreams: Emigration or Exile in Contemporary Irish Fiction?', *Éire-Ireland* 49, nos. 3–4 (2014), 60–94.

[8] See McWilliams, *Women and Exile in Contemporary Irish Fiction*, 172–3 and Cullingford, 'American Dreams', 70–1, 83.

[9] Aamer Hussein, '*Brooklyn*, by Colm Tóibín', *Independent*, 30 April 2009.

O'Brien's (1897–1974) and Laverty's (1907–66) works (although they are set in the 1920s, not the 1930s) than has previously been acknowledged. Because of the privileged position afforded the Ireland–USA relationship in discussions of Irish transnationalism, the echoes of O'Brien's and Laverty's novels in the extant scholarship on *Brooklyn* have been missed. This is surprising given that Tóibín has cited and anthologized O'Brien's work, spent three years living in Barcelona himself, owns a home in Spain, and continues to set some of his fiction there.[10]

Drawing on Amanda Tucker and Moira E. Casey's definition of Irish transnational literature as 'writing that places Irish identity in dialogue with other cultural, national, or ethnic affiliations',[11] the larger concern of this chapter is to dislodge Irish America as the dominant referent in discussions of Irish transnationalism and investigate a substantial tradition that positions Spain as an important space in the Irish transnational imagination. This genealogy is associated particularly with novels by women writers of the 1930s and 1940s: O'Brien's *Mary Lavelle* (1936) and *That Lady* (1946) and Laverty's *No More Than Human* (1944) are all set in Spain. Early drafts of Maeve Brennan's (1917–93) *The Visitor* (composed in the mid-1940s but not published until 2000) have Anastasia King returning to Ireland from Barcelona, rather than Paris, after six years.[12] Meanwhile, in Dorothy Macardle's (1889–1958) *The Uninvited* (1942), which first appeared as *Uneasy Freehold* in 1941, Spain is a significant imagined space because of the way it pits Englishwoman Mary Meredith against Spanish Carmel in profoundly racialized ways. Later in the century, Edna O'Brien's *The High Road* (1988) and Tóibín's *The South* (1990) share several affinities in their treatment of the Irish woman artist in Spain. Intriguingly, whereas *The South* is a 'straight' novel preoccupied with Katherine Proctor's heterosexual relationships, Tóibín produces a queer reworking of it in 'Barcelona, 1975', a short story from his 2011 collection, *The Empty Family*. Spain is also an important queer destination in *Nights Beneath the Nation* (2008) by first-time novelist Denis Kehoe (1978–).

The following discussion will pay particular attention to *Brooklyn*'s relationship to Kate O'Brien's and Laverty's novels, arguing that by displacing the USA and focusing on Spain instead, we begin to see that *Brooklyn*—through its associations with *Mary Lavelle* and *No More Than Human*—re-routes the iconic Irish-American transatlantic relationship through a much more capacious cis-Atlantic frame of reference. Reading the novel as a 'sly, mid-Atlantic appropriation' of O'Brien's and Laverty's novels positions *Brooklyn* as an invitation to readers to interrogate the overwhelming preoccupation with the *trans*atlantic, in both fiction and scholarship, and consider instead crossings and

---

[10] One example of Tóibín citing O'Brien is a talk he delivered eight days before the 2015 Irish same-sex marriage referendum, the title of which he borrowed from the sentence in *The Land of Spices* (1941) that ensured the novel's banning in Ireland. See Colm Tóibín, 'The Embrace of Love: Being Gay in Ireland Now', Trinity College Dublin, 14 May 2015, https://www.youtube.com/watch?v=qYzyHtayywE&feature= youtube. Accessed 24 April 2018.

[11] Amanda Tucker and Moira Casey, 'National and Transnational Irish Literatures', in Amanda Tucker and Moira Casey (eds), *Where Motley is Worn: Transnational Irish Literatures* (Cork: Cork University Press, 2014), 2.

[12] Unpublished drafts of *The Visitor*, Maeve Brennan Papers, 1940–1993, Stuart A. Rose Manuscript, Archives, and Rare Book Library, Emory University.

journeys between Ireland and other Atlantic-facing spaces, in Tóibín's own work and that of other Irish writers. The chapter is divided into two sections. The first provides an overview of some of the existing and emerging critical voices relating to Irish transnational fictions. It emphasizes the centrality of Irish America in extant discussions of transnationalism and points to alternative ways of conceptualizing how Ireland's cultural, historical, economic, and environmental circumstances are enmeshed, literally and imaginatively, with those of other spaces and places. The second part focuses more specifically on how we might productively read Tóibín's novel in relation to *Mary Lavelle* and *No More Than Human*. Identifying echoes and reverberations across the works that are suggestive and speculative rather than emphatic and categorical, the chapter reads the three works together with a view to expanding the parameters of current research on, and understandings of, Irish transnational fictions.

IRISH TRANSNATIONAL FICTIONS: IRISH AMERICA AND BEYOND

It is important to note that the very term 'transnational' in Irish studies privileges the relationship between Ireland and the USA, to the extent that the phrase—when applied specifically in literary and cultural studies rather than in disciplines such as business, sociology, or anthropology—is overwhelmingly associated with a US American studies context. In November 2004, the 'transnational turn' was the subject of an address to the American Studies Association by its then president, Shelley Fisher Fishkin. Fishkin argued that 'understanding the multiple meanings of America and American culture in all their complexity' requires 'looking beyond the nation's borders, and understanding how the nation is seen from vantage points beyond its borders'.[13] For Fishkin and other scholars, the importance of challenging US nationalism and exceptionalism was a particularly urgent project, given the aggression that characterized US foreign policy in the aftermath of the attacks of 11 September 2001. If the 'transnational turn' in American studies gained momentum through a commitment on the part of Americanist scholars to revealing 'the workings of the [US] nation's unilateral projection of power and hegemony over the rest of the world',[14] transnationalist scholarship in Irish literary and cultural studies has tended to focus on Ireland's diaspora and, most particularly, on Irish America. This is not surprising given that, as Khachig Tölölyan declared in the inaugural issue of the journal *Diaspora*, diasporas are the 'exemplary communities of the

---

[13] Shelley Fisher Fishkin, 'Crossroads of Cultures: The Transnational Turn in American Studies—Presidential Address to the American Studies Association, November 12, 2004', *American Quarterly* 57, no.1 (2005), 20.

[14] Ibid., 21.

transnational moment'.[15] Irish studies has, since the 1990s, responded with enthusiasm and commitment to the 'diasporic turn' and much of this work is compelling, important, and profoundly enabling.[16]

However, scholarly work on Irish transnationalism(s) that is not obviously engaged with the Irish diaspora in the USA and Britain has been much slower to develop. The necessity of expanding transnational modes of inquiry beyond the diaspora is underscored by Tucker and Casey who, in their introduction to the first collection of essays devoted to transnational Irish literatures, argue that because diaspora has functioned as 'a sort of de-territorialised nationalism' it risks allowing Irish studies 'to be global in theory and insular in practice'.[17] They further maintain that 'Irish Studies as a field of study has been curiously resistant to new approaches and areas of inquiry',[18] and this has certainly been the case with modes of transnational scholarship that are not diaspora-oriented. This resistance is due, at least in part, to Irish literary scholars' tenacious attachment to postcolonialism and their suspicion of modes of inquiry that depart from postcolonialism's most established critical iterations. As Andrew Kincaid observes in the same volume, 'to think through the term "transnationalism" inevitably requires paying attention to those other terms, such as postcolonialism, modernism and globalisation, that hover around it, draw on its energies'.[19]

One of the most pressing debates in contemporary postcolonial studies asks whether the 'global' is a more appropriate frame of reference in today's transnational world. As Alfred J. López and Robert P. Marzec observed in 2010, 'What has arguably changed over the past quarter century is not the "post" but its referent: that is, the futures toward which the field known as "postcolonial studies" think and work. This new referent... is the global'.[20] In other words, if scholars of Irish studies have been slow to embrace non-diaspora-oriented transnational frameworks, this may be attributed to the perceived suspicious proximity of transnationalism to globalization, which would move critics further away from postcolonialism as more traditionally conceived. This is not to say that there is no compelling scholarly or creative work that links the global, the transnational, and the postcolonial in Ireland. Rather, it is to highlight that the ongoing privileging of postcolonialism as a critical framework in Irish studies has implications not

---

[15] Khachig Tölölyan, 'The Nation-State and Its Others: In Lieu of a Preface', *Diaspora: A Journal of Transnational Studies* 1, no. 1 (1991), 5.

[16] Landmark publications in this area include *Irish Review. Special Issue: Memoir, Memory and Migration* 44 (2012); *Éire-Ireland. Special Issue: New Approaches to Irish Migration* 47, nos. 1–2 (2012); *Irish Studies Review. Special Issue: Texts and Textures of Irish America* 23, no. 2 (2015); and *Éire-Ireland. Special Issue: Beyond the Nation: Transnational Ireland* 51, nos. 1–2 (2016). In addition, important studies by Liam Harte, Jack Morgan, and Tony Murray, and a volume edited by Oona Frawley, are listed in the Further Reading section at the end of the chapter.

[17] Tucker and Casey, 'National and Transnational Irish Literatures', 4.   [18] Ibid., 13.

[19] Andrew Kincaid, 'Subverting the Waves of Global Capital: Piracy and Fiction in the Wake of the Union', in Tucker and Casey (eds), *Where Motley is Worn*, 181.

[20] Alfred J. López and Robert P. Marzec, 'Postcolonial Studies at the Twenty-Five Year Mark', *Modern Fiction Studies* 56, no. 4 (2010), 677–8.

only for that set of paradigms but also for a concatenation of others, including trans-nationalism, 'that hover around it, draw on its energies'.

One rich and productive site of transnational literary scholarship is the 'archipelagic turn' evident in the work of a number of critics of British and Irish literatures, including John Brannigan, Claire Connolly, Nick Groom, and Jos Smith, and emerging, to a significant extent, from the Atlantic Archipelagos Research Consortium (AARC), which involves academics in Irish, British, and American universities.[21] The referenda on Scottish independence in 2014 and on UK membership of the European Union in 2016, as well as the extensive interest they generated in the archipelago more broadly, testify to the ongoing negotiation of questions of political sovereignty, affective bonds, and regional distinctions or similarities between Scotland, England, Wales, Ireland, and Northern Ireland and their peoples. As Smith points out, archipelagic approaches to the literature and the culture of the British Isles arose in the late 1990s out of 'a growing political and national uncertainty over precisely what was meant by the obviously Anglocentric implications of the terminology in titles such as "Great Britain" or the "United Kingdom"'.[22] Meanwhile, Brannigan has recently argued that an emphasis on archipelagic relations between Britain and Ireland 'implies a plural and connective vision' that challenges both 'the cultural and political homogenisation' of the unionist project and the 'exceptionalism and insularity' that have characterized Scottish, Welsh, and Irish nationalisms.[23]

Taking its cue from this body of work—which is 'Atlanticist' to the extent that it seeks 'to imagine, map, and develop the identities, cartographies and cultural ecologies of the Atlantic Archipelago'[24]—this chapter aims to think more transnationally about Atlantic space. One of the ironies of scholarship in transatlantic literary studies is that despite its assault on critical frameworks that took for granted the primacy of the nation-state, it has itself been characterized by a number of telling assumptions and exclusions. For one thing, it has been dominated historically by an exceptionalist idea of what the 'transat-lantic' is: the Anglo-American relationship. As Christopher Cusack notes, despite the fact that Ireland, 'an island in the Atlantic ocean, has been a conspicuous presence in the Atlantic world in various ways', it constitutes a 'lacuna' in the field of Atlantic studies.[25]

---

[21] See https://willson.uga.edu/research/associations/aarc/. Accessed 24 April 2018.

[22] Jos Smith, 'An Archipelagic Literature: Re-framing "The New Nature Writing"', *Green Letters: Studies in Ecocriticism* 17, no. 1 (2013), 8–9.

[23] John Brannigan, *Archipelagic Modernism: Literature in the Irish and British Isles, 1890–1970* (Edinburgh: Edinburgh University Press, 2015), 6. Recent research in the area of archipelagic literary studies includes Claire Connolly's comparative work on 'Four Nations Fiction' and a 2015 workshop at University College Cork on comparative coastal topographies which focused on 'shared codes and conventions in the depiction of coastal landscapes in Ireland, Wales, Scotland and the West Indies'; 'The Irish Sea' and 'Women and the Sea' symposia at Dun Laoghaire in, respectively, 2014 and 2015; and Nicholas Allen, Nick Groom, and Jos Smith (eds), *Coastal Works: Cultures of the Atlantic Edge* (Oxford: Oxford University Press, 2017).

[24] Atlantic Archipelagos Research Project (AARP), University of Exeter, http://humanities.exeter .ac.uk/english/research/projects/aarp/. Accessed 24 April 2018.

[25] Christopher Cusack, 'Beyond the Emerald Isle: Studying the Irish Atlantic', *Atlantic Studies* 8, no. 3 (2011), 381.

Two recent examples of the opening up of this field of inquiry to Irish perspectives are the special issues of, respectively, *Atlantic Studies* (2014) on 'Irish Global Migration and Famine Memory' and *Symbiosis: A Journal of Transatlantic Literary and Cultural Relations* (2015) on 'The Irish Atlantic'. Meanwhile, in an Irish studies context, it could be argued that the transatlantic relationship between Ireland and North America (but usually the USA) has overshadowed all other kinds of inter-Atlantic engagement. Of David Armitage's influential 'three concepts of Atlantic history', this chapter is interested particularly in his delineation of a 'cis-Atlantic' approach that 'studies particular places as unique locations within an Atlantic world and seeks to define that uniqueness as the result of the interaction between local particularity and a wider web of connections and comparisons'.[26]

There are deeply suggestive literal and imaginative connections between Ireland and Spain. As Gayle Rogers observes, Spain has long occupied a position of 'internal other' in Europe. Its 'European marginality and its proximity to Africa have been geographical features that fed myths such as its allegedly sanguinary Catholicism and its "qualified Westernness" throughout its cultural history'.[27] In its perceived position on the (Atlantic) periphery of European modernity, with its predominantly Catholic population and having undergone a bloody civil war which was viewed by some disaffected Irish republicans as 'a reincarnation of the Irish Civil War of 1922–23',[28] it certainly bears similarities to Ireland in the first half of the twentieth century. The forging of literary affinities, to echo the literal ones, between Ireland and Spain is not at all unusual. Indeed, as Rogers further argues, Joyce's *Ulysses* (1922) posits similarities between 'the marginal states of Ireland and Spain' through its positioning of Molly Bloom as a 'Spanish type' who was born and grew up in Gibraltar.[29] Meanwhile, Ute Anna Mittermaier suggests that, between the 1930s and the 1970s,

> Irish and Spanish society and culture were marked by the dominant influence of the Catholic Church and its state supported propagation of a patriarchal family model, the idealization of the nation and the glorification of its history, governmental efforts to promote one language (Irish and Castilian respectively) over another (or several others in the case of Spain), the exaltation of rural life and tradition above urban life and modernity, and the cultural isolation from the modern world by means of rigid censorship.[30]

---

[26] David Armitage, 'Three Concepts of Atlantic History', in David Armitage and Michael J. Braddick (eds), *The British Atlantic World, 1500–1800* (Basingstoke: Palgrave Macmillan, 2002), 21.

[27] Gayle Rogers, *Modernism and the New Spain: Britain, Cosmopolitan Europe, and Literary History* (Oxford: Oxford University Press, 2012), 9, 12.

[28] Daniel Gomes, '*Good-Bye, Twilight*: Ireland, Spain, and the Ballad Resurgence', *Éire-Ireland* 50, nos. 3–4 (2015), 36.

[29] Rogers, *Modernism and the New Spain*, 25.

[30] Ute Anna Mittermaier, 'Kate O'Brien's Subtle Critique of Franco's Spain and de Valera's Ireland, 1936–46', in Dorothea Depner and Guy Woodward (eds), *Irish Culture in Wartime Europe, 1938–48* (Dublin: Four Courts Press, 2015), 117–18.

Mittermaier contends that Kate O'Brien 'repeatedly used Spain as a reference point for her indirect critique of socio-political conditions in Ireland'.[31] For example, in *Pray for the Wanderer* (1938), the novel that immediately succeeded *Mary Lavelle*, censored writer Matt Costello reflects, in a description that evokes General Franco, that Éamon de Valera is 'a more subtle dictator than most—though he also, given time, might have the minds of her people in chains. He did not bring materialism out for public adoration, but materialistic justice controlled by a dangerous moral philosophy, the new Calvinism of the Roman Catholic.... A clever man, Dev.'[32]

For many other writers, the internal political, religious, and linguistic divisions of both Spain and Ireland offer fruitful comparative possibilities. Tóibín's first novel, *The South*, follows Katherine Proctor, an Irish Protestant, from 1950, when she leaves her Wexford-based husband and son and travels to Barcelona, hoping to become a painter, to the early 1970s, by which time she has left Spain, returned to Ireland, reconnected with her estranged son, and enjoyed some modest success with her painting career. For Ellen McWilliams, the setting of the novel in Catalonia is significant because 'it amplifies the meaning of the title of the novel; it holds up a mirror to Irish Catholic culture but also, importantly, forges a direct connection between Irish nationalisms current and past and the nationalist zeal of the Catalan community in which Katherine settles'.[33] When Katherine meets a fellow Wexford native in Barcelona, she tells him she is from an area 'Between Newtownbarry and Enniscorthy', to which he replies, 'they don't call [Newtownbarry] that any more. I'm from Enniscorthy'.[34] This brief exchange between an Irish Protestant and Irish Catholic, who were born and raised within ten or fifteen miles of each other, conjures up in a couple of sentences the fraught colonial history inscribed upon their shared landscape.

Newtownbarry was the name of a landed estate that came to attach itself to the estate's adjoining village (previously known as Bunclody) from about the mid-seventeenth century. After independence in 1922, efforts were made to change the name of the village back to Bunclody, efforts that came to fruition in 1950 when Newtownbarry was officially renamed by Local Government Order.[35] The implied connection between 'nationalisms current and past' in *The South* echoes Delia Scully's claim of 'a close kinship between the Catalonians and the Irish' in *No More Than Human*: 'Their long fight for independence, their yearning for individualism as expressed in the way they clung to their language and customs, and their love of liberty as shown in their demand for republican status—all these things made a brother-bond for us.'[36] It also recalls other internal nationalisms in Spain. On a day trip to Altorno (Bilbao), Mary Lavelle is amused to hear the names ' "Arthur Griffiths" [sic] and "Patrick Pearse" '[37] mentioned in

[31] Ibid., 114.   [32] Kate O'Brien, *Pray for the Wanderer* (Harmondsworth: Penguin, 1958), 30.

[33] McWilliams, *Women and Exile in Contemporary Irish Fiction*, 160.

[34] Colm Tóibín, *The South* (London: Picador, 1992), 36.

[35] S.I. No. 281/1950 Local Government (Change of Name of Non-Municipal Town) Order, 1950, available online via irishstatutebook.ie. Accessed 24 April 2018.

[36] Maura Laverty, *No More Than Human* (London: Virago, 1986), 189.

[37] Kate O'Brien, *Mary Lavelle* (London: Virago, 2006), 112.

the oration of a Basque nationalist. Meanwhile, when Juanito's beautiful wife Luisa tells Mary that she 'admire[s] the Irish-Spanish hero, de Valera, thought the civil war in Ireland tragic but inevitable, and the Treaty compromise a grave mistake', Mary immediately interprets her views on Ireland as an indirect comment on Spain, and asks her, 'Do you then sympathise with the nationalist ambitions of the Catalans and the Basques?'[38]

Kate O'Brien, Maura Laverty, and 'Unlooked-for Spain'

As Tucker and Casey state, 'Transnational Irish literature is invested in the multiple points of identification and belonging that result from a writer's commitment to Ireland, to other countries, and to the world at large.'[39] In the novels by O'Brien and Laverty under discussion here, Spain features as one node that connects Ireland and the wider world. O'Brien's *Mary Lavelle* charts four months in the life of the eponymous twenty-two-year-old 'Miss', who decides to spend a year governessing in Spain (specifically, the area around Portugalete and Bilbao in the Basque country), while her fiancé back in Mellick (Limerick) earns enough money to set them up in a comfortable married life. However, Mary returns to Ireland to break off her engagement after embarking on a doomed affair with Juanito, the married son of the family for whom she works. The novel's emotional area is further complicated by the presence of a lesbian character, Agatha Conlan, a fellow governess who eventually confesses her desire for Mary. Laverty's *No More Than Human* is the sequel to *Never No More* (1942), which describes the experiences of a teenage girl, Delia Scully, growing up in the home of her cherished grandmother in Ballyderrig, County Kildare. After her grandmother's death in 1924, and aged just seventeen, Delia secures a position as a governess (and subsequently works as an English-language instructor and clerk) in Madrid. Her professional and romantic adventures in Spain are the subject of *No More Than Human*, at the conclusion of which she returns to Ireland and marries local Ballyderrig man and her long-time correspondent, Michael Walsh.

Published over six decades later, Tóibín's novel sees Eilis Lacey emigrate reluctantly to the USA in the early 1950s to work in a Brooklyn department store. For several months, before the sudden death of her sister Rose precipitates a return visit to Ireland, Eilis dates Tony, an Italian-American plumber, who persuades her to marry him prior to her departure. Back in Enniscorthy, Eilis is wooed by local publican Jim Farrell and contemplates leaving Tony and returning to live permanently in Ireland. However, she sails back to Brooklyn after her former employer hints that she is aware of—and will reveal—the fact that Eilis is already married. In all three novels, oppositions between home place and cosmopolitan experience are deconstructed; they trace what Eve Walsh Stoddard,

---

[38] Ibid., 132.   [39] Tucker and Casey, 'National and Transnational', 2.

writing about *Brooklyn*, calls 'a dialectic of parochial sameness in difference'.[40] If the *trans*atlantic crossing is often framed as a journey from the Old World to the New, from economic and political backwardness to progressive modernity, from monoculture to multiculture, routing *Brooklyn* through Spain allows for a consideration of the relationship between gender, sexuality, and cis-Atlantic journeying in much more complex and multifaceted ways.

There are a number of evocative overlaps and intersections between the three novels in terms of character and event. As McWilliams notes, Eilis's 'apparent passivity and lack of agency [is] an aspect of the character that has been commented on with some frequency and with some frustration in reviews of the novel'.[41] Indeed, the narrator tells us early on that

> Eilis had always presumed that she would live in the town all her life, as her mother had done, knowing everyone, having the same friends and neighbours, the same routines in the same streets. She had expected that she would find a job in the town, and then marry someone and give up the job and have children.[42]

Eilis even contemplates suggesting that Rose, who is more extroverted and energetic than she is, go to Brooklyn in her place. Her passivity is better understood, perhaps, when she is viewed as a latter-day Mary Lavelle who, similarly, has 'a modest estimate of herself and [has] no very urgent desire to hurl a lance against the vague and mighty world'.[43] Even before meeting her fiancé, she 'realised the limitations of Mellick, and of her place in it, were she to be married or single—nothing glamorous or amazing'.[44] Just as *Mary Lavelle* was, until relatively recently, dismissed as an inconsequential romance, so too has Tóibín's centralizing of romance in *Brooklyn* puzzled some reviewers and irked others.[45] However, as Siobhan Somerville observes, 'Questions of citizenship and national belonging have long been understood to be embedded within structures of desire and affect. For better or worse, in the words of Benedict Anderson, "nations inspire love, and often profoundly self-sacrificing love." '[46] Equally, as Stoddard observes, while the cosmopolite finds in migration 'an expanded sense of belonging', some nations 'demand of their citizens a monogamous attachment, a choice'.[47] In other words, the romance framework is a useful vehicle for interrogating questions of migration,

[40] Stoddard, 'Home and Belonging', 154.

[41] McWilliams, *Women and Exile in Contemporary Irish Fiction*, 172.

[42] Colm Tóibín, *Brooklyn* (London: Viking, 2009), 27–8.   [43] O'Brien, *Mary Lavelle*, 24.

[44] Ibid.

[45] On the critical tendency to dismiss O'Brien's work because she writes in the genres of family saga and romance, see Aintzane Legarreta Mentxaka, *Kate O'Brien and the Fiction of Identity: Sex, Art and Politics in 'Mary Lavelle' and Other Writings* (Jefferson, NC: McFarland, 2011), 102. On the labelling of Tóibín's novel as 'chick lit', see John Spain, 'Colm Tóibín's "chicklit" novel makes him No. 1', *Irish Independent*, 23 May 2009.

[46] Siobhan B. Somerville, 'Notes Toward a Queer History of Naturalization', *American Quarterly* 57, no. 3 (2005), 659.

[47] Stoddard, 'Home and Belonging', 155.

displacement, and exile, and O'Brien's and Tóibín's novels evidence a keen awareness of this fact. Both Mary and Eilis engage in forbidden romances that symbolize larger betrayals of, respectively, home (Mary's fiancé in Mellick) and adopted home (Tony in Brooklyn), and both women end up questioning their national attachments as a result of these illicit, and eventually thwarted, relationships. In both novels, the poignant 'what-ifs' of their forbidden affairs are memorialized in cherished items. During their passionate day trip to Toledo, Juanito buys a postcard and inscribes it to Mary. While she is packing for her return to Ireland and worrying about the postcard's safety, it is swept out of the window by a sudden gust of wind and Mary is devastated that her 'one sweet treasure'[48] has disappeared. In *Brooklyn*, while Eilis prepares to return to Tony, she conceals photographs of her seaside outing with Jim, George, and Nancy in the bottom of her suitcase, knowing that on some future date she will 'look at them and remember what would soon, she knew now, seem like a strange, hazy dream to her'.[49]

Laverty's Delia is a more spirited protagonist than either Eilis or Mary. Nonetheless, there are some striking echoes of Laverty's novel in *Brooklyn*, notably in the deployment of the boarding-house setting to foreground the tensions and complementarities of local, national, and diasporic attachments. Two parallel scenes in *No More Than Human* and *Brooklyn*—which depict the challenges of on-board self-fashioning prior to Delia's and Eilis's arrivals in Madrid and New York respectively—speak to the ways in which the novels imagine the particularly gendered negotiations of space and place required of single female migrants leaving Ireland. In *No More Than Human*, lipstick and dress connote Delia's mistaken assumption that she will enjoy freedoms in Spain that were unavailable to her in Ireland. Before leaving the boat at Santander, Delia dons 'the light blue satin dress' her grandmother had bought for her to wear to a local dance the previous Christmas, thinking that 'Madrid deserved the best in [her] wardrobe'.[50] Her cabin mate, a young Jewish woman from Liverpool, gives her a box of white powder and a lipstick, which Delia applies in the lavatory of the train from Santander to Madrid before meeting her new employer. Señora Basterra (an Irishwoman and former governess herself) is unimpressed, however, and promptly informs her that to wear lipstick or rouge as a governess is entirely inappropriate. Forced to 'deglamourize' herself by taking off her blue satin dress and make-up, Delia notes ruefully that 'so far as appearances went I might be going to sit down to bacon-and-cabbage in Ballyderrig instead of high lunch in Madrid'.[51]

A comparable scene in *Brooklyn* seems to allude quite explicitly to Laverty's novel, except that Eilis's cabin mate, a stylish blonde Englishwoman called Georgina, mentors Eilis more effectively with regard to suitable dress and appearance. Still, both Eilis and Delia encounter difficulties with the limitations of primping at sea. Speculating that there must have been 'something wrong with the water on that boat' or with the shampoo she used, Delia recalls that her hair—'never what could be called tractable'—now 'stood up on [her] head like a furze bush and pushed [her] navy straw hat up into the

---

[48] O'Brien, *Mary Lavelle*, 255.   [49] Tóibín, *Brooklyn*, 251.
[50] Laverty, *No More Than Human*, 6.   [51] Ibid., 9.

air.'[52] Meanwhile, Georgina counsels Eilis against washing her hair again before disembarking and, on the Englishwoman's advice, does not make the same sartorial blunders that Delia does. Georgina recommends that Eilis wear 'nothing fancy' when disembarking, to avoid 'looking like a tart'; nonetheless, it is important that Eilis not look 'too innocent'.[53] Although Eilis 'almost never' wears make-up at home, Georgina spends twenty minutes 'applying a thin cake of make-up and then some rouge, with eye-liner and mascara'.[54] Eilis is struck by the confidence with which her mask of make-up equips her: 'It would be easier, she imagined, to go out among people she did not know... if she could look like this', but it would also make her nervous because 'people would look at her and might have a view on her that was wrong if she were dressed up like this every day in Brooklyn'.[55] Unlike Delia's arrival in Madrid, Eilis's entrance to the USA sees her balance successfully the need to look 'plain' or unobtrusive alongside the necessity of not looking 'too innocent'.

For Delia, the journey to Spain is not experienced as liberation from Irish mores. She observes ruefully how similar Spain is, in its multiple prohibitions, to Ireland. As Delia recounts: 'A governess must wear her skirts well below the knees. A governess must not use cosmetics. A governess must never be seen in male company. A governess must not smoke.'[56] She eventually concedes that whereas she had 'visualized Spain as a laughing bare-shouldered girl with a rose in her hair', she had 'turned out to be a bleak-eyed, forbidding wardress, with a bunch of keys in one hand, a penal code in the other'.[57] Time and again, Delia's (sexually) transgressive behaviour is linked to her sartorial choices, none more so than when, in Madrid, she purchases a scarlet swimsuit which, her fellow governesses warn her, she will not be allowed to wear when she travels to her employer's holiday home at Neguri in the Basque country. The Marquesa de la Roja duly confirms that unless she furnishes herself with more appropriate bathing attire, Delia will not be permitted to swim on the beach. Delia compares the proscription on her sartorial choices with conservative attitudes to dress in Ireland, just as she does when her attire upon arrival in Madrid meets with her first employer's disapproval. The preferred bathing suit, as described by her employer, is 'identical with the creation which [Delia's] poor mother had preserved from her Tramore honeymoon—a bloomer-legged, long-sleeved, befrilled garment of navy serge and white braid'.[58] Delia trades her scarlet swimsuit for the regulation one, thus dashing her hopes of attracting the attention of wealthy young men who visit the beach in the mornings. However, after befriending a young Scot called Art McBain, Delia goes swimming with him and wears the forbidden swimsuit. When her behaviour with Art is observed by her employer, she loses her job.

The swimsuit motif is enlarged upon in *Brooklyn* in an important scene that alludes to both *No More Than Human* and *Mary Lavelle*. Tóibín's deployment of the swimsuit as a signifier of transgressive sexuality is reminiscent of Laverty; however, for the scene's queer undertones, Tóibín is likely indebted to O'Brien. In a compelling analysis of *Mary*

---

[52] Ibid., 6.   [53] Tóibín, *Brooklyn*, 49.   [54] Ibid., 50.   [55] Ibid.
[56] Laverty, *No More Than Human*, 75.   [57] Ibid.   [58] Ibid., 76.

Lavelle, Katherine O'Donnell argues that the novel invites the careful reader to interpret Mary's (apparently heteronormative) desire for Juanito as a transfer of affections from Luisa, Juanito's wife. 'For a number of pages at the heart of *Mary Lavelle*', O'Donnell writes, 'it appears that the central love affair is to be between [Mary and Luisa]: their meeting is dramatic, intense and immediately intimate.'[59] As such, the novel 'houses queer desires'[60] beyond those that Agatha Conlan confesses to harbouring for Mary. In this context, and given the other similarities between Mary and Eilis, the note-trading on their Italian-American boyfriends between Eilis and her immediate superior at Bartocci's, Miss Fortini, is deeply suggestive. In one especially provocative passage, Miss Fortini orders swimming costumes for Eilis to try on, after the store has closed, with a view to Eilis purchasing one for her forthcoming outing to Coney Island with Tony:

> She walked around Eilis so that she could inspect how it fitted from behind and, moving closer, put her hand under the firm elastic that held the bathing suit in place at the top of Eilis's thighs. She pulled the elastic down a fraction and then patted Eilis twice on the bottom, letting her hand linger the second time.[61]

Several times, Miss Fortini undertakes this ritual of touching Eilis close to her genitalia. She also encourages Eilis to try on different costumes several times over, ostensibly to assess their suitability. As a result, Eilis's breasts are exposed to Miss Fortini and, on one occasion, she is entirely naked. Eventually, Eilis puts an end to the encounter but is in no doubt about what it meant: 'there was in the way [Miss Fortini] stood and gazed at her something clear that Eilis knew she would never be able to tell anyone about.'[62] When Eilis subsequently goes swimming with Tony at Coney Island, and feels 'his erect penis hard against her', the thought 'come[s] into her mind of telling him who the last person to touch her bottom was'.[63] It is as though Tóibín here overwrites *Mary Lavelle* in the kind of homoerotic episode that O'Brien herself did not dare to commit to print until she published her final novel, *As Music and Splendour* (1958), featuring a year-and-a-half long romantic relationship between Irish Clare Halvey and Spanish Luisa Carriaga.[64]

While the romance framework performs useful cultural work by raising larger questions about national (un)belonging, gender, and sexuality, all three novels are also explicitly engaged with cis-Atlantic geography. At the outset of *Mary Lavelle*, the similarities between Mary's home place and new environment, Cabantes (Portugalete), are framed in terms of their Atlantic locations.[65] Mary notes in a letter to her fiancé soon

---

[59] Katherine O'Donnell, '"But Greek... Usually Knows Greek": Reading Sexuality in Kate O'Brien's *Mary Lavelle*', in Patricia Boyle Haberstroh and Christine St. Peter (eds), *Opening the Field: Irish Women, Texts and Contexts* (Cork: Cork University Press, 2007), 79.

[60] Ibid., 80.   [61] Tóibín, *Brooklyn*, 153.   [62] Ibid., 154.   [63] Ibid., 160.

[64] See, for example, the overt treatment of Clare and Luisa's physical relationship in the twelfth chapter of *As Music and Splendour* (London: Penguin, 2005), 239–76.

[65] For the 'real-life' equivalents of *Mary Lavelle*'s place names, I am indebted to Éibhear Walshe, *Kate O'Brien: A Writing Life* (Dublin: Irish Academic Press, 2006), 62 and Mentxaka, *Kate O'Brien and the Fiction of Identity*, 174.

after her arrival that 'it is not a bit like my idea of Spain': 'Perhaps it's the sea under my window that gives me the illusion—because now the tide is out, and the smell of sea-weed is coming into the room exactly as if I were in Kilbeggan. I suppose that makes me feel less strange.'[66] Since the 'real' Kilbeggan is a landlocked town in the Irish midlands, it is likely that O'Brien's Kilbeggan is a fictionalized version of one of County Clare's Atlantic coastal villages—Kilkee, Lahinch, or Spanish Point—that are within easy reach of Limerick (Mellick).[67] In a moment of nostalgia, Mary reflects on her new surround-ings and finds the view 'had no proclamation in it. In that it was—surprisingly—like Mellick.'[68]

If Mary is surprised by the unexpected similarities between Mellick and the Basque country, the connectedness of Cabantes, 'a little fishing village', to global trade routes is emphasized at the outset: 'Ships from everywhere—and fairly big ones, about as big as come into Mellick—sail past my windows up to Altorno. The children say that I will get to know all the flags of the world from watching the ships.'[69] In addition, the mining industry in Altorno (Bilbao) and its surrounding areas not only draws in foreign work-ers ('there is a large English colony in Altorno') but the area's iron-rich mountains are the 'fertile womb' from which are eventually produced luxury goods that are, presumably, exported all over the world.[70] Mary's is a touristic gaze as she looks upon mining villages and thinks they are 'sadder and wilder than any poverty she knew in Ireland'.[71] This is 'an unlooked-for Spain. Busy, rich, common and progressive on the one hand—on the other, grave and pitiful. Where were the castanets and the flowers in the hair?'[72]

The very same landscape—the seaside towns around Bilbao, specifically Neguri and Las Arenas—also causes Delia to make rather unexpected connections between rural life in her home place and new location. While reading to her charges at her employer's villa by the sea, she likes to watch the peasants who come in from the country to do their shopping in Las Arenas. Despite the notable physical differences between these 'Indian-brown men' and 'sun-dried women' and her own 'light-skinned heavy-suited friends who at that very moment were making ready to save the turf and earth the potatoes', there is still 'a similarity between them' that expresses itself in their shared 'easy-going walk'.[73] The sight of the Basque peasants transports Delia imaginatively to Ballyderrig, reminding her of 'how the gorse would be scattering its golden sovereigns at home, and how the banks along the Monasterevin road would be cream-splashed with primroses'.[74] Her imagination assumes 'a restlessness that had no way of easing itself except in a poem',[75] the publication of which captures the attention of Michael Walsh and thus begins their extensive correspondence.

On several occasions, the connections Delia forges between Spain and Ireland prove both aesthetically and financially fruitful. On Michael's advice, she researches the

---

[66] O'Brien, *Mary Lavelle*, 6.

[67] In a further historical connection between Ireland and Spain, Spanish Point is named for the ill-fated ships of the Spanish Armada that were wrecked off Ireland's west coast in 1588.

[68] O'Brien, *Mary Lavelle*, 19.   [69] Ibid., 1, 7.   [70] Ibid., 7, 64.   [71] Ibid., 64.

[72] Ibid.   [73] Laverty, *No More Than Human*, 65.   [74] Ibid., 66.   [75] Ibid.

similarities between Irish and Spanish folktales and thereafter receives payment when she publishes English translations of Spanish legends in the Irish Catholic magazine, *Our Boys*. Travelling 'to and from Tablada between the arid Castilian acres', she feels 'a great longing to rest [her] eyes on the rich freshness of an Irish wheatfield'; the resulting poem is published in an Irish magazine.[76] Finally, while recovering from scarlet fever, Delia manages to finance her return to Ireland by writing twelve stories with a Spanish setting for *Our Boys*.

In *Brooklyn*, too, seaside locations provide important 'mirror scenes' through which Wexford and Brooklyn are mutually reflected and refracted. At first glance, the scenes seem to function in terms of contrasts.[77] However, closer inspection reveals, as with other mirror scenes in *Brooklyn*, that what Wexford's Irish Sea (the comforts and limitations of home) and New York's Atlantic shoreline (the anxieties and opportunities of an alien environment) represent are ultimately not all that different from one another. During one of her bouts of homesickness, Eilis becomes lost in a reverie about her home county's coastal locations: 'She was flying, as though in a balloon, over the calm sea on a calm day. Below, she could see the cliffs at Cush Gap and the soft sand at Ballyconnigar. The wind was propelling her towards Blackwater, then the Ballagh, then Monageer, then Vinegar Hill and Enniscorthy.'[78] When Eilis returns to Wexford and goes on a seaside outing with her friends, they eschew Curracloe, fearing that it might be too crowded, and opt instead for Cush Gap. This idealized setting could not be more different from Eilis's experience of Coney Island: she and Tony travel on a teeming subway train, only to arrive at a beach that is similarly overcrowded. Despite the fact that the water, when compared with that of the Irish Sea, seems warm to Eilis, she realizes, in a none-too-subtle passage, 'that she would have to be careful not to swim too far out of her depth in this unfamiliar sea. Tony, she saw, was afraid of the water, hated her for swimming away from him.'[79]

Before Eilis leaves Brooklyn, Tony shares with her his plans to build family houses on a plot of land by the sea on Long Island. Despite the apparent opportunities offered by 'this unfamiliar sea', Eilis realizes that her life on the Atlantic seaboard will not be all that different from what it would have been had she not emigrated in the first place. Prior to leaving Enniscorthy, she expected 'she would find a job in the town, and then marry someone and give up the job and have children'.[80] After marrying Tony, she acknowledges that, despite the fact that she would like to keep working, 'she would stay at home, cleaning the house and preparing food and shopping and then having children and looking after them as well'.[81]

---

[76] Ibid., 211.

[77] On mirror scenes in *Brooklyn*, see Sinéad Moynihan, ' "We Are Where We Are": Colm Tóibín's *Brooklyn*, Mythologies of Return and the Post-Celtic Tiger Moment', in Leslie Elizabeth Eckel and Clare Frances Elliott (eds), *The Edinburgh Companion to Atlantic Literary Studies* (Edinburgh: Edinburgh University Press, 2016), 88–102.

[78] Tóibín, *Brooklyn*, 68.   [79] Ibid., 160.   [80] Ibid., 28.   [81] Ibid., 220.

CODA

If *Brooklyn* is 'a sly, mid-Atlantic appropriation' of elements of *Mary Lavelle* and *No More Than Human*, Tóibín's *The Empty Family* challenges readers to look beyond the transatlantic by explicitly rewriting aspects of the novel that immediately preceded it. Most of the stories in the collection thematize various forms of displacement and exile, with one in particular engaging very provocatively with *Brooklyn*. In the title story, set in the contemporary moment, the unnamed narrator returns to County Wexford from California. The story's mode of address, to a male 'you' who is implicitly the estranged lover of the narrator whom s/he left behind in Ireland, recalls the 'what if' of Eilis Lacey's thwarted romance with Jim Farrell. Like Eilis, who only understands as she walks through the Enniscorthy graveyard 'the extent to which she had been dreading' visiting Rose's grave, the narrator of 'The Empty Family' realizes that 'Home [is] some graves where my dead lay outside the town of Enniscorthy.'[82] However, the story reworks *Brooklyn*'s Irish Sea/Atlantic mirror scenes by replacing the Atlantic with the Pacific Ocean: the narrator returns to Ireland when s/he realizes that s/he was taking repeated day trips to Point Reyes on the Pacific coast because s/he missed the views of Rosslare Harbour and Tuskar Rock lighthouse that the family home at Ballyconnigar afforded: 'I went out to Point Reyes every Saturday so I could miss home.'[83] S/he therefore returns to 'my own forgiving sea, a softer, more domesticated beach, and my own lighthouse, less dramatic and less long-suffering'.[84] At the family graves, the narrator leaves stones they have carried from California, stones that have been 'washed by the waves of the Pacific'.[85] This chapter has suggested that one productive way of reading *Brooklyn* is to re-route it through Spanish-set Irish fictions of the 1930s and 1940s. *The Empty Family* further invites readers to consider Tóibín's recycling of certain locations, motifs, and scenarios as a formal complement to his capacious engagement with forms of transnationalism that both flirt with and reject the 'grand narrative' of Irish America.

FURTHER READING

Appadurai, Arjun. *Modernity at Large: Cultural Dimensions in Globalization*. Minneapolis, MN: University of Minnesota Press, 1996.

Armitage, David. 'Three Concepts of Atlantic History'. In David Armitage and Michael J. Braddick (eds), *The British Atlantic World, 1500–1800*. Basingstoke: Palgrave Macmillan, 2002: 11–25.

Brannigan, John. *Archipelagic Modernism: Literature in the Irish and British Isles, 1890–1970*. Edinburgh: Edinburgh University Press, 2015.

Doyle, Laura. 'At World's Edge: Post/Coloniality, Charles Maturin, and the Gothic Wanderer'. *Nineteenth-Century Literature* 65, no. 4 (2011): 513–47.

---

[82] Ibid., 209; Colm Tóibín, *The Empty Family* (New York: Scribner, 2012), 30.
[83] Tóibín, *The Empty Family*, 29.   [84] Ibid.   [85] Ibid., 30.

Fishkin, Shelley Fisher. 'Crossroads of Cultures: The Transnational Turn in American Studies—Presidential Address to the American Studies Association, November 12, 2004'. *American Quarterly* 57, no. 1 (2005): 17–57.

Frawley, Oona (ed.). *Memory Ireland, Volume 2: Diaspora and Memory Practices.* Syracuse, NY: Syracuse University Press, 2012.

Harte, Liam (ed.). *The Literature of the Irish in Britain: Autobiography and Memoir, 1725–2001.* Basingstoke: Palgrave Macmillan, 2009.

McWilliams, Ellen. *Women and Exile in Contemporary Irish Fiction.* Basingstoke: Palgrave Macmillan, 2013.

Morgan, Jack. *New World Irish: Notes on One Hundred Years of Lives and Letters in American Culture.* Basingstoke: Palgrave Macmillan, 2011.

Murray, Tony. *London Irish Fictions: Narrative, Diaspora and Identity.* Liverpool: Liverpool University Press, 2012.

Tucker, Amanda and Moira Casey (eds). *Where Motley is Worn: Transnational Irish Literatures.* Cork: Cork University Press, 2014.

Vertovec, Steven. 'Conceiving and Researching Transnationalism'. *Ethnic and Racial Studies* 22, no. 2 (1999): 447–62.

PART IX

CONTEMPORARY IRISH FICTION

CHAPTER 30

....

DUBLIN IN THE RARE NEW TIMES

....

DEREK HAND

THE economic crash that signalled the end of the Celtic Tiger period in 2008 brought with it some very real dilemmas, as the traditional narratives by which Irish people lived and understood themselves, their society, and their culture began to weaken or vanish. The city of Dublin was one of the major crucibles of this moment of transition, the location where the impact of sudden change was registered most conspicuously at the material and cultural level. The fourteen years of accelerated economic growth and prosperity prior to 2008 brought into being entirely new commercial, leisure, and living spaces. For example, the International Financial Services Centre (IFSC) transformed Dublin's docklands area on the north and south banks of the River Liffey, as did the regeneration of the city-centre Temple Bar area as a cultural quarter. But although it has been argued that Dublin remade itself as 'a new place in an old space'[1] during this period, the experience of transformation was a complex, anxious, and uncertain one in retrospect. As new buildings and housing estates sprung up, and the old city of Dublin expanded well beyond its traditional borders, there was a concurrent reconfiguration of the grand defining narratives of modern Ireland and Irish identity. This was a time which saw the demise of many of the categories by which many Irish people had come to understand themselves. Catholicism, nationalism, a romantic ideology associated with rural space—each came under pressure and were transformed, if not done away with completely. The inherent instability and malleability of the novel form made it a particularly suitable vehicle for capturing this time of transformation, ambivalence, and contradiction, and for giving expression to the anxieties that perplexed many Dubliners during this unprecedented period in the history of their city and country.[2]

Published four years after the implosion of the Irish economy, Spanish novelist Enrique Vila-Matas's *Dublinesque* centralizes the fiction of James Joyce (1882–1941) as the touchstone for any fictional engagement with the city of Dublin. Joyce's work is an

---

[1] Gerry Smyth, *Music and Irish Identity: Celtic Tiger Blues* (London: Routledge, 2017), 64.
[2] See Declan Kiberd, 'The City in Irish Culture', *City* 6, no. 2 (2002), 219–28.

emotional and cultural map for Samuel Riba, Vila-Matas's central protagonist, insofar as it offers him a means of understanding not just Dublin in the modern moment but modernity itself, for everyone everywhere. The narrator informs us: 'It's the characteristic of the imagination always to consider itself to be at the end of an era. For as long as he can remember he's heard it said that we are in a period of maximum crisis, a catastrophic transition towards a new culture.'[3] Thus, *Ulysses* (1922) becomes for Riba an elaborate means of waking, in funerary terms, both the twentieth century and the age of print as the digital era looms into view.

What *Dublinesque* acknowledges is how endings can lead to beginnings and vice versa. Importantly, the novel suggests that while the contemporary moment is extraordinary—or seemingly so to those in the midst of it—it is also the case that such times of momentous change and transition are a historical constant. A peculiar feature of much contemporary Irish writing is its remarkable self-consciousness about the 'newness' and exceptionalism of the present and its attendant dilemmas. This overt knowingness is also evident in the fictional configuring of the city of Dublin in a time of globalization. It is remarkable how many contemporary novelists self-reflexively ponder the role of art in general, and the novel in particular, in rendering their versions of metropolitan Irish modernity. The anxiety of literary influence is certainly a factor but so too is an apprehension about the viability of the novel form itself in a modern world dominated by ever-evolving digital modes of expression and communication, from Twitter to Snapchat.[4]

One of the consequences of the pre-eminence of Joyce as the literary chronicler of Dublin is that many literary and cultural critics misread the city as a unitary space, homogeneous and easily accessible. Although Joyce, as arch-modernist, attempted to register all experience and all facets of city life, the task was self-evidently impossible: his rendering of the city in writing obviously disconnects the space from itself in the moments of its being written and subsequently read. As Franco Moretti observes, 'if the city of *Ulysses* were the real Dublin of the turn of the century, it would not be the literary image par excellence of the modern metropolis.'[5] A unitary understanding of the city can never be applied to a reality that is in constant flux. Walter Benjamin suggests that an element of any city's presence is how this reality of movement and change is counteracted by the 'unconquerable power in names of streets, squares, and theaters, a power which persists in the face of all topographic displacement'.[6] This interplay between past and present, stasis and flux, centre and periphery, is what marks the modern city, and

---

[3] Enrique Vila-Matas, *Dublinesque*, trans. Rosalind Harvey and Anna McLean (London: Harvill Secker, 2012), 110. The novel was first published in Spanish as *Dublinesca* in 2010.

[4] On the question of influence, see, for example, Ferdia Mac Anna, 'The Dublin Renaissance: An Essay on Modern Dublin and Dublin Writers', *Irish Review* 10 (1991), 14–30 and Roddy Doyle, 'Overlong, overrated and unmoving: Roddy Doyle's verdict on James Joyce's *Ulysses*', *Guardian*, 10 February 2004.

[5] Franco Moretti, *Signs Taken for Wonders*, trans. Susan Fischer, David Forgacs, and David Miller (London: Verso, 1983), 190.

[6] Walter Benjamin, *The Arcades Project*, trans. Howard Eiland and Kevin McLaughlin (Cambridge, MA: Belknap Press of Harvard University Press, 2002), 516.

Dublin is no exception. Furthermore, the contemporary era in Ireland, particularly from the 1980s onwards, has been marked by an intense interrogation of monolithic and singular thinking in terms of personal, communal, and national identity. The colonial and post-colonial models that fitted the Irish experience of oppression and under-achievement no longer applied as financial wealth and economic success became the new means of measuring value and worth. As Liam Harte contends, this is a palpable turning point between the past and the future, a moment when writers 'find deficiencies in totalizing narratives of the past'.[7] The result is that writers, particularly novelists, eschew the received grand narrative of Dublin to embrace the myriad possibilities that 'the cities of Dublin'[8] might produce.

The following discussion will examine novelistic responses by writers from different generations to the social, cultural, attitudinal, and behavioural changes that have characterized life in Dublin during and after the years of economic uplift. The first part of the chapter will explore portrayals of changing personal, moral, and artistic value systems at a time when the forces of globalization were altering the distinctive culture of a city whose demographic expansion was accompanied by an increase in cultural and ethnic diversity and widening disparities between the affluent and the poor. This will be followed by a consideration of the treatment of history in some recent Dublin-set novels, with a particular focus on works that explore the interplay between previous eras and the present one, including the devastating legacies of hidden trauma. If the novels under discussion have a unifying thread, it lies in the questions they pose about how one relates to, lives among, and makes coherent sense of one's surroundings in a time of rapid, technology-driven change. A keen attention to place, not merely as a passive backdrop but as a shaper of experience and identity, coexists in these works with a sustained attempt to identify, whether by means of social realism or satire, what it is that defines Dubliners and their city in the era of globalization. While the answers vary from novelist to novelist, all understand the city's identity to be fluid and mobile, a work in progress where the evolving combinations of the local and the global present fresh challenges to those who live and work there, challenges that pose unsettling questions about the meaning and constitution of self and community in these rare new times.

NEW DUBLIN(S)

One novelist in particular is closely associated with the Dublin of the contemporary moment: Roddy Doyle (1958–). His exploration of this territory began with his Barrytown trilogy, comprising *The Commitments* (1987), *The Snapper* (1990), and *The Van* (1991), which focuses on the working-class inhabitants of a recently-built suburban estate on the city outskirts. Unlike Dermot Bolger (1959–), whose subject in novels such

---

[7] Liam Harte, *Reading the Contemporary Irish Novel 1987–2007* (Oxford: Wiley Blackwell, 2014), 3.
[8] Keith Ridgway, *The Parts* (London: Faber and Faber, 2003), 42.

as *The Woman's Daughter* (1987) and *The Journey Home* (1990) is the ancient village of Finglas being swallowed up by the ever-expanding city, Doyle's fictional Barrytown is not a village in that traditional sense but is instead emblematic of the numerous satellite towns created as part of the modernizing project of the 1960s and 1970s. Few of the inherited signifiers of Irish identity and meaning have any purchase in this world; the civic and religious institutions of the state mean little to the Rabbittes, the family at the centre of the trilogy, or to their friends and neighbours. Instead, the inhabitants of this community embrace the possibilities of self-reliance. In *The Commitments*, this manifests itself in the creation of soul band by Jimmy Rabbitte, while in *The Van* his father starts a local business with his best friend. That the band eventually splits up and Jimmy's business venture ends in failure does not really matter. Such abortive attempts at working-class entrepreneurship are a commonplace in a community where there are no easy solutions to entrenched social problems, nor are there any happy endings. What does emerge, however, is a portrait of resilience and survival in which displaced individuals and socially disenfranchised communities with few traditions to sustain them are forced to live by their wits and improvise by creating new modes, new rules, and new rituals by which to live.

Doyle's Booker Prize-winning novel, *Paddy Clarke Ha Ha Ha* (1993), further develops these themes by exploring the 1960s expansion of the northside suburbs. Paddy Clarke's physical and emotional growth runs in parallel to the birth of sprawling housing estates and the attendant transition to a more secular, consumerist society. Having a child protagonist, while a staple in much twentieth-century Irish fiction, is an effective way of emphasizing the inherent, unstable novelty of this place. Tellingly, the significant landmarks in Paddy's Dublin are not those politically symbolic locations such as College Green or the General Post Office but intimate and local spaces such as the newsagent's shop and the public library. These are the points of reference that bind his world and his narrative as he negotiates and adapts to an alien territory. Indeed, Doyle's characters' intense attachment to their immediate environment means that they are instinctively wary of the centre of the city and feel out of place there.

A recurring image in Doyle's work, subsequently amplified in the movie versions of his novels, is that of the DART (Dublin Area Rapid Transport), the electrified train service that began operating in 1984 and which links the capital's northside and southside. Famously, in George Eliot's *Middlemarch* (1871), the railway is a signifier of progress, a machine to be feared because it had the potential to bring change and destruction to traditional communities. In Doyle's fiction, the DART is a positive image of modernity, mobility, and connection: a symbol of a forward-looking city reimagining itself. The presence of the DART and later the Luas—Dublin's light rail system, launched in 2004— enables suburban outposts to prosper economically and also opens up new leisure choices, as evidenced in *Paula Spencer* (2006) by the title character's resolution to take a trip to Tallaght on the 'gorgeous'[9] Luas. Such responsiveness to the possibilities heralded by new transport modes and routes within the city is mirrored by the characters'

---

[9] Roddy Doyle, *Paula Spencer* (London: Vintage, 2007), 103.

readiness to exploit the economic opportunities afforded by their access to relatively inexpensive air travel. The scene in which Paula's sister Carmel seeks to persuade her of the benefits of buying an apartment in Bulgaria encapsulates the effects of this new culture of monetized market forces:

> – It's an investment, Paula.
> – Oh. Yeah.
> – When Bulgaria joins the EU the value of those apartments will go through the fuckin' roof. An investment.
> An investment. They used to talk about *Eastenders* and their husbands.[10]

Again and again in his post-1995 fiction, Doyle allows characters to articulate a response of bemused bewilderment to the changes wrought by the sudden prosperity of the boom years, self-consciously signalling how everyday experience was being transfigured, including people's relationships to the concepts of home and place. This impulse to reimagine the spaces of the city in response to the burgeoning forces of globalization is also registered in his earlier fiction, notably in *The Commitments*, where the band members reinterpret the lyrics of the song 'Soul Train', so that the train becomes the DART and all the stations from Killester and Kilbarrack to Sutton and Howth are name-checked. The global and local can sit happily alongside each other here, the moral being that the means to self-discovery and self-expression are to be found in the most surprising—even uninspiring—of locations. This playful act of appropriation speaks to the continual need to reimagine the home place and re-energize the ways in which different generations can connect with it.

Doyle's achievement, like that of the cultural revivalists who rehabilitated Irish rural space for literature and drama a century before him, is to make Dublin suburbia and the lives lived there a worthy subject of fictional representation. In the process, he represents modern Dublin as a place open to the nuances and complexities of everyday life, replete with problems, certainly, but also home to boundless potential. It is this city of possibility and energy that the economic boom brought to the fore and which novelists attempted to render in a variety of ways, none more so than Keith Ridgway (1965–). His *The Parts* (2003) is a black comedy which gloriously dissects the foibles of Celtic Ireland Dublin or, rather, a plurality of Dublins. The novel repeatedly underscores the evolving diversity of the contemporary city, from its many different subcultures to its contrasting moods and shifting impressions:

> Working Dublin, queer Dublin, junkie Dublin, media Dublin, party Dublin, executive Dublin, homeless Dublin, suburban Dublin, teenage Dublin, gangland Dublin, Dublin with the flags out, mother Dublin, culchie Dublin, Muslim Dublin . . .
>   Dublin is friendly they'd say. Dublin is stubborn. And he knew that what they were saying was that Dublin had friendly people in it—that Dublin had stubborn people in it. And he'd heard people talk about the city itself—the buildings and the

---

[10] Ibid., 29.

streets and the river. Dublin is dirty. Dublin is squalid. Dublin is too small. . . . Dublin is wet and windy and cold. Dublin is bitter. . . . Dublin is cruel. Dublin eats your heart out. Dublin kills you. Dublin is great. Great fun. Great craic.[11]

As the plot unfolds across three sections, the heterogeneity of city life is echoed in the respective narratives of six characters whose stories slowly merge. Ridgway's characters know *where* they live, but they don't know *how* to live. Technological change, in the form of the internet and the mobile phone, demonstrates how objects designed to aid communication and connection can, for some, exacerbate dislocation and alienation. Others revel in the sense of contemporary Dublin as a mosaic of worlds, a place where people no longer have to be grounded in any one specific space or identity but can be whoever they want to be, or at least maintain the illusion that such choices are possible.

The Parts' hyper-awareness of place is shared by other novels of the period, as is Ridgway's emphasis on plural identities and their myriad possibilities. Two such works are Barry McCrea's (1974–) *The First Verse* (2005) and Belinda McKeon's (1979–) *Solace* (2011). Both are set in Trinity College and foreground the university's geographical centrality and accessibility by making it the pivot around which the life of the city circulates. The early chapters of *Solace* capture a glimpse of a Dublin social life that is carefree and fun: 'On warm summer evenings a crowd always surrounded the pub on the corner of South Anne Street, not trying to get in, but taking pleasure in being outside, drinks in hand, soaking up the last of the sun.'[12] But the sense of perpetual summer cannot last, and the main character's disintegrating doctoral project on Maria Edgeworth, coupled with the death of his partner, points to a beckoning adult world of responsibility. If *Solace* is ultimately a sombre piece, *The First Verse* cleverly entertains its readers with a postmodern plot revolving around Trinity students becoming involved in a cultish group devoted to reading the future through *sortes*, the practice of randomly choosing passages from any text to foretell the future.[13] Focalized through the eyes of middle-class Dubliner Niall Lenihan, who has left home to go to college, the mundane world of the undergraduate student—making friends, partying, studying—is juxtaposed with the surreal and utterly fantastic. Yet this latter aspect disguises the far more interesting story that is at the heart of the novel, that of being young and gay in Celtic Tiger Dublin. *The First Verse* offers the reader a map of gay life in the city through its naming of places and landmarks. For Niall, such naming is an act of making the entire city his own: naming is an act of possession and ultimate ownership.

The problem broached in *The Parts*, that of how to live in a time of unprecedented, accelerated socio-economic change, is revisited from a satirical perspective in two early twenty-first-century novels that examine the fate of artistic endeavour in a culture increasingly defined by consumption and commodification. Éilís Ní Dhuibhne's (1954–)

[11] Ridgway, *The Parts*, 41, 47–8.

[12] Belinda McKeon, *Solace* (London: Picador, 2011), 109.

[13] See Michael G. Cronin, '*The Parts* by Keith Ridgway & *The First Verse* by Barry McCrea', *The Stinging Fly* 24, no. 2 (2013), https://stingingfly.org/2013/02/01/parts-keith-ridgway-first-verse-barry-mccrea/. Accessed 28 September 2018.

Fox, Swallow, Scarecrow (2007) skewers the foibles and vanities of the Dublin literati and asks pointed questions about the place and value of fiction in this affluent milieu. It takes as its starting point striking images of a newly gentrified Dublin from the perspective of a southside tram's journey into the city centre. The panorama takes in 'the new glass bridge which spanned the inscrutable waters of the Grand Canal', 'chic apartments, their balconies rubbing shoulders with almost equally chic corporation houses', and the reno-vated streetscape of Adelaide Road, 'all windows and transparency, where once there had been high hedges and minority religions'.[14] As persuasively argued by Susan Cahill, all this glass becomes a grand reflecting mirror, throwing back on those who wander the streets images of success and confidence.[15] Yet for all the cultural and economic divi-dends yielded by the Celtic Tiger, palpable urban class distinctions still persist:

> Travelling by tram, at least on the Green Line, had a bit of cachet. Being seen on it was not necessarily a bad thing, whereas being seen on a Dublin bus, even a most respectable bus like the 7 or the 11, was an abject admission of social and economic failure. Only the young, the old and the poor used the bus.[16]

In the novel's central protagonist, Anna Kelly Sweeney, Ní Dhuibhne fashions a char-acter who is the very personification of a culture in which style and surface overwhelm substance and depth. A writer of children's fiction and the wife of a wealthy property developer—a nexus that highlights the interdependency between commerce and art in this opportunistic new world—Anna is, we are told, a woman of 'no beliefs whatsoever':

> She was vaguely agnostic, vaguely socialist, vaguely capitalist, vaguely materialistic, vaguely spiritual. The only thing she really believed in was her ambition to be a suc-cessful writer, by which she meant some sort of mixture of famous, bestselling and good. But she had never considered why she wrote or why she wanted to write a 'good' book, or what good such a book could do for its readers. Such questions—questions regarding the meaning of literature, or of writing—were never discussed in her literary circles. Similarly, questions as to the meaning of life were never dis-cussed in her social or family circles.[17]

A similar displacement of personal and artistic integrity by moral vacuity and narcissis-tic ambition is prominently on show in Anne Haverty's (1959–) *The Free and Easy* (2006), which lampoons a Dublin art world in which an artwork's physical size is a key determinant of its worth in the marketplace. Land development and the buying and sell-ing of property, at home and abroad, provide the backdrop to this story of New Yorker Tom Blessman who comes to Dublin on a mission to spend the fortune of his Irish

---

[14] Éilís Ní Dhuibhne, *Fox, Swallow, Scarecrow* (Belfast: Blackstaff Press, 2007), 1.
[15] See Susan Cahill, *Irish Literature in the Celtic Tiger Years 1990–2008: Gender, Bodies, Memory* (London: Continuum, 2011), 163ff.
[16] Ní Dhuibhne, *Fox, Swallow, Scarecrow*, 2.
[17] Ibid., 75–6.

émigré great-uncle on the unspecified perceived needs of the Irish people. Haverty's use of the trope of the traveller to Ireland, which is central to many nineteenth-century Irish novels, allows her to present an outsider perspective on a fast-changing society. But whereas the Victorian tourist typically discovers an Ireland and an Irishness that are always already exotic and strange, Blessman finds only dull sameness, a people 'exactly the same as everyone else', as one acquaintance remarks, apart from 'the theme park aspect. That's an area that's really thriving.'[18]

What *The Free and Easy* captures particularly well is how staggeringly self-conscious some Dubliners have become about *this* moment of success and how keen many are to 'jettison the past'.[19] As a film director puts it in an interview that Blessman reads, 'The rain, the drunken father . . . all that sob stuff, the mangy dogs, all that shite, it's over. It's over historically, it's over cinematically. . . . We're global now, we're multicultural, let's celebrate. We're done with whingeing, right?'[20] Evidently, it is not enough for some to be the beneficiaries of sudden wealth and prosperity; they must insistently display and broadcast their largesse. This changed Dublin (and Ireland) demands a fresh story, one that emphasizes the newness of everything. The very act of telling that story makes it real, as real as the golf courses springing up all over the city and its swiftly gentrifying environs.

The economic crash of 2008 brought such narratives of breezy success (and the golf course developments that accompanied them) to an abrupt halt. Paul Murray's (1975–) third novel, *The Mark and the Void* (2015), takes up the task of attempting to dissect, through a metafictional and satirical lens, the causes and ongoing catastrophic consequences of the global financial crisis and its implications for Ireland. The plot centres on the lives of investment bankers and traders of different nationalities based at the headquarters of a European bank in Dublin's IFSC, the construction of which in the late 1980s heralded the city's emergence as an international financial services hub. As a place that exists to service the global world of capital and its virtual movement, the IFSC is depicted as a signifier for the dissonance caused by an incompatibility between the amoral individualism encouraged by free market capitalism and the humane communalism that traditionally sustained local neighbourhoods. The IFSC is one of the voids to which the novel's title alludes, being 'a shadow-place', 'a kind of legal elsewhere: multinationals send their profits here to avoid tax, banks conduct their more sensitive activities with the guarantee of a blind eye from the authorities'.[21]

But *The Mark and the Void* is also self-reflexively concerned with literary matters. Its central conceit involves a black-clad character called Paul attempting to write a novel about the world of high finance, using as his everyman figure a French banker named Claude Martingale, whom Paul thinks of as a modern-day equivalent of Leopold Bloom. By shadowing Claude, Paul hopes 'to discover the humanity inside the corporate machine' and 'write something that genuinely reflects how we live today. Real, actual

---

[18]   Anne Haverty, *The Free and Easy* (London: Vintage, 2008), 112.
[19]   Ibid., 113.   [20]   Ibid., 37.
[21]   Paul Murray, *The Mark and the Void* (London: Penguin, 2015), 23.

life, not some ivory-tower palaver, not a whole load of *literature*.'[22] Claude soon discovers, however, that Paul is not all he purports to be. Unlike Murray's previous novel,
Skippy Dies (2010), *The Mark and the Void* never rises above farce. As in *Fox, Swallow,
Scarecrow*, we are immersed in a culture where story rivals substance, for bankers as
much as for novelists. Just as the latter need a narrative frame for their fictions, the former 'turn companies into characters, quarterly reports into events, the chaos of global
business into a few simple fables ending in a buy or sell recommendation which, if followed, will hopefully result in a profit. The truth is fine in principle, but stories are what
we sell.'[23]

Yet the seriousness of *The Mark and the Void*'s satirical takedown of an amoral global
capitalist system is unmistakeably piercing. The novel's relentless evisceration of a world
in which anonymous, unaccountable individuals, whose actions can determine the fate
of whole nations, no longer recognize a distinction between truth and fiction, or
between the actual and the virtual, or between right and wrong, is both comically absurd
and profoundly tragic. The novel's moral critique of this culture is crystallized in a pivotal set-piece scene towards the end of part one, in which Claude emerges from the IFCS
and suddenly comes face to face with a reality so overwhelming that he must avert his
eyes:

> And here, on the teeming road, are the Irish: blanched, pocked, pitted, sleep-
> deprived, burnished, beaming, snaggle-toothed, balding, rouged, raddled, beaky,
> exophthalmic; . . . to walk among them is to be plunged into a sea of stories, a human
> comedy so rich it seems on the point of writing itself. For a moment I wonder, hope-
> lessly, what the International Financial Services Centre can offer to compare—then
> I remember that this was [Paul's] very point, that the storyless, faceless banks are the
> underwriters of all this humanity, that we are the Fates who weave the fabric of the
> day . . .[24]

Claire Kilroy's (1973–) *The Devil I Know* (2012) further unpicks this woven fabric,
combining the modes of social realism and fantasy to expose the recklessness of
those who sold their souls for the trappings of wealth and success—the cars, the houses,
the trophy spouses. The year is 2016 and the setting is Howth, its literary history referenced by oblique nods to W. B. Yeats (1865–1939) and Joyce, the latter's *Finnegans Wake*
(1939) supplying the novel's epigraph. The novel comprises the testimony given to a
judge-like interlocutor over ten days by one Tristram St Lawrence, the thirteenth Earl of
Howth and a globe-trotting interpreter by profession. If this scenario calls to mind the
workings of the many tribunals of inquiry that have in recent decades exposed corrupt
practices in Irish political and civic life, so too does the nature of Tristram's 'evidence':
his business partnership with a Dublin property developer, forged during the boom
years at the instigation of the shadowy Monsieur Deauville, who turns out to be a truly
diabolical sponsor.

[22] Ibid., 16, 15. Original emphasis.
[23] Ibid., 96–7.   [24] Ibid., 112–13.

The story that unfolds describes the destruction of a millennia-long family lineage and a twenty-first-century national economy by boorish greed and hubris. The novel's powerful critique of a culture and society that has lost its way is underlined by having St Lawrence's narrative culminate in the spring of 2016, on the eve of the centenary of the foundational event of the Irish state:

> I set off on foot up the Quays along the silver Liffey. *riverrun, past Eve and Adam's, from swerve of shore to bend of bay, brings us by a commodius vicus of recirculation back to Howth Castle and Environs.* Do you remember? It used to be written on the tenner back when we still had our own currency.
>
> On O'Connell Street preparations were afoot outside the GPO for the celebration of the Centenary of the Easter Rising. One hundred years since the Proclamation of the Irish Republic and our sovereignty had been hocked. It was Holy Thursday and the panic-drinking was already under way, what with the pubs shutting to mark Good Friday. It would get messy on the streets of Dublin that night.[25]

In a narrative dominated by intricate testimony, there is arresting force in the narrator's muted allusion to the spectacle of a newly economically enslaved nation celebrating the centenary of the insurrection that led to its independence from colonial rule. Just as the denizens of Doyle's Barrytown were compelled to improvise their way through the legacies of earlier economic crises, the millennial generation must contrive ways of living in the wake of the most recent. In the new Dublin as in the old, the commodius vicus of recirculation determines that surviving in the city is a perpetual work in progress.

DUBLIN'S PAST(S)

We have already identified Roddy Doyle as the pre-eminent chronicler of the lives of contemporary working-class Dubliners. Yet it would be a mistake to regard him as a wholly present-centred novelist. On the contrary, his exploration of Dublin's early twentieth-century history in *The Last Roundup*, his trilogy of novels featuring Henry Smart, which comprises *A Star Called Henry* (1999), *Oh, Play That Thing!* (2004), and *The Dead Republic* (2010), revisits the past in order to uncover the backstory of the working-class communities that inhabit the city of his novels set in more recent times. *A Star Called Henry*, the more successful of these novels, focuses on the revolutionary period, portraying the rebels of 1916 as members of sectarian bourgeois elites with little concern for the true liberation of the poor and the dispossessed. In this class-based analysis of the Rising, the isolation and alienation of the inhabitants of modern-day Barrytown can be traced to this defining moment of disenfranchisement, which means that, for Doyle, the revolutionary past and its legacies are a disaster to be overcome. His

---

[25] Claire Kilroy, *The Devil I Know* (London: Faber and Faber, 2012), 354.

view of the country's historical development since independence is that it is has produced a society based on an ideologically narrow and socially conservative Catholic nationalist ethos that bears little relevance for the people of Barrytown, and which must therefore be jettisoned in order for a more positive future for them to be realized.

This mining of history is of particular note in recent Dublin-set fiction.[26] Certainly, many contemporary Irish novelists approach the past as a troubling site of contention, whether by meditating upon its contours and legacies in the present or by offering different interpretations and reimaginings of it. For some, this backward look suggests development and growth and serves to clarify the distinction between 'then' and 'now'. Writers define the past out of which they, and we, have come. In so doing, they shape a narrative (or particular parts thereof) of how we as a people have arrived in the present moment. For example, John Banville (1945–), writing as Benjamin Black, uses 1950s Dublin in novels such as *Christine Falls* (2006) and *Elegy for April* (2010) as a backdrop against which the plots of his *noir* thrillers unfold. Even as the complexities of the modern city evaporate in the stylized, perhaps clichéd, images of smoke-filled bars and rain-washed pavements, the present-day reader may derive pleasure from savouring the contrast between the seemingly grim days of the past and the apparently brighter, freer present.

Other novelists suggest that similarity rather than difference is the key to understanding our relationship to history. Joseph O'Connor's (1963–) *Ghost Light* (2010) focuses on dramatist J. M. Synge (1871–1909) and his love affair with Abbey Theatre actress Molly Allgood in the early 1900s. What is interesting about this novel is how, in order to dramatize an intimate human story, O'Connor ignores any self-consciousness about the nature of history and how it is made and told. The character of Synge, always the most elusive of the Irish Revival writers, emerges as complex and fully rounded. The intensity of his relationship with Molly transcends any specific historical moment, so much so that what at first might appear as a straightforward deployment of nostalgia—Edwardian Dublin in 'the rare ould times'—actually has the potential to render the present moment strange because O'Connor's characters appear as our contemporaries. Rather than being distant, different, and disconnected from us, these characters provide the reader with a shock of recognition, disturbing the dichotomy between their time and our own.

A concern with strangeness centred on time suffuses the recent work of Antrim-born Deirdre Madden (1960–), who has lived in Dublin for many years. Time and perceptions of time are *the* great tropes of modernist and postmodernist fiction.[27] This self-consciousness suggests that the real question of contemporary fiction is not *where* one lives but *when*. In novels such as *Authenticity* (2002) and *Molly Fox's Birthday* (2008), Madden dwells on the quiet lives of middle-class Dubliners in red-brick houses in the older parts of the city, places with a 'history', such as Drumcondra and Portobello. Her

---

[26] This trend has not been without its critics. See, for example, Alison Flood, 'Julian Gough slams fellow Irish novelists as "priestly caste" cut off from the culture', *Guardian*, 11 February 2010.

[27] See Peter Boxall, *Twenty-First-Century Fiction: A Critical Introduction* (Cambridge: Cambridge University Press, 2013), 1–18.

locations register socio-economic change across the generations: what were once the cottages of workers and artisans are now the homes of affluent urban professionals. In *Time Present and Time Past* (2013), Fintan Buckley, a successful legal advisor living in the plush environs of Howth, is experiencing a midlife crisis. His crisis produces moments of disconnection and defamiliarization in the midst of the hustle and bustle of city life, a plot twist that recalls Declan Kiberd's observation that the contemporary urban environment is too ordered and predictable to accommodate the chance street encounters that propel *Ulysses*, for example.[28] In a café, Fintan is suddenly struck by the arbitrariness of the words on a menu and this feeling of disorientation expands to encompass other people, including his own family: 'if people who are close to him are becoming strange, he is also beginning to see strangers in an intimate and overly familiar way'.[29] His disconcerting sense of the ambiguous interplay of past and present, the known and the strange, is deepened by his son's remark that 'we tend to think that the past was more interesting than it really was, and my point is that it was more banal than we give it credit for, but also more complicated'.[30] Time and perceptions of time, the novel suggests, are seldom singular and never stable.

Time Present and Time Past also suggests that *how* one lives is as important as when or where. This is underscored by the story of Fintan's sister Martina, who had a successful career in London until she abruptly returned to Dublin without offering a full explanation to her family. The reason, it transpires, is because she was violently beaten by a man with whom she was beginning a relationship. Madden shows, however, that this trauma does not necessarily have to become the defining, paralysing event of this woman's life, and that her return home can allow her to begin again. While this outcome is positive for Martina Buckley, her response to personally injurious experience is not shared by all Dubliners in contemporary fiction. A more common trope is that of the traumatized subject trapped in a painful psychic state, consumed by a catastrophic event that is continually replayed or relived through memory.[31]

Trauma fiction focuses not only on the past but also on the act of memory itself. The consequences of this manoeuvre are manifold, not least of which is the acknowledgement of the personal human responses to the grand movements and oppressions of history. Anne Enright's (1962–) Man Booker Prize-winning novel, *The Gathering* (2007), provides a powerful example of this dynamic, moving as it does between the prosperous capital of the late 1990s and the city of the early 1900s, when the effects of poverty and deprivation were more conspicuously pervasive.[32] The past in the novel is associated

---

[28] Declan Kiberd, 'Bloom in Bourgeois Bohemia: A Moment of Perpetual Possibility for Joyce—and for Dublin', *Times Literary Supplement*, 4 June 2004, 15.

[29] Deirdre Madden, *Time Present and Time Past* (London: Faber and Faber, 2013), 69.

[30] Ibid., 112–13.

[31] For analyses of the treatment of traumatic experience and memory in recent Irish fiction, see Robert F. Garratt, *Trauma and History in the Irish Novel: The Return of the Dead* (Basingstoke: Palgrave Macmillan, 2011) and Kathleen Costello-Sullivan, *Trauma and Recovery in the Twenty-First-Century Irish Novel* (Syracuse, NY: Syracuse University Press, 2018).

[32] See Carol Dell'Amico, 'Anne Enright's *The Gathering*: Trauma, Testimony, Memory', *New Hibernia Review* 14, no. 3 (2010), 59–73 and Harte, *Reading the Contemporary Irish Novel*, 217–42.

with a traditional Dublin, epitomized by a two-up, two-down house in Broadstone in the inner city. It is here that Veronica Hegarty's grandmother Ada Merriman lived and where her brother Liam was sexually molested as a child by Ada's landlord, Lamb Nugent. The story told by Veronica is prompted by her brother's suicide, which has forced her to reconsider the frailties of her dysfunctional family. Her voice, at once disoriented and knowing, suggests a measure of power and authority that is deceptive: she is able to put others in their place, yet she struggles to fit the fragments of her life into a coherent narrative. Veronica lives in a comfortable, if bland, housing estate and her jaded narrative voice is inflected by her underlying disaffection for the place. Her tone is a form of defence, of self-evasion; her tendency to ironize every experience constitutes a deferral of real feeling. This self-evasion also manifests itself in her preoccupation with what became a national obsession during the years of economic boom: the buying and selling of property. Referring to her grandmother's home, Veronica quips, 'When I have beaten the shit out of the place and made it smell, in a wonderfully clean but old-fashioned way, of wood soap and peonies, I will sell it on for twice the price.'[33]

One way of overcoming the past, it seems, is to sell it to the highest bidder. Overweening confidence was one of the chief qualities that defined the Celtic Tiger era. The past was a problem only if one allowed it to be and the present could be remade with enough capital investment. In Veronica Hegarty, Enright creates a character who registers the insidious effects of the new materialistic values sweeping the city, the growing tendency to equate emotional well-being with the pursuit of wealth and possessions. Tellingly, Veronica's inventory of her life conflates material and human belongings, as if they occupy the same moral and emotional plane: 'husband, car, phone bill, daughters'.[34] That the cumulative sum of such possessions falls far short of happiness is confirmed in chapter eleven when Veronica recalls a mundane moment before her brother's death, when she glimpsed her reflection in her car window: 'The sun was breaking through high-contrast clouds, the sky in the window pane was a wonderful, thick blue, and in my dark face moving past was a streak of a smile. And I remember thinking, "So, I am happy. That's nice to know."'[35] If such symptoms of anomie and self-alienation predate Liam Hegarty's suicide, his loss multiplies their intensity and lays bare the full extent of her estrangement from her own life:

> I was living my life in inverted commas. I could pick up my keys and go 'home' where I could 'have sex' with my 'husband' just like lots of other people did. This is what I had been doing for years. And I didn't seem to mind the inverted commas, or even notice that I was living in them, until my brother died.[36]

Like Fintan Buckley, Veronica Hegarty is in the throes of a midlife crisis, with the crucial difference that hers is overlaid by the anguish of bereavement and a belated response to childhood trauma. While both characters must reassess the past and its relationship

---

[33] Anne Enright, *The Gathering* (London: Vintage, 2008), 238.
[34] Ibid., 10.   [35] Ibid., 68.   [36] Ibid., 181.

to the present, Veronica is compelled by her loss to dredge up that which had been hidden, or evaded, or misread. By dramatizing Veronica's painful, protracted attempt 'to bear witness to an uncertain event' that is 'roaring inside' her, and come to terms with its manifold ramifications, *The Gathering* reveals the extent to which her life and relationships have been blighted by unacknowledged and unprocessed trauma.[37] She thus emerges not only as an alienated product of 1990s Ireland's eager embrace of consumer capitalism, the confident front merely disguising a yawning emptiness within; she is also an emblematic survivor of a pre-capitalist Ireland in which the victimization of the vulnerable was endemic: 'This is the anatomy and mechanism of a family—a whole fucking country—drowning in shame.'[38] Novels like this, even ones built round trauma, provide further evidence that the contemporary moment may not be quite so exceptional after all.

All cities are, by definition, evolving entities; there is always something more to be built, done, said, and, indeed, revealed. In *The House of Ulysses*, a novel originally published in Spanish in 2003, Julián Ríos recognizes this when he observes how in Joyce's writing 'revelations and knowledge emerge gradually ... as so often is the case in cities'.[39] This remains true of the city of Dublin a century after Joyce memorialized it in fiction. While the panoramic perspectives embraced by Joyce are perhaps in some ways still longed for, the multiple stories encompassed by the Dublin-set novels of the Celtic Tiger era and after tell of a city busily refashioning itself for the twenty-first century, as the reach and pace of globalization and consumer capitalism expand and intensify. The notion of a common Dublin experience is thoroughly deconstructed in the work of recent novelists, as are monolithic views of the city's history and its meaning. Furthermore, the boundary between the old and the new is shown to be neither absolute nor stable. The past remains alive in a mutating present and remains capable of exerting a formative influence on the new narratives of place that are continually coming into being. Form, too, is subject to interrogation and redefinition. Fundamental questions about the capacity of the novel form itself to capture and render the multiplicity of these new narratives are a feature of much contemporary Dublin fiction, indicating that the challenges for the novelist are as they have always been: to be relevant to the moment and to be engaged with the realities of lives that are being lived in the here and now.

Further Reading

Bauman, Zygmunt. *Liquid Modernity*. Cambridge: Polity Press, 2000.

Cahill, Susan. *Irish Literature in the Celtic Tiger Years 1990–2008: Gender, Bodies, Memory*. London: Continuum, 2011.

Foster, John Wilson (ed.). *The Cambridge Companion to the Irish Novel*. Cambridge: Cambridge University Press, 2006.

Hand, Derek. *A History of the Irish Novel*. Cambridge: Cambridge University Press, 2011.

---

[37] Ibid., 1.   [38] Ibid., 168.

[39] Julián Ríos, *The House of Ulysses*, trans. Nick Caistor (Dublin: Dalkey Archive Press, 2010), 136.

Harte, Liam. *Reading the Contemporary Irish Novel 1987–2007*. Oxford: Wiley Blackwell, 2014.

Harte, Liam and Michael Parker (eds). *Contemporary Irish Fiction: Themes, Tropes, Theories*. Basingstoke: Macmillan, 2000.

Jeffers, Jennifer M. *The Irish Novel at the End of the Twentieth Century: Gender, Bodies, and Power*. Basingstoke: Palgrave Macmillan, 2002.

Moretti, Franco (ed.). *The Novel, Volume 1: History, Geography, and Culture*. Princeton, NJ: Princeton University Press, 2006.

Moretti, Franco (ed.). *The Novel, Volume 2: Forms and Themes*. Princeton, NJ: Princeton University Press, 2006.

O'Brien, George. 'Contemporary Prose in English: 1940–2000'. In Margaret Kelleher and Philip O'Leary (eds), *The Cambridge History of Irish Literature, Volume 2: 1890–2000*. Cambridge: Cambridge University Press, 2006: 421–77.

O'Brien, George. *The Irish Novel 1960–2010*. Cork: Cork University Press, 2012.

Peach, Linden. *The Contemporary Irish Novel: Critical Readings*. Basingstoke: Palgrave Macmillan, 2004.

Roche, Anthony (ed.). *Irish University Review. Special Issue: Contemporary Irish Fiction* 30, no. 1 (2000).

Smyth, Gerry. *The Novel and the Nation: Studies in the New Irish Fiction*. London: Pluto Press, 1997.

St Peter, Christine. *Changing Ireland: Strategies in Contemporary Women's Fiction*. Basingstoke: Macmillan, 2000.

CHAPTER 31

....

NORTHERN IRISH
FICTION AFTER THE
TROUBLES

....

FIONA McCANN

THERE is general consensus that the conflict in the North of Ireland began in 1969 and ended in 1998 with the Good Friday/Belfast Agreement, but these landmark dates discount sectarian or political violence perpetuated before and after this period. The definitive compendium of Troubles-related deaths, *Lost Lives*, first published in 1999, begins with the murder of John Patrick Sullivan in June 1966 and ends with that of James McMahon in November 2003, thus drawing attention to the permeability of the temporal limits of the conflict.[1] While it is fair to say that the violence has certainly abated, one might still question the extent to which we can justly speak of a 'post-conflict' Northern Ireland, especially when dissident republican paramilitary activity and power-sharing tensions, disruptions, and suspensions are factored in. Indeed, it is one of the many ironies of the post-1998 era that some highly conspicuous physical manifestations of division, such as the so-called 'peace walls' in Belfast, continue to proliferate.[2] With these caveats in mind, this chapter will focus on works of fiction published in or after 1998, many of which continue to engage in innovative ways with the causes and ideological characteristics of the conflict, without in any way suggesting that those tensions have somehow magically disappeared as a result of the Good Friday Agreement. Indeed, the sustained interest in the Troubles in contemporary novels and short stories suggests that literature is one of the places where these tensions can be teased out and interrogated without necessarily being fully resolved.

---

[1] David McKittrick, Seamus Kelters, Brian Feeney, Chris Thornton, and David McVea, *Lost Lives* (Edinburgh: Mainstream, 1999). This book has since appeared in revised and updated editions.

[2] According to one commentator, there were 99 barriers of various kinds dividing neighbourhoods in Belfast in December 2013, many of which had sprung up since the ostensible end of the Troubles. See Henry McDonald, 'Belfast "peace walls" will come down only by community consent—minister', *Guardian*, 3 December 2013.

The opening pages of a policy document entitled *A Shared Future*, published in 2005 by the Office of the Northern Ireland First Minister and Deputy First Minister, highlight the necessity of encouraging 'understanding of the complexity of our history, through museums and a common school curriculum' and of supporting 'cultural projects which highlight the complexity and overlapping nature of identities and their wider global connections'.[3] The premise from which I will be working in this chapter is that many cultural productions in the literary, artistic, and cinematic arenas which evoke the past do not adequately manage to address these complexities, and that this is regrettable as no shared future can emerge from a superficial engagement with the past. By superficial I mean a tendency to reduce the Troubles to an atavistic conflict with little or no reference to the social, political, and economic factors which engendered and sustained it.[4] I will be suggesting that it is in the departures from the usual script that dissensus, a concept I explain below, can emerge and encourage different ways of thinking about the past. In short, I argue that, like politics, artistic and literary practices construct what cultural philosopher Jacques Rancière terms 'material rearrangements of signs and images, relationships between what is seen and what is said, between what is done and what can be done'.[5]

Dissensus in this context means more than mere dissent (although that is part of its meaning). It involves creating a breach in the established or 'sensible' order—what Rancière glosses as 'a given state of things'[6]—and pushing into the open what has until that point been invisible. As translator and critic Gabriel Rockhill explains it, 'dissensus is not a quarrel over personal interests or opinions. It is a political process that . . . creates a fissure in the sensible order by confronting the established framework of perception, thought, and action with the "inadmissible."'[7] Literary fiction, I will argue, is a privileged space in which the 'inadmissible' can be imagined. Dissensus, then, dovetails to some degree with genres such as postcolonial fiction, postmodern fiction, and queer fiction, in which untold stories are imagined and written into being and well-known stories (fictional or otherwise) reimagined and rewritten from various viewpoints. However, Rancière cautions against any attempt to establish a cause-and-effect relationship between 'the intention realized in an art performance and a capacity for political subjectivation'.[8] Fiction is at best 'a way of changing existing modes of sensory presentations and forms of enunciation; of varying frames, scales and rhythms, and of building

[3] Office of the First Minister and Deputy First Minister, *A Shared Future: Policy and Strategic Framework for Good Relations in Northern Ireland* (Belfast: Office of the First Minister and Deputy First Minister, 2005), 10.

[4] Examples of this type of cultural production include the novels *Divorcing Jack* (1995) by Colin Bateman, *Eureka Street* (1996) by Robert McLiam Wilson, and *The Twelve* (2009) by Stuart Neville. See also Owen McCafferty's play, *Mojo Mickybo* (1998), Terry Loane's film adaptation of it, entitled *Mickybo and Me* (2005), and *Good Vibrations*, the 2013 film based on the life of the Belfast punk impresario Terri Hooley, directed by Lisa Barros D'Sa and Glenn Leyburn.

[5] Jacques Rancière, *The Politics of Aesthetics*, trans. Gabriel Rockhill (London: Continuum, 2004), 39.

[6] Jacques Rancière, *Dissensus: On Politics and Aesthetics*, trans. Steven Corcoran (London: Bloomsbury, 2013), 143.

[7] Rancière, *The Politics of Aesthetics*, 85.   [8] Rancière, *Dissensus*, 141.

new relationships between reality and appearance, the individual and the collective'.[9] In attempting to do this, literature acts politically.

In order to frame this discussion, I will be referring to Rancière's concept of *le partage du sensible*, which roughly translates as 'the distribution or sharing out of the sensible'. Paraphrasing Rancière, Rockhill explains the philosopher's defining concept in the following terms:

> [It is] the implicit law governing the sensible order that parcels out places and forms of participation in a common world by first establishing the modes of perception within which these are inscribed. The distribution of the sensible thus produces a system of self-evident facts of perception based on the set horizons and modalities of what is visible and audible as well as what can be said, thought, made, or done. Strictly speaking, 'distribution' therefore refers both to forms of inclusion and to forms of exclusion. The 'sensible', of course, does not refer to what shows good sense or judgement but to what is *aisthēton* or capable of being apprehended by the senses.[10]

Rockhill also emphasizes the need to attend to both meanings of the verb *partager*—to share and to divide—and as such invites us to be aware of the ways in which allotted roles are apportioned and accounted for in a certain time and place. For Rancière, politics, the essence of which is dissensus, 'exists wherever the count of parts and parties of society is disturbed by the inscription of a part of those who have no part', and is not so much 'a confrontation between interests or opinions' as 'the demonstration (*manifestation*) of a gap in the sensible itself'.[11] Bearing all of this in mind, I will offer a brief panorama of post-Troubles Northern Irish fiction (which includes the work of one novelist born in the Republic, close to the border) and investigate the manner in which the present discourse of shared futures has influenced contemporary literary representations in both positive and negative ways. In some cases, this discourse serves a conservative agenda of consensus at all costs; in others, it supports a more radical agenda of dissensus in which uncomfortable questions (and not always those we might expect) are enshrined as central to narrative aesthetics.

Nihilism and Nostalgia

This section will consider two dominant poles of expression in post-Agreement fiction: nostalgia and nihilism. I will argue that it is in the interstices between them that dissensus is best expressed; that is to say, where hidden otherness is rendered visible or audible, thus redistributing the sensible (or that which is self-evident) and foregrounding a more

---

[9] Ibid.   [10] Rancière, *The Politics of Aesthetics*, 85.
[11] Jacques Rancière, *Disagreement: Politics and Philosophy*, trans. Julie Rose (Minneapolis, MN: University of Minnesota Press, 1999), 123; Rancière, *Dissensus*, 38.

radical politics of change. Once the Good Friday Agreement was signed and violence began to abate, an opportunity to reimagine the past from a more politically stable standpoint emerged. Among those who seized this opportunity were Anna Burns (1962–) and Glenn Patterson (1961–), two Belfast authors whose respective fictional engagements with the troubled past are anchored in specific ethno-national groups: the working-class and mainly Catholic enclave of Ardoyne in north Belfast for Burns, and the middle-class Protestant districts of south and east Belfast for Patterson.[12] The two novels under scrutiny here, Burns's *No Bones* (2001) and Patterson's *The Rest Just Follows* (2014), are similar insofar as they focus on the evolution of friendship groups over a period that stretches from the beginning of the Troubles through to the peace process and beyond. I wish to suggest that while Burns's artistic endeavour is dissensual, precisely because it adopts a quite radical aesthetic, Patterson's novel, in spite of its evident aesthetics of nostalgia, also manages to accommodate an exposure of that which resists, what Rancière would call the 'inadmissible'.

Our collective difficulty in addressing the recent past in Northern Ireland in a constructive, holistic, and honest way haunts the present, with many unresolved issues continuing to resurface periodically, all in the name of a shaky and perpetually embryonic 'shared future'. A good deal of contemporary fiction from the North also operates from within a self-perpetuating distribution of the sensible which reinforces a politically expedient consensus. Glenn Patterson is arguably Northern Ireland's best-known novelist. To date, he has written ten novels, three works of non-fiction, and co-authored a screenplay.[13] His first three novels were published before the end of the Troubles, in 1988, 1992, and 1995 respectively, and he has consistently attempted to find ways in which to reassess the recent and more distant past. Parts of *Fat Lad* (1992) were already historical in their scope, as Drew Linden, the main character, muses over three generations of his family, and *The Mill for Grinding Old People Young* (2012) is entirely set in industrializing nineteenth-century Belfast. His most recent novels, however, return to the Troubles era and beyond. *The Rest Just Follows* is a particularly nostalgic account of a sort of paradise lost, one far removed from the traumatic loss of innocence endured by the protagonist of his debut novel, *Burning Your Own* (1988). Patterson has asserted that *The Rest Just Follows* deals with 'alternative histories' and that he does not believe 'any of

[12] While this is the case for the novels analysed here, it would be reductive to describe all of their fictional output in these terms. Burns's *Little Constructions* (2007) and *Mostly Hero* (2014) are both set in an indeterminate and somewhat dystopian time and place, while her most recent novel, the Man Booker Prize-winning *Milkman* (2018), is set in an unnamed but clearly recognizable Belfast. The prolific Patterson has varied the temporal and geographical settings of his novels, as evidenced by the non-Irish locales of *Black Night at Big Thunder Mountain* (1995) and *The Third Party* (2007).

[13] The screenplay in question is *Good Vibrations*, which is overtly nostalgic in its view of the past. In the film, punk is presented in an idealized way as a means of transcending sectarian conflict. The film's subtext is that the Troubles were merely provoked by tribal warring factions and could have been prevented, or ended, if only people had embraced the power of punk. Although there is a certain irony in using the profoundly anti-establishment phenomenon of punk music to express consensus, the scriptwriters evidently saw no incongruity in their presentation of an 'Alternative Ulster' in which British soldiers and music-makers are benevolent onlookers in the midst of a putatively nonsensical conflict.

those official versions' of the past which, he suggests, 'need to be undercut slightly, because it's all a lie. So many of those neat versions of the past are either lies of omission or commission.'[14] As he sees it, 'ideological straight lines' do not 'express the chaotic nature, the opportunistic nature' of the years of conflict.[15]

Despite Patterson's antagonism towards received narratives of the Troubles, there is a discrepancy between this stance and what actually transpires in *The Rest Just Follows*. This is evident in the novel's most problematic and ambiguous aspect. One of the three central characters, Craig Robinson, develops a friendship with his history teacher, Alec Harrison, which grows into a deep interest in history, even after Alec is shot dead by the Provisional IRA, ostensibly because of an article in which he criticized the republican leadership's weaponization of the Maze hunger strikes of the early 1980s. Asked years later by St John Nimmo, a childhood friend, to participate in a television programme in which Alec's alleged association with loyalists comes to light, Craig prefers to let the past lie. Patterson, on the surface, appears to endorse this position in his presentation of the recorded interview between the two men, which is abruptly terminated when St John asks Craig whether Alec's 'connection to some pretty shadowy people' affects his memory of him:

> CRAIG
>
> Yes, but, you see, the problem, revisiting the past, is that you can't really control it once you start. Let's say for instance someone was to get hold of something else about you from when you were growing up . . . something like stealing money from the filling station where you used to work. . . . Remember you did that? Just up the road there at the back of the school.
>
> ST JOHN (*to camera*)
>
> Can we stop there, please?[16]

Ostensibly a rejection of 'neat versions of the past' and a plea for 'compassionate leave from history',[17] this passage is revealing of Patterson's wider agenda, which, paradoxically, appears to embrace both the belief that hoking around in history is somehow disrespectful and the idea that it is precisely through interrogating the past that dissensus can emerge. Craig, who has become a sort of spin doctor for a local liberal unionist party, endorses the view that his preferred interpretation of history should not be questioned, but his puerile attempt to draw moral equivalence between sectarian killing and petty theft undermines his position.

Yet Patterson also introduces a note of ambiguity by, on the one hand, highlighting how personal loyalties can collide with more dispassionate historical investigations and, on the other, underscoring the necessity of acknowledging and engaging with the

---

[14] Quoted in Declan Burke, 'Review: *The Rest Just Follows*', *Irish Examiner*, 16 March 2014.
[15] Ibid.
[16] Glenn Patterson, *The Rest Just Follows* (London: Faber and Faber, 2014), 337.
[17] Ibid., 140.

ongoing dissonance caused by complex historical legacies. In a telling moment just before the passage cited above, the sound engineer who is recording the interview is 'displeased with something in the atmosphere' but is unable 'to pinpoint the source of his irritation'.[18] His 'picking up a bit of buzz from somewhere'[19] neatly signifies the fact that while there will always be interference when it comes to examining the past in post-conflict societies, it must be accommodated in the name of a viable future. The engineer's remarks prefigure the way the dredged-up past interferes with the on-camera reminiscences of St John and Craig and expands to encompass the whole peace process era. Consensus thus begins to rupture and dissensus emerges, however tentatively, in both the recognition of the 'bit of buzz' and the presence of counter-narratives of the past. This is not to suggest that Patterson's novel is non-consensual. The distribution of the sensible is almost completely intact, with all the usual parties, except for the British Army, making a stereotypical appearance, thus reinforcing once again the representation of the conflict as an atavistic one. The interference is not even put into language yet; for now, it is merely an irritating 'buzz'. Yet precisely because Patterson is not trying to write a political novel, the cracks (or interference) in the sensible narrative must be noted, and with it the reality that any sabbatical from history can only ever be temporary.

The temporal scope of *The Rest Just Follows* is quite similar to that of Anna Burns's first novel, *No Bones*, the action of which ends slightly earlier, in 1994, the year of the paramilitary ceasefires. There is no 'compassionate leave from history' available in Burns's hyperbolic and extremely disturbing story of Amelia Lovett's battle with psychological, physical, sexual, and political violence. This is partly because Burns's characters are from the socio-economically deprived area of Ardoyne and therefore find themselves on the front line of the Troubles, unlike Patterson's more shielded middle-class protagonists. It is also because *No Bones* is more challenging in its style than the naturalistic *The Rest Just Follows*, not only in terms of its shifting sands of narrative focalization but also in its systematic use of hyperbole and the grotesque.

The novel begins comically with the announcement of the Troubles as a form of entertainment by one of young Amelia's friends, although that humour quickly fades as the 1969 pogroms are described from the viewpoint of a terrified child barricaded inside her house. Gradually, the dysfunctional private sphere becomes more important than the equally dysfunctional public sphere, and the emphasis is placed on the impact of the Troubles on one Belfast enclave rather than on the macropolitics of the crisis. Although many of the chapter titles borrow from the vocabulary of war, the most egregious forms of violence in the novel—rape, incest, murder, abuse, sexism, punishments, suicide—are those carried out within the family and in the disempowered community. This disjunction is a strong indication that Burns is suggesting that the Troubles engender other, lesser acknowledged forms of conflict and tension. The devastating black humour which accompanies these representations of violence is disconcerting, such that if this novel

---

[18] Ibid., 330.   [19] Ibid.

can be described as 'critical art', then it is, in line with Rancière, 'not so much a type of art that reveals the forms and contradictions of domination as it is an art that questions its own limits and powers'.[20]

An especially interesting feature of *No Bones* is its refusal to embrace closure in the final chapter entitled 'A Peace Process'. Like many of the preceding chapters, there is a tension between the implications of the title and the chapter content since there is little to suggest that peace is imminent. The accent is on process rather than resolution. Tentatively recovering from sexual assault, anorexia, alcoholism, and complete psychological breakdown, Amelia and her friends take a day trip to Rathlin Island, only to find themselves under threat from the locals and exposed to insular mindsets. Nevertheless, the very fact that they have undertaken the trip, accompanied by the Japanese wife of one of Amelia's friends, suggests that the process of recovery and opening out (as opposed to looking inwards) has begun. This lightening mood provides a qualified counterbalance to the pervasive nihilism of much of the novel, which depicts extreme violence and offers little solace other than a disconcerting use of black humour.

In contrast to *The Rest Just Follows*, there is no trace of nostalgia in *No Bones*. Burns's recreation of the period between 1969 and 1994 shows Amelia and other characters being exposed to numerous forms of violence in both the public and private spheres. The hyperbolic and often grotesque episodes make for difficult reading, particularly in the chapter entitled 'Troubles, 1979', in which Amelia's brother Mick and his girlfriend attempt to sexually assault her, only to be thwarted by another sister and her group of friends, who end up tearing Mick to pieces in a parody of Dionysian maenads. As there are too many disturbing moments in this chapter to be dwelled on here, I will limit myself to one, which occurs towards the end. In the scene in question, the focalization shifts to Amelia to reveal her distress at her body's involuntary physiological reaction to the assault and her anxiety that the physical signs of sexual arousal may indicate that she was in some way complicit in it. In writing this scene, Burns is naming and making visible what is rarely spoken of in sexual assault cases. Furthermore, by titling this chapter 'Troubles, 1979', Burns is clearly indicating the blurring of private and public forms of violation, and calling attention in passing to the inappropriateness of the euphemism of 'troubles' for either sphere. All actors in the conflict, from republican paramilitaries to RUC wives, are revealed to be incompetent, suffering in various ways from their own traumas and making others suffer too. Far from a nostalgic account of growing up largely oblivious to the conflict, *No Bones* presents a devastating picture of a carnivalesque society where mental health problems are the norm. This is about as far as one can get from the sanguine imagery on the poster promoting the 1998 referendum on the Good Friday Agreement.[21] As the novel's inconclusive ending confirms, Burns is utterly uninterested in promoting a facile discourse of reconciliation and much more

[20] Rancière, *Dissensus*, 149.
[21] The poster showed an archetypal nuclear family facing a picturesque dawn, which looked more like a sunset, accompanied by the words 'It's your decision'.

concerned with uncovering the ugliness of the past, lest it be shoved aside and allowed to fester.

The Rest Just Follows and *No Bones* thus contribute in complementary ways to reassessing the Troubles. For Patterson's characters, the conflict is largely incidental as their lives are mostly unaffected by it, whereas Burns presents violence as central to the development of dysfunctional family and community relationships. Their narrative moods and tones may differ—nostalgia predominating in *The Rest Just Follows*, nihilism in *No Bones*—but both novels present scripts which diverge from the common one by refusing closure and exposing oblique or overt 'interference' as a dissensual breach in the sensible order. *No Bones* is particularly ambitious in this regard since it starts out as a *Bildungsroman* before unexpectedly giving way to narrative disintegration in the chapter entitled 'Mr Hunch in the Ascendant, 1980', which reads as a series of carnivalesque vignettes reflecting one minor character's psychological breakdown. Dissensus, in both texts, serves not so much a political agenda as a cultural one, presenting readers with alternative histories of both banal and horrifying experiences which jar with the idea of a 'shared future'.

Gender Politics and the Ethics of Terrorism

This section will consider two other forms of counter-narrative which have emerged in the wake of the Good Friday Agreement and the ostensible end of paramilitary violence, one centred on an interrogation of gender politics and the other on the ethics of terrorism. If, in a chapter devoted to post-Troubles fiction, there is a certain irony in referring to novels which tackle the representation of violence, it is perhaps the relative peace (notwithstanding persistent tensions) which enables novelists to imagine a redistribution of the sensible or the self-evident in relation to the conflict and its aftermath. The two novels analysed in this section, Patrick McCabe's (1955–) *Breakfast on Pluto* (1998) and Mark Mulholland's *A Mad and Wonderful Thing* (2014), question hegemonic norms of masculinity in multiple ways: by undermining and rewriting the mythologies that sustain them, by stimulating gender trouble, and by reflecting upon the morality of violence. Both narratives jettison the culture and mystique of the 'hard man', as identified by Allen Feldman, in favour of dissensual narratives of masculinity.[22] *Breakfast on Pluto* does this by queering the stereotypes of paramilitarism, *A Mad and Wonderful Thing* by attenuating them. Both texts' interrogatory approaches extend to attitudes to violence: rather than condemn or dismiss violence outright as inherently wrong, they seek to open up alternative ways of understanding it.

---

[22] See Allen Feldman, *Formations of Violence: The Narrative of the Body and Political Terror in Northern Ireland* (Chicago, IL: University of Chicago Press, 1991), 46–56.

Monaghan-born Patrick McCabe has written many novels which expose the dark and disturbed underbelly of rural Irish society. He is also one of the few novelists from the Republic to engage with the troubled North, sometimes glancingly, as in *The Dead School* (1995), and sometimes more overtly, as in *Breakfast on Pluto*, which was published in May 1998 within days of the all-Ireland referendum that ratified the Good Friday Agreement. The latter is one of several of his works set in the liminal territory of the border that divides Ireland into two jurisdictions. The arbitrary and contested nature of this territorial boundary, which does not belong entirely to either Northern Ireland or the Irish Republic, inflects the text in several ways, including narrative unreliability and the use of linguistic pastiche, both of which features resonate strongly with how Rancière perceives dissensus. But it is through the central motif of transgressive gender performance that *Breakfast on Pluto* ruptures the sensible order and pushes to the fore a more fluid understanding of identity in the context of contemporary Ireland and the Troubles. If, as Feldman asserts, 'Transgression of moral order occurs when bodies are out of place, when they occupy territory to which they have no organic contiguity or shared iconic historical or spatial codes,'[23] then *Breakfast on Pluto*'s central protagonist is an exemplary example of this thesis.

Patrick Braden, McCabe's narrator, informs us that he was conceived in the border town of Tyreelin in 1955 as a result of the rape of a local teenager by the parish priest. But Patrick is also Pussy Braden. Born male but elaborately feminine in dress and behaviour, she/he flamboyantly writes and performs an identity that is both transgendered and queer, lurching between masculine and feminine personae. The novel's two short prefatory chapters set the tone for the hyperbolic and parodic comic narrative that follows, entitled 'The Life and Times of Patrick Braden'. The iconoclastic irreverence of the black humourist characterizes the responses of Patrick/Pussy to sectarian violence throughout, such as when, on hearing of the Bloody Sunday massacre of 1972, she/he thinks not 'about the dead victims or their relatives but what combination of my luscious goodies I should go and try on first!'[24] Pussy's own role in acts of violence, particularly the IRA's London bombing campaign, is rendered deliberately ambiguous. Braden's account finely balances the possibility that she is responsible for planting an explosive device against the possibility that she has been traumatized by the atrocity. Ultimately, however, it hardly matters, for it is in the sending up of caricature and stereotype that the importance of the chapters devoted to Pussy's London life lies.

McCabe's parodic intent is signalled by the discordance between chapter titles ('It's Bombing Night and I Haven't Got a Thing to Wear', 'Up West!', 'Dancing on a Saturday Night') and their content. 'Up West!' is entirely written in cockney English and describes a bomb attack, accompanied by a series of racial slurs against the Irish. The tone blends cartoon-like onomatopoeia ('BANG!') and understatement ('Cor, it don't arf try your patience, I'll tell you!') with gory detail ('Poor bloke didn't even get the steak as far as 'is marf, blew his fackin' 'ead off!').[25] Pussy's ventriloquism of this exaggerated accent reads

---

[23] Ibid, 59.   [24] Patrick McCabe, *Breakfast on Pluto* (London: Picador, 1999), 39.

[25] Ibid., 86.

as another performance and is perhaps best understood as a response to the renewed racialization of Irish people in Britain and the attribution to them of pro-IRA sympathies in the wake of atrocities such as the 1974 Birmingham and Guildford pub bombings. The discovery that Pussy is, in her own words, 'an ordinary transvestite prostitute' only serves to reinforce this narrative of deviant treachery peddled by the British press, which promptly characterizes her as 'a wicked little fucker who would stop at nothing in his determination to mutilate and maim, even going so far as to disguise himself as a tart'.[26]

This media discourse displaces political action onto the level of psychological and sexual deviance and dovetails with the age-old tendency to perceive the (native) Irish as barbaric, irrational, and feminine.[27] By choosing feminization in full agency, Pussy/Paddy thwarts this othering process and, potentially, uses it as a disguise behind which she can carry out a 'terrorist' attack. One may perceive here a tension between the possibility that Pussy actually plants the bomb and the novel's anti-racializing agenda. However, only *readers* know that Pussy is perhaps responsible because she hints at this (and even then the issue is never resolved). The only reason she is singled out by the police is because of her nationality and her transgressive gender and behaviour. Pussy's potential guilt does not erase the racializing agenda of the authorities.

McCabe also debunks loyalist paramilitary hypermasculinity when Pussy takes revenge on the leader of a paramilitary unit which has tortured and killed a fellow Tyreelin man. Playing on the double meaning of the leader's 'big pistol' and 'great big gun' in a manner reminiscent of British feminist artist Margaret Harrison's paintings and sketches of the early 1970s, Pussy seduces and kills the ironically named hypermasculine Vicky.[28] McCabe is clearly muddying gender conventions here. Virile masculinity is ridiculed before being dispatched by a transgender assassin who exudes skittish coquettishness. One could hardly imagine a more disruptively unassimilable—and therefore dissensual—riposte to the entrenched political binaries of ethno-nationalist ideology.

Mark Mulholland's *A Mad and Wonderful Thing* presents paramilitary violence and its relationship to masculinity in a very different fashion. Unlike McCabe, Mulholland's agenda is not so much situated in the realm of gender politics. Rather, the novel interrogates the possible accommodation of violence within the everyday and subverts the usual separation (*partage*) of state-endorsed soldiers from 'illegitimate' guerrillas and paramilitaries. The narrator-protagonist, Johnny Donnelly, is a republican sniper who operates outside the movement on the orders of a high-ranking IRA volunteer, acting as a lone ranger figure who has vowed to kill ten British soldiers, one for each of the hunger

---

[26] Ibid., 142–3.

[27] See David Lloyd, *Irish Culture and Modernity 1800–2000: The Transformation of Oral Space* (Cambridge: Cambridge University Press, 2011), 85–115.

[28] McCabe, *Breakfast on Pluto*, 172.

strikers who died in 1981.[29] Donnelly is also an outlier among male republican paramilitaries in contemporary fiction, who tend to be depicted as bloodthirsty, egotistical killers whose ideological affiliations are a mere pretext for personal advancement.[30] Donnelly stands in sharp contrast because of the contextualized exposition of his ideological commitment and the evocation of the inner conflict engendered by his decision to take up arms in the name of a cause—effects enhanced by the novel's use of first-person narration. Here is a character who, when he is not killing people, is generally witty, intelligent, helpful, caring, and obliging, at least until his lover is killed in an accident. This is not to suggest that Mulholland mythologizes violence, however. Johnny's paramilitary activity is described in crude detail, most notably in the moment where he opens a car door to kill an informer and, although shocked to find his brother inside, kills him nevertheless and shows little remorse afterwards. Yet because the character is likeable, Mulholland's agenda, and it is a welcome one, is to introduce a note of dissensus into the literary status quo. Donnelly thus provokes more complex responses in readers than the one-dimensional characters cited above. It is this very complexity (cold-blooded and caring, in equal measure) which is innovative and potentially dissensual in the sense that Mulholland uses his fiction to reappraise the figure of the republican paramilitary and to 'inven[t] new trajectories between what can be seen, what can be said and what can be done'.[31]

A Mad and Wonderful Thing also has a fabular dimension, frequently establishing links between tales of war and battles enshrined in ancient Irish mythology (particularly the Táin Bó Cúailgne) and the Troubles. Unlike Tara West, who in her novel, Fodder (2002), recycles myths so as to queer loyalism and empty the signifier so that it cannot be recuperated by contemporary paramilitaries, Mulholland cultivates his protagonist's links with mythological heroes in order to question the morality of war and show how perceptions of violence are altered by circumstance and perspective. A cursory reading of Augusta Gregory's (1852–1932) Cuchulain of Muirthemne (1902) reveals that the eponymous warrior was renowned for being ingenious in his deployment of various ways of killing, all in the name of defence. Yet he is celebrated as an icon, not only within republicanism but also among some loyalists, precisely because of his status as a supreme warrior. As Johnny points out during a discussion of Cúchulainn, 'Those who challenge the ordinary and familiar are viewed as a greater threat than any oppressor. Right and wrong are unfixed: they are conditional on time and place.'[32] This clearly amounts to moral relativism, but it pinpoints the paradox of celebrating the bloody deeds of a distant mythological figure, famed for his single-handed defence of his community, and

---

[29] The implication is that Donnelly is the notorious south Armagh sniper, to whom the deaths of several members of the security forces were attributed during the 1990s. It is commonly accepted that these killings were the work of teams of snipers rather than a single gunman.

[30] Figures such as Cow Pat Coogan in Bateman's Divorcing Jack, Gerry Fegan in Neville's The Twelve, and Freddie Scavanni in Adrian McKinty's The Cold, Cold Ground (2012) all spring to mind.

[31] Rancière, Dissensus, 149.

[32] Mark Mulholland, A Mad and Wonderful Thing (London: Scribe, 2016), 108.

abhorring the murderous actions of those who embody a similar stance in the contemporary era.

Donnelly is also characterized as an excellent marksman and, after his partner Cora Flannery dies in a tragic accident, an inveterate lover. The bulk of the action is set in Dundalk in County Louth, a town that lies close to the border, built on the remains of Dún Dealgan, the legendary fortress of Cúchulainn and Emer. 'Cúchulainn' predictably becomes Johnny's code name for military activity and, in a twist on the mythological story, he kills his informer-brother rather than his son. Whereas in the mythic tale Cúchulainn does not realize he has killed his son Conlaí until it is too late, Johnny's realization comes before he pulls the trigger. His proceeding to murder his own kin bespeaks a cold-bloodedness that is absent from his mythological antecedent, as does his quoting Hemingway as he lies in wait to ambush a soldier: '*There is no hunting like the hunting of man*.'[33] Johnny also functions as the living memory of Irish history, reciting verbatim the 1916 Proclamation and Robert Emmett's 1803 speech from the dock. Furthermore, he is the embodiment of Irish geography, literally walking the four corners of the country and commenting on the topographical specificities and history of the land and its coastline. Thus, Johnny Donnelly evolves into a personification of the nation and, as the peace process dawns, significantly decides to bow out of military involvement, only to find it impossible to do so.

In a dream sequence towards the end of the novel, Donnelly has a hellish nightmare in which he faces a grotesque, frail old woman whose 'eyes are colourless and blind, and when she opens her mouth, her teeth are a rotten yellow and black'.[34] After asking him, in Irish, to fill her cup, she pushes Johnny into a pit of screaming naked bodies, only to pull him out again when he begs for mercy. The sequence ends with the hag repeating words uttered by Cora before she died: ' "You wouldn't do a bad thing" she asks. "Would you Johnny?" '[35] This episode overtly references the *puella senilis* motif of Celtic tradition, which received its most iconic expression in W. B. Yeats's (1865–1939) *Cathleen Ni Houlihan* (1902), in which a decrepit crone is spectacularly restored to youthful beauty by the sacrificial blood of a young man. However, Mulholland plays a telling variation on the cultural and political symbolism of this motif by showing the dishevelled old woman whom Johnny encounters to be depleted *because* of the shedding of blood in Ireland's name. It is not more sacrificial deaths she needs but fewer.

Yet this encounter between ancient and contemporary embodiments of the nation is not necessarily to be read as a complete disavowal of twenty-first-century republican militancy. Rather, it should be understood as a rejection of the romanticization of nationalist struggle. Mulholland, through the figure of Johnny Donnelly, foregrounds the pragmatic and ugly aspects of paramilitary involvement, even as he presents it as an ethically valid choice. However, for all that it introduces a different perspective on paramilitarism, the novel is firmly constructed upon heteronormative grounds, with Johnny's hypersexuality and irresistible sex appeal to women being unproblematically

---

[33] Ibid., 140. Original italics.   [34] Ibid., 221.   [35] Ibid., 222.

celebrated throughout. Unlike Yeats's Cuchulain in *On Baile Strand* (1904), who has been read as 'a figure of gender subversion' and a threat to 'the integrity of gender categories themselves', this latter-day Cúchulainn manqué offers no dissensus in the realm of gender politics.[36]

Following the Cúchulainn motif through to its end, albeit in an ironic fashion, the novel shows Johnny Donnelly dying in the act of fighting 'the men of Ireland'. In a barely disguised reference to the 1998 Omagh bombing by the Real IRA, Johnny, disgusted by the random violence of the conflict, attempts to prevent the explosion of an IRA bomb in the centre of Banbridge, County Down. He thus finds himself in the ironic position of defending Ulster against militant republicans and, like Cúchulainn, dies in the process, having first prevented several deaths. Although many of the signifiers of the mythological hero's death are present—a loss of power in the left side of his body, a pillar of the gate which he rests against, a raven—this contemporary Hound of Ulster dies knowing that he will most likely be blamed for the explosion. In other words, he will not be a hero. This message is central to Mulholland's agenda, which simultaneously deglorifies violence and places it in its political context. The final chapter completes the fable and sees Johnny reunited with Cora in Tír na nÓg, the mythical land of the ever young. While one might well read this conclusion sceptically as being gratuitously idyllic, thus undoing the pragmatism which underpins the novel's fabular flights of fancy, it can also be understood as an effort by Mulholland to accommodate the moral relativism of the narrative. Johnny is not judged for his paramilitary activities but is rewarded with a fairytale ending. This outcome deviates from the dominant realistic setting and undermines the notion of an everlasting cycle of violence, placing the emphasis instead on the possibility of regeneration through myth. This pointed departure from mainstream portrayals of paramilitarism is akin to McCabe's provocative subversive approach to the same subject in *Breakfast on Pluto*.

Accordingly, both novels can be said to 'fashion and sustain new subjects' and 'create new forms of perception' that reconfigure the sensible order by allowing marginalized voices to be heard.[37] As Joseph J. Tanke in his analysis of Rancière's work reminds us, 'Provided they do not appear in scripted ways, art allows the part of those without part to manifest a voice they were thought not to possess.'[38] Patrick McCabe, by queering the Troubles narrative, and Mark Mulholland, by recycling mythologies, foreground alternative ways of envisaging terrorism which eschew the hackneyed ideological paradigms of republicanism and loyalism and refuse to take easy sanctuary on the moral high ground. While neither novel makes for comfortable reading, each forces us to take notice of the excluded, 'the radical other, the one who is separated from the community

---

[36] Joseph Valente, *The Myth of Manliness in Irish National Culture, 1880–1922* (Urbana, IL: University of Illinois Press, 2011), 173, 174.

[37] Joseph J. Tanke, *Jacques Rancière: An Introduction* (London: Continuum, 2011), 103.

[38] Ibid., 104.

for the mere fact of being alien to it, of not sharing the identity that binds each to all, and of threatening the community in each of us'.[39]

BEYOND THE TROUBLES

Perhaps the best indication that the troubled past is really receding is its absence from several recent novels and short stories. For authors such as Lucy Caldwell (1981–) and David Park (1953–), the conflict often exists only in the background of their fiction, if at all. Eoin McNamee (1961–), for his part, has developed a marked preference for delving into a pre-Troubles era, as evidenced by his *Blue* trilogy (2001–14). I would like to conclude this chapter by offering some remarks on another contemporary Northern Irish writer, Jan Carson (1980–), whose artistry arguably represents the most radical attempt to disrupt the sensible order. A relative newcomer to the field of fiction, her output to date comprises two novels, *Malcolm Orange Disappears* (2014) and *The Fire Starters* (2019), and two short story collections, *Postcard Stories* (2017) and the volume that will be the focus of my discussion here, *Children's Children* (2016).

Carson's short stories are particularly provocative and dissensual, both in their style and content. Many of the stories in *Children's Children* are concerned with stasis, which acts as a general metaphor for the situation in the present-day North and the profound challenges facing the post-Troubles generation. For example, the title (and final) story in the collection is a fable about a partitioned island which is so depleted by emigration that its very survival is threatened. The last remaining inhabitants, a young man from the North and a young woman from south of the border, accept the urgent need for them to marry and procreate. However, their wedding plans are scuppered by their inability to agree where to cohabit: 'They could not settle upon a side, for the land changed shape the moment you crossed the border. Ten minutes before their wedding day they realised that the island was asking more of them than they could ever manage.'[40] The story's inconclusive ending leaves it unclear whether the couple will manage to love the island 'enough to be neither north nor south, foreigner or familiar, but rather a brave new direction, balanced like a hairline fracture in the centre of everything.'[41] The poised syntax of this line, reinforced by the alliterative 'f' and the allusion to the 'brave new world' of Shakespeare's naïve Miranda and Huxley's dystopian vision, convey mixed messages about what lies ahead. The comparison of the fragile future to a very thin but very fundamental dividing line, combined with the earlier image of the couple's unclasping hands, tips interpretation away from hoped-for communion towards static separation.

---

[39] Jacques Rancière, *Aesthetics and its Discontents*, trans. Steven Corcoran (Cambridge: Polity Press, 2009), 116.

[40] Jan Carson, 'Children's Children', in *Children's Children* (Dublin: Liberties Press, 2016), 190.

[41] Ibid.

These themes of stasis and retreat also animate the quirky yet poignant 'Still', the narrator of which is 'a man who'd prefer to be made of concrete', so wedded is he to his 'calling' of being a human statue.[42] His obsession with remaining as still as possible puts his relationship with his pregnant partner in jeopardy and when she eventually leaves him his withdrawal into stasis is complete: 'No part of me is moving now, not even my heart. I might as well be a wall, I think, or a solid oak staircase. I am happy as I have never been in transit.'[43] Like 'Children's Children', this fable-like story is freighted with metaphorical import. Applied to the post-Troubles North, the story's emphasis on an unwillingness to change, even in the most basic of ways, and a refusal to feel can be taken to imply a preference for paralysis over progress. It is almost a form of locked-in syndrome, willingly embraced. In this respect, one cannot overlook the other, adverbial meaning of 'still': enduring, ongoing, unfinished. Read thus, the title anticipates the futility of the narrator's retreat from movement (which is after all fundamental to the human condition) since although he may have achieved complete stasis, he 'still' exists.

Other stories thematize seclusion and isolation in an equally oblique and suggestive way. In 'More of a Handstand Girl', the narrator's mother has immolated herself, leaving her alone with a brother who is 'allergic to people'[44] and convinced he will die if outsiders lay eyes on him. The narrator responds to his condition by partitioning their shared apartment with 'a trash-bag wall',[45] through which they communicate using phones made from soup cans. After four years of intimate separation, the boy builds a homemade suit of armour. Meanwhile, his sister develops a suffocating loneliness. The story ends on a characteristically opaque note with the narrator using a tin opener to 'slice my brother wide open in his sleep',[46] after which she retreats to the charred spot on the living room floor where their mother died and contemplates following her example. On the surface, 'More of a Handstand Girl' has no necessary connection to Northern Ireland since neither the place nor the protagonists are given localized identities. Yet read from a post-conflict perspective this tale of a dysfunctional family could be taken to be representative of the experiences of an unknown number of people in the North who continue to endure their anguish in secret.

The more magical realist and wryly humorous 'Floater' also features a non-normative family unit, through which lens it explores themes of ambivalent maternity and single motherhood. The narrator is the mother of a daughter whom she conceived as a result of sex with a stranger in an airplane toilet. Altitude continues to be a feature of the six-year-old girl's childhood. Resistant to gravity, she hovers in mid-air, tethered to the garden fence by a ribbon, except when it rains and her mother puts her in the attic. Surface comedy and profound sadness commingle in this surreally metaphorical evocation of a young mother's mixed feelings towards a daughter she loves yet literally keeps at arm's length:

---

[42] Jan Carson, 'Still', in *Children's Children*, 39.
[43] Ibid., 44.
[44] Jan Carson, 'More of a Handstand Girl', in *Children's Children*, 80.
[45] Ibid., 82.   [46] Ibid., 90.

'I love you,' I say, tugging on the end of your purple ribbon to make a point, 'but I'm not quite sure how to make this work.'

'Don't worry, Mama,' you shout, turning upside down to look me in the eye, 'I'm going to pray that God gives you wings so you can come up here too.'[47]

The narrative culminates in the mother finally snipping the ribbon and watching her daughter disappear into her 'home'[48] in the sky. Afterwards, she feels not remorse but relief, and contemplates having 'a brand new baby with ordinary feet'.[49] The mother's last thoughts are less about the fate of the little girl from whom she is now irrevocably severed and more about her own repressed anger towards the man who impregnated her: 'if, in the instance before evaporation, your very last thought is anger, do not blame me. Do not blame yourself. Blame the airplane bathroom and your father, who was only there for the easy part.'[50]

As these readings suggest, Jan Carson's short stories offer original and disconcerting perspectives on contemporary lives in the North, bringing an iconoclastic literary sensibility to the sphere of intimate relations and a defamiliarizing gaze to everyday social interactions. In this, they are dissensual narratives that render visible the banalities of the quotidian in rather extraordinary ways. As Rancière reminds us, 'Literary dissensus works on changes in the scale and nature of individualities, on deconstruction of the relationships between things and meanings.'[51] In *Children's Children*, Jan Carson shifts the emphasis from a specific time-space ('post-Troubles' Northern Ireland) to an indeterminate one, thus renewing the sometimes jaded coordinates of Northern Irish fiction and constructing new 'relationships between things and meanings' through frequent use of the fantastic. In this way, 'existing modes of sensory presentation and forms of enunciation' are sidelined and replaced with fresh and 'varying frames, scales and rhythms' which map out welcome new directions in Northern fiction.[52]

This survey clearly cannot do full justice to the diverse body of post-Troubles Northern Irish fiction. It also raises questions about just how relevant it is to apply the term 'post' to this literary corpus since all of the authors mentioned here engage to some extent with the violent past and its ongoing legacies in a still deeply divided society. The texts discussed above should be seen as representative of various new departures, new politics, and new poetics in Northern Irish fiction. They also register writers' diverse attempts to grapple with the complexities of the post-conflict period and shake up the established frameworks of thought and perception, thus participating, in Rancierian terms, in a redistribution of the sensible order. But since the redistribution of the sensible is a process that is always in flux, this discussion of dissensual fictional narratives can only really function as a snapshot of a particular moment. 'Political and artistic fictions introduce dissensus by hollowing out [the] "real" and multiplying it in a polemical way', writes Rancière. 'The practice of fiction undoes, and then re-articulates,

[47] Jan Carson, 'Floater', in *Children's Children*, 123.
[48] Ibid., 126.   [49] Ibid., 127.   [50] Ibid.
[51] Jacques Rancière, *The Politics of Literature*, trans. Julie Rose (Cambridge: Polity Press, 2011), 43.
[52] Rancière, *Dissensus*, 141.

connections between signs and images, images and times, and signs and space, framing a given sense of reality, a given "commonsense".[53]

I have suggested here some of the ways in which contemporary Northern Irish writers have been engaging in these processes of evacuation, multiplication, and re-articulation. Veering away from barren discourses and exhausted antagonisms, they variously direct their energies towards exploring the ethics of presenting alternative narratives of the past (Patterson); exposing harsh truths about the constitutive nature of violence (Burns); queering clichéd representations of paramilitarism (McCabe); questioning the morality of war by reviving ancient Irish myths (Mulholland); and evoking trauma and dysfunction by means of absurdist allegories and magical realist fables (Carson). As the political institutions of twenty-first-century Northern Ireland continue to display a marked fragility, fiction may, for the foreseeable future, be the most productive space in which radical reappraisals of the past and audacious visions of the future can be imagined.

FURTHER READING

Fadem, Maureen E. Ruprecht. *The Literature of Northern Ireland: Spectral Borderlands*. Basingstoke: Palgrave Macmillan, 2015.

Jeffers, Jennifer M. *The Irish Novel at the End of the Twentieth Century: Gender, Bodies, and Power*. Basingstoke: Palgrave, 2002.

Kennedy-Andrews, Elmer. *Fiction and the Northern Ireland Troubles since 1969: (De-)constructing the North*. Dublin: Four Courts Press, 2003.

Lehner, Stefanie. *Subaltern Ethics in Contemporary Scottish and Irish Literature: Tracing Counter-Histories*. Basingstoke: Palgrave Macmillan, 2011.

Lloyd, David. *Irish Culture and Modernity 1800–2000: The Transformation of Oral Space*. Cambridge: Cambridge University Press, 2011.

McCann, Fiona. *A Poetics of Dissensus: Confronting Violence in Contemporary Prose Writing from the North of Ireland*. Bern: Peter Lang, 2014.

Magennis, Caroline. ' "Titanic Men and Special Powers": Re-Writing Protestant History in the Novels of Glenn Patterson'. *Irish Studies Review* 22, no. 4 (2015): 348–60.

Mahon, Peter. *Violence, Politics and Textual Interventions in Northern Ireland*. Basingstoke: Palgrave Macmillan, 2010.

Mulhall, Anne. 'A Cure for Melancholia? Queer Sons, Dead Mothers and the Fantasy of Multiculturalism in McCabe's and Jordan's *Breakfast on Pluto*(s)'. In Noreen Giffney and Margrit Shildrick (eds), *Theory on the Edge: Irish Studies and the Politics of Sexual Difference*. New York: Palgrave Macmillan, 2013: 221–40.

Persson, Åke. 'Crossing Boundaries: Transgenderism as Resistance in Patrick McCabe's *Breakfast on Pluto*'. *Nordic Irish Studies* 12 (2013): 41–58.

Rancière, Jacques. *Disagreement: Politics and Philosophy*, trans. Julie Rose. Minneapolis, MN: University of Minnesota Press, 1999.

Rancière, Jacques. *Aesthetics and its Discontents*, trans. Steven Corcoran. Cambridge: Polity Press, 2009.

Rancière, Jacques. *The Emancipated Spectator*, trans. Gregory Elliott. London: Verso, 2009.

Rancière, Jacques. *Dissensus: On Politics and Aesthetics*, trans. Steven Corcoran. London: Bloomsbury, 2013.

---

[53] Ibid., 149.

CHAPTER 32

....

'OUR NAMELESS DESIRES'

The Erotics of Time and Space in Contemporary Irish Lesbian and Gay Fiction

....

MICHAEL G. CRONIN

LIKE all such literary categories, 'contemporary Irish lesbian and gay fiction' demands some explication. Initially, we can approach this from three perspectives: chronology, aesthetics, and authorship. Chronologically, this category can be said to relate to fiction published since 1993, the year in which sex between consenting adult men was decriminalized in the Republic of Ireland. This momentous development stimulated lesbian and gay subculture and led to a period of intensive political activity, artistic creativity, and sexual experimentation, concentrated in, but not confined to, Dublin city.[1] Decriminalization was part of a conjunction of local and global currents that contributed to this vibrancy. Other contributory factors included the therapeutic advances that gradually made HIV a medically manageable rather than fatal condition, the ascendance of a political orthodoxy that combined neoliberal economics and socially liberal policies (Clintonism; Blairism; the Fianna Fáil/Labour and 'Rainbow' coalition governments), and an increase in funding for urban regeneration projects, particularly in Dublin, during the first wave of the 1990s economic boom.

Yet 1993 is also a somewhat arbitrary starting point, in that decriminalization was the culmination of a lesbian and gay activist movement dating back to the 1970s, which had spawned a vibrant social scene and sustained networks of support (most notably in the wake of the 1980s AIDS epidemic). From a literary historical perspective, then, focusing on the watershed year of 1993 blinds us to earlier Irish fiction that thematizes same-sex desire between women and men, by authors such as Oscar Wilde (1854–1900), Kate

---

[1] For an overview from the time, see Íde O'Carroll and Eoin Collins (eds), *Lesbian and Gay Visions of Ireland: Towards the Twenty-first Century* (London: Cassell, 1995). For an engaging retrospective account, see Rory O'Neill, *Woman in the Making: A Memoir* (Dublin: Hachette Books, 2014), 106–50.

O'Brien (1897–1974), Molly Keane (pseudonym of M. J. Farrell, 1904–96), Brendan Behan (1923–64), John Broderick (1924–89), and Desmond Hogan (1950–). The fiction examined in this chapter exhibits continuities with that tradition, chiefly through its imaginative engagement with same-sex passions within a realist aesthetic. However, there are two significant reasons why contemporary lesbian and gay fiction is distinctive. First, this writing gives expression to a historically new form of consciousness that, as shorthand, we can term 'post-Stonewall', which initially emerged in Anglo-American culture and spread rapidly throughout the West from the early 1970s.[2] Second, this fiction is written by authors who publicly identify as lesbian and gay, and who have varying degrees of affiliation to lesbian and gay subculture. Thus, to take two contrasting examples, Colm Tóibín's (1955–) literary reputation was initially consolidated entirely independently of gay subculture, whereas Mary Dorcey's (1950–) was closely associated with her lesbian feminist activism. Nevertheless, authors, publishers, and distributors actively assume the existence of this subculture as at least one component of the potential readership being addressed by this fiction, and the author's persona is one element of this.

Combining these perspectives, we can identify lesbian and gay fiction as the literary form of a historically distinct late twentieth-century political formation. Building on, while also marking a decisive break with, earlier homophile movements, this formation has had two major strands or currents. One is a universalizing, liberationist, and utopian political imaginary that took its coordinates from the writings of Herbert Marcuse and variants of Marxism, feminism, anti-colonialism, and the New Left. From this gay liberation and lesbian feminist perspective, the struggle against the oppressive stigmatization of homosexuality is necessarily inseparable from the struggle for a revolution in which social institutions—notably marriage and the family—and all social relations—gender, race, class—would be radically transformed. Paradoxically, since this revolution aimed to undermine wholesale the modern sex-gender system, it would of necessity bring about 'the end of the homosexual', as Denis Altman predicted in his pioneering manifesto of the 'gay lib' position.[3]

The other strand is a reformist or assimilative liberal/social democratic project seeking recognition, protection, and civil rights for a lesbian and gay minority. This is predicated on a formative connection between erotic desire and identity, the notion that each of us 'has' a 'sexuality', as well as the relative autonomy of sexuality from other social relations. It assumes the continued existence of a fundamental hetero-homo binary, albeit one more tolerantly mediated by cultural norms and, where that fails, actively policed by the state to ensure parity. In short, freedom from oppression for lesbians and

---

[2] The 1969 Stonewall riots in Manhattan, New York comprised a series of demonstrations by members of the gay and lesbian community against discrimination and police harassment. They marked a seminal moment in the emergence of the gay liberation movement.
[3] Dennis Altman, *Homosexual: Oppression and Liberation* (London: Serpent's Tail, 1971), 241.

gay men can, in this view, be secured within the existing social order; indeed, can only really be secured within the dominant liberal democratic and capitalist order.[4]

Aside from brief periods of subcultural efflorescence in the early 1970s and early 1990s, the first current has had little manifest impact on the historical evolution of the lesbian and gay (latterly LGBT) political movement. Moreover, even those sympathetic to the radical conception of sexual freedom essayed in the now residual gay liberation and lesbian feminist positions must concede that the reformist LGBT rights movement has, as politicians nowadays like to say, delivered. At the end of the 2010s, many lesbians and gay men living in Ireland and other First World societies hold a secure freedom to fulfil their emotional and erotic needs that would have been scarcely imaginable in 1976. Nevertheless, queer libertarian and, in particular, Marxist critiques of the dominant trajectory of LGBT politics remain compelling. To take one example, the symbolic centrality of family imagery in the Irish campaign for same-sex marriage in 2015 may have been strategically effective, but it also exemplifies how pursuing this political objective reinforces heterosacramentalism, which term David Alderson, drawing on Marcuse, defines as the long-standing view that 'sexual pleasure stands in need of redemption, whether conceived in religious or humanistic terms, and that this endows the sacramental relationship with a qualitative moral and emotional superiority over all others'.[5] As Alderson argues, 'couched in egalitarian terms', the demand for same-sex marriage 'represents the extension of the principle under liberalised conditions: sacramentalism for all'.[6] Likewise, the conception of equality in the 'marriage equality' campaign was quite narrowly formalist and contractual. The rhetoric of the Yes campaign conjured a vision of lesbian and gay households 'equally' free to compete as privatized units of consumption and to strive to manage their resources. This political objective was simultaneously progressive and conservative; it promoted inclusivity and pluralism while adhering to the prevailing neoliberal political rationality.[7]

The radical gay liberation and lesbian feminist positions, then, are not just historical relics. Although absent from organized LGBT politics, they still offer nourishing sustenance to the political imagination. Indeed, it is as relics that they are most powerful; ghostly reminders that other futures were once possible and may still be. For this reason, it may be unhelpful to describe radicalism/liberation and reformism/assimilation as two internally coherent but mutually exclusive positions. Rather, as Les Brookes argues, we can envisage a dynamic oscillation between radicalism and assimilationism as the defining ideological struggle within LGBT politics—not only a conflict *between* those

[4] See Steven Seidman, 'Identity and Politics in a "Postmodern" Gay Culture: Some Historical and Conceptual Notes', in Michael Warner (ed.), *Fear of a Queer Planet: Queer Politics and Social Theory* (Minneapolis, MN: University of Minnesota Press, 1993), 105–42 and Rosemary Hennessy, *Profit and Pleasure: Sexual Identities in Late Capitalism* (London: Routledge, 2000), 42–9.

[5] David Alderson, *Sex, Needs and Queer Culture: From Liberation to the Post-Gay* (London: Zed Books, 2016), 71.

[6] Ibid., 72.

[7] See Jaye Cee Whitehead, *The Nuptial Deal: Same-Sex Marriage and Neo-Liberal Governance* (Chicago, IL: University of Chicago Press, 2011).

supporting same-sex marriage and its gay affirmative/queer critics but also *within* an apparently unified political project such as the marriage equality campaign.[8] To approach lesbian and gay fiction as the literary form of post-Stonewall sexual politics, therefore, is not to adjudicate whether an individual work is liberationist or assimilationist; rather, it is to consider the fiction as a literary terrain on which a persistent problem—how we envisage sexual freedom—is imaginatively confronted but not resolved.

Here we must briefly address the specificity of the Irish situation. From its beginnings, with the foundation of the Irish Gay Rights Movement in 1974, lesbian and gay politics in the Irish Republic confronted a dominant ideology that combined capitalism with a fusion of Catholicism and conservative nationalism. Since the post-Famine decades, this formation placed an oppressive emphasis on controlling the body, the emotions, and all expressions of human sexual needs and pleasures.[9] Maintaining such control was held to be a moral as well as an economic and political imperative. With the creation of the two confessional states on the island after 1922, the cultural stress on such control was given further legislative force. In the first two decades of its existence, the Irish Free State retained the legislation, inherited from the imperial parliament, that outlawed abortion and sex between men (criminalized as 'gross indecency' since 1885) and imposed bans on birth control (and information on it) and divorce. Confronting this still hegemonic formation in the 1970s, the Irish lesbian and gay movement battled powerful opposition on unyielding terrain. Thus, the law annulled in 1993 had been significantly reformed in England and Wales twenty-six years earlier, and the Irish state fought a long legal battle to resist change.

Nevertheless, in retrospect this situation also created political opportunities. In the Irish context, the lesbian and gay struggle was part of a broader battle, fought on various fronts, to assert the autonomy of individuals over their bodies and enhance their freedoms. Women were to the forefront, since the key issues (access to birth control and pregnancy termination; support for single mothers; reform of the archaic marriage laws and divorce) had the most immediate effect on their health, well-being, and liberty. For this reason, lesbian and gay politics in Ireland did not evolve into the 'ethnic' model of identity politics—dominated by the interests of white, middle-class men—that quickly replaced gay liberation in the United States.[10] Instead, it remained a social movement working in coalition with other left-leaning progressive movements and liberal politicians.[11] While this political environment created opportunities for alliance building, it also presented an ideological problem. The Catholic Church's dominant position as

---

[8] Les Brookes, *Gay Male Fiction Since Stonewall: Ideology, Conflict, and Aesthetics* (London: Routledge, 2009) 12–40.

[9] See Tom Inglis, *Moral Monopoly: The Rise and Fall of the Catholic Church in Modern Ireland* (Dublin: University College Dublin Press, 1998), 17–38.

[10] Seidman, 'Identity and Politics in a "Postmodern" Gay Culture', 117.

[11] See Paul Ryan, 'Coming Out of the Dark: A Decade of Gay Mobilisation in Ireland, 1970–1980', in Linda Connolly and Niamh Hourigan (eds), *Social Movements and Ireland* (Manchester: Manchester University Press, 2006), 86–105 and 'The Pursuit of Lesbian and Gay Citizenship Rights, 1980–2011', in Máire Leane and Elizabeth Kiely (eds), *Sexualities and Irish Society: A Reader* (Dublin: Orpen Press, 2014), 101–26.

hegemonic arbiter of sexual morality meant that social progress was exclusively equated with secularization and liberalism. In these circumstances, the space for radical materialist interpretations of sexual regulation and freedom was restricted. There is a lost history of leftist, left-republican, and gay liberation groupings from the 1970s and early 1980s to be recuperated—the Cork and Dublin Gay Collectives, for example, and Gays Against Imperialism—but their apparitional presence in the archive attests to the infertile territory on which they were optimistically formed.

COMING OUT

Surveying the development of Irish lesbian and gay fiction since 1993, we can distinguish two significant compositional principles: plots that are structured temporally and those that are structured spatially. The former are by far the most common and can be further subdivided into plots structured around biographical time and plots involving historical time. The defining trope of gay and lesbian novels structured around biographical time is that of 'coming out'. The belief that self-disclosure is simultaneously personally liberating and politically transformative is a core principle of the post-Stonewall lesbian and gay social movement. It is where the 'personal' imbricates most powerfully with the 'political'. Unsurprisingly, then, a large proportion of Irish lesbian and gay fiction adapts the conventions of the coming-out romance.

The literary careers of Tom Lennon (a pseudonym) and Emma Donoghue (1969–) have followed starkly divergent trajectories. After two novels, Lennon disappeared from view, whereas Donoghue went on to achieve considerable commercial and critical success internationally. Yet these writers began their careers by producing similar versions of an Irish coming-out romance, Donoghue with *Stir-fry* (1994) and *Hood* (1996), and Lennon with *When Love Comes to Town* (1993) and *Crazy Love* (1999). Despite a charming comic tone, Lennon's first novel is aesthetically debilitated by the urgency with which it addresses 'issues'. In the space of a few weeks, the young protagonist, Neil, comes out to his friends and family; begins socializing on the gay scene; befriends a number of older gay men, including two married cross-dressers; visits another of his new friends who is (rather suddenly) dying of AIDS; is unconscious for three days after being gay-bashed; attempts suicide; has his first relationship; begins a second—and gives an emotional interview on Irish national radio. Although mediated through comic irony and gentle satire, Donoghue's novels are similarly sociological in their references to lesbian feminist subculture. In *Stir-fry*, this is facilitated through Maria's arrival in Dublin from a small town to begin university, where she becomes the housemate of a lesbian couple, Ruth and Jael. Naïve but sharply observant, Maria is our proxy in her voyage of discovery through this unknown social world. But there is also an inner journey of discovery as Maria is drawn into the intensity of her friendship with the two women. By the end, Ruth and Jael's relationship has collapsed, and Maria and Ruth are in love.

While the first novels of Lennon and Donoghue pivot on teenage self-exploration and identity formation, their second novels focus on relationship crises. In *Hood*, the thirty-year-old narrator Pen grieves for her lover Cara, killed in a car accident. The novel's present unfolds in the week after the accident. Pen's narration of this week reveals that she and Cara had been lovers since they were schoolgirls, despite Cara's affairs with other women and men. But nobody, aside for some of Cara's lesbian activist friends, knows about their relationship, which means that Pen's grief is exacerbated by the lack of public acknowledgement, although the chirpy, comic tone of her narrative voice, which sits awkwardly with the tragic action, undermines any sense of Pen as victim. Pen comes out to various characters about her relationship and in the closing chapter she returns to her mother's house to talk to her. In *Crazy Love*, narrated in the second person, Paul is a successful young executive and the married father of a small child. His closeted life collapses when he begins a passionate affair with a younger male colleague. Balancing two lives precipitates a nervous breakdown for Paul, but out of this crisis a happy ending smoothly materializes—an amicable break-up with his wife, which means he can still be a father, and a new (equally comfortable) domestic life with Johnny.

These plots hinge on the value of subjective coherence and authenticity, and what Eve Sedgwick describes as 'people's sense of the potency, magnetism, and promise of gay self-disclosure'.[12] Donoghue has some of her lesbian characters attest to the fluidity of their sexual desires; the narrative voice passes no obvious judgement, but the fully drawn, sympathetic protagonists—Maria, Ruth, and Pen—are distinguished by their fidelity to one woman. Lennon's narratives rigidly affirm that an authentic gay identity lies fully formed beneath the artificiality of his protagonists' dissembling performance of heterosexuality. Both authors' narrative styles, which variously comprise first-, second-, and third-person narration focalized around the consciousness of a young protagonist, reiterate this emphasis on sexual desire and self-knowledge. Biographical temporal structures and the (sometimes melodramatic) use of crises as plot devices convey the urgency of achieving identity validation; it is the only viable route to psychic well-being. In sum, these novels gave imaginative shape to the conception of sexuality identity underpinning the LGBT political project that, at that point in Ireland, had just been fortified by the success of decriminalization. Moreover, these texts' sociological current suggests a pressure to be representative—not merely to construct a narrative but to stake a claim for recognition.

As such, these novels were significant pioneering works, creating a space in Irish writing for imagining richer possibilities for sexual self-expression and a more pluralist, humane society. Nevertheless, their imaginative construction of a lesbian or gay identity is troubling. Donoghue's playful, satirical jabs at lesbian feminist activism demonstrate her indebtedness to its intellectual legacy. These ideas circulate in the voices of some of her characters, even if those 'characters' are closer to 'caricatures', but never in the voice of her main protagonists. By contrast, Maria and especially Pen (steering clear of the lesbian scene; dutifully going to her unglamorous teaching job; tending to domestic

---

[12]   Eve Kosofsky Sedgwick, *Epistemology of the Closet* (London: Penguin, 1990), 67.

chores) attest to the value of the ordinary—the value of reconciling oneself to reality and getting on with it.

Lennon's fiction is notably conservative in its conception of class and gender relations. *Crazy Love* satirizes the acquisitiveness, the competitiveness, and the hollow consumerism of Paul's Celtic Tiger generation. But while mocking the cultural obsession with wealth, both *Crazy Love* and *When Love Comes to Town* insistently remind us of their protagonists' social and material success. In many respects, the narrative imperative is to imagine how the conventional markers of such success, for a privileged, privately educated white man, can be efficiently married with a gay identity. In the same way that both novels invite us to condemn the homophobic views of those characters who equate being gay with effeminacy and a 'failed' masculinity, the narrative perspective of *When Love Comes to Town* encourages sympathetic identification with the two cross-dressing characters and the wise-cracking 'Daphne', a working-class gay man who actively accentuates his effeminate persona. Nevertheless, the novel counters this homophobia with its own anxious effeminophobia. The determining feature of the characterization of Neil and Paul is the reiteration of just how conventionally manly a gay man can be. Ultimately, Lennon's novels demand a peculiarly narrow form of pluralism: the right of a young, middle-class white man to be gay, without losing any of the patriarchal dividend and inherited class power to which he is entitled by birth, gender, and skin tone.

Mary Dorcey is best known as a poet and author of an acclaimed short story collection, *A Noise from the Woodshed* (1989). *Biography of Desire* (1997) is less successfully constructed, since the formal strengths of the lyric poem and the short story—crystallized experience over character development; evocation of mood and tone over plot—weaken when stretched across the frame of a realist novel. While Dorcey's lyrical evocation of the distinctive emotional density, sensuality, and eroticism of lesbian relationships, which made her stories so groundbreaking in Irish writing, is present, it is attenuated by exposition and an over-accumulation of descriptive detail. Like Edna O'Brien (1930–) in the final volume of *The Country Girls* trilogy, Dorcey uses first- and third-person narration in alternate chapters, thus giving us two perspectives. Katherine is writing a journal while waiting in County Clare for her lover Nina to arrive. Meanwhile, Nina is in Dublin, painfully deciding between staying with her partner Elinor and their daughter or starting a new life with Katherine (who has left her husband and two children). Formally, the novel incorporates the consciousness-raising central to second-wave feminism: dialogic double consciousness. This is reflected in Katherine's confessional journal, in which she strenuously interrogates her motivation for marrying Malachy, her desire for Nina, and her relationship with her parents, and in Dorcey's emphasis on understanding Nina and Katherine's relationship within the longer trajectory of their respective lives from childhood, as telegraphed in the titular reference to 'biography'.

This commitment to a feminist hermeneutic is reiterated through the comparison between the limitations of Malachy and Katherine's marriage and the erotic mutuality and emotional intensity of the relationships between the women. Yet, since the story turns on

Katherine and Elinor waiting passively for Nina's decision, the novel also suggests that lesbian relationships are not immune to possessiveness and asymmetries of power. This oscillation between idealization and a more nuanced portrayal of lesbian relationships reveals an unresolved tension. The novel's feminist politics are affirmed through exposition rather than being sensuously realized through the story itself; even though the narrator *tells* us that their shared political activism is central to Nina and Elinor's relationship, the primary dramatic and emotional interest remains intensely focused on the texture of the interactions between two people in love. So while Dorcey's novel consciously strives to imagine more sustaining forms of human relationships by challenging the damaging personal/political binary and affirming the feminist possibilities for self-realization of passion between women, it must finally settle for the unsatisfactory solution of shifting the inherited symbolic weight of sacramentalism from heterosexual to lesbian relationships. Nevertheless, Dorcey's fiction affirms the persistent attraction of the liberationist imaginary and, crucially, challenges the reformist/assimilative model of sexuality as autonomous from power relations.

In a similar fashion, Jarlath Gregory's (1978–) comic coming-out romances, *Snapshots* (2001) and *G.A.A.Y: One Hundred Ways to Love a Beautiful Loser* (2005), situate power as constitutive of sexual desire between men. Set in the Catholic nationalist community of Crossmaglen in County Armagh, where Gregory comes from, *Snapshots* alternates between the first-person perspectives of Oisín and Jude, interspersed with brief third-person 'snapshots'. Episodic, picaresque, and written in an energetically mannered prose style (staccato sentences; speech rhythms; extensive use of dialect and slang; darkly camp tone), the action is mostly a sequence of dismal parties characterized by boredom, too much alcohol, and desperate sex. There are painful encounters with parents about being gay, and the plot leads, circuitously, towards the possible beginnings of a romantic relationship between Oisín and Jude. However, Gregory dispenses with a key convention of the coming-out romance by revealing that neither coming out nor the promise of romance bring resolution or catharsis. Oisín's and Jude's sexual encounters at the parties are not with each other but with straight men from among their acquaintances. Thus the novel oscillates between two positions. On one side, it affirms the cultural connection between truth, authenticity, and sexual identity—unlike Oisín and Jude, these other men, in this view, are dissembling or in denial. On the other, it challenges the coherence demanded by the dominant sex-gender system and the reductive framework of discrete sexual identities by posing the question: to be legitimate, must sex between men always be 'meaningful' and deliver some truth about ourselves?

Coming out does not provide resolution in *Snapshots* because being closeted about one's sexuality is not the primary problem. Beneath the comic surface there is a darker undertow, that of a war held at bay by a brittle ceasefire and a legacy of violence, loss, and bitterness. Specifically, the crisis in Oisín's life—he is overwhelmed by depression and inertia—is not precipitated by disguising or revealing his sexuality but by reverberations of a familial and political tragedy. The novel ends with Oisín and Jude sharing a beer at the grave of Sean, Oisín's older brother who was killed accidently some years before while transporting explosives for the IRA. His death may not have been accidental, however; a chapter narrated by Sean suggests it may have been suicide. Standing at the grave, Jude plucks petals from a wreath and throws them at Oisín, who wryly describes them as 'confetti'.[13] Hardly subtle, the symbolism is nevertheless redolent. Juxtaposing that futurity promised by a romance sacramentalized in marriage with the persistent nullity of death and war, Gregory's ending scrambles the temporality of the coming-out narrative—the trajectory towards maturity and authenticity—as well as the political temporality central to liberal sexual politics: a model of progress where the conflicts inherent to capitalism are transmuted into 'differences' to be gradually reconciled through the chimera of neoliberal 'equality'.

As Alan Sinfield notes, the view that the ideal gay and lesbian relationship is inherently egalitarian, free from hierarchies of gender, age, or class, has been a central thematic of lesbian and gay fiction and cinema since the 1970s. That this must be so anxiously reiterated reveals the degree to which such hierarchies persist (we have already noted this anxiety as a structuring feature of Dorcey's fiction). As Sinfield argues, however, the 'prevailing sex/gender system . . . is geared to the production of hierarchy and, as part of that, to the production of anxious, unhappy, and violent people. It produces us and our psychic lives—straights and gays—and it is not going to leave us alone'.[14] The hierarchal power relations of the capitalist social order structure what we believe to be most intimate and private: our sexual desires, fantasies, and pleasures. To believe otherwise is 'a liberal-bourgeois delusion'.[15] Yet the rights-based model of LGBT politics has been strategically committed to this ideological position, which, in Sinfield's view, ignores the reality that 'all power is about command over the means of life' and

the intense commitments that we call 'love' may, ultimately, be intricately mediated versions of a will to survive, ontologically as well as materially. This may lead us into interpersonal opportunities which seem to afford a reassuring exercise of our own power. Equally, it may draw us into the orbit of people who appear powerful and may protect us.[16]

Narrated by a young gay man living with his family in a council flat, G.A.A.Y is unusual in having a working-class character as its central protagonist rather than as a tokenistic bringer of narrative 'colour'. Since Anto is ostentatiously open about his sexual identity, the generic crisis of dissimulation and revelation focuses on his two potential lovers, Khalid, a British Asian man working in Dublin, and Cathal, a neighbour whose sporting prowess gives the novel its punning title. At first glance, we appear to be on familiar territory as Anto wonders if he has 'backed two losers in the coming-out race'.[17] The biographical narrative of courage needed to attain psychic coherence is overlaid with a cultural one which suggests that some cultures—here, Asian immigrant

---

[13] Jarlath Gregory, *Snapshots* (Dublin: Sitric Books, 2001), 197.
[14] Alan Sinfield, *On Sexuality and Power* (New York: Columbia University Press, 2004), 82.
[15] Ibid.   [16] Ibid., 143.
[17] Jarlath Gregory, *G.A.A.Y: One Hundred Ways to Love a Beautiful Loser* (Dublin: Sitric Books, 2005), 203.

and Irish Catholic—place barriers across the route to subjective coherence, and so the trajectory of the self towards authenticity is complicated by the trajectory of the culture toward modernity. However, as their homophonous names suggest, perhaps Khalid and Cathal are not to be read as literary characters, representative of a closeted subjectivity, but rather as interchangeable avatars, emblems of a masculinity which is politically troubling (misogynistic, homophobic, violent, competitive, emotionally repressed) but erotically irresistible.

Gregory's novel suggests that this erotic enthrallment to embodiments of patriarchal masculinity is not necessarily a fetish of gay men but symptomatic of contemporary culture more broadly. It achieves this through its rendering of Anto's infatuation with Cathal—rather than an obstacle to consummation, perhaps his troubled performance of 'straightness' is precisely what makes him so desirable—as well as through its paratext: the title and cover image of a young man photographed from behind, a Dublin GAA jersey and jeans framing his pert body for our gaze. In this regard, the novel forms an interesting comic counterpoint to Donal Óg Cusack's celebrated memoir, *Come What May* (2009), in which the prominent Cork hurler courageously wrote about being gay, while emphatically distinguishing between the homosociality of organized sport and the emotional, erotic texture of his homosexual encounters. *G.A.A.Y* queries this devoutly held ideological fiction. By setting the novel in its working-class milieu— including a parodic concern with the ethics and aesthetics of social mobility— Gregory insists that this cultural eroticization of the male sporting body should not be conceived in psychosexual terms but, rather, as materially determined. His novel reiterates how living under a cultural dominant that constitutively engenders anxiety and precariousness, as we all do, must invariably lead us to form strong libidinal investments in symbols of strength and invulnerability. In contemporary culture, the finely honed—and heavily commodified—body of the male sports star functions as just such an object of cathexis.

Historical Romances

In this section, I wish to turn from biographically structured novels to historical romances. Jamie O'Neill's (1962–) *At Swim, Two Boys* (2001) and Denis Kehoe's (1978–) *Nights Beneath the Nation* (2008) use fiction to unearth, and imaginatively recreate, an archaeology of same-sex passions between men in pre-1970s Ireland. These tragic romances speak powerfully to a yearning to make the silences of history speak; both novels are propelled by a belief that fiction can work an alchemy on the past that is inaccessible through other modes of history writing. The difficulty with which they must contend, then, is the creation of a style of narration which can imaginatively encounter, without condescending to, the alterity of the past.

Kehoe confronts this challenge by alternating between 1990s Dublin, to which his narrator Daniel has returned after living in the US for forty years, and the story Daniel recounts of his passionate love affair with another young man in the city in the 1950s, the tragic ending of which precipitated his flight to New York. In this way, the novel fore-grounds the act of storytelling, the conscious activity of narratively reconstructing the past. This narrative self-consciousness is underscored by having Daniel, in the novel's present, befriend a young man writing a novel about bohemian, theatrical, and homo-sexual culture in 1950s Dublin. Unfortunately, this formal self-awareness is inconsist-ently applied. Daniel tells his story with the fluent assurance of an omniscient narrator and a scholar's attention to historical detail, so that the complex problematic of human memory, its creative dynamism and fragility, is never broached. Kehoe diligently recre-ates the geography of the 1950s cityscape and evokes its bohemian *demi-monde*. But fac-tual accuracy is less vital in historical fiction than storytelling which vividly animates the sensuous, intellectual, and emotional experience of living in another time. The chal-lenge to the historical imagination is to capture the essential difference of the past and avoid reducing it to a simulacrum shaped by our present preoccupations. Fusing the love story with the generic conventions of a crime thriller, as Kehoe does, only exacer-bates this problem. The sombre mood and inevitable tragic dénouement reduces the historical experiences of the men who lived in those pre-Stonewall times to one-dimensional victimhood.

O'Neill, whose novel has attracted considerable commercial success and critical attention, attempts to circumvent this problem of the historical imagination through extensive intertextuality. Along with the titular nod to Flann O'Brien (1911–66), there are recurring Joycean stylistic pastiches and allusions to E. M. Forster, Oscar Wilde, and the poetry of Douglas Hyde (1860–1949). Furthermore, as Joseph Valente points out, O'Neill's gay reworking of the *Bildungsroman* explicitly acknowledges its debt to Irish antecedents, notably *The Picture of Dorian Gray* (1891), *A Portrait of the Artist as a Young Man* (1916), and *The Last September* (1929).[18] *At Swim, Two Boys* also combines histor-ical figures with fictional characters. Through these techniques, the novel self-consciously draws our attention to its project: registering the volatile, multivalent emergence of male homosexuality as a form of subjectivity in the decades around the imprisonment and death of Wilde.

Set in a Dublin suburb in the year leading up to the 1916 Rising, the narrative centres on a love story between two teenage boys, Jim and Doyler, who become involved in the militant nationalist movement and fight together in the rebellion. Thus the novel analo-gizes sexual identity and national identity. Through its historical and fictional figures and types, embodying and expressing heterogeneous political discourses, *At Swim, Two Boys* suggests that in this period both gay identity and Irish identity were in flux. On one side, we have Wildean dandyism, elite Hellenism, and the manly comradeship and socialism of Walt Whitman and Edward Carpenter, as well as the pathologizing, crimin-alizing apparatus that fatally imprisoned Wilde for gross indecency (and Dermot MacMurrough, one of O'Neill's fictional protagonists). On the other, we have

---

[18] Joseph Valente, 'Race/Sex/Shame: The Queer Nationalism of *At Swim, Two Boys*', *Éire-Ireland* 40, nos. 3–4 (2005), 63–5.

middle-class Catholic unionists, conservative Home Rulers, clericalist militant nationalists, radical, idealistic cultural nationalists, and socialist republicans (the latter embodied by Doyler).

Valente and other critics affirm the radical potential in O'Neill's correlation of the affective and erotic with the communal and national, and the 'narrative parallelism'[19] between the boys' *Bildungsroman* and that of the Irish nation. Specifically, these critics believe, the novel powerfully queers, in a deconstructionist rather than erotic sense, the national narrative. Valente celebrates the novel's 'articulation of an Irish nationalism that, far from reifying some ethnically proper spirit, orientation, or form of life, would fulfil the queer mandate of instituting an "oppositional relation to the [social/sexual] norm" or "resistance to the very idea of the norm as such"'.[20] But it is not entirely clear how well this postmodern political objective chimes with the socialist republicanism articulated by James Connolly and his fictional comrade Doyler, since it is towards Doyler and Jim that our political as well as emotional sympathies are directed. Moreover, this queer reading underplays how the idealized relationship of Jim and Doyler is explicitly cast as monogamously egalitarian and contrasted favourably with the non-monogamous and asymmetrical cross-class liaisons of MacMurrough's older generation. From our post-Stonewall perspective, their relationship is actually quite close to the sacramentalized 'norm'. And, as I have argued elsewhere, viewed from the perspective of 2001 rather than 1916—that is, as a historical novel which discloses more about the era of its creation than the era it represents—O'Neill's narrative offers an alliance of identity and national politics that affirms more than it destabilizes the current hegemonic neoliberal conception of Ireland as a country that is at once tolerant, pluralist, and fundamentally committed to a financialized global economy.[21]

The historical romance risks offering a lesbian and gay supplement—here is 'our' history to add to 'yours'—to that narrative of modernity underpinning the dominant ideology but without fundamentally querying, or queering, the structure of thought that shapes that narrative.[22] Positioning a pre-Stonewall *Weltanschauung* as a tragically imperfect stage on the trajectory towards our post-Stonewall world, such fiction reiterates the inevitability of the concept of sexual freedom articulated in mainstream LBGT politics. In other words, while this fiction may usefully enrich our perspective on the past, it might do little to dislodge our perspective on the present and future. It may in

[19] Ibid., 58.

[20] Ibid., 60. Valente is citing here the work of David Halperin and Tim Dean. See also Jodie Medd, '"Patterns of the Possible": National Imagining and Queer Historical (Meta)Fictions in Jamie O'Neill's *At Swim, Two Boys*', GLQ 13, no. 1 (2007), 1–31 and Patrick R. Mullen, *The Poor Bugger's Tool: Irish Modernism, Queer Labour, and Postcolonial History* (Oxford: Oxford University Press, 2012), 147–79.

[21] See Michael G. Cronin, '"He's My Country": Liberalism, Nationalism and Sexuality in Contemporary Irish Gay Fiction', *Éire-Ireland* 39, nos. 3–4 (2004), 250–67.

[22] On 'queer temporality', see Heather Love, *Feeling Backward: Loss and the Politics of Queer History* (Cambridge, MA: Harvard University Press, 2007), José Esteban Muñoz, *Cruising Utopia: The Then and There of Queer Futurity* (New York: New York University Press, 2009), and Elizabeth Freeman, *Time Binds: Queer Temporalities, Queer Histories* (Durham, NC: Duke University Press, 2010).

fact reinforce our complacent sense that present arrangements, of political economy as much as of sexual and gender relations, are the best we can achieve.

An interesting exception here is Colm Tóibín's *The Master* (2004). Focalized around the consciousness of the writer Henry James, as speculatively reconstructed by Tóibín, the novel apparently affirms our sense of the inhibited, restrictive homophobic past. An early chapter focuses on Henry's intense fascination with Wilde's trial, suggesting that the terrifying example of the Irish playwright's spectacular shaming and punishment definitively solidifies the American novelist's deliberate repression of his homoerotic desires.[23] Henry's consciousness is shaped by the dialectic of powerful passions incited by male bodies and an equally powerful control exercised over those passions. His suppression of homoerotic desires is on a spectrum of emotional repression, coldness, and betrayal—particularly towards the women in his life. But, the novel insinuates, the costly maintenance of this emotional distance is essential for the creative exploitation of Henry's relationships and the transmutation of suppressed emotions into his fiction. Thus, the closet, as a historical condition, could be as creative as it was destructive.

Tóibín's fiction has a distinctive structure of feeling: the homoerotic as most truly absorbing when tragic. His novels are notable in Irish fiction for their representation of gay men living with HIV, and the presence of HIV has considerably shaped erotic and emotional reality for two generations of gay men. Tóibín's pellucid prose minutely conveys the dismaying, shattering effects of diagnosis—Richard Garay and Pablo Canetto in *The Story of the Night* (1996)—and the terrifying physiological effects, psychic debilitations, and banal humiliations of dying—Declan Breen in *The Blackwater Lightship* (1999). Tóibín's naturalist aesthetic reiterates the material and historical specificity of HIV. His fiction is attuned to how this pandemic came about from the early 1980s onwards because a virus met with new opportunities for dissemination provided by a globalizing world. In *The Story of the Night*, for instance, the movement of people and capital takes Pablo to San Francisco while also bringing IMF bankers, CIA agents, and investors to 1980s Argentina to reap the benefits of privatization.

At the same time, symbolically overdetermined routes of transmission (blood, semen) coincided with stigmatizing structures of power (poverty, race, sexuality). Tóibín's novels specifically reiterate how homophobia, psychic and social, was amplified by the arrival of the disease, while also portraying HIV as simultaneously physical and metaphysical. In a similar manner to the Irish coastal landscape, the virus generates moments in the text which, in the words of Matthew Ryan, 'draw the characters out from the present into contemplation of timelessness and absolute isolation', reminding them of 'a lack of connection to the world, a consciousness of alienation'.[24] Merging sexual pleasure and mortality, Eros and Thanatos, HIV is for Tóibín another iteration of that tragic and existential—as opposed to historical—condition inhabited by Henry. As

---

[23] See Colm Tóibín, *The Master* (London: Picador, 2004), 67–82.
[24] Matthew Ryan, 'Abstract Homes: Deterritorialisation and Reterritorialisation in the Work of Colm Tóibín', *Irish Studies Review* 16, no. 1 (2008), 26.

such, HIV is a disease overdetermined by homophobia, while simultaneously offering a symbolic rebuke to the progressive historicism of the gay and lesbian movement.

This often unsettling sexual politics merges in Tóibín's fiction with an ambivalence towards the prevailing narrative of modernization, a narrative to which Tóibín as journalist and commentator is unambiguously committed. This is most strongly felt in *The Story of the Night*. Richard's first-person narrative is a self-cancelling *Bildungsroman*. His affirmative story of material success and sexual and emotional fulfilment with Pablo, after childhood isolation and poverty, clashes with the concluding news of his and Pablo's infection, and this intimation of early death imbues the foregoing narrative with an air of grieving retrospection. Richard's story is interwoven with that of Argentina in the 1970s and 1980s; but again, optimism about the transition from the generals' dictatorship to democratic freedom is undermined. Although wilfully politically naïve, even Richard begins to grasp that the emergent Argentinean democracy is effectively a stratagem of US power—embodied by his shadowy employers Susan and Donald Ford—and while it may enrich some local allies, its principal beneficiaries will be elsewhere in the global financial system. The view that history might be cyclical rather than progressive, and that exploitation and oppression are mutating forces, is reiterated through the entwinement of biography and history. Richard's maternal grandfather came to Argentina from Britain; his Anglophile mother's obsession with 'the emblems of empire'[25] intensifies as she declines. To what degree, the novel asks, is the emerging neoliberal, globalizing order, in which Richard can apparently secure material and sexual freedom, merely a new phase in the same capitalist world system, a different hegemony exercising a different style of power?

At first glance, *The Blackwater Lightship* and Keith Ridgway's *The Long Falling* (1998) offer optimistic perspectives on modernization in Ireland at the end of the twentieth century. In the first, Declan travels from his hospital bed in Dublin to his grandmother's house in Wexford for a final visit, and is cared for by his grandmother, mother, and sister Helen, along with his gay friends Paul and Larry. Ridgway's novel centres on Grace, who murders her abusive husband and escapes to Dublin where her son Martin lives with his partner Henry. The novels share a formal structure, interweaving biographical and generational time with the time of national history. The younger generation is confidently assured—Helen is a highly regarded teacher, Paul and Henry work for the EU—and capable of forming healthy, emotionally honest, sexually compatible relationships. That Tóibín's characters are women and gay men suggests that these successful lives can be read allegorically, indicating the social change wrought in Ireland since the 1970s by feminist and lesbian/gay social movements. However, these political movements are given no diegetic space, thus implying that individual effort is primarily responsible, with one exception.

While telling the story of coming out to his parents, Larry refers to a symbolically powerful meeting in 1993 between President Mary Robinson and a group of lesbian and gay activists at Áras an Uachtaráin, the official residence of the President of Ireland, thus aligning the

---

[25] Colm Tóibín, *The Story of the Night* (London: Picador, 1996), 3.

younger generation with the promise of tolerant pluralism signalled by her presidency. An analogous note of hope is registered in *The Long Falling* through its subplot, a significant part of which centres on the 'X' case of 1992, when the Irish state attempted to prevent a pregnant fourteen-year-old rape victim from leaving the country to access a termination. The novel ends with Grace participating in a mass demonstration in February 1992 to protest the government's actions, an artistic choice that emphasizes the control still maintained by Church and state in 1990s Ireland, and the persisting limits on personal autonomy, while at the same time signifying that this religious-juridical control would now be met by democratic opposition, and that its hegemony was eroding.[26]

Nevertheless, the past cannot be easily overcome. Helen's and Martin's assured poise is fragile. The emotionally debilitating legacies of family trauma—the early death of Helen's father and her estrangement from her mother; the childhood death of Martin's brother and his parents' abusive marriage—sweeps them back into its currents. Hence the shape of Tóibín's narrative structure: the unfolding of the current family trauma oscillates with the recounting of that earlier trauma through Helen's reignited memories. Tóibín attempts to symbolically reconcile the demands of tradition and modernity through the tentative rapprochement between Helen and her mother, although this is overshadowed by Declan's impending death, and through Paul's story of his secret marriage ceremony by a maverick Catholic priest, although this story has the quality of fable, a 'lavish piece of Catholic homosexual wish-fulfilment' that provides a 'magical catharsis of Ireland's moral woes'.[27] By contrast, Ridgway subjects emerging liberal Ireland to as much withering scepticism as its conservative adversaries. If Martin's moral failings are a legacy of the bleak past, those of his gay friend Sean, a journalist eager to exploit the 'X' case and betray Grace to further his career, are thoroughly modern, symptoms of the cynicism and alienation of competitive individualism.

SPACES OF DESIRE

Ultimately, the historical imagination in the novels discussed above is weakened by a schematic distinction between a reified 'tradition' and 'modernity'. Counter-intuitively, we find a more complex, dialectical historical sense in three novels where space rather than time is the primary compositional principle: Ridgway's second novel, *The Parts* (2003), Micheál Ó Conghaile's (1962–) *Sna Fir* (1999), and Barry McCrea's (1974–) *The First Verse* (2005). In the final section of this chapter, I will examine common patterns in these linguistically and stylistically distinctive novels. I will pay particular attention to these writers' experimentation with the conventions of realism, to the thematic and structural significance of the motif of mobility, and to the ways in which homoerotic desire is shown to infuse the collective geography of the city rather than inhere in individual identity.

---

[26] Keith Ridgway, *The Long Falling* (London: Faber and Faber, 1998), 284–305.
[27] Terry Eagleton, 'Mothering', *London Review of Books*, 14 October 1999, 8.

My purpose is to show how through their use of two interconnected chronotopes—the city and the gay sauna—these novels map an imaginative space where erotic and political desires meet and challenge us to reflect on our understanding of sexual freedom.

With their student narrators, *Sna Fir* (which can be translated as 'Among Men') and *The First Verse* initially conform to the conventions of the coming-out romance. Ó Conghaile's John Paul Mac Donncha travels between his family home in Connemara and the gay scenes of Dublin and, briefly, London. Generically, this should precipitate a crisis in which John Paul, as a gay *gaeilgeoir* (Irish speaker), negotiates competing cultural and sexual identities projected onto different social geographies. But the episodic rhythm, along with an emphasis on movement and conversation over action (listening to the men in his family pub; chatting to the men he meets cruising; listening to the folklore of his elderly friend for a college project), unexpectedly subvert these generic conventions. A picaresque tale of going 'ag crúsál', the narrative situates John Paul in what Bakhtin terms 'adventure time', rather than in the biographical time of the modern novel, and the generic crisis of identity—our expectation that a conflict between homoerotic desire and culture must be resolved comically or tragically—is thus undermined.[28]

In *The First Verse*, McCrea's Niall Lenihan leaves home to study at Trinity College Dublin, thus opening a door into a new social and intellectual world, including his first forays into the Dublin gay scene and his first relationship. However, it quickly becomes apparent that the central drama lies elsewhere. Niall is increasingly absorbed in a cult-like relationship with two characters. Together they practise a form of bibliomancy or *sortes virgilianae*, which entails interpreting randomly chosen lines of text to answer questions. They also ritualistically reread selections of randomly chosen passages to induce hallucinogenic states. After a while, Niall's life consists of nights spent at these occult rituals and days spent wandering the city.

Composed of six plotlines, *The Parts* is divided into sections, each narrated in the third or second person but focalized around one of six characters. These sections are of varying length without a discernible pattern to their sequence. Ridgway uses typographical devices (ideograms, different font styles) to indicate which character is the focus of the narrative at any given point. Playing with conventions of narration and presentation in this way, Ridgway displaces the unique individual perspective and, significantly in the context of contemporary Irish writing, dislodges the family as the basic plot unit. The six stories become entwined in various complicated, random, comic, and tragic ways, as the novel gleefully plays with different genres, from Irish Big House Gothic to the crime thriller. Dublin acts as the fulcrum on which the plots turn, and the intricate geography of the city's class relations and wealth disparities is well captured. Our view shifts dramatically from the mansion in the Dublin mountains of Delly, widow of a billionaire tycoon, to the quays where Kez works as a rent boy. As well as being shown how patterns of consumption ceaselessly generate unquenchable desires, we see how

---

[28]   Micheál Ó Conghaile, *Sna Fir* (Indreabhán: Cló Iar-Chonnachta, 1999), 43; Mikhail Bakhtin, *The Dialogic Imagination: Four Essays*, trans. Caryl Emerson and Michael Holquist (Austin, TX: University of Texas Press, 1981), 87–110.

transnational circuits of affluence embed the city in the inequities of global capitalism, the movement of capital and wealth that connects Delly to Paris, London, Zurich, and New York being the obverse of those movements of poverty and migration that bring Nigerians to Dublin.

McCrea's distinctive prose style features recurring descriptions of Niall wandering through Dublin and Paris, with the listing of place names and landmark buildings creating a rhythmic, incantatory affect. We do not merely observe Niall on his travels but inhabit as part of the reading experience something of the *flâneur*'s ambiguous perspective, caught between the soothing reassurance of place names, with their promise of solidity and permanence, and the discombobulating effects of movement and ceaseless flux. As with John Paul's encounters in the Phoenix Park and Soho in *Sna Fir* and Kez's working life in *The Parts*, mobility in *The First Verse* is both melancholic and erotic. At the mercy of random events, coincidences, and synchronicities, the cruising gay man balances vertiginously between freedom and alienation.[29] Since randomness and control are thematically as well as structurally important, all three novels suggest that these qualities are not necessarily confined to a minority community but are emblematic of late capitalist subjectivity.

If the city is both setting and chronotope in these novels, another notable chronotope is the gay sauna. The exhilarating erotic possibilities and distinctive gloomy mood of this space features in earlier novels, including *The Story of the Night*. Keith Ridgway's fiction, even in the comic mode of *The Parts*, tends to emphasize protagonists' feeling of squalor and self-loathing in sauna-based episodes. By contrast, Ó Conghaile's handling of John Paul's sauna experience in *Sna Fir* is emblematic rather than idiosyncratic or pathological. On the threshold of the changing room and the cruising area, John Paul stops to think about himself as he stands naked, apart from a small towel. His nakedness delivers a sudden, anxious, exhilarating sensation of liberation which he describes as 'saoirse iomlán',[30] a full or total freedom. However, the epiphanic resonances of this scene are complicated by what comes before and after it. In the preceding paragraph, Ó Conghaile shows John Paul handing over his sauna entry fee, thus framing his revelatory moment within a commercial, consumerist context. Later, John Paul describes television screens, visible from every direction, showing porn, the emblem of an insistent, wearying technological incitement to sexual desire and its ever-expanding commodification in an age of corporate capitalism.

These chronotopes, city and sauna, are symbolic spaces where the novels of contemporary Irish gay writers contend imaginatively and dialectically with a central paradox of sexual freedom in the late capitalist era. Achieving new sexual rights and challenging patriarchal domination and compulsory heterosexuality has, over the last forty years, proceeded simultaneously with the deepening penetration of consumerism into every facet of our emotional and sexual lives, making potential new freedoms inextricable

---

[29] The poetics and erotics of cruising also feature in stories by Tóibín and Ridgway in *The Empty Family* (2010) and *Standard Time* (2001) respectively.
[30] Ó Conghaile, *Sna Fir*, 63.

from new forms of regulation.[31] Yet by means of their dynamic plotting and subtle subversion of realist convention, the novels of Keith Ridgway, Micheál Ó Conghaile, and Barry McCrea eschew naturalist denunciation or pessimism; the new freedom is compromised for sure, but, like cruising, it is not without its glamour and spaces of joy. And, as with the effect of Niall Lenihan's bibliomancy rituals or John Paul Mac Donncha's transcendent sauna moment, these novels fuse critique with an openness to, and a recognition of, that utopian desire we used to, and may again, call liberation.

FURTHER READING

Barron, Michael. 'Advocating for LGBT Youth: Seeking Social Justice in a Culture of Individual Rights'. *Irish University Review* 43, no. 1 (2013): 23–30.

Costello-Sullivan, Kathleen. *Mother/Country: Politics of the Personal in the Fiction of Colm Tóibín*. Bern: Peter Lang, 2012.

Cronin, Michael G. 'Clubs, Closets and Catwalks: GAA Stars and the Politics of Contemporary Irish Masculinity'. In Conn Holohan and Tony Tracy (eds), *Masculinity and Irish Popular Culture: Tiger Tales*. Basingstoke: Palgrave Macmillan, 2014: 13–26.

Delaney, Paul (ed.). *Reading Colm Tóibín*. Dublin Liffey Press, 2008.

Ging, Debbie. 'Gay in the GAA: The Challenge of Dónal Óg Cusack's 'Coming Out' to Heteronormativity in Contemporary Irish Culture and Society'. In Rosie Meade and Fiona Dukelow (eds), *Defining Events: Power, Resistance and Identity in Twenty-First-Century Ireland*. Manchester: Manchester University Press, 2015: 218–35.

Jeffers, Jennifer M. *The Irish Novel at the End of the Twentieth Century: Gender, Bodies, and Power*. Basingstoke: Palgrave, 2002.

Madden, Ed. 'Queering Ireland, in the Archives'. *Irish University Review* 43, no. 1 (2013): 184–221.

Mulhall, Anne. 'Queer in Ireland: Deviant Filiations and the (Un)holy Family'. In Lisa Downing and Robert Grillett (eds), *Queer in Europe*. Farnham: Ashgate, 2011: 99–112.

Mulhall, Anne. '"What's Eating Victor Cusack?" *Come What May*, Queer Embodiment, and the Regulation of Hetero-Masculinity'. *Éire-Ireland* 48, nos. 1–2 (2013): 282–308.

O'Donnell, Katherine. '*The Parts*: Whiskey, Tea and Sympathy'. In Pilar Villar-Argáiz (ed.), *Literary Visions of Multicultural Ireland: The Immigrant in Contemporary Irish Literature*. Manchester: Manchester University Press, 2014: 188–200.

Peach, Linden. *The Contemporary Irish Novel: Critical Readings*. Basingstoke: Palgrave Macmillan, 2004.

Ryan, Paul. *Asking Angela MacNamara: An Intimate History of Irish Lives*. Dublin: Irish Academic Press, 2012.

Smyth, Gerry. *The Novel and the Nation: Studies in the New Irish Fiction*. London: Pluto Press, 1997.

Walshe, Éibhear (ed.). *Sex, Nation and Dissent in Irish Writing*. Cork: Cork University Press, 1997.

Walshe, Éibhear. *A Different Story: The Writings of Colm Tóibín*. Dublin, Irish Academic Press, 2013.

---

[31] See Alderson, *Sex, Needs and Queer Culture*, 83–93 and Hennessy, *Profit and Pleasure*, 107–13. See also Nancy Fraser, *Fortunes of Feminism: From State-Managed Capitalism to Neoliberal Crisis* (London: Verso, 2013), 209–26.

CHAPTER 33

....

CONTEMPORARY
IRISH-LANGUAGE
FICTION

....

PÁDRAIG Ó SIADHAIL

THE characters in Máirtín Ó Cadhain's (1906–70) modernist novel, *Cré na Cille* (Graveyard Clay, 1949), are dead. Robert Schumann's *Kinderszenen* (Scenes from Childhood, 1987) takes matters a step further, declaring: 'Cé mhéad de seo atá fíor? Tá Robert Schumann marbh. Tá údar an leabhair seo marbh. Ní mise Robert Schumann' (How much of this is true? Robert Schumann is dead. The author of this book is dead. I'm not Robert Schumann).[1] Thus, the Irish-language novel meets postmodernism in the guise of Roland Barthes's famous insistence that the author must die for the reader to live. Colm Breathnach's (1961–) *Con Trick 'An Bhalla Bháin'* (Con Trick 'of the White Wall', 2009) ups the ante, mischievously dispatching not only 'Fear uasal…darb ainm Rólann de Beart' (A gentleman…named Roland Barthes)[2] to the guillotine but also the reader. *Kinderszenen* and *Con Trick* represent one distinctive strain in Irish-language fiction that dates back to the 1980s. In reality, however, the contemporary novel in Irish is as heterogeneous in its genres, themes, narrative styles, and settings as its equivalents in world literature. It ranges from experimental literary works to conventional crime fiction, from historical tales to futuristic parables, and from highbrow philosophical meditations to light reading and graphic novels. Beyond locations in Ireland, settings include mainland Europe, Africa, Asia, North America, and the Caribbean—and versions of the otherworld. However, the position of Irish as an endangered minority language, albeit one with official status and state support, directly impacts its literature.

Since the novel was introduced early in the twentieth century during the Gaelic Revival, most Irish-language novelists writing for adult readers have been male, although that is slowly changing with the recent emergence of a small cadre of female novelists. Few writers have focused exclusively on the novel—in fact, a significant number have published only one novel—and increasingly, novelists have acquired Irish as a

---

[1] Robert Schumann, *Kinderszenen: Radhairc ar Shaol an Pháiste* (Baile Átha Cliath: Taibhse, 1987), 139.
[2] Colm Breathnach, *Con Trick 'An Bhalla Bháin'* (Indreabhán: Cló Iar-Chonnacht, 2009), 146.

second language, rather than being from the Gaeltacht (Irish-speaking areas considered the cultural heartland of the language) or from non-Gaeltacht Irish-speaking backgrounds. Overwhelmingly, the novelists who have made their mark have been born in Ireland and have remained there, although at present almost as many Irish-language novelists live outside Ireland as in the Gaeltacht.

As a limited number of novels and novellas are published annually—usually no more than fifteen titles across all genres—there are opportunities to publish and freedom to experiment with theme and form. Yet there are also creative pressures on, and critical expectations of, writers who are aware that their readers have access to the full spectrum of world literatures in English or through English translation, including translations of a selection of Irish-language works. Readership, outside the education system, is modest, comprising networks of keen individuals and adult learners or returnees to the language. In addition, fears about declining literacy standards in Irish highlight the challenge of ensuring a market for texts deemed linguistically 'difficult', even for university students. Inevitably, a central feature of contemporary fiction in Irish is the issue of language itself—playing with it, code-mixing for comic or dramatic effect, drawing on readers' knowledge of at least one other language (usually English), tailoring the language so as not to overtax some readers' Irish-language vocabulary, or including a glossary aimed at learners.

There is also the shadow cast by the literary giant, Ó Cadhain, whose creative writings and linguistic command inspired and intimidated his peers and immediate successors. Ó Cadhain's death in 1970 left a major gap in Irish literature, and the passing during the 1980s of three other prominent writers—Eoghan Ó Tuairisc in 1982, Diarmaid Ó Súilleabháin in 1985, and Dónall Mac Amhlaigh in 1989—appeared to signal the close of a perceived golden era for Irish-language fiction. Indeed, one current writer, Liam Mac Cóil (1952–), has argued that Ó Cadhain's literary heirs have not built on the foundations laid down by the master.[3] Nevertheless, novels from the 1970s and 1980s revealed a vitality to Irish-language fiction and evidenced the emergence of a new generation of writers. The two genuine popular successes were *Lig Sinn i gCathú* (Lead Us into Temptation, 1976) by Breandán Ó hEithir (1930–90), an irreverent account of a university student, Máirtín Ó Méalóid, and his extracurricular antics in Galway, just as the Irish state proclaims the establishment of a republic in 1949; and Pádraig Standún's (1946–) *Súil le Breith* (Expecting, 1983), a Gaeltacht tale about a priest and his relationship with his pregnant housekeeper that foreshadowed revelations about taboo subjects such as clerical celibacy and anticipated the Irish culture wars of the last three decades. In addition, Alan Titley (1947–) and Breandán Ó Doibhlin (1931–) set a high standard for literary fiction in their respective second novels. Titley's *Méirscrí na Treibhe* (The Tribe's Fissures, 1978) explored the personal and political dilemmas confronting Paul Lodabo, a young Western-educated black man, after he returns home to Zanidia, a fictional country in war-torn postcolonial sub-Saharan Africa. In Ó Doibhlin's *An Branar gan Cur* (Untilled

---

[3] Seosamh Ó Murchú and Antain Mag Shamhráin, 'Ar an Imeall i Lár an Domhain: Alan Titley, Bríona Nic Dhiarmada agus Liam Mac Cóil ag caint le hOghma', *Oghma* 4 (1992), 44.

Grassland, 1979), the central character Fergus ponders his past, his beliefs and aspirations, and the future course of his life while on a train from Dublin to Derry in the 1950s. As such, the idea of a journey works on two levels, the physical and the philosophical.

The most striking early post-Ó Cadhain novel was Séamas Mac Annaidh's (1961–) *Cuaifeach Mo Londubh Buí* (The Blackbird's Whirlwind, 1983) in which four narrative threads merge: a day in the life of a newly-minted university graduate in Enniskillen; a reworking of the Gilgamesh myth; the weird world of an Irish-lite version of Dr Strangelove; and the graduate's experiences at a Gaeltacht summer college. Just as *An Béal Bocht* (The Poor Mouth, 1941) by Myles na Gopaleen—a pseudonym of Brian O'Nolan (1911–66)—and Ó Cadhain's *Cré na Cille* had electrified and, in some instances, shocked their 1940s readers, *Cuaifeach Mo Londubh Buí*, with its riff 'Is cuma faoin scéal' (The story doesn't matter), challenged 1980s Irish-language writers and readers to imagine a new direction for fiction in Irish, to move beyond the pursuit of the then holy grail, the realistic urban novel, and to embrace the potential of experimental fiction. A year before the publication of *Metafiction*, Patricia Waugh's seminal study of self-reflexive fiction, *Cuaifeach Mo Londubh Buí* previewed the metafictional novel in action and signalled not just the arrival but the mainstreaming of experimental writing in Irish.

Ó hEithir was a talented journalist and broadcaster rather than a novelist, whose eagerly anticipated sequel to *Lig Sinn i gCathú*, *Sionnach ar mo Dhuán* (A Fox on my Hook, 1988), proved structurally unwieldy and disappointing. The recent publication of Ó Doibhlin's third novel four decades after its predecessor is an unexpected pleasure. *Sliocht ar Thír na Scáth* (Offspring in the Land of Shadows, 2018) purports to be an unnamed Ulster bardic poet's testimony, freshly discovered in the former Irish College in Paris, about the collapse of his private and public worlds with the defeat of Hugh O'Neill and his allies in early seventeenth-century Ireland. The novel is a notable achievement, particularly in its depiction of the cultural and political institutions that sustained Gaelic society in Tyrone and the local rivalries that contributed to the downfall of that society's elites. Mac Annaidh is the Cú Chulainn of modern Irish-language fiction, one assured of enduring fame on account of his boyhood deeds but apparently fated to pass prematurely as a creative and innovative force. *Cuaifeach Mo Londubh Buí* appeared to herald the arrival of an outstanding talent. Indeed, he quickly announced that the novel was merely the first instalment in a trilogy. *Mo Dhá Mhicí* (My Two Mickies, 1986) and *Rubble na Mickies* (1990) duly appeared, reacquainting us with some of the themes, characters, and narrative techniques in the first book and adding fresh ingredients. The trilogy was an ambitious undertaking, but as it developed there was a sense of flagging energy on the author's part and flagging engagement on the reader's. Nevertheless, the trilogy remains a signal achievement by a young writer. Regrettably, Mac Annaidh's three subsequent novels are laboured works of social realism. In contrast, Standún and Titley have made substantial contributions to fiction in Irish over several decades. It is instructive, therefore, to focus on their works, not only because of their inherent merit but also for the light they cast on the dominant strands of contemporary Irish-language fiction.

THE MAJOR STRANDS OF CONTEMPORARY
FICTION IN IRISH

Having published more than a dozen books, Mayo-born Pádraig Standún, who has spent his adult life serving as a priest, mainly in Gaeltacht communities, is the most pro-lific contemporary novelist in Irish. His trademark style of writing is narrative-driven social realism. Early novels portrayed in an unvarnished manner the lives and relation-ships of characters in rural Ireland, especially the Gaeltacht, with the figure of the priest playing a central narrative role. Standún's priests are not the stern authority figures of a bygone era. They challenge elites, including church leaders, deal with their communi-ties' social problems and domestic dramas, and struggle with their own personal demons. *A.D. 2016* (1987) sees an ex-priest on a pilgrimage to Dublin, contemplating how the Ireland of 2016 measures up to the Christian message of Easter and the idealism of the leaders of the 1916 Easter Rising. In *Stigmata* (1994), the priest shelters a local woman, ostracized for her reputed lifestyle as a prostitute, and *Cion Mná* (A Woman's Part, 1993) features a lesbian couple.

Importantly, as evidenced by *Súil le Breith*, Standún's work helped to bring into the literary mainstream issues and characters previously marginalized in Irish literature. His early novels attracted curious readers, not least of all in the Gaeltacht, an area trad-itionally resistant to reading fiction in Irish. To his credit, Standún sought to evolve as a novelist and remain topical by, for example, moving his setting from Ireland to Crete in *Saoire* (Holidays, 1997). Later novels tackle television soap opera, sexual abuse scandals, and, in novels set in Venice and Amsterdam respectively, the aftershocks of the Troubles and dementia. Yet while Standún has always been a good storyteller, his work increas-ingly suffers from a sense of repetition in its narrative style. He continues to write and publish, but the fact that one recent book was for young readers and another featured a teenage hero suggested that Standún may be seeking to refresh his writing in the latter phase of his career. In *Mac Dé Cé Hé* (The Son of God, Who is He?, 2017), however, he returns to a familiar setting, showing how a Gaeltacht community, including its priest, reacts to a visiting film crew tasked with reinterpreting the life of Christ.

Cork-born Alan Titley, the most accomplished contemporary Irish-language prose writer, has published novels, short stories, plays, and poetry, as well as works of literary criticism. *Eiriceachtaí agus Scéalta Eile* (Heretics and Other Stories, 1987) breathed new life into the short story in Irish as Titley led readers on a zany journey from the origins of man to the Day of Judgement. His novels published since the aforementioned *Méirscrí na Treibhe* in 1978 are impressive works. *An Fear Dána* (The Poet, 1993) recreates the life of the thirteenth-century poet Muireadhach Albanach Ó Dálaigh, whose travels reputedly took him beyond the Gaelic world to the Crusades. Narrated in the first person, *An Fear Dána* is a work of high art, drawing on conventions of Irish syllabic poetry and laced with linguistic puns and literary allusions. More recently, in his short novel, *Gluaiseacht* (Movement, 2009), a young black African recounts the horrific events and experiences that compelled him to flee his homeland and seek refuge in an unwelcoming unnamed European state. *Gluaiseacht* is a story of our times, stark and pointed in its telling, that appeals to young and adult readers alike. *An Bhean Feasa* (The Witch, 2014), the first novel in verse form in Irish, reimagines the life, trial, and death by hanging of Goody Glover, reputedly an Irish-speaking woman convicted of witchcraft in seventeenth-century Boston. While an array of characters steps forward to testify against her, the story loses some of its dramatic effect because the format limits interaction between characters. Only once does Glover herself speak, to curse those who judge and condemn her. Like Titley in his best work, she yields not an inch.

The popular novel, as evidenced by Standún's works, and the literary novel, represented by Titley's, form the two main strands of modern fiction in Irish. Neither is mutually exclusive of the other; each has its own substrands and range of genres. However, in recent years, funding agencies, some publishers, and Oireachtas na Gaeilge through its annual literary competitions have sought to promote the writing of more accessible forms of popular fiction in order to boost reading in Irish, amidst concerns about declining literacy levels. Caoilfhionn Nic Pháidín, co-director of Cois Life, one of the four established publishers of fiction in Irish, has argued against the publication of literary novels for which there is little demand, declaring: 'Má tá rún againn dáiríre an gnáthphobal a chur ag léamh, ní ar an ardlitríocht go príomha ba chóir an bhéim a leagan. Ní mór seánraí nua a shaothrú, ficsean bog, eachtraíocht, agus bleachtaireacht, na cineálacha leabhar is coitianta a léitear in aon teanga' (If we are serious about getting ordinary people reading, the emphasis should not be primarily on highbrow literature. It is necessary to cultivate new genres: light fiction, adventure and detective material, the sorts of books most commonly read in any language).[4] It is too early to assess the long-term results of this strategy. Meanwhile, for writers inclined towards popular fiction and social realism, it remains business as usual. Notable Gaeltacht examples include Kerry's Maidhc Dainín Ó Sé (1942–2013) and Joe Steve Ó Neachtain (1942–2020) from Conamara, personalities not only in their home communities but in the broader Irish-speaking world. Ó Sé and Ó Neachtain, who have published extensively across different genres, share a preference for narrative-driven fiction. Ó Sé published a handful of novels, especially historical and contemporary thrillers set in his native Kerry and in Chicago, where he lived for years, with love, lust, greed, and murder as staple ingredients. His writing style displays more energy in the telling of stories than craftsmanship in framing the narrative or exploring characters' interior lives. Ó Neachtain's style is more carefully honed than that of Ó Sé. In his first novel, *Scread Mhaidne* (Dawn of Day, 2003), a young woman named Sorcha journeys to Conamara and on to England in search of her mother and the truth about her family background. The follow-up novel, *Lámh Láidir* (By Force, 2005), is a multigenerational Conamara tale of high emotions, low deeds, and class and language tensions. Ó Neachtain's storytelling is first rate,

---

[4] Caoilfhionn Nic Pháidín, '"Cén Fáth Nach?"—Ó Chanúint Go Críól', in Róisín Ní Mhianáin (ed.), *Idir Lúibíní. Aistí ar an Léitheoireacht agus ar an Litearthacht* (Baile Átha Cliath: Cois Life, 2003), 129. Regrettably, Cois Life ceased publishing in 2019.

though occasionally predictable. Linguistically, he adopts a procedure that is increasingly common in Irish-language realist writing: to convey authenticity, characters from whom one would not anticipate hearing Irish—foreigners and Irish-born monolingual Anglophones—speak English.

There is a surprising dearth of successful comic novels in Irish, with the enjoyable exception of *Cáibín an Phápa* (The Pope's Old Hat, 1992) by Eoghan Mac Cormaic, which imagines John F. Kennedy, Elvis Presley, and Pope John Paul II roaming around Derry and Donegal. Conversely, romance narratives abound, with novels in which characters' relationships cause them to move abroad noteworthy. Manchán Magan's (1960–) *Bí i nGrá* (Be in Love, 2008) deals with a troubled young woman who flees her native New Hampshire after her lover's death, eventually reaching Ireland and finding herself and happiness there. The journey is in the opposite direction in *Aiséirí* (Resurrection, 2011) and *An Tearmann* (The Sanctuary, 2016) by the Dutch-born and now Brazil-based Alex Hijmans (1975–). In the former novel, Rebekka leaves Holland to live in Galway, where she encounters a visiting Lakota Indian and follows him to North America; in the latter, Eoin, a human rights' activist who has abandoned his pregnant lover in Belfast, becomes entangled in a deadly confrontation between natives and non-indigenous people in Brazil. Hijmans' writings, which include non-fiction and short stories, exemplify the international nature of the contemporary Irish-speaking literary world, as does the work of Finnish-born Panu Petteri Höglund (1966–), whose *Tachtaimis an Grá Sin* (Let's Strangle that Love, 2009) deals with relationships that involve erotic sexual twists in a fictional Finnish town. Höglund expands his range in his more recent novel, *An tSlaivéin* (Slavenia, 2013), a story about a young Scandinavian's travels to a fictional post-Soviet eastern European state.

GAEILGE *NOIR*

The most popular form of light reading in Irish at present is crime fiction. English-born Cathal Ó Sándair (1922–96) holds an honoured place in Irish-language literature due to his prolific output, most notably his *Réics Carló* detective series for young readers, published between the 1950s and the 1970s. Until recently, however, there had been limited new crime fiction. In the last decade, most likely as a result of the moves to encourage popular fiction, the crime novel in Irish has had such a resurgence that one can legitimately speak of a Gaeilge *noir* subgenre, of which there are two distinct strands. First, there are novels with a contemporary Irish setting. The Dublin-born and USA-based Seán O'Connor has produced three instalments of the exploits of Detective Inspector Seán Ruiséal. Geared to adult learners, Pól Ó Muirí's (1965–) Garda Paloma Pettigrew series of short novels is well written and entertaining. T. S. Ó Maoilriain—likely a pen name—has produced *Bean na Ciotóige* (The Left-handed Woman, 2005), a well-constructed and well-paced whodunit, and the poet Liam Ó Muirthile (1950–2018) published a stylish thriller, *Sceon na Mara* (Terror of the Sea, 2010), which features Detective

Inspector Jack Hennessey, a former Kilkenny hurler, and his police team in pursuit of a serial killer.

Women novelists have also made their mark in this area. The established English-language writer Éilís Ní Dhuibhne (1954–) penned commissioned plays in Irish in the mid-1990s before turning to the novel. Her bestselling Gaeltacht murder mystery, *Dúnmharú sa Daingean* (Murder in Dingle, 2000), introduced the amateur sleuth Saoirse Ní Ghallchóir, who returned in *Dún an Airgid* (The Fort of Money, 2008), the title of which refers to a Celtic Tiger-era town, with its glossy veneer and criminal underbelly. By then, however, Ní Dhuibhne had changed tack. Her 2003 novel, *Cailíní Beaga Ghleann na mBláth* (The Little Girls of the Valley of Flowers), which is presented through the lens of an adult recalling her experiences in an Irish-language summer camp, is a companion piece to *The Dancers Dancing* (1999), her English-language novel set in the Gaeltacht. Ní Dhuibhne has since embarked on a series of novels exploring the lives of young people, especially female characters, in Dublin. *Aisling Nó Iníon A* (Aisling or Ms A, 2015) tackles the contentious issue of abortion as a fifteen-year-old girl, raped by a colleague of her pro-life mother, chooses to travel to England for a termination. The novel was timely in light of a string of horrific incidents in Ireland that highlighted not just the question of access to abortion but also the implications of enshrining a pro-life amendment in the Irish Constitution.[5]

Dublin-born Anna Heussaff (1957–) has taken on the mantle of female crime novelist from Ní Dhuibhne, with novels showcasing the crime-solving skills of former journalist Aoife Nic Dhiarmada. *Bás Tobann* (Sudden Death, 2004) and *Buille Marfach* (A Deadly Blow, 2010) are set in west Cork. In *Scáil an Phríosúin* (The Prison Shade, 2015), Aoife visits her daughter in Dublin in the vicinity of Kilmainham Gaol, only to find herself investigating two related murders, one historic, one contemporary. Heussaff's novels are intelligent, well constructed, and enjoyable. The series has the potential to continue and evolve.

The second strand of Gaeilge *noir* plays on distinctive aspects of the Gaelic tradition and includes fictional narratives with diverse historical settings. Seán Ó Dúrois (1960–) recreates the tensions of Victorian-era Belfast and its environs as his Irish-speaking Royal Irish Constabulary detective, William Watters, and his sidekick, Constable Cameron, follow the trails of blood and leads in *Crann Smola* (Blighted, 2001) and *Rí na gCearrbhach* (King of the Gamblers, 2003). Unfortunately, Ó Dúrois has not built on the foundations of a strong series that challenges simplistic views about language and identity in 1860s Ulster. The most notable one-off crime novel in this strand is Proinsias Mac a' Bhaird's (1973–) *Rún an Bhonnáin* (The Secret of the Bittern, 2010), which is about a killer, motivated by a secret linked to an eighteenth-century poet, who is murdering *sean-nós* (old-style) singers: in it, the worlds of Dan Brown, the master of cults, and Seosamh Ó hÉanaigh, the master *sean-nós* performer, collide. *Rún an Bhonnáin* is an entertaining action-driven read. In addition, it illustrates the potential

---

[5] In May 2018, the Irish electorate voted overwhelmingly to repeal this amendment and to permit legislators to introduce a law regulating access to abortion.

for works by talented writers that marry popular genres, such as the crime novel or thriller, with the Gaelic tradition. In fact, within this Gaeilge *noir* strand, the poet Biddy Jenkinson (1949–) has published two fine collections of tales about the lexicographer Father Patrick S. Dinneen, whose dictionary, first published in 1904, occupies pride of place on most contemporary writers' desks. Jenkinson's Dinneen engages in much play and wordplay as he solves mysteries and crimes in early twentieth-century Ireland.

LITERARY FICTION

Kerry-born Siobhán Ní Shúilleabháin (1928–2013) was the most prominent (verging on the only) female Irish-language novelist in the second half of the twentieth century writing for adults and young readers. *Aistriú* (Move, 2004), a late novel, explored the beginnings of the Gaeltacht colony of Ráth Chairn in County Meath from the perspective of women settling there in the 1930s. Ní Shúilleabháin's daughter, Tina Nic Enrí, is also a writer and has published two novels, a romance and an exploration of the life of a victim of violence. Romance and its complexities are also explored in Éilís Ní Anluain's (1963–) *Filleann Seoirse* (Seoirse Returns, 2011), an unusual version of the *ménage à trois*, told from the perspective of the woman involved. But despite these writers' contribution, and that of Ní Dhuibhne and Heussaff, the conundrum of the absence of sizeable numbers of women novelists writing for adult readers persists. Accordingly, the literary novel in Irish remains largely the domain of men.

This form has long held special status within the Irish-reading community, reflecting the influence and interests of a literary class who were and are products of, and in some instances academic employees in, Irish third-level institutions. Recently, however, there are signs that practitioners of literary fiction are on the defensive as a consequence of the push to publish lighter fare. Certainly, as Máirín Nic Eoin has noted, there is evidence of a growing divergence between, on one side, 'an art literature…whose core audience is highly educated and academic' and, on the other, popular fiction 'directed at a larger, younger and less academic audience'.[6] Some Gaeltacht writers have sought to straddle this divide, notably Diarmaid Ó Gráinne (1950–2013) and Pádraic Breathnach (1942–). Breathnach returns to childhood, the scene of many of his best short stories, in his first novel, *Gróga Cloch* (Heaps of Stones, 1990), while another rite of passage, retirement, is the subject of his *Deargadaoil i mBád fó Thoinn* (Beetles in a Submarine, 2012), in which a university lecturer bids a not-so-fond adieu to colleagues. Ó Gráinne's early novels, *Brionglóidí Briste* (Broken Dreams, 1991) and *An Traimp* (The Tramp, 1991), contain a large autobiographical component; more recently, he broke new ground by presenting a Conamara family's struggle through the eyes of a female character in *Muintir na Coille*

---

[6] Máirín Nic Eoin, 'Contemporary Prose and Drama in Irish: 1940–2000', in Margaret Kelleher and Philip O'Leary (eds), *The Cambridge History of Irish Literature, Volume 2: 1890–2000* (Cambridge: Cambridge University Press, 2006), 298.

(The People of the Forest, 2011). But to evaluate the significance of a more overt Gaeltacht literary strand we must turn to the fiction of Micheál Ó Conghaile (1962–), Beairtle Ó Conaire (1939–), and Pádraig Ó Cíobháin (1951–).

A Conamara native, Ó Conghaile has played a pivotal role in contemporary Irish-language literature as an accomplished short story writer and, especially, as a publisher since 1985, the year in which he founded Cló Iar-Chonnacht, the main Gaeltacht-based publishing company. His one novel to date, *Sna Fir* (Manhood, 1999), is a *Bildungsroman* about a young Conamara man, John Paul Mac Donncha, as he comes to terms with his homosexuality. The novel treats sensitively Mac Donncha's emotional and psychological journey from the closet into the open, although the book's explicit descriptions of his sexual exploits in Dublin and London likely made some readers uncomfortable. Indeed, this unsettling element continues in *Seachrán Jeaic Sheáin Johnny* (Jeaic Sheáin Johnny's Delusion, 2002), his novella about an elderly *sean-nós* singer and his obsession with a young girl. The lines between reality and fantasy in Jeaic's rambling mind are blurred. It may be no more than Jeaic confusing the present with the past, when the girl's grandmother abandoned him at the altar, but the portrayal of the sexual encounter between him and the young woman is disturbingly realistic. As with Ó Conghaile's work in general, the writing is first-rate, as is his skill in handling references to folksongs and storytelling devices that reflect Jeaic's cultural currency. One of Ó Conghaile's gifts is his mastery of different registers, whether it is *cruachaint*, the language of an elderly character steeped in his community, or the linguistic hybridity of young Gaeltacht men such as John Paul's peers in *Sna Fir*.

Beairtle Ó Conaire, who belongs to an older Conamara generation than Ó Conghaile, has also demonstrated a strong command of language in *Fonn na Fola* (Desire of the Blood, 2005) and *Iad Seo Nach bhFaca* (Those Who Did Not See, 2010). The respective settings of these novels are distinctive: a nursing home in Scotland where a Conamara man spends his last days, and Conamara itself, to which Aibhistín and his family have returned to live after years away, and where he meets an old school friend who never left home. In both books, the tone is introspective and the action is secondary to the exploration of character and motives as the main figures contemplate and revisit the choices they made and the subsequent direction of their lives.

Kerry-born Pádraig Ó Cíobháin is the foremost contemporary exponent of an 'art literature', having ambitiously declared his mission to be 'Mo stampa eitneach féin d'fhágaint ar dhán litearadh na cruinne' (To leave my own ethnic stamp on the literary art of the world).[7] Although relatively late in publishing his first book in 1991 at the age of forty, Ó Cíobháin proved to be prolific over the next fifteen years, during which time he often alternated between issuing a novel and a short story collection. To date, he has published five novels and a novella. *An Gealas i Lár na Léithe* (Brightness in the Midst of Greyness, 1992), his first novel, is an enjoyable *Bildungsroman* and fictional autobiography modelled on James Joyce's (1882–1941) *Portrait of the Artist as a Young Man* (1916). The unnamed narrator, an aspiring writer who shares a family name with the author,

---

[7] Aifric Mac Aodha, 'Ní hAnsa. Pádraig Ó Cíobháin Faoi Agallamh', *Comhar* 71, no. 4 (2011), 15.

recreates his youth in the Kerry Gaeltacht, his years at boarding school in Anglophone Killarney, and formative romantic and sexual experiences. At the core of the text are the various forms of *ealaín* (art) that the narrator encounters—including that of his stone-mason grandfather—as he progresses towards 'ealaín na bhfocal' (the art of words).[8] The stonework image and metaphor recur throughout Ó Cíobháin's writing. The apprentice learns his craft from the master before striking out on his own.

Ó Cíobháin's Irish is rooted in the language of his home community, augmented by his reading of older literary texts, modern literary and critical lexicons, and linguistic borrowings. Just as he moved away physically from Kerry, Ó Cíobháin has shifted thematically from lightly disguised portrayals of that community to challenging philosophical discussions of life and in-depth character portrayals. His second novel, *Desiderius a Dó* (Desiderius Two, 1995), which borrows its title from a translation of a Spanish Counter-Reformation text, provided a template for his subsequent works. It charts the emotional relationship between Cork university students Peadar and Súsan, including their time together in London, their decision to separate, which leads Peadar on a spiritual quest to a monastery in France, and their apparent reconciliation. On such a slight narrative framework Ó Cíobháin hangs weighty contemplations on love, relationships, and the search for an understanding of life. In *Ar Gach Maoilinn Tá Síocháin* (There is Peace on Every Hillock, 1998), characters either demur to personal circumstances and societal expectations or rebel against them. *Faightear Gach Laoch in Aisce* (Age Conquers All, 2001) has parallel narratives about the heroic, one set in contemporary Ireland, the other in medieval Spain. *Ré an Charbaid* (Chariot-course, 2003) is nominally a Galway campus novel.

Each of these works is a self-reflexive literary construct in which Ó Cíobháin—like the stonemason—builds his text layer upon layer: a skeleton plot, a dash of drama, bouts of character introspection, intertexual reworkings of Irish myth and folktales, references to world literature, and authorial interjections. Central to this writing style are Ó Cíobháin's rejection of realist conventions and his invitation to the reader to participate in a circuitous narrative experience. Ó Cíobháin has been relentless in his vision of the role of the artist and he is equally demanding of his readers. However, in light of the absence of a new novel for more than a decade, the publication in 2014 of *Novella Eile* (Another Novella), an early work that captures the lives, loves, and pastimes of his Kerry community at Christmastide in 1988, as well as the release of previously unpublished short stories in 2015, point to a hiatus in his literary mission and may hint at its winding down. Certainly, it brings us full circle.

Dublin-born Tomás Mac Síomóin (1938–) shares Ó Cíobháin's interest in the novel of ideas, although he provides a more solid dramatic framework for his philosophical musings. A talented writer who has made a genuine contribution to writing in Irish, Mac Síomóin is the most prolific twenty-first-century Irish-language novelist and an unapologetic left-wing voice in the contemporary canon. He was already an established poet when he published *Ag Altóir an Diabhail: Striptease Spioradálta Bheartla B* (At the

---

[8] Pádraig Ó Cíobháin, *An Gealas i Lár na Léithe* (Baile Átha Cliath: Coiscéim, 1992), 310.

Devil's Altar: Beartla B's Spiritual Striptease) in 2003. The novel's format is the first-person confession. Beartla B appears to be a dissident who is warehoused and medicated in a care institution, while a global conglomerate and its local surrogate take over his Gaeltacht community. However, things are not as they seem, as a nameless editor has subsequently 'improved' Beartla B's confession, thereby compelling us to question the authenticity of that which we presumed to be factual. By turns a satire on Celtic Tiger Ireland's preoccupation with material advancement at the expense of the individual and tradition, a send-up of the brave new world of artificial intelligence (specifically, mail-order robotic sex companions), and a parody of the world of letters, *Ag Altóir an Diabhail* has sufficient political bite, narrative flair, and black humour to sustain it.

The retrieved manuscript ploy recurs in *In Inmhe* (Growing Up, 2004), but in contrast to the playfulness and satire of *Ag Altóir an Diabhail* its theme is strangely traditional: the coming of age of an orphan in 1940s Ireland. Mac Síomóin returned to contemporary themes in subsequent works, notably in *An Tionscadal* (The Project, 2007), which won the main Oireachtas literary award. Subtitled 'a fable for the new age', the novel is set in a Catalan mountain village where Irish scientist Daithí Ó Gallchóir discovers a modern Tír na nÓg, whose community does not age. When a subsidiary of the multinational company responsible for the robots in *Ag Altóir an Diabhail* seeks to acquire global rights for the elixir of life, Gallchóir is confronted with a crisis of conscience, forced to choose between his responsibility to the villagers, the pursuit of scientific enquiry, and the potential for untold profits for him and the multinational.

Although as ambitious in concept as *Ag Altóir an Diabhail* and *An Tionscadal*, Mac Síomóin's more recent novels, *Ceallaigh* (The Kellys, 2009) and *An Bhfuil Stacey ag Iompar?* (Is Stacey Pregnant?, 2011), are less successful, perhaps suggesting that the author rushed publication. *Ceallaigh* links the stories of two namesakes, James J. O'Kelly, an Irish journalist (and later an Irish Party MP) who reported on the Cuban war of independence in the 1870s, and Séamas S. Ó Ceallaigh, a fictional journalist dispatched to Cuba by an American newspaper to report on contemporary events. Mac Síomóin skilfully interweaves their respective experiences, although his refusal to disguise his political support for the Castros and their Cuban revolution mars the novel as it edges towards propaganda. A dystopian futuristic work set in the Ireland of 2517, *An Bhfuil Stacey ag Iompar?* repeats the well-worn device of a found manuscript (in this case unearthed and edited by twenty-sixth-century scholars) that casts cold light on the end of the world as we know it in the early twenty-first century, through humankind's failure to engage with issues such as global warming. As civilization collapses, the characters amuse themselves with gossip about a soap opera star who may or may not be pregnant. The satire is pointed, although it is difficult to maintain the outrage over 250 pages.

Having lived in Catalonia for many years, Mac Síomóin best exemplifies the transnational nature of contemporary Irish-language fiction, as evidenced by his series of short historical novels, published under the heading *Gaeil i gCéin* (Gaels Abroad) in dual-language (Irish and Spanish) format, about the exploits of Irish adventurers in the Spanish-speaking world. In this respect he is heir to Pádraic Ó Conaire (1882–1928), the most important Irish-language writer of the Gaelic Revival, who lived and wrote in

London between 1899 and 1914. Like Ó Conaire, Mac Síomóin has done his best writing outside Ireland, suggesting that, far from being an obstacle to creativity, distance from homeland may well provide the stimulus and freedom to write one's heart out.

Pádraig Ó Siadhail (1957–), a Derry-born academic who lives in Nova Scotia (and the author of this chapter), has also contributed to the contemporary Irish-language novel, especially in its transnational guise. His second novel, *Éagnairc* (Requiem, 1994), uses the Bloody Sunday killings in Derry in 1972 as a starting point for an exploration of how the Troubles affect two childhood friends and the different paths they follow. The novel also examines the political alienation of some nationalists in Northern Ireland from their counterparts in the Republic. Unsurprisingly, due to his time abroad, Ó Siadhail's fiction has increasingly focused on diasporic themes. *Peaca an tSinsir* (Original Sin, 1996) satirizes North American political correctness and obsession with family roots. Forced into early retirement from his university position in western Canada following allegations of sexual impropriety, a professor's unhealthy fascination with historical death penalty cases, including that of his Irish grandfather, results in predictably dire consequences. *Beirt Bhan Mhisniúla* (Two Brave Women, 2011) recreates the friendship in London between Pádraic Ó Conaire and Canadian Katherine Hughes. Taking its title from an Ó Conaire short story, Ó Siadhail constructs his novel around the few known facts about the Ó Conaire–Hughes relationship, as well as drawing on his research into Hughes's high-flying public and literary career in pre-suffrage Canada and her political transformation from self-styled Canadian imperialist to Irish republican.

Liam Prút, Ciarán Ó Coigligh (1952–), and the late Seán Ó Siadhail (1950–2006) have contributed to the literary novel across different genres. However, as with that strand of crime fiction that specifically draws on Irish-language literature and culture, several literary novels merit mention for successfully tapping into the same resource. Lorcán S. Ó Treasaigh (1957–) has explored the world of the Dublin-born Irish speaker in the allegorical *Bás san Oirthear* (Death in the East, 1992) and, in a more realistic vein, in *Céard é English?* (What's English?, 2002), a fictional autobiography that predated Hugo Hamilton's (1953–) English-language expositions of the reputed horrors of a Dublin Irish-speaking upbringing in *The Speckled People* (2003) and *The Sailor in the Wardrobe* (2006). Notable Irish-language texts provide the inspiration for both Antain Mac Lochlainn's (1965–) *Ruball an Éin* (The Bird's Tail, 2005) and Dáibhí Ó Cróinín's (1954–) *An Cúigiú Díochlaonadh* (The Fifth Declension, 1994). Mac Lochlainn rises to the challenge of completing Seosamh Mac Grianna's (1900–90) abandoned political novel of 1930s Ireland, *Dá mBíodh Ruball ar an Éan* (If the Bird had a Tail, 1940), while Ó Cróinín presents a surreal twist to the long-established autobiographical genre in Irish that dates back to Tomás Ó Criomhthain's (1856–1937) *An t-Oileánach* (The Islandman, 1929) in *An Cúigiú Díochlaonadh*, which begins: 'Cuirim romham sa leabhar so scéal mo bháis a insint don phobal' (I propose to tell the public in this book the story of my death).[9] But it is *An Béal Bocht*, Myles na Gopaleen's parody of that genre, that provides the novel's true

---

[9] Dáibhí Ó Cróinín, *An Cúigiú Díochlaonadh* (Indreabhán: Cló Iar-Chonnachta, 1994), unpaginated foreword.

reference point. Echoing the satire aimed at Gaelic elites in *An Béal Bocht*, *An Cúigiú Díochlaonadh*'s narrator awakens, after his murder by a fellow robber, to encounter the Gaelic establishment in a hellish otherworld. The satire lacks force at times, but Ó Croinín's book, with its anti-hero, its energetic folkloric narrative style, and, especially, its fantastical otherworld atmosphere, fits into the magic realist tradition more commonly found in the short story in Irish, especially works by Micheál Ó Conghaile. That shift from realistic to fantastical setting also anticipates Robert Welch's (1947–2013) *noir* novel, *Tearmann* (Refuge, 1997), and Daithí Ó Muirí's (1977–) anti-story, *Ré* (Era, 2012), in which characters find themselves in otherworlds of sorts.

HISTORICAL FICTION

If the crime novel currently reigns supreme amongst popular Irish-language fiction, the historical novel has emerged as literary fiction's primary genre. The 1960s was an earlier high point for the genre, but the 1970s and 1980s saw a dramatic fall-off, with a mere three historical novels being published in this period.[10] It was Alan Titley's aforementioned 1993 novel, *An Fear Dána*, that signalled renewed interest in the genre. In the years since then, the corpus of quality novels featuring historical characters or set in the past has increased steadily. Unsurprisingly, the twists and turns of Irish history provide the main creative stimulus. For authors, there is an attraction to historical fiction beyond the challenge of seamlessly blending factual and invented detail. Readers' familiarity with the subject matter also plays a part, as does, in some cases, the opportunity to treat a topic from the perspective of the Gaelic world at a time when Irish was still spoken widely. A common narrative device is that of the rediscovered eyewitness account that conveys a sense of historical authenticity and permits the author to play with older registers or dialects. Apart from Ó Doibhlin's *Sliocht ar Thír na Scáth*, prime examples of such work include Colm Mac Confhaola's *Ceol an Phíobaire* (The Piper's Music, 1997), set during the 1798 United Irish rebellion in Wexford, and *Cogadh 'gus Cathú* (War and Conflict, 2002), which centres on Cromwell's Irish sojourn in 1649. Both novels are full of drama, romance, violence, and a cast of real and fictional characters.

A number of works focus on fictional characters in a historical setting or on the fictional recreation of historical lives. *Hula Hul* (2007) by Seán Mac Mathúna (1936–), a talented short story writer in Irish and English, is set at the tail end of the Irish Civil War and features an anti-Treaty officer escorting a prisoner through the back roads of Kerry to avoid Free State patrols. While the book's title, which is a fox-hunting call, is a metaphor for the fratricidal war, the emphasis is on the personal and one couple's happy ending.

---

[10] Breandán Delap, *Úrscéalta Stairiúla na Gaeilge* (Baile Átha Cliath: An Clóchomhar Tta., 1993), 127. The most noteworthy of these is Aodh Ó Canainn's *Léine Ghorm* (Blue Shirt, 1984), which explores post-partition Ireland and Irish links with the Spanish Civil War through the story of a Derryman who samples and ultimately rejects the dogmas and ideologies of the time.

When Máire Mhac an tSaoi (1922–) turned to fiction, she selected as subjects fellow poets Piaras Feiritéar (d. 1652) and Gearóid Iarla FitzGerald (c.1338–98), historical figures who bridged two worlds, Feiritéar linking the Irish and the English in the seventeenth century and FitzGerald the Hiberno-Norman and the Gaelic in the fourteenth. In *A Bhean Óg Ón* (Dear Young Woman, 2001), Feiritéar rescues Meg Russell, about whom he had composed love poems, from her abusive husband in London and returns her to her family. *Scéal Ghearóid Iarla* (The Story of Gearóid Iarla, 2011) recreates the flesh-and-blood eponymous figure rather than the one-dimensional character of Irish folklore, depicting transitional moments in FitzGerald's life, from his being an illegitimate son to his becoming an earl, his messy domestic situation, the occasions of his poetry making, and his violent death as his own illegitimate son's stepfather seeks the earldom for that son. With her richly textured Irish, Mhac an tSaoi skilfully captures each moment and whets the reader's appetite for more.

Liam Ó Muirthile added to his body of prose fiction in 2014 with *An Colm Bán: La Blanche Colombe* (The White Dove). In it, a contemporary Cork writer named William Driscoll—likely the same Driscoll who goes on a journey of recovery and self-discovery after a psychiatric breakdown in Ó Muirthile's *Ar Bhruach na Laoi* (On the Banks of the Lee, 1995)—travels to Paris to research the story of Corkwoman Nóra Buckley, a dancer in the Folies Bergère during the interwar years. We encounter one city, two epochs, two lives, and two voices as Driscoll's first-person narrative alternates with the third-person recreation of Buckley's experiences. Throughout, Ó Muirthile taps his imaginative and linguistic resources to recreate a bygone Paris and its lively nightlife, and to give a strong flavour of the present-day multiracial city. Ultimately, a certain mystery remains about Buckley, with the author speculating that she may have died in a Nazi concentration camp. Nevertheless, *An Colm Bán* is an evocative literary work that spotlights an Irish dimension to the political maelstrom and popular culture of early twentieth-century continental Europe.

The two major historical novels of recent years are Liam Mac Cóil's *Fontenoy* (2005) and Darach Ó Scolaí's *An Cléireach* (The Clerk, 2007). Like Ó Doibhlin's *Sliocht ar Thír na Scáth* and Mac Confhaola's novels, *Fontenoy* and *An Cléireach* are epistolary in form, while being more sophisticated in their goals. *Fontenoy* initially appears a straightforward work, comprising Captain Seán Ó Raghallaigh's first-hand recollections of the 1745 battle between the victorious French, including Ó Raghallaigh's Irish Brigade, and the British and their allies. The Irishman had originally narrated his testimony to a French scribe. However, the latter, none other than Voltaire, is less interested in recording accurately Ó Raghallaigh's experiences than in producing a version that serves his own agenda. Ó Raghallaigh prepares another account, one subsequently 'improved' by a contemporary editor correcting limitations in the text. Consequently, *Fontenoy* becomes a postmodernist exploration of history and historiography, their accuracy, their lacunae, their ownership, and their use and misuse. Amongst the strengths of this multilayered novel are Mac Cóil's weaving together of the competing versions of the narrative and his recreation of eighteenth-century Irish in Ó Raghallaigh's vivid descriptions of a bloody battle and its horrific aftermath.

In *An Cléireach*, Ó Scolaí revisits the drama and trauma of Cromwellian Ireland. The primary narrative device is once again the first-hand account, in this case by Tadhg Ó Dubháin, a clerk and quartermaster in the Confederate Army in 1650. We sample the hardships, the friendships, the tensions, the rivalries, and the petty jealousies amongst comrades in arms, including remnants of the Gaelic literary class, as the Confederate soldiers, increasingly a rabble more than a cohesive unit, retreat in advance of Cromwell's forces. *An Cléireach* concludes with the narrator and his family in exile in continental Europe. But along the retreat route, and central to the novel, members of the Confederate Army camp, rest up, and tell versions of a story about the keeper of a treasured manuscript, 'Saltair an Easpaig' (The Bishop's Psalter). Their versions raise issues about memory construction, the limitation of individual perspectives, personal agendas, and how minor changes in the telling of a story can alter our understanding of history. Thus, *An Cléireach* complements *Fontenoy* in moving beyond mere realistic recreation of a historical event or period to interrogate the notion of history as construct.

Like Titley's *An Fear Dána*, *Fontenoy* is a literary gem, and Mac Cóil has continued to mine Irish history in *An Litir* (The Letter, 2011) and *I dTír Strainséartha* (In a Foreign Land, 2014), the first volumes in a planned trilogy set in 1612. Lúcas Ó Briain, a young Galway scholar, must deliver an important letter to the exiled Hugh O'Neill in Rome, a letter that may determine the future of Gaelic Ireland. *An Litir* sets the scene, ending with Lúcas's dramatic escape from Ireland as an apparent spy nicknamed 'An Sionnach' (the Fox) closes in. *I dTír Strainséartha* depicts Lúcas's travel through England, his deadly encounter with the spy, who turns out to be an ally of sorts, and his safe departure from England, thus preparing the ground for his final adventures. The framing of the novels is excellent, as are *An Litir*'s recreation of seventeenth-century Galway, with its dank taverns, dangerous alleyways, and learned schools, and *I dTír Strainséartha*'s depiction of the covert world of English Catholics in Reformation-era Bristol. The Lúcas Ó Briain series is a prime example of crossover fiction. Its youthful hero and swashbuckling action appeal to both young and adult readerships, and the numerous literary references provide an extra dimension for the initiated. There is a buzz of anticipation about this series not seen in Irish since that period in the 1980s when readers awaited the sequel to Séamas Mac Annaidh's *Cuaifeach Mo Londubh Buí*.[11]

EXPERIMENTAL IRISH-LANGUAGE FICTION

Undoubtedly, Mac Annaidh's trilogy paved the way for other postmodernist novels, chief among them the aforementioned *Kinderszenen*, central to which is the issue of authorship. The name Robert Schumann is a pseudonym, borrowed from the

---

[11] *Bealach na Spáinneach* (The Way of the Spaniards), the final volume in Mac Cóil's trilogy, was published in 2019.

nineteenth-century German composer of 'Kinderszenen', a series of thirteen pieces for piano. With its short scenes, the novel mirrors both the structure of Schumann's composition and elements of the composer's life, one marked by mental illness and eventual institutionalization. The novel charts the story of multiple generations within a family, with the youngest member undergoing a course of medication and treatment in a psychiatric hospital. The fragmentary narrative captures the patient's mental state, while also emphasizing the novel's rejection of realist story-telling conventions and its refusal to concede the premise of authorial control or even to countenance the existence of fact over fiction. Explicit in all of this is the agency of the reader to fill in the gaps between the fragments.

Similarities abound between *Kinderszenen* and Liam Mac Cóil's *An Dochtúir Áthas* (Doctor Joy, 1994), the introduction to which sets the scene: the referral of the unnamed narrator by his doctor to a psychoanalyst for treatment for an undisclosed illness. However, the closing sentence of the introduction—'Ba mar sin a thosaigh an scéal seo; más scéal é' (That's how this story started; if it is a story)[12]—signals that the narrator is recalling his unusual encounters with one Séamas Áthas MD and, in the process, subverting the reader's expectations of social realism. We learn little about the external lives of the narrator or Áthas. Instead, bookended by 'An Chéad Seisiún' (The First Session) and 'An Seisiún Deireanach' (The Final Session), we embark on a strange journey without a clear destination, in which physical Dublin landmarks may be familiar but where little else is easily recognizable or decipherable. Along the way, there is much intellectual, literary, and linguistic playfulness, including an exquisite parody of the Freudian theory of penis envy. In the final psychoanalysis, *An Dochtúir Áthas* is less about the destination than the journey, less about the story than its telling, and not so much a literary whodunit as a psychological whodunwhat.

The latest of these well-written and impressive experimental texts, Colm Breathnach's *Con Trick 'An Bhalla Bháin'*, declares its intent with an introductory extract from Barthes's landmark 1968 essay, 'The Death of the Author'. Ostensibly a story about a writer and the novel he is working on, *Con Trick* is in fact a self-styled metafictional novel fully stocked with postmodernist self-reflexive devices that emphasize the reader's centrality and agency. But the book's significance lies less in what it is or does than in the fact that the Irish-reading public has not responded to it. In the early 1980s, Mac Annaidh's *Cuaifeach Mo Londubh Buí* struck a chord not solely for its artistic strengths but because it coincided with a realization that Irish-language fiction must escape the shackles of social realism to prosper. Almost forty years later, and irrespective of its liter-ary merit, *Con Trick* is evidently out of step with the current direction of that fiction and the interests of a large part of the Irish-reading community.

There have been almost as many Irish-language novels published in the last quarter century as in the previous 100 years. It takes dedicated effort to keep abreast of these works; equally, it has never been easier to choose to read that fiction, whether in

---

[12] Liam Mac Cóil, *An Dochtúir Áthas* (Indreabhán: Leabhar Breac, 1994), 7.

traditional or electronic format. These developments are genuine causes for celebration. Of course, the overall standard of contemporary fiction is uneven, with a limited number of excellent novels, many more of modest value, and not a few poor ones. For native Irish speakers, the decision to write in their first language may be an obvious one; it is less so for secondary bilinguals. For all, writing in Irish is an act of faith in the language and in its future. A strength of Irish-language fiction since the 1980s has been writers' freedom to experiment, largely independent of trends and practices in mainstream publishing. This can also become a weakness, insofar as writers may self-indulge rather than serve their readers. This raises a question central to the future of the novel in Irish: for whom are the writers writing and the publishers publishing? There is no simple answer to this complex question. Nevertheless, recent developments—the increased emphasis on popular fare, the publication of literary works that not only challenge but entertain, and the continuing commitment of talented writers such as Alan Titley, Liam Mac Cóil, Tomás Mac Síomóin, and Anna Heussaff—place the Irish-language novel on as tentatively secure a footing as any lesser-used language can hope to be in order to cater to its diverse readership.

Further Reading

de Brún, Sorcha. '"Sinne Laochra Fáil": Heroism and Heroes in the Work of Pádraig Ó Cíobháin'. In Sandrine Brisset and Noreen Doody (eds), *Voicing Dissent: New Perspectives in Irish Criticism*. Dublin: Irish Academic Press, 2012: 226–40.

Doherty, Ronan, Brian Ó Conchubhair, and Philip O'Leary, (eds). *Úrscéalta na Gaeilge*. Indreabhán: Cló Iar-Chonnacht, 2017.

Keefe, Joan Trodden. 'Dwelling in Impossibility: Contemporary Irish Gaelic Literature and Séamas Mac Annaidh'. *World Literature Today* 63, no. 1 (1989): 46–51.

McCann, Anthony. '"Ar Lorg na Gaoithe": The Impossibility of Translating Séamas Mac Annaidh's *Cuaifeach Mo Londubh Buí* into English'. In Patricia A. Lynch, Joachim Fischer, and Brian Coates (eds), *Back to the Present, Forward to the Past: Irish Writing and History since 1798, Volume 2*. Amsterdam: Rodopi, 2006: 175–86.

Ní Dhonnchadha, Aisling and Máirín Nic Eoin. 'Ar an gCoigríoch: Migration and Identity in Twentieth-Century and Contemporary Irish-Language Literature'. *Irish Review* 44 (2012): 60–74.

Nic Eoin, Máirín. 'Contemporary Prose and Drama in Irish: 1940–2000'. In Margaret Kelleher and Philip O'Leary (eds), *The Cambridge History of Irish Literature, Volume 2: 1890–2000*. Cambridge: Cambridge University Press, 2006: 270–316.

Nic Eoin, Máirín. 'Prose Writing in Irish Today'. In Caoilfhionn Nic Pháidín and Seán Ó Cearnaigh (eds), *A New View of the Irish Language*. Dublin: Cois Life, 2008: 131–9.

Nic Eoin, Máirín. 'Interdisciplinary Perspectives on Transnational Irish-Language Writing'. *Breac: A Digital Journal of Irish Studies*, 12 April 2013.

Ó Conchubhair, Brian. 'The Novel in Irish Since 1950: From National Narrative to Counter-Narrative'. *The Yearbook of English Studies* 35 (2005): 212–31.

O'Leary, Philip. 'Teanga gan Teorainn: The Novels of Alan Titley'. In Brian Ó Conchubhair (ed.), *Why Irish? Irish Language and Literature in Academia*. Galway: Arlen House, 2008: 91–130.

Ó Siadhail, Pádraig. '"Beidh sé Crap": Bilingualism and Pidginisation in Éilís Ní Dhuibhne's Irish Language Writings'. In Rebecca Pelan (ed.), *Éilís Ní Dhuibhne: Perspectives*. Galway: Arlen House, 2009: 197–219.

Ó Siadhail, Pádraig. 'Odd Man Out: Micheál Ó Conghaile and Contemporary Irish Language Queer Prose'. *Canadian Journal of Irish Studies* 36, no. 1 (2010): 143–61.

Titley, Alan. *An tÚrscéal Gaeilge*. Baile Átha Cliath: An Clóchomhar Teoranta, 1991.

Titley, Alan. 'The Irish Prose of the Twentieth Century'. In *Nailing Theses: Selected Essays*. Belfast: Lagan Press, 2011: 218–40.

Titley, Alan. 'The Novel in Irish'. In *Nailing Theses: Selected Essays*. Belfast: Lagan Press, 2011: 300–17.

CHAPTER 34

··

POST-MILLENNIAL IRISH FICTION

··

SUSAN CAHILL

THIS chapter explores the ways in which Irish fiction has engaged with some of the defining developments in the Republic of Ireland since the turn of the millennium, pre-eminently the transition from a period of transformative growth—the socio-economic phenomenon known as the Celtic Tiger, which lasted from approximately 1994 to 2008—to one of economic collapse and recession. The opening years of the twenty-first century were characterized by a still-vibrant economic climate and the ongoing absorption of the effects of the far-reaching changes ushered in by the 1990s. Then, with alarming suddenness, the ground shifted under the seismic impact of the 2008 financial crisis, which triggered a severe recession, during which the Republic was forced to surrender its economic sovereignty as part of an International Monetary Fund-led bailout programme. The imaginative responses of Irish novelists to this crisis took different forms, from Claire Kilroy's (1973–) satirical take on the property boom in *The Devil I Know* (2012), to Donal Ryan's (1977–) affecting account of the effects of the recession on rural Irish psyches in *The Spinning Heart* (2012), to Paul Murray's (1975–) dark critique of free market capitalism in *The Mark and the Void* (2015). The period under discussion also saw the inauguration of the Ireland Chair of Poetry in 1998, the appointment of a Children's Laureate in 2010, and the establishment of a Fiction Laureate in 2015, developments that displayed a coming of age and a confidence in the public value and significance of Irish writing.

Claims that a new fictional renaissance was afoot were heard in many quarters during these years, with accolades and awards being heaped on audacious debut novels, notably Kevin Barry's (1969–) *City of Bohane* (2011), Eimear MacBride's (1976–) *A Girl is a Half-formed Thing* (2013), Lisa McInerney's (1981–) *The Glorious Heresies* (2015), Sara Baume's (1984–) *Spill Simmer Falter Wither* (2015), and Sally Rooney's (1991–) *Conversations with Friends* (2017). These and other talents were nurtured by independent publishing houses like Tramp Press, New Island Books, and Lilliput Press, and by a plethora of literary journals launched in the midst of economic austerity, *Banshee*, *The Bohemyth*, *The Moth*, and *The Penny Dreadful* among them. The recession that laid waste to so much that had been accumulated during the years of growth also proved conducive to the emergence and consolidation of a wealth of Irish literary talent.

The following discussion will chart the experiments in form and content that define much of Ireland's recent fiction, as well as the ways in which writers refine and revisit the traditions of the Irish novel. In addition to tracing changes and continuities in the work of established authors such as Anne Enright (1962–), Sebastian Barry (1955–), and Colm Tóibín (1955–), the chapter will examine the formal and thematic choices of the newer generation that has come to prominence since the turn of the century. A good deal of the fiction of the period under discussion addresses the profound changes that Ireland and Irishness have recently experienced, although much women's writing in particular cautions against an uncritical acceptance of the discontinuities that before-and-after narratives imply. Another significant strand is marked by a desire and a readiness to reconsider the defining stories of the Irish nation in ways that register anxieties about memory, history, and narrative itself. Fiction of this period also exhibits a preoccupation with the changes wrought by mobility and migration, and displays an attention to the transformation of the natural landscape that is informed by concerns about environmental protection and sustainable development. Unifying these strands and tendencies is a prevalent desire by contemporary novelists to cultivate a sense of empathetic understanding and humane connection with others as a means of counter-ing the moral indifference and isolationist perspectives of neoliberal ideologies and policies.

One of the key concepts of the millennium was the idea of the new. The opening years of the century revealed an Ireland that, in many ways, was radically different to the country of just twenty years earlier. Here was a changed nation—wealthy, progressive, globalized, increasingly secular—that bore little similarity to the conservative, inward-looking society of previous decades. The period of accelerated growth that began in the mid-1990s coin-cided with, and was partly fuelled by, the rise of the information society, driven by the transformative power of the internet, which revolutionized the personal, social, and work-ing lives of millions across the globe.[1] As has been well rehearsed, the substantial changes to Ireland's economic climate also brought about significant socio-political shifts, such that by the year 2000 there was much evidence to suggest that conservative Catholicism had loosened its stranglehold on the populace.[2] Here was a country that had recently decriminalized homosexuality (1993), legalized divorce (1995), closed the last Magdalene

---

[1] As Gerry Smyth notes, the significant presence of information technology in the Republic's socio-economic landscape has had profound effects on the country's relationship to both information and technology. See his 'Tiger, Theory, Technology: A Meditation on the Development of Modern Irish Cultural Criticism', *Irish Studies Review* 15, no. 2 (2007), 125. See also Claire Lynch, *Cyber Ireland: Text, Image, Culture* (Basingstoke: Palgrave Macmillan, 2014), which details the ways in which this techno-logical revolution has influenced Irish writing.

[2] See, for example, Claire Bracken, *Irish Feminist Futures* (New York: Routledge, 2016), 4–5, Patricia Coughlan, 'Irish Literature and Feminism in Postmodernity', *Hungarian Journal of English and American Studies* 10, nos. 1–2 (2004), 175–202, and Michael Parker, 'Changing History: The Republic and Northern Ireland since 1990', in Scott Brewster and Michael Parker (eds), *Irish Literature since 1990: Diverse Voices* (Manchester: Manchester University Press, 2009), 3–15.

laundry (1996), and elected successive female presidents—Mary Robinson (1990–97) and Mary McAleese (1997–2011)—all of which landmark events suggested profound transformations in relation to issues of gender, sexuality, equality, and diversity.

These decades were also marked by revelations of chronic corruption and abuse perpetrated by the two elites that had dominated Ireland throughout the post-independence period: the Catholic Church and the country's political and financial leaders. Yet despite many state tribunals and official inquiries since the 1990s, the political landscape has remained largely unchanged since 2000 and the Church still dominates schooling and healthcare.[3] Furthermore, the Irish electorate voted in 2004 to remove the automatic entitlement of all those born in Ireland to citizenship at birth, revealing a racism attributable to the Republic having become a net recipient of migrants during the Celtic Tiger era. Thus, narratives of socio-economic progress must be carefully parsed and attention paid to the persistence of deep-rooted prejudices and inequalities that affect ethnic minorities, women's reproductive rights, and expressions of non-normative sexualities and gender identities.

Speaking in 2015 about Ireland's recent literary renaissance, Fiction Laureate Anne Enright commented on how today's writers are writing 'about anything at all, and that includes contemporary Ireland. That fictional sense of "Grand Ireland", which happened in the past and was rural, has gone almost entirely.'[4] She went on to point to 'a confidence in female voices that I haven't seen ever before—a hugely important thing. Traditionally, Irish writing has been about breaking silences. The biggest silence has continued to be about the real lives of women.'[5] Crucially, fiction by women writers in particular has cautioned against taking an overly idealistic view of the socio-economic changes apparent in the new century, especially where women's bodily autonomy is concerned. The Irish Constitution still inscribes women's place within the home and, until the country voted in 2018 to repeal Article 40.3.3 (known as the Eighth Amendment), made it illegal to procure an abortion within the state. Ireland, moreover, lacks a legal definition of consent and has a 1 per cent rate of conviction for cases of rape, making this substantially the lowest rate in the EU.[6]

Fiction by women writers has continued to draw attention to these inequities, none more so than that by Enright herself, whose literary project has been to interrogate the

---

[3] See Claire McGing and Timothy J. White, 'Gender and Electoral Representation in Ireland', *Études Irlandaises* 37, no. 2 (2012), 33–48. According to recent figures, 97 per cent of state-funded primary schools in the Republic are Church-run. Many hospitals are also run by religious orders and state-funded hospitals express a Catholic ethos.

[4] Quoted in Justine Jordan, 'A new Irish literary boom: the post-crash stars of fiction', *Guardian Review*, 17 October 2015.

[5] Ibid.

[6] Hannah McGee, Rebecca Garavan, Mairead de Barra, Joanne Byrne, Ronán Conroy, *The Sexual Abuse and Violence in Ireland (SAVI) Report: A National Study of Irish Experiences, Beliefs and Attitudes Concerning Sexual Violence* (Dublin: Liffey Press in association with Dublin Rape Crisis Centre, 2002); Linda Regan and Liz Kelly, *Rape: Still a Forgotten Issue: Briefing Document for Strengthening the Linkages—Consolidating the European Network Project* (London: London Metropolitan University, 2003), 10.

gendered occlusions of the Irish cultural imaginary, particularly when those gaps and silences relate to the maternal body. Her 2000 novel, *What Are You Like?*, for example, begins with a pregnant woman whose life is deemed less important than that of her unborn twins due to a unilateral decision made by her husband not to treat her brain tumour. Enright's representation of the female body here is a powerful statement about the positioning of woman as vessel and the lack of status accorded to her in the Irish state. It also registers a profound criticism of the Eighth Amendment, in which the right to life of the unborn was legally privileged over that of the mother.[7] *The Pleasure of Eliza Lynch* (2002) also places a pregnant woman's consciousness at the centre of the narrative and combines the tropes of motherhood and migration to speak back to the strident rhetoric that preceded the Irish Citizenship referendum of 2004, which positioned the pregnant migrant body as a threatening presence and as an 'arch manipulator of the nation state'[8] in the eyes of the powerful. The oppression of mothers and children is also one of the governing themes of *The Gathering* (2007), which confronts child sex abuse and the public and private failures to protect the most vulnerable members of society.

Such concern for the silences and the occlusions of historical narratives permeates the fiction produced during the first decade of this century. Indeed, Tara Harney-Mahajan's analysis of Sebastian Barry's work as 'preoccupied with reviving the lost, or deeply unpopular, stories of marginalized figures embedded in Irish history'[9] can be extended to the historical fiction that dominated the early 2000s. Much of this work focused on the years that are the subject of the 'Decade of Commemorations' initiative, the state-sponsored commemorative programme marking the many significant centenaries that fall during the period from 2012 to 2022.[10] Among the most notable works are Roddy Doyle's (1958–) trilogy comprising *A Star Called Henry* (1999), *Oh, Play That Thing* (2004), and *The Dead Republic* (2010), Jamie O'Neill's (1962–) *At Swim, Two Boys* (2001), William Trevor's (1928–2016) *The Story of Lucy Gault* (2002), Sebastian Barry's *A Long Long Way* (2005), Mary Morrissy's (1957–) *The Rising of Bella Casey* (2013), and Lia Mills's *Fallen* (2014). Common to all of these novels is an intense fictional renegotiation of the Republic's founding moments, driven by a desire to recover lost voices, raise awareness of multiple historical perspectives, and generate fresh narratives with which to structure new formulations of nation and identity. Mills's and Morrissy's novels, for example, focus on women's involvement in revolutionary politics in 1916, an aspect that

---

[7] The novel's plot was prescient for the case in which a pregnant woman, who was pronounced dead, was kept on life support despite her family's wishes. See Mary Carolan, 'Open verdict on pregnant woman taken off life support', *Irish Times*, 22 September 2015.

[8] Bracken, *Irish Feminist Futures*, 119. The vote came in the wake of a wave of racist discourse targeting pregnant African women who were accused of taking advantage of the law to remain in Ireland to care for their Irish-born offspring. See Ronit Lentin, 'From Racial State to Racist State: Ireland on the Eve of the Citizenship Referendum', *Variant* 2, no. 20 (2004), 7–8.

[9] Tara Harney-Mahajan, 'Provoking Forgiveness in Sebastian Barry's *The Secret Scripture*', *New Hibernia Review* 16, no. 2 (2012), 54.

[10] See https://www.decadeofcentenaries.com/. Accessed 8 October 2018.

was largely invisible in historical and literary narratives of the Rising until the recent recovery work undertaken by feminist historians and writers.[11]

Such historical fiction is particularly invested in exploring what Tina O'Toole refers to as the 'alterity' of the revolutionary period, which is being re-evaluated as part of 'ongoing critical attempts to trouble…complacent versions of our histories'.[12] O'Neill's *At Swim, Two Boys* aligns homosexual desire with revolutionary politics and posits same-sex love as an alternative nation by having central protagonists Jim and Doyler make a pact to swim to a cluster of rocks off the Dublin coast called the Muglins on Easter Sunday 1916, where they will claim the island for themselves by planting a green flag there. This is the place where they consummate their relationship, thus expressing the need for non-normative sexualities to be cherished equally in the hoped-for new republic. However, the death of Doyler during the fighting of Easter week prefigures the inhospitality of the future nation to such relationships. Barry's *A Long Long Way* also situates itself in the years leading up to the Rising and approaches the moment from another occluded perspective, that of a Catholic Dubliner, Willie Dunne, serving in the British Army during the First World War. Several of his novels (and plays) excavate once-unspoken histories, from *The Whereabouts of Eneas McNulty* (1998) to *The Temporary Gentleman* (2014), whose protagonist is Eneas's brother. The McNulty family also feature in *The Secret Scripture* (2008), which focuses on the life of Rosanne Clear, incarcerated in a mental institution for giving birth to a child out of wedlock, and whose testimony in the novel highlights the traumas enacted on women by the state. Barry's decision to revisit the same family in his novels draws attention to the recursive dynamics of historical legacies at the level of the individual psyche.

The Secret Scripture alternates between the voice of Rosanne and that of her psychiatrist Dr Grene, who attempts to assess her mental state before the imminent closure of the institution. She, meanwhile, secretly writes her life story, hiding the pages in the floorboards, a poignant metaphor for the forgotten stories of women like her. However, Barry also highlights the difficulties inherent in accessing such histories. Rosanne admits her failures of memory and draws attention to her unreliability as narrator, while Dr Grene constructs an alternate narrative from official documents (including testimony from a Catholic priest) which contradicts her version. Dr Grene's attempt to piece together Rosanne's story puts official history in tension with personal memory, and his recognition of the tenuous and dubious nature of official narrative and its relationship to constructs of nation is a concern that is echoed elsewhere in the post-millennial Irish novel:

> I am beginning to wonder strongly what is the nature of history. Is it only memory in decent sentences, and if so, how reliable is it?…And yet I recognise that we live our lives, and even keep our sanity, by the lights of this treachery and this unreliability, just as we build our love of country on these paper words of misapprehension and untruth.[13]

[11] Historical novels set outside the revolutionary period, such as Anne Haverty's *The Far Side of a Kiss* (2000) and Emma Donoghue's *Slammerkin* (2000), *Life Mask* (2004), and *The Sealed Letter* (2008), have also tended to explore women's hidden histories.

[12] Dominic Bryan, Mike Cronin, Tina O'Toole, and Catriona Pennell, 'Ireland's Decade of Commemorations: A Roundtable', *New Hibernia Review* 17, no. 3 (2013), 65–6.

[13] Sebastian Barry, *The Secret Scripture* (London: Faber and Faber, 2008), 293.

Rosanne Clear is not alone in her forgetfulness and fallibility. Mary Morrissy's *The Pretender* (2000), Claire Kilroy's *All Summer* (2003), and Jennifer Johnston's (1930–) *Foolish Mortals* (2007) all revolve around amnesiac protagonists, thus highlighting concerns about the reliability of memory, secrets, and revelations—pervasive themes of the contemporary canon. In the last paragraph of Colm Tóibín's novel about Henry James, *The Master* (2004), James happily walks through his empty house after the departure of his brother's family. The rooms now 'belonged to an unrecoverable past, and would join...all the other rooms from whose windows he had observed the world, so that they could be remembered and captured and held'.[14] The tension here between a past which is 'unrecoverable' and one that can be 'remembered and captured' is a particular preoccupation of the twenty-first-century Irish novel. At the novel's close, James becomes simultaneously a ghost and a historian, haunting his rooms while cataloguing them. Mike McCormack's (1965–) *Solar Bones* (2016) extends this conceit, charting in one sentence the thoughts and memories of its recently dead narrator who has returned to his family home in County Mayo on All Souls' Day, a day for commemorating the dead. As he stands at the kitchen table, narrator Marcus Conway's thoughts range associatively over the major and minor moments of his life, so that the entire novel becomes a patchwork of memories, a life told with its dying breaths, in an attempt to capture the fleeting and the temporary. These and other recent Irish novels accentuate the tentative and provisional nature of representation and the creative potential of memory to release new energies and perspectives that can transform the present.

Several of these works draw attention to their own processes of construction and pose broader philosophical questions about narrative and storytelling. What is an Irish novel? What does an Irish novel do? How does the contemporary novel speak back to the orthodoxies of the past? How does it account for the potentials that can be drawn from recognizing the alterities of the past? Enright's *The Gathering*, for example, is engaged in a sustained conversation with James Joyce's (1882–1941) *Dubliners* (1914), as source, influence, and intertext, and as a means of reimagining the dead and their relationship to the past and the present. As Enright commented in an interview:

> You think of history as what happens after people are dead, but it is the story that is told when there is no one left who remembers, no one there to contradict it. And yet history is something that has to be broken open again and again and retold, even though officially it's something that has stopped. But as we continue, history shifts and changes all the time.[15]

A persistent theme of *The Master* relates to Henry James's moments of inspiration for his novels, the ways in which he curates often painful events and memories into art. However, the novel, which is full of imagery of silence, darkness, and liminality (James is often positioned at windows or at a physical or emotional distance from the action),

---

[14]   Ibid., 359.

[15]   Claire Bracken and Susan Cahill, 'An Interview with Anne Enright', in Claire Bracken and Susan Cahill (eds), *Anne Enright* (Dublin: Irish Academic Press, 2011), 31.

queries easy access to, and representation of, the past. Tóibín shows us the actual erasure of the past—left in charge of her papers, James burns Constance's letters from him and his sister without rereading them, anxious that any intimations of intimacy be effaced—and yet also registers the persistence of its energies. This project of repeatedly returning to and reformulating the narratives that have shaped and constructed contemporary identities is one of the unifying preoccupations of twenty-first-century Irish novelists.

As well as this preoccupation with historical narratives and their undoing, many post-2000 Irish novels stage critiques of the social and cultural changes wrought by the years of rapid economic growth and prosperity. Whereas the dominant mode of earlier engagements with the boom tended toward satire and the comic—particularly evident in Anne Haverty's (1959–) *The Free and Easy* (2006), Éilís Ní Dhuibhne's (1954–) *Fox, Swallow, Scarecrow* (2007), Murray's *Skippy Dies* (2010), Enright's *The Forgotten Waltz* (2011), and Kilroy's *The Devil I Know*—a more melancholy tone was adopted by writers like Donal Ryan and Sara Baume. All of these novelists critique the drive towards commodification and unthinking consumption and the structures of late capitalism that create atomized subjects. As the recession deepened, literature increasingly arraigned neoliberalism and the austerity measures that governed the political sphere.[16]

Ryan's *The Spinning Heart*, arguably the first recession novel, takes a small town in rural Ireland as its setting, mapping the effects of economic collapse and changing demographics on an insular community. The subjects of the novel, such as construction foreman Bobby Mahon, are not the big bankers or developers pilloried in *The Devil I Know*, nor are they the urban elite of *The Free and Easy* and *Fox, Swallow, Scarecrow*. Rather, they are the vulnerable and ordinary members of society whose lives have been profoundly damaged by the downturn. Structured to allow twenty-one different voices to each contribute to the story, the novel evokes a sense of the unconscious of a community, the energies running below the surface of everyday interactions, so that the narrative becomes a medium through which characters express thoughts and emotions that cannot be publicly articulated in their daily lives. The voices operate in an almost confessional mode, collectively comprising an oral history of the boom years and their catastrophic aftermath, while also charting histories of abuse, violence, betrayal, solipsism, and mental illness. These multiple perspectives also highlight a pervasive sense of fracture and alienation, and register the persistence of unreconciled histories. As Jim, a policeman, remarks, 'Madness must come around in ten-year cycles.'[17]

Ryan depicts a community built on misogyny and the repression of emotion, beneath which lies the violence and rage which is registered in the chorus of anguished voices. In one example, a young girl attempts to negotiate the viciousness of the language that surrounds her though a fascination with curse words, illustrating a representational system obsessed with violence. Ryan's novel is a highly ethical meditation on the trickledown consequences of sudden and severe economic disruption. The spinning heart of

---

[16] See Claire Bracken and Tara Harney-Mahajan, 'A Continuum of Irish Women's Writing: Reflections on the Post-Celtic Tiger Era', *Lit: Literature Interpretation Theory* 28, no. 1 (2017), 1–12.

[17] Donal Ryan, *The Spinning Heart* (London: Doubleday Ireland, 2013), 137.

the title becomes a metaphor for the emotional effects that move the community. The titular heart swings, rusting and creaking, on the gate of one of the least likeable characters, Bobby's abusive, murdered father Frank, whose consciousness from beyond the grave is included in the polyphony of voices. Positioned thus, this 'mocking symbol'[18] of the heart, locked in place and aimlessly spinning in repetitive cycles, functions as a comment on the deterioration of this community's compassion. However, the spinning heart also points to the emotional connections between characters and mimics the way the narrative itself spins through the inner thoughts of the various members of a community.

Representations of disordered families, fractious intergenerational relationships, and the fraught positionings of the maternal continue to be dominant concerns in early twenty-first-century fiction. Writing in 2006, Eve Patten noted the contemporary novel's alertness to 'a haunted or traumatized Irish society and deep-seated disturbances in the national psyche. The dysfunctional family, and within it the child—abused, victimized or emotionally stunted—continued to provide staple metaphors of cultural crisis.'[19] This fictional thread has been notably enriched by Eimear McBride's *A Girl is a Half-formed Thing* and *The Lesser Bohemians* (2016), which immerse the reader in the tangled dynamics of sex, power, and victimization, filtered through a pre-articulate, poetic stream-of-consciousness style. Indeed, Jacqueline Rose has hailed McBride as 'the writer of sexual abuse, now recognised as one of the hallmarks of the new century'.[20]

Both novels chart the inner lives of teenage girls, particularly as they become sexually aware and active in ways that are often self-destructive. *A Girl is a Half-formed Thing* is particularly alert to the difficulties of articulation for its young female protagonist in a suffocating patriarchal culture. The unnamed narrator details her experiences of growing up in the rural west of Ireland in the 1980s and 1990s with her excessively religious mother and beloved brother who has been brain damaged due to a tumour that almost killed him as a child. As the novel progresses, we witness the girl's experience of rape by her uncle and the ways in which her sexuality becomes tied up in self-harm and illusory moments of power. More than any other writer, McBride forces the abuse to be articulated, dismantling and restructuring language and representation in order to do so. As she herself explains, in order to 'express a natural, prismatic experience of life through words…language had to work differently. Be broken, reformed, have its grammar mauled and punctuation recalibrated.'[21] Violence is inflicted on both the sentence and the word, and there is an almost complete absence of the connecting comma in favour of the abruptness of the full stop.

The Lesser Bohemians begins in the consciousness of Eily (who is named halfway through the novel), an eighteen-year-old Irish girl in her first year of drama school in London, where she loses her virginity and begins an affair with a much older actor,

---

[18] Ibid., 148.
[19] Eve Patten, 'Contemporary Irish Fiction', in John Wilson Foster (ed.), *The Cambridge Companion to the Irish Novel* (Cambridge: Cambridge University Press, 2006), 259.
[20] Jacqueline Rose, 'From the Inside out', *London Review of Books*, 22 September 2016, 11.
[21] Eimear McBride, 'How I wrote *A Girl is a Half-formed Thing*', *Guardian*, 10 September 2016.

Stephen. London, with its attendant freedoms and promiscuities, stands in contrast to the Ireland of *A Girl is a Half-formed Thing*, and indeed *The Lesser Bohemians* reads in many ways as a counterpoint to its predecessor. As Rose comments, 'One way of reading *The Lesser Bohemians* would be as girl given a second chance',[22] as Eily has also suffered abuse at the hands of an older man known to her family and yet finds a way through the damage to embark on a complicated and messy (but all the more real for this) relationship with Stephen, abused by his own mother and separated from his daughter, who is the same age as Eily. If the home and the family are metaphors of nation, McBride's work is a damning portrait of the sexual health of both Ireland and Britain.

What is remarkable about the novel is its powerful drive towards forgiveness and its celebration of sex and love, even in the wake of destructive experiences. The bond that develops between Eily and Stephen is damaged and damaging, yet it is also expansive and restorative. Characters' names are revealed once Stephen has told Eily his seventy-page-long life story, in a move that insists on the articulation of abuse and the intimacy that shared stories bring. With this, the style begins to knit itself back together. Contrast the novel's last sentence—'I take one last look at him there against the evening sky then go naked to him, open to him, full of life'—with its opening lines: 'I move. Cars move. Stock, it bends light. City opening itself behind. Here's to be for its life is the bite and would be start of mine'.[23] The novel's style is also notable for the unparalleled ways it captures the dynamics of heterosexuality from the perspective of a young girl encountering and growing into desire, then experiencing the intense physicalities and affects of sexual activity, as what is happening to her body and the language of her inner world inform and stimulate each other.

Irish recessionary fiction is vibrant both in the wealth of its production and its stylistic innovation. While Patten could claim in 2006 that contemporary Irish fiction remained 'formally conservative' with a 'prevalent social realism', the same cannot be said for more recent literary debuts.[24] Indeed, the Goldsmiths Prize, established in 2013 to 'reward fiction that breaks the mould or extends the possibilities of the novel form',[25] was awarded to Irish writers in three of its first four years (Eimear McBride in 2013, Kevin Barry in 2015, and Mike McCormack in 2016). Barry's prose is an anarchic demotic, described by one reviewer as a 'formidable pastiche of Irish slang mixed with perhaps a reggae-meets-"chav" spin on what is a ghetto-gypsy-globalized patter',[26] whereas McCormack's *Solar Bones* is composed of one unbroken sentence, of which the novelist himself remarked: 'It seemed obvious to me…that the prose would proceed as a continuous outpour because that is the way a ghost would think…continuous, never stopping for fear that, as a ghost, he might dissipate or falter'.[27] These and other contemporary Irish novelists are interested

---

[22] Rose, 'From the Inside out', 11.

[23] Eimear McBride, *The Lesser Bohemians* (London: Faber and Faber, 2016), 312, 3.

[24] Patten, 'Contemporary Irish Fiction', 259.

[25] See https://www.gold.ac.uk/goldsmiths-prize/about/. Accessed 9 October 2018.

[26] John L. Murphy, review of *City of Bohane*, *Estudios Irlandeses* 7 (2012), 194.

[27] Derek Flynn, '"A Stream of Post-Consciousness": Mike McCormack on *Solar Bones*', *writing.ie*, 1 September 2016.

in immersive experiences, in breaking boundaries between the reader and the consciousness of the novel in order to enhance compassionate understanding. As McBride observes of her writing in *A Girl is a Half-formed Thing*, 'I didn't want the reader to feel separate from her or in a position to pass judgment on her actions. I wanted them to feel they *were* her, and that what was happening to her, and inside her, was also happening within themselves.'[28] Similarly, Sara Baume's *Spill Simmer Falter Wither* and *A Line Made by Walking* (2017) make us privy to the inner conversations that the narrators have with themselves, as does Caitriona Lally's *Eggshells* (2015) and Claire-Louise Bennett's linked short story collection, *Pond* (2015), whose first-person narrators share an eccentricity of voice. The immersive quality of the stylistic techniques of thought associations, broken syntax, and stream-of-consciousness narration all speak to a desire to create empathetic connections in contemporary Irish fiction that runs counter to the isolationist imperatives of neoliberalism. We are asked to spend time in other people's heads, in other people's lives, and engage with them humanely because of this extended exposure to their thoughts and emotions.

This desire for empathetic connection also expresses itself through writers' affinity for what Lally identifies as 'oddball narrators…, outsiders who don't fit into boom-time society and who remain alienated during the bust', whom she links to 'a pervading sense of loneliness and alienation from society, which is heightened by the growing gap between rich and poor, the haves and have nots. There is also a sense of foreboding; as readers, we fear for these misfits who are vulnerable in their solitariness, without the back-up of a group.'[29] Lally cites as examples Ray in *Spill Simmer Falter Wither*, Johnsey in Donal Ryan's *The Thing About December* (2013) (and we could also include several of the narrative voices in *The Spinning Heart*), as well as Vivian in her own *Eggshells*, a woman who believes herself to be a changeling and who spends her days attempting to cross over into the otherworld. Many of these eccentric narrators, moreover, share mental health difficulties; Frankie in *A Line Made by Walking*, for instance, experiences a breakdown in Dublin and moves into her dead grandmother's house in the country, where her recovery is never quite effected. The ubiquity of such marginalized loners can be read as symptomatic of a pervasive sense of disconnection from the public performances of life and a resigned estrangement from traditional sources of institutional power and authority in twenty-first-century Ireland.

The dominant mode of these novels tends towards explicit critique of the neoliberal policies governing the Irish economic and political sphere, while also registering anxieties about the efficacy of literature to counter such forces in a climate in which art has become increasingly commodified. Haverty's *The Free and Easy* and Ní Dhuibhne's *Fox, Swallow, Scarecrow* make this anxiety particularly explicit as they indict the production of art as commodity in the Celtic Tiger years, appealing instead for an ethically engaged artistic practice that would challenge the economic and capitalist ethos of post-millennium Ireland. *Solar Bones* features an artwork composed of texts of court reports

---

[28] McBride, 'How I wrote *A Girl is a Half-formed Thing*'. Original emphasis.
[29] Caitriona Lally, 'The oddball narrators of 21st-century Irish literature', *Town Crier*, 28 August 2015.

written in the artist's own blood, and the novel itself turns the ordinary rituals of a life into art. Similarly, *A Line Made by Walking* meditates on the relationships between conceptual art and small everyday acts.

Other critiques of Celtic Tiger culture choose the teenager as their focal point, such as Murray's *Skippy Dies* and Rob Doyle's *Here Are the Young Men* (2014). Recessionary fiction is no different, with a strong teenage presence in Ryan's *The Spinning Heart* and McInerney's *The Glorious Heresies* and its sequel, *The Blood Miracles* (2017). The satisfaction of individual desire, so indicative of burgeoning teenage subjectivity, readily maps onto a society invested in hyper-consumerism and self-interested neoliberal ideologies, while teenage experience also resonates with the powerlessness and angst that have characterized public responses to successive governments' harsh austerity measures. Additionally, the transitory nature of the teenage years speaks powerfully to a culture undergoing major transformative change. As Alison Waller notes, 'Adolescence is, after all, a less stable and more fluid concept, defined by its "in-between-ness", its transitory position between childhood and adulthood, and its dependence on fleeting popular culture.'[30]

The bravado and vulnerability of the teenager are particularly well wrought in McInerney's novels, which are populated with characters who work outside the systems of power. Social exclusion, alienation, and the legacies of emotional damage are major themes. In *The Glorious Heresies*, Maureen—haunted by her narrowly-escaped fate in a Magdalene laundry, sent to England instead while her parents raise her illegitimate son—reflects on how 'Decisions taken on her behalf forty years ago had anchored her to a moment doomed to repeat itself, over and over', leaving her mired in desolation: '*And shame on you, Ireland, . . . You think you'd at least look after your own?*'[31] McInerney repeatedly shows the ways in which state and society remain indifferent to characters such as Ryan, a teenage drug-dealer who eventually attempts to take his own life. The novel is deeply concerned with legacies that are both familial and national, as shown by Maureen's question when she encounters Ryan about to jump in the River Lee: 'Ah. You're suffering from something inherited, is it?'[32] This focus on troubled adolescence extends to a concern with the impact of a blighted youth on the possibilities of the future, which, of course, the young are poised to inherit.

These teenage protagonists point towards another phenomenon of twenty-first-century Irish fiction: the rise to prominence of fiction aimed at young adults. This trend is evidenced by the success of writers such as Louise O'Neill (1985–), author of *Only Ever Yours* (2014), which centres on a feminist dystopia in which young girls are manufactured to the specifications of a patriarchal culture, and *Asking for It* (2015), which explores contemporary rape culture. Other significant voices in Ireland's burgeoning Young Adult canon include Sarah Crossan (1981–), Paul McVeigh, Sarah Moore Fitzgerald, Moïra Fowley-Doyle, Claire Hennessy (1986–), Sarah Bannan (1978–), Deirdre Sullivan, Elske Rahill (1982–), and

---

[30] Alison Waller, *Constructing Adolescence in Fantastic Realism* (New York: Routledge, 2009), 6.
[31] Lisa McInerney, *The Glorious Heresies* (London: John Murray, 2015), 363. Original italics.
[32] Ibid., 369.

Sheena Wilkinson (1968–), as well as the more established figures of Roddy Doyle and John Boyne (1971–). A dominant concern across representations of the Irish teenager is the effects of harm and neglect on their emotional and psychological development, which often expands to an indictment of the failure of state and society to nurture and accommodate the potential of the young.

Resonating with these depictions of troubled and vulnerable youth, much post-2000 fiction bears witness to the changing realities and effects of emigration, a theme that connects novels such as Colm Tóibín's *Brooklyn* (2009), Colum McCann's (1965–) *Let the Great World Spin* (2009) and *TransAtlantic* (2013), Anne Enright's *The Green Road* (2015), and E. M. Reapy's (1984–) *Red Dirt* (2016). The ways in which migrations come into tension with the legacies of home animate many of these works. For example, the action of *The Green Road* circulates around a Christmas gathering of the Madigan family in 2005, when Rosaleen, the mother, announces that she is going to capitalize on the property boom by selling the family home, much to the dismay of her children. Enright's representation of the house as disjointed and fragmented registers its ambivalent status as both resonant symbol of attachment and marketable commodity: 'It all looked strange and unconnected: the turn of the bannisters at the top of the stairs, the small study with its light bulb gone, the line of damp on the dining room wall paper inching up through a grove of bamboo.'[33] The fragmentation of the family is expressed in the structure of the novel, which is composed of snapshots of the siblings' lives at disparate moments—Hanna in Clare in 1980, Dan in New York in 1991, Constance in Limerick in 1994, Emmet in Mali in 2002.

The Green Road is about empathy and selfishness, and the ways that we fail at compassion, especially within the spaces that generate and shape us, the family and the nation. As Enright has observed, all of the characters 'have a challenge to their compassion.'[34] We see this in Emmet's failure to invite Denholm, his Kenyan flatmate, to Christmas dinner in his mother's house, despite his 'sudden mortification at the fact that he was leaving Denholm alone.'[35] The excuse he silently offers himself—'*I can not invite you home for Christmas because I am Irish and my family is mad*'—masks deeper prejudices that highlight the social exclusion faced by migrants of colour in Ireland: 'It was not a question of colour (though it was also a question of colour).'[36] Denholm's financially dictated lack of mobility contrasts starkly with the ease of movement that the Madigans enjoy.

Recent literature and criticism has also begun to engage with questions of race and ethnicity in the context of Ireland's rapidly changing demographics. Roddy Doyle's short story collection, *The Deportees* (2007), attempted to chart the tensions of race and nation in the new century, although Maureen Reddy rightly points out the problematics of 'Doyle's own positionality—white, Irish, settled, male, economically secure . . .: he is the

---

[33] Anne Enright, *The Green Road* (London: Jonathan Cape, 2015), 13.
[34] Diane Prokop, 'What it is to be alone: *The Millions* interviews Anne Enright', *The Millions*, 21 May 2015.
[35] Enright, *The Green Road*, 211–12.   [36] Ibid., 212.

one ventriloquizing blackness, so to speak'.[37] Sara Martín-Ruiz also cautions against privileging white Irish writers on the subject, arguing that 'while representations of the so-called "New Irish" in fiction...have received widespread media and scholarly attention, it is high time that the literary voices of immigrants themselves are finally heard'.[38] Several of these voices, particularly those of immigrant writers of colour that have emerged in recent years, offer powerful critiques of Ireland's structures of exclusion, such as the inhumanity of Direct Provision, the state's system for processing asylum seekers, which isolates them from mainstream society.[39] Notable examples include three Nigerian-born authors, Melatu Okorie (1975–), who came to Ireland as an asylum seeker in 2006 and whose 2017 short story, 'This Hostel Life', is set in a Direct Provision centre; Ifedinma Dimbo, who has written both short stories and a novel, *She Was Foolish?* (2012), which deals with migration, asylum seekers, and sex work; and Ebun Akpoveta (1970–), whose novel, *Trapped: Prison Without Walls* (2013), is attentive to the difficulties of the female immigrant facing racist discrimination heightened by the 2004 Citizenship referendum, as well as gendered expectations from her home community. Initiatives such as Women Writers in the New Ireland network, founded in University College Dublin in 2007, and the Migrant Writers and Performing Artists Ireland group, initiated in 2010 by Theophilus Ejorh, are important collectives to support the work of migrant authors. Similarly, the annual Intercultural Writing Competition, a collaboration between *Metro Éireann* and Duke University's Kenan Institute of Ethics, aims to foster a new generation of writers. Furthermore, the ways in which new poets are challenging the formal and aesthetic conventions of Irish poetry speaks in exciting ways to the potentials of new Irish fiction.[40]

This emphasis on migration, both inward and outward, leads us to a consideration of place and landscape in twenty-first-century Irish fiction. Landscape in the post-2000 novel frequently functions as a marker of the excesses of the boom years and the losses of the recession. This trend is particularly embodied in the image of the house, which is often depicted in commodified form, as a piece of real estate, as in *The Green Road*, and the so-called 'ghost estate', which features prominently in *The Spinning Heart*. Ghost estates—unfinished housing developments, of which there were almost 3000 by late 2011—are perhaps the most arresting physical manifestations of the Republic's precipitous economic collapse.[41] Home to a few isolated people, these abandoned structures stood as a stark illustration of the devastation wrought by unchecked neoliberal

---

[37] Maureen T. Reddy, 'Reading and Writing Race in Ireland: Roddy Doyle and "Metro Eireann"', *Irish University Review* 35, no. 2 (2005), 386.

[38] Sara Martín-Ruiz, 'Melatu Okorie: An Introduction to her Work and a Conversation with the Author', *Lit: Literature Interpretation Theory* 28, no. 2 (2017), 173.

[39] See Anne Mulhall and Gavan Titley, '"Direct Provision" is a holding pen where people are kept for efficient deportation', *thejournal.ie*, 15 October 2014.

[40] See Alice Feldman and Anne Mulhall, 'Towing the Line: Migrant Women Writers and the Space of Irish Writing', *Éire-Ireland* 47, no. 1 (2012), 201–20.

[41] See Rob Kitchin, Cian O'Callaghan, and Justin Gleeson, 'The New Ruins of Ireland? Unfinished Estates in the Post-Celtic Tiger Era', *International Journal of Urban and Regional Research* 38, no. 3 (2014), 1069–80.

capitalism, embodying both the crises of boom-and-bust economics and the squandered potential of so many ordinary lives. As commentators have noted, these new geographical features, which dotted the post-crash landscape, represented 'the remainder and reminder of Celtic Tiger excess', symbolizing 'a new form of ruin that is not constituted through an abandoned past but rather an abandoned future.... As the ruins of the Celtic Tiger they recast that period as one of "chaotic" excess rather than "rational" progress, while also signifying the ruined future promised by the Celtic Tiger.'[42]

A keen awareness of the devastating environmental as well as social impact of rapid economic expansion since the mid-1990s, followed by abrupt economic contraction, is noticeable in many recent post-crash novels. Kilroy's *The Devil I Know*, for example, takes us back to the sources of this ruination, to the greed and corruption that fuelled the property boom, which is reimagined as a Faustian pact between the hubristic masses and avaricious property developers. The novel articulates the dominant attitude towards land during the Celtic Tiger period through the voice of Hickey, a crooked builder, who gleefully boasts: 'I knew there was treasure buried around here somewhere. I could smell it, so I could. An now I've found it. It was right under me nose all the time. Land. Or what happens to land when a man like me changes it into *property*. I've transformed a heap a muck into gold.'[43]

In critiquing the commercial exploitation of a precious, shared resource, twenty-first-century Irish fiction asks us to reverse Hickey's transformation by turning property back into land. This manifests in two ways: first, in a tendency towards post-apocalyptic depictions of Ireland and its landscapes, and secondly, in an emphasis on attention and slowness. The British writer David Mitchell (1969–), who has been living in Ireland since 2004, set the last of the six parts of *The Bone Clocks* (2014) in a post-apocalyptic west Cork landscape, skilfully refusing a nostalgic return to the land while simultaneously imagining the effects of climate change on rural Ireland in 2043. Kevin Barry's *City of Bohane* is set in a futuristic dystopian city in the west of Ireland in 2053, a place devoid of technology and subject to gangland anarchy. The present is known as 'the lost time', inaccessible to memory and history due to a mysterious and presumably disastrous event. Barry's landscape combines a labyrinthine crumbling city with a malevolent bog, known as the Big Nothin', and a malodorous river known mostly as a suicide location. In this and in his second novel, *Beatlebone* (2015), landscape is almost palpably sentient, animistic, and not friendly.

McCormack's *Solar Bones*, set just before the recession, depicts an Ireland suffering the consequences of a compromised water supply: 'viral infection and contamination, a whole city puking its guts up, the stuff of a B-movie apocalypse seventy miles up the road.'[44] The novel is deeply concerned with citizenship and the imbrications between a

[42] Ibid., 1069, 1076–77. See also Jason Buchanan, 'Ruined Futures: Gentrification as Famine in Post-Celtic Tiger Irish Literature', *Modern Fiction Studies* 63, no. 1 (2017), 50–72.

[43] Claire Kilroy, *The Devil I Know* (London: Faber and Faber, 2013), 142.

[44] Mike McCormack, *Solar Bones* (Dublin: Tramp Press, 2016), 30. This scenario contains an ironic nod to the water charges controversy in the Republic that was a persistent source of public and political concern in the period between 2014 and 2016. See 'The sorry history of Ireland's water charges', *Irish Independent*, 26 April 2016.

human life and the larger civic structures within which that life is built. Marcus Conway is a civil engineer who is as resistant as he can be to the demands of politicians and developers, yet the virus in the water supply—'a virus derived from human waste which lodged in the digestive tract, so that…it was now the case that the citizens were consuming their own shit, the source of their own illness and there was something fatally concentric and self-generating about this'[45]—implicates the entire nation in its destruction. The fact that the only responsible voice belongs to a ghost suggests a bleak future, yet the novel also reveals Marcus to be a narrator whose fears about the precarity of planetary life reach far back into his childhood. Near the beginning of the novel, he recalls his father disassembling a tractor, the sight of which he took as 'proof of a world which was a lot less stable and unified than my childish imagination had held it to be,…the whole construct humming closer to collapse than I had ever suspected'.[46] Forty years later, the sight of a dismantled wind turbine being driven through his town reactivates his existential anxiety, to the point where this dismembered turbine seems to symbolize not only the corpse of environmental sustainability but also that of 'God himself or some essential aspect of him being hauled through our little village on the edge of the world, death or some massive redundancy finally caught up with him'.[47]

Wind turbines also feature prominently in Baume's *A Line Made by Walking*, where they are again linked to themes of impermanence and relativity. The solitary turbine near the bungalow inhabited by artist Frankie reminds her of 'a thing that had been shot down from space',[48] yet she appreciates its aesthetics, seeing it almost as sculpture. In the novel, art and environmentalism become intertwined, as signalled by Baume's title, which refers to a 1967 artwork by Richard Long, which Frankie describes thus:

> A short, straight track worn by footsteps back and forth through an expanse of grass. Long doesn't like to interfere with the landscapes through which he walks, but sometimes he builds sculptures from materials supplied by chance. He specialises in barely-there art. Pieces which take up as little space in the world as possible. And which do little damage.[49]

This brief commentary encapsulates a moral as well as an artistic stance that is endorsed by both the narrator and the author.

A Line Made by Walking and other recent Irish novels stage a counterpoint to the excesses of the affluent years and the austerity politics of the recession by means of a pared-back aesthetics and a sustained interiority, accompanied by an ethical and environmental drive audible in the close attention the narrative voice pays to the landscape and its seasonal transformations. *Spill Simmer Falter Wither* exemplifies this in its characterization of Ray, a lonely middle-aged man living in isolation in a small seaside town with his adopted rescue dog, with whom he converses over the course of a year. Ray's monologue directs the reader's attention to 'the smallest, quietest things. A chewing-gum

---

[45] McCormack, *Solar Bones*, 108.   [46] Ibid., 26.   [47] Ibid., 29.
[48] Sara Baume, *A Line Made by Walking* (Dublin: Tramp Press, 2017), 14.
[49] Ibid., 235.

blob in the perfect shape of a pterodactyl. A two-headed sandeel coiled inside a cockle shell. The sliver of tungsten in every incandescent.'[50] Such imaginative attentiveness forces us to contemplate along with him the minutiae of nature's transformations in a slow, quiet, and non-invasive way, which is pointedly at odds with the reckless disregard for environmental sustainability exhibited by some during the Celtic Tiger era. Through the use of a sustained second-person conversation with dog, landscape, and reader, Baume's novel promotes a kind of affective environmentalism that preaches care and respect for human and nonhuman others alike.

In conclusion, the opening two decades of the twenty-first century have witnessed an extraordinary renaissance in Irish fiction, featuring novels that are stylistically experimental, ethically engaged, and pointed in their social, cultural, and political critiques. Women's writing in particular stands at the forefront of the innovations in the field. Anne Enright's final lecture as Fiction Laureate, before handing over to her successor Sebastian Barry in early 2018, ends on a cautiously hopeful note in this regard:

> They [women writers] are publishing in a time of cultural change, and into a new awareness, one that is fed by social media, acknowledged in print, supported by publishers and encouraged by festival curators. At least I hope they are. I hope we will finally sit side by side—in the newspapers, on the stage, up on the damn poster— men and women together. There is plenty of room.[51]

Enright's appeal for inclusivity and diversity resonates with a predominant concern of the contemporary Irish novel, which is to make room for the marginalized, the silenced, the alienated, and the discriminated against, including those whose voices and experiences have been elided from standard accounts of the nation's past. In carrying out their acts of revision, contemporary novelists are wary of replacing one exclusionary narrative with another, which makes for works of fiction that are informed by a self-reflexive awareness of the provisional nature of representation, be it literary or historical. As the impact of the neoliberal policies that govern the Irish economic and political sphere become ever clearer, much contemporary fiction is aligned with those who seek to resist such policies and the ideologies from which they spring, not least by stimulating empathetic understanding and humane connection with human and nonhuman others. Furthermore, post-millennial Irish fiction sounds a battle cry for the value of art in an increasingly commodified world, and a privileging of a particular type of attention—to the small, the ordinary, the overlooked—which tends to be deeply entwined with an environmental focus. As it moves into the third decade of the new millennium, Irish fiction is committed to an aesthetics of experiment and inclusion, eager to remap the contours of the literary and ecological landscapes, and determined to diversify the narratives of gender, race, and belonging embedded in the Irish cultural imaginary.

---

[50] Sara Baume, *Spill Simmer Falter Wither* (Dublin: Tramp Press, 2015), 43.
[51] Anne Enright, 'Diary', *London Review of Books*, 21 September 2017.

FURTHER READING

Bracken, Claire. *Irish Feminist Futures*. New York: Routledge, 2016.

Bracken, Claire and Tara Harney-Mahajan. 'A Continuum of Irish Women's Writing: Reflections on the Post-Celtic Tiger Era'. *Lit: Literature Interpretation Theory* 28, no. 1 (2017): 1–12.

Bracken, Claire and Tara Harney-Mahajan. 'A Continuum of Irish Women's Writing II: Reflections on the Post-Celtic Tiger Era'. *Lit: Literature Interpretation Theory* 28, no. 2 (2017): 97–114.

Brewster, Scott and Michael Parker (eds). *Irish Literature since 1990: Diverse Voices*. Manchester: Manchester University Press, 2009.

Cahill, Susan. *Irish Literature in the Celtic Tiger Years 1990–2008: Gender, Bodies, Memory*. London: Continuum, 2011.

Cahill, Susan. 'Celtic Tiger Fiction'. In Heather Ingman and Cliona Ó Gallchóir (eds), *A History of Modern Irish Women's Literature*. Cambridge: Cambridge University Press, 2018: 426–44.

Harte, Liam and Michael Parker (eds). *Contemporary Irish Fiction: Themes, Tropes, Theories*. Basingstoke: Macmillan, 2000.

Lehner, Stefanie. *Subaltern Ethics in Contemporary Scottish and Irish Literature: Tracing Counter-Histories*. Basingstoke: Palgrave Macmillan, 2011.

Lynch, Claire. *Cyber Ireland: Text, Image, Culture*. Basingstoke: Palgrave Macmillan, 2014.

McWilliams, Ellen. *Women and Exile in Contemporary Irish Fiction*. Basingstoke: Palgrave Macmillan, 2013.

Meaney, Gerardine. *Gender, Ireland, and Cultural Change*. New York: Routledge, 2010.

Patten, Eve. 'Contemporary Irish Fiction'. In John Wilson Foster (ed.), *The Cambridge Companion to the Irish Novel*. Cambridge: Cambridge University Press, 2006: 259–76.

Pine, Emilie. *The Politics of Irish Memory: Performing Remembrance in Contemporary Irish Culture*. Basingstoke: Palgrave Macmillan, 2010.

Roche, Anthony. 'Introduction: Contemporary Irish Fiction'. *Irish University Review. Special Issue: Contemporary Irish Fiction* 30, no. 1 (2000): vii–xi.

PART X

CRITICAL
EVALUATIONS

CHAPTER 35

....

THE IRISH NOVELIST AS CRITIC AND ANTHOLOGIST

....

EVE PATTEN

In an 'Autobiographical Note' drafted in the 1940s but never published, Elizabeth Bowen (1899–1973) wrote of her literary career: 'I do not really consider myself a critic—I do not think, really, that a novelist *should* be a critic; but, by some sort of irresistible force, criticism seems to come every novelist's way.'[1] Bowen excelled as a critic and her distinguished essays, such as 'Notes on Writing a Novel' (1945) and 'The Bend Back' (1950), combine with her various prefaces, introductions, and reviews to form a substantial audit of both British and Irish literary landscapes in the mid-twentieth century.[2] Propelled by the same 'irresistible force', many other Irish novelists have served as critics of their own craft and tradition. Some, such as Frank O'Connor (1903–66) and Edna O'Brien (1930–), have published full-length scholarly works; others, like John McGahern (1934–2006) and John Banville (1945–), make only occasional forays into literary criticism and non-fiction. A current generation of novelists, meanwhile, continues to cross into the critic's terrain, with John Boyne (1971–), Anne Enright (1962–), Colm Tóibín (1955–), and numerous others serving regularly as international reviewers or professional commentators on contemporary literature.

While modern Irish writers have always engaged in *belle-lettristic* activity and the reviewing of each other's work, they have also cast a critical eye more generally on their own *metier*—the writing of fiction itself. This reflexivity is of particular interest given the troubled history of the novel genre in Ireland, where it has frequently been presented as the 'poor relation' of the national literary family, overshadowed by the luminaries of

---

[1] Quoted in Allan Hepburn, 'Introduction', in Elizabeth Bowen, *People, Places, Things: Essays by Elizabeth Bowen*, ed. Allan Hepburn (Edinburgh: Edinburgh University Press, 2008), 5. Original emphasis.

[2] For these and other Bowen essays, see *The Mulberry Tree: Writings of Elizabeth Bowen*, ed. Hermione Lee (London: Vintage, 1999).

poetry, drama, and the short story. In their critical essays and memoirs, Irish novelists themselves have often written negatively of long-form fiction—and specifically social realist fiction—as a misfit genre for the Irish nation. In *The Backward Look: A Survey of Irish Literature* (1967)—one of the most important accounts of Ireland's literary-political interface after independence—Frank O'Connor sees the Irish novelist as a belated bridesmaid, trailing a flamboyant Irish revivalism on one side and an assertive international modernism on the other, and languishing permanently in their wake. In the same vein, O'Connor's contemporary Seán O'Faoláin (1900–91), whose admiring readings of various international novelists of the 1920s furnish his 1956 essay collection, *The Vanishing Hero: Studies in Novelists of the Twenties*, recalls in his autobiography, *Vive Moi!* (1964), his personal struggle to write about an Ireland which lacked what he described as 'the complexity of manners and types'[3] required to fuel the realist novel.

Recently, much attention has been given to querying a critical narrative of the Irish novel's essential weakness and, indeed, to the (re)discovery of its de facto resilience between the 1890s and 1960s.[4] Despite this, pessimism about Irish fiction often re-emerges, and not least in the criticism applied by contemporary Irish novelists to their own chosen genre. In the discussion to follow, I examine this tendency further by looking to a key decade for the Irish novel, the 1990s, when a much-celebrated pre-millennial Irish fiction frequently evolved an internal critical commentary on its own fragility, a practice heavily reliant on the metafictional device of the 'novelist within the novel', and one arguably influenced by postcolonial theorizing on the long-term failure of Irish realism. Brought into this focus, the contemporary Irish novel maintains a tendency to be 'constantly interrogative of the genre as a whole',[5] as critic James Cahalan has observed, and to convey a strategic scepticism towards the novel tradition, even as that tradition flourished on an international stage.

Additionally, as a counter-balance of sorts to the argument posed above, this chapter will show how the same decade of the 1990s witnessed the positive consolidation of an Irish fictional lineage, this time through the compilation of influential literary anthologies. Just as it had done towards the close of the Victorian period, the prose anthology of the late twentieth century became a seminal critical force—an important instrument for the calibration of Irish fiction and for the endorsement of the novel as a mainstay of Irish cultural and literary life. I explore this direction in two major anthologies of the 1990s: *The Picador Book of Contemporary Irish Fiction*, first published in 1993 and edited by novelist, playwright, poet, and publisher Dermot Bolger (1959–), and *The Penguin Book*

---

[3] Seán O'Faoláin, *Vive Moi! An Autobiography* (London: Hart Davis, 1965), 242; see also O'Faoláin's remarks on his conflict with his editor and mentor, Edward Garnett, on the writing of realist fiction in Ireland, 254–5. *The Vanishing Hero* contains expert commentaries on writers including Evelyn Waugh, Graham Greene, Virginia Woolf, and William Faulkner.

[4] For examples of this recovery work, see in particular John Wilson Foster, *Irish Novels 1890–1940: New Bearings in Culture and Fiction* (Oxford: Oxford University Press, 2008) and Frank Shovlin, 'From Tucson to Television: Irish Reading, 1939–69', in Clare Hutton and Patrick Walsh (eds), *The Oxford History of the Irish Book, Volume V: The Irish Book in English 1891–2000* (Oxford: Oxford University Press, 2011), 128–51.

[5] James Cahalan, *The Irish Novel: A Critical History* (Dublin: Gill and Macmillan, 1988), xxi.

of Irish Fiction, first published in 1999 and edited by the novelist, short story writer, and critic Colm Tóibín. Both collections convey in their substantial critical introductions the strength of the Irish novel in the late twentieth century but show too how the genre remained beset by the political pressures of the national context and a problematic Irish literary inheritance.

FICTION AS CRITIQUE: THE AUTOCRITICAL TRADITION

In their contributions to a special Irish issue of the British literary journal *Horizon* in 1942, both Frank O'Connor and Seán O'Faoláin expressed their fears that Ireland's political isolation during the Second World War would have a damaging effect on the Irish creative imagination, and particularly on the writing of novels. The poverty of the country's social fabric was exacerbated by neutrality, O'Connor argued. Having imagined that he and O'Faoláin would succeed in establishing a prose tradition in the mould of the Russians, they now confronted only 'thinness'—a diminished society which languished 'under the weather' in terms of providing material for a solid realist portrayal.[6] With the war over, the novelist Benedict Kiely (1919–2007) echoed these views in his 1950 study, *Modern Irish Fiction: A Critique*. Comparing the weakness of a domestic literary tradition to a British lineage bolstered by titans such as D. H. Lawrence, he concluded that the Irish novel represented a missed opportunity for the new nation. 'Thirty years ago', Kiely wrote, 'a man with a feeling for the literary might have been excused for thinking that the novelist, particularly the realist novelist, was in Ireland about to come into his Kingdom.'[7] Instead, the reluctance of his generation to capitalize on this 'open country' had resulted in decades of stagnation, with the novel 'a road not taken' in Ireland's literary landscape.[8]

In such terms Irish authors writing in the long wake of the Literary Revival maintained a discernible anxiety about the novel's role in modern Ireland, effectively spearheading a mid-century campaign of critical defeatism with regard to Irish long-form fiction in general and social realist fiction in particular. With hindsight we can argue that such commentary obscures the grassroots evidence of literary production: from the 1940s to the early 1960s, the realist novel of rural or small-town, working-class or petty-bourgeois Irish life, frequently framed by the family romance or saga, was in fact thriving in the work of writers such as Walter Macken (1915–67), Maurice Walsh (1879–1964), Maura Laverty (1907–66), Francis MacManus (1909–65), Michael McLaverty (1904–92), and a

---

[6] Frank O'Connor, 'The Future of Irish Literature', *Horizon* 5, no. 25 (1942), 61. See also O'Faoláin's observations on the imaginative poverty of the mid-century literary community in Ireland in 'Yeats and the Younger Generation', *Horizon* 5, no. 25 (1942), 43–54.

[7] Benedict Kiely, *Modern Irish Fiction: A Critique* (Dublin: Golden Eagle, 1950), vi.   [8] Ibid.

young John McGahern.[9] Nonetheless, the critical narrative of Ireland's novelistic poverty proved resilient and, as many critics have observed, it served a concomitant ideological purpose, the crisis of faith in the novel suggesting, by proxy, a scepticism towards the narratives of the new nation as it moved beyond independence and through a difficult, even fraught, process of maturation.[10] Conceived of as a failed genre of the evolving Republic, the fragile Irish novel spoke eloquently to—and damned—a regime of censorship, clerical interference, isolationism, and ideological conservatism. In this equation, Irish writers who excelled at the short story saw themselves as struggling with structured, longer narratives because Ireland's mid-century evolution was itself riddled with structural and ideological fractures.[11]

If the counter-Revival era was marked by scepticism on the part of author-critics towards their own novelistic profession and output, it might then be expected that Irish writers would gain confidence in the novel as the genre achieved solidity and influence in the final years of the twentieth century. Indeed, for many commentators and reviewers the genre seemed finally to come of age in the flourishing of the so-called 'New Irish Fiction' of the 1990s.[12] In tandem with the economic upswing of that decade, and stimulated by the political changes heralded by the liberal reformist presidency of Mary Robinson, who held office between 1990 and 1997, pre-millennial Irish novels— and particularly those of urban realists such as Dermot Bolger and Roddy Doyle (1958–)—became the primary indices of a contemporary and increasingly secular Ireland. Gaining a representative function above and beyond the rival forms of poetry and drama, Irish fiction offered a barometer for the changing conditions of Church, state, family, ideology, and sexuality. Moreover, the Irish novel became a recognized and successful commodity in both domestic and overseas markets, its high profile secured by award-winning writers such as Anne Enright and Colm Tóibín, and bolstered by the interest of British and North American publishers in Irish creativity.

This heightened international profile served to restore an external critical confidence in the role and calibre of Irish fiction. Internally, however, celebrity brought renewed insecurities. Some writers conveyed their unease at the extent to which Irish fiction—now

[9] For an overview of writers at this time, see Derek Hand, *A History of the Irish Novel* (Cambridge: Cambridge University Press, 2011), chapter five. For an earlier but still useful recuperative survey, see Sean McMahon, 'The Realist Novel after the Second World War', in Augustine Martin (ed.), *The Genius of Irish Prose* (Dublin: Mercier Press, 1985), 145–54.

[10] One of the most cogent overviews in this respect is John Kenny, ' "No Such Genre": Criticism and the Contemporary Irish Novel', in P. J. Mathews (ed.), *New Voices in Irish Criticism* (Dublin: Four Courts Press, 2000), 45–52.

[11] Critics identifying this corollary include James Cahalan, who suggests that 'It may be that the conventional novel is a form for a made society, whereas the short story and unconventional novels that bear the strong stamp of the short story are forms for a society in the making' (*The Irish Novel*, xxiii). The centrality of the short story in Irish tradition was consolidated by Frank O'Connor's landmark critical study, *The Lonely Voice: A Study of the Short Story* (1962).

[12] For usage and definition of this category and its relation to Mary Robinson's presidency, see Gerry Smyth, *The Novel and the Nation: Studies in the New Irish Fiction* (London: Pluto Press, 1997), 1–7. For an analysis of the decisive context of the 1990s for Irish fiction writers, see Jennifer M. Jeffers, *The Irish Novel at the End of the Twentieth Century: Gender, Bodies, and Power* (Basingstoke: Palgrave, 2002).

released from the strictures of censorship—remained too tightly bound to a political agenda, geared to a concerted revisionist critique of the ideals of Éamon de Valera's Republic and hobbled by this responsibility. The novelist Julia O'Faoláin (1932–), daughter of Seán, makes this point in her 1997 essay, 'The Furies of Irish Fiction', wherein she usefully surveys the major authors of the contemporary landscape in relation to their shared and defining 'angers'[13] against the common evils of patriarchy, clerical abuse, and paramilitary violence. The pressure to write against this inheritance risked becoming a limitation, O'Faoláin suggests, with the 'energising anger' a distraction from the novel's capacity to report on the actual conditions of a 'protean and pluralist reality'.[14] As a result, contemporary Irish fiction was homogenized by a series of well-worn tropes: 'It can hardly be accidental that self-laceration in the form of suicide, madness, murder, alcoholism and dysfunctional families should recur in Irish fiction of the last decade, as do symbolic venues such as slaughter houses and reform schools'.[15] From the perspective of one of its own practitioners, therefore, the Irish novel of the 1990s remained a reductive, backward-looking, and formulaic genre, still struggling to achieve a novelistic realism adequate to Irish society at large.

At the same time, some Irish authors of the 1990s turned their anxieties inwards, maintaining a pervasive line of self-doubt that appeared *within* the works themselves. A recurring fictional construction of the period is that of the troubled author-protagonist who tries but fails to write a novel, or who struggles with the process of realist representation. The 'novelist-within-the-novel' conceit was far from new, of course: Dermot Trellis, protagonist of Flann O'Brien's (1911–66) *At Swim-Two-Birds* (1939), for example, is in the process of writing a novel which collapses under the weight of its kaleidoscopic source material. But the particular inflection of the device in 1990s fiction is worth noting, its usage no doubt incentivized by that decade's rampant fictional postmodernism but inheriting, too, an Irish critical tradition of resistance to the realist novel's purchase in Ireland. In this respect, we can suggest that pre-millennial Irish fiction became a distinctly 'autocritical' phenomenon, whereby the genre's frequent engagement of failing author-protagonists, combined with an overarching turn to pastiche, became a means of perpetuating an ingrained critical self-doubt about the role of the realist novel in narrativizing the Irish nation.

Published in 1994, Michael Collins's (1964–) *The Life and Times of a Teaboy* is a useful example of this trait. The novel's protagonist, Ambrose Feeney, sits in the canteen of a Dublin mental hospital struggling to write one of many abortive beginnings to his great unfinished novel. After several false starts in imitation of Dostoevsky, and a panicked switch between first- and third-person voice, he admits to the futility of his project. The problem with writing an Irish novel is not only one of style but also of subject, as Feeney realizes on confronting the flimsiness of his raw material:

---

[13] Julia O'Faoláin, 'The Furies of Irish Fiction', *Graph* 3, no. 1 (1998), 6. This essay was originally published online in the *Richmond Review* in 1997.

[14] Ibid., 11.   [15] Ibid., 10–11.

[I]f pressed, as he was now, Ambrose saw himself as a metaphor of a backward nation, which had to forego the spectacle of World War Two—for budgetary concerns. A nation which did not participate in great wars, fighting with itself, no Battle of Britain, no D-Day, no collective horror, no Auschwitz. His national destiny was just plain madness.... The long and short of it was, Ambrose could not write the sociological novel of his dreams, Irish life was too alien. It reflected nothing of the world outside.[16]

In highlighting the country's lack of substance for the writer of realist fiction, Collins's protagonist parrots the literary diagnosis of Frank O'Connor's generation almost half a century later, the metafictional frame-break rehearsing a now familiar concept of the Irish novel's compositional handicaps alongside a national failure to secure a healthy tradition of narrative realism.

Late twentieth-century Irish fiction writers frequently engage versions of the incapacitated or inadequate author-protagonist, in novels ranging from Jennifer Johnston's (1930–) *The Illusionist* (1995) to Ronan Bennett's (1956–) Africa-set *The Catastrophist* (1997), and in this way consolidate a line of authorial self-doubt with regard to the fundamental task of narrative representation. Without over-reading this reflex, we can relate it nonetheless to long-term perceptions of the novelist as a 'freak'[17]—in critic Augustine Martin's 1965 description—within Ireland's cultural landscape. One of the most successful of the New Irish Fiction generation, Patrick McCabe (1955–), author of the landmark black comedy, *The Butcher Boy* (1992), is also one of the most self-referential (and ironic) in this respect. McCabe's 2003 novel, *Call Me the Breeze*, features in first-person narrative a small-town Irish writer who, despite the benefits of endless creative writing classes and cross-border creativity grants, cannot complete his 'true-life' novel about a local act of brutality. Instead, McCabe's internal author, Joey Tallon, comes up with *Doughboy*, a chaotic and whimsical pastiche much lauded by its credulous London publishers. McCabe's author-character fails in his bid for authentic realism and his resultant psychotic disintegration represents both literary and individual collapse: having offered nothing more than parody, Tallon now contemplates a future living off his advances as a dud novelist—'"Mr Failed Writer", the man no one wants to bring to the party'[18]—and existing in a permanent state of writer's block.

McCabe's metafictional convolutions in this text inevitably refer to the broader postmodern turn of Irish novels published towards the end of the twentieth century, and this theoretical context adds to the Irish author's self-critical slant. Arguably, it was not until the 1990s that Irish fiction fully absorbed the impact (just as its British counterpart had done during the 1980s) of postmodern discourses circulating within, and then beyond, academia. A sideways glance at the British fiction landscape is perhaps useful here in showing how this discursive spillover further complicates the critical hinterland of the contemporary novel. In his introduction to *After Bakhtin: Essays on Fiction and*

[16] Michael Collins, *The Life and Times of a Teaboy* (London: Phoenix, 1994), 229.
[17] Augustine Martin, 'Inherited Dissent: The Dilemma of the Irish Writer', *Studies* 54 (1965), 12.
[18] Patrick McCabe, *Call Me the Breeze* (London: Faber and Faber, 2003), 305.

Criticism, published in 1990, novelist and academic David Lodge observes that whereas thirty years previously the relationship between fiction and criticism had been relatively uncomplicated, with the latter a 'second-order discourse'[19] to the former, in more recent times the gradual collision of the two genres had become exposed. Encouraged by post-structuralist moves to dissolve the boundaries between creative and critical texts, he suggests, British novelists increasingly displayed a theorized self-consciousness in their work. The British novel of the 1980s thus developed the specific capacity to incorporate and address academic discourses, in what Mark Currie has uneasily but pertinently described as a 'mutual contamination'.[20]

By extension, the autocritical turn of the pre-millennial Irish novel highlights the proximity of the New Irish Fiction to a parallel academic theorizing on the novel genre and tradition in Ireland. To what extent did Irish fiction writers of the 1990s not only inherit the insecurities of a post-Revival generation with regard to their chosen genre but also redeploy the critical discourses rehearsed at this time by their university coun-terparts and colleagues? If British novelists such as Angela Carter and Salman Rushdie were indeed writing to a visible academic agenda, as suggested by the historian of the British novel, Dominic Head, were Irish novelists caught in the same bind a decade later?[21] These questions (which also address the Irish novelist's frequent crossover into the domain of the public intellectual) probe the impact of academic literary theory dur-ing the 1990s on an adjacent fictional landscape and, above all, highlight the intersection of the Irish novel with a persuasive postcolonialism, the critical discourse which domin-ated Irish academic debate at this time.[22]

Postcolonial theorists tended to position the classic realist novel as the 'calling card' of a white imperialism invested in ideas of imposed chronology, civility, and homogen-eity.[23] This contention was calibrated within an Irish academic context during the early 1990s but largely in relation to *nineteenth-century* literary history. In an Ireland suffering under a Victorian colonial regime, the novel is seen to provide a convenient discursive metaphor—that of an evolved and bourgeois social realism awkwardly and illegitim-ately imposed on a violent, transitional culture naturally given to the Gothic, the fantas-tic, and the short tale adapted from a peasant storytelling tradition. Two important critical (and political) readings of the novel genre in nineteenth-century Ireland were

[19] David Lodge, *After Bakhtin: Essays on Fiction and Criticism* (London: Routledge, 1990), 11.

[20] Mark Currie, *Postmodern Narrative Theory* (London: Macmillan, 1998), 66. See also Patricia Waugh, *Metafiction: The Theory and Practice of Self-Conscious Fiction* (London: Routledge, 2002).

[21] See Dominic Head, *The Cambridge Introduction to Modern British Fiction, 1950–2000* (Cambridge: Cambridge University Press, 2000), 3–4.

[22] For a commentary on the prominence of postcolonial discourse within Irish arts and humanities criticism during the 1990s, see Glenn Hooper, 'Introduction', in Glenn Hooper and Colin Graham (eds), *Irish and Postcolonial Writing: History, Theory, Practice* (Basingstoke: Palgrave Macmillan, 2002), 15–17.

[23] As outlined, for example, in Homi Bhabha's alliance of classic realist fiction and 'homogenous time' in 'DissemiNation: Time, Narrative, and the Margins of the Modern Nation', in Homi K. Bhabha (ed.), *Nation and Narration* (London: Routledge, 1990). For further useful commentary on the novel genre and postcolonial resistance, see Peter Hitchcock, 'The Genre of Postcoloniality', *New Literary History* 34, no. 2 (2003), 299–331.

particularly influential in this regard. The first, David Lloyd's 'Violence and the Constitution of the Novel' in his *Anomalous States* (1993), reads the Irish novel in Bakhtinian terms as atypical of classic realism and as 'symptomatic of the resistance of an anomalous Irish culture to modes of representation emerging into dominance'.[24] The second, Terry Eagleton's 'Form and Ideology in the Anglo-Irish Novel', included in his 1995 collection, *Heathcliff and the Great Hunger*, similarly argues that nineteenth-century Ireland was essentially inimical to the polished workings of classic narrative realism. Instead, the Irish novels of the period are formally incoherent, often rooted in folklore, and identified as a recalcitrant form which, in Eagleton's description, 'continually plays havoc with realist figuration and narrative continuity', representing through this generic disturbance 'a deeper contention of national cultures, between English convention and Irish experience, a language given and a language heard'.[25]

Postcolonial critiques of the nineteenth-century novel and Ireland offered a highly attractive formula for academic criticism, and also, we can suggest, a portable rationale for the metafictional and autocritical instincts of Irish fiction produced in the late *twentieth* century. These critiques form an important critical backdrop to the emergent strand of a distinctive 'self-policing' Irish novel, one highlighting its own compositional and generic fragility, or its atypicality in relation to realist convention, in keeping with a postcolonial schematic. On occasion, the crossover from critic to novelist is overt: for example, in Joseph O'Connor's (1963–) celebrated 2002 historical novel, *Star of the Sea*—a work which specifically lists Eagleton's *Heathcliff and the Great Hunger* among its source texts—the American writer Grantley Dixon lambasts 'that idiot Dickens' but also admits his own failure to document a famine-ravaged Irish society which 'deserved no place in printed pages, in finely wrought novels intended for the civilized'.[26] Other writers make looser gestures towards the same theme. 'You must read *Pride and Prejudice*,...that at least',[27] insists the long suffering wife of the autodidact sergeant in Dermot Healy's (1947–2014) *A Goat's Song* (1994), but her pleas are in vain to a husband who knows that his bookshelf of nineteenth-century English classics has no relevance to his understanding of Ireland's turbulent and fantastical history.

Inevitably, this argument for a theoretical determinism in pre-millennial Irish fiction relies on a degree of cherry-picking from the many and varied novels published at that time. There is no mistaking a 'mutual contamination' between Irish fiction and postcolonial criticism in one of the most celebrated Irish novels of the 1990s, however: Seamus Deane's (1940–) autobiographical *Reading in the Dark* (1996). In this text, novelist and critic coalesce systematically and almost seamlessly. Deane's text illustrates what might be viewed as a critical vested interest in the Irish novel's undermining of its own legitimacy. In its resistance to generic definition—is it autobiography or fiction, a long episodic narrative or a series of Gothic *petits recits*?—the work frustrates the characteristics of

---

[24] David Lloyd, *Anomalous States: Irish Writing and the Post-Colonial Moment* (Dublin: Lilliput Press, 1993), 129.

[25] Terry Eagleton, *Heathcliff and the Great Hunger: Studies in Irish Culture* (London: Verso, 1995), 203.

[26] Joseph O'Connor, *Star of the Sea* (London: Vintage, 2002), 131.

[27] Dermot Healy, *A Goat's Song* (London: Harvill, 1997), 115.

classic narrative realism while simultaneously claiming a novelistic identity.[28] 'Reading in the Dark', one of the sub-sections of the first chapter, self-consciously adds to the ambiguity of this critical self-positioning. Absorbed in reading a historical romance of the 1798 rebellion, and having subsequently littered his school essay with exotic vocabulary culled from the dictionary, Deane's autobiographical child-protagonist becomes the incapacitated internal author, 'embarrassed' at his own novelistic ambitions when his elaborate homework composition is set beside a very different kind of narrative, the simple tale, little more than a prose poem, submitted by a fellow pupil:

> The English teacher read out a model essay which had been, to our surprise, written by a country boy. It was an account of his mother setting the table for the evening meal and then waiting with him until his father came in from the fields. She put out a blue-and-white jug full of milk and a covered dish of potatoes in their jackets and a red-rimmed butter dish with a slab of butter, the shape of a swan dipping its head imprinted on the surface.... 'Now that,' said the master, 'that's writing. That's just telling the truth.'[29]

This careful juxtaposition is simultaneously engaging and disingenuous. Deane ruptures his own ersatz novel with a vision of an authentic Irish literary tradition ('That's just telling the truth') harnessed to the rural idiom and approximating to the short tale. This is a covert displacement of 'novelistic' narrative within a novel which, in its entirety, challenges the genre. *Reading in the Dark* represents the high watermark of a fictional/critical symbiosis—Deane, like David Lodge, occupying both creative and critical roles in his career—and as such usefully illustrates how the Irish novel 'makes its own contribution to theoretical discussion',[30] as Linden Peach suggests, functioning as part of, rather than anterior to, a critical discourse.

The New Irish Fiction of the 1990s inhabits, in this regard, a zone of paradox, its authors securing credibility while simultaneously compromising the genre in which they achieved eminence. Despite this postmodern inflection (and its related postcolonial subtexts), the Irish novel of the late twentieth century *did* achieve not only a commercial stability but also a sense of national pre-eminence. It gained this primarily through the increased anthologizing of fiction at this time. While anthologies themselves were inevitably fraught with issues of exclusion and bias (as shown by the multivolume Field Day endeavour of 1991, of which Deane was general editor), the collation of Irish fictional texts during the 1990s served to consolidate and re-position the novel genre, with practitioners taking a leading role. In the second half of this chapter, I turn to

---

[28] In its formal resistance to novelistic narrative Deane's novel perhaps plays on Walter Benjamin's 'The Storyteller: Reflections on the Work of Nikolai Leskov' in his *Illuminations*, trans. Harry Zohn (New York: Schocken Books, 1968), 83–109. On the postcolonial and political context of the text in this regard, see Liam Harte, 'History Lessons: Postcolonialism and Seamus Deane's *Reading in the Dark*', *Irish University Review* 30, no. 1 (2000), 149–62.

[29] Seamus Deane, *Reading in the Dark* (London: Vintage, 1997), 20–1.

[30] Linden Peach, *The Contemporary Irish Novel: Critical Readings* (Basingstoke: Palgrave Macmillan, 2004), x.

the work of the novelist as anthologist, exploring two major Irish fiction collections, edited and prefaced by Dermot Bolger and Colm Tóibín respectively, to comment further on this process.

STRATEGIC REALIGNMENTS: ANTHOLOGIZING IRISH FICTION IN THE 1990S

The Picador Book of Contemporary Irish Fiction, published in 1993, with a revised edition appearing the following year, was edited and introduced by Dermot Bolger, whose 1990 novel, *The Journey Home*, was regarded by many as a defining text of the New Irish Fiction. The novel's focus on the existence of an alienated Irish underclass caught up in a daily reality of inner-city Dublin drug abuse and social alienation, in counterpoint to an increasingly corrupt post-nationalist Irish political hierarchy, offered a gritty vernacular realism characteristic of the author's work in different literary genres. Bolger also brought professional literary experience to the Picador anthology: in 1977, he set up Raven Arts Press and co-founded the successful imprint New Island Books in 1992. His approach to the task of selecting and framing a representative display of contemporary fiction thus combined personal commitment to the craft with the more detached eye of a professional (and commercially attuned) editor, alert to significant changes in the landscape of Irish writing generally at this time.

This background helps shape the particular generational ethos of the Picador collection. Although Bolger's selection dates from the later work of Samuel Beckett (1906–89) and includes several well-established senior Irish authors, his emphasis is on the emergence of a younger cohort of writers born after the Second World War and shaped by the iconoclastic, liberationist attitudes of the 1960s. In his editorial introduction, he pays a prefatory homage to the concept of an Irish literary tradition, but his real focus is on ideas of creative and thematic *dis*continuity. While contemporary writers have inherited elements of the landscape which formed their predecessors, including a self-confidence in their art and a connection to Europe gained through the precedence of Beckett and James Joyce (1882–1941), they represent in more precise terms, Bolger suggests, a point of fracture with the past. 'The problems would include the fact that if, as Joyce said, history was a nightmare from which we were trying to awaken, then frequently Joyce and others are shadows that newer Irish writers are trying to avoid being pushed under.'[31] The ensuing selection is therefore a means of writing out of, rather than into, a recognized Irish literary inheritance.

Bolger's disavowal of Joyce clears the ground for his anthology to address, purposefully, what he regards as three disabling myths that continue to dog the evolution of a

---

[31] Dermot Bolger, 'Introduction', in Dermot Bolger (ed.), *The Picador Book of Contemporary Irish Fiction* (London: Picador, 1993), viii.

contemporary Irish fictional output, and in this respect the Picador anthology offers a distinct (not to say brave) political and cultural statement. First, Bolger turns to content, asserting that the major themes which preoccupied the Joycean generation are no longer the staples of Irish prose writers, who must therefore write against the grain of critical expectation:

> It is not just a case that we are presumed to share a city or country with Joyce, but those themes which obsessed him and his generation—Catholicism and Nationalism and the role of the artist—are somehow supposed to be central to our own work, so that at times our work can be judged on how we handle subjects which are, in fact, absent from them.[32]

Indeed, the idea of a Joycean inheritance is itself a fault, Bolger continues, given that writers of his own generation rarely had access to *Ulysses* (1922) and the stylistic pursuits of modernism. Nor were they products of the decades of mid-century economic stagnation and emigration that produced, in Seán O'Faoláin's generation, a political complacency. 'Often these writers chose to keep the realities of their country at bay in their work, to create an aesthetic of a hackneyed version of Ireland (loved by foreign literary editors) to hide behind',[33] he suggests. A new generation is therefore seen as having been released from Joycean paternity, with all it implied, and liberated too from a more localized conformity imposed by mid-century torpor and literary censorship.

Aided by the impact of free second-level education, which was introduced in the Republic in 1968, and the emergence of an indigenous Irish publishing industry, the fiction writers of the 1990s are seen by Bolger as being well prepared to challenge orthodox versions of Irishness linked closely to a rural, conservative, and Catholic ideology, and to engage their art for critical and oppositional purposes. Following in the footsteps of three influential writers whose works had fallen foul of either the state censor or the board of the Abbey Theatre in the 1960s—John McGahern, Tom Murphy (1935–2018), and Eugene McCabe (1930–)—Bolger characterizes contemporary Irish writers as an instinctively rebellious generation, whose struggle is 'to write in their own way and to have that work recognized on its own merit—both inside and outside Ireland'.[34] This lineage, coupled with the politicized role expected of the contemporary Irish writer, leads Bolger to offer a second important realignment of contemporary Irish fiction: a rejection of the widespread perception (largely stemming from outside Ireland itself) that all Irish writing since the early 1970s has necessarily been dominated by the Northern Troubles. While accepting that the Troubles have informed the work of several major writers, from Benedict Kiely to Glenn Patterson (1961–), Bolger argues that the effect of political violence on literary expectations and reception has been out of proportion, and has thereby served

---

[32] Ibid.   [33] Ibid., x.   [34] Ibid.

to reinforce the notion that the North was central to all Irish writing, so that, as a writer from the Republic of Ireland—which is three times the size of the North—one frequently felt that you were writing about a society which had been rendered invisible. The genuine changes and struggles and the separate reality of people's lives in the South seemed to count as nothing for academics, editors and critics with their own agendas.[35]

These sentiments, published just before the first Provisional IRA ceasefire in August 1994, need careful consideration. Bolger's defence of a distinct fictional corpus devoted to issues relevant to the Republic tackles first, and implicitly, the literary and political impact of the conflict in Northern Ireland as it was filtered largely through poetry, in the work of Seamus Heaney (1939–2013), Michael Longley (1939–), Derek Mahon (1941–), Ciaran Carson (1948–2019), and others. The idea of the Republic suffering a resultant 'invisibility' is particular interesting in throwing responsibility not simply onto a different political, social, and constitutional landscape but, indeed, onto a different genre: prose fiction. What the Troubles did for Northern Irish poetry must now, it seems, be matched in terms of impact by what prose fiction can do in registering the continuing and comparatively unrecognized issues affecting the Republic.[36] Furthermore, the theoretical and political structures which have by default been extended from the situation in Northern Ireland to contextualize the island as a whole should be dismantled and rejected since, Bolger insists, 'it is simply not possible to allow a phrase like "postcolonial literature" still to wander about like a decomposing chicken in search of its head, and to have it foisted on the backs of younger writers'.[37] Nationalism and its legacies are thus pushed to the background for a contemporary generation of writers who, like Bolger himself, address more immediate concerns of family, city, and state before the now-distant pressures of 'nation'.

This is a key directive of Bolger's preface, not a depoliticization as such but a strategic realignment of Irish fiction around the core themes of social realism—urban life, the family, the workplace or lack of it—and a concomitant distancing of it from political violence and paramilitary activity, which had, by default, come to signify Irish writing as a whole. If there is a hint of resentment from the anthologist towards a supposed Northern monopoly on the reading public's attention, that sentiment is kept in check, and the volume's contents imply respect for those Northern Irish writers who have worked to find formal narrative strategies appropriate to the vexed condition of their home territory. But the inclusiveness is nuanced, the anthology integrating Northern Irish writers into the mainstream of the collection while signalling an end to their perceived dominance of the creative field.

---

[35] Ibid., xi–xii.

[36] On the identification of genre with political constituencies, see Eve Patten, ' "Flying to Belfast": Audience and Authenticity in Recent Northern Irish Fiction', in Tony Brown and John Russell Stephens (eds), Nations and Relations: Writing Across the British Isles (Cardiff: New Welsh Review, 2000), 30–42.

[37] Bolger, 'Introduction', xiii. For commentary on Bolger's anthology, see Ray Ryan, 'The Republic and Ireland: Pluralism, Politics, and Narrative Form', in Ray Ryan (ed.), Writing in the Irish Republic: Literature, Culture, Politics, 1949–1999 (Basingstoke: Macmillan, 2000), 84–9.

In keeping with the iconoclasm of the anthology's preface, Bolger also addresses issues of genre and form, aware of the politicized literary history attendant on these since the counter-Revival generation, as discussed in the first half of this chapter. The hallmark of the younger generation of Irish writers is, he suggests, their capacity to move across and between genres: six of the writers included in his anthology born after 1955 began their careers as poets and five are also playwrights, a category which includes the author himself. Their distinction, however, has been their ability to exploit the longer prose narrative form, to become novelists of a new generation and, in doing so, to break the stranglehold of the short story as the default Irish mode. Moreover, as he observes, many celebrated Irish short stories have been subsequently reworked by their authors as novels, including Aidan Higgins's (1927–2015) 'Killachter Meadow', later developed into the 1966 novel, *Langrishe, Go Down*, and Eoin McNamee's (1961–) 'If Angels had Wings' (1988), which became the novella, *The Last of Deeds* (1989), and which the anthology includes. Several of the leading post-Revival writers excel more as novelists than short story writers, Bolger argues, including the accomplished John McGahern and John Banville.

Bolger's point here goes beyond the technicalities of literary craftsmanship, for he clearly reads the expansion of novel publication in modern Ireland as a sign of national maturity, the country having left behind an era of censorship, mediocrity, and confessionalism which imprinted itself on the devices of the short format and curtailed longer narrative development. His emphasis is on the present generation's ability not only to escape the clutches of a supposed national tradition in favour of a contemporary modern ethos but also to match the generic standards of the rest of Europe. Thus, it is with confidence that Bolger includes in his selection several novel extracts, and concludes that 'the major achievements of contemporary Irish fiction in recent years have been most frequently in the novel form'.[38] There is a note of defiance here which, in contradiction to the structured hesitations over the novel detailed in the first part of this chapter, wills the genre into pre-eminence.

The overall tone of the Picador anthology is therefore defiant and celebratory. Bolger is rightly attentive to commercial changes, pointing out that progress in Irish writing has been enabled by the recent emergence of a fertile Irish publishing industry and the commitment to new writing from a range of outlets, such as the *Irish Press*, the *Sunday Tribune*, and the *Irish Times*, all of which helped to confound the sometimes sterile expectations of London and American publishers looking for the rural idiom and traditional form. The explosion in Irish writing over the preceding two and a half decades has encompassed a diversity of place—with writers taking on international settings and stories—and of theme, particularly in the treatment of gender and sexuality, as writers openly addressed the subject of homosexuality.

Bolger's anthology, then, is an important statement in praise of Irish literary evolution in general and a defence of a new urban realist voice in particular, one invested in the ironies of a modern-day Irish society largely detached from traditional pieties of Church

---

[38] Bolger, 'Introduction', xv–xvi.

and nationhood. It raises questions, however, as to the extent to which any critic can, at this juncture, attribute a *national* distinctiveness—an 'Irish quality', as it were—to Irish writing, while at the same time applauding an ethos of diversity and formal liberation. The anthologies of the 1980s and 1990s were important testing grounds for this issue. They frequently exhibit a tension between the push of individual literary ambition and the pull of national affiliation, with 'Irish' increasingly a flag of convenience for a set of younger writers whose work is almost wholly detached from recognizable markers of place, state, language, and nation.

One means of resolution to this problem lies in the catch-all identity of 'European', to which Bolger ultimately turns, aligning his own work and that of his contemporaries with a 'young European literature'.[39] This is, on the one hand, a seemingly smooth resolution to the dilemmas of Irish identity politics: like Ireland as an independent state within the European Union, the Irish-European writer retains an effective federal distinctiveness, while benefiting from the aura of cosmopolitanism, longevity, and philosophical capacity vaguely conveyed by the concept of 'Europe'. On the other hand, however, it strikes a false note. Even a cursory reading of Seán O'Faoláin, Elizabeth Bowen, or—it goes without saying—Samuel Beckett reveals that a previous generation of Irish writers was much more closely tied to, and influenced by, continental authors and culture than their contemporary descendants. Indeed, one could argue that the label 'European' was introduced rather lazily in many discussions of new Irish writing in the 1990s, reflecting little more than an aspirational continentalism suggested (rather than substantiated) by a range of 'travel' novels—usually of the Irish *ingénue* abroad variety—which appeared around this time.

An attempted resolution to the contemporary Irish novelist's identity problem—the split between national distinctiveness and international anonymity—is offered in a second prose anthology of the 1990s, *The Penguin Book of Irish Fiction*, published by Viking Penguin in 1999 and reissued in 2001. This collection is edited by Colm Tóibín, the journalist-turned-*litterateur* whose novels of the 1990s, including *The Heather Blazing* (1992), *The Story of the Night* (1996), and *The Blackwater Lightship* (1999), established him as a major figure within the New Irish Fiction category. His Penguin selection, which covers writers from Jonathan Swift (1667–1745) to Emma Donoghue (1969–), is prefaced by a critical introduction addressing the need for Irish fiction writers to retain a local sensibility while accessing and aspiring to belong to the best of European and world literature. It is almost a response to Bolger's dilemma of national categorization. Tóibín's anthology aims not to recuperate lost writers or justify obscure outriders but rather to position recognized and well-established Irish authors securely within a two-way relationship, connecting the local and international without compromising either category. The collection foregrounds, therefore, a tradition of Irish fiction which is self-aware and mobile, responsive to international influences while at the same time being attentive—albeit somewhat conservatively—to the importance of a communal national lineage.

[39] Ibid., xxvi.

The anthology is framed by Tóibín's negotiations not only with Irish fiction but, cru-cially, with the political investments of Irish criticism in the twentieth century and the continuing pull of the national question on writing. It addresses a perennial problem in Irish fiction: that individual concerns and incentives are sublimated to, or read as repre-sentative of, a broader national condition. In the absence of a revolutionary political culture, Tóibín suggests, it is the role of the writer to gesture, through stories of individ-ual suffering, to the wider political landscape. 'We have no communards, no rabble in the streets', he writes. 'Instead, we have personal sacrifice as a metaphor for general sacrifice.'[40] This Romantic reading of an Irish literary culture is by no means new. Tóibín follows (with due acknowledgement) a line of critics and writers from Daniel Corkery (1878–1964) onwards in exposing the determinist relationship between Irish culture and Irish society, a representative weight that has pulled heavily on prose fiction (including his own) for generations.

The resolution to this stranglehold lies not in plot but in formal device, and in the achievements of a ground-breaking modernist coterie which, led by Joyce, found revo-lutionary potential and effect in language itself, thereby avoiding the pitfalls of their stolid realist contemporaries. Tóibín again follows a previous generation of critics in exposing the lack of fit between the placid realist genre and a turbulent, recalcitrant Irish story, illustrating his point in a comparison between George Moore (1852–1933)—read as a stalwart realist—and Joyce, praised for his dazzling experimental register of indi-vidual consciousness. Whereas a novel such as Moore's *Esther Waters* (1894) succeeds as the appropriate form for England, a 'settled' society, and one lacking any ongoing polit-ical distractions, Joyce's *Ulysses* represents the struggle of its author to find (as Joan Miró and the modernists had done) 'a new beginning in the creation of fiction'.[41] And in this struggle, Joyce produces in his epic work not only a radical stylistic departure but also 'a deeply patriotic and liberating book'.[42] *Ulysses* marks a fresh beginning for Irish fiction and also confirms a quintessential national difference—'the fact of feeling Irish',[43] as the Argentinian writer Jorge Louis Borges, whom Tóibín quotes, puts it—through its innov-atory role within English culture.

Thus, where Bolger detached contemporary Irish fiction from its Joycean moorings, Tóibín recuperates them. But if the Penguin anthology follows familiar lines in rehears-ing the modernist-versus-realist debate as a formal proxy for the terms of an Irish–English relationship, it breaks new ground by recognizing a key facet of Irish fiction writing, in Tóibín's admission that an Irish fictional 'tradition' is in many regards a mis-nomer. Rather, Irish fiction collectively foregrounds a series of distinct tropes—the father/son conflict; the dance; destruction by fire; the killing of women by men; the stranger returned from exile—which help shape a lineage. While this view maintains the Irish novel's origin myths in the superior and stronger constitution of the Irish short

---

[40] Colm Tóibín, 'Introduction', in Colm Tóibín (ed.), *The Penguin Book of Irish Fiction* (London: Viking Penguin, 1999), x.
[41] Ibid., xv.   [42] Ibid., xiv.   [43] Ibid., xvii.

story, which is typically based on a very similar set of tropes, it successfully avoids the pressure for the anthologist either to define a tradition in the first place or to force connections between a wide variety of writers. It also allows Irish stories grounded in local detail to aspire to universality, and in this respect the argument lays the groundwork for Tóibín's elevation of a writer often overlooked in surveys of Irish fictional development, Mary Lavin (1912–96), whose work combines a composed attention to the recurrent Irish tropes with a quiet trust in the narrative of individual life. 'Love, memory, family, age, death, hope and hopelessness became her themes', he observes, adding: 'She is prepared to dramatize the small details, the moments of pure truth. Her stories tell you very little about "Irish society" and a great deal about the human heart.'[44]

This defence of a 'small details' writer is perhaps the most significant aspect of the Penguin anthology, and Tóibín's preface reflects his own writing practice in its careful and astute positioning of such an author in relation to the world. Where Bolger struggled to make sense of the 'European' label beyond a convenient shorthand for diversity, Tóibín offers a confident validation of those 'small details' writers such as Lavin and Kate O'Brien (1897–1974), seeing them as engaging the European 'knowingness' of a Miró or a Picasso while retaining the material and settings of the local and the intimate. What appears perhaps as the conservatism or even the *quaintness* of their limited landscapes is informed by their view of a wider fictional and social canvas, recognized and absorbed from a safe distance. In this, Tóibín takes his lead from Borges, whose 1932 essay, 'The Argentine Writer and Tradition', illuminates the split perspective of the hinterland or colonial writer, detached from the metropolitan centre and writing back to it from within the pressurized grip of the margins:

> For Borges and his generation in Buenos Aires, the real world was elsewhere: they spoke and read French and English, and in their imagination they belonged to Europe, but when they lifted their heads from books, or came back from abroad, they were in a cultural backwater, and they had no intention of becoming chroniclers of their half-formed time or their badly formed country. They realized that they had no choice but to invent their own time and their own country. They believed as many Irish writers came to believe (and later writers García Márquez in Colombia and Amos Tutuola in Nigeria came to believe), that you cannot write social realism in an underdeveloped country.[45]

In this adaptation of Borges, Tóibín provides a generous, even capacious stage for Irish literary tradition: the Irish fiction writer is always, by default, an artificer, engaged in a self-conscious process of national invention (never simply a pedestrian representation) and elevated by virtue of this fact into an international confederacy of stylists, working creatively between the complex layerings of domestic theme and cosmopolitan form. In Tóibín's formulation, therefore, the modern Irish author is always 'writing back' to a homeland, rather than simply writing *from* it. This nuanced positioning successfully

---

[44] Ibid., xxvii.   [45] Ibid., xix.

updates the problematic hybrid of 'Anglo-Irish Literature' with a charismatic version of a contemporary Irish fiction responsive to the 'matter of Ireland' but attractive and accessible to an Anglo-American literary academy as a whole.

This bifocalism also facilitates, finally, the grouping of a younger generation of Irish fiction writers for whom North American literary influences have been more significant than the legacies of continental European or even British authors. The writers who came of age in the 1970s, Tóibín suggests, were completely open to a transatlantic cultural influence:

> Ireland lay down and let America wash over it. Thus in the 1980s and 1990s it was possible to detect the spare poetic realism of Raymond Carver and Richard Ford, or the eccentric voices of Flannery O'Connor and Grace Paley, in many of the younger writers, but more than that the influence of American cinema and American music.[46]

This openness is borne out by the many younger writers in the Penguin collection, such as Colum McCann (1965–), Patrick McCabe, and Emma Donoghue, whose Irish idiom is glossed by the narrative structures, settings, or popular culture of North America. *The Penguin Book of Irish Fiction* thus introduces a more flexible and viable currency for the writer than the vague identity of 'Irish-European' proposed as a convenient default by Bolger, and indeed, heralds the emergence in the current period of a new school of Irish-American criticism.

For both anthologists, finally, the instinct to hybridize the Irish author in the first place indicates a pressing concern that the boundaries of Irish literary nationhood have, by the 1990s, eroded well beyond the point of repair. The anthology of Irish prose fiction becomes, in this regard, not a reflection of common trends or developments but rather the strategic reconstitution of a writing community which has already begun to drift from the recognized moorings of a national sensibility. In both anthologies discussed here, therefore, if in slightly different ways, the Irish novelist's recalcitrance gives way to international confidence and to a strength of purpose which validates idiosyncrasies as much as continuities and communities. The problems of an inherited tradition of the Irish novel, meanwhile—a tradition which sustained, as we have seen, an autocritical investment in the genre's instability—are overturned in the collective project of the anthology, and the Irish novelist placed firmly at the political and cultural vanguard of the changing nation.

FURTHER READING

Cahalan, James. *The Irish Novel: A Critical History*. Dublin: Gill and Macmillan, 1988.
Ellmann, Maud. 'The Irish Novel 1914–1940'. In Patrick Parrinder and Andrzej Gasiorek (eds), *The Oxford History of the Novel in English, Volume 4: The Reinvention of the British and Irish Novel 1880–1940*. Oxford: Oxford University Press, 2011: 451–72.

---

[46] Ibid., xxxii.

Foster, John Wilson (ed.). *The Cambridge Companion to the Irish Novel*. Cambridge: Cambridge University Press, 2006.

Hand, Derek. *A History of the Irish Novel*. Cambridge: Cambridge University Press, 2011.

Harte, Liam. *Reading the Contemporary Irish Novel 1987–2007*. Oxford: Wiley Blackwell, 2014.

Head, Dominic. *The Cambridge Introduction to Modern British Fiction, 1950–2000*. Cambridge: Cambridge University Press, 2000.

Jeffers, Jennifer M. *The Irish Novel at the End of the Twentieth Century: Gender, Bodies, and Power*. Basingstoke: Palgrave, 2002.

Peach, Linden. *The Contemporary Irish Novel: Critical Readings*. Basingstoke: Palgrave Macmillan, 2004.

Smyth, Gerry. *The Novel and the Nation: Studies in the New Irish Fiction*. London: Pluto Press, 1997.

Smyth, Gerry. *Decolonisation and Criticism: The Construction of Irish Literature*. London: Pluto Press, 1998.

Index

Note: The method of alphabetical ordering used is letter-by-letter. Titles of works are listed alphabetically under the name of the author. Bibliographical and passing references are omitted. Footnote references are included only where they amplify the discussion in the main text.